The Mississippi Valley Historical Review

VOLUME XLIV

June, 1957, to March, 1958

Published Quarterly by the Mississippi Valley Historical Association

Contents of Volume XLIV

ARTICLES

The Great Visitation to American Democracy. By Thomas D. Clark . . . 3

Fulfilling American Democracy: The Conservation Movement, 1907 to 1921. By J. Leonard Bates . . . 29

Objectives and Methods in Intellectual History. By John C. Greene . . . 58

The National Progressives of America, 1938. By Donald R. McCoy . . . 75

Was Jackson's Kitchen Cabinet a Cabinet? By Richard P. Longaker . . . 94

Woodrow Wilson and His Interpreters, 1947-1957. By Richard L. Watson, Jr. . . . 207

The Origins of the Teapot Dome Investigation. By Burl Noggle . . . 237

The South and the Blair Education Bill. By Allen J. Going 267

"Fifty-four Forty or Fight"—An American Political Legend. By Edwin A. Miles . . . 291

The Fiftieth Annual Meeting of the Mississippi Valley Historical Association. By Oscar O. Winther . . . 310

Religious Benevolence as Social Control, 1815-1860. By Clifford S. Griffin . . . 423

A Scheme in Regard to Cyrenaica. By James A. Field, Jr. . 445

The Brownsville Episode and the Negro Vote. By Emma Lou Thornbrough . . . 469

The Semicentennial of the Mississippi Valley Historical Association. By James L. Sellers . . . 494

Under Our Strange Device: A Review of the "Review." By John W. Caughey . . . 519

ANDREW JACKSON VERSUS THE HISTORIANS. By Charles Grier Sellers, Jr. 615

THE DISMISSAL OF LORD SACKVILLE. By Charles S. Campbell, Jr. . 635

BOOKS AND READING ON THE OHIO VALLEY FRONTIER. By Howard H. Peckham 649

BUSINESS DISUNITY AND THE PROGRESSIVE MOVEMENT, 1901-1914. By Robert H. Wiebe 664

THE LOUISVILLE AND PORTLAND CANAL COMPANY, 1825-1874. By Paul B. Trescott 686

BOOK REVIEWS 109, 335, 536, 709

BOOK NOTES 172, 385, 579, 766

HISTORICAL NEWS AND COMMENTS . . 181, 393, 585, 777

COMMUNICATIONS 202

DIRECTORY OF CONTRIBUTORS . . . 204, 420, 612, 794

The Mississippi Valley Historical Review

PUBLISHED QUARTERLY BY THE MISSISSIPPI VALLEY HISTORICAL ASSOCIATION

VOL. XLIV, NO. 1 — JUNE, 1957

Correspondence concerning contributions, books for review, and all editorial matters should be addressed to William C. Binkley, Managing Editor, Tulane University of Louisiana, New Orleans 18, Louisiana. Annual membership dues are $5.00. Student membership dues are $3.00 annually. Correspondence concerning membership dues and all business matters should be addressed to the Secretary, William D. Aeschbacher, 1500 R Street, Lincoln, Nebraska. The *Review* is sent to all members of the Association. Single numbers and back files may be obtained from the Secretary.

The Mississippi Valley Historical Association disclaims responsibility for statements whether of fact or of opinion made by contributors.

Entered as second-class matter, May 22, 1914, at the post office in Cedar Rapids, Iowa, and Lincoln 8, Nebraska, under the Act of August 24, 1912. Printed by The Torch Press, Cedar Rapids, Iowa.

Contents

THE GREAT VISITATION TO AMERICAN DEMOCRACY. By Thomas D. Clark . . . 3

FULFILLING AMERICAN DEMOCRACY: THE CONSERVATION MOVEMENT, 1907 TO 1921. By J. Leonard Bates 29

OBJECTIVES AND METHODS IN INTELLECTUAL HISTORY. By John C. Greene . 58

THE NATIONAL PROGRESSIVES OF AMERICA, 1938. By Donald R. McCoy . . 75

WAS JACKSON'S KITCHEN CABINET A CABINET? By Richard P. Longaker . 94

BOOK REVIEWS

Pochmann, *German Culture in America*, by H. F. Peters 109
Ellis (ed.), *Documents of American Catholic History*, by Harvey Wish . . . 113
Quattlebaum, *The Land Called Chicora*, by Richard K. Murdoch 114
The Bay Psalm Book: A Facsimile Reprint of the First Edition of 1640, and Haraszti, *The Enigma of the Bay Psalm Book*, by Louis B. Wright 116
Miller, *Errand into the Wilderness*, by John E. Pomfret 117
Wright, *The Cultural Life of the American Colonies*, by Clifford K. Shipton . . . 120
Still, *Mirror for Gotham: New York as Seen by Contemporaries*, by Nelson Manfred Blake . 121
White, *The Beekmans of New York in Politics and Commerce, 1647-1877*, and *The Beekman Mercantile Papers, 1746-1799* (3 vols.), by James B. Hedges 123
Buranelli, *The Trial of Peter Zenger*, by John A. Schutz 125
Easterby (ed.), *The Colonial Records of South Carolina: The Journal of the Commons House of Assembly*, by Robert H. Woody 126
Charles, *The Origins of the American Party System*, by Manning J. Dauer . . . 127
Nye, *A Baker's Dozen: Thirteen Unusual Americans*, by Wood Gray . . . 129
Nichols, *Advance Agents of American Destiny*, by W. Donald Beatty . . . 130
Bond (ed.), *The Intimate Letters of John Cleves Symmes and His Family*, by John D. Barnhart 131
Ferguson, *Truxtun of the Constellation*, by William W. Jeffries 132
Malone, *Cherokees of the Old South*, by Angie Debo 133
Siegel, *A Political History of the Texas Republic, 1836-1845*, and Hollon and Butler (eds.), *William Bollaert's Texas*, by Jim Dan Hill 134
Shanks (ed.), *The Papers of Willie Person Mangum*, Vols. III-V, by Culver H. Smith . 138
Franklin, *The Militant South, 1800-1861*, by Fletcher M. Green 140
Coulter, *Auraria: The Story of a Georgia Gold-Mining Town*, by T. Conn Bryan . . 141
Gara, *Westernized Yankee: The Story of Cyrus Woodman*, by Irene D. Neu . . 142
Chandler, *Henry Varnum Poor: Business Editor, Analyst, and Reformer*, by Paul W. Gates . 143
Randall, *The Courtship of Mr. Lincoln*, by Mary Elizabeth Massey . . . 144
Cornish, *The Sable Arm: Negro Troops in the Union Army*, by Benjamin Quarles . . 146
Govan and Livingood, *A Different Valor: The Story of General Joseph E. Johnston*, by John P. Dyer 147
Williams, *Lincoln Finds a General*, Vol. IV, by D. A. Brown 148
Barrett, *Sherman's March through the Carolinas*, by Richard E. Yates . . . 150
Vandiver, *Rebel Brass: The Confederate Command System*, by John Bennett Walters . 151
Conner, *Joseph Reddeford Walker and the Arizona Adventure* (ed. by Berthrong and Davenport), by Andrew F. Rolle 152
Lively, *Fiction Fights the Civil War*, by Lawrence S. Thompson 153
Simpson, *The Cokers of Carolina*, by Margaret DesChamps Moore 154
Athearn, *William Tecumseh Sherman and the Settlement of the West*, by Raymond L. Welty . 155
McVaugh, *Edward Palmer: Plant Explorer of the American West*, by Samuel W. Geiser . 157
Frink, Jackson, and Spring, *When Grass Was King*, by Joe B. Frantz 158
Sage, *William Boyd Allison: A Study in Practical Politics*, by Jeannette P. Nichols . 159
McKelvey, *Rochester: The Quest for Quality, 1890-1925*, by Bayrd Still . . . 161
Beale, *Theodore Roosevelt and the Rise of America to World Power*, by Julius W. Pratt . 162
Gibb and Knowlton, *The Resurgent Years, 1911-1927: History of the Standard Oil Company (New Jersey)*, by Harold F. Williamson 164
Kennan, *Soviet-American Relations, 1917-1920*, Vol. I, *Russia Leaves the War*, by Fred H. Harrington 165
Sindler, *Huey Long's Louisiana: State Politics, 1920-1952*, by Charles P. Roland . 167
Dupree, *Science in the Federal Government*, by Kendall Birr 168
Hurst, *Law and the Conditions of Freedom in the Nineteenth-Century United States*, by Leonard W. Levy 170

BOOK NOTES 172

HISTORICAL NEWS AND COMMENTS 181

COMMUNICATIONS 202

DIRECTORY OF CONTRIBUTORS 204

The Great Visitation to American Democracy

By Thomas D. Clark

If no American had ever written a book about his country there would still be an appreciable body of American literature. From the moment the first European adventurer set foot on American soil this vast continent has held great fascination for travelers. They came searching for answers to vital personal questions, for freedom, and to refute accounts of earlier travelers.[1]

The first Europeans to visit America were essentially travelers, and even yet foreign archives are believed to contain untouched materials left by early observers. One of the first published accounts was that of Alvar Núñez Cabeza de Vaca. Cast ashore on the Texas coast, this wanderer crossed an enormous stretch of territory, much of it semi-arid, to reach western central Mexico. De Vaca's experiences were published in the *Relacion* in 1542.[2] In time this foundation travelogue was followed by enough descriptive books to stock a respectable library.

John Smith was the first major Englishman to approach the New World pen-in-hand. He required three sizable volumes to exhaust his personal experiences along the Atlantic seaboard.[3] In

Editor's Note: — This paper was presented as the presidential address at the Fiftieth Annual Meeting of the Mississippi Valley Historical Association in Lincoln, Nebraska, on May 2, 1957.

1 Sources referred to in this paper represent only a fractional part of the materials used in this field. The following bibliographies and collections indicate something of the voluminous travel literature pertaining to America: Frank Monaghan, *French Travellers in the United States, 1765-1932: A Bibliography* (New York, 1933); Jane L. Mesick, *The English Traveller in America, 1785-1835* (New York, 1922); Max Berger, *The British Traveller in America, 1836-1860* (New York, 1943); E. Merton Coulter, *Travels in the Confederacy: A Bibliography* (Norman, 1947); Thomas D. Clark (ed.), *Travels in the Old South: A Bibliography* (2 vols., Norman, 1956).

2 Fanny Bandelier (trans.), *The Journey of Alvar Núñez Cabeza de Vaca and His Companions from Florida to the Pacific, 1528-1536* (New York, 1905).

3 John Smith, *The General Historie of Virginia, New England, and the Summer Isles, with the Names of the Adventurers, Planters, and Governours from Their First*

these he described his involvements with natives and nature, one of which became a foundation piece of American melodrama. Chief Powhatan, Pocahontas, and Captain Smith were the original characters in the great American romantic story,[4] which in time came to include other Indian maids, cowboys, highwaymen, bankers' daughters, and schoolteachers.

A motley procession of travelers came on John Smith's heels to praise, scoff, or grumble, and to offer unsolicited advice. Among the first of these were Thomas Glover, Baron Christoph von Graffenried, George Fox, and Father Louis Hennepin.[5] They recorded impressions of European beginnings in the New World. These early journals were often fragmentary and geographically vague. Of necessity early travelers gave less attention to human factors than did subsequent accounts. There is present in them, however, the exciting element of virginal exploration. Occasionally there are limited bits of geographical information, elementary listings of plants, scales of distances, and glimpses of Indian life.[6]

Possibly the most distinct contribution made by seventeenth-century visitors was their concept of the continent's staggering challenge. Never before did transient observers have opportunity to make available fresh information to so many people anxious to begin their lives anew. Publishers welcomed travel manuscripts, and readers bought their books. So popular were early American travels that many were translated into several different languages and published in numerous editions.[7]

Beginning, An: 1548 to the Present, 1626 (London, 1632); *A True Relation of Such Occurrences and Accidents of Noate as Hath Happened in Virginia since the First Planting of that Collony, which is now Resident in the South Part Thereof, till the Last Returne from Thence* (London, 1608); and *A Map of Virginia: With a Description of the Country, the Commodities, People, Government, and Religion* (Oxford, 1612).

[4] Smith, *General Historie*, 48-49.

[5] Thomas Glover, "An Account of Virginia, Its Situation, Temperature, Productions, Inhabitants, and Their Manner of Planting and Ordering Tobacco," reprinted from the *Philosophical Transactions of the Royal Society* (Oxford, 1676); Baron Christoph von Graffenried, *Account of the Founding of New Bern*, ed. by Vincent H. Todd and Julius Goebel (Raleigh, 1920); George Fox, *A Journal or Historical Account of the Life, Travels, Sufferings, Christian Experiences and Labour of Love in the Work of the Ministry, of that Ancient, Eminent and Faithful Servant of Jesus Christ, George Fox* (London, 1694); Louis Hennepin, *Description de la Louisiane: Nouvellement Decouverté aux Sud Ouest de la Nouvelle France* (Paris, 1683).

[6] Hennepin, especially, made extensive claims of discovery. A good example of this kind of account is that of William Hilton, *A Relation of a Discovery Lately Made on the Coast of Florida* (London, 1664).

[7] Fox went through fourteen editions. Hennepin was translated into German,

No one can say with certainty what positive effects travel accounts in three centuries had upon immigration to America. They were important mediums of publicity. As travel in America increased, eighteenth-century presses enlivened the stream of journals and personal observations. Merchants, colonial agents, and shipowners advertised new outlets for trade. Scientists found abundant varieties of fauna which enlarged possibilities for study. They came to examine geological formations, collect plants and animals, measure giant trees, taste strange fruits and nuts, observe marine life, and combat reptiles and insects.[8]

As immigrants moved beyond established social bounds they were considered to have removed their souls into outer darkness. Ministers and missionaries followed them to propagate the gospel, and later to attend religious conferences.[9] They rambled between infant settlements weighted down with burdens of spiritual care, scarcely taking opportunity to observe life about them. Indian traders, James Adair among them, exchanged European goods for furs and skins, and in time pursued the children of the woods to the last fur bin on this continent.[10] Priest and trader alike recorded their adventures and these bore eloquent witness to conditions of life on the outer fringes of civilization.

At a date earlier than that assigned by some historians, foreign travelers revealed sectional influences in America. This phenomenon was noted in agricultural variations, attitudes toward land ownership and use, social behavior, conditions of climate, distances between settlements, the presence of slaves in the South, and in visual evidences of progress.[11] Added to these were differing politi-

Dutch, English, and Italian, and went through six editions. John Woolman's *Journal* (Philadelphia, 1774) was translated into several languages, and went through twenty-two editions.

8 J. F. D. Smyth, *A Tour in the United States of America* (2 vols., London, 1784), 35-64; Thomas Cooper, *Some Information Respecting America* (London, 1794), 144-77; François A. Michaux, *Travels to the Westward of the Alleghany Mountains* (London, 1805), 40-43; Gilbert Imlay, *A Topographical Description of the Western Territory of North America* (London, 1792), 203-28.

9 John Burnyeat, *The Truth Exalted in the Writings of that Eminent Servant of Christ* (London, 1691); Thomas Bray, *Apostolick Charity* (London, 1698); Samuel Bownas, *An Account of the Life, Travels, and Christian Experiences in the Work of the Ministry of Samuel Bownas* (London, 1756).

10 James Adair, *The History of the American Indians* (London, 1775), gives a personal view of the early Indian trade, including considerable information on the traders themselves.

11 The first "Grand Tour" was from Boston to New York, to Philadelphia, Baltimore, Williamsburg, Charleston, and Savannah. In time this was expanded to include

cal attitudes. Some historians might have profited in this area by more judicious reading of travel accounts. Emergence of sectional patterns was recorded by later travelers more as an intensification of regional influences than as the development of new forces in American life.[12]

Foreigners moving southward from New England before 1800 noted social and environmental changes with almost thermometric precision. In this respect they made a dependable record of varying conditions in the expanding colonial system. In the northern colonies where social life was more intensively organized there was a cohesiveness of religion, politics, and economics; but this changed as travelers approached the South. The sharp stratifications in social life in America could hardly be explained by background references to European orgins.[13]

It was in this changing phase of colonial life that travelers most readily detected the processes of Americanization. An initial question asked by scores of visitors was, "What influences in the New World produced change?" Or more accurately, what responses did immigrants make to conditions of life where resources were plentiful and there were few restrictions upon individual aspirations? Land, timber, minerals in undetermined varieties and quantities, wild life, and favorable climatic conditions helped convert Europeans into Americans.[14]

Many travelers expressed beliefs that climate lifted human spirits to new heights in America.[15] Englishmen laboring in their

many of the smaller towns. The early tour kept close to the seaboard, with the trip from Baltimore to Norfolk, Wilmington, and Charleston being made often by boat. The same thing was true of the trip from New York to Boston.

[12] Thomas Anburey, *Travels through the Interior Parts of America* (2 vols., London, 1789), 259-314.

[13] Edward A. Kendall, *Travels through the Northern Parts of the United States in the Years 1807 and 1808* (3 vols., New York, 1809); Robert Sutcliff, *Travels in Some Parts of North America, in the Years 1804, 1805, and 1806* (York, Eng., 1811), 88-130. Andrew Burnaby, *Travels through the Middle Settlements in North America, in the Years 1759 and 1760* (3rd ed., London, 1798), is a highly revealing view of sectional differences.

[14] Harry Toulmin, *The Western Country in 1793*, ed. by Marion Tinling and Godfrey Davies (San Marino, 1948), 49, 74-75; Frederick Marryat, *A Diary in America with Remarks on Its Institutions* (3 vols., London, 1839), II, 3; Smyth, *Tour in the United States*, I, 188-203; Adam Hodgson, *Letters from North America* (2 vols., London, 1824), II, 25-42.

[15] Thomas Cooper, *Some Information Respecting America* (London, 1794), 233; Charles Lyell, *A Second Visit to the United States* (2 vols., London, 1849), I, 154; Burnaby, *Travels through the Middle Settlements*, "Diary of the Weather," Appendix 5, pp. 215-51; William E. Adams, *Our American Cousins* (London, 1883), 52-59.

summer humidity or chilling winter dampness could not expend so much energy and keep their poise. The same thing was true for Europeans. In America, New Englanders came to regard work as moralistic. Poor Richard codified a simple authoritarian doctrine of the virtue of labor, and many Americans were scarcely able to distinguish between Franklin's homely proverbs and the Scriptures.

Though resources existed in variety and abundance, their exploitation required great physical exertion. To rob forest and land of their riches and to adapt civilization to primitive conditions required inexhaustible human vigor and persistence. Possibly at no other time in history did so many people by their own effort shed so quickly the yoke of peasantry and serfdom to become landowners and tradesmen. Constantly travelers attempted to ascertain the stages in this evolutionary process. Frequently visitors saw immigrant families making congenial responses to American environment. Back of them in Europe might be generations of ancestors subjected to economic poverty, if not serfdom. In America they faced, said the travelers, a more certain future. It was not so much evidence of economic progress which interested observers as expressions of new social attitudes and anticipations. American optimism often made people appear bumptious if not foolish. Knowing immigrant backgrounds, travelers jumped to the conclusion that such a bubbling spirit of optimism was nothing more than gross immaturity.[16]

Aside from physical advantages, some eighteenth-century travelers believed Americans began their national existence at the proper moment to profit from the industrial revolution. New machines and factories in England and Europe supplied cheap goods on this side of the Atlantic.[17] Others explained American progress by the fact that colonials had none of Europe's historic handicaps. No state church, feudal aristocracy, mercantile monopoly, or ancient political forms needlessly sapped human energy in emotional campaigns for reform.[18]

Extended international rivalries in mid-eighteenth century

16 Captain Marryat's Diary was a good example of this point of view. So were Frances M. Trollope, *Domestic Manners of the Americans* (2 vols., London, 1832), and Thomas H. Hamilton, *Men and Manners in America* (2 vols., Philadelphia, 1833).

17 An analysis of colonial trade to indicate this fact appears in Burnaby, *Travels through the Middle Settlements*, reprint of 3rd ed. (New York, 1904), 164-88.

18 Alexander Mackay, *The Western World: or, Travels in the United States in 1846-47* (2 vols., Philadelphia, 1849), I, 243-60.

brought many visitors to America. Frenchmen wandered over their empire from Gulf to Lakes, recording in true Gallic style long historical and statistical accounts which gave little heed to contemporary details. Indians appeared in their accounts as noble men of the forest dressed like Roman senators. Even a voluptuous maiden tied to the stake was portrayed as a classic Venus of full stature, gracefully surrendering life before a gladiatorial torchbearer.[19] If Frenchmen were sometimes defective observers of the contemporary social scene, they did leave good descriptions of natural conditions.

Hardly had Britain won the power struggle against France before travelers noted a rising conflict between colonials and the Crown. More thoughtful travelers endeavored to determine sources of this friction. Though this record was an uneven one, many observers appreciated the changes which reflected an inevitable course of empire history. Others plodded on, obstinately refusing to understand what they saw and heard. In their descriptions of natural and social conditions, in collecting an appreciable amount of statistical data, and in noting colonial political views, the travelers created a creditable body of information. British military and political officials had at their command in 1775 a body of strategically significant material which was indispensable in planning American campaigns. Ignoring this information was possibly one of the Crown's most serious blunders in the American Revolution.

In the latter half of the eighteenth century travelers discovered new American personalities. Washington, Jefferson, Adams, Franklin, Hamilton, and others attracted attention. Tom Paine was a marked man, not so much because of his radical writings as for his unorthodox religious views. Unfriendly Englishmen constantly arrived before his door to irritate him and to record their preconceived impressions.[20]

Foreigners, up to 1850, generally believed American maturity had to be measured on the fallacious time scale of ancient Europe. This partly accounted for an intense interest in Indian culture. Travelers were curious about the ancient origins of the Indians. Somewhere, they believed, there must be stones which held clues to the riddle of human existence in America. Burial mounds and monu-

[19] Pierre J. B. Nougaret, *Beautés de l'Histoire des Etats-Unis de l'Amérique Septentrionale* (Paris, 1817), 132.

[20] John Melish, *Travels through the United States of America in the Years 1806 and 1807, and 1809, 1810, and 1811* (2 vols., Philadelphia, 1815), I, 129-31.

ments, ceremonial pillars, and confused legend hinted at antiquity. This somewhat explains interest in strange geological formations, stones of unusual conformations, and landmarks which might indicate ancient associations. Even the hackneyed Welsh Indian legend stimulated more than its rightful share of speculation.[21]

Thoughtful visitors found it difficult to conceive of a permanent and stable human institutional system without an aged foundation. Visitors directly from Europe failed to understand that American thinking and society, even with slavery, had by-passed feudalism. "As if by special order of providence," wrote one traveler, "mankind are invited into the most distant regions of the country by the advantages of soil and climate, nowhere exceeded in the world. Sprung from the only country, which at the period of settlement of America, possessed anything like a rational freedom, the principles of the *popular branch* of the British Constitution came into practical operation unalloyed by the feudal system." [22]

Early in the nineteenth century choleric Captain Thomas Hamilton cared not about America's past; his concern was for its present. To him Americans were imitative and incapable of escaping the thraldom of the English language and literature. Their optimism and energy might breach the barriers of nature, but intellectually they remained captive to an Old World past. There were no native examples of excellence to which they could appeal although they were surrounded by an original world of untried images. Still they imitated the experiences of a people who denied them praise for skillful imitation.[23]

Visitors were too often concerned with the superficialities of travel and their own preconceptions to comprehend the fundamental structure of American society. Many expected to find British and European social and political systems planted in a fresh environment without change. Failure to plumb the depths of adaptability of the people themselves led to fundamental misunderstandings of the basic strengths of American civilization. Nevertheless, by the outbreak of the American Revolution it was clear to many travelers that few traditional ties obscured future anticipations.

Travelers emphasized the belief that Americans after 1776 were

21 Adair, *History of the American Indians,* 16-230; Kendall, *Travels through the Northern Parts of the United States,* I, 243-49.

22 Melish, *Travels through the United States,* I, Preface, iv.

23 Hamilton, *Men and Manners in America,* II, 49.

committed to a doctrine of equality. Implications of the Declaration of Independence provoked extensive comment on conditions of American society. Doubtless travelers approached the United States with idyllic notions of its economic, social, and political conditions. If the Declaration of Independence set men free, in what way had they facilitated their freedom? How had they applied the fundamental doctrine of leveling equality? Under the subsequent Bill of Rights, how had they further ordered their institutions? American experiences in these areas gravely concerned visitors. They tried to analyze the processes of government at all levels. British travelers were able to use simple descriptions of variations in the American system, but French and German observers made broad structural analyses. Local government, from the New England town meeting to the loosely administered southern county, including state legislatures, were, for many, political anomalies.

Britishers never fully comprehended the detailed workings of the federal system so far as it related to state legislative processes. State governments were largely ignored, or were regarded as more primitive and therefore more easily corrupted. Even Alexis de Tocqueville believed that "the chief cause of superiority of the Federal Constitution lay in the character of the legislators who composed it," and there was a low opinion of state legislators. Some travelers described the national government as though they had just made an original political discovery.[24]

Judgments of American democracy were as varied as were individual observers and the time in which they made their observations. With practical unanimity travelers thought Congress represented in kind the rabble of the people. Critics who sat in the House gallery trying to understand what was happening on the floor were hopelessly confused. Before them was an unruly, tobacco-chewing, hat-wearing, desk-slapping, mannerless collection of country bumpkins who sat with their feet propped atop their desks desecrating the dignities and liberties of the people. The system of electing these representatives and their short tenure of office were blamed for lack of statesmanship. The people were thought incapable of making intelligent choices of congressmen. A visiting member of Parliament suggested that there was too much floor

[24] Alexis de Tocqueville, *Democracy in America,* trans. by Henry Reeve (2 vols., New York, 1889).

space in the House to keep order. Remove the desks and scurrying pages, crowd the members together on long benches and they would have to pay attention to debates.[25]

There were few "tall sycamores" among the soiled-shirt friends of the people in Congress before 1860, believed the travelers. Henry Clay, John C. Calhoun, and a few others enjoyed the favor of the visitors. They generally expressed friendly attitudes toward those congressmen whom they met in Washington boarding houses, but others they believed unstatesmanlike.[26]

Often the House gallery was crowded by tittering women, assembled, it seemed, to irritate serious foreigners who wished to understand American democracy. In this light the House was frequently presented as an aimless, confused body which obscured the purposes of deliberative government. Travelers little understood the work of committees and conferences, or pork barrel legislation, to say nothing of the subtle sectional interests which shaped the course of legislation.

The United States Senate presented sharp contrast to the seeming disorder and confusion of the House. Its proceedings were calm and orderly except when some orator pounded his knuckles bloody in spread-eagle debate. Generally senators maintained a dignified decorum, their dress bore less the stamp of hinterland byways and hedges, and members kept their feet on the floor. Debates were more scholarly, and statesmanship was more evident. Universally, travelers believed that senators were superior to representatives because of their mode of election and tenure of office.[27]

The administrative and judicial branches of the government likewise came under visitorial scrutiny. No respectable traveler could publish his book until he had sat before the robed but wigless judges of the Supreme Court, visited with cabinet members, and had grasped the hand of the President.

George Washington deserves more credit than he has received in textbooks and biographies for being a patient host. He was the

[25] H. Hussey Vivian, *Notes of a Tour in America* (London, 1878), 205.

[26] Joseph Gurney, *A Journey in North America* (Norwich, 1841), 79-84; Mackay, *Western World*, I, 177-96; Tyrone Power, *Impressions of America* (2 vols., London, 1836), I, 260-83; Charles A. Murray, *Travels in North America* (2 vols., London, 1839), I, 130-39.

[27] Mackay, *Western World*, I, 189-94; Vivian, *Notes of a Tour in America*, 203-205; Hamilton, *Men and Manners in America*, II, 18-19; [Anon.], *Across the Atlantic* (London, 1851), 163-74.

best-known American of his day, and to Englishmen, especially, he symbolized transplanted British aristocratic dignity. Classically he was the Cincinnatus of freedom and independence. Many travelers regarded him as a personal symbol of world freedom. As a result of this exalted esteem, the Master of Mount Vernon endured insufferable boredom from idolizing visitors. They pursued him in New York and Philadelphia, and followed him into retirement to Mount Vernon. It seems that the Washington family was scarcely ever without traveler under roof and at table. After Washington's death, travelers visited his family, and stood before his tomb in silent worship. They fussed because the old tomb was allowed to fall into decay, and they criticized the new one for lack of aesthetic taste. Washington's popularity with the foreign traveler is one of the curiosities of American history. He could hardly be called an expansive host, and certainly he was an indifferent conversationalist.[28]

Rivaling George Washington as host was Thomas Jefferson. Monticello, like Mount Vernon, became a touchstone for foreigners. Every liberal-minded traveler who reached America with a glimmer of a democratic idea hastened to Virginia to discuss it with the author of the Declaration of Independence. If Jefferson had collected tavern rates for his hospitality he would have died a wealthier man.[29]

From George Washington to Dwight D. Eisenhower foreigners have lingered in Washington hoping to get a glimpse of the President, an invitation to a public reception, and to savor republican society. Before the President came under the solicitous watch care of the Secret Service it was astonishingly easy to visit with him. All a traveler had to do was ring the White House doorbell, and a butler or maid ushered him into a parlor. The President came out to greet his guest like any friendly householder. One traveler admitted to Jefferson that frankly he had come by to see what he looked like. Lady Emmeline Stuart Wortley and her young daughter called on General Zachary Taylor and spent an hour engaged in folksy conversation with him. When they were ready to go, the bow-legged old man accompanied them to their carriage lamenting that he too was not going to his Mississippi plantation.[30]

28 Benjamin H. Latrobe, Manuscript Journal, quoted by Talbot Hamlin, *Benjamin Henry Latrobe* (New York, 1955), 76-79.

29 Hodgson, *Letters from North America*, I, 313-20.

30 Emmeline Stuart Wortley, *Travels in the United States* (New York, 1851), 86-87.

Sometimes cabinet meetings were interrupted so the President could greet a visitor. Foreigners were ever amazed that the President of the United States dressed plainly, rode his horse about the countryside either alone or accompanied by a servant or a cabinet member, sat in a commoner's pew in church, and passed along the streets being greeted like other citizens.[31] Earlier presidential receptions attracted much attention because of their simplicity and cordiality. There were no glittering uniforms except those worn by stray naval and military officials, little pomp, no ranking of guests, and few other formalities to be observed abroad. Even the common people crowded into receptions and behaved like neighbors. Perhaps no major traveler made an adverse personal comment about a president on whom he called.[32]

If official Washington was subjected to constant inspection, so was physical Washington. Earlier every mudhole in Pennsylvania Avenue harbored a foreigner struggling across the "magnificent distances." Government buildings were examined and criticized — not one of them escaping critical comment. The Capitol made a reasonably favorable impression, though to some it seemed too imitative for a republican nation. One visitor believed the half-finished Washington Monument should be crushed into rubble to fill the chuckholes in Pennsylvania Avenue before it was too late to help either.[33]

Most intelligent travelers realized that heartland America lay beyond the confines of New York and Washington. The behavior of federal officials, the physical appearance of Washington, and urban social strivings were manifestations only of the democratic system — not the system itself. One had to visit the hinterland to judge the application of principles enunciated in the Declaration of Independence and the Bill of Rights. Almost unanimously, foreigners were unable to reconcile the existence of slavery among a people who made such positive expressions of freedom. Attitudes, if not facts, concerning slavery can be summarized. The Union

31 Power, *Impressions of America*, I, 277-81; Hodgson, *Letters from North America*, I, 69-76; James Silk Buckingham, *America, Historical, Statistic, and Descriptive* (3 vols., London, 1841), I, 287-90.

32 Basil Hall, *Travels in North America in the Years 1827-1828* (3 vols., Edinburgh, 1830), III, 1-33; Gurney, *Journey in North America*, 391-92; Power, *Impressions of America*, I, 200-83; Hector Bolitho, *Haywire: An American Travel Diary* (New York, 1939), 158-61.

33 William H. Charlton, *Four Months in North America* (Hexam, Eng., 1873), 44.

could not remain suspended between the extremes of slavery and freedom. Slavery contained the fatal germ of dissolution, and if the Republic was to survive it would have to purge itself of the germ.[34]

Long before James D. B. De Bow and Hinton Rowan Helper compared statistically progress and welfare between slave and free states, foreign travelers noted sectional differences. To them the institution of slavery clogged the South, a fact noted almost instantly upon entry to the region. Characteristically one traveler noted: "The South, I feel sure, if she would maintain her place in the race of nations, must modify her social system; she cannot advance with the clog of slavery at her foot. And this I say in no unkindly spirit, but rather with the most heartfelt wishes for her prosperity and perfect appreciation of the difficulties of her position. Still the fact is there, stern and immovable — admitted too, by the South in her secret heart, that slavery is a curse to the land." [35]

The South has ever been on the "Grand Tour." Nearly every major traveler arriving before 1860 visited the region. They visited the great plantations, entered into conversations with masters and slaves, heard attacks upon abolitionism, examined instruments of punishment, attended slave religious services, and saw families torn apart in auction sales.[36] At the same time they accepted the comfortable hospitalities offered in handsome plantation houses by black hands; and, sometimes, in the enjoyment of these physical comforts they became confused as to their moral reactions. One visitor observed after a pleasant visit in low-country South Carolina that "These two days' experience have not taught me to love slavery, though I am impressed more than ever with the practical difficulty of the subject." [37]

As important as is the voluminous detail pertaining to slavery in

[34] Michel Chevalier, *Lettres sur l'Amérique du Nord* (2 vols., Brussels, 1837), I, 272-74; Hall, *Travels in North America*, III, 171-72; Alexander Marjoribanks, *Travels in South and North America* (London, 1853); James Stirling, *Letters from the Slave States* (London, 1857), 302-33; William G. Bek (trans.), *Gottfried Duden's "Report," 1824-1827* ([Columbia, Mo.], 1919; reprinted from *Missouri Historical Review*, Vols. XII-XIII), 71-75; Fredrika Bremer, *The Homes of the New World*, trans. by Mary Howitt (New York, 1853), 527-45.

[35] Stirling, *Letters from the Slave States*, 236.

[36] Gurney, *Journey in North America*, 376-77; Marjoribanks, *Travels in South and North America*, 341-45.

[37] William Ferguson, *America by River and Rail* (London, 1856), 139.

travel accounts, the real significance of this material is to be found in the general impressions which must have been made upon readers. Few immigrants wishing to escape social and economic problems of their homelands would be attracted southward after reading travel comments upon slavery. In the minds of travelers, slavery came nearer reproducing serfdom than did any other American institution. The political influence of southern slaveowners closely paralleled that of privileged classes in Europe.

Few travelers believed that slavery and its accompanying race problem could be solved by either colonization or narrow legislation. The Negro, like the Germans, Irishmen, and Scandinavians, was in America to stay. Once he was freed, placing him in democratic society would be a major problem. The Civil War did not disrupt the "Grand Tour," the South was of greater interest than ever. Reconstruction with its chaotic economic and social conditions, race problems, and political disorganization attracted traveler attention.

Later, in the twentieth century, fresh crops of travelers came South to see tenant farmers, Jeter Lesters, and Stribling and Faulkner characters on their home grounds. Many came to reconstruct for themselves the bleak romance of *Gone with the Wind.* After 1930 the Tennessee Valley Authority became host to thousands of foreign visitors, many of whom sought information to correct problems in their homelands. They wished to know how a great river's flood was controlled, how land and human beings were reclaimed, and to study the production of tremendous hydro-electric power.[38]

Foreign service personnel in India, Pakistan, Indonesia, and Thailand have faced knotty problems in the last decade. They have been forced to plan American tours for visitors with full knowledge of the dangers of their becoming involved in unfortunate race incidents. Not even subtle suggestions that Hindus wear turbans have reduced their anxieties. The prospective visitor was "Grand Tour" conscious, and he wanted to see those parts of America about which he had read, and description of the southern scene was an important part of travel literature. Thus the information

[38] There are hundreds of these books. Some of them are: Odd Hølaas, *Nederst ved Bardet* (Oslo, 1936); Ilya Ilf and Eugene Petrov, *Amérique sans Etages* (Paris, 1946); Morgan P. Price, *America after Sixty Years* (London, 1936); Sudhindra Bose, *Fifteen Years in America* (Calcutta, 1920); Ursula Branston, *Let the Band Play "Dixie"* (London, 1940); Jean Carn, *Villes et Paysages d'Amérique* (Paris, 1937); André Demaison, *Terre d'Amérique* (Paris, 1939).

services can only await the inevitable stream of letters to families and newspapers, and the travel books describing life in the United States.

On the reverse side of the ledger was the important visitation to the post-Civil War cities. Primarily, foreign visitors were city-conditioned, and most of them were better oriented to compare urban growth with that in their own countries than to appraise conditions in rural America. New York, Boston, Philadelphia, Charleston, Cincinnati, Louisville, St. Louis, and San Francisco were major stopping places. Generally travelers found older seaboard urban centers to be modified European cities. Nineteenth-century New Orleans was an exception. To Frenchmen it was a pallid imitation of La Havre and Paris combined, but for more puritanical Englishmen it was a dumping ground for the dregs of civilization. They failed to find social direction or culture beyond that of its bagnios.[39]

Chicago symbolized for travelers raw, expanding America. To visitors it was different from other large cities. Here was the heartland of trade and transportation, it was even a great international trade center. The rawness of Chicago's rapidly changing climate, its sprawling position alongside Lake Michigan, its constant disorder of expansion and change, and its frantic bustle baffled travelers. To many, like pompous Bishop S. Reynolds Hole, it was truly "murky-grimy-choky Chicago." The Bishop believed it unfortunate that Lake Michigan did not have the seasonal characteristics of the Nile.[40] Abbé Felix Klein repeated the story of the man from the Loop, who, upon arriving in the next world, joyously exclaimed that "Heaven is no different from Chicago! 'Excuse me,' said a doleful bystander, 'You are not in Heaven'."[41] There were others who felt that Mrs. O'Leary's legendary cow deserved permanent tenure.

Despite wry, and often unfair, observations about Chicago, it was here that travelers felt most distinctly the heart throb of American industry. They felt it in towering grain elevators, amidst mazes of rails, on the frantic grain exchange, and in the stockyards and

[39] Hodgson, *Letters from North America*, I, 151-81; M. Perrin du Lac, *Travels through the Two Louisianas* (London, 1807), 87-101; Marjoribanks, *Travels in South and North America*, 356-58; Buckingham, *America*, II, 202.

[40] S. Reynolds Hole, *A Little Tour in America* (London, 1895), 249.

[41] Felix Klein, *America of Tomorrow* (Chicago, 1911), 67.

packing houses. The spirit of progress was evident in hotel lobbies and club rooms, and in the parlors of merchant princes, railway barons, and packing-house tycoons.[42] High on the list of places to see were the stockyards and packing houses. Travelers in continuous procession stood in awe and watched streams of pigs being hoisted to slaughter. They were transfixed by executioners who slashed throats with murderous blades, or they watched killers with fiendish grins on their faces whetting their blades to razor keenness.[43] The "jungle" was a fierce place where bloodthirsty men might run amuck and carry their killing to people on the streets. No wonder those who accumulated fortunes from pigs and range steers had to wait a generation to be accepted into "bluebook" society.

After listening to discussions of Chicago's cultural advances in 1910, a visitor observed that despite the influence of President William R. Harper, "dilettantism in Chicago seems out of place, and somehow suggests one's cab driver turning from his box to tell what Ruskin has to say about sunsets, or a laundress turning from her washtub to discourse on the chemistry of soap bubbles. . . . Pork not Plato has made Chicago, and Chicago people have not so far arrived at that stage of culture at which they can feel justified in seriously changing their allegiances." [44] Seven years later Sir Frederick E. Smith charged into Chicago on a World War I propaganda mission to exclaim over the city's cultural attainments. His descriptions of the city itself were in marked contrast to those of other travelers who looked upon it as an exciting place with its fine public buildings, homes, museums, and public parks.[45]

The American city presented to travelers interesting studies in American life. Unlike those of the Old World those in America were without ancient pasts and had few established landmarks. There were few legends about them beyond the fact that they had mushroomed about crossroads stores and stagecoach taverns, at steamboat landings and railway sidings, or at strategic points on bays and lakes. Rows of buildings standing today would be crushed into rubble tomorrow to permit expansion and progress.

42 Adams, *Our American Cousins*, 34-47; Hamil Grant, *Two Sides of the Atlantic* (London, 1917), 96; Hole, *Little Tour in America*, 257-60; Sisly Huddleston, *What's Right with America* (Philadelphia, 1930), 172-85.

43 Adams, *Our American Cousins*, 47-48.

44 Grant, *Two Sides of the Atlantic*, 96.

45 Frederick E. Smith (Lord Birkenhead), *My American Visit* (London, 1918).

Travelers were impressed by frame houses, and often they saw them being moved through the streets.[46] To them this meant that America's social and economic forms were unsettled and impermanent.

There were few monuments comparable to those which adorned ancient European cities; there was no room for them, and even those in existence blocked progress. It was not the past that appealed to modern American city-dwellers but bigness, efficiency, and future prospects. City populations reflected the effects of immigration. In the 1890's there were more populous Irish cities in America than in Ireland, little Italies in New York and Boston rivaled Rome and Florence, and Berlins, Munichs, and Viennas existed in Cincinnati, Louisville, St. Louis, and Milwaukee, while little Chinas flourished in San Francisco and New York. The American city had not succeeded in these later years in assimilating its immigrant populations.[47]

To travelers it seemed that democratic principles had broken down in the big cities. They saw unabsorbed masses of poor, ignorant, and manageable immigrants as means for political corruption. Briefly the cities were efficient places where commercialism flourished. Spiritually and politically they were degenerate places, devoid of the simple moral standards of humanity considered so necessary to survival of a democratic civilization.[48] Though they were seats of fine art galleries, museums, libraries, universities, and theaters, cities still lacked warmth of souls and depth of humanity.

Closely paralleling the rise of towns and cities was the growth of the newspaper press. Once the printing press appeared in America, travelers never ceased to be interested in the multiplicity of journals. They never understood fully the role of the weekly paper, the great passion of Americans for getting their names in print, or political editorials. Even more baffling was the country editor's florid style, and his failure to distinguish between casual bits of news and that of major importance.[49] The yeomen of the printer's

[46] Timothy Dwight, *Travels in New England and New York* (4 vols., London, 1823), I, 448-57, II, 444-49; Hole, *Little Tour in America*, 175-92, 249.

[47] Adams, *Our American Cousins*, 208; Hugo Münsterberg, *The Americans*, trans. by Edwin B. Holt (New York, 1904), 115-84. An economic summary of America which bears upon American population is to be found in Rudolf H. Meyer, *Ursachen der Amerikanischen Concurrenz* (Berlin, 1883), 720-815.

[48] Philip Burne-Jones, *Dollars and Diplomacy* (New York, 1903), 43-45; Peter Neilson, *Recollections of Six Years Residence in the United States of America* (Glasgow, 1830), 25; Adams, *Our American Cousins*, 34-38.

[49] Francis J. Grund, *The Americans in Their Moral, Social, and Political Rela-*

stool incurred almost as much ridicule for their reckless use of fact and language as did James Gordon Bennett, William Randolph Hearst, and Colonel Robert McCormick.

Foreigners found the American dailies mixtures of unadorned commercialism and gossipy news reporting, with some good editorial writing. Extravagant advertising seemed incompatible with the idea that newspapers were organs of opinion. Newspaper jingoism and expansionism provoked many a foreigner into believing that the United States was at heart an imperialistic nation. In the area of foreign news, however, much of the press seemed extremely provincial and nationalistic.[50]

Many travelers failed to discover a consistency in American newspapers. T. S. Hudson was impressed by this when he read in one column of a New York paper that Wendell Phillips had made the eagle scream in a Fourth of July oration by proclaiming equality the greatest blessing that God had bestowed upon America: "Our fathers announced this sublime, and, as it seemed, the foolhardy declaration, that God intended all men to be free and equal — *all* men, without restriction, without limit." In a parallel column a story said a colored colonel was refused a room in the Revere Hotel in Boston, and that a Negro preacher was not allowed to eat dinner at a public table on a Hudson River steamboat.[51]

The irresponsible tabloid with its gossipy and mischievous reporting was, it seemed to travelers, a misuse of the freedom of the press. Like the cities in which they were published, papers sometimes seem to lack integrity. Reporters corrupted the language, mocked good taste, and mistook license for freedom. But travelers marveled at the mechanical proficiency of American newspaper plants.[52]

If travelers were baffled at times by American newspapers, the same thing was true of education. Eighteenth-century visitors gained favorable impressions of American educational beginnings.

tions (2 vols. in one, Boston, 1837), 121-23; James Boardman, *America and the Americans* (London, 1833), 75-79.

50 Kendall, *Travels through Northern Parts of the United States*, I, 146-48; Adams, *Our American Cousins*, 115-20; Grant, *Two Sides of the Atlantic*, 20-85; A. Maurice Low, *America at Home* (London, 1905), 200-18; Huddleston, *What's Right with America*, 186-92.

51 T. S. Hudson, *A Scamper through America* (London, 1882), 214-15.

52 Hole, *Little Tour in America*, 175-92; Price Collier, *America and the Americans from a French Point of View* (New York, 1897), 267-85; Grund, *The Americans*, 112-23; Anthony Jenkinson, *America Came My Way* (London, 1936), 220-28.

In later years, however, there was more uncertainty as to the standards of universal education. As foreigners began comparing American universities after 1870 with those abroad there was further doubt. There was a general feeling that American youths matured earlier and were more able to apply training, but that those of England and Europe were more soundly and liberally educated.[53]

Many twentieth-century travelers were professors and special lecturers who visited universities and colleges or attended educational conferences. To them American educational objectives seemed as vague as party politics. The preciseness with which education was administered was beyond their comprehension. For instance, the idea of constant examination of students in certain fields of learning was abhorrent. How could a student learn to appreciate literature if he were forever preparing for irrelevant examinations?[54]

In broader areas of social growth other American institutions attracted the travelers' attention. There seems to have prevailed some notion among the travelers that a democratic society would have only a limited crime problem. To more sensible observers the question was one of treatment of criminals. Large numbers of them inspected jails and penitentiaries. Four major prisons might be considered as on the early "Grand Tour"; these were Auburn, Charlestown, Sing Sing, and Philadelphia. The various systems of discipline were appraised for their effectiveness. The Swedish traveler, Frihere Axel Klinkowström, like many of his fellows, expressed the belief that American prisoners were held for security reasons rather than for punishment.[55]

Klinkowström was pleased on his approach to Sing Sing. The prisoner at the gate, he said: "Is not met with the insidious glances from the guards who secretly enjoy getting a new inmate on whom they can practice their sadism. He does not hear the rattle of chains; he does not see filth and despair; and his first view of the prison is not as horrifying as with us. In the American prisons the criminal has hope that his sentence will be shortened for good be-

[53] Lawrence P. Jacks, *My American Friends* (New York, 1933), 164-65; Francis Lieber, *The Stranger in America* (2 vols., London, 1835), I, 18.

[54] This point of view has been expressed many times on the lecture platform. For a specific reference see Jacks, *My American Friends*, 158-72; Huddleston, *What's Right with America*, 108-14.

[55] Franklin D. Scott (trans. and ed.), *Baron Klinkowström's America, 1818-1820* (Evanston, 1952), 100-101; Buckingham, *America*, II, 50-61.

havior."[56] Hopes for redemption of American prisoners rested upon finding means by which men might be disciplined without the sadism of lash and club. In Auburn discipline was by rule of silence, while at Philadelphia prisoners were confined to solitary cells.

Travelers often lacked common sense and honesty, and their observations were narrow and malicious. A small army of special pleaders aired their prejudices and irritations. Many of these saw everything which confirmed their preconceptions. Some visitors brought with them to America stereotypes which they nourished throughout their visits, and went home with them still intact. Often petty human annoyances became more important than the maturity of society. Frequently travelers were people of routine habits who forgot that proscriptive routine is the most provincial of human characteristics. Thus it was natural that some travelers stepped out of their environments expecting everybody to conform with their eccentric personal wishes. When an American tavern maid, waiter, stage coach driver, or other service person reacted independently, they impudently offered an affront to an older social order.[57] Few travelers who viewed functional American democracy failed to be startled at the rugged independence of the people. They seemed unaware that social democracy had really broken academic constrictions to become a common assumption.

Much of the material in large numbers of travel accounts is highly valid. Some accounts are classics in kind.[58] Many an observant traveler was able to distinguish American characteristics in those areas where natives were incapable of observing them. Often in viewing casual everyday behavior the real differences in American life were revealed. Foreigners seem to have witnessed the occurrence of every dramatic event in our history. They saw battles in progress, attended major political meetings, witnessed tragedies of all sorts, saw presidents inaugurated, met presidential funeral processions in streets, plowed through Patent Office records informing themselves about American inventiveness.[59] They published an

[56] *Klinkowström's America*, 100-101.

[57] Lieber, *Stranger in America*, I, 88; Grund, *The Americans*, 403; Adams, *My American Cousins*, 97, 102-103; Neilson, *Recollections*, 28, 154-55, 167.

[58] Among these there are those by Mackay, Hodgson, Tocqueville, Bremer, Lyell, Michaux, Duden, Grund, Marryat, and Hall, previously cited.

[59] William Priest, *Travels in the United States of America* (London, 1802), 83, 87; Mackay, *Western World*, I, 96; Ramon de la Sagra, *Cinq Mois aux Etats-Unis de l'Amérique du Nord*, trans. by René Baisas (Paris, 1837), 138-57.

astonishing volume of factual detail. For instance, Captain Thomas Anburey said that on August 4, 1779, he saw a cotton gin in operation on the Jones plantation near Charlottesville, Virginia. The machine described is considered even today to be more efficient than Whitney's.[60]

The mere fact that travelers spent much time on the road enabled them to see what went on in public. They traveled in every way imaginable and were subjected to unusual experiences at almost every turn of the road. They jostled both shoulders and bed sheets with a milling, restless public. They wandered through hotel lobbies and steamboat decks, crowded up to tavern bars, snatched at food and ice water *table d'hote*, and listened to constant conversation and gossip. Strolling up and down dust-laden streets or churning mud on back-country trails, they saw a vigorous America coming of age. They sensed people on the move; nothing in the new Republic was static; Americans were wedded to the future.

A good amount of detail quoted by travelers is dependable. Fortunately for historians the travelers rendered considerable critical judgment of others' books in justifying the publication of their own. At the same time much travel material is worthless trash.[61] Historians have no business using travel accounts unless they have more gumption than the traveler, plus judgment and parallel sources enough to validate both fact and probability. Certainly they should have fewer biases and nationalistic tendencies than the travelers. Every travel source must be held accountable for its own dependability, and scholars need to understand both the author's background and the conditions under which he traveled.

The basic importance of the travel account does not lie entirely within the confines of factual reporting, but rather in the larger area of concepts of America abroad. Few people in western Europe were unfamiliar with travelers' views of America. The truth of this is substantiated by simple collation of this material, a task which yet awaits completion. American stereotypes created by Englishmen often became those of other countries. Since they maintained the same institutional patterns and subscribed basically to the same

[60] Anburey, *Travels through the Interior Parts of America*, I, 425.

[61] Some good examples of the more dependable books are those by Hodgson, Kendall, Grund, Neilson, Michaux, Bremer, Lieber, Mackay, and William Archer, *Through Afro-America* (London, 1910).

political principles, it was assumed that their descriptions were trustworthy.

Descriptions of institutions often revealed gross misunderstandings of America by travelers. The same thing was true when they discussed personal characteristics of the people. Foreign stereotypes of Americans were weird and fugitive things. They were represented as having an ephemeral and contradictory character. Collectively they were polite and rude; generous, hospitable, and penurious; they were modest and boastful; tobacco-chewers all; and they swore loudly, but were remarkable for swearing moderately. They drank heavily but temperately; they were intensively religious without religious form. They thrived on ice water, bolted their food, were ignorant and gracious, yet hostile to foreigners, fond of muddy roads, swollen streams, bedbugs, and steamboat disasters. They willingly endangered their lives in competition, were always in a hurry, yet somehow spent long hours patiently answering foreigners' questions. Americans always sought the main chance, but were neighborly; they were intimately personal, even in the use of communal hairbrushes and combs, were rampant nationalists, expansionists, and isolationists who sought a world market for their products.

Foreigners were never able to cast American character in a rigid mold. The internationally accepted "Brother Jonathan" caricature failed them when they viewed Yankee society in the flesh.[62] Yankees did not all talk with rasping nasal twangs, have hawksbill noses, whittle on sticks, nor appear with outstretched hand to snatch the last "almighty dollar." Brother Jonathan was nothing more than a piece of European stage property. There was no such thing as a single personal type or stratum of American society. Americans spoke with their own peculiar accents, making such modifications and adaptations as they pleased. Some retained old English speech forms while others were influenced by those of non-English-speaking immigrants. Travelers often found the American personality, so far as it seemed English, only a façade. Actually Americans reflected their diverse national origins.[63]

62 Mackay, *Western World*, I, 247; Paul Blouëtt, *Jonathan and His Continent* (New York, 1889), 1-16; Hudson, *Scamper through America*, 55; Hugo Playfair, *Brother Jonathan and His Continent* (3 vols., London, 1844). The contents of these three volumes are, in fact, stereotype descriptions of Americans.

63 Collier, *America and the Americans*, 136-68; Grund, *The Americans*, 13-30; Low,

In the latter part of the nineteenth century when excitement over the Civil War had abated and the last foreigner had visited the battlefields to sigh over the bloody struggle,[64] travelers renewed their search for *homo Americana.* Their hunting grounds were changed. The "Brother Jonathan" cliché was abandoned in favor of those of industrial America. The paunchy capitalist with the dollar-mark vest, the diamond stickpin, plug hat, and oversized cigar was the new stereotype. His consort was the bejeweled fur-bearing Mrs. Orelië. These minions of frenzied capitalism haunted exclusive clubs, expensive restaurants, Pullman cars, and hotel lobbies chasing dollars. Bloated robber barons went abroad to boast of their material accomplishments and to sniff at inefficient and profitless European antiquity. Daughters of this new era ceased to be demure members of domesticated families and became décoletté club women who sinned without vice, and were good, if good at all, by the grace of God.[65]

Often late nineteenth and twentieth century travelers found themselves imprisoned aboard Pullman cars with noisy throngs of businessmen, or plumed knights of fraternal orders, bound for conventions.[66] They were pressed into hotel lobbies amidst tipsy, belabeled delegates who were assembled to discuss selling such diverse articles as sewing machines, egg-laying mash, and ladies' foundation garments. To foreigners it seemed more likely they had come to slip the marriage halter and escape small town social taboos.[67] Solid old rural types described by earlier travelers had disappeared with the Indians. Few if any backwoodsmen spat on the feet of sophisticated Pullman travelers, and farmers came in sight only as fixtures on the landscape that whizzed by train windows.

As for the traveler himself, he too had changed. Few honest-to-goodness old line "bellyachers" plodded along muddy roads, complained about sleeping with strange snoring natives, or ate at common tables. Many modern visitors were important governmental officials, distinguished literary and theatrical personalities, political

America at Home, 219-28; André Siegfried, *America Comes of Age,* trans. by H. H. and Doris Hemming (New York, 1927), 3-32.

64 William H. Dixon, *New America* (2 vols., London, 1867), 264-369.

65 Low, *America at Home,* 70-83; Emily Faithfull, *Three Visits to America* (New York, 1884), 336-54; Huddleston, *What's Right with America,* 214-19.

66 Hudson, *Scamper through America,* 210.

67 Bolitho, *Haywire,* 148-51.

scientists, ministers, and merchants. Many came bearing golden messages of "what was really happening over there." [68] They were darlings of women's literary and culture clubs all the way from Brooklyn Navy Pier to the Golden Gate, and from the foot of Canal Street to the high school auditorium in Green Bay. These minions of culture dashed across country obeying booking agent commands with the docility of trained seals. They fattened lean purses on fees for indifferent lectures, and confirmed their notions as to what was wrong with overfed and overheated America.

Of all the books written by the thousands of travelers many of those by the supercilious "kept" men of the twentieth-century lecture bureaus were the trashiest. Sir Phillip Gibbs stumbled over the country, in what one reviewer said appeared to be a constant state of intoxication, grabbing frantically at names and bits of misinformation to rush home and publish his non-sensical *America Speaks*.[69] Hector Bolitho dashed about in pursuit of lecture funds and a decent cup of tea, and in his ephemeral book, *Haywire: An American Travel Diary*, he bit many of the generous hands that "fee'd" him.[70]

These later accounts spread abroad a fascinating story of American travel. The American railroad, with its long open-aisle communal passenger cars, was a captivating institution. Some foreigners liked these cars where they could see large numbers of fellow passengers, while others regarded them as unreasonable invasions of privacy.[71] Conductors, flagmen, porters, and news butchers received almost as much attention as the railroad companies. The Pullman car never failed to attract attention. Some travelers marveled at the mechanical ingeniousness of the berths, and they admired the skill of porters in converting daytime coaches into cozy canvas hotels. A member of Parliament described the Pullman car as having the general appearance of a rolling Gothic church which served as both club and hotel.[72]

68 There were literally hundreds of these. Characteristic of these were Low, Jacks, Bolitho, Branston, and Cecil Roberts, *And So to America* (London, 1946).

69 (London, 1942).

70 (New York, 1939).

71 Burne-Jones, *Dollars and Diplomacy*, 66-78; Collier, *America and the Americans*, 169-78; Arthur G. Puller, *Notes on a Journey to the United States* (High Cross, 1879), 31-33; Mackay, *Western World*, I, 31-32.

72 Vivian, *Notes of a Tour in America*, 269-72.

There were those, however, who disliked this famous American traveling facility. Many pretended modesty and were horrified to think that within the canvas jungle were sleeping men and women. Some of them wakefully sped through the night thinking somberly about their entrapment in ambulatory coffins. If travelers were not concerned with sleeping arrangements, then they disliked the heat of coaches, and some Britishers, especially, soon learned not to throw windows open because, as one traveler said, "Americans are shivery people." [73]

Wherever they traveled, foreigners noticed social climbing. No royal family or titled aristocracy set a central pattern of behavior. Presidents of the United States behaved largely like middle-class yeomen, leaving social leadership to the wealthy families who pulled and hauled through social seasons at resorts, using the same tactics and competitive spirit that characterized American business. In this striving for position many families sought to establish distinguished ancestry for themselves. Travelers read with amazement advertisements offering to create, for reasonable fees, distinguished lineages to be documented by impressive coats of arms.[74]

American families who claimed lofty parchment descent were the Vanderbilts, dePeysters, and Watts. The last traced family relationships with Alfred the Great; the dePeysters fortified their social position by taking in Charlemagne; the Hammersleys established a vested interest in the House of Stuart; the Van Rensselaers preempted the House of Nassau; and the Jays traded long on Philip the Hardy, whoever he was.[75]

Travelers often overlooked the fundamentals of American society in discussing the snobbishness of the wealthier classes. Few of them indicated that they comprehended in abstract terms the hard labor involved in the conquest of the land and resources, or the willingness of Americans to make arduous efforts in the present to prepare for a more pleasant future. One traveler wondered how an active American ever fell in love. It was hard for him to conceive of a businessman hustling about city streets and dashing across the continent in pursuit of dollars being able to settle down long enough to

[73] Blouëtt, *Jonathan and His Continent*, 269-73.

[74] Charlton, *Four Months in North America*, 34; Low, *America at Home*, 41-54; William Chambers, *Things as They Are in America* (London, 1854), 178.

[75] Grant, *Two Sides of the Atlantic*, 107.

give reins to the subtleties of romantic emotions.[76] Romance and American commercialism impressed foreigners as being rudely contradictory.

American feelings were deeply hurt many times by travelers whom they entertained hospitably. Several books left gaping wounds in national pride and provoked defendants to rush into print with more vituperation than judgment.[77] They often saw travelers in the same dubious light as did Francis Lieber in 1835: "They [travelers] are next to Bedouins, the most dangerous class of people to deal with, and I no longer permit one of them to approach me with his pencil unsheathed. 'Lay down your arms,' I cry, 'come like an honest man, but no stabbing in the back, and you are welcome; don't drink my wine, and go many thousand miles off and say you drank cider; and put things in my mouth which never dropped from my lips'." [78]

The traveler has become a fixed part of American life. We welcome them by hundreds and thousands at this time in the twentieth century. If they do not come of their own volition we subsidize their visits as exchange students, professors, mechanics, engineers, government officials, businessmen, farmers, housewives, and scientists. Americans strive mightily to convince other peoples that we are committed irrevocably to the propositions of freedom embodied in the Declaration of Independence and the Bill of Rights. We have also undertaken to convince them that we have not exploited vast resources for purely selfish reasons. Our record in this area is highly contradictory. We send forth tons of slick magazines and movies representing the American way of life as one of lavish living on the one hand, and as a violation of everybody's moral code on the other. We encourage these foreign visitations to disprove our lack of morals, and to display our material accomplishments without emphasizing materialism.

In the broader area Americans profited even from adverse traveler comments. They gained some perspectives which might not have been possible under other conditions. The tremendous volume of

[76] A. P. Day, *Life and Society in America* (2 vols., London, 1889), I, 33.

[77] Books which possibly offended Americans most were: Thomas Ashe, *Travels in America Performed in 1806* (3 vols., London, 1808); Hamilton, *Men and Manners in America*; Trollope, *Domestic Manners of the Americans*; Charles Dickens, *American Notes* (New York, 1842); and Marryat, *A Diary in America.*

[78] Lieber, *Stranger in America*, I, 18.

descriptive material now available on America not only constitutes a significant collection of books of varying historical importance but also important tangible evidence that the American democratic system has never avoided free public inspection. Many travelers may have provoked a blinding wrath by their malicious comments, but they have never provoked a desire to deny free visitation to America and its institutions.

Fulfilling American Democracy: The Conservation Movement, 1907 to 1921

By J. Leonard Bates

"Conservation," as related to an evolving government policy in the twentieth century, has not been a clearly defined term. For average citizens it has meant in a general way the prevention of waste. For scholars and government administrators it has frequently meant a little more definitely the careful management of natural resources. Herbert Hoover as food administrator in World War I and as secretary of commerce in the early 1920's helped to popularize such a concept, with emphasis on efficiency of use.[1] There is much to be said for this construction. The acceptance of conservation in a broad sense represents a considerable advance from the nineteenth century when with a few notable exceptions squandering of public and private resources went on recklessly and often cynically. Moreover, its acceptance was a tribute to a group of men whose concept of official responsibility for conservation was not a loose, vague theory, nor a matter of efficiency as such, but a fighting, democratic faith.

Historians of modern reform have given scant attention to a rationale of conservation or to conservation as a democratic movement.[2] In fact the program associated with Theodore Roosevelt

[1] Herbert Hoover, *Memoirs: Years of Adventure, 1874-1920* (New York, 1951). 244 and *passim*; Mark Sullivan to Philip P. Wells, September 30, 1926, and Wells to Sullivan, October 26, 1926, Gifford Pinchot Papers (Division of Manuscripts, Library of Congress), Box 1676; Herbert Hoover, "The Part of the Federal and State Authorities in Promoting the Interstate Electric Super-Power Project," Address of October 13, 1923, *Economic World* (New York), XXVI (October 20, 1923), 544-46.

I am indebted to the Social Science Research Council and to the University of Illinois for grants in aid of research; also to Robert M. Albert of the University of Illinois for assistance in research and for helpful insights.

[2] See George E. Mowry, *Theodore Roosevelt and the Progressive Movement* (Madison, 1946); Arthur S. Link, *Woodrow Wilson and the Progressive Era* (New York, 1954); Eric F. Goldman, *Rendezvous with Destiny* (New York, 1952); Richard Hofstadter, *The Age of Reform* (New York, 1955).

and Gifford Pinchot is occasionally disparaged as largely sound and fury. Doubtless the ambiguity and complexity of "conservation" have tended to obscure its democratic implications. Then too, this policy was both a product of and a stimulant to the larger, so-called Progressive Movement; it shared in certain weaknesses of this epoch of reform and has shared in the criticism. The usual interpretation today is that the Progressive Movement was essentially an uprising of the middle class, protesting against monopoly and boss control of politics, stressing heavily the virtues of competition, freedom, and morality.[3] With respect to conservation this view leads to the criticism that there existed a fundamental inconsistency between the ideas of protecting natural resources and the dominant beliefs in individualism and competition with the resultant low prices, heavy consumption, and waste.[4]

There was another side to the Progressive Movement — perhaps the most significant side: the decline of laissez faire, the development of a social conscience, the repudiation of Social Darwinism. Most leaders of progressivism believed in a positive state. Some came to believe in the sort of factory and social legislation, welfare action, utility regulation, and limited government ownership that is associated with the New Deal. A few wished to go farther than the New Deal ever went.[5] While the conservationists, like others progressively inclined, differed among themselves, nevertheless they had a program which may be described as limited socialism in the public interest. Influenced by Henry George, Edward Bellamy, Lester Ward, William James, Arthur Twining Hadley, Thorstein Veblen, Charles A. Beard, and others, these protectors of the public lands were far removed from classical economics.

[3] See for example George E. Mowry, "The California Progressive and His Rationale: A Study in Middle Class Politics," *Mississippi Valley Historical Review* (Cedar Rapids), XXXVI (September, 1949), 239-50; Hofstadter, *Age of Reform*, 143-48.

[4] Erich W. Zimmermann, *World Resources and Industries* (New York, 1933), 786-87, 789, and *passim*; Hofstadter, *Age of Reform*, 6, 93, and *passim*.

[5] Walter E. Weyl, *The New Democracy* (New York, 1914), 160-62, 320-23; Link, *Wilson and the Progressive Era*, 224 ff.; Mowry, *Roosevelt and the Progressive Movement*, 380-81. See also letters of Harry A. Slattery, one of those closely associated with Gifford Pinchot: for example a "platform" written by Slattery for the Committee of Forty-eight, August, 1919, in Pinchot Papers, Box 1860. The Socialist party, which in 1912 received 5.97 per cent of the total vote, had a considerable influence on the left wing of the progressives. See David A. Shannon, "The Socialist Party before the First World War: An Analysis," *Mississippi Valley Historical Review*, XXXVIII (September, 1951), 279.

The organized conservationists were concerned more with economic justice and democracy in the handling of resources than with mere prevention of waste. One aspect of the matter was the price and income situation, the actual monetary rewards from the marvelous wealth of this land. Conservationists believed that somehow the common heritage, the socially created resources and institutions, had passed into the hands of vested interests and that the benefits were siphoned into the hands of a few. There were several ways in which this situation might be remedied, as they saw it: first, to hold on to the remaining public lands, at least temporarily, preventing further monopolization; second, to attempt to give the people a fuller share of opportunities and profits; and finally, in that period of low income to keep prices proportionately low. The monopolists who jacked up prices were anathema, even though their methods might contribute to conservation by reducing consumption. Conservation through penalizing the public was something which democratically motivated leaders were not prepared to accept.

The conservationists' approach was broad. They believed in government studies and safeguards for the preservation of irreplaceable resources such as petroleum; they recognized and struggled with problems which remain today only partially solved. They understood the need for federal leadership in an organic structure based on the unity of nature itself. As early as 1910 Gifford Pinchot proclaimed, "Every river is a unit from its source to its mouth." [6] They made mistakes, of course. Like most progressives, they concluded easily that the opposition on a particular issue consisted of "robber barons," conspirators, and frauds. Yet at times they were capable of a surprising detachment; a key conservationist, for example, referred admiringly to a "very scholarly and fine" argument that the public domain should be turned over to the states.[7]

[6] Gifford Pinchot, *The Fight for Conservation* (New York, 1910), 54, 110-13; Wells to Max W. Ball, July 25, 1917 (copy), and Wells memorandum for Pinchot at the bottom of above letter, with respect to enclosure, Max W. Ball, "Memorandum for the Director [Geological Survey]," March 30, 1916, concerning a mineral leasing bill; also Wells to Slattery, August 16, 1917, all in Pinchot Papers. J. O. Richardson, "Naval Petroleum Reserves No. 1 and No. 2," *Proceedings of the United States Naval Institute* (Annapolis), XLII (January-February, 1916), 94-97; Irvine L. Lenroot in *Cong. Record*, 66 Cong., 1 Sess., 4111-12 (August 21, 1919), and Robert M. La Follette, *ibid.*, 4733-36 (September 3, 1919); Henry S. Graves, "Public Welfare in Relation to the Conservation of Natural Resources," *Annals of the American Academy of Political and Social Science* (Philadelphia), CV (January, 1923), 11-12.

[7] Slattery to Pinchot, October 7, 1919, Pinchot Papers, Box 1842.

In a sense the conservation movement was a nonpartisan, statesmanlike cause, winning support from scientists, politicians, and others all over the country. But a fact of long-range significance was its Republican origin; Republicans led by Pinchot and Roosevelt were the main inspiration of this program. These men were proud of their work, many of them almost fanatically devoted to Roosevelt. They did not easily dissociate the Republican party or the "Republican Roosevelt," who had first given them their chance,[8] from the body of their accomplishments. Politics and personalities help appreciably to explain the conservation fight from 1907 to 1921.

In tracing the growth of a new attitude toward public resources it would be inaccurate to give credit only to the Republicans. This enlightenment was evolutionary, like reform in general, and Grover Cleveland, William A. J. Sparks as land commissioner, Hoke Smith as secretary of the interior, and other Democrats in later years made important contributions.[9] Even so, the concern here is with the full-fledged movement to which was given in 1907 the name "conservation." There is no doubt that progressive Republicans were the main actors.

Albert J. Beveridge of Indiana, United States senator, 1899-1911, a Republican and a progressive, was among those who witnessed the beginnings of the conservation policy. In 1921 he wrote to Gifford Pinchot:

> So, time, and time, and time again I thought of you, and the notable work you began more than twenty years ago, and have steadily pursued ever since, to save the country's woodland resources; and it suggested to me again your magnificent statesmanship known as the Conservation policy. For it is statesmanship, real statesmanship of the highest order. You may recall that after breakfast at your house, when you had developed your idea and before you presented it to President Roosevelt, you outlined it to me, and I said to you that forenoon that it was the biggest piece of constructive statesmanship that I had run across. . . . The whole Conservation system is yours, dear Gifford. I honestly think that you have done more than any other man for the future well-being of the Republic; and I have said this publicly as well as privately on every appropriate occasion — and I intend to go on saying it.[10]

[8] John M. Blum, *The Republican Roosevelt* (Cambridge, 1954), is discerningly appreciative of Roosevelt's inspirational qualities.

[9] An interesting inquiry is Gifford Pinchot, "How Conservation Began," *Agricultural History* (Washington), XI (October, 1937), 255-65.

[10] Albert J. Beveridge to Pinchot, September 2, 1921, Pinchot Papers, Box 236.

Pinchot remembered "with keen interest and satisfaction" the beginnings of this movement as described by Beveridge, and in 1937 he recalled further: "The idea was so new that it did not even have a name. Of course it had to have a name. Our little inside group discussed it a great deal. Finally Overton Price suggested that we should call it 'conservation' and the President said 'O. K.' So we called it the conservation movement."[11]

Allowing for exaggeration on the part of Pinchot and his friends, it is doubtless true that he and Roosevelt inspired this movement.[12] Gifford Pinchot, the son of a Pennsylvania landowner, businessman, philanthropist, and patron of the arts, was stimulated to an early interest in forestry. His father, James W. Pinchot, recommended forestry as a profession, having seen it practiced in Europe but not in this country. The young Pinchot was captivated by the idea. Finding no genuine forestry course in the United States after his graduation from Yale in 1889, he went to Europe to study. On returning, he became forester at George Vanderbilt's Biltmore Estate, near Asheville, North Carolina.[13] In 1896 he was appointed to the National Forest Commission and assigned the task of surveying United States forest resources. His reputation now established, in 1898 he became "forester" of the Forest Division (later the Forest Service) in the Agriculture Department, the position he held while in government service. Pinchot had boundless energy and enthusiasm; "tree mad" some had called him at Yale. Although not a systematic thinker, and sometimes annoyingly platitudinous, he possessed unusual qualities of intellect, character, and leadership. He was cultured and receptive to ideas. He was an aristocrat devoting himself to public service, passionately concerned about economic injustice — a fighter, a likable fellow, a good companion. Former Congressman William Kent of California referred in 1923

11 Pinchot to Beveridge, September 8, 1921, *ibid.*, and Pinchot, "How Conservation Began," *Agricultural History*, XI (October, 1937), 262-63.

12 In opening the White House Conference of Governors (May 13, 1908), Theodore Roosevelt declared: "Especial credit is due to the initiative, the energy, the devotion to duty, and the farsightedness of Gifford Pinchot, to whom we owe so much of the progress we have already made in handling this matter of the coordination and conservation of natural resources. If it had not been for him this convention neither would nor could have been called." Newton C. Blanchard *et al.* (eds.), *Proceedings of a Conference of Governors in the White House* (2 vols., Washington, 1909), I, 10.

13 Pinchot, "How Conservation Began," *Agricultural History*, XI (October, 1937), 261. For a good sketch of James W. Pinchot see Joseph A. Arnold, "James Wallace Pinchot," *Yearbook of the United States Department of Agriculture, 1907* (Washington, 1908), 495-97.

to one of Pinchot's best qualities, his "inherent modesty" and "desire to work in harmony with others." [14]

Pinchot owed much to older men who pioneered in the scientific study of resources, and whose influence was personal and forceful; notably John Wesley Powell (1834-1902) and W J McGee (1853-1912). Powell is well remembered as a naturalist, explorer of the Grand Canyon, director of the United States Bureau of Ethnology, and director of the Geological Survey. McGee, a remarkably versatile and influential man, had a fascinating career as anthropologist, geologist, ethnologist, hydrologist, inventor, philosopher, author, and public servant. He was in the Geological Survey while Powell was its head, later headed the Bureau of Ethnology (1893-1903), and then went on to hold numerous posts of importance. While director of the St. Louis Public Museum, he was among those in 1907 who instigated a study of inland waterways and thereby called attention to the physiology of natural resources — water, land, plants, and their interrelationships.[15] Roosevelt promptly appointed him to the Inland Waterways Commission. While at Memphis, during a tour of the Mississippi River, McGee, Pinchot, and others made up their minds that the President ought to call a conference; in this way they could dramatize their ideas and objectives. Thus the famous White House Conference; and, as Pinchot said, "the fight was on." [16]

Prior to this conference Pinchot's Forest Service already had been fighting effectively for some of the principles of unified resource management: for a sustained yield in the national forest lands; for grazing within the forest areas on payment of a fee; for leasing of water power sites, rather than giving them up permanently to private control. In other ways as well the activities of the Forest Service were expanded; not the least influential was a skillful, vigorously conducted publicity campaign.[17]

[14] William Kent to Pinchot, March 19, 1923, Pinchot Papers, Box 249. See also Roy M. Robbins, *Our Landed Heritage* (Princeton, 1942), 337.

[15] Whitney R. Cross, "W J McGee and the Idea of Conservation," *Historian* (Bloomington, Ind.), XV (Spring, 1953), 148-62; Charles R. Van Hise, *The Conservation of Natural Resources in the United States* (New York, 1913), 5; William C. Darrah, *Powell of the Colorado* (Princeton, 1951), 398-400 and *passim.*

[16] Pinchot, "How Conservation Began," *Agricultural History*, XI (October, 1937), 263. See also Theodore Roosevelt, *Autobiography* (New York, 1926), 408-409 and *passim.*

[17] Roosevelt, *Autobiography*, 399-407; Gifford Pinchot, *Breaking New Ground* (New York, 1947), 304-305.

It was not accidental that many of the leaders associated with Pinchot after 1908 were lawyers. There were for instance James R. Garfield, son of the former president, and Walter L. Fisher of Chicago. Garfield served the Roosevelt administration first in the Department of Commerce and Labor and in 1907 became secretary of the interior, doing much to establish the conservation system. Fisher succeeded Richard A. Ballinger as secretary of the interior during the Taft administration and moved within the inner circle of conservationists.[18] Other lawyers of importance were Philip P. Wells, George W. Woodruff, and Harry A. Slattery. These three in particular were experts in their understanding of knotty legal problems that arose from land withdrawals and impending legislation. Conservation was entering a phase by 1910 in which legal minds grappled over words and phrases or over decisions of almost appalling magnitude. Its opponents had been able to retain the finest advice; but with expert legal talent now arrayed in its support, no longer, as in the past, would the public wealth go by default.[19]

Philip Wells and George Woodruff, like Pinchot, were graduated in the Yale class of 1889. Wells was a man of unusual attainments. After taking the bachelor's degree he went ahead to do graduate work at Yale in economics and history, and in 1900 he received his Ph.D. Not satisfied with this, he had begun the study of law at Yale and continued at Columbian (later George Washington) University in Washington, D. C. His career for a time was centered at Yale as instructor in and librarian of the Law School, as well as a lecturer in history. In 1906 Pinchot brought him to Washington where he served first as chief law officer with the Forest Service and later in the same capacity with the Reclamation Service. Both in and out of government he acted as a special adviser to Pinchot. Woodruff was a former Yale football great and a genial and able friend whom Pinchot brought into the Forest Service as his first law officer. He was soon called, however, on a special assignment to the Interior Department as an assistant attorney general. For a few months in 1907 he functioned as acting secretary of the interior. Slattery came later into the Pinchot circle.

18 "Jim" and Helen Garfield were intimate friends of the Pinchots. See, for example, Pinchot to Garfield, November 9, 1921, Pinchot Papers, Box 238. On Fisher's appointment, see Mowry, *Roosevelt and the Progressive Movement*, 86.

19 See Pinchot, *Fight for Conservation*, 25, 90.

Good friends and brilliant lawyers, these men worked effectively for the principles of the conservation program.[20]

After 1909 the rallying point for conservationists became the National Conservation Association, with headquarters in Washington, D. C. This organization grew out of the struggle between the President and Congress over executive authority in appointing commissions. Specifically, a Commission on National Conservation appointed by Roosevelt as a result of the White House Conference undertook an inventory of all resources. Its work was comprehensive and its findings significant; but the Sixtieth Congress consented to publish only a few copies of the report and declared that such executive commissions were unconstitutional. Roosevelt denounced this view, and when President Taft, as his successor, decided in 1909 that Congress perhaps was right and that the Commission should do its work indirectly the forces of Pinchot and Roosevelt decided that action was demanded.[21] They formed the National Conservation Association, a private body, with Charles W. Eliot, former president of Harvard, serving briefly as president before being succeeded by Pinchot, with Harry Slattery as secretary,[22] and with Philip Wells as one of its counsel. Typical directors in the period 1916-1917 were Jane Addams, Carrie Chapman Catt, Samuel Gompers, Judge Ben Lindsey of Denver, and Irvine L. Lenroot of the House of Representatives.[23]

The National Conservation Association's effectiveness stemmed in large part from the great abilities of Harry Slattery as executive secretary, with headquarters near the Capitol. According to Roosevelt, the Association had first to prevent bad legislation in order to protect public resources from monopoly control, and second to guide through Congress the best of conservation measures. According to McGee, it had become the "legitimate repository and exponent of conservation doctrine, and the accepted leader of the Conservation

[20] See especially Pinchot, *Breaking New Ground*, 302-304.

[21] W J McGee, "The Conservation of Natural Resources," Mississippi Valley Historical Association, *Proceedings for the Year 1909-1910* (Cedar Rapids, 1911), 374-75; Roosevelt, *Autobiography*, 368-69, 416-17; Pinchot to Howard B. Gill, September 19, 1921, Pinchot Papers, Box 1846; Van Hise, *Conservation of Natural Resources*, 11-12; *Presidential Addresses and State Papers of William Howard Taft, March 4, 1909, to March 4, 1910* (New York, 1910), *passim.*

[22] Slattery was preceded by Thomas R. Shipp. Pinchot referred to Overton Price, his associate forester, as the mainstay of the National Conservation Association until Price died in 1913. *Breaking New Ground*, 302.

[23] Pinchot Papers, Box 1838.

Movement, more especially in its moral aspect," and Charles R. Van Hise saw it as the propaganda agent of the movement.[24] With understandable prejudice, Pinchot reviewed its work in 1921 and concluded that "no other Association has exerted anything like so large an influence in proportion to its membership and expenditures. It has overcome, not once, but many times, the efforts of the greatest lobbies ever assembled in Washington."[25] Each of these evaluations was essentially true. Slattery in some respects was better qualified than Pinchot to fight the lobbies, to make the rounds of Congress, to grind out publicity and propaganda, and when necessary to work night and day poring over legislation looking for ambiguities and loopholes, drawing up legislation as he and Wells, or Lenroot, or Senator Robert M. La Follette, or others thought it ought to be.[26]

A native of South Carolina, Slattery completed his education at Georgetown University and George Washington University and remained in the Washington area. In 1909, still in his early twenties, he became secretary to Pinchot. A short time later he took over the job with the National Conservation Association. Slattery was an informal, amiable sort of person, folksy in his speech but sharp of mind. People liked him and relied upon him. He was informed on history, law, and economics, but most especially on politics and personalities — the Washington scene. Liberal if not radical, he conceived of himself and the Association as the "watchdog" of conservation.[27] When Slattery resigned as secretary in 1921 (to remain with the Association as counsel) Pinchot remarked on his "intimate knowledge" of and close contact with Congress. In this, he thought, Slattery stood "alone among the secretaries of associations with headquarters in Washington." And the result had been Slattery's "controlling part" in writing conservation principles of

24 Pinchot to Howard B. Gill (quoting Roosevelt), September 19, 1921, Pinchot Papers, Box 1846; McGee, "Conservation of Natural Resources," Mississippi Valley Historical Association, *Proceedings, 1909-1910*, p. 375; Van Hise, *Conservation of Natural Resources*, 12.

25 Pinchot to Gill, September 19, 1921, Pinchot Papers, Box 1846.

26 Admiration of Slattery and his work was well-nigh universal among the progressives and conservationists. See Raphael Zon, of the Forest Service, to Pinchot, June 14, 1919, Pinchot Papers, Box 1843, and William Kent to Pinchot, May 18, 1922, *ibid.*, Box 457; also Robert M. La Follette, quoted in Belle C. and Fola La Follette, *Robert M. La Follette* (2 vols., New York, 1953), II, 942-43.

27 Slattery to Pinchot, February 28, 1921, Pinchot Papers, Box 1846.

"immense value" into the laws of the land.[28] It was a generous tribute to the kind of man who so often serves the public, with little publicity and no public recognition.

The developing rationale of the conservationists is of the utmost importance in explaining their conduct and influence. By no means were they all alike, but people such as Roosevelt, Pinchot, and La Follette believed that a larger amount of governmental interference and regulation in the public interest was required. They were especially concerned about the remaining public lands, which, according to principles grounded in the Homestead and other acts, belonged to all. Millions of acres had been given away or sold to corporate interests for a trifling price or had been actually stolen. This record of carelessness and exploitation could not be expunged. However, to conserve and use wisely that which remained, to show that civilized man could profit from mistakes of the past, to democratize the handling of a common heritage, would be a genuine consolation. A crisis, they felt, existed. Such an attitude was a compound of idealism, passion, and sober analysis. These men realized that American society in the twentieth century must be increasingly one of co-operative and collective gains.

As progressives they agreed passionately on the need for honesty and a social conscience in the administration of resources. Declared Pinchot in 1910: "There is no hunger like land hunger, and no object for which men are more ready to use unfair and desperate means than the acquisition of land." Americans had to make up their minds whether their political system was to be devoted to "unclean money or free men." [29] It was fortunate, he believed, that special interests were afflicted with a "blindness" because of their "wholly commercialized point of view." [30] Conservationists were convinced that hostility toward materialism and toward money men and special interests usually was warranted, that history afforded ample justification for suspicion. If nothing else united the conservationists, there was this hatred of the boodler, the rank materialist, the exploiter.

[28] Pinchot to Slattery, April 6, 1921, *ibid.*, Box 242. See also Wells to Slattery, October 31, 1919, *ibid.*, Box 1843. In the early 1920's Slattery played an important part in the oil leasing investigation; in 1933 he joined Harold Ickes as a special assistant; and later he headed the Rural Electrification Administration.

[29] Pinchot, *Fight for Conservation*, 92-93.

[30] *Ibid.*, 69.

Intellectually there was much that drew these men together. McGee, whom Pinchot called "the scientific brains" of the conservation movement, provided a rationale for action. "Every revolution," said McGee, "whatever its material manifestations . . . is first and foremost a revolution in thought and spirit." [31] Believing that Americans had largely lost their rights in the land, McGee felt that knowledge of how this had occurred might yet insure the "perpetuity" of the people.

From the early beginnings of the United States there had been confusion and carelessness in the administration of "land," a word identified with resources generally: "When Independence was declared and the Constitution was framed, no resources were reckoned except the Men who made the nation and the Land on which they lived." [32] Trees were considered an obstacle to be burned or girdled; little attention was paid to natural growth above or minerals below. The "Fathers," filled with their dreams of a freehold citizenry rooted in the soil, proceeded to dissipate values other than the land itself. The results were both good and evil. So far as certain farsighted or favored individuals were concerned, the way was opened to wealth, power, and monopoly. McGee wrote: "the resources passed under monopolistic control with a rapidity never before seen in all the world's history; and it is hardly too much to say that the Nation has become one of the Captains of Industry first, and one of the People and their chosen representatives only second." Moreover, "the free gift" of resources "under the title of land" defeated the original purpose of creating a free independent citizenry. The people had become "industrial dependents." [33] Incidental to this process of resource appropriation was waste.

"Ample resources" remained, it was true, but what was to be done with them? Should the "People," whose work and travail had created this wealth, receive the benefits? Or should they go

[31] McGee, "Conservation of Natural Resources," Mississippi Valley Historical Association, *Proceedings, 1909-1910,* p. 378. See also Pinchot, *Breaking New Ground,* 359-60.

[32] McGee, "Conservation of Natural Resources," Mississippi Valley Historical Association, *Proceedings, 1909-1910,* p. 364.

[33] *Ibid.,* 367. Pinchot observed (1910) that the average family income was only $600, and he showed a deep concern over the "tragedies" resulting from "the lack of a little money." *Fight for Conservation,* 110-13 and *passim.* Hofstadter, *Age of Reform,* Chap. I; Henry Nash Smith, *Virgin Land: The American West as Symbol and Myth* (Cambridge, 1950), 258-60.

"into the hands of the self-chosen and self-annointed [*sic*] few, largely to forge new shackles for the wrists and ankles of the many?" Deliberately and thoughtfully, McGee argued, American freemen must proceed "to reclaim their own." [34] Theodore Roosevelt's opening address at the White House Conference expounded on the same theme — the right of the people to public wealth and, moreover, their right to control *private* property for the common weal. He quoted the high authority of Justice Holmes, speaking for the Supreme Court with respect to state protection of water, forests, and the atmosphere: "This public interest is omnipresent wherever there is a State, and grows more pressing as population grows." And Roosevelt added emphatically that the dictum was to be carried farther than the forests and the streams.[35]

McGee's indebtedness to Henry George is obvious. As a product of the exciting generation in which Social Darwinism was elaborated and then repudiated, as an associate of such men as John Wesley Powell and Lester Ward, it was not strange that McGee emphasized economic justice. The Bill of Rights must be purified, he said, through equal opportunities and equal rights in the common resources. He stressed the "trinity" of liberty, equality, and fraternity. The keynote was fraternity. There remained to be established "full brotherhood among men and generations." [36] Pinchot, advancing similar arguments, thought that the answer lay in the conservation movement, the most democratic that the country had known in a generation.

Philip Wells became more explicit about the ideas and hopes which had driven him and his associates "in the conservation fight." They had been concerned with economic justice and incidentally with waste because if the resources were destroyed nothing remained upon which the principle of justice could operate. In the light of

[34] McGee, "Conservation of Natural Resources," Mississippi Valley Historical Association, *Proceedings, 1909-1910*, pp. 369-70.

[35] Blanchard *et al.* (eds.), *Proceedings of Conference of Governors*, I, 10-12.

[36] McGee, "Conservation of Natural Resources," Mississippi Valley Historical Association, *Proceedings, 1909-1910*, pp. 377-79. See also Pinchot, *Fight for Conservation*, 81 and *passim*. Cross, "McGee and the Idea of Conservation," *Historian*, XV (Spring, 1953), 162, concluded that "McGee was largely responsible for conveying the theoretical, positive, social Darwinism of the late nineteenth century into the realm of practical political action in the conservation movement of the twentieth century." It is noteworthy, however, that McGee's own ideas had changed appreciably since 1899. See W J McGee, "National Growth and National Character," *National Geographic Magazine* (Washington), X (June, 1899), 185-206.

the American system, he said, they conceived of economic justice as meaning that "so far as possible within the general limitations fixed by popular opinion as to fundamentals, and within the specific limitations fixed by constitutional provisions, the 'economic rent,' present and future ('unearned increment') in natural resources should be retained by the public which should also see that the resources are not wasted in order that the benefits of the new policy may be prolonged as far into the future as possible." While at Yale, Wells had studied under William Graham Sumner, who once remarked that every man was either a socialist or an anarchist. Actually, Wells believed, most people were somewhere between these two poles. "Now the conservationists as to specific natural resources (water power, forests, the mineral fuels and mineral fertilizers) inclined to the socializing pole; that is, they sought to enlarge the public control of these resources . . . both for the prevention of waste and, more essential, for the socializing of the raw resource value including unearned increment."[37]

Wells went ahead to discuss Henry George, "a constructive economist of very high order" rather than a crank, as some maintained, and to compare his philosophy with that of the conservationists. They differed in that George was essentially an individualist, of the "Neo-Manchester School." They had agreed in "trying to socialize raw resource value," George attempting to do this through his single tax on unearned increments and with slight regard for constitutional problems. The conservationists, on the other hand, were interested primarily in "selected resources exhaustible or subject to great waste, suitable for development only or chiefly by large aggregations of capital and peculiarly open to monopolistic abuse." They differed further as to ideas of management, Wells continued. "The conservationists want to socialize to a certain extent the management of their selected resources (as the Forest Service does in selling standing timber in a National Forest by restrictions imposed on logging methods to secure a new timber crop); whereas George would anarchize the management of all natural resources by turning them over to unrestricted private ownership."[38]

[37] Wells to Mark Sullivan, September 22, 1926, Pinchot Papers, Box 1676.

[38] *Ibid.* At the top of this copy of the letter is a notation: "GP read and approved this — Sept 23/26."

Pinchot and his group therefore believed in using the authority of federal and state government to compel conservation practices ("socialization of management"), even aiming to do this on *private* forest lands.[39] With respect to the alternatives of federal or state action Pinchot once remarked: "I have very little interest in the abstract question whether the nation is encroaching upon the rights of the states or the states upon the nation. Power falls naturally to that person or agency which can and does use it, and . . . the nation acts . . . [while] the states do not."[40]

The influence of these ideas and the impact of the Pinchot organization cannot be minimized. Nevertheless, Pinchot and his friends did not constitute the entire conservation movement. There were issues which inevitably divided the conservationists as a whole: the clashing of personalities and ambitions, disagreement over methods if not over goals, disputes between Democrats and Republicans, and economic sectionalism especially as it arose between the West and the East. Any issue or event could impinge upon conservation with divisive results or with diverse and complicating effects — for example World War I. In general, one accepting the designation of "conservationist" was a progressive, believing in the necessity of strong executive leadership and federal action. He might be a radical or an outright socialist. Frequently, on the other hand, he emphasized as heavily as did President Taft the authority of Congress, the statutory system that must be erected, the quieting of any doubts as to constitutionality.[41] And it was not strange for a conservationist to consider himself a conservative; one who believed in honest government and orderly processes, who hated boodling, who watched vigilantly for the sly steals that special interests might perpetrate. Representative James R. Mann of Illinois, for example, might be linked politically with "Uncle Joe" Cannon's Old Guard, but the Pinchot forces treasured him as one of their most dependable allies.[42] Regionally speaking, the southerner who

[39] Wells to Sullivan, October 26, 1926, *ibid.* Wells concluded: "I could write a volume to prove and explain Pinchot's policy." As to control of forest lands, see Pinchot to Liberty H. Bailey, June 6, 1921, *ibid.*, Box 236, and Gifford Pinchot, "What About Forestry?" *Saturday Evening Post* (Philadelphia), June 4, 1921, p. 73.

[40] Statement of August 11, 1924, Pinchot Papers, Box 255.

[41] See, for example, Taft to William Kent, June 29, 1909, quoted in Henry F. Pringle, *The Life and Times of William Howard Taft* (2 vols., New York, 1939), I, 480.

[42] Slattery to Pinchot, August 21, 1919, Pinchot Papers, Box 1842. See the sketch of Mann in *Dictionary of American Biography* (21 vols., New York, 1928-1944), XII,

favored conservation differed from the northerner or from the westerner. Southerners were much influenced by traditions of agrarianism and anti-monopoly action as well as by the fact (acidly noted by Pinchot) that the lands to be conserved and "saved" were mostly outside their region.[43]

There was one charge endlessly repeated against the conservationists with the effect of creating cleavages in the ranks. Time and again their foes, or those who called themselves moderate and reasonable conservationists, asserted that the Pinchot policy resolved itself into keeping resources in cold storage, or under lock and key, or hermetically sealed up. They implied or even declared that Pinchot and his adherents had no interest in jobs and opportunities for the people of the West; that they cared nothing for necessary development. Senator Charles S. Thomas (Democrat) of Colorado expressed this point of view in 1919:

> The average conservationist — I will not say it applies to all of them — is very much concerned about conserving other people, but when it comes to a personal application of the doctrine he is not so enthusiastic. I believe the gentleman who claims to be the great progenitor, the father of conservation is the Hon. Gifford Pinchot, at one time chief adviser to President Roosevelt, forester of the United States, and one of the founders and leaders of the late lamented Progressive Party. He it was who discovered that the way to conserve was to reserve, and that the way to develop was to keep everything petrified and stagnant. To him, so far as his actions are concerned, the American Indian . . . was the ideal conservationist.[44]

Pinchot, Slattery, and others denied or sought to make light of such accusations and in turn directed much of their criticism against such conservationist ideas and practices as those of Hoover while food administrator and secretary of commerce.[45] In their own defense

244. As a legislator of intellectual force and courage but also of curious contradictions, Mann deserves a careful study.

43 Pinchot, *Breaking New Ground*, 89.

44 *Cong. Record*, 66 Cong., 1 Sess., 4255-56 (August 23, 1919). See also Representative Sylvester C. Smith of California in *Cong. Record*, 61 Cong., 2 Sess., 5062 (April 20, 1910); Senator Thomas J. Walsh of Montana to R. S. Hamilton, October 19, 1918, Thomas J. Walsh Papers (Division of Manuscripts, Library of Congress); Hoover, Address of October 13, 1923, *Economic World*, XXVI (October 20, 1923), 544-46.

45 See, for example, Pinchot to Los Angeles *Herald*, April 13, 1920, Pinchot Papers, Box 1941; Pinchot to Mark Sullivan, February 24, 1921, *ibid.*, Box 242; Pinchot to Hoover, November 22, 1923, *ibid.*, Box 1701; and Wells to Sullivan, October 26, 1926, *ibid.*, Box 1676.

they could point to the fact that Pinchot in heading the Forest Service as well as in later years advocated and practiced conservation through use. Nevertheless, it was true that the Roosevelt-Pinchot-Taft withdrawals of land, the study for purposes of classification, and the shaping of new laws meant some delay. How much of this delay was to be charged to them and how much was to be charged to their enemies among state righters and special interests remained an open question.

From 1910 to 1912 two dramatic events had the effect of both quickening the conservation movement and causing its reorientation; and World War I, following shortly, added complications. First, there was the famous Ballinger-Pinchot controversy, in which Pinchot, becoming a critic of the Secretary of the Interior, was fired from his job as chief United States forester. Pinchot and the progressives convinced themselves that President Taft had been a traitor to their cause; that the Secretary of the Interior, Richard A. Ballinger of Seattle, had yielded to the big interests; and that the majority report, after a congressional investigation, was a "whitewash." [46] Democrats were delighted to echo these charges. It was indeed true that Ballinger had served as private adviser to the same interests that he favored as a government official, and that from 1910 to 1912 he and his counsel seemingly put themselves on record as sworn enemies of conservation. He seems also to have been weak or changeable in the formulation and execution of departmental policies, and in retaining him the President strengthened the suspicions and resentment of the Pinchot group.[47] Whatever the exact meaning of this affair, many progressives never forgave Taft; nor doubted that Ballinger was in league with the Guggenheims; nor forgot that such a man as Edwin Denby (later secretary of the navy under Harding) had been among the "whitewashers" in Con-

[46] See George W. Norris to Pinchot, March 11, 1921, *ibid.*, Box 240; Pinchot to Harold J. Howland, October 3, 1921, *ibid.*, Box 238; Mowry, *Roosevelt and the Progressive Movement*, 73-87.

[47] For discussions of some of the reactions to the controversy see Alpheus T. Mason, *Bureaucracy Convicts Itself: The Ballinger-Pinchot Controversy of 1910* (New York, 1941), 178-80 and *passim*, and Mowry, *Roosevelt and the Progressive Movement*, 80 ff. An examination of Ballinger's departmental correspondence as compared with that of Walter L. Fisher, who succeeded him, reveals the weakness of Ballinger's administration. Compare, for example, George Otis Smith (director of the Geological Survey) to Ballinger, December 22, 1910, and Ballinger to Attorney General George W. Wickersham, December 24, 1910, with Charles Hilles to Fisher, March 1, 1913, and Fisher to President Taft, March 1, 1913, Files of the Secretary of the Interior, General Land Office, Oil Lands (National Archives).

gress.[48] And on the other side, Taft was reported as believing that Pinchot was "a socialist and a spiritualist . . . capable of any extreme act." [49]

All of this helped to precipitate the second event, the revolt of Republican progressives, and the formation of the Roosevelt "Bull Moose" party in 1912. As a result of this schism Woodrow Wilson came to the White House, and for the first time a Democratic administration had to cope with twentieth-century problems, including conservation. The relations between Republicans who had inaugurated this policy and the polyglot Democrats who tried more or less to carry it out were well-nigh predictable. Prospects of mutual satisfaction were scant.

In the meantime the Republicans remained seriously divided; and the career of Robert M. La Follette affords an illustration of their confusion during these years. La Follette had led the progressive forces in 1910-1911, had aspired to the Republican nomination for the presidency, and had been dropped by the progressive members of his party because they believed Roosevelt to have a greater dramatic appeal and thus a better chance to win. He felt that he had been betrayed by a number of men such as Pinchot, who initially had promised their support, and as a result he and the Roosevelt men were never to become fully reconciled. In Wisconsin the struggle among Republicans stemming from the split of 1912 brought a break between La Follette and Irvine L. Lenroot. These two had worked closely and cordially from 1900 to 1912, with Lenroot supporting "Fighting Bob's" progressive policies and coming to Washington himself in 1909 as a representative. By 1911 La Follette depended upon Lenroot's support in seeking the presidential nomination; but Lenroot, like most progressives, went over to Roosevelt. The La Follettes were stricken by this defection. Mrs. La Follette wrote to a friend: "Nothing that has happened has been so hard for me. We have managed to keep the personal relation but I realize that Bob and Irvine can never be the same to each other as before." [50]

[48] Amos Pinchot to Gifford Pinchot, February 26, 1921, Pinchot Papers, Box 241. See also Gifford Pinchot to Samuel M. Lindsay, March 6, 1921, *ibid.*, Box 239; Norris to Pinchot, March 11, 1921, *ibid.*, Box 240; Gustavus Pope to Pinchot, March 6, 1924, *ibid.* For an expression of La Follette's contempt for Taft, see *Cong. Record,* 66 Cong., 1 Sess., 4747 (September 3, 1919).

[49] Archie Butt to Clara Butt, April 12, 1910, in *Taft and Roosevelt: The Intimate Letters of Archie Butt, Military Aide* (2 vols., New York, 1930), I, 327-28.

[50] La Follette, *Robert M. La Follette,* I, 420-24.

Each of the two Wisconsinites had a strong record on conservation. But after 1912, increasingly, they went their separate ways, Lenroot becoming an "internationalist," while La Follette was exceedingly critical of Wilsonian diplomacy.[51] It was Lenroot who worked closely with the National Conservation Association. As a member of the House Committee on Public Lands he was the more likely to sponsor bills for these organized conservationists; and after transferring to the Senate in 1918 he continued as one of their contact men.[52] Pinchot and Lenroot on one side and La Follette on the other had not forgotten their differences when Lenroot campaigned in 1920 for re-election to the Senate. Pinchot came to Wisconsin to help. He assailed La Follette as an autocrat who had selfishly refused to follow Roosevelt in the Bull Moose campaign and who now in the same selfish way was doing all he could to block Lenroot's ambitions.[53]

At the same time, however, the forces of La Follette and Pinchot could work together in February-March, 1919, to defeat the so-called Pittman mineral leasing bill, an anti-conservationist measure which they considered peculiarly obnoxious. On matters of principle, they could unite; but Slattery, Wells, and company of the National Conservation Association took pains not to "get the wires crossed" between La Follette and Lenroot when needing so keenly the help of both.[54] It was La Follette finally, not Lenroot, who saved them in the petroleum fight, La Follette who argued and filibustered successfully against the mineral leasing bill with materials supplied by the Association.[55] And two years later it was

[51] "Lenroot and La Follette: A Contrast," *Outlook* (New York), CXV (April 18, 1917), 691; Irvine L. Lenroot, "The War Loyalty of Wisconsin," *Forum* (New York), LIX (June, 1918), 699.

[52] Slattery regretted Lenroot's departure from the House, where his "influence for good" had been so powerful. Slattery to Mrs. Pinchot, September 11, 1919, Pinchot Papers, Box 1841. See also a eulogistic statement in "Suggestions for Sec. of Interior," December 11, 1920, probably written by Slattery, *ibid.*, Box 1941; Wells to Lenroot, May 21, 1919, and Wells to George W. Woodruff, May 22, 1919, *ibid.*, Box 1700; and Slattery to Pinchot, December 4, 1918, *ibid.*, Box 1838. Senator Paul O. Husting (a Democrat), who died in 1917 and was replaced by Lenroot, had also worked closely with the Pinchot group.

[53] Address by Pinchot at Racine, Wisconsin, October 25, 1920, *ibid.*, Box 1948.

[54] Wells to Woodruff, May 22, 1919, and Wells to John J. Hannan (La Follette's assistant), August 20, 1919, *ibid.*, Box 1700.

[55] See especially National Conservation Association "News Letter on Conservation," March, 1919 (written by Slattery for approval by Pinchot and release to newspapers), *ibid.*, Box 1842, and Wells, "Analysis of Pittman Conference Bill, 1919," *ibid.*, Box 1859. La Follette's speech is in *Cong. Record*, 65 Cong., 3 Sess., 4713-16 (March 1, 1919) and *passim.*

La Follette, again assisted by Slattery and Wells, who instigated the Teapot Dome investigation.[56]

La Follette and Pinchot operated differently, and this was no discredit to either. The Wisconsinite had neither the disposition nor the opportunity for bartering favors with Wilson (after 1916), nor with Harding, Coolidge, and others of the Republican Old Guard. His forte was to attack, to filibuster, to block "giveaways," to tack on remedial amendments, to force concessions, to rally the left wing. With Pinchot it was a different story. In each Congress, in each administration, Pinchot as president of the National Conservation Association would try to place his men, would distribute his propaganda, would try to win support. Just as the special interests lobbied to control or influence policy, so would he. As an additional moderating influence there were without doubt Pinchot's political ambitions. He was available, for instance, for a place in Harding's cabinet, and a conciliatory course was sometimes prudent.[57] He would agitate from within if possible, or he would attack from without if necessary.

In their proposals for control of public lands, the two men differed only slightly. In La Follette's opinion there had been only one great issue in all of history: a struggle "between labor and those who would control, through slavery in one form or another, the laborers." [58] Uppermost in his consideration, therefore, was justice for the exploited. With respect to public resources in general, he argued that there must be a policy of continuing public ownership, of leasing where possible, of price controls, and a degree of govern-

[56] See speeches by Robert M. La Follette, Jr., George W. Norris, Basil Manly, and others, at a dinner in honor of Harry Slattery, Cosmos Club, Washington, D. C., June 25, 1932, quoted in *Cong. Record*, 72 Cong., 1 Sess., 15456-62 (July 15, 1932). Senator Norris said: "Without such a man [Slattery] to back us up, without such a man to furnish evidence and information and documents, lots of times it would have been physically impossible for us to get results. Without such a man, those who have tried to fight the peoples' causes in the last ten years . . . would nearly always have failed." See also E. C. Finney (first assistant secretary of the interior) to Wells, June 7, 1921, and copy of draft of resolution prepared by Wells for Senator La Follette via Slattery, March 11, 1922, Pinchot Papers, Box 1700; and Slattery to Pinchot, June 21, 1921, *ibid.*, Box 242.

[57] See extensive correspondence between Pinchot and Slattery, 1920-1921, in Pinchot Papers, Boxes 1841 and 1846. Slattery and Pinchot had genuine hopes of converting Harding to the conservationist faith. When Pinchot grew discouraged Slattery urged him on. Otherwise, he wrote, "you would not be able to work with Harding at all, and would undo everything you have done." Slattery to Pinchot, February 16, 1921, *ibid.*, Box 1846.

[58] *Cong. Record*, 66 Cong., 1 Sess., 4755-56 (September 3, 1919).

ment operation depending upon the monopoly situation. Basic raw materials, even though privately owned, must sell at a reasonable price and if they did not he advocated government appropriation. Quite early he had called for leasing rather than selling government properties, and in the conservation fight of the late Wilson years he stressed a leasing system for coal and oil and other nonmetalliferous minerals but not without adequate safeguards for democratic development and prevention of waste. He believed, for example, that evidence of collusive bargaining and fixing of prices among the lessees should warrant government cancellation of the lease.[59] There were some who charged that La Follette hoped actually to destroy the leasing bills and in time to substitute his own "socialistic" schemes.[60]

The coming of a Democratic administration in 1913 produced a reorientation affecting everyone in the fight for conservation. This was due partly to the status of the withdrawal question; nonmetallic mineral lands and water power sites no longer were being sold or given away and had to be made available under some scheme for development. Prior to 1913, Republicans had argued mostly among themselves; they could now sit back and watch the Democrats undertake the direction of policy, and could wait for an appropriate occasion to assail and expose them. Wilson believed in conservation, and the policy of his administration was directed toward formulation of a leasing system.[61] But on the question of how this should be done his own advisers were often in sharp disagreement,[62] thereby giving the Republicans their opportunity for

[59] *Ibid.*, 65 Cong., 3 Sess., 4715 (March 1, 1919), and 66 Cong., 1 Sess., 4754-58 (September 3, 1919).

[60] "Interview" given out by Senator Walsh, March 12, 1919, and Walsh to Hattie Grace, March 26, 1919, Walsh Papers. See also Walsh in *Cong. Record*, 66 Cong., 1 Sess., 4112 (August 21, 1919), and La Follette's explanation that his purpose was constructive; that to improve rather than destroy the leasing bill was his aim. *Ibid.*, 4251-52 (August 23, 1919).

[61] For Wilson's views on conservation see his statement of October 7, 1912, quoted in *Cong. Record*, 63 Cong., 2 Sess., 14948 (September 10, 1914), and his Inaugural Address, March 4, 1913, Ray S. Baker and William E. Dodd (eds.), *The Public Papers of Woodrow Wilson* (6 vols., New York, 1925-1927), III, 1-6. See also Scott Ferris to Wilson, May 27, 1918, and Wilson to Ferris, May 28, 1918, Woodrow Wilson Papers (Division of Manuscripts, Library of Congress), Box 505.

[62] Pinchot, "Open Letter to the Honorable Franklin K. Lane . . . Concerning the Navy's Oil Lands," August 12, 1916, Pinchot Papers; Wilson to Thomas W. Gregory, February 19, 1917, Gregory to Wilson, February 26, 1917, Josephus Daniels to Gregory, February 26, 1917, Gregory to Claude A. Swanson, February 26, 1917, Wilson Papers, Box 505.

criticism. In the beginning, La Follette, Pinchot, and many Republicans of a progressive mind were sympathetic to Wilson's program. A few turned against him by 1916;[63] many others by 1918; and by 1920 their abandonment was almost complete.

World War I and industrial mobilization were largely responsible for this time of trouble. Of deepest concern to the organized conservationists was this question: How disinterested, how patriotic, were the businessmen who came streaming into Wilson's government for the purpose of preparing the nation for war? In the attitude of conservationists toward dollar-a-year men one finds new evidence that their aims went far beyond the mere prevention of waste. They were concerned with problems of men against money, with profiteering, with economic justice, with maintaining democracy. By these standards Wilson qualified, at the least, as a moderate conservationist. He believed that leasing laws opening western lands to development must be passed; that the war (creating new demands for petroleum and other resources) made a solution most urgent; and that a compromise doing justice to all parties could be effected. Wilson was cautious and showed a wariness about the possibility of profiteering and corruption under cloak of war.[64]

Wilson's secretary of the navy, Josephus Daniels, going beyond wariness, was absolutely convinced that the special interests were using the war emergency for purposes of grabbing resources belonging to all the people.[65] La Follette, Pinchot, and most of the progressive Republicans agreed. Slattery, writing from Washington, expressed the attitude of the National Conservation Association when he referred to that "National Council of Defense outfit." "We have been surrounded with them . . . and I have from the start had my strong suspicions about the whole bunch." Slattery and Gifford Pinchot feared that Secretary of the Interior Franklin K. Lane was "going to give away every thing in sight" before the war

63 See Pinchot, "Open Letter to 5,000 Editors," September 7, 1916, and replies, Pinchot Papers, Box 1943.

64 Memorandum of Norman Hapgood letter to Wilson, July 31, 1916, Wilson to Gregory, August 2, 1916, and Wilson to Hapgood, August 2, 1916, Wilson Papers, Box 505; Thomas J. Walsh to Wilson, June 22, 1917, and Wilson to Walsh, June 29, 1917, *ibid.*, Box 371.

65 See for example Daniels to Wilson, June 20, 1917, Wilson Papers, Box 505; Daniels to Franklin D. Roosevelt, July 7, 1943, and January 28, 1944, Josephus Daniels Papers (Division of Manuscripts, Library of Congress), Box 17.

had ended, unless they stopped him.[66] Slattery picturesquely summed up the whole situation: It looked as though "these bushwhacking gentlemen," while good people had their faces turned to the war, were going to "raid the 'smokehouse and hen-roost' as of border-war days." [67] Slattery and his associates had in mind particular bushwhackers, such as John D. Ryan and C. F. Kelley of the Anaconda Copper Company and Edward L. Doheny of the Pan-American Petroleum Company.[68]

One effect of the southern leadership in the Wilson administration was to stimulate sectional rivalries, with some important effects upon conservation. The western states resisted at first a federal program for the public lands while eastern and southern leaders were forcing the issue. But the native South of Woodrow Wilson differed somewhat from the East of Gifford Pinchot. In brief, the East-West division over conservation was accompanied in the Wilson years by a flare-up of North-South animosities. There had been nothing like it since the 1890's, perhaps since Reconstruction. Some applied the term of Reconstruction days, "waving the bloody shirt," to the divisive strategy of Republican politicians, who urged their constituents to vote for Republicans since only in that way could the power of southern Democrats be broken.[69] To measure the importance of these sectional feelings is difficult, but that they

[66] Slattery to Amos Pinchot, September 22, 1917, Slattery to Gifford Pinchot, August 16, 1917 (enclosing "Memorandum for the Press," from Department of Interior, July 26, 1917), and Pinchot to Slattery, undated, Pinchot Papers, Box 1838. Slattery had marked portions of Lane's Memorandum to emphasize "giveaways": the rapid classification of lands and restoration to private entry.

[67] Slattery to Wells, August 3, 1917, *ibid.*

[68] Slattery to Pinchot, February 28, 1918, Pinchot Papers, Box 1838; Wells to Pinchot, December 6, 1919, *ibid.*, Box 1700; Amos Pinchot to Conference Committee of Senate and House of Representatives, September 18, 1917 (copy), *ibid.*, Box 1859. Some of the official correspondence seemed to indicate a growing cordiality between leaders of government and business. See for example George Otis Smith (director of the Geological Survey) to Ballinger, December 22, 1910, and Smith to Lane, September 4, 1917, Files of the Secretary of the Interior, General Land Office, Oil Lands; statement by Mark Requa of the Fuel Division, September 30, 1918, on the world struggle for oil, and Van H. Manning (director of the Bureau of Mines) to Newton D. Baker (copy, undated, but early 1920), Files of the Secretary of the Interior, Administration General, Oil Situation (National Archives).

[69] For some of the reactions to southern leadership see A. Maurice Low, "The South in the Saddle," *Harper's Weekly* (New York), February 8, 1913, p. 20; T. J. Hocking in Helena *Montana Record-Herald*, October 16, 1918; Slattery to Pinchot, June 21, 1921, Pinchot Papers, Box 242; Walsh to W. M. Johnston, November 12, 1918, Walsh Papers; and Seward W. Livermore, "The Sectional Issue in the 1918 Congressional Elections," *Mississippi Valley Historical Review*, XXXV (June, 1948), 29-60.

existed and exerted an influence of subtle though powerful proportions is certain.

The organized conservationists from the start had resisted as best they could the regional prejudices that might reduce their influence on policy or disrupt their plans in Congress. Nevertheless, as advocates of a withdrawal policy they had to face intrenched hostility from many western interests. The conservationists were of course convinced that their policies benefited the western people, as distinguished from the big interests. They were correct in asserting, as Pinchot did, that "monopolistic control was infinitely more potent in the West . . . than in the East." [70] It was in this region of the enterprising pioneer and the free individual that the special interests attained their most ruthless power. The Southern Pacific Railroad, the Standard Oil Company of California, Colorado's corporate interests or "the Beast" (as described by Judge Ben Lindsey), the Phelps Dodge corporation in Arizona, and the Anaconda Copper Company of Montana (Standard Oil) were notorious examples. Edward L. Doheny's Pan-American Petroleum Company and Harry Sinclair's Mammoth Oil Company were worthy inheritors of at least a portion of this tradition — that the United States government was fair game.

The West, however, was always divided. Men like Representative William Kent and Governor George C. Pardee of California, Judge Ben Lindsey of Colorado, Senator John B. Kendrick of Wyoming, and Governor Joseph M. Dixon of Montana were in the conservationist camp. The trend in the Progressive Era was conservationist. Roosevelt's dramatic flair was combined with Pinchot's incessant labors for the cause. It was formidable propaganda for the justice, wisdom, and democracy of the federal government's program. Western senators and representatives, who had been almost unanimous against the land withdrawals, who favored the old policy of gift and sale, slowly had to recognize the handwriting on the wall. Public sentiment had come to favor the forest reserves, the government retention of mineral areas and water power sites, and an active federal policy. As Senator Walsh of Montana saw the situation in 1919, it was "useless" to declaim against leasing. "Almost every western Senator has protested loud and long and

70 Pinchot, "How Conservation Began," *Agricultural History*, XI (October, 1937), 264-65.

often. It is a condition and not a theory that confronts us." If these lands were to be developed, he concluded, Congressmen had better compromise on a leasing bill.[71] One incentive to compromise was the probability that western states would share handsomely in royalties accruing from federal lands within their borders. To some, compromise seemed in the air; sectionalism seemed on the decline.

Though the West and the South have often been allied in politics, they seldom were allied on conservation policy. Slattery suggested that the South's residue of state-rights feeling accounted for its apparent lack of interest in the support of federal measures to regulate resources,[72] but as a matter of fact the anti-conservationists got little comfort from below the Mason and Dixon line. Edward T. Taylor, a Democratic representative from Colorado and one of the die-hards opposing conservation, took note of this fact in 1914. Referring to the southern failure to help the West by resisting "carpetbag control" from Washington, Taylor said: "I want to say to my genial friends from the sunny South that during my six years of service in this House I never yet have been able to understand why the members from the Southern states, that had such a long and serious experience in being governed by appointive officials from Washington, controlled by nonresident officers, can not only complacently vote for but work for propositions controlling our western states . . . from Washington." [73]

Among the Democrats who contributed importantly to the promotion of the Roosevelt-Pinchot program or its continuation under Wilson were such southerners or border-state men as Representatives William B. Craig (Alabama), Scott Ferris (Oklahoma), and Asbury F. Lever (South Carolina), Attorneys General James C. McReynolds (Tennessee) and Thomas W. Gregory (Texas), Secretary of the Navy Josephus Daniels (North Carolina), and Senator Claude A. Swanson (Virginia).[74] Some co-operated with the

[71] Walsh to Senator Charles B. Henderson (Nevada), September 2, 1919, Walsh Papers. See also Robbins, *Our Landed Heritage*, 394-95.

[72] Slattery to Pinchot, enclosing "News Letter on Conservation," March 19, 1919, Pinchot Papers, Box 1842.

[73] *Cong. Record*, 63 Cong., 2 Sess., 15053 (September 12, 1914). A year later Taylor observed that the "conservation sentiment of the North and of the South" was almost "unanimously" in favor of a federal leasing program. Address at Conference of the Mining Society of America, December 16, 1915, printed in *Senate Docs.*, 64 Cong., 1 Sess. (1916), No. 233, p. 21.

[74] For comments by Ferris and Craig on early phases of the program, see *Cong.*

National Conservation Association, dominated by Pinchot; and Ferris, chairman of the House Committee on Public Lands from 1913 to 1919, enjoyed the confidence of both President Wilson and the Association. In 1918, however, Slattery wrote: "Ferris has recently been made Chairman of the Democratic Congressional Committee, which is certainly an unfortunate thing for us. Politics will begin undoubtedly to have quite a sweep with him, and we will certainly have to watch him from now on."[75] Secretary Daniels and Attorney General Gregory enjoyed good relations with the Pinchot group as well as with La Follette. Their principles were much the same,[76] and all contributed toward forcing a compromise on leasing, in which the special claimants to public lands, some of them fraudulent, would be granted a minimum of their demands.

The Northeast and the Southeast, in effect, were able at last to force a leasing system upon the West. The passage of the Water Power Act and the Mineral Leasing Act of 1920 inaugurated a new policy of continuing public ownership and federal trusteeship in which conservation and the national interest seemed to be the winners. These laws, said Senator Walsh, would be regarded in the future as a landmark no less important to western people than the Homestead Act of 1862 or the Mining Act of 1872.[77] Pinchot declared that the major portion of the Roosevelt program had now been achieved. Slattery, Wells, La Follette, and Daniels were among those who in spite of a few doubts indicated general satisfaction with the compromise.[78] Undoubtedly they had won something of a victory and the way had been prepared for a larger federal role in

Record, 61 Cong., 2 Sess., 5062, 5081-82 (April 20, 1910); for Lever's defense of Pinchot, *ibid.*, 63 Cong., 2 Sess., 15068 (September 12, 1914). See also Pinchot, "Open Letter to the Honorable Franklin K. Lane," August 12, 1916, Pinchot Papers.

75 Slattery to Wells, March 16, 1918, Pinchot Papers, Box 1838.

76 La Follette in *Cong. Record*, 65 Cong., 3 Sess., 4715-16 (March 1, 1919); *ibid.*, 66 Cong., 1 Sess., 4750 (September 3, 1919).

77 Helena (Mont.) *Independent*, August 3, 1924. See also Robbins, *Our Landed Heritage*, 394-97.

78 Pinchot to Slattery, February 24, 1920, Pinchot Papers, Box 1841; Pinchot to Theodore Roosevelt, Jr., February 18, 1921, and Slattery to Pinchot, April 3, 1921, *ibid.*, Box 242; Wells to Slattery, February 19, 1920, *ibid.*, Box 1700; Daniels to T. Spellacy, April 12, 1920, Daniels Papers, Box 239. Former Attorney General Gregory expressed the most serious reservations. Gregory to Daniels (for transmittal to the President), February 23, 1920, Thomas W. Gregory Papers (Division of Manuscripts, Library of Congress). In Wells's opinion, this compromise was "about the least harmful" that could be obtained. Wells "Memorandum," February 19, 1920, Pinchot Papers, Box 1700.

the future. The leasing laws of 1920 grew, however, from a long struggle, involving many people who remembered clearly the controversies of the recent past. To separate this and other conservation issues from the pall of suspicions and hatreds in 1918-1921 is impossible.

There was a special rancor after the passage of the leasing acts. Democrats claimed this legislation as an achievement for their party. The Republican conservationists retorted that they had originated this program; that without the vigilance of Pinchot and La Follette bad bills would have passed; and that the Sixty-sixth Congress, in which the compromise had been attained, was a Republican Congress elected in 1918.[79]

Progressive Republicans of the Pinchot variety developed a distrust for "southern reactionaries" and others in the Wilson administration.[80] They regarded as exceptions such men as Josephus Daniels or Thomas W. Gregory. Even President Wilson, they believed, had betrayed them at a critical point in the leasing fight by giving his support to the notorious Pittman bill in February, 1919.[81] Those for whom conservationists reserved a special contempt were Secretary Lane, A. Mitchell Palmer (who succeeded Gregory as attorney general in 1919), and Albert S. Burleson, the postmaster general. Certain Democratic senators were almost in the same class — the "western crowd" including Key Pittman of Nevada, James D. Phelan of California, Charles S. Thomas of Colorado,

[79] Slattery to Pinchot, June 5, 1920, Pinchot Papers, Box 1841; Pinchot to Theodore Roosevelt, Jr., February 18, 1921, *ibid.*, Box 242; Republican National Committee, "Questionaire [*sic*] on Conservation of National Resources," 1920, *ibid.*, Box 1860.

[80] Expressions of discontent and bitterness among progressive Republicans could be multiplied almost indefinitely. Pinchot, in announcing for Harding as the Republican nominee, declared that the country must be taken out of the hands of southern reactionaries. New York *Times*, August 30, 1920. See also Robert D. Carey (governor of Wyoming) to Harold Ickes, September 6, 1920, Harold Ickes Papers (Division of Manuscripts, Library of Congress), and Wells to Stephen W. Phillips, March 7, 1919 (marked "not sent"), Pinchot Papers, Box 1676.

[81] It seems probable that Wilson, concerned with problems of the peace, had yielded temporarily to western pressure and sanctioned the passage of this bill. See *Cong. Record*, 65 Cong., 3 Sess., 4490 (February 27, 1919); Pinchot wireless to Wilson, aboard U. S. S. *George Washington* [copy, undated, but February, 1919], Pinchot Papers, Box 1859, and Pinchot to Slattery, February 26, 1919, *ibid.*, Box 1842; Gregory, quoted in *Cong. Record*, 65 Cong., 3 Sess., 4492 (February 27, 1919); Daniels, quoted, *ibid.*, 4396 (February 27, 1919); La Follette analysis, *ibid.*, 4713-16 (March 1, 1919); Wells to Phillips, March 7, 1919 (marked "not sent"), Pinchot Papers, Box 1676, and Slattery to Pinchot, with enclosure of "News Letter on Conservation," March 19, 1919, *ibid.*, Box 1842.

and Walsh of Montana (coupled with Republicans like Reed Smoot of Utah and Albert B. Fall of New Mexico).[82]

Lane and Palmer were favorite targets, regarded as being worse than Richard Ballinger. Lane's administration was, and will continue to be, controversial; for he was a complex personality, and his seven years in office were critical for the conservation movement and for the security of the nation itself. Conservationists were convinced quite early in the Wilson years that Lane had turned out to be a dissembler, coming to Washington as a progressive from California, talking the language of an idealist and a conservationist, but siding in fact with special business interests. It is clear, however, that Lane did change after 1913, becoming pro-business in outlook, and though he often played the role of conservationist his heart lay with "the American Pioneer."[83] Palmer became persona non grata to progressives of both parties because of his role in the "Red Scare"; but more than that, as attorney general he assumed authority over the disposition of many public land cases, including petroleum cases in California, and was regarded as having failed to protect the public interest.[84] The progressive Republicans who had initiated conservation came to feel, therefore, that the Wilson administration had badly deteriorated and was no longer to be trusted. They hoped that their own party, after winning the election of 1920, would do better.

Conservation had arrived at a crisis in 1920-1921 more serious than its adherents suspected. Their achievements were not quite so momentous nor so unshakeable as they liked to believe. Political partisanship had become intensified; co-operation between north-

82 Slattery to Pinchot, August 19, 1919, Pinchot Papers, Box 1842. See also Slattery to Pinchot, August 2, 1917, *ibid.*, Box 1838; Pinchot to Samuel M. Lindsay, March 6, 1921, *ibid.*, Box 239; Slattery to Pinchot, January 16, 1917, and Pinchot reply, undated, *ibid.*, Box 1838.

83 See for example Ernest Knaebel (assistant attorney general) to A. I. McCormick, June 18, 1913, and Lane to Knaebel, July 3, 1913, enclosing letter from M. V. McQuigg to Lane, May 27, 1913, Department of Justice, Record Group 60 (National Archives); Lane, *Reports of the Department of the Interior, 1915* (2 vols., Washington, 1916), I, 17-18; Lane, "The American Pioneer," address at San Francisco Exposition, February 20, 1915, in Pinchot Papers, Box 1856; Pinchot, "Open Letter to the Honorable Franklin K. Lane," August 12, 1916, *ibid.*

84 Statement of William Kent in Los Angeles *Record*, March 2, 1920 (clipping in Daniels Papers, Box 235); Daniels to A. Mitchell Palmer, December 6, 1919, quoted in R. G. Tracie, "History of the Naval Petroleum Reserves," MS. in Daniels Papers, Box 264; Daniels to Senator Walsh, May 20, 1924, *ibid.*, Box 582; John Ise, *The United States Oil Policy* (New Haven, 1926), 291-94.

erners and southerners in behalf of conservation had been rendered more difficult. Albert B. Fall and others who shared his views were moving into positions of responsibility. Many honest men during the 1920's declared for a watered-down version of conservation almost synonymous with business efficiency or gave serious consideration to plans for turning public lands over to the states. Business organizations appropriated, with more or less sincerity, the word "conservation." If ever an opportunity afforded itself for the rejection of Pinchot's ideals concerning democracy in resource use, this was the time.

Conservation not only survived the 1920's; it emerged in some respects stronger than ever. William Kent had observed in 1919 that the conservation principles were gaining acceptance all over the West and that, moreover, many of the ideals growing out of this movement were affecting sentiment in all directions. His own work in conservation had been of all his efforts the most satisfying and constructive.[85] In 1923 Governor Joseph M. Dixon of Montana, the old "Bull Mooser" then engaged in a bitter struggle against the Anaconda Copper Company, remarked on the growing popularity of the conservation policy. Even its enemies in the West were being converted, he wrote to Pinchot. "It would surprise you to know with what unanimity the people of the West now acquiesce to your own far-sighted vision of thirty years ago. The old crowd that fought so viciously against any governmental regulations of the forest and range are now your most pronounced friends. On several occasions during public talks, I have taken some satisfaction in 'rubbing it in' by telling them that 'Gifford Pinchot saved us [Westerners] from ourselves'." [86] At the height of the Teapot Dome scandal in 1924 Pinchot declared: "So far the only clear thing about it all seems to be that the conservation policy has once more completely defeated its enemies, and is more strongly in-

[85] Slattery to Pinchot, August 14, 1919, Pinchot Papers, Box 1842. See also Senator John B. Kendrick to Wilson, June 19, 1918, in which Kendrick asserted his conviction that "public sentiment during the past decade has undergone a very great change and . . . the country is now practically unanimous in the belief that the great resources on the public domain should be held for the benefit of the many rather than sequested [*sic*] by a few for the benefit of a few." Records of the Department of Justice, Record Group 60 (National Archives).

[86] Joseph M. Dixon to Pinchot, August 17, 1923, Pinchot Papers, Box 245. See also J. Leonard Bates, "Senator Walsh of Montana, 1918-1924" (Ph.D. dissertation, University of North Carolina, 1952).

trenched in the public confidence and consideration than ever before." [87]

In spite of its complexity, in spite of its ambiguity, the conservation policy contained an inner vitality that could not be obscured or destroyed. Here was an effort to implement democracy for twentieth-century America, to stop the stealing and exploitation, to inspire high standards of government, to preserve the beauty of mountain and stream, to distribute more equitably the profits of this economy. From McGee, to Pinchot and La Follette, to George Norris and Harold Ickes, to Wayne Morse and Lister Hill — there has burned a democratic zeal, a social faith. The faith was genuine; the propaganda effective. Though a careful evaluation of the impact upon this country remains to be made, it is difficult to escape the conclusion that a fighting band of conservationists has made the United States much richer in material wealth and in the democratic spirit and faith of its people.

87 Pinchot to Sir Horace Plunkett, February 27, 1924, Pinchot Papers, Box 252. See also J. Leonard Bates, "The Teapot Dome Scandal and the Election of 1924," *American Historical Review* (New York), LX (January, 1955), 303-22; Robbins, *Our Landed Heritage*, 401-402, 412-17; E. Louise Peffer, *The Closing of the Public Domain* (Stanford, 1951), 288-90.

Objectives and Methods in Intellectual History

By John C. Greene

The rapid rise of intellectual history to prominence in the world of American scholarship has occasioned considerable comment in recent years. Most observers of this development have found it more remarkable for vitality and scope than for clarity as to aims, methods, and subject matter. In 1949 Merle Curti reported "much stirring and productivity" in the new domain of history but conceded that "basic methodological problems" remained largely unsolved.[1] In 1951 John Higham described American intellectual history as "still seeking coherence, still eluding confinement."[2] In a similar vein, Charles A. Barker attributed three main characteristics to the growing movement in both social and intellectual history: "its newness, its bigness, and its unorganized — that is to say its little-interpreted — condition."[3] More recently Henry L. Swint reported "an extreme looseness of definition and disparity of emphasis" in the courses offered in social and intellectual history in various institutions throughout the country. Although he disclaimed any intention to establish rigid boundary lines or to limit the free play of the mind, Swint nevertheless concluded that "Free discussion of terms, concepts, areas, and purposes should . . . result in a better understanding of the general purpose or goals of social history and of intellectual history and should to some extent clarify the confusion which apparently exists among specialists in the field."[4]

The consensus of these observers — specialists themselves — is

[1] Quoted in Thomas C. Cochran, "A Decade of American Histories," *Pennsylvania Magazine of History and Biography* (Philadelphia), LXXIII (April, 1949), 153.

[2] John Higham, "The Rise of American Intellectual History," *American Historical Review* (New York), LVI (April, 1951), 453.

[3] Charles A. Barker, "Needs and Opportunities in American Social and Intellectual History," *Pacific Historical Review* (Berkeley), XX (February, 1951), 3, 7.

[4] Henry L. Swint, "Trends in the Teaching of Social and Intellectual History," *Social Studies* (Philadelphia), XLVI (November, 1955), 243, 249.

that intellectual historians need to exchange ideas concerning aims and methods in their field of study. By way of contributing to such a discussion, the following pages offer a provisional definition of intellectual history, explain and illustrate the method of research implied in the definition, and argue the advantage to be gained by a wider application of this method in American intellectual history. No particular originality is claimed for the views presented. On the contrary, the author's debt to such writers as Alfred North Whitehead, Max Weber, Arthur O. Lovejoy, and Perry Miller should be obvious.[5] If the ensuing reflections contain anything new, it is the suggestion that the methods employed so successfully by these writers be applied more generally and more consistently in the study of American thought. It should be emphasized, however, that the author does not aim to construct a Procrustean bed in which everyone who would call himself an intellectual historian must lie. Every definition, every method, has its advantages and disadvantages. Doubtless the approach recommended here has its limitations, but in a field characterized by "extreme looseness of definition and disparity of emphasis" almost any definition is better than none. At the very least it may challenge others to formulate a more adequate one.[6]

In the view of the present writer, the primary function of the intellectual historian is to delineate the presuppositions of thought in given historical epochs and to explain the changes which those presuppositions undergo from epoch to epoch. All history is intellectual history in some sense, but it is the peculiar province of the intellectual historian to search for and describe those most general ideas, or patterns of ideas, which inform the thought of an age, define its intellectual problems, and indicate the direction in which solutions are to be sought. The historian of science, for example, may study the origins of the doctrine of organic evolution, the stu-

[5] Grateful acknowledgment is also made to the following persons for stimulating and helpful criticism of the present article: Merle Curti, Crane Brinton, Richard H. Shryock, Bert J. Loewenberg, Henry F. May, Charles A. Barker, George L. Mosse, Roy H. Pearce, Stow Persons, Arthur Bestor, Robert A. Lively, Charles G. Sellers, John W. Ward, Thomas LeDuc, Arthur M. Schlesinger, Sr.

[6] For other recent attempts to define intellectual history and its problems see, for example, Crane Brinton, *Ideas and Men: The Story of Western Thought* (New York, 1950), Introduction; Franklin L. Baumer, "Intellectual History and Its Problems," *Journal of Modern History* (Chicago), XXI (September, 1949), 191-203; John Higham, "Intellectual History and Its Neighbors," *Journal of the History of Ideas* (New York), XV (June, 1954), 339-47.

dent of political philosophy the development of natural rights theory, the religious historian the debate concerning revealed and natural religion, but it is the intellectual historian whose special task it is to delineate the general conceptions of nature which informed men's thinking on all of these topics in a given era. Particular philosophies, ideologies, and scientific or artistic theories interest the student of the history of philosophy, politics, science, art, or literature. The more general patterns pervading the thought of an age are the object of the intellectual historian's attention. If he can delineate those patterns, he will have rendered a valuable service to all who study particular developments in the period, and it will be a service which he best can render.

But how does one discover the presuppositions of thought in a given age? The process involves both analysis and synthesis. This process might be illustrated in many ways, but it will be best to give one extended illustration from a period in which the author feels at home. Suppose, then, that one's aim is to delineate the dominant view of nature in the eighteenth century. One can dive in almost anywhere in either European or American sources — by examining the great debate between the friends of revelation and the advocates of natural religion, by reading the works of natural scientists, or by studying the poetry or political philosophy of the age. All that is needed is a wide coverage of material and a capacity to penetrate to implicit major premises. One soon discovers that these premises are related to each other and that an effort of synthesis is required to display their relations. It becomes apparent, moreover, that there was not just *one* pattern of thought in the epoch, but that there were several, some dominant, the others subdominant, incipient, or vestigial. These general modes of thought often coexisted in the mind of a single individual even when they were not entirely compatible with each other. They manifested themselves simultaneously in a single paragraph of his writings. They were not the particular views of particular individuals or even of particular groups of individuals; they were tendencies or patterns which the intellectual historian, aided by hindsight, discerns in the thought of the age.

To drive this point home it may be worth while to analyze in detail the underlying views of nature in the eighteenth century, defining that century broadly so as to include the period from

Newton, whose *Principia* was first published in 1687, to Laplace, whose *Traité de Mécanique Céleste* was completed in 1825. After reading widely in writings on natural history and on natural and revealed religion in this period, the present writer arrived at the following formulation of the dominant view of nature.[7] Nature was conceived primarily as a framework of rationally contrived structures fitted as a stage for the activities of intelligent beings. The words *framework*, *structures*, and *stage* all express the dominant sentiment of the stability and permanence of the great features of nature: the fixed stars, the everlasting hills, the eternal seas, the created species. Change was recognized as a real aspect of nature, but a superficial aspect. It contributed variety to nature's panorama, but it could not alter her fundamental structures. Change might take the form of decline from original perfection, of cyclical movement serving to maintain the status quo, or of random variation about a norm, but in no case could it produce real novelty.

Closely linked to the idea of the permanence of the basic structures of nature was the conviction of their intelligent design. The framework of natural structures was regarded as divinely contrived

[7] The following titles selected from various fields of thought afford a sample of the kinds of source materials from an examination of which the present delineation of views of nature in the eighteenth century was constructed: John Ray, *The Wisdom of God Manifested in the Works of the Creation* (3rd ed., London, 1701); William Paley, *Natural Theology: or, Evidences of the Existence and Attributes of the Deity, Collected from the Appearances of Nature* (3rd ed., London, 1803); William Smellie, *The Philosophy of Natural History* (Dover, N. H., 1808); Timothy Dwight, *Theology Explained and Defended, in a Series of Sermons* (12th ed., 4 vols., New York, 1846); William M. Van der Weyde (ed.), *The Life and Works of Thomas Paine* (10 vols., New York, 1925); Ethan Allen, *Reason the Only Oracle of Man: or a Compendious System of Natural Religion* (New York and Philadelphia, 1836); Carolus Linnaeus, *A General System of Nature*, tr. by William Turton (7 vols., London, 1806); Georges Cuvier, *The Animal Kingdom Arranged in Conformity with its Organization*, tr. by M. M'Murtrie (4 vols., New York, 1831); Pierre Simon Laplace, *The System of the World*, tr. by Henry H. Harte (2 vols., Dublin, 1830); Immanuel Kant, *Kant's Cosmogony as in His Essay on the Retardation of the Rotation of the Earth and His Natural History and Theory of the Heavens*, tr. and ed. by William Hastie (Glasgow, 1900); Saul K. Padover (ed.), *The Complete Jefferson* (New York, 1943); Jedidiah Morse, *The American Geography* (2nd ed., London, 1792); Samuel Stanhope Smith, *An Essay on the Causes of the Variety of Complexion and Figure in the Human Species* (2nd ed., New Brunswick, 1810); Peter Shaw (ed.), *The Philosophical Works of the Honourable Robert Boyle, Esq.* (2nd ed., 3 vols., London, 1738); Georges Louis Le Clerc (Comte de Buffon), *Natural History, General and Particular*, tr. by William Smellie (2nd ed., 9 vols., London, 1785); Jared Sparks (ed.), *The Works of Benjamin Franklin* (10 vols., Chicago, 1882), Vol. VI. Specific illustrations of the dominant view of nature may be found in the present writer's "Some Early Speculations on the Origin of Human Races," *American Anthropologist* (Menasha, Wis.), LVI (February, 1954), 31-41, and "Some Aspects of American Astronomy 1750-1815," *Isis* (Cambridge), XLV (December, 1954), 339-58.

to support the activities of intelligent, moral beings. Design and permanence went together, as did their antitheses, chance and change. The earth, since it was intended as a habitation for man, must have the stability and conformation requisite in a well-designed stage, however much accidental vicissitudes might alter the details. The same must be true of the planets and of all the other globes distributed throughout space. To the eighteenth-century mind, whether deist or Christian, it was axiomatic that matter existed to sustain mental and moral activity. The realms of space *must* be inhabited by intelligent beings, otherwise all those celestial bodies would have been created in vain. So it seemed to Sir William Herschel and to Tom Paine as well as to Archdeacon Paley and to the American clergyman and educator Timothy Dwight.

The perfect balance of nature was still another corollary of this general view of things. Whether in the motions of the solar system, or in the mutual preying of animals on each other, or in the cycle of geological processes on the surface of the earth, change in one direction was thought to be compensated by change in another, while nature as a whole remained unchanged. So fixed was this idea that when the evidence for the extinction of species and the disappearance of stars became too strong for disbelief, the breach in traditional attitudes was repaired by the calm assumption that nature had made provision for replacing these losses.

This is not to say that all of the elements of this pattern of thought were peculiar to the eighteenth century. On the contrary, many of them can be traced back to the Greeks, and not a few have survived to the present day. It was the combination, or general pattern, of ideas that was peculiar to the Newtonian period broadly defined. It would be possible to describe this pattern more fully and to illustrate its ubiquity by examples drawn from various fields of thought. One thinks, for example, of the notion of linguistic decay, of the myth of the social contract, of Blumenbach's theory of race formation by degeneration from the original model of the human species, of Linnaeus' contempt for varieties as the "sports of nature," of Paine's conception of the solar system as a schoolroom designed by the Almighty Lecturer, of Jefferson's bland assurance that God would not place man on earth without giving him a moral sense, of Newton's argument for the divine origin of the solar system, and of many other manifestations of the same habit of thought.

The main argument will be better served, however, by considering the relations of this dominant view of nature to a subdominant, or incipient, view of nature which took root in the seventeenth century, developed in uneasy subordination to the dominant view for nearly two centuries, and eventually emerged dominant itself, though in a somewhat modified form, in the late nineteenth century. This was the conception of nature as a law-bound system of matter in motion, the cosmology elaborated in the seventeenth century by the founders of the science of mechanics — Galileo, Descartes, Huyghens, and Newton — and neatly summarized in Newton's speculation that "God in the Beginning form'd Matter in solid, massy, hard, impenetrable, moveable Particles, of such Sizes and Figures, and with such other Properties, and such Proportion to Space, as most conduced to the end for which he form'd them." [8]

The bearing of this cosmology on the doctrine of special providence is well understood; not so its bearing on the view of nature just described. In some respects the mechanical cosmology bore the imprint of the dominant view of nature. Newton's impenetrable atom was an example par excellence of a permanent structure which participated in the world of change without being altered thereby. The atom simply was what it was because God had designed it a certain way and intended it to stay that way. But however immutable the atom might be, the idea that visible nature is produced by the combinations and permutations of a system of material particles in motion had disturbing implications for the dominant view of nature, the view expressed in John Ray's definition of the works of the creation as "the Works created by God at first, and by him conserved to this Day in the same State and Condition in which they were first made." [9] There was nothing in the idea of a law-bound system of matter in motion to suggest the stability of the structures produced by its functioning. Mutability, not stability, was the logical outcome of such a system, and, since every state of the system proceeded by rule from the preceding state, it was hard to see why any state should be regarded as initial or as final. As Kant was to show in the following century, the argument from design could

[8] Isaac Newton, *Opticks: or, A Treatise of the Reflections, Refractions, Inflections, and Colours of Light* (4th ed., London, 1730), 375-76. See also Robert Boyle, *The Origin of Forms and Qualities; Serving as an Introduction to the Mechanical Philosophy*, in Shaw (ed.), *Philosophical Works of Robert Boyle*, I, 214-15.

[9] Ray, *The Wisdom of God Manifested in the Works of the Creation*, Preface.

be saved only by supposing that the Creator had planned the history of nature *ab initio*.[10] But these implications of the new science and cosmology were slow to develop. Newton and Boyle were aware of them, but they managed to reconcile the conception of nature as a system of matter in motion with the dominant view of the stability and wise design of the fundamental structures of nature by supposing that God had so contrived the properties of matter and the laws of motion that they would perpetually produce the stable world required for His moral purpose.[11] A long road stretched from Robert Boyle's *Origin of Forms and Qualities*, published in 1666, to Charles Darwin's *Origin of Species*, and on every mile of that road the progress toward an evolutionary view of nature was impeded by the deeply ingrained conviction that nature was a framework of rationally contrived structures adapted to support the activities of intelligent beings. The dominant view did not yield its supremacy without a severe and protracted struggle.

Almost imperceptibly the discussion has shifted from the problem of delineating the presuppositions of thought in a given period to the problem of explaining how and why a dominant view ceases to be dominant and a subdominant view achieves dominance. This is as it should be, for only by describing the patterns of thought at two different moments in history can the historian mark out a movement of thought. Before one can explain an intellectual development, one must be able to define it by indicating the *terminus a quo* and the *terminus ad quem*. This task of definition requires of the historian a broad exposure to the relevant source materials, a logical

[10] "Matter, which is the primitive constituent of all things, is . . . bound to certain laws, and when it is freely abandoned to these laws it must necessarily bring forth beautiful combinations. It has no freedom to deviate from this perfect plan. Since it is thus subject to a supremely wise purpose, it must necessarily have been put into such harmonious relationships by a First Cause ruling over it; and there is a God, just because nature even in chaos cannot proceed otherwise than regularly and according to order." Immanuel Kant, *Universal Natural History and Theory of the Heavens*, in Hastie (ed. and tr.), *Kant's Cosmogony*, 23.

[11] See Newton, *Opticks*, 377-78, for evidence of his uneasiness about the temptation to derive the structures of nature, including the solar system, from the combinations and permutations of the system of matter in motion: "For it became who created them [the ultimate particles of matter] to set them in order. And if he did so, it's unphilosophical to seek for any other Origin of the World, or to pretend that it might arise out of a Chaos by the mere Laws of Nature." See also Boyle, *Excellence and Grounds of the Mechanical Philosophy*, in Shaw (ed.), *Philosophical Works*, I, 187: "nor do I suppose, when God had put into the whole mass of matter, an invariable quantity of motion, he needed do no more to make the universe; the material parts being able, by their own unguided motions, to throw themselves into a regular system."

habit of mind, and a keen eye for the recurrence of the telltale words and phrases which unlock the thought habits of a bygone age. When an eighteenth-century writer uses the adjectives *fixed*, *appointed*, *assigned*, or, conversely, *accidental* or *adventitious*, that is when he unconsciously shows his hand. It makes little difference for this purpose whether he is a "great thinker" or just a country parson grinding out a sermon. Noah Webster's *History of Animals* or Jefferson's *Notes on Virginia* will do quite as well as Linnaeus' *System of Nature* or Kant's *Natural History and Theory of the Heavens*. The greater the range and variety of source materials, the more certain one is that the pattern which emerges is indeed a general pattern, the pattern of the age.

But when, after defining a movement of thought, one seeks to explain how and why it took place, the problem becomes infinitely more complicated. It is no longer a simple matter of textual analysis, for a great many non-logical factors play a part in transitions of thought. True, there is an internal development of thought arising out of the intellectual effort of successive generations of thinkers. In this development the great thinker plays a peculiarly important part, the analysis of which will always be one of the major tasks of the intellectual historian. But the intellectual discoveries and mythopoeic creations of men of genius are only single strands in the complicated web of causes which produces a movement of thought. World view exerts an enormous influence, ideology speeds or delays the transitions of thought in behalf of partisan purpose, and technology alters drastically the conditions of life, thereby changing human receptivity to certain ideas and attitudes. To ascertain the exact force of these and other causal influences in producing a major change of intellectual habit seems impossible, but the intellectual historian must make as close an approximation as he can.

Here again an example is in order. If one attempts to explain the great movement of thought which led from John Ray's *The Wisdom of God Manifested in the Works of the Creation*, published in 1691, to Herbert Spencer's *First Principles*, and from Boyle's *Origin of Forms and Qualities* to Darwin's *Origin of Species*, one must take into consideration a great many causal factors. One must consider, for example, the cumulative effect of the growth of empirical knowledge concerning the earth and its inhabitants, the discoveries resulting from technical innovations, and the contribution of scientific genius, whether, as in the case of Linnaeus and Cuvier, the contribution was made within the context of received ideas concerning nature, or whether, as in the case of Buffon, Erasmus Darwin, and Lamarck, it consisted in a restless search for a new key to old problems, involving a determined attempt to throw off the omnipresent influence of the dominant view of nature by exploring the implications of the subdominant view. One must also consider the extent to which ideological conflict drew out the implications of the new science and cosmology. The reformers of the eighteenth century found in the Newtonian system of matter in motion a convenient symbol of the kind of society they hoped to usher in — a society in which the activities of innumerable individuals, each pursuing his own happiness, would eventuate by divine contrivance in the general welfare of mankind. In Newton's demonstration of the motions of the solar system these reformers found a perfect physical model of their social ideal, a model which seemed to vindicate that ideal by proving it "natural." At the same time the conception of nature as a law-bound system of matter in motion could be used to discredit the Scriptural sanctions invoked by conservatives in defense of antiquated institutions, for did it not exclude the possibility of miracles, including those miracles which were supposed to prove the divine origin of the Bible and of the Christian dispensation? Clearly, the world-machine had its polemical uses in the struggle for reform in the eighteenth century. In the next century the Marxians would push its logic even further in an attempt to discredit not only Christianity but liberal bourgeois society as well. Materialism and mutability would be extended to the realm of social thought. It was Marx, it will be recalled, who declared that "the present society is no solid crystal, but an organism capable of change and . . . constantly changing." [12]

The drawing out of the implications of the seventeenth-century cosmology undermined many traditional conceptions — the doctrine of the plenary inspiration of Scripture, the conviction of the stability of nature, the notion that matter is subordinate to mind, the cosmological argument from design — but it could not in itself suggest the idea of evolution, or progressive improvement, in na-

[12] Karl Marx, *Capital: A Critical Analysis of Capitalist Production*, tr. from 3rd German edition by Samuel Moore and Edward Aveling (New York, 1890), "Preface to the First Edition," 16.

ture. The advance of this idea in biology resulted from a variety of causes, too numerous and complex to discuss fully here. The gradual uncovering of the fossil record was one factor, but an earlier and more pervasive influence on biological thought was the general sense of progressive improvement in society; and this in turn had economic and technological, as well as intellectual, roots. The extension to the cosmic order of the growing social and historical optimism is illustrated in Erasmus Darwin's suggestion "that all nature exists in a state of perpetual improvement by laws impressed on the atoms of matter by the great CAUSE OF CAUSES." "This idea," he declared, "is analogous to the improving excellence observable in every part of the creation; such as in the progressive increase of the wisdom and happiness of its inhabitants; and is consonant to the idea of our present situation being a state of probation, which by our exertions we may improve." [13]

Many other factors in the transition to an evolutionary conception of nature deserve attention, but those already mentioned should suffice to indicate the types of investigation involved in a causal analysis of a major intellectual movement. It should be recognized, however, that abstract analysis is not the final goal of the intellectual historian's labors. The end product of research in intellectual history, as in all history, should be a narative which not only tells what happened and how and why it happened but makes it happen again for the reader. To accomplish this task the intellectual historian must pay attention to the affective tone of general ideas and to their concrete manifestations in language, literature, art, and popular myth. He must realize, for example, that every world view involves an emotional as well as an intellectual apprehension of nature. When nature is conceived as an artifact contrived by a transcendent God, the contemplation of nature evokes delight and wonder at the divine ingenuity. But when God is thought to be immediately present in nature, admiration gives way to rapture: "God, I can push the grass apart, And lay my finger on thy heart." Thus, sensitivity to affective tone is as requisite in the study of intellectual history as analytical acumen. Without it the historian can never reach beyond description and causal analysis to re-create the past and make it live again in men's imaginations.

So much concerning intellectual history in general. What of

[13] Erasmus Darwin, *Zoonomia: or, the Laws of Organic Life* (4th Amer. ed., 2 vols., Philadelphia, 1818), I, 400-401, 437.

American intellectual history in particular? At first blush it may seem that investigations of the kind described have little to do with American intellectual history. They belong, it may be urged, to the general history of Western thought and concern developments in Europe more than those in America. They may provide useful background material for studies in American intellectual history, but they are not of its essence, hence they should be left to students of European thought. America for the Americans; Europe for the Europeans.

This Monroe Doctrine in intellectual history is entirely untenable. The peculiarity of general ideas is their ubiquity in time and place. Western thought is all of a piece. It cannot be chopped up into centuries and countries without rendering it lifeless and meaningless. American thought is but an aspect of Western thought, inseparable from it in any effective sense. The truth of this proposition should be apparent from what has already been said about views of nature in the eighteenth century. By way of more concrete illustration, however, it may be worth while to consider a specific development in American thought, such as, for example, the conflict between science and religion. Now the conflict between science and religion has undoubtedly had some special features in America which were not present in the same degree in a predominantly Catholic country like France or in a Protestant country with an established church, such as England, nor is there any question that these and other national peculiarities require special study. But surely one should try to understand the general nature of the conflict between science and religion before undertaking to study its distinctive manifestations in the American environment. How is one to know what is peculiar and unique until one knows what is common and general? Here is a pitfall into which many have stumbled by trusting to secondary accounts or to a brief survey of European writers to form their ideas of the general state of knowledge and opinion. Some historians, for example, have thought to find distinctively American causes for ideas and attitudes in Jeffersonian America without realizing that these thought patterns were common in the Western world long before Jefferson's time.

But to return to the conflict between science and religion, how can the general nature of this conflict be understood without a searching inquiry into the structure of Western thought? Consider, for example, the overwhelming importance in this conflict of the doctrine of the plenary inspiration of Scripture, the doctrine which maintains that the Bible is of divine origin and that everything in it, properly understood, is substantially true.[14] The influence of this doctrine in American thought has been insufficiently appreciated. One looks in vain in most books on American intellectual history for a satisfactory exposition of the doctrine. One reads, of course, that the Bible was very important in American thought, that it was regarded as divinely inspired, that the progress of natural science and Biblical criticism did much to impair belief in Scripture, but, except in a very few books, one fails to learn in what sense it was believed to be inspired, what rules were laid down for its interpretation, what were the "internal" and "external" evidences supporting the belief in its divine origin, what arguments were advanced to show the inherent probability that God would make such a revelation to man, or what grounds were alleged for expecting such a revelation to be mysterious to human reason. Still less does one form any conception of the influence of the doctrine, or of the intellectual and spiritual consequences of its decline.

To illustrate. The assumption of plenary inspiration by the friends of revelation dictated their way of conceiving the conflict between science and religion. What was science from their point of view? It was the study of God's truth as revealed in His works. What was theology? It was the study of God's truth as revealed in His Word. But surely God's truth could not conflict with God's truth, hence there could be no real conflict between science and reli-

14 "The true definition of inspiration, then, is SUCH A DIVINE INFLUENCE UPON THE MINDS OF THE SACRED WRITERS AS RENDERED THEM EXEMPT FROM ERROR, BOTH IN REGARD TO THE IDEAS AND THE WORDS. This is properly called PLENARY inspiration. Nothing can be conceived more satisfactory. Certainty, infallible certainty, is the utmost that can be desired in any *narrative*; and if we have this in the sacred Scriptures, there is nothing more to be wished in regard to this matter." Archibald Alexander, *Evidences of the Authenticity, Inspiration, and Canonical Authority of the Holy Scriptures* (Presbyterian Board of Publication, Philadelphia, n.d.), 230. Alexander was a professor of theology at the Presbyterian Seminary in Princeton in the mid-nineteenth century. For a Congregationalist view of plenary inspiration see Timothy Dwight, "On Revelation," *Sermons* (2 vols., New Haven, 1828), II, 61-78. The classic work on the evidences of Christianity, used for many years in American colleges, was William Paley's *A View of the Evidences of Christianity*, first published in London in 1794. It should be emphasized that the discussion in the present article refers only to the belief in the *plenary* inspiration of Scripture. Unitarians, such as Joseph Priestley and William Ellery Channing, believed in the inspiration of Scripture, but not in plenary inspiration. See William E. Channing, *A Discourse on the Evidences of Revealed Religion, Delivered before the University in Cambridge, at the Dudleian Lecture, March 14, 1821* (Boston, 1821).

gion. Any apparent conflict must result either from faulty science or from a faulty interpretation of Scripture. So the argument ran, and it is impossible to understand the wearisome series of reconciliations of science and the Bible by eminent scientists like Benjamin Silliman, James Dwight Dana, and Edward Hitchcock without first grasping their reasons for believing that science and Scripture must agree.[15]

The decline of belief in the plenary inspiration of Scripture had important intellectual and spiritual consequences. The point to be stressed is that the Bible so conceived provided a key to the great problem of man's origin, duty, and destiny, a problem to which most men feel the need of some answer. Believers in plenary inspiration might disagree as to the interpretation of Scripture, but they were united in the conviction that the Bible, properly interpreted, could teach man categorically and infallibly what it most concerned him to know. The decay of belief in plenary inspiration thus precipitated a search for a new key to the problem of human destiny. The deists thought to find it in nature and reason, but what their reason found in nature was little more than what Christian natural theology had taught them to expect to find there. The transcendentalists were the pietists of natural religion. They, too, looked to nature for the key to man's situation in the universe, but not to nature conceived as a system of matter in motion. For them, nature was the immediate manifestation of the divine presence, the garment of the living God. As the implications of the mechanical cosmology for the dominant view of nature were progressively revealed, both deists and transcendentalists were thrown on the defensive. Some men turned to history to find a clue to the meaning of human life; others to psychology; others made a religion of

[15] Thus, the oceanographer Matthew F. Maury laid it down as a rule of conduct "never to forget who is the Author of the great volume which nature spreads out before us, & always to remember that the same Being is also the Author of the book which Revelation holds up to us; & though the two works are entirely different, their records are equally true; & when they bear upon the same point . . . it is as impossible that they should contradict each other as it is that either should contradict itself. If the two cannot be reconciled, the fault is ours, & it is because, in our blindness & weakness, we have not been able to interpret aright, either the one or the other or both." Letter to "My dear Sir," Washington, D. C., January 22, 1855, Maury Collection (Division of Manuscripts, Library of Congress). It is interesting to observe how many of the ablest American scientists of Maury's day were evangelical in their faith and believers in the plenary inspiration of the Bible. The view of nature implicit in such a faith seems to have been more conducive to the study of natural science than that which informed transcendentalism.

science. Whatever the direction, the quest was the same. It was a search for a key such as that which had once been provided by a book believed to be divinely inspired and infallibly correct in everything it said.

If we probe still deeper into the conflict between science and religion, the hopelessness of attempting to study it in a purely American context becomes even more apparent. Not only the doctrine of plenary inspiration but also the dominant view of nature was crumbling before the onslaught of science. This process, already under way in the eighteenth century, developed rapidly in the nineteenth, affecting Christians, deists, and transcendentalists alike. Unfortunately, most writers have paid little attention to this development in the pre-Darwinian era. As a result, the treatment of Darwinism itself has been inadequate.

On its profoundest level, the conflict between science and religion involves an issue concerning the meaning and possibility of knowledge and the reliability of various ways of knowing. It is on this level that the conflict is taking place today. Surely our intellectual histories should acquaint the student with the general outlines of this great issue. They should cut beneath the bare exposition of pragmatism, instrumentalism, and other isms to the underlying tensions in Western thought, tensions which have manifested themselves in a thousand forms and contexts from the time of Plato and Aristotle to the present day. In short, the American intellectual historian must be first and foremost an intellectual historian and only secondarily an American historian.

Certain advantages may be expected to follow from a wider application of this approach to intellectual history. First, it gives to the intellectual historian a definite field of his own, with a clearly defined subject matter related in an intelligible way to the subject matter of surrounding disciplines. Although the intellectual historian works with the same materials that are used by the political historian, the student of literature, and the historian of science, he handles them in a different way with a different object in view. His findings, far from competing with those of scholars in related disciplines, should prove very useful to them. How thankful would the student of Progressivism be for a clear delineation of the most general presuppositions of thought regarding nature, human nature, and society in the world of the late nineteenth century! He himself may contribute to such a delineation, of course, but that is not his main concern. He must look to the intellectual historian for a general orientation in Western thought.

The second advantage follows from the first. It consists in helping to place American ideas in proper perspective and thus to set off their uniqueness and originality where they have any. It guards against naïve attempts to explain intellectual developments solely in terms of the frontier or some other peculiarly American influence. It places a damper on chauvinism and discourages parochialism.

Thirdly, it makes for a more balanced approach to American intellectual history. Anyone concerned with discovering the presuppositions of American thought and explaining their transformations will find it difficult to neglect religious thought as, in general, it has been neglected except for certain phases which have excited interest because of their bearing on literature, politics, or reform. The failure of American intellectual historians to reckon adequately with the doctrine of the plenary inspiration of Scripture is relevant in this connection. It is noteworthy, also, that the vast majority of Americans in the mid-nineteenth century belong to churches which described themselves as evangelical; yet, although we have many studies of transcendentalism, we have no general intellectual portrait of evangelical orthodoxy. It is natural, of course, that the directions of research in intellectual history should be dictated to a considerable extent by the personal interests of the researcher, but these cannot be his sole guide. Account must also be taken of the interests of the people whom he is investigating. If he is looking for the presuppositions of thought in seventeeth, eighteenth, or nineteenth century America, he cannot avoid prolonged study of religious writings, theology included.

Fourthly, the search for basic presuppositions demands and encourages an analytical habit of mind which is much needed in American intellectual history. There are several comprehensive descriptive accounts of American thought, but of works which attempt to analyze the structure of thought in given periods and to account in a systematic fashion for fundamental shifts of intellectual outlook there have been all too few. Notable exceptions, such as Perry Miller's studies of Puritanism, come to mind, but the fact remains that most writers on American intellectual history have been content to describe the surface of American thought.

These accounts are highly useful, but they need to be supplemented and illuminated by studies which penetrate to fundamental presuppositions, delineate the dominant and subdominant patterns of thought, and thus prepare the way for attempts at causal explanation. Thus, for example, simple descriptive accounts of mesmerism, spiritualism, adventism, hydropathy, and similar mid-nineteenth century phenomena are much to be desired, but studies of this kind in no way obviate the necessity for an approach which treats these phenomena collectively and undertakes, by a close analysis of the writings associated with them, to discover their lowest common denominator and thus to reveal some basic relations between new and old patterns of thought. This kind of undertaking requires careful training in textual analysis, training aimed at developing an analytical habit of mind. The practice required is in close examination of source materials for the underlying premises, with special attention to the connotations of words and to the recurrence of stock phrases and of situations in which the writer seems to be trying to adhere simultaneously to mutually incompatible patterns of thought. Training of this sort is extremely valuable for the teaching and writing of all forms of history. In intellectual history it is indispensable. Some historians suppose that simple descriptive studies can provide building blocks for reconstructing the general patterns of thought in a given period, but this is not the case. Such studies may yield a general impression of their subject and some occasional insights, but unless the author has attempted to discover underlying presuppositions, the reader is left with nothing but vague hunches and speculations to the effect, for example, that mesmerism, hydropathy, and similar phenomena may have been related to the frontier experience, to the mobility of American life, or to the insecurity of such and such a class. Hunches of this kind are valuable, but their verification requires systematic studies of the kind indicated.

Finally, the adoption of a more analytical approach to intellectual history should enable the intellectual historian to participate more effectively in cross-disciplinary projects. Historians have been urged to adapt the methods and tools of the social sciences to the study of history, but seldom have they seemed to realize that they have a contribution to make in return, especially in the field of intellectual history. For why should not the type of analysis that enables the intellectual historian to reconstruct the thought patterns of past ages prove equally serviceable in discovering the tensions in modern thought? It is true, of course, that the presuppositions of thought in the present age are those of the intellectual historian himself, and that he will therefore have difficulty in recognizing them for what they are. Nevertheless, it should be possible for an intellectual historian steeped in the thought of earlier periods and rendered sensitive by long practice to the underlying assumptions of written discourse to assist modern scientists, social scientists, historians, and others by calling attention to the thought patterns implicit in their writings. This may seem more a task for a logician than for an intellectual historian, but the time dimension is all-important. The tendencies and habits of thought which are dredged up by analysis have a long history, and the understanding of that history is relevant to the clarification of thought in the present. No other person is so well equipped for this task as the intellectual historian, for he specializes in describing patterns of thought and explaining their transformations.

The possibilities for intellectual collaboration of this kind are enormous. Social scientists in particular would benefit greatly from a systematic analysis of their writings by well-trained intellectual historians, nor is there any doubt that the historians themselves would learn something in the process. But intellectual history must have its own discipline before it can contribute much to cross-disciplinary studies. It must place less emphasis on encyclopedic coverage and more on the search for basic patterns and for the factors which produce change in those patterns. What it sacrifices in scope it will gain in clarity and force. These considerations apply to all intellectual history but especially to American intellectual history, which, as Professor Higham puts it, is "still seeking coherence, still eluding confinement."

In conclusion, it should be re-emphasized that no single approach to the study of the history of ideas is sufficient in itself. Tastes vary, problems vary, and every individual makes his contribution in his own way. To the present author it seems that a wider application of the approach here recommended would have beneficial effects on the study and writing of American intellectual history. But mere prescriptions and recipes do not constitute intellectual history. The proof of the pudding is in the eating, the proof of intellectual history in the reading.

The National Progressives of America, 1938

By Donald R. McCoy

Rarely has a period in American history been the subject of so much published history so soon afterward as that of the 1930's. Treatment of the politics of the decade, however, has been confined almost exclusively to the activities of the Democratic and Republican parties. Actually, independent political groups scored impressive victories in Minnesota, Nebraska, New York, and Wisconsin, and were astir with varying degrees of success in many other states. These movements also contributed significantly to the make-up of the New Deal in personnel, ideas, electoral support, and pressure for more advanced action.[1] Equally important, they posed a standing political threat to the Democratic party. The question as to why they remained only a threat may be answered in part by a study of the National Progressives of America, an organization which represented one of the more significant attempts to amalgamate these independent political groups into a new national party.

Rooted in the tradition of Wisconsin progressivism, the National Progressives of America was founded in 1938 by Philip F. La Follette, the younger son of Robert M. La Follette, Sr. Basic to the formation of the National Progressives were the political successes achieved by independent political groups in 1936. Not only had they gained important victories in their own right, but they believed that they had played an indispensable role in the re-election of President Roosevelt. In Minnesota, Farmer-Labor gubernatorial candidate Elmer A. Benson received a plurality, with a record-breaking total of about 680,000 votes. Progressive Philip La Follette, running successfully for re-election as Wisconsin's governor, received almost 600,000 ballots. The American Labor party

1 For an account of some of the contributions made by independents and third party leaders, see Donald R. McCoy, "The Progressive National Committee of 1936," *Western Political Quarterly* (Salt Lake City), IX (June, 1956), 454-69.

of New York polled some 275,000 votes for Roosevelt, while the Progressive National Committee and Labor's Non-Partisan League claimed to have attracted or held millions of voters for the President.[2]

These successes at the polls encouraged more and more independents to talk of going it alone on the national level. In late 1936 and 1937, considerable interest in forming a new national party of liberals and radicals was shown by the Minnesota and Wisconsin third parties, as well as by the socialists and communists.[3] Even Labor's Non-Partisan League and the American Labor party hinted that a new party might have to be organized to extend the gains made by labor and agriculture during Roosevelt's first term as president.[4]

Interest in a new political party was not confined to the leadership of the existing independent political movements. A large segment of the American public was also attracted to the idea. In an American Institute of Public Opinion poll, taken in December, 1936, 18 per cent of those questioned said that they would join a new farmer-labor party; by July, 1937, 21 per cent said that they would join.[5]

The appeal of new party action was strengthened by the development of several problems which harassed the Roosevelt administration in 1937 and early 1938. Dissension between labor leaders and the New Deal was quite apparent in 1937 because of the President's seeming impartiality in the bitter struggles between labor and industrial management, and the administration's tendency to ignore labor's advice on public policy.[6] Some labor leaders, particularly

[2] *Common Sense* (New York), VI, No. 1 (January, 1937), 24; *The Legislative Manual of the State of Minnesota* (Minneapolis, 1937), 206; *The Wisconsin Blue Book, 1937* (Madison, 1937), 420; Sidney Lens, *Left, Right, and Center: Conflicting Forces in American Labor* (Hinsdale, Ill., 1949), 316-19.

[3] Ernest Lundeen to the Chairman of the Minnesota Farmer-Labor Convention, January 28, 1937, and Minutes of the Minnesota Farmer-Labor Association's Executive Committee, July 17, 1937, Papers of the Minnesota Farmer-Labor Association (Minnesota Historical Society, St. Paul); Gordon Sinykin to Fred Bettelheim, Jr., November 11, 1936, Papers of Philip F. La Follette (State Historical Society of Wisconsin, Madison); New York *Times*, November 6, p. 6, November 24, 1936, p. 16; Earl Browder, *The People's Front* (New York, 1938).

[4] New York *Times*, November 7, pp. 1 and 8, November 12, 1936, p. 3; Stephen B. Sarasohn, "The Struggle for Control of the American Labor Party, 1936-1948" (M.A. thesis, Columbia University, 1948).

[5] Hadley Cantril and Mildred Strunk (eds.), *Public Opinion, 1935-1946* (Princeton, 1951), 576.

[6] New York *Times*, August 21, p. 1, August 24, p. 14, November 7, 1937, Sec. IV, p. 7.

John L. Lewis of the United Mine Workers, openly discussed the possibility of a third party.[7] Sharp reductions in the number of recipients of public works employment and relief after the 1936 elections also disillusioned many political supporters of the New Deal. These economy measures placed a severe burden on state and local emergency aid programs because industry could not absorb all those persons cut off from federal aid.[8]

Another disillusioning factor was the strong congressional opposition which confronted the President in 1937 and early 1938. The defeat of Roosevelt's proposals for executive and judicial reorganization, the emasculation of his slum clearance plan, and the delays encountered in the passage of crop control and wages and hours legislation, led many to conclude that he had lost control of Congress. Moreover, the administration's apparent inability to cope with the economic recession of 1937-1938 contributed significantly to liberal and radical dissatisfaction.[9] The ranks of the dissidents were further swelled when the President demanded increased naval and military expenditures. The sensitivity of many liberals and radicals to rearmament, especially its potential threat to civil liberties and economic stability, was heightened by Roosevelt's sudden interest in international collective security as revealed in his October, 1937, "Quarantine" speech.[10]

It was against the background of this apparent upsurge of dissatisfaction with the New Deal and the recent independent political successes that Philip La Follette undertook to organize the National Progressives of America. Since the political activities of the

[7] John L. Lewis, "The Struggle for Industrial Democracy," *Common Sense*, VI, No. 3 (March, 1937), 5-8; New York *Times*, August 21, p. 1, August 28, p. 3, September 4, 1937, p. 1.

[8] These reductions in the federal government's relief and public works programs were vigorously protested by a group of liberal governors including Elmer A. Benson of Minnesota, Henry Horner of Illinois, Philip La Follette of Wisconsin, Herbert H. Lehman of New York, and Frank Murphy of Michigan. New York *Times*, March 1, p. 1, March 2, 1937, p. 1.

[9] In late 1937 and early 1938, disgruntlement and disillusionment characterized commentaries on the national administration's recession policies and defeats in Congress in liberal periodicals like the *New Republic*, *Nation*, *Christian Century*, and *Common Sense*. These attitudes were also mentioned or reflected in the later writings of some of President Roosevelt's associates in their discussions of the period. See James A. Farley, *Jim Farley's Story: The Roosevelt Years* (New York, 1948), 91-150; Harold L. Ickes, *The Secret Diary of Harold L. Ickes* (3 vols., New York, 1953-1954), II, 260-340; Frances Perkins, *The Roosevelt I Knew* (New York, 1946), 302; Samuel I. Rosenman, *Working with Roosevelt* (New York, 1952), 169, 181.

[10] Arthur A. Ekirch, Jr., *The Civilian and the Military* (New York, 1956), 246-51.

National Progressives were to be so closely intermingled with those of the Wisconsin Governor, the part he played in this new party venture requires closer examination. La Follette had been elected Wisconsin's chief executive on the Republican ticket in 1930 at the age of thirty-three. After being defeated in the Republican primary election two years later, he assumed a passive political role until the establishment of the Wisconsin Progressive party in 1934. He gained virtual control of the new state party immediately upon its formation. With the aid of his brother, Senator Robert M. La Follette, Jr., he was able to bring it to electoral success, winning the governorship as a Progressive in the elections of 1934 and 1936.[11]

Prior to 1938, Governor La Follette generally had supported the Roosevelt administration, although on occasion he vigorously quarreled with New Deal policies. While the party which he headed theoretically proclaimed its intention to expand into a national party in conjunction with independent liberal forces elsewhere, La Follette eschewed such action until 1938. He held that other independent state and local groups were, with few exceptions, too weak politically to establish a significant new national party. "Any sound political realignment must be built state by state," he said. "We learned in my father's campaign in 1924 that it can't be done overnight in the nation, but must be developed in the states after a great deal of organization work."[12] This conclusion was realistic in view of President Roosevelt's attractiveness to most of the nation's liberals, and in view of the patronage and financial aid which the New Deal had extended to the Wisconsin Progressives.

Soon after the 1936 elections, however, the Governor became convinced that the President had abandoned any idea of effecting permanent measures to solve the nation's basic economic problems. La Follette contended that the large-scale discharge of Works Progress Administration personnel in 1937 constituted the first proof of this abandonment. As Roosevelt was increasingly plagued by new domestic and foreign problems in 1937, the Governor concluded that not only was the President unable to deal with them,

[11] For a study of the beginnings of the party, see Donald R. McCoy, "The Formation of the Wisconsin Progressive Party in 1934," *Historian* (San Francisco), XIV (Autumn, 1951), 70-90.

[12] Philip F. La Follette to Edwin Hadfield, Jr., October 7, 1937, P. La Follette Papers.

but, as a result, was losing the support of liberal leaders.[13] Another probable factor in La Follette's disaffection with Roosevelt was the possible loss of political strength to the Democratic party. La Follette feared that his party adherents, in voting for the Democrats nationally, might decide to desert the Wisconsin Progressive party altogether. In addition, the friendliness that had been manifest between Roosevelt and the Wisconsin third party had not been carried over into relations between the state's Democrats and Progressives. One Democratic party field agent, for example, protested to National Committee Chairman James A. Farley in 1936 that Wisconsin's Democratic leaders ignored the state's Republicans, but continually attacked the La Follette brothers, who were friendly to Roosevelt.[14]

With these considerations in mind, Philip La Follette decided to work toward the formation of a new political movement in the United States. His own role in the movement, according to his conception of it, would be to help crystallize sentiment, to offer advice, and to interest independent liberal leaders in doing the detailed organizational work required to lay the basis for a new party. Starting in the spring of 1937, he began to lay the groundwork by corresponding and conferring with hundreds of possible new party leaders.[15]

La Follette's first public step toward forming a new movement was taken at the May, 1937, celebration commemorating the third anniversary of the founding of the Wisconsin Progressive party. At that time, he urged the country's liberals to co-operate with the Wisconsin Progressives in building a new major party. "The Progressive party has just begun to fight," he declared. "It looks forward to a national existence and to a national realignment. The time is close at hand for the formation of a new political realignment in the nation which will defeat the reactionary forces of the nation just as the Progressive party has defeated the reactionary

13 Statement by P. La Follette, personal interview, April 4, 1952.

14 Otto La Budde to James A. Farley, July 20, 1936, Papers of the Democratic National Committee (Franklin D. Roosevelt Library, Hyde Park, N. Y.). The antagonism between the two parties was well illustrated by the successful move of Wisconsin's Democrats and Republicans to wrest patronage control from the Progressives for the appointment of some 20,000 election officials. Madison *Capital Times*, March 2, 1938, p. 1.

15 P. La Follette to Hadfield, October 7, 1937, P. La Follette Papers; statement by P. La Follette, personal interview, April 4, 1952.

forces of Wisconsin."[16] Later, Governor La Follette asserted in a speech in Des Moines that Roosevelt's "progressive leadership has been hamstrung by the swarm of reactionaries that infest the Democratic party."[17] Addressing a Labor Day celebration in Omaha, he lashed out at the "tweedledum and tweedledee politics [which] will destroy democracy in America," and asserted that a new political realignment must arise from "the vitality and liberalism of the middle west." Progress, he declared, would never result from a political party system in which liberals and conservatives were mixed helter-skelter in the two major parties; this could lead only to governmental inaction or some form of fascist dictatorship.[18]

In the summer of 1937, La Follette began to look for possible new party affiliates in other states. Through the efforts of Professor Paul H. Douglas, of the University of Chicago, he was put in touch with Raymond Haight, the leader of the California Progressive party. Haight, who had polled over 300,000 votes in the 1934 California gubernatorial election, was eager to expand the influence of his group through association with a national third party of liberals. After a good deal of investigation, La Follette concluded that the California Progressives would be welcome allies.[19] He also worked to gain the support of Mayor Fiorello La Guardia of New York, and to inspire the development and co-operation of the Iowa Farmer-Labor and Progressive movements. Meanwhile, La Follette continued to discuss economic ideas and new party action during the fall and winter of 1937-1938 with grass roots farm, labor, white collar, and small business leaders.[20] With the exceptions of Douglas, Haight, and La Guardia, however, he avoided consulting recognized independent and third party leaders on his political plans.

A clean break between Governor La Follette and the national

16 Madison *Capital Times*, May 19, 1937, pp. 1 and 8.

17 "La Follette Speech at Riverview Park, Des Moines," July 31, 1937, P. La Follette Papers.

18 Omaha *World Herald*, September 7, 1937, p. 7.

19 Paul H. Douglas to P. La Follette, July 16, La Follette to Douglas, July 19, Douglas to La Follette, July 21, and La Follette to Douglas, August 2, 1937; and La Follette to John R. Richards, August 11, Richards to La Follette, November 26, and La Follette to Richards, December 15, 1937; P. La Follette Papers.

20 John F. Wirds to P. La Follette, September 17, 1937, P. La Follette to Wirds, September 20, H. P. Fagan to Gordon Sinykin, September 12, P. La Follette Papers. Governor La Follette's attempts to enlist La Guardia's aid led him to suggest, on a visit to New York City, that Senator Robert La Follette, Jr., and the Mayor might well be the presidential and vice-presidential candidates of a new Progressive party. New York *Times*, March 1, 1938, p. 14.

administration came in April, 1938, when he vehemently attacked the New Deal's economic policies in a series of four radio talks. Referring to the existing recession, he declared that something was fundamentally wrong when after nine years of depression half of the American people were no better off than they had been in 1931. He recalled that after the election of 1936 the Progressives had urged upon the government the need for a sound, comprehensive, and carefully planned program. But "the national administration believed that the war on the depression had been won and that we were out of the woods," he declared. "Instead of a comprehensive program, it began to break camp, and to disband its army." [21] Condemning the policy of paying millions of people not to produce, La Follette called for a reorganization of the national economy to give the unemployed an opportunity to support themselves and thereby to add to the country's total wealth. He asserted that unified Progressive action was essential to make up for the failure of the New Deal.[22]

Senator Robert La Follette meanwhile had been persuaded to join his brother in working for a new political movement. Late in 1937 and continuing into 1938, Senator La Follete had been sharply critical of the government's economic policies, and had indicated his basic disagreement with the administration's military program and foreign policies. Typical of much of his criticism was his statement of April 24, 1938, in which he declared his opposition to Roosevelt's billion dollar naval expansion plan, and predicted that if the country geared its productive machinery to an expanding arms program, the worst depression in the world's history, and probably revolution, would occur when that expansion was stopped. He pleaded for a greater concentration on constructive internal improvements to replace the defeatist attitude "which says that we can do nothing but prepare for the inevitable war," and argued that a huge, low-cost housing program, for example, would be far more beneficial than building battleships, and would provide more employment.[23]

These April speeches and statements by the La Follette brothers served as the immediate fanfare for the establishment of the Na-

21 Madison *Capital Times*, April 21, 1938, pp. 3 and 10; New York *Times*, April 21, 1938, p. 3.

22 New York *Times*, April 22, p. 4, April 23, 1938, p. 2.

23 *Ibid.*, April 25, 1938, p. 7; Madison *Capital Times*, April 25, 1938, p. 1.

tional Progressives of America. Governor La Follette announced at the conclusion of his series of radio talks that a conference would be held in the University of Wisconsin Live Stock Pavilion on April 28, 1938, for the purpose of considering a reorganization of the liberal and progressive forces of the nation. Senator La Follette added that "a national third party is inevitable and now is the time to form one." [24]

The Live Stock Pavilion meeting, compared with other Progressive conferences, was unusual in its trappings. The gathering was "protected" by national guardsmen in shiny steel helmets and was marked by the display of a red, white, and blue cross-and-circle emblem.[25] A capacity crowd of 3,500 people attended the meeting. In an introductory speech, Judge Alvin Reis stressed that the liberal gains of the last five years would surely be lost if, as seemed probable, both the Democrats and the Republicans nominated conservative candidates for president in 1940. Progressives were urged by Judge Reis to prepare for such an event.[26] Governor La Follette gave the main address of the conference. The Governor decried the world-wide retreat of democracy as evidenced by the "rise of dictators, the destruction of democracy and the spectre of another world war." "The failure to produce enough real wealth" had been at the base of this retreat because it had compelled people to support authoritarian-type governments to regulate the division of wealth. In the United States, he declared, the significance of these facts should be plain. The nation had to regain an economy of abundance in order to save traditional American liberties and to maintain and improve the standard of living.

In the course of his address the Governor dismissed, one by one, the current economic ideologies as instrumentalities incompetent to do the job. Economic plenty and security, he said, could not be derived from socialist share-the-wealth schemes or from the rugged individualism of classic capitalism. The first doctrine contradicted

[24] New York *Times*, April 26, 1938, p. 5.

[25] The cross-and-circle symbol was seen by Governor La Follette as representing the unity of the nation, the power of the ballot, equality, and the need for multiplication of wealth and organized social action. Many people, undoubtedly to the detriment of the National Progressives, likened the emblem to Nazi and Fascist insignia. *Life* magazine reproduced the symbol under a half-page photograph of the Governor standing on a podium with his hand held up as if in the act of giving a Nazi salute. *Life* (New York), May 9, 1938, p. 9.

[26] Russel B. Nye, *Midwestern Progressive Politics, 1870-1950* (East Lansing, 1951), 372.

human nature in its impossible demand for absolute equality; the second was impractical in a society lacking a surplus of undeveloped natural resources. He also rejected Fascism and Communism as possible solutions to America's problems, because of their autocratic and coercive characteristics. In short, he insisted, the nation was not at a crossroad where it could turn to any one of these four ideologies. "*We are near the end of the road.* The time has come when a *new* trail must be blazed — a trail that will take fundamental teachings of the past and apply them to the modern world as we know it. . . . We [must] have the right to try new ways, or to retain the old." He called for modernization of the present form of government by giving the executive branch the power "to get things done." This could be accomplished, without threatening the people's liberties, by strengthening — as had been done in Wisconsin — the safeguards against abuse of power by government officials.

In discussing the actions which a reinvigorated American government should take to achieve national economic security, Governor La Follette cautioned that a perfected blueprint for action could not be devised in advance. The nation could aim in the "right direction," however, and learn from experimentation and practical experience how to deal with the details and contingencies. One of the first steps would be "to suppress . . . those stupid people who deny others access to materials that they themselves do not know rightly how to use." Then, the power of government would be used — regardless of cost — "to restore to every American the opportunity to help himself. After that he can sink or swim." This process, he said, would involve undertaking a series of projects which would not only give capital and men the chance to work, but would improve the nation's standard of living.

Using the nation's housing problem as an example, La Follette indicated the path which he thought could be followed in working on specific projects. He suggested that the procedures used in building streets and laying sewers might be adapted for improving the country's housing standards. First, an engineering and architectural plan would be drawn up, subject to the approval of the family affected. Second, the government would order that the plan be implemented. Third, easy financing arrangements would be made by the government between private capital and the family involved.

Lastly, the construction work would be done, in so far as possible, by small contractors hired on the basis of a merit bid. The actual work should be done by private enterprise, he said, because "no government on earth can successfully manage, regulate and direct the numerous details that make for healthy families or successful business."

The address further contended that it was not difficult to think of or agree upon a series of national improvements which could put people back to work. The difficulty was in securing a government that had the resourcefulness and courage to act. The Governor charged that the two old parties had proved their inability to accomplish the job. The Republican party, he held, was bankrupt in providing ideas and methods to enable democratic principles of economics and government to be maintained or to thrive. The Democrats, despite Roosevelt's "brilliant leadership," had been unable to cope with the tasks before the nation because of intra-party sabotaging and bickering. "When there are basic issues to be met, leadership alone, no matter how great, can not mix political oil and water."

Governor La Follette then proclaimed the formation of the National Progressives of America, the organization which he claimed could solve the nation's economic problems in an effective yet democratic fashion. "This is no 'popular front,' no conglomeration of conflicting, opposing forces huddled together for temporary expediency." The new movement would seek "only those who come with complete conviction, and without reservation. The movement that unites America, must be itself united. . . . Definitely and irrevocably we are in the lists to stay until the American people recapture their heritage. Make no mistake, this is NOT a *third* party. As certain as the sun rises, we are launching THE party of our time." [27]

The establishment of the new organization immediately caught the attention of the press; the National Progressives of America was front-page news throughout the country. This publicity was probably responsible for the sizable amount of public and political reaction to the movement. Within a month after its organization

[27] "For Release, Thursday, April 28, 1938, at 8 P.M., Speech by Philip F. La Follette," P. La Follette Papers. For a printed version in pamphlet form see Philip La Follette, *A New Movement . . . The National Progressives of America . . . Is Under Way* (Madison, 1938).

was announced, Governor La Follette's office received some 25,000 letters concerning the proposed party, most of them praising it. The American Institute of Public Opinion conducted a survey in May and found that 64 per cent of those interviewed had heard of the National Progressives of America. One out of every ten of those who were familiar with the movement indicated interest in joining it.[28]

The reaction of liberal and radical leaders who were expected to lend the movement support was generally not encouraging. Typical of the response of agricultural leaders was the comment of K. W. Hones, the head of the Wisconsin branch of the National Farmers' Union: "I don't believe the rank and file of farmers are going to give up what they have, no matter how little it is, unless they are cocksure of something better." Hones indicated that his apathy was prompted partly by the fact that "We and Labor have not been asked to sit in on the inside to discuss it." [29] The labor press and major labor leaders, in the main, avoided comment, although the letters Governor La Follette received from minor trade union officials usually revealed sympathy with the organization's aims.[30] Senator George W. Norris, the elder statesman of Progressivism, voiced the fears of many liberals when he stated that the new organization might split liberal forces.[31] Herbert Hoover gave support to Norris' concern when he expressed the hope that the National Progressives might serve as a divisive element in the New Deal coalition and thereby aid the Republicans to return to power.[32]

The major magazines of liberal persuasion differed in their estimates of the National Progressives. The *New Republic* believed that Governor La Follette's criticisms contained much merit, but

28 New York *Times*, May 29, 1938, Sec. IV, p. 10; Cantril and Strunk (eds.), *Public Opinion*, 577.

29 *Farmers' Equity Union News* (Madison), May, 1938, p. 2.

30 The general silence of major labor leaders and organs might be explained largely by two factors. First, they were concentrating much of their time and resources on the battle between the American Federation of Labor and the new Congress of Industrial Organizations. Second, in view of President Roosevelt's renewed campaign to secure legislation favorable to labor, especially the Fair Labor Standards bill, they were in no position to break with the New Deal leaders. Had the President failed to gain passage of the measures desired by organized labor, many labor leaders would conceivably have shown interest in new party action later in the year. This was illustrated by the threat of David Dubinsky of the International Ladies' Garment Workers to declare in favor of a new party if the Democrats repudiated the New Deal program. New York *Times*, May 1, 1938, Sec. II, p. 6.

31 *Ibid.*, April 30, 1938, p. 3.

32 *Ibid.*, May 2, 1938, p. 17.

added that "it is obviously too early to say whether a third party will be either desirable or necessary in the 1940 election." The magazine saw the organization as a weapon which would operate to exert pressure on the Democratic party for more liberal action.[33] *Common Sense* called upon liberals to try to reinvigorate the New Deal. It hoped that the National Progressives would not interfere with this attempt, but rather would stand as a reserve organization for liberals should the New Deal collapse.[34] *Christian Century* analyzed the La Follette maneuver as serving "notice on Mr. Roosevelt that if his party adopts a conservative or equivocal course in 1940 it must prepare to suffer the loss of vitally important liberal votes." The periodical lauded the National Progressives' objectives as constituting "a liberal program which is neither Marxist nor fascist in its origins, but which gives promise of attacking the roots of our economic problem as the New Deal has never done." [35] On the other hand, the *Nation* was disturbed because it could find "no indication of a genuine farmer-labor base for [La Follette's] program." This magazine branded the National Progressives "middle class," and declared that it would regard the new organization with "critical sympathy." [36]

Caution or outright rejection characterized the reaction of other third party groups. Spokesmen for the American Labor party were skeptical of the program. Moreover, they saw no necessity for a new national party so long as President Roosevelt fought for liberal legislation.[37] The Minnesota Farmer-Laborites announced that although they would continue to support President Roosevelt's program, they would watch the development of the National Progressives with "sympathy and friendship." The Minnesota group appointed a committee of five to study the organization.[38] Norman Thomas, the 1936 Socialist candidate for president, hailed La Follette's analysis of the defects of the New Deal, and remarked

[33] *New Republic* (New York), XCIV (May 4, 1938), 382-83; XCV (May 11, 1938), 3-4.

[34] *Common Sense*, VII, No. 6 (June, 1938), 3.

[35] *Christian Century* (New York), LV (May 11, 1938), 8.

[36] *Nation* (New York), CXLVI (April 30, 1938), 492-93, (May 7, 1938), 519-20. The *Nation's* comments were confirmed for many observers when the National Advisory Organization of Little Business indicated its interest in the National Progressives of America's program. Cleveland *Plain Dealer*, May 1, 1938, p. 7.

[37] New York *Times*, April 30, p. 3, May 4, p. 11, May 12, 1938, p. 12.

[38] St. Paul *Minnesota Leader*, May 7, 1938, p. 4; Minutes of the Minnesota Farmer-Labor Association's State Committee, May 21, 1938, Minnesota Farmer-Labor Association Papers.

that his party would view the movement sympathetically.[39] The Socialist party executive committee, however, later charged that the new organization represented a move toward Fascism. The committee labeled the new party's program "a shocking disappointment," which "offers the workers and farmers no more than the Republicans, [and] less than the New Deal." [40] The Communist response was understandably more vigorous. Calling the National Progressives' objectives "reactionary" and "phony," the Communist party declared that the new group would split America's progressives.[41] Mayor La Guardia, in commenting on La Follette's proposals, indicated that there was not so much need for a new party as for progressive unity.[42] The only enthusiastic response to the formation of the National Progressives from a third party leader came from Representative William Lemke, the Union party's 1936 presidential candidate.[43]

President Roosevelt showed no public concern over Governor La Follette's new venture. Privately, however, the President revealed interest in the development of the movement. He was well aware that the National Progressives could injure state and national Democratic election efforts in 1938 and 1940 by siphoning off liberal votes.[44] Moreover, he told Secretary of the Interior Harold Ickes that unless La Follette went too far, the National Progressives would demonstrate to Democratic leaders that they were in danger of losing the liberal support necessary to victory in 1940.[45] Commenting further on the organization in a personal letter to Ambassador William Phillips, the President wrote:

> Did you know that Phil La Follette started his Third Party with a huge meeting in Wisconsin, the chief feature of which was the dedication of a new emblem — a twenty foot wide banner with a red circle and a blue cross on it? While the crowd present was carried away with the enthusiasm of the moment, most of the country seem to think that this was a feeble imitation of the Swastika. All that remains is for some major party to adopt a new form of arm salute. I have suggested the raising of both

39 *Socialist Call* (New York), April 30, 1938, p. 5.

40 New York *Times*, May 15, 1938, p. 2.

41 See Central Committee, Communist Party, U. S. A., *The La Follette Third Party* (New York, 1938).

42 New York *Times*, April 30, 1938, p. 3.

43 *Common Sense*, VII, No. 6 (June, 1938), 23.

44 Miscellaneous memoranda, n.d., President's File and Papers of the Democratic National Committee (Roosevelt Library).

45 Ickes, *Secret Diary*, II, 379.

arms above the head, followed by a bow from the waist. At least this will be good for people's figures![46]

Despite the discouraging initial response of independent political groups to the National Progressives, its leaders set out to build the movement into a strong national political force. Many challenging problems confronted them. Funds had to be raised, a headquarters established, lieutenants recruited and disciplined, literature written, mailing lists compiled, correspondence answered, hostile election laws complied with, and, of greatest importance, voters had to be attracted.

The work of attacking these problems began immediately after the formation of the National Progressive party. Governor La Follette began the campaign by making a series of speeches in Iowa, including one in Des Moines which was broadcast over a national radio network. In an address in Cedar Rapids he declared that the party hoped to have congressional candidates in ten states by fall. He urged the people of Iowa to support the formation of a united Progressive party in that state, but pointed out that such an organization could come only from the people and not from leaders.[47] Throughout the summer and fall of 1938, the Wisconsin Governor continued to speak on behalf of the National Progressives in the Middle West and the East. Senator Robert La Follette in his speeches and radio addresses also gave support to the new organization, as did General Ralph Immel, its executive director. An office was established in Madison to handle mail and the raising of funds. The Progressive party of California, running Raymond Haight for governor, became the affiliate in that state. In Iowa, a Farmer-Labor ticket, representing the National Progressive forces there, was entered in the 1938 election contests. By September, groups in Idaho, North Dakota, and Oregon were connected with the La Follette organization, and factions of liberals in Illinois and Texas were negotiating for the establishment of connections.[48]

Early in the fall, however, it was apparent that the new party was not meeting with signal success. Raymond Haight received only about 254,000 votes out of over two million cast in California's

[46] Roosevelt to Phillips, May 18, 1938, Elliott Roosevelt (ed.), *F. D. R.: His Personal Letters, 1928-1945* (2 vols., New York, 1950), II, 785.

[47] Madison *Capital Times*, April 29, p. 1, April 30, pp. 1 and 3, May 1, 1938, p. 1; New York *Times*, May 1, 1938, p. 1.

[48] New York *Times*, September 25, 1938, Sec. IV, p. 7.

August primaries, and this did not augur victory in that state.[49] In Iowa, there was little popular enthusiasm for the National Progressives. The other state groups declared that they were not yet ready to enter the electoral lists.[50] These difficulties seemed to indicate that the party's potential appeal to liberals had been greatly reduced by the endeavors of the national administration to offset the liberal dissatisfaction which had developed in 1937 and early 1938. The enactment in 1938 of the second Agricultural Adjustment Act and of legislation regulating wages and hours, combined with a spectacular upsurge in federal public works employment and the New Deal's trust-busting program, worked to restore liberal confidence in President Roosevelt. The President endeared himself to many other liberals by his intensive, although unsuccessful, efforts to purge the Democratic party of conservative officeholders.

Meanwhile, Governor La Follette seemed to be losing political strength in Wisconsin. Although most of the state's Progressives gave either tacit or enthusiastic support to his organization, an important minority refused to endorse it. The widely read Madison *Capital Times*, the semiofficial newspaper of the Wisconsin Progressive party, announced that "if repudiation of Pres. Roosevelt is to be a requisite of joining this new venture, the *Capital Times* is frank in saying that it will not go along." [51] The newspaper also called the National Progressive program vague, and even suggested that the methods used in staging the Live Stock Pavilion meeting were comparable to Nazi and Fascist techniques.[52] The powerful Farmer-Labor Progressive Federation, which included the organized farm, labor, and socialist supporters of the Wisconsin Progressive party, adopted a "hands off" policy toward the new organization.[53] Eleven prominent Progressives, including Paul R. Alfonsi, the speaker of the lower house of the state legislature, charged that the National Progressives tended "to split the unity of the people." This group noted with alarm that the new party,

49 Secretary of State (California), *Statement of Vote at Primary Election Held on August 30, 1938 in the State of California* (Sacramento, 1938), 5-6.

50 Statement by P. La Follette, personal interview, April 4, 1952.

51 Madison *Capital Times*, April 28, 1938, p. 1. The editor of the *Capital Times*, William T. Evjue, also served as editor of the *Progressive*, the official newspaper of the Wisconsin Progressive party. While the *Progressive's* editorials supported the National Progressive program, its pages devoted very little space to news coverage of the organization.

52 Madison *Capital Times*, May 1, 1938, p. 26.

53 *Ibid.*, May 22, 1938, p. 1.

"While making no attack on Wall Street monopolies, makes sharp attacks on the standards of organized labor and on relief and the W.P.A." [54]

Other problems embarrassed the Progressives at home. William T. Evjue, the editor of the *Capital Times*, laid the foundation for effective Republican and Democratic attacks against his own party by his forthright criticisms of the conduct of party and governmental affairs in Wisconsin. Evjue's disagreement with Progressive leaders stemmed from Governor La Follette's attempts to secure passage of his 1937 legislative proposals. When the regular session of the legislature adjourned without enacting the Governor's program for social and economic welfare, he called a special session to meet in September, 1937. Again the members procrastinated in considering the proposed legislation, and a week before the scheduled adjournment date, he demanded that action be taken on the controversial measures. Legislative leaders, therefore, with the Governor's encouragement, abandoned some of the customary parliamentary procedures. Evjue unrestrainedly characterized this portion of the session as "a week in which we had legislation by executive decree," and charged La Follette and his capitol supporters with using "tactics of the Huey Long variety." Although the editor declared that he favored the measures enacted, he warned that "two can play this game," and that the incident afforded reactionaries an undesirable precedent.[55] From this time on, Evjue's editorials continued to be extremely critical of the expediency and personal ambition which he felt increasingly marked Progressive government and politics in Wisconsin.[56]

Many other incidents occurred which not only allowed the opposition parties to make political capital, but created unrest within the Wisconsin Progressive party. Important among these were the summary dismissal of the popular president of the University of Wisconsin, Dr. Glenn Frank; the conviction of one of La Follette's aides of manslaughter in connection with an automobile mishap;

[54] *Ibid.*, May 25, 1938, p. 1; Janesville *Daily Gazette*, May 25, 1938, p. 1.

[55] Madison *Capital Times*, October 19, 1937, p. 20. For a discussion by the Governor of the problems of legislative procedure, see P. La Follette, *Democracy Functions in Wisconsin: A Record of Achievement of the 1937 Legislature* (Madison, 1937), 7-8.

[56] Evjue explained the reasons for his editorial attacks on his party in a personal letter to James A. Stone, December 14, 1937. Papers of James A. Stone (State Historical Society of Wisconsin).

charges of political coercion of Works Progress Administration employees by the Progressive party; accusations of illegal use of old-age beneficiary lists for political purposes; and the doubtful Wisconsin residency of the 1938 Progressive candidate for United States senator. The virtual snubbing of the Progressive Youth League and the Farmer-Labor Progressive Federation in determining party policies antagonized those groups, and the Federation tried to defeat the Governor for renomination in the 1938 primary election. While its candidate was beaten by a four-to-one margin, its activities revealed an amount of dissatisfaction that had not been apparent in previous Progressive gubernatorial primaries. Governor La Follette's inadequacy in dealing with these situations resulted largely from the difficulty involved in trying to serve effectively both as governor and as head of a national political organization. Not only was the administration of government and party affairs in Wisconsin consequently impaired, but his efforts on behalf of the National Progressives of America also suffered.

The misfortunes and mistakes of the Governor and the Wisconsin Progressives in 1937 and 1938 heartened the state's Democrats and Republicans. Powerful factions in these two parties ran gubernatorial candidates in the 1938 primary elections on coalition or "Stop La Follette" platforms. They agreed that the old party nominee who received the least number of primary votes would withdraw in favor of the other. In compliance with this bargain, the Democratic gubernatorial nominee renounced his candidacy and endorsed Republican Julius P. Heil.[57] This maneuver, combined with exploitation of the many charges against the state administration and disgruntlement within Progressive ranks, led to Governor La Follette's defeat in the November election. Heil received 543,675 votes to 353,381 cast for the incumbent. La Follette's decisive rejection at the hands of the Wisconsin voters was accompanied by an equally clear repudiation of the state's Progressive party. The party lost control of the other four state-wide elective offices and retained only two of its seven seats in the national House of Representatives. The Progressive delegation in the state legislature dropped from forty-nine to thirty-two in the assembly, and from eighteen to eleven in the senate.[58]

57 William F. Raney, *Wisconsin: A Story of Progress* (New York, 1940), 369.

58 *The Wisconsin Blue Book, 1940* (Madison, 1940), 606-20. A substitute Democratic candidate for governor, Harry W. Bolens, received only 78,446 votes, which

The fate of the National Progressive affiliates in Iowa and California in 1938 was even more dismal. In California, the Progressive program for economic reconstruction failed to divert public attention from the battle waged between Republican and Democratic forces over old-age benefits. Progressive gubernatorial candidate Raymond Haight polled only 64,418 ballots out of over 2,600,000 cast in the California election.[59] In Iowa, the National Progressive candidates failed to obtain the two per cent minimum of the total vote which was necessary to qualify their party for a permanent place on the ballot.[60]

Although faced with these severe defeats, Governor La Follette declared his intention of going on with the National Progressives of America. He saw the reverses that liberals in general suffered in the 1938 elections as proving "more than ever the vital necessity for a new national movement. Both the old parties are firmly in the control of reactionaries. A few years practical demonstration will again show the incapacity of reactionaries to meet the problems of our day. . . . The National Progressives of America goes forward today. Around it, liberals and progressives throughout the nation will rally." [61] Despite these optimistic words, the party was maintained only as a paper organization, held in reserve for independent liberal action in the event that both major parties should nominate conservative presidential candidates in 1940. With the nomination of Roosevelt for a third term, however, the movement was completely abandoned.

In form, if not in goals, the National Progressives of America seemed to represent something new on the American scene. It was an attempt by Progressives to unite for constructive political action the nation's liberals and moderate conservatives, those who thought that private enterprise merited a future in American society, but who believed in more government action to control it. In this respect, therefore, it was conceived as a means of perpetuating the power of independent liberal politicians. That the movement failed

illustrated the appeal of the coalition idea. It is also interesting to note that Governor La Follette received 38 per cent of the ballots cast for governor in 1938 as compared with 39 per cent in 1934 and 46 per cent in 1936. Compare *The Wisconsin Blue Book* for 1940 (p. 606) with those of 1935 (p. 613) and 1937 (p. 420).

[59] Secretary of State (California), *Statement of Vote at General Election Held on November 8, 1938, in the State of California* (Sacramento, 1938), 4.

[60] Secretary of State (Iowa), *Official Register, 1939-1940* (Des Moines, 1939), 571-75.

[61] Madison *Capital Times*, November 9, 1938, p. 12.

was due only incidentally to the political mismanagement from which it occasionally suffered. More important was the fact that as long as independent liberals could achieve some of their goals by co-operating with the Democratic party they would be unwilling to surrender their influence in order to make the hazardous attempt to gain complete control of the government. They might threaten to withdraw their support from the Democratic party, but this was a tactical maneuver designed to force the Democrats to accede to their demands. This is not to suggest that as an organization the National Progressives of America did not serve a purpose in 1938. Though it failed to unite even the various state Progressive movements, it dramatically called the attention of Democratic leaders to the fact that the liberal aspects of their administration must continue if they were to retain the support of independent liberals.[62]

62 President Roosevelt was certainly aware of this. In a letter to Ambassador Josephus Daniels after the 1938 elections, he exulted in the elimination of "Phil La Follette and the Farmer-Labor people in the Northwest as a standing Third Party threat. They must and will come to us *if* we remain definitely the liberal party." Roosevelt to Daniels, November 14, 1938, Elliott Roosevelt (ed.), *F. D. R.: His Personal Letters, 1928-1945*, II, 827.

Was Jackson's Kitchen Cabinet a Cabinet?

By Richard P. Longaker

Every serious student of the American presidency has faced in some form the problem of identifying the actual formulators of policy for some particular presidential administration or for the upper reaches of the executive branch of the government in general. Because influence is difficult to measure, because the advice of confidants is by definition confidential, and because the channels of opinion and counter opinion within the president's circle are not always clearly defined, the real source of influence in any administration usually lies in the shadows. The areas of obscurity thus created have provided fertile ground for the nurture of legends which frequently attribute influence to individuals who did not wield it and overlook others whose influence may have been decisive. A persistent minor legend of the American presidency, born and fostered in inadequate or faulty information, dates back to the 1830's and concerns Andrew Jackson's "Kitchen Cabinet."

It is not mere antiquarian interest that compels a review of the Kitchen Cabinet legend, for the phrase "Kitchen Cabinet" is very much alive in the literature of public administration, and it has always had a prominent place in commentaries on the Jackson administration. In the nineteenth century — and frequently today — the phrase symbolized a clandestine method of making policy decisions in the Jacksonian era. To the anti-Jackson men who coined the term it signified also that "King Andrew" was not the reigning monarch but was, instead, a heroic figurehead for conspiring political opportunists. These assumptions need to be tested against existing evidence; and in order to cast more light on the origins of policy in the Jackson administration it is necessary to seek the answers to two basic questions. First, was the Kitchen Cabinet an institutional entity — in the words of an authority on this period, "a continuing and active group"?[1] Second, is the com-

[1] Leonard D. White, *The Jacksonians: A Study in Administrative History, 1829-1861* (New York, 1954), 95. White also repeats the common but erroneous generaliza-

panion concept that Jackson served as a façade for his advisers in the Kitchen Cabinet a sound one?

Before dealing with these two questions, however, it is perhaps desirable to settle one lesser historical ghost. While it is an accepted truism that Jackson did not rely upon his officially constituted cabinet for conciliar advice, this does not mean that he wished to destroy, or to subvert, or even to ignore the cabinet as an institution. That he did not use it extensively was in part the result of political circumstance, since political demands rather than his free choice dictated the cabinet membership in the early years of his administration. Furthermore, he seems to have thought primarily of the cabinet officer as the administrative agent of an executive department through whom the president should act in matters relating to that department. Such officers might express their opinions on any question on which their advice was sought, but he believed that in cases of difference of opinion between the president and the cabinet the will of the president as the responsible head of the administration must be expected to prevail.[2] While it is true that Jackson preferred to consult with department heads individually, available evidence shows that it is an unwarranted simplification to contend that his cabinet did not meet.[3] That it did meet sporadically is clearly shown by the following tabulation of dates of meeting, subjects discussed, and references to sources of information.

September, 1829, the Eaton affair. James A. Hamilton, *Reminiscences of James A. Hamilton during Three Quarters of a Century* (New York, 1869), 146.

January, 1830, the Eaton affair. Jackson's Memorandum, not dated, in John Spencer Bassett (ed.), *Correspondence of Andrew Jackson* (7 vols., Washington, 1926-1935), IV, 123; Jackson to David Burford, July 28, 1831, *ibid.*, 318.

November 28, 1830, the French imbroglio. Hamilton, *Reminiscences*, 227.

tion that the members of the Kitchen Cabinet were "primarily concerned with patronage and party manipulation."

2 William MacDonald, *Jacksonian Democracy, 1829-1837* (New York, 1906), 226-28. For further light on Jackson's relations with his cabinet, see John C. Fitzpatrick (ed.), *The Autobiography of Martin Van Buren* (American Historical Association, *Annual Report*, 1918, Vol. II, Washington, 1920), 231, 250-51, and John Spencer Bassett, *The Life of Andrew Jackson* (2 vols., New York, 1911), II, 475-76.

3 See, for example, Mary L. Hinsdale, *A History of the President's Cabinet* (Ann Arbor, 1911), 86; Marquis James, *Andrew Jackson: Portrait of a President* (Indianapolis, 1937), 227; and Frederic A. Ogg, *The Reign of Andrew Jackson* (New Haven, 1919), 129-30.

August, 1831, the Bank question. Louis McLane to Van Buren, August, 1831, Fitzpatrick (ed.), *Autobiography of Martin Van Buren*, 579; Carl B. Swisher, *Roger B. Taney* (New York, 1935), 161.

September 3, 1831, the French imbroglio. Hamilton, *Reminiscences*, 227.

March 6[?], 1832, Netherlands indemnities. Jackson to Van Buren, March 6, 1832, Papers of Martin Van Buren (Division of Manuscripts, Library of Congress).

July 3[?], 1832, the Bank question. Marquis James, *Andrew Jackson: Portrait of a President* (Indianapolis, 1937), 302.

November, 1832, the Bank question. Roger B. Taney, Bank War Manuscript (Division of Manuscripts, Library of Congress), pp. 149-50; Swisher, *Roger B. Taney*, 210.

March 19, 1833, the Bank question. Jackson's Memorandum to the Members of the Cabinet, March 19, 1833, Bassett (ed.), *Correspondence of Jackson*, V, 32-33.

April, 1833, diplomatic appointments. Patrick McCauley to Nicholas P. Trist, April 29, 1833, Papers of Nicholas P. Trist (Division of Manuscripts, Library of Congress).

May 4, 1833, Maine boundary dispute. Nicholas P. Trist Memorandum, May 4, 1833, Trist Papers.

September 10, 1833, removal of the deposits. William J. Duane, *Narrative and Correspondence Concerning the Removal of the Deposits* (Philadelphia, 1838), 97.

September 17, 1833, removal of the deposits. Duane, *Narrative and Correspondence*, 99.

September 18, 1833, removal of the deposits. James D. Richardson (comp.), *Messages and Papers of the Presidents, 1789-1897* (10 vols., Washington, 1899), III, 36.

August 10, 1836, Specie Circular. Thomas H. Benton, *Thirty Years' View* (2 vols., New York, 1854-1856), I, 678.

November 15, 1836, Pageot question. Jackson's Memorandum Respecting A. Pageot, November 15, 1836, Bassett (ed.), *Correspondence of Jackson*, V, 436.

This list is undoubtedly incomplete; but it provides definite evidence that on at least sixteen occasions Jackson called the cabinet together to consider some specific question in which public policy was involved. On the other hand, the absence of any systematic record of its deliberations would seem to suggest that the significant innovation under Jackson was not so much the reduction in the number of meetings as the fact that he used the cabinet differently. Even though he sometimes professed high respect for the views of its members, it seems clear that there were no meetings of equals to discuss and determine policy. Some meetings were apparently held merely to enable him to hear their arguments and then come to his own decision.[4] In several characteristic instances, such as the meetings on the Peggy Eaton affair, the Bank veto, and the removal of deposits, the cabinet gathered to receive a presidential ultimatum based on a policy previously determined. According to Thomas H. Benton's account of the cabinet and the Specie Circular, "He did as he had often done in councils of war — called the council together to hear a decision. He summoned his cabinet — laid the case before them — heard the majority of adverse opinions: — and directed the order to issue." [5]

In view of the circumstances which had determined the selection of the individual members of the cabinet during the early years of the Jackson administration, it was perhaps to be expected that the relationship between them and the president would not always be harmonious or even one of mutual respect. His first cabinet was little more than an anti-Clay group thrust together by an inexperienced president to satisfy sectional demands and to pay political debts incurred in the campaign of 1828. It dissolved under the pressure of the celebrated Peggy Eaton affair and the next group was shattered by the controversy over the second Bank of the United States. Not until 1834 did Jackson's difficulties with his cabinet subside, and only then did his official advisers attain a substantial degree of harmony. Until 1834, therefore, there were compelling reasons for him to depend upon unofficial advisers.

According to legend, the Kitchen Cabinet both contributed to the weakening of the regular cabinet and filled the vacuum created by its decline. The picture is sometimes embellished by a caricature of the President sitting senseless in the midst of the Kitchen Cabinet's wily maneuvering. Actually, the facts are somewhat different. The cabinet did decline — at least it moved away from the Jeffersonian image of a group of equals seated in mutual harmony to advise with the president on questions of policy — and concurrently with its decline came the rise of a new and amorphous advisory pattern. It was this amorphous and fluctuating system which came to be called the Kitchen Cabinet.

That the Kitchen Cabinet was not an institutionalized entity is

[4] In an address entitled "General Jackson and the Present Times," delivered in February, 1862, Amos Kendall said: "He never took a vote in his Cabinet. Questions were submitted and discussed; but, when it came to the decision, 'he took the responsibility'." William Stickney (ed.), *Autobiography of Amos Kendall* (Boston, 1872), 635.

[5] Benton, *Thirty Years' View* (2 vols., New York, 1854-1856), I, 678.

indicated in the difficulty of compiling a list of its members at any given time. Traditionally, the membership list included William B. Lewis of Tennessee, Amos Kendall, Francis P. Blair, Isaac Hill, Duff Green, and Roger B. Taney.[6] Jackson's influential advisers were more numerous, however, and he drew them from a wide variety of sources. Some were also members of the traditional cabinet: for example, John H. Eaton when he was secretary of war, Taney as attorney general, and two secretaries of state, Martin Van Buren and Edward Livingston. Others, particularly Thomas H. Benton and James K. Polk, came from Capitol Hill, and after Taney's appointment to the Supreme Court the judiciary was also represented.

When it was politically impossible to appoint a trusted confidant to the cabinet the President arranged for positions in the Treasury Department or elsewhere to sustain his friends while they rendered advisory assistance in his household. Andrew Jackson Donelson, the President's nephew and private secretary and a figure of considerable importance on policy and patronage questions, held a sinecure as a clerk in the General Land Office. William B. Lewis and Amos Kendall served as second and fourth auditors in the Treasury Department, and Lewis was at one time custodian for "the renewal and repair" of the furniture of the Executive Mansion,[7] but received no higher appointment. Kendall, on the other hand, subsequently became postmaster general. Francis P. Blair, the nineteenth-century equivalent of the presidential press secretary, received his income from printing contracts awarded to the administration newspaper, the Washington *Globe*.

Other figures had an important but transitory influence on the President and may be listed as fringe members of the ever-changing Kitchen Cabinet. Isaac Hill of New Hampshire, extravagantly styled the "Marat of the Kitchen Cabinet" by one writer on the Jackson era,[8] served as comptroller in the Treasury Department from 1829 to 1830. Duff Green, a Calhoun partisan and editor of the *United States Telegraph*, was an important presidential adviser

[6] See, for example, Edward C. Smith and Arnold J. Zurcher (eds.), *A Dictionary of American Politics* (Rev. ed., New York, 1955), 216; J. Franklin Jameson, *A Dictionary of American History* (Boston, 1894), 354; White, *The Jacksonians*, 95; and Claude G. Bowers, *The Party Battles of the Jackson Period* (New York, 1922), 144-70.

[7] For Jackson's explanation of this odd appointment see Jackson to Richard G. Dunlap, August 29, 1831, Bassett (ed.), *Correspondence of Jackson*, IV, 337.

[8] Bowers, *Party Battles of the Jackson Period*, 158.

in the formative days immediately following Jackson's first inauguration. Finally, mention should be made of Senator Hugh L. White, who led several administration battles in the Senate and frequently advised the President until his break with the Jackson party in 1834. In their time all of these men were consulted by the President and exercised influence in his policy decisions.

These observations suggest that the traditional membership list of the Kitchen Cabinet should be revised. Some names, such as Benton, Polk, White, Van Buren, Donelson, and Livingston, should be added, while others should be deleted. There is no evidence, for example, that Isaac Hill was notably influential in presidential conclaves after 1832. Duff Green soon deserted the Jacksonian camp; and William B. Lewis, frequently touted as the head chef in the Kitchen Cabinet, has retained a reputation for sustained influence and a position in the presidential councils which he does not deserve. Although Lewis was not repudiated by Jackson, his influence waned as the train of events outran his political acumen.[9]

It is extremely difficult to assign more influence to any one of these presidential advisers than to the others, because they were not all consulted on the same issues. Some of them might hold the President's attention on one issue while he was turning at the same time to some of the others for advice on another question. Although Kendall, Donelson, Taney, Van Buren, and Blair seem to have constituted the innermost ring of the circle, it is doubtful that they ever met as a group, and it is certain that they did not always agree upon questions of policy or even upon the question of their own relative importance. Van Buren considered himself "the individual destined to occupy the first place in his [Jackson's] confidence";[10] but Blair maintained in a self-congratulatory letter that Van Buren was no more influential than other advisers and that Jackson "values my opinion in some things, and those nearest to him, more than he does the magician's."[11]

9 See Louis R. Harlan, "Public Career of William Berkeley Lewis," *Tennessee Historical Quarterly* (Nashville), VII (March-June, 1948), 3-37, 118-51.

10 Fitzpatrick (ed.), *Autobiography of Martin Van Buren*, 232. It is clear that Jackson was strongly influenced by Van Buren's maneuverings in the struggle for power with Calhoun, particularly during the Peggy Eaton affair and the reorganization of the cabinet. Caught in the turmoil of strong personal feelings during the Eaton affair, he was uncharacteristically pliable; and it was at this time that he described Van Buren as "a *true* man with no guile." Jackson to John Coffee, May 31, 1831, Bassett (ed.), *Correspondence of Jackson*, IV, 260.

11 Francis P. Blair to Mrs. Benjamin Gratz, March 2, 1831, in Thomas Clay, "Two Years with Old Hickory," *Atlantic Monthly* (Boston), LX (August, 1887), 192.

If there was a first position in the hierarchy of influence, it probably belonged to Amos Kendall, for his influence was the most pervasive and his talents the most widely used by the President. He assisted in the preparation of at least ten of Jackson's messages to Congress and was constantly available to give political advice or to serve as amanuensis in the composing of statements for public use.[12] Other members of the group seem to have had their own special policy areas, partly through Jackson's choice. Van Buren, for example, helped to form the President's attitude toward internal improvements;[13] Edward Livingston and Kendall were the principal architects of the President's famous proclamation on nullification; Donelson and Senator Benton worked together in drawing up the Specie Circular;[14] and Taney's role in the Bank controversy is well known.[15]

Actually, however, there was no hierarchy of advisers, just as there was no institutionalized entity — a Kitchen Cabinet — meeting regularly with a firmly established membership. The evidence suggests that decisions were made by the President in a haphazard manner with the assistance of those who had his ear at a particular time and who could, in turn, convince him of the wisdom of their position. Often he called upon those who were sympathetic toward a predetermined policy, or prejudice, to articulate and rationalize his beliefs for congressional and public consumption. In spite of stories of his short and violent temper to the contrary, those who disagreed with Jackson seldom fell from favor unless their disagreement was basic and of long standing. Those who disagreed with

[12] Henry A. Wise reported that Jackson held "private conferences at night, in which Amos Kendall was his chief scribe and amanuensis, to write the broadside editorials of the *Globe* under his dictation and instruction, but not with his diction. He was a better thinker than his scribe, his scribe a better writer than he. He would lie down and smoke and dictate his ideas as well as he could express them, and Amos Kendall would write a paragraph and read it. That was not the thing; many times the scribe would write and rewrite again and again, and fail to 'fetch a compass' of the meaning. At last, by alteration and correction, getting nearer and nearer to it, he would see it, and be himself astonished at its masterly power. General Jackson needed such an amanuensis, intelligent, learned, industrious as Mr. Kendall was. He could think, but could not write; he knew what nerve to touch, but he was no surgeon skilled in the instrument of dissection. Kendall was." *Seven Decades of the Union* (New York, 1872), 117.

[13] Van Buren to Jackson, November 5, 1834, Bassett (ed.), *Correspondence of Jackson,* V, 305-306. See also Fitzpatrick (ed.), *Autobiography of Martin Van Buren,* 306-38.

[14] Benton, *Thirty Years' View,* I, 678.

[15] See especially Swisher, *Roger B. Taney,* 185-206.

him on one issue might find themselves shunted aside only to be called upon for advice on another problem. Even strong differences between the President and his cabinet were tolerated if the differences did not touch upon intense personal feelings, as in the Eaton affair, or did not involve a basic conflict, such as occurred between the President and Secretary of the Treasury William J. Duane over the removal of the government deposits from the Bank of the United States.[16] The general rule was that dissenting advisers were not discharged; they simply were not consulted further on the question at issue.

It is this aspect of the question, the varying personnel of the group of advisers as well as the lack of certainty that their advice would be followed, which leads to the conclusion that a Kitchen Cabinet, as a stable and regularized institution, did not exist. The term describes a procedure, the random choice of a variety of advisers, rather than a specific, organized body of men.

The charge that Jackson was an upstairs captive in his own house is frequently a corollary of the Kitchen Cabinet legend. Manufactured by his opponents in the 1830's, the legend has continued to persist in various forms. In the 1830's the story portrayed the President as the victim of "political intriguers" who were using his "name and popularity to advance their own projects."[17] A century later the author of a popular biography of Van Buren described Jackson's unofficial advisers as "camp followers [who] had inveigled the Conqueror," and stated that "Left to their mercies he became little more than a gullible old man."[18] Although Jackson was understandably dependent upon more experienced political hands like Van Buren, Lewis, and Duff Green in the first year or two of his presidency, his dependence slackened as he became more familiar with the problems and pressures of his new role. After the first few months the political lieutenants arrived and departed as the President willed and did not constitute a united group of self-appointed guardians of the executive bedchamber. When it be-

16 For an example of Jackson's forbearance see Jackson to Van Buren, December 6, 1831, Bassett (ed.), *Correspondence of Jackson*, IV, 379. For his attitude toward Duane see especially Jackson to Duane, July 17, 1833, *ibid.*, V, 131-40; and "Paper Read to the Cabinet," September 18, 1833, *ibid.*, 192-203.

17 *The Conduct of the Administration* (an anonymous political pamphlet published in 1832), p. 21. See also Harriet Martineau, *Retrospect of Western Travel* (2 vols., New York, 1838), I, 155-56.

18 Holmes Alexander, *The American Talleyrand: The Career and Contemporaries of Martin Van Buren* (New York, 1935), 250.

comes clear that the Kitchen Cabinet was not an organized and stable unit, that there was no settled body of men to whom he turned for advice, it becomes easier to document Jackson's independence of his unofficial advisers. Information on the extent of his activity in executive affairs and the testimony of the advisers themselves should throw new light on this persistent allegation that his policies were molded by "political intriguers" for their own ends.

Jackson's theory of executive responsibility, his training as a military commander, and, in the early years at least, his distrust of members of his cabinet propelled him into an active role in administrative affairs and policy making. His diligence ran the gamut from the faithful execution of the laws in the nullification crisis to minor appointments and inconsequential budgetary matters.[19] The recollections of his aides and his own complaints of weariness depict a man who was president twenty-four hours a day.

The President's participation in the preparation of his messages illustrates his vital concern with the affairs of state, and his control over the formulation of policy.[20] He wrote the first draft of many of his messages to Congress and he prepared drafts, either partial or complete, of other important state documents, including the proclamation on nullification.[21] There was no set pattern in the preparation of presidential messages. Jackson certainly did not submit the drafts to a kitchen cabinet group; instead the impression is one of advisers contributing to the message as circumstances permitted and as Jackson's inclination dictated. If an adviser were on hand and sympathetic toward the project under discussion, he was consulted for ideas and phrasing. Amos Kendall was the most frequent contributor, but he always worked in collaboration with the President and others.

[19] The extent of Jackson's absorption in administrative affairs is thoroughly discussed by Albert Somit in "New Papers: Some Sidelights upon Jacksonian Administration," *Mississippi Valley Historical Review* (Cedar Rapids), XXXV (June, 1948), 91-98, and "Andrew Jackson as Administrator," *Public Administration Review* (Chicago), VIII (Summer, 1948), 188-96.

[20] See, for example, "Rough Draft of the First Inaugural Address," Bassett (ed.), *Correspondence of Jackson,* IV, 10-13; "Draft of the First Annual Message," *ibid.,* 97-104; and James Parton, *Life of Andrew Jackson* (3 vols., New York, 1860), III, 455-56.

[21] Jackson handled much of the presidential correspondence either in his own hand or by preparing an outline reply to be used by his secretary, Andrew J. Donelson. At one time or another Nicholas P. Trist, William B. Lewis, or Francis P. Blair assisted the President in this task. See Bassett (ed.), *Correspondence of Jackson,* IV, 382, 450-51; V, 461.

The following tabulation of the individuals — so far as they can be determined from available evidence — who gave advice or assistance in the preparation of each of Jackson's formal state papers will perhaps serve to throw light on the extent to which any single individual or any small group may be considered to have influenced the formulation of his policies.

First Inaugural Address, March 4, 1829: Lewis, Donelson, James A. Hamilton, Henry Lee. Bassett (ed.), *Correspondence of Jackson*, IV, 10 n.; Lewis to Jackson, October 6, 1839, *ibid.*, VI, 31; Hamilton, *Reminiscences*, 104-106; Parton, *Life of Jackson*, III, 164.

First Annual Message, December 8, 1829: Kendall, Hamilton, Van Buren. Bassett (ed.), *Correspondence of Jackson*, IV, 97 n.; Dorothy G. Fowler, *The Cabinet Politician: The Postmasters General, 1829-1909* (New York, 1943), 23.

Maysville Road veto, May 27, 1830: Van Buren. Bassett (ed.), *Correspondence of Jackson*, IV, 137 n.; Fitzpatrick (ed.), *Autobiography of Martin Van Buren*, 320-24.

Second Annual Message, December 6, 1830: Kendall, Van Buren. Jackson to Van Buren, November 1, 1830, and November, 1830, Bassett (ed.), *Correspondence of Jackson*, IV, 198, 209; Fowler, *Cabinet Politician*, 23.

Third Annual Message, December 6, 1831: Kendall, Van Buren. Jackson to Van Buren, June 23, 1831, Bassett (ed.), *Correspondence of Jackson*, IV, 301-302; Fowler, *Cabinet Politician*, 23.

Bank veto, July 10, 1832: Taney, Donelson, Kendall, Levi Woodbury (secretary of the navy). Swisher, *Roger B. Taney*, 194-95; Charles W. Smith, "Roger B. Taney and Mr. Biddle's Bank," *Maryland Historical Magazine* (Baltimore), XXXI (March, 1936), 4-5.

Fourth Annual Message, December 4, 1832: Advisers not known.

Nullification Proclamation, December 10, 1832: Livingston, Kendall, Donelson, Lewis Cass (secretary of war). Jackson to Livingston, December 4, 1832, Bassett (ed.), *Correspondence of Jackson*, IV, 494-95; Fowler, *Cabinet Politician*, 23; Samuel Tyler, *Memoir of Roger Brooke Taney* (Baltimore, 1872), 188; Charles H. Hunt, *Life of Edward Livingston* (New York, 1864), 371-81.

Second Inaugural Address, March 4, 1833: Kendall. Fowler, *Cabinet Politician*, 23.

Paper Read to the Cabinet, September 18, 1833: Kendall, Taney, Donelson. Bassett (ed.), *Correspondence of Jackson*, V, 192 n.; Swisher, *Roger B. Taney*, 232; Fowler, *Cabinet Politician*, 23.

Fifth Annual Message, December 3, 1833: Advisers not known.

Public Lands Bill veto, December 4, 1833: Van Buren. Jackson to Van Buren, July 30, 1833, Bassett (ed.), *Correspondence of Jackson*, V, 144-45.

Protest to the Senate, April 15, 1834: Benjamin F. Butler (attorney general), Kendall. Bassett, *Life of Jackson*, II, 650.

Sixth Annual Message, December 1, 1834: Kendall. Fowler, *Cabinet Politician*, 23.

Seventh Annual Message, December 7, 1835: Kendall, Taney. Jackson's Notes, Bassett (ed.), *Correspondence of Jackson*, V, 377-79; Frederic Hudson, *Journalism in the United States* (New York, 1873), 248.

Specie Circular, July 11, 1836: Benton, Donelson. Benton, *Thirty Years' View*, I, 678.

Eighth Annual Message, December 5, 1836: Advisers not known.

Farewell Address, March 4, 1837: Taney. Jackson to Taney, October 13, and Taney to Jackson, October 15, 1836, Bassett (ed.), *Correspondence of Jackson*, V, 429-31; "Letters of Andrew Jackson to Roger Brooke Taney," *Maryland Historical Magazine*, IV (December, 1909), 304.

Except for the fact that Kendall's name appears in connection with the preparation of ten of these eighteen messages, this list seems to offer little evidence of sustained or unified efforts by either official or unofficial groups to influence the content and form of Jackson's statements of the policies of his administration. Of the other eleven men who are known to have served as advisers, six were members of the official cabinet at the time of their participation. Seven of the advisers, including four cabinet members, were consulted for only one document each, and there is only a single instance of the same three men working together more than once (Kendall, Taney, and Donelson on the Bank veto message and the paper read to the cabinet). Van Buren assisted in the preparation of five documents, and Taney and Donelson in four each. Of the other reputed members of the Kitchen Cabinet, Lewis participated only in the preparation of the first inaugural address, and the names of Blair, Hill, Eaton, and Green do not appear.

Such additional information as is available concerning the way in which the assistance of these men was actually given indicates also that it was Jackson rather than they who made the selection of advisers on any particular subject and determined the nature of their participation. In general, his practice was either to prepare a tentative outline or draft, which was then submitted to selected individuals for their comment, or to ask the prospective advisers to present their ideas in written or oral form before the initial draft was prepared.[22] Although it is not possible to recover the full story

[22] For examples of such requests see Jackson to Van Buren, July 30, 1833, Bassett (ed.), *Correspondence of Jackson*, V, 144-45, and Jackson to Taney, October 13, 1836, *ibid.*, 429-30.

of the drafting of the proclamation on nullification, what is known of it may be used to illustrate the first of these procedures. The document represented the joint effort of the President, who possibly wrote the first draft, Secretary of State Edward Livingston, Secretary of War Lewis Cass, Kendall, and Donelson, and the final product bore the imprint of Jackson's thought tempered by the close legal scrutiny of Livingston. As the document was nearing completion the President sent Livingston a trial draft of a closing paragraph with the following note: "I submit the above as the conclusion of the proclamation to your amendment and revision. Let it receive your best flight of eloquence to strike to the heart and speak to the feelings of my deluded Countrymen of South Carolina." [23] Livingston incorporated the sentiment but not the language of Jackson's suggestion, and the President apparently accepted the adjustment.

That Jackson had the last word on the proclamation as a whole, however, is shown in a statement made later by Lewis. According to this account, Livingston's completed draft was referred to the President for final review, and upon reading it he "remarked that Mr. Livingston had not correctly understood his notes — there were portions of the draft, he added, which were not in accordance with his views, and must be altered. He then sent his messenger for Mr. Livingston, and, when he came, pointed out to him the passages which did not represent his views, and requested him to take it back with him and make the alterations he had suggested. This was done, and the second draft being satisfactory, he ordered it to be published." [24]

A good illustration of the second plan of procedure as well as of Jackson's guiding role in the preparation of his state papers appears in the case of the Bank veto message. The first draft was written by Kendall at Jackson's request and was turned over to Donelson for revision; but while the revision was in progress Jackson asked Taney, who was then the attorney general in the cabinet,

[23] Jackson to Livingston, December 4, 1832, *ibid.*, IV, 494-95.

[24] Parton, *Life of Jackson*, III, 466, Lewis added that when he suggested the omission of a section to avoid antagonizing the state-rights group Jackson replied: "Those are my views, and I will not change them nor strike them out." See also Wise, *Seven Decades of the Union*, 145-46, for a statement that on another occasion when Secretary of State John Forsyth and Donelson attempted to change Jackson's meaning in a final draft of a message dealing with France, he declared: "That, sir, is not my language; it has been changed, and I will have no other expression of my own meaning than my own words."

to assist in putting the manuscript into better legal form. The procedure from that point has been described by Taney himself.

> I passed three days in this employment [he said], the President frequently coming in, listening to the reading of different portions of it from time to time as it was drawn up, and to the observations and suggestions of Mr. Donelson and myself, and giving his own directions as to what should be inserted or omitted. . . . Mr. Donelson told me when I came in that no member of the cabinet had been in the room or offered any aid to him, since Mr. Kendall's draft had been placed in his hands. I saw none of them the first day; and it is possible that none of them knew I had returned. . . . Upon the second day Mr. Woodbury came in, and took part in the work, and continued with us until it was completed, when a fair copy was made, which after being examined by the President and approved and read in the cabinet, was transmitted to Congress.[25]

The President, in sum, was not an idle figurehead or a "gullible old man" who remained passive and unknowing as clever and more literate political lieutenants embedded their words and ideas in his messages. If Jacksonian policies were shortsighted, as frequently they were, there is still not the slightest doubt that the President's eyes, ears, and often his pen were active in policy formulation.

The testimony of his friends, of course, should not be conclusive in judging the question of the independence of Jackson's thinking. Some will claim influence, others deny it. But even persons unfriendly to the President attested to his dominance in the formulation of policy. A decade after Jackson's departure from the Executive Mansion, John McLean, Supreme Court justice, conceded that even though Jackson was "chiefly influenced by his friends" it was generally true "that he dictated the course of his administration."[26] The President, aware of the accusations of subservience, took pains to emphasize that the acts of the presidency were the acts of the President. Writing to John Randolph he declared: "In regard . . . to these complaints and others of a similar character founded on a pretended distrust of *influences* near or around me, I can only say that they spring from the same false view of my character. I should loath myself did any act of mine afford the slightest colour for the insinuation that I follow blindly the judgement of any friend in the discharge of my proper duties as a public or private individual."[27]

[25] Taney's Bank War Manuscript, pp. 125-26, as quoted in Swisher, *Roger B. Taney*, 194.

[26] John McLean to John Teasdale, December 10, 1848, "Letters of John McLean to John Teasdale," *Bibliotheca Sacra* (Oberlin, Ohio), LVI (1899), 736.

[27] Jackson to John Randolph, November 11, 1831, Bassett (ed.), *Correspondence of Jackson*, IV, 372.

The advisers themselves thought of Jackson as a successful and jealous guardian of presidential independence, and in this respect, at least, their testimony was unanimous. Van Buren stated in his *Autobiography* that although the President received suggestions openly the final decision was invariably Jackson's own. According to John C. Rives, also a friend of the administration, "General Jackson consulted with his friends as frequently and as fully as any other President ever did, *before* he undertook any measure of great moment, and heard their opinions patiently, whether they coincided with his own or not; but if, *after* hearing them, he was 'of the same opinion still,' as he usually, if not invariably, was, then it was useless to talk to him — he was inflexible and immovable." [28]

But such evidence is inconclusive unless supplemented by considered reflection on Jackson's view of his constitutional and political role. His experience as a frontier general had impressed upon him the necessity of drawing the crucial but cloudy distinction between advisory and decision-making functions. His habits as a military leader did not change when he captured the presidency; they were merely set in a different framework. His interpretation of his executive responsibilities [29] and his ability to predict public reaction, together with his characteristic independence, freed him from advisers' bounds. The advisers respected the political judgment of their constitutional superior and his intuitive grasp of the limits of public and party support. They deferred to the President, once their views were submitted, because he demanded it and because his decisions had the reputation of political soundness. Ideas and tactical proposals came from many sources, but all passed through the complex filter of the President's mind.

Thus the driving force of the Jacksonian presidency was rooted in the policies and decisions of the political and constitutional leader rather than in a Kitchen Cabinet — partly because, as a result of the President's administrative method, such a body did not exist, either formally or informally. In actual practice the ad-

[28] Quoted in Hudson, *Journalism in the United States*, 349.

[29] The best statement of Jackson's view of his executive responsibility appears in his Protest to the Senate, April 15, 1834, Richardson (comp.), *Messages and Papers of the Presidents*, III, 80. James A. Hamilton quoted him as having said in 1828: "I have accustomed myself to receive with respect the opinion of others, but always take the responsibility of deciding for myself and acting on my own opinion, if I think it correct. That I believe to be not only the wisest but the safest course; if I err the blame thus attaches to him to whom it belongs." Hamilton, *Reminiscences*, 77.

visory procedure was carried on not through the agency of an organized or unified group but through the exchange of advice by an informal and ever-changing roster of advisers selected by and operating under the influence of the President himself. The legend of a Kitchen Cabinet operating without authority to dictate the formulation of Jackson's policies would seem, therefore, to have been based upon little more than a concept created by his political opponents for propaganda purposes.

Book Reviews

German Culture in America: Philosophical and Literary Influences, 1600-1900. By Henry A. Pochmann. (Madison: University of Wisconsin Press, 1957. xvi + 865 pp. Tables, notes, and index. $7.50.)

It is impossible to do justice, within the limits of a review, to the scope and the scholarship of this remarkable work which represents the findings of a quarter of a century of research. Suffice it to say that no scholar interested in intercultural penetrations, more specifically in the course of German influences on America, can disregard it. Mr. Pochmann and his collaborators have set a standard of excellence in a complex and difficult field that will long remain unchallenged.

To give some idea of the scope of his labors, Mr. Pochmann informs us that for the sake of economy he subjected the manuscript to two drastic revisions, reducing its length from 2,800 to 1,000 typewritten pages. I judge that even after this reduction the text and notes (but excluding the index) of his book run to well over half a million words.

German Culture in America is divided into two parts. Book I deals with German thought in America, Book II with German literary influences. Mr. Pochmann is, of course, aware that it is not always easy to distinguish between the two and, occasionally, he includes material in one section which might more properly be included in the other; but, on the whole, his classification is sound. It is true that although the book purports to deal with German influences in three centuries almost 90 per cent of the material falls into the nineteenth. The reason for this imbalance, as Mr. Pochmann points out, is not the lack of German influences on colonial America but the paucity of scholarly investigations of the earlier period. He suggests that "early German-American intellectual interrelations cannot be appraised until sixteenth and seventeenth-century German-English relations are studied more exhaustively" (p. 20). The book abounds in such suggestions some of them tailor-made for doctoral candidates in search of a thesis.

In tracing the cumulative impact of German thought on nineteenth-century America, Mr. Pochmann elaborates two main themes: German scientific methodology and German philosophic speculation. He makes a convincing case for the statement often heard but rarely proved that German techniques of research have left a lasting imprint on American scholarship. Starting with such early champions of the German system of higher education as Ticknor,

Everett, Cogswell, Bancroft, and others who initiated what has been called the "German craze" in Boston in the 1820's, Pochmann examines the role of Francis Lieber, "the first scholar of note widely to introduce German scientific methods of research into American colleges and universities" (p. 126). What Bancroft did for American historiography, Lieber did for American political science. In lexicography it was the German-trained George Martin Lane who led the way. Careful documentation, close study of original texts, elaborate footnotes and bibliographies: these research techniques, German in origin, have prevailed and continue in use.

The impact of German philosophy has not been as permanent although, at times, it has been considerable. In a detailed and brilliantly written chapter Mr. Pochmann analyzes the subtly pervasive influence of Kant and post-Kantian idealism on Emerson and the New England transcendentalist movement. He points out that the term "transcendentalist philosophy" was first used in America by Frederic Henry Hedge in the *Christian Examiner* for March, 1833. It was Hedge who said in 1870 that he was "a German by intellectual descent." Being thoroughly familiar with German, Hedge — unlike most of the other Transcendentalists who got their knowledge of German philosophy second-hand through Coleridge or Carlyle — had read Kant, Fichte, and Schelling in the original. His enthusiasm for their ideas was infectious and his influence considerable, although it has "never been evaluated" (p. 144).

The longest essay in the book deals with the growth and development of Emerson's thought. All his life Emerson was in love with philosophy, but he was not a philosopher. He lacked the patience to discipline his mind and failed to grasp the subtle epistemological distinctions upon which the systems of Kant and his followers rest. Whether he indeed overcame the most serious crisis in his life by successfully synthesizing Goethean self-reliance with Kantian metaphysics, as Mr. Pochmann says, is debatable. I am more inclined to agree with the conclusion that "the question of precisely to what extent Emerson was indebted to philosophy generally and to German philosophy specifically remains, in some respects, an open one" (p. 206).

In contrast to Kant's idealistic philosophy Hegel's triadic doctrine left a deeper imprint on the American mind; not only because of the efforts of such devoted St. Louis Hegelians as William Torrey Harris and Denton Snider, but because it was better suited to the American temperament and the needs of American society. The conviction that life in society is a continuous compromise of conflicting interests — perhaps the most basic American trait — found support in Hegel's concept of "synthesis." Here was a practical philosophy, substantiated by American experience and applicable to American realities. Hegel's dictum that "the history of the world is the unfolding of liberty" was in complete accord with the American credo.

Whether it is true that Hegel was better understood in America than in Germany, as Mr. Pochmann thinks, is debatable. But there is no doubt that Hegel's influence was considerable and may be detected even in such practical developments as the kindergarten movement and the founding of communal universities.

The rise of pragmatism at the turn of the century marked the end, at least temporarily, of German philosophic infiltration in America. In trying to assess the significance of that infiltration, Mr. Pochmann says that through German philosophy Americans "became acquainted with ideas until then unfamiliar to them" (p. 321). This may be true. But equally true, it seems to me, is his earlier statement that "Americans took to Germany what they sought there" (p. 119).

Book II of Mr. Pochmann's study, which deals with German literary influences, supports a similar conclusion: foreign writers are most likely to find an appreciative native American audience when they conform to existing levels of taste. The changing response of the American public toward Goethe and Schiller is a case in point. During the first half of the nineteenth century Schiller was generally held in higher esteem than Goethe, more of his poems appeared in American publications, and his ethical idealism was contrasted favorably with Goethe's amoral naturalism. It is easy to understand that the Transcendentalists felt more at home with Schiller's uncompromising defense of all that is morally noble than with Goethe's frank indifference to traditional morality. Bancroft and Norton wrote openly hostile articles against the Weimar poet, while Emerson, Longfellow, and Parker expressed but qualified approval. It is true that Emerson included Goethe in his *Representative Men*, "perhaps the greatest single monument to Goethe yet produced in American criticism" (p. 331), but even Emerson was uneasy about Goethe's lack of moral conscience.

With the rise of the anti-idealistic trend in American society after the Civil War the position of the two German poets was reversed. Schiller who ranked first before the war dropped to fifth place in the last decades of the nineteenth century. He was outranked by Goethe, Uhland, Heine, and Rückert.

A similar observation can be made with regard to the vogue of German fiction in America. In the first half of the nineteenth century Jean Paul Richter, that whimsical forerunner of the Romantics, was the favorite German prose writer, followed by Fouqué and Zschokke. After the war American readers preferred Auerbach, Spielhagen, Gerstäcker, and the "damned mob of scribbling women" who wrote for the *Gartenlaube.* Gustav Freytag's novels depicting the "more smiling aspects" of life of the German middle-class likewise were popular. The American public evidently sought in German literature what it was accustomed to at home. It neither knew nor cared for the work of such great literary figures as Mörike, Kleist, Grillparzer, Hebbel, Ludwig, Stifter, Keller, Storm, Meyer — not to mention Schopenhauer or Nietzsche.

But popular taste is not the only yardstick to measure the impact of German literature of America; more significant is the influence of Germanic materials and motifs on that literary genre which has long been regarded as distinctly American: the short story. That the first practitioners of that genre — Irving, Hawthorne, and Poe — made extensive use of German sources is well known. It was noted at the time and frequently criticized. The charge was even made that the American writers were plagiarizing German authors. Mr. Pochmann subjects that charge to a searching analysis and concludes that many well-known American short stories, *Rip Van Winkle* for example, are clearly derivative as regards subject matter and plot. By printing parallel passages of Irving's story and the old German legend of Peter Klaus, Mr. Pochmann shows how closely Irving followed the German original. At the same time, however, in narrative technique and style Irving's story is clearly his own. The same is true of Hawthorne, sometimes called the "American Tieck." "In style Hawthorne owes nothing to Tieck" (p. 382). And, finally, Poe used E. T. A. Hoffmann's motifs more effectively than the German. He concentrated the story line, omitted lengthy didactic passages, and created a work of art distinct from the German "Erzählung." Here the matter rests. Mr. Pochmann's presentation of the complex interrelationship between German themes and American style could hardly be improved upon.

The final chapter of the book treats the extent of German influences on individual American authors of the nineteenth century. It should be required reading of any student of American literature. That Longfellow was "deeply imbued with the spirit of German sentiment and song" (p. 410) has often been said but rarely been presented so convincingly. More surprising is the evidence here assembled of Walt Whitman's indebtedness to German, in particular Hegelian, thought. It is indeed an "irony of history . . . that the 'Prussian State and Court Philosopher' should find among his most notable disciples the American poet who called himself the poet of democracy" (p. 474).

Insights of this kind make the reading of *German Culture in America* a stimulating and rewarding experience. In addition, the book is a work of reference which, in conjunction with the author's previously published *Bibliography of German Culture in America to 1940*, offers the student of German-American cultural relations an indispensable tool. One can only hope that a scholar of equal distinction will some day tackle the reverse aspect of the problem: the impact of America on Germany.

Reed College H. F. PETERS

Documents of American Catholic History. Edited by John Tracy Ellis. (Milwaukee: The Bruce Publishing Company, 1956. xxvi + 677 pp. Notes and index. $8.75.)

The classroom needs for one-volume documentary readings in history have stimulated the output of many useful anthologies, including documentary histories of the Negroes and the Jews. American Catholic history is now fully represented in this new collection by Monsignor Ellis, whose monumental biography of Cardinal Gibbons has earned him distinction. Teachers in American social history as well as those offering courses in Catholic history will benefit from this discriminating, well-edited volume of selections which appear in large, clear print. Each reading is prefaced by an informative introduction which includes bibliographical references. Although the arrangement is strictly chronological and thus occasionally breaks up the logical topical unity, this is partly offset by a full table of contents and an adequate index. There are 163 items, many of full essay length, taken from Catholic archives, learned religious and secular journals, printed letters, autobiographies, newspapers, Catholic literary writings, and other sources, most of them inaccessible in the average college.

Although the editor states that he had no precise rules of selection, there is sufficient organic unity to make it possible for the reader to peruse the volume from cover to cover, beginning with the famous Papal Bull of 1493 and ending with such contemporary events as the founding of the *Catholic Worker* in 1933 and the 1939 encyclical of Pope Pius XII on the sesquicentennial of the American hierarchy. Monsignor Ellis adds that "A conscious effort was made to have the principal churchmen and laymen of the American Catholic past represented, and to include sample material that would give some idea of the chief organizations and institutions of the Church."

Among the more striking reports of famous Catholic leaders are those of Father Kino on the Arizona missions, Junípero Serra on the Mission of San Carlos de Monterey, the concordat between the Franciscans and Dominicans dividing the California missions, the trials of the Jesuits in the French colonies, the various landmarks of religious freedom such as the Maryland Act of Toleration and the Quebec Act. The church itself struggled with internal factionalism such as the dispute over lay trusteeism and the divisive tendencies of new immigrant groups demanding their own priests and separate organizations. Monsignor Ellis uses his own recent researches into the careers of Cardinal Gibbons and Archbishop Ireland to make available some very significant documents which throw light on the efforts of the hierarchy to protect the Knights of Labor from the same type of papal condemnation that the Canadian branch had suffered as a result of its secret organization and activities. Again the editor's sympathetic attitude toward the American principle of the separation of church and state is reflected in the selection of some of the relevant letters.

Considerably less adequately represented are the lay leaders of Catholicism, who would be of particular interest to non-Catholic historians. Occasionally one meets with a figure like Thomas Fortune Ryan, who is neither representative nor (as far as the selection goes) significant in the story of the American Catholic. Much more important are the passages from Tocqueville pointing out the blend of Catholic ideas with American democracy, the informal explanation of Roger B. Taney regarding slavery, the decision of Chief Justice Edward D. White on divorce, and Governor Alfred E. Smith's defense of his record in office against religious bias. The reviewer would have preferred more items on Fenianism, the impact of Sinn Fein, and even more material from the influential Boston *Pilot*. Inevitably, some will wonder why the distinguished magazine *Commonweal* and its contributors are omitted.

There is a fair question as to whether a book of readings on Catholic history might not be strengthened by more selections from non-Catholic but pivotal sources. It is certainly advantageous to find here examples like General George Washington's interesting letter banning the celebration of Guy Fawkes Day in the army, President Jefferson's reassurance to the Louisiana Ursulines regarding their future under the American government, and John Adams' impression of a Catholic service. But these are very few. Monsignor Ellis, although following a most enlightened attitude in handling controversial issues, could have enhanced this quality by including Terence Powderly, unorthodox leader of the Knights of Labor, and Father Edward McGlynn, the single taxer who courted excommunication by refusing to go to Rome to explain his ideas. Instead, their critics, along with the editor of the volume, are alone represented. No volume of selections, however, could be expected to satisfy everyone completely, and Monsignor Ellis deserves congratulations for making this outstanding documentary collection available. It will serve historical scholars of all faiths.

Western Reserve University HARVEY WISH

The Land Called Chicora: The Carolinas under Spanish Rule with French Intrusions, 1520-1670. By Paul Quattlebaum. (Gainesville: University of Florida Press, 1956. xiv + 153 pp. Illustrations, appendixes, bibliography, and index. $3.75.)

The old admonition, "If at first you don't succeed, try, try again," applies to the efforts of Spain in the sixteenth and seventeenth centuries to maintain a foothold along the Atlantic coast from Florida northward to Chesapeake Bay, a region considered vital to the protection of her successful Caribbean establishments. Relatively little is known of most of these colonizing efforts as the documents are either scattered or lost. Although few historians have undertaken the painstaking search required to piece the story together, excellent studies such as the one by Mark F. Boyd, Hale G. Smith, and John W. Griffin, *Here They Once Stood: The Tragic End of the Apalachee Mission*, and that by Clifford M. Lewis and Albert J. Loomie, *The Spanish Jesuit Mission in Virginia, 1570-1572*, have appeared recently, each dealing with a fragment of the larger story. Now Paul Quattlebaum has added his book, *The Land Called Chicora*, which describes Spanish activities near present-day Charleston.

Mr. Quattlebaum has combined a study of the original documents whenever available locally with the most widely accepted secondary works on the subject, and has produced an interesting account of exploration and settlement, beginning with the expedition of Lucas Vázquez de Ayllón, one of the early Caribbean conquistadors, and ending with the permanent appearance of the English in 1670. The Spanish faced one disaster after the other: the numerous Indian tribes, initially friendly, later were alienated by the invaders' excesses; French and English privateers took an unpleasantly active interest in the settlements; harvests were poor and food always scarce; and, above all, nature and geography conspired to frustrate the Spanish. Supply vessels were wrecked with monotonous regularity on shoals along the coast. The early settlements at Santa Elena (1520), San Miguel de Gualdape (1526), and Fort San Felipe (1566) lasted but a few years.

The author mentions certain well-known occurrences, such as the successful St. Augustine settlement in Florida, to explain events taking place along the coast. He goes to great pains to discuss many lesser points of geography still in dispute. His footnotes bear witness to his stated desire to resolve these controversies if possible and to point out errors and omissions in earlier secondary works.

Several statements of fact are open to question: Hernando Cortés married twice, once in Cuba and once in Spain, but neither wife was the daughter of Governor Velázquez of Cuba (p. 5, note 7); the famous dogs used by the Spanish may have been bloodhounds or mastiffs but not greyhounds (p. 35); Philip II could not have received or replied to letters in 1600 as he died on September 13, 1598 (p. 81); and the *Mayflower* of Pilgrim fame could hardly have been the ship on which Sir Robert Heath's colonists reached Virginia in the summer of 1630 as it was one of the ships in the fleet of eleven bringing John Winthrop and his Puritan followers to Massachusetts. Although the style is generally clear, there is a tendency to be repetitious especially in the last few chapters. Full personal names are used too often on a single page, and paragraphs often are concluded with *non sequiturs*. Although the format of the book is handsome, as are most of those from the University of Florida Press, one blemish that cannot be charged against the author is the inclusion of two sets of Plates V and VI, and no set of Plates I and II. These are minor points, however, and do not detract from the over-all contribution of the book to the growing knowledge of Spain's activities along the Atlantic coast in the years prior to English settlement.

University of Georgia RICHARD K. MURDOCH

The Bay Psalm Book: A Facsimile Reprint of the First Edition of 1640. With a companion volume, *The Enigma of the Bay Psalm Book*, by Zoltán Haraszti. Two volumes. (Chicago: University of Chicago Press, 1956. Vol. I: pages not numbered; Vol. II: xiv + 144 pp. Notes, appendixes, and index. $10.00 the set.)

The first book printed in the British colonies in North America was *The Whole Booke of Psalmes Faithfully Translated into English Metre*, otherwise known as "The Bay Psalm Book," which Stephen Day produced at the little press in Cambridge, Massachusetts, in 1640. Of the seventeen hundred copies printed by Day, only eleven copies in varying degrees of completeness survive, and of these only one copy is still in private hands. The others are in institutional libraries. The price paid for the last recorded sale of a Bay Psalm Book, in 1947, was announced as $151,000. That copy is now at Yale.

Two copies are to be found in the Prince Collection at the Boston Public Library, and these two copies are the source of the present facsimile edition with an accompanying volume, *The Enigma of the Bay Psalm Book*, by Zoltán Haraszti. The two volumes are handsomely produced by the University of Chicago Press.

The process used in making the facsimile was line offset. Because the original printing was very poor, with splotches, over-inking, show-through, and other blemishes, the editor explains that "In making the present facsimile these blemishes have been removed by careful opaquing, without retouching the negative otherwise." Furthermore, because of the bad printing of some pages in all copies, Mr. Haraszti has chosen the best pages in the two copies in the Boston Public Library for reproduction. Consequently what we have is a "made up" copy for facsimile, reproduced by a method that eliminates much of the appearance of the original in the interest of legibility. Although this facsimile will answer most needs for a text of the Bay Psalm Book, austere bibliographers will not be satisfied with this method of reproduction. Others, however, who know Mr. Haraszti's own meticulousness will take comfort in his assurance that "The proofs were compared letter by letter, with the original pages. For the correctness of the reproduction, the writer testifies."

Mr. Haraszti in *The Enigma of the Bay Psalm Book* provides a succinct account of the Puritan's need for a new version of the Psalms, new evidence about the identity of the translators, the Puritan interest in music and in

Psalm singing, the history of the Bay Psalm Book's printing and its influence, and other pertinent information.

Ever since Cotton Mather published in his *Magnalia* a verse jingle by Thomas Shepard poking fun at the varying talents of Thomas Welde, John Eliot, and Richard Mather, these three worthies have had credit for the new translation of the Psalms printed in the Bay Psalm Book. Mr. Haraszti corrects this traditional view by proving that other leading ministers of the Bay Colony, including John Cotton, John Wilson, and others, translated some of the Psalms. Furthermore the Preface, previously attributed to Richard Mather, is now proved to be from the pen of John Cotton. The manuscript of this Preface exists in the Boston Public Library.

The Puritans of Massachusetts Bay wanted a fresh translation of the Psalms because the version by Sternhold and Hopkins, long in use, was not sufficiently literal. The Puritans believed that a translator had no right to tamper with Holy Writ. In the interest of versification, previous translators had departed too far from the meaning of the Hebrew originals and the Puritans' religious concept of the literal truth of the Scriptures now required them to prepare an exact translation. They also had to cast the Psalms into metrical forms suitable for singing. The two objectives were not always compatible, but the translators somehow managed to wrench the texts into rhymes and meters. Mr. Haraszti manfully struggles to prove that the poetry is not so bad as earlier critics have made it out, but not even an age accustomed to the jawbreaking jangles of some of our *avant-garde* poets will be easily persuaded that the Bay Psalm Book is much better than Moses Coit Tyler described it, a compilation of battered verses "hammered out on an anvil by blows from the blacksmith's sledge."

Mr. Haraszti has provided a careful and scholarly discussion of the problems of the Bay Psalm Book that will deserve the gratitude of all scholars in the field.

The Folger Library LOUIS B. WRIGHT

Errand into the Wilderness. By Perry Miller. (Cambridge: The Belknap Press of Harvard University Press, 1956. xii + 244 pp. Notes and index. $4.75.)

This volume derives its name from the first of ten essays on American Puritanism written by Perry Miller between 1931 and 1955, and includes his briefer contributions "to the massive narrative of the movement of European culture into the vacant wilderness of America," except for those pieces recast as chapters in *The New England Mind.* The preface should be read because it explains Mr. Miller's early determination to seek the innermost propulsion of this country's history. The mind of man, he contends, is the basic factor (but not the only one) in human history. Seeking a coherence "with which I could coherently begin," he found it in a body of Protestant doctrine in the seventeenth century and particularly seventeenth-century New England. Though the meaning of America is still far from being explained historically, the riddle of Puritan New England, thanks to Mr. Miller and his co-workers, has been vigorously assaulted in its own terms — intellectual and theological.

The title essay of the volume embodies a provocative speculation that caused considerable soul-searching among second and third generations in the Bay Colony. Had the elect failed to fulfill the terms of the original covenant that would have wrought a model for Protestant Europe or, in view of shifts in England, had the need of "A City upon a Hill" become outmoded by 1680? Though preachers lamented and synods railed, the question by the end of the century was not one of default, but one of attaining a new identity. Though the air was rent with cries of repentance, the Puritans had unknowingly launched themselves upon a process of Americanization. Out of their travail, then, came lamentations caused in large measure by the inner tensions set in motion in attempting to redefine their errand. In "Thomas Hooker and the Democracy of Connecticut" the author refutes the views of Parrington and James Truslow Adams that Connecticut was a "democratic" secession from "theocratic" Massachusetts. Under Mr. Miller's scrutiny the flowering of democracy in the "river towns" does not hold up and he is persuaded that the personal rivalry between Hooker and Cotton was a large factor in the removal. By and large the concepts of the "river towns" followed those of the Bay. "The Marrow of Puritan Divinity," by far the longest essay, is too detailed a treatment to discuss here. The thesis of the article has been reworked "into less aggressive formulations" in the author's *The New England Mind*. As the title specifies, it embodies "a constellation of ideas basic to any comprehension of the American mind."

In "Religion and Society in the Early Literature of Virginia" the author shows that this colony had many similarities with Puritan New England. Both were legatees of the Reformation, and Virginia's outlook was so thoroughly Protestant as to be virtually indistinguishable from the Puritan. Mr. Miller finds ample evidence to support the view that the Virginia Company could justify its errand into the wilderness only by an appeal to the Protestant theology of the seventeenth century. Virginia's governance was formed with the conscious and powerful intention to merge that society with the purposes of God. It was a business, in Captain John Smith's words, "most acceptable to God." The dissolution of the Company changed Virginia from a holy experiment to a commercial plantation.

In "The Puritan State and the Puritan Society" the author analyzes the particularism of New England Puritanism — the close relation of church and state, and its rejection of both toleration and democracy. As early as

1681 the Reverend Samuel Willard felt called upon to explain that the business of the founders "was to settle, and secure Religion to Posterity, according to that way which they believed was of God." New forces were undermining the citadel, and to these currents the old Puritanism could not adjust. John Wise in 1717 pointed the way, and Jonathan Mayhew in 1750 virtually completed the revolution. Mr. Miller in "Jonathan Edwards and the Great Awakening" sees in the latter phenomenon a blaze that consumed the theological universe of the seventeenth century. He regards Edwards as the most literate theorist of the Awakening. It was Edwards' conviction that the minister must, by actual participation, bring the people into an experience that was no longer privileged, but social and communal. The real leader, regardless of his authority and dogma, must adapt himself to the public good. Henceforth men were prepared to contend that the guiding rule of society was its welfare — a clear rejection of the old scholastical axiom that men were incapable of recognizing what was their own welfare. This was the crisis of the Great Awakening.

The last four pieces are relatively brief: "The Rhetoric of Sensation" is an explanation of Edwards' recognition of the power of the word and of his resolution "to present ideas naked"; "From Edwards to Emerson" is an attempt to show that the gulf between the two "is not so deep nor so wide as a strictly doctrinal definition would lead us to believe"; "Nature and the National Ego" reveals mid-nineteenth-century America's, and Emerson's, preoccupation with Nature as the last sure bastion between us and the impending crass civilization, which would indeed be an unspeakable ending to the errand into the wilderness. And finally, "The End of the World" deals with the changing cosmology of universal destruction from the time of Michael Wigglesworth's *The Day of Doom*. The greatest artist of the apocalypse, Jonathan Edwards, an admirer of Newtonian nature, insisted, despite some qualms, that the need of a Judgment had not been removed by scientific discovery. The end will come, he wrote defiantly, "as a cry at midnight."

Students of American history and literature will be happy to have this group of essays so readily available in this volume. They reveal to us in even greater compass than *The New England Mind* the mind of Perry Miller. It is to be regretted that the jacket does not do justice to the book and that the proofreading is no credit to the art of publishing (e. g., pp. 186, 191, 194, 198, 206, and 211).

Huntington Library JOHN E. POMFRET

The Cultural Life of the American Colonies, 1607-1763. By Louis B. Wright. *The New American Nation Series.* Edited by Henry Steele Commager and Richard B. Morris. (New York: Harper and Brothers, 1957. xvi + 292 pp. Illustrations, notes, bibliography, and index. $5.00.)

To those of us who were weaned on the American Nation Series, and who as graduate students cut our teeth on the American Life Series, the New American Nation Series, and particularly this volume by Mr. Wright, is an exciting demonstration of the vast stride taken by historiography in our generation. There was no volume of social history corresponding to this in the American Nation Series, and that in the American Life Series was poor, chiefly because the monographs on which it should have been based had not then been written. Mr. Wright's problem, on the other hand, has been the culling of fruits from the lush jungle of new books and articles, and the selection and interpretation of the best topics for his purpose. It is typical of the changed situation that he lets Salem witchcraft off with a half-dozen words.

Such is the mass of new material available that an adequate criticism of Mr. Wright's selection and interpretation would be as long as the book itself. Since one of his chief sources has been his own long list of excellent books and articles on literature and on the South, a reviewer can well pass over those fields, no matter how inclined he might be to make a different selection or interpretation. The obvious weakness of the volume is in its treatment of the northern colonies. The emphasis on the South is useful in that the scholarship in this field is newer, and in that it corrects the list toward the North in most earlier volumes, but it does result in crowding off the page much that is important. Mr. Wright discusses life in the South freshly and at length, but is inclined to dismiss life in the North with the remark that it was urban, as if that made closer examination unnecessary. Nowhere does he discuss the development of those characteristics of New England town and church life which mark the northern states as far west as Iowa, and have so shaped our ideas and culture.

When the corresponding volume in the American Life Series was written, the standard theory of American cultural evolution, as held by men like James Truslow Adams, Parrington, and Beard, was "up from Puritanism" — from a kind of Puritanism which existed only in their interpretations. Mr. Wright makes no such mistakes. He knows his English Puritanism thoroughly, but unfortunately he is not so familiar with the literature of the cultural history of New England. He is keenly aware of the place of religion in colonial society, but, so far as New England is concerned, at the theological level and not that of everyday life. The chapter on religion is the poorest in this volume. It repeats the old tale, exploded twenty years ago, that in Massachusetts "the civil magistrates carried out the instructions of the clergy" until the Theocracy was overthrown by the revocation of the Charter (pp. 80-84).

Another thesis taken from the obsolete books which were broken reeds when Beard and Parrington leaned on them is that "the famous triangular trade between New England, the West Indies, and the coast of Africa . . . was the basis of New England's prosperity in the eighteenth century" (p. 33). I have examined the records of hundreds of voyages to or from the ports of Massachusetts and Connecticut, and not one which I have chanced to find has been in the hypothetical "triangular trade." The Yankees usually paid for their sugar and molasses with their own fish and timber. This false idea of the New England economy is behind the unfair emphasis in the characterization of Peter Faneuil as "the successful slave trader" (p. 33). Similar obsolete bibliography makes the sections on dancing and music less satisfactory than one would wish.

Because the world is today faced with the choice between American and Communist culture, the question of the origin and development of our ideas of democracy and toleration is vital, but Mr. Wright in this area does little more than retell the stories of Anne Hutchinson and Roger Williams. The omission of such a chapter in a work which the publishers say is devoted to the "ideas, manners, and institutions" of the colonies is disappointing.

People who know Mr. Wright and his wonderful fund of southern lore and stories will wonder if a man so imbued with the culture of one area can be fair in his treatment of the other colonies. The fact is that he has been objective. Such unfortunate statements as that Cotton Mather would gladly have exterminated the Quakers and Indians (p. 161) arise not from prejudice but from a lack of familiarity with the monograph and source material of New England. The number of obvious factual errors in the book is small. Its faults, and they are few for a work of such scope, warn us that the mass of knowledge now accumulated in the colonial field cannot be mastered by any scholar who devotes less than full time to it, and that more chairs in early American history are desperately needed.

American Antiquarian Society CLIFFORD K. SHIPTON

Mirror for Gotham: New York as Seen by Contemporaries from Dutch Days to the Present. By Bayrd Still. (New York: New York University Press, 1956. xx + 417 pp. Illustrations, notes, bibliography, and index. $7.50.)

By drawing upon more than six hundred different contemporary descriptions found in travelers' accounts, letters, diaries, and the like, Professor Still has been able to portray New York City as it appeared in consecutive periods from New Amsterdam days to the present. Each of the ten chapters contains a synthesis of the materials for a particular period, followed by a generous selection of two- or three-page excerpts from the sources themselves.

Unlike such cities as Paris or London where travelers are drawn to old historic buildings, New York's memorable sights have always been its new structures. "In reality," exclaimed the architect Le Corbusier in 1947, "the city is hardly more than twenty years old." The feeling that New York was forever being torn down and rebuilt runs through the descriptive literature of many decades. Despite this extraordinary tendency to change, Professor Still believes that there have been "virtually constant fundamentals of the city's personality and growth." These he identifies as the magnificent port, the cosmopolitan society with its "flair for entertainment," and the dynamism of the community's daily activities.

By providing a perceptive and well-written description of New York's physical and social evolution, Professor Still has made a valuable contribution to the still sparse literature of American urban history. Particularly interesting are the more than eighty excerpts from the sources. Taken largely from travel books, these have the characteristic virtues and shortcomings of their genre. They give vivid pictures of the city in its outward aspects, but tell much less of its inner life. Occasionally they reveal more about the author than the subject. It does not surprise us that Walt Whitman should thrill to New York's "hurrying, feverish, electric crowds of men," or that Mark Twain should find the city "a splendid desert — a domed and steepled solitude, where a stranger is lonely in the midst of a million of his race."

Although travelers are often prosy and repetitious, the best of them by a turn of phrase or a few lines of penetrating comment permit us to view even familiar things with fresh perspective. The simplicity of much New York society, even as late as the 1880's, is thus illuminated by Lady Hardy's observation that on a warm summer's evening one might see the gas burning low in elegantly furnished homes while the inhabitants were taking the air on their doorsteps after the old Knickerbocker custom. The quaint turn of phrase in a foreign description can be amusing. A speak-easy, in the definition of the French diplomat, Paul Morand, was "a clandestine refreshment-bar selling spirits or wine." Through the Marx-Leninist eyes of two Soviet visitors, the coffee machine in the automat appeared as "something humiliating, something insulting to man."

In as rich a collection of materials as this, each reader will have his own favorites. The reviewer read with particular pleasure Basil Hall's portrayal of a midnight fire, George Templeton Strong's diary notes on how the city reacted to news of the capture of Richmond, H. G. Wells's reaction to the after-work exodus across Brooklyn Bridge, and Anthony Willis' hilarious account of his misadventures in the subways.

In format Professor Still's book is attractive with a readable type-face, excellent illustrations, and well-organized notes, bibliography, and index.

Many readers will wish, however, that a few simple maps had been added to show the location of important points of interest for the various periods.

Syracuse University NELSON MANFRED BLAKE

The Beekmans of New York in Politics and Commerce, 1647-1877. By Philip L. White. (New York: The New-York Historical Society, 1956. xxxii + 705 pp. Illustrations, notes, tables, appendix, bibliographical note, and index. $10.00.)

The Beekman Mercantile Papers, 1746-1799. Three volumes. Edited by Philip L. White. (New York: The New-York Historical Society, 1956. Vol. I: *Gerard G. Beekman: Letter Book, 1746-1770.* x + 526 pp. Vols. II and III: *James Beekman: Mercantile Correspondence, 1750-1799*, pp. 527-1485. Appendixes and index. $25.00.)

The declared purpose of the author of this book is "to trace and evaluate the role of the Beekmans as a representative family of New York's old aristocracy." To this end he has conducted investigations into four members of the family who were "Public Servants" in the years 1647-1758; three who were "Merchants," 1744-1799; and one whom he terms "the Philanthropist," 1815-1877.

The first section of the book, based primarily on printed rather than manuscript materials, makes it clear that various members of the family were prominent in the affairs of Provincial New York as legislators, landholders, administrators, and protagonists of self-government. Although none was outstanding or spectacular, every one of them played a substantial part and left his mark upon the colony.

Part three relates the aristocratic James William Beekman to State politics, to reform, and to civic affairs in the years 1848 to 1877.

The middle section is devoted to the mercantile members of the family. Gerard G. Beekman was engaged in diversified commercial activity at one time or another. Yet, his chief concern was with commission business, and his most persistent interest was the flaxseed trade with Ireland in the period 1746-1770, when the linen industry in that country was approaching its peak.

Dr. William Beekman made the transition from "Generalist to Specialist" as he increasingly concentrated upon the importation of dry goods from England.

James Beekman, beginning about 1750, was involved in many kinds of business on a small scale. But over the long pull he was predominantly an importer of dry goods. Taking advantage of the flush times attending the Seven Years' War, James imported goods to the amount of £27,497 Sterling in the three years 1757-1759, goods for which he remitted not in kind but in specie or bills of exchange. As the author remarks, James exemplifies the fact that specialization of function was more common in the business structure of New York than of New England at that time. Specialization, the author tells us, was made possible by the "greater abundance and the wider distribution of money in New York." But the trend toward specialization was seriously checked by the Currency Act of 1764 which had a constricting effect upon the money supply of the province.

After 1759 the volume of James Beekman's business declined rather abruptly. For the sixteen years 1760-1775 his importations averaged slightly less than £2,000 Sterling per year. The impact of the Revolution upon him was catastrophic. After gorging himself on British wares in 1784-1785, he never again imported goods on his own account.

It is a bit hard to understand why the author chose to spin out to such length the anticlimactic story of the diminishing significance of James Beekman's business. An account of the importation of dry goods can never make exciting reading; but the chronicle of decline, decade by decade, over a period of thirty-five years becomes dreary and trying.

The author has drawn some comparisons between the Beekmans and other business families of the same period. But there are other comparisons which he has not taken the trouble to make. Judged by the scale, continuity, and longevity of their business, the Beekmans were eclipsed by others of their time. Richard Pares has remarked that Gerard G. Beekman "was no merchant prince." The same could be said of the other Beekmans in business. How do the Beekmans compare with their contemporaries in imagination, daring, innovation, and versatility? The reader of this book cannot fail to be impressed by the helplessness of James Beekman as he viewed the changing conditions which were causing his importing business to wither and die. A more resourceful man would perhaps have made those changing conditions the occasion to develop other types of business activity. Such men actually lived in those years!

The author's consideration for his reader has prompted him to include "A Glossary of Eighteenth-Century Trade Terms." But in some other respects he is less solicitous of the reader's convenience and understanding. He refers (p. 490) to a business transaction of 1780 involving "$80,375 — Continental Money." As he makes no mention of depreciation of the "continentals," the unwary reader could be completely deceived by the figure given. The author should, for the benefit of the reader, state the specie equivalent of the almost worthless paper.

Because his "Key to Abbreviated Citations" is faulty and incomplete, some of the author's citations are utterly meaningless.

Evidently the author became more and more enamored of the Beekmans as his composition progressed. The last sentence of the text tells us that James W. Beekman, "more even than his conscientious forbears, exemplified the family motto, *mens conscia recti*, a mind conscious of rectitude." But this tribute to the "conscientious forbears" is strangely at variance with his earlier statement (p. 121) concerning one of them: "He was a vigorous opponent of corruption in government yet he was clearly involved in bribery at the time the Bolting Act was passed and it is difficult to believe that his enormous land grants required no quid pro quo." Perhaps he should allow the reader to draw his own conclusions in regard to the rectitude of the family.

In *The Beekman Mercantile Papers* the editor has printed, with a minimum of editorial comment and explanation, copies of Gerard G. Beekman's letters, 1746-1770, to his correspondents in Rhode Island, Ireland, England, the Caribbean, and the southern colonies; letters received by James Beekman from Europe, 1750-1799; and his own letters to European correspondents for the years 1766-1799. More extended annotation would have rendered the *Papers* more generally useful.

Brown University JAMES B. HEDGES

The Trial of Peter Zenger. Edited by Vincent Buranelli. (New York: New York University Press, 1957. viii + 152 pp. Illustration, appendixes, notes, and index. $3.75.)

In a seventy-five page introduction that is followed by an edited version of the trial, Mr. Buranelli describes the Peter Zenger case in sharp lines of white and black, of hero and villain, and of popular government versus creeping despotism. It is an intensely absorbing account that makes use of journalistic devices to arouse emotion for the embattled hero. Peter Zenger, a German immigrant and former apprentice to William Bradford, fell into the company of Governor Cosby's opposition, becoming the editor of a newspaper that waged an unusually bitter war on the administration and brought him into the colonial courts of New York on charges of libel. Defended by the greatest lawyer of the time, Andrew Hamilton, Zenger won a verdict from the jury that Mr. Buranelli says "touched off reactions throughout the other Colonies. The published account of the trial was hailed as a notable addition to the documentation of freedom — something to be referred to whenever the liberties of the subject were endangered."

Mr. Buranelli is a professional newswriter for radio, who became interested in the Zenger trial some years ago through graduate work in journalism. He approaches the subject almost entirely from his interest in the maintenance of a free press.

From the literary point of view the book has some value as an example of journalistic style in historical writing, with its clear outlines of controversy, issues, and personalities, and its successful devices for sustaining interest. As a product of historical research, however, it has many shortcomings and probably adds nothing to present knowledge of the trial, though some confusion will be created by the interpretations. The strong shades of evil and goodness in the controversy between William Cosby and Lewis Morris are too heavily drawn. Cosby may have been arbitrary and self-seeking, but he was fighting a group of politicians who were letting nothing interfere with their aspirations for power. The Morris party of landowners and merchants was using the assembly and the courts to fight the exercise of royal authority. There were offices, legislative acts, land distribution, Indian trade, and countless other things that would be controlled by the successful party. With the stakes high, politics were dirty on both sides. Alured Popple of the Board of Trade was not fooled at all by the opposition to Cosby and pressed Colden to explain the actions of the Morris party: "I cannot help being Surpriz'd that you who was so strenuous for it as appears by the Minutes of Council of the 5th of Decemr 1727, should now oppose the holding that Court [of Chancery]."

Because these issues of politics have not been carefully analyzed, the reader has no way of judging the real issues of the trial. One suspects that Cosby was more sinned against than sinning and that another person as governor would have suffered nearly as much hostility. The popular party in New York was not a democratic party. It was using the press and the opposition to the governor to establish its own control of the economic, social, and political life of the colony.

Whittier College JOHN A. SCHUTZ

The Colonial Records of South Carolina: The Journal of the Commons House of Assembly, September 10, 1745–June 17, 1746. Edited by J. H. Easterby. (Columbia: South Carolina Archives Department, 1956. xii + 291 pp. Illustration and index. $8.00.)

This volume of the South Carolina *Colonial Records* covers only one year because the Election Act of 1745 reduced the legislative term from three years to one, and longer sessions could not be held until the Act was disallowed in 1748. The Act made other changes: persons who received salaries from the General Assembly were excluded from membership in the Commons House, and the property qualifications were increased both for members of the House and for voters. It is calculated that the property qualification for members was increased some fivefold; the change in the suffrage requirement was mainly in the direction of favoring the inhabitant whose land was settled rather than vacant. The effects of these changes are obscure, and may not have been significant, but one gets the impression that more than the usual number of elected members declined to serve. Some parishes failed to elect the number of representatives to which they were entitled.

As usual, the Commons was concerned with bills of both local and provincial importance. One finds petitions with respect to roads, ferries, parish churches; legislation to establish a market, and "for preventing engrossing, forestalling, regrating, and unjust exactions," or to "prevent frauds and deceits in selling rice, pitch, tar, rosin, turpentine, beef, pork, shingles, staves, and firewood." Fiscal matters loomed large: appropriations, accounts, counterfeiting, bills of credit, interest rates, and what to do about "Woods Half Pence," small copper coins in three denominations in the hands of the late treasurer, Gabriel Manigault. These coins had been received in the time of Governor Francis Nicholson to be used for small change, "but the Assembly at that time refused to have anything to do with them, because they had been sent over without their first being acquainted or having given any Direction for that Purpose."

Affairs with the Indians again needed close attention. For the settlement of the back country a bill was brought in to exempt from provincial taxes for fifteen years "all Persons who come from the back Parts of Pennsylvania and Virginia or any other of his Majesty's Northern Colonies . . . when one hundred Families shall arrive and become Settlers." Questions of the relations among Indian tribes, trade, the danger of some Indians being drawn from the Carolina interest by the promises of other provinces, the designs of the French "to debauch those Indians from the British Interest," the need to send special agents among the Cherokees to keep them from joining "the Northern Indians" against the Catawbas ("a very brave active People and always ready at the Call of this Government") received attention. Several Indians, including the Chickasaw chief, Squirrel King, who had expressed a desire to go to Great Britain, were to be invited to Charles Town in order to go to England in the next "Man of War." Three "Independent Companies" were sent from the mother country for the protection of the province.

There is not space to discuss the successful development of indigo culture and the consequent repeal of the provincial bounty, or the "unprecedented Case" of the Negro wench, Kate, who had committed a murder but could not be brought to trial because she had lost her reason, or the strained relations between the governor and the assembly.

The journals in this series constitute the most important single source for the history of colonial South Carolina. They are invaluable.

Duke University ROBERT H. WOODY

The Origins of the American Party System: Three Essays. By Joseph Charles. (Williamsburg: The Institute of Early American History and Culture, 1956. viii + 147 pp. Notes and index. $2.50.)

The Institute of Early American History and Culture has published three essays from a manuscript by the late Joseph Charles on party origins of Jeffersonian Democracy. These essays, reprinted from the *William and Mary Quarterly*, shed important light on and raise additional questions concerning the formative period of American political parties, after the adoption of the

Constitution and prior to the election of Jefferson in 1800. Mr. Charles examined a great mass of new material in the manuscript collections of leaders of the Federalist period in both political parties. His principal point of view is that the development of parties, on the national scale, was not expected by either the framers of the Constitution or the writers of the *Federalist Papers*. He also believes that the customary point of view as to the constitutional dichotomy between Jefferson and Hamilton is too simple a frame of reference for the analysis of the period or for the point of view of the leaders of the time: Hamilton, Jefferson, Washington, and Adams. For example, Hamilton's objectives have to be measured in terms of a continuing effort to strengthen the role of his own group. Consequently his position in the *Federalist Papers* is hardly compatible with some of his statements at the time of the Constitutional Convention, or his actions as legal leader of the Federalist party. This last point is one of the fundamental questions the author raises in the first essay. Concerning Washington and the party conflict he takes the position that Washington's role as president and in the party picture has never been completely analyzed and developed. In this regard Washington has never been fortunate in the biographers who have treated him.

The second essay is on Adams and Jefferson and points out the difference between Adams and Hamilton. In regard to Jefferson, Charles concludes that John Beckley, first clerk of the House of Representatives, was the actual organizer of the Republican party rather than Jefferson. While not denying the importance of Beckley's contribution, this reviewer is not so convinced that Jefferson came as late to the party struggles as Mr. Charles has indicated.

The third essay is on the impact of the Jay Treaty in the formation of parties. Here Charles views the treaty from a different perspective from that of Samuel Flagg Bemis in his *Jay's Treaty*. Charles regards the treaty, both at the time and in its aftereffects, as a deliberate attempt on the part of the Federalists to fit the United States back into England's sphere of influence in commerce, and to separate the United States from France. At the same time the objective of the Federalists in domestic politics was to limit the scope of the opposing Republican party.

Despite the brevity of these essays the many questions raised by Mr. Charles are of the first level of importance for the understanding of the formative years of the American Union. One can readily agree with the preface by Frederick Merk that this is "a brilliant piece of original analysis."

University of Florida MANNING J. DAUER

A Baker's Dozen: Thirteen Unusual Americans. By Russel B. Nye. (East Lansing: Michigan State University Press, 1956. xii + 300 pp. Notes. $5.00.)

This book, directed at the general reader and non-specialist, is designed to rescue thirteen interesting, even bizarre, personalities from varying degrees of oblivion. John Fries of Pennsylvania was a tavern loud-mouth who opposed John Adams' naval war against France and only fortuitously escaped being the first American hanged for treason — with imponderable consequences for later developments in the nation. Harman Blennerhassett, romantic and myopic, brought from Ireland a young wife and one hundred thousand dollars to build an island Eden in the Ohio River. For having listened to the Mephistophelean blandishments of Aaron Burr he was banished to a wandering mendicancy. Globe-circling John Ledyard of Connecticut was born with an itching foot under the curse of Tantalus and failed repeatedly in his dream of opening the fur trade with the northwest coast. Edward Bonney, conscientious Iowa lawyer, followed a more modest but successful odyssey to destroy a network of thieves and murderers that covered the Midwest. Simon Girty had lost his humanity as a boy captive of the Indians and became the most famous of the frontier renegades. Unctious John A. Murrell plotted a shadowy outlaw and slave uprising in the Old Southwest. He, like Girty, died in bed. Through many of these stories, in fact, runs the theme of frontier violence, one of the darkest in all American history.

Among the brighter portraits is that of patriarchal John Humphrey Noyes. His perfectionist community — the nation's one successful example of group eugenics — lasted until the irresistible currents of American conformity engulfed it. James Strang, the Mormon who would be king, briefly ruled a petty monarchy in Lake Michigan until his reign was brought to an abrupt end by a brutal and blatantly unpunished murder in which the civil authorities connived. Arrogant, stubborn self-righteousness carried Clement L. Vallandigham to, or over, the edge of treason and to an ironically appropriate self-inflicted death by shooting. Jacob Coxey began with a sensible idea for combining the need for better roads with a public works program that might be a depression cure. From that point he digressed into bypaths of financial heresy and took the road to Washington, where his shabby and cowardly reception symbolized the decline in executive leadership that had taken place in the White House since Lincoln's day. Dr. Nye indicts the institution of slavery as the real culprit in the tragedies of Nat Turner and Elijah Lovejoy. Lovejoy's death opened the eyes of many northerners to the truth that acquiescence in the denial of one human right leads to the repudiation of all; but Nat Turner died in vain, he says, because the South could not bring itself to face that inescapable fact. For good measure the author includes Phineas

Quimby, follower of the ancient practice of faith healing and forerunner of a well-known religious group and of the modern lay doctrine of self-help.

In all of them the scholarship is impeccable if not exhaustive. The author has an unusual insight into character and the significance of events and a flair for the apt phrase which he has demonstrated in his earlier publications. In this work his powers of conciseness are also brought most successfully into play. Enlightenment and enjoyment are offered to the reader.

George Washington University WOOD GRAY

Advance Agents of American Destiny. By Roy F. Nichols. (Philadelphia: University of Pennsylvania Press, 1956. 254 pp. Illustration, maps, appendixes, bibliographical notes, and index. $5.00.)

The exploits of neglected or almost forgotten Americans who figured in the early development of our foreign policy are the subject of Professor Nichols' book. Among these first agents were a number of men who sought personal advantage and were only incidentally servants of the nation. Others were prompted by curiosity or were impelled to herald the superiority of our system, while some were devoted primarily to the service of the state. Whatever their motives, they visited places near and far and sent back information which influenced policy then and today.

The first part of this compact and colorful book deals with the problems and frustrations which the representatives of the new nation met when attempting to establish commercial and diplomatic connections with other powers. Spain in particular, as Americans were quick to discover, had no intention of being agreeable except during periods of emergency. Even when trade was permitted, our representatives met with infuriating restrictions which seemed to have no rational basis. Perhaps the most enterprising of the "advance agents" was William Shaler, who represented the United States either officially or unofficially in the West Indies, South America, Central America, Mexico, the Pacific, Europe, and Africa. The account of Shaler's adventures not ony sheds light on Spanish manners and customs but also calls attention to Shaler's own prophetic observations that California would fall readily to the United States and that Cuba would be the last of the Spanish colonies to seek freedom.

A second major division of the book centers about the quest for guano islands during the middle and later part of the nineteenth century. During this period alert mariners and businessmen searched for bits of coral in the Pacific and the Caribbean — small islands not yet formally claimed — where the prized fertilizer might be found. This interest led to an 1856 statute which authorized the registration of discoveries and recognition of the right to take guano. Subsequently, after various requirements of the statute had been met, a number of islands were treated as "appertaining to the United States." Thus, the island of Navassa in the Caribbean (1859) became the first noncontiguous area to be added to the United States. By the same method our ownership of Johnston, Sand, Palmyra, Baker, Howland, and Jarvis islands was established, and it was the guano activity which led in time to our agreement with Great Britain concerning joint use of Canton and Enderbury islands.

This is both a useful and an entertaining volume. The absence of footnotes is perhaps compensated for by an extensive bibliography. The author did not intend to change the general picture. He sought instead to draw attention to a neglected aspect of our diplomacy. This he has done in a well-organized account which is pleasant reading, especially for those who during World War II were stationed on those vital dots in the Pacific which first were visited a century or more ago by the advance agents of American destiny.

University of Minnesota W. DONALD BEATTY

The Intimate Letters of John Cleves Symmes and His Family, Including Those of His Daughter Mrs. William Henry Harrison, Wife of the Ninth President of the United States. Edited by Beverley W. Bond, Jr. (Cincinnati: Historical and Philosophical Society of Ohio, 1956. xxxiv + 174 pp. Illustration, notes, and index. $4.50.)

One of the highlights of this little volume is an unfavorable evaluation by John Cleves Symmes of his newly acquired son-in-law, William Henry Harrison: "If I knew what to make of Capt Harrison, I could easily take [*sic*] proper arrangements for his family. he can neither bleed, plead, nor preach, and if he could plow I should be satisfied. his best prospect is in the army, he has talents, and if he can dodge well a few years, it is probable he may become conspicuous" (p. 82). Symmes, a pioneer colonizer in Ohio, was equally devastating in his analysis of the reasons Governor Arthur St. Clair was unsuccessful in his campaign of 1791 against the Indians (pp. 114-23). A third letter is important enough to mention individually; a letter of Symmes and Judge George Turner to Acting Governor Winthrop Sargent, July 10, 1790, criticizing the judiciary of the Northwest Territory (pp. 110-14).

Most of the other letters are intimate family letters, often showing fine sentiment and personal affection, but being generally of little importance to the historian. Local historians and biographers of Symmes, or of his daughters and sons-in-law, will find much to interest them.

The letters are not arranged in chronological order, but in groups which are associated with members of the family and friends. The first group is composed chiefly of communications of John Cleves Symmes to his two grandsons, Charles Wilkins Short and John Cleves Short. The editor, Beverley W. Bond, Jr., feels rather strongly that they may be compared with the letters of Lord Chesterfield. The second part, which is made up of letters to the parents of the above grandsons, reveals some details of pioneer life in Ohio and Kentucky. Mrs. Susan Livingston Symmes, the third wife of John Cleves Symmes, spent some fourteen years on the Miami frontier but did not adjust herself to its hardships, although a fine new home was built for her. The letters of the third part are chiefly concerned with her dissatisfaction.

A list of books sold for Symmes and a small group of letters chiefly between Symmes and Robert Morris of New Jersey, which give some information about the financial difficulties of the former, constitute the fourth part of the volume. Part five contains miscellaneous letters which include two of those already referred to. A final part of the volume contains letters from and to Mrs. William Henry Harrison. They reveal her as a lady of deep religious faith, strong family affection, quiet persistence, and, perhaps, of carelessness in money matters. The editor's brief but charming introduction equals the best of the letters. The few typographical errors scarcely mar the work.

Indiana University JOHN D. BARNHART

Truxtun of the Constellation: The Life of Commodore Thomas Truxtun, U. S. Navy, 1755-1822. By Eugene S. Ferguson. (Baltimore: The Johns Hopkins Press, 1956. xiv + 322 pp. Notes, bibliography, and index. *$5.25.*)

A reviewer always finds pleasure in a book that makes a real contribution to historical knowledge. *Truxtun of the Constellation* is just such a book. Although many short sketches have been written about Commodore Thomas Truxtun, Eugene S. Ferguson's biography is the first complete study of the man. Seldom does one find a near-definitive biography of a somewhat obscure person in American history that is so interpretive of the person, his period, and his significance.

Undeservedly, Thomas Truxtun is not well known, and his real significance is too seldom appreciated. The one fact that is commonly known about Truxtun is that he commanded the *Constellation* in its glorious single-ship-action victory over *L'Insurgente* in the Naval War with France. But what of the man himself, his earlier and later careers, and his lasting influence? All these are described so effectively and interestingly by Mr. Ferguson that this book may well become recognized as a classic in the field of naval history.

In a sense, Thomas Truxtun was typical of so many of the captains of the early American navy. That is, he had little real naval experience, but was trained in the merchant marine as a seaman and as commander of merchantmen and later of privateers in the Revolutionary War. As a shipowner and captain he made voyages to the Far East at a time when that trade was just beginning to blossom. With this background and experience, and since he served in the United States Navy only from 1794 until 1802, it is remarkable that Truxtun could become generally recognized among naval historians as the "Father of the United States Navy." Only John Paul Jones could compete for such a title, but Jones is known primarily as the father of naval traditions.

Truxtun was a student of the sea; a navigator at a time when navigators were rare; a writer of books on navigation, seamanship, signals, and organization and training of a ship's company; a true leader of men; and a skillful tactician in battle. Although a petty despot aboard ship, he was a fair one, popular with both the public and his officers and crews.

Mr. Ferguson sums up Truxtun very effectively on his concluding page: "Throughout the naval service, although his name might be forgotten by younger officers, was the indelible stamp of Commodore Truxtun. He had established a system where no system existed. By precept and example, he had founded a tradition of command. His attributes of personal bravery, audacity, and tenacity were being encouraged within the service. His tradition was being carried on and preserved for generations of naval officers yet unborn." And, the author concludes, "The tradition of Thomas Truxtun still lives. His concept of command at sea has stood the test of a century and a half of time."

Truxtun of the Constellation is an unusually well-written study that will appeal to general readers and historians alike. Mr. Ferguson's research is careful and penetrating, and it has taken him into a wide variety of sources, including Truxtun family papers.

United States Naval Academy WILLIAM W. JEFFRIES

Cherokees of the Old South: A People in Transition. By Henry Thompson Malone. (Athens: University of Georgia Press, 1956. xiv + 238 pp. Maps, illustrations, notes, bibliographical note, and index. $4.50.)

Seldom does a reviewer have the opportunity of evaluating a book as satisfactory on all scholarly counts as Henry Thompson Malone has produced in *Cherokees of the Old South.* Many books have attempted to trace the history of these remarkable Indians; but nearly all, even those that express the opposite aim, have been restricted to their external relations, to what was done to the Cherokees. This one tells the story from the inside.

Mr. Malone begins with their native social and political institutions, and traces their progress — slow at first, then brilliantly accelerated — in what the white man defines as "civilization." He describes their acceptance of new economic techniques; their gradual conversion to Christianity; their quickening interest in education, by which the whole nation became literate in their own language and their leaders became skilled in the learning of the English-speaking world; and their adoption of a constitutional government, functioning successfully through written laws, enforcement machinery, courts, and an informed electorate. The account stops, as the title indicates, on the eve of their expulsion from their homeland just as they reached the highest stage in their development. It barely hints of the appalling loss of life, the economic desolation, and the internal strife that was their subsequent fate.

The writer of this monograph has special qualifications for a work of this scope. Born in Georgia, reared in South Carolina, and trained in research — master's and doctorate — at Emory University, he is at home in the physical and historical setting. As consultant on Cherokee history for the Georgia Historical Commission, and a member of the advisory committee for the New Echota-Cherokee Foundation he has become familiar with sources never explored before. In addition he has learned clearness of expression through a varied experience in journalism and education.

His research is a model of completeness. He seems to have missed none of the many scholarly secondary works in this field; or of the published diaries, memoirs, and travelers' accounts stretching over three centuries. He has explored all the usual manuscript sources from Georgia to Oklahoma, and from Washington to Boston; and he has examined numerous out-of-the-way collections available only through family and neighborhood contacts. He has carefully read and evaluated obscure contemporary periodicals, including religious journals, and — this is of immense importance — a complete file of the *Cherokee Phoenix*, the bilingual newspaper published by the tribal government, made available to him in microfilm.

All this material has been organized and interpreted to form a clearly written, smoothly running narrative. The style is objective, but the cumulative effect is strangely moving. Within its own carefully fixed boundaries of time and space the study deserves to be ranked as definitive, and it deals with a phase of American history that ought to be better known.

Marshall, Oklahoma ANGIE DEBO

A Political History of the Texas Republic, 1836-1845. By Stanley Siegel. (Austin: University of Texas Press, 1956. xiv + 281 pp. Maps, illustrations, bibliography, and index. $5.00.)

William Bollaert's Texas. Edited by W. Eugene Hollon and Ruth Lapham Butler. (Norman: University of Oklahoma Press, in co-operation with the Newberry Library, Chicago, 1956. xxiv + 423 pp. Maps, illustrations, notes, appendixes, bibliography, and index. $5.00.)

The unusual narrative that is Texas history has been substantially expanded through these two books. The one by Dr. Siegel is a present-day account — long overdue — of the political history of the Texas Republic. The second presents a view of the Republic in the years 1842-1844 through the eyes of a rover, William Bollaert, who, before he saw Texas, had run through a series of brief careers as laboratory assistant to Michael Faraday, geologist in South America, and soldier of fortune in the dynastic civil wars of Spain. Perhaps it has been Texas' fortune to attract men like Bollaert.

The first of the books corrects a lack of balance in the historiography of the Republic. There have been economic, social, military, naval, and diplomatic treatments that took cognizance of the significant political groupings and leaders within the powder-burnt Republic, but such political references were necessarily background to another story. Likewise, there have been numerous biographies, but until the recent and superb *Anson Jones; The Last President of Texas*, by Herbert Gambrell, not one provided a strong, unbroken thread through the Republic's tapestry of domestic politics. Actually the more conventional treatments of the Texas story have ignored the Republic as such. Most historians treat in some detail the Mexican chaos and American westward movement that put Americans in Texas, which in turn created the clash of cultures and of interests which lead to San Jacinto. They seem to consider the "Treaty of Velasco" a valid document that but for post-treaty perfidy had ended a war; and thereafter their Texas story passes rapidly toward the climax of annexation, with the affairs of the Republic hinged to larger questions of American-English diplomacy and slavery expansion. This has been the conventional path for by-passing some most engrossing, though often confused, phases of Texas independence.

Dr. Siegel's history of the Republic recognizes the presence of non-political elements in Texas history, but subordinates everything to politics. In tracing the political path to revolution he gives conventional recognition to the presence of a war party led by William H. Wharton and another party, under the leadership of Stephen F. Austin, looking for peaceful progress within the terms of the Mexican Constitution of 1824. Austin died in the early days of independence, while Wharton passed from the scene — initially by diplomatic appointment, and soon thereafter by the accidental discharge of a pistol. Wharton, however, had already been displaced as the war-party leader by the military hero of San Jacinto, Sam Houston. But in the years that followed San Jacinto, it was Houston who became the hope of the peace party, with annexation as the solution to all problems, while San Jacinto's cavalry hero, Colonel Mirabeau B. Lamar, became the voice for militant action against Mexico. Diplomatic failures and the disastrous Santa Fe expedition might well have killed the war party for good, had not raids by Mexicans resulting in a twice recaptured San Antonio stirred the Texans toward new fears and mounting anger. Thus Houston in his second term was forced to talk tough at the same time he was using his executive powers to sabotage the retribution schemes of those who hoped to coerce a peace with Mexico.

The author does not accentuate the foregoing pattern of party conflict after San Jacinto as much as he perhaps should have. It is present in his book, but in a somewhat incidental manner. To him the party politics of the Republic are essentially clashes of personalities — between those for or against Houston, or those for or against Lamar. He suggests that party conflict within the Lone Star Republic was thus no more than the personal politics of America's Jacksonian era projected west of the Sabine. This is not in conflict with the analysis suggested above, for certainly he is right in the opinion that within the Republic there did not develop well-defined party organizations with definite labels, periodic conventions, and platforms, or with a recognized, continuing leadership. Thus to the political scientist, the brief era of the Republic might well be a barren period, but Dr. Siegel's narrative makes good reading that correlates many well-known episodes and explores sundry dark corners.

A more informal view of the Republic, though confined to but two years of its history, is afforded by *William Bollaert's Texas.* Bollaert had lead a strenuous life before he arrived in February, 1842, but at the same time was cultivating an interest in writing. He became an incurable note taker, developed an interest in journalism, eventually authored magazine articles, a book or two in his declining years, and died in 1876 with adequate notes for considerably more. Among other publications, mention may be made of his article in Volume XXXII, *Littell's Living Age*, 1852, for example, which is a frequently cited source for most that is known of the New Orleans and Gulf pirate, Jean Lafitte. The present edition of Bollaert's Texas papers had its point of origin some fifty years ago when Edward E. Ayer acquired Bollaert's writings — notes, diaries, and sketches — and presented them to the Newberry Library in 1911. The Library has co-operated in the present publication, edited by two capable historians, W. Eugene Hollon and Ruth Lapham Butler.

This reviewer first learned of Bollaert's writings while preparing a history of the Texas navy some twenty-five years ago. This experience with Texas naval history raises one or two questions with Bollaert's editors. The reviewer must disagree, for example, with the impression they give that Bollaert enlisted in the Texas navy and did a brief cruise aboard a Texan man-of-war. Internal evidence alone is sufficient to reveal him as a sergeant in a militia company self-styled the "Coast Guards." Second only to "Sea Fencibles," perhaps, the title was then the most popular name for seaport National Guard units from Maine to Texas. The modern usage of the term "Coast Guards," referring to crewmen for wartime naval ships, stems from the consolidation of the Revenue Cutter Service with the coastal Life Saving Service in 1915. In time of peace they are an arm of the Treasury Department. It thus appears the editors made a plausible error in thinking of Bollaert, the coast defense national guardsman, as a member of a wartime naval service. Moreover, the existence of a muster roll in Texan Archives does not identify the S. S. *Lafitte* as a Texas navy warship as the editors seem to think. Had she been such, her name would not be so conspicuously absent from Bollaert's own ship list of the Lone Star navy among his notes on that subject. He does not even include the *Lafitte* as a privateer, though he does list a few vessels as such. The legal status of the ship on her "cruise" to the vicinity of Corpus Christi, with the "Coast Guards" and "Fusileers" aboard, appears to have been that of a merchantman under charter as a troop transport. The filing of a roster of active duty (which might serve to validate a future land claim) for such a locally inspired and presidentially authorized expedition to checkmate reported enemy troop movements and to "give confidence to the people down the coast" was in keeping with Texan practice. The accident of geography made Bollaert's military excursion seaborne instead of the more conventional horse-borne operation; otherwise there was no difference.

And while we are bickering over petty details, it may be pointed out that technicians in reproducing the lower drawing opposite page 72 most likely reversed a negative, or the equivalent of such. The original from which the reproduction was made, as this reviewer recalls, showed "Galveston, Tex" written in ink on the reverse side of rather porous paper. These words showed through the paper and so should appear backwards on the printed sketch. Little harm is done except that the technician, in making the script conform to reading habits, has reversed the sloop in the foreground so that it heads up the bay instead of the opposite direction, and the town of Galveston, such as it was in 1842, is completely reversed.

These quibbles notwithstanding, Eugene Hollon and Ruth Butler's edition of Bollaert's papers relative to Texas is a major contribution to Texas history, and to exploration and travel in the American West. One lays the book aside with deep regret — sorrow that Bollaert seems to have been so narrowly short of the time, literary skill, industry, or all three, essential for him to have written one of the truly great contemporary accounts in American history. With an occasional broader touch and a somewhat stronger hyperbole, some of his situations could have been from the pen of Mark Twain. He saw, met, and conversed with all the high and the low in the Texas of his two years and had a good reporter's eye for detail.

The editors have been most generous with footnotes identifying every significant person met and further correlating Bollaert's notes with the tide of events as of the day he wrote them. They and their publisher merit warm commendations for rescuing these materials from the dusty files in which they have lingered too long.

Wisconsin State College at Superior JIM DAN HILL

The Papers of Willie Person Mangum, Volumes III-V. Edited by Henry Thomas Shanks. (Raleigh: State Department of Archives and History, 1953-1956. Vol. III [1953]: *1839-1843*. xxiv + 521 pp. Vol. IV [1955]: *1844-1846*. xxviii + 579 pp. Vol. V [1956]: *1847-1894*. xxxviii + 812 pp. Illustrations and indexes. $3.00 per volume.)

The publication of the fifth volume of the Mangum Papers concludes a praiseworthy and notable undertaking. Together the five volumes of this set make a first-rate contribution to the historical literature of nineteenth-century America. Willie Person Mangum, one of North Carolina's ablest sons, spent most of his adult life in public affairs. In a congressional career of twenty-two years, most of them in the Senate, he distinguished his state and himself, holding his own with the better advertised political figures of the time. In these volumes there are few historical personages in the American scene of his time who are not included by letter or by reference. There are estimates of character, revelations of plans and purposes, examples of the inner workings of the political machinery, as well as material on many other aspects of American life — education, newspapers, travel, health, and housing. The specialist will determine the contribution of the papers to his own particular field, but no researcher in the period can hereafter safely ignore the collection.

Volume III, published in 1953, covers a period of great significance in Mangum's career, the years 1839-1843. The Whig party, of which he was a leader, won the election of 1840, and shortly, upon Harrison's death and Tyler's accession, Mangum's colleagues elected him permanent president of the Senate, thus putting him in line for succession to the presidency. In the papers one finds some of Mangum's friends speculating about Tyler's health and Mangum's prospects of succeeding him. Mangum was now at the center of Whig politics of the Clay label. His letters in this period — there are 47 in the volume — are probably the most significant letters in the entire collection, according to the estimate of the editor himself. One revealing letter is a long one to Duncan Cameron in June, 1841, confidentially detailing top-level politics and the woes of the Whigs as the leaders tried to keep Tyler in Whig dress.

Volume IV, published in 1955, contains 379 items, 45 of them by Mangum, and covers the short period of 1844 through 1846. Mangum was still president of the Senate, and he headed the Whig Senate committee for the campaign of 1844, leading the movement in the South for Clay's nomination. The correspondence reflects the excitement of the campaign and Whig chagrin at Clay's failure. It reveals, too, speculations about prospects in 1848 and some interesting evaluations of Henry Clay. The annexation of Texas — a move which Mangum opposed — is another subject touched on in these pages. There are a few letters from Clay, Webster, Reverdy Johnson, Thurlow Weed, Winfield Scott, Calvin Colton, Memucan Hunt, and several from James Watson Webb.

The fifth and final volume covers Mangum's last term in the Senate, 1847-1853, and his declining years as a private citizen and as justice of the peace, to the time of his death in 1861. Later years covered by the volume are devoted mainly to memorials and reminiscences. The latter part of the book is made up of three special groups of papers: (1) twenty undated manuscripts, identified with the period 1819 to 1850; (2) about a score of items discovered after the publication of the volumes in which they logically belonged; (3) twelve of Mangum's longer speeches, most of them delivered in the Senate. In the earlier pages of the volume are 72 Mangum letters— more than in any previous volume but only about 17 per cent of the 416 items (excluding speeches) printed. It is one of the regrets of the editor that the number of Mangum manuscripts could not be a larger proportion of the whole. For the series the proportion is about 13 per cent. There are two letters from Webster and two from Clay in this volume; also one from Abraham Lincoln seeking Mangum's help for a federal appointment.

This last volume focuses attention upon Whig politics as related to the Mexican War, the election of 1848, the Compromise of 1850, and the campaign of 1852. Mangum supported the war after it got started, but he opposed a military man for president, although he worked for Taylor's election after his nomination. He served with Clay and Webster on the Senate Committee of Thirteen which prepared the compromise measures of 1850, and he is credited with having persuaded Webster to make his famous Seventh of March speech. He apparently dominated the Whig convention of 1852. "The nominations," he wrote his wife, "I may say, are mine." Mangum was a nationalist who feared dissolution of the Union, but when the break came he followed his state; and his only son, whom he had encouraged to volunteer, was killed in the first Battle of Manassas.

Volume V, like all the others, contains a number of good illustrations, including many pictures of Mangum's contemporaries. All five volumes are uniform in format, as are the editorial devices. The indexes are full and well arranged. The footnote annotations are generous and most helpful. The printing is remarkably free from slips or bungling. Thanks are due both to Professor Shanks and to the North Carolina Department of Archives and History for their completion of a highly commendable and useful publication project.

University of Chattanooga CULVER H. SMITH

The Militant South, 1800-1861. By John Hope Franklin. (Cambridge: The Belknap Press of Harvard University Press, 1956. xiv + 317 pp. Bibliographical essay and index. $5.00.)

Americans whether professional historians or laymen never seem to grow weary of telling the story of their Civil War and of attempting to explain its coming. In this book Professor Franklin has chosen to give us a new interpretation of the coming of that conflict. While recognizing the influence of such factors as "the controversial question of the autonomy of the states and the concept of liberty," the rivalry of a "commercial-industrial" North and a "predominantly agricultural" South, and the conflicts between a North "committed to the view that universal freedom was the proper foundation for improving the social order" and a South that "insisted that its half-free, half-slave society needed only to be let alone," the author finds the major cause of the war in the tendency of southerners "to resort to violence for the settlement of any dispute, whether personal, social, or political." Professor Franklin does not claim that "all Southerners, or even almost all of them, were bellicose or militant." On the contrary, he recognizes that there were southerners who "regarded violence and other forms of precipitate action as revolting." But the latter, says he, "were shouted down, voted down, and fought down by those Southerners who . . . subscribed to the code of conduct and a plan of action that was the antithesis of moderation and conciliation. These created the climate of militancy."

In support of this thesis the author organizes his descriptive story around such topics as love of soldiering, Indian fighting, disciplining slaves, dueling, manifest destiny and filibustering, and military schools. These he marches across his pages with the precision and effectiveness of a platoon sergeant drilling his troops. In this descriptive story the author demonstrates beyond any doubt that a spirit of militancy pervaded all classes of society. And yet the story gives a one-sided, exaggerated, and distorted picture of southern life. Unique and bizarre incidents are recounted as if they were the usual and commonplace and one gets the impression that the entire South was in a perpetual state of militarism. Sweeping generalizations also make for an inaccurate picture. For instance the statement that "only in the ante-bellum South did men in public life persist in defending their honor by dueling" ignores the fact that as late as the 1850's some northern and western men in public life defended their honor in personal encounters and even gave up their lives in so doing. Again in his effort to develop the militant spirit of southerners the author omits an essential part of the story. Such is the case where he fails to recognize that a major factor in the establishment of the state military schools was the need for trained engineers.

A major weakness of much of the writing on the South is that it ignores the fact that the South was after all a part of the nation. The writings tend to overemphasize the differences between the sections (differences in degree and not in kind) and to ignore their similarities. Such a criticism can legitimately be leveled against *The Militant South.* Nearly every facet of life which Professor Franklin explores in developing his story — soldiering, Indian fighting, military schools, rioting, manifest destiny, and the others — had its counterpart in the North and West, some to a lesser others to a greater degree. Hence to give a balanced picture and to explain properly the coming of the Civil War other factors than southern militancy must be explored.

University of North Carolina FLETCHER M. GREEN

Auraria: The Story of a Georgia Gold-Mining Town. By E. Merton Coulter. (Athens: The University of Georgia Press, 1956. x + 149 pp. Illustrations, notes, bibliography, and index. $3.00.)

Auraria is the history of a gold-rush town which flourished more than a century ago and then declined until it was virtually forgotten. The importance of this book lies in its graphic description of social, economic, and political activities in a gold-mining community which antedated the mining settlements of the West. Although the author has made no attempt to write a history of gold mining in the South, or even in Georgia, the narrative goes beyond a mere local study and includes pertinent historic developments of the Jacksonian era and of western migration.

Twenty years before the cry of "Gold!" resounded in California, rich deposits of the precious ore were discovered in the hills of northern Georgia. As a horde of adventurers invaded lands claimed by the Cherokees, America's first gold-mining town — Auraria, Georgia — sprang into existence. In 1833 the village had a cosmopolitan population of a thousand inhabitants, but Auraria's period of greatness was short-lived. Gold became more difficult to strike, Aurarians began moving away, and the town gradually dwindled until it became little more than a memory.

Professor Coulter's latest book was made possible by his discovery of a complete file of the *Western Herald*, a newspaper published in Auraria when the town was reaching its zenith. Although the *Western Herald* lasted only a few months (April 9, 1833, to January 31, 1834), its editor made the paper a remarkable reflector of a unique period in Georgia's history. By using the *Western Herald* as a basic source, the author has presented a realistic view of life in a southern gold-mining center.

A maze of legends and distorted tales concerning Auraria has been dispelled by Professor Coulter's research. He discloses that the name of Auraria was not selected by John C. Calhoun, as was previously thought, but by a Major John Powell. The author refutes the notion that Auraria was an extremely lawless community resembling a "wild West" town. "In the period of Auraria's greatness, only one murder took place" (p. 47). Yet a letter written by a prospector at Auraria in 1833, a copy of which is in possession of the reviewer, asserts that not all Aurarians were law-abiding: "I have never before been amongst such a complete sett [*sic*] of lawless beings. I do really believe, that for a man to be thought honest here, would be a disadvantage to him, or at least he would be set down for a fool and treated accordingly."

Written with feeling and understanding, this significant monograph enriches our knowledge of a dramatic phase of history.

North Georgia College T. CONN BRYAN

Westernized Yankee: The Story of Cyrus Woodman. By Larry Gara. (Madison: State Historical Society of Wisconsin, 1956. xii + 254 pp. Illustrations, notes, bibliographical note, and index. $4.50.)

A conspicuous person on the American frontier during the nineteenth century was the land agent, a man who typically filled three roles. As an agent he acted for absentee investors, but at the same time he speculated in lands on his own account and played the part of moneylender to settlers. Such a characteristic figure was Cyrus Woodman.

As the title of Dr. Gara's book implies, Woodman was a native New Englander. A graduate of Bowdoin College and a member of the Massachusetts bar, he went west in 1839 as an agent of the Boston and Western Land Company. When the company was liquidated in 1843 he remained in the West and the following year went into partnership with Cadwallader C. Washburn, who had a law office and land agency in Mineral Point, Wisconsin. This partnership was to continue for eleven years and was perhaps the most significant phase of Woodman's career.

The "money and land grabbing firm of Washburn and Woodman" (so Woodman jokingly referred to the old partnership in 1864) followed the usual pattern of such concerns. The partners cared for and sold lands for absentee owners and collected debts for creditors living at a distance. They also speculated in lands, at one time attempting a monopoly of the Wisconsin-Minnesota pineries. Their most profitable source of income, however, was the lending of money to settlers at high rates of interest. Most of the money was advanced in the form of so-called time-entries. Title to a desired parcel of land was entered in the name of Washburn and Woodman (or of the capitalist for whom they were acting), and the borrower was given a bond promising transfer of title at the end of a year upon payment of the purchase price plus 25 per cent. Thus the lender could lose nothing and Wisconsin's usury law was circumvented.

The firm of Washburn and Woodman was dissolved in 1855, but for another decade Woodman spent most of his time in the West caring for his lands and looking for new opportunities for speculation and investment.

After 1862 he was land agent of the St. Mary's Falls Ship Canal Company. In 1869 he emerged from semi-retirement in Massachusetts to supervise the building of a branch line of the Burlington and Missouri River Railroad in Nebraska. He died in Cambridge in 1889.

Westernized Yankee meticulously sets forth Woodman's day-by-day activities, evidence of the months its author devoted to a study of the Woodman Papers, the book's principal source. Perhaps it is understandable that in the course of such concentrated research Dr. Gara became a partisan of his subject. Throughout the book he emphasizes that Woodman's business ethics were superior to those of most of his contemporaries. He fails to prove his contention, however, by documented comparison. A wider use of the papers of nineteenth-century businessmen would have revealed that in that period, if not in this, business and personal ethics seldom coincided and that the interlarding of a man's letters with high-minded sentiments was not necessarily proof that he was any less aggressive than his fellows when it came to sharp business practices. In this connection, it must be said that throughout the book Dr. Gara has made but slight use of available monographic material. The work of Paul Wallace Gates on the role of the land speculator in western development comes first to mind, but at no point in the volume is it cited. However, *Westernized Yankee*, in providing a detailed study of a western land agent has helped to sharpen the historian's focus on an important frontier figure.

Southeast Missouri State College IRENE D. NEU

Henry Varnum Poor: Business Editor, Analyst, and Reformer. By Alfred D. Chandler, Jr. (Cambridge: Harvard University Press, 1956. 362 pp. Illustration, map, notes, appendix, bibliography, and index. $6.50.)

Henry Varnum Poor made the *American Railroad Journal*, of which he was editor from 1849 to 1861, an outstanding industrial journal of far-reaching influence in railroad and financial circles and indispensable to economic historians of a later day. His penetrating criticisms and constructive suggestions, while not always consistently presented, won serious consideration and, at times, reform. They also subjected him to harsh attacks. Badly located lines, failure to set up reserves for depreciation on property and for the retirement of bonds, failure to make cost accounting studies, and inefficient operation were pointed out and remedies suggested. While he found no merit is Asa Whitney's impractical suggestion for a railroad to connect Lake Superior with Puget Sound he strongly advocated railroad extension in the South and West wherever local groups were sufficiently interested and able to begin construction with local capital. State aid for sound enterprises he favored, but he had doubts about the wisdom of federal aid.

Poor abandoned the emphasis of the early *Journal* upon engineering and technical aspects of railroading to concentrate more on financial practices, such as the proportion of stocks and bonds in the capital structure of a railroad and the methods of marketing securities both at home and abroad. His belief that the details of railroad operation and policies should be made public led him to favor compulsory publicity through reports made regularly to a state commission. This same belief in the salutary effects of publicity led him to devote much space to analyses of the reports of the railroads, meager as some of them were.

Mr. Chandler has succeeded remarkably well in this study in tracing the career of a leader in the field of industrial and financial journalism. The influence of Poor's rural background, his short legal career, his brother's part in developing the railroad network of Maine, and the intellectual and reform circles into which marriage brought him are all linked up with the editorial and business advice he offered at a later date. The author has not hesitated to show inconsistencies in Poor's analyses and criticisms, his inclination to favor certain railroads whose securities were being handled by banking houses he trusted, and to point out that some of his suggestions were quite impractical. He shows that a Michigan Central official thought it wise to advertise in the *Journal* because of Poor's influence in financial circles abroad. He might have added that the Illinois Central Railroad also found it expedient to advertise its lands in the *Journal*, though few or no prospective land buyers could be expected to see such displays. Poor's Whiggish notions on the tariff had to be abandoned as he came to feel the need of the railroads to buy their iron rails as cheaply as possible.

After retiring from the editorship of the *Journal* at the age of forty-nine, Poor, who lived to ninety-three, wrote briefly on financial matters for other journals, became government director of the Union Pacific, and was a lobbyist for the railroads in their fight against higher tariff rates on steel rails. He also undertook the preparation of his *Manual of the Railroads of the United States* and with his son organized a commission house. Mr. Chandler is less interested in this period of Poor's career and gives serious attention only to his lobbying activities and the management of the *Manual*. This is as it should be, for Poor's significance is in his services as a critic and counselor to railroads and as a business journalist. Both Henry Varnum Poor and historians have fared well at the hands of Mr. Chandler.

Cornell University PAUL W. GATES

The Courtship of Mr. Lincoln. By Ruth Painter Randall. (Boston: Little, Brown and Company, 1957. xvi + 219 pp. Illustrations and bibliographical note. $3.75.)

In the restudy and reinterpretation of the Lincoln era, many legends of the man have melted away under the glaring lights of new historical evidence.

It is one of these legends that Ruth Painter Randall has undertaken to disprove for all time: William H. Herndon's "fabrication," as she terms it, that Lincoln failed to appear at his scheduled wedding to Mary Todd in early 1841, and that when the ceremony eventually did take place in late 1842, it was not followed by a marriage based on deep, mutual love. Mrs. Randall emphasized that the Herndon story was incorrect in her earlier study, *Mary Lincoln: Biography of a Marriage*, but she was not satisfied with the cursory treatment the courtship period was forced to receive in that volume. Therefore, she has chosen to write more fully of the stormy, mysterious months preceding the marriage, and the result is *The Courtship of Mr. Lincoln.*

Mrs. Randall presents Mary Todd and Abraham Lincoln against the backdrop of the Illinois frontier of the 1830's and 1840's. So successful is she in conveying the spirit of the place and time, so understanding is she of the people involved (and of human nature in general), and so warm and smooth-flowing in her style of writing, that the reader has no difficulty in imagining himself on the scene of activity. Herein is the greatest strength of this volume.

Concentrating on the Mary Todd–Abraham Lincoln romance, Mrs. Randall deals with the earlier romantic interest of each briefly and only to the degree she feels necessary to give the reader an understanding of the couple's own courtship. She recognizes the long-accepted fact that there were contrasts in the backgrounds, personalities, social interests, and attitudes of the plump Miss Todd and the lanky Mr. Lincoln. But, rather than conclude, as many earlier writers did, that these differences made impossible a happy marriage, she believes they afforded a proper balance. She emphasizes that Mary Todd was more interested in politics than "became" a lady of that age, that she shared Lincoln's political ideas, that she appreciated her suitor's abilities more than she disliked his lack of polish, and that she recognized his potentialities despite her family's belief that he would not make her a suitable husband. In the author's opinion these positive ideas of Miss Todd's (and she *was* positive), coupled with her implicit faith in and love for Mr. Lincoln, more than counteracted their differences.

The period from January, 1841, when the couple parted company (for reasons even Mrs. Randall can only surmise), until their marriage in November, 1842, was filled with frustration for Miss Todd and torment for Mr. Lincoln. The author shows that neither could have been happy with the state of affairs in these months, for when mutual friends brought them together, the courtship resumed and the marriage took place shortly thereafter.

Mrs. Randall has chosen a very difficult, though interesting subject for a study, which she assures the reader is not "fictionalized." In final evaluation, however, it is well to remember the numerous obstacles inevitably encountered in rendering an accurate, historical account of so intimate a subject.

Although she made use of many letters written by and to the principals during the turbulent courtship period, there is not yet sufficient evidence to knit together an uncontestable account of what really happened. Chances are strong that the complete story was never recorded by either party; maybe it was never spoken to anyone. Certainly, the whole story is not yet told; and, because of its personal nature, it may never be. But Mrs. Randall has written the most exhaustive account to date.

There is much interpretation in this volume, as there would have to be when writing a continuous account without the necessary facts to substantiate every statement. The book is not documented, but Mrs. Randall writes that she has the fully documented manuscript in her possession. It is regrettable, also, that it has no index, an omission scarcely reconcilable with a volume of history. There is a bibliography, however, which enhances the value of the work as a whole for the student of the period.

Winthrop College MARY ELIZABETH MASSEY

The Sable Arm: Negro Troops in the Union Army, 1861-1865. By Dudley Taylor Cornish. (New York: Longmans, Green and Company, 1956. xiv + 337 pp. Notes, bibliography, and index. $6.00.)

As its title implies, this book holds that the Negro soldier comprised a valuable addition to the Northern forces in the Civil War. If, instead of bearing arms, the Negro had sat the war out, "the history of the American people in general and of the American Negro in particular must have been far different from what it was." If this phrase from the foreword seems to overstate the case, a sober reading of the entire volume is certainly an eye-opener. Bristling with footnotes, this solid study contributes markedly to Civil War combat history, particularly in so far as military history is a reflection of influences economic, social, and psychological.

The Sable Arm supplies a full complement of revealing statistics. One learns that the generally accepted total figure for enlisted Negroes is 178,895, not including 7,122 officers. Thus although the recruiting of colored troops did not begin in earnest until the spring of 1863, Negroes were to make up between nine and ten per cent of the Union soldiery. Death took 68,178, or more than one-third, of these Negro volunteers. Desertions in colored troops ran to 14,887, out of a total of over 200,000 in the Union army. In an instance in which there were conflicting figures — as in the number of engagements in which Negroes fought, ranging from 250 to 449 — the author furnishes an explanatory word (pp. 264-65).

In evaluating their battle performance, Mr. Cornish relies heavily on the word of commanding officers who observed them in action. While these comments are mainly commendatory, recorded also is the opinion of Colonel Charles Francis Adams, Jr., "that the negro was wholly unfit for cavalry service." Despite the discriminations against them in pay, in promotions, and in duties assigned, the Negro soldiers fought well, concludes Cornish, because they fought not only for the flag and the Union, but for their personal freedom and to refute the contention that they lacked soldierly qualities. A notable backdrop of *The Sable Arm* is the inclusion of sketches of generals who were advocates of colored troops. David Hunter in the Sea Islands comes more out of the shadows, as does John W. Phelps, who without authorization sought to organize five companies of Negroes in the Department of the Gulf. Justly enough the lion's share of attention is given to Lorenzo Thomas for his groundwork in the organizing of seventy regiments of former slaves in the Mississippi Valley.

On occasion the author applies modern terminology to Civil War maneuvers, with telling effect: a small-scale operation undertaken up the Bell and Sapelo rivers by the First South Carolina regiment is viewed as "a reconnaissance in force, a commando raid, a recruiting drive, and a training problem with live ammunition, all rolled into one."

This work unravels so much that it may seem gratuitous to note that little is said of the Negro sailor and of the civilian Negro military laborer; the former is given one paragraph and the latter even less. The existence of each of these groups, however, substantially reduced the army's black potential; moreover, to slight them is to risk leaving the impression that the Negro's role on the battle fronts was one-dimensional. Whether these omissions are justifiable may be debatable, but there can be no disagreement that *The Sable Arm* is an exceptionally meritorious work.

Morgan State College BENJAMIN QUARLES

A Different Valor: The Story of General Joseph E. Johnston, C. S. A. By Gilbert E. Govan and James W. Livingood. (Indianapolis: Bobbs-Merrill Company, 1956. 470 pp. Maps, illustrations, notes, bibliography, and index. $6.00.)

For years Civil War historians have been nodding gravely to each other, agreeing that some time someone would write a biography of General Joseph E. Johnston. Now one has been written. Gilbert Govan and James Livingood have produced a book which, except for the lack of studies of Braxton Bragg and Albert Sidney Johnston, fills the gap previously existing in the long shelf of biographies of leading Confederate military figures.

Perhaps one reason why a book about Johnston has been so long delayed is that he is a difficult subject, somewhat lacking in "color" and in any really notable successes to show for his four years of service as a Confederate general. In the defense of Richmond during the Peninsular campaign his orders were not properly carried out, and at Seven Pines he was wounded and replaced by Lee, who went on to glory. As a department commander in the

West in 1863 he displayed little imagination and again his orders were not well executed, with the result that Vicksburg fell. As commander of the Army of Tennessee he carried out the controversial strategic retreat from Dalton to Atlanta in 1864. Though considered a brilliant officer by many of his peers and greatly admired by his soldiers, it is difficult to isolate and pin down the direction his brilliance took. Was it in strategy? In tactics? In logistics? In organization and administration? The answer is not clear.

Perhaps there might be a more satisfying answer if it had not been for Johnston's private war with Jefferson Davis. This war within a war was a major factor in Johnston's career; and it becomes the major theme of this biography. Actually at times it appears that the book lacks balance because the authors have devoted so much effort to showing what a scoundrel Jefferson Davis was. At the same time there are instances when the serious personality defects of Johnston are glossed over. Particularly, it seems to this reviewer, have the authors failed properly to take into account the influence of Mrs. Johnston in keeping the fires of conflict with Davis burning brightly in her "poor, dear" husband's breast. She hated bitterly and vindictively, and never for a moment let the General forget that Davis was persecuting him.

From the above it must not be inferred that this is not a good book. It is good and in many respects excellent. Perhaps nothing short of psychoanalysis could completely explain the vendetta which these two men carried on to the detriment of the Confederate cause; and the authors are not psychoanalysts. So far as this reviewer knows they have utilized all available source material on Johnston. The facts appear to be accurate and are well organized, though it is impossible to decipher the last paragraph on page 169. (This must be a printer's error.) Having worked through much of the controversial material, this reviewer knows how difficult it is to keep from taking sides for or against Johnston. In spite of that, however, he wishes there were a little more about Johnston's shortcomings. On the other hand perhaps Davis *was* an unmitigated scoundrel. The reader will get excellent material to substantiate this conclusion.

Tulane University JOHN P. DYER

Lincoln Finds a General: A Military Study of the Civil War. By Kenneth P. Williams. Volume IV, *Iuka to Vicksburg.* (New York: The Macmillan Company, 1956. xviii + 616 pp. Maps, illustrations, appendix, notes, bibliography, and index. $7.50.)

In this fourth volume of his magnificent study of General Grant's Civil War career, Kenneth P. Williams centers his story on Vicksburg and the year of conflict preceding that mighty bastion's fall. The reader moves with Grant and his armies through Kentucky, Tennessee, and down the Mississippi Valley during the hard and discouraging winter of 1862-1863. As the time approaches for the final and major assault on Vicksburg, Mr. Williams brings in peripheral incidents, including such important but usually neglected actions as Colonel Benjamin Grierson's raid into the heart of Mississippi.

This period was the testing time for Grant, when events and his own abilities moved him from a minor to a major status among the Union's military leaders. A lesser general would have grown reckless or timid in the face of what seemed to be continuous frustration, but we see Grant's character hardening. One of the most difficult forms of historical writing is to show such development of character, and it is to the author's credit that he has accomplished this feat most skillfully, presenting the maturation of Grant as a man and a military leader from carefully documented records. In fact, this volume is probably the most thoroughly documented study of Grant in the West, almost one quarter of the volume being devoted to notes, appendixes, and bibliography.

In one of the most entertaining sections of the book, Part III of the appendix, "The Cadwallader Story of June 6 and 7, 1863," the author attacks the currently snowballing legend of Grant's drinking sprees, and virtually demolishes one of the originators of the stories, Sylvanus Cadwallader, whose "lost" memoirs were only recently published. Sometimes using a rapier, sometimes a bludgeon, Mr. Williams also goes after General John A. McClernand, who for some reason seems to be the preferred villain of current Grant biographers. Actually — and Mr. Williams is aware of this of course — McClernand was not the only general who corresponded out of channels with President Lincoln, nor the only one who was an ambitious schemer. Indeed, it would seem from leafing through Lincoln's war correspondence and the *Official Records* that almost every officer in the Union army at one time or another wrote a letter out of channels to Mr. Lincoln, and most of them were bent on gaining some profit from the war. That is the way wars are, and McClernand was no worse than many others among the political generals.

Mr. Williams has a particular scorn for historians who tend to exploit the sensational without careful investigation of the truth of their sources, and reminds us of a timely warning given by Douglas Southall Freeman shortly before his death, a warning against "records of events made after a prolonged interval." Anyone who has worked with Civil War materials knows there is nothing trickier than the memory of an old warrior. Mr. Williams believes that history in essence is drama, and that it needs no spectacular garnishing to make it readable. He has already proved his thesis with this continuing study of Grant, which has three volumes yet to come.

University of Illinois D. A. Brown

Sherman's March through the Carolinas. By John G. Barrett. (Chapel Hill: University of North Carolina Press, 1956. x + 325 pp. Bibliography and index. $6.00.)

This excellent book tells the story of General Sherman's theory of total war and the implementation of that theory in the march from Savannah to Raleigh. Although he entered the conflict with the conventional notion that war should not be waged against barns, smokehouses, haystacks, and other property of noncombatants, Sherman had changed his mind by the fall of 1862. In the Civil War, he declared, there were no noncombatants. "The entire South, man, woman, and child are against us, armed and determined." The southern people "cannot be made to love us," he further asserted, "[but they] can be made to fear us, and dread the passage of troops through their country."

But as Dr. Barrett unfolds in full-bodied detail the sequence of events in the march through the Carolinas, it becomes evident that the General could never quite throw off the restraints imposed by his early military training. He had no explicit compunction about waging total war, but apparently he felt it was not altogether decent to avow it. Indeed, the army marched under orders that strictly forbade putting into practice the commanding general's most recent theories. But the author makes it clear that Sherman was a lax disciplinarian only when he wanted to be. Threats were made to burn Raleigh, but prompt and effective measures removed the threats. Threats against Columbia had been even clearer. No efforts were made to take effective measures, and Columbia burned.

Dr. Barrett has presented a most restrained and objective treatment, generally being content to let the reader form his own interpretation of the events. True, he does describe the rape and murder of Negro women in Columbia as "detestable," but in that context the word is merely descriptive. The unusually extensive sources enable the author to give such a vivid and detailed account of arson and theft that the tale needs no further adorning. It is proper to remark, however, as the author does, that the destruction of private property by Sherman's soldiers probably had no appreciable effect upon the outcome of the war.

So far as the reviewer can detect, no fault of any consequence mars this solid and readable book. One question, however, does deserve more attention than it has received. From the day Sherman left Atlanta in November, 1864, until one of his columns collided with Johnston at Bentonville in March, 1865, the Confederacy assembled no force that impeded the progress of the Yankee intruder. This long delay in concentrating forces to oppose Sherman is not adequately explained. But this is a matter that lies along the periphery of the author's main story, and it detracts little from the high praise this work merits.

Hendrix College RICHARD E. YATES

Rebel Brass: The Confederate Command System. By Frank E. Vandiver. (Baton Rouge: Louisiana State University Press, 1956. xviii + 143 pp. Illustrations, bibliography, and index. $3.00.)

Some thirty years ago the late Frank Owsley pointed out in his *State Rights in the Confederacy* that the very foundation stone of the Confederacy, state sovereignty, was its weakest point. Throughout its brief span of years the Confederate States of America struggled with no real success to reconcile the demands of state sovereignty with the need to enforce increased controls and greater centralization. War in a new dimension — total war — demanded centralized control, but from the outset Confederate command was dispersed and supply services disorganized.

This question of centralization forms an important topic in Professor Vandiver's study of the Confederate command system. He has examined this system, not only with regard to military leadership in the field, but in the larger framework of co-ordination between the civil and military direction of the war. He points out the failure of the Confederate government to comprehend the nature of the war — that everything in the war effort, including the importance of civilian morale to soldier morale, represented a command problem. Total war could not be waged piecemeal, and the South's failure testified to a tragic lack of comprehension of the vital place of logistics. At the very least, the logistics of war fought on the scale of the Civil War demanded a central purchasing agency, co-ordination between supply services, and transportation, in addition to centralized command in the field.

Professor Vandiver emphasizes Jefferson Davis' inability to delegate authority, and his failure to establish harmonious relations with the Congress. Excellent evaluations of Confederate cabinet officers point up the lack of co-ordination between their essential departments, which resulted in duplication of efforts and in ruinous competition for vital supplies and services. The author believes the inefficient direction of the South's war effort resulted, in large part, from the inadequacy of executive leadership — a leadership which was itself the victim of the very system which it had helped create, and which it tried so nobly to defend.

There is nothing new or startling in this book. The material with which the author deals is so well known to Civil War students that he saw no need for documentary support, and there are no footnotes. Professor Vandiver states in the foreword that this is only an introduction to the study of Confederate command, and he expresses the hope that it will draw the criticism of Civil War students. One needs only to read the statement on page 123 that "had all of the economic and human resources of the South been managed for a total war effort, the Rebels could have won the war," to feel that the author's fondest hopes for criticism will be realized. In his introduction to this book Professor T. Harry Williams well states its contribution when he describes Vandiver's accomplishment as "a sound job of thinking." And a thorough job of thinking it is — brief, concise, and effectively written, it leaves no doubt about the author's familiarity with the subject matter. The book brings into sharp focus a great deal of scattered thinking on the subject, and the reviewer heartily recommends it to every student of the Civil War.

Alabama College JOHN BENNETT WALTERS

Joseph Reddeford Walker and the Arizona Adventure. By Daniel Ellis Conner. Edited by Donald J. Berthrong and Odessa Davenport. (Norman: University of Oklahoma Press, 1956. xxii + 364 pp. Map, illustrations, bibliography, and index. $5.00.)

Each year continues to see the publication of significant memoirs that enhance our knowledge of the American West. This book is such a reminiscence. Written in the late nineteenth century by Daniel Ellis Conner, it is an account of an expedition through New Mexico and Arizona in 1862-1863 under the command of the renowned fur trapper and trader, Captain Joseph Reddeford Walker. Conner's story of thirty-odd men and fifty animals traversing the wilderness sheds new light upon Walker, then described as a magnificent specimen of manhood between sixty and seventy years old with "a luxuriant growth of hair" flowing over his shoulders. Before the publication of this book very little was known about the later career of this man who, like Jedediah Smith, almost symbolized the trapping West.

This book is also rich in describing the arid country traversed and conditions encountered between the Raton Pass in northern New Mexico, Fort Yuma in western Arizona, and Sonora in Mexico. But it is not only a volume of travel. Conner introduces his reader to such varied phenomena as soapweed, the operation of Mexican plows and gristmills, the "side-lining" of mules, how to bait beaver traps, the use of Indian smoke signals, and, above all, the incessant atmosphere of conflict with the Indians.

The expedition constantly needed to outsmart hostile Indians who in the middle of the night would fire volleys at the intruders or in broad daylight drive off stock. The tension became particularly intense when both Indians and whites were forced to drink from the same water hole. As bitterness reached a climax, savages lurked around campfires like fleeting ghosts, picking off whites whenever they dared. Frequent torture, the burning of the bodies of captured whites, and death by strangulation are only a few of the harrowing cruelties Conner describes.

In this conflict the white man appears in scarcely more noble light than his opponent, a fact well illustrated by Conner's description of the capture and ultimate betrayal of Mangus Coloradas, "great chief of all the Apache tribes which roamed the territories of New Mexico and Arizona and a portion of Old Mexico." By an act of treachery Walker and his men, Conner included, captured this chief and turned him over to the soldiers of General Joseph R. West, who tortured him with red hot bayonets. When Mangus resisted he was shot dead on the pretext that he had attempted to escape.

About this sort of butchery Conner remarks that as "it was the order of the day to kill, and to do nothing else but kill, there was but little attention paid to the manner of doing it." Conner's experiences verged on the incredible. They took place during the emergence of Arizona from a frontier wilderness to the threshold of civilization, often at campsites that would become modern cities.

The diary is attractively printed and competently edited, with only a few minor typographical errors. It is a notable narrative of high adventure on the Arizona trail.

Occidental College ANDREW F. ROLLE

Fiction Fights the Civil War: An Unfinished Chapter in the Literary History of the American People. By Robert A. Lively. (Chapel Hill: University of North Carolina Press, 1957. x + 230 pp. Notes, bibliography, and index. $5.00.)

University presses would do well to leave the business of publishing doctoral dissertations to University Microfilms. Robert A. Lively's 1951 dissertation, "The Novelist as Historian of the Civil War: A Survey and an Evaluation," contains some useful material; but after five years of revision, it is still the exercise of a graduate student rather than a significant critical work.

Lively's approach, probably dictated by his graduate adviser, is that of the historical analyst who is dealing with material of tertiary value. He reviews Civil War fiction according to themes, characters, and biographical backgrounds of the authors. He compares fictional accounts of historical events with the known facts and studies the North's self-criticism and the South's self-admiration. The most worth-while portion of the book is the chapter dealing with the rather sterile effort of the novelist to be a historian, and it can serve as fair warning to history teachers who attempt to sugar-coat collateral reading lists by loading them with fiction.

The historical novel is basically a subject for the literary historian and should be treated with his techniques. A study of the Civil War novel with its couple of dozen outstanding titles, some hundred or so mediocre titles, and perhaps eight or nine hundred sub-literary works could be handled most effectively in terms of a comparison with the main streams of American literature. We need to see the incongruous wit and wickedness of De Forest's Knickerbocker lieutenant in contrast with other fiction published during the Reconstruction period. James Lane Allen's *Sword of Youth* is best viewed as a wobbling example of the twilight of local color (surely not one of Lively's bold selection of the fifteen best Civil War novels). Faulkner's *The Unvanquished* is, to be sure, a significant tale of southern decadence, but one understands it most clearly when it is seen through the spectacles of Freudian psychology and New Deal economics so important to novelists of the thirties.

Lively's gravest weakness is as a bibliographer. He lists 512 titles, apparently selected at random from the institutional collection with which he worked, but including all of the better titles. He would have performed a real service to have included the some 500 additional titles comparable in subject matter and scope. (The University of Kentucky Library catalog shows 808 comparable titles in his period, ending with 1949.) There are misspelled names, e. g., Helen H. Gard[e]ner, Mari[a]n Calhoun Legar[é] Reeves, Paul Str[a]hl, and R. J. C[a]rothers. Other names are wrong, e. g., Lydia [Cope] Wood, [Jane] Franc[e]s Swallow, and A[il]sa Page. Some married women are entered under maiden names with no cross-references, e. g., Florence J. O'Connor [Willard] and Frances Courtenay Baylor [Barnum]. Lively does not know that "A Lady of Warrenton, Va.," was Cora S. Ives or that Ida Glenwood is the pseudonym of Mrs. C. M. R. Garton. He cites the New York edition of *Raids and Romance of Morgan and His Men* rather than the memorable first issued by S. H. Goetzel in Mobile. He confounds two different pseudonymous authors who use the pen name "An American." Some interesting perspectives might have been gained by comparison with foreign Civil War novels such as Eneroth's *Manne Mobergs farer och äfventyr* and *Alabama*, H. av Trolle's *Utkastad i verlden*, Heinrich Schmidt's *Aus einer blutigen Beit*, and Herbert Patira's *Für die schöne blaue Flagge*; but perhaps the idea of a reading knowledge of foreign languages is only a prejudice of the old-fashioned graduate schools. The most practical use for bibliographies such as Lively's is to turn them over to library school students as examples of what a bibliography should not be.

University of Kentucky Library LAWRENCE S. THOMPSON

The Cokers of Carolina: A Social Biography of a Family. By George Lee Simpson, Jr. (Chapel Hill: University of North Carolina Press, 1956. xvi + 327 pp. Map, illustrations, bibliography, and index. $5.00.)

The Cokers were prominent in South Carolina before the Civil War; in the half century that followed they became outstanding economic and cultural leaders. In that era the family produced many well-known citizens, including notable scholars and a respected legislator. But the achievements of these men are overshadowed by the contributions which James Lide Coker and his sons made to southern industry, agriculture, and education.

James Lide Coker was born in 1837 into a prosperous family who educated him at The Citadel and Harvard. After serving with distinction as a major in the Confederate army, he returned home to find that his fortune had vanished in the smoke of Sherman's fires. With a small country store and his farm land, he set out to repair his losses. Before his death in 1918, he, his sons, and associates had built in Hartsville a large mercantile establishment, a pulp mill, a paper factory, a textile-cone manufacturing plant, a cottonseed oil mill, a seed-breeding business, and a four-year college for women. These enterprises, some of them merged and all of them expanded, have remained in the hands of the Major's descendants who today operate Sonoco Products Company, Hartsville Oil Mill, Coker Pedigreed Seed Company, and Coker College.

The scope of the family's operations and services to the Southeast defy coverage in three hundred pages. The author, a sociologist, limits his subject by studying the Cokers as an example of a family which has held together during times of great social change. He does not attempt to relate them to the "New South" industrial movement; nor does he investigate their business enterprises from the viewpoint of the economic historian. For his sources he depends largely on personal papers. Students of the Civil War will be glad to find that he has included much of Hannah Lide Coker's *A Story of the Late War*, hitherto printed only for the family and considered by Douglas S. Freeman one of the best of the wartime narratives written by women. Historians and economists will doubtless wish that more space has been devoted to the Coker enterprises, for one learns more about the men than about the extent and influence of their businesses. Yet the author has told an interesting story of a family whose ingenuity, pioneering zeal, and faith in southern economic progress deserved to be recorded.

University of Mississippi MARGARET DESCHAMPS MOORE

William Tecumseh Sherman and the Settlement of the West. By Robert G. Athearn. (Norman: University of Oklahoma Press, 1956. xx + 371 pp. Illustrations, maps, notes, bibliography, and index. $5.00.)

The pacification of the Indians and the development of transportation were essential to the rapid settlement of the West in the two decades following the Civil War. Professor Robert G. Athearn has written an interesting and informative study of General William Tecumseh Sherman's contributions toward the achievement of these ends. For four years as commanding officer of the Military Division of the Missouri and for fourteen years as General of the Army, Sherman was largely responsible for army policies in the defense of the frontier. At the close of the Civil War, many of the western Indian tribes were dissatisfied and a few were hostile. The rush of settlers westward, the laying out of overland trails, the construction of railroads, and the killing of the buffalo often contrary to Indian treaties or without the consent of the Indians, were the principal reasons for Indian hostilities. In this situation the small regular army under Sherman protected both the settlers and the Indians.

The frontier population favored a more aggressive Indian policy that would either force the Indians out of the desired areas to small reservations or liquidate them. Friends of the Indians insisted that the Indians be protected even at the expense of rapid settlement of the West. The Indian Bureau officials usually favored this latter view. General Sherman's position was about halfway between the two extremes. The military men advocated the army's control of the Indians on the frontier and confinement of the Indian Bureau's supervision to Indians who lived peacefully on their reservations. This conflict in policy was never completely settled and caused much of the trouble with the Indians.

The author brings out clearly General Sherman's view that the principal function of the army on the frontier was to protect the building of the railroads rather than the protection of isolated settlements. He believed that the completion of the railroads would end the hostile Indian problems, and that as the buffalo were killed and the settlers came in the Indians would have no alternative but to retire to reservations and give up their hunting way of life. His policy was considered too harsh in the East; but the West wanted the Indians removed at once and demanded that he protect the settlements without respect for Indian treaties. The General had much confidence in the army's policies, its honesty, and its fairness, and he found it hard to take abuse from both sides. Even his old friend President Grant sided against him in support of the political pressure, however, and in his private letters Sherman was bitter in his criticism of politicians, political considerations, and pressure groups who opposed him.

Weaknesses of the book are few. The author is not too critical of Sherman's attitude toward the Indians and their rights under the treaties. The few errors — such as the mixing of Sherman's and Sheridan's names on page 100 — do not detract from its value. Better selection of place names might have improved the maps. Professor Athearn used many unpublished materials from the National Archives and the Library of Congress. He depended largely upon the Sherman Papers and government documents of the War Department, Indian Bureau, and Congress, and made good use of contemporary frontier and eastern newspapers. This book has made an important contribution on the historical significance of the army's activities and General Sherman's role in the settlement of the West.

Fort Hays Kansas State College RAYMOND L. WELTY

Edward Palmer: Plant Explorer of the American West. By Rogers McVaugh. (Norman: University of Oklahoma Press, 1956. xviii + 430 pp. Illustrations, notes, appendixes, bibliography, and index. $6.00.)

The botanist Edward Palmer, British-American field collector in the southwestern United States and northern Mexico, was one of a trio of distinguished botanical collectors in that area in the last century, ranking with C. G. Pringle and Charles Wright. In addition to his botanical work (perhaps 2,000 species of plants are based on his collections over sixty years, and some 100,000 dried plant specimens were collected and distributed in the period 1859-1911), he was also for several years a collector of archaeological and other materials for the United States Bureau of Ethnology.

The present work is the partial fruit of Mr. McVaugh's sixteen years of study on the life and work of Palmer, at all possible sources: Washington, Yale, Harvard, the New York and Missouri botanical gardens, Iowa State College, and at more remote places where field lists, diaries, specimens of plants, and other available material could be consulted. To say that this life of Palmer has been done with high competence is superfluous to all who know at first hand earlier historico-botanical publications of the author.

In an introductory chapter, McVaugh has given a clear historical view of the situation of plant study in America in the early nineteenth century, and a very good summary of Palmer's personality, including an exposition of his excellent qualities as well as his shortcomings as a collector. The book as a whole is a highly factual account (a desideratum for the botanist who has worked or shall work with Palmer's plants), but is replete with illuminating sidelights on the men with whom and the conditions under which Palmer worked in the long period of his botanical activity.

The first part (some 120 pages) of the book is a running account of Palmer's life in America. This is followed by a Geographical Index (230 pages, 1,239 entries) which gives carefully worked and accurate indications of Palmer's localities and itineraries. This is not a mere gazetteer; it includes all dates at which Palmer visited a given locality, and the nature and extent of his collecting and collections there. Some of the items are very extended (e. g., "Colorado," "Kansas," "Indian Territory") and give a succinct but complete, dated overview of all explorations made by Palmer in the larger areas. The Geographical Index is much to be commended for its completeness and usefulness.

Five appendixes of exceptional value to the systematic botanist follow the Geographical Index, and an 18-page section on "References and Sources" locates those materials, manuscript and printed, that were consulted extensively in the preparation of the work. The list is selective, and does not include perhaps a hundred sources (whose use to McVaugh was of secondary importance) listed in the 249 footnotes scattered through the book. In the appendixes are given such significant matters as chronologies of Palmer's plant collections; locations of known sets of field notes; lists of herbaria which have considerable collections taken by Palmer; and his botanical field notes made in Colorado, May and June, 1861, and in the Indian Territory, March to September, 1868.

McVaugh's work is packed with detailed, well-digested, and adequately indexed information; and it will be indispensable to any botanist who is concerned with Palmer's plants, or to anyone interested in the history of botanical exploration of the West. Five portraits of the naturalist, and well-nigh perfect typesetting and presswork contribute to make this one of the most attractive books that have appeared on the history of botanical exploration in America.

Southern Methodist University SAMUEL W. GEISER

When Grass Was King: Contributions to the Western Range Cattle Industry Study. By Maurice Frink, W. Turrentine Jackson, and Agnes Wright Spring. (Boulder: University of Colorado Press, 1956. xvi + 465 pp. Illustrations, notes, bibliography, and index. $8.50.)

In these days of all sorts of package deals here comes a literary package that is intriguing, and even curious. It consists of three independent studies, tied together only by being concerned with the range cattle industry north of Texas. Maurice Frink leads off with a 123-page essay on — and assay of — the range cattle industry as a business. W. Turrentine Jackson follows with a 200-page study of "British Interests in the Range Cattle Industry," and Agnes Wright Spring concludes with a 100-page analysis of that Colorado-Wyoming " 'Genius for Handling Cattle': John W. Iliff."

Frink is concerned with whether as a generality it can be said that the range cattle industry paid its way. His affirmative conclusion is perforce based in part on fragmentary evidence and in part on opinion. In 1886, for instance, *The Stock Grower* of Las Vegas, New Mexico, concluded from a study of thirty-one ranchers that a rancher who practiced good management techniques ought to show an average annual gain of nearly 15 per cent. But, as Frink points out, thirty-one ranchers here, a dozen elsewhere, and an isolated one scattered about do not make a complete economic picture. The result, says Frink, is that the only positive statement which can be made has to be couched in terms of human experience rather than in cold statistics. The range cattle industry definitely paid in the heritage it left succeeding generations of cattlemen. Beyond that, the historian is merely hazarding intelligent guesses.

On more solid ground is Jackson, for the British kept rather complete syndicate records. They were playing, as the Edinburgh *Courant* pointed out in 1884, "poker on joint-stock principles," with all the opportunities for huge profits and huge losses that a protracted poker-fest can produce. On the whole the nineteenth-century British experience is one of financial loss, aggregating perhaps seventeen million dollars. But at the same time the British freed American capital for other expansive endeavors and helped improve breeding, transportation, and marketing conditions throughout the industry. If the British lost, the United States gained considerably by that loss. The British, incidentally, recouped their losses, at least in part, in the twentieth century by rises in both land and cattle prices.

Mrs. Spring brings a story of contrast to Jackson's. Whereas the British began their spreads with considerable corporate capital, John W. Iliff, a youth in his twenties, came west with only five hundred dollars and no experience. When he died two decades later, he had built an empire that nowadays causes him to be paired with Charles Goodnight as the western cattleman most deserving tribute. By way of sour grapes it might be added that many a cattleman will agree that neither Goodnight nor Iliff could hold a hackamore for half a dozen other western cattle "hosses," but Goodnight had the advantage of a perceptive biography by Evetts Haley, and now Iliff gets a rather full treatment from Mrs. Spring. One suspects that as generations move on and personal recollections fade the men whose reputations endure will be those with the best biographers.

University of Texas JOE B. FRANTZ

William Boyd Allison: A Study in Practical Politics. By Leland L. Sage. (Iowa City: State Historical Society of Iowa, 1956. xiv + 401 pp. Illustrations, notes, bibliography, and index. $6.50.)

This biography was written by a historian for historians and for political scientists. It is devoted chiefly to narrating how an Iowan won ten elections to federal office, getting and keeping places in the House (1863-1871) and Senate (1873-1908). The author has meticulously studied many pertinent, available manuscript sources in Iowa and the Library of Congress besides others in libraries located at Boston, Chicago, Fremont (Ohio), Madison, New Haven, New York City, Princeton, and Springfield (Illinois). Also much secondary literature has been combed. This wealth of data has been coalesced into 334 pages of text and 1,104 remarkably accurate notes.

As it happens that this reviewer was (as far as she knows) the first historian granted unrestricted use of the Allison papers in Des Moines, she has perused text and notes — every line of both — with intense interest and, it must be confessed as respects the notes, with continual aggravation. These notes must be used by the strenuous "fore and aft technique": left thumb and forefinger desperately clutching front pages, right ditto clutching rear pages, and woe betide the reader if either clutch is released. Alternate note pages are cruelly headed "William Boyd Allison" and "Footnotes"; these pages are kept sternly bare of any pampering heading, such as bracketed page-numerals revealing to what pages of text a page of footnotes is wed. Some pitying authors are using the bracket device; they earn the undying gratitude of hapless readers in this epoch of "Notes in the back" books.

Yet, I am deeply grateful to Mr. Sage, for he has done a "bang-up" job of political sequences; it should be a long time indeed before any student of Allison's job-keeping can hope to do anything better, and all of us tackling similar subjects may well study his achievements. His book is particularly distinguished for forthrightness, persistent avoidance of hero worship, eschewing of oversimplification of issues, keen awareness of the infinite complexity of political situations, unwillingness to claim that the last word has been said, and some readiness to make positive alternate guesses as to what may have motivated a decision. Surely such qualities are invaluable and far from easy for biographers to maintain.

Since a reviewer is expected to dilute enthusiastic praise with at least a modicum of criticism, I continually punctuated my perusal with wary queries. At thirty-five not-quite-clinched political junctures, I wished that the author had found space either to reveal the final response to a proposition or to state frankly that the existing evidence leaves it up in the air, where in fact many such matters must remain suspended till the end of time. On Allison-Sherman relations, Sage refers to a "most closely attached . . . most enduring" friendship (p. 127), an imputation of warmth for which I have yet to find much evidence. In the difficult art of making and keeping warm friendships with people of all sorts, Allison was a past master, but Sherman, unluckily, could hardly take the first degree.

On important federal legislation — to which a biography of this brevity and political emphasis cannot frequently allot detailed exposition — the biographer sometimes uses diction which seems to impute to Allison an authorship or a responsibility which he actually shared with several others and which the context as a whole demonstrates that he shared. In such cases, readers are likely to prefer the author's endorsement that "Whoever wrote it, Allison guided it" (p. 304), with reference to such verdicts concerning Senate legislation. This problem is encountered with the Bland-Allison Bill, with the 1888 Senate amendments to the Mills Bill, with Senate amendments to the Dingley Bill, and with the Hepburn Railroad Act.

The road-blocks which intricate matters erect before the progress of biographers are illustrated by the currency issue. Allison is a "convinced" bimetallist on page 242, an "international" bimetallist on page 254, and a stockholder in Dorsey's silver mine on page 360, note 16. Having encountered the fliers of numerous congressmen (not excluding Bland) in mining investments, I suspect Allison got little from his; in any case Iowa had spoken out loudly for silver and the legislature would vote on Allison's retention of his Senate seat in January, 1878. It seems to this reviewer that the political connotations of the issue, more than "opinions of his own" (p. 156), determined Allison's currency stances from time to time, especially as Sage repeatedly and conclusively demonstrates that this highly astute estimator-of-how-the-political-cat-would-jump was "never one to go out on a crusade" (p. 132), "was a politician, not an economist" (pp. 157, 162), and again and again "successfully played the role of a compromiser" (p. 290). Like all other politicians who manage to retain public office over long periods of changing times, Allison astutely weighed the opinions of the Iowa electorate over against those of his more conservative business associates and wealthy friends and came out strongly and ably for a compromise most favorable to the side he considered most important to him at that juncture. To impute such a role to Allison is not to denounce him. In time of dire emergency, democracy needs such senators as Grimes of Iowa; but for the ordinary, day-to-day business of legislation the symbol of compromise is indispensable for preserving representative processes.

Middle-western politicos, often compromisers par excellence, have had their own peculiar significance in the political and economic kaleidoscope of American development. Workers in this vineyard owe a debt of gratitude to anyone who, like Mr. Sage, has cultivated a sector of it intensively and well.

University of Pennsylvania JEANNETTE P. NICHOLS

Rochester: The Quest for Quality, 1890-1925. By Blake McKelvey. (Cambridge: Harvard University Press, 1956. xvi + 432 pp. Illustrations, bibliography, and index. $6.00.)

Over the years, multi-volume sets have been less the exception than the rule in the writing of urban history, most of them heavy with uncritical biographies and the contributions of many untrained hands. Hence there is still a degree of novelty in the kind of voluminous urban record represented by Blake McKelvey's *Rochester: the Quest for Quality*, which brings to a total of three volumes his continuing chronicle of the upstate New York community. The present work — an admirably digested and remarkably comprehensive coverage of the period from 1890 to 1925 — is a fit companion for the two which preceded it: *Rochester: the Water-Power City, 1812-1854*, and *Rochester: the Flower City, 1855-1890.* Indirectly, like its predecessors, it does credit to a city which has had the wisdom to employ the full-time services of a professional, as well as official, historian.

Dr. McKelvey sees the "Quest for Quality" as the key to Rochester's behavior in the generation from 1890 to 1925, both because of the ardor with which many of its citizens sought to achieve civic improvement, social reform, and the cultural enrichment of the community in these years and because of the efforts of its industrial leaders to counter with quality products the competition of cities economically better suited to large-scale manufacturing. In documenting this theme, he has made a solid contribution not only to the history of Rochester and urban history in general but also to the social and economic history of the nation at large. This is especially true of the chapters which deal with civic and political reform, the response of the church to contemporary problems, the local manifestations of industrial growth and the consequent tension between labor and management, and the impact on the community of the Panic of 1893 and World War I. This is local history which properly avoids involvement in the discussion of developments on the national scene but which, nevertheless, contributes significantly to an understanding of them.

The reader may be less satisfied with Dr. McKelvey's treatment of the ethnic ingredients of the community, especially in connection with the question of why and how the foreign-born were drawn to Rochester in these years. He may feel that there is excessive detail on the activities of the almost countless clubs and societies which flourished in this era of organization. He would welcome, on occasion, a fuller identification of persons and institutions originally introduced in earlier volumes. He will nevertheless be impressed with the careful diligence with which the author has mastered local discussion of the widest range of issues and events, indeed to the point that his interpretation has the flavor and the insight, though fortunately not the bias, of that of a participant. This comprehension of the material and comprehensiveness of the coverage more than anything else lend the work a "quality" that comports well with the aspirations of the Rochester of the generation with which the volume deals.

New York University BAYRD STILL

Theodore Roosevelt and the Rise of America to World Power. By. Howard K. Beale. *The Albert Shaw Lectures on Diplomatic History, 1953.* (Baltimore: The Johns Hopkins Press, 1956. xxiv + 600 pp. Notes and index. $6.00.)

Professor Howard K. Beale, who has for many years been gathering material for a biography of Theodore Roosevelt, gives us in this meaty volume an important foretaste of his projected *magnum opus.* Perhaps the first feature of this study to impress the critical reader is the vast amount of source material that has gone into its composition. Professor Beale's researches through all relevant manuscript collections have been untiring. He has drawn not only from Roosevelt's own voluminous correspondence and that of his wide circle of friends, but also from a great variety of peripheral material, and has woven the product together into a readable and often exciting narrative.

In his preface the author mentions a number of questions about trends in American foreign policy for which he has been in search of answers. Those to which the volume most successfully provides answers are two. First, how important was Roosevelt's actual role in events in which he participated? Second, what was the general character of his impact on world affairs? The answer to the first seems established beyond question by the evidence presented. For example, Roosevelt's direct and continuous participation in the negotiations which resulted in the treaties of Portsmouth and Algeciras is made perfectly plain. Of special interest is Professor Beale's detailed analysis of Roosevelt's part in the Venezuela crisis of 1902-1903. While conceding that Roosevelt's later accounts were inexact, the author concludes that on at least three occasions "an urgent warning was actually delivered to Germany," though "the implication that the 'ultimatum' was violent and unpleasant is partly an addition of the war years . . . and partly a false assumption by historians" (p. 430).

Roosevelt's impact upon world affairs and upon the course of American foreign policy Professor Beale regards as for the most part unfortunate, or at best negative. Roosevelt failed in his objectives of establishing a permanent balance of power in the Far East and a secure peace in Europe. He envisioned a future built largely upon Anglo-American co-operation, failing to foresee the decline of British power. As a result of his racial theories — especially his failure to understand Chinese potentialities — he contributed to the growth of an imperialism that was later to produce tragic results. Some of these conclusions are open to debate, but Mr. Beale argues his case persuasively.

In one respect the book will disappoint some readers. The treatment is highly selective. There is, for example, much about the Hay-Pauncefote treaties and the Venezuela episode but nothing about the Panama revolution and a mere mention of the Roosevelt Corollary; much about the Russo-Japanese War and an almost forgotten Chinese boycott of American trade in 1905-1906 (which led Roosevelt to threaten to send an army to China) but nothing about the San Francisco school controversy or the Root-Takahira agreement. Presumably the author either considered these neglected episodes of minor significance in "the rise of America to world power," or found nothing to alter materially the existing accounts of them. It is to be expected that such aspects of the Roosevelt foreign policy will receive appropriate space when the complete biography appears, let us hope in the near future.

University of Buffalo JULIUS W. PRATT

The Resurgent Years, 1911-1927: History of the Standard Oil Company (New Jersey). By George Sweet Gibb and Evelyn H. Knowlton. (New York: Harper and Brothers, 1956. xxxii + 754 pp. Illustrations, charts, appendixes, notes, and index. $7.50.)

Second in the series sponsored by the Business History Foundation, *The Resurgent Years* covers the history of Standard Oil Company (New Jersey) from the dissolution decree (1911) to the time when the company had readjusted its operations as a world-wide industrial organization. Like the first volume in the series, this work is "predominantly an administrative" history with primary focus upon the holding company and major operating policies and only secondarily upon the implementation of these policies at lower levels. As the authors point out, it is only a part of a broader study, one that can best be understood in conjunction with the one that preceded it and the one that is to follow.

While the dissolution severed Jersey Standard from a substantial portion of its domestic production, transportation, and marketing operations, the company retained extensive domestic tidewater refineries along with major producing and marketing properties outside the United States. As might be expected, the dominant focus of the management turned to foreign operations. For some years, however, Jersey Standard was slow to readjust its operations and policies largely because, under the dissolution decree, it was allowed to continue business relations with former affiliates. Events during World War I demonstrated the basic weakness of such informal affiliations, especially when a growing independence on the part of producers and shippers threatened supplies of crude to the organization's domestic refineries. It was not until after World War I that the company, under the leadership of W. C. Teagle, developed a clear-cut policy of reintegrating its domestic production and transportation operations with refining and of expanding its crude production to cover all parts of the world. By 1927 these goals were largely achieved.

In terms of their objectives and the limitations of relating the history of an exceptionally complicated business in one volume, the authors have done a most creditable job. The study contributes much to a better understanding of the management evolution of large industrial concerns. Economists and economic historians will be interested in how a former monopoly adjusted to a new competitive pattern. Students of the petroleum industry will find it a welcome addition to the literature in the field.

At the same time, the authors have not entirely escaped from the "occupational hazard" of business historians of viewing events too much from the point of view of the management. This is the case, for example, in their treatment of how Jersey Standard met the threat by the German government to nationalize the company's affiliate in the Reich. Much is made of the lack of support by the United States State Department to Standard in this struggle, but on a basis of the evidence given, there is little to indicate that the company needed such support to force the German government to back down on its proposal. Treatment of the disastrous strikes that affected Jersey Standard's Bayonne refineries in 1915 and 1916 is especially unsatisfactory. The various elements that contributed to labor unrest are indicated, but heavy emphasis on the "non-English speaking workers," "immigrants," and "eastern Europeans" in the labor force and on the role of "professional agitators" gives an undue emphasis to the management's position and virtually obscures the authors' concluding observation that "No official excuses could hide the fact that working conditions in some of the departments at Bayonne were very bad."

It may also be pointed out that by concentrating on the administration of the holding company the authors were forced to neglect other important phases of the company's history. This is particularly noticeable in respect to the role played by large affiliates, such as Standard of Louisiana, Imperial (Canada), Carter Oil, and Humble Oil and Refining, that dance in and out of the narrative. It is intriguing but not revealing to be told, for example, that Imperial underwent a complete reorganization and that the administration of the Carter Oil Company "was reported to be tinged with favoritism and lacking in drive" when the significance of these observations is not given a more thorough analysis.

Despite these limitations, on balance the assets of *The Resurgent Years* clearly exceed liabilities by a comfortable margin. Few readers will be dissatisfied with the dividends that a careful examination of the material will repay.

Northwestern University HAROLD F. WILLIAMSON

Soviet-American Relations, 1917-1920. Volume I, *Russia Leaves the War.* By George F. Kennan. (Princeton: Princeton University Press, 1956. xiv + 544 pp. Maps, illustrations, appendix, bibliography, and index. $7.50.)

This volume launches an important series, based on manuscripts as well as published works. Other volumes are to follow — several, probably, for Kennan here handles four months, and has thirty still to go.

The focus is indicated by the jacket subtitle, "The Americans in Petrograd and the Bolshevik Revolution." Kennan follows Americans stationed elsewhere in Russia, and studies Washington developments. Emphasis, however, is on a day-by-day, often hour-by-hour, examination of the activities of Americans who were in the Russian capital during and immediately after the November revolution.

By choosing this approach, Kennan puts Raymond Robins at the center of the stage. Robins was a politician-businessman-Red Cross official who backed

Kerensky; then, when the Bolsheviks triumphed, he tried to work with the new men of power. Since Ambassador Francis and Secretary Lansing would not recognize the Bolsheviks, Robins provided informal liaison. Most American officeholders took a dim view of Robins. But there was need for contact, so Robins was allowed to continue, and was once or twice encouraged. The government did not, however, support Robins' main proposal — to provide aid for the Bolsheviks in the hope that Russia would not make a separate peace with Germany.

Robins is the central figure of the volume, but not the hero. While acknowledging Robins' patriotism and vigor, Kennan feels that this unofficial agent was wrong in judgment, tactics, and recollection of events; wrong in assuming he had official backing in January, 1918; wrong in believing it possible to deal with Lenin and Trotsky.

Actually, Kennan puts these interpretations on a broader basis: (1) He feels that diplomatic reporting and policy suggestions should come from professional diplomats; that reliance on amateurs is not in the national interest. (2) He believes it was absurd even to consider dealing with the Bolsheviks. Thus, his view of Robins is more harsh than his view of amateurs who took strong anti-Bolshevik positions — say the fumbling Francis and Sisson, who fell for the forged papers. (But Kennan does make distinctions among those who favored working with the Bolsheviks, as in treating General Judson more favorably than Robins.)

Is Kennan right? Given the decision not to recognize the Bolsheviks — a decision Kennan approves — it was necessary to use informal channels, or none. Granted, Robins was an overenthusiastic amateur who made grave mistakes while engaged on a hopeless or near-hopeless mission. But was it wrong to try? Was the first State Department policy better (do-nothing-until-the-dust-settled)? Or the second (intervention-on-a-tiny-scale)?

Or take the part about professional diplomats. We should have had more in 1917-1918. But would they have changed things fundamentally? Kennan believes Wilson and Lansing made the right decisions. Presumably, then, these decisions would have been about the same if there had been more professional advice. This is a puzzling point. Puzzling, too, is the question of the influence of State Department officials on Lansing-Wilson policies. This *does* involve the question of influence of men with experience in diplomacy (Miles, for example); but Kennan does not pursue this matter. His treatment of the thinking of Wilson and Lansing, both on European Russia and on Siberia, also leaves something to be desired.

Clearly, all readers will find a rich store of material in *Russia Leaves the War*. But, detailed though it is, the book does not contain all the information future historians will need; and interpretations will continue to differ, in the future as in the past.

University of Wisconsin FRED HARVEY HARRINGTON

Huey Long's Louisiana: State Politics, 1920-1952. By Allan P. Sindler. (Baltimore: The Johns Hopkins Press, 1956. xviii + 316 pp. Maps, tables, notes, bibliographical essay, and index. $5.50.)

Mr. Sindler provides a close analysis of Louisiana politics immediately before, during, and after the advent of Huey P. Long. Rejecting as only partially accurate Huey's explanation that the key to his spectacular success lay in his own personality — that he was *sui generis* — the author has wisely sought the roots of Longism in the history of the state. He concludes that the rise of Long represented the culmination of an abiding class hostility, the successful revolt of the farmers, supported by urban citizens of similar economic and social status, against the long-dominant alliance of conservative planters and city merchants and professional classes.

Long's program reflected portions of the old Populist and Progressive assault on the corporate interests — especially Standard Oil — in addition to an imposing array of state services, including among others the granting of textbooks free of charge to students in both public and parochial schools, construction of a modern system of paved highways, expansion of the state university, creation of a new medical school, and building of a new state capitol. Intoxicated by power, Long became increasingly dictatorial, and on September 8, 1935, an assassin's bullet cut him down.

Longism did not die with Huey P. Long, for his successful challenge of the long-intrenched political forces in Louisiana created a virile bifactionalism that faithfully reflected the state's ancient economic cleavage and represented to a considerable degree a true two-party system in local affairs. But the Kingfish's political heirs overreached themselves and the Richard W. Leche administration disintegrated in a carnival of corruption. In 1940 a combination of the old conservative alliance and those citizens interested in cleaning house capitalized the opportunity provided by the "scandals" and elected Sam Houston Jones governor. Jones did as much as could have been expected under the circumstances in the way of assuring honest government, but there could be no return to the parsimony — or conservatism — of an earlier day, and the reform administration borrowed heavily from Long's economic liberalism.

The last dozen years of the state's political history have been marked by a fierce and continuing bifactionalism, in which the victory has fallen first to one side and then the other, to anti-Long Governors Jimmie Davis in 1944 and Robert F. Kennon in 1952, and to the "buccaneering liberalism" and prodigious taxation of Earl Long in 1948 and 1956. Mr. Sindler believes that this is the logical end of a historical process as old as the state. Much can be said for this interpretation, which applies the thesis of agrarian revolt to the emergence of Longism. Partially formulated by a number of other scholars, it is here stated in complete form and buttressed by a painstaking analysis, by parishes, of the voting behavior of the people of Louisiana during the entire period.

But this reviewer would raise certain questions. Has not the thesis of class conflict been brought into too strong relief, with insufficient emphasis on the flamboyant personality and relentless energy of the Longs? The author appears to come close to saying as much in explaining the defeat of the opposing faction in the 1948 governor's race: "Perhaps most basically, compromise government lacked the spectacular flavor by which Huey Long was able to command the loyalties of thousands of citizens." Many aspects of the role of the Negro in Louisiana politics are discussed with insight, but the author seems to have missed a generalization that is implicit in his evidence, which is that the determination to maintain "white supremacy" has overshadowed all other factors in the thinking of a majority of white Louisianians. This impulse is treated as something of a counterfeit issue that during the nineteenth century perversely deflected what was "by objective standards" the true course of Louisiana history, that of class struggle. Is it not significant that the triumph of Longism was possible only after "white supremacy" had been assured by the virtually complete disfranchisement of the Negroes in the constitution of 1898? Finally, are not the great issues that stir a people always fully as "subjective" as they are "objective," and therefore incapable of being demonstrated statistically?

Whether or not one fully agrees with Mr. Sindler's thesis, he is to be congratulated on his thorough research, cogent analysis, and readable though hardly epigrammatic presentation. This book can be studied with profit by all who aspire to a better understanding of the vicissitudes of twentieth-century Louisiana politics.

Tulane University CHARLES P. ROLAND

Science in the Federal Government: A History of Policies and Activities to 1940. By A. Hunter Dupree. (Cambridge: The Belknap Press of Harvard University Press, 1957. xii + 460 pp. Bibliographic note, references, and index. $7.50.)

Since World War II, Americans have become increasingly aware of the existence of a "mighty edifice of government science" which has "universally inspired admiration, wonder, and fear." The growth of this edifice is the theme of Professor Dupree's first-rate study. Science in the federal government had its origins in the Constitution itself, but governmental scientific accomplishments before 1830 hardly matched the expansive visions of Jefferson and John Quincy Adams. In the three decades preceding the Civil War, however, a new generation of professional scientists began to man the government's first permanent scientific agencies, inaugurated despite congressional constitutional compunctions. The rise of American technology revived the Patent Office and persuaded Congress to support briefly the newly invented telegraph. The needs of commerce brought support for the Coast Survey and the *Nautical Almanac*, while an Englishman's will provided a reluctant United States government with the Smithsonian Institution. Most important, an expanding nation sponsored an extraordinary array of exploring expeditions at home and abroad.

The post-Civil War period saw the establishment of most of the important government scientific agencies. Politically astute scientists developed the problem approach to research, wheedled organic acts out of a reluctant Congress by attaching riders to appropriation bills, and built powerful scientific groups in the Department of Agriculture and the Geological Survey. The conservation movement stimulated work in irrigation, forestry, and wildlife, while the rise of industry inspired the establishment of such agencies as the National Bureau of Standards. Meanwhile government medical groups, particularly the Army, contributed spectacularly to the medical revolution of the late nineteenth century. The Civil War and World War I tested the ability of the government and the scientific community to mobilize science for war. The twenties saw government science survive the complacency of prosperity and adjust its activities to a changing scientific world, while the subsequent depression challenged the whole social role of science. Certain themes — government control versus scientific independence, relations of government science with Congress and other scientific groups, the relative roles of applied and basic research, and the co-ordination of the nation's scientific activity — persistently recur. Answers to these problems shaped the history of science in the federal government.

Professor Dupree has handled his subject superbly. His engrossing narrative is clearly and non-technically written. Judgments are incisive, generally sound, and buttressed by extensive research. If the study emphasizes organization and administration, the broader interplay between the developing scientific establishment and a changing American society is not neglected. Nor is the human element missing. Leaders such as Bache, Henry, Powell, Pinchot, and Millikan play important roles; personalities and cliques helped shape the organization of American science.

The work has its limitations, of course. The discussion of the period since 1918 seems thin compared with the earlier chapters. The book would have benefited from a few pages on the colonial background, and its judgments would have been enriched by more comparisons between federal scientific activities and those in the states and in European countries. Since the emphasis is on administration, the description and evaluation of the actual scientific work is not always complete. Some of the author's judgments may be modified or supplemented in the future, for he made only sparing use of manuscripts in the National Archives and elsewhere. Yet most of these limitations reflect the lack of good secondary accounts in the history of science and technology rather than the author's shortcomings. In the final analysis this volume should stimulate new research and will prove interesting and instructive to both the general reader and the specialist in the history of science or public administration.

Amherst College KENDALL BIRR

Law and the Conditions of Freedom in the Nineteenth-Century United States. By James Willard Hurst. (Madison: University of Wisconsin Press, 1956. x + 139 pp. Notes and index. 2.50.)

This slim volume by Professor Hurst of the Law School of the University of Wisconsin contains the most suggestive thinking yet published about the functions of American law. His achievement is the greater when one considers that his broad synthesis lies in a neglected field of scholarship. The writing of American legal history, excepting federal constitutional law, has hardly begun despite the fact that the United States reveals itself no less in its law than in its politics, literature, or economy. The prime question of legal history is: How does the law of a given time and place meaningfully connect with the society of which it is a part? American legal history shows in striking fashion how law is shaped by and in turn shapes the thought, experiences, and needs of the American people. The relation of the individual to the state and of the state to the economy; the private and public interests deemed important enough to secure in authoritative form; the comparative valuations placed on different activities and goals, and upon liberty and order; the points of tension, growth, and power; and prevailing conceptions of rights, duties, and liabilities — all these are exposed in our law. Professor Hurst presents considered and stimulating reflections on all.

Unlike the formal legalists who delight in tracing the evolution of legal doctrines or of philosophies about law, Hurst is concerned with our law as a social instrument embodying public policy. What interests him are the uses of law and its interplay with other social institutions and with liberty, which he defines as the possession of a wide range of choices leading to self-fulfillment for individuals.

The point of departure for Hurst's analysis is the principle, central to our legal order as deduced from popular attitudes and action, that law exists for people and not people for the law. The promise of material abundance in the United States created an imperative that law be used to help realize deep-seated beliefs in the social desirability of broad opportunities for personal self-expression and for the possession of liberty, thereby enhancing the chances of a meaningful life. Accordingly, the American legal order, as Hurst discerns, revealed two working principles concerning the uses of law: it should promote "the release of individual creative energy to the greatest extent possible" — the subject of his first chapter — and should "mobilize the resources of the community to help shape an environment which would give men more liberty by increasing the practical range of choices open to them and minimizing the limiting forces of circumstances" — the subject of chapter two. In the third and last chapter, Hurst explains how and why our law entered a new stage in its evolution after about 1870. The social costs of rapid industrial and urban development provoked legal as well as political policy shifts, which were to emerge more fully in our own century, expressing a search for a new balance of power and a concern for the functional soundness of our society.

In the course of his analysis, Hurst effectively rejects the notion that nineteenth-century legal policy was laissez faire in character. He shows how the positive power of the state was resorted to in many ways where necessary to "release energy" and master the environment, particularly in economic affairs. He also stresses the primacy of contract law, especially as to corporations, in encouraging private initiative and activity, at the same time the sanctions of contract law set a definite framework for the security of entrepreneurial ventures. Property in action — at risk in new ways, not secure and at rest — enlisted the law's benevolent protections. As Hurst observes, we may be surprised by the "limits the nineteenth century put on protection of vested rights" unless we note that "what we did in the name of vested rights had less to do with protecting holdings than it had to do with protecting ventures," a fact explained by the scarcity of venture capital, the expansion of business, and the necessity of opening the continent.

This is a highly conceptualized book, richly documented, and filled with bold generalizations (though sometimes lacking in finesse of expression, for example, at p. 89). Hurst has traversed a huge field and a tremendous variety and number of sources ranging from Wisconsin's judicial and legislative records, of which he makes particularly effective use, to historical monographs and the literature of sociology and psychiatry. He has something instructive and interesting to say to all historians regardless of specialization. Doctoral candidates searching for worth-while, original topics will find suggestions by the dozen. I regret that I did not have the benefit of Hurst's ideas when writing my own book on Chief Justice Lemuel Shaw. In 1950 Professor Hurst published *The Growth of American Law*, a book which bore the subtitle *The Law Makers.* The present volume, modestly described as a report of "work in progress," seems to this reviewer to form the basis for a worthy companion volume for which the subtitle might be "The Functions of Law."

Brandeis University LEONARD W. LEVY

Book Notes

Index to the Writings on American History, 1902-1940. Compiled by David Maydole Matteson. (Washington: American Historical Association, 1956. viii + 1115 pp. $5.00 for members of the Association, $10.00 for non-members.) The publication of this volume is a major event for students and research workers in the field of American history. For more than half a century they have depended upon the annual volumes of *Writings on American History* as a guide to the literature of their subject, but in the absence of a general index it has been necessary to follow the cumbersome procedure of searching through the indexes of the individual volumes to find what has been published on a given subject. It was in recognition of the need for a more convenient finding medium that Mr. Matteson conceived the idea some thirty years ago for the compilation of a cumulative index and persistently carried it forward as a labor of love until his death in 1949. His work has now been brought to completion by others with the aid of a fund which he bequeathed to the American Historical Association for that purpose. Actually, the finished product is not simply a consolidation or cumulation of the indexes of the individual volumes through 1940; it also contains references and subject classifications which will not be found in those indexes. All told, there are more than 300,000 entries, covering both subjects and authors, and it seems safe to assert that few, if any, topics or individuals in American history fail to appear somewhere in its pages. One finds it easy to agree with the closing sentence of the Foreword: "This volume will be a lasting memorial to a great scholar and an indispensable guide for all other scholars in American history."

The New-York Historical Society's Dictionary of Artists in America, 1564-1860. By George C. Groce and David H. Wallace. (New Haven: Yale University Press, 1957. xxx + 759 pp. Key to sources. $15.00.) This documented biographical dictionary includes entries on "painters, draftsmen, sculptors, engravers, lithographers, and allied artists, either amateur or professional, native or foreign-born, who worked within the present continental limits of the United States between the years 1564 and 1860." The authors have considered the term "artist" in a broad sense so as to exclude in the main only actors, musicians, and photographers. Over ten thousand artists are listed alphabetically in double-columned pages which contain on the average about seven or eight entries to a column. The length of an entry, however, is not intended to indicate the importance of the subject, since some lesser persons about whom little has been published may have relatively larger entries. As an indication of the allocation of space, 21 lines are devoted to Jacques Le Moyne, chronologically the first artist listed; 106 lines to

Benjamin West; 9 lines to Benjamin Franklin; 20 lines to Paul Revere; 41 lines to Benjamin Henry Latrobe; and 38 lines to John James Audubon. One of the more valuable parts of the dictionary is the inclusion of the lesser artists (there are over a hundred entries under "Smith") for some of whom even the first name is unknown. For each artist the authors have aimed to include "as much as possible of the following information: full name, dates and places of birth and death, media and subject matter of his work, chronology of residences and exhibitions, pupils, and in some instances locations and reproductions of representative works." All entries are documented and are based on research in both primary and secondary sources. Among the primary sources consulted were city directories and business directories, census records, and exhibition catalogues. The range of the dictionary makes it a useful work of reference for a wide variety of researchers as well as for historians of art.

A True Discourse of the Present State of Virginia. By Ralph Hamor. Reprinted from the London Edition, 1615, with an introduction by A. L. Rowse. (Richmond: Virginia State Library, 1957. xxviii + 74 pp. Index.) Published as Number 3 of Virginia State Library Publications, this volume presents a facsimile reproduction of a rare pamphlet about the colony of Virginia in its formative years. The author emigrated to Virginia in 1610, and spent the next four years there, part of the time as a clerk to the Council. He returned to England in 1614 and published his *Discourse* the next year. The pamphlet affords a contemporary insight into such topics as the prospects of the colony, its early troubles and discords, the administration of Sir Thomas Gates, and the story of John Rolfe and Pocahontas. It is pointed out in a prefatory note that although Hamor's *Discourse* was "not primarily a promotional piece, it served a propagandistic purpose in addition to giving the public news from the Colony." Mr. Rowse terms the *Discourse* "a reliable account of events in the Colony."

Bacon's Rebellion: The Contemporary News Sheets. Edited by Harry Finestone. (Charlottesville: University of Virginia Press, 1956. 40 pp. Map and bibliographical note. $2.60.) Published in collaboration with the Tracy W. McGregor Library at the University of Virginia, this slim volume is one of a series of source books in seventeenth-century Virginia history. It reproduces two contemporary English accounts, by an unknown author, of Bacon's Rebellion of 1676. The first of these accounts, published in 1677, bears a long title which begins: *Strange News from Virginia; Being a Full and True Account of the Life and Death of Nathanael Bacon, Esquire, Who Was the Only Cause and Original of All the Late Troubles in That Country.* The second, *More News from Virginia*, was composed by the same author, who states that "In our Last we gave you an Account of part of the Life and the last *Exit* of *Bacon*, the Grand Opposer of the *Royall Party* in *Virginia*; but then our Intelligence reached no farther than his Death." The sequel reaches further to report "The Names and Characters of those Persons who have been lately executed for their Rebellion." The editor points out that both pamphlets "are cloudy and uncertain in details, as such reports were likely to be, and somewhat fragmentary because of the author's obviously incomplete knowledge of the events he was describing."

Daring Diplomacy: The Case of the First American Ultimatum. By Andor Klay. (Minneapolis: University of Minnesota Press, 1957. xiv + 240 pp. Illustrations, notes, and index. $5.00.) *Daring Diplomacy* is a book about the case of Martin Koszta, a Hungarian refugee who claimed the protection of American citizenship on the strength of having previously signed a declaration of intention to become a citizen. Koszta was abducted by Austrians while he was traveling in Turkey in 1853 for an American firm. The incident became an important international issue when Commander Duncan Ingraham of the United States Navy demanded and secured Koszta's release from an Austrian warship. Although the narrative is overly dramatized, the author does not fail to give a valuable, detailed account of the case and its subsequent ramifications in international law and diplomacy. Documentation has been purposely kept to a minimum.

California Gold Rush Merchant: The Journal of Stephen Chapin Davis. Edited by Benjamin B. Richards. (San Marino: The Huntington Library, 1956. xviii + 124 pp. Notes and index. $5.00.) Stephen C. Davis spent less than three years in California, but his carefully kept diary is a valuable source for gold-rush history. Davis left his native Massachusetts for the gold regions in 1850 at the age of seventeen. Unsuccessful at first both at mining and business he returned home, only to be lured to California again in 1852. This time he became the successful operator of a store in Coultersville, where he stayed two years before returning to the East. Davis' observations on his four isthmian voyages are as important as his account of his business activities in California and take up approximately the same amount of space. The journal is filled with details, yet the comments are brief. According to the editor, "In making four Panama crossings he never fails to mention a passing ship; he tells us the cost of goods and services, and he speculates, however briefly, on the prospects and present condition of business in the many places he visits." A careful editing job and frequent informative notes increase the value of the book.

Filings from an Old Saw: Reminiscences of San Francisco and California's Conquest by "Filings"—Joseph T. Downey. Edited by Fred Blackburn

Rogers. (San Francisco: John Howell, 1956. viii + 170 pp. Illustration, appendix, notes, and index. $10.00.) The eighteen articles reprinted in this book originally appeared in the San Francisco *Golden Era* from January 9 to July 3, 1853. They furnish a colorful and valuable account "of the California of 1845-1847 by a person who was either present at, or learned soon of the exciting doings of that period." Vignettes of Commodore Robert F. Stockton, Captain John C. Frémont, General Stephen W. Kearny, and other figures of importance in the conquest of California are candidly though subjectively drawn. The author of the articles, which were signed with the pseudonym, "Filings," has been identified by the editor as Joseph T. Downey, an enlisted man who served on the *Portsmouth* under Commodore Stockton. Although Downey emphasizes the role of the Navy in the Conquest he devotes much attention to land battles and relations with the Mexicans.

Sitting Bull, Champion of the Sioux: A Biography. Revised Edition. By Stanley Vestal. (Norman: University of Oklahoma Press, 1957. xxii + 349 pp. Illustrations, appendix, bibliographical essay, and index. $5.00.) The first edition of *Sitting Bull* was published in 1932. It has now been "updated and revised in the light of fresh evidence" to be published as the forty-sixth volume in the University of Oklahoma Press Civilization of the American Indian series. The emphasis of this book is necessarily on Sitting Bull's life as a warrior, but the Sioux Chief's rôles as "diplomat, organizer . . . patriot, statesman, and prophet" are also described. Besides the usual source materials use has been made of numerous interviews with Indians who knew Sitting Bull as a relative, friend, or enemy. By this means Mr. Vestal hopes to counterbalance the unfavorable legends concerning Sitting Bull, which he believes to have been "largely the creation of personal enemies."

Fifty Years on the Old Frontier as Cowboy, Hunter, Guide, Scout, and Ranchman. By James H. Cook. (Norman: University of Oklahoma Press, 1957. xxvi + 253 pp. Illustrations and index. $4.00.) First published in 1923 by the Yale University Press, this book has been out of print for several years. It is essentially a book of reminiscences of many hunting, scouting, cattle driving, and ranching experiences, covering principally the last quarter of the nineteenth century. Cook's activities ranged from New Mexico, where he scouted during the Apache War, to Texas, where he drove cattle and managed a ranch, to Wyoming, where he was a big-game hunting guide. Among the Indian tribes about which Cook contributes information are the Northern Cheyennes, the Apaches, the Comanches, and the Sioux. As J. Frank Dobie points out in the Foreword to this new edition, Cook's narrative was written with greater perspective, sensitivity, and maturity than the average western reminiscences.

Studies in Southern History. Edited by J. Carlyle Sitterson. *The James Sprunt Studies in History and Political Science,* Volume 39. (Chapel Hill: University of North Carolina Press, 1957. xii + 168 pp. Notes. $2.50.) This group of essays has been prepared in memory of Albert Ray Newsome by a group of his former students at the University of North Carolina. Each of the essays — which range chronologically from the colonial period to the present — demonstrates "the interdependence of state, regional, and national history which was fundamental in the research and writing of Professor Newsome." Of the ten essays, six deal primarily with North Carolina subjects: the churches of Granville County, the North Carolina Whigs (1765-1775), William Blount, David Lowry Swain, North Carolina agriculture, and business leaders in post-Civil War North Carolina. The remaining essays are entitled: Confederate Literature and Its Publishers; The Cotton Crisis, the South, and Anglo-American Diplomacy, 1914-1915; Hoke Smith and the New Freedom, 1913-1917; and Governor Eugene Talmadge and the New Deal.

Tidewater Maryland Architecture and Gardens. By Henry Chandlee Forman. (New York: Architectural Book Publishing Company, Inc., 1956. xvi + 208 pp. Illustrations, drawings, appendix, bibliography, and index. $10.00.) The author, a practicing architect, has written the text, made the drawings, and taken most of the photographs for this generously illustrated work, a sequel to his *Early Manor and Plantation Houses of Maryland.* Not intending it as an architectural history, he has presented rather "a series of concise monographs of Maryland gardens and buildings" in order to record "the beauty of a time and place which have changed." Dr. Forman is clearly interested in the preservation of Maryland's architectural heritage, and the work shows a close familiarity with the structures described. A helpful discussion of early building terms is included in the introduction. A few sections of the work are reprinted, with changes, from the *Maryland Historical Magazine.*

From Slavery to Freedom: A History of American Negroes. Second Edition, Revised and Enlarged. By John Hope Franklin. (New York: Alfred A. Knopf, 1956. xvi + 639 + xlii pp. Illustrations, bibliographical notes, and index. $5.50 text, $7.50 trade.) The greater part of this second edition of a distinguished history of American Negroes is substantially the same as the first edition published in 1947. The publisher points out, however, that "The entire text has been reviewed and, where necessary, altered." Most of these changes appear in the last two chapters, reflecting the comment by Dr. Franklin in his new preface that "The nine years that have elapsed since this work first appeared have been among the most momentous in the history of the American Negro." The bibliographical notes at the end are printed largely as they appeared in the first edition, supplemented on pages 637-39 by a "Bibliographical Note, 1956." The last chapter of the book, "Mid-Century Inventory," includes brief mention of current (1956) events specially concerning the Negro, and an evaluation of his position in America at mid-century.

The Negro and Southern Politics: A Chapter of Florida History. By Hugh D. Price. (New York: New York University Press, 1957. xviii + 133 pp. Maps, tables, notes, bibliography, and index. $5.00.) This book describes and analyzes the voting behavior of Negroes in Florida from 1944, when white primaries were declared illegal by the Supreme Court, to 1956, when Negro voters constituted 10 per cent of the total Florida electorate. It is a political science case study based on extensive interviews of Negro voters and examination of local election statistics. Florida is not presented as a typical southern state, but the author believes that the conclusions of this study will illuminate Negro participation in politics in the South. The author concludes that the evidence "demonstrates the growing ability of the Southern Negro to use the ballot with traditional American aims and values in mind and within the framework of traditional American party and political institutions."

The Negro in the United States. Revised Edition. By E. Franklin Frazier. (New York: The Macmillan Company, 1957. xxxiv + 769 pp. Tables, maps, diagrams, notes, bibliography, and index. $6.40.) In the preface to the first edition of this work, published in 1949, the author, a sociologist, stated that he would be concerned "with the emergence of the Negro as a minority group and his gradual integration into American life." The same emphasis is continued in the present edition, since the "events during the past seven or eight years have brought into clearer focus the trends toward the integration of the Negro into American society as well as the nature of the forces which are opposed to his integration." The first two parts of the book, comprising 168 pages, are largely historical and have undergone little revision. Statistics and analyses of Negro family and community life in the last three parts have been revised and material on Negro education has been added. The maps and tables, however, are still based on the 1940 census.

Norwegian-American Studies and Records, Volume XIX. Edited by Carlton C. Qualey. (Northfield, Minnesota: Norwegian-American Historical Association, 1956. x + 217 pp. Notes and bibliography. $2.50.) Nine articles on Norwegian immigrant history make up this new volume of the *Norwegian-American Studies and Records* series. The opening article is a reprint of the first chapter of *Land of Their Choice*, by Theodore C. Blegen, former editor of the series. Some of the other articles are: "Boyesen and the Norwegian Immigration"; "Norwegian Forerunners among the Early Mormons"; "'Snowshoe' Thompson: Fact and Legend"; and "Norwegian-Danish Methodism on the Pacific Coast." The series of bibliographical reports on Norwegian-American history is continued in this volume by Clarence A. Clausen.

Pioneers in Service: The History of the Associated Jewish Philanthropies of Boston. By Barbara Miller Solomon. (Boston: Associated Jewish Philanthropies, 1957. xviii + 197 pp. Illustrations, note on the sources, appendixes, and index. $3.00.) The Associated Jewish Philanthropies was organized in 1930, but its predecessor, the Federated Jewish Charities, was organized in 1895, and the roots of Boston Jewish charities go back to the 1840's. "This book," as the author says, "analyzes the process by which the Boston federation came into being and went through successive stages before attaining its modern form. The first four chapters preserve in considerable detail even obscure charitable enterprises; the fifth [final] chapter gives only a panoramic view of the later accomplishments without attempting historical evaluation." *Pioneers in Service* contributes a good deal to the history of the Americanization of the Jewish immigrant, for one of the main concerns of the Jewish charitable organizations was to help immigrants find jobs and help them adjust to American life. The unity of effort represented in the organization of the Federated Jewish Charities in 1895 reflected the greater complexity of the problem of charity created by the vast increase of Jewish immigrants in the 1880's and 1890's. Although there are no footnotes, the "Note on Sources" is comprehensive and the style is scholarly.

Victory in Papua. By Samuel Milner. *United States Army in World War II: The War in the Pacific.* (Washington: Office of the Chief of Military History, 1957. xvi + 409 pp. Maps, illustrations, notes, bibliographical note, glossary, and index. $6.00.) This volume, the seventh to be published of *The War in the Pacific* series, covers the campaign for the recapture of the Papuan Peninsula of New Guinea in the latter half of 1942. According to the author the campaign was strategically important because it blunted "the Japanese thrust toward Australia" and "put General MacArthur's forces in a favorable position to take the offensive." It was also of major tactical significance, "for it was . . . the first time in World War II [that the Allies] encountered and reduced an area fortified and defended in depth by the Japanese."

Political Party Patterns in Michigan. By Stephen B. and Vera H. Sarasohn. (Detroit: Wayne State University Press, 1957. x + 76 pp. Appendixes and notes. $1.75.) In this work the authors attempt to get behind the legal and statutory framework of political parties and analyze factional politics within the Republican and Democratic parties of Michigan. The period covered is from 1900 to 1956, but the emphasis falls on the period after the depression, when the Democratic party began effectively to challenge Republican dominance in the state. Much of the narrative centers on the political power of the major automobile manufacturers and the United Automobile Workers of America, "The two greatest concentrations of economic power in the state." Michigan newspapers are the principal sources for the study.

Fable, Fact, and History. By Willis Thornton. (New York: Greenberg, 1956. xiv + 242 pp. Illustrations and index. $4.50.) Willis Thornton, a journalist, here records his version of a number of historical episodes which have been distorted by false or inadequate information. The Boston Massacre, the Mecklenburg Declaration of Independence of 1775, Pocahontas and John Smith, the Connecticut "Blue Laws," the "escape" of John Wilkes Booth, and Wilson's "Sunrise Conference," are typical of the items discussed. The author attempts to strip these episodes of their fictional embellishment, believing that the stories are more worth telling as they actually happened, and that greater instruction is gained from the true version. Although the scope of the book is not limited to the United States, the episodes chosen are primarily American. Other chapters deal with notable historical forgeries and hoaxes, the supposed reappearances of famous figures, and the relationship between history and literature.

Common Frontiers of the Social Sciences. Edited by Mirra Komarovsky. (Glencoe, Illinois: The Free Press, 1957. viii + 439 pp. Notes. $6.00.) The essays in this book do not discuss in general terms interdisciplinary research; they were chosen to exemplify the uses of sociological research techniques in the work of historians and economists. Most of the seventeen contributors are sociologists or economists. In a seventy-page essay called "Research Problems in American Political Historiography," Lee Benson provocatively demonstrates how little information historians have on presidential elections. He focuses attention "upon problems of interpretation which result from lack of detailed voting data over time and space, and from the present unsystematic techniques of handling available data." In another section of interest to American historians there is a set of three short essays on the importance of public opinion polls to present and future historians.

The Presidency in the Courts. By Glendon A. Schubert, Jr. (Minneapolis: University of Minnesota Press, 1957. xii + 391 pp. Notes, appendixes, table of cases, and subject guide. $5.50.) In introducing his subject the author asks a number of concise questions: "Do American courts exercise judicial review of the official acts of the President of the United States? Do they restrain Presidents from committing illegal and unconstitutional acts? How? And when?" It is these topics which the author analyzes, finding his answers in the opinions not only of the United States Supreme Court but in those of inferior courts as well. The book is "a study in the powers of the Presidency, as seen through the eyes of the courts." Arrangement of material in large part follows the theme of presidential function, the four major divisions bearing the titles: chief administrator, chief of state, commander in chief, and chief magistrate (under the last heading the author discusses the legal sources of presidential power, due process in presidential lawmaking, and the scope of judicial review of presidential action). The principal appendix is a listing of cases which have held presidential decisions unconstitutional; the cases range in point of time from 1804 to 1956 with the greatest concentration in the decades of the 1860's and 1930's. A major contribution of the book is its presentation of the view that "the most significant aspect of judicial review of presidential orders is its ineffectiveness."

The American Conscience. By Roger Burlingame. (New York: Alfred A. Knopf, 1957. x + 420 + xv pp. Notes, bibliography, and index. $6.75.) Mr. Burlingame's versatility as a writer becomes more evident with his current survey of *The American Conscience.* Perhaps best known among historians for his interpretations of industrial America, and more recently for his works on Henry Ford and Benjamin Franklin, he now presents "an inquiry into three centuries of American behavior and the moral judgments of the people upon themselves." He begins his story of the American conscience with the Pilgrims and carries it chronologically through the close of the nineteenth century, with a concluding survey of the America of Warren G. Harding and Al Capone. Professional historians, who may find much of the survey of American behavior a familiar account of American history, may bear in mind that the book "is not written for scholars." Scholars, however, will take interest in the author's effort to view American history in the light of the growth of the American conscience, although, as the author observes, the history of the American conscience "is scarcely separable" from the rest of American history. Mr. Burlingame explains this close relationship by pointing to "the peculiar American compulsion to assign moral values to every historical event, economic theory, or social trend. There is hardly a thought or deed in our story that has not been clothed with virtuous or vicious intent or religious significance."

Historical News and Comments

Official Notice to Members

In compliance with the mandate of the Constitution, notice is given that the Nominating Committee of the Mississippi Valley Historical Association invites, and will receive until October 15, 1957, suggestions for nominations to the following prospective vacancies:

Vice-President
Executive Committee (3 positions)
Executive Committee Teachers Section (2 positions)
Nominating Committee (3 positions in 1958)

In accordance with the provisions of the Constitution, this Committee plans to nominate for the presidency the Vice-President currently in office.

Suggestions should be addressed to Norman A. Graebner, Department of History, University of Illinois, Urbana, Illinois.

Arthur Bestor
Carl Bridenbaugh
Joe B. Frantz
Bennett H. Wall
Norman A. Graebner, *Chairman*

The Prize Monograph Series

At its mid-year meeting in December, 1956, the Executive Committee of the Mississippi Valley Historical Association approved the recommendations of a special publications committee for the establishment of a series of prize monographs in American history to be published under the imprint of the Association. To carry out this program, the Association has created a standing committee on publications composed of the following members: J. Merton England, University of Kentucky; Fletcher M. Green, University of North Carolina; Edward C. Kirkland, Bowdoin College; Richard W. Leopold, Northwestern University; and Chase C. Mooney, Indiana University (chairman).

This committee has announced the establishment of an award of $1,000 to be made to the author of an unpublished monograph in the field of American history. The study selected by the committee will be published by the University of Kentucky Press without the payment of a subsidy by the author. It is expected that one award will be made each year, beginning in 1959; but the committee is authorized to withhold the award in any year in which no acceptable manuscripts have been submitted.

Manuscripts to be considered for the first award will be received by the committee from June 1 to August 31, 1958, and the committee's selection will be announced at the annual meeting of the Association in 1959; and the same schedule will apply for each succeeding year.

The following requirements and rules governing the competition have been established by the committee:

The manuscript must:

a. be not more than 100,000 words (including notes and bibliography)
b. deal with some phase of American History of wider scope and significance than traditional local history (genealogical studies are not acceptable)
c. be typed, double-spaced, on a good white bond paper (8½ x 11) with ample margins
d. be submitted in duplicate — a clean ribbon copy and a clear first carbon copy
e. be written in English
f. have the pages numbered consecutively throughout (including notes and bibliography)
g. have a working table of contents
h. have a preface without acknowledgments
i. have a title page with the name of the author
j. be accompanied by a submittal sheet (to be obtained from the chairman)

(If any substantial portion of the manuscript has been previously published, it should not be submitted. If *any* portion has been published or accepted for publication, such should be indicated on the submittal sheet. The manuscript must be boxed and should be sent by MANUSCRIPT EXPRESS. All manuscripts will be returned MANUSCRIPT EXPRESS COLLECT.)

Footnotes must:

a. be numbered consecutively throughout each chapter — beginning each chapter with 1
b. be double-spaced and assembled on separate sheets at the end of the text
c. conform to the MLA Style Sheet and an accompanying sheet of exceptions

(All questions of style in text, documentation, and bibliography are governed by the MLA Style Sheet and the stated exceptions.)

Bibliography must:

a. be a critical and analytical essay, with materials classified according to the nature of primary and other sources
b. show the name and location of manuscript collections

Maps and illustrative materials

(If such are to be used, those on hand that are suitable for reproduction should accompany the manuscript. On a separate sheet the author should indicate the other materials which he will furnish — at his own expense — if his manuscript is chosen for publication.)

Inquiries and requests for forms should be addressed to Chase C. Mooney, Chairman, MVHA Publications Committee, Department of History, Indiana University, Bloomington, Indiana.

OTHER ASSOCIATION ACTIVITIES

At its annual business meeting in Lincoln, Nebraska, on May 3, the Association elected Wendell H. Stephenson of the University of Oregon to serve as president for the year 1957-1958, and William T. Hutchinson of the University of Chicago as vice-president. The three new members of the Executive Committee, elected by mail ballot for terms ending in 1960, are Robert G. Athearn, University of Colorado, Thomas C. Cochran, University of Pennsylvania, and Robert E. Riegel, Dartmouth College. James A. Barnes of Temple University and W. Eugene Hollon of the University of Oklahoma were elected to the executive committee of the Teachers Section. Thomas D. Clark of the University of Kentucky was elected chairman of the Executive Committee of the Association for the ensuing year.

The next annual meeting will be held in Minneapolis on April 24, 25, and 26, 1958. Philip D. Jordan, of the University of Minnesota, will serve as chairman of the committee on local arrangements. The program committee consists of Gilbert C. Fite of the University of Oklahoma, chairman, Harold W. Bradley of Vanderbilt University, Rodman W. Paul of the California Institute of Technology, W. Stitt Robinson of the University of Kansas, David A. Shannon of Teachers College, Columbia University, and Irvin G. Wyllie of the University of Missouri (University of Wisconsin after July 1). Members of the Association are urged to send to any member of this committee suggestions for session topics, subjects for papers, and persons prepared either to present papers or to discuss major problems of historical importance for the 1958 meeting.

George L. Anderson of the University of Kansas, Charles A. Barker of Johns Hopkins University, and Eugene H. Roseboom of Ohio State University were appointed as members of the board of editors of the *Review* for three-year terms ending in 1960, and George E. Mowry of the University of California, Los Angeles, was made a member of the Pelzer Memorial Committee for the term ending in 1961.

The Pelzer Memorial prize, given annually for the best publishable essay submitted by a graduate student, has been awarded for 1957 to Clifford S. Griffin, a doctoral candidate in history at the University of Wisconsin, for his essay, "Religious Benevolence as Social Control, 1820-1860." Honorable mention went to Robert H. Wiebe, a doctoral candidate at the University of Rochester, for his essay on "Business Disunity and the Progressive Movement, 1901-1914." Both essays will be published in the *Review*.

Essays to be considered for the 1958 Pelzer award must be submitted to the managing editor of the *Review* not later than January 15, 1958. For a summary of the requirements, see the June, 1956, issue of the *Review* (Vol. XLIII, p. 158).

Personals

Walter Prescott Webb of the University of Texas delivered the nineteenth series of the Walter Lynwood Fleming Lectures in Southern History at Louisiana State University on March 25 and 26, 1957. The theme of the series was "Some Aspects of American Sectionalism," and the titles of the individual lectures were: "The North: Its Power and Its Party"; "The South: Before and After the New Deal"; and "The West: Desert and Arid Civilization."

Lewis Leary of Columbia University has been appointed to a Huntington Library Fellowship for the year beginning July 1, 1957, to carry on his study of the beginnings of literature in the United States, 1783-1820. Similar fellowships have also been awarded to V. H. Galbraith, Oriel College, Oxford University, and F. P. Wilson, Merton College, Oxford; and grants-in-aid for historical research have been made to George R. Abernathy, Jr., of the University of Alabama, and Howard R. Lamar, of Yale University.

Walter Johnson, professor of history in the University of Chicago, has been selected to serve as the Harmsworth Professor of American History at Oxford University for 1957-1958.

Carl Bode, executive secretary of the American Civilization program at the University of Maryland, has been given a leave of absence until February, 1959, to serve as cultural attaché in the American Embassy to Great Britain.

Leonard W. Levy, assistant professor of American history at Brandeis University, has been appointed to the newly established Chief Justice Earl Warren Chair of American Constitutional Studies.

Thomas B. Alexander of Georgia Teachers College has accepted a one-year appointment as visiting associate professor of history at the University of Alabama.

At Colorado College, Paul P. Bernard has been promoted to assistant professor of history. Donald P. Greene of Indiana University has been appointed instructor in history, replacing Earland I. Carlson, who resigned to accept an appointment as dean of North Park College, Chicago. Harvey L. Carter has been designated as John and Harriet Parker Campbell Professor of American History and will continue as chairman of the department. Carroll B. Malone, emeritus professor of history, is on a two-year appointment as professor of history in Tunghai University, Taiwan.

Douglas R. Spitz, a doctoral candidate at the University of Nebraska, has been appointed instructor in history at Monmouth College, effective in September, 1957.

Daniel M. Smith of Stanford University has accepted an appointment as assistant professor of history at the University of Colorado.

Frederick M. Binder has been promoted to the rank of professor of history at Thiel College.

At Occidental College, Raymond E. Lindgren has been promoted to professor of history, and Andrew F. Rolle to associate professor.

Dorothy O. Johansen has been promoted to professor of history at Reed College.

Wayne State University, in Detroit, has announced the promotion of Milton Covensky, C. Norman Guice, and Richard D. Miles to the rank of associate professor and the appointment of Franklin W. Wallin as assistant professor of history.

David M. Ellis has been promoted to professor of history at Hamilton College.

Claude Carson Smith, professor of history and political science at the University of Nevada, died on December 12, 1956, at the age of sixty-two. Born in Tennessee, he was graduated from Carson-Newman College in 1921, and received the Ph.D. degree at Stanford University in 1947. He had been a member of the faculty at Nevada since 1929, and was best known for his effectiveness as a teacher of undergraduate students.

Ralph Hyden Records, retired professor of history at the University of Oklahoma, died on January 4, 1957, at the age of sixty-eight. He received his B. A. (1922) and M. A. (1923) degrees from the University of Oklahoma, and the Ph.D. degree from the University of Chicago in 1936; and he taught at the University of Oklahoma from 1926 until the fall of 1945, when he suffered a stroke which incapacitated him for active service. He was the author of several articles on ranching in the Southwest, published in state historical society journals.

Thomas Waverly Palmer, Jr., associate professor of history and co-ordinator of Latin American studies at Boston University, died on January 12, 1957, at the age of thirty-six. A graduate of Amherst College (1941), he received the Ph.D. degree at Columbia University in 1950, and he had taught at Yale University and at the Fletcher School of Law and Diplomacy before going to Boston University. He had recently completed a book on the Latin American policy of the United States.

Peter Masten Dunne, S. J., chairman of the department of history at the University of San Francisco, died on January 15, at the age of sixty-seven. He was graduated from Gonzaga University in 1914 and received the Ph.D. degree at the University of California in 1934. After teaching at Santa Clara College in the 1920's he went to the University of San Francisco in 1930 and made this an important center for the study of Jesuit history in the American Southwest. His published works include *Black Robes on the West Coast* (1940), *Pioneer Jesuits in Northern Mexico* (1944), *Black Robes in Lower California* (1952), and more than fifty articles in scholarly journals. He had served on the executive council of the American Catholic Historical Association, as a member of the board of editors of the *Pacific Historical Review*, and in 1956 as president of the Pacific Coast Branch of the American Historical Association.

Morris L. Wardell, professor of history at the University of Oklahoma since 1925, died on February 5, at the age of sixty-seven. A native of Illinois, he was graduated from the University of Oklahoma in 1919, received the M. A. degree at Harvard in 1922, and the Ph.D. degree at the University of Chicago in 1936. He was the author of *A Political History of the Cherokee Nation* (1938), and joint author with Edward E. Dale of *A History of Oklahoma* (1948).

Henry Raup Wagner, best known to historians as the bibliographer of the early American West, died in San Marino, California, on March 28, at the age of ninety-four. Born in Philadelphia and graduated from Yale (1884), he had a long and successful career as a mining engineer and promoter before turning to historical and cartographical research. In 1920 he published *The Plains and the Rockies: A Contribution to the Bibliography of Original Narratives of Travel and Adventure, 1800-1865*, and in 1924 *The*

Spanish Southwest, 1542-1794: An Annotated Bibliography, both of which were republished in greatly enlarged new editions in 1937 and became basic guides for research workers. Other important works by him include monographs on Spanish explorations along the west coast of North America, his two-volume *Cartography of the Northwest Coast of America to the Year 1800* (1937), numerous articles in historical journals, and his autobiography — *Bullion to Books* (1942) — a revealing account of his transformation from businessman to scholar.

William Orlando Lynch, professor emeritus of history at Indiana University and former president of the Mississippi Valley Historical Association, died in Bloomington on March 29, 1957, at the age of eighty-six. A native of Indiana, he taught for several years in the public schools of that state; and after receiving the B. A. degree at Indiana University in 1903, he divided his time between teaching in Indiana State Teachers College (Terre Haute) and graduate study at the University of Wisconsin and at Harvard. He became professor of history at Ball State Teachers College in 1918, and in 1920 he joined the history department faculty at Indiana University where he remained until his retirement in 1941. Among his best-known published works are *Fifty Years of Party Warfare, 1789-1837* (1931), and his interpretative essays on population movements in the Mississippi Valley and in the South which appeared in historical periodicals between 1930 and 1945.

In addition to serving as president of the Mississippi Valley Historical Association in 1938-1939, Professor Lynch was chairman of its executive committee from 1943 to 1946, a member of the board of editors of the *Review*, 1924-1928, and acting managing editor of the *Review* from July to December, 1946. He was the managing editor of the *Indiana Magazine of History* from 1928 to 1941; president of the Indiana Historical Society, 1946-1950; a member of the board of editors of the *Journal of Southern History*, 1936-1939; and member of the executive council of the Southern Historical Association, 1949-1951.

Generous, tolerant, and unostentatious in his relations with colleagues and professional associates, Professor Lynch won their respect and admiration for his strong sense of responsibility, his unselfish service, and his sound judgment. He was a stimulating and effective teacher; and for more than a score of younger men and women who earned the doctorate under his guidance his gentleness of spirit and his exacting standards of scholarship will constitute an enduring influence.

Historical Activities

The Library of Congress has received the personal and professional papers of John Franklin Jameson as a gift from his son, Francis Christie Jameson, and the Carnegie Institution of Washington. Numbering about 78,000 pieces, these papers cover his work as teacher, editor, director of historical research at the Carnegie Institution, and chief of the Library of Congress Division of Manuscripts, and include family correspondence and diaries for the years 1867-1921 (available only by special permission, which should be requested through the Chief of the Manuscript Division).

Some 17,500 papers of General Henry T. Allen have been presented to the Library by his son. These cover his military service in Alaska (1885-1886), as military attaché in St. Petersburg (1890-1895) and Berlin (1897-1898), in the Philippines (1901) and Mexico (1916), as a division commander on the Western Front in World War I, and as commander of American Forces of Occupation on the Rhine following the war, and extensive correspondence pertaining to the Alfred E. Smith presidential campaign of 1928.

Among recent additions to the Library's collection of foreign reproductions are microfilm copies of the following manuscripts in the Public Record Office in London: 618 additional volumes of British embassy and consular correspondence, which completes the Library's holdings of Class 115 of Foreign Office records through the year 1901; 20 volumes of miscellaneous materials, dated between 1783 and 1828, in Class 6 of the records of the Board of Trade; all of Class 12 (146 volumes) of Audit Office records, concerned with claims of American Loyalists; and 20 volumes of original correspondence of the Secretary of State, 1720-1761, and intercepted letters, 1775-1783, in Class 5 of the Colonial Office records.

Other important collections recently received by the Library include: the papers of Grover Cleveland Leoning, prominent aircraft engineer, covering the years from 1910 to 1940 (about 11,000 pieces); a portion of the papers of Colonel Henry Breckinridge, consisting primarily of correspondence and speeches connected with his service as assistant secretary of war, 1913-1916, his campaign for a seat in the United States Senate in 1934, and his part in the 1936 presidential campaign of the Republican party (about 2,000 pieces); the papers of Vice-Admiral Emory Scott Land, covering the period from 1903 to 1952 and including correspondence, speeches, diary notes, and other data relative to his service as assistant chief of the Navy Bureau of Aeronautics, 1926-1928, as chief of the Bureau of Construction and Repair, 1932-1937, as chairman of the United States Maritime Commission, 1938-1946, and as administrator of the War Shipping Administration during World War II (about 5,000 pieces); a small addition to the Josephus Daniels papers, relating mainly to his career as editor of the Raleigh *News and Observer* (about 500 pieces); and three additions to the collection of James A. Garfield diaries — two of them kept by Garfield between 1866 and 1871, and the third by Mrs. Garfield during the first seven weeks of her husband's service as President.

The Mills College Library, Oakland, California, has recently acquired the Hitchcock-Coit collection of manuscripts, consisting of about 3,000 letters and various personal diaries which fill fifty journal books. The earliest papers, which belonged to the James Hunter family in Virginia, include correspondence from General Nathanael Greene, James Madison, and James Monroe, as well as copies of letters from Hunter to important Virginians between 1782 and 1787. The diaries of Captain Nathaniel Wyche Hunter describe the Seminole War, 1839-1840, and the papers of Dr. and Mrs. Hunter deal with his service as a surgeon in the Mexican War. The more recent papers include impressions of California from 1850 to 1875 by members of the Hitchcock family, and from 1890 to 1911 by Lillie Hitchcock Coit.

The American Historical Association has announced the establishment of the Moses Coit Tyler Prize, to be awarded for the first time at the annual meeting of the Association in December, 1957. The award will be $1,500 plus publication, for the best manuscript in American intellectual history, including biography. The Cornell University Press is providing the funds out of money available to it and will publish the manuscript. The manuscripts may range from 50,000 to 125,000 words in length and must be the author's first or second book. The committee in charge of this award consists of Merle Curti, University of Wisconsin, chairman; Charles A. Barker, Johns Hopkins University; Ralph H. Gabriel, Yale University; Stow Persons, State University of Iowa; and Frederick Rudolph, Williams College. Communications concerning the prize should be sent to the Association office, 400 A Street, S. E., Washington 3, D. C., or to Professor Curti. Manuscripts will be received until September 1, 1957.

At the seventy-first annual meeting of the American Historical Association, held in St. Louis, December 28-30, 1956, William L. Langer, Harvard University, was elected president for the current year, Walter P. Webb, University of Texas, vice-president, and Solon J. Buck, Washington, D. C., re-elected treasurer. New members of the Executive Council are James B. Hedges, Brown University, to fill an unexpired term, and Crane Brinton, Harvard University, and Stanley Pargellis, Newberry Library, for the full terms ending in 1960.

Awards and prizes in the field of American history were announced as follows: the Albert J. Beveridge Award, to Paul W. Schroeder of the University of Texas for his manuscript, "The Axis Alliance and Japanese-American Relations, 1941," with honorable mention to Clark C. Spence of Pennsylvania State University for his manuscript, "British Investment and the American Mining Frontier, 1860-1901"; the John H. Dunning Prize, to John Higham of Rutgers University for his book, *Strangers in the Land:*

Patterns of American Nativism, 1860-1925 (Rutgers University Press), with honorable mention to John William Ward of Princeton University for his *Andrew Jackson: Symbol for an Age* (Oxford University Press), and to Joseph F. Wall of Grinnell College for his *Henry Watterson: Reconstructed Rebel* (Oxford University Press).

The 1956 Bancroft Prizes of $2,000, given annually by Columbia University "for distinguished writings in American history," have been awarded to George F. Kennan for *Russia Leaves the War* and to Arthur S. Link for *Wilson: The New Freedom.* Both books were published by the Princeton University Press.

At the twentieth annual meeting of the Society of American Archivists, held in Washington, D. C., October 10 and 11, 1956, the following officers were elected for the year 1956-1957: president, Lester J. Cappon, Institute of Early American History and Culture; vice-president, Herbert E. Angel, The National Archives; secretary, Dolores C. Renze, state archivist of Colorado; and treasurer, William D. Overman, Firestone Archives. G. Philip Bauer of The National Archives was named editor of the *American Archivist* to succeed Karl Trever, who had submitted his resignation after six years of service. The next meeting of the Society will be held in Columbus, Ohio, on October 3 and 4, 1957, with Erwin Zepp, director of the Ohio Historical Society, in charge of local arrangements.

The fifth Conference on Early American History — the first in the Far West — held at the Henry E. Huntington Library, San Marino, California, on February 9, 1957, dealt in general with the American Revolution. Papers presented were: "British Politics Preceding the American Revolution," by John W. Wilkes of Pomona College; "The Anglican Bishoprics and the American Revolution Re-examined," by Carl Bridenbaugh of the University of California, Berkeley; "Democracy in the Revolution," by Merrill Jensen of the University of Wisconsin; and "Hamilton, Madison, and Hume," by Douglass Adair of the Claremont Graduate School. John E. Pomfret, director of the Huntington Library, served as chairman of the conference.

The program of the twenty-seventh annual meeting of the South Carolina Historical Association, held in Clinton on April 6, included an address by Bell I. Wiley, Emory University; a paper on "The Repossession of Georgia, 1782-1784," by Robert S. Lambert of Shorter College; one on "Secretary of War Calhoun and the Removal of the Choctaw Indians," by Arthur H. DeRosier, Jr., of The Citadel; and a discussion of the place of history in the liberal education program, by Elizabeth H. Davidson of Coker College.

The officers of the Association for 1957-1958 are: Thomas B. Alexander of Georgia Teachers College, president; Anne King Gregorie of Charleston, vice-president; and Jack K. Williams of Clemson College, secretary-treasurer.

At the annual meeting of the Mississippi Historical Society, held in Natchez on February 15 and 16, Frank Freidel, Harvard University, delivered the dinner address on "Franklin D. Roosevelt and the South." Luncheon speakers were Walter B. Posey, Agnes Scott College, on "Chewing Tobacco, Bolting Food, and Drinking Whisky in the Old South," and James P. Coleman, governor of Mississippi, on "The Origins of the Constitution of 1890." Two general sessions dealt with "Mississippi in the Early Nineteenth Century" and "Natchez in the Civil War."

The British Association for American Studies is undertaking a survey of sources, both printed and manuscript, for American studies in the United Kingdom. The project is made possible by a generous grant from the United States Information Service in the United Kingdom. It is hoped that a reference work will result which will be a definitive guide to the location and general nature of all possible source and research materials connected with the history, politics, economics, and literature of the United States, and of British material that bears on them. The committee for the project is particularly anxious to locate previously uncatalogued material and dormant printed material which, even if not directly relevant to American studies, may yet contain some relevant matter — for example, family and business papers including correspondence to and from America, and local newspapers and magazines which are especially rich in articles on the prospects of investment in and migration to the United States.

Obviously many American scholars who have worked in British libraries and archives will have knowledge of some such materials unknown to British historians. It would greatly help the completeness and accuracy of the proposed survey if such American scholars would write to the director, Mr. H. L. Beales, or to the assistant director, Mr. B. R. Crick, Survey of Sources for American Studies in the United Kingdom, care of Institute for Historical Research, University of London, London W. C. 1.

The University of Wisconsin has received a grant of $100,000 from the Ford Foundation to be used over a five-year period for the promotion of studies in the history of American philanthropy. The program will be under the direction of Merle Curti, of the University of Wisconsin, assisted by Irvin G. Wyllie, formerly of the University of Missouri, who will transfer to Wisconsin on July 1 and will devote half time to research in the history of

American philanthropy. The project is intended to encourage monographic research, in part through fellowships to graduate students who will prepare dissertations at the University of Wisconsin.

Recent Articles of General Interest

Agricultural History — October, 1956: "Gathering the Grass [development of hayrakes]," by Clarence H. Danhof.

January, 1957: "The Cincinnatus Image in Presidential Politics," by W. Burlie Brown; "T. P. Gore and Agricultural Legislation," by Monroe Billington.

American-German Review — February-March, 1957: "Carl Schurz and Conservation," by Hildegard Binder Johnson; "The Kolping Society in America," by Alphonse L. Ellerkamp.

American Historical Review — January, 1957: "We Shall Gladly Teach," by Dexter Perkins; "Hamilton's Notes in His Pay Book of the New York State Artillery Company," by E. P. Panagopoulos; "The History of American Philanthropy as a Field of Research," by Merle Curti.

American Political Science Review — March, 1957: "American Political Thought and the Study of Politics," by Robert G. McClosky.

American Quarterly — Winter, 1956: "Berkshire's Golden Age," by Richard D. Birdsall; "Crane's 'Real' War in His Short Stories," by E. R. Hagemann; "The Stamp Act in Satire," by Bruce Ingham Granger.

Catholic Historical Review — January, 1957: "The Moral Laws of History," by Oscar Halecki.

Historian — February, 1957: "Alexander Hamilton, His Friends and Foes," by Broadus Mitchell; "The Report on Manufactures," by Louis M. Hacker; "The Papers of Alexander Hamilton," by Harold C. Syrett and Jacob E. Cooke; "Chancellor Kent's 'Brief Review of the Public Life and Writings of General Hamilton' — A Newly Identified Document," ed. by Douglass Adair.

Iowa Journal of History — January, 1957: "David B. Henderson: Speaker of the House," by Willard L. Hoing.

Journal of Negro History — January, 1957: "Herman Melville and the American National Sin: The Meaning of Benito Cereno," by Sidney Kaplan.

Journal of Politics — November, 1956: "Woodrow Wilson and Collective Security Today," by D. F. Fleming.

February, 1957: "An American Paradox: The Emergency Detention

Act of 1950," by Cornelius P. Cotter and J. Malcolm Smith; "Cruel and Unusual Punishments," by David Fellman; "Woodrow Wilson as Legislative Leader," by Marshall E. Dimock.

Journal of Southern History — February, 1957: "Blueprint for Radical Reconstruction," by John S. Sproat.

Journal of the Illinois State Historical Society — Winter, 1956: "Lorado Taft and Theater," by Genevieve Richardson; "Spelling Bothered Lincoln, Too," by Charles H. Coleman.

Journal of the Presbyterian Historical Society — March, 1957: "The History of North American Presbyterianism," by Gaius Jackson Slosser; "Archibald Alexander, Winsome Conservative (1772-1851)," by John Oliver Nelson.

Maryland Historical Magazine — March, 1957: "The Battle of South Mountain [Civil War]," by Warren W. Hassler, Jr.

Mid-America — January, 1957: "Terence V. Powderly and the Knights of Labor," by Gerald N. Grob.

Military Affairs — Winter, 1956: "Air Arm Doctrinal Roots, 1917-1918," by Thomas H. Greer; "Origins of the Chemical Corps," by Leo P. Brophy.

Minnesota History — December, 1956: "Frank B. Kellogg's View of History and Progress," by Charles G. Cleaver.

Oregon Historical Quarterly — December, 1956: "Woodrow Wilson: The End of His First Century," by Earl Pomeroy.

Pacific Historical Review — February, 1957: "The Work of the Indian Claims Commission under the Act of 1946," by Thomas LeDuc.

Political Science Quarterly — March, 1957: "The Demands of Politics and Job-Centered Unions," by James W. Kuhn; "The Basic Democrat: A Version of Tocqueville," by Marvin Meyers.

Register of the Kentucky Historical Society — January, 1957: "Mexican War Journal of Leander M. Cox," ed. by Charles F. Hinds.

Review of Politics — January, 1957: "The Birth of Democracy," by Christopher Dawson.

Social Studies — January, 1957: "The Meaning of the Zenger Case," by Vincent Buranelli.

Southwestern Historical Quarterly — January, 1957: "The Historian in America," by Boyd C. Shafer.

Southwestern Social Science Quarterly — March, 1957: "The Sunrise Conference: Myth or Fact?" by Monroe Billington.

West Virginia History — January, 1957: "The Early Empire Days of the United States," by A. T. Volwiler.

William and Mary Quarterly — January, 1957: "The American Revolution: Revisions in Need of Revising," by Edmund S. Morgan; "Amelia Simmons Fills a Need: *American Cookery*, 1796," by Mary Tolford Wilson; "The Army Contractors for the Niagara Campaign, 1755-1756," by Theodore Thayer; "Early Political Handbills in the United States," by Noble E. Cunningham, Jr.; "Thomas Paine's Plan for a Descent on England," by Alfred Owen Aldridge.

World Affairs Quarterly — January, 1957: "New Trends in Foreign Policy: A Criticism of the 'Kennan Thesis'," by Dwight J. Simpson.

Recent Articles Concerning the East

Connecticut Historical Society Bulletin — January, 1957: "The Circus in Connecticut," by Phyllis Kihn; "The Old State House," by Newton C. Brainard; "Some Aspects of Early Eighteenth-Century Connecticut Trade," by Glenn Weaver.

Delaware History — March, 1957: "The Restoration of the Courthouse in New Castle," by Daniel F. Wolcott; "Shipbuilding in Delaware," by David B. Tyler; "The Political History of Delaware during the Civil War — Part II, The Coming of the War," by Harold Bell Hancock; "Favorite Wilmington Plays before the Civil War," by Jack and Margaret Neeson.

Maryland Historical Magazine — March, 1957: "Maximilian and Eliza Godefroy," by Dorothy Mackay Quynn; "The Old Wye Mills, 1690-1956," by Edwin M. Barry; "The Chesapeake Pottery Company," by Nancy R. FitzPatrick.

New England Social Studies Bulletin — March, 1957: "The Vermont Marble Company: An Entrepreneurial Study, 1869-1939," by Robert C. Gilmore.

New-York Historical Society Quarterly — January, 1957: "The Western Campaign of 1779: The Diary of Quartermaster Sergeant Moses Sproule of the Third New Jersey Regiment in the Sullivan Expedition of the Revolutionary War, May 17–October 17, 1779," ed. by R. W. G. Vail.

Pennsylvania History — January, 1957: "Sources for Pennsylvania History in the Department of Internal Affairs," by Genevieve Blatt; "Jeffersonians in Local Politics along the Pennsylvania-Maryland Border," by

Frederic Shriver Klein; "James Logan: The Political Career of a Colonial Scholar," by E. Gordon Alderfer; "The Historical Society of York County," by Henry J. Young.

Pennsylvania Magazine of History and Biography — January, 1957: "Trial and Error at Allegheny: The Western State Penitentiary, 1818-1838," by Eugene E. Doll; "The Pennsylvania Railroad's Southern Rail Empire," by John F. Stover; "The Sea Captains Club," by William Bell Clark; "Scull and Heap's Map of Philadelphia," by Nicholas B. Wainwright.

RECENT ARTICLES CONCERNING THE SOUTH

Agricultural History — October, 1956: "Free Land, Free Labor, and the Freedmen's Bureau," by Martin Abbott; "Mechanizing the Cotton Harvest," by James H. Street.

Alabama Review — January, 1957: "Gold Mining in Alabama before 1860," by Robert A. Russell; "Bibb Graves as a Progressive, 1927-1930," by William E. Gilbert; "Alabama's Yellow Fever Epidemic of 1878," by Robert Partin; "Mary Gordon Duffee's 'Sketches of Alabama'," Part IV, ed. by Virginia Pounds Brown and Jane Porter Nabers.

Arkansas Historical Quarterly — Spring, 1957: "Cadron: An Early Town that Failed," by Margaret Smith Ross; "The Mountain Meadows Massacre and its Completion as a Historic Episode," by Ralph R. Rea; "Matthew Lyon's Last Frontier," by George L. Montagno; "The Confederate Attempt to Counteract Reunion Propaganda in Arkansas, 1863-1865," by Robert F. Smith; "Pioneers of Ashley County," by Y. W. Etheridge; "Valley Springs Academy," by Mrs. Fount G. Hollabaugh; "The Story of Tontitown, Arkansas," by Thomas Rothrock; "A Witch Trial in Carroll County," by Vance Randolph; "Arkansas Confederates among the Immortal Six Hundred," by Robert R. Logan; "The Story of Mockingbird Lane, 1856-1956," by Mary Katherine Watson; "Documents Relating to Elisha Baxter's Imprisonment," ed. by Ted R. Worley.

Field and Laboratory — January, 1957: "William H. von Streeruwitz (1833-1916), Geologist on the Dumble Survey of Texas," by Samuel W. Geiser.

Filson Club History Quarterly — January, 1957: "Cassius M. Clay, 'Lion' of White Hall: Some Unpublished Letters Of and About," ed. by Cassius M. Clay; "Pikeville College: Its Contribution to the Educational and Spiritual Life of Eastern Kentucky," by A. A. Page; "Three Letters of Charles S. Todd to Henry B. Dawson," ed. by Franklin A. Smith.

Florida Historical Quarterly — January, 1957: " 'The Florida Plan': An Ante-Bellum Effort to Control Cotton Sales," by Weymouth T. Jordan;

"Alabama and West Florida Annexation," by Hugh C. Bailey; "The 1913 Campaign for Child Labor in Florida," by Emily Howard Atkins; "Dudley Warren Adams, Pioneer" by Harriet M. Bryant; "The Trials of Captain Don Isidoro De Leon," trans. and ed. by Lucy L. Wenhold, with an introduction and notes by Albert C. Manucy; "The Call to Arms: Secession from a Feminine Point of View," ed. by Samuel Proctor; "Horace Greeley, Presidential Candidate: A Floridian's View," ed. by Willard E. Wight.

Georgia Historical Quarterly — March, 1957: "The Peace Movement in the Confederate Congress," by Wilfred B. Yearns; "The Georgia Wine Industry on the Eve of the Civil War," by James C. Bonner; "William Gilmore Simms and the *Cosmopolitan*," by John C. Guilds, Jr.; "Birdsville," by C. D. Hollingsworth; "The Letter Book of Thomas Rasberry, 1758-1761," Part III, ed. by Lilla M. Hawes; "Nathaniel Pendleton's 'Short Account of the Sea Coast of Georgia in Respect to Agriculture, Ship-building, Navigation, and the Timber Trade'," ed. by Theodore Thayer; "Reconstruction in Georgia: Three Letters by Edwin G. Higbee," ed. by Willard E. Wight.

Journal of Mississippi History — January, 1957: "The Mississippi Press in the Jackson Era, 1824-1841," by Edwin A. Miles; "The Vicksburg River Defenses and the Enigma of 'Whistling Dick'," by Edwin C. Bearss; "Some Notes on Hugh Miller Thompson, Second Episcopal Bishop of Mississippi," by Nash K. Burger; "A Bibliography of Theses and Dissertations Relating to Mississippi, 1956," comp. by James H. McLendon.

Journal of Negro History — January, 1957: "Sources of the History of the Negro in Texas, with Special Reference to Their Implications for Research in Slavery," by George R. Woolfolk; "The Mississippi Slave Insurrection Scare of 1835," by Edwin A. Miles.

Journal of Southern History — February, 1957: "Facets of the South in the 1850's," by James W. Patton; "Albert Sidney Johnston and the Loss of Forts Henry and Donelson," by Charles P. Roland.

North Carolina Historical Review — January, 1957: "Cherokee-White Relations on the Southern Frontier in the Early Nineteenth Century," by Henry T. Malone; "The Cotton Textile Industry in Ante-Bellum North Carolina," by Diffee W. Standard and Richard W. Griffin; "Organization and Early Years of the North Carolina Bar Association," by Fannie Memory Blackwelder; "The Colored Industrial Association of North Carolina and Its Fair of 1886," by Frenise A. Logan; "Civil War Letters of Henry W. Barrow to John W. Fries," ed. by Marian H. Blair.

Register of the Kentucky Historical Society — January, 1957: "The Barlow Planetarium," by Dwight L. Mikkelson; "Stock Raising in the Ante-Bellum Bluegrass," by Richard Laverne Troutman.

South Carolina Historical Magazine — January, 1957: "Autobiography of Daniel Stevens, 1746-1835," ed. by Anne King Gregorie; "Letters of Thomas Pinckney, 1775-1780," ed. by Jack L. Cross; "Wappetaw Congregational Church," by Petrona Royall McIver.

Southwestern Historical Quarterly — January, 1957: "James Bowie, Big Dealer," by J. Frank Dobie; "Major Whitfield Chalk, Hero of the Republic of Texas," by Olive Todd Walker; "The Abduction of Free Negroes and Slaves in Texas," by Earl W. Fornell; "Calendar of the Letters of Antonio Martinez, Last Spanish Governor of Texas, 1817-1822," Part V, ed. by Virginia H. Taylor.

Tennessee Historical Quarterly — March, 1957: "The Line of Blood: Lincoln and the Coming of the War," by David Rankin Barbee; "Outline of the Organization of the Medical Department of the Confederate Army and Department of Tennessee by S. H. Stout," ed. by Sam L. Clark and H. D. Riley, Jr.

Virginia Magazine of History and Biography — January, 1957: "Mulberry Trees and Silkworms: Sericulture in Early Virginia," by Charles E. Hatch, Jr.; "A Voyage of Fishing and Discovery, 1609," ed. by Martha W. Hiden; "Green Spring Plantation," by Louis R. Caywood; "News from Virginny, 1644," ed. by Joseph Frank.

West Virginia History — January, 1957: "Petitions of Western Virginians to Their General Assembly in Richmond," by W. Edwin Hemphill; "West Virginia Estate Settlements," by Ross B. Johnston.

William and Mary Quarterly — January, 1957: "Landon Carter and the Pistole Fee Dispute," by Jack P. Greene; "The Structure of Politics in Georgia, 1782-1789," by William W. Abbot.

Recent Articles Concerning the Middle West

Agricultural History — October, 1956: "Six Decades of Rugged Individualism: The American National Cattlemen's Association, 1898-1955," by Charles A. Burmeister; "Journal of F. and W. Renick on an Exploring Tour to the Mississippi and Missouri Rivers in the Year 1819," ed. by Paul C. Henlein.

January, 1957: "Shifting Range-Feeder Patterns in the Ohio Valley before 1860," by Paul C. Henlein; "An Historical Consideration of the Terms 'Corn' and 'Corn Belt' in the United States," by William Warntz.

Bulletin of the Historical and Philosophical Society of Ohio — January, 1957: "Westward Ho: Removal of Ohio Shawnees, 1832-1833," by Carl G. Klopfenstein; " 'Let the Men and Women Sit Apart' [Ohio Methodists]," by Paul H. Boase; "The Farmers' Party," by Ernest I. Miller.

Chicago History — Winter, 1956-1957: "The Gilpin Fund," ed. by Paul M. Angle; "A German Family in Chicago, 1856," ed. by Paul M. Angle.

Chronicles of Oklahoma — Winter, 1956-1957: "The Great Seal of the Chickasaw Nation," by Muriel H. Wright; "Jessie Elizabeth Randolph Moore of the Chickasaw Nation," by Muriel H. Wright; "Missionary Tour in the Chickasaw Nation and Western Indian Territory," by Hilary Cassal; "The Balentines, Father and Son, in the Indian Territory," by Carolyn Thomas Foreman; "Carl Sweezy, Arapaho Artist," by Althea Bass; "The Story of an Oklahoma Cowboy, William McGinty, and His Wife," by Leslie A. McRill; "A Spanish 'Arrastra' in the Wichita Mountains," by W. Eugene Hollon; "The Osage Indians and the Liquor Problem before Oklahoma Statehood," by Frank F. Finney; "Notes on Events Leading to the Chickasaw Treaties of Franklin and Pontotoc, 1830 and 1832," by Muriel H. Wright.

Indiana History Bulletin — February, 1957: "Our Capitols," ed. by Dorothy L. Riker.

Indiana Magazine of History — March, 1957: "Western War Aims, 1811-1812," by Reginald Horsman; "The Twain-Cable Readings in Indiana," by Paul Fatout; "Cyrus Nutt Becomes a Hoosier," ed. by Eleanore A. Cammack; "Smithson College Circular, 1871," contributed by Helen Lennox Tidrick, ed. by Donald F. Carmony.

Iowa Journal of History — January, 1957: "A History of Company D, Eleventh Iowa Infantry, 1861-1865," ed. by Mildred Throne.

Journal of Economic History — March, 1957: " 'Profits' and the Frontier Land Speculator," by Allan G. Bogue and Margaret Beattie Bogue.

Journal of the Illinois State Historical Society — Winter, 1956: "Shelby M. Cullom: Presidential Prospect," by William A. Pitkin; "The Destruction of an Early Illinois Library," by John T. Flanagan; "Chicago and the War between Greece and Turkey in 1897," by E. P. Panagopoulos.

Kansas Historical Quarterly — Winter, 1956: "Annals of Quindaro: A Kansas Ghost Town," by Alan W. Farley; "The Journal of an 1859 Pike's Peak Gold Seeker," ed. by David Lindsey; "Old Fort Solomon at Lindsey," by Theodore H. Scheffer; "Dodge City Varieties — A Summer Interlude of Entertainment, 1878," by James C. Malin; "Jefferson Davis and Kansas Territory," by Eugene T. Wells; "Touring Kansas and Colorado in 1871: The Journal of George C. Anderson," concluded, ed. by Nyle H. Miller.

Michigan History—March, 1957: "An Archaeological Reconnaissance of Isle Royale," by Fred Dustin; "Isle Royale National Park Movement, or A Study in Frustrations," by Martha M. Bigelow; "Agricultural Trends in the Upper Peninsula," by Henry S. Heimonen; "Apologia of a Republican Office Seeker, 1854," ed. by Philip P. Mason; "The Carp in Michigan," by Robin A. Drews and Eugene T. Petersen.

Minnesota History—December, 1956: "Moses N. Adams: A Missionary as Indian Agent," by Everett W. Sterling; "Fort Snelling: From Military Post to Historic Site," by Russell W. Fridley.

March, 1957: "Bishop Ireland's Connemara Experiment," by James P. Shannon; "When Minnesota Was Florida's Rival," by Helen Clapesattle; "Books for Pioneers: The Minneapolis Athenaeum," by Betty L. Engebretson.

Missouri Historical Review—January, 1957: "Fort Orleans: The Heritage of Carroll County," by Floyd C. Shoemaker; "David Rice Atchison: 'Faithful Champion of the South'," by William E. Parrish; "The Morrill Lands of the University of Missouri," by John J. Jones; "Missouri in Crisis: The Journal of Captain Albert Tracy, 1861," Part II, ed. by Ray W. Irwin.

Nebraska History—December, 1956: "Arts and Sciences on the Early American Frontier," by Thomas D. Clark; "Opportunities in Local History," by Howard H. Peckham; "Nebraska and the Presidential Election of 1912," by Donald F. Danker.

New-York Historical Society Quarterly—January, 1957: "Three Ornaments Worn by Upper Missouri Indians a Century and a Quarter Ago," by John C. Ewers; "A New York Girl Plays Cards with Mr. Lincoln: Life in Springfield, Illinois, a Century Ago," by Kenneth Scott.

North Dakota Quarterly—Winter, 1957: "The Midland Continental Railroad," by James D. Johnson.

Northwest Ohio Quarterly—Winter, 1956-1957: "The People's Schools: Popular Foundations of Toledo's Public School System," Part I, by Randolph C. Downes; "Indian Land Cessions in Northern Ohio and Southeastern Michigan (1805-1808)," by Dwight L. Smith; "Early Musical Life in Wooster, Ohio, and Vicinity (1830-1870)," by Donald I. Sonnedecker; "The Old Northwest in 1841: A Study in Development and Depression," by Kenneth R. Walker.

Ohio Historical Quarterly—January, 1957: "Faith vs. Economics: The Marietta and Cincinnati Railroad, 1845-1883," by John E. Pixton, Jr.; "The Steubenville and Indiana Railroad: The Pennsylvania's Middle Route to the Middle West," by Walter Rumsey Marvin; "Ethan Allen Brown and Ohio's Canal System," by John S. Still; "A Surgeon's Mate at Fort Defiance: The Journal of Joseph Gardner Andrews for the Year 1795," ed. by Richard C. Knopf.

Palimpsest—January, 1957: "The Fairfield *Ledger*," by Wallace E. Sherlock.

Wisconsin Magazine of History—Winter, 1956-1957: "Settling the Wisconsin Cutovers," by Lucile Kane; "A Half-Century of University Extension," by Lorentz H. Adolfson; "A King Sleeps in Wisconsin [James J. Strang]," by Conan Bryant Eaton; "Peter Hotaling Brings a Steamboat to Lake Winnebago," by Marcus A. McCorison; "The Irish of the North Country," by M. Justille McDonald.

Spring, 1957: "Political Loyalties, Immigrant Traditions, and Reform: The Wisconsin German-American Press and Progressivism, 1909-1912," by Gerd Korman; "The Birth of the St. Croix Octopus," by William G. Rector; "Belmont," by William E. Lass; "The Sugar River Valley," by Melchior Koch; "The City Beautiful: The Madison Park and Pleasure Drive Association, 1892-1938," by Helen H. and Harold M. Groves.

Recent Articles Concerning the Far West

Agricultural History—October, 1956: "Correcting Nature's Error: The Colorado-Big Thompson Project," by Oliver Knight.

Colorado Magazine—January, 1957: "Wireless Was Developed in Colorado (1904-1907)," by E. N. Pickerell; "Nathaniel P. Hill Inspects Colorado," ed. by Agnes Wright Spring; "Colorado's Terrible Mine: A Study in British Investment," by Clark C. Spence; "George Hooper Taylor," by John Taylor Wilson; "Colorado-Big Thompson Initiation, 1933-1938: The Story of a Gigantic Irrigation Project in Embryo," by William R. Kelly.

Journal of the Presbyterian Historical Society—March, 1957: "Letters of Amanda R. McFarland," Part III, ed. by Charles A. Anderson.

Mid-America—January, 1957: "A Note on Early Sonora and Arizona: Father Kino's *Chomites*," by Alberto Francisco Pradeau.

Military Affairs—Winter, 1956: "Army Life on the Frontier, 1865-1898," by Edward M. Coffman.

New Mexico Historical Review — January, 1957: "Famous Fugitives of Fort Union," by Elma Dill Russell Spencer; "The *Apuntes* of Father J. B. Ralliere," by Florence Hawley Ellis and Edwin Baca; "Seventeenth Century Navaho-Spanish Relations," by Frank D. Reeve; "John Simpson Chisum, 1877-84," by Harwood P. Hinton, Jr.

New-York Historical Society Quarterly — January, 1957: "A Grandfather in the Gold Rush: Isaac Annis Writes Home from Auburn Dry Diggins," ed. by John E. Parsons.

Oregon Historical Quarterly — December, 1956: "Mostly Division 'R' Days: Reminiscences of the Stormy, Pioneering Days of the Forest Reserves," by Harold D. Langille; "Pioneer Pastimes," by Dan E. Clark.

March, 1957: "The Founding of Camp Watson," by Judith Keyes Kenny; "The Oregon Donation Act and the National Land Policy," by James M. Bergquist; "Portland Remedial Loan Association: Organization, Growth, and Final Liquidation," by E. B. MacNaughton; "The War on the Webfoot Saloon," by Malcolm H. Clark, Jr.

Pacific Historical Review — February, 1957: "Oregon Territory's Movement for Self-Government, 1848-1853," by Robert W. Johannsen; "Quicksilver at New Almaden," by Henry Winfred Splitter.

Pacific Northwest Quarterly — January, 1957: "More Land for Industry: The Story of Flood Control in the Green River Valley," by Howard A. Hanson; "Anderson's Landing: Life in the Early Settlements on Hood Canal," by Patricia J. Hanley; "Ranald MacDonald: The Sailor Boy Who Visited Japan," by Joel E. Ferris; "Drafting Washington's State Constitution," ed. by Charles M. Gates; "The Washington Library Association, 1931-55," by William H. Carlson.

Recent Articles Concerning Canada

Canadian Historical Review — March, 1957: "The Round Table Movement in Canada, 1909-1920," by James Eayrs; "The Heir and Devisee Commission of Upper Canada, 1797-1805," by Lillian F. Gates; "John A. Macdonald on Raising Troops in Canada for Imperial Service, 1885," by C. P. Stacey; "The Independent Member for Kent Reports, 1853," by J. M. S. Careless.

Mid-America — January, 1957: "Troops to Red River," by R. E. Lamb.

Communications

To the Managing Editor, *Mississippi Valley Historical Review*:

Professor Harold J. Bingham's review of my book *Lincoln and the Tools of War* (December, 1956, pp. 495-96) is generally all I could wish, and I thank him for it. Nevertheless he has not won me over to his view of the Civil War breechloader question; and since this is one of the more important themes in my book, I should like to answer the questions he raises in that connection.

Professor Bingham says first that my case for the overwhelming superiority of Civil War breechloaders over muzzle-loaders is based largely on postwar testimony. On tallying the independent sources my book cites on that point, I find that twenty-four of them date from before 1865 and only nine after. Statistics aside, I would be quite content, if anyone objects on principle to postwar testimony, to rest my entire case on the twenty-four wartime sources alone. Professor Bingham next says that European nations were not sold on breechloaders until after the Austro-Prussian War. This strikes me as beside the point, but in any case (as my book points out) it was in 1864, when the Austro-Prussian War was but a gleam in Bismarck's eye, that the British War Office recommended the adoption of breechloaders for all British troops — largely on the basis of American experience. Professor Bingham then says that a proper metal cartridge was essential to a successful breechloader. But, as my book demonstrates, the Sharps was highly successful with a paper cartridge; and even if good metal cartridges were necessary, they were at hand — the Spencers used them with great success all through the war.

Finally, Professor Bingham turns to what my book describes as the "strongest argument" of Lincoln's conservative Chief of Ordnance, Brigadier General James W. Ripley, that breechloaders could not have been turned out in time to do any good. Waiving the question of how soon American manufacturers could have turned them out in significant numbers, I contend that Ripley should have at least considered the opinion of the Chief of Navy Ordnance, Andrew Harwood, in May, 1861, that "facilities [for making breechloaders] can be found abroad — especially in the great manufacturing towns of Belgium." I believe that if Ripley had acted quickly on Harwood's suggestion, enough breechloaders — say a hundred thousand — might have been ready by the middle of 1863 to shorten the war by a year or more.

On this last point, I do not claim and never have claimed final authority; and if anything in my book implies otherwise, it was not so intended. I suspect that Professor Bingham is in about the same position. The question, in fact, probably belongs among those eternally arguable issues that are the salt and spice of Civil War history. I merely wish to suggest here that my own view of the case is not altogether groundless.

Robert V. Bruce
Boston University

To the Managing Editor, *Mississippi Valley Historical Review*:

The *Review* and Professor Bruce have offered me the opportunity to state again that *Lincoln and the Tools of War* is interesting and well told. It remains my opinion, however, that the sharp contrast between Lincoln and Ripley is overdrawn and is based on an over-simplification of a perennial problem of logistics.

Contrary to Bruce's assertion in his rejoinder, the "case for the overwhelming superiority of Civil War breechloaders over muzzle-loaders" was not questioned in the review. The question was whether or not "by 1863 the effectiveness of the breechloader was generally recognized by the Union Army." The point and date are important in evaluating Bruce's contrast of Lincoln as the agent of progress and Ripley as the symbol of obstruction. The date is important since Ripley's tenure of office ended in September, 1863, and Lincoln lost interest in ordnance affairs shortly thereafter. The point is important since Bruce, in part, condemned Ripley for obstinately opposing prevailing opinion. A second reading of Bruce's book did not reveal, on this point, evidence that I can regard as substantial or contemporary.

The recommendation for British adoption which was made in 1864 by a committee appointed by the British War Office did not result in the adoption by the War Office of a method of conversion until 1866. Even in 1867 competitions and tests to enable the selection of a model for adoption for manufacture were still in progress. As indicated by discussion in *Cornhill Magazine* in that year, "the intimate relation which exists between the cartridge and the gun" was generally recognized and consideration was being given to the possibility of substituting coiled sheet brass for the "absolutely inadmissible" paper cartridges and for the imperfect copper ones.

Bruce's belief that significant numbers of breechloaders could have been secured in Europe requires more support than the statement of Harwood, whom Bruce, himself, describes as "inexpert." The most readily available pertinent information is that upon which Harwood most likely based his suggestion: a report of a "Military Commission to Europe in 1855 and 1856" (*Sen. Exec. Docs.*, No. 60, 36 Cong., 1 Sess.). This commission recognized the potential of the breechloaders; discussed European manufacturing, especially that in Liége; noted that production was largely by hand; and concluded that improvement of firearms was in a state of transition. There was attached to this report a treatise by J. Schön on "Rifled Infantry Arms"

(Dresden, 1855), translated by the one man who, we are reasonably sure, was familiar with the theory and potential supply of breechloaders, Josiah Gorgas, later the Confederate Chief of Ordnance. Although the Confederacy depended almost entirely upon the European market, it did not secure an appreciable number of breechloaders. It does seem that the possibility of securing 100,000 from Europe in two years is highly conjectural.

Each generation of scholars contrives methods whereby the South could have won the war or the North could have shortened it — an advantage, obviously, that historians hold over military commanders.

HAROLD J. BINGHAM
Teachers College of Connecticut

Directory of Contributors

Thomas D. Clark is professor of history and chairman of the department of history in the University of Kentucky.

J. Leonard Bates is assistant professor of history in the University of Illinois.

John C. Greene is associate professor of history in Iowa State College, Ames.

Donald R. McCoy is associate professor of social studies in the State University of New York, Teachers College, Cortland.

Richard P. Longaker is associate professor of political science in Kenyon College.

The Mississippi Valley Historical Review

PUBLISHED QUARTERLY BY THE MISSISSIPPI VALLEY HISTORICAL ASSOCIATION

VOL. XLIV, NO. 2 — SEPTEMBER, 1957

Correspondence concerning contributions, books for review, and all editorial matters should be addressed to William C. Binkley, Managing Editor, Tulane University of Louisiana, New Orleans 18, Louisiana. Annual membership dues are $5.00. Student membership dues are $3.00 annually. Correspondence concerning membership dues and all business matters should be addressed to the Secretary, William D. Aeschbacher, 1500 R Street, Lincoln, Nebraska. The *Review* is sent to all members of the Association. Single numbers and back files may be obtained from the Secretary.

The Mississippi Valley Historical Association disclaims responsibility for statements whether of fact or of opinion made by contributors.

Entered as second-class matter, May 22, 1914, at the post office in Cedar Rapids, Iowa, and Lincoln 8, Nebraska, under the Act of August 24, 1912. Printed by The Torch Press, Cedar Rapids, Iowa.

Contents

WOODROW WILSON AND HIS INTERPRETERS, 1947-1957. By Richard L. Watson, Jr. 207

THE ORIGINS OF THE TEAPOT DOME INVESTIGATION. By Burl Noggle . . . 237

THE SOUTH AND THE BLAIR EDUCATION BILL. By Allen J. Going . . . 267

"FIFTY-FOUR FORTY OR FIGHT" — AN AMERICAN POLITICAL LEGEND. By Edwin A. Miles 291

THE FIFTIETH ANNUAL MEETING OF THE MISSISSIPPI VALLEY HISTORICAL ASSOCIATION. By Oscar O. Winther 310

BOOK REVIEWS

Echeverria, *Mirage in the West: A History of the French Image of American Society to 1815*, by Alfred O. Aldridge 335
Wittke, *The German-Language Press in America*, by Henry A. Pochmann . . 336
Fenton, *American Indian and White Relations to 1830: Needs and Opportunities for Study*, by Allen W. Trelease 337
Hartley, *Ironworks on the Saugus*, by Bernard Bailyn . . . 339
Scheer and Rankin, *Rebels and Redcoats*, by Charles S. Grant . . . 340
Russell, *Guns on the Early Frontiers*, by Robert G. Athearn . . . 342
Hacker, *Alexander Hamilton in the American Tradition*, by Noble E. Cunningham, Jr. . . 343
Smith, *Freedom's Fetters: The Alien and Sedition Laws and American Civil Liberties*, by Adrienne Koch 344
Bruchey, *Robert Oliver, Merchant of Baltimore, 1783-1819*, by Clarence P. Gould . . 347
Brant, *James Madison, The President, 1809-1812*, by Bradford Perkins . . 348
Greene and Smith (eds.), *The Journals of Welcome Arnold Greene*, by John H. Reinoehl . . 349
Fuller and Hafen (eds.), *The Journal of Captain John R. Bell*, by Harvey L. Carter . . 350
Smith, *Professors and Public Ethics*, by Louis Filler . . . 352
Teeters and Shearer, *The Prison at Philadelphia, Cherry Hill*, by Blake McKelvey . . 353
Stevens, *The Early Jackson Party in Ohio*, by Eugene H. Roseboom . . . 355
Eaton, *Henry Clay and the Art of American Politics*, by Joseph G. Tregle, Jr. . . 356
Sellers, *James K. Polk, Jacksonian, 1795-1843*, by Norman A. Graebner . . 357
Field, *Prairie and Mountain Sketches* (ed. by Gregg and McDermott), by Walker D. Wyman . 359
Levy, *The Law of the Commonwealth and Chief Justice Shaw*, by Carl B. Swisher . 360
Oliphant and Eaves (eds.), *The Letters of William Gilmore Simms*, Volumes IV and V, by Joseph P. Roppolo 362
Vandiver, *Mighty Stonewall*, by Dudley T. Cornish . . . 363
Hassler, *General George B. McClellan, Shield of the Union*, by Edwin B. Coddington . 365
Howe, *Justice Oliver Wendell Holmes: The Shaping Years, 1841-1870*, by Robert J. Harris . 366
Smith and Anderson (eds.), *Mark Twain of the Enterprise*, by Rodman W. Paul . . 368
Erickson, *American Industry and the European Immigrant, 1860-1885*, by Rowland T. Berthoff . 369
Pierce, *A History of Chicago.* Volume III, *The Rise of a Modern City, 1871-1893*, by Wyatt W. Belcher 371
Bonner, *Medicine in Chicago, 1850-1950*, by Philip D. Jordan . . . 372
Mechem (ed.), *The Annals of Kansas, 1886-1925* (2 vols.), by Charles L. Stansifer . . 373
Dulles, *The Imperial Years*, by Dexter Perkins . . . 374
Damon, *Sanford Ballard Dole and His Hawaii*, by Harold W. Bradley . . 375
Hughes and Patterson (eds.), *Robert Russa Moton of Hampton and Tuskegee*, by E. David Cronon 377
Peterson and Fite, *Opponents of War, 1917-1918*, by Howard H. Quint . 378
Schlesinger, *The Age of Roosevelt: The Crisis of the Old Order, 1919-1933*, by Clarke A. Chambers 379
McNeil, *The Fight for Fluoridation*, by Thomas N. Bonner . . 381
Handlin, *Race and Nationality in American Life*, by Edward N. Saveth . 382
Cooke, *Frederic Bancroft, Historian*, by Thomas J. Pressly . . 383

BOOK NOTES 385

HISTORICAL NEWS AND COMMENTS 393
Report of the Secretary-Treasurer for the Year 1956-1957. By William D. Aeschbacher . 411

DIRECTORY OF CONTRIBUTORS 420

Woodrow Wilson and His Interpreters, 1947-1957

By Richard L. Watson, Jr.

During the last decade, and particularly in 1956, the centennial of Woodrow Wilson's birth, so much new Wilson material appeared in print that even a specialist in twentieth-century American history has difficulty in keeping the titles clearly in mind.[1] A number of edited selections or reprints of Wilson's writings, biographies or biographical sketches, and a host of monographs and periodical articles have given solid backing to Wilson's stature as one of the most written-of Americans. A large part, but not all, of this writing reflects the interests of professional historians and political scientists. A part has been the recollections of those who knew Wilson. Some

[1] This article represents the enlargement of an original design to prepare a group review of the following five book-length studies of Woodrow Wilson, published in 1956:

Wilson: The New Freedom. By Arthur S. Link. (Princeton: Princeton University Press, 1956. xiv + 504 pp. Illustrations, notes, bibliography, and index. $7.50.)

Woodrow Wilson and the Politics of Morality. By John Morton Blum. *The Library of American Biography*. Edited by Oscar Handlin. (Boston: Little, Brown and Company, 1956. viii + 215 pp. Note on the sources and index. $3.50.)

Woodrow Wilson: A Great Life in Brief. By John A. Garraty. (New York: Alfred A. Knopf, 1956. x + 206 + vi pp. Index. $2.50.)

Woodrow Wilson and Colonel House: A Personality Study. By Alexander L. George and Juliette L. George. (New York: The John Day Company, 1956. xx + 362 pp. Illustration, notes, bibliography, and index. $6.00.)

A Crossroads of Freedom: The 1912 Campaign Speehes of Woodrow Wilson. Edited by John Wells Davidson. (New Haven: Yale University Press, for the Woodrow Wilson Foundation, 1956. xviii + 570 pp. Illustrations, source notes, description of sources, and index. $6.00.)

The decade since 1947 seems to represent a convenient period for this survey because other bibliographical studies have discussed the Wilson literature prior to that year. See especially the bibliography in Arthur S. Link, *Wilson: The Road to the White House* (Princeton, 1947); Link, "A Decade of Biographical Contributions to Recent American History," *Mississippi Valley Historical Review* (Cedar Rapids), XXXIV (March, 1948), 637-52; Laura Shearer Turnbull (comp.), *Woodrow Wilson: A Selected Bibliography of His Published Writings, Addresses, and Public Papers* (Princeton, 1948); and Richard W. Leopold, "The Problem of American Intervention, 1917," *World Politics* (New Haven), II (April, 1950), 405-25.

of it has appeared in print as revisions of doctoral dissertations, while another part is the work of professional scholars long expert in the subject of Wilson or his times. The latter is true particularly of a number of the biographical studies. The most productive of the present-day Wilson scholars, Arthur S. Link, published his *Wilson: The Road to the White House* in 1947 and the second volume of this major biographical study, *Wilson: The New Freedom*, in 1956.[2] Other book-length biographical studies of Wilson which have appeared since 1947 are: *Woodrow Wilson and American Liberalism*, by E. M. Hugh-Jones, a British study published in 1948; and three American works, all published in 1956: *Woodrow Wilson and the Politics of Morality*, by John M. Blum; *Woodrow Wilson and Colonel House: A Personality Study*, by Alexander L. and Juliette L. George; and *Woodrow Wilson*, by John A. Garraty. Biographical studies, however, comprise the smaller part of publications about Wilson during the decade. The greater productivity has been in the field of critical monographs and periodical articles dealing with some phase of Wilson's administration or policy. Here, more noticeably than in the biographical works, the publications reflect not only the widespread interest in Wilson, but a particularly fertile field of activity in graduate training in history and political science.

These numerous publications of the last decade, as would be expected, have not united in presenting a consistent portrait of Wilson. Some parts of his character and policies have become less of an enigma, but in some other respects he continues to ignite controversial interpretations among scholars. Moreover, the writers themselves project their own individuality into the interpretation. As John A. Garraty has pointed out: "The great man's permanent fame is dependent upon his biographers. The image he casts into the future is almost as much the product of their work as his own." [3] And in the case of Wilson, one other factor which has colored the interpretation is the general feeling toward him — and particularly toward his foreign policies — which has been shaped in part by contemporary conditions, attitudes, and partialities. Charles Seymour, the dean of the present generation of Wilson scholars, has

[2] Among other publications by Professor Link in this decade, one of the most notable was his volume in the New American Nation Series, entitled *Woodrow Wilson and the Progressive Era, 1910-1917* (New York, 1954).

[3] Garraty, *Woodrow Wilson*, 196.

suggested in an article in the *Virginia Quarterly Review* a correlation between the character of the times and the differing appraisals of Wilson's activities at Paris. First came the eulogy or the hostile criticism of his contemporaries. Then the number of eulogists dwindled as the League failed to solve the international crises of the late 1920's and the 1930's. With World War II, however, the popularity of Wilson and his ideal of world organization increased; but as war gave way to cold war the advocates of a greater realism in diplomacy again criticized him as one who had ignored practical considerations of power in a war-torn world.[4]

The image of Wilson in the last decade, however, has been modified less by way of interpretative bias — whether on the part of the writer or the character of the contemporary world — than it has by more extensive research into sources not previously utilized. It is possible that some of the newer Wilson publications were occasioned by centennial zeal, but the larger number represent primarily the results of more mature research, not only in the Wilson Papers, at the Library of Congress, but in government archives and in the papers of Wilson's influential friends and contemporaries. Among printed sources, *The Public Papers of Woodrow Wilson*, edited by Ray S. Baker and William E. Dodd (6 vols., New York, 1925-1927), has remained the principal point of departure for studies of Wilson. No other extensive collection has appeared in recent years, although the reader who wants to sample Wilson's writings and speeches now has a choice of several one-volume collections. One of the most valuable of these is the volume edited by John W. Davidson which revises our knowledge of Wilson's 1912 campaign speeches. A selection by Donald Day presents chronologically a number of Wilson's public and private writings, with conventional comments.[5] A less popular, but more penetrating, selection was prepared by August Heckscher, of the New York *Herald Tribune*, and published as *The Politics of Woodrow Wilson*.[6] Organized

4 Charles Seymour, "The Paris Education of Woodrow Wilson," *Virginia Quarterly Review* (Charlottesville), XXXII (Autumn, 1956), 578-81. See also D. F. Fleming, "Woodrow Wilson and Collective Security Today," *Journal of Politics* (Gainesville, Fla.), XVIII (November, 1956), 611-24, and Earl Pomeroy, "Woodrow Wilson: The End of His First Century," *Oregon Historical Quarterly* (Portland), LVII (December, 1956), 315-32.

5 *Woodrow Wilson's Own Story*, selected and edited by Donald Day (Boston, 1952).

6 *The Politics of Woodrow Wilson: Selections from His Speeches and Writings*, edited with an introduction by August Heckscher (New York, 1956).

topically and including Wilson's earliest significant article, published in 1879 in the *International Review*, and concluding with an *Atlantic Monthly* article of 1923, this volume is concerned with "political principles and opinions." Heckscher takes issue with those who argue that Wilson was basically a conservative who was led to support moderate reforms by force of circumstance, and concludes that "at his best, Wilson had an instinctive grasp of realities which enabled him to preserve the vital balance between ideals and practice." [7]

A different sort of anthology, gathering together a number of fresh essays about Wilson, was prepared by Mrs. Em Bowles Alsop under the authorization of the Woodrow Wilson Centennial Commission.[8] Mrs. Alsop, appointed by President Eisenhower and the Commission, revealed a sense of mission in her work: to present to the people of the United States "an immediate re-evaluation of Woodrow Wilson as our first world leader." She decided upon a book "introduced by the President of the United States, concluded by the Secretary-General of the United Nations, with chapters of specific chronological authority by the greatest living Wilsonians." The result is a work which, though uneven in quality, has several chapters which compensate for the uncritical nature of the others. For example, Arthur Link contributes an excellent distillation of some of his views in a chapter on "The Progressive"; Luis Quintanilla compares Wilson to Bolivar and sees in Wilson's Pan-Americanism certain precedents for the League of Nations; [9] and Walter Lippmann provides a suggestive analysis of Wilson's political philosophy.[10]

In honor of the centennial, too, several professional journals, de-

[7] *Ibid.*, xiv, xvi, xxi-xxii.

[8] *The Greatness of Woodrow Wilson, 1856-1956*, arranged and edited by Mrs. Em Bowles Alsop (New York, 1956). *The Wilson Reader*, selected and edited by Frances Farmer (New York, 1956), includes several excerpts from essays about Wilson, originally published elsewhere, and a small selection of his speeches, principally on foreign policy.

[9] Scholarly support for Quintanilla's point may be found in Charles H. Carlisle, "Woodrow Wilson's Pan-American Pact," *South Carolina Historical Association Proceedings* (Columbia), XIX (1949), 3-15.

[10] An excellent commentary by Katharine E. Brand on the Woodrow Wilson Papers in the Library of Congress is reprinted from the *Library of Congress Quarterly Journal of Current Acquisitions* (Washington), XIII (February, 1956), 61-72. Other contributors (either directly or by reprints) include Clifford Dowdey, Virginius Dabney, Frank Bell Lewis, Harold W. Dodds, Edgar E. Robinson, Madame Chiang Kai-shek, Boguniel Vosnjak, Thomas Connally, and William Allen White.

voting an entire issue to Wilson, have published numerous articles of real merit. Among such journals are the *Virginia Quarterly Review* and a newer publication, *Confluence*, published under the auspices of the Harvard Summer Session.[11] In addition, Florida State University has published a special issue of its *Studies*, consisting of three articles based upon printed sources dealing with Wilson's presidential role in national politics.[12]

Most of the research of the past ten years has concentrated upon the presidency, with relatively little coverage of Wilson's formative years. Both Garraty and the Georges are exceptions to the general statement, for in their effort to make more effective use of psychology in historical interpretation they have shown a special interest in the influence of home, family, and early life. Most other scholars seem to have endorsed Link's opinion, expressed in his *Wilson: The Road to the White House*, that Ray Stannard Baker had "done for Wilson's early personal life a job that will not have to be done again, except in so far as the origins and development of Wilson's political thought are concerned" (p. xi). Among the few specialized works of the past ten years dealing with Wilson's earlier life are Helen W. Thackwell's "Woodrow Wilson and My Mother," a somewhat sentimental article which throws some light on Wilson's love for the companionship of women, and McMillan Lewis' *Woodrow Wilson of Princeton*.[13] The latter was designed to fill the gap left

11 *Virginia Quarterly Review* (Charlottesville), XXXII (Autumn, 1956). Particularly stimulating articles in this issue are: "Wilson the Domestic Reformer," by Marshall E. Dimock; "A Portrait of Woodrow Wilson," by Arthur S. Link; "The Paris Education of Woodrow Wilson," by Charles Seymour; and "The Price of Woodrow Wilson's Illness," by Perry Laukhuff. Two issues of *Confluence* (Cambridge), V (Autumn, 1956, and Winter, 1957), contain articles by such scholars as William L. Langer, Max Beloff, Robert E. Osgood, McGeorge Bundy, and John M. Blum.

One of the most unusual publications of the centennial year is *Lectures and Seminar at the University of Chicago, January 30-February 3, 1956, in Celebration of the Centennial of Woodrow Wilson, 1856-1956* (Chicago, 1956), published by the University of Chicago in co-operation with the Woodrow Wilson Foundation. This consists of lectures by Raymond Fosdick, Francis B. Sayre, Jonathan W. Daniels, Alben W. Barkley, and Louis Brownlow; and seminar sessions led by Arthur S. Link, Thomas J. Wertenbaker, Arthur W. MacMahon, Marshall E. Dimock, and Edward H. Buehrig.

12 Elston Roady, "Woodrow Wilson's Role as Party Leader: Trust Legislation"; Paul J. Piccard, "The Electoral Colleges of President Wilson"; Gregg Phifer, "Woodrow Wilson's Swing around the Circle in Defense of His League," *Florida State University Studies*, No. 23, *Woodrow Wilson Centennial Issue*, edited by Victor S. Mamatey (Tallahassee, 1956).

13 Helen W. Thackwell, "Woodrow Wilson and My Mother," *Princeton University Library Chronicle* (Princeton), XII (Autumn, 1950), 6-18, is a summary of letters written between Harriet Woodrow and Wilson, giving an account of an early

by Link's failure to discuss in much detail Wilson as a teacher. The most useful work on the Princeton years, however, is *Woodrow Wilson: Some Princeton Memories*, by William Starr Myers and others of Wilson's Princeton colleagues. One of the essays, by J. Duncan Spaeth, at that time a professor of English at Princeton, is especially provocative in view of more recent critical appraisals of Wilson. Spaeth points to the "feminine note in Wilson's genius": his intuitiveness, his "immediate awareness of affinity in fundamental attitudes." More importantly Spaeth resolves the paradox of Wilson who refused to compromise and Wilson the opportunist: "There is such a thing as an opportunism of conviction. To swim with the current does not prove a man wrong, any more than swimming against it proves him right. . . . The fact that Wilson did not change his *direction* when the tide turned against him, should be sufficient proof of his sincerity when he swam with the current." [14]

Spaeth's discussion of opportunism is central to any interpretation of Wilson's career, and it is one to which recent historical writing has devoted considerable attention. It is a topic which has special bearing on Wilson's relationship to Progressive thought, a troublesome question confronting historians who have sought to pinpoint the motivation behind Wilson's presidential, domestic policies. To what extent was the change in Wilson's views from the Manchester liberalism of undergraduate and graduate days to that of Progressive reformer the result of political opportunism? The book which has become a basic work on this subject was published in 1943: *The Economic Thought of Woodrow Wilson*, by William Diamond (Baltimore, 1943). But the question has continued to attract both Wilson scholars and writers in the larger fields of the Progressive movement and of American thought. Henry Steele Commager's interpretation is that "with Wilson the story of the formal repudiation of laissez-faire . . . reached a climax and . . . shifted somewhat uncertainly from negative interposition to positive action." [15] Ralph H. Gabriel has found Wilson a leading progressive, and one who conformed to the doctrines of the

love affair and later relationships. McMillan Lewis, *Woodrow Wilson of Princeton* (Naberth, Pa., 1952), is based largely on solicited letters from Princeton alumni of the 1890-1915 period.

[14] Spaeth, "Wilson, As I Knew Him and View Him Now," in William Starr Myers, *Woodrow Wilson: Some Princeton Memories* (Princeton, 1946), 69-91.

[15] Henry Steele Commager, *The American Mind* (New Haven, 1950), 218-19; see also pp. 322-25, 349-51.

American "democratic faith," in that he believed in the fundamental moral law, the free individual, and the mission of America. At the same time, according to Gabriel, Wilson believed that the state should be used to make competition free.[16]

What Wilson believed about the role of the state — what he believed at one time and what he believed at another — is the core of the problem. It is a problem, too, which grows more complex when seen in the light of a broader but related subject, the difference between Wilson's New Freedom and the Roosevelt-Progressive New Nationalism, a difference which came into focus in the election of 1912. Too frequently the difference has been considered inconsequential, whereas actually the choice between the two posed a dilemma to twentieth-century reformers. As Eric Goldman has succinctly pointed out about the election of 1912: "for the first time a major split in reform doctrine was being argued before a national audience." [17]

More recently Richard Hofstadter, although he takes a different approach to the Progressive movement from that of Goldman, has come to essentially the same conclusions as to the significance of the campaign of 1912.[18] Wilson's program for a "New Freedom," launched in this campaign, showed agreement in principle with the thinking of Brandeis, La Follette, and Bryan, "that a real effort should be made to restore, maintain, and regulate competition rather than regulate monopoly" as Roosevelt in the New Nationalism would have it. Hofstadter asserts, furthermore, that Wilson in 1912 gave "magnificently articulate expression" to his own views; yet he concludes that Wilson soon fudged by asserting that only business that grew big because of "illicit competition" was bad, and that he was "for big business, and . . . against the trusts." [19]

16 Ralph H. Gabriel, *The Course of American Democratic Thought* (2nd ed., New York, 1956), 362-65.

17 Eric F. Goldman, *Rendezvous with Destiny* (New York, 1953), 214-19.

18 Richard Hofstadter, *The Age of Reform, from Bryan to F. D. R.* (New York, 1955), 214. To Hofstadter, "the Progressive Movement was the complaint of the unorganized against the consequences of organization," a "revolt against industrial discipline." The economic order of the nineteenth century stimulated and rewarded "certain traits of personal character." Success was a reward of virtue. The protest movement of the twentieth century, according to Hofstadter, saw the organization becoming greater than man, and thus "contrary to all the principles of progress."

19 *Ibid.*, 222, 246-51. A brief article which scratches the surface of this problem is Jack Kenney Williams, "Roosevelt, Wilson, and the Progressive Movement," *South Atlantic Quarterly* (Durham), LIV (April, 1955), 207-11. See also Daniel Aaron, *Men of Good Hope: A Story of American Progressives* (New York, 1951), 281-86,

Stimulating as these interpretations of Wilson's part in the Progressive movement are, Link's work on Wilson requires their substantial revision. In his *Woodrow Wilson and the Progressive Era*, Link, like Goldman, highlights Roosevelt and Wilson in the election of 1912 as representatives of diverging philosophies of government "far-reaching in . . . implications for the future development of governmental policies in the United States." Link emphasizes that Roosevelt's New Nationalism meant not only accepting and regulating the trusts but recognizing federal responsibility for "social justice" legislation concerning such questions as child labor, workmen's compensation, and conservation. Although Wilson had made "a general commitment to the ideal of social justice" by 1912, Link continues, he was still fundamentally a Jeffersonian liberal. At heart his faith lay in state rights: "He believed the federal power should be used only to sweep away special privileges . . . and to preserve or restore competition in business. The idea of the federal government's moving directly into the economic field, by giving special protection to workers or farmers, was as abhorrent to Wilson in 1912 as the idea of class legislation in the interest of manufacturers or shipowners." [20]

To this point Link's interpretation is not particularly novel; but with the first administration Link plows new ground. He believes that within a comparatively few months after Wilson came into office factors that were largely political forced him to change his objectives, and that he took over a program that was essentially that of the New Nationalism. The Wilson of the Underwood Tariff, Federal Reserve, and Clayton Anti-Trust acts gave way to the Wilson of rural credits, child labor, workmen's compensation, seamen's, and Adamson eight-hour-day legislation.

The first of these two phases is covered in more detail in Link's *Wilson: The New Freedom*, which, significantly, covers only the

and Arthur M. Schlesinger, Jr., *The Age of Roosevelt: The Crisis of the Old Order, 1919-1933* (Boston, 1957), 27-45.

[20] Link, *Woodrow Wilson and the Progressive Era*, 18-20. Good summaries of Link's views are contained in his *American Epoch: A History of the United States since the 1890's* (New York, 1955) and in the following articles: "The Enigma of Woodrow Wilson," *American Mercury* (New York), LXV (September, 1947), 303-13; "The South and the New Freedom: An Interpretation," *American Scholar* (Richmond), XX (Summer, 1951), 314-24; "Woodrow Wilson and the Democratic Party," *Review of Politics* (Notre Dame), XVIII (April, 1956), 146-56; "A Portrait of Woodrow Wilson," *Virginia Quarterly Review*, XXXII (Autumn, 1956), 524-40.

first two years of the presidential administration. It is excellent historical scholarship, with certain particular qualities which merit special emphasis. Too frequently the historian of American politics loses sight of the nature of the American party system. Pressed for space and the need for generalization, he passes over lightly the activities at the grass roots, so basic for an understanding of the president's role; furthermore, he is tempted to neglect crucial questions such as patronage and relations with Congress. A third problem, almost insoluble in political history, is to keep a proper balance between a topical and chronological organization. It is conventional, for example, to separate the problems of foreign from those of domestic policy even though history does not move that way. Frequently, indeed, one affects the other to a significant degree. Yet some believe that to arrange all parts of the story chronologically may create a greater confusion in the mind of the reader than is actually justified by the events.[21]

Link is obviously quite conscious of these questions. He is, understandably because of the space at his disposal, much more successful in *Wilson: The New Freedom* than in *Woodrow Wilson and the Progressive Era* in keeping an eye on local politics while at the same time concentrating on the national scene. He is somewhat less successful in maintaining a balance between a chronological and topical treatment, his technique being to treat major issues such as the tariff, the Federal Reserve system, and Latin American policy separately but within a broad chronological framework.

The chapters which show Link at his best are those on Wilson himself, on his closest advisers, and on the presidential office. A character sketch of Wilson, for example, reflects the sense of assurance that familiarity with the records gives: "his craving for affection and his refusal to give on equal terms, his love of the people en masse and his ordinary disdain for individuals, the warm idealism of his speeches and the coolness of many of his official relationships, the bigness of his political visions and the pettiness of his hatreds."

Link apparently believes that Wilson's "expansion and per-

[21] Frederic L. Paxson attempted an organization of this kind, and it makes for meaty reading; yet a student who worries his way through Paxson's pages may have a better understanding of what happened than those who have confined themselves to volumes with a less involved approach. Frederic L. Paxson, *American Democracy and the World War* (3 vols., Boston, 1936-1948).

fection of the powers of the presidency" will be "his most lasting contribution." [22] Discussing first of all Wilson's developing theory on the presidential office, Link is in agreement with Edward S. Corwin in asserting that "the revivification of the presidency by Theodore Roosevelt" had convinced Wilson by 1908, when his *Constitutional Government* was published, that strong leadership by the president was possible.[23] Coming to the presidency with a theory and administrative experience which equipped him for leadership, he took advantage of a favorable situation in Congress and in the country. By his oratory and public messages, by his use of the caucus system and the patronage, he demonstrated his understanding of practical politics. In the process he gave up some of his reform ideals, but he "won the larger goal of mastery over the Democratic forces in Congress and in the nation." Those who are still teaching Wilson as the idealist stubbornly refusing to compromise should read this chapter.

The techniques described in general by Link are well illustrated specifically in two clear-cut Wilson victories—the Underwood Tariff and the Federal Reserve Act, two successful legislative measures of the New Freedom. Most significant in the tariff controversy was the fact that the President's leadership had enabled the Democrats to honor past promises "precisely because he was determined, resourceful, and, above all, bold." Link arrives at a similar conclusion regarding the Federal Reserve Act, which he describes as "the greatest single piece of constructive legislation of the Wilson

22 Link puts this rather oddly: ". . . historians a century hence will probably rate his expansion and perfection of the powers of the presidency as his most lasting contribution." *Wilson: The New Freedom*, 145. Scholars already seem to be of that mind. See, for example, Wilfred E. Binkley, "The President and Congress," *Journal of Politics*, XI (February, 1949), 72; Edward S. Corwin, "The Presidency in Perspective," *ibid.*, 11-12; Corwin, "Woodrow Wilson and the Presidency," *Virginia Law Review* (Charlottesville), XLII (October, 1956), 761-83; Arthur W. MacMahon, "Woodrow Wilson as Legislative Leader and Administrator," *American Political Science Review* (Menasha, Wis.), L (September, 1956), 641-75; Henry A. Turner, "Woodrow Wilson: Exponent of Executive Leadership," *Western Political Quarterly* (Salt Lake City), IV (March, 1951), 97-115; Turner, "Woodrow Wilson as Administrator," *Public Administration Review* (Chicago), XVI (Autumn, 1956), 249-57; and Marshall E. Dimock, "Woodrow Wilson as a Legislative Leader," *Journal of Politics*, XIX (February, 1957), 3-19.

23 Link, *Wilson: The New Freedom*, 146; Corwin, "Woodrow Wilson and the Presidency," *Virginia Law Review*, XLII (October, 1956), 761-66. There seems to be good evidence that Cleveland's presidency played a part in Wilson's changing theory. Walter Lippmann, "Woodrow Wilson's Approach to Politics," *New Republic* (New York), December 5, 1955, pp. 15-18; Arthur P. Dudden to the *New Republic*, *ibid.*, December 26, 1955, p. 23.

era and one of the most important domestic Acts in the nation's history."

These integral elements of the New Freedom, however, were not enough for the "advanced progressives," a numerous but miscellaneous group of reformers who, according to Link, "shared a common faith in the efficacy of legislation and in the superiority of collective over individual remedies." Link acknowledges that Wilson shared some of the views of the "advanced progressives," but that on significant issues by late 1913, his differences with them were making the legislative path far from smooth. Among these was Wilson's implicit support for Negro segregation in government departments, and "the ambiguity of his relationship" to labor legislation, a woman-suffrage amendment, and federally financed rural credits.

Issues of this nature raised the critical problem of the extent to which Wilson was willing to accept the solutions of the New Nationalism. At first, for one reason or another, he was not at all willing to accept them. On antitrust legislation, however, Link argues that the President began to shift his position. Support increased for the establishment of a stronger trade commission than Wilson at first favored. Even Brandeis by late 1913 was advocating one. This helped to decide Wilson. He threw his prestige behind a potentially powerful commission, and it was authorized in September, 1914. In the meantime, according to Link, Wilson allowed the antitrust act to drift, and a rather innocuous bill, the Clayton Act was allowed to pass. To complicate further the interpretation of this part of the New Freedom, Wilson's appointees to the Federal Trade Commission and to the Federal Reserve Board were far more acceptable to the business world than to the "advanced progressives."[24]

Thus ends the second volume of the Wilson biography; but Link's approach to subsequent events may be found in his earlier, single-volume study, *Woodrow Wilson and the Progressive Era.* Here the key event is the election of 1916, since, as Link suggests, the period of appeasement of business ended as the election approached. Wilson was convinced that the only hope for "progressive" change lay with the Democratic party. The party could

[24] For a detailed legislative history of this episode, see Elston Roady, "Woodrow Wilson's Role as Party Leader: Trust Legislation," *Florida State University Studies,* No. 23 (1956), 1-27.

stay in power only by gaining Progressive votes. Thus under Wilson's leadership, concludes Link, "a Democratic Congress enacted the most sweeping and significant progressive legislation in the history of the country up to that time."

Link's interpretation of the Wilson administration means essentially that there are three phases of domestic legislation — the New Freedom, the New Nationalist phase, and World War I. This analysis, reminiscent of the concept of the first and second New Deals, explains much that has been hitherto passed over without explanation. Link's documentation is substantial, and it would be difficult to find major flaws in his argument. Like the concepts of the two New Deals, however, there is some danger in making the distinction too clear-cut, and perhaps also of misinterpreting motivation.

One question important to the interpretation, for example, is the extent to which Wilson was an advocate of "social justice" legislation by the time he was elected to the presidency. Although Link has been cautious on this point, he has perhaps not given Wilson quite his due. But new light has been thrown on the subject by the publication of *A Crossroads of Freedom: The 1912 Campaign Speeches of Woodrow Wilson*, which contains the full texts of most of Wilson's "major speeches, as well as sections of many minor ones," of the 1912 campaign. The editor, John W. Davidson, believes that the evidence indicates that Wilson had strong inclinations toward social justice legislation by the time of that campaign. Davidson shows that previously published compilations of the campaign speeches are inadequate.[25] Conscientious historians such as Link have made use of newspapers, but, as Davidson points out, newspaper texts were not satisfactory because Wilson usually spoke extemporaneously and the advance texts with which newspapers were furnished were thus frequently inaccurate. Fortunately for the historian, a nineteen-year-old shorthand expert, Charles L. Swem, accompanied Wilson and kept notes. The tracking down of these notes and the preparation of a new edition of the speeches from the various sources is a fascinating example of skillful editing.[26]

[25] Compare, for example, the speeches in Woodrow Wilson, *The New Freedom* (Garden City, 1913), and in Ray Stannard Baker and William E. Dodd (eds.), *The Public Papers of Woodrow Wilson* (6 vols., New York, 1925-1927), with the record of the same speeches in Davidson's volume.

[26] Davidson (ed.), *Crossroads of Freedom*, 4-7.

The speeches show that the primary issues of the campaign were those of the New Freedom — the tariff, the bank, and the anti-trust laws. At the same time the speeches make it equally clear that Wilson in the 1912 campaign did not deny the responsibility of the federal government to insure social justice to its citizens.[27] "No law," he said in his speech of acceptance, "that safeguards . . . [the lives of the working people], that makes their hours of labor rational and tolerable, that gives them freedom to act in their own interest, and that protects them where they can not protect themselves, can properly be regarded as class legislation or as anything but as a measure taken in the interest of the whole people." [28] Actually, in this campaign he showed agreement with many of Roosevelt's objectives. He argued strongly, however, that the Democrats were the ones to put them into effect.[29] It is possible, in short, that Wilson's conversion to the social justice of the New Nationalism was perhaps more evolutionary than Link implies.

A question may be raised about another point in interpretation, that of the influence of southern congressmen in the New Freedom phase of the Wilson program. Link divides this group "roughly into two factions." First of all were administration stalwarts, conservative in viewpoint, such as Oscar W. Underwood and Carter Glass; the other group consisted of radical agrarians who, according to Link, "helped to make Wilson an advanced progressive and helped to commit his administration to a broad program of welfare legislation." [30] Link makes it clear that the interest of these southern agrarians was in agrarian "reform" rather than in legislation related to industrialism or urbanism, but it is not clear what part the southerners played in the latter legislation.

Richard M. Abrams has helped to clarify the role of southerners by analyzing the part they played in several important legislative

27 John W. Davidson, "Woodrow Wilson and 1912," *Saturday Review of Literature* (New York), December 22, 1956, p. 39-40.

28 Davidson (ed.), *Crossroads of Freedom*, 30-31.

29 Davidson points out how confusion on this point resulted from inadequate reporting of one of Wilson's major speeches. The New York *Tribune* reported Wilson as having said that "the history of liberty is a history of limitation of governmental power, not the increase of it." Swem's notes of the speech show that prior to this statement Wilson had said that "in past decades the government had not been free to act in the interest of all of us," that it had had "special connections" from which it should be made free. Once free it would be in a position to "save civilization and humanity." *Ibid.*, 7-8, 124-25, 130.

30 Arthur S. Link, "The South and the 'New Freedom'," *American Scholar*, XX (Summer, 1951), 316.

battles.[31] He and Link are actually not far apart on most points, but he questions Link's use of the term "radical" or "radical faction." According to Abrams those southerners whom Link terms "radicals" were merely those who opposed Wilson at various points. They were not a coherent faction, and the "stable core was very small." Frequently they included conservatives and reactionaries. Most of the southern opposition to Wilson's policies was, in fact, conservative rather than radical. And with regard to the rural credits legislation, in which the southern agrarian was most concerned, Abrams concludes that Wilson's support did not result from any need of southern votes — he could always rely on them in a national election — but because of the need for mid-western votes.[32]

Finally, in spite of Link's careful evaluation of the situation in Congress, there is still a question as to whether he has paid sufficient attention to other circumstances which might have influenced Wilson's course of action. For example, might not Wilson's lack of energy in pushing certain social justice reforms in the early months have been a means of working with conservative committee chairmen? Moreover, the death of Mrs. Wilson on August 6, 1914, after several months' illness, was a major disaster for Wilson, as Link sensitively suggests. At the same time, the Mexican imbroglio and the European War were requiring more of his attention. Given such a combination of circumstances, it is perhaps surprising that Wilson won as much as he did.[33]

[31] Richard M. Abrams, "Woodrow Wilson and the Southern Congressmen, 1913-1916," *Journal of Southern History* (Lexington, Ky.), XXII (November, 1956), 417-37.

[32] Abrams is particularly persuasive in arguing that the "impulse" toward the New Nationalism came from Wilson and that southerners played a subordinate role. *Ibid.*, 436-37. For another account of this same question see Dewey W. Grantham, Jr., "Southern Congressional Leaders and the New Freedom, 1913-1917," *Journal of Southern History*, XIII (November, 1947), 439-59, and especially Grantham, "Hoke Smith and the New Freedom, 1913-1917," J. Carlyle Sitterson (ed.), *Studies in Southern History in Memory of Albert Ray Newsome* (*James Sprunt Studies in History and Political Science*, Vol. XXXIX: Chapel Hill, 1957), 139-51. Much confusion can result from the use of terms. In *American Epoch*, Link, more successfully than most textbook writers, explains the difficulties in defining the Progressive movement. His own treatment of the Wilson administration, however, well illustrates this difficulty. He cites Wilson's implicit support of segregation in government departments and his opposition to immigration restriction to indicate the administration's lack of sympathy for "social justice" legislation. Yet there was certainly less than unanimity among "progressives" in favor of integration; and as for immigration restriction, Wilson made a good case for his veto's being a "progressive" act.

[33] For other complicating factors, see Abrams, "Wilson and the Southern Congress-

After the war broke out in Europe, Wilson's attention was understandably attracted away from domestic affairs. Foreign affairs did not shunt aside all legislative proposals for domestic change, but inevitably the increasing likelihood of being drawn into the war channeled the administration's interests more toward world affairs. Traditionally, too, the role of Wilson in foreign affairs and as a war president seems to have held the greater interest of the public and attracted the larger number of scholars. Before World War II numerous monographs were published on Wilson's foreign policy, of which those of the most general interest were probably Charles Seymour's *American Diplomacy during the World War* (Baltimore, 1934) and Harley Notter's *The Origins of the Foreign Policy of Woodrow Wilson* (Baltimore, 1937). During the Second World War there appeared several studies of special interest, among the most important of which were Thomas A. Bailey's *Woodrow Wilson and the Lost Peace* (New York, 1944) and *Woodrow Wilson and the Great Betrayal* (New York, 1945), and the excellent brief biography by Herbert C. F. Bell, *Woodrow Wilson and the People* (Garden City, 1945).

Link's *Wilson: The New Freedom* is itself not entirely concerned with domestic affairs. It has excellent, highly critical chapters on "New Freedom Diplomacy, 1913-1914," Latin American policy, and the Mexican crisis; and it describes the Bryan-Wilson policies as "missionary diplomacy" which assumed that "they knew better how to promote the peace and well-being of other countries than did the leaders of those countries themselves." The record to the fall of 1914 "was marked more by contradiction and failure than by consistency and success." This failure, according to Link, was the result of inexperience on the part of Wilson, an insufficient staff of trained bureaucrats, Wilson's lack of confidence in traditional channels and techniques of diplomacy, and most especially the naïveté of the assumptions that moral force and reason would lead to an "orderly and righteous international society." [34]

men," *Journal of Southern History*, XXII (November, 1956), 429; Dewey W. Grantham, Jr., "Oscar W. Underwood and Henry D. Clayton: Leaders in Enacting the Tariff and Trust Legislation of the New Freedom," *Alabama Historical Quarterly* (Montgomery), VII (Winter, 1945), 594; Marshall E. Dimock, "Wilson, the Domestic Reformer," *Virginia Quarterly Review*, XXXII (Autumn, 1956), 557-58. In a later article Dimock takes direct issue with Link. See his "Woodrow Wilson as a Legislative Leader," *Journal of Politics*, XIX (February, 1957), 7-8. The Mexican problem is excellently covered by Link, but the reader of *Wilson: The New Freedom* will find little more than that the European War has broken out.

34 William Diamond characterizes "The New Freedom in Foreign Policy," in

Link is similarly critical of those phases of Wilson's Far Eastern activities which fall within the chronological limits of his published volumes.[35] This is the area of Wilson's foreign policy, however, which has probably been most carefully explored by other historians in the decade from 1947 to 1957, and their appraisals differ rather markedly. For example, Roy Watson Curry's *Woodrow Wilson and Far Eastern Policy, 1913-1921* (New York, 1957), the only one of half a dozen volumes which covers the entire Far Eastern question during both administrations, appears to approach foreign policy with Wilson's predispositions. Tien-yi Li, in *Woodrow Wilson's China Policy, 1913-1917* (New York, 1952), points out how Wilson by the time he reached the presidency envisaged the possibility of fulfilling a democratic and Christian mission in China. He was not, however, unrealistic in the development of his policy. He saw the need for a long process of education and the development of internal unity before a democratic China could appear. He stressed practical matters — stability, prevention of foreign intervention — in arriving at specific decisions. Yet on other matters he was quite impractical. On the question of the Consortium, for example, Tien-yi Li concludes that Wilson's repudiation of dollar diplomacy was "morally faultless" and succeeded in winning the heartfelt gratitude of the Chinese; but that it was a "precipitate decision" based upon "imperfect knowledge" and in the long run harmful to the Chinese. When Wilson became worried about the growing predominance of Japan, he was unprepared to do more than give moral support to China.[36]

A complicated question which injects itself into a consideration of Far Eastern policy at this point was the worsening of relations

similar terms but emphasizes another factor, that of Wilson's aggressive determination to develop foreign trade. *Economic Thought of Woodrow Wilson*, 131-61. William Appleman Williams apparently believes that this is a decisive factor. "Reflections on the Historiography of American Entry into World War II," *Oregon Historical Quarterly*, LVII (September, 1956), 274-79. A sympathetic analysis of Wilson's foreign policy is Herbert C. F. Bell, "The Genesis of Wilson's Foreign Policy," *Thought* (New York), XXIII (December, 1948), 657-64. Somewhat more critical is Harold P. Ford, "Centennial Thoughts about Wilsonian Diplomacy," *Christianity and Crisis* (New York), XVI (December 24, 1956), 176-78.

[35] See especially *Wilson: The New Freedom*, 283-304, and *Woodrow Wilson and the Progressive Era*, 82-90.

[36] Tien-yi Li, *Woodrow Wilson's China Policy*, 82, 203-205, 209-13. Cf. Curry, *Wilson's Far Eastern Policy*, 19-27; and especially, for the aggressiveness of the "American group" in the Consortium, Charles Vevier, "The Open Door: An Idea in Action, 1906-1913," *Pacific Historical Review* (Berkeley), XXIV (February, 1955), 49-62.

with Japan because of the discriminatory land laws being considered in the state of California.[37] To Link the passage of legislation in 1913 restricting alien ownership of land represented a major "failure of New Freedom diplomacy." But Link's treatment here contains some inaccuracies and his usually incisive arguments are weaker and less convincing than Thomas A. Bailey's analysis of the subject. Bailey admits that Wilson failed in his avowed object of preventing passage of a discriminatory measure, but points out that "in diplomacy the object sought is not always the object avowed." Wilson "had little hope of preventing [discriminatory] legislation," according to Bailey, but hoped to relieve the tension "by such an open gesture of friendliness as the sending of Bryan to California." This, Bailey concludes, was successful and "did more than any other one thing to avert a serious crisis."[38]

The monographs which deal with the later phases of Wilsonian Far Eastern policy are in general favorably inclined toward the President's course of action. Roy W. Curry, whose well-documented volume ties together prewar and wartime policy, sets the tone for such appraisals. Curry agrees with those who stress the idealism of Wilson's aims in the Far East, but at the same time he insists that the question which Wilson posed about each individual problem was: "What can be done?"[39] On the Shantung question Curry's general view of Wilson's action is amplified by Russell H. Fifield in *Woodrow Wilson and the Far East: The Diplomacy of the Shantung Question* (New York, 1952). Fifield discusses the Twenty-one Demands and the Second Consortium as background for the climax of his book in the negotiation over the Shantung issue at Versailles.[40] Throughout he is sympathetically critical of Wil-

[37] See Curry, *Wilson's Far Eastern Policy*, 43-63, for a narrative indicating the numerous facets to this story.

[38] Thomas A. Bailey, "California, Japan, and the Alien Land Legislation of 1913," *Pacific Historical Review*, I (February, 1932), 55-56. Link does not cite Bailey in either footnotes or bibliography.

[39] See also Roy W. Curry, "Woodrow Wilson and Philippine Policy," *Mississippi Valley Historical Review*, XLI (December, 1954), 435-52. Link and Curry agree that during these years Wilson was not fundamentally opposed to Japan's economic aims on the mainland and believed that Japan as an "expanding nation must be permitted the wherewithal for her national development." Curry, *Wilson and Far Eastern Policy*, 312-13, 315, 318-19; Link, *Woodrow Wilson and the Progressive Era*, 90. This, of course, did not imply a disposition to undermine the Open Door or the political integrity of China. These conclusions are approximately the same as Tien-yi Li, *Wilson's China Policy*, 128-29, 210-11.

[40] Fifield's treatment of the New Consortium of 1918 is somewhat foreshortened, and its documentation leaves something to be desired. Curry, on the other hand, has

son's position. Wilson, according to Fifield, was fully aware of the complexities of the Shantung issue, and hoped, as did his advisers, to support China. But he was faced with the fact that Lloyd George and Clemenceau considered themselves bound by the secret treaties, and also with Japan's threat not to join the League. Unwell and forced to make numerous decisions on complex subjects, he took too much on himself. He compromised with Japan, therefore, believing that Japan was not bluffing and that her membership was essential to make the League a universal organization. The League, he assumed, could correct the world's injustices to China.[41] Fifield, too, concludes that the Japanese were not bluffing, but he believes that Wilson exaggerated the importance of their being in the League, "was unduly optimistic" about the usefulness of that organization, and did not adequately explain the settlement to those most interested.[42]

The story of another important episode, the Siberian intervention, is told briefly by Fifield and Curry, but can be supplemented by several other monographs. Of these the most useful for Wilson's role is Betty Miller Unterberger's *America's Siberian Expedition, 1918-1920: A Study of National Policy* (Durham, 1956).[43] Mrs. Unterberger's narrative is clear, concise, and well documented. She believes that the actual reason for American intervention was Wilson's desire to restrain Japan and "preserve the open door in Siberia and North Manchuria." She insists that his objective was not anti-Bolshevik, but that he could not keep troops there without aiding Kolchak and the anti-Bolshevik forces, and when Wilson became ill "underlings in the State Department," who favored Kolchak, assumed control. According to Mrs. Unterberger, America's participation provided a "moderating influence" upon the

exploited Secretary Lansing's desk diary and an important memorandum by Breckinridge Long. These documents would not change but would have thrown more light on some of Fifield's conclusions. Curry, *Wilson and Far Eastern Policy*, 191-95; cf. Fifield, *Wilson and the Far East*, 48, 96-97.

41 Fifield, *Wilson and the Far East*, 222-29, 240-41, 288-92.

42 *Ibid.*, 292-93, 308, 316, 333. See also Russell H. Fifield, "Japanese Policy toward the Shantung Question at the Paris Peace Conference," *Journal of Modern History* (Chicago), XXIII (September, 1951), 265-72. Curry essentially agrees with Fifield, and argues that China did receive some specific concessions. *Wilson and Far Eastern Policy*, 282-83.

43 See also Betty Miller Unterberger, "President Wilson and the Decision to Send American Troops to Siberia," *Pacific Historical Review*, XXIV (February, 1955), 63-74, and "The Russian Revolution and Wilson's Far-Eastern Policy," *Russian Review* (New York), XVI, No. 2 (April, 1957), 35-46.

Allies and restrained somewhat Japanese expansion in the Far East.[44]

In view of the growing interest of the United States in the Far East in the decade following World War II, it is quite understandable why historians of the time have explored so intensively the development of American Far Eastern policy during the First World War. It is less clear why they have not emphasized more the European phases of that struggle. Perhaps the availability of sources on World War II and the increasing prestige of "recent" history persuaded most historians to concentrate on the later period. Whatever the reason, since Richard W. Leopold's important bibliographical article of 1950 on "American Intervention, 1917" comparatively few monographs have appeared on the problem of American entry into World War I, or on American diplomacy during the war. Leopold mentioned a number of "untilled areas," such as the global problem, public opinion, the role of Congress, the need for biographical studies, and numerous other critical topics, and in some of these additional work has been done.[45]

44 Unterberger, *America's Siberian Intervention*, 230-34. See also Curry, *Wilson and Far Eastern Policy*, 213-48; Pauline Tompkins, *American-Russian Relations in the Far East* (New York, 1949); John A. White, *The Siberian Intervention* (Princeton, 1950). A broad survey of the Siberian intervention into March, 1918, appears in George F. Kennan, *Russia Leaves the War* (Princeton, 1956), 275-329, 458-85. William Appleman Williams argues that economic expansionism and anti-Bolshevism were more important than would appear in Mrs. Unterberger's study. See his review in *Mississippi Valley Historical Review*, XLIII (March, 1957), 700-702. See also William A. Williams, *American-Russian Relations, 1781-1947* (New York, 1952), 116-18, 158-59, 163.

45 Leopold, "The Problem of American Intervention, 1917," *World Politics*, II (April, 1950), 423. Thomas A. Bailey, *A Diplomatic History of the American People* (5th ed., New York, 1955), is especially useful because of the excellence of its bibliographies. Among the biographies which have thrown light on this problem, Frank Freidel, *Franklin D. Roosevelt: The Apprenticeship* (Boston, 1952), is useful for Roosevelt's political connections with Wilson, the preparedness agitation, and wartime mobilization. It is particularly interesting if read with Jonathan Daniels, *The End of Innocence* (Philadelphia, 1954), which gives the point of view of Secretary of the Navy Josephus Daniels on many of the same questions. Belle C. and Fola La Follette, *Robert M. La Follette* (2 vols., New York, 1953), contains primary source material on certain aspects of Wilson's domestic policy as well as the neutrality, wartime, and postwar foreign policies of the Wilson administration. Richard W. Leopold, *Elihu Root and the Conservative Tradition* (Boston, 1954), has two excellent chapters on the relationships between Wilson and Root during the war and on the League question. Lee Meriwether, *Jim Reed, "Senatorial Immortal": A Biography* (Webster Groves, Mo., 1948), is an unscholarly, highly partisan biography of this anti-Wilson Democrat. A brief chapter on Wilson's wartime powers is in Clinton Rossiter, *Constitutional Dictatorship: Crisis Government in the Modern Democracies* (Princeton, 1948), 241-54. Several studies of public opinion in which Wilson is featured have been made: for example, John C. Crighton, *Missouri and*

Edward H. Buehrig and Arthur Link are perhaps the two scholars who, during the last decade, have developed the subject of Wilsonian neutrality in most detail.[46] Link's *Woodrow Wilson and the Progressive Era* contains an excellent treatment of why the United States became involved in World War I. It touches upon many of those questions that Leopold suggested as "untilled areas": sectional and hyphenate blocs, advocates of preparedness and pacifists, and especially the role of Congress. He is particularly successful in clarifying points which other writers have left obscure.

Link concludes that the Wilsonian neutrality was marked both by major success and by immaturity and confusion. To the end, according to Link, Wilson hoped that the United States would not have to fight. Thus his fears caused him to avoid a showdown with Germany on the submarine question. This angered Britain, and by late 1916 relations became worse with her than with Germany.[47] Worried about this dilemma, he worked in vain for a negotiated peace. Link insists, however, that even after diplomatic relations with Germany were severed, Wilson had not given up hope for peace until the Zimmermann note and the sinking of American ships forced the decision.[48] This is not to say that Link endorses Wilson's

the World War, 1914-1917: A Study in Public Opinion (*University of Missouri Studies*, Vol. XXI, No. 3: Columbia, 1947); Cedric C. Cummins, *Indiana Public Opinion and the World War, 1914-1917* (Indianapolis, 1945); Arthur S. Link "The Middle West and the Coming of World War I," *Ohio State Archaeological and Historical Quarterly* (Columbus), LXII (April, 1953), 109-21.

[46] Edward H. Buehrig, "Wilson's Neutrality Re-Examined," *World Politics*, III (October, 1950), 1-19; *Woodrow Wilson and the Balance of Power* (Bloomington, Ind., 1955); "Idealism and Statecraft," *Confluence*, V (Autumn, 1956), 252-63. Another book which points to the importance of the press in confusing relationships between England and the United States is Armin Rappaport, *The British Press and Wilsonian Neutrality* (Stanford, 1951). The view of one who was Washington correspondent of the London *Times*, secretary of the British War Mission, and representative of the Ministry of Information in Washington is Arthur Willert, *The Road to Safety: A Study in Anglo-American Relations* (New York, 1953).

[47] See also Rappaport, *The British Press and Wilsonian Neutrality*, 94-127. A persuasive article is Arthur S. Link, "The Cotton Crisis, the South, and Anglo-American Diplomacy, 1914-1915," in Sitterson (ed.), *Studies in Southern History*, 122-38.

[48] Link provides a succinct summary of this in *American Epoch*, 195-96. For the analysis of Link's treatment of Wilsonian neutrality, I have drawn heavily from my "American Political History, 1900-1920," *South Atlantic Quarterly*, LIV (January, 1955), 112-13. See also Samuel R. Spencer, Jr., *Decision for War, 1917: The Laconia Sinking and the Zimmermann Telegram as Key Factors* (Rindge, N. H., 1953). Daniel M. Smith, "Robert Lansing and the Formulation of American Neutrality Policies, 1914-1915," *Mississippi Valley Historical Review*, XLIII (June, 1956), 59-81, is an important study which takes issue with Link at several points. Smith presents a careful argument and persuasive documentation for the thesis that Lansing's role in shaping American foreign policy was more important than generally granted. Es-

policies. Apparently he feels that the United States was justified in entering the war because of the threat to the balance of power posed by a German victory, but that Wilson refused to talk in these terms, and that the reasons he gave "had no realistic meaning." [49]

Edward Buehrig in his various writings on Wilsonian neutrality has attempted to relate the United States involvement in World War I to the historical movements which resulted in the rise of new powers. World War I was one of the landmarks because it "signalized the decline of Europe from its former pre-eminence in world politics." It was the "first major challenge to the pattern of 19th century American policy," and, according to Buehrig — who perhaps underemphasizes Theodore Roosevelt — Wilson's was the first important attempt to adjust to the twentieth-century situation. The war thrust the European problem to the fore, but American precedents "offered only deceptive guidance" for the development of a policy. In these circumstances, Buehrig contends, Wilson was not dogmatic, but developed a policy of sustaining Britain for reasons of security. He was realistic, moreover, in feeling that "stability is to be found in an equilibrium of forces." This belief, according to Buehrig, led Wilson to the movement for a negotiated peace, and this in turn to the endorsement of the League, which "was to be a device for injecting American influence into international politics." Buehrig believes, however, that Wilson succumbed to Lansing in presenting the war in terms of a struggle between autocracy and democracy; and that he was led to do this not only because of his own "temperamental leanings" but also because of his sensitivity to American public opinion so responsive to "expressions of hope, pride, and sentiment." [50]

pecially does he show that Lansing was quite sensitive to the possibilities of a hostile coalition among Germany, Japan, and Russia if Germany should win the war.

49 Link, *American Epoch*, 175. According to Smith, Lansing thought in these terms and "successfully presented to the idealistic Wilson courses of action already clothed in moralistic and ideological terms." Smith, "Lansing and American Neutrality Policies," *Mississippi Valley Historical Review*, XLIII (June, 1956), 81. Link's position is essentially that of George F. Kennan, *American Diplomacy, 1900-1950* (Mentor edition, Chicago, 1951), 64-65, 72. Important because of its place in a consideration of the moralistic-legalistic bases of twentieth-century American foreign policy is Robert E. Osgood, *Ideals and Self-Interest in America's Foreign Relations* (Chicago, 1953). Osgood devotes one third of his book to Wilsonian foreign policy.

50 Buehrig develops these views in detail in his *Wilson and the Balance of Power*, but a convenient summary is found in "Idealism and Statecraft," *Confluence*, V (Autumn, 1956), 252-63. Robert E. Osgood takes issue with the idea that Wilson was inspired by "balance of power" notions. Wilson's idea, according to Osgood, was "a community of power, built upon universal obligations, as the indispensable alterna-

It is apparent from the variety of interpretations offered that scholars differ as to the extent to which a moralistic-legalistic approach characterized Wilsonian foreign policy, and also the extent to which ignorance of diplomatic techniques and conditions in other countries complicated solutions to problems in foreign policy. These differences are equally apparent in writings on Wilsonian policy toward various European countries during the war. One of the comparatively few scholarly monographs on Wilsonian diplomacy during World War I written in the decade after the Second World War is by George F. Kennan, who, with Hans Morgenthau, has been primarily responsible for raising questions concerning the moralistic-legalistic approach. In *Russia Leaves the War*, however, Kennan places major stress on Wilson's lack of understanding of Russian affairs together with his failure to make use of normal diplomatic channels.[51] On the other hand, John L. Snell, in a series of significant articles on Wilson's propaganda campaign in Germany during the war, makes it clear that he does not view Wilson as an "ivory tower idealist," and indicates that, on German problems, Wilson does not seem to have been badly advised.[52] Moreover, Snell suggests that although "idealistic internationalism" was at the root of Wilson's appeals, they were realistically designed as psychological warfare. They failed in some of their objectives. Yet the appeals, because of their idealistic internationalism, inspired the Allied peoples to sacrifice, loosened the ties binding Germany together, and perhaps made the German revolution liberal and "Western in its orientation."[53]

tive to the outmoded system of the balance of power." The stress was upon law and justice rather than power politics. This was not surprising; in fact Osgood points out, "it would have been truly implausible for Wilson to have demonstrated a political sophistication which — if one excludes the early years of independence — has only appeared in the United States on a significant scale during the past decade or two." Osgood, "Woodrow Wilson, Collective Security, and the Lessons of History," *ibid.*, V (Winter, 1957), 341-54.

51 Kennan, *Russia Leaves the War*, 28 ff, 140 ff, 149 ff, 190, 260-64.

52 "German Socialist Reaction to Wilsonian Diplomacy: From Neutrality to Belligerency," *Journal of Central European Affairs* (Boulder, Colo.), IX (April, 1949), 61-79; "Wilson's Peace Program and German Socialism, January-March, 1918," *Mississippi Valley Historical Review*, XXXVIII (September, 1951), 187-214; "Benedict XV, Wilson, Michaelis, and German Socialism," *Catholic Historical Review* (Washington), XXXVII (July, 1951), 151-78; "Wilsonian Rhetoric Goes to War," *Historian* (Bloomington, Ind.), XIV (Spring, 1952), 191-208.

53 Snell adds the interesting observation: "Wilson's words by no means won the war alone, but they hastened the victory which guaranteed an Allied interpretation of their semantics. That this is an inescapable result of victorious ideological warfare

The same differences that distinguish Kennan's and Snell's interpretations of Wilson's ability and understanding in foreign relations are apparent in several of the writings on central Europe. Louis L. Gerson, for example, vigorously argues that Wilson's policies indicated that he did not know much about Poland, but desired to build "a brave new world" in which Poland would share. After 1916, however, his ardor cooled as political pressures from Polish-Americans mounted, but "under the pressure of his pro-Polish advisers he played out his role as patron saint of Poland."[54]

In the case of the dissolution of Austria-Hungary, on the other hand, American policy, expressed most often as a policy of "self-determination," seems to have been formulated for highly realistic reasons. Victor S. Mamatey has concluded that the basic factor in blotting out Austria-Hungary was the fear that Germany would continue to control that empire after the war. The goal of self-determination for the peoples of Austria-Hungary was thus primarily a war measure.[55] Max Beloff and Robert H. Ferrell, who agree with these conclusions, go even further in endorsing Wilson's position. Beloff takes direct issue with those who have complained that Wilson destroyed a great area of "free political and economic cooperation" when the Hapsburg empire was broken up, and Ferrell concludes that Wilson "neither invented national self-determination nor advocated it beyond the bounds of expediency."[56]

No additional material of a basic nature on the subject of Wilson at Versailles or on his subsequent foreign policy has appeared in any special monographic studies published in the decade after World War II.[57] Such studies may be forthcoming, for it is apparent from the review of Wilson literature of the decade that his policies, both domestic and foreign, continue to attract scholars in large numbers.

many have failed to learn." *Mississippi Valley Historical Review*, XXXVIII (September, 1951), 214.

54 Louis L. Gerson, *Woodrow Wilson and the Rebirth of Poland, 1914-1920: A Study in the Influence on American Policy of Minority Groups of Foreign Origin* (New Haven, 1953).

55 Victor S. Mamatey, "The United States and the Dissolution of Austria-Hungary," *Journal of Central European Affairs*, X (October, 1950), 255-70. In the Adriatic question, Mamatey concludes that Wilson's aims were "sound and reasonable" but his diplomatic method unrealistic. "The United States and the Origins of the Adriatic Question (1918)," *Florida State University Studies*, No. 4 (1951), 45-60.

56 Max Beloff, "Self-Determination Reconsidered," *Confluence*, V (Autumn, 1956), 195-203. Ferrell is particularly persuasive, "Woodrow Wilson: Man and Statesman," *Review of Politics*, XVIII (April, 1956), 138 ff.

57 One should note here Paul Joseph Mantoux, *Les Délibérations du Conseil des Quatres (24 mars — 28 juin 1919): Notes de l'Officier Interprete* (2 vols., Paris, 1955).

Even those monographs which had the appearance of exhausting a particular feature of Wilson's policy or administration did not preclude later research and interpretation. A similar observation may be made in the larger field of Wilson biography. This had been fairly well tilled ground prior to 1947 when the publication of Link's multi-volume study was begun. The earlier biographies, however, have not dulled interest in Link's work. Nor has his work closed the field to other biographical studies. Three new biographies, published during the centennial year, are alike in presenting a relatively brief, one-volume appraisal of Wilson, and thus, in form at least, are not in competition with Link's lengthier and more detailed work.[58] In addition, these biographies add to the study of Wilson another dimension which had not been stressed in other writings. This is the approach of the psychologist. To be sure, writers at least since the time of William Allen White have seen in Wilson's personality an intriguing subject and have used the psychological approach to some extent.[59] It may be that an essay by Richard Hofstadter, first published in 1948, suggested the course which writers inspired with a new interest in the behavioral sciences might follow. Hofstadter referred to the compulsions that inspired Wilson, and stated that "a deep sense of isolation, a cramped capacity for personal communication, tortured and stunted his emotional life." [60]

Both John M. Blum and John A. Garraty, in their recent writing, have developed an unusual interest in the use of psychology in historical interpretation. Indeed, both have strongly implied that the historian who does not make use of psychological concepts in interpreting his subject has failed to meet the obligations of scholarly research.[61] Blum's life of Wilson is well proportioned with a sur-

[58] John M. Blum, *Woodrow Wilson and the Politics of Morality* (Boston, 1956) in the "Library of American Biography"; John A. Garraty, *Woodrow Wilson* (New York, 1956) in "Great Lives in Brief" Series; Alexander L. and Juliette L. George, *Woodrow Wilson and Colonel House: A Personality Study* (New York, 1956). A penetrating, sympathetic earlier biography of Wilson, included in the British "Teach Yourself History Library," is E. M. Hugh-Jones, *Woodrow Wilson and American Liberalism* (New York, 1948).

[59] William Allen White, *Woodrow Wilson: The Man, His Times and His Task* (Boston, 1924).

[60] Richard Hofstadter, *The American Political Tradition and the Men Who Made It* (New York, 1948 [Vintage edition, 1954]), 238-82. A hostile evaluation of Wilson using this approach is Edward Ryerson, "The Leadership of Woodrow Wilson," *American Scholar*, XXI (July, 1952), 301-308.

[61] See Blum's review of *Red Scare: A Study of National Hysteria, 1919-1920*, by Robert K. Murray, in *Mississippi Valley Historical Review*, XLII (June, 1955),

prising amount of detail in less than two hundred pages. His interpretation parallels Link in descriptions of the evolution of Wilson's thought and the domestic legislation of his presidency. The conclusion he reaches on Wilson's domestic program is that it was a "magnificent performance," yet "distinguished by its scope rather than its originality," dependent to a considerable extent upon "a political and intellectual foundation" laid by others, and satisfied the yearnings of the past rather than "the needs of the future." Blum extends his interpretation beyond the Wilson era and concludes, rather unnecessarily, that certain of the administrative practices of the New Freedom phase were "in the 1920's to become the pattern of normalcy," and that they contained "something of the spirit that was, years later, to lead many of its apostles to the Liberty League."

In Blum's treatment of Wilson's foreign policy stress is upon the thesis implied in the title of his book — the politics of morality. The meaning of the thesis is clear: Wilson believed that law governs relations among nations, and that moral principle required obedience to the law. Blum, with some reason, differs fundamentally from those who see Wilson motivated by a calculating intent to provide for American security. But Blum seems to overstress the role of morality, certainly if one considers the extent to which Wilson came to grips with the realities of politics in the situation in the Far East and elsewhere.

Blum's chapter on the war is one of the best of the book, and the chapters on the peace treaties are skillful summaries. At the same time, they contain more than the normal number of generalizations which are at times suggestive and thought-provoking, but at other times are open to serious question. Wilson's dilemma, for example, is well described: he was "at once the keeper of a rigid conscience and the creature of a political system that worked only when he bent that conscience to conform to the narrow set of public tolerances." Yet what do those sentences mean which read: "Wilson's was a nineteenth-century intelligence, obsolescing at a rapid rate, and

144-45; and Garraty's review of Link's *Wilson: The New Freedom*, in *Journal of Southern History*, XXIII (May, 1957), 260-62. Blum's earlier researches uniquely prepared him for writing a biography of Wilson. As associate editor of the eight-volume *The Letters of Theodore Roosevelt* (Cambridge, 1951-1954), he contributed a series of brilliant, interpretative essays, later incorporated into his *The Republican Roosevelt* (Cambridge, 1954). Equally important is his biography of Wilson's secretary, *Joe Tumulty and the Wilson Era* (Boston, 1951). See also John M. Blum "Woodrow Wilson: A Study in Intellect," *Confluence*, V (Winter, 1957), 367-75.

this obsolescence the war accelerated. Conscience and intellect, stern, bright, intrinsically even dear, stood still while the race of time transfigured the world they understood"? There is enough of this sort of writing to suggest that Blum has fallen into the trap of letting a naturally colorful style run away, to the point where it at times becomes purple and at other times leads to generalizations which can confuse the unwary reader. Perhaps Blum's interest in probing Wilson's personality encourages the tendency to generalization and leads him to use language like the following: Wilson "had to maintain some electric identity between his intuitive self and the elusive consensus that is the resultant of conflicting political attitudes."[62]

John A. Garraty, like Blum, was already well grounded in the general field when he came to a study of Wilson.[63] His biography is less balanced than that of Blum's since the amount of space devoted to the treaty and the League struggle is out of proportion to that devoted to the domestic problems of the first administration and economic mobilization during the second. At the same time, Garraty makes up for this in part by a gift for condensation. He has accepted in general the Link version of the change in Wilson's program from that of the New Freedom to the New Nationalism, but is justifiably more cautious in ascribing this to political opportunism. He differs with Blum at several points in detail, but they agree in the general outline of their appraisals.[64] For example, both agree that Wilson could have had a good treaty with reservations if his tactics had been more skillful; both treat his physical collapse sympathetically as a partial explanation for his political failure; and both mention his aspirations for a third term.[65]

[62] Blum, *Woodrow Wilson and the Politics of Morality*, 43, 157, 158.

[63] John A. Garraty, *Henry Cabot Lodge: A Biography* (New York, 1953), has five perceptive chapters on the relationship between Lodge and Wilson. Garraty has devoted some time to post-doctoral study of psychology, and has given considerable thought to biographical writing. See for example his "How to Write a Biography," *South Atlantic Quarterly*, LV (January, 1956), 73-86.

[64] Blum, for example, places more emphasis on the election of 1918. Undoubtedly he has profited from his own study of Tumulty on this question. See for example *Joe Tumulty and the Wilson Era*, 157-68, and especially Seward W. Livermore, "The Sectional Issue in the 1918 Congressional Elections," *Mississippi Valley Historical Review*, XXXV (June, 1948), 29-60, which de-emphasizes Wilson's appeal for a Democratic Congress.

[65] A persuasive article is Perry Laukhuff, "The Price of Woodrow Wilson's Illness," *Virginia Quarterly Review*, XXXII (Autumn, 1956), 598-610. See also Gregg Phifer, "Woodrow Wilson's Swing around the Circle in Defense of His League," *Florida State University Studies*, No. 23 (1956), 65-102. Lee Meriwether describes

In any short biography of an influential figure such as Wilson, obvious dangers exist because of the need for generalizing. Garraty overcomes these dangers remarkably well. His literary style, moreover, is clear, simple, and direct. At no point is it overwritten. It has psychological overtones, but there is no jargon, and conclusions are judiciously presented. In a very recent article Garraty demonstrates more clearly than in the biography his interest in exploring personality. Writing in the *South Atlantic Quarterly*, he makes the "highly tentative" suggestion that some of Wilson's difficulties "lie in his childhood experiences, possibly in the fantastically high standards set for him by his father." This training, concludes Garraty, "may well have left him with a sense of inadequacy, irrational, but deep-seated."[66]

This tentative thesis is significant, particularly in view of a comparable approach developed at length by Alexander L. and Juliette George in their study of Woodrow Wilson and Colonel House. These authors have attempted "a developmental analysis" of Wilson, drawing upon their specialized knowledge of personality development. They believe in general that "a variety of early childhood experiences" and experiences well into the adult years shape personality. The "developmental biographer" strives to study "chronologically and cross-sectionally" the "interaction between personality and situational factors"; he studies intensively "important episodes" for which "the individual's previous life history is regarded as a set of learning experiences which have structured predispositions operative in the present situation."[67]

With regard to "the dynamics of Wilson's political behavior," the Georges' "basic hypothesis . . . is that power was for him a compensatory value, a means of restoring the self-esteem damaged in childhood." He craved power, but must at the same time feel virtuous. Consequently his "constructive strategy" was to support

how he organized the "campaign of education" against the League and the opposition to Wilson's "swing around the circle." *Jim Reed, Senatorial Immortal*, 67-69, 77-79. A careful analysis of the positions of the twenty-two southern senators during the League fight is in Dewey W. Grantham, Jr., "The Southern Senators and the League of Nations, 1918-1920," *North Carolina Historical Review* (Raleigh), XXVI (April, 1949), 187-205. See also Wesley M. Bagby, "Woodrow Wilson, a Third Term, and the Solemn Referendum," *American Historical Review* (New York), LX (April, 1955), 567-75. David H. Stratton, "President Wilson's Smelling Committee," *Colorado Quarterly* (Boulder), V (Autumn, 1956), 164-84, uses the Albert B. Fall Papers.

[66] John A. Garraty, "Woodrow Wilson: A Study in Personality," *South Atlantic Quarterly*, LVI (April, 1957), 176-85.

[67] George and George, *Woodrow Wilson and Colonel House*, 317-19.

only those popular reform projects which seemed possible of accomplishment. His "constructive strategy proved unavailing," however, because of his "demand for *immediate* compliance," his "insatiable" and "compulsive" ambition, and his inability to resolve his "conflicts with the legislature before disruptive anxieties, which opposition to his will generated, came into full play."[68] House's relationship to Wilson helps to demonstrate the validity of this hypothesis because, "being an astute psychologist" according to the authors, he had at least partially diagnosed the complexity of Wilson's personality and saw how he could "exert political influence" in collaboration with Wilson.[69]

The Georges, fortunately for some readers, have restricted their technical vocabulary largely to a research note at the end of the book. Moreover, at several points they acknowledge that "personality factors" alone are not enough to explain "any man's political action," and that their interpretation "will be more credible" to some than to others. They have used extensive printed sources, particularly the writings of Link and Bailey, together with some manuscript collections, especially those of Colonel House and Ray Stannard Baker. The bibliographical note states that "the study was almost complete when permission to examine the Wilson Papers was granted."[70] They have made a major contribution in interpreting the relationship between House and Wilson, an interpretation based largely upon unpublished portions of the House diary. At the same time the fact that the book is so much more concerned with Wilson than with House raises a question as to whether the title is an accurate one.

A more important question in appraising the Georges' work is the extent to which it contributes to an understanding of Wilson. This depends upon the acceptability of their basic thesis, which, put briefly, is that Wilson's "compulsive" search for power resulted from a sense of inadequacy produced by a stern and ambitious father. The Georges go further than this. They contend that his father bred in Wilson hostile feelings. Under such circumstances, continue the Georges, a child may be "so terrified that he dares not even recognize the existence of such feelings within himself but, rather, seeks constantly to persuade himself of a surpassing devo-

68 *Ibid.*, 114-23, 320-21.

69 *Ibid.*, 123-32.

70 Consequently they have been used only "sparingly." *Ibid.*, xvii, 12, 114, 323.

tion to his parent. This seems to have been Wilson's method of handling the anxiety engendered by his hostile feelings." It would appear that the weakness of the hypothesis is the difficulty of proving the existence of lasting anxieties and particularly of hostility toward the father. There is certainly as much evidence to show devotion as hostility, a fact which the Georges readily admit.[71] Moreover, a danger which the Georges have not entirely avoided is that of seeing in the hypothesis an explanation for actions which conceivably could be explained by a combination of such factors as a religiously inspired sense of duty, a politician's sensitivity to a developing situation, or the effect of overwork and deteriorating health, climaxed by a cerebral thrombosis in the fall of 1919. In short, a danger of the psychological approach is to generalize without sufficient examination of alternative hypotheses.[72] Statements such as the following, for example, can be more disturbing than clarifying, especially since they are almost impossible to substantiate:

> It mattered little to him that deferring to the Senate might save the substance of the program. The substance of his program, although sustained by a variety of personal needs and intellectual convictions which sincerely committed him to it, was in the last analysis the external vehicle of his need to dominate. His paramount requirement — though he would literally rather die than recognize the fact — was to vanquish the Senate for personal, "selfish" reasons. He must not defer to the Senate. It must defer to him. He must not surrender to Lodge. Lodge — another Dean West, another *father*! — Lodge must surrender to him. His very integrity was at stake![73]

[71] *Ibid.*, 9-13. On this subject George C. Osborn, "The Influence of Joseph Ruggles Wilson on His Son Woodrow Wilson," *North Carolina Historical Review*, XXXII (October, 1955), 519 ff., indicates that there were two years shortly before the father's death in which relations were strained, but that otherwise they were devoted to one another. Garraty balances the effect of the father's influence and concludes that some "self-doubt" remained. *Woodrow Wilson*, 4-5; cf. Blum, *Woodrow Wilson and the Politics of Morality*, 5-9, and Link, *Wilson: Road to the White House*, 1-3. Robert H. Ferrell in briefly acknowledging the influence of Wilson's father concludes that childhood is "a treacherous area" which psychology "has done little to clarify." See "Woodrow Wilson: Man and Statesman," *Review of Politics*, XVIII (April, 1956), 132 ff.

[72] This is not to say that the Georges do not discuss the importance of Wilson's religion, but simply that they favor father-hostility as a cause. For a brief account of Wilson's church activities in Washington see James H. Taylor, *Woodrow Wilson in Church: His Membership in the Congregation of the Central Presbyterian Church, Washington, D. C., 1913-1924* (Charleston, S. C., 1952). For a discussion of the illness see especially Blum, *Joe Tumulty and the Wilson Era*, Ch. XII, note 35.

[73] George and George, *Woodrow Wilson and Colonel House*, 208.

There is another danger in using the psychological approach in biographical writing. Almost inevitably it results in stressing idiosyncrasies. One does not see the effect of one incident upon another, the difficult alternatives, the complexity of situations. One remembers words like compulsiveness, anxieties, and frustration. One forgets to make comparisons with what went on before and what happened afterwards. And one may fail to compare Wilson's problems with those faced by other strong presidents. A stress upon personality can violate the historical approach. Yet, the cautious use of psychological concepts, keeping in mind historical perspective, can open new vistas of interpretation.

Although the historians in the decade after the Second World War have made a beginning in opening these new vistas in studying Wilson, the most important contributions have been in the traditional areas of exploring new sources of information or different aspects of his career. We know much more about his relationship to the Progressive movement and his use of the presidential office. We know more about aspects of his foreign policy. We have seen enough evidence of the way in which he functioned to know that some of the generalizations which have been applied to him simply do not stand up. He was an idealist, but not an idealist who constantly refused to accept the realities of a situation. He was stubborn at times, but he made many significant compromises in his career.

Almost forty years after his first book on Wilson, Charles Seymour made a penetrating re-evaluation by finding Wilson "eminently educable." His whole political career, according to Seymour, was marked by development, and although to the end he did not learn some important things, his education was continuing, even at Paris.[74] A useful volume could perhaps be written entitled "The Education of Woodrow Wilson." One wonders how different the historical interpretations might be today had Wilson himself had the opportunity or the desire to write such a book.

[74] Seymour, "The Paris Education of Woodrow Wilson," *Virginia Quarterly Review*, XXXII, 581 ff., 592-93. See also Seymour, "Woodrow Wilson in Perspective," *Foreign Affairs* (New York), XXXIV (January, 1956), 175-86; William L. Langer, "Woodrow Wilson: His Education in World Affairs," *Confluence*, V (Autumn, 1956), 183-94; and Ferrell, "Woodrow Wilson: Man and Statesman," *Review of Politics*, XVIII (April, 1956), 145. See for characteristic observations of Carl Becker on Wilson and Versailles, Phil L. Snyder, "Carl Becker and the Great War: A Crisis for Humane Intelligence," *Western Political Quarterly*, IX (March, 1956), 1-10.

The Origins of the Teapot Dome Investigation

By Burl Noggle

About fifty miles north of Casper, Wyoming, a formation of eroded Parkman sandstone looms up out of the bare sagebrush flats. Although it resembles a disfigured human hand, this geologic fault is called Teapot Rock. It overlooks a nine-thousand-acre expanse of land containing an important oil deposit which was set aside in 1915 as United States Naval Oil Reserve Number Three. Men in the oil business, associating the pool with the landmark, have long referred to this reserve as Teapot Dome. In the 1920's this designation became much better known as the name of one of the major political scandals in American history. Before it became a national scandal, however, the Teapot Dome oil reserve was one part of a continuing dispute between a small, dedicated group who advocated conservation of natural resources and a secretary of the interior who did not. Much of the historic debate over conservation in the United States was summed up in this battle, with two of the protagonists, Gifford Pinchot and Albert B. Fall, personifying the forces for and against conservation. Oil reserves constituted one issue, timber reserves and the forestry service another, in a running battle between the conservationists and Secretary Fall, which began soon after he entered the cabinet in 1921. This dispute, which came to focus finally on Teapot Dome, has not hitherto been made part of the narrative of the scandal.

In June, 1920, at its national convention in Chicago, the Republican party nominated Warren G. Harding for president of the United States. To Gifford Pinchot, a great and luminous name in the American conservation movement, as well as to many other friends of conservation, Harding seemed entirely acceptable as a candidate. One of these conservationists, a key figure in the Teapot Dome story, was a Washington lawyer named Harry A. Slattery.

A bachelor all his life, Slattery married himself to conservation, bestowing upon it fidelity and loving care from an early career with the Inland Waterways Commission to the very day he died. From 1909 to 1912, he was secretary to Pinchot. From 1912 to 1917, he was secretary of the National Conservation Association, "the organized voice of the Conservation Movement in America." [1] Throughout his career, Slattery was investigator, counsel, legislative draftsman, and confidant for numerous friends of conservation in Congress, as well as for others in private life. In 1920, Slattery was practicing law in Washington, but still burrowing, as had been his custom, through the *Congressional Record* and other government publications, and through a variety of metropolitan daily newspapers. He was corresponding regularly with Gifford Pinchot, with numerous friends of conservation, and with a selected circle of newspaper reporters and columnists.[2]

As the 1920 presidential campaign opened, Slattery felt that the Republicans were firm supporters of conservation. Harding's platform had "emphasized the Republican devotion to . . . conservation." It was "no secret," said Slattery, "that this plank in the platform was written by the conservationists." [3] In the late summer Harding's publicity man, Judson Welliver, a close acquaintance of Slattery's, invited him to come to Marion, Ohio, where Harding was conducting a front-porch campaign. There Slattery helped to prepare an address on conservation for Harding. Slattery later described the speech as "a direct commitment for the conservation policies — strong and clear-cut." [4]

At about this same time Slattery arranged a meeting between Pinchot and Harding. To Harding's campaign manager, Slattery wrote: "Just before he left Washington, Senator Harding was anxious to have Mr. Pinchot come [to Marion] and go over with

[1] Slattery's description of the Association, in a statement to Consolidated Publishing Company, Washington, D. C., June 12, 1921, Harry A. Slattery Papers (Duke University Library, Durham, N. C.).

[2] For biographical information on Slattery, see his unpublished autobiography, "From Roosevelt to Roosevelt," and his voluminous personal papers, Duke University Library.

[3] Harry Slattery, "The Story of the Teapot Dome Scandal" (unpublished manuscript, Slattery Papers), pp. 19-20. The Republican platform stated, in part: "Conservation is a Republican policy. It began with the passage of the Reclamation Act signed by President Roosevelt." See Republican National Committee, *Republican Campaign Text-Book, 1920* (n.p., n.d.), 95.

[4] Slattery, "From Roosevelt to Roosevelt," 74-75.

him the conservation, agricultural and other progressive matters in which GP had worked." Pinchot agreed to make the trip, and Slattery's suggestion was accepted by the Marion headquarters.[5] Late in August, Pinchot, following his visit to Marion, publicly endorsed Harding's candidacy. As one newspaper phrased it, Pinchot was "much pleased" with Harding's views on conservation.[6]

Gifford Pinchot, in 1920, was a private citizen of Milford, Pennsylvania, who thought of himself as a Roosevelt Republican. Indeed, he had made the first of several annual pilgrimages to the Rough Rider's grave, perhaps to live again those days of the Roosevelt administration when the conservation movement reached its first fruition and Pinchot enjoyed a power he had never since held. In 1910-1911, during the heated clashes of the Ballinger-Pinchot controversy, President William H. Taft had demanded and received Pinchot's resignation as chief forester of the United States. To many of the public, and certainly to his numerous close followers, Pinchot was a martyr to conservation. And in private life he continued to dominate the conservation movement, providing it with an inspirational leadership.[7] In a lifetime of devoted

[5] Slattery to Elijah Hanson, July 13, 1920; Slattery to John C. McCarl, July 17, 1920; Slattery to John Snure, July 17, 1920; Hanson to Slattery, July 23, 1920; McCarl to Slattery, July 26, 1920; Snure to Slattery, July 28, 1920, Slattery Papers.

[6] Charlotte (N. C.) *Observer*, August 31, 1920. See also Philadelphia *Public Ledger*, August 31, 1920.

[7] A former chief of the Forest Service, William B. Greeley, who worked with Pinchot for many years, has written that Pinchot made his associates "feel like soldiers in a patriotic cause," and that he brought to this cause "a fervor of religious intensity and a magnetic personal leadership . . . rarely equaled in the American drama." William B. Greeley, *Forests and Men* (Garden City, 1951), 58, 82. There is no published biography of Pinchot, and scholarly studies of any kind specifically about him are rare. For the estimates of Pinchot offered throughout this article, I have relied upon portions of the Gifford Pinchot Papers (Division of Manuscripts, Library of Congress), numerous items in the Slattery Papers, and, among published sources, the following: Gifford Pinchot, *Breaking New Ground* (New York, 1947); Gifford Pinchot, *The Fight for Conservation* (New York, 1910); John T. Ganoe, "Some Constitutional and Political Aspects of the Ballinger-Pinchot Controversy," *Pacific Historical Review* (Berkeley), III (September, 1934), 323-33; Alpheus T. Mason, *Bureaucracy Convicts Itself: The Ballinger-Pinchot Controversy of 1910* (New York, 1941); Harold L. Ickes, *Not Guilty: An Official Inquiry into the Charges Made by Glavis and Pinchot against Richard A. Ballinger, Secretary of the Interior, 1909-11* (Washington, 1940); and Whitney R. Cross, "W J McGee and the Idea of Conservation," *Historian* (Bloomington, Ind.), XV (Spring, 1953), 148-62. A superior unpublished study is Harold T. Pinkett, "Gifford Pinchot and the Early Conservation Movement in the United States" (Ph.D. dissertation, American University, 1953). For a survey of the movement, published after this article was written, see J. Leonard Bates, "Fulfilling American Democracy: The Conservation Movement, 1907 to 1921," *Mississippi Valley Historical Review* (Cedar Rapids), XLIV (June, 1957), 29-57.

labor, he, as much as any single man, made conservation a crusader's program and over the years revealed consummate skill in promoting and protecting the movement that he considered, in large measure, his peculiar creation. In 1920, one of his great fights lay immediately ahead.

When Harding swept into office with ease in November, receiving over sixteen million votes out of the twenty-five million votes cast, the friends of conservation had reason to feel secure. The campaign had assured them that Harding would support their policies. Furthermore, soon after the victory Pinchot was called to Marion again. There he talked about forestry with Harding, who also had him submit a list of five men as possible candidates for the post of secretary of the interior. Harding said that he was anxious to support a conservation program, and wanted a man for the office who would promote conservation as an administration policy.[8] To R. C. Bryant at Yale Forestry School, Pinchot wrote that his talk with Harding was "most satisfactory." And he added: "Altogether I am much better pleased with the situation than I expected to be a month ago." [9] But even as Pinchot was writing to Bryant, the political scene was changing with the appearance of a new actor.

Late in the afternoon of November 15, 1920, Senator Albert B. Fall of New Mexico arrived at Brownsville, Texas. That night he dined and talked with his old Senate companion, President-elect Harding, who was spending a brief vacation with friends near Brownsville.[10] Fall, who was chairman of the Senate subcommittee on Mexican Affairs, had been an acidulous critic of President Woodrow Wilson's policy toward Mexico, and at the 1920 Republican Convention he had written the party plank on Mexican policy. Behind Fall when he settled in New Mexico Territory in 1886 lay a Kentucky childhood and education, and several years of rough toil and gold-prospecting in Texas and northern Mexico. In New Mexico, he had waxed rich and strong and acquired a goodly share of that broad land. In 1907, he had opened a law office in Las Cruces and had gone into politics. Until William Jennings Bryan "muddied the pond," as Fall expressed it, he had been a Democrat.

[8] John Lathrop to Pinchot, March 11, 1924, Pinchot Papers, Box 236.

[9] Pinchot to R. C. Bryant, January 4, 1921, *ibid.*

[10] New York *Times*, November 16, 1920, p. 1.

As Democrat, and then as Republican, he held several political offices in the Territory, and when New Mexico became a state in 1912 he was elected as a Republican to the United States Senate.[11] In Washington, this frontier baron with his wide-brimmed hat and easy drawl soon became a conspicuous figure. His background hinted of a hard but lucrative struggle for wealth and of a strong political ambition, nurtured by frontier individualism. As a senator, Fall created close friendships as well as bitter enmities. One of his more intimate cronies was the colleague who sat next to him in the Senate, Warren G. Harding of Ohio.[12] Perhaps it was this friendship that had brought Fall to Brownsville during Harding's winter of indecision, when the President-elect struggled to select a cabinet.

Perhaps it was friendship, also, that took Fall to Marion in mid-December, when he again conferred with Harding, after which he told reporters that Harding did not bring up cabinet matters. "But," added Fall, "whether I said anything about the cabinet is another question."[13] A week later, the Chicago *Tribune* reported that Harding had decided upon at least three cabinet appointments, one of whom was Fall for secretary of the interior.[14] Late in January, 1921, Harding went to Florida as a guest of Senator Joseph S. Frelinghuysen of New Jersey, and with him was Fall. The press wires from Miami on January 30 reported that Fall was in line for the Interior Department post. Finally, on March 1, Harding announced from Marion that he was choosing Fall as secretary of the interior.[15] Meanwhile he had been filling in the other cabinet names,

11 For biographical information on Fall, see obituary note in *New Mexico Historical Review* (Santa Fe), XXI (January, 1946), 78-80; William A. Keleher, *The Fabulous Frontier* (Santa Fe, 1945); Owen P. White, "Five El Paso Worthies," *American Mercury* (New York), XVIII (December, 1929), 433-40; and William G. Shepherd, "How Carl Magee Broke Fall's New Mexico Ring," *World's Work* (New York), XLVIII (May, 1924), 29-40.

12 Harry Daugherty wrote that Fall and Harding were accidentally thrown into "intimate friendship by the assignment of seats in the Senate . . . which placed them side by side for six years." Harry M. Daugherty, *The Inside Story of the Harding Tragedy* (New York, 1932), 76-80.

13 New York *Times*, December 16, 1920, p. 9.

14 Chicago *Tribune*, December 23, 1920.

15 See Walter E. Edge, *A Jerseyman's Journal* (Princeton, 1948), 120-21. Edge, a senator from New Jersey, considered himself "particularly fortunate" in being "the only companion of the President-elect while he was resting at the Hotel Ponce de Leon at St. Augustine" in February. According to him, Harding's appointments of such close personal friends as Fall and Harry M. Daugherty (attorney general) "were, as he often said, personal appointments and obligations." *Ibid.*, 121-22.

and when he appeared before the Senate on Inauguration Day to present the nominations, his old chums and former colleagues cheered him tumultuously. The burst of applause which followed the reading of Fall's name seemed to show that his Senate friends approved his selection.[16]

The friends of conservation, however, were aroused. While Harding had fished and golfed and gradually put together his cabinet, they had consulted each other in growing anxiety. A telegram to Gifford Pinchot in late February asked: "How is Fall on Conservation?" Pinchot replied: "Don't quote me yet on Fall. Want to go carefully over his record in Senate and other records not immediately available. He has been with exploitation gang, but not a leader. Has large personal holdings in mining and other resources in this country and Mexico. Trouble ahead." [17] His examination of the record was not reassuring, and two days after the inauguration he wrote: "On the record, it would have been possible to pick a worse man for Secretary of the Interior, but not altogether easy." [18] This judgment was later to be expressed more specifically by another conservationist, who pointed out that the position of secretary of the interior "called for a man with a strong appreciation of public rights and interests," and said: "Fall was condemned as absolutely unfit for such a post by every detail of his record in the Senate. He had been an exploiter, and a friend of the exploiters. He had always opposed the conservation movement." [19]

To Harry Slattery, thinking back to the Republican campaign and his own contacts with it, "announcement of the Harding Cabinet . . . came as something of a shock." The appointment of Fall, he said, "placed in the key conservation post in the Cabinet one who for years had bitterly opposed the conservation program as a Senator." [20] Both Slattery and Pinchot also expressed concern over the selection of Edwin Denby as secretary of the navy. Pinchot recalled that as a congressman from Michigan during the Taft administration Denby had been a member of the committee which reported in favor of Ballinger. "I went to Detroit afterwards," he

[16] *Cong. Record*, 67 Cong., 1 Sess., 7 (March 4, 1921); New York *Times*, March 5, 1921, pp. 1, 9.

[17] Walter Darlington to Pinchot, and Pinchot to Darlington, February 24, 1921, Pinchot Papers, Box 237.

[18] Pinchot to Samuel McCune Lindsay, March 6, 1921, *ibid.*, Box 239.

[19] John Ise, *The United States Oil Policy* (New Haven, 1926), 365-66.

[20] Slattery, "From Roosevelt to Roosevelt," 75.

said, "and helped beat him for re-election. Why he should have been appointed, nobody seems to know." Furthermore, according to Slattery, the conservationists were also worried over the fact that "several assistant secretaries were appointed in the Navy and Interior Departments and in the Department of Justice who were not likely to be friends from their past records and affiliations."[21]

Spurred by their fears and suspicions, the conservationist leaders went to work almost at once to preserve the cause of conservation from the despoiling hands of the new secretary of the interior. They realized, however, that until they could produce positive evidence relating to a more or less specific issue it would be necessary to proceed with caution, and their first attention was directed toward the maintaining of a close watch upon developments which might affect the conservation program. Thus when, soon after Harding's inauguration, Slattery received a request from *The Survey*, a liberal fortnightly magazine, for an article of "1,000 words on Fall and the Department of the Interior" which would be "a straight fact story," he first procrastinated and, two months later, finally declined to contribute the article.[22] At that time he was still seeking the "straight facts" about Fall, still searching for more substantial evidence than he had yet uncovered.

Not long after Fall took over the Interior Department, Slattery heard that he was moving out "many trained and zealous public servants" and surrounding himself with his personal friends, and that as a result a "lowering tone was going down through the whole Department." Soon afterwards there came the unbelievable rumor that Fall had by executive order secured the transfer of the naval oil reserves from the Navy Department into his own hands. "This was so bold a move," Slattery said, "that it at first did not sound true."[23] If true, this might mean that Fall was preparing the way for a direct assault on one of the most important conservationist gains of the two preceding presidential administrations.

During the Taft administration, a concerted drive by the Navy Department and the friends of conservation had brought about the creation of two great naval oil reserves on government lands in

21 Pinchot to Lindsay, March 6, 1921, Pinchot Papers; Slattery, "From Roosevelt to Roosevelt," 75.

22 S. Adele Shaw to Slattery, March 21 and April 14, 1921; Slattery to Shaw, April 4, April 5 and June 2, 1921, Slattery Papers.

23 Slattery, "From Roosevelt to Roosevelt," 81-82.

California. Then in 1915 President Wilson had set aside the Teapot Dome tract in Wyoming as Naval Oil Reserve Number Three.[24] Taft and Wilson had specifically designated these three areas as oil reserves for the exclusive use of the United States navy, but throughout the Wilson administration, conservationists, determined to maintain them as reserves, were engaged in a contest with private oil interests who were equally determined to obtain rights to lease portions of the government oil lands. Harry Slattery expressed a common viewpoint of the conservationists when he referred to the oil in these reserves as "a supply laid up for some unexpected emergency," and insisted that it should be left underground, intact, and safe "as an insurance policy for national defense." [25] During the Wilson years, Secretary of the Interior Franklin K. Lane alienated Pinchot and his friends over the leasing issue. In the cabinet itself a running fight developed between Lane and Secretary of the Navy Josephus Daniels, who was backed by Pinchot, Senator Robert M. La Follette of Wisconsin, and a number of naval officers. Daniels wanted the naval oil reserves entirely closed to leasing. Lane felt that individuals with claims filed upon the oil lands before they were withdrawn had a legitimate complaint. Wilson usually sided with Daniels, but there was bickering within the administration, and at least one interdepartmental feud.[26]

Finally, in 1920, Daniels managed to acquire control of the reserves. Working through the House Naval Affairs Committee, he pushed through a special amendment to the 1920 naval appropriations bill. The amendment directed the secretary of the navy to

[24] Max W. Ball, *Petroleum Withdrawals and Restorations Affecting the Public Domain* (U. S. Geological Survey, Bulletin 623: Washington, 1916), 283-84, 291, 333. For a recent study that places these withdrawals in historical perspective, see John A. DeNovo, "Petroleum and the United States Navy before World War I," *Mississippi Valley Historical Review*, XLI (March, 1955), 641-56. Ise, *United States Oil Policy*, is basic for any study of oil conservation; see especially pp. 274-356 for discussion of oil withdrawals. E. Louise Peffer, *The Closing of the Public Domain* (Stanford, 1951), is likewise an admirable study which encompasses much besides oil reserves.

[25] Harry Slattery, "Conservation of Public Oil Lands" (unpublished memorandum dated March, 1924, Slattery Papers), p. 10.

[26] Peffer, *Closing of the Public Domain*, 127-28; Ise, *United States Oil Policy*, 335 ff; J. Leonard Bates, "Josephus Daniels and the Naval Oil Reserves," *Proceedings of the United States Naval Institute* (Annapolis), LXXIX (February, 1953), 171-79; Slattery, "Story of the Teapot Dome Scandal," 19. See Daniels to William C. Redfield, February 2, 1924, Josephus Daniels Papers (Division of Manuscripts, Library of Congress), Box 578, for Daniels' statement that "Wilson stood with me throughout the whole controversy when Lane and I disagreed."

take possession of the naval oil reserves, and "to conserve, develop, use and operate the same in his discretion, directly or by contract, lease or otherwise." [27] Thus the administration of the three reserves passed into the willing hands of a stubborn conservationist, and the friends of conservation felt that their precious oil reserves were secure. But when Harding came into office and Josephus Daniels returned home to North Carolina, Edwin Denby was moved in as head of the Navy Department. It was only about a month after he assumed office that Slattery heard the rumor that control of the reserves was being shifted, by executive order, from Denby to Fall.

About the same time that Slattery first caught this rumor, he also read a *Navy News* release of April 16, in which Secretary Denby made an announcement that gave him added concern. It was stated that Denby had decided to lease drilling rights in one of the California naval oil reserves to private oil companies, and that bids were to be opened soon. Denby admitted that this was the first time such rights were being granted and justified his decision by asserting that government oil was being drained by the wells of private companies operating on the rim of the naval oil reserve. In Slattery's view, whether or not the transfer rumor proved to be true, the reserves were evidently in danger from Denby's new policy. He quickly sent off a note to Pinchot: "Some good might come out of it if you would give me a note of introduction to TR, Jr. [Theodore Roosevelt, Jr., assistant secretary of the navy under Denby], and I could discuss this briefly with him." Pinchot promptly addressed a note to "Dear Ted," introducing Slattery as "a man in whom you may have complete dependence from every point of view. Not only will whatever he tells you be true, but you will find him thoroughly posted on whatever . . . he desires to take up with you . . . He is especially interested, as I am, in the oil policy of the Navy Department." [28]

Slattery allowed the letter to Roosevelt to lie idle for a few weeks. Then, just three months after Harding came into office, the White

27 For the text of the amendment see *Cong. Record,* 66 Cong., 2 Sess., 6214-15 (April 28, 1920). The House agreed to the appropriation bill, with this amendment included, on June 1, 1920 (*ibid.,* 8101), and the Senate approved it on the following day (*ibid.,* 8162-63).

28 Slattery to Pinchot, April 25, 1921, and Pinchot to Theodore Roosevelt, Jr., April 28, 1921, Slattery Papers. A copy of the *Navy News* release of April 16, 1921, is also in Slattery Papers.

House announced on June 1 that the President had signed an executive order transferring the naval oil reserves from the Navy Department to the Department of the Interior. The action had been recommended jointly by Secretaries Denby and Fall, the announcement said, and the secretary of the interior now possessed authority to grant drilling rights in Reserve Number One in California, the only reserve thus far opened to drilling. Although this transfer gave Fall the reserves, Slattery still had confidence in the Roosevelt name. He went to the Navy Department, carrying Pinchot's letter with him. He told Roosevelt of the old "naval oil fights and of my knowledge of them, and the vital necessity of oil for the Navy." Roosevelt, according to Slattery, began showing irritation. When Slattery spoke of Fall's poor conservation record, Roosevelt "hit the ceiling." He told Slattery that Fall had been in his father's Rough Riders and that Slattery must not "say anything derogatory of this great good friend." Slattery recalled that he and Roosevelt "sparred back and forth" for awhile, until Roosevelt "finally admitted he himself had carried the Executive Order, written by Fall and with Denby's approval, to President Harding . . . [who] then signed it." Slattery predicted to Roosevelt that Fall would "turn over the Naval reserves to private interests in the oil industry." Roosevelt, in anger, showed Slattery the door.[29]

The New York *Times* had placed the oil transfer story on page twelve, in a small block entitled "Fall Takes Over Navy Oil." [30] But Slattery thought the executive order worthy of much more attention. He paid a visit to Senator La Follette, the old crusader, who had a reputation as a friend of conservation, and who had backed Secretary of the Navy Daniels in his successful efforts to secure naval control of the reserves. La Follette and Slattery had worked together on conservation problems in the past. Now once again they began a co-operative venture. La Follette, first learning of the oil transfer when Slattery told him about it, was disturbed at the news and encouraged Slattery to investigate the transfer.[31]

[29] See Slattery's account of this visit, "From Roosevelt to Roosevelt," 82-83. In the early 1930's, Slattery told Ralph Sucher, a former secretary of La Follette's, of his visit with Roosevelt. See Sucher memorandum, February 24, 1932, and Sucher to Slattery, February 24, 1932, Slattery Papers. The executive order is reprinted in Senate Committee on Public Lands and Surveys (68 Cong., 1 Sess.), *Leases upon Naval Oil Reserves* (3 vols., Washington, 1924), I, 177-78.

[30] New York *Times*, June 2, 1921, p. 12.

[31] See statement by Robert M. La Follette, Jr., at a dinner in honor of Slattery,

Urged on partly by La Follette and partly by his own interests, Slattery began a lengthy study of Fall's conservation record. For ten months, quietly and exhaustively, he probed. During this time it became apparent that the oil transfer was only one part of a series of policies planned or inaugurated by Fall, which looked to Slattery like a major anti-conservation campaign. The oil transfer tended to shrink in importance as Slattery discovered evidence of plans in the Department of the Interior to enlarge private exploitation of resources in Alaska and to bring all or part of the Forest Service — then in the Department of Agriculture — under control of the Department of the Interior.[32] As Slattery probed Fall's maneuverings he began reporting periodically to Pinchot, who eagerly spurred on the search, for when Fall touched the forest reserves he all but literally touched Pinchot's soul.

From the time of his appointment as the first chief forester of the United States in 1905, Pinchot had looked upon the Forest Service as the seed-bed of the conservation movement. At the time of his appointment it constituted a bureau in the Department of the Interior, but under him it was soon transferred to the Department of Agriculture, and for the rest of his life he labored to keep it out of the hands of what he considered to be a predatory Interior Department. The controversy with Secretary of the Interior Richard A. Ballinger in 1910, leading to Pinchot's dismissal, served to fix his impressions more indelibly, and as Slattery reported evidence of Fall's new plans, the former chief forester — whom Harold Ickes called "Sir Galahad of the Woodlands"[33] — prepared again for battle with the Interior Department, aiming now at Fall.

Already Pinchot had tried to stop the oil transfer by Harding. Immediately after learning that "powerful oil interests were seek-

Cosmos Club, Washington, D. C., June 25, 1932, quoted in *Cong. Record,* 72 Cong., 1 Sess., 15457-58 (July 15, 1932).

32 Slattery to Pinchot, June 6, 1921, Slattery Papers. Forest Service Chief William B. Greeley recalled that the Harding administration "was not three months old when Secretary [of Agriculture] Wallace told me gravely that we must be on our guard," because a scheme was brewing to turn the national forests back to the Interior Department, "and the scheming centered in the Secretary of the Interior." Greeley, *Forests and Men,* 96.

33 Harold L. Ickes to Pinchot, May 18, 1940, copy in Slattery Papers. Written while Ickes was secretary of the interior, as part of a controversy between him and Pinchot over a current effort to transfer the Forest Service to the Interior Department, this letter was a blistering criticism of Pinchot's long series of activities against that Department. See also Ickes, "Not Guilty: Richard A. Ballinger — An American Dreyfus," *Saturday Evening Post* (Philadelphia), May 25, 1940, pp. 9-11, 123-28.

ing to obtain through executive action what they had failed to accomplish through congressional action," he made an urgent personal appeal to the President not to sign the executive order. His protest failed, said Pinchot, because Harding did not believe that he could arouse the country in the interests of oil as effectively as he had done earlier in the interests of forest conservation.[34] But with the national program of forest conservation now jeopardized by Fall, Pinchot became an active and influential force behind the growing conservationist opposition to the new policies forming in the Department of the Interior.

Secretary Fall was clearly showing interest in more than oil reserves in California and Wyoming. Soon after his appointment he began talking about the resources of Alaska. He culled through old reports and data. He had several conferences with President Harding, who finally, according to the New York *Times*, "told the Secretary . . . to go ahead and carry out the program which both are convinced will mean a greater Alaska." The *Times* reported that Fall was impressed by the vast coal fields, the oil of high quality, and "the wonderful forests of Alaska, with, we hope, a future that is bright for the wood pulp and paper industries." To Fall, Alaska's greatest handicap was its decentralized administration. Division of authority led to conflict of authority. There was, he said, "just one way to develop Alaska, and that is to vest absolute authority in a single head . . . the President himself."[35] But Fall also had other solutions for the Alaskan bureaucracy. In particular, he had ideas about the forests in the Territory, as well as those in the states. He wanted to transfer the Forest Service to the Interior Department, or else have the functions of Interior moved over to Agriculture. Naturally, he preferred to preserve his own domain, and two months after he took office he had drawn up for Harding's signature an executive order to transfer the Forest Service to the Interior Department. Later, in July, he supported an alternative procedure of effecting the transfer by congressional action.[36]

[34] Remarks of Pinchot, reported and quoted in Philadelphia *Public Ledger*, March 5, 1924. Also reported in New York *Times*, March 5, 1924, p. 2.

[35] *Ibid.*, July 17, 1921, Sec. VII, p. 2. Scott Bone, appointed by Harding as governor of Alaska, agreed with Fall: "A simplified and centralized system brought closer home to Alaska is urgently and obviously needed to speed the progress of the Territory." Department of the Interior, *Report of the Governor of Alaska to the Secretary of the Interior*, 1923 (Washington, 1923), 2-3.

[36] Secretary of the Interior, *Annual Report*, 1921 (Washington, 1921), 7; Slattery,

At Slattery's suggestion, Pinchot sought a conference with Fall, who agreed to a meeting on July 29. Pinchot reported afterwards that at the meeting Fall was "most gratified that I had asked to see him, and expressed himself generally in a most friendly manner." According to Pinchot, Fall "specifically and definitely" did not want the administration of Alaskan forests transferred to his Department. He merely wanted "control of the business end of timber sales," leaving with the Forest Service in Agriculture "the marking of timber, and other details of the management on the ground." During the conversation, Pinchot was given a confidential copy of a congressional bill which included Fall's views on Alaskan development.[37]

Pinchot had mixed reactions to his talk with Fall. To Frederick H. Newell, a conservation pioneer, he wrote immediately about "a long and very satisfactory conference." But to an old Bureau of Fisheries expert, John N. Cobb at Juneau, Alaska, Pinchot dispatched a less optimistic note. He related to Cobb the gist of his conversation with Fall, pointing out that Fall did not want the forests transferred to Interior, but did want "to take control of the business end of timber sales." Pinchot thought that "such a separation would not work well for fairly obvious reasons," and asked Cobb to do what he could "to promote the keeping of the whole forest problem in the hands of the men who are best able to handle it — very obviously, the Forest Service men themselves." [38] To Frederick E. Olmsted, consulting forester at Stanford University, Pinchot sent notes on his interview with Fall, as well as those from

"Conservation of Public Oil Lands"; and New York *Times*, November 10, 1921, p. 23. For the suggested executive order, see Russell Lord, *The Wallaces of Iowa* (Boston, 1947), 227.

37 Slattery to Pinchot, July 20 and July 23, 1921; Pinchot to Slattery, July 22 and July 25, 1921, Slattery Papers. A copy of "Confidential Committee Print, 67 Cong., 1 Sess., House Bill," given to Pinchot on July 29, 1921, by Fall, and "Notes of G. P.'s talk with Secretary Fall, on Friday afternoon, July 29, 1921," are in the Slattery Papers. Pinchot sent these to Slattery "for the files of the Conservation Association," with an explanation that "These notes were made immediately after the talk, and accurately represent the position taken by the Secretary." Pinchot to Slattery, September 26, 1921, Slattery Papers.

38 Pinchot to Frederick H. Newell, August 1, 1921, Pinchot Papers, Box 240; Pinchot to John N. Cobb, August 1, 1921, *ibid.*, Box 237. Pinchot began his note to Cobb with a parenthetical complaint over mistreatment by Harding: "The President evidently forgot his promise to consult me on the appointment of a Governor of Alaska. I knew nothing of Scott Bone's appointment until it was made, and am very far from being pleased with it. It is clear that Bone's position approaches far more closely that of the Seattle exploiters than . . . that of the real Alaskans like yourself."

a subsequent conversation with Harding. Olmsted found them "most instructive," and predicted: "Off hand, I should say it looks like a fight, for I doubt if anything else will knock sense into their big business heads. I haven't the slightest doubt . . . that the lumber interests are behind Fall and coaxing him along." Olmsted thought that "an open fight on the whole conservation business would be an excellent thing. With the . . . present administration . . . out and out for big business, there is bound to be a lot of damage done secretly, anyway; why not have a show-down?"[39]

Pinchot already had decided to look for a showdown. By late summer of 1921 he evidently had become convinced that Fall was attacking the government's entire conservation program. When Pinchot reached this stage in his thinking he set in motion a maneuver which he had used successfully fifteen years earlier as chief forester. He began enlisting the aid of the press, this time in a publicity war on Fall. Slattery was a key figure in the propaganda campaign, and by September he had managed to place in the *Christian Science Monitor* the first of four stories on forestry, written by E. A. Sherman, associate forester of the United States. Essentially, the articles defended the status quo in Alaska. Slattery thought they had "a good slant." Ten days later, Slattery reported to Pinchot: "In addition to . . . the Monitor . . . I have got NEA, Chicago Tribune, New York Tribune, Federated Press, and Consolidated folks to use a part or all of it. It is good stuff."[40]

In early December, 1921, as Fall continued with his plans, Pinchot began calling out new reserves and adopting new tactics. On August 10, Senator Harry S. New of Indiana had introduced a bill to implement some of Fall's Alaskan proposals; and on November 16, Senator William H. King of Utah had proposed a bill to transfer the national forests to Interior.[41] Pinchot mustered the state forestry associations against both bills. He wired a friend in Massachusetts that "Efforts to transfer Forest Service . . . is [*sic*] serious and threatening. Suggest Massachusetts Forestry Association take strong action [against the proposed forestry bills], and communicate with all Massachusetts Senators and Representatives, also with President." He informed R. C. Bryant at Yale Forestry

[39] Frederick E. Olmsted to Pinchot, December 5, 1921, Pinchot Papers, Box 240.
[40] Slattery to Pinchot, September 22 and October 2, 1921, Slattery Papers.
[41] *Cong. Record*, 67 Cong., 1 Sess., 4805 (August 10, 1921), and 7746 (November 16, 1921).

School that he was going to write to all the forestry associations. "Generally," he said, "I am starting to stir things up. The situation is thoroughly serious, and while we are going to beat them in the end, it is going to take some fighting." Pinchot hoped that the executive committee of the Society of American Foresters could take action. "If so, what they say ought to be sent to every Senator and Congressman, and to all members of the Cabinet." Bryant replied: "As President of the Society . . . I have been trying to stir up opposition to the King Bill. . . . You will be the leader in the fight . . . as you have always been and . . . you may rely upon our support in any way that you need it."[42]

From the state forestry associations, as well as from any other source, Pinchot wanted pressure put upon the administration to prevent the Forest Service transfer. As he told a close friend, "Fall has made up his mind to get the Service, and Harding is on the fence." As a result, Pinchot himself was "seriously disquieted by the situation." In his opinion, of course, Fall had no justification for the transfer: "The argument our way is . . . overwhelming, but argument as compared with letters from the folks back home is a mighty ineffective means of persuasion."[43]

By mid-December, 1921, Pinchot could write that the fight was "going merrily on." Furthermore, Secretary of Agriculture Henry C. Wallace had "at last got his fighting clothes on" and Pinchot was confident of success.[44] By Christmas, he was even more optimistic. To his brother Amos, he wrote: "I think we have won our fight on the transfer."[45] Certainly his press campaign was booming. The American Forestry Association was able to publish a news sheet, made up largely of excerpts from newspapers throughout the

[42] Pinchot to Bryant, December, 1921, and Bryant to Pinchot, December 6, 1921, Pinchot Papers, Box 236.

[43] Pinchot to Philip Wells, December 8, 1921, *ibid.*, Box 243. Wells was a counsel of the National Conservation Association, and a long-time legal adviser and friend of Pinchot's.

[44] Pinchot to Olmsted, December 12, 1921, *ibid.*, Box 240. Pinchot had called Harding's selection of Henry C. Wallace as secretary of agriculture "the best appointment" in the cabinet (Pinchot to Lindsay, March 6, 1921, *ibid.*, Box 239), and he understood and sympathized with Wallace's desire to avoid an open break with Fall at this particular time. See especially Pinchot to Barrington Moore, December 20, 1921, *ibid.*, Box 240, in which he said: "We do not want to put the President into a position of backing the transfer [of the Forest Service] as a necessary incident of defending Fall."

[45] Pinchot to Amos Pinchot, December 23, 1921, *ibid.*, Box 240.

country, all of them attacking Fall, the proposed transfer, or both.[46] On March 8, 1922, the Association sent directly to President Harding, to Congress, and to newspapers throughout the country, a special sheet, captioned "The Case of the People vs. the Proposal to Transfer the U. S. Forest Service to the Department of the Interior," in which it presented "a resumé of the editorial opinion of the country denouncing the proposed plan to take the Forest Service out of the Department of Agriculture." In April, *American Forestry* magazine claimed that "As a result of widespread information, the opposition [to the transfer] has become most pronounced. The newspapers are practically a unit in protesting against the proposal and scores of influential organizations have condemned it."[47]

Whatever their effect upon Congress and the President, the conservation crusaders finally pierced Fall's armor. Vigorously, he struck back. He complained to Harding about the "impropriety" of the "vicious and unwarranted attack" by Pinchot and by the Forest Service itself upon "the head of a coordinate department of the Government," and he accused the Department of Agriculture and Secretary Wallace of fathering "vicious propaganda" against him and his policies.[48] In a "Memorandum to the Press," a twelve-page document which he had drawn up, Fall strongly defended his forest and general conservation policies and scathingly denounced "Pinchotism." Toward Alaska he remained obdurate; the country must be opened up, and its natural resources exploited.[49] When portions of this memorandum appeared in the press, Slattery joyfully clipped them and sent them to Pinchot, saying: "You will note by these . . . that Mr. Fall has been having a nice time digging himself in a hole that he won't be able to get out of so easy. You will get some laughs out of some of it." Slattery thought that

[46] See copy of News Sheet, American Forestry Association, Washington, D. C., undated, in Slattery Papers. Excerpts came from papers in San Francisco, Salt Lake City, Grand Rapids, Washington, and other cities.

[47] *American Forestry* (Washington), XXVIII (April, 1922), 200, with a photographic reproduction of the special sheet, which included comments from *Country Gentleman*, the *Christian Science Monitor*, the Pittsburgh *Post*, the Pueblo *Journal*, and various other papers and magazines.

[48] *Wallaces' Farmer* (Des Moines), March 24, 1922, p. 8; New York *Times*, March 7, 1922, p. 2, quoting a letter from Fall to "Chairman of one of the principal committees of the House."

[49] Copy of Fall's memorandum, dated March 4, 1922, Slattery Papers.

Pinchot now should "sit tight just like the Secretary [Wallace] and let the heathen rage." [50]

President Harding apparently was bewildered by all the noise over conservation, and wondered which side to support. Loyal to Fall as friend, the President, after having supported him in the Alaska proposals, had now become silent about forestry. Aware of his many limitations, and lonely for the press room of his old newspaper at Marion, Harding was, nevertheless, trying to be a president. About the same time that Fall was striking back at the conservationists, the New York *Times* reported "a widening in the gulf" between the President and his Secretary of the Interior. There were "surface indications" that Fall might soon resign. The *Times* said nothing about the conservation struggles, but observed that during the first year of the Harding administration, the President had "become attached to the point of view and the counsel of Secretary Hughes and Secretary Hoover." Fall, meantime, had become "a mere member of the Cabinet." [51]

The conservationists' relentless pressure upon Fall continued to tighten, but it soon began to focus more on oil than on forests. On March 10, Slattery made a prepared speech at a luncheon at the Ebbitt House in Washington, where he spoke before a forum of the National Popular Government League. Judson King, the executive secretary and driving force of the League, had asked Slattery to present the "facts" on the current controversy over the Forest Service. Slattery made a robust speech. He struck hard at Fall, and argued strongly for leaving the Service in Agriculture. Having covered his subject, he spoke further, almost parenthetically, about the naval oil reserves. "I think Mr. Fall will be asked a few questions about his stewardship," he said. "And one of these . . . will be about the leasing of the oil lands in Naval Reserve Number One . . . to . . . a Doheny interest." Although it is not entirely clear from the speech, it is likely that the reference was to a lease granted by Fall on July 12, 1921, shortly after he acquired control of the reserves from the Navy Department, in which he awarded to Edward L. Doheny the right to drill offset wells in Reserve Number One. There had been little criticism of this lease, since the drainage by

[50] Slattery to Pinchot, March 7, 1922, *ibid.* See also "Secretary Fall Appeals for Help," *American Forestry*, XXVIII (April, 1922), 207.

[51] New York *Times*, March 12, 1922, Sec. VII, p. 1. See also the intimate portrait of Harding in *The Autobiography of William Allen White* (New York, 1946), 615 ff.

adjoining wells was evident and the bidding for the lease had been open and competitive. Slattery gave it as his opinion, nevertheless, that Congress would be inquiring about Fall's private leases of the reserves, since "we have heard stories about Mr. Fall being quite friendly with large interests of an oleaginous nature." [52]

Immediately after the forum, a slow fuse began to burn under Harding's cabinet. Secretary Wallace had sent a stenographer to the luncheon to take notes on Slattery's remarks, and Wallace himself carried these notes to the President. But Harding evidently was not going to give full support to one cabinet member against another. He would not alter the action taken some nine months earlier which transferred control of the naval oil reserves to Fall, but he did postpone decision on the proposed transfer of the Forest Service. Wallace then stirred up a row in a cabinet meeting by broaching the question of Fall's conservation policies; and he was reported to have told the cabinet that if the Forest Service was transferred, he would resign, call public meetings in large cities of the Midwest, and put before the country "the case against Fall and his colleagues — forests, oil, and everything." [53]

The month of March, 1922, which saw Wallace taking a more vigorous role in opposition to Fall, marked also a change in direction of the conservationists' attack on Secretary Fall's policies. Since the summer of 1921 the major target had been that part of his program which contemplated change in the Forest Service, with the oil conservation issue temporarily on the shelf. After March the relative importance of forests and oil began to shift, and oil conservation policies soon made the forestry issue a secondary question. The change is marked, too, by Pinchot's announcement, two days after Slattery's March speech, of his candidacy for the governorship of Pennsylvania. Pinchot's energies were now turned mainly to state politics, and he seemed content in the belief that the Forest Service was safe from Fall. Slattery and other conservationists, however, did not slacken their drive. The "Fall war" was still going on. By the end of March, Slattery was writing to Philip Wells that although "the transfer scrap has died down . . . I am still afraid that

[52] Quotations from the speech appear in a copy of a National Popular Government League Bulletin, March 10, 1922, in the Slattery Papers. For the Doheny lease, see Ise, *United States Oil Policy*, 372.

[53] Lord, *The Wallaces of Iowa*, 227-28. The quotation is Lord's version of Wallace's sentiment. See also Slattery, "From Roosevelt to Roosevelt," 88.

Harding is going to side with Fall." It was not encouraging news, he said, "to hear that Fall has been to White House twice lately and had long pow-wows with Harding." To another conservationist, Slattery wrote: "Something must be done. . . . Our friends in American Forestry evidently fear to offend the Powers that Be — and GP is all absorbed with his Pa. campaign. You and I could conspire together to throw a few brickbats — certainly the situation is going to need it." [54]

But where find the brickbats? For more than a year the conservationists had been probing for weaknesses in Fall's defenses; yet their latest barrage had merely forced him to cover — and perhaps only temporarily. Then Slattery stumbled upon an opening, one that caused the campaign against Fall to soar off into new dimensions.

Although Fall had controlled the naval oil reserves since the executive order of May 31, 1921, Slattery had discovered little overt activity in the Interior Department which would document his anxiety. True, Fall had granted Doheny the right to drill offset wells in Reserve Number One, but this was not major exploitation of the reserve. Fall was also reopening old hearings on certain oil claims decided against great oil companies during the Wilson administration, and was rendering decisions now in their favor. Yet this knowledge brought only frustration to the conservationists; Fall's behavior was highly suspect in their eyes, yet it was legal. Some time in early March, 1922, Slattery decided to search for fire beneath the oil smoke. His speech at the Ebbitt House luncheon had indicated a growing interest in the oil question, though, as he had stated there, the forest transfer was "the real issue." Perhaps he decided that Fall could be brought to bay on the Forest Service through a flanking attack on oil. Whatever his thoughts, on March 15 he sent Senator La Follette a noteworthy letter.

Slattery had it "on reliable authority," he reported, that Fall had just leased a large acreage within Reserve Number One to the Doheny oil interests, the same group which had earlier been granted the limited right to drill offset wells. He reminded La Follette that this reserve "was the one the naval experts said was best fitted to store oil underground for naval use." Fall had also recently re-

[54] Slattery to Wells, March 30, 1922; Slattery to H. H. Chapman, March 15 and March 31, 1922, Slattery Papers.

opened another oil claim case; and the naval coal reserve in Alaska, also transferred to Fall, was "known to be up for private leasing." Slattery had drawn up a proposed Senate resolution that would direct the secretary of the interior to send to the Senate a list of all oil leases made by Interior within Naval Reserves One and Two, with full details on them; all executive orders and other papers in Interior files authorizing or regulating such leases; and "all correspondence, papers, and files showing and concerning the application for such leases and the action of . . . Interior . . . thereon." Slattery told La Follette that he would be glad to go over the resolutions with the Senator at any time. La Follette replied soon afterwards: "I am interested in this . . . and hope you will take it up at your earliest convenience." [55] Actually, Slattery had little more than hunches at this point, and his letter to La Follette represented an effort to seize the initiative in another skirmish in the "Fall war." As he informed Philip Wells in Connecticut, "We still have our scheme to launch a few bolts at Mr. F. under cover — and I hope you will hear it clear to Middletown when it comes through." [56]

Early in April, 1922, Slattery had a long talk with La Follette. They decided "that a Senate resolution would be the only way to get at the facts," and they began to gather data to incorporate in a resolution calling for information from Fall. On April 6, La Follette wrote to Josephus Daniels, whose protection of the reserves while secretary of the navy had won La Follette's approval. He told Daniels of his intentions to bring the question before the Senate "at the first opportunity." It had surprised him that no naval officer connected with the reserves and aware of their significance had made any adverse comment on Fall's oil policy. Would Daniels offer an opinion on the situation? [57] The same day La Follette began searching for necessary documents. Harding's executive order of May 31, 1921, transferring the reserves, had never been published and was not filed in the customary section at the State Department. La Follette wrote to Secretary of State Charles Evans Hughes "asking for copies of the President's orders relating to naval oil

[55] Slattery to La Follette, March 15, 1922; La Follette to Slattery, March 20, 1922, *ibid.*

[56] Slattery to Wells, March 30, 1922, *ibid.*

[57] La Follette to Daniels, April 6, 1922, quoted in Sucher memorandum, February 24, 1932, Slattery Papers.

and coal reserves."[58] Without replying, Hughes sent the letter to Fall, who, La Follette claimed, did not reply.[59] La Follette managed to procure a copy of the executive order and upon reading it decided that it was illegal and that Harding had no authority to issue it.

Gradually, more evidence began to filter in to La Follette. Daniels, replying to La Follette's letter of April 6, suggested that La Follette consult Rear Admiral Robert S. Griffin, who had been Chief of the Navy's Bureau of Engineering for over eight years, and who had opposed the naval oil reserve transfer.[60] La Follette gave Slattery letters of introduction to Admiral Griffin and to several other naval officers, including Captain John Halligan, "one of the Navy's experts on oil." Slattery saw them all. The Admiral, though retired, was still a member of the Naval Consulting Board; thus, wrote Slattery, he was "in a delicate position, since . . . Denby was his chief, but he clearly indicated his hope that the Senator would force an investigation." He told Slattery: "If they get into this thing, they will find stranger things in heaven and earth than we have dreamed of." Slattery reported the interview to La Follette, "and the significance of Admiral Griffin's remark was not lost upon him."[61] La Follette was also soliciting viewpoints of other naval officers, "men, who, he knew had stood staunchly against the transfer or leasing of the reserves"; but he learned that they had all been ordered to distant stations. This news, too, aroused his suspicions.[62]

58 La Follette to Charles E. Hughes, April 6, 1922, cited in Belle C. and Fola La Follette, *Robert M. La Follette* (2 vols., New York, 1953), II, 1045.

59 The Sucher memorandum of February 24, 1932, indicates that La Follette never received an answer from Fall, and that when Fall produced the supposed reply eighteen months later, La Follette decided that it had been drafted at a later period to avoid any charges of concealment. See Sucher memorandum, Slattery Papers. On the other hand, La Follette, *Robert M. La Follette*, II, 1045, refers to a letter from Fall to La Follette, dated April 12, 1922, without questioning when it may have been written. Fall's letter, whenever written, is printed in *Leases upon Naval Oil Reserves*, I, 265-66.

60 Daniels to La Follette, April 15, 1922, cited in La Follette, *Robert M. La Follette*, II, 1048.

61 The quotations are from Slattery, "From Roosevelt to Roosevelt," 87.

62 Sucher memorandum, February 24, 1932, Slattery Papers. On April 8, 1922, Slattery, still in his role as publicist, wrote to John E. Lathrop of the New York *World*: "You have no doubt noticed a war that has begun on Secretary Fall along the Potomac. . . . I want to ask if you can put a few spikes in the schemes of this gent . . . and if I might take the liberty of furnishing you some 'dope' now and then." Two days later, Lathrop replied that he would be glad to receive news about Fall's conservation plans. Slattery to Lathrop, April 8, 1922; Lathrop to Slattery, April 10, 1922, Slattery Papers.

Perhaps the conservationists forced Fall's hand; or, conceivably, he was preparing the way for other announcements to follow later. At any rate, on April 7, he announced the adoption by the Interior Department of a policy for protecting the government against further losses of oil in the California reserves. He estimated that around twenty-two million barrels of oil had been lost through failure of the Wilson administration to drill protective offset wells there. This loss was irrecoverable, and Interior could only inaugurate a drilling campaign to save the oil that still remained in the ground. This campaign already had started. Fall announced leases on Reserve Number Two to companies with preferential rights to drill, based upon claims held prior to withdrawal of the land by President Taft. No definite contracts, other than the limited one to Doheny of July 12, 1921, had yet been made for Reserve Number One, but a permanent policy was "being rapidly formulated" whereby the government would receive a portion of the oil produced, and would store it in steel tanks for future needs by the navy.[63]

In his statement Fall committed a sin of omission. He failed to announce that on this same day, April 7, he had leased the entire area of Teapot Dome to oil man Harry Sinclair. Slattery learned of the lease three days later.[64] On April 14, Slattery's private information became public, when the *Wall Street Journal* carried a front-page report that Fall had leased Teapot Dome to Sinclair's Mammoth Oil Company. Interior officials, the paper reported, had indicated that "the arrangement . . . marks one of the greatest petroleum undertakings of the age and signalizes a notable departure on the part of the government in seeking partnership with private capital for the working of government-owned natural resources." [65]

In the meantime, the investigation of Fall's conservation policy had begun to slip from the hands of the conservationists into those of the United States Senate and the public press. At the same time that La Follette was writing to Daniels and Hughes, Senator John B. Kendrick of Wyoming began receiving telegrams and letters from his constituents, asking him to inquire into rumors that Teapot Dome had been, or was about to be, leased to private interests. Kendrick asked the Interior Department for information, and on

[63] New York *Times*, April 8, 1922, p. 19.

[64] Memorandum by Slattery, dated April 10, 1922, Slattery Papers.

[65] *Wall Street Journal* (New York), April 14, 1922, pp. 1 and 8.

April 10 received a reply that no contract for a lease had been made. The rumors echoed beyond Wyoming, and newspapers tried to get a verification. They, too, learned nothing.[66] But they, as did Kendrick, began to dig. On April 15, the day after the *Wall Street Journal* story appeared, Kendrick rose in the Senate and introduced a resolution. He proposed that the secretaries of the Navy and Interior departments "inform the Senate, if not incompatible with the public interests," about "all proposed operating agreements" upon the Teapot Dome reserve. The Senate agreed to Kendrick's resolution without comment and without a roll call vote.[67]

While Kendrick's call for this information on Teapot Dome was evidently motivated largely by pressure from his own constituents, he was standing, consciously or not, against a background erected by the friends of conservation, who had labored steadily since the day Fall was named secretary of the interior. In time, Kendrick alone might have instigated a full-dress investigation of Fall's oil leasing policy. Yet, until April 15, he had not entered the "Fall war"; and even then he merely questioned, rather than attacked, Fall's policy. In late April, however, his position would be greatly reinforced by La Follette, demanding an exhaustive investigation of "this entire subject of leases upon naval oil reserves." La Follette was incited to activity by Slattery, who, with the encouragement and aid of Gifford Pinchot, had kept alive a continuing campaign, already over a year old, against Secretary Fall.

On April 18, while Fall was on an inspection tour of Reclamation Bureau projects in the West, acting Secretary of the Interior Edward C. Finney formally announced the leasing of Teapot Dome.[68] Three days later, in response to Kendrick's resolution, Finney officially notified the Senate and sent it a copy of the contract by which Sinclair's Mammoth Oil Company had been given a lease on the entire area of Naval Oil Reserve Number Three. Under the terms of this contract the government was to receive royalties of 12½ to 50 per cent on the production of the wells. The lease was for twenty years and, in customary oil lease language, "so long thereafter as oil or gas is produced in paying quantities from said

[66] See *Cong. Record,* 67 Cong., 2 Sess., 11785 (August 25, 1922), for Kendrick's account of his activities concerning Teapot Dome in early April, 1922. See also New York *Times,* March 12, 1924, p. 6, and Ise, *United States Oil Policy,* 357.
[67] *Cong. Record,* 67 Cong., 2 Sess., 5567-68 (April 15, 1922).
[68] New York *Times,* April 19, 1922, p. 31.

lands." An unusual provision stipulated that the government was not to receive its royalty in oil or in cash payment, but in oil certificates. These could be exchanged for fuel oil and various petroleum products, could be redeemed in cash, or could be exchanged for oil storage tanks — all such exchanges to be with the Mammoth Oil Company.[69]

When Finney announced the Teapot Dome lease, he also indicated that Edward L. Doheny's Pan-American Petroleum and Transport Company was being awarded a contract on parts of the California oil reserves. By April 25 the terms were arranged. The navy's royalty oil from the reserves was to be exchanged for storage tanks that Doheny would construct at Pearl Harbor, along with docks, wharves, and other facilities for fueling the fleet. The Doheny contract also stipulated that if future leases should be given for any or all of the California reserve, Doheny's company would have a preference right to the lease.[70]

The two contracts received little publicity. Finney's announcement, as did Kendrick's resolution, raised hardly a ripple outside conservation and oil circles. The Democratic New York *World* merely criticized the administration's secretiveness over the new oil policy, saying: "The whole transaction lends color to the theory of underground government . . . and the Harding administration can thank only itself for standing in a bad light before the country." [71] But the country, and evidently the press, knew little about any mysterious maneuverings in the Interior Department. John Lathrop of the *World* asked Slattery for facts, "and I don't care whom they hit," he added. "If you have . . . provable facts — fire them along." [72]

Slattery, too, wanted some facts. He had a surplus of hunches, and every day was picking up rumors and opinions to support them. Soon after his talk with Admiral Griffin he was visited by Captain John Halligan, one of the naval officers he had seen earlier. Slattery described their conversation in his diary: "We had a long talk. He showed me that Griffin, [Commander Nathan H.] Wright, and [Commander H. A.] Stuart, including himself, protested Executive Order on Naval Reserves, also data showing Stuart knew nothing

69 The contract is printed in *Leases upon Naval Oil Reserves*, I, 6-21.
70 *Ibid.*, I, 296-98.
71 New York *World*, April 19, 1922.
72 Lathrop to Slattery, April 21, 1922, Slattery Papers.

of Teapot Dome; that Wright was out on Naval Reserve in California, knew nothing of Doheny deals—also letter of Stuart in protest . . . to Admiral John K. Robison, and long one to Denby. . . . This is going to be a national scandal before all is over."[73]

Slattery conveyed whatever information he possessed, as well as his fears, to La Follette. On April 21, a week after the news of the Teapot Dome lease had appeared in the *Wall Street Journal*, La Follette introduced in the Senate a resolution which, with one major addition, was almost a carbon copy of the one Slattery had suggested to him in the middle of March. Since the Teapot Dome lease had now been added to the book of suspicions, the original resolution was adjusted to include it in the call for information. La Follette asked that the secretary of the interior be directed to send to the Senate all the facts about the leasing of Naval Oil Reserves One, Two, and Three to private persons or corporations. He wanted a list of all oil leases, all executive orders and papers authorizing or regulating those leases, and all correspondence, papers, instructions, requests, arguments, and actions relating to them in the files of the Interior Department. As with Kendrick, the Senate offered no objection, and the Vice-President ordered that the resolution be printed, and lie upon the table, as La Follette had requested. This resolution called only for information, not an investigation; but, as Slattery noted, it "could not be met with any brief perfunctory reply such as had been given in response to the Kendrick resolution. Nor could the excuse be put forward that the Department did not know what information was desired by the Senate."[74]

On April 28, Josephus Daniels' Raleigh *News and Observer* offered the editorial opinion that "Every day since the reserves were created there has been a well oiled propaganda to open them—and the recent action, wholly indefensible, promises to be the subject of congressional investigation."[75] La Follette and Slattery had already set out to make the promise fact. As Slattery expressed it, "the war on Fall goes merrily on." And he wrote to Pinchot's secretary in Milford, Pennsylvania, explaining an inability to make

[73] Extract from Slattery diary, quoted in Slattery, "From Roosevelt to Roosevelt," 87.

[74] *Cong. Record*, 67 Cong., 2 Sess., 5792 (April 21, 1922); Slattery, "From Roosevelt to Roosevelt," 84.

[75] Raleigh *News and Observer*, April 28, 1922.

a visit there: "I could not . . . leave [Washington] just when the Fall resolution was coming up. Confidentially, it would have completely bogged down because I know most of the facts." [76] The "Fall resolution" about which Slattery wrote referred to the new action which La Follette was to take in the Senate, amending and amplifying his resolution of April 21. Since Fall had failed to explain or justify his recent oil leases in any way, La Follette decided that he must try to smoke him out by calling for an investigation. Just before noon on April 28, as he left his office to go to the Senate floor, La Follette said: "I am going just as far as I can in the charges I make. . . . I can't prove that there has been corruption but if we get this investigation I am confident it will be shown." [77]

La Follette's afternoon speech to the Senate was a strong performance. In scathing language he sketched a history of the oil reserves, recalling past exploitation and subterfuges used to gain private entry. He referred to the 1921 transfer of the reserves by executive order, and warned his party colleagues that "we can not afford to permit a record to be made here which will parallel the record of Mr. Ballinger." He condemned the Interior Department as "the sluiceway for a large part of the corruption to which this Government of ours is subjected." The leases which had followed the transfer of the oil reserves to this department had come "as a distinct shock to the country." La Follette asked the Senate why it should not inquire "who were the real organizers of the Mammoth Oil Co. who were to be favored by the Government with a special privilege in value beyond the dreams of Croesus?" A great national policy had been reversed, and the nation was endangered. Congress and the public should have the facts. For these reasons, he was amending his resolution of April 21, and now asking that the Senate Committee on Public Lands and Surveys "be authorized to investigate this entire subject of leases upon naval oil reserves . . . and to report its findings and recommendations to the Senate." La Follette asked for unanimous consent that his resolution be taken up immediately for adoption. Reed Smoot, Republican, of Utah, objected; he wanted to study the proposal first. La Follette replied that it was nothing more than a request for an inquiry. Smoot still

[76] Slattery to H. H. Chapman, April 28, 1922, and Slattery to Philip Stahlnecker, April 27, 1922, Slattery Papers.

[77] La Follette, *Robert M. La Follette*, II, 1048.

wanted to read it. On that note, the day's session ended.[78] The next afternoon, following a brief debate, the Senate adopted the resolution by a unanimous vote — fifty-eight to none, with thirty-nine Republicans voting for an investigation of their party's administration.[79] Perhaps by coincidence, that same afternoon the Senate received a copy of the Teapot Dome contract from Secretary Fall himself, in further response to the Kendrick resolution.

When the Senate adopted La Follette's resolution, the initiative passed to the Senate Committee on Public Lands and Surveys. The conservationists, who had initially led the campaign against Fall, withdrew to the position of observers, though occasionally they scurried back with aid and suggestions. Hearings did not begin until eighteen months after the Senate had approved the investigation. Slattery believed that Reed Smoot and his Republican cohorts on the committee delayed any investigation until after the congressional election in the autumn of 1922; but Senator Thomas J. Walsh, the Democratic prosecutor on the committee, later commented: "It is scarcely fair to Smoot to charge him with the delay." [80] Nevertheless, the committee dallied, and the explanation for their behavior is not clear. Perhaps Smoot did procrastinate from partisan motives. Possibly feeling about Teapot Dome, except among those directly involved, bordered on unconcern. Senator Walsh himself seemed unaware of the sensations implicit in Teapot Dome, and perhaps therein lies the better explanation for the delay.

Once his resolution had passed, La Follette, looking for a bellwether among the Public Lands Committee members, had urged Walsh to "take the leadership in investigating." Senator Kendrick joined La Follette in his plea. Walsh, already holding more committee assignments than any man in the Senate, accepted with reluctance and hesitation.[81] Even months later, on the very eve of the committee's first hearing, duty, more than interest, appeared to

[78] *Cong. Record*, 67 Cong., 2 Sess., 6041-50 (April 28, 1922).

[79] *Ibid.*, 6097 (April 29, 1922). The Democrats provided the remaining 19 affirmative votes. There were 38 senators not voting: 21 Republicans and 17 Democrats.

[80] Slattery, "Story of Teapot Dome," 52; Walsh to Lewis Gannett, June 9, 1928, Thomas J. Walsh Papers (Division of Manuscripts, Library of Congress).

[81] La Follette, *Robert M. La Follette*, II, 1051-52; Thomas J. Walsh, "The True History of Teapot Dome," *Forum* (New York), LXXII (July, 1924), 1-12; J. Leonard Bates, "Senator Walsh of Montana, 1918-1924: A Liberal under Pressure" (Ph.D. dissertation, University of North Carolina, 1952), 309-10.

be motivating him. To a Montana correspondent he wrote: "I am handling this Teapot Dome matter at his [La Follette's] special insistence and urgent request." [82] In addition Walsh realized that Smoot and other Republican members of the committee were unsympathetic to the probe, and this helped to persuade him to take informal command of a committee chaired by a Republican and containing a Republican majority.

La Follette gave Walsh all the evidence that he had gathered on Fall. Then in June, 1922, Walsh suddenly received more material than he could handle. Fall, in response to the resolution, sent to the Senate a truckload of documents. Slattery had anticipated that Fall would try to swamp the committee with a mass of material too voluminous to permit a full analysis of all items. Soon after Fall's documents arrived at the committee rooms, La Follette and Slattery held a conference at Walsh's office, where they agreed that Slattery should work through the great mass during the summer, "and be ready for the hearings on the oil leases in the fall." [83]

Slattery went through the material, and occasionally La Follette also turned a hand to the analysis. But their hopes for hearings in the fall had to be abandoned. Instead of beginning the hearings, Walsh started what he later called "a laborious study" of the evidence. Between June, 1922, and October, 1923, a period of some sixteen months, he made "a critical analysis of the lease itself"; he studied past legislation relevant to the leasing; and he sent letters to "all journals which had exhibited any special interest in the subject," asking for the sources of statements they had made in their columns.[84] Most of this activity he crammed into the summer and fall of 1923, for he had been slow to suspicion, and not until then did his distrust of Fall fully develop. It was characteristic of Slattery and Pinchot to see corruption at once in any program endangering conservation. Walsh, however, did not react like Pinchot, and unless Fall's policy was positively shaded with corruption, Walsh was not the man to oppose it. But by March 12, 1923, Walsh was becoming "very much interested" in the hearings, then scheduled to begin in the fall when the next session of Congress opened.[85]

[82] Walsh to J. T. Carroll, October 10, 1923, Walsh Papers, Box 374.

[83] Slattery, "From Roosevelt to Roosevelt," 90; Walsh, "True History of Teapot Dome," *Forum*, LXXII (July, 1924), 1-12; *Leases upon Naval Oil Reserves*, I, 24-68.

[84] Walsh, "True History of Teapot Dome," *Forum*, LXXII (July, 1924), 1-12.

[85] Walsh to Hamilton Holt, March 12, 1923, cited in Bates, "Senator Walsh of Montana," 310. For Walsh's record on conservation, see *ibid.*, 29, 292-303.

Meantime, Fall resigned as secretary of the interior. On January 2, 1923, eight months after the Senate had approved La Follette's resolution, the White House announced that Fall had entered the cabinet at great financial sacrifice; now he was resigning, effective March 4, in order to devote his time to business affairs in the Southwest. Although he and Harding still were friends, Fall reportedly was piqued over several acts and shortcomings of the Harding administration and Congress. One source of his vexation, his friends asserted, was the "long undercover controversy" over proposals "to transfer to the Department of Agriculture many bureaus now under the Interior Department," and the failure to accomplish his plans for reorganizing Alaska.[86]

If Fall included the pending oil investigation among his grievances, the *Times* did not report it. Nevertheless, Harry Slattery believed that "the threat of the coming . . . investigation . . . drove Fall out of the . . . Cabinet." Slattery was in upstate New York on his way home when he heard of Fall's resignation; and he wrote in his diary: "His demise gave me satisfaction all the way to New York." For Slattery, Fall's resignation marked "the end of one phase of the oil fight." [87] Pinchot saw a connection between Fall's resignation and his feud with the conservationists, and wrote in one letter: "I had a good deal to do, I think, with the decision of Fall to resign." [88] Several friends wrote to Pinchot, asking him to propose various names to Harding for successors to Fall, and to one of them he replied: "President Harding credits me with having had something to do with forcing Fall's resignation, which I am by no means disposed to deny, and, therefore, any action I might take would hurt rather than help the man I would recommend."[89]

As Fall retired, he revealed his chagrin over the accusations lately thrown at him. In an article which the New York *Times* called "Secretary Fall's Soliloquy on Quitting Harding Cabinet," he wrote of the obligations facing persons in government service and the obstacles which worked against a full public understanding of their actions. By implication his own career was clearly in his thought. "The public mind," he said, without full information on decisions

[86] New York *Times*, January 3, 1923, pp. 12, 19.

[87] Slattery, "From Roosevelt to Roosevelt," 90-91, including quotations from his diary.

[88] Pinchot to John E. Ballaine, February 15, 1923, Pinchot Papers, Box 244.

[89] Pinchot to Marshall McLean, February 5, 1923, *ibid.*, Box 250.

and actions taken, cannot "crystallize into judgments unless information is conveyed to it thereafter." To Fall, history had shown "that such information is often never acquired, or, if so, [it is] after the object of this public attack has not only gone out of the public service, but has departed from life." [90]

Fall would not have to wait so long for a judgment. On October 22, 1923, hearings before the Senate Committee on Public Lands and Surveys began. Thereafter, the Teapot Dome investigation, rooted in a conservation feud and nourished for eighteen months past by political caretakers, began to bloom in profusion.

[90] New York *Times*, March 4, 1923, Sec. VII, p. 14.

The South and the Blair Education Bill

By Allen J. Going

In the period following the Civil War the question of a national program for improvement of the country's educational system came to be an important issue in the gradual trend toward enlargement of federal governmental activities. Numerous proposals in Congress to strengthen the public schools through the use of federal aid brought various reactions which shed considerable light on political and regional attitudes of that day. One of the most persistent of these pioneer efforts to provide federal aid was a proposal which bears the name of a Republican senator from New Hampshire, Henry W. Blair. In the 1880's the Blair bill was the center of the controversy over the question of federal assistance to public schools. Although its supporters were never able to secure approval of the bill by both houses of Congress, the discussions to which it gave rise, extending through most of the decade both in the states and in Congress, illustrate the political questions which complicated such a policy in that period.

From a regional viewpoint, the Blair bill was of peculiar importance to the South. Since it provided for the distribution of federal funds to the states in proportion to the illiteracy rate in each, the southern states, with their higher illiteracy, stood to benefit more than others. Out of a proposed annual allotment of fifteen million dollars, the former Confederate states would have received almost two thirds of the total. It is not surprising, therefore, that the Blair bill received a more thorough analysis and provoked more argument in the South than in any other region. The proposal frequently became an issue in southern state politics, and reactions to it illustrate the basic cleavage among southern Democrats between the Bourbon (or Redeemer) faction and the older, agrarian order. The Redeemers usually supported Blair's plan, while the agrarians opposed it on grounds of unconstitutionality, extravagance, the high taxes required, and for other reasons.

The Blair bill has received little attention from historians, despite the fact that its discussion contained important political, sectional, and social implications. The most comprehensive treatment may be found in Gordon C. Lee's *The Struggle for Federal Aid, First Phase*, which embraces the whole story of federal aid to education from 1870 to 1890. Although some attention is given to southern reactions, the author treats his subject as a national problem, with particular emphasis on its significance as background for the twentieth-century phase of the controversy.[1] The southern reaction to the bill, however, is a study in itself, revealing more clearly the divisions of thought in the postwar South and the sectional factors which affected congressional action on Senator Blair's proposals.

The different congressional proposals for federal aid which were made in the 1880's were new answers to a problem which had become specially burdensome to southerners. Following the Civil War, educational leaders and civic-minded persons in both North and South increasingly realized that something should be done to improve southern schools and in particular to reduce the high rate of illiteracy, especially among the newly freed Negroes. Although Reconstruction governments had established elaborate public school systems in the South, depressed economic conditions and other factors prevented adequate financial support for these systems in the 1870's and 1880's. As late as 1880 the sixteen former slave states appropriated approximately $12,000,000 to education, and one third of this amount was accounted for by two states, Missouri and Maryland. The twenty-two northern states appropriated over five times as much. In the sixteen southern states in 1881 the average annual expenditure for each child of school age ranged from a low of 87 cents in North Carolina to a high of $5.56 in Delaware, with only six states (Delaware, Kentucky, Maryland, Missouri, Texas, and West Virginia) showing $2.00 or more. Similar per capita expenditures in the former free states ranged from a high of

[1] Gordon C. Lee, *The Struggle for Federal Aid, First Phase* (Teachers College, Columbia University, Contributions to Education, No. 957: New York, 1949). C. Vann Woodward, *Origins of the New South, 1877-1913* (Baton Rouge, 1951), 63-64, recognizes the importance of the bill and implies, without fully explaining, the divided reaction in the South. The only article dealing with reactions in the individual southern states is Daniel M. Robison, "Governor Robert L. Taylor and the Blair Educational Bill in Tennessee," *Tennessee Historical Magazine* (Nashville), Second Series, II (October, 1931), 28-49.

$18.47 in Massachusetts to a low of $4.65 in Wisconsin, with only two other states, Vermont and Minnesota, showing less than $5.00.[2] J. L. M. Curry, one of the more active proponents of federal aid, estimated that the South actually needed from $30,000,000 to $40,000,000 annually to support adequately its public schools.[3]

Although philanthropic agencies, such as the Peabody Education Fund, created specifically for the promotion of teacher training in the South, rendered some assistance, those who were working for the improvement of southern education became increasingly interested in the idea of national aid for common schools in the late 1870's and early 1880's. With Radical Reconstruction overthrown and the compromise arrangement of 1877 stimulating co-operation between southern Democrats and northern Republicans, southerners looked more favorably upon schemes of national assistance in educating the Negroes. The Forty-fifth Congress, in 1877-1879, received sixty petitions and memorials calling for such aid, and all but six of these originated in southern states.[4]

Early in 1878 a special conference, called by Gustavus J. Orr, Georgia commissioner of education, and by other Georgia leaders, met in Atlanta for a discussion of southern education. One hundred delegates from nine states agreed that the wants of southern states were "immediate and pressing" and memorialized Congress for federal assistance in the form of public land revenues.[5] Commissioner Orr in a later address to the National Education Association, in 1880, stated that the South believed that the duty of providing for Negro education belonged to the whole country. This was the viewpoint, too, of Senator Joseph E. Brown of Georgia, who said at the Atlanta meeting of the Association the next year, "In this matter of education . . . we must have the aid of the United States." The Association, representing the opinion of professional educators

[2] Statistics from "Support of Common Schools," *House Reports*, 48 Cong., 1 Sess., No. 495, Pt. 1, p. 3; Bureau of Education tables in *Cong. Record*, 49 Cong., 1 Sess., 1277-78 (February 20, 1884). For general discussions of the educational plight of the South, see Edgar W. Knight, *Public Education in the South* (Boston, 1922), 415-28; Ellis P. Oberholtzer, *A History of the United States since the Civil War* (5 vols., New York, 1917-1937), IV, 536-41.

[3] "Statements and Testimony . . . before the Committee of the Senate on Education and Labor," *Senate Misc. Docs.*, 48 Cong., 1 Sess., No. 55, p. 85.

[4] Lee, *Struggle for Federal Aid*, 61.

[5] "Statements and Testimony," *Senate Misc. Docs.*, 48 Cong., 1 Sess., No. 55, pp. 39-40; Judson C. Ward, "Georgia under the Bourbon Democrats, 1872-1890" (Ph.D. dissertation, University of North Carolina, 1947), 445-46, 464.

throughout the nation, unanimously adopted a resolution at this meeting, as it did at later meetings, to petition Congress for aid to education.[6] In the spring of the following year a committee of the National Education Association appeared before a joint committee of Congress in support of national aid. Of the six educators, four, including Orr, were southerners.[7]

The trustees of the Peabody Education Fund also contributed to the growing sentiment for national educational assistance to the South. Under pressure from its chairman, Robert C. Winthrop, and Barnas Sears, its field agent, this group in 1879 designated a special committee headed by Alexander H. H. Stuart of Virginia to study the subject. At the next annual meeting, after hearing an elaborate report describing the urgent needs of the South, the trustees addressed a memorial to Congress requesting "such aid as may be deemed proper in furtherance of education in the Southern States." [8] J. L. M. Curry, the newly appointed agent of the Peabody Fund and himself a southerner, presented the memorial to Congress and followed it by a special memorial of his own and by frequent appearances before Senate and House committees. Senator Blair later said that the movement for national aid received its "first and most powerful impetus" from the Peabody trustees.[9]

The figures on illiteracy released in the 1880 census added impetus to the movement, highlighting especially the need to improve the literacy rate among southern Negroes. These figures were quoted, studied, and interpreted at length in the ensuing debates on federal aid. For the country as a whole, the actual number of illiterates increased between 1870 and 1880 from 5,658,000 to 6,239,000, but the ratio of illiterates to the total population decreased from 20 per cent to 17 per cent. The same general trend characterized the

[6] *The Addresses and Journal of Proceedings of the National Education Association* (Salem, Ohio, 1880), 89; *ibid.* (1881), 158-60; *ibid.* (1882), ix-x.

[7] "Notes on the Hearings before the Committees on Education and Labor," *Senate Misc. Docs.*, 47 Cong., 1 Sess., No. 72. United States Commissioner of Education John Eaton, who had been Republican superintendent of education in Tennessee, throughout the 1870's consistently urged the necessity of some form of federal aid. *Report of the Commissioner of Education for 1871* (Washington, 1872), 7; *ibid.* (1872), lxxxvii; *ibid.* (1873-1880), *passim.*

[8] *Proceedings of the Trustees of the Peabody Education Fund* (6 vols., Boston and Cambridge, 1875-1916), II, 203, 208, 244, 270-301.

[9] *Cong. Record*, 50 Cong., 1 Sess., 5121 (June 11, 1888). See also J. L. M. Curry, *A Brief Sketch of George Peabody and a History of the Peabody Education Fund* (Cambridge, 1898), 138-39.

South, but there the percentage remained shockingly high in comparison with figures for the rest of the country. The total number of illiterates in the South increased from 4,189,972 in 1870 to 4,714,-173 in 1880, and while the percentage declined, it was from a high 42 per cent to a high 37 per cent. Within the South, the highest was 55 per cent, in South Carolina, the lowest was 13 per cent, in Missouri, and eight of the states showed a figure of over 40 per cent. Negroes accounted for a large majority of southern illiterates, 3,168,905 in 1870 and 4,085,571 in 1880. And although the proportion of illiterate Negroes in the whole Negro population of the South was declining, it was from 85 per cent in 1870 to 75 per cent in 1880.[10] Such figures could not help but be disturbing.

Continued interest from southerners and from educational organizations plus the statistics of the 1880 census increased the likelihood that national aid to education would become a political issue in the 1880's. The movement had begun in 1870 with a proposal by Representative George F. Hoar of Massachusetts for the establishment of a national system of education; but his bill incurred so much opposition both from the South and from professional educators that it never came to a vote. Both the public and Congress looked with more favor upon proposals to use proceeds from the sale of public lands to aid state school systems. In 1872 the House passed such a bill which had been introduced by Representative Legrand W. Perce, a Republican from Mississippi, but it was not given serious consideration in the Senate. A similar measure, introduced by Republican Senator Ambrose E. Burnside of Rhode Island, passed the Senate in 1880 but was not voted upon in the House. Nine other federal aid bills were introduced during the decade, but none was seriously considered.[11] By 1880, however, the Republican party had moved toward a position favoring federal aid, declaring in its national platform that it was the duty of the central

10 Charles Warren, *Illiteracy in the United States in 1870 and 1880* (U. S. Bureau of Education, Circular of Information No. 3: Washington, 1884), 71-75. Warren, who was statistician of the Bureau of Education, based his tables on returns from the Ninth and Tenth Censuses. Illiteracy was at that time generally defined as an inability to write; smaller percentages were given for those unable to read.

11 For a full discussion of the Perce and Burnside bills, see Lee, *Struggle for Federal Aid*, 57-60. Southern Democrats had generally considered the Perce bill as another piece of Reconstruction folly; the affirmative voters included all southern Republicans but only four southern Democrats. By 1880, however, the situation had changed, and only four southern Democrats voted against the Burnside bill. Edward McPherson, *A Handbook of Politics* (Washington, 1872), 122; *ibid.* (1882), 37.

government to aid education "to the extent of its constitutional power." The Democratic platform declared that common schools should be "fostered and protected" but included this statement in the plank that opposed centralization in government.[12] Republican Presidents Grant, Hayes, and Garfield either approved in principle or specifically recommended federal aid. President Arthur in his first message to Congress recommended that education be aided by setting apart proceeds from public land sales "or by some other course."[13]

The growing surplus in the federal treasury suggested a new approach to the education problem, a direct appropriation from the national government. Such an idea had a particular appeal for Republicans and high-tariff Democrats who feared that an excessively large surplus would encourage tariff reduction. Senator Henry W. Blair of New Hampshire assumed the leadership of this new approach. A Union veteran, Blair demonstrated his party regularity by supporting high tariff rates and increased pensions for veterans, but he also showed interest in such reforms as prohibition and woman suffrage.[14] The first Blair bill, introduced in December, 1881, called for an appropriation of $105,000,000 to be distributed among the states on the basis of illiteracy and over a period of ten years, beginning with $15,000,000 the first year and decreasing by $1,000,000 each year thereafter. In April, 1882, the Senate Committee on Education and Labor, of which Blair was chairman, reported the bill favorably along with one by Senator Justin S. Morrill which called for school aid from public land revenues. Blair alone discussed his bill in the Senate, and no action was taken at that session.[15] In the second session of the Forty-seventh Congress a parliamentary clash between Blair and Morrill as to which bill

[12] Kirk H. Porter and Donald B. Johnson, *National Party Platforms, 1840-1956* (Urbana, Ill., 1956), 56, 61.

[13] James D. Richardson (ed.), *A Compilation of the Messages and Papers of the Presidents* (10 vols., Washington, 1890-1899), VII, 203, 479, 506, 626, VIII, 58; Garfield quoted in *Cong. Record,* 47 Cong., 2 Sess., 3258 (February 24, 1883).

[14] Allen Johnson and Dumas Malone (eds.), *Dictionary of American Biography* (21 vols., New York, 1928-1937), II, 334-35; McPherson, *Handbook of Politics* (1882), 63, 65; *ibid.* (1886), 78; *ibid.* (1888), 82, 83; *ibid.* (1890), 72, 73. According to his own statement, Blair was the real author of the earlier Morrill bill for the support of agricultural colleges. Blair to J. L. M. Curry, [1884], Curry Papers (Division of Manuscripts, Library of Congress).

[15] *Cong. Record,* 47 Cong., 1 Sess., 70 (December 12, 1881), 226 (December 20, 1881), 270-71 (January 9, 1882), 4820-33 (June 13, 1882). For the full text of the original Blair bill, see *ibid.,* 227.

should have precedence prevented the consideration of either.[16]

A number of similar plans were proposed in the House of Representatives. A substitute for all of these, reported by John C. Sherwin, Republican of Illinois, provided annual appropriations of $10,000,000 for five years distributed to the states on the basis of illiteracy. Since this Sherwin bill lacked the elaborate provisions for federal inspection called for in the Blair bill, some thought that it had a better chance of becoming law.[17] Despite strong support from southern Democrats, however, the opposition group, by a close margin, blocked a vote on the measure.[18]

Before Blair reintroduced his proposal in the next Congress, interest had spread, particularly in the South. An Interstate Educational Convention met concurrently with the Louisville Exposition in September, 1883, and appointed a commission to draft a federal aid bill. The resulting proposal, later submitted to Congress, differed from the original Blair bill in providing for a smaller total appropriation and in vesting more control in the hands of state officials.[19] Although this proposal never received formal consideration, it undoubtedly influenced the new education bill as reported to the Senate in January, 1884.

This second Blair bill provided for virtually complete control over the funds by state officials rather than the joint control by federal and state officials specified in the original bill.[20] During March and the first week of April, 1884, the Senate devoted much time to debating the proposal. Numerous changes were made, the most important of which reduced the total appropriation to $77,000,000 distributed over a period of seven years. Some amendments pleased

16 *Ibid.*, 47 Cong., 2 Sess., 1014-15 (January 9, 1883). Senator Morrill later complained that the Senate committee would not permit his bill to come up until the Blair bill had passed both houses. *Ibid.*, 49 Cong., 1 Sess., 1480 (February 16, 1886).

17 Amory D. Mayo, *National Aid to Education* (Boston, 1883), 4. For a copy of the bill, see "Support of Common Schools," *House Reports*, 47 Cong., 1 Sess., No. 1214, pp. 5-7.

18 *Cong. Record*, 47 Cong., 1 Sess., 6354 (July 22, 1882), 6573-75 (July 27, 1882), Appendix, 582-91; *ibid.*, 47 Cong., 2 Sess., 1202-1205 (January 15, 1883), 3253-60 (February 24, 1883), Appendix, 173, 281-87.

19 "Support of Common Schools," *House Reports*, 48 Cong., 1 Sess., No. 495, Pt. 2, pp. 6-12.

20 Senator James L. Pugh of Alabama played an important part in revising this second bill. *Cong. Record*, 49 Cong., 1 Sess., 1479 (February 16, 1886); *ibid.*, 50 Cong., 1 Sess., 870-71 (February 1, 1888). For copies of the various versions of Blair's proposal, along with his speeches and tables of educational statistics, reprinted from the *Congressional Record*, see Henry W. Blair, *The Education Bill* (Washington, 1887).

northerners, such as that by Senator Benjamin Harrison imposing stiffer restrictions against racial discrimination in distributing the funds. Satisfactory to southerners was the provision that separate schools would not be interpreted as discrimination. The bill finally passed on April 7 by a vote of 42 to 21, with the greater support coming from the Republicans, but with substantial support from a group of Democrats.[21]

The Blair bill itself was not reported or discussed in the House of Representatives, but a number of similar measures were introduced. In February, 1884, Kentucky's Albert S. Willis reported from the Committee on Education a substitute for all of these; it was essentially the same as Blair's proposal but appropriated a smaller sum, $55,000,000 over a ten-year period. Although referred to committee of the whole, the measure never came up for consideration in an open session of the House.[22]

The controversy over federal aid for education reached a climax early in 1886. As expected even by its critics, the third Blair bill, after lengthy debate, passed the Senate on March 5 in essentially the same form as the second Blair bill two years earlier. The vote showed a slightly larger favorable majority, 46 to 22, with the greater support still coming from the Republicans.[23] In spite of widespread opinion that this bill or a similar measure would pass the House in 1886,[24] the Committee on Education failed to act. In vain did Democrats James W. Reid of North Carolina and Joseph Wheeler of Alabama propose resolutions requiring the committee to report. At the suggestion of Representative Willis the House on March 29 decided to transfer the bill to the Committee

[21] *Cong. Record*, 48 Cong., 1 Sess., 2100-2719 (March 20 to April 7, 1884), *passim*, 2724 (April 7, 1884); McPherson, *Handbook of Politics* (1884), 146-47. The vote showed 24 Republicans and 18 Democrats for the bill; 15 Democrats and 6 Republicans against.

[22] *Cong. Record*, 48 Cong., 1 Sess., 1066 (February 12, 1884), 1174 (February 15, 1884), 1359 (February 25, 1884). The minority of the Committee on Education favored a measure similar to that proposed by the Interstate Educational Commission. "Support of Common Schools," *House Reports*, 48 Cong., 1 Sess., No. 495, Parts 1 and 2.

[23] The vote for the bill was 28 Republicans and 18 Democrats; against, 12 Democrats and 10 Republicans. An amendment was added, appropriating an additional $2,000,000 for the first year on a matching basis for school construction. *Cong. Record*, 49 Cong., 1 Sess., 2105 (March 5, 1886).

[24] See for example *The Nation* (New York), XLII (January 21, 1886), 51-52; Raleigh *State Chronicle*, February 25, 1886; Raleigh *News and Observer*, March 7, 1886.

on Labor which was thought to be more favorably disposed. A month later, however, that committee reported a substitute which returned to the idea of an educational fund derived from public land sales. Although at no time during the decade in which the Blair bill was before the Senate did the House take a formal vote on a comparable measure of its own, the vote to transfer to the Committee on Labor can be considered in the nature of a test vote. Those voting in favor of the transfer were likely to favor a Blair-type proposal. On this vote, passed by a margin of 139 to 113, it was apparent that Democratic support was proportionately slightly greater in the House than in the Senate.[25]

After 1886, support for the Blair bill in the Senate diminished, and supporters of such a measure in the House were unable to bring it up for consideration on the floor. No assistance could be looked for from President Cleveland, in office since 1885, since he was becoming even stronger in his demands for tariff reduction and his opposition to surplus-reducing schemes sponsored by Republicans. When the third Blair bill again came to a vote in the Senate, early in 1888, it was passed by a vote of 43 to 33, with somewhat less support this time even from Republicans.[26] Two years later, in 1890, although Republicans controlled both houses of Congress, the fourth and last Blair bill was defeated in the Senate by a vote of 42 to 36.[27] With a growing increase through the decade in both Republican and Democratic opposition to the proposal, the Blair bill after 1890 was no longer a live issue, although southern educational needs were no less urgent than before.

The defeat of the fourth Blair bill, ending the effort which had been begun in 1881 to secure congressional approval of Senator Blair's proposals for federal aid, terminated a decade of southern

[25] The vote for the transfer was 80 Republicans and 59 Democrats; against, 27 Republicans and 86 Democrats. *Cong. Record,* 49 Cong., 1 Sess., 2410 (March 16, 1886), 2633 (March 22, 1886), 2881-82 (March 29, 1886), 3888 (April 27, 1886); *ibid.*, 49 Cong., 2 Sess., 777-78 (January 18, 1887); "Establishment and Temporary Support of Common Schools," *House Reports,* 49 Cong., 1 Sess., No. 1993; New York *Times,* March 30, 1886.

[26] The vote for was 26 Republicans and 17 Democrats; against, 13 Republicans and 20 Democrats. *Cong. Record,* 50 Cong., 1 Sess., 268-1050 (January 1 to February 8, 1888), *passim,* 1223 (February 15, 1888).

[27] *Ibid.,* 51 Cong., 1 Sess., 1067-2436 (February 5 to March 20, 1890), *passim.* Although one House bill received a favorable committee report, it did not come up for consideration on the floor. "Establishment and Temporary Support of Common Schools," *House Reports,* 51 Cong., 1 Sess., No. 2605.

controversy over the proposals. The South had a great deal more to gain from them than did the North, yet opinion in the South and among southern congressmen had been divided. Perhaps the readiest method of analyzing this division within the South is to observe first the character and interests of those individuals or groups who favored the proposals.

In Congress the Blair bill was consistently supported by both senators from Georgia, Mississippi, Louisiana, Florida, Arkansas, North Carolina, and Virginia, and by one senator each from Alabama and South Carolina.[28] Some southern senators gave perfunctory support to the bill, perhaps acting only in response to instructions from their legislatures, while others, such as James Z. George of Mississippi, James L. Pugh of Alabama, Joseph E. Brown of Georgia, Augustus H. Garland of Arkansas, Wade Hampton of South Carolina, Charles W. Jones and Wilkinson Call of Florida, and Harrison H. Riddleberger of Virginia, vigorously supported the bill in open debate. In the House of Representatives strenuous but futile efforts to bring the Blair bill or similar measures to the floor for a clear-cut vote were made by such southern representatives as Albert S. Willis of Kentucky, Joseph Wheeler of Alabama, Judson C. Clements of Georgia, Clement Dowd and James W. Reid of North Carolina, John F. King of Louisiana, and John W. Daniel and George D. Wise of Virginia.

Southern educational leaders and those interested in the cause of southern education almost solidly backed Blair's plan. In addition to support from the National Education Association numerous southern teachers' associations, both Negro and white, passed resolutions in favor of the Blair bill and often sent petitions to Congress. In 1886 the superintendents of education in thirteen southern states as a group memorialized Congress for "speedy action in aid of education." [29] The two men who held the office of United

[28] In some states, such as Tennessee, Kentucky, and West Virginia, the senators did not vote consistently in the different Congresses.

[29] *Cong. Record*, 49 Cong., 1 Sess., 2410 (March 16, 1886). For typical petitions see *ibid.*, 48 Cong., 1 Sess., 425 (January 16, 1884), 1743 (March 10, 1884), 3514 (April 23, 1884); *ibid.*, 48 Cong., 2 Sess., 465 (January 5, 1885), 845 (January 19, 1885), 1987 (February 20, 1885); *ibid.*, 49 Cong., 1 Sess., 134 (December 9, 1885), 345, 398 (December 21, 1885), 2572 (March 19, 1886), 7667 (July 28, 1886); *Report of the Commissioner of Education* (1887-1888), 424. Between 1881 and 1891 thirty-two public educational organizations in the South petitioned Congress as compared with fourteen from all the rest of the country. Lee, *Struggle for Federal Aid*, 95. The *Proceedings of the Department of Superintendence of the National Education Association* during the

States commissioner of education in the 1880's, John Eaton, who had been state superintendent of education in Tennessee, and N. H. R. Dawson of Alabama, endorsed the idea of federal aid, and specifically the Blair bill.[30] Amory D. Mayo, a northern preacher particularly prominent in the cause of southern education, was one of Blair's most effective supporters, emphasizing the point that the South both needed and deserved the aid.[31] Although the trustees of the Peabody Fund took no formal action on the question of federal aid after 1880, Chairman Winthrop in private and Agent J. L. M. Curry in public vigorously supported Blair's efforts.[32]

Southern newspapers were somewhat divided on the issue; for example, forty-one Tennessee papers have been listed as approving the bill in 1887 and forty-three opposed.[33] But the daily papers in the larger cities almost unanimously supported the bill prior to 1889. Among the leading advocates were the Richmond *Dispatch*, the Charleston *News and Courier*, the New Orleans *Picayune*, the Jacksonville *Florida Times-Union*, the Raleigh *News and Observer*, the Raleigh *State Chronicle*, the Montgomery *Advertiser*, and papers under the influence of Colonel Arthur S. Colyar of Nashville, such as the Nashville *Union*, the Chattanooga *Times*, the Atlanta *Constitution*, the Birmingham *Age*, and the Mobile *Register*. Negro, Republican, and independent newspapers in the South appear to have consistently favored the bill.[34]

Senator Blair's proposal also stirred up strong reactions in

1880's (Bureau of Education, Circulars of Information, Washington, 1882-1888), record more speeches in favor of the Blair bill than against it from southern delegates to its annual meetings. See also "Support of Common Schools," *House Reports*, 48 Cong., 1 Sess., No. 495, Pt. 1, pp. 22-32.

[30] *Report of the Commissioner of Education* (1883-1884), cclxx-cclxxi; *ibid.* (1884-1885), cccxiii; *ibid.* (1887-1888), 33.

[31] "Notes on the Hearings," *Senate Misc. Docs.*, 48 Cong., 1 Sess., No. 72, pp. 14-18; Mayo, "Last Words from the South," *Proceedings of the National Education Association* (1884), 117-24; Mayo, *National Aid to Education.*

[32] Robert C. Winthrop to Hamilton Fish, February 13, 1890, Hamilton Fish Papers (Division of Manuscripts, Library of Congress); Jessie P. Rice, *J. L. M. Curry: Southern Statesman and Educator* (New York, 1949), 141, 152-54.

[33] Robison, "Governor Taylor and the Blair Bill," *Tennessee Historical Magazine*, Second Series, II (October, 1931), 36, 44-45. In the previous year in North Carolina twenty-one papers were listed as favorable and seven as opposed. Raleigh *State Chronicle*, April 1, 15, 1886; Fayetteville (N. C.) *Observer and Gazette*, February 2, 1886.

[34] As examples, see Winston (N. C.) *Union Republican*, February 25, March 11, 1886, January 12, 26, 1888; Huntsville (Ala.) *Gazette*, April 15, 22, 1882; Huntsville *Advocate*, October 27, 1884; Montgomery *Colored Citizen*, May 3, 1884.

southern state legislatures that sometimes resulted in resolutions instructing senators and requesting representatives to support the bill. A survey of state legislative documents shows that petitions of support passed the North Carolina legislature four times, the Louisiana legislature three times, Georgia, Mississippi, and Virginia twice each, and Alabama and Florida once each. In 1886 a Blair supporter in the House of Representatives stated that the legislatures of ten southern states had at one time or another passed such resolutions.[35]

The Blair bill often served, too, as a key issue in southern state elections in the mid-1880's. In Virginia, the Republicans made political capital by accusing the Democratic party of blocking the measure in the House. The gains of Republicans in Kentucky were attributed to the fact that state Democrats had opposed the Blair bill.[36] In Tennessee, Robert L. Taylor, both in the gubernatorial election of 1886 and during his first term as governor, was compelled to steer a difficult middle-of-the-road course on the Blair bill between the diametrically opposed positions of the two Democratic factions in his state.[37] Other southern governors also generally took equivocal positions because of divided opinion within their states, but open support did come from Governors Thomas Seay of Alabama and Alfred M. Scales of North Carolina.[38] Although national Democratic platforms avoided the issue of the Blair bill, a number of southern state Democratic platforms endorsed it. These were sometimes qualified in a manner similar to the North Carolina plank which specified that the funds be "disbursed by State agents and not accompanied by objectionable features." Southern Republican state platforms usually gave unqualified endorsement.[39]

Among nonpolitical groups, farm and labor organizations in the

[35] *Cong. Record*, 49 Cong., 1 Sess., 2410 (March 16, 1886). Many more such resolutions came from southern legislatures than from those in all the rest of the country combined. See table of petitions to Congress, in Lee, *Struggle for Federal Aid*, 95.

[36] Richmond *Dispatch*, March 9, 12, 1886; *Nation*, XLV (August 25, 1887), 145.

[37] Daniel M. Robison, *Bob Taylor and the Agrarian Revolt in Tennessee* (Chapel Hill, 1935), 83-90.

[38] *Report of the Commissioner of Education* (1887-1888), 167-68; Raleigh *State Chronicle*, March 25, 1886. For the local significance of the Blair bill in Alabama, see Allen J. Going, *Bourbon Democracy in Alabama, 1874-1890* (University, Ala., 1951), 156-57.

[39] *Appletons' Annual Cyclopaedia* (New York, 1884), 424, 529, 594; *ibid.* (1886), 10, 619, 656; *ibid.* (1888), 619; Richmond *Dispatch*, January 15, 1888.

South did not generally take definite stands on the bill. At least one religious denomination, the Methodist, actively supported it, both in the *Southern Christian Advocate* and through the writings and speeches of Bishop Atticus G. Haygood. In literary circles, George Washington Cable, a caustic critic of southern conditions but vitally concerned with the Negro's welfare, ardently advocated the measure.[40] It is impossible to say what percentage of the southern people as a whole supported Blair's proposal. The *Congressional Record* lists a total of 593 petitions from private citizens in the South as compared with 771 from all other sections of the country. Senator Blair stated that there was unanimous support for his bill among the people of South Carolina. A more judicious appraisal, made of North Carolina opinion, concluded that "public endorsement" was "widespread." [41]

The arguments employed by Blair's southern supporters ranged widely. Southern advocates usually began by pointing out that a treasury surplus existed, that educational need was admitted, and that federal aid was the obvious and unanswerable solution. The census figures on illiteracy were quoted repeatedly to prove that the South alone could not cope with the existing emergency. The South should receive its share, argued one newspaper, or otherwise Congress would continue "to make extravagant appropriations . . . to be distributed in the North in the way of pensions and monuments to soldiers." [42] At the same time, it was often pointed out, southern states were doing everything within their power to carry an impossible financial burden. "I ask the nation," said Rev. Amory D. Mayo, "to help the Southern people beause no people, under similar disadvantages, has done so big a job of helping itself." And J. L. M. Curry, after citing a mass of figures on taxable wealth and educational appropriations, concluded that "What the South has done for free education is marvellous." [43]

40 Hunter D. Farish, *The Circuit Rider Dismounts* (Richmond, 1938), 203-204, 248-49; Atticus G. Haygood, *If Universal Suffrage, Then Universal Education* (Bureau of Education, Circular No. 3: Washington, 1883); George W. Cable, *The Negro Question* (New York, 1890), 59-65.

41 *Cong. Record*, 49 Cong., 1 Sess., 1259 (February 9, 1886), 1481 (February 16, 1886); Joseph F. Steelman, "The Progressive Era in North Carolina" (Ph.D. dissertation, University of North Carolina, 1955), 73.

42 New Bern (N. C.) *Daily Journal*, April 6, 1886.

43 Amory D. Mayo, *Building for the Children in the South* (n.p., 1884), 163; J. L. M. Curry, *National Aid to Education* (Bureau of Education, Circular of Information No. 3: Washington, 1884), 91.

The burden of educating the Negroes, however, seemed overwhelming, and it was argued strongly that it particularly was a burden which the nation as a whole must share. "In asking the passage of the Blair bill," said one newspaper, "it [the South] only demands that the General Government should recognize an obligation which rests . . . equally upon all the sections, and which the South has so far borne alone." [44] Among other commentators, George W. Cable wrote that federal aid must be supplied, "not as a national condescension or charity, but as the one final payment of a national obligation." [45] A corollary to this argument was the point often made that since the North forcibly enfranchised the Negro, it should assist in making him a literate voter. "As this illiterate citizenship is protected by the Constitution in the suffrage," said Senator Howell E. Jackson of Tennessee, "why should not the General Government . . . aid in preparing them for its wise and intelligent exercise?" [46] And a North Carolina newspaper summed up the views of many southerners in its statement that the Blair bill "simply proposes to pay a debt the country as a whole owes this section." [47]

Southern advocates gave particular attention to several of the more common objections made to the bill. In reply to the charge of its unconstitutionality, they cited the precedents of land-grant aid to education as well as federal appropriations to Indian and Alaskan schools. "Can you vote money to educate Indians," asked Senator George of Mississippi, "and not have the power to vote money to educate negroes and white men?" And Senator Jackson defended the bill "as warranted by the express language of the Constitution . . . approved by the unquestioned weight of high authority, and . . . sanctioned by the contemporaneous and continued practice of the government." [48] If the Constitution permitted assistance to Chicago

[44] New Orleans *Picayune*, February 19, 1886.

[45] Cable, *The Negro Question*, 61.

[46] *Cong. Record*, 49 Cong., 1 Sess., 1475 (February 16, 1886). Senator James Z. George of Mississippi summarized the plight of his region by saying: "I see in the South millions of unlettered children; I see in the South, wasted and desolated by war, an inability to educate them. . . . I see on the part of the propertied classes of the South a willingness to help them; but . . . there is in many of the states . . . an inability to meet the demand." *Ibid.*, 48 Cong., 1 Sess., 2514 (April 2, 1884). As evidence of the seriousness of the situation, one report claimed that illiterate voters held the balance of power in ten northern and all southern states. "Support of Common Schools," *House Reports*, 49 Cong., 1 Sess., No. 495, Pt. 1, p. 21.

[47] Raleigh *News and Observer*, March 9, 1886.

[48] *Cong. Record*, 49 Cong., 1 Sess., 1474 (February 16, 1886), 1768 (February 25,

after the fire, and to flood victims in the Mississippi Valley, argued a southern editor, then certainly it should permit aid to the South in its critical emergency.[49]

Blair's southern supporters also emphasized repeatedly that under the terms of the bill, with control vested in the hands of state officials, there would be little danger of unwarranted federal influence. "The government," said Senator Randall L. Gibson of Louisiana, "parts from its jurisdiction when it parts with the property by executing the donation." [50] Finally, the proponents of federal aid accused their opponents of using arguments like that of unconstitutionality simply to conceal a fundamental opposition to publicly supported education. When Senator John T. Morgan of Alabama intimated that some of the best people, both Negro and white, had no formal education, a Birmingham paper stated: "Senator Morgan is perfectly sincere in his views of public education, but he is a century and a half behind the age in which he lives." [51] A Charleston paper assailed those who were attempting to keep the Negro in a servile position by denying him access to knowledge; and a Florida editorial writer concluded that opposition to the Blair bill really came from two sources: "penurious Northerners who want to close the treasury to all hands but their own, and those who want to keep the Negroes uneducated." [52]

Opponents of federal aid to education were numerous in the South but not quite so outspoken as the supporters. On the three roll call Senate votes between 1884 and 1888, both senators from Texas, Delaware, Missouri, and Maryland, and one senator each from Alabama, South Carolina, Tennessee, and Kentucky voted

1886). See also Senator Pugh's arguments upholding constitutionality. *Ibid.*, 50 Cong., 1 Sess., 869-73 (February 1, 1888).

[49] Charleston *News and Courier*, January 31, 1888.

[50] *Cong. Record*, 48 Cong., 1 Sess., 2593 (April 4, 1884). This guarantee of state control provoked considerable northern opposition and prompted a number of qualifying amendments, some of which passed. McPherson, *Handbook of Politics* (1884), 146; *ibid.*, (1886), 160; *Cong. Record*, 49 Cong., 1 Sess., 1240 (February 9, 1886), 1993-94 (March 3, 1886), 2085 (March 5, 1886); Louisville *Courier-Journal*, March 4, 1886.

[51] Birmingham *Age*, February 13, 1886. Morgan publicly expressed his doubts about education for the Negro when he said, "He [the Negro] belongs to a class. . . . Do for him what we may, we have not the moral power or the political or physical power to elevate that man out of that groove." *Cong. Record*, 48 Cong., 1 Sess., 2635 (April 5, 1884).

[52] Charleston *News and Courier*, January 31, 1888; Jacksonville *Florida Times-Union*, February 12, 1886.

against the Blair bill.[53] Senator Morgan of Alabama led the opposition on the Senate floor and became so bitter that he and Blair were reportedly the only two senators who did not speak when they met.[54] Also outspoken in their criticism were Senators Samuel B. Maxey and John H. Reagan of Texas, Matthew C. Butler of South Carolina, and Thomas F. Bayard and Eli Saulsbury of Delaware.

Since no debate on the bill ever occurred on the floor of the House, it is impossible to say which southern representatives would have joined the opposition. There is no doubt, however, that Speaker John G. Carlisle of Kentucky effectively blocked the consideration and possible passage of the Blair bill. He unalterably opposed what he considered reckless spending of the treasury surplus, a practice that he feared might lead to tariff increases. His opposition to the bill or any similar measure was common knowledge, and he would recognize no one for the purpose of calling it up for consideration.[55] By packing the Committee on Education with those known to be opposed to federal aid, he condemned the bill to inevitable death in committee. Of the thirteen members of the committee in 1886, only four favored the bill in the test vote on the floor.[56] In 1888 a newspaper interview with the chairman of the committee, Allen D. Candler of Georgia, reported that Candler, who was more favorably disposed than any other member, believed that the Senate version required too much federal supervision.[57]

In the southern states opponents of the Blair bill usually concentrated their efforts on defeating legislative resolutions of approval rather than attempting to sponsor resolutions of disapproval.[58] In the late 1880's, however, after opposition had considerably increased, the legislatures of Kentucky and Arkansas did

[53] Both senators from Tennessee and Kentucky voted against the bill in 1888.

[54] Birmingham *Age-Herald*, January 23, 1889.

[55] James A. Barnes, *John G. Carlisle* (New York, 1931), 137, 152-53. One ardent supporter wrote another, "Carlisle's violent course in resisting even the consideration of it [Blair bill] by a Commee leaves me no hope of anything being accomplished." Winthrop to Curry, February 7, 1888, Curry Papers.

[56] All three northern Democrats opposed the bill, along with two southern Democrats, James F. Miller of Texas and James N. Burnes of Missouri. The favorable votes came from two southern Democrats and two northern Republicans. *Cong. Record*, 49 Cong., 1 Sess., 2882 (March 29, 1886); *Congressional Directory*, 49 Cong., 1 Sess., 108.

[57] Raleigh *State Chronicle*, January 12, 1888.

[58] For example, in 1885 the Tennessee legislature failed to adopt a favorable resolution by one vote. Robison, "Governor Taylor and the Blair Bill," *Tennessee Historical Magazine*, Second Series, II (October, 1931), 38.

formally petition their senators and representatives to oppose the bill.[59] The Kentucky and Texas state Democratic platforms also included opposition planks.[60] Both Governor Edward A. O'Neal and former Governor Rufus W. Cobb of Alabama privately supported Senator Morgan in his fight against the bill.[61] Organized groups of citizens in the South appear to have supported, rather than opposed the bill. The *Congressional Record* does not list a single unfavorable petition from any such group. A few private individuals, however, did put their opposition on record. Among these were Oscar H. Cooper, Texas state superintendent of public instruction; General Samuel C. Armstrong, president of Hampton Institute; and Woodrow Wilson, who had in 1882, as a lawyer in Atlanta, witnessed a debate on the subject in the Georgia legislature.[62]

Although most newspapers in the larger southern towns approved Blair's proposal, there were a few notable exceptions. The Baltimore *Sun* questioned its constitutionality. The Galveston *News* bitterly denounced it and quoted other Texas newspapers in a similar vein. And the Nashville *American* stated that there were many other matters of more pressing importance.[63] Just as the New York *Evening Post* and the *Nation* headed the fight against the Blair bill in the North, the Louisville *Courier-Journal* led the journalistic attack in the South. Editor Henry Watterson utilized every conceivable argument, combining sledgehammer blows with biting satire against the "vicious plan of Granny Blair" backed by "political demagogues, tricksters, charlatans . . . and professional philanthropists." When the Senate defeated the bill in 1890, Watterson exulted: "The bait is refused, the snare has been laid in vain. . . . The sham philanthropy of the day was rebuked . . . and a most insidious attack on the common school system of the country was

59 Arkansas General Assembly, *Acts* (Little Rock, 1889), 190; Kentucky General Assembly, *Acts* (Frankfort, 1888), 229-30.

60 Louisville *Courier-Journal*, January 20, 1888; *Cong. Record*, 49 Cong., 1 Sess., 1481 (February 16, 1886).

61 Rufus W. Cobb to John T. Morgan, March 11, 1886, John T. Morgan Papers (Division of Manuscripts, Library of Congress); *Cong. Record*, 49 Cong., 1 Sess., 1606 (February 18, 1886).

62 Galveston *News*, February 13, 1888; "Georgia Rejects," *Nation*, XLIX (August 1, 1889), 84; Winthrop to Curry, February 7, 1888, Curry Papers.

63 Baltimore *Sun*, March 6, 1886, February 15, 1888; Galveston *News*, February 15, 1888, February 28, 1890; Nashville *American*, March 4, 8, 1886.

repelled."[64] By 1890, too, some of the southern papers that previously had supported the measure were opposing it.[65]

The argument most frequently employed in opposing the Blair bill was its alleged unconstitutionality. It was contended that no clause in the Constitution warranted such an appropriation, and that the provisions of the bill undermined the basic theory of the division of powers between the federal and the state governments. Senator Bayard of Delaware believed that measures of such a nature would "lead inexorably to the overthrow of the whole theory of our form of government."[66] Senator Morgan and others pressed this point at great length, citing innumerable precedents and authorities. As an example of what he considered the ridiculous extremes to which such an interpretation of the Constitution might lead, Morgan mentioned national prohibition, pure food and drug laws, abolition of penitentiaries, requirement of higher wages for workers, and socialized medicine.[67] One newspaper editor conceived of the bill as beginning "the gradual extension of the National Government to supercede State Government and even municipal government."[68]

A related argument held that even if the purpose of the aid was only temporarily to alleviate an emergency situation, it tended to destroy the self-reliance and the educational efforts of the southern states themselves. Senator Butler of South Carolina contended that the effects of the Blair bill would be "to induce . . . a very great many men who are now earnestly struggling to build up their own local institutions to put their hands in their pockets and say, 'The General Government is going to educate everybody'."[69] Editor Watterson stated this point of view in greater detail. "We recognize the Blair Bill," he said, "as the chief obstacle to the growth of the common-school system in the South. We know that it has destroyed self-reliance; we know that many communities have postponed the question of local taxation, deluded with the idea that

64 Louisville *Courier-Journal*, February 22, 1886, January 24, 1888, March 22, 1890.

65 Jacksonville *Florida Times-Union*, March 24, 1890; Charleston *News and Courier*, February 8, 1890; Atlanta *Constitution*, March 7, 1890.

66 *Cong. Record*, 48 Cong., 1 Sess., 2584 (April 4, 1884).

67 *Ibid.*, 2106 (March 20, 1884), 2460-68 (April 1, 1884), 2581-84, 2595-98 (April 4, 1884); *ibid.*, 49 Cong., 1 Sess., 1340-41 (February 11, 1886); *ibid.*, 50 Cong., 1 Sess., 269-72 (January 5, 1888).

68 Galveston *News*, quoted in Louisville *Courier-Journal*, March 1, 1886.

69 *Cong. Record*, 48 Cong., 1 Sess., 2290 (March 26, 1884).

Federal appropriations would make it unnecessary to resort to local aid." [70] Watterson's paper often referred to Blair's proposal as "a bill to promote mendicancy," a phrase employed by many other critics. It was argued that public education in the southern states had made and was making great strides forward without federal aid.[71]

The opposition frequently contended, also, that in spite of the provisions in the bill for local administration the inevitable result would be federal control leading to a nationalized educational system. "I regard this measure," said Senator James B. Beck of Kentucky, "as a Pandora's box. . . . It is the entering-wedge to absolute Federal domination over education in the States." [72] Senator Beck believed that such "federal domination" would be climaxed by a demand for mixed schools, although no dominant part of the southern argument in these years centered about the issue of integrated schools. Restrictive amendments proposed by northerners and their remarks in the Senate implying suspicion and distrust of the South [73] led some southerners to view Blair's proposal as an attempted revival of the Reconstruction pattern. "The Blair bill," said an unidentified former slaveholder, "is simply . . . the old hallucination, 'fifty acres and a mule,' which has caused more briers and sassafras bushes to grow in Southern fields than all else." [74] Some southerners, in a similar frame of mind, were suspicious of a proposal pushed so vigorously by a New England refomer, and they sometimes resorted to personal ridicule. The *Courier-Journal* referred to Blair as "the most visionary and ridiculous old granny in the Senate. . . . It is as necessary for him to make speeches as it is for gas to rise upward, and it is simply an impossibility for him to make a sensible speech on a sensible subject." [75]

[70] Louisville *Courier-Journal,* February 17, 1888. The paper criticized such proponents of federal aid as Senators George and Jackson, Representative Willis, and Colonel Colyar for failing to make any efforts for increased state and local support for schools. *Ibid.,* February 27, 1886, February 9, 1888.

[71] *Ibid.,* February 23, 1886.

[72] *Cong. Record,* 48 Cong., 1 Sess., 2540 (April 3, 1884). See also Galveston *News,* February 20, 1886, February 28, 1890; Baltimore *Sun,* February 24, 1886; Fayetteville (N. C.) *Observer,* January 19, 1888.

[73] See especially remarks of Senators John Sherman and Charles H. Van Wyck and Representative John C. Sherwin. *Cong. Record,* 47 Cong., 2 Sess., 3257 (February 24, 1883); *ibid.,* 48 Cong., 1 Sess., 2062-63 (March 19, 1884), 2514 (April 2, 1884).

[74] Quoted in *Nation,* XLII (January 21, 1886), 52. See also Louisville *Courier-Journal,* February 22, 1886.

[75] Louisville *Courier-Journal,* March 3, 1886, January 24, 1888. Southerners were

Another strong opposition argument centered around the problem of financing the federal aid. Although a treasury surplus existed at the time, it was argued, Congress should not commit future funds that might necessitate increased taxation. "It is assistance so bestowed," said the *Courier-Journal*, "as to make continued assistance . . . essential. There is no way of turning back once we have entered on this path."[76] Both Senators Beck and Morgan vehemently argued that the money which was available had been accumulated by "oppressive taxation" and that the proposal would impose even heavier future burdens on the common people of the country.[77] Time and again southern opponents contended that the primary objective, a Republican one, was not to aid education or to reduce illiteracy but simply to reduce the surplus as a prerequisite to the Republican aim of maintaining or raising protective tariff rates. As Watterson saw the situation, the supporters of the bill were "willing to accept any excuse, however transparent, for reducing the surplus in the Treasury"; and time and again it was pointed out that Blair himself was an ardent protectionist as well as the author of the treasury-depleting dependent pension bill.[78] Very frequently those southern newspapers advocating a protective tariff policy were also supporters of the Blair bill, while many of the papers opposed to the bill, like the *Courier-Journal*, vigorously fought for tariff reduction.

The whole Blair bill controversy rather clearly illustrates the divided mind of the post-Civil War southern Democrats. It seems clear that the proposal received its most vigorous political support,

not alone in ridiculing Blair. The New York *Times*, February 21, 1890, said: "Senators may come and Senators may go, as they commonly do when he [Blair] has the floor, but he will go on forever."

[76] Louisville *Courier-Journal*, March 11, 1886.

[77] *Cong. Record*, 48 Cong., 1 Sess., 2539-40 (April 3, 1884), 2595 (April 4, 1884); *ibid.*, 49 Cong., 1 Sess., 1337-38 (February 11, 1886), 1438 (February 15, 1886). Similar feelings prompted Senators Butler and Maxey to propose unsuccessful amendments specifying more definitely where the money should come from. *Ibid.*, 48 Cong., 1 Sess., 1562 (February 17, 1886).

[78] Louisville *Courier-Journal*, February 27, 1886. For Blair's connection with the pension bill, see *Nation*, XLII (May 27, 1886), 435; *Cong. Record*, 49 Cong., 2 Sess., 1072-75 (January 27, 1887). In debating the Blair bill Senator Beck spent most of his time denouncing protection, which, he said, "is the main object of the Republican advocates of this bill." *Cong. Record*, 48 Cong., 1 Sess., 2540-52 (April 3, 1884). And an Alabama legislator explained what many southern opponents meant by "the Blair bribe" when he described the bill as "a bribe to keep us quiet about the excessive taxes and tariffs of the Federal government." J. W. John, quoted in Montgomery *Advertiser*, February 11, 1887.

among southern congressmen and in the South at large, from the Redeemer, or Bourbon, faction who placed their faith in business-industrial development and in alliance with the East, while the opposition generally came from the more agrarian-minded faction that emphasized the traditional Democratic virtues of state rights and low taxes. The two Georgia senators, Joseph E. Brown and Alfred H. Colquitt, belonged to their state's famous Redeemer triumvirate and consistently supported the bill. Mississippi had a similar triumvirate, and all three of its members, James Z. George, Lucius Q. C. Lamar, and Edward C. Walthall, who succeeded Lamar in 1885, supported it.[79] In Tennessee, Senator Howell E. Jackson, spokesman for the Colyar-industrial wing of the Democratic party, vigorously promoted the bill until his resignation in 1886, while Isham G. Harris and Jackson's successor, William B. Bate, members of the agrarian, state rights wing, consistently opposed it. Senator James B. Beck of Kentucky, who strongly opposed Blair, was originally elected by an agrarian-controlled legislature.[80] "New South" newspapers denounced the opposition to federal aid as "old fogyism" and as "sentimental, unpractical, and out of joint with progressive times." [81] There were some special considerations, of course, in this general pattern. The almost unanimous opposition of Texas senators and representatives may be best accounted for on the grounds that Texas public land holdings were considered entirely adequate to support the state schools without outside aid. And Henry Watterson, who generally espoused the Redeemer-New South program, put tariff reduction above all other considerations at this time and considered the Blair bill merely a political scheme to retain high protective rates.

Although the South had more at stake than did other parts of the country in the success or failure of the Blair bill, the ultimate de-

[79] Woodward, *Origins of the New South,* 14-17; Albert D. Kirwan, *Revolt of the Rednecks: Mississippi Politics, 1876-1925* (Lexington, Ky., 1951), 9, 48.

[80] Robison, *Bob Taylor and the Agrarian Revolt in Tennessee*, 16, 56; Thomas D. Clark, *A History of Kentucky* (New York, 1937), 589. In South Carolina and Alabama, where no clear-cut factions existed, the differing opinions of their senators cannot be so readily explained. In Alabama, Senator Pugh may have been influenced by his ante-bellum Whig connections, and Morgan advocated a political alliance between West and South rather than the Southern-Eastern alliance favored by most Redeemers. See John T. Morgan, "The Political Alliance of the South with the West," *North American Review* (New York), CXXVI (March, 1878), 309-22.

[81] Richmond *Dispatch,* March 17, 1886. See also Atlanta *Constitution,* December 20, 1884.

feat of the bill cannot be attributed to any one section of the country, or, for that matter, to either political party alone. It is true that in the four Senate votes more Democratic than Republican votes were cast against the bill, but in each vote except the last well over one third of the favorable votes were Democratic. The party division on each of these four occasions may be conveniently summarized in tabular form:

PARTY VOTING IN SENATE ON BLAIR BILL

	For		Against	
Year	*Republicans*	*Democrats*	*Republicans*	*Democrats*
1884	24	18	6	15
1886	28	18	10	12
1888	26	17	13	20
1890	26	10	18	24
	104	63	47	71

The table illustrates one additional fact about Democratic support, namely, that in the first two votes the Democrats favoring the measure outnumbered those opposing it. As the following table shows, the bulk of this Democratic senatorial support came from the former Confederate states, and the bulk of the Democratic opposition from the border and northern states.

DEMOCRATIC VOTING IN SENATE ON BLAIR BILL

	For		Against	
Year	*Former Confederate States*	*Former Union States*	*Former Confederate States*	*Former Union States*
1884	14	4	5	10
1886	14	4	5	7
1888	15	2	6	14
1890	9	1	11	13
	52	11	27	44

Southern Democrats, it is evident, provided the main strength of the Democratic support for the bill in the Senate. And, in addition, all of the southern Republican senators supported the bill. Thus, the limited pattern of senatorial voting that emerges is one which shows that the Republican senators provided numerically the greater support, but that they were aided by a substantial number of Democrats; and regionally, at least in earlier votes, southern senators, Republican or Democratic, offered proportionately greater support than did the senators from any other region.

In the House of Representatives the test ballot of 1886 indicated a distribution of votes very similar to the 1886 senatorial vote shown in the first table above. More Democrats than Republicans in the House opposed the bill, but slightly over two fifths of the support came from Democrats. And so far as the Democratic vote itself was concerned, the division between former Confederate and non-Confederate states was similar to the senatorial division shown in the second table above. In the House in 1886, of the 39 supporting Democratic votes, 30 came from the former Confederate states; and of the 86 opposition votes, the great bulk, 68, came from the border or northern states. The eleven Republican representatives from the South all voted in support of the proposal.

In the vote in this year, 1886, the Blair bill came closer to passage than at any other time, and the vote in Congress was a fairly accurate index to regional reactions to the measure. The South was stronger in its support than was the North. Although the bill had the appearance of being a northern, Republican measure, active support and assistance in committees, on the floor, and outside of Congress came largely from southern Democrats.[82] In the Senate debates Blair himself bore almost the entire burden of northern support for his measure. Indeed, the opposition press in the North indicated that many northern Republicans did not particularly favor this method of expending the surplus, and Senator Preston B. Plumb, Republican of Kansas, was quoted as saying that he could count on his fingers the senators who really believed the bill good.[83]

It may be concluded that federal aid to education along the lines of Blair's proposal apparently was acceptable to the dominant leadership of the lower South, where the largest Negro concentration existed. It was opposed by a combination of border and northern

[82] Of the sixty-five bills proposing federal aid to public schools introduced in the House of Representatives between 1881 and 1890, fifty-two came from southerners.

[83] *Nation,* XLII (March 11, 1886), 208. Southerners often suggested that the northern opposition stemmed in part from resentment that much of the money would go to the South, and that this prompted some of the amendments which were objectionable to southerners. Raleigh *News and Observer,* March 16, 1886; Raleigh *State Chronicle,* May 13, 1886; New Bern (N. C.) *Journal,* March 2, 1886.

Democrats, by agrarian, state rights southerners, and ultimately by Republican leadership. It is interesting to note that southern opposition to the Blair bill emphasized the economic and constitutional arguments more than the question of mixed schools or federal control. Southern supporters of the measure likewise emphasized in their arguments not the general educational needs of their section but rather the responsibility of the nation as a whole to share the burden of Negro education. The failure of the bill left the problem of public education in the South still unsolved. In 1900, the statistics on southern education compared no more favorably with those for other states than they had in 1880.[84]

For southern Negroes the defeat of the bill meant generally less money for their own schools. In 1890 Senator John S. Barbour of Virginia in making a last desperate plea for federal aid asked whether it was not "expecting too much of us . . . that we should go on and tax ourselves to support unaided this colored . . . uneducated class."[85] His question was subsequently answered by the increasing tendency of legislatures and school authorities to allocate smaller sums to Negro schools or to restrict their financial support to revenue received from Negro tax payments. And finally the lack of progress and of hope for Negro education may have furthered measures to disfranchise the Negro. Representative Sherwin had warned in 1883 that "Means will be found for subverting the citizen's right to vote if ignorance exists."[86] Certainly the Negro's illiteracy proved to be an effective argument to justify depriving him of the ballot.

The defeat of the Blair bill also served as an additional indication that northerners had abandoned their efforts to rehabilitate the Negro. The only positive good for the South growing out of this decade of controversy over federal aid was the publicity given its educational plight. Such publicity helped to develop the understanding between northern philanthropy and southern leaders that took shape around the turn of the century in the Southern Education Movement.

84 For an analysis of southern education in 1900, see Woodward, *Origins of the New South*, 398-400.

85 *Cong. Record*, 51 Cong., 1 Sess., 1935 (March 5, 1890).

86 *Ibid.*, 47 Cong., 2 Sess., 3257 (February 24, 1883).

"Fifty-four Forty or Fight"—An American Political Legend

By Edwin A. Miles

One of the best-known "facts" concerning United States political history is that "Fifty-four forty or fight" was a campaign slogan that virtually won the presidential election of 1844 for James K. Polk and the Democratic party. Historians have drilled its importance into the minds of American youth: "Democrats won away thousands of Clay's supporters" by chanting it; "lusty Democrats . . . yelled" it; "great crowds cheered Democratic orators who shouted" it; it "proved to be a telling campaign slogan with the western voters"; "schoolboys chalked this alliterative bluster on fences"; "it was one of the most effective campaign slogans in all American history." [1]

Yet there is nothing in the contemporary evidence concerning the events of 1844 to indicate that "Fifty-four forty or fight" was used at all in the campaign. Instead, the evidence shows clearly that the slogan did not gain currency until approximately one year after Polk's inauguration, and thus it could not have played an important

Editor's Note: — This paper was read at the annual meeting of the American Historical Association in St. Louis on December 28, 1956. Since that time an article entitled "'Fifty-four Forty or Fight': Facts and Fictions," by Hans Sperber, professor of German in Ohio State University, has been published in *American Speech* (New York), XXXII (February, 1957), 5-11. Although the conclusions drawn by Professor Sperber and the present writer are in general agreement, neither author was aware of the researches of the other.

[1] These quotations are from the following textbooks or reference works, listed in the order in which they are quoted above: Leland D. Baldwin, *The Stream of American History* (2 vols., New York, 1953), I, 700; Fred W. Wellborn, *The Growth of American Nationality* (New York, 1943), 720; Ray A. Billington, Bert J. Loewenberg, and Samuel H. Brockunier, *The United States: American Democracy in World Perspective* (New York, 1947), 201; Homer C. Hockett, *Political and Social Growth of the American People, 1492-1865* (3rd ed., New York, 1940), 631-32; Thomas A. Bailey, *A Diplomatic History of the American People* (4th ed., New York, 1950), 233; Preston W. Slosson, "The Hundred Years of Peace among English Speaking Peoples," *Independent* (New York), LXXXI (March 1, 1915), 317.

part in his victory. This means, also, that the incorrect association of the slogan with the Democratic victory has caused historians to overemphasize the role of Oregon in the 1844 election. The evidence simply does not support the statement of Albert J. Beveridge, for example, that "the American title to the Oregon country was quite as strong a political force in the campaign of 1844 as the annexation of Texas."[2] The soundness of such an assertion can perhaps best be tested by means of a closer examination of both the Oregon question and the slogan itself in their relationship to the events and discussions of 1844-1846.

As the first sizable groups of pioneers from the United States poured into the Pacific Northwest during the 1840's, the ownership of Oregon became a matter of deep concern to many Americans. For twenty-five years the United States had been willing to continue the so-called joint occupation arrangement with Great Britain under conventions signed in 1818 and 1827. Although British and American diplomats had advanced the respective claims of their nations to the entire area between 42 degrees and 54 degrees, 40 minutes, north latitude, west of the Rocky Mountains, each nation had expressed a willingness to divide the territory. On four separate occasions the United States had proposed to compromise by establishing the boundary at the forty-ninth parallel from the Rocky Mountains to the Pacific Ocean, and the British had suggested that the forty-ninth parallel line be extended only to the Columbia River, with the international boundary to follow that river westward to the Pacific Ocean.[3]

In 1843, however, a movement for "all of Oregon" began in the United States. In July, an Oregon convention, presided over by former Vice-President Richard M. Johnson of Kentucky and attended by 113 persons from six states, was held in Cincinnati. The delegates passed resolutions asserting that the right of the United States "to the Oregon Territory from 42 to 54 degrees 40 minutes north latitude is unquestionable." They also approved resolutions urging the federal government to extend its jurisdiction over the territory and to establish a line of forts from the Missouri River to

[2] Albert J. Beveridge, *Abraham Lincoln, 1809-1858* (2 vols., New York, 1928), I, 368.

[3] The American offers were made in 1818, 1824, 1826, and 1843. See Hunter Miller (ed.), *Treaties and Other International Acts of the United States of America* (8 vols., Washington, 1931-1948), V, 5-101.

* accounts for following (body of whole)

the Pacific Ocean to provide protection for American settlers en route to the Northwest.[4]

During the first session of the Twenty-eighth Congress, which met in December, 1843, both the Senate and the House considered the question of giving the one-year notice required for the termination of the joint occupation with England, but the proposal found few adherents. One such measure, presented by Representative Robert Dale Owen of Indiana, never reached a vote in the House, while the Whig Senate defeated a similar resolution sponsored by Senator David R. Atchison of Missouri. In defending his resolution, Atchison assumed a bellicose tone: "Our object is not to bring on war; it is to occupy the land we are entitled to; and if war follows our doing so, why, let it come. Before we yield an inch by negotiation, let our common country sink — let all be lost."[5]

Frank P. Blair, editor of the Washington *Globe*, supported Atchison and Owen by opening his columns to "the friends of Oregon." Blair predicted that the people of the United States "will go to Oregon in spite of conventions, and they will possess that country in spite of England." But he did not expect war. "They will conquer it, not by arms, but by that inflexible law of nature which enables a growing blade of grass to raise a stone — the law of expansion." He questioned the idea that Great Britain might be offended: "We understand John Bull well enough to know that it is not by succumbing to him, by fawning and flattering appeals to his forbearance, his good will is to be won." Blair and other Democratic editors denounced the Whig senators for their unanimous opposition to the notice resolution.[6]

The demand for the entire Oregon Country appeared to be gaining momentum, but it was still only the pet project of a small clique of Democratic politicians. The annexation of Texas was the foremost political issue of the day, and the right stand on that question promised to determine the Democratic nomination for the campaign of 1844. Democratic advocates of the whole of Oregon realized that in order to thrust their favorite issue into the campaign they must couple Oregon with Texas. Thus expansionist Democrats

[4] C. S. Kingston, "The Oregon Convention of 1843," *Washington Historical Quarterly* (Seattle), XXII (July, 1931), 163-71.

[5] *Cong. Globe*, 28 Cong., 1 Sess., 103 (January 4, 1844), 307 (February 22, 1844), 418 (March 21, 1844).

[6] Washington *Daily Globe*, February 16, March 23, March 27, 1844.

from the Northwest joined with expansionist Democrats from the South to combine the "reoccupation of Oregon" with the "reannexation of Texas." Among the leading aspirants for the nomination, Martin Van Buren had alienated the expansionists by announcing his opposition to the immediate annexation of Texas, and Lewis Cass had declared himself in favor of annexation but had not mentioned Oregon. But James K. Polk, originally an active candidate for the vice-presidential nomination on a ticket with Van Buren, had said: "Let Texas be reannexed, and the authority and laws of the United States be established and maintained within her limits, as also in the Oregon Territory, and let the fixed policy of our government be, not to permit Great Britain or any other foreign power to plant a colony or hold dominion over any portion of the people or territory of either."[7]

At the Democratic National Convention, which met in Baltimore in May, 1844, the Ohio delegation, headed by Samuel Medary, editor of the Columbus *Ohio Statesman*, took the lead in bringing the Oregon question into the discussion. Medary, who has been called the author of the "Fifty-four forty or fight" slogan,[8] had played a conspicuous role four months earlier in a state Democratic convention which had declared that it was "the duty of the American government to take formal and immediate possession" of Oregon, "and to meet with stern denial, and if necessary, with indignant rebuke, the insolent pretensions of England to that part of our soil." [9] At Baltimore, the Ohioans "distinguished themselves by tremendous efforts for Van Buren" and opposed the adoption of the two-thirds rule which sealed his doom.[10] Frustrated in their support of their favorite candidate, they then sought recognition of the Oregon issue. Medary asked the convention to give the people of his state "a candidate who was right on the Oregon question, and who would carry forward the interests of the democracy."

[7] Quoted in *Niles' Weekly Register* (Baltimore), LXVI (June 8, 1844), 229. For Cass's statement see Washington *Daily Globe*, May 16, 1844.

[8] "It has been said that he [Medary] was the originator of the popular slogan '54°—40′ or fight,' but the claim is as yet not proved." Helen P. Dorn, "Samuel Medary — Journalist and Politician, 1801-1864," *Ohio State Archaeological and Historical Quarterly* (Columbus), LIII (January, 1944), 19.

[9] *Proceedings and Address of the Democratic State Convention of the State of Ohio Held in the City of Columbus on the Eighth and Ninth Days of January, 1844* (Columbus, 1844), 7.

[10] Cincinnati *Morning Herald*, June 3, 1844; James C. N. Paul, *Rift in the Democracy* (Philadelphia, 1951), 147-48.

He assured the delegates that "he was a friend to the annexation of Texas; and should they give Ohio a candidate in favor of that object, and of extending the protecting aegis of our flag over Oregon, he would pledge that the 'lone star' of Texas should be blazoned on the democratic standard in Ohio, and that under it they would lead on to certain victory." This opened the way for Gideon J. Pillow, Polk's unofficial floor manager at the convention, to exploit the Tennessean's earlier statement on the Oregon question; and after the nomination he announced that Polk was "for resisting at the threshold British aggression and British intrigue. He is utterly opposed to letting the foot of the British lion tread upon one inch of our rightful soil in Oregon or of the Texian republic." [11]

The expansionists also prevailed in the writing of the party platform. According to George Bancroft, a delegate from Massachusetts, the platform contained "a strong Texas, & still stronger Oregon, resolution: with hits at Calhoun in both." [12] The resolution stated that "our title to the whole of the territory of Oregon is clear and unquestionable; that no portion of the same ought to be ceded to England or any other power; and that the re-occupation of Oregon and the re-annexation of Texas at the earliest practicable period are great American measures, which this convention recommends to the cordial support of the democracy of the union." [13] Curiously enough, the principal author of the platform was Silas Wright, the loyal Van Buren senator from New York. Senator William Allen of Ohio, another so-called author of "Fifty-four forty or fight," strongly approved the Oregon stand.[14]

The Baltimore resolution set the stage for Oregon to play an important role in the campaign of 1844. At a ratification meeting in the District of Columbia, an Indiana Democrat predicted that "the prairies of the whole west will ring with loud shouts for Polk and Texas, Dallas and Oregon." [15] But the fears of a Pennsylvania

11 The statements by Medary and Pillow appeared in Washington *Daily Globe*, June 6, 1844.

12 George Bancroft to Martin Van Buren, May 25, 1844, quoted in Robert S. Lambert, "The Democratic Party, 1841-1844" (Ph.D. dissertation, University of North Carolina, 1950), 179.

13 *Niles' Weekly Register*, LXVI (June 8, 1844), 227.

14 See Reginald C. McGrane, *William Allen: A Study in Western Democracy* (Columbus, 1925), 104, for a statement that although both Medary and Allen have been named as possible authors of the slogan, "There is no definite information that either of them actually coined the phrase."

15 Washington *Daily Globe*, June 1, 1844.

Democrat that "this *Oregon* question will not be urged with that zeal to which its great importance entitles it" appear to have been justified.[16] Few Democrats emphasized "the whole of the territory of Oregon" claimed by the party platform: the cry (when given) was "Oregon," not "all of Oregon." Polk's advocates made surprisingly little of the charge that while Clay was secretary of state the United States had offered to divide the Oregon territory along the forty-ninth parallel.[17]

Even in the Northwest, Texas held priority over Oregon. In Ohio, the home of Medary and Allen, "the Texas question and the national bank absorbed the interest of the two parties," according to one student of the state's political history.[18] "We hear no bold assertion of our rights — of the paramount claims of the Oregon question," declared the editor of the Cincinnati *Morning Herald*, an advocate of James G. Birney, the Liberty party candidate. "The song of the party is *Texas* and Polk. . . . Look at your papers, at the North, — in the twinkling of an eye, they have stopped all declamation about Oregon, our *own* territory, and gone a whoring after Texas, a *Slaveholding* territory, to which we have no right!"[19] As the campaign progressed, Medary and others realized that the balance of power in Ohio lay with the abolitionists, who opposed the annexation of Texas, and since Oregon was so intimately connected with Texas, they said little about expansion during the late stages of the campaign.[20] Although Indiana and Illinois Democrats

[16] *Ibid.*, June 7, 1844. "Although Polk had identified himself completely . . . with the 'whole of Oregon' platform, the lack of enthusiasm for that issue in the campaign of 1844 might have raised some doubt in his mind as to its wide acceptance even within the Democratic party." Norman A. Graebner, "Polk, Politics, and Oregon," East Tennessee Historical Society, *Publications* (Knoxville), XXIV (1952), 11. For a contrary view see Frederic H. Soward, "President Polk and the Canadian Frontier," Canadian Historical Association, *Report of the Annual Meeting of 1930* (Ottawa, 1930), 73-74.

[17] In his campaign newspaper, the *Ohio Coon Catcher* (Columbus), August 24, 1844, Medary pointed out that Oregon was "the country which Mr. Clay, while Secretary of State under J. Q. Adams, after the bargain, offered, in part, to give to the British." See also speech of B. F. Hallett, in Washington *Daily Globe*, October 3, 1844, and "Fifty Reasons Why Henry Clay Should Not Be President of the Union," *ibid.*, September 6, 1844.

[18] Edgar A. Holt, "Party Politics in Ohio, 1840-1850," *Ohio Archaeological and Historical Quarterly*, XXXVIII (January, 1929), 92.

[19] Cincinnati *Morning Herald*, June 29, 1844.

[20] Medary to Polk, October 28, 1844, and D. T. Disney to Polk, October 28, 1844, James K. Polk Papers (Division of Manuscripts, Library of Congress). In the *Ohio Coon Catcher*, Medary devoted considerably less attention to Oregon than to such topics as Clay's dueling, card-playing, and use of profanity; the coalition of Whigs

may have shown a greater interest in Oregon, even in those states the Texas question was still paramount.[21]

Whatever influence the Oregon issue may have had in the northwestern states, Polk could have lost all of them and still have won the presidency.[22] His narrow plurality over Clay in New York, the pivotal state in the election, was due not so much to his position on the Oregon question as to the fact that the vote of the anti-Texas majority was divided between Clay and Birney. According to one student of the election in New York, "it is surprising to note that Oregon was excluded so completely from public discussion. There was little interest, either expressed or implied, in the solution of the Northwest's difficulties." [23] One of the few eastern Democrats who sought to stress the Oregon issue was George Bancroft, who

and Native Americans; the "corrupt bargain" between Clay and John Quincy Adams; and Clay's alleged duplicity toward the abolitionists. On August 24, 1844, the paper printed a map of the Oregon territory and declared: "*Oregon is ours!* let us not elect a party to power that will forever give it, or a part of it, to the enemy." In the succeeding numbers, however, Oregon was almost completely ignored. In *Facts for the People* (August, 1844), another publication sponsored by Medary, the issues of the campaign were enumerated: "A National Bank — the Great Issue"; "The Tariff Question"; "Distribution Question"; and "The Texas Question." It stated, however, that "Texas is a minor question in comparison even with the single issue of a United States Bank." It made no reference to Oregon. The *Ohio Coon Catcher* and *Facts for the People* are bound together in one volume in the Rare Books Collection of the Library of Congress.

[21] At an Indianapolis Democratic rally in June, resolutions were adopted in favor of Texas and Oregon — Texas to be annexed "at the earliest practicable period," but with no immediacy indicated in the case of Oregon. The meeting adjourned with "three cheers for 'Polk, Dallas, Texas, and democracy'." Washington *Daily Globe*, June 28, 1844. On June 19, Senator Sidney Breese of Illinois spoke on "Oregon and Texas" to a Democratic rally in New York City, but his remarks on Texas generated much more enthusiasm. Shouts of "Three Cheers for Texas" resounded throughout the audience at the conclusion of his speech. Springfield *Illinois State Register*, July 12, 1844. Likewise, on September 16, "Three Cheers for Polk, Dallas, and Texas" followed an address by Representative Stephen A. Douglas of Illinois to a gathering in St. Louis. *Ibid.*, September 27, 1844. A search of the files of the *Illinois State Register* has failed to uncover evidence that the Oregon question aroused much interest among Illinois Democrats in the campaign.

[22] Polk received the 26 electoral votes of Michigan, Illinois, and Indiana; his margin of victory over Clay was 65 votes — 170 to 105.

[23] George W. Roach, "The Presidential Campaign of 1844 in New York State," *New York History* (Albany), XIX (April, 1938), 167. Horace Greeley attributed Polk's slender plurality in New York to his ambiguous position on the tariff and the arguments by New York Democrats that the annexation of Texas would not lead to a rupture with Mexico or to the assumption of the Texan debt. New York *Weekly Tribune*, November 16, 1844. The Washington *Daily National Intelligencer*, November 26, 1844, blamed the Whig defeat in New York on the interference of "dependents upon Executive patronage," fraudulent naturalization of immigrants by Democrats, misrepresentations of Clay's Texas views, and misrepresentation of Polk's tariff views.

had served on the platform committee of the Baltimore Convention. In accepting the Democratic candidacy for governor of Massachusetts, Bancroft declared that "Oregon shall ever be American soil," [24] yet in the closing days of the campaign, the Boston *Courier*, which supported Bancroft and Polk, issued a long list of the party's principles, in which the Oregon question was not even mentioned.[25]

Whigs also avoided discussion of the Oregon issue. Many northern members of the party undoubtedly agreed with one Vermont editor who declared that Oregon had been "wrapped round" Texas, "just as the nurse disguises a nauseous dose in honey to cheat the palate of a rebellious patient. They think thus to seduce the North and West into support of Polk and into the election of another locofoco Congress; *then* Texas will be admitted, and we venture to predict that the Oregon fever will straitway subside." [26] Later in the campaign the Whig national organ ridiculed the manner in which the Oregon resolution had been adopted by the Democrats: "What did one out of ten of them know, for example, of the grounds of our title to Oregon, or of the extent or limits of 'the whole of the Territory' of Oregon?" [27] From the point of view of the northern Whigs, however, the less said about Oregon the better, for it might work to their disadvantage no matter what position they adopted. To dispute the American claims would appear to be unpatriotic; to champion them might well alienate their southern colleagues, already embarrassed by Clay's opposition to the annexation of Texas. But if the Oregon question had become a significant campaign issue the Whigs would have been forced to discuss it. Their silence indicated that Oregon had failed to arouse widespread interest. Late in the campaign, Clay felt it necessary to hedge on the Texas issue, but he continued to ignore the Oregon question.[28]

After the election, both the Whig and the Democratic press omitted mention of Oregon as a factor in Polk's victory. In its analysis of the Indiana election returns, the Whig Cincinnati *Atlas*

[24] New Bedford *Register*, August 20, 1844.

[25] Boston *Courier*, November 14, 1844.

[26] Montpelier *Watchman and Journal*, June 28, 1844.

[27] Washington *Daily National Intelligencer*, October 5, 1844.

[28] Senator John M. Berrien of Georgia, one of the few Whigs who attempted to challenge the position of the Baltimore platform, favored a continuation of the policy of "masterly inactivity" which Secretary of State John C. Calhoun had sponsored. Berrien argued that the "tide of emigration which is tending in that direction will ere long people the country with American citizens, and lead eventually to the quiet surrender of the territory to us." *Ibid.*, October 4, 1844.

declared that "the Hoosier State has cast her electoral vote for Polk, Texas, and Free Trade." The Hudson (New York) *Republican* lamented the fact that "*Polk, Dorr, Free Trade, Texas, War* [with Mexico], *Slavery, and Foul Dishonor are the inheritance of the People for the next four years.*" The Alexandria (District of Columbia) *Gazette* attributed the Whig defeat to "Abolitionists at the North — ultra Texas men at the South — Protection in Pennsylvania — free trade in Alabama — religious prejudice in Maine, and Mormonism in Illinois — and *foreigners* every where." [29]

"What Has the Election Decided?" was the headline inquiry of the campaign organ of the District of Columbia Democrats. The editor answered by discussing the issues one by one: the bank, tariff, assumption of state debts, executive veto, and the annexation of Texas. Oregon was not mentioned.[30] A brief item in *Niles' Register* only a few days after the November election further indicates the lack of interest that the Oregon issue had generated during the campaign. "Other topics have so monopolized the attention of both government and people for some time past," it reported, "that we have almost forgotten that a minister reached this country some months since from Great Britain, especially charged with the duty of negotiating in relation to the differences which exist between that country and the United States in relation to the boundaries of the northwestern line separating the two countries." [31]

In his annual message to Congress in December, 1844, President Tyler declared that the question of the annexation of Texas had been "presented nakedly" to the consideration of the American people, who had "decisively manifested" their approbation by the election of Polk. In his discussion of the Oregon controversy with Great Britain, however, the President, while looking forward to a "happy and favorable termination to the existing negotiation upon terms compatible with the public honor," made no reference to Oregon as an issue in the campaign.[32]

With both of the major parties apparently relegating the Oregon

[29] All quoted in Washington *Daily National Intelligencer,* November 15 and 16, 1844.

[30] Washington *Young Hickory,* November 23, 1844.

[31] *Niles' Weekly Register,* LXVII (November 23, 1844), 179.

[32] James D. Richardson (comp.), *A Compilation of the Messages and Papers of the Presidents, 1789-1897* (10 vols., Washington, 1896-1899), V, 2191, 2196-97.

question to the background during the campaign of 1844, there would seem to have been little occasion for the coining or the use of such a slogan as "Fifty-four forty or fight" to stir the voters. That it either was not used or had not become generally known, even to some Democratic leaders, was interestingly demonstrated early in the next session of Congress. On December 23, 1844, Representative Aaron V. Brown of Tennessee, the congressman from Polk's home district and chairman of the House Committee on Territories, reported a bill which provided for the extension of the jurisdiction of the United States over the Oregon Territory — from 42° to 54° 49′. It was not until one month later that Representative John Quincy Adams called to his attention the fact that the northern claim of the United States was 54° 40′. Brown explained that the error was due to a "mistake in copying, or otherwise" at the last session, implying an unfamiliarity with the exact American claim.[33] If "Fifty-four forty or fight" had been a campaign cry during the previous months, apparently it had made no impression on him. It is significant that a year later northwestern Democrats in accusing their southern colleagues of abandoning the platform of the Baltimore Convention reminded them of such campaign slogans as "Texas and Oregon," but not once did they declare that "Fifty-four forty or fight" had been one of those slogans.[34]

If, then, "Fifty-four forty or fight" was not a campaign slogan in 1844,[35] when did it originate? For the answer to this question,

[33] *Cong. Globe*, 28 Cong., 2 Sess., 63 (December 23, 1844), 202 (January 27, 1845).

[34] Representative Charles W. Cathcart of Indiana, for example, declared that "from prairie and wood, hill and dale, the Democracy sent up their battle cry — Texas and Oregon, Oregon and Texas. Texas we have — Oregon we look for"; and Representative Orlando B. Ficklin of Illinois asserted that "'Texas and Oregon' were cradled together in the Baltimore convention, were inscribed on our banners, and were flung to the breeze in every portion of the Union." *Cong. Globe*, 29 Cong., 1 Sess., 323, 325 (February 6, 1846). And to these a southerner, Representative Jacob Thompson of Mississippi, added: "Upon almost every flag in the Union were inscribed 'Oregon and Texas'; and James K. Polk was elected." *Ibid.*, 295 (February 2, 1846).

[35] For indications that the present writer is not alone in the conclusion that the slogan played no part in the 1844 campaign, see Roach, "The Presidential Campaign of 1844 in New York State," *New York History*, XIX (April, 1938), 167, for the statement that "a fairly intensive scanning of a large group of source materials has failed to reveal any trace, in New York State, of the use of '54-40 or Fight' as a campaign slogan, although that ringing cry has come to symbolize the campaign for many historians"; Lester B. Shippee, "Federal Relations of Oregon," *Oregon Historical Quarterly* (Portland), XIX (December, 1918), 329, where it is suggested that "it had not played an important or even conspicuous part in the contest"; and Lambert, "The Democratic Party, 1841-1844," for the statement that he had discovered "no

it is necessary to examine the subsequent history of the Oregon controversy.

Although the Oregon question had not been an important factor in the campaign of 1844, the Baltimore platform committed the Democratic party to the policy of asserting the nation's title to the entire Oregon Country. The "friends of Oregon" did not hesitate to remind the party of its obligation. In so doing, they magnified the role of Oregon in Polk's victory. In January, 1845, Representative Jacob Thompson of Mississippi declared that "at the last canvass, the subjects of Texas and Oregon occupied as large a space in the public mind as any other subjects that were brought in issue." [36] One year later Representative Robert Smith of Illinois made an even more extravagant claim when he contended that "the election of Mr. Polk was owing more to his opinions on the Oregon question, than to all other considerations put together." [37]

During the last session of the Twenty-eighth Congress, which passed the joint resolution that led to the annexation of Texas, the House passed a bill to extend the jurisdiction of the United States over the Oregon Territory and to give notice of the termination of joint occupation, but the Senate refused to act on the matter.[38] The northwestern Democrats looked to the incoming Polk administration for a favorable settlement of the Oregon question. In his inaugural address, Polk reaffirmed the position of the Baltimore Convention, declaring that it was his duty to "assert and maintain by all constitutional means the right of the United States to that portion of our territory which lies beyond the Rocky Mountains." He also stated that "our title to the country of the Oregon is 'clear and unquestionable'." [39] Assertion of the American claim to all of Oregon was no longer a mere party pledge; it was the official policy of the new administration.

Despite this pronouncement, Polk instructed Secretary of State James Buchanan to suggest to British Minister Richard Pakenham

evidence which would tend to prove the use of the slogan, 'Fifty-four-forty or fight,' in the campaign of 1844." It was Professor Lambert and the late Professor Albert Ray Newsome who first aroused the interest of the present writer in searching for the origins of the slogan.

[36] *Cong. Globe*, 28 Cong., 2 Sess., 221 (January 30, 1845).

[37] *Ibid.*, 29 Cong., 1 Sess., 335 (February 7, 1846).

[38] *Ibid.*, 28 Cong., 2 Sess., 236-37 (February 3, 1845), 387 (March 3, 1845). Senator Allen of Ohio bitterly protested the Senate's failure to take action on the House bill.

[39] Richardson (comp.), *Messages and Papers of the Presidents*, V, 2231.

that the Oregon Territory be divided by the forty-ninth parallel, explaining that he was committed by the acts of his predecessors to offer such a compromise. When Pakenham declined this overture without referring it to his government, Polk then withdrew the offer and reasserted the claims of the United States to the entire territory. Even when he learned that the British had been displeased with Pakenham's abrupt action, he refused to renew his compromise proposal or to invite the British to make a similar offer.[40]

On November 6, 1845, the new Democratic organ, the Washington *Union*, edited by Thomas Ritchie, summed up the administration's official position in an editorial entitled "The Whole of Oregon, or None."[41] Ritchie's article, which asserted that the claims of the United States to the Oregon Country applied to all the territory up to 54° 40′, led to the popular slogan, "All of Oregon or none," which has also been erroneously attributed by many secondary writers to the campaign of 1844.

When Congress met in December, 1845, the Oregon question immediately assumed considerable importance. In his annual message Polk outlined the history of the negotiations with Great Britain and recommended that Congress approve a notice terminating joint occupation. He declared that the rights of the United States in Oregon "cannot be abandoned without a sacrifice of both national honor and interest."[42] With Texas already in the Union, the northwestern Democrats were determined to secure a fulfillment of the Oregon pledges of the Baltimore Convention.

The debate in Congress centered around the manner in which the notice should be given. Should the United States assert that it intended to extend its jurisdiction over the entire territory? Or if Great Britain should offer to settle at the forty-ninth parallel, as it was rumored she would, should the offer be rejected? Early in the session, Senator William Allen of Ohio advised Polk that if Britain should offer such a compromise he should "submit it confidentially to the Senate for their previous advice."[43] But the northwestern Democrats, urged on by instructions and requests from

[40] Milo M. Quaife (ed.), *The Diary of James K. Polk during His Presidency, 1845 to 1849* (4 vols., Chicago, 1910), I, 1-6, 62-65, 77-80.

[41] The editorial was reprinted in *Niles' Weekly Register*, LXIX (November 15, 1845), 164. According to the Cincinnati *Daily Commercial*, November 20, 1845, it was "creating a great sensation in this country."

[42] Richardson (comp.), *Messages and Papers of the President*, V, 2247.

[43] Quaife (ed.), *Diary of James K. Polk*, I, 139.

their state legislatures and public meetings of their constituents, insisted that there should be no compromise. Allen soon joined this group of ardent "friends of Oregon" and perhaps regretted that he had made his suggestion to Polk; but the President was unkind enough to remind him of it on more than one occasion.[44]

As early as July, 1845, Senator Sidney Breese of Illinois had told a gathering in his state that any statesman "who shall advise the surrender to England of one foot of its [Oregon's] soil or one drop of its water is a *doomed man*."[45] Shortly after Congress met, Senator Hopkins L. Turney of Tennessee informed Polk that some of the western Democrats were "almost mad on the subject of Oregon."[46] The recognized leader of these "ultra friends of Oregon," Senator Edward A. Hannegan of Indiana, declared on December 30, 1845, that he "never would consent to a surrender of any portion of the country north of 49°, nor one foot, by treaty or otherwise, under 54° 40′."[47] One week later, he proposed this toast for a meeting in Philadelphia: "Oregon — Every foot or not an inch; 54 degrees and 40 minutes or *delenda est Britiania* [*sic*]."[48] Hannegan and his followers adopted the language of Ritchie's editorial, and made "The whole of Oregon or none" or "All of Oregon or none" their rallying cry.[49]

On February 9, the House of Representatives approved a resolution giving notice of the termination of joint occupation.[50] In the Senate, however, the debate continued for two months. The "54 40 men" vigorously opposed all amendments which suggested that the American and British claims to Oregon might be resolved by a compromise. On the other hand, a large majority in the Senate favored a settlement along the forty-ninth parallel, if Great Britain should propose that boundary. Senator Thomas Hart Benton of

[44] *Ibid.*, 274.

[45] *Niles' Weekly Register*, LXVIII (August 9, 1845), 364.

[46] Quaife (ed.), *Diary of James K. Polk*, I, 140.

[47] *Cong. Globe*, 29 Cong., 1 Sess., 110 (December 30, 1845). On March 12, 1846, Senator Atchison referred to the "54° 40′ men, at the head of whom stood his friend from Indiana [Mr. Hannegan] — he believed that was generally conceded on all hands." *Ibid.*, 490 (March 12, 1846).

[48] Daniel Wait Howe, "The Mississippi Valley in the Movement for Fifty-four Forty or Fight," Mississippi Valley Historical Association, *Proceedings for the Year 1911-1912* (Cedar Rapids, 1912), 104.

[49] For examples of their use of these slogans, see *Cong. Globe*, 29 Cong., 1 Sess., 133 (January 3, 1846), 212 (January 15, 1846), 267 (January 28, 1846), Appendix, 72-74, 83 (January 5, 1846), 107 (January 7, 1846), 276 (January 8, 1846).

[50] *Cong. Globe*, 29 Cong., 1 Sess., 349 (February 9, 1846).

Missouri had made clear his opposition to the "ultra friends of Oregon." John C. Calhoun, once again representing South Carolina in the Senate, at first favored a continuation of the policy of "masterly inactivity," which he had sponsored as secretary of state, but he soon abandoned this position in favor of a compromise along the forty-ninth parallel.[51] When Calhoun, Senator George McDuffie of South Carolina, and other senators talked of a resolution requesting the President to reopen negotiations, Polk informed them that he would probably submit any offer from Great Britain to the Senate for its previous advice. In vain the "54 40 men" attempted to get assurances from Polk that he would reject any such proposal.[52]

On March 4, Senator William H. Haywood of North Carolina threw a bombshell into the ranks of the "ultra friends of Oregon" when he stated — apparently with authority — that Polk would probably ask the Senate for its previous advice in case of a British offer to compromise at the forty-ninth parallel. The "54 40 men," he said, were attempting to force the President to adopt the unreasonable position of rejecting an offer he had once made. In effect, Haywood continued, compliance with their demands would require the President to say: " 'Should the offer of my predecessors already adopted by me, as that of the *nation* itself, happen to be returned upon me, I will not entertain it!' 'There shall be no compromise' — 'No consultation with the Senate' — 'All of Oregon or none' — '54° 40′, fight or no fight!' " "Oh, my God," the Senator cried, "what an attitude is this for a man's friend to assume for him!"[53]

The "54 40 men" were incensed by the apparent desertion of the President. If Haywood's representation of Polk's position were accurate, Hannegan declared, "so long as one human eye remains to linger on the page of history, the story of his abasement will be read, sending him and his name together to an infamy so profound, a damnation so deep, that the hand of resurrection will never be able to drag him forth."[54] On the evening following Haywood's speech, Hannegan rushed to the White House. Polk, who had been expecting him, informed him that no one was authorized to speak

[51] Quaife (ed.), *Diary of James K. Polk*, I, 69-70, 131, 159-62.

[52] *Ibid.*, 248-49, 250-51. As early as December 27, 1845, the cabinet had agreed that any proposal from Great Britain should be submitted to the Senate.

[53] *Cong. Globe*, 29 Cong., 1 Sess., Appendix, 372 (March 4, 1846).

[54] *Cong. Globe*, 29 Cong., 1 Sess., 460 (March 5, 1846).

for the President, but he did not repudiate Haywood's representation of his views. Two days later, after a caucus of the "ultra friends of Oregon," Hannegan, accompanied by Senator Atchison, called on the President and asked him bluntly whether he planned to "go for the whole of Oregon up to 54° 50′" or to compromise at the forty-ninth parallel. Polk's reply that he could make no promise concerning his future actions gave little comfort to the two senators.[55]

As the senatorial debates progressed, the "ultra friends of Oregon" adopted the battle cry of "54° 40′" (or simply "54 40"). "Patriotic members of Congress" procured "seals engraven with the strange device of 54° 40′." Levi D. Slamm, editor of the New York *Globe*, carried the figures on the top of his gold-headed cane as well as below the masthead of his journal.[56] On March 23 the Washington correspondent of the New York *Morning Express* reported that "in the course of two or three nights of the last week, these Cabalistic figures were written apparently four or five thousand times upon the windows, doors, street-corners, houses, public buildings, stores and fences of the different avenues and streets of the city."[57] Senator Jacob W. Miller of New Jersey, who had observed the figures chalked "on doorways and fences . . . from one end of Pennsylvania avenue to the other," suggested that "these new muniments of our title might perhaps overcome the weight of official records, and our title to '54 40' be made 'clear and indisputable' by party resolutions, by dinner toasts, by wax stamps, and by chalked doors and fences."[58] Senator Ambrose H. Sevier of Arkansas predicted that "before the summer is over, 54° 40′ are appellations

55 Quaife (ed.), *Diary of James K. Polk*, I, 262, 270.

56 New York *Evening Post*, March 28, 1846; New York *Daily Globe*, April 7, 1846; New York *Daily Tribune*, June 20, 1846. As early as April 13, 1846, the Philadelphia *Daily Keystone* also headed its columns with "54° 40′."

57 The writer continued that "this little trick, which appears to have been designed very deliberately, has consumed half the chalk of the city and all the brains of those who directed the work to be done. I hear of stamps and seals, made also to represent the one idea of the radical democracy and upon which also appear the same figures '54-40'." New York *Morning Express*, March 25, 1846. A correspondent for a Philadelphia newspaper reported on June 4 that "a little incident leaked out to-day, which proves that the 54 40 members of Congress had something to do with the chalking of that number upon the doors and walls all over the principal cities, so as to give an impetus to public opinion. There is no doubt but that men were paid to 'chalk up the marks'." Philadelphia *Pennsylvania Inquirer and National Gazette*, June 6, 1846.

58 *Cong. Globe*, 29 Cong., 1 Sess., Appendix, 569 (March 26, 1846).

which will be given to favorite objects, and by many, bestowed as names, upon their children."[59]

Apparently the phrase "Fifty-four forty or fight" did not originate with the champions of that boundary line but with the Senate moderates whom Senator Lewis Cass once referred to as the "un-ultra friends of Oregon."[60] Senator Haywood had characterized the position of his opponents as that of "54° 40′, fight or no fight!";[61] Senator George Evans of Maine spoke of those who favored "54° 40′ at all hazards";[62] Senator Alexander Barrow of Louisiana talked of the men who advocated "54° 40′, *war or no war*";[63] Senator Benton spoke of the folly of "54° 40′ or war."[64] And on March 11, Senator Reverdy Johnson of Maryland, according to some press accounts, referred to Senators Allen and Hannegan, the "Hotspurs of the Senate," as gentlemen who "were all for 54, 40 or fight."[65] Perhaps the chalk-bearers of Washington occasionally scribbled the words "or fight" along with "54 40."[66] At any rate, a few weeks later, the St. Louis *Republican* reported that emigrants leaving for Oregon decked their wagons with banners demanding " 'Oregon 54° 40′ — all or none!' and they say they are willing to fight for it if necessary."[67] On April 8, the Philadelphia *Dollar Newspaper* suggested that the abbreviation "P. P. P. P." might be used to stand for "Phifty-Phour Phorty or Phight."[68] Oddly enough, it was in this unphonetic dress that the slogan generally appeared in the year of its origin.

On April 16, after an extended debate, the Senate passed a resolu-

[59] *Ibid.*, Appendix, 390 (March 25, 1846).

[60] *Ibid.*, Appendix, 423 (March 30, 1846).

[61] Haywood used the phrase "fight or no fight" several times in his speech. *Ibid.*, Appendix, 372, 375, 376 (March 4, 1846).

[62] *Ibid.*, Appendix, 572 (March 9, 1846).

[63] *Ibid.*, Appendix, 589 (March 30, 1846).

[64] *Ibid.*, 570 (March 30, 1846).

[65] Philadelphia *Pennsylvania Inquirer and National Gazette*, March 14, 1846. According to the New York *Daily Tribune*, March 13, 1846, Johnson used the phrase "54° 40′ or fight." The Philadelphia *American Sentinel* reported that "he said these gentlemen were all for 54 40, or for fight." In *Cong. Globe*, 29 Cong., 1 Sess., 482 (March 11, 1846), his words were recorded as "54° 40′ or a fight."

[66] "The figures are often accompanied by the strong terms of the radicals, — 'the whole of Oregon is ours,' — 'whole or none,' or some phrase or other caught from the speeches or conversation of those who design to make political capital, or manufacture public opinion out of this grave and serious question." New York *Morning Express*, March 25, 1846.

[67] Quoted in *Niles' Weekly Register*, LXX (July 4, 1846), 281.

[68] Quoted in Mitford M. Mathews (ed.), *A Dictionary of Americanisms on Historical Principles* (2 vols., Chicago, 1951), I, 603.

tion of notice, but with a conciliatory amendment, proposed by Reverdy Johnson, expressing the hope that the United States and Great Britain might reach an "amicable settlement of all their differences and disputes in respect to" Oregon.[69] After a conference between House and Senate committees, both houses agreed on April 23 to a resolution embodying the Senate's view; and President Polk approved the resolution five days later.[70] With this action it was apparent that a treaty providing for the international boundary along the forty-ninth parallel would secure the necessary two-thirds vote for ratification. When on June 10 Polk submitted a British draft of such a convention for the consideration of the Senate, the United States was engaged in a war with Mexico. Two days later the Senate advised its acceptance by a vote of 38 to 12, and the final vote on ratification of the treaty, on June 18, was 41 to 14.[71]

"Where now is the Watchword of the four Ps 'Phifty-Phour Phorty or Phight' [?]" asked the Washington correspondent of the New York *Tribune*.[72] As if in reply, the New Orleans *Tropic* asserted that " 'Phifty Phour Phorty or Phight' has now phortunately phallen to phinal phlat phooted phixing at 'Phorty nine' without the 'Phight' against a phoreign phoe." [73] In a widely reprinted editorial entitled "Phifty Phour Phorty or Phight," the Cleveland *Plain Dealer*, which had championed the extreme American claim, declared that "as we have been despoiled of the 'Phifty Phour Phorty,' by a traitorous alliance of Southern Democrats with Tory Whigs, we have nothing left us now but 'Phight,' and this, although originally intended for the British lion, shall now be directed to those trembling souls who lie crouching at his feet." The editorial then continued: "Had the President showed 'Phight' to Great Britain as valiantly as he showed 'Phifty Phour Phorty' to the people of this country, we should have had the whole of Oregon ere now." [74]

The tone of ridicule and the implications of betrayal contained in this editorial and other commentaries are perhaps a reflection of part of the process by which the slogans "Fifty-four forty or fight"

69 *Cong. Globe*, 29 Cong., 1 Sess., 680, 683 (April 16, 1846).

70 *Ibid.*, 716-17, 720-21 (April 23, 1846); Quaife (ed.), *Diary of James K. Polk*, I, 363.

71 *Senate Journal*, 29 Cong., 1 Sess., 547-50, 555.

72 New York *Daily Tribune*, June 20, 1846.

73 Quoted in Philadelphia *Spirit of the Times*, July 15, 1846.

74 Quoted in Washington *Daily National Intelligencer*, June 29, 1846.

and "All of Oregon or none," which arose in the Oregon debates of 1845-1846, came to be attributed to the presidential campaign of 1844. During the course of the arguments in Congress concerning the termination of joint occupation the "ultra friends of Oregon" referred often to the resolution of the Baltimore Convention as the basis for their demand for "all of Oregon," but in the heat of debate they did not always distinguish carefully between what had been said during the campaign and what was being said in the subsequent discussion. And now, in condemning the President for what they chose to call abandonment of campaign promises, they were still inclined to overstate the part which the Oregon question had played in that campaign. Two days after the ratification of the treaty, for example, Democratic Representative William Sawyer of Ohio made the extravagant assertion that during the campaign he "had seen on many a flag the figures 54° 40′, at least two feet in height, and the Democracy of the West rallying under them from all quarters. This cry of 'the whole of Oregon' resounded from every stump and every schoolhouse, and every cross-road." [75] No one contradicted the statement, perhaps because the Whigs had nothing to gain by doing so, and the supporters of the Polk administration wished to drop the whole matter as quietly as possible.

In the absence of a formal refutation, therefore, the association of the slogans with the 1844 campaign was able to survive unchallenged in the popular mind; and within a few years the Whigs themselves had incorporated it into their own campaign propaganda against the Democratic party. During the presidential campaign of 1852, for example, an article entitled "The Democratic Convention," published in the *American Whig Review*, stated:

> Previous to the election of 1844, both Mr. Polk and the Convention which nominated him were committed, as unequivocally as the English language could commit them, to the policy of "*fifty-four forty, or fight.*" This was another of the inscriptions which graced the banners of the Democracy, both North and South, in that memorable campaign. "*The whole or none*" of Oregon was the popular war-cry with which the ears of the nation were stunned. The patriotic sentiment graced the columns of the whole Democratic press. It was emblazoned, in conspicuous letters, on all their banners, as they gaily floated in the breeze. The capacious lungs of the party were put in requisition, to make it resound through the land, and ambulatory orators shouted it from every stump. Indeed, the sentiment was set to music, so universally was it adopted.[76]

[75] *Ibid.*, June 22, 1846.
[76] *American Whig Review* (New York), XVI (July, 1852), 3.

In thus linking "Fifty-four forty or fight" and "all of Oregon or none" to the campaign of 1844 the Whigs contributed the finishing touch in the creation of an erroneous explanation of the origin and application of those phrases. First used by moderate Democrats to characterize the demands of the "ultra friends of Oregon" in 1846, they were distorted into expressions of ridicule by newspapers seeking to discredit the Polk administration, while they became enmeshed at the same time in the efforts of the champions of the fifty-four-forty boundary to show that their demands of 1846 were based on campaign commitments of 1844. With the establishment of the boundary at the forty-ninth parallel, the slogans became to members of the last group symbols of the extent to which they claimed to have been betrayed; and when the administration, having obtained a peaceful settlement of the Oregon question and now occupied with the conduct of the Mexican War, permitted their implications to go unchallenged, the opportunity was left open for the Whigs to place these slogans in the context of the 1844 campaign as an unqualified statement of fact. And despite numerous corrective studies based on thorough research by specialists in the field, the legend thus created has continued to lead writers of general histories of the United States into errors of fact and interpretation concerning the place of the Oregon question in the political developments of the mid-nineteenth century.

The Fiftieth Annual Meeting of the Mississippi Valley Historical Association

By Oscar O. Winther

On May 2-4, 1957, the Mississippi Valley Historical Association met at Lincoln to hold its semicentennial annual meeting. It was at Nebraska's capital city that the Association had been tentatively organized on October 18, 1907. Now, fifty years later, sunny skies and balmy air greeted the first arrivers, and pleasant weather prevailed for the duration of the meeting. A friendly and efficient committee on local arrangements, of which James C. Olson was chairman, had provided well for the comfort and enjoyment of the members, their wives, and friends of the Association. Hotel Cornhusker served as headquarters, and the hotel management offered its guests friendly service, good "board and keep," and highly satisfactory accommodations for the general activities of the meeting. There were 565 registrants. Special arrangements were made for the wives in attendance. A coffee hour brought the women together on Thursday morning, a tea was scheduled for them that afternoon, and a special ladies' luncheon was held at the Lincoln University Club on Friday. For all those attending the meeting the Nebraska State Historical Society held Open House on Friday afternoon in its new and resplendent home at 1500 R Street. This occasion gave guests an opportunity not only to view the Society's magnificent building and its rich treasures, of which our secretary-treasurer, William D. Aeschbacher, is Director, but to visit as well the home office of the Association. And for all who had the time and inclination to observe places of special historical interest, the printed program called attention to "Fairview" (the home of William Jennings Bryan), the University of Nebraska College of Agriculture gardens, the State Capitol in which Nebraska's unicameral legislature was then in session, the new Pershing Memorial

Auditorium with its imposing mosaic façade (a touch of modern Mexico in the corn belt), and the University's art galleries and museum.

The gold-covered printed programs accented the commemorative character of this Fiftieth Annual Meeting of the Association. In recognition of the anniversary event, the program committe had arranged two meetings fittingly devoted to overviews of the past half-century. The first, a Thursday morning plenary meeting, was on "The Mississippi Valley Historical Association in Retrospect"; the second, scheduled for the following morning, was a critique of "A Half Century of American History." Aside from these two special features, the program committee simply aimed at providing those in attendance with an intellectual menu sufficiently varied in its listings to satisfy the conventional as well as a selected few esoteric appetites. Thus, in conjunction with five participating historical societies and Phi Alpha Theta, the committee offered a series of sessions suggesting a chronological sequence in American political, economic, and regional history. Additional provision was made for sessions of one or more topics each concerned with intellectual, diplomatic, urban, and Mexican history. Also offered was a program dealing with the tools and problems of the history teacher.

A near-capacity audience gathered in the Ball Room for the opening meeting. Presiding was Oliver M. Dickerson of Colorado State College of Education, whose membership and devoted loyalty began in the formative years of the Association. The first of two papers presented was by James L. Sellers, University of Nebraska. Basing his paper on the Association's files, Mr. Sellers recounted how, in 1907, at the instigation of Clarence Sumner Paine, secretary of the Nebraska State Historical Society, representatives from six middle-western states had met at Lincoln to organize tentatively the Mississippi Valley Historical Association. Actually, the first annual meeting offering a scheduled program was held at Lake Minnetonka, Minnesota, during June of the following year. The published *Proceedings* of that meeting, edited by Benjamin F. Shambaugh, constituted the Association's first publication. The establishment of the *Review* was authorized at the Omaha meeting (1913) and a board of editors was chosen by the Executive Committee, with Clarence W. Alvord as managing editor. The first number of the *Review* appeared in June of the following year.

The death of Paine immediately following the 1916 meeting was a serious blow to the Association. President Frederic L. Paxson bridged the emergency by appointing Mrs. (Clara S.) Paine as clerk in charge of the business until the following annual meeting. At this meeting Mrs. Paine was elected secretary-treasurer of the Association, a position she held without break until 1952. Meantime the Executive Committee was reconstituted with a chairman selected from its own members, as had been suggested by the late Secretary Paine. The resignation of Managing Editor Alvord in 1923 raised new problems. But these, including the successive selection of five managing editors, were largely resolved by the Executive Committee.

Mr. Sellers concluded his paper by noting that the remarkable growth of the Association is indicated by a present membership in excess of three thousand, and by the fact that the committees of our organization carry on a wide range of activities and that *The Mississippi Valley Historical Review* is recognized as the leading publication devoted to the entire range of United States history. "The growth and activity of the Association," said Sellers, "is less the fulfillment of a dream than the adaptation to the consciously felt needs of the membership over the years. It is a fitting appreciation for the work of the founders that this fiftieth anniversary meeting is held at Lincoln."

Mr. Sellers was followed by John W. Caughey, University of California, Los Angeles. In an unusually fast-paced presentation Mr. Caughey presented a review of the Association's journal, *The Mississippi Valley Historical Review.* Stopping short of the present editorship, the speaker presented a keen, critical, as well as taxonomic, analysis of the contents of the first forty volumes of the *Review.* He noted how the character of articles and book reviews has changed over the years. He credited all the editors with excellent craftmanship and the contributors with reasonably good and meaningful scholarship. Following these two careful and sharp appraisals of our record, comment was offered by Clarence E. Carter of the National Archives and by Edward E. Dale, University of Oklahoma. Both of these long-standing members recalled additional highlights of the Association's history. Mr. Carter reminisced about his work with Alvord, and paid tribute to the latter's sound scholarship and guiding influences upon the Association. Mr. Dale, on the other hand, emphasized the fine fellowship he has found at meetings, a factor which, over the past fifty years, has contributed immeasurably to the remarkable growth of the Association. At high noon, a note from the hotel caterer tactfully reminded the chairman that the time had come to feed the inner man, whereupon the meeting adjourned.

At the luncheon conference which followed within a few minutes, Chairman Dwight L. Dumond introduced Chancellor Clifford M. Hardin of the University of Nebraska, who in behalf of the host institution extended warmest greetings to his guests. The principal luncheon speaker was Max Savelle, University of Washington, who addressed his remarks to the question: "Is Liberalism Dead?" He asserted that liberalism, conceived as a self-conscious ideology resting upon the concept of the free and autonomous individual intelligence, is a peculiarly Western and modern phenomenon. That this ideology has lived through its life cycle is believed by such contemporary thinkers as J. H. Hallowell, Thomas Neill, Arnold Toynbee, Jacques Maritain, and Reinhold Niebuhr. Moreover, Karl Mannheim and B. F. Skinner have presented many studies to show that the concept of the free, autonomous individual intelligence is a myth. The conditions of fact in modern society seem to bear out testimony of these students and observers. There have, of course, been protests to such lines of thinking, but these have been based chiefly upon logic. And when, asked Savelle, has the logic of philosophy prevailed against the logic of events? The fact is that the most powerful evidence that the basic premises of liberalism are still valid is to be found in the science of biology, notably in the works of Julian Huxley, Hermann J. Muller, and N. J. Berrill. This mutually contradictory evidence, behavioral as opposed to biological, poses a dilemma for the historian. If he accepts the one set of evidence, history itself has no validity; if he embraces the other, all history becomes the record of the animal man using its "mind," including its free intelligence, as a set of mechanisms for achieving success in the struggle to survive and to find the good life.

Thus stranded on two horns of a dilemma, the individual members went their separate ways to any of four Thursday afternoon meetings. At the one on colonial history, presided over by Aubrey C. Land of the University of Nebraska, attention was focused upon the office of governor. "His Excellency, the Governor, before and after 1776," a paper read by Lynn W. Turner of Indiana University, contained some conclusions about the less obvious effects of the American Revolution on the institutions of state government derived from studying general developments in the governor's office in New Hampshire before 1820. The experiences of John Wentworth, New Hampshire's last royal governor, 1767-1775, were compared with those of William Plumer, the governor of this same state in 1812-1813 and again in 1816-1819. Even though both were native New Englanders, Wentworth's authority came from the United Kingdom, in contrast to that of Plumer, which was derived directly from the people of New Hampshire. While the executive authority of the colonial governor was regarded with intense suspicion, it is to be observed that Plumer, governor by the will of the people, actually exercised more triumphant power than colonial Governor Wentworth would have dared to wield. The hypothesis was advanced that the Revolution interrupted a natural political evolution toward parliamentary and cabinet government in the colonies by establishing legislative dictatorships, and finally, through the inevitable reaction to this form of tyranny, eventuated in restoring the independent executive to a position of even greater importance than he had enjoyed in colonial times.

How one became a colonial governor was explained, with special reference to Thomas Hutchinson, in a paper by Malcolm Freiberg of the Pennsylvania State University. Position, service, point of view, and desire all combined to make Thomas Hutchinson governor of Massachusetts in 1771. Great-great-great-grandmother Anne had been the only Hutchinson to cause trouble; all others had been, on the whole, sedate and respectable. But Thomas Hutchinson inherited more than respectability from his Bostonian father and through marriage came into business and wealth. Just but stern in business, Hutchinson carried those traits over into private and public affairs. Starting in 1737 Hutchinson held an astonishing variety of governmental posts — both mean and lofty — before finally becoming governor. As early as 1757 Hutchinson had been hankering for the governorship; he was awarded the lieutenant-governorship instead. As second in command he was unhappy, and both his activities and correspondence reveal a continuing desire for the governorship. In 1769 he accepted an opportunity to serve as acting governor. And then a year later came, at long last, the offer of the highest appointive post in Massachusetts. Outwardly nonchalant over the arrival of his governor's commission in 1771, he was inwardly nervous as he made all manner of preparations. They served him ill; Thomas Hutchinson's governorship was the bitterest, if not the shortest, served by any eighteenth-century native son of the Bay Province.

The case of Hutchinson provided an excellent basis for listening to John A. Schutz, Whittier College, point out that the appointments of colonial governors in Massachusetts were nearly always due to a climax of intrigue in the local and imperial community that depended upon the patronage of their office. The succession of governors in 1741 caused more than the usual plotting; in fact, secret alliances were formed by so many groups trampling upon each other that it became necessary to resort to the use of governmental authority to save themselves from disaster. While such tactics were dirty and slippery, the stakes were great enough to cause even people of principle to resort to ruthless measures. With spoils possible from the redistribution of offices in Massachusetts and from the creation of an independent government in New Hampshire, political groups developed a rapacious desire that could be satisfied only through the control of the local patronage. And in securing patronage the favor of the colonial governor was always essential. How to manipulate the appointment of the governor was a problem facing spoils-seeking Bostonians, inasmuch as the governorship was filled by the ruling classes in the United Kingdom. While these facts concerning appointment were well understood by Bostonians, they nevertheless hoped to circumvent the system by finding a man with connections in both Boston and London who could satisfy the grasping aspirations of controlling groups in both aristocracies. Governor William Shirley was such a person.

In commenting upon these three papers Thomas P. Abernethy, University of Virginia, observed that in New Hampshire, the shift noted by Mr. Turner, namely, from less to more executive power which accompanied the change from colonial to sovereign state status was generally true in New England. It was, however, not the situation in Virginia, where, after the governorship of Henry ("Light-Horse Harry") Lee, there was no real challenge to the domination of the Jeffersonian Republicans. Because of this lack of acute rivalry in politics, Virginia did not find it necessary to change her constitution between 1776 and 1830 despite the marked weakness of the executive authority. Mr. Abernethy expressed surprise at the pattern of colonial politics attributed to Governors Hutchinson and Shirley by Messrs. Freiberg and Schutz. Abernethy said he was not aware that any such thing existed in Virginia. Before being confronted with these papers Mr. Abernethy had come to the conclusion that Virginia had not produced the species which we recognize as professional politicians. In Virginia the governor received a handsome salary, but he usually resided in England and took no part in colonial administration. The lieutenant governor, who did the actual work, was assisted by a few royally appointed officials, mostly concerned with revenues of the Crown, who were paid modest salaries. But neither the members of the governor's council, the burgesses, nor the justices of the peace who ruled the counties, received any salary. Under the governor, the administration was carried on by amateurs who performed their arduous services because of the prestige which public service conferred. And since no native Virginian ever attained the office of governor, politics, in the modern manner as practiced by Governors Hutchinson and Shirley, was not known in the Old Dominion. All of this tends to show that each colony was a law unto itself and that it is unsafe to formulate too many general conclusions about them.

Politics, but of a late nineteenth century vintage (more appropriately politics and business) was the subject of a concurrent meeting chaired by Herbert Heaton of the University of Minnesota. An audience occupying all seats and all the standing room greeted the speakers. Fletcher M. Green, University of North Carolina, spoke first; his subject, the background and origin of the Credit Mobilier. The origin of this company, began Mr. Green, has always been something of a mystery, even to the Union Pacific Railroad. The parent organization was the Pennsylvania Fiscal Agency, chartered by the state legislature in 1859. It was an organization which evolved out of a long series of financial transactions by Duff Green, who had left politics and had devoted himself to business enterprises and railroad construction during the 1840's and 1850's. After a series of somewhat abortive promotional schemes, Green became interested in the idea of a Southern Pacific Railroad connecting New Orleans with Mazatlan. For this he secured charters from the Texas and Mexican governments, organized a holding company for expediting the project, established contact with English bondholders, and finally applied for and secured a charter for the "Pennsylvania Fiscal Agency." Green's major purpose in organizing the Agency, of which he had controlling interest and served as president, was to provide capital for financing his Southern Pacific Railroad. Work on this project was begun, but it was cut short by the outbreak of the Civil War, in which war Green became a rebel. Ignoring Green, the company reorganized in 1863, and in 1864 sold the Agency to Vice-President Thomas C. Durant of the Union Pacific Railroad Company. Shortly thereafter the Pennsylvania legislature changed the Agency's name to The Credit Mobilier. Even though pardoned by President Andrew Johnson, Green failed to recover his interests in the company. Green had failed to carry out his plan for a Southern Pacific railroad, but he had succeeded in organizing an agency to provide corporate capital, based on land grants and government bonds, working through a construction company with limited liability, that as the notoriously corrupt Credit Mobilier built the Union Pacific Railroad.

In the second paper of this session, Hal Bridges, University of Colorado, pointed out that in treatments of the idea of the robber barons in American historical writing, these business leaders for the period from about 1865 to 1900 are widely represented as a set of avaricious rascals who habitually cheated and robbed investors and consumers, corrupted government, and fought ruthlessly among themselves. Some revisionist interpretations, however, have been offered, such as those by Charles Francis Adams, Jr., Frederick Jackson Turner, and Allan Nevins. The robber baron idea has also been challenged in the re-study of the Standard Oil Company by Ralph and Muriel Hidy, and in railroad histories, such as those by James B. Hedges, Richard C. Overton, Edward C. Kirkland, and an analysis of the mind of American railroad leaders, 1845-1890, by Thomas C. Cochran. These revisionist views, however, are not flawless, yet the revisionist interpretations do seem to reveal the inadequacy of the robber barons.

A robber baron of a different stripe was portrayed in a paper by David H. Stratton, Baylor University, dealing with Albert B. Fall and the Teapot Dome controversy. While recognizing that Fall's acceptance of money from E. L. Doheny and H. F. Sinclair was clearly wrong, Mr. Stratton raised these questions: Were the oil deals a sinister, well-conceived plot to rob the nation of valuable natural resources affecting national security? Or was Fall simply guilty of a serious indiscretion? The former is doubtful; the answer to the latter is obvious. Today the Republicans have outlived the worst effects of Teapot Dome, but as long as the Democrats can use it to identify the Republican party with corruption; and certainly as long as Herbert Hoover stands as a living link with the Harding administration, Teapot Dome will live in political folklore.

Fred A. Shannon, in discussing these papers, deplored the tendency of faddists in historical writing who swing, pendulum-like, from one extreme to another, with no new evidence to support the oscillations. He congratulated the audience on having heard two papers dealing with robber barons without rancor or bias, and another paper stressing the need of a balanced approach by the historian between the exposures of the muckrakers and the inordinate glorifications of business written by persons who would deny that there ever were any robber barons. He expressed the hope that this meeting was the harbinger of the return of sanity to discussions of the subject, and that it would endure at least throughout his remaining years.

Also during Thursday afternoon a modestly sized, but intensely interested group met in the Lincoln Room to hear papers concerned with the Kansas City History Project. Period sketches of our host metropolis adorned the walls of the meeting place and thereby provided an appropriate backdrop for the urban theme. George L. Anderson of the University of Kansas presided over an across-the-board University of Chicago panel. A paper by A. Theodore Brown described two distinct approaches to interpreting Kansas City's past which, by their contrasting emphasis, reflect changing patterns in the city's historiography. The first is the "written" tradition promulgated largely by Robert T. Van Horn, an early Kansas City editor, and subsequently expounded by W. H. Miller. The second, or "oral" tradition, traces back to the reminiscences of John C. McCoy, a pioneer settler. The former finds in the city's history the materials which make it consistent with its present economic power and future ambitions, whereas the latter reveals little hope in the future and is filled with overtones of bitterness and nostalgia for a kind of vanished golden age. Both traditions are the source of common attitudes held by residents of the city, and they have helped to shape points of view on the meaning of urban life in Kansas City which still flourish.

A portrayal of Kansas City's business community during the 1840's and 1850's was presented by Charles N. Glaab. Business wealth then owed much to earlier New Mexican trade, to Indian annuities, and to government freighting contracts. Land values rose with trade expansion, and fortunes were made. Within this business community one observes two rough groupings, namely, the mercantile element and dealers in real estate. The Civil War caused a temporary setback to Kansas City, but most of those who had been prominent in this business community before the outbreak of hostilities were able subsequently to rceoup their fortunes.

With the Kansas City Project in mind, Mildred C. Cox explored the subject of development and management of historical materials for urban history. She revealed that the use of very manageable microfilm copies of newspapers was preferred to the handling of bulky originals. The summary notes taken down from newspaper sources serve a better purpose than printed indexes, for they can be sorted and re-sorted in ways most convenient to the investigator. In this form the data is provided with the added virtue of retrievability. One useful purpose served by this kind of local research is that much permanently valuable historical material is made readily available for future scholars. In short, the guiding principles in the development and management of materials for urban history are the provision of enhanced accessibility, flexibility, and retrievability of the data.

Professor Bayrd Still of New York University expressed his gratification that a middle-western city was being studied in detail, emphasized the necessity of evaluating critically the written record of a city's early years, and singled out for special comment the fact that two of the papers delineated the relationship of the towns to the westward advance. He also suggested a number of ways in which Kansas City's experience paralleled that of other western cities. In his comments, Professor Thomas C. Cochran noted the desirability of more comparative studies and urged that those associated with the study of Kansas City make greater use of statistics and measurements in order to determine the rate of growth of the city. Professor Cochran thought that a quantification of this evidence would make it possible to contrast in more specific terms the carriers of the oral and written traditions. He called attention, also, to the significance of federal expenditures in the early years of Kansas City.

The fourth session on Thursday afternoon was one held jointly with the Southern Historical Association and presided over by Harris G. Warren, University of Mississippi. Expansion and diplomacy in southern politics respecting New Orleans and the Caribbean, 1845-1860, was discussed by C. Stanley Urban of Park College. Public opinion on this subject at New Orleans has passed through no less than five well-defined stages. One observes a period when New Orleans was content with its regional status; an era of Democratic minority opposition to the Compromise of 1850 but in favor of Cuban annexation; a time when first Whigs and then Know Nothings fought a holding action against ultra-expansionist Democrats; then a period when, regardless of party label, public opinion stiffened in support of the Democratic dogma, becoming increasingly resentful against the North for its territorial frustrations; and, lastly, there emerged an apparent will to terminate a Federal Union which opposed the expansion of slavery. That such a process from conservatism of the majority to radicalism of the majority occurred in New Orleans, admittedly a Yankee city reluctant to accept the tenets of the agrarian South, suggests that a like process occurred in other key cities of the Gulf states. Verification of the working hypothesis, namely, that it was the Democratic party in New Orleans which was identified with the southern expansionist cause, and that both the Whigs and the Know Nothings eventually accepted Democratic sectional dogma concerning the right and necessity of slavery to expand, regardless of its impact upon the Federal Union, suggests the possibility of a similar hypothesis for regional study.

Brainerd Dyer, University of California, Los Angeles, dealt with a post-Civil War topic, namely, the United States claims to Confederate property abroad, 1865-1887. He indicated that at the close of the Civil War, the United States government claimed all assets of the defunct Confederate government wherever such existed. Abroad such property consisted mainly of military supplies, cotton, ships, and funds in the hands of Confederate agents. Most of it was in England, but some was found in France, the West Indies, and Canada. Recovery of the property involved court proceedings, the primary purpose being to settle the principles involved and to obtain evidence that could be useful in larger matters — presumably American claims for damages resulting from Britain's unneutral services to the Confederacy. But, concluded Mr. Dyer, the persistent efforts of the United States to recover Confederate property abroad accomplished little.

The discusser, Charles G. Summersell, University of Alabama, felt that the subjects of these two papers had much in common: both are based on much new source material; both focus attention on the Civil War; and each is a chronicle of failure by Americans, both North and South, in contests with foreign powers. Ideas appear in both papers which could lead to a discussion of American foreign policy today, but Mr. Summersell forthwith resisted the temptation.

The annual Association dinner Thursday evening was distinguished in many ways. All available tables were taken, and many persons unable to secure reservations gathered in assorted nooks and crannies following the repast to hear Vice-President Wendell H. Stephenson, University of Oregon, in good wry, dry humor introduce President Thomas D. Clark for what he said was about the fourteenth time during his career and to hear the presidential address, "The Great Visitation to American Democracy." President Clark responded to Mr. Stephenson with appropriate wit, and then delivered his excellent address in exactly sixty minutes. Since this address appeared in the June number of the *Review* it suffices to say here that the large and friendly audience present on this occasion was a genuine expression of affection which all members of our Association hold for the "President of the Year."

Friday morning the program moved relentlessly forward on four fronts, not counting special reunion breakfasts and general visitations either in or about the lobby. The main morning attraction, "A Half Century of American History," was the second and only other session inspired by the Association's fiftieth anniversary. Once again the Ball Room was filled to near-capacity as John D. Hicks of the University of California introduced William B. Hesseltine, University of Wisconsin. Mr. Hesseltine kept his audience interested, amused, and enlightened as he expounded with verve and vehemence upon a half-century of political history. Recalling Freeman's dictum — "History is past politics. Present politics is history" — he declared that while Clio was confined in academic cloisters and preoccupied with constitutionalism and politics, there was going on outside the walls of "academia" the production of local and popular works which, though scorned by the academicians, had a broadening influence upon historical studies. Yet in the half-century since the Mississippi Valley Historical Association came into existence political history has shown a sturdy capacity to survive assaults. While past politics has remained the central core of history, political history has itself changed in character, has grown, widened in scope, and improved with the passing years.

Mr. Hesseltine's remark that the multi-volume *History of American Life* is a hodgepodge of social items, but never a basic synthesis, set the stage for Philip D. Jordan, University of Minnesota, who presented a retrospective view of social history. This type of history resulted from the work of James Harvey Robinson, Arthur M. Schlesinger, Dixon Ryan Fox, and others. He pointed out that social history was a part of the "new" history — a history that was to broaden its base by including social and cultural data, a history that stressed the continuity of civilization and extended the time concept into the remote past. Almost overnight social history became a vogue. But interpretation has been the yawning pit into which social historians have tumbled; failure at interpretation is the great weakness of *A History of American Life*. The mere collection of data without interpretation in social history is no more justifiable than is the massing of evidence without interpretation in political history. Perhaps, said Mr. Jordan, it would be well to declare a moratorium on new research in this area and begin to devote time and thought to the interpretation of what has been written thus far. Certainly the social historian must not forget that his segment is a part of all history, that he cannot ignore European backgrounds, that social history may not be significant merely because it is interesting.

Fifty years of economic history was evaluated by Thomas C. Cochran, University of Pennsylvania. Mr. Cochran indicated that the early twentieth-century faith in factual knowledge as the first step in perfecting society led logically to an American discipline of economic history. The development of German historical or institutional thought in economics made history a necessary adjunct of economics. Meanwhile, some writing on economic subjects was being done by such historians as Katherine Coman, John B. McMaster, and Ellis P. Oberholtzer, who had little interest in economic theory. Thus there emerged a division of forces between history and theoretical economics. But gradually "economic" and other historians were coming to see all problems as parts of a complex, indivisible culture. More than ever they doubted the utility of simplifying real relationships into models having only a few variables. But whatever the disciplinary uncertainties may have been, energetic American scholars kept on producing an immense quantity of literature on the history of economic situations. No comment had been arranged for this meeting but there was general agreement that all three papers were well done and stimulating.

Devotees of the West could choose between the trans-Allegheny West and the Spanish American Southwest. Alfred L. Burt, University of Minnesota, was chairman of an excellent program called the "Old West," at which the first paper was presented by Colin B. Goodykoontz, University of Colorado, on the Constitutional Convention of 1787 and the West. While the West was not the chief concern of the delegates to this convention, it entered significantly into their deliberations on the framework of the new government, methods of compelling states to fulfill their obligations in the union, the perils of democracy, rivalries among various economic and sectional interests, and all calculations as to the future balance of power. The paper was chiefly concerned with the admission of new states and their future role in the affairs of the nation. There was agreement that new states should be admitted but disagreement as to the conditions of admission. The views of one group were restrictionist in character, those of another were generally sympathetic with the aims of the westerners. Long ago the balance of power in the nation crossed the Alleghenies. The results, by and large, have shown how groundless were the fears of those who sought to safeguard some inherent superiority of East over West; events have justified the faith of those who, in the words of James Wilson, conceived "that all men wherever placed have equal rights and are equally entitled to confidence."

Reginald Horsman, Indiana University, explained British Indian policy in the Old Northwest, 1807-1812. Much as the British agents have been exonerated of late of plotting to stir up Indian discontent in the West, it remains to determine to what extent the British took advantage of the Indian situation. British interests in the Indians revived following the *Chesapeake* affair due to fear of war and invasion of Canada. Following the theory that in the event of war the Indians would not be idle, and that if England did not use the Indians, the Americans would, "Governor-General" Sir James Craig established, in 1807 and 1808, what was in effect a dual policy to be pursued by the Indian Department. He urged that nothing should be said in public council to offend the United States; but in private, selected chiefs were to be urged to join the British interest. Craig's interest vacillated but in 1810 he warned the Americans that an Indian war was near. This conduct was above reproach, but it seems that Craig in the early months of 1811 was desperately trying to avert hostilities toward which his own policy had contributed. Then in the second half of 1811 and the first half of 1812, energetic preparations were made for a war now regarded as inevitable. By this time, therefore, Craig's policy of perfect neutrality began to crumble. Finally, came the efforts of Brock and the members of the Indian Department to enlist the Indians for the coming war. As a result, at the outbreak of war in June, 1812, friendly Indians were converging on the British posts in the West.

Ronald E. Shaw, Miami University, spoke on the Erie Canal and American nationalism. The Canal, he said, was by its very nature a national enterprise. The nationalism of the Erie Canal was related most directly to western development in the prevalent belief that it would serve as a bond of union to prevent the detachment of the West from the East. The completed canal fulfilled many of the prophecies made for it, and its commerce exceeded the wildest dreams.

In commenting on these three papers, Francis P. Weisenburger, Ohio State University, referred to the fears of the older states expressed in Mr. Goodykoontz's paper, namely, that legislation might be passed to their disadvantage if new states had equal power, and said these were not wholly unfounded. The acceptance of the basic idea of majority rule came to mean that the "have nots" would share in some of the assets of more favored individuals in other areas. He declared Mr. Horsman's paper a careful analysis of the problems of British officials, and he concurred in the point of view expressed by Mr. Shaw, stating that pioneers saw the Erie Canal as an indispensable aid to a united country, much as a generation later American leadership saw the imperative need for transcontinental railroads to bind the nation together by bands of iron or steel.

If a prize had been offered to the one who traveled farthest especially to attend the Lincoln meeting, it would have gone to John A. Hawgood, from the University of Birmingham, England. Mr. Hawgood served in double capacity as chairman of the meeting on the Spanish Southwest, and subsequently as a reader of a paper of his own making. Carlos E. Castañeda, University of Texas, was prevented by illness from delivering his paper on Spain's reaction to French incursions on the Mississippi, but it was read by Joe B. Frantz, a colleague. La Salle's incursions aroused Spain to frantic action which resulted in the temporary occupation of East Texas but this still left the Mississippi, claimed by Spain, unsettled. French settlement along the lower Mississippi further provoked Spain and resulted in an energetic protest of the Council of the Indies against this French intrusion. The traditional importance of Spain and the inexperience of Philip V, not yet Spanish at heart, defeated Spain's efforts. Torn by war and dissension, Spain could do little more than protest. In time she became reconciled to the loss of the Mississippi, limiting her efforts until 1763 to the containment of the French from penetrating into northern and eastern New Spain.

Harry R. Stevens, Duke University, spoke on Hugh Glenn and expansion of the southwest frontier, 1817-1822. Glenn was one of the principal pioneers in the Santa Fe trade, but in most respects he was a failure. A re-examination of Glenn's interesting career nevertheless helps us to recapture some of the variety, complications, and richness of frontier experience. In keeping with this thought, John P. Bloom, Texas Western College, made his contribution by discussing how American soldiers viewed life along the Rio Grande, 1846-1848. As revealed in letters and diaries, soldiers then were chiefly interested in the appearance of the countryside, the towns (especially Matamoros) and buildings, Mexican men and, in particular, women. Other interests included Mexican religious practices, business relations between Mexico and the invaders, and foods of the Rio Grande Valley. Ivie E. Cadenhead of Tulsa University, the commentator, wondered if soldier opinion varied with individual economic and educational background. Mr. Cadenhead also raised a general question: Are well-written, well-documented, well-delivered papers — such as these — good regardless of subject? He questioned the extent to which these three papers may or may not have contributed something new to historical knowledge.

The last of the four Friday morning sessions was a joint program with the Agricultural History Society. It concerned the agricultural press. Earle D. Ross, Iowa State College, acted as chairman of this session, which featured papers by George F. Lemmer, Falls Church, Virginia, on the early agricultural editors and their philosophies; John T. Schlebecker, Iowa State College, on the dairy press — studies in useful farm journalism; and one by Homer E. Socolofsky, Kansas State College, on the famed Capper farm press in the Missouri Valley. Mr. Lemmer revealed that until well after the Civil War the editors of farm journals directed most of their efforts toward the improvement of agriculture and the raising of professional standards. The *Prairie Farmer*, under the direction of John S. Wright, secretary of the Union Agricultural Society, became the outstanding farm journal in the West, and survives today as an important agricultural periodical. In addition to patronizing agricultural reform, Wright played a leading role in promotions of teacher training, became a successful land speculator, and an important manufacturer of reapers. Mr. Schlebecker stated that well over fifty farm journals were started between 1852 and 1857 but only a handful lasted more than five years. The reasons for success and failure were given. The development of the dairy interests and the changes in editorial policy were also traced to show how the editors kept abreast of changing circumstances. Mr. Socolofsky described the Capper press as a farm-paper syndicate which began with the acquisition of the *Missouri Valley Farmer* by Arthur Capper in April, 1900. Capper's successful formula in a newspaper enterprise was to work hard, improve his publication to attract increased circulation and advertising, and to develop a personal loyalty among his staff. After 1912 Capper became more involved in politics, and beginning in 1915 he held elective state and national offices for thirty-four years. Late in 1956 the entire enterprise was sold to Stauffer Publications which plans no fundamental or immediate changes in the make-up of the Capper farm press.

Commenting on this program, Gilbert C. Fite, University of Oklahoma, made the observation that this was the best agricultural history session he had ever attended. Mr. Fite, however, raised a basic question pertaining to the subjects under discussion: Is it actually a fact that agricultural reforms and better farming practices resulted from the publication and distribution of agricultural journals? Perhaps farm papers were equally, or even more, important for their cultural value to rural, isolated people. And for his part, Robert G. Dunbar, Montana State College, sought to set these three studies in the larger framework of those economic changes which are often referred to as the Agricultural Revolution.

Following an expeditious and good-humored business session luncheon, four Friday afternoon meetings were held, again concurrently. At one meeting devoted to mid-nineteenth-century political history, over which Walter Johnson, University of Chicago, presided, a paper was presented by Donald W. Riddle, University of Illinois, Navy Pier, on Lincoln and the birth of the Republican party in Illinois. Strictly speaking, Lincoln had nothing to do with the birth of the Republican party in Illinois. When the party was organized in Illinois in 1854, Lincoln declined to join it; and even though he sought Republican support in 1855, Lincoln ran for the state senate as a Whig candidate. When Lincoln did affiliate with the new party in February, 1856, it had divested itself of its earlier abolitionist leadership and had taken a moderate position on slavery. But even though Lincoln had nothing to do with the birth of the Republican party in Illinois, his role in its early life was significant. By keeping the party moderate, by his influence among Whigs and Know Nothings, by awarding places in the party to former members of these parties — and to Democrats as well — Lincoln managed the party skillfully and effectively.

Stephen A. Douglas, on the other hand, has fared worse in the hands of posterity, according to Gerald M. Capers, Newcomb College, than any great American statesman. Douglas' unsavory reputation is chiefly due to the uncritical acceptance by historians especially of James Ford Rhodes, who in turn accepted charges made by enemies. Mr. Capers thinks that the "Little Giant" properly ranks with Clay and Webster as a national leader who worked in vain for compromises to preserve the Union. Illness in his family unfortunately kept Reinhard H. Luthin, Trinity College (Hartford), from attending the meetings and from reading a scheduled paper "Demagogues in the Early Republican Party." Eugene H. Roseboom, Ohio State University, and Maurice G. Baxter, Indiana University, both contributed critical comments which greatly enhanced the value and interest of this meeting. Mr. Roseboom viewed the Republican party as basically a fusion of humanitarian idealism and Whig concern for the rights of property. The Republican party's history has been shaped as much by continuing intra-party antagonisms as by co-operation. He felt that the paper by Mr. Capers went too far in assuming that present-day historians have generally followed Rhodes in their critical treatment of Douglas. Mr. Baxter expressed the opinion that Lincoln's appeal to the abolitionists in his "House-Divided" speech has been overemphasized, for the necessity to make concessions to this element of the party was never great. And as for Douglas' historical reputation, Mr. Baxter did not think it as bad as Mr. Capers would lead one to believe.

The never-lagging interest in Progressivism was further demonstrated by the overflow attendance at the session presided over by Charles A. Barker, Johns Hopkins University. At this meeting Martin Ridge discussed Ignatius Donnelly as a Greenbacker, a role which offered the movement nationally recognized leadership. Viewed as a case study, Donnelly's Greenback experience indicates that much of the writing concerned with the appeal of the movement is out of focus. Donnelly's record indicates that the accepted idea which represents the Greenbackers as debt-ridden farmers seeking to escape from their obligations through inflation does not hold in Minnesota, the reformer's home state. Paul W. Glad, Coe College, gave William Jennings Bryan a fresh look. Inasmuch as the Commoner served as the effective spokesman for the rural wing, his career should be viewed within the context of the urban-rural dichotomy within Progressivism. In his interpretation of agrarian discontent, Bryan accepted the emotionally charged Populist analysis. By contrast, the urban Progressives emphasized reasoned, scientific humanism. Bryan, with his faith in the common man, held that wrong was the work of a vicious few; the urban Progressives thought that evil-doing was universal and that society as a whole was responsible for social injustice. Peter J. Coleman, Park College, gave a still newer perspective to the general subject by noting some facets of the progressive movement in New Zealand.

He suggested that it might be useful to study the impact of the entire Australasian progressive movement on the United States. In offering comment, Paolo E. Coletta, United States Naval Academy, suggested that a fuller consideration of Mr. Glad's topic would include the urban reception of Bryan's agrarian reforms and how agrarian and urban reforms merged during the Progressive era. Theodore Saloutos, University of California, Los Angeles, agreed that greenbackism was not farmer-inspired originally. He believed that Donnelly's many shifts reflected shifts in views of the farmers. Mr. Saloutos believed that Mr. Glad had oversimplified his thesis and expressed doubts that the differences between the rural and the urban Progressives can be reduced to an evaluation of the beliefs, the techniques, and the actions of a Theodore Roosevelt and a William Jennings Bryan.

A joint session with the American Studies Association on "Mainstreet, Middletown, Revisited" featured two papers, one by Frederick D. Kershner, Jr., Ohio University, on the role of the small town in midwestern urbanization; another by Charles T. Miller, State University of Iowa, on the midwestern small town in literature. These papers served as a reconsideration of the cultural role of the midwestern small town during the late nineteenth and early twentieth centuries. Mr. Kershner demonstrated that, at least statistically, the small town has survived the flight of population from the countryside and has resisted the magnetic attractions of the larger cities. Mr. Miller noted the ever-increasing extent to which writers have made the small town their appropriate locales for the examination of perennial human experiences. Without having received these papers in time for preparing comment, Harold E. Briggs, Southern Illinois University, chose instead to discuss the early theater on the middle-western frontier, a subject he knows so well. The western theater, he pointed out, was at its best in its earlier years.

A change of locale for railroad devotees was graciously offered by the Nebraska State Historical Society. The Society's auditorium housed the joint meeting with the Lexington Group, attended by approximately seventy-five people. With Thomas LeDuc, Oberlin College, as chairman, this session's always enthusiastic audience heard C. Clyde Jones, University of Illinois, detail the agricultural development work of the Burlington Railroad, 1918-1933 — a subject which has received little attention from historians. The group also heard Stanley N. Murray, North Dakota Agricultural College, discuss railroads and agricultural development of the Red River of the North. In his comments Earle D. Ross of Iowa State College commended the objectivity of both speakers in treating railroad promoters neither as "robber barons" nor as benevolent "empire builders."

By Friday evening a light touch seemed in order, and this was charmingly provided by J. Harvey Young, Emory University, at the Phi Alpha Theta dinner, over which Chase C. Mooney, Indiana University, presided. The subject: "From Hooper's Female Pills to Hadacol." Hooper's pills had their inception in colonial times, but the American public has been surfeited with nostrums and their testimonials ever since. Henry T. Helmbold and his Bechu was cited to represent the genus patent medicine promoter in the portrait gallery of self-made men during the Gilded Age. Dudley J. LeBlanc, with his Hadacol and his Kary-On, illustrates the merry side of contemporary tonic promotion.

Attendance at the final Saturday morning meetings remained good. Scheduled for this period was the perennial meeting on the trans-Mississippi West, this time presided over by Ray A. Billington, Northwestern University. It was at this meeting that John A. Hawgood, University of Birmingham (England), presented his provocative paper, "The Pattern of Yankee Infiltration in Mexican Alta California, 1821-1846." Mr. Hawgood described in some detail "The Larkin Plan," which had as its aim the bringing of Alta California, with the consent and if possible at the initiative of the Mexican and Spanish Californians, into closer connection with the United States. If Larkin's plan had succeeded, asserted the speaker, there need have been no United States military intervention. Among the rival plans to Larkin's was that of the overland pioneers who impatiently intrigued for an American *coup d'etat*. Another interesting and moving paper was one delivered by LeRoy R. Hafen on the subject of the Mormon handcart migration to the Great Basin. Most critics of the handcart plan see only the terrible tragedy of the late companies of 1856; few recognize that the plan, though it had limitations, was an economical and effective means of overland travel. The last of the papers read was by Everett Sterling, University of South Dakota, on the Sioux Indians in the early reservation period. It dealt chiefly with the efforts of Joseph R. Brown, a prominent Minnesota pioneer, in making possible the Sisseton-Wahpeton Treaty of 1867. Paul F. Sharp, University of Wisconsin, one of the commentators, recognized Mr. Hawgood's paper as challenging and sparkling, but he submitted that on three major points Hawgood's reinterpretations lack conviction: one, Larkin's concept of popular sovereignty has not been clearly defined; two, "The Larkin Plan" needs further documentary evidence; and three, Mr. Hawgood appears to underestimate the effectiveness of the overland push for California as much as he exaggerates the maritime aspects of the dynamics of Manifest Destiny. Mr. Sharp thought that Mr. Hafen's paper adds little to our present knowledge, but that Mr. Sterling's case study adds considerable to our understanding of the solving of Indian problems on the frontier. Edwin R. Bingham, University of Oregon, viewed the Hafen and Sterling papers as competent and as falling clearly within the traditional pattern of writing on western history. Mr. Bingham did not think that the title of Mr. Hawgood's paper fitted the subject matter, and he suggested that the term "infiltration" was used loosely. In conclusion the chairman offered a general summary and a few pointed observations of his own.

National Mexico was also represented on the program and the meeting on this topic was ably managed by John F. Bannon, S. J., St. Louis University. A widening approach to American-Mexican relations of the mid-1820's was revealed by C. Harvey Gardiner, Washington University. He pointed out that the pattern of this subject is now firmly established, but he indicated areas that can add dimensions of understanding to this early critical period. "Mexico Opens the Door to American Capital, 1877-1880" was the subject of a paper by David M. Pletcher, Hamline University, in which American-Mexican relations were further explored with special reference to a three-year period which led to the granting of the first concessions for American railroad-building in Mexico. Lastly, Stanley R. Ross, University of Nebraska, presented a historical evaluation of Ambassador Dwight W. Morrow's delicate mission to Mexico in 1927. Ross regards Morrow as the precursor of that policy which was generalized and dramatized by Franklin D. Roosevelt under the designation of "Good Neighbor." Discusser Robert W. Delaney, Nebraska State Teachers College, offered many helpful suggestions which might enrich the studies represented at the meeting.

The Teachers Section of the Mississippi Valley Historical Association offered a varied fare under the heading, "The History Teacher: Tools and Problems." Not without the skillful chairmanship of Philip D. Jordan could so many participants (including the audience) have performed significantly within an allotted two-hour period. First, E. McClung Fleming of the Henry Francis DuPont Winterthur Museum gave an informative illustrated talk on the decorative arts as social documents of importance to American studies. Objects produced by the decorative arts should hold an important place, said Mr. Fleming; they are concrete data which can be handled, examined, verified. They constitute material evidence — as against circumstantial evidence — of the outer and inner character of a culture. Next, J. Cutler Andrews, Chatham College, presented the fruits of his experience in teaching a non-credit adult education course in United States history over Pittsburgh's community educational television station. He felt that his experience with an adult audience does not throw much light on the feasibility of closed-circuit television as a means of providing instruction for the greatly expanding college student population. However, television can hardly fail to enhance one's effectiveness as a classroom teacher, if for no other reason, through the accumulation of suitable visual materials that it makes possible.

The final lively feature of this session was a round table discussion on the subject of the history major, 1957. It had been organized by Cedric C. Cummins, University of South Dakota, who shared the panel discussion with Max P. Allen, Northern Michigan College, and Otis E. Young, Bradley University. Mr. Jordan served as moderator. Mr. Cummins began the discussion with two theses: first, the numbers of history majors, unlike history enrollments, are not increasing as fast as the health of the departments and of society in general demand; and second, too many graduates of our Ph.D. programs enter college teaching without a knowledge of the facts of life as concerns the handling of survey courses and of becoming satisfactory members of college and town communities. Mr. Allen briefly reviewed certification problems he had encountered in administrative work, asserting that it is becoming increasingly difficult to fulfill both the Education and History requirements.

He analyzed some of the possibilities and difficulties in general education programs, pointing out the vexing problem of securing adequately trained staff members to handle these interdisciplinary courses. Mr. Young expressed a particular interest in the survey course. He felt that one problem in such courses was the presence of many students with a preconceived indifference toward historical study. It was his belief that the discussion approach was superior to the lecture method in dealing with these courses but that rapidly increasing enrollments would probably necessitate more lecture teaching. Perhaps the most significant aspect of this program was the very interested and extensive participation by the audience, suggesting that more Association sessions might be organized in a manner to encourage such participation. Comments from the audience indicated a general interest in the problem of covering a lengthening American history in six semester hours. Solutions suggested included raising the traditional three-hour survey course to one of four or five hours each semester, selection of material, and the ending of the survey course at approximately the First World War. The session closed on an optimistic and agreeable plea by one member of the group that the college teacher of history abandon assumptions that his subject is uninteresting to many.

As a final crowning touch to this golden anniversary, the Nebraska History and Social Studies Teachers Association sponsored a luncheon meeting at Tillman's Cafeteria in Hotel Lindell which was further concerned with history teaching. William D. Tallichet, Irving Junior High School at Lincoln, presided, and presented as speaker Walter P. Webb, University of Texas, whose challenging and talk-provoking article, "The American West, Perpetual Mirage" had had so recent and untimely an appearance in the midst of unprecedented rainfall in Mr. Webb's so-called "desert West." In his talk Mr. Webb gave an account of a very excellent job of history teaching that he had seen done by a sixth-grade teacher. This teacher had used such varied techniques as public speaking, folk dancing, art appreciation, and several other skills; all were brought together into an integrated whole.

The success of this program, to which so many generously testified, may be attributed to the chairman's imaginative, hard-working, and co-operative fellow-committee members: Robert G. Athearn, Gilbert C. Fite, Aubrey C. Land, H. Gresham Toole, and James W.

Silver. It was also due to the splendid response from the Association membership, and likewise to the participants, without whom there would have been no program. And certainly, without the support of my University, the splendid help and co-operation of President Clark and the Executive Committee, James C. Olson's committee on local arrangements, and Secretary William D. Aeschbacher, and many hours generously given by Mrs. Mary J. Schriver, administrative secretary of the Graduate School at Indiana University, the probable results had best be left uncontemplated.

Book Reviews

Mirage in the West: A History of the French Image of American Society to 1815. By Durand Echeverria. (Princeton: Princeton University Press, 1957. xviii + 300 pp. Notes, bibliographical note, and index. $5.00.)

The present-day Frenchman is likely to admire American business and technical efficiency, but to disparage the cultural, intellectual, or ethical standards of the United States, if he recognizes that they even exist. Immediately before the French Revolution the opposite attitude prevailed. The *philosophe* and *homme moyen* alike regarded America as a utopian land of exemplary virtue, political liberty, and intellectual genius. The simplest explanation for these divergent attitudes is to assume that both of them are correct — that it is the United States itself which has changed fundamentally in character. It began as a noble experiment in political liberty guided by statesmen of genius and probity, but has developed into a society of mechanics, technicians, and businessmen indifferent to moral and esthetic values. The foreigner — French or otherwise — has merely observed and recorded his impressions of national changes. Obviously this is fallacious. Regardless of the internal changes which have taken place, the foreign observer is influenced by principles, presuppositions, fears, and loyalties which have no connection with the United States. Take, for example, the attitude toward Benjamin Franklin. Practically every eighteenth-century Frenchman agreed with Mirabeau that he was "one of the greatest men who have ever served philosophy and liberty." Yet a century later Renan viewed him as a "soul deprived of religion and poetry." Obviously Franklin himself underwent no changes. The difference existed in the notions of Mirabeau and Renan — in their sentiments, ideals, prejudices, and the climates of opinion with which they were surrounded.

Durand Echeverria's masterful study proves that even before 1815 widely divergent French opinions concerning America existed concomitantly. Some Frenchmen considered it a political and social utopia; others, a chaos of political anarchy, backwoods crudity, and commercial dishonesty. Contrary to general belief, the earliest notion of America was pejorative rather than complimentary. De Pauw, Buffon, and others had circulated the concept of biological degeneration in America — the notion that the insalubrious climate of the New World was so baleful that animals and men inevitably degenerated and successive generations of stock transplanted from Europe became physically, morally, and intellectually inferior to their ancestors. Despite refutations by Franklin, Jefferson, and others, this notion was never entirely eradicated. With the outbreak of the American Revolution and the advent of Franklin upon French soil, however, the *philosophes* to a man regarded America as a land of liberty, virtue, prosperity, and enlightenment. Their military brethren who crossed the Atlantic to participate in the Revolution had a somewhat less glowing, but still favorable, impression.

The reaction against America came in the last decade of the century—caused in part by the internal politics of the French Revolution, in part by the diplomatic relations between the United States and England, and in part by the national pride of Americans themselves. The latter phenomenon was notably reflected in the debate of a congressional committee in 1796 on whether the United States should officially be designated "the most enlightened nation in the whole world." The disenchantment of the travelers to America during the Empire makes less interesting reading than the impressions of their predecessors during the Revolution, for they either possessed less literary skill or spent their time on the frontier rather than in the centers of intellectual and cultural activity on the eastern seaboard.

The author's analysis of these trends in French thought is brilliant. His scholarship is precise, thorough, and comprehensive; his literary style, brisk and appealing. Without exaggeration, this is an important book on an important question.

The author has exhausted printed materials on his subject. The only significant primary source which he has not used consists of the manuscript reports of French diplomats to the home government, which are available in the Ministère des Affaires Etrangères. Those of Louis Otto are particularly revealing. One might also observe that some of the enthusiasm for the United States after 1789 came as part of the temper of the times. Just as Washington, Franklin, and Adams became heroes of the French Revolution, so did Priestley, Bentham, David Williams, and a host of other Europeans. Indeed Priestley, Paine, and Anacharsis Cloots were elected to the National Assembly, an honor not accorded to anyone born in North America although Joel Barlow apparently sought it.

University of Maryland ALFRED OWEN ALDRIDGE

The German-Language Press in America. By Carl Wittke. (Lexington: University of Kentucky Press, 1957. viii + 311 pp. Notes and index. $6.50.)

Professor Wittke's *German-Language Press in America* adds another essential volume to what is already the most considerable contribution made by one man to the immigration history of the United States. His most comprehensive book, *We Who Built America: The Saga of the Immigrant*, appeared in 1939; in it he not only surveyed the external history of all the major immigrant strains but analyzed with remarkable insight the complex inner history of their acculturation. Books in which he focused his attention more closely upon the German element include *German-Americans and the World War* (1936), *Against the Current: The Life of Karl Heinzen* (1945), *The Utopian Communist: A Biography of Wilhelm Weitling* (1950), and *Refugees of Revolution: The German Forty-eighters in America* (1952). His latest contribution is, as the American historian has come to expect of whatever comes from Dr. Wittke's study, perceptive, considered, definitive.

The story of German-language journalism that he relates is a long, complex one. Beginning with the short-lived *Philadelphische Zeitung* on May 6, 1732, it proceeds through a remarkable period of efflorescence that attended the activities of the Forty-eighters and the ever-growing hordes of immigrants to the 1890's, when some eight hundred German newspapers were published in the United States, and finally to the present day when a handful of weeklies and a sole daily survive. The surviving daily is the *New Yorker Staats-zeitung und Herold*, founded in 1834.

Dr. Wittke's thorough orientation in all the various and complex phases of immigration history enables him to tell much of the inside story of German journalism in the United States that would escape any other historian not similarly oriented, involving currents and cross-currents peculiar to the Germans, editorial personalities and bias, factional frictions, political issues and alignments, international complications, religious prepossessions, economic stringencies, racial alliances and differences, reader reactions, and a hundred other factors that affect journalists, journals, and their readers. Thus this volume becomes more than a history of German journalism in the United States; it is a vital chapter in the larger cultural history of the United States. Nowhere is this more apparent than in Dr. Wittke's skillful documentation of what is the basic thesis of the book, namely, that for more than two centuries the German-language newspapers in the United States served as a stabilizing force and an agency of Americanization during the transition from an Old World culture to the new traditions of a strange land.

University of Wisconsin HENRY A. POCHMANN

American Indian and White Relations to 1830: Needs and Opportunities for Study. By William N. Fenton, with a bibliography by Lyman H. Butterfield, Wilcomb E. Washburn, and William N. Fenton. (Chapel Hill: University of North Carolina Press, for Institute of Early American History and Culture, 1957. xii + 138 pp. Bibliography and index. $3.00.)

This is the second volume to emerge from a series of conferences held at Williamsburg in 1952-1953 under the auspices of the Institute of Early

American History and Culture. Its purpose, like that of Whitfield J. Bell's *Early American Science* (1955), is "to encourage a broadening of historical studies into fields where relatively little original research has been carried on or where new approaches to old problems challenge investigators." In this case the intention is to stimulate greater interest and more comprehensive research in what has become a sadly neglected field of early American history.

The present book consists of two parts, the first being an essay by Dr. Fenton on Indian-white relations as "a common ground for history and ethnology." As one of the nation's ranking ethnologists he argues eloquently and convincingly that increased co-operation and a mutual awareness of the other's doings are needed by students of both disciplines if the story of Indian and white relations is to be handled intelligently. To this end he describes not only the quantity and quality of ethnological research to date on the Indians of eastern North America, but also the methods used by his fellow practitioners, especially the historical approach. The field to which this approach leads they have termed ethnohistory.

The remaining pages (nearly a hundred in all) comprise an annotated bibliography of the most important literature and source materials bearing on Indians east of the Mississippi and on Indian-white relations in that area prior to 1830. It is divided into sections on ethnological literature, historical literature (limited to Indian-white relations), periodicals, manuscript sources, documentary publications, and special topics such as Indian portraiture, biography, captivity narratives, and government policies toward the Indian. Within these groups no attempt has been made to achieve completeness; but so far as the reviewer can judge, the compilers have succeeded admirably in pointing out the main sources of information and the means of reaching others. The notations, though brief and perhaps too few, are usually adequate, and the book is furnished with a good index.

It is implied in the Foreword that this volume will facilitate the study of interracial contacts for students of both disciplines. For the historian wanting to investigate the complexities of Indian society this is certainly true. The ethnologist, however, will look in vain for corresponding sections on early white civilization which would help explain the motivations of a John Eliot or the pressures inducing white penetration of the Ohio Valley. Although he will find many suggestions here, the book is aimed primarily at historians.

An adequate account of Indian-white relations must portray the cultures and motivations of both peoples as organic parts of a single theme. It remains to be seen whether either historians or ethnologists can sufficiently master both disciplines to do the job effectively. The body of available knowledge is far greater today than it was in the time of Parkman. But the challenge should be taken up. Fenton has polished the chain of friendship between practitioners of the two disciplines, and historians must not let it rust by neglecting his wise words.

Wells College ALLEN W. TRELEASE

Ironworks on the Saugus: The Lynn and Braintree Ventures of the Company of Undertakers of the Ironworks in New England. By E. N. Hartley. (Norman: University of Oklahoma Press, 1957. xvi + 328 pp. Illustrations, notes, bibliographical note, and index. $4.50.)

It is much less surprising that this is a good book than that it could have been written at all. To anyone familiar with the printed sources of early Massachusetts history and the Ironworks Papers in the Baker Library at Harvard, three hundred pages on the Saugus (Massachusetts) Ironworks, in active operation scarcely two decades in the mid-seventeenth century, would seem unlikely. But Professor Hartley has gone far beyond the obvious sources. He has culled material not only from every relevant manuscript collection here and abroad, from genealogical writings and studies of ironmaking, but he has used as well the archeological lore amassed by the Saugus Restoration, under whose auspices he began his researches. The result is an extraordinarily detailed description of a remarkable venture.

The familiar outlines of the Ironworks history has not been altered by Professor Hartley's research, but the story has been enormously enriched. The Company of Undertakers of the Ironworks in New England, with plants at Braintree and what is new Saugus, capitalized, according to the author's careful calculations, at about £12,000, was originally a child of the fertile brain and vast energy of that Puritan virtuoso, John Winthrop, Jr., and was financed by a group of Puritan sympathizers and influential entrepreneurs in England. The integrated iron manufactory established by the company near the Saugus River, large by any contemporary standard, included not only a blast furnace and fineries, but a slitting mill at a time when "there were less than fifteen slitting mills on which data have survived in the world," a small fleet of vessels, a sophisticated water power system, and a labor force of not less than 185 men. At the height of production in the early 1650's the plant produced 144 tons of iron a year, worth about £2,600.

One is struck repeatedly, in reading this full account, by the magnitude of the company's undertaking, by the great obstacles surmounted, and by the ingenuity and determination of the enterprisers. One is struck also by the magnitude of the failure. Within a decade of the founding the entire operation was bankrupt, and though for at least a decade thereafter attempts were made to revive operations, nothing approaching full success was attained. By the 1670's the works were in ruins, capable of restoration but not of revival. The causes of the collapse pose the central problem of interpretation. Professor Hartley concludes that profits were unattainable, ground away between high production costs on the one hand and price limitations imposed by a paternalistic government and competitive imports on the other. His careful analysis of costs, prices, and profits fully bears out this conclusion. The point is illustrated also by his treatment in the final chapter of a half-dozen later seventeenth-century colonial ironworks whose personnel bear some relationship to that of Saugus. Almost without exception these plants, too, failed despite the variations in local conditions. The causes were the same: "inadequate capitalization, high wage bills, and, above all, the competition of imported iron."

Professor Hartley raises other questions of interpretation, but the book as a whole is descriptive, and as such it is thorough to a fault. We now know all we are ever likely to know — and more than one would ever have expected to know — of the people involved in the Ironworks, of the relationship of the enterprise to the surrounding community, and especially of the management and technology of the plants — topics, these last, treated splendidly by Professor Hartley in two chapters full of completely original material.

The weaknesses of the book, if they may be called that, flow from an excess of virtues. Professor Hartley's enthusiasm for his subject leads him into digressions which, though conveniently summarizing and in places adding to information on a range of related topics such as the abortive projects for ironmaking in early Virginia (a full chapter), tend to distract the reader's attention from the main theme and make the book diffuse and unwieldy. The author's fondness for his subject leads also to an almost antiquarian search for "firsts" associated with the Ironworks, part of an effort to locate the venture as a forerunner of "American industrial civilization." Anachronisms inevitably result, for historically the differences between this seventeenth-century enterprise and the problems of modern industry are more important than the similarities.

But these are minor points in a work of exhaustive scholarship. Anyone interested in the history of the colonies or of American economic development will profit from a careful study of this book.

Harvard University BERNARD BAILYN

Rebels and Redcoats. By George F. Scheer and Hugh F. Rankin. (Cleveland: The World Publishing Company, 1957. 572 pp. Maps, notes, bibliography, and index. $7.50.)

Rebels and Redcoats gives us another excellent volume for our Revolutionary War shelf. The authors of this work have dealt exclusively with campaigns and battles, and by quoting at length from diaries, letters, reports, and recollections they have put us in the midst of the fighting men. The men appear neither heroic nor cowardly but generally confused about the action and adept at rationalization. This emphasis on men rather than on tactics is all to the good. Most Revolutionary fights were won when the militia stood fast and lost when they ran. It behooves us to know the attitude of the soldier and not where he was stationed.

Scheer and Rankin escape most of the pitfalls that endanger this technique of relying on long quotations. First, the reader is not lost in the minute details but is kept abreast of the main currents of battle and war; indeed, two thirds of the book comprise a straight military history somewhat more detailed than Willard M. Wallace's *Appeal to Arms* and more compact than Christopher Ward's two-volume study. Second, the danger of abrupt transitions is usually surmounted. For example, at the Battle of Long Island the most dramatic action occurred as Howe completed an end-run around Washington's left flank at Jamaica Pass. But unfortunately no diarist happened to be present at Jamaica and the most colorful account of the day's fighting (by Private Joseph Martin) dealt with action back at the less crucial right flank. Fortunately, the authors tell us enough about the main action in their own words and then skillfully ease us back to the point where the diarist happened to be taking notes. Finally the problem of the dramatic but misleading excerpt is well handled. The reader is treated to Ethan Allen's account of his accomplishments at Ticonderoga but is appropriately put on guard first. "Typically, where Allen told the story, he made himself the hero."

Unlike Lynn Montross, who with *Rag, Tag, and Bobtail* used a similar mixture of military history and lengthy quotation, Scheer and Rankin do little special pleading. Where Montross was a strong Gates advocate, it is difficult to say where the present writers stand. In general they tend toward understatement. The militia are not as hopeless as John Miller made them; Howe seems a little faster in his movements; even the soldiers' feet at Valley Forge seem less bare and frozen.

There are a few criticisms. The authors occasionally ask too much of their evidence. "What manner of man made up the army . . . ? Washington's soldier was David How . . . he was also Daniel McCurtin . . . Aaron Wright." Actually, these soldiers were diarists, relatively sensitive and articulate men, a handful out of ten thousand and hardly typical. The footnotes are especially important in this work, and scholars would appreciate having them at the foot of the page. Undoubtedly some purists will object to the corrected spelling and punctuation although I for one applaud this cleanup.

Middlebury College CHARLES S. GRANT

Guns on the Early Frontiers: A History of Firearms from Colonial Times through the Years of the Western Fur Trade. By Carl P. Russell. (Berkeley: University of California Press, 1957. xvi + 395 pp. Illustrations, notes, bibliography, and index. $8.50.)

From the beginning of the American frontier movement, down to its blazing exit in the latter part of the nineteenth century, none of the white man's inventions played a more prominent part than the gun. It was the most important possession of the trapper and soldier; as time went by it became equally so to the Indian. To all three the gun spelled the difference between life and death from enemies and often from starvation in the wilderness. Strangely enough, the Indian, who treasured his gun above all other things he could acquire by trade from the whites, was careless and even abusive of it. "The tendency of the Indian was to try coercion upon his rifle if it seemed to fail him. With fire and water and brute force he was apt to abuse his weapon, or simply to ruin it through neglect and rough handling" (p. 141). Yet he was perfectly aware of its worth to him and would make any sacrifice to own one.

While Mr. Russell is primarily interested here in the arms used in the West in the first half of the nineteenth century, he spends a considerable amount of time discussing their antecedents on earlier frontiers and the contribution of European gunsmiths. His first chapter, "Arming the American Indian," in which he tells how the natives came by the gun, is sixty-one pages long. More interesting is his chapter on the personal weapons used by the trappers and traders. Since these men literally lived with their guns, the selection of firearms was to them of prime importance and they were quick to adopt the latest improvements offered by manufacturers, something that cannot be said of the military. Russell repeats and underscores the old story of the army's reluctance to accept improvements, much to the frustration of inventors and manufacturers like Samuel Colt.

The best chapter in the book deals not with guns but with powder, ball, and accessories. The story of the development of various kinds of missiles and their methods of propulsion, down to the cartridge, is fascinating. In a well-written account the reader learns of various "recipes" for making the most effective and highly explosive gunpowder and something of its history in the United States. One reason the chapter is appealing is because throughout the rest of the book there is a tremendous amount of antiquarian detail about who presently owns this particular gun or that one and where it can be found. In discussing powder and ball there is not much opportunity to incorporate this kind of information. About the only real criticism that might be leveled against the book is the author's lack of some concluding words telling of the general significance of firearms on the frontier and illustrating the point with a few examples where firearms proved to be a determining factor in its history.

University of Colorado ROBERT G. ATHEARN

Alexander Hamilton in the American Tradition. By Louis M. Hacker. (New York: McGraw-Hill Book Company, 1957. xiv + 273 pp. Notes, bibliography, and index. $4.75.)

The place of Alexander Hamilton in American history, never above controversy, appears today in a state of marked fluidity of interpretation and evaluation. The present essay seeks to inquire into Hamilton's intentions and contributions, to examine his political and economic ideas, and to interpret Hamilton for present-day Americans.

Professor Hacker challenges the recent interpretations by Russell Kirk and Clinton Rossiter in which Hamilton has been rejected as a conservative spokesman. He also seeks to reopen Merrill Jensen's disposition of the "critical period." Writing with the conviction that Hamilton has a message for the present, he offers a determined defense of Hamilton as representative of the best of American statesmanship and a reasoned brief for the acceptance of Hamilton as "a real conservative."

Hamilton is seen as devoted essentially to the establishment of stability and enduring government. His fiscal policies, his stand on foreign relations, his bid for the support of the government by the classes of wealth and order were all directed toward that end. He viewed the 1790's as a time of national emergency requiring extraordinary energy on the part of the government. Professor Hacker feels strongly that to call Hamilton a monarchist or an aristocrat in the European sense is unjust; and as for seeking to undermine democracy, "Hamilton was distrustful of democracy only in its equalitarian sense." A great statesman, a great administrator, "his public life one of sacrifice and rectitude, he labored unceasingly to establish the integrity of the government, to assure the welfare of the American people, and to guarantee the endurance of republican institutions." His advocacy of a foreign policy favoring "self-interest as against a crusading zeal, of narrow and clearly defined objectives as against broad principles," has, when followed, stood America in good stead. Where Dumas Malone has concluded that Hamilton "more than any other major American statesman of his time, lusted for personal as well as national power," Professor Hacker views Hamilton's ambition, in the words of Washington, as "of that laudable kind which prompts a man to excel in whatever he takes in hand."

Considerable attention is given to Hamilton's economic ideas. Rejecting the mercantilist label for Hamilton, the author stresses Hamilton's reliance on Adam Smith. Government intervention to stimulate manufactures was but a short-run policy adopted to advance the security and the prosperity of an infant nation in a world not yet prepared to live in a "system of perfect liberty." Although the influence of Smith on Hamilton has been previously recognized, this facet of Hamilton's thought has never before been so clearly demonstrated.

Professor Hacker is more at home with Hamilton in the economic realm than in the political. He has not gone behind the economic theorist, the policy maker, and the statesman, to Hamilton the politician. The depth to which Hamilton was enmeshed in the partisan politics of the period is not at all clear, and even such a crucial development as Hamilton's break with Adams is passed over with little effort to explain the action.

Interpretative in character, the volume makes no pretense of new discoveries or exploitation of unused sources but seeks to contribute to a reappraisal of Hamilton.

University of Richmond NOBLE E. CUNNINGHAM, JR.

Freedom's Fetters: The Alien and Sedition Laws and American Civil Liberties. By James Morton Smith. (Ithaca: Cornell University Press, in cooperation with the Institute of Early American History and Culture, 1956. xvi + 464 pp. Notes, appendix, bibliographical note, and index. $5.00.)

It is fashionable in political science circles to regard political principles as merely the verbal mask behind which the eternal power battle of "Ins" and "Outs" pursues its relentless course. Like all other oversimplifications, this one robs us of the full-bodied texture of history and reduces great men (and momentous issues) to uniform, creaturely size. The complex human adventure, with its phases of courage and vision, and its occasional redirection of the actual by the ideal, is stripped of significance in order to substitute a more manageable, supposedly more "scientific," reality. No incident, and no conjunction of human powers and human values, is better able to test the limitations of this approach than the alien and sedition system, enacted and enforced in the period 1798-1800 — the close of the first decade of life for the American Republic.

Mr. Smith is responsible for calling these reactionary "laws" a system, and his terminology appears choice and just in the light of the careful story he tells. There is little doubt that *Freedom's Fetters* is the fullest study to date of this repressive Federalist legislation. It is the first of a projected two-volume study, the second to deal with the Republican response in the form of the Kentucky and Virginia Resolutions — a response creative enough, though certainly not free of its own embarrassments for the future. The author believes that the two volumes together will constitute "a chapter in the evolution of the American civil liberties tradition . . . for the questions involved go to the very heart of the concept of intellectual freedom." Those who believe further that intellectual freedom goes to the very heart of the ground rules for any putatively free society, might agree in substance with this statement, only preferring to strengthen its claim.

What was at stake in the "alien and sedition system" was actually government by consent of the governed. After an exhaustive examination of the Sedition Law, correlating its wording with the manner of its enforcement by the courts, the author concludes that it "reduced the limits of speech and press in the United States to those set by the English common law in the days before the American Revolution," and that this was equivalent to the bad-tendency test typical of an age of authority "antirepublican to the core." Thus, the American "experiment" in government, that began with the repudiation of the idea that government was the master of the people, an expression of political faith given its classic formulation in the Declaration of Independence and re-enforced by the Virginia Act for Establishing Religious Freedom and the First Amendment to the Constitution, was invaded and seriously threatened with destruction.

While strict and systematic enforcement of the Sedition Law worked to silence or intimidate every important Republican journal in the country, concentrating in the key political areas of the the Federalist-dominated New England and Middle States, the companion legislation of the Alien Friends Act remained "a dead letter from enactment to expiration." But lack of enforcement in this companion law must not be taken at face value, as the author patiently shows. In its design it was indeed that "libel on legislation" that Jefferson named it. Nourished by the spirit of xenophobia, this act, as Gallatin argued in Congress, allowed more stringent procedures in peacetime against alien friends than would have been authorized in case of war for enemy aliens. In fact, Republican argument against the contemplated alien bill was so strong that it may have had something to do with President John Adams' reluctance to use the sweeping deportation powers it could authorize. Being a skilled lawyer and constitutional theorist, Adams could not be insensible to the Republican denunciation of the bill as a wanton attack on the guaranties of civil rights in the Constitution — exposing any suspected stranger to removal without presentment by a grand jury, without a speedy and public trial by an impartial jury, without information of the nature and cause of the accusation, without confrontation and examination of witnesses, and without counsel.

The arch-Federalist, Secretary of State Timothy Pickering, pressed for extensive use of the Alien Law, eager to enforce it against incoming aliens, diplomatic personnel, and alien writers who criticized the administration, as well as against virtually every French resident in the United States. Adams wavered, conceding in principle far more than he could ever confess to, but determined to give the law a much stricter interpretation in action than the Federalist zealots in his cabinet desired. The most revealing sample of the anti-foreign hysteria that infected even moderate Federalists like Adams is seen in the reasoning he used to justify his unwillingness to grant passports to the famous French philosopher Du Pont de Nemours and his companions from the National Institute: to wit, "we have had too many French philosophers already and I really begin to think, or rather to suspect, that learned academies, not under the immediate inspection and control of government, have disorganized the world, and are incompatible with social order." It is also to the great John Adams' discredit that when he included the name of the scholar and bookseller, Moreau de St. Méry, in his list of Frenchmen to be deported under the Alien Act, and was queried by a senator about the nature of the charge against him, replied, "Nothing in particular, but he's too French." These, however, are expressions of the prevailing Federalist mood. The most solid reason behind the administration's lack of "enforcement" of the Alien Friends Law was the mass exodus of frightened foreigners that took place even before the law was passed, but as soon as the spirit of that law was reliably reported.

Thus, Jefferson's claim that turning the Federalists out and putting a different party into office was "The Revolution of 1800," is substantiated. Scholarly studies prior to Mr. Smith's have established the essential import of this great crisis in democratic government. They have scored the attempted identification of the government of the United States with the administration of it by the Federalists and they have properly assessed the Republicans' fight, against what looked like overwhelming legal odds and bigoted opinion in full swing, to reaffirm the right to government by consent, by public criticism and scrutiny, and in the interest of personal liberty, security, and intellectual freedom. Mr. Smith's elaborate consideration of every individual case, or each attempted enforcement, and of the Federalist-Republican arguments for and against each measure provides a better-stocked armory of information on the opinion, the strategy, the personnel, and the state and local as well as federal methods of handling these peculiar cases. That the narrative could be better organized and the information offered thus made more easily available is true. But this is a book for historians, and they will have to mine it as their interest dictates. It might be that Mr. Smith will write a smoother and more sharply-limned story when he turns to the second volume, where there is both greater room for original consideration (of the Kentucky and Virginia Resolutions) and where the specific and multiple legal trials and proceedings will not contribute to what is perhaps an inevitably gritty slowing-up of pace.

University of California, Berkeley ADRIENNE KOCH

Robert Oliver, Merchant of Baltimore, 1783-1819. By Stuart Weems Bruchey. *The Johns Hopkins University Studies in Historical and Political Science*, Series LXXIV, No. 1. (Baltimore: The Johns Hopkins Press, 1956. 412 pp. Illustrations, notes, tables, appendixes, bibliography, and index. $5.00.)

This volume is an intimate study of the business affairs of a very successful Baltimore merchant engaged in foreign trade in the years following the Revolution. Ledgers and letter books of his companies were available for most of the period and adequate use has been made of other contemporary records. The work is drawn from unquestionably reliable sources.

Oliver's various partnerships dealt almost entirely in importing and exporting. Some of the imports of course remained in Baltimore and some Baltimore products appear among the exports; but the mass of the goods handled had a foreign origin and a foreign destination. The largest items were coffee and sugar obtained from Central and South America, the Caribbean, and frequently from the East Indies, and disposed of mostly in Holland, Germany, and Italy. Ships to the Orient seem to have gone largely in ballast, or carrying European goods. Textiles, chiefly linens, from the Dutch and German ports were marketed at home and in the Caribbean. Cargoes to England were infrequent, but a great deal of banking was done there. Deviations from these general patterns were of course numerous.

The cargo lots in which goods were handled followed no regular sequence and were often shifted from port to port until a sale was found. The captain or the supercargo exercised wide discretion in the foreign dealings. Similarly, unexpected shipments came to Oliver from foreign merchants. These goods were sometimes for wholesale purchase and sometimes for disposal on a commission basis.

The fortunes of such a widely dispersed business constitute an excellent mirror for the economic conditions of those troubled and shifting years. The period from 1783 to 1785, in which business consisted largely of imports from England for sale in Baltimore, was very dull. Oliver's firm accumulated only about £1,000 in approximately two years. The next four years brought improvement but still not sufficient to draw Oliver and his partners away from the commission business into any considerable adventures of their own. Prosperity increased after the beginning of the European war, and by 1800 Oliver himself was worth about $60,000.

Despite a business recession about 1801 the company's dealings grew enormously in the following years. Here is a concrete example of the rich neutral trade that flourished in spite of belligerent captures. Shipments between April, 1806, and May, 1807, cost for cargo $1,440,972 and, although two ships were lost, returned a net profit of $1,004,673. Much of this business grew out of a lucrative contract to participate in extracting the wealth of the Spanish government from Mexico. In this operation enough trade with Vera Cruz was opened to Oliver's firm to keep eight vessels busy.

The Continental System on one side of the water and the Embargo on the other put an end to this bonanza, but Oliver managed from time to time to get a ship through both hazards. The difficulties were such, however, that in 1810, then a millionaire, he resolved to give up his business, and only occasionally thereafter did he buy a parcel of goods or send out a cargo.

To an economic historian the book is both enlightening and very interesting. References to complex exchange rates, however, may at times tax the comprehension of the reader.

Youngstown University CLARENCE P. GOULD

James Madison, The President, 1809-1812. By Irving Brant. (Indianapolis: Bobbs-Merrill Company, 1956. 540 pp. Illustrations, notes, and index. $6.50.)

This volume, the fifth in a monumental and provocative biography, follows Madison's career from his inauguration through the declaration of war against England. Once again, Mr. Brant has preferred frank advocacy to a pose as mere observer. Since Madison, as president, has been harshly treated by many historians — notably Henry Adams, whose apparently intentional distortions Mr. Brant demonstrates anew — an aggressive defense of the Virginian is welcome.

Two central themes, blending and rising to a crescendo in the spring of 1812, dominate *Madison, The President.* One is that, particularly after Canning's rejection of the Erskine agreement, Madison, though retaining hope that the Orders in Council would be repealed, moved steadily and consistently toward war with England as the only possible alternative. His French policy, legally correct and politically astute, was aimed primarily at forcing affairs with Britain to a climax. With pressure upon Britain apparently failing, the President carried the nation into war in June, 1812. Closely connected with this theme is the second, that Madison, while certainly not infallible, was in general the master of events and central figure in the coming of war. His importance has been concealed by Federalist propaganda and his own view of the president's role, but in effect the nation and the War Hawks did Madison's bidding. In thus emphasizing the consistency and strength of the President, Mr. Brant is of course challenging the interpretations, not only of Adams, but also of such scholars as Burt, Mayo, and Pratt.

Although Mr. Brant supplies impressive evidence to support his interpretations, they are still open to challenge, notably in his discussion of the winter of 1811-1812. Madisonian leadership, if it existed, was concealed, not only from Federalists, Smith-Giles Republicans, and War Hawks, but even from the President's own faction. Surely the War Hawks were more responsible for war than the Executive; they provided the spirit and drive until the very end, when first Secretary Monroe and then the President stepped from the wings to aid them. Furthermore, the argument for presidential leadership depends upon the assertion that Madison followed a consistent success-by-coercion-or-war line. Yet, during the war session, the Navy bill failed by a narrow margin for want of presidential support; Madison permitted Gallatin to submit financial recommendations that temporarily crushed the war spirit; he did not use the most powerful coercive instrument available, an embargo upon grain shipments to Wellington in the Peninsula; and the President used language with the English minister that was certainly unclear if not irresolute, although Mr. Brant criticizes Foster rather than Madison for the failure of communication. Each of these points, and others, may be singly explained away. Taken together, however, they do not seem to show a courageous and decided leader in action.

Nevertheless, in this volume Mr. Brant has performed a useful service. He has examined a large number of manuscript collections and a fair sample of eastern newspapers, and he has approached these materials with imagination and a proper unwillingness to accept blindly the conclusions of others who have gone before him. By ruthlessly pushing aside such topics as the role of the West, the vagaries of British policy, and most aspects of Madisonian America not related to diplomacy, Mr. Brant has been able to expose the statesmanship of Madison to a study whose intensity has not before been equaled. The result is a portrait that, though perhaps partially unconvincing to some, can certainly not be ignored. Irving Brant has enlivened once again the perennially interesting problems presented by the coming of "the second war for independence."

University of California, Los Angeles BRADFORD PERKINS

The Journals of Welcome Arnold Greene: The Voyages of the Brigantine Perseverance, 1817-1820. Edited by Howard Greene and Alice E. Smith. (Madison: State Historical Society of Wisconsin, 1956. xiv + 221 pp. Illustrations, notes, and index. $5.00.)

The two sections of *The Journals of Welcome Arnold Greene* are comprised, first, of the observations kept by Greene during two voyages, and secondly, of selections from the correspondence between Greene and the owners of the vessel *Perseverance* as she traveled from North American ports to those of Europe and then to South America.

Welcome Greene traveled on the *Perseverance* as supercargo, the agent for the merchants who owned the vessel, responsible for the cargo she carried. Only twenty-one when he started the first voyage, Greene recorded in his journal his opinions of the customs and sights that he saw at Richmond,

Norfolk, Bergen, Gibraltar, Cadiz, Rio de Janeiro, Montevideo, and Havana. His youthful curiosity led him to notice and to comment upon subjects ranging from fire prevention methods in Bergen (two casks of water in front of each house) to bribery in Cadiz (an office is only desired as it enables the individual to line his pockets with cash for permitting violations of law). Quaker Greene disliked a variety of things his curiosity led him to observe, and his candor made him comment unfavorably on Jefferson, statues raised to military leaders, Roman Catholic ritual, and gambling.

The business letters that passed between Greene and the S. G. Arnold Company in Providence told of a commerce that had ceased to be profitable but still struggled on. American commercial houses had not known prosperity since 1807, when as neutral carriers they had become wealthy as suppliers to the warring European continent. Commercial restrictions, embargo, and war had snuffed out this bonanza, and the attempt to revive trade following the War of 1812 was not successful. Greene's vessel carried staves and tobacco to Norway; fish, flour, and sugar to Gibraltar; brandy and wine to South America; beef to Havana; and sugar and molasses to Providence. At no time did he report favorable trading conditions and his problems included those attendant upon doing business in an oversupplied port: glutted import markets, impossibility of obtaining specie, heavy discounts on drafts, and overpriced services and return cargoes. Neither Greene nor the *Perseverance* sailed again after the end of the second voyage in 1820.

The editors, one of whom is a grandson of the writer of the Journals, have modernized the spelling and punctuation throughout. Explanatory footnotes are used where needed although they are occasionally poorly placed: for example, the term "pipe" is used throughout the letters, but is not explained until a note on page 150. The index is excellent.

Michigan State University JOHN H. REINOEHL

The Journal of Captain John R. Bell, Official Journalist for the Stephen H. Long Expedition to the Rocky Mountains, 1820. Edited with introductions by Harlin M. Fuller and LeRoy R. Hafen. *The Far West and the Rockies, 1820-1875*, Volume VI. (Glendale: The Arthur H. Clark Company, 1957. 349 pp. Maps, illustrations, notes, and index. $9.50.)

The Long expedition had two historians, Dr. Edwin James and Captain John R. Bell, both of whom joined the party in 1820 as replacements for Dr. Baldwin, who had died, and Major Biddle, who had withdrawn from the venture. The account by Dr. James was published in 1823. Captain Bell's *Journal* has not previously been published. Indeed, it was not known to be extant until Harlin M. Fuller, while a student at Stanford University in 1932, discovered it in the possession of the family of his roommate, Edwin B. Saunders. The Saunders family had brought it with them when they moved from New York to California, but they did not know how it came to be in their possession. Mr. Fuller edited and annotated it, and the original was deposited at Stanford University, where it presently may be found. Mr. Fuller's work, enlarged by the expert editorial notes of Dr. Hafen, forms the basis of the present volume.

Captain Bell, instructor in tactics at the United States Military Academy, was assigned to the expedition at his own request. His motive was adventure. Beginning his *Journal* upon leaving West Point, he joined Major Long and Dr. James in Pittsburgh, traveled with them by boat to St. Louis, and thence by horseback to Council Bluffs, where the rest of the party awaited them. Dr. Charles D. Humberd has furnished detailed notes and a map for the Missouri portion of the journey.

Captain Bell's *Journal*, although not so long as that of Dr. James (which occupies three volumes in Thwaites, *Early Western Travels*), is a more readable account for the average person, since it contains no botanical excursions. Points of actual disagreement with the James account are few but one is of great importance. James presented a confused narrative of the portion of the journey lying between present Denver and Colorado Springs which Bell's account makes perfectly clear, both as to time and route. In identifying Elephant Rock, near Palmer Lake, Colorado, as the "Castle Rock" of the explorers, Dr. Hafen has cleared up a long-standing puzzle concerning apparent geographical inaccuracies in the James report. There is not the slightest doubt of the correctness of this identification.

The editors' observation that Bell provides the first record of the names of the men who accompanied Dr. James on the first ascent of Pikes Peak is only partially correct. The James account does give the name of Wilson as one of them, but fails to mention Verplanck as the other. Bell gives the names of both men. But Samuel Seymour, the artist who served Long's expedition, remains an elusive figure concerning whom the present editors have been unable to supply biographical information.

Captain Bell does not make the "Great American Desert" statements, for which both James and Long have been taken to task, although he does refer to the region between Cañon City and Pueblo, Colorado, as a desert. His account of how the group of which he had charge made the descent of the Arkansas River while Long and James descended the Canadian River, although of value and interest, is handicapped by the fact that he had no map with him and so fell into geographical errors. These errors the editors have carefully corrected in their notes. Bell's observations concerning his return to Washington, D. C., across Illinois, Kentucky, Tennessee, Virginia, and Maryland will be of some use to social historians. The editors have not attempted much annotation of this portion of the narrative, since it falls outside the scope of *The Far West and the Rockies* series. Captain Bell's *Journal* is a welcome and notable addition to the literature of western exploration.

Colorado College HARVEY L. CARTER

Professors and Public Ethics: Studies of Northern Moral Philosophers before the Civil War. By Wilson Smith. (Ithaca: Cornell University Press, for the American Historical Association, 1956. viii + 244 pp. Notes, appendixes, bibliography, and index. $4.00.)

This monograph might seem of primary concern to specialists in intellectual history, or even more particularized nineteenth-century developments. It can, however, serve broader purposes. Professor Smith's view, I believe, is that men have not lived by bread alone, and that the rationales for action provided by the moral philosphers of the pre-Civil War decades implemented, where they did not merely supplement, those offered by economic, sectional, and other motivations.

The author's subject would easily have responded to no more than descriptive treatment of his selected moral philosophers (mostly clergymen) and the major tenets of their faith. Francis Lieber and Francis Wayland are well-known figures whose views and relationships can serve any number of historical projects. Others, like Professor John Daniel Gros of Columbia College, author of *Natural Principles of Rectitude* (1795), James Walker, president of Harvard, and Charles B. Haddock, the "Horace Mann of New Hampshire," enjoyed somewhat more circumscribed careers, but can readily be fitted into the constellation of moral philosophers. Professor Smith has been concerned, however, with understanding the bases of their fame, and estimating their actual and changing influence, and has brought to his work a sense of the subtle relations between action and ideas.

He traces the "pattern of moral philosophy" out of its European background, distinguishing between Locke's version of democracy and that of the Reverend William Paley, whose utilitarianism, weighted with Christian ethics, so deeply satisfied the dominant American outlook early in the century. Nevertheless, by the 1840's, principled opinion respecting the critical anti-slavery issue had mounted so high as to impugn the value of Paley's expedient version of ethical conduct, offending as it did, to a degree, both southern and northern opinion. Professor Smith makes much of "Whig ethics," with which he largely identifies his moral philosophers: a combination of doctrinaire Christian principles which assumed social responsibilities, though too often with limited perspectives and conservative presumptions. The Jacksonians were more aggressive in behalf of the "common man," but their capacity for expedient conduct ranged from sacrificing Indian rights to accepting fellowship from slaveholders. The moral philosophers were sometimes not relevant to the needs of their constituents, but they were often not offensive to those needs, and could thus more logically than the Jacksonians sustain their role of official public conscience.

Lieber and Wayland were among the most famous of the moral philosophers of the ante-bellum period, and the author comments perceptively upon them. He includes an interesting essay on the Dorr War which reveals Wayland's Hamletesque veerings between duty and legal rights. Lieber is presented as the most impressive of the gallery: a forerunner of William Graham Sumner, Albion W. Small, John W. Burgess, and even Thorstein Veblen, among others. But contrasting Lieber's work with theirs sharply exposes his limitations. His studies and interests were wide and interrelated, but rarely deep and searching; and his influence waned with the Civil War as certainly as did that of the other moral philosophers.

Why did it wane? Professor Smith has it that the war unleashed forces which could no longer use the premises and approach of these clergymen and professors. The Darwinian hypothesis did not help them. James Walker wished to see science accompany religion into realms "where nothing is to be feared [and] everything is to be hoped." But this was tepid fare to the pilots of the new industrial dispensation. The immediate result of their demands would take the form of Social Darwinism, rather than moral philosophy.

Professor Smith does not here have occasion to discuss later moralists who, like Woodrow Wilson, defied the challenge of evolution and were not necessarily rendered ineffective. His own thesis might have gained additional dimensions by including contrasts between his subjects and moralists less academic in substance. Thus, it appears inadequate to notice Theodore Dwight Weld only as a "ubiquitous slavery scandal-monger of the Old Northwest" (p. 190). But the author's treatment of the delicate web of feelings and attitudes which his protagonists sustained gives *Professors and Public Ethics* a substantial place among other studies which help set the background for the men of action of the period.

Antioch College LOUIS FILLER

The Prison at Philadelphia, Cherry Hill: The Separate System of Penal Discipline, 1829-1913. By Negley K. Teeters and John D. Shearer. (New York: Columbia University Press, for Temple University Publiations, 1957. xviii + 249 pp. Illustrations, notes, appendixes, and index. $5.50.)

Historians as well as students of penology will welcome this informative account of the rise and decline of Pennsylvania's famous "separate" or "solitary" prison system. The authors, one a professor of sociology and a writer on penal history, the other director of the Eastern Pennsylvania Diagnostic and Classification Center, have made good use of the rich documentary sources at Cherry Hill and have thrown fresh light on several aspects of its development.

The story of this historic penitentiary is full of conflict, as well as significance, and the authors have neglected neither. After a suggestive review of earlier theories and practices, they plunge into the controversies that divided the several proponents of the solitary system during the long years of planning and show how some issues were resolved during the hectic period of construction. They note the special contributions of Robert Vaux and the elder Dr. Benjamin Rush, of John Haviland the architect, of Thomas Bradford and other board members, most notably Richard Vaux, and of the wardens whose practical interpretations of the system did not always conform to those of the inspectors. They review in one chapter the findings of three major investigations ordered by the state. The next chapter presents in striking parallel the indictment of the system by Charles Dickens in his *American Notes* and the answer prepared by William Peter, the British consul general stationed in Philadelphia, as well as an abstract of the record on each prisoner visited by the English novelist. The authors describe with great detail the disciplinary practices and policies and relate the successive escape attempts and other incidents of succeeding administrations. Finally they endeavor to place the contributions of this institution in the larger setting of prison history.

While the authors pay several tributes to the earlier study by Harry Elmer Barnes on the *Evolution of Penology in Pennsylvania* and quote his characterization of the system at Cherry Hill as "sterile," they apparently do not subscribe fully to that view. They recognize the failure, first of the solitary and then of the separate systems, but retain a hope for the individual treatment philosophy evolved in later years. Meanwhile they feel impelled to comment with some asperity on the follies of that penal gadfly, as they describe Louis Dwight, whose zealous labors in behalf of the rival Auburn or "silent" system assured its early triumph in America and thus provided at least the setting in which penology has made its limited progress. However, if this book treats Cherry Hill's "nemesis" somewhat shabbily, it is perhaps for that very fact a more accurate presentation of this great experiment which not only won world-wide fame for Philadelphia and its penal reformers but also adhered stubbornly to its ways in the midst of contending and often more popular doctrines until its penal rivals had made sufficient modifications in their programs to appropriate and give new vitality to the individual treatment concept long dormant in the separate system.

Rochester, New York BLAKE MCKELVEY

The Early Jackson Party in Ohio. By Harry R. Stevens. (Durham: Duke University Press, 1957. xiv + 187 pp. Map, bibliographical note, appendixes, and index. $4.50.)

The question of how a state unit of the Jackson party was created is answered in Mr. Stevens' study of the emergence of the party in Ohio in the election of 1824. The campaign itself is not discussed but an analysis of the results of the election is included for evidence of the party's achievements.

The birth of the party in Ohio, its infancy, and its surprising growth into vigorous youth are covered in detail. No type of political activity is overlooked. Prenatal influences take up over a third of the book, for Moses Dawson, parent or godfather, does not exhibit the baby until Chapter VI. The relevance of much of this section and of some other parts of the book is open to question: for example, the descriptions of the physical appearance and business life of Cincinnati, the biographical sketches of so many figures, including non-Jacksonians, accounts of Fourth of July celebrations, and the details of local elections — as early as 1817.

The bibliography seems to have been sacrificed to local color and personalities. A bibliographical note of two pages attests to the author's thorough research by listing various types of sources. He attributes to lucky accidents his discovery of valuable manuscripts in unlikely places, but the reader is left in the dark as to what and where they are. Footnotes are given only for quotations, and these are nearly all from familiar sources. An appendix provides a table of votes by counties, a map of Ohio in 1824, and a list of some 1,200 names of active party figures, grouped under candidates and counties, an amazing compilation.

In the final chapter the author compares the Jackson, Clay, and Adams parties and reaches conclusions that are difficult to summarize here, as they are sometimes tentative, sometimes conjectural, and occasionally even obscure. In general, he believes that there were no social, economic, or geographical factors or important issues to set off the Jacksonians from their rivals. This leaves "the imponderable element of personality and the more definable element of prior political affiliation" as explanations. Thus men "with a given outlook on life" might prefer one candidate rather than another: the aggressive, Jackson; the reflective, Adams; those skilled in what the author quotes as "wire-working," Clay. The measurement of these imponderables is something else.

Issues are dismissed as unimportant, as all parties were in substantial agreement. The sharp newspaper battles over candidates' attitudes on protective tariff and internal improvements are ignored. Were the voters' "outlooks on life" unaffected by reading newspapers?

All parties used familiar methods of arousing voter interest, with the Jacksonians more effective at the county level and in their use of a party press but seemingly more laggard in developing professional politicians. State and local elections as yet had slight relationship to the presidential struggle, though the same individuals might be active in all three.

In a brief comparison of the Ohio Jacksonians with those of other states, the author concludes that each group was unique, that there was no uniform pattern. This, along with his emphasis on the individual and the personal in his Ohio synthesis, makes one wonder whether too careful an examination of so many trees has obscured for him the patterns of the forest.

Ohio State University EUGENE H. ROSEBOOM

Henry Clay and the Art of American Politics. By Clement Eaton. *The Library of American Biography.* Edited by Oscar Handlin. (Boston: Little, Brown and Company, 1957. xii + 209 pp. Note on the sources and index. $3.50.)

If compromise is indeed the essence of the art of American politics, then Henry Clay must certainly be granted his place as one of the consummate craftsmen of our political history. It is this conviction which gives direction to Professor Eaton's study of the Kentucky nationalist, in a highly readable and remarkably concise survey of a long and complex career.

More than perhaps any other man of his time, Clay was constantly engaged in political practice. He has left behind a wealth of correspondence, now fortunately being gathered together at the University of Kentucky, and Mr. Eaton has drawn generously from this lode. But little is changed thereby from the traditional interpretation of Clay's character or of his place in the American story.

Mr. Eaton sees him as beset with an ambition for public office which would prove to be his "Achilles heel"; as a Jeffersonian humanitarian who looked to Madison for his political code; and as a pragmatist who understood the need of a national response to the industrial and economic revolution of his time, though he frequently misjudged the effects of this revolution upon the political aspirations of the mass of American citizenry. Indeed, Clay's major weakness, Mr. Eaton believes, was his inability to see beyond the institutional or governmental issues confronting the nation and into the minds and desires of the "little people." His concern for national strength, economic as well as political, drove him into identification with the "business community," whose champion he was to become. "In his speeches and letters he does not say much about the working man," Mr. Eaton tells us — "his main concern was for the manufacturer and the wealthy planter." As payment for this failure, Clay was to be the most frequently frustrated presidential candidate in American history.

Clearly, then, Mr. Eaton's Clay cannot qualify as a master practitioner of the art of politics if the winning of sought-after office is the mark of quality.

His great attainments were in the field of bending his congressional colleagues to the necessities of compromise, to the acceptance of "the possible." In this he had no peer, and it was here that the true marks of his political genius were to be found. Unfortunately, Mr. Eaton is not given sufficient scope to develop this central idea to a point at which it might make a real contribution to our understanding of the basic techniques of early American politics. His book falls between biography and interpretative essay, with the result that we are told a great many things that we already know and denied that exposition of the main theme which would make it meaningful. No author can do much to demonstrate the vitality of Clay's political art, for example, when space limitations squeeze his analysis of party alignments into such barren equations as the familiar "Jacksonians equal the common man," "Whigs equal the wealthy business aristocracy." As a result, we come away still ignorant of the real processes of Clay's political accomplishments.

Objective balance and judicious evaluation are maintained throughout this book, and it is clear that Mr. Eaton admires the great westerner, though one suspects that he would not have joined the Clay camp. The picture of Clay's unwavering optimism in his presidential campaigns is somewhat overdrawn, however, giving the impression of a simple-minded blindness to realities. Actually, it is certain that Clay was convinced as early as December, 1831, for example, that he had no chance of toppling Jackson from the presidency the next year, and that he remained in the race only because of his concern for the fate of his adherents in local contests in Louisiana and Maryland.

The political chapters are complemented by brief essays on Clay as a Kentucky planter, humanitarian, and "early Victorian gentleman." Perhaps it is indicative of some flaw in Clay's political personality that these pages on his unofficial pursuits are the most attractive in the book.

Loyola University, New Orleans JOSEPH G. TREGLE, JR.

James K. Polk, Jacksonian, 1795-1843. By Charles Grier Sellers, Jr. (Princeton: Princeton University Press, 1957. xiv + 526 pp. Illustrations, notes, bibliography, and index. $7.50.)

"Who is James K. Polk?" demanded Whig orators with feigned astonishment during the presidential campaign of 1844. These men knew better, but they were exploiting a dilemma that has always dogged Polk's political career. Except among his close political associates he was unappreciated in his own day; succeeding generations of Americans have all but ignored him. Perhaps the reason is obvious. Men are remembered for their unique characteristics and Polk had none. In oratory he lacked the distinction of Daniel Webster or Thomas Hart Benton, in intellect that of John C. Calhoun, and in personality and leadership that of Henry Clay. His failure to seize the attention of his and later generations, however, has never denied the fact that he was a man of substantial qualities.

Whatever doubt may have remained regarding Polk's significance to American history has been dispelled by Charles G. Sellers' distinguished first volume of his projected two-volume study of this noted Tennessean. Those historians who have long felt that Polk has deserved a better fate and that his successful years in the White House were no accident will find their impressions vindicated. James was born into the Polk clan in the environs of old Mecklenburg, North Carolina, in the days when the "Great Speculation" was perennially tempting North Carolinians to move westward. Eventually the fever caught Sam Polk, James's father, and brought him to Carter's Creek in Middle Tennessee. This frontier state was then undergoing a veritable demographic revolution, and when James returned from his studies at the University of North Carolina in 1818, Tennessee was becoming a major political factor in the nation, capable of projecting its favorite sons into the national limelight.

Polk had imbibed the philosophy of Thomas Jefferson as a backwoods youth and he never compromised with those convictions. For him political realism did not demand it. In agricultural Tennessee the middle-class economic pressures that eventually splintered his own Democratic party and drove many of its leaders toward paternalism never encroached on his standards. He entered political life an enemy of Clay's American System, and never ceased to condemn the protective tariff, the national bank and credit system, internal improvements, and the distribution of federal surpluses among the states. "I would keep no surplus revenue there to scramble for, either for internal improvements, or for any thing else," he once said. "I would bring the Government back to what it was intended to be, a plain economical Government."

Polk first achieved political prominence in Congress when he joined the vanguard in the Jacksonian attack on the Maysville Road bill and the United States Bank. His close addiction to Jeffersonianism led him eventually into the camp of Martin Van Buren and a successful term as speaker of the House of Representatives. Polk followed his congressional career with a term as governor of Tennessee. For him life consisted of politics and he forced himself to the limit of his abilities to maintain his political power at home and in Congress. Without a captivating personality, he schooled himself in "a rather ceremonial affability" which permitted him to cultivate some lasting friendships. He developed the techniques of stump speaking, and during his arduous speaking tours in the Tennessee canvasses of 1839, 1841, and 1843 he gradually mastered the art of wit, sarcasm, and facial expression. A vigorous campaigner, a thorough Jacksonian, and a man of parts in national Democratic circles, Polk had become a man marked for the vice-presidency as early as 1842. If his nomination and election to the White House two years later might not have been anticipated, his "availability" was clear.

Professor Sellers' prodigious research is evidenced by his careful detail and measured judgment. If the author's devotion to his subject is explained in part by his own boyhood in Mecklenburg, it is a devotion that has not been misplaced. This volume is at once a detailed analysis of an ambitious and successful politician and a vigorous account of Jacksonian democracy in action. As such it will be useful and exciting to students of ante-bellum America. Historians will anticipate with pleasure the publication of the second volume of this sympathetic and noteworthy biography.

University of Illinois NORMAN A. GRAEBNER

Prairie and Mountain Sketches. By Matthew C. Field. Edited by Kate L. Gregg and John Francis McDermott. (Norman: University of Oklahoma Press, 1957. liv + 239 pp. Illustrations, notes, appendix, and index. $4.50.)

In the spring of 1843 the Trans-Mississippi West attracted several organized groups of adventurers besides the usual fur traders who made their way west with the annual supply of goods. At the bend of the Missouri River Lieutenant John C. Frémont prepared to lead his second expedition into the mountain country. John James Audubon waited for the American Fur Company to take his small party upstream. A large contingent of emigrants, mostly Missourians, waited in Independence for the grass to grow while they settled their quarrel over the number of cattle each family could take to Oregon. A few Jesuits waited for their overland journey to the Flatheads on the Snake River. There was also another group present that spring, a group which this book rescues from continued oblivion.

Prairie and Mountain Sketches is the record of a pleasure-seeking party under the leadership of Sir William Stewart, a Scottish sportsman who had made his first trip west in 1833-1835, his second in 1836, his third in 1837, and his fourth in 1838. It was on his fourth expedition that he took along the artist, Alfred Jacob Miller, to perpetuate on canvas this fascinating West. In 1843, this sportsman, now wealthy, gathered a polyglot group of adventurers interested in pleasure alone and started out the Platte River in search of good hunting and interesting sights. In the party was Matt C. Field, assistant editor of the New Orleans *Picayune,* seeking renewed health as well as thrills. It was Field who kept diaries, wrote letters, and sent reports to his newspaper about the trip, and these writings constitute the material of this attractive book, published as Volume 23 in the University of Oklahoma "Exploration and Travel Series." The writings were first located by Clyde and Mae Reed Porter, who made them available to Professor Kate L. Gregg for editing. Following her untimely death, the skilled editorial hand of

John Francis McDermott gave considerable unity to these diverse records, wrote the introduction, and inserted explanatory notes. His greatest task was to integrate the story into a readable running account.

The adventurers' pleasure jaunt took them to the Wind River Mountains in Wyoming between May 8 and October 27, 1843. The account is not a day-to-day chronology, but covers the whole period either as a daily entry or as a newspaper story. Sir William Stewart does not emerge as an important character who hunts and drink and eats, but others do. In the main, episodes of the trip having a human interest do emerge as central to the overland jaunt. It is interesting to note, for example, that Sir William kept for himself special privileges even among the hardy democratic spirits of his party, and that Field and others were impatient when the expedition stopped one day while Sir William's Indian companion gave birth to a baby.

The contribution of this volume lies in its narrative of the experiences of a pleasure-seeking group of early travelers. It adds little to the geographic knowledge of the West, to the history of overland travel and exploration, or even to the hunting of the buffalo. It does, however, provide glimpses into the character and behavior of some of the men attracted to the frontier.

Wisconsin State College, River Falls WALKER D. WYMAN

The Law of the Commonwealth and Chief Justice Shaw. By Leonard W. Levy. (Cambridge: Harvard University Press, 1957. x + 383 pp. Illustration, notes, appendix, bibliography, table of cases, and index. $6.50.)

This study of the professional career of Lemuel Shaw is one of the few significant analyses of the work of judges of the highest state courts in the United States. Legal history is a vital part of general history, and in our legal history the work of the courts at the peaks of state judicial systems has been extremely important. Yet little has been done in the way of writing the history of these courts or the biographies of their leading judges. One reason has been the extremely technical character of the private law materials with which state courts and state judges have been primarily concerned and the difficulty of clarifying the significance of these materials for general readers. Another reason has lain in the fact that, because there have been so many state courts and so many state judges, neither the courts nor individual judges have become generally known as has the Supreme Court of the United States and as have its justices; there has not, in other words, been the initial popular impetus to analysis and biographical writing.

This study of the judicial opinions of Chief Justice Shaw, of the Supreme Judicial Court of Massachusetts from 1830 to 1860, demonstrates the historical richness of such materials. Shaw was adept not merely at getting cases decided but also at tracing legal issues to their roots in public policy.

In this respect he seems to have made to the constitutional and statute and common law of Massachusetts much the same kind of contribution that Chief Justice Marshall made to the constitutional law of the United States, with a carry-over of important influence from the Massachusetts court to the area of federal jurisprudence as well. Although other state judges lived through the same rich period in legal development as did Shaw without in the same degree sensing or being able to meet the need for judicial creativity, Shaw, like Marshall, stood at the threshold of a tremendous unfolding in American law and took advantage of his opportunities to articulate legal principles in terms of the changing contours of society.

The range of Shaw's judicial work included the following areas. He dealt with the legal issues of the relations of church and state. He handled important cases involving the rights of Negroes in Massachusetts, giving protection where possible but deserting the abolitionists to uphold the federal fugitive slave law of 1850. In interpreting the common law of Massachusetts he launched the "separate but equal" doctrine which spread to other states and was at first accepted and later rejected by the Supreme Court of the United States in interpreting the Fourteenth Amendment. He aided in the development of the law of common carriers as railroads changed the pattern of transportation and the relations between shippers and carriers. To the benefit of employers he aided in the development of the law of negligence and the fellow-servant rule and the concept of assumption of risk. He aided labor, however, by rejecting the concept of the union as conspiracy. In a long series of cases he helped in developing the concept of police power as a category of legitimate activity of the state in behalf of its citizens.

While disapproving of the separate-but-equal concept and the doctrines reducing the responsibility of employers for injuries to employees, the author finds that although Chief Justice Shaw might be classified as a conservative he was conservative in an intelligent fashion and not blindly so. The author disagrees with Professor Corwin's appraisal of the Shaw court as a court concerned primarily with the protection of vested rights, insisting that it was "oriented toward the public interest, not vested interests." However that may be, Professor Levy has given us a well-written study of the work of an able and influential judge during an important period in American history. It is to be hoped that the book will set an example for the writing of others of its kind.

The Johns Hopkins University CARL BRENT SWISHER

The Letters of William Gilmore Simms. Volumes IV and V. Edited by Mary C. Simms Oliphant and T. C. Duncan Eaves. (Columbia: University of South Carolina Press, 1955-1956. Vol. IV [1955]: *1858-1866*. xvi + 643 pp. Illustrations, list of letters, and index. Vol V [1956]: *1867-1870*. xxiv + 571 pp. Illustrations, notes, appendixes, general index, and index of Simms's works. $8.50 per volume; $31.25 the set of five.)

With something of the symmetry and intensity of fiction, the story of William Gilmore Simms reaches a bitter climax in Volume IV of his letters and then moves swiftly in Volume V through scenes of suffering, sacrifice, and fortitude toward the death of the author. The two volumes complete the five-volume series of *The Letters of William Gilmore Simms*. The same high standards of scholarship are maintained throughout, even to the inclusion in Volume V of an appendix devoted to errata and addenda for Volumes I through IV. Footnotes, as before, supply historical context and identifications which both the casual reader and the scholar will find helpful. Of more importance, perhaps, is the General Index in Volume V which, finally, makes a unit of the entire series.

Volume IV of *The Letters* is concerned largely with what Simms and his editors call the Confederate War. Simms here reveals himself as both strategist and prophet. He warns his northern friend James Lawson of the probability of secession and attempts to reason out "the projects and plans" of the United States government. He discusses psychological warfare and the uses of propaganda, and he offers detailed plans for defense and offense. With rare exceptions his suggestions and prophecies are ignored.

Although he could complain that "The North takes away from me, and the South has never given," Simms was an ardent southron, likely to be blinded by patriotism and optimism. He crowed to Lawson in 1861, "Three years of war will be the making of our people"; but after three years of war Simms was writing to Paul Hamilton Hayne: "We are made daily to sup on horrors. The war will probably be of continued duration till both parties are exhausted, — unless God shall more emphatically interpose."

Blow follows dramatic blow in the sequence of letters in Volume IV. Gilmore, Simms's son, is wounded, and deaths within the family occur with remarkable frequency. "Woodlands," Simms's plantation home, is burned not once but twice, the second time under the torches of stragglers with Sherman's army. The famous library of some 10,700 volumes is destroyed ("My books! My books! My heart is ready to break when I think of them!"). At war's end Simms is a penniless widower with only six of his fifteen children alive. But he is not broken. He has his land, and he has his brain. With these, and with his children and grandchildren as assets and liabilities, he faces the rigors of reconstruction.

In Volume V, Simms's courage and ingenuity come into strong focus. For the purpose of keeping his family alive and housed, he shuttles between Woodlands and Charleston and between Charleston and New York, writing, supervising the cultivation of a few acres, and attempting to re-establish connections with northern publishers. And always he is ill and suffering. ("Terrible," he writes, "that a man's brains should be at the mercy of his bowels.")

Simms emerges at the end of Volume V as an admirable — and very human — character, with elements of the superman that leave the reader echoing Richard Henry Wilde. "What you have effected under the most unpromising auspices," Wilde wrote Simms in 1843, "moves my wonder and despair." There are more than 1,500 letters in the five volumes, including "letters of uncertain date" (Vol. V, Appendix I) and "supplementary letters of certain or probable date" (Vol. V, Appendix II) — no mean output even for a literary man. In addition the index to Simms's works occupies forty-six columns of fine print in Volume V (pp. 548-71). Of these works eighty-two were book-length and were published in Simms's lifetime.

So prolific a writer — as the editors themselves point out in the introduction to Volume I of *The Letters* — necessarily suffers from unevenness; but one must regret — again with the editors — that more of the novels have not been reprinted and that some have not appeared in book form at all.

There is hope now that Simms will receive the attention that is his due. Successful completion of the five volumes of his letters is assurance of that, for the letters, along with the great mass of scholarly material that accompanies them, constitute at once both an achievement and a challenge.

Tulane University JOSEPH P. ROPPOLO

Mighty Stonewall. By Frank E. Vandiver. (New York: McGraw-Hill Book Company, 1957. xii + 547 pp. Maps, illustrations, notes, bibliography, and index. $6.50.)

In the pantheon of Confederate heroes Thomas Jonathan "Stonewall" Jackson stands beside Robert E. Lee; like him he has become more than a Confederate hero, the property of the whole nation. Partly because of his meteoric rise from obscure major to lieutenant general in less than two years, in part because of his sudden death at the peak of his powers, but most of all because of his military genius and baffling personality, Stonewall has been the subject of a galaxy of biographies, monographs, and military studies. With all that has been written on him, by contemporaries, fellow soldiers, historians, it would seem temerity to attempt another biography of him. But despite the volumes on Jackson he remained a shadow looming larger than life, an enigma defying understanding, an authentic American "character" but one whose springs of thought and action were sometimes obscure. Colonel

Henderson's classic study of the war and Jackson's role in it stood alone for nearly two generations. Burke Davis' recent biography freshened the picture and brought "Lee's right arm" into clearer focus. Now at last comes a fresh, clear, and complete picture. Frank E. Vandiver has written the definitive biography of Stonewall Jackson.

Definitive is a strong word, but for organization, scope, careful research, critical analysis, and character delineation this study goes beyond anything earlier and turns the idealized equestrian statue on the field of Bull Run into a credible human being. With painstaking care, Professor Vandiver has mined Jackson materials all across the South and out of them produced a full-length portrait. Jackson's whole life comes under inspection: youth in the Virginia hills, cadet days at West Point, baptism of fire in Mexico, post-war duty in Florida, professor at Virginia Military Institute, tragic first marriage to Ellie, travels here and abroad, idyllic union with Mary Anna. The author's use of family letters is particularly effective and provides important insights into Jackson's relations with the men and women nearest him. Certainly this treatment of Jackson's pre-Civil War life (seven chapters) is most thorough and well related to the maturation of Lee's most valued corps commander.

But Vandiver's best writing and most judicious analysis are of the war years (twelve chapters): lucid, logical narrative and exposition of Jackson's development from stiff martinet, leading VMI cadets to war, to the Stonewall at Manassas, the rock of the Confederate left at Sharpsburg, the brilliant tactician of the Valley Campaign and Chancellorsville. This is superb military history, and the author's earlier researches into the relatively fresh field of Confederate logistics serve him well. More than that, this is superb biography presenting the most complete explanation of Jackson's complicated nature. The many-sided man shines forth: ambitious junior officer, conscientious professor (but not much of a teacher), devoutly religious layman, precise disciplinarian beloved by his troops (if not by his brigade commanders), inspiring leader, loyal friend, loving husband and father, dedicated soldier. Here is Jackson as he must have looked and felt to his contemporaries: calm, determined, exacting but kind, furious in combat, impatient when his troops were in motion, prayerful before action, secretive, trusting of those who could be trusted, humbly grateful to the God of Battles for whatever came.

The maps are unfortunately of uneven quality, hardly comparable to those in Henderson. Larger, provided with scale and clearly oriented, they might have been more helpful. It is also regrettable that the publishers have not given the volume a more durable binding.

Professor Vandiver has successfully written his way into the front ranks of Civil War scholarship. Readers should not accept the panegyric overtones of the opening pages as typical of the book or conclude from the frequent repetition in early chapters that here is one more academic plodder. For when Jackson goes into action, whether in the Valley, the Peninsula, or the Wilderness, the pace quickens and the reader is swept along with the Stonewall Brigade from Harper's Ferry to Manassas, from White Oak Swamp to Port Republic, from Fredericksburg to Chancellorsville and the end. The author demonstrates that there is no substitute for thorough research and that scholarship and readability are not mutually exclusive. He has made a major contribution to Civil War literature.

Kansas State Teachers College, Pittsburg DUDLEY T. CORNISH

General George B. McClellan, Shield of the Union. By Warren W. Hassler, Jr. (Baton Rouge: Louisiana State University Press, 1957. xvi + 350 pp. Illustrations, notes, critical essay on authorities, and index. $6.00.)

General George B. McClellan, one of the most important and controversial figures of the Civil War, has long deserved a careful study of his military career. In this monograph Dr. Hassler attempts to determine whether "McClellan was not only a most able organizer, drillmaster, and disciplinarian, but . . . also a soldier of superior strategic and tactical ability as compared with many of the other prominent generals on both sides" (p. xvi). The account begins with McClellan's appointment on April 23, 1861, as major general of volunteers and commander of all Ohio troops, and ends with his dismissal from active service, November 10, 1862, as major general in the regular army and commander of the Army of the Potomac. During this period of approximately nineteen months McClellan had the distinction of winning for the Union the "first land battle of the war," of fashioning a defeated mob of volunteers after Bull Run into the famous Army of the Potomac, of succeeding the great Winfield Scott as general in chief of the armies, of approaching within five miles of Richmond in the Peninsular campaign, and finally of gaining an advantage over Lee at the crucial battle of Antietam. Yet with all his achievements Lincoln fired him. Dr. Hassler feels that McClellan did not deserve removal at this time, if ever, and that perhaps by this act Lincoln "unwittingly extended the duration of the war for a year longer" (p. 323).

This conclusion in defense of McClellan's military record comes from an examination of a great variety of historical materials. Certainly McClellan deserves more credit than many students of the war have been willing to accord. In doing justice to McClellan this latest study should silence these critics once and for all — but it will not, and rightly so. A basic defect is the biographical approach, which tends to make the author see events through McClellan's eyes and lessens the objectivity of a study in command. As a result the failures of the Lincoln administration receive too much emphasis and McClellan's shortcomings too little. The author admits that the "Union commander was a circumspect man, with a tendency to magnify difficulties at times, and [that] he hesitated to take what he considered to be an unnecessary risk of serious defeat" (p. 88), but refuses to consider these characteristics as sometimes fatal. McClellan's propensity to estimate the size of the enemy's forces as many times larger than his own was not just a handicap, it was a basic weakness. In explaining McClellan's failures at critical times the author very properly stresses a long list of circumstances which contributed to his undoing. They range from Lincoln's concern for the safety of Washington, Stanton's malevolence, and Halleck's incompetency to mistakes made by Hooker, Sumner, and Burnside at Antietam. To dwell, however, on these influences while underplaying McClellan's weaknesses leads to questionable conclusions.

Many questions which have been raised in other works were either ignored or overlooked in this study. One wishes the author had gone more deeply and extensively into these matters, for he has made an excellent start. In the meantime it is impossible to decide whether McClellan was a great general and whether Lincoln committed a fatal blunder when he relieved him of his command.

Lafayette College EDWIN B. CODDINGTON

Justice Oliver Wendell Holmes: The Shaping Years, 1841-1870. By Mark DeWolfe Howe. (Cambridge: The Belknap Press of Harvard University Press, 1957. xiv + 330 pp. Illustrations, notes, and index. $5.00.)

Shortly before the Second World War, Justice Holmes's executor, John G. Palfrey, asked Professor Howe of Harvard Law School to prepare a biography of Holmes and made all of the great jurist's personal papers available. Since that time Professor Howe has edited and published the *Holmes-Pollock Letters* (2 vols., 1941); *Touched with Fire: Civil War Letters and Diary of Oliver Wendell Holmes, Jr.* (1946); and the *Holmes-Laski Letters* (2 vols., 1953). After this substantial editorial preparation, Professor Howe has now turned to the biography itself, and in this, the first volume, presents "the shaping years," 1841-1870. They are presented with careful attention to detail, partly because Holmes's "years of education were years in which his convictions and his doubts took their permanent shape," and partly because of the biographical material available. Since the Holmes papers include diaries for the earlier years, the author has decided to treat these years by days and months and Holmes's later life in terms of years and decades. The first reason is valid; the second is questionable.

Within this general plan of organization Professor Howe presents an excellent account of Holmes's education. He emphasizes the influence of family environment upon his intellectual development and traces his formal education from a Dame's school (where he was taught among other things to close his papers with a biblical quotation), through a Latin school, and then on to Harvard. At Harvard, which was conducted like "a primary school, on a grand scale," and where the faculty was as much of a police court as an agency of instruction, Holmes did well enough scholastically to overcome demerits for conduct and make Phi Beta Kappa. As an undergraduate he began to display something of a rebellious mood against religion, and, despite the orthodoxy of Harvard, began to develop the speculative, inquiring, and skeptical intellectual outlook that was to mature in his later life and to become the distinguishing characteristic of his professional career. Before graduation in 1861, at the age of twenty, Holmes enlisted in the Massachusetts volunteers and was soon commissioned a first lieutenant. Whether he was prompted by sympathy for abolition or his desire to save the Union is obscure, but in the hardships of war, during which he was wounded three times, Holmes began to have doubts about abolition and "causes" generally, and to make duty, gallantry, and chivalry his ideals.

Mustered out as a lieutenant colonel in 1864, Holmes enrolled in the Harvard Law School. Once again Professor Howe offers an admirable account of education at Harvard. He describes the law school faculty, the courses, textbooks, and methods of instruction, along with the nature of Holmes's independent reading. After three terms of law school and a few months in a law office, Holmes was awarded his degree and then set out on a trip to Europe. On his return he entered a leading Boston law firm which included among its partners James Bradley Thayer, whose subsequent ideas on judicial review closely paralleled those that Holmes was to develop. In 1870 Holmes was named University Lecturer on Constitutional Law in Harvard College and become co-editor of the *American Law Review*.

Stimulated by a consuming ambition "to beat the whole crowd" (p. 283), Holmes devoted his time intensely to work, so much so that William James complained that Holmes, like a planing machine, would "gouge a self-beneficial groove through life." Achievement was not enough; he desired praise and more praise, not from the crowd, however pleasant its adulation might be, but from the discerning elect, and Thayer, though alert to his better qualities, found him "selfish, vain, thoughtless of others" (p. 282). The picture of Holmes as an ambitious, vain, and arrogant young man emerges clearly in the pages of this volume in contrast to much of what Holmes would have called the "sentimental drool" that has been written about him in such a way as to make him a legend.

Perhaps the most important contribution of Professor Howe is the meticulous manner in which he traces Holmes's intellectual development from Unitarianism, combined with the vestigial Puritanism of his childhood, through evolution and positivism in his early manhood. Outside the law Holmes was largely a dilettante, swayed by Comtian positivism, Malthusian and Spencerian economics, and Darwinian evolution. He accepted uncritically the scientific method as a way to all knowledge. He attributed to science an omniscience it did not have and dogmatized about politics, economics, religion, literature, art, and philosophy in a manner that hardly became the author of the epigram that "certitude is not the test of certainty." That Holmes changed his views on particulars after 1870 is certain, but Mr. Howe makes it clear that the basic contours of his thought had been clearly formulated before he was thirty years old.

Professor Howe's first volume of Justice Holmes's life has been written with thorough and loving care. Sometimes the author's meticulous attention to detail has become excessive, which perhaps contributes to the fact that in some portions of the volume the vital Holmes does not seem to come alive. He seems more lifelike in those pages in which he speaks for himself, and the author is wise enough to let him speak often. But in many respects the volume has the qualities of great biography; its portrayal of the warts and moles as well as of the beauty in the character of the young Holmes, and its narration of his intellectual development combine to make it a notable contribution to history and biography. On the basis of the present work, as compared with others on Holmes, it appears that Professor Howe, a Yankee like Holmes and one of his former secretaries, has beaten "the whole crowd."

Vanderbilt University ROBERT J. HARRIS

Mark Twain of the Enterprise: Newspaper Articles and Other Documents, 1862-1864. Edited by Henry Nash Smith with the assistance of Frederick Anderson. (Berkeley: University of California Press, 1957. 240 pp. Illustrations, notes, biographical directory, and index. $6.00.)

The biggest obstacle to understanding Mark Twain's life on the Comstock Lode has always been the strange lack of any known file of the Virginia City *Territorial Enterprise* for 1862-1864. The *Enterprise* was, of course, the newspaper that made a professional writer out of Sam Clemens. In its columns there must have appeared several hundred news stories and letters by the young reporter who was then metamorphosing into Mark Twain. As Henry Nash Smith remarks in his excellent introduction to the present volume, hitherto "not one single article written by Clemens for the *Enterprise*" has "been known in its original form." All that we have had until now has been a scattering of articles (about twenty in number) that survived because they were reprinted by other newspapers of the day.

Upon the death in 1952 of a grandniece of Mark Twain, the University of California purchased four scrapbooks of clippings that had been compiled, for the most part, by Mark Twain's brother, Orion. In these family scrapbooks Mr. Smith found thirty additional letters and dispatches to the *Enterprise*. What is more, the new articles had been clipped from the *Enterprise* itself, so that at long last it was possible to see some of Mark Twain's journalistic pieces in the original type in which they were set. It is these newly discovered items that form the bulk of the present volume. To them Mr. Smith has added a twenty-page section that prints all known correspondence dealing with the question of whether Mark Twain had to leave Virginia City in order to avoid fighting a duel. By way of scholarly aids, Mr. Smith has provided a careful and very illuminating general introduction, special prefatory remarks preceding each individual item, fifteen pages of notes at the end of the volume, and a useful biographical directory of persons mentioned in the text. Mr. Smith and his assistant, Frederick Anderson, have gone to infinite trouble to date each article and to identify the innumerable proper names and obscure local references.

Most of the materials printed here are humorous in some degree at least. Few of the routine, factual, daily "local items" that Mark Twain must have written have survived. Some of the articles are outright burlesque, of none too original a sort, while others are "straight" reporting salted with occasional witticisms or satirical remarks aimed at a local official or custom. Professor Smith remarks, "The political reporting reproduced here shows a much greater quantity of serious, disciplined work than Mark Twain has traditionally been credited with at this period." It becomes apparent that in studying Mark Twain, the uninhibited humorist, one must not overlook Sam Clemens, the competent professional journalist. On the other hand even the best of these *Enterprise* articles can hardly stand comparison with Mark Twain's autobiographical account of the same events in *Roughing It*. *Roughing It* is a work of art; these articles are samples of a man's day-to-day journalistic output.

California Institute of Technology RODMAN WILSON PAUL

American Industry and the European Immigrant, 1860-1885. By Charlotte Erickson. (Cambridge: Harvard University Press, 1957. xii + 269 pp. Appendixes, notes, and index. $4.75.)

Those oddly-matched twins, the Contract Labor Act of 1864 and the Anti-Contract Labor Act of 1885, bound a confusing episode in the history of immigration to America. Miss Erickson's workmanlike study of contract labor dispels the confusion.

The term "contract labor" was applied to two different processes. One of these, immigration under contract, was widely condemned but relatively unimportant. The few workingmen whom American employers imported under contract were highly skilled hands. The masses of unskilled newcomers did not come under such agreements and so were not, in the usual sense, contract laborers at all.

The other process was more complex, more common, but less publicized. Both before and after the Act of 1885 — in the era of the "old" Northwestern European immigrants no less than in that of the "new" Southern and Eastern Europeans — mass emigration from a particular country or district might be started by ticket agents for steamship companies and thereafter kept in motion by the letters which the emigrants themselves wrote from America. There was an approximation to emigration under contract in the form of mortgage-secured loans which the European ticket agents sometimes advanced to individuals to cover the fare to America. Then in a quite separate transaction after the immigrants reached America, one of the many private labor agencies might send them out in job lots to industrial employers, not infrequently as strikebreakers.

With the latter process the Anti-Contract Labor Act had nothing to do. The Act was passed as a sop to the craft unions, who resented recent importations of a few hundred skilled strikebreakers. But to gain broader support, it was represented as a means of keeping out of the country vast hordes of "inferior" Italians and Hungarians — men like the unskilled strikebreakers whom American labor agencies had been supplying. Since the Act was only a trifling barrier to this sort of "contract labor" between 1885 and 1914, its principal effect, Miss Erickson concludes, was to set organized labor on the "track of prejudice and fear" leading to the racialist quota legislation of the 1920's.

It might be re-emphasized that the abuses of immigrant contract labor were more than mere fantasies. Legal prohibition in 1885 of immigration under contract was no doubt misguided as a method of dealing with these abuses, just as in 1924 legal discrimination among immigrants on a racial basis was an irrelevant way to deal with the problems which ethnic diversity posed for American society. These social problems, we now understand, were not racial but cultural; they were nonetheless real. Likewise, even though immigration under contract was negligible, the many cases of strikebreaking which Miss Erickson adduces were real enough and were a form of contract labor. Thus to say that the Acts of 1885 or 1924 were formed by prejudice and fear does not mean that unregulated immigration involved no palpable social problems.

This useful study should serve to discourage students from plowing further the sterile field of "immigration promotion" by employers. We need to know more about the European conditions which made men susceptible to steamship company advertising and also about the place of the new arrivals in the American industrial society into which labor agencies dispatched them.

Princeton University Rowland T. Berthoff

A History of Chicago. Volume III, *The Rise of a Modern City, 1871-1893.* By Bessie Louise Pierce. (New York: Alfred A. Knopf, 1957. xvi + 576 + xxxvi pp. Illustrations, notes, appendix, bibliography, and index. $8.50.)

The long-awaited third volume of Professor Pierce's engaging history of Chicago continues the high standards of scholarship established in the first two volumes of this distinguished work in urban history. This book follows the pattern developed in the second volume, published in 1940, and gives a composite view of the economic, political, social, and cultural aspects of the highly diverse and complex history of a rapidly growing city fast maturing into a metropolis. Admittedly, this is a formidable task, but the author succeeds reasonably well in bringing balance and giving perspective to the various factors that entered into the making of Chicago from the Great Fire of 1871 through the World's Columbian Exposition of 1893, two epochal events in the city's history.

Primary attention is given to Chicago's "economic empire." The quick rebuilding of the city after the disastrous fire of 1871 was convincing proof of its favorable geographical and economic position as the leading entrepôt of the Middle West. Professor Pierce deftly sets forth the economic developments that propelled Chicago forward to become the second largest city in the United States by 1890. Chicago was nourished by industrial capitalism and bold, imaginative business leadership. Unrivaled transportation facilities made the city a leader in the grain, lumber, and livestock trade and a center for meat packing, manufacturing, and merchandising. Large specialized units were organized with borrowed capital to exploit business opportunities and often went through a speculative stage before achieving stabilized success. This maturing economy produced a restive labor movement which sought a more satisfactory adjustment to industrial capitalism. The "Great Strikes" in 1877 and the Haymarket Riot in 1886 were symptomatic of the embittered relations between labor and management before a better understanding prevailed in the more prosperous years from 1887 to 1892.

The political story is rather condensed but well organized and provides many insights into the practices of urban politics. Here was the battleground not only for hard-fought contests between the two major parties, but also a fertile field for sporadic third parties and militant reform groups such as the Citizens' Association and the Municipal Reform Club. Perennial issues, complicated by the fast growth of the city, centered around law enforcement, election frauds, fire protection, city improvements, economy in government, and sanitary measures. It was the usual case of the People *versus* Themselves working through the medium of democracy trying to solve their own problem. This stormy political vortex brought to the fore two well-known mayors,

Joseph Medill and Carter Henry Harrison, and one leader of state and national prominence, John Peter Altgeld.

The social and cultural aspects are treated in a more discursive manner. This material is too heterogeneous to fit into a well-organized synthesis. The social fabric, composed as it was of so many ethnic groups with diverse backgrounds living in an overcrowded city, had to withstand many tensions that made for a difficult period of social adjustment. Education, religion, and culture are traced as evolving social movements with changing patterns as the city matured. The selection of Chicago as the site for the World's Columbian Exposition over such contenders as New York, Washington, and St. Louis was a fitting tribute to the "I will" spirit of the Windy City.

Professor Pierce has made a major contribution in the field of urban history in setting critical standards that are lacking in other works on metropolitan areas. She has examined a tremendous amount of source material, her research has been thorough, and the text is well written with careful documentation. An appendix of useful tables, a selective bibliography, and a good index add to the value of the work.

Wisconsin State College, Superior WYATT W. BELCHER

Medicine in Chicago, 1850-1950: A Chapter in the Social and Scientific Development of a City. By Thomas Neville Bonner. (Madison: American History Research Center, 1957. xviii + 302 pp. Illustrations, notes, bibliography, and index. $5.00.)

Before the history of medicine and public health in the United States can be written, there must be prepared innumerable monographs and single volumes that delineate the progress of medical science and practice on local, state, and regional levels. And particular attention must be paid to urban communities. All this, it is gratifying to note, is being accomplished.

Mr. Bonner's descriptive analysis of a hundred years of medicine in Chicago, made possible in part by a grant from the committee on medical history of the Chicago Medical Society, supplements a two-volume history of medicine in Illinois and complements similar studies for Milwaukee and other American cities. It is a book of genuine value not only because it traces the history of medicine in Chicago but also because it integrates the medical aspects with the general culture of the community. This is no easy task, and the author accomplishes it with grace and balanced judgments.

After sketching the growth of medicine in early Chicago, Mr. Bonner explores generally the five decades from 1850 to 1900. Perhaps these two chapters are of most interest to the general historian who is not overly fascinated by the purely professional aspects of medical history. And they seem a little better written than some later chapters. Discussion next turns to an explanation of the rise of modern medical science, to the development of medical schools, to professional societies and their publications. Other sections deal with medical education in the twentieth century, a history of the Chicago Medical Society, a discriminating explanation of socio-medical problems in the half century prior to 1950, and to public health practices and philosophies. The final chapter may evoke varying reactions. This deals with the medical profession and the public.

Mr. Bonner, for example, makes the point that the medical profession did not enjoy a large measure of public confidence in the last half of the nineteenth century. He adds that the Chicago Medical Society, in the next century, opposed contract care, fought against health insurance programs, hammered away "incessantly" at the evils of state medicine, was reluctant to accept the need for reform. The Society called the Murray-Wagner-Dingell health bill, introduced in 1945, "a further extension, pure and simple of outright collectivism." The author states frankly that only the threat of a federal system of health insurance made the Society institute a voluntary medical insurance program which was co-ordinated with the local Blue Cross plan. He admits also that much remains to be accomplished by the medical profession before the "problem of medical economics has been solved for Chicago's citizens." He refrains from adding that public confidence in the profession today may not be much greater than it was in the nineteenth century.

All in all, however, this volume is marked by candor and more frankness than might be expected in a project financed in part by a medical organization. In general, the sections dealing with medical history and personalities prior to 1900 seem stronger and less biased than those that interpret the later period.

University of Minnesota PHILIP D. JORDAN

The Annals of Kansas, 1886-1925. Two volumes. Edited by Kirke Mechem. (Topeka: Kansas State Historical Society, 1954-1956. Vol. I, *1886-1910*: x + 526 pp. Vol. II, *1910-1925*: vi + 551 pp. Illustrations, tables, and index. $7.50 per set.)

The Kansas State Historical Society presents in these two volumes a detailed, day-by-day listing of events in Kansas history from 1886 to 1925. The work serves as a continuation, though with many differences in content and style, of Daniel W. Wilder's 1886 publication, *Annals of Kansas, 1541-1885.* Better balanced and more authoritative than Wilder's work, the present *Annals* bring together thousands of news items and over a hundred contemporary photographs to portray the daily life and interests of the people of Kansas in a forty-year span of history. The people of Kansas, as shown by the record in the *Annals*, were occupied periodically with politics, football, rainmaking experiments, visiting celebrities, and woman suffrage, and always with agricultural improvements, road conditions, and prohibition.

Although most items are condensed or paraphrased into three or four lines of text, a few get more space. William Allen White's more famous editorials, for example, are printed in full. The bulk of the items have been culled from the major Kansas daily newspapers (although the names of the papers are not regularly provided), with numerous selections from the extensive collection of local journals in the Society's files at Topeka. In addition to the news items, statistics on agriculture, population, education, and industry, and the names of state government officials have been compiled from state records and appended to each year's December 31 entry.

Inevitably in a work of this kind, selections of exclusively local interest are numerous. The reader discovers, for example, that on August 8, 1903, "In a berry-picking contest near Troy, Matilda Euler, 18, picked 240 quarts, breaking all records." Such information may seem unimportant but reflects the purpose of the compilers to show exactly what Kansans were thinking and doing. This purpose explains and perhaps justifies the fact that references to rabbits and rabbit-hunting outnumber references to Populists in the index.

The *Annals* is not only a chronological list of Kansas events; it is also a valuable statistical and pictorial reference and serves to some extent as a guide to topics and materials for the further study of Kansas history. A clear and detailed index, 114 pages long, is included. Reminiscing Kansans will doubtless pay most attention to this work, but many historians will find it of interest.

Tulane University CHARLES L. STANSIFER

The Imperial Years. By Foster Rhea Dulles. (New York: Thomas Y. Crowell Company, 1956. x + 340 pp. Illustrations, bibliographical notes, and index. $5.00.)

There are at least three kinds of historical works (probably more, but three will do for the purpose of this review). There are books which represent a genuine contribution to knowledge and add significantly to our understanding of the past by unearthing new and important data; there are books which purport to do the same thing, but really deal with the minute and the trivial, and fail to say anything that is important; and there are books which are frankly a synthesis, and which, by their skillful selection of facts, and by their effective interpretation and insight, give to the general reader, as distinguished from the specialist, something of real value.

Professor Dulles' book is of the third type. It deals with the development of the imperial impulse in the United States, and covers the period from 1885, when Grover Cleveland first took office, to the end of the second Theodore Roosevelt administration, with the accent on the period since 1895. It is lively in tone; it gives due emphasis (as works on diplomatic history are fortunately coming more and more to do) on ideas as well as on the incidents of policy; and it also skillfully combines an interest in individuals with concern for the larger forces that help to make up policy. There is room for more of this kind of studies.

There are, of course, questions that the specialist may raise. The impulse of American imperialism was not exhausted in 1909, when one considers the occupation of three Caribbean republics in the years that followed, and it is possible to take the view that Professor Dulles' study should have been extended to cover this period.

There are also some specific questions on which the reviewer would slightly change the emphasis. It has not been commonly enough observed that in the Venezuela dispute of 1895 the terms of reference of the arbitration agreement which ended the controversy were so framed that they were bound to give the British a large part of what they wanted, by fixing on the principles of prescription as the basis for the award.

The reviewer feels, too, that Professor Dulles is too cautious in his judgment on the Roosevelt legend with regard to the German blockade of Venezuela in 1902. Though a recent work, like many previously, attempts to find some substance of truth in the Roosevelt narrative, it still seems significant that there is not a word in the German archives to substantiate the story of an ultimatum, and almost incredible that if any ultimatum were given there should be no trace of the fact in Berlin. It is also significant that the Germans accepted arbitration in principle only a few days after the blockade began, and that they had even then discarded any idea of the occupation of Venezuelan territory.

Nor does it seem any more likely that Roosevelt's talk in 1905 about entering the Russo-Japanese war on the side of Japan in case the French or the Germans intervened has any real substance, since nothing has ever been found to confirm it.

But these are matters of detail. In its broad lines this is a useful synthesis on a period of very great interest, and one that links itself to the whole development of American foreign policy in the twentieth century.

Cornell University DEXTER PERKINS

Sanford Ballard Dole and His Hawaii. By Ethel M. Damon. (Palo Alto: Pacific Books, for the Hawaiian Historical Society, 1957. xiv + 394 pp. Illustrations and index. $5.00.)

Sanford B. Dole was a very important figure in the history of a very small nation. He was born in the Hawaiian Islands, the son of American missionary parents. He was a graduate of Williams College and selected the law as a profession partly because it would be "a possible stepping stone to influence and power in the Government." In 1893, he was invited by a group planning a revolution to become their titular leader, and three days later he was president of the Provisional Government of Hawaii. During the ensuing ten years, he held office also as president of the Republic of Hawaii, and first governor of the Territory of Hawaii.

In his later years, Dole prepared two sets of memoirs. The first dealt with events leading to the Revolution of 1893 and was published as one volume of the two-volume *Memoirs of the Hawaiian Revolution*, edited by Andrew H. Farrell. The second set, covering his entire life, was more personal than political in character and was enlivened by numerous anecdotes of life in the Islands and by references to activities of other members of his family. This second set seems to have been written for the specific use of a biographer, and Dole expressed the hope that Miss Damon would be that biographer.

Any biography of Dole must give considerable attention to his political career. This one does so only to the extent required to provide a portrait of Dole the man. Approximately 100 of the 375 pages of text deal with the ten years in which Dole was the chief executive of Hawaii. This is the story of the personal life of Dole and of the environment in which he grew to manhood and lived as an adult. Readers will gain an insight into the character and personality of the man, and they will find much to help them understand the leisurely life of nineteenth-century Hawaii. They will learn less of Dole the statesman. In those chapters where Miss Damon does discuss Dole's political activities, she is obviously an admirer of her subject. By her emphasis upon Dole as a man of integrity and good will — qualities which few would deny Dole possessed in abundant measure — Miss Damon tends to overlook the fact that his political opponents also regarded themselves as honest and well-intentioned. There is no clue in this book as to why many persons in the Islands did not welcome the Revolution, or accepted the Republic and annexation with reluctance. In particular, the book does less than justice to Grover Cleveland, who certainly believed that he acted honestly in taking a politically unprofitable position in denouncing the Revolution of 1893 and in opposing subsequent efforts to achieve annexation.

Miss Damon is well known to students of Hawaiian history as the author of several useful works dealing with missionaries or missionary families. Like Dole, she is the descendant of an early Christian worker in the Hawaiian Islands and she is a part of the closely-knit group of missionary descendants in the Islands who still occasionally refer to each other as "Cousin." It is obvious that she remembers Dole with affection and respect, and that bias is reflected in the book she has written. It is important to note, however, that Miss Damon is one of the very few living persons who combine a personal acquaintance with Dole and an insight into Hawaiian history adequate to the task of writing the account of the personal character and qualities of the man who became Hawaii's only president. She frankly disclaims any thought that this is the definitive biography; and in the context in which she planned and wrote her volume it will be welcomed as an important contribution by all who are interested in the history of the Hawaiian Islands.

Vanderbilt University HAROLD WHITMAN BRADLEY

Robert Russa Moton of Hampton and Tuskegee. Edited by William Hardin Hughes and Frederick D. Patterson. (Chapel Hill: University of North Carolina Press, 1956. xii + 238 pp. Illustrations. $4.00.)

The name Robert Russa Moton is sure to appear on any list of outstanding Negro Americans. Born in Virginia in 1867, Moton grew up in a rural plantation environment not greatly different from that of his parents under slavery, a fact that no doubt conditioned his later views on race relations, especially his faith in the basic good will of southern whites. Throughout his life he moved in the shadow of Booker T. Washington, beginning at Hampton Institute in the late 1880's where after graduation he became the first Negro commandant of cadets and an influential member of the administrative staff. When Washington died in 1915, Moton was the obvious choice to succeed him as principal of Tuskegee Institute in Alabama, for he not only shared Washington's faith in the Hampton-Tuskegee stress on vocational training for Negroes, but also possessed Washington's patience, tact, his willingness to accept half a loaf rather than none, and perhaps most important, his contacts with northern and southern white philanthropists. More quiet and reserved than his predecessor, Moton never attained Washington's unique position as national spokesman for the Negro people, but he none the less exerted considerable influence over Negro and white Americans who approved his pragmatic, conservative approach to racial problems. Before he retired in 1935, he had greatly expanded Tuskegee's plant and endowment and had raised it from a modest trade school to a degree-granting teacher and technical college.

This book, which contains three chapters from Moton's long-out-of-print autobiography, *Finding a Way Out*, and a collection of warm tributes from his Negro and white associates, indicates that in some respects Moton's leadership has been underrated. He is portrayed as a man willing to compromise in order to win limited gains for his people, as when he helped to secure a training camp for Negro army officers in World War I, but agreed that it should be located in the North lest white southerners be outraged. He was likewise willing to temporize in the face of grave provocation, as when he kept silent during the bloody wave of postwar lynchings and race riots and saw to it that his faculty and students did nothing to give the powerful Ku Klux Klan an excuse to destroy Tuskegee as both a useful institution and a symbol of Negro hope. Yet he is also pictured as a man of simple dignity and rare courage, who firmly insisted that colored doctors and nurses be permitted to serve in the Negro Veterans Administration hospital built adjacent to Tuskegee, and quietly defied a delegation of local Klansmen who threatened him with death if he did not agree to an all-white staff.

As is doubtless inevitable in any volume of tributes, the book makes no pretense of offering a balanced evaluation of its subject. Moton's life and contributions are described in his own words and by his friends and associates, who largely share his views on Negro education and race relations. There is scarcely a hint of the bitter opposition of some Negroes to the Hampton-Tuskegee type of vocational training, which allegedly fostered a servant psychology, or of the complaints that Moton's counsel of co-operation and moderation often amounted to toadying Uncle Tomism. The editors have sought to secure essays on representative aspects of Moton's career and personality, but the selections are of varying quality and sometimes overlap, and the absence of an index makes it difficult to find specific information or to compare different versions of the same event. Still, this is an illuminating account of an interesting and important figure, and it will serve both as a useful source and as a reminder that here is a fine subject for a scholarly biography.

Yale University E. DAVID CRONON

Opponents of War, 1917-1918. By H. C. Peterson and Gilbert C. Fite. (Madison: University of Wisconsin Press, 1957. xiv + 399 pp. Illustrations, notes, bibliography, and index. $6.00.)

After reading this truly frightening book one might be constrained to say that the American people had become somewhat more civilized in the twenty-odd years between World Wars I and II. For surely, public behavior toward opponents of the war in the years between 1941 and 1945, while not completely enlightened, was nonetheless a considerable improvement over that of the World War I period when professional patriots, anti-union employers, and plain ordinary citizens sometimes fiendishly persecuted those who opposed the great crusade to make the world safe for democracy.

We of the World War II generation do not have completely clean hands, as was attested by our treatment of thousands of loyal Japanese-Americans. Yet aside from this one outstanding and shameful aberration, there was comparatively little by way of the suppression of free speech, dismissals of teachers and professors, outrageously severe prison sentences and fines for those convicted under the Espionage and Sedition acts, tar-and-featherings, beatings, yellow-paint treatments, and even murders that were committed in the name of patriotism during 1917-1918 and immediately after. Our own witch-hunting, indeed, came after the war, and as bad as McCarthyism was, it was in no way comparable to what transpired during the earlier period.

But have we become more civilized? Perhaps so, though our use of the atomic bomb gives cause to wonder. And if radicals were not hounded and persecuted in World War II, as were the IWW men and Socialists during 1917-1920, could this not be in part because the Soviet Union was our war-time ally and our American Communists staunch supporters of the war? Too, World War II did not catch us on the crest of a crusade to reform the world in the democratic image and this conceivably provided us with a sufficient degree of cynicism to resist the excesses committed in the names of loyalty and democracy. Finally, the recent war had distinct racial overtones and our hatred was so focused on the unfortunate Japanese-Americans that we had little time for ferreting out the real dissidents.

This exceedingly impressive monograph by the late Professor Peterson, edited and prepared for publication by Professor Fite, provides ample documentary evidence to those historians who habitually talk and write in highly generalized terms about World War I persecutions. Also, I should think, they call into question the objectivity, and hence reliability, of such a paper as the New York *Times*, on which historians have traditionally depended for sound reporting and balanced editorial judgments. The *Times* was distinguished for neither. Not a few reputations are severely damaged by this study. For example, the late Judge Kenesaw Mountain Landis, the first commissioner of baseball, is depicted as a narrow-minded twentieth-century Torquemada whose excessively harsh sentences on those convicted of violating the Espionage and Sedition acts made a travesty of justice. And the authors tend to confirm what many have long maintained, namely, that our unbending President emerged from the war as a badly tarnished liberal hero. The test of a liberal, after all, is under fire; here Wilson failed miserably.

University of South Carolina HOWARD H. QUINT

The Age of Roosevelt: The Crisis of the Old Order, 1919-1933. By Arthur M. Schlesinger, Jr. (Boston: Houghton Mifflin Company, 1957. xvi + 557 pp. Notes and index. $6.00.)

Arthur Schlesinger's prefatory apology that this may be "a bad time to be writing about Franklin Roosevelt" because "the reputation of a commanding figure is often at its lowest in the period ten to twenty years after his death" need not concern us deeply or long. Edgar E. Robinson's attack upon the Roosevelt leadership from the conservative right, and the critiques from the liberal, sophisticated left by Richard Hofstadter, Eric Goldman, and James Burns have been balanced by the more objective, but still sympathetic, analyses of Bernard Bellush, Daniel Fusfeld, and, most notably, Frank Freidel. Professor Schlesinger sets out, in this volume, candidly and with passion, as an advocate of his protagonist; and although his enthusiasms often get out of control (as in the peroration, for example), he usually has them on the leash.

The organization of the volume is artfully conceived; the style is lively and precise, even though it occasionally assumes the sonorous tone of the epic;

the research is thorough. The author's understanding of the wellsprings of behavior, his grasp of the dramatic moment, his ability to evoke the mood of the past — all may be counted as assets. But most significantly, Mr. Schlesinger's participation in contemporary politics at the highest levels has given him the knowledge that American politics embraces the whole of American life, a sense of the significance of the intimate detail of practical politics, and a wide acquaintanceship with many of the leading and peripheral actors of the era whose history he tells. This volume is political history in the broadest and best sense of the term.

Mr. Schlesinger writes with such verve that one is almost persuaded to believe, with him, that in the years he describes America was saddled with an ancient regime, and the "old order's" Deer Park located, symbolically perhaps, on Wall Street. The hero is rarely permitted to lose command of the situation; thus, while the author recognizes the dilemma which Tammany corruption posed for the Democratic candidate in 1932, one must look elsewhere to realize that Roosevelt behaved badly and clumsily in handling this delicate situation. The Republican platform of 1932, probably no more evasive and no less candid than that of the Democrats, is treated with gratuitous cynicism whereas the glaring contradictions in the Democratic pledge are presented without criticism, either explicit or implicit. The latter form of presentation is to be preferred; one objects only to the double standard. With Roosevelt, to explain is too often to condone; with Hoover, to condemn.

Moreover, the book's epigraph: "Every revolution was first a thought in one man's mind," can be made to apply to any era, even including the Age of Roosevelt in which the man loomed large, only by a mis-weighting of the evidence. In fact, the author's brilliant and sensitive analysis of the complicated root structure of the Roosevelt personality, philosophy, and program would tend to contradict his inclination to exaggerate the influence of "one man's mind." Emerson's dictum is an insufficient guide to the interpretation of great historical events; Mr. Schlesinger's own text offers abundant evidence that the underlying assumption is a weak one.

The Whig historians of earlier generations carried all things before them because their postulates were widely accepted as the common sense of the matter, because they were men of affairs as well as first-rate scholars, because they were clever, because they wrote eloquently, because they rode their prejudices hard and proudly. The influence of this book, and of the volumes still to come, will undoubtedly be of the same high order of political and historical significance.

University of Minnesota CLARKE A. CHAMBERS

The Fight for Fluoridation. By Donald R. McNeil. (New York: Oxford University Press, 1957. xii + 241 pp. Notes, essay on the sources, and index. $5.00.)

It all began in 1901 when a dentist named Frederick McKay became interested in the stained and mottled teeth of the children of Colorado Springs. His indefatigable efforts over the next three decades to define the geographical limits of this "Colorado Stain" and stimulate professional interest in it form the fascinating prologue to the most lively public health drama of our times.

In his epochal paper of 1916 (written with G. V. Black), Dr. McKay proved that Colorado Stain disregarded nationality, social position, and general bodily health, and he prophetically concluded that "these waters contain something that is not commonly detected in the standard water analyses." The break-through came in 1930-1931 with the identification of fluorine as the responsible agent. Then the quantitative surveys which confirmed an old suspicion that mottled teeth were good teeth and the first guarded suggestions that fluoridation of water supplies would inhibit tooth decay. In the 1940's came the large-scale trials at Grand Rapids and Newburgh, the zealous pushing of fluoridation by the bold "Wisconsin group," and the widespread public confusion as opposition developed.

The fight over fluoridation which raged in the late 1940's and the 1950's raised the old public health question of what degree of caution should be exercised by promoters of new and promising discoveries in medicine. Is it better to "err on the side of caution," as one group advised regarding fluoridation, or should minimal risks be taken so that the present generation may benefit? Certainly the statements of advocates of caution were later wrenched out of time and context by the fanatical fringe groups which joined and later dominated the fight against fluoridation. Dr. McNeil identifies the present leaders of the anti-fluoridation group as a few dentists and physicians who are convinced that fluoridation is harmful, Christian scientists, health food advocates, many old foes of pasteurization and vaccination, chiropractors who are fighting the medical profession as much as fluoridation, and those who profess to see in the adding of fluorides a Communist plot to weaken America or a Jewish conspiracy to control the world. Fluoridation is today endorsed by virtually every professional body concerned with medicine, dentistry, or public health, which raises the question of the role of the scientific expert in a democracy. Professional men have deplored the transfer of the fluoridation question from the laboratory and the learned journals to the political arena, yet they have been focred to turn for implementation to popularly elected officials sensitive to any current of criticism among their constituents.

Dr. McNeil has done an exellent job of reporting on the historical dimension of a current public health question. There are places where one might wish for more analysis and interpretation and less straightforward reporting, especially on the anti-fluoridation movement, its strategy, support, and parallels with similar movements in the past, but information here is admittedly difficult to come by. It is sometimes difficult, too, to maintain perspective when dealing with the very recent past but there are offsetting advantages. Dr. McNeil was able to establish contact with a number of the principals in the fight over fluoridation and he makes considerable use of the information thus acquired. The work is well documented throughout. The author has used the professional literature extensively as well as the collected papers of a number of the stalwarts in the controversy. In addition he had access to American Medical Association and American Dental Association files, the papers of several state and local health departments, and the records of the two hearings by congressional committees on the subject. Newspapers in the cities where sharp battles took place were used to good effect. The style throughout is lively and readable.

University of Omaha THOMAS N. BONNER

Race and Nationality in American Life. By Oscar Handlin. (Boston: Atlantic-Little, Brown, 1957. xiv + 300 pp. Notes and index. $4.00.)

This book is less all-embracing than the title suggests in so far as it treats only special aspects of immigration and race problems in the United States. Many of the chapters have appeared in identical or similar form as articles in popular or scholarly magazines or in memoranda prepared by the author for the President's Commission on Immigration and Naturalization (1952). Some new essays have been included, and the style has been shaken down so that the transition of the reader from a section of the book which appeared originally in the *William and Mary Quarterly* to one which was first published in the *Atlantic* or *Commentary* is relatively, if not entirely, easy.

Handlin considers the emotional and ideological aspects of racism more important than the economic, and he treats the former more fully. His account of the history of race thinking is rather sketchy, particularly in its concern with American *Rassentheoretikers.* He might, for example, have included race concepts developed by American historians in the late nineteenth century which had important impact upon the restrictive immigration legislation of the 1920's. On the other hand, there is an admirable presentation of the fallacies, ethnic and other, that entered into the forty-two volume report of the Immigration Commission of 1910. This is very different from the respectful consideration given the work of the Immigration Commission by Roy Garis. "The Horror" is the most impressive chapter in this section of the book, with its association of prejudice with what information Handlin has been able to assemble concerning the inner emotional life of the American people. This chapter represents Handlin at his best — which is very good, indeed.

Having dealt with phases of the economic, ideological, and emotional aspects of racism, Handlin next turns his attention to a summary of those factors which contributed to the transition — nay "revolution" — from the "tightly meshed pattern of discriminatory practices [that] put substantial portions of the American population at an enormous disadvantage in almost every aspect of life" in 1918 to the greater equality of today. Here his most important section is an account of science's assault upon the race concept. He rounds out the book with several brief and diversified chapters on the theme of immigrant and ethnic integration into the larger American pattern.

Handlin's writing in the field of immigration is invariably provocative and interesting. If his recent books, including this one, lack the rich documentation and trail-blazing character of his memorable *Boston's Immigrants*, the scholar as well as the general reader are indebted to him for consistent mastery of a complex and difficult field.

The New School for Social Research EDWARD N. SAVETH

Frederic Bancroft, Historian. By Jacob E. Cooke, with an introduction by Allan Nevins and three hitherto unpublished essays on "The Colonization of American Negroes from 1801 to 1865," by Frederic Bancroft. (Norman: University of Oklahoma Press, 1957. xiv + 282 pp. Illustrations, notes, bibliographies, and index. $4.00.)

This volume consists of two distinct sections. The first is a biographical sketch of Frederic Bancroft, by Jacob E. Cooke (approximately 140 pages in length), while the second section consists of three hitherto unpublished essays by Bancroft himself on the colonization of American Negroes from 1801 to 1865, essays edited by Dr. Cooke and covering some 112 pages. In addition, there is an introduction by Professor Allan Nevins which contains some interesting observations concerning Bancroft.

Dr. Cooke's biographical essay is one of the very few published studies of Frederic Bancroft, and it is based on the manuscripts in the Bancroft Collection in the Columbia University Library. These reasons alone are sufficient to give interest and value to the essay. In Dr. Cooke's view, Bancroft "was not a figure of central importance in American scholarship" (p. 139), and in the light of that evaluation one can understand and approve the limitation of the biography to its present length. Bancroft's life (1860-1945) spanned most of the period in which the modern profession of historian has existed in the United States, and Dr. Cooke describes his position in the ranks of United States historians as that of "a human bridge connecting the old with the new; he was a charter member of that select company, most of them university professors, who in the two decades prior to 1900 attempted to make the study of history a profession, and a member as well of that small group of men who carried on the tradition of history as a study for gentlemen of leisure, approaching it as an absorbing avocation" (p. 140).

Bancroft, in both a social and intellectual sense, was part of a group of financially independent "gentlemen scholars" — including, among others, Henry Adams, Charles Francis Adams, Jr., and James Ford Rhodes — who pursued the study of history largely outside the academic world. Dr. Cooke describes the actions and ideas of Bancroft in a straightforward, thorough, and conscientious fashion; his approach has its virtues, but it is least satisfactory, in the opinion of this reviewer, in the discussion of Bancroft's ideas concerning history. Dr. Cooke makes it clear that Bancroft was not himself interested in the question of "philosophy of history" and that Bancroft did not make systematic statements explaining his ideas on history, but this reader was left with the impression that a more subtle and more intensive analysis would have benefited the discussion of this ever-old, ever-new, and ever-important question.

The three essays by Bancroft which are published in this volume for the first time (with, we are told, "minor changes" by the editor) are characterized both by clarity of expression and by wide research in the sources. The essays are, so far as this reviewer knows, among the most extensive and authoritative discussions in print of their three subjects: "The Early Antislavery Movement and African Colonization," "Schemes to Colonize Negroes in Central America," and "The Ile à Vache Experiment in Colonization." These essays were completed in 1917 and were written as part of a large-scale history of the South, the plans for which Bancroft made as early as 1900; even Bancroft's best-known work, *Slave Trading in the Old South* (1931), was but a fragment of this large history on which Bancroft worked for decades but which was never completed and published. Some historians may be surprised to find that Bancroft published as many articles and book reviews as he did — Dr. Cooke has compiled a useful bibliography of the published writings of Bancroft which includes, in addition to the volumes on Seward, on Calhoun, and on slave trading which are generally known to historians, some seventeen articles and thirty-nine book reviews. Even so, one can agree with Dr. Cooke's implication that there is a striking disparity between the decades of research and the relatively few major publications of this bachelor who, from the age of thirty-seven, was financially independent and free of teaching duties, and who lived to the age of eighty-five with his mind remaining alert and vigorous until his death. Bancroft was exempt from some of the usual pressures for publication and he was also a perfectionist who was never quite satisfied with his research and with the preliminary drafts of his writings. One can sympathize with his explanation and defense of perfectionism:

Experience has taught me that there is always need of relentless self-

> criticism and that it is worth more than it costs. Unfortunately there is not much "bread and butter" in the method, and it offers no guarantee of "glory" but it will always save one from doing very poorly. The world has no means of knowing what has been merely written and what has been re-written. . . . It is no slight gain to be able to keep everything but one's best an entire secret. That's the pith of my creed" (p. 139).

Yet one can also sense the note of tragedy in the entry in Bancroft's diary in which he recorded an observation and prediction made by James Ford Rhodes in 1908, "that I knew more history and would write less, than anyone he could name" (p. 48).

University of Washington THOMAS J. PRESSLY

Book Notes

The Soldier and the State: The Theory and Politics of Civil-Military Relations. By Samuel P. Huntington. (Cambridge: The Belknap Press of Harvard University Press, 1957. xvii + 534 pp. Notes and index. $7.50.) The primary purpose of political scientist Huntington is to present a theory of civil-military relations. To achieve his purpose he ranges widely, in Part I of this work, through the history of Western civilization describing and analyzing major developments in theory and practice that have contributed to the rise of the military profession, the military mind, and civil-military relations. A good two thirds of the book, however, will be of immediate interest to American historians. This portion (Parts II and III) concentrates upon the American experience. While Mr. Huntington disclaims any attempt at "historical description of civil-military relations in the United States," inescapably a goodly amount of Part II, "Military Power in America: The Historical Experience, 1789-1940," involves this sort of scholarship. If this were the only reason for calling this volume to the attention of the guild, it would be necessary to point out that Bernardo and Bacon in their *American Military Policy* (1955) and Arthur Ekirch in his *The Civilian and the Military* (1956) have done this job in greater detail. Huntington has, however, added new material, a thoughtful analysis, and a fresh and provocative synthesis. Throughout, his concern is with the current of ideas and belief as it shaped American thought on matters of military policy. He finds that the prevailing climate of liberalism in American thought has been the chief determinant of our policy in regard to the role of the military. The Constitution, on the other hand, he points out, is the major institutional stumbling block to effective civilian control of the military. Against the background of these two constants he charts the course of the development of civil-military relations in the United States.

The last third of the book (Part III) is devoted to the deep change that has come about since World War II. Mr. Huntington confirms the general belief that a major shift in American ideas about the military has developed. In this portion of the book he explores in detail the roles of the Joint Chiefs and the departmental structure of civil-military relations. Finally, he offers a new theory of civil-military relations which he contends is more pertinent to our present needs for security and our position in world affairs.

The Bill of Rights and What It Means Today. By Edward Dumbauld. (Norman: University of Oklahoma Press, 1957. xvi + 242 pp. Illustrations, notes, bibliography, and index. $3.75.) The author, a practicing attorney and a Jefferson scholar, points out in his preface that "Amazingly little scholarly literature has been published dealing with the Bill of Rights embodied in the first ten amendments to the Constitution." Going beyond the limits of Robert A. Rutland's study of *The Birth of the Bill of Rights, 1776-1791* (1955), the author discusses not only the circumstances leading to the adoption of the Bill of Rights but also the "current judicial interpretation" of the amendments themselves. A concluding section treats of the "Value of the Bill of Rights," and the appendixes contain a variety of relevant documents. In some respects the work is comparable to the author's 1950 publication, *The Declaration of Independence and What It Means Today.* The publisher points out that the present work "is designed to fill a long-felt need as the first single convenient source for detailed study of the Bill of Rights." A special feature of the author's work is his citation and analysis of the numerous cases in which the Supreme Court has interpreted the first ten amendments.

Alexander Hamilton: Selections Representing His Life, His Thought, and His Style. Edited by Bower Aly. (New York: Liberal Arts Press, 1957. xxvi + 261 pp. Bibliography and index.) A variety of selections from Hamilton's writings, ranging in time through most of his life, make up the bulk of this volume, published as Number 20 in the *American Heritage Series.* The editor, who is also the author of *The Rhetoric of Alexander Hamilton* (1941), has chosen from available documents those which will exhibit "Hamilton's typical methods of utterance as well as the substance of his thought." Some modifications have been made by the editor in transcribing, chiefly with regard to spelling and punctuation, in accordance with his purpose to provide "an edited text rather than a transcription." One of the later chapters, entitled "Apotheosis," is comprised of brief quotations from a large number of judgments or appraisals which have been made of Hamilton.

Empire of the Columbia: A History of the Pacific Northwest. By Dorothy O. Johansen and Charles M. Gates. (New York: Harper and Brothers,

1957. xvi + 685 pp. Illustrations, maps, notes, and index. $6.00.) *Empire of the Columbia* is a textbook covering all of the Oregon Country before 1846, and all the area comprising the present states of Oregon, Washington, and Idaho after that date. It is divided into four parts of approximately equal length: Part I deals with the original inhabitants and early European explorations, and necessarily concentrates on the fur trade; Part II is concerned with migrations to the Oregon Country, diplomatic adjustment of the boundaries, and the establishment of territorial and state governments; Part III, which covers the period from 1880 to World War I, has railroads, mining, and lumber as its central themes; Part IV centers on industrialization and particularly on conservation. Nowhere, except perhaps in Part II, has politics been emphasized; the emphasis is on the economic development of the region and the exploitation of its natural resources. Taking into account the diversity of the Pacific Northwest, the authors have "attempted to recognize the individuality of each of the geographic localities or provinces that make up the Pacific Northwest, and at the same time to emphasize how each one has contributed to the development of the region as a whole." Interesting illustrations, helpful footnotes, and an attractive, readable style enhance the value of the work as a textbook.

Political Tendencies in Louisiana, 1812-1952. By Perry H. Howard. (Baton Rouge: Louisiana State University Press, 1957. xx + 231 pp. Maps, tables, notes, bibliography, and index. $3.75.) This is an analysis of Louisiana politics from the origin of the state through the 1952 gubernatorial and presidential elections. Mr. Howard seeks to explain Louisiana politics through the processes of political ecology — a study of the history and voting behavior of the people as influenced by the state's physical characteristics. He finds the key to be class conflict — a struggle largely submerged during the ante-bellum period, deflected by the Civil War and reconstruction, overt in the Populist movement, and obvious as the buoyant medium of Longism in the twentieth century.

Messages of the Governors of Tennessee. Volume IV, *1845-1857.* Edited by Robert H. White. (Nashville: Tennessee Historical Commission, 1957. x + 741 pp. Illustrations, map, notes, bibliography, appendix, and index. $4.00.) Continuing the plan established in the earlier volumes of this work, Dr. White presents not only the executive messages but also numerous other documents and commentaries which throw light on the implementation of the governors' recommendations. The intensity of party rivalry in Tennessee during the period covered is suggested in the fact that the governorship alternated between Democratic and Whig incumbents, each of whom held office for a single two-year term until Andrew Johnson broke the pattern by winning re-election in 1855. Yet so far as state matters are concerned the messages reveal remarkably little difference between the two parties, and it is interesting to find Whig and Democratic governors urging similar measures on such questions as state banking problems and state support of internal improvements and public education. In internal improvements, especially, the material reflects the shift in emphasis which occurred within the period from improvement of rivers and turnpikes to promotion of railroad construction by the state. The editorial work maintains the high standards of the earlier volumes, and the indebtedness of students of Tennessee history to the editor and to the Tennessee Historical Commission greatly increases as each new volume appears.

A Navy Surgeon in California, 1846-1847: The Journal of Marius Duvall. Edited by Fred Blackburn Rogers. (San Francisco: John Howell, 1957. xiv + 114 pp. Illustrations, appendix, notes, and index. $10.00.) Marius Duvall was an assistant surgeon in the United States Navy, assigned to duty aboard the *Portsmouth* when that ship took part in the conquest of California. His journal, written at least every week, covers the period from April, 1846, to May, 1847. The editor states: "In Dr. Duvall's journal pass in review Californians, adopted Californians, and visitors, both civilian and of the services. His mention of these varies from a mere naming to discussions of their characteristics. Examples of the latter are his descriptions of Frémont, Stockton, Sutter, General Vallejo and his family, Dr. John Marsh, Merritt, and Neal. Outstanding are the narrations of the trip of the *Portsmouth's* launch to Frémont with supplies, of Sutter's establishment . . . and of the 'battle' of Santa Clara." According to the editor, Duvall's observations "agree substantially" with those made by Joseph T. Downey, whose comments were published in *Filings from an Old Saw* (1956), the first of the John Howell series on the United States Navy in old California. The present work is the second in the series.

The Coming of the Civil War. Second edition revised. By Avery Craven. (Chicago: University of Chicago Press, 1957. xii + 491 pp. Notes and index. $5.00.) When this work was first published in 1942 (New York: Charles Scribner's Sons) the reviews ranged from fulsome praise to biting criticism; and in the controversy which was stirred up by the critics its importance as an effort to present a more balanced view of the sectional conflict of the 1850's was all but overlooked. In answer to some of his critics Mr. Craven emphatically declares in his preface to the new edition that he had "no intention of saying categorically that the war was a 'needless war' . . . [and] no desire to defend slavery." He believes that "the writing of Civil War history has changed profoundly since the book appeared, and most scholars have accepted the general point of view that it suggests." The revisions consist largely of a rephrasing of some of the language for purposes of clarification, and the correcting of typographical errors. The general emphasis of the earlier edition has not been changed.

X. Beidler, Vigilante. Edited by Helen Fitzgerald Sanders in collaboration with William H. Bertsche, Jr. (Norman: University of Oklahoma Press, 1957. xviii + 165 pp. Illustrations, notes, appendixes. $2.00.) John Xavier Beidler, known as X. Beidler, was a frontier scout, prospector, and deputy United States marshal whose career centered in Montana in the 1860's. His yen for justice led him to found (with Wilbur F. Sanders) a Montana Vigilante Committee and made him a famous frontier character. Beidler's exploits are told in this book by means of his reminiscences, newspaper clippings, and miscellaneous accounts of certain incidents by others. The introduction and foreword provide only a bare outline of Beidler's life.

Marks of Lincoln on Our Land. By Maurine Whorton Redway and Dorothy Kendall Bracken. (New York: Hastings House, 1957. 121 pp. Illustrations and bibliography. $3.75.) The numerous Lincoln statues and memorials are the principal subjects of this book. In addition to describing and sketching the history of the memorials, the authors use them as a unifying thread to construct a brief biography of Lincoln. The three purposes of the book are: "to serve as a guide book . . . to relate in its essential outline the story of Lincoln's life . . . and finally, to stimulate its readers to travel in person the historic trail of the Lincoln monuments." It is a better-than-average book of its kind.

The Dark Missouri. By Henry C. Hart. (Madison: University of Wisconsin Press, 1957. xviii + 260 pp. Maps, tables, illustrations, notes, and index. $6.00.) Utilizing the knowledge of the Missouri River basin accumulated by geologists, climatologists, hydrologists, agriculturalists, and historians, Mr. Hart ably describes the problem of water development in the Missouri Valley. His treatment is largely historical — he describes chronologically the settlement and growth of population in the Valley and the numerous plans for controlling and utilizing the waters of the Missouri — yet the emphasis is on the present status and future possibilities of water control in the region. It is Mr. Hart's thesis, expounded in the chapter called "Their Own Minds," that despite a deeply ingrained love of autonomy the people of the Missouri Valley have failed to look upon themselves as comprising a region. He pleads for "a sense of community in the basin," and for a new, comprehensive basin program to resolve the problem of the conflicting interests of irrigation, navigation, flood control, municipal water supply, and water power, which has hampered Missouri Valley development in the past.

Pioneers for One Hundred Years: San Jose State College, 1857-1957. By Benjamin Franklin Gilbert. (San Jose: San Jose State College, 1957. xii + 243 pp. Illustrations, bibliographical essay, appendix, and index. $3.25.) Based on ample local records and interviews with past and present college officials, *Pioneers for One Hundred Years* is essentially a factual narrative of the academic and material expansion of San Jose State College from its beginnings as a normal school to the present multipurpose state college. Brief biographical sketches of important administrators and faculty members and numerous photographs of college officials and student activities are included. In the forty-page appendix Professor Gilbert "presents a brief history of the eleven divisions and thirty departments of the college, the ROTC units, and the library."

California Social Welfare: Legislation, Financing, Services, Statistics. By Vaughn Davis Bornet. (Englewood Cliffs, New Jersey: Prentice-Hall, 1956. xxiv + 520 pp. Tables, notes, note on sources, and index. $5.00.) The publishers expect this monograph to "appeal to volunteer workers for agencies, trained social workers, those who contribute funds to soliciting groups, taxpayers, and all concerned with people in need." It is an attempt to describe the contemporary status of social welfare organizations, both governmental and voluntary, in California. Separate sections describe laws governing welfare organizations, fund raising and expenses, and services provided to those in need of financial or institutional assistance, such as the unemployed, the blind, the aged, and victims of crippling diseases. One hundred and ten tables supply statistics concerning all phases of welfare activity in California. Although the aim of the book is to describe organized social welfare in the entire state, the study centers on four counties in the San Francisco Bay area — San Francisco, Alameda, San Joaquin, and Sonoma. The author does not attempt to draw sweeping conclusions; his purpose and that of the sponsoring institution, the Commonwealth Club of California, was to make the study "entirely objective and factual."

Southern Race Progress: The Wavering Color Line. By Thomas J. Woofter. (Washington: Public Affairs Press, 1957. xii + 180 pp. Index. $3.50.) "I review," the author states in the preface, "my fifty years of close contact with and observation of issues and movements in race relations and write about the people and events which, in retrospect, impress me as having been significant in shaping the present and likely to influence the future." In addition to these personal observations Dr. Woofter, a sociologist born in Macon, Georgia, presents conclusions drawn from his research on cotton plantation sharecropping and Negro migrations from farm to city and from South to North. Dr. Woofter attributes the gradual rise in status of the southern Negro to "the quiet unspectacular cooperation of men of good will," and he believes that such co-operation is increasing.

Enterprise in Oil: A History of Shell in the United States. By Kendall Beaton. (New York: Appleton-Century-Crofts, 1957. xvi + 815 pp. Illustrations, maps, drawings, notes, appendixes, and index. $7.50.) The early pages of this comprehensive history of Shell Oil Company in the United States trace the formation and growth of the Royal Dutch-Shell interests in other parts of the world, but the main bulk of the work is confined to the development of Shell interests in the United States. This development began in 1912 when Shell gained "a toehold in a new country through a small marketing organization in the Pacific Northwest and a small oil-producing company in Oklahoma." A relatively obscure company until the 1920's, Shell expanded in that decade "into an organization blanketing the 48 states," and after a curtailment of operations during the depression, expanded after World War II to reach a position "in the first rank, not only of American oil companies, but of American industry." The author of this history is "a member of the company's staff, has had full access to all company records and has been assisted by company personnel." He points out, however, that the "book is 'official' only in that the company willingly sat for its portrait and paid the painter's fee; it does not necessarily endorse the result." A number of professional historians, who have worked in the field of oil history, have afforded the author editorial and critical assistance. The "Citations of Sources" indicate extensive research conducted not only in documentary sources but also by way of personal interview, and the history of Shell which emerges is a detailed and intimate one. Organizational and statistical information of interest to a limited number of readers has been confined to appendixes. The illustrations are numerous and enhance the reader's understanding of the company and of the times.

Public Addresses, Letters, and Papers of William Kerr Scott, Governor of North Carolina, 1949-1953. Edited by David Leroy Corbitt. (Raleigh: North Carolina Council of State and the Department of Archives and History, 1957. xxxiv + 626 pp. Illustrations, notes, and index.) Governor Scott's numerous public addresses make up approximately half of this volume. Proclamations, statements and articles for the press, letters and telegrams, and a list of Scott's appointments make up the rest. Partly because Scott did not always fully write out his addresses, the editor has deemed it necessary "to change the capitalization, punctuation, phraseology, and sentence arrangement" in some cases. Robert W. Redwine, "an active supporter of Governor Scott," is the author of the brief, laudatory biographical sketch which precedes Scott's papers. The volume may be obtained without cost upon application to the North Carolina Department of Archives and History.

The Signal Corps: The Test (December 1941 to July 1943). By George Rayner Thompson, Dixie R. Harris, Pauline M. Oakes, and Dulany Terrett. *United States Army in World War II: The Technical Services.* (Washington: Office of the Chief of Military History, 1957. xvi + 621 pp. Illustrations, notes, bibliographical note, and index. $4.50.) Beginning with the attack on Pearl Harbor, this volume, the second in the series on the Signal Corps, covers a time span of only eighteen months. The period is largely one of confusion and frustration caused by the rapid expansion of the Corps together with the inevitable shortages of men, training facilities, and equipment. The emphasis falls on administrative organization and technical communications developments rather than on field operations, though the latter is not neglected. According to the authors, the Signal Corps in mid-1943 "was fulfilling its mission relatively well" and Major General Dawson Olmstead, Chief Signal Officer, was performing well in a very difficult assignment. Yet there was much dissatisfaction with the Corps in higher Army circles, resulting in the firing of General Olmstead in June, 1943, and the beginning of a new phase in the history of the Corps in World War II. One more volume in the series on the Signal Corps remains to be written.

The Transportation Corps: Operations Overseas. By Joseph Bykofsky and Harold Larson. *United States Army in World War II: The Technical Services.* (Washington: Office of the Chief of Military History, 1957. xviii + 671 pp. Maps, illustrations, notes, bibliographical note, guide to footnotes, glossary, and index. $6.50.) With the publication of *The Transportation Corps: Operations Overseas*, the United States Army series on the Transportation Corps is complete. The previous two volumes dealt with administrative and organization problems and with moving troops and equipment within and from the United States. "The present work deals primarily with the Army transportation organizations in the several overseas commands, the operations for which they were responsible, their relation to transportation matters that were not directly their responsibility, and their position in the theater structure." Well-known transportation operations on the Burma Road, in the Persian Corridor, and in the invasion of Normandy are adequately described. But the authors show that lesser known and less glamorous activities of the Corps, such as making maximum use of damaged and inadequate overseas ports, contributed equally to the war effort.

Historical News and Comments

Personals

John D. Hicks has retired from active duty at the University of California, Berkeley, effective July 1, and will spend the next year in travel in Europe. His successor as the May Treat Morrison professor of history at California is Kenneth M. Stampp.

Richard M. Brace has been promoted to professor of history at Northwestern University. Leaves of absence have been granted to Leften S. Stavrianos and Roger F. Hackett for the year 1957-1958, and to Franklin D. Scott for the fall quarter. John T. Meskill and Alfred J. Rieber have been appointed visiting lecturers in history for the year.

Richard B. Schlatter has been chosen chairman of the history department at Rutgers University, succeeding L. Ethan Ellis. Richard P. McCormick and James R. W. Leiby will be on partial leaves of absence for research during the year. George F. Frick has joined the department as an instructor.

Walter S. Sanderlin has been promoted to professor of history at Washington and Jefferson College, and John A. Carpenter has been appointed assistant professor of history.

Glover G. Hatheway, a doctoral graduate of the University of Minnesota, has been appointed assistant professor of history at Purdue University.

At the University of Oregon, Earl Pomeroy has been appointed chairman of the department of history for a three-year term, succeeding Gordon Wright, who has accepted an appointment as professor of history at Stanford University. Edwin R. Bingham has been promoted to associate professor and John E. Selby to assistant professor. Val R. Lorwin of the University of Chicago has been appointed professor of history and has been granted a leave of absence for 1957-1958 to do research in Belgium as a Social Science Research Council Fellow. William O. Shanahan of Notre Dame University will serve as acting professor of history and Paul A. Varg of Ohio State University as acting associate professor at Oregon in 1957-1958. Stanley A. Pierson of Wesleyan University has been appointed assistant professor, and William M. Bowsky of Princeton has been named instructor.

David H. Pinkney has been promoted to professor of history at the University of Missouri, and James N. Primm and Lewis W. Spitz to associate professors. Gilman M. Ostrander of Ohio State University has been appointed assistant professor and Stephen B. Baxter of Dartmouth College has been named visiting assistant professor for 1957-1958. Charles F. Mullett will be on leave of absence to serve as visiting professor at Columbia University in 1957-1958.

Charles P. Roland has been promoted to associate professor at Tulane University, and Hugh F. Rankin, formerly with Colonial Williamsburg, has been appointed instructor in history. In the Newcomb College for Women of Tulane, Francis G. James has been promoted to professor of history and Raymond A. Esthus of the University of Houston has been appointed assistant professor.

Dudley T. Cornish has been promoted to professor of history at Kansas State Teachers College, Pittsburg.

Larry Gara of Eureka College has been appointed professor of history at Grove City College, Pennsylvania.

Samuel Davis has been appointed assistant professor of history at Kansas State College for the year 1957-1958 in place of William F. Zornow, who will be on leave of absence for the year.

Henry B. Webb has been promoted to professor of history at San Antonio College.

Harold Seymour of the University of Buffalo has been appointed professor of history at Finch College in New York City.

At Wake Forest College the department of social science has been reorganized into a department of history and a department of political science. Henry S. Stroupe has been named chairman of the department of history and Percival Perry has been promoted to the rank of professor in the department. Associate Professors Forrest W. Clontz and Wilfred B. Yearns, Assistant Professors David L. Smiley and Lowell R. Tillett, and Instructor John K. Huckaby of the former social science department have been transferred to the new history department. Robert G. Gregory, a doctoral graduate of the University of California, Los Angeles, and Frank B. Josserand, a doctoral graduate of the University of Texas, have been added to the department as assistant professors, and Thomas E. Mullen, a doctoral candidate at Emory University, has been appointed instructor in history.

Robert W. Shoemaker has been promoted to assistant professor of history at Rensselaer Polytechnic Institute, and Assistant Professor William H. Pease will be on leave of absence for 1957-1958 to teach at Case Institute of Technology.

Delber L. McKee has been promoted to professor of history and Arthur L. Jensen to associate professor at Westminster College (Pennsylvania).

Arthur L. Throckmorton has been appointed chairman of the department of history at Lewis and Clark College, and Richard C. Dales has been promoted to assistant professor.

Lawrence L. Graves has been promoted to associate professor of history at Texas Technological College, and Lowell L. Blaisdell, who was on a temporary appointment at the University of Oklahoma in 1956-1957, has been appointed assistant professor. Associate Professor David M. Vigness has received a Fulbright appointment to teach at the University of Santiago, Chile, during 1957-1958.

Allan J. McCurry has been promoted to associate professor and Robert F. Erickson to assistant professor in the department of history and political science at Butler University.

William E. Smith has retired from the chairmanship of the department of history at Miami University (Ohio) to devote full time to his duties as dean of the Graduate School. Harris G. Warren of the University of Mississippi has accepted an appointment as professor of history and chairman of the department at Miami.

At the University of Chicago, Richard J. Storr has been promoted to associate professor of history and Eric W. Cochrane, a doctoral graduate of Yale University, has been added to the staff as instructor. Daniel J. Boorstin was on leave during the spring and summer terms to lecture at the University of Kyoto. Walter Johnson will be on leave for 1957-1958 to serve as Harmsworth Professor at Oxford University, and Louis Gottschalk has been given a year's leave of absence for work in the Institute of Behavioral Sciences at Stanford University.

Ralph W. Hidy of New York University has been appointed to the Isidor Straus professorship of business history at Harvard University.

Godfrey Davies, chairman of the research staff of the Henry E. Huntington Library, died on May 28, 1957, at the age of sixty-five. A native of England, he was educated at Oxford University and until 1924 was engaged in teaching at Oxford. He came to the United States in 1925 and for the next five years was a member of the history department of the University of Chicago. He joined the research staff of the Huntington Library in 1930 and became its chairman in 1949. From 1937 to 1948 he was the editor of the *Huntington Library Quarterly*, and he also lectured for some years at the University of California, Los Angeles, and at the California Institute of Technology. Through his published works he came to be recognized as a leading authority in seventeenth-century English history, and through his innumerable services to British and American students who have worked in the Huntington Library during the past quarter of a century he made a lasting contribution not only to his own but also to many other fields of historical scholarship.

Historical Activities

The papers of George Fort Milton, editor, historian, and federal official, have been presented to the Library of Congress by Mrs. Milton. Numbering about 15,000 items in the period 1927-1945, the bulk of the material is concentrated in the 1930's. The papers include correspondence, lectures, and manuscripts of Milton's books, and they reflect to a remarkable degree a concept of the interrelation of history and current affairs. Many of the letters concern his research in the writing of his books on the Civil War period. When the papers have been organized they will be available for research in the Manuscript Division.

The Library has recently received from the New York office of Pinkerton's National Detective Agency seven manuscript volumes of the letters and papers of Allan Pinkerton, the founder of the agency. These consist of letters written from the New York office from 1869 to 1873, letter books of Pinkerton himself for the years 1872 to 1883, and a journal of interviews, telegrams, and assignments of operatives kept between October, 1865, and November, 1866. They are available for consultation in the Manuscript Division, but the use of their contents is subject to specific restrictions which may be waived only by the Pinkerton Agency.

Other important collections recently received by the Library include: small additions to the papers of Robert Lansing, to those of Bainbridge Colby, and to those of Cordell Hull; several pieces of correspondence of Joseph Holt, written in the 1870's, concerning the trial and execution of Mrs. Mary Surratt; a collection of letters written by Edwin O. Wentworth as a soldier in a Massachusetts volunteer regiment during the Civil War; and a manuscript journal entitled "An Army Wife's Forty Years in the Service, 1862-1902," written by Elizabeth Reynolds (Mrs. Andrew S.) Burt, which records her experiences at most of the forts established in the West during the period of westward expansion.

Additions to the Naval Historical Foundation collections deposited in the Library of Congress include the journal of Midshipman William T. Rodgers for the years 1813-1818, which describes his services on board the U. S. sloop-of-war *Peacock*, the U. S. brig *Boxer*, and the merchant brig *Wilson* in the Atlantic trade.

The Bancroft Library of the University of California has recently received as a gift the papers of Count Revilla-Gigedo, viceroy of Mexico, 1789-1794, and one of the ablest of the Spanish viceroys who served in America. The collection, which includes his correspondence with the government in Spain, contains thirty-seven folio volumes of about 18,000 pages, of which twelve volumes are monographs prepared as reports by explorers and scientists in government employ, and twenty-five are the Viceroy's hitherto unedited and unpublished correspondence with the Spanish ministries (about 5,000 letters). Notable among the monographs is the unpublished diary of the leader of the Nootka Expedition of 1792, including drawings and maps long believed to have been lost. Among the letters are more than two hundred about the Nootka explorations and almost as many on the California missions and presidios and on Spanish activities in New Mexico, Texas, and Louisiana.

The congressional letters and papers of Arthur Capper, governor of Kansas from 1915 to 1919 and United States senator from 1919 to 1949, have been placed on deposit with the Kansas State Historical Society in Topeka. Because of Senator Capper's interest in agricultural legislation this collection provides a valuable source for students of political and agricultural history. Although the papers have not yet been catalogued they are open for research.

The Southwest Collection, Texas Technological College, has recently received the home office records of the Matador Land and Cattle Company, Ltd., from Dundee, Scotland. Added to the archival material from the American offices of the company, this acquisition brings to approximately 400,000 the number of manuscript pieces bearing on the career of the Scottish syndicate now in the possession of the Collection.

The Institute of Early American History and Culture sponsored a Symposium on Seventeenth-Century Colonial History, April 8-12, as part of its participation in the 350th Anniversary Celebration at Jamestown. Discussions centered on "The Indian in Seventeenth Century America," based on papers by Wilcomb E. Washburn of the Institute and Nancy O. Lurie of the University of Michigan; "People and Classes," based on papers by Mildred Campbell of Vassar College and Bernard Bailyn of Harvard;

"Church and State," based on papers by Philip N. Haffenden of the University of Toronto, William H. Seiler of Kansas State Teachers College (Emporia), and Emil Oberholzer, Jr., of the College of the City of New York; and "History in the Seventeenth Century," based on a paper by Richard S. Dunn of the University of Michigan. A final evening lecture, "The Place of the Seventeenth Century in the History of the United States," was presented by Oscar Handlin of Harvard University. In addition to those giving papers, the following visiting scholars participated in the symposium: Wesley Frank Craven, Princeton University; Frederick B. Tolles, Swarthmore College; Raymond P. Stearns, University of Illinois; Edmund S. Morgan, Yale University; John E. Pomfret, Henry E. Huntington Library; Alan Simpson, University of Chicago; and Max Savelle, University of Washington.

The Permanent Committee for the Oliver Wendell Holmes Devise to write the history of the Supreme Court that was authorized by an act of Congress in 1955 has outlined plans for a chronological approach to the Court's history with a volume to be prepared on each of seven broad periods. According to a preliminary announcement, "The work as a whole is expected to portray the Court as a living institution, to trace the vital growth and development of the Court, and to show and interpret the interactions between it and its cultural environment over more than a century and a half. Every element in the work will be tested against primary source materials, and the history will be, in effect, an entirely original treatment of the subject."

The authors of six of the proposed volumes have been chosen as follows: Antecedents and Beginnings, 1787-1801, Julius Goebel, Jr., professor of law at Columbia University; The Taney Period, 1836-1864, Carl B. Swisher, professor of political science at Johns Hopkins University; Reconstruction and Reunion, 1864-1888, Charles Fairman, professor of law at Harvard University; National Expansion and Economic Growth, 1888-1910; Phil C. Neal, professor of law at Stanford University; Responsible Government and the Judiciary, 1910-1930, Alexander M. Bickel, associate professor in the Yale Law School; and Depression, New Deal, and the Court in Crisis, 1930-1941, Paul A. Freund, professor in the Harvard Law School, who will also serve as editor in chief of the history. An author has not yet been named for the volume on the Marshall period, 1801-1835.

The Devise Fund established by Congress for this project consists of Justice Holmes's original bequest of the residue of his estate to the United States Government in 1935 together with a 1955 appropriation in lieu of interest on the original gift. It is administered by a Permanent Committee, which is authorized to spend the income from the Fund and as much of the principal as necessary to have the history prepared and published under its general supervision. Members of the Permanent Committee are the Librarian of Congress, who is designated by law to be the chairman; Charles T. McCormick, representing the Association of American Law Schools; Edward S. Corwin, representing the American Philosophical Society; George L. Haskins, representing the American Historical Association; and Virgil M. Hancher, representing the Association of American Universities. The last four were appointed by the President of the United States.

The Spring meeting of the Upper Midwest History Conference was held at the Minnesota Historical Society Building in St. Paul on April 27, with one hundred members in attendance. At the dinner session, presided over by Walker D. Wyman of Wisconsin State College, River Falls, President James P. Shannon of the College of St. Thomas presented a paper on "Catholic Colonization on the Western Frontier."

The Texas State Historical Association held its sixty-first annual meeting in Austin on April 26 and 27 with a program which included three sessions of three papers each, two luncheon meetings, and the annual dinner, in addition to two sessions of the Junior Historians. Ralph W. Steen of the Texas Agricultural and Mechanical College was elected president for the ensuing year.

The annual meeting of the Council of the Institute of Early American History and Culture was held in Williamsburg on May 3 and 4, 1957. Members newly elected to the Council are Richard B. Morris of Columbia University, Alan Simpson of the University of Chicago, Max Savelle of the University of Washington, Lyman H. Butterfield, editor of the Adams Papers, and Edmund S. Morgan of Yale University. Walter M. Whitehill of the Boston Athenaeum was re-elected chairman of the Council and of the Executive Committee. The newly elected vice-chairman of the Council is Richard H. Shryock of the Institute of the History of Medicine at Johns Hopkins University; John R. Alden of Duke University was re-elected secretary of the Council.

Lester J. Cappon, director of the Institute, announced that the Lilly Endowment of Indianapolis has awarded $60,000 to the Institute to promote the expansion of its book publication program. An annual grant of $20,000 for the next three years will assist the Institute in subsidizing scholarly publications of high caliber without financial obligation by the authors.

The University of Chicago and the University of Virginia are sponsoring the publication of a new and complete edition of the papers of James Madison. The editors will appreciate information about the location of letters by or to James Madison or his wife, especially letters in private possession or among uncalendared manuscripts in the collections of public or private institutions. Please address: The Papers of James Madison, 1126 East 59th Street, Chicago 37, Illinois.

Grants and Awards

The New England Quarterly and Houghton Mifflin Company have established the *New England Quarterly* Literary Fellowship Award in American Studies. The award will be given annually for work in progress, and is designed to encourage the writing of books of general interest in the fields of American history, literature, and the social sciences. The award, which will amount to $2,400, is intended primarily for writers who need financial aid, though it is not completely limited by that intention. Further information and application blanks may be obtained from The Editor, Houghton Mifflin Company, 2 Park Street, Boston 7, Massachusetts.

The annual Book Prize of the Institute of Early American History and Culture for 1956 has been awarded to I. Bernard Cohen of Harvard University for his *Franklin and Newton: An Inquiry into Speculative Newtonian Experimental Science and Franklin's Work in Electricity as an Example Thereof*, published by the Philosophical Society as Volume 43 of its *Memoirs.*

In 1958 the Institute will replace the annual Book Prize with a newly-established Institute Manuscript Award to be given annually for the best unpublished work in early American history. The amount of the award will be $500 and assurance of publication of the award-winning manuscript. A committee chosen from the Council of the Institute will judge the entries in association with James M. Smith, Editor of Publications. To be eligible for the 1958 Award, manuscripts must be sent before December 31, 1957, to the Editor of Publications, Box 1298, Williamsburg, Virginia.

Walter N. Trenerry has received the Solon J. Buck Award of the Minnesota Historical Society for 1956, for an article on "The Minnesota Rebellion Act of 1862: A Legal Dilemma of the Civil War," published in the September, 1956, issue of *Minnesota History*. The Award, which carries with it a prize of fifty dollars, is given each year to the author of the best article appearing in the Society's quarterly.

The Society of American Historians has announced that the second annual Francis Parkman Prize will be awarded during the winter of 1958 for a book published in 1957. This award of $500 has been established by the Society "to stimulate the writing of history as literature, thus emphasizing literary distinction in historical writing." The prize is to be awarded in the field of American history or biography, and the books submitted for consideration may deal with any aspect of the colonial or national history of what is now the United States. Colonial history would admit of a treatment of the English, French, or Spanish background if definitely connected with the colonies. Literary, religious, economic, political, scientific and technological, legal and constitutional history, and the history of foreign relations would fall within the field. For further information address: Dr. Rudolf A. Clemen, Executive Vice-President, The Society of American Historians, Princeton University Library, Princeton, New Jersey.

The first annual award, for books published in 1956, has been made to George F. Kennan for his book, *Russia Leaves the War*, published by the Princeton University Press. Citations of honorable mention were also given to Alpheus T. Mason, for his *Harlan Fiske Stone: Pillar of the Law*, and David L. Cohn, for *The Life and Times of King Cotton.*

The Social Science Research Council has announced the award of faculty research fellowships to six applicants, including the following two in history: Bradford Perkins of the University of California, Los Angeles, for research on certain aspects of Anglo-American relations, 1805-1825; and Marc Raeff of Clark University, for research on the professional intelligentsia in Russia and in Western Europe.

Research training fellowships have been awarded to the following persons in the field of history: Robert F. Berkhofer, Jr., Ph.D. candidate at Cornell University, for training and research on the history of the Seneca Indians; William W. Dusinberre, Ph.D. candidate at Columbia University, for research on the southern question in Philadelphia politics, 1856-1870; Jack D. Forbes, Ph.D. candidate at the University of Southern California, for research in Spain on Apache-Spanish relations on the frontier of New Spain; Thomas Naff, Ph.D. candidate at the University of California, Berkeley, for training at the London School of Oriental Studies and for research on Ottoman-British relations in the sixteenth century; and Henry A. Turner, Jr., Ph.D. candidate at Princeton University, for research in Europe on the German People's party, 1918-1930.

Grants-in-aid for research projects in American history have been awarded to Thomas B. Alexander, Georgia Teachers College, for research in the northeastern United States on the American Whigs, 1860-1900; Joseph J. Mathews, Emory University, for research on the career of George W. Smalley; Edward H. Phillips, Rice Institute, for research on Timothy Pickering and the Federalist party; George W. Smith, University of New Mexico, for research on the northern states during the Civil War; and David S. Sparks, University of Maryland, for research on General Henry W. Halleck and military command in a democracy. Similar grants for research in other fields of history were also made to the following: William A.

Bultmann, Arkansas State Teachers College; John C. Cairns, University of Toronto; Charles Jelavich, University of California, Berkeley; William F. Kahl, Simmons College; Henry C. Meyer, Pomona College; Ramon E. Ruiz, University of Oregon; Richard B. Schlatter, Rutgers University; Marion C. Siney, Western Reserve University; and Dorothy A. Williams, Principia College.

Faculty research grants were awarded to Lewis E. Atherton, University of Missouri, for research on the role of the businessman on the American frontier; Joel Colton, Duke University, for research on Leon Blum and French socialism since 1919; George A. Lensen, Florida State University, for research on Russo-Japanese relations before 1875; James B. Parsons, University of California, Riverside, for research on the governing bureaucracy of China in the Ming Dynasty; Thomas C. Smith, Stanford University, for research in Japan on its agrarian background; Bernard D. Weinryb, Dropsie College, for research on the economic and social history of Jews in Eastern Europe; Bertie Wilkinson, University of Toronto, for research in England on fifteenth-century English history.

Grants for research on the history of American military policy have been made to Richard H. Fraser, Ph.D. candidate at the University of Oklahoma, for research on the foundations of American military policy, 1783-1815; Harold M. Hyman, Arizona State College, for research on the policies and functions of the Army provost marshal and resulting problems in civil-military relations, 1774-1920; Thomas LeDuc, Oberlin College, for research on the use of federal armed forces in support of civil power, 1789-1939; Louis Morton, deputy chief historian, Department of the Army, for research on naval war plans, 1919-1938 (renewal); and Raymond G. O'Connor, Stanford University, for research on the role of the Navy General Board in American naval policy, 1900-1922.

Recent Articles of General Interest

Agricultural History — April, 1957: "William Ewing, Agricultural Agent to the Indians," by Donald Jackson; "Letters of Philander H. Standish (1835-1918)," ed. by C. Clyde Jones; "Fig History in the New World," by Ira J. Condit; "English Agricultural Methods and the American Institute, 1871-1872," by Thomas L. Bushell; "The Development of Short Courses at the Land Grant Institutions," by Vernon C. Larson.

American-German Review — April-May, 1957: "German Craftsmen in Jamestown," by Klaus G. Wust.

American Historical Review — April, 1957: "Jackson Men with Feet of Clay," by Charles Grier Sellers, Jr.

American Jewish Archives — April, 1957: "The Kidnapped and the Ransomed (How the Friedman Brothers Liberated an Alabama Slave)," by Kate E. R. Pickard.

American Political Science Review — June, 1957: "The Morris Committee Assignment Controversy: A Study in Senate Norms," by Ralph K. Huitt; "The Coming of Age of America," by Louis Hartz.

Catholic Historical Review — April, 1957: "Hawthorne and Confession," by Henry G. Fairbanks.

Historian — May, 1957: "Early American Relations with Formosa, 1849-1870," by Leonard Gordon.

Huntington Library Quarterly — February, 1957: "Mark Twain's Social Darwinism," by Sherwood Cummings.

Journal of Negro History — April, 1957: "The New Negro History," by John Hope Franklin; "The Protestant Churches and Lynching, 1919-1939," by Robert Moats Miller.

Journal of Politics — May, 1957: "Dred Scott One Hundred Years After," by Carl Brent Swisher.

Journal of Southern History — May, 1957: "The Gosport Affair, 1861," by John Sherman Long; "The First-Class Hotel and the Age of the Common Man," by Doris Elizabeth King.

Journal of the History of Ideas — April, 1957: "History as Art: The Psychological-Romantic View," by Floyd W. Matson.

Journal of the Presbyterian Historical Society — June, 1957: "The Irish Background of Francis Makemie," by Clifford M. Drury.

Maryland Historical Magazine — June, 1957: "Documents Relating to the Colonial Tobacco Trade," ed. by John M. Hemphill, II.

Mennonite Quarterly Review — April, 1957: "The Mennonite Book and Tract Society, 1892-1908," by John A. Hostetler.

Mid-America — April, 1957: "American Liberalism: Its Meaning and Consistency," by John J. Whealen.

Military Affairs — Spring, 1957: "Robert Matteson Johnston and the Study of Military History," by Alexander Baltzly; "The Problem of Writing about the Guerrillas," by Virgil C. Jones; "Hampton's Cattle Raid, September 14-17, 1864," by Richard Lykes.

Museum Echoes — April, 1957: "Charles Farrar Browne ('Artemus Ward')," by Walter Rumsey Marvin.

May, 1957: "David Ross Locke ('Petroleum V. Nasby')," by Watt P. Marchman.

June, 1957: "Mary Hartwell Catherwood," by Robert Price.

Pacific Historical Review — May, 1957: "Bryan, McKinley, and the Treaty of Paris," by Paolo E. Coletta; "As the Russians Saw Our China Policy," by John Albert White; "A Philosophical Appraisal of the Christian Interpretation of History," by Theodore M. Greene; "MacArthur's Blockade Proposals against Red China," by John Norman.

Political Science Quarterly — June, 1957: "The Revolution in the Presidential Nominating Convention," by William G. Carleton.

Social Studies — April, 1957: "The Attitudes of the Major Protestant Churches in America toward War and Peace, 1929-1939," by Robert Moats Miller.

Tennessee Historical Quarterly — June, 1957: "The Chickasaw, the English, and the French, 1699-1744," by Dawson A. Phelps; "Letters from a Canadian Recruit in the Union Army," ed. by Doris Fleming.

William and Mary Quarterly — April, 1957: "The French Farmers-General in the Chesapeake: The MacKercher-Huber Mission of 1737-1738," by Jacob M. Price; "The American Dream: John Tabor Kempe's Rise from Poverty to Riches," by Catherine Snell Crary; "Jefferson, the Napoleonic Wars, and the Balance of Power," by Lawrence S. Kaplan.

Wisconsin Magazine of History — Summer, 1957: "On the Nature of Local History," by James C. Malin.

Yale Review — Summer, 1957: "The Legacy of John Adams," by Clinton Rossiter.

Recent Articles Concerning the East

American Jewish Archives — April, 1957: "Jewish Immigrant Life in Philadelphia: From *The Sunday Mercury*, August 10, 1890," by Louis Edward Levy.

Connecticut Historical Society Bulletin — April, 1957: "Some Afterthoughts on the Moulthrop Exhibition," by Samuel M. Green, II; "Aaron Roberts: His Life and Times," by Houghton Bulkeley.

Maryland Historical Magazine — June, 1957: "Kent Island: Part I, The Period of Settlement," by Erich Isaac; "Henri Herz' Description of Baltimore," ed. by Henry Bertram Hill and Larry Gara; "Reminiscences of Judge Richard Henry Alvey," by Alexander Armstrong; "The Post Office Department in St. Mary's County in the War of 1812," by Arthur Hecht.

New England Quarterly — June, 1957: "The Reverend Thomas Allen: Jeffersonian Calvinist," by Richard D. Birdsall; "Labor Conditions at the Old York, 1831-1900," by Roy P. Fairfield; "Thomas Hutchinson and the Province Currency," by Malcolm Freiberg.

New England Social Studies Bulletin — May, 1957: "Enter Pitt Fessenden," by Charles A. Jellison.

New-York Historical Society Quarterly — April, 1957: "The Recollections of John Ferguson Weir (1841-1926): Painter and Teacher," ed. by Theodore Sizer.

Pennsylvania History — April, 1957: "The Religion of Joseph Priestley," by Ira V. Brown; "James Logan: Patron and Natural Philosopher," by E. Gordon Alderfer; "The Small Arms Industry of Lancaster County, 1710-1840," by Carlton O. Wittlinger; "Employment of Paupers at Philadelphia's Almshouse before 1861," by Benjamin Joseph Klebaner.

Pennsylvania Magazine of History and Biography — April, 1957: "The Culture of Early Pennsylvania," by Frederick B. Tolles; "William Penn, Classical Republican," by Mary Maples; "John Redman, Medical Preceptor, 1722-1808," by Whitfield J. Bell, Jr.; "Governor William Denny in Pennsylvania," by Nicholas B. Wainwright.

Susquehanna University Studies — May, 1957: "The Economic Impact of Pennsylvania upon the Nation," by William A. Russ, Jr.

Western Pennsylvania Historical Magazine — Spring, 1957: "Forerunners in American Glass: The New Gorley Case," by Lowell Innes; "The Rise of Philanthropic Agencies in Pennsylvania in 1861," by Edward G. Everett; "Descent of the Allegheny, 1818," by J. Bennett Nolan; "Painting in Pittsburgh from the Frontier Settlement to the Industrial Development," by Walter Read Hovey; "Buchanan and Western Pennsylvania in 1856," by Robert E. Carlson.

Recent Articles Concerning the South

Agricultural History — April, 1957: "The Pendleton [S. C.] Farmer's Society," by Clyde E. Woodall and George H. Aull.

Arkansas Historical Quarterly — Summer, 1957: "Arkansas Post — Its Human Aspects," by Ray H. Mattison; "An Arkansas Fugitive Slave Incident and its International Repercussions," by Roman J. Zorn; "The Third Arkansas Regiment from Formation to Fredericksburg," by Orval E. Allbritton; "Three Letters of Cephas Washburn," ed. by Margaret Smith Ross; "The Governor of Georgia Urges the Secession of Arkansas," ed. by Willard E. Wight; "Major Josiah H. Demby's History of Catterson's Militia," ed. by Ted R. Worley.

Catholic Historical Review — April, 1957: "Some Wartime Letters of Bishop Lynch," ed. by Willard E. Wight.

Filson Club History Quarterly — April, 1957: "John Breckinridge's Bluegrass Plantation Agreement to Operate, 1806," ed. by Lowell H. Harrison; "Fontaine Fox as I Have Known Him," by W. Wayne Wilson; "Cassius M. Clay, 'Lion' of White Hall: Some Unpublished Letters of and About," Part II, ed. by Cassius M. Clay; "General John Hunt Morgan: The Great Indiana-Ohio Raid," by James Bell Benedict, Jr.

Florida Historical Quarterly — April, 1957: "Florida's Overseas Railroad," by David L. Willing; "Early Newspapers of Ocala," by Eloise Robinson Ott; "The Early Sugar Industry in Florida," by Wilbur Siebert; "A Guide to Spanish Florida Source Material," by Charles Arnade; "Indian Presents: To Give or Not to Give. Governor White's Quandary," by Richard K. Murdoch.

Georgia Historical Quarterly — June, 1957: "Ulrich B. Phillips, the University of Georgia, and the Georgia Historical Society," by Wendell H. Stephenson; "Woodrow Wilson as a Young Lawyer, 1882-1883," by George C. Osborn; "John Abbot, Pioneer Naturalist of Georgia," by Elsa G. Allen; "The Letter Book of Thomas Rasberry, 1758-1761," Part IV, ed. by Lilla M. Hawes; "From Spotsylvania Courthouse to Andersonville: A Diary of Darius Starr," ed. by E. Merton Coulter.

Journal of Mississippi History — April, 1957: "The Origin of the Constitution of 1890," by James P. Coleman; "Paul Bunyan Comes to Mississippi," by James W. Silver.

Journal of Negro History — April, 1957: "Three Years among the Freedmen: William C. Gannett and the Port Royal Experiment," by William H. Pease.

Journal of Southern History — May, 1957: "The Southern Education Board and the Race Issue in Public Education," by Louis R. Harlan; "Toward a Reinterpretation of Booker T. Washington," by August Meier.

Journal of the Presbyterian Historical Society — June, 1957: "Colonial Presbyterianism in the Valley of Virginia, 1727-1775," by Robert F. Scott.

Mid-America — April, 1957: "The Bishop of Natchez and the Confederate Chaplaincy," by Willard E. Wight; "Towns of the Alabama Black Belt," by Glenn N. Sisk; "General O'Reilly's Arrival at New Orleans," ed. by Donald G. Castanien.

Mississippi Quarterly — Spring, 1957: "Literature and Southern Cities," by Edd Winfield Parks; "The Agrarian Manifesto: A Generation Later," Robert B. Holland; "The Urbane Bourbon," by John K. Bettersworth.

North Carolina Historical Review — April, 1957: "The Cotton Textile Industry in Ante-Bellum North Carolina: Part II, An Era of Boom and Consolidation, 1830-1860," by Richard W. Griffin and Diffee W. Standard; "A Bibliography of the Published Writings of Benjamin Griffith Brawley," by John W. Parker; "Dare County Belles-Lettres," by Richard Walser; "Roanoke Colonists and Explorers: An Attempt at Identification," by William S. Powell.

Register of the Kentucky Historical Society — April, 1957: "The Established Churches and Slavery, 1850-1860," by Will Frank Steely; "Captain Thomas Henry Hines and His February, 1863, Raid," by Edward M. Coffman; "Justice John Marshall Harlan of Kentucky," by John S. Goff; "Manuscript Accessions in Kentucky for 1956," by G. Glenn Clift.

South Carolina Historical Magazine — April, 1957: "The Death of Alexandre Placide," by Sylvie Chevalley; "Letters of Thomas Pinckney, 1775-1780," Part II, ed. by Jack L. Cross; "Wappetaw Congregational Church," Part II, by Petrona Royall McIver.

Southwestern Historical Quarterly — April, 1957: "The Texas State House: A Study of the Building of the Texas Capitol," by Frederick W. Rathjen; "The Diary of Eliza (Mrs. Albert Sidney) Johnston: The Second Cavalry Comes to Texas," ed. by Charles P. Roland and Richard C. Robbins; "Texas Pioneer Surveyors and Indians," by Forrest Daniell; "Trade Goods for Texas: An Incident in the History of the Jeffersonian Embargo," by C. Norman Guice; "The Report of the Expedition of Major Robert S. Neighbors to El Paso in 1849," ed. by Kenneth F. Neighbours; "Calendar of the Letters of Antonio Martinez, Last Spanish Governor of Texas, 1817-1822," Part VI, ed. by Virginia H. Taylor.

Tennessee Historical Quarterly — June, 1957: "Building a Tennessee Army, Autumn, 1861," by Peter Franklin Walker; "Davy Crockett: The Genesis of Heroic Myth," by Stuart A. Stiffler; "A Student at the University of Nashville: Correspondence of John Donelson Coffee, 1830-1833," ed. by Aaron M. Boom.

Virginia Magazine of History and Biography — April, 1957: "The Devil in Virginia in the Seventeenth Century," by Richard Beale Davis; "Early Cemetery on 'Third Ridge' at Jamestown," by Joel L. Shiner; "Some Jefferson Manuscript Memoranda of Colonial Virginia Records," by Harry Clemons; "The Jamestown Tercentennial Exposition of 1907," by Robert T. Taylor; "John Martin, Ancient Adventurer," by Samuel M. Bemiss.

West Virginia History — April, 1957: "A Half Century of Educational Progress in West Virginia: A Historical and Statistical Study," by Roy

C. Woods; "Alleghany Collegiate Institute of Alderson, West Virginia," by Nat G. Barnhart; "Kanawha Trails," by Robert Hurley.

William and Mary Quarterly — April, 1957: "The Revolutionary Militia in the Southern Campaign, 1780-1781," by Robert C. Pugh.

Recent Articles Concerning the Middle West

Bulletin of the Historical and Philosophical Society of Ohio — April, 1957: "Dan Rice, Circus Man," by John C. Kunzog; "A Western Chapter in the History of American Transcendentalism," by Frank R. Shivers, Jr.; "Cincinnati & Westwood Railroad Co.," by John H. White, Jr.; "Historical Collecting: Letters of A. Randall to Lyman Copeland Draper, 1846-1855," ed. by William B. Hesseltine and Larry Gara.

Chicago History — Spring, 1957: "One Hundred Twenty Years Ago," ed. by Paul M. Angle.

Chronicles of Oklahoma — Spring, 1957: "The Seal of Cimarron Territory," by Muriel H. Wright; "The History of No-Man's-Land, or Old Beaver County," by Morris L. Wardell; "Shade's Well," by Laura V. Hamner; "Memoirs of Oklahoma," by Kittie M. Harvey; "The Butterfield Overland Mail One Hundred Years Ago," by Muriel H. Wright; "Dr. and Mrs. Richard Moore Crain," by Carolyn Thomas Foreman; "Health Conditions in Indian Territory, 1830 to the Civil War," by Bernice Norman Crockett.

Indiana Magazine of History — June, 1957: "New Albany: Mid-Nineteenth Century Economic Expansion," by Victor M. Bogle; "Thomas R. Marshall's Victory in the Election of 1908," by Keith S. Montgomery; "William Orlando Lynch, 1870-1957," by John D. Barnhart; "Letters of John Traub, Twenty-ninth Indiana Infantry," ed. by Paul Fatout; "An Indiana Volunteer Advises His Neighbors," ed. by Charles G. Talbert.

Iowa Journal of History — April, 1957: "The Development of the Iowa Constitution of 1857," by Russell M. Ross; "Contemporary Editorial Opinion of the 1857 Constitution," ed. by William J. Petersen; "State Support of Higher Education in Iowa," by Irving H. Hart; "The Diary of a Law Student, 1853-1855," ed. by Mildred Throne.

Journal of Southern History — May, 1957: "An Oklahoma Indian Trader as a Frontiersman of Commerce," by Oliver Knight.

Journal of the Illinois State Historical Society — Spring, 1957: "Three Galena Generals," by Elmer Gertz; "Sources of Early Antislavery

Thought in Illinois," by Merton L. Dillon; "Lincoln's Tomb: Designs Submitted and Final Selection," by William J. Hosking.

Journal of the Presbyterian Historical Society — June, 1957: "Love Letters and Journal of Comfort I. Slack," ed. by Charles A. Anderson; "Minutes of the Nebraska Presbytery, 1849-1851 and Minutes of the Presbytery of Highland, 1857-1858," ed. by Guy S. Klett.

Kansas Historical Quarterly — Spring, 1957: "The Invention and Development of the Dial Telephone: The Contribution of Three Lindsborg Inventors," by Emory K. Lindquist; "Manhattan's Oldest House Was Built by David A. Butterfield," by C. W. McCampbell; "Theatre in Kansas, 1858-1868: Background for the Coming of the Lord Dramatic Company to Kansas, 1869," by James C. Malin.

Minnesota History — June, 1957: "Gateway to the Northwest: St. Paul and the Nobles Expedition of 1859," by Willoughby M. Babcock; "Pioneer Teachers: The Benedictine Sisters at St. Cloud," by Sister Grace McDonald; "Commercial Fishing on Lake of the Woods," by John Dobie.

Missouri Historical Review — April, 1957: "Hermann: A Bit of the Old World in the Heart of the New," by Floyd C. Shoemaker; "Congressional Opinion in Missouri on the Spanish-American War," by James Warren Neilson; "St. Louis and the Union Baseball War," by Harold Seymour; "Missouri in Crisis: The Journal of Captain Albert Tracy, 1861," Part III, ed. by Ray W. Irwin.

Nebraska History — March, 1957: "The Nemaha Half-Breed Reservation," by Berlin B. Chapman; "Young Radicals of the Nineties," by Mary Louise Jeffery; "Some Effects of the Introduction of the Automobile on Highways and Land Values in Nebraska," by Clinton Warne.

June, 1957: "Imprisoned at Andersonville: The Diary of Albert Harry Shatzel, May 5, 1864-September 12, 1864," ed. by Donald F. Danker; "Indian Missions and Missionaries on the Upper Missouri to 1900," by Ray H. Mattison; "A Tempest in a Teapot? — Governor Poynter's Appointment of William V. Allen to the United States Senate," by Paolo E. Coletta.

North Dakota History — January, 1957: "The Siege at Fort Abercrombie," by Roy P. Johnson.

Northwest Ohio Quarterly — Spring, 1957: "The Scott Nearing Controversy in Toledo, 1916-1917 (Part I)," by Elliott J. Anderson; "A Memorial to Major William G. Oliver — Pioneer of Port Lawrence," ed. by Irene McCreery; "The People's Schools: Popular Foundations of Toledo's Public School System," Part II, by Randolph C. Downes.

Ohio Historical Quarterly — April, 1957: "The Removal of the Wyandots from Ohio," by Carl G. Klopfenstein; "Indian River and Place Names in Ohio," by August C. Mahr; "A Surgeon's Mate at Fort Defiance: The Journal of Joseph Gardner Andrews for the Year 1795," Part II, ed. by Richard C. Knopf; "Marching through South Carolina: Another Civil War Letter of Lieutenant George M. Wise," ed. by Wilfred W. Black.

Susquehanna University Studies — May, 1957: "The Reaction of Franklinton, Ohio, to the Northwestern Army, 1812," by Lyder L. Unstad.

Western Pennsylvania Historical Magazine — Spring, 1957: "My Trip across the Plains," by Margaretta Faber McClintock, ed. by Charles A. McClintock.

Wisconsin Magazine of History — Summer, 1957: "Lincoln and the Mayor of Chicago," by Don E. Fehrenbacher; "The Beloit College Agency," by Helen L. D. Richardson; "A Frontier Smithy in Wisconsin Territory," by Evan A. Hart; "The Story of the Black Hawk War," by Elizabeth B. Rooney.

Recent Articles Concerning the Far West

Colorado Magazine — April, 1957: "'His Turbulent Excellency,' Alexander Cummings, Governor of Colorado Territory, 1865-1867," by William Hanchett; "About Towns: Del Norte," ed. by Agnes Wright Spring; "Ranching in Rio Blanco County," by J. N. Neal; "Nathaniel P. Hill Makes Second Visit to Colorado, 1865," ed. by Agnes Wright Spring; "Relations between the Colorado Central Railroad and the Union Pacific," by Ralph N. Traxler, Jr.; "More about Bent's Old Fort," ed. by Agnes Wright Spring.

New Mexico Historical Review — April, 1957: "The Southern Overland Mail and Stagecoach Line, 1857-1861," by Oscar O. Winther; "Spanish Transportation in the Southwest, 1540-1846," by Max L. Moorhead; "Military Transportation in the Southwest, 1848-1860," by Averam B. Bender; "Railway Development in the Southwest," by William S. Greever; "Stagecoaching in Territorial New Mexico," by William S. Wallace.

Oregon Historical Quarterly — June, 1957: "British Investment and Oregon Mining, 1860-1900," by Clark G. Spence; "The Oneida Toll Road Controversy, 1864-1880," by Donald N. Wells and Merle W. Wells; "When the Train Reached Seaside . . ." by Inez Stafford Hanson; "The Ilwaco Railroad," by Thomas E. Jessett.

Pacific Northwest Quarterly — April, 1957: "Frederic G. Young, Regionalist and Historian," by George A. Frykman; "The Location of Flathead Post," by Allan H. Smith; "Hospitality at the Punch Bowl: An Astorian's Recollections of an Evening with Count Baranoff," ed. by John Francis McDermott; "The State Archives of Washington," by Robert W. Nesbit.

Recent Articles Concerning Canada

Canadian Historical Review — June, 1957: "*Le Canadien* and the British Constitution, 1806-1810," by Lawrence A. H. Smith; "The Change in Liberal Party Leadership, 1887," by Margaret A. Banks; "A Note on the Red River Hunt by John Norquay," by Margaret Arnett MacLeod.

Journal of Politics — May, 1957: "Civil Service Commissions in the Canadian Provinces," by Howard A. Scarrow.

REPORT OF THE SECRETARY-TREASURER FOR THE YEAR 1956-1957

By William D. Aeschbacher

One of the most important activities of the Association during the year has been the completing of plans for its Publications Award Program. The special committee to plan this program held a meeting in St. Louis on June 16, 1956, and accepted the proposal of the University of Kentucky Press for the implementation of the publications program. To forward the program the chairman of the Executive Committee twice queried the members of that committee during the fall to obtain suggestions for the membership of the committee to administer the program. The make-up of this committee was discussed at length in a preliminary meeting of the finance committee on the evening of December 27, prior to the American Historical Association meeting at St. Louis, December 28-30, 1956. The finance committee then in its regular meeting nominated the members of the committee and these nominations were ratified by the Executive Committee.

The Association held its regular mid-year meeting in conjunction with the St. Louis meeting. At the morning session, Elwood R. Maunder of St. Paul, Minnesota, presented a paper on "The Forest History Foundation" and Stanley F. Horn of Nashville, Tennessee, presented one on "Seventy-Five Years of *The Southern Lumberman*." Comment was by John H. Moore of the University of Mississippi. At the dinner session, presided over by Wendell H. Stephenson of the University of Oregon, vice-president of the Association, Jeannette P. Nichols, University of Pennsylvania, presented a paper entitled "A Half Century of Evolution in American Diplomacy."

The Executive Committee met at 8:30 A.M., December 29, 1956, with the following members present: George L. Anderson (chairman), Thomas P. Abernethy, Lewis E. Atherton, Ray A. Billington, William C. Binkley, Thomas D. Clark, Merle Curti, James L. Sellers, Fred A. Shannon, Paul F. Sharp, Kenneth M. Stampp, Wendell H. Stephenson, Walter P. Webb, T. Harry Williams, and William D. Aeschbacher (secretary-treasurer). Reports were heard from Oscar O. Winther, chairman of the program committee; Roy M. Robbins, chairman of the membership committee; Bennett H. Wall, chairman of the nominating committee; James C. Olson, chairman of the local arrangements committee, and George L. Anderson, chairman of the finance committee. A publications committee, consisting of Chase C. Mooney, chairman, Richard W. Leopold, J. Merton England, Edward C. Kirkland, and Fletcher M. Green, was established as previously indicated. It was suggested that the Secretary's Annual Report should include a tabulation of the number of members by states to stimulate interest in membership. On recommendation of the managing editor, the title of Philip F. Detweiler was changed from editorial assistant to associate editor of the *Review*. The interim appointment of the new director of the Nebraska State Historical Society, William D. Aeschbacher, as secretary-treasurer of the Association was confirmed. The Executive Committee voted to accept an invitation from Minneapolis for the 1958 annual meeting.

The Fiftieth Annual Meeting of the Association was held in Lincoln, Nebraska, May 2, 3, and 4, 1957. The Executive Committee met in the University Club on the evening of May 1, with the following members present: Anderson (chairman), Abernethy, Atherton, Billington, Binkley, Clark, Curti, W. Stull Holt, Sellers, Shannon, Sharp, Stephenson, and Aeschbacher (secretary-treasurer). The minutes of the December 29 meeting were approved as submitted to the members of the committee by mail. Reports were heard from James C. Olson, chairman of the local arrangements committee; Roy M. Robbins, chairman of the membership committee; Oscar O. Winther, chairman of the program committee, and Bennett H. Wall, chairman of the nominating committee. Action was taken to have the program committee for the annual meeting each year arrange the program for the ensuing joint session with the American Historical Association. The suggestion of the nominating committee that it pass on its files of the past three years to the succeeding committee and deposit the fourth year's files in the Association office was approved. It was voted that the chairman of the nominating committee be authorized to open and count the ballots prior to the annual meeting, and be instructed to report the results to the business session at the annual meeting, and to turn the ballots over to the secretary-treasurer for confirmation and to be preserved for one year. The recommendation of the executive committee of the Teachers Section that the Association should not affiliate with the Council for Basic Education was accepted.

Chase C. Mooney, chairman of the publications committee, reported on the plans for the establishment of the Prize Monograph Series and presented the requirements and rules agreed upon by the committee to govern the competition for the annual award. The report was approved.

Mr. Binkley, chairman, reported for the Pelzer Memorial Committee that the winner of the Pelzer Award for 1957 was Clifford S. Griffin, a doctoral candidate at the University of Wisconsin, and that Robert H. Wiebe, a doctoral candidate at the University of Rochester, had been given honorable mention. Mr. Binkley also made an informal report as managing editor of the *Review*. On his nomination, George L. Anderson, Charles A. Barker, and Eugene H. Roseboom were elected members of the board of editors of the *Review* for the term ending in 1960. The Executive Committee approved an informal proposal to renew the arrangement with Tulane University concerning the editorship of the *Review* for another five-year period, and expressed its appreciation to Tulane for its continued manifestation of interest in and support of the affairs of the Association.

The offer of Mr. Shannon to give his file of the Association's publications to the Association in return for a life membership was accepted. Mr. Anderson reported for the finance committee and the action of that committee in accepting a budget for 1957-1958, authorizing the transfer of the Association membership records to IBM records, handling of the investment of surplus funds, establishing a policy on the number of *Reviews* to print, and action in regard to surplus publications was approved. Mr. Atherton submitted a report on newspaper microfilming, and the following resolution to be presented to the Association of Research Libraries was adopted:

> The Mississippi Valley Historical Association, with a membership of 3,119 American historians and libraries, urges the Association of Research Libraries to establish a newspaper microfilm pool of American newspapers along the lines of the Foreign Newspaper Microfilm Project which is now in operation. Such action would greatly facilitate research in the field of American history, and we feel sure that many educational institutions and research libraries would join such a project. We also urge that in developing such a pool attention be given to the possibility that institutions joining the pool might be willing to lend to it part of their holdings of microfilm of back issues of newspapers.

The annual business meeting of the Association was called to order on Friday, May 3, at 1:10 P.M. with President Thomas D. Clark presiding. The President announced that if there were no corrections to the minutes of the last annual meeting, held in Pittsburgh, April 20, 1956, as they appeared in the September, 1956, *Review*, they would stand approved. No corrections were offered. The secretary-treasurer's report as presented by W. D.

Aeschbacher was approved. The report of Elfrieda Lang, chairman of the auditing committee, was accepted, as was the report of the Executive Committee, made by the chairman, George L. Anderson.

Roy M. Robbins, chairman of the membership committee, reported that 394 new members had been added during the period from April 1, 1956, to March 31, 1957. Of these, 26 were from foreign countries; and of the 368 within the United States, 329 were individual and 39 were institutional memberships. Mr. Robbins explained the plan of operation of the committee through state sub-chairmen, and he attached to his report a table showing the number of new members in each state. The five states showing the greatest numerical gains were: New York, with 72 new members; Pennsylvania, with 23; Louisiana, with 21; California, with 18; and Iowa, with 17. "It is significant to note," he said, "that for the first time the Association has boosted its membership above the three thousand mark," the total as of March 31, 1957, being 3,119 — distributed as follows:

Alabama	43	Maine	4	Oklahoma	56
Arizona	14	Maryland	54	Oregon	32
Arkansas	28	Massachusetts	94	Pennsylvania	144
California	176	Michigan	108	Rhode Island	7
Colorado	42	Minnesota	77	South Carolina	22
Connecticut	40	Mississippi	32	South Dakota	34
Delaware	6	Missouri	89	Tennessee	84
Dist. of Columbia	53	Montana	12	Texas	129
Florida	24	Nebraska	63	Utah	7
Georgia	44	Nevada	3	Vermont	8
Idaho	10	New Hampshire	8	Virginia	74
Illinois	193	New Jersey	55	Washington	44
Indiana	140	New Mexico	18	West Virginia	30
Iowa	80	New York	300	Wisconsin	91
Kansas	52	North Carolina	55	Wyoming	9
Kentucky	59	North Dakota	23	Foreign	99
Louisiana	84	Ohio	166		

Russell K. Nelson, acting chairman of the committee to co-operate with the National Park Service, presented the following report and recommendations, which were approved:

(1) The Federal Government program for the survey and salvage of historic sites in Missouri Valley Reservoir areas, begun in 1946, is approaching completion. At this time the National Park Service is anticipating a revival of the nation-wide Historic Sites Survey beginning July 1, 1957. It is recommended, therefore, that the purpose of this committee be changed from assistance in the salvage of historic sites in the Missouri

River Basin to assistance in the investigation and preservation of significant historic sites throughout the United States.

(2) Consistent with the above, it is recommended that the name of this committee be changed to the Historic Sites Committee.

(3) Also consistent with the above, it is recommended that membership in this committee, now limited to the Upper Mississippi Valley area, be expanded to include representation from all major geographical regions of continental United States.

(4) The Committee will continue its efforts to interest graduate students in research and writing in the historic sites field.

(5) The Committee will seek other opportunities to give support to the cause of historic sites preservation, such as the proposed salvage of historic values threatened by the new federal interstate highway program.

Bennett H. Wall, reporting for the nominating committee, presented the names of Wendell H. Stephenson for president and William T. Hutchinson for vice-president. As no additional nominations had been made as provided by the constitution, they were unanimously elected. Mr. Wall further reported:

The nominating committee certifies that during the annual meeting of the Mississippi Valley Historical Association held at Lincoln, beginning May 2, 1957, we opened the sealed ballots delivered by the chairman of the nominating committee, counted the votes on the individual ballots, determined and hereby announce the election of the following:

To the Executive Committee — Robert G. Athearn, Thomas C. Cochran, and Robert E. Riegel;

To the Executive Committee of the Teachers Section — James A. Barnes and W. Eugene Hollon;

To the Nominating Committee — Arthur Bestor and Carl Bridenbaugh.

The report was accepted.

Howard H. Peckham, chairman of a special resolutions committee, presented the following report:

In the past year this Association has suffered the loss of three of its former presidents.

Isaac J. Cox, president of the Mississippi Valley Historical Association in 1914-1915, died on October 31, 1956. Born in New Jersey in 1873, he earned his A. B. from Dartmouth and his Ph.D. from Pennsylvania. He taught at the University of Cincinnati from 1904 to 1919, when he went to Northwestern. There he became chairman of the history department in 1927 and served until his retirement in 1941. He was a Latin-American scholar, author, and translator, whose chief work was on the West Florida controversy.

Eugene C. Barker, president of the Mississippi Valley Historical Association in 1923-1924, died on October 22, 1956. He obtained his bachelor's and master's degrees from the University of Texas and his doctor's degree from Pennsylvania in 1908. Meanwhile he had begun teaching at Texas in 1901 and remained there more than fifty years. He wrote a school history of Texas, a biography of Stephen Austin, a book on Mexico and Texas, and edited the Austin Papers and the writings of Sam Houston. Professor Barker also served as editor of the *Southwestern Historical Quarterly* from 1910 to 1937. As a result of his collecting activities, the Regents of the University established the Eugene C. Barker Texas History Center, named in his honor.

William O. Lynch, president of the Mississippi Valley Historical Association in 1938-1939, died on March 29, 1957. He held degrees from Indiana University and the University of Wisconsin. After work in secondary schools, he began his college teaching at Indiana State Teachers College in 1903. He joined the history department of Indiana University in 1920 to teach American history. From 1928 to 1941 he edited the *Indiana Magazine of History* and was president of the Indiana Historical Society from 1946 to 1950. He was the author of a well-known work on party warfare in the United States, and he served as acting managing editor of the *Mississippi Valley Historical Review* in 1946.

In adopting these resolutions the members stood in silent tribute to these scholars.

T. Alfred Larson, chairman of the resolutions committee, presented the following resolutions, which were adopted:

Be it resolved, that the members of the Mississippi Valley Historical Association, convened in Lincoln, Nebraska, for their Fiftieth Annual Meeting, give thanks to the following:

President Thomas D. Clark and Secretary-Treasurer William D. Aeschbacher for their over-all planning and supervision of the meeting;

Oscar O. Winther, chairman, and the other members of the Program Committee for their devoted and successful efforts to present a stimulating program;

The University of Nebraska, the Nebraska State Historical Society, and the Local Arrangements Committee, under the chairmanship of James C. Olson, for their careful attention to important details that have contributed to the comfort and enjoyment of the membership;

The Hotel Cornhusker for the completeness and courtesy of its services.

And, finally, *Be it further resolved*, that the Association offer its deep appreciation to Tulane University for its continuing support of the *Review*.

Chase C. Mooney, chairman of the publications committee, reported on the plans and program of that committee, and announced the establishment of the Prize Monograph Series, after which the meeting adjourned.

Following the annual business meeting of the Association, the Executive Committee convened again with the following members present: Anderson (chairman), Abernethy, Robert G. Athearn, Atherton, Billington, Binkley, Clark, Thomas C. Cochran, Curti, Holt, William T. Hutchinson, Robert E. Riegel, Sellers, Shannon, Sharp, Stephenson, Webb, and Aeschbacher (secretary-treasurer). Thomas D. Clark was elected chairman of the Executive Committee to succeed Mr. Anderson, whose term as a member of the Committee expired with this meeting. George E. Mowry was appointed a member of the Pelzer Memorial Committee for the term ending in 1961. Invitations were presented for future meetings from Detroit, Denver, Colorado Springs, and Milwaukee. It was decided to defer a decision on the 1959 meeting place until the mid-year meeting in December.

Mr. Billington presented the following resolution, which was adopted:

> In view of the growing shortage of teachers of history in the colleges and universities of the United States, and with the prospect of a more serious shortage in the near future:
>
> *Resolved*: that the Mississippi Valley Historical Association suggest to the American Historical Association the desirability of a joint effort to secure foundation support for a major fellowship program that would attract graduate students into the area of historical studies.

It was voted that a committee be appointed to restudy the organization and functions of the executive committee of the Teachers Section of the Association. Suggested revisions of the regulations adopted in 1948 as rules of procedure for the Executive Committee were amended and approved. The Committee adopted a resolution expressing its appreciation to George L. Anderson for his service as chairman of the Executive Committee for the past two years.

Statement of Cash Receipts and Disbursements for the Year Ending March 31, 1957

Cash on hand and on deposit, April 1, 1956		$23,200.76
Receipts:		
New memberships — institutional	$ 350.00	
New memberships — individual	690.00	
New memberships — student	560.00	
Sustaining memberships — institutional	4,750.00	
Sustaining memberships — individual	7,586.50	
Sustaining memberships — student	198.00	
Life membership	100.00	
Foreign postage	77.75	
Index, Volume III, sales	72.00	
Review sales	759.25	
Advertising — *Review*	1,211.88	
Miscellaneous publications	19.75	
Annual meeting — registration and miscellaneous	406.44	
Annual meeting — advertising	1,219.10	
Interest received on bonds and savings accounts	869.90	
Redemption of matured Series F bond	74.00	
Redemption of matured Series G bond	500.00	
Subsidy	2,000.00	
Other income	6.02	21,450.59
		$44,651.35

Disbursements:	
Clerical salaries	$ 1,592.30
Office supplies and expense	301.48
Postage and express	330.92
Miscellaneous printing	386.08
Printing of *Review*	12,406.71
Travel expense	772.20
Annual meeting expense	904.47
Legal and professional	275.00
Taxes — general and payroll	12.98
Retirement annuity — Mrs. C. S. Paine	1,200.00
Refunds of membership	16.00
Telephone and telegraph	27.83
Surety bonds — employees	195.10

Book binding	150.05	
Miscellaneous expense	51.20	
	18,622.32	
Cost of U. S. Treasury bonds purchased	2,405.47	21,027.79
Cash on hand and on deposit, March 31, 1957		$23,623.56

SECURITIES OWNED (March 31, 1957)

Description	*Interest Rate*	*Maturity*	*Cost*
United States Savings Bonds, Series G	2½%	May 1, 1957	$ 2,000.00
United States Savings Bonds, Series G	2½%	November 1, 1957	2,000.00
United States Savings Bonds, Series G	2½%	December 1, 1957	8,500.00
United States Savings Bonds, Series G	2½%	March 1, 1959	1,000.00
United States Savings Bonds, Series G	2½%	November 1, 1959	1,000.00
United States Savings Bonds, Series G	2½%	November 1, 1960	1,000.00
			$15,500.00
United States Treasury Bonds	2½%	November 15, 1961	$ 2,405.47

Directory of Contributors

Richard L. Watson, Jr., is associate professor of history in Duke University.

Burl Noggle is assistant professor of history in the New Mexico College of Agriculture and Mechanic Arts.

Allen J. Going, who was associate professor of history in the University of Alabama when his article went to press, is now associate professor of history in the University of Houston.

Edwin A. Miles is associate professor of history in the University of Houston.

Oscar O. Winther is professor of history and associate dean of the Graduate School in Indiana University.

The Mississippi Valley Historical Review

PUBLISHED QUARTERLY BY THE MISSISSIPPI VALLEY HISTORICAL ASSOCIATION

VOL. XLIV, NO. 3 — DECEMBER, 1957

Correspondence concerning contributions, books for review, and all editorial matters should be addressed to William C. Binkley, Managing Editor, Tulane University of Louisiana, New Orleans 18, Louisiana. Annual membership dues are $5.00. Student membership dues are $3.00 annually. Correspondence concerning membership dues and all business matters should be addressed to the Secretary, William D. Aeschbacher, 1500 R Street, Lincoln, Nebraska. The *Review* is sent to all members of the Association. Single numbers and back files may be obtained from the Secretary.

Entered as second-class matter, May 22, 1914, at the post office in Cedar Rapids, Iowa, and Lincoln 8, Nebraska, under the Act of August 24, 1912. Printed by The Torch Press, Cedar Rapids, Iowa.

Contents

Religious Benevolence as Social Control, 1815-1860. By Clifford S. Griffin 423

A Scheme in Regard to Cyrenaica. By James A. Field, Jr. 445

The Brownsville Episode and the Negro Vote. By Emma Lou Thornbrough 469

The Semicentennial of the Mississippi Valley Historical Association. By James L. Sellers 494

Under Our Strange Device: A Review of the "Review." By John W. Caughey 519

Book Reviews

Allen and Hill (eds.), *British Essays in American History*, by Louis M. Hacker . . 536
Wharton, *The Life of John Smith, English Soldier* (trans. by Striker), by Jarvis M. Morse . 537
Tolles, *James Logan and the Culture of Provincial America*, by Clarence L. Ver Steeg . . 539
Klingberg (ed.), *The Carolina Chronicle of Dr. Francis Le Jau, 1706-1717*, by J. H. Easterby . 541
Scott, *Counterfeiting in Colonial America*, by Carlos Richard Allen, Jr. 542
Aldridge, *Franklin and His French Contemporaries*, by Verner W. Crane 543
Roche, *Joseph Reed: A Moderate in the American Revolution*, by Elisha P. Douglass . . 544
Uhlendorf (trans.), *Revolution in America: Confidential Letters and Journals, 1776-1784, of Adjutant General Major Baurmeister of the Hessian Forces*, by Hugh F. Rankin . . 546
Cohn, *The Life and Times of King Cotton*, by Bennett H. Wall 547
Davis, *Homicide in American Fiction, 1798-1860*, by Alexander C. Kern . . 549
Carter (ed.), *The Territorial Papers of the United States*, Vol. XXII, *The Territory of Florida, 1821-1824*, by Kathryn Abbey Hanna 550
Shepperson, *British Emigration to North America*, by Roger V. Clements . . . 552
Yates, *William T. Porter and the "Spirit of the Times,"* by Eugene Current-Garcia . . 553
Blair and Meine (eds.), *Half Horse, Half Alligator: The Growth of the Mike Fink Legend*, by Mody C. Boatright 554
Smith, *Revivalism and Social Reform in Mid-Nineteenth-Century America*, by Henry Lee Swint . 555
Younger (ed.), *Inside the Confederate Government: The Diary of Robert Garlick Hill Kean*, by Rembert W. Patrick 557
Miers (ed.), *When the World Ended: The Diary of Emma Le Conte*, and Hoole, *Vizetelly Covers the Confederacy*, by John G. Barrett 558
Roland, *Louisiana Sugar Plantations during the American Civil War*, by Herbert Weaver . 559
Silver, *Lincoln's Supreme Court*, by Winfred A. Harbison 561
Baxter, *Orville H. Browning: Lincoln's Friend and Critic*, by William F. Zornow . . 562
Singletary, *Negro Militia and Reconstruction*, by Horace W. Raper 563
Hughes, *Pioneer Years in the Black Hills* (ed. by Spring), by Edgar I. Stewart . . 565
Campbell, *Anglo-American Understanding, 1898-1903*, by Richard W. Van Alstyne . . 567
Shryock, *National Tuberculosis Association, 1904-1954*, by Donald R. McNeil . . . 568
Hargreaves, *Dry Farming in the Northern Great Plains, 1900-1925*, by Robert G. Dunbar . 569
Hutchinson, *Lowden of Illinois: The Life of Frank O. Lowden* (2 vols.), by George F. Howe . 570
Draper, *The Roots of American Communism*, by Stow Persons 572
Divine, *American Immigration Policy, 1924-1952*, by Oscar Handlin 573
Perkins, *The New Age of Franklin Roosevelt, 1932-45*, and Agar, *The Price of Power: America since 1945*, by L. Ethan Ellis 574
Stern, *Imprints on History: Book Publishers and American Frontiers*, by J. H. Shera . . 576
Kohn, *American Nationalism: An Interpretative Essay*, by Boyd C. Shafer . . . 577

Book Notes 579

Historical News and Comments 585

Directory of Contributors 612

Religious Benevolence as Social Control, 1815-1860

By Clifford S. Griffin

In the years between 1815 and the Civil War the United States was in a ferment of great and fundamental social, economic, and political change. Thousands of families were rushing westward, occupying land, and creating cities and states from forests and prairies. Native-born and immigrant factory workers, laborers, shopkeepers, and artisans were crowding the new centers of industry and the older cities, and creating new economic and social problems. Western settlers and enterprising eastern business pioneers were repeatedly crossing new horizons only to find that beyond lay seemingly boundless areas for expansion. While Federalism declined and new political parties remained ill-defined, men were casting about for other alliances which would embrace the expanding frontier and the growing electorate. Some welcomed changes that seemed to promise greater heights in the "rise of the common man" and wider vistas for "Young America." Others feared new forces in American life, worried about political and social upheavals, and deplored new moral standards. To many of those who could not accept the changing America, evangelical Protestantism seemed an excellent means of keeping the nation under control.

Between 1815 and 1826 many Presbyterians and Congregationalists, aided by a smaller number of Methodists, Baptists, and Episcopalians, seeking to supply the religious needs of the expanding country, joined to form five great national interdenominational societies.[1] The American Education Society, organized in Boston

Editor's Note: — This article received the Mississippi Valley Historical Association's Pelzer Award for 1957.

[1] The American Education Society was formed in Boston, August, 1815; the American Bible Society in New York, May, 1816; the American Sunday School Union in Philadelphia, May, 1824; the American Tract Society in New York, May, 1825; and the American Home Missionary Society in New York, May, 1826.

in 1815, subsidized future ministers in colleges and seminaries. From its offices in New York the American Home Missionary Society helped poor congregations pay their pastors and sent men to new settlements.[2] Between 1816 and 1861 the American Bible Society distributed millions of copies of the Bible; and the American Tract Society supplemented and extended religious and moral reading by issuing before 1861 almost 200,000,000 books and tracts. From Philadelphia the American Sunday School Union sent missionaries to establish schools and then furnished the young scholars with lessons, religious volumes, and moral stories.[3] Held together by the idea of benevolence toward man as the highest Christian virtue and united in promoting what they considered the fundamentals of evangelical Protestantism, these societies worked outside regular church organizations to convert the nation to God.

From the changing Calvinism of an earlier age, the managers of the societies[4] inherited a religion which retained elements of the Genevan master's theology, but altered his idea of a predestined elect of God. Presbyterians and Congregationalists, together with men of other churches who claimed to be propagating only the essence of Christianity, accepted the Calvinistic stress on the original and

[2] The American Home Missionary Society and the American Education Society were almost exclusively for the benefit of Presbyterians and Congregationalists. See Absalom Peters to William Cogswell, January 31, 1834 (copy); Charles Hall to Washington Thacher, January 26, 1850 (copy); David B. Coe to S. Sawyer, April 12, 1855 (copy), American Home Missionary Society Papers (Chicago Theological Seminary). Also, American Education Society, *Annual Report* (Andover and Boston), XX (1836), 72-73. After the Old School-New School schism in the Presbyterian church in 1837 and 1838, the societies aided New School Presbyterians and Congregationalists. After 1861 both societies existed to help Congregationalists alone.

[3] Although the American Bible Society and the American Sunday School Union had members of several denominations on various boards and committees, the largest single number was Presbyterian. See Joseph Holdich to H. Brownson, February 15, 1858 (copy), American Bible Society Papers (American Bible Society, New York); American Sunday School Union, *Annual Report* (Philadelphia), VIII (1832), 32 n. The constitution of the American Tract Society stipulated that each member of the five- or six-man publishing committee, which alone decided what the society would publish, should be of a different denomination. American Tract Society, *Annual Report* (New York), I (1826), 6. Subsequent annual reports until 1841 gave the denominations of the members; that this distribution generally continued is obvious from the lists of officers in later reports.

[4] The Bible Society and Sunday School Union were operated by boards of managers; the Tract and Home Missionary societies by executive committees; the Education Society by a board of directors. Meeting once or twice a month, these voluntary and unpaid boards and committees decided policy; between meetings, paid, full-time secretaries implemented the decisions. The word "managers" is used in this article to indicate the members of these variously named governing boards, plus the secretaries and presidents of the societies, who were members of the groups.

actual sins of man and his evil in God's sight. But the late eighteenth and early nineteenth centuries finally saw the modification of the idea that Christ had died only for God's elect; instead, heirs of Calvinism emphasized that Christ had died for all mankind. More than man's sins, the societies stressed Christ's atonement, the mercy which God offered, and the grace which God would grant to those who repented and believed. Although this general theology emphasized that only God could bestow sanctifying grace — that man could not win it for himself — the managers believed that in forsaking sin and believing in Christ man could put himself in an excellent position to merit mercy and forgiveness. The societies' aim was to get the people into this state.[5]

In striving toward this goal, the managers believed themselves to be expressing in action the idea of benevolence to man which the societies held was the essence of all Protestantism. This idea was not new. Colonial Puritans, for example, had been familiar with Cotton Mather's *Essays to Do Good.* But in the late eighteenth century the Congregational minister Samuel Hopkins, who preached in Newport, Rhode Island, in his later years, gave the concept great currency.[6] It quickly became popular in several denominations. As interpreted by the societies, benevolence — or, as it was often called, charity, or love for man — was the idea that certain persons, having received God's sanctifying grace, were obliged to extend to all men the means of obtaining that grace. The managers reasoned that God's mercy was the greatest gift anyone could receive, that love, which was the fulfilling of the Law, directed the sanctified to share this gift, and that the societies' activities were the best ways to help sinners. Believing that most of the people in the United States were living in original and actual sin and that many of them were not aware of it, the managers considered it their duty, as sanctified men, to make sinners realize their evil, to

[5] For typical expressions of the societies' theology and its practical workings, see American Tract Society, *Annual Report,* I (1826), 9-10; letter from Sunday School Union Secretary Frederick A. Packard in New York *Observer,* March 17, 1838; American Home Missionary Society, *Report* (New York), VIII (1834), 9-10; *Home Missionary* (New York), XXXI (May, 1858), 8-15; American Bible Society, *Annual Report* (New York), VIII (1824), 48.

[6] See Oliver Wendell Elsbree, "Samuel Hopkins and His Doctrine of Benevolence," *New England Quarterly* (Baltimore and Boston), VIII (December, 1935), 534-50, especially 540-42. Also Joseph Haroutunian, *Piety versus Moralism: The Passing of the New England Theology* (New York, 1932), 82-87.

persuade them to repent, and thus to help God's saving work. Benevolence was an infinite concern for other people's souls.[7]

These men who were vitally interested in their fellow citizens' salvation were heirs of more than a modified Calvinistic theology. Out of the colonial past came the concept, equally strong in political and social spheres, that the sanctified of God had the right and duty to govern. Nurtured by the Calvinistic theocrats, especially in New England, the idea had passed into the philosophy of Federalism which supplemented the heritage by adding to the elect of God the elect of men. Both Puritans and Federalists claimed that a minority of special attainments should supervise the majority. This assertion harmonized well with the concern which men of benevolence had for the souls of others, for the test of an individual's conversion from sin was his secular action. All of these ideas came together in the benevolent societies. Their leaders, at first Federalists and afterward those who continued the Federalist traditions, asserted the right not only to guide men along God's narrow path, but also to direct proper political and social conduct.

The effort to mold a nation attracted both laity and clergy. Ministerial representation was considerable and, as befitted religious societies, ministers frequently expressed the aims of the organizations. But most of the more than five hundred officers who served in the period from the organization of the societies until 1861 were laymen. All of the lay officers were of rising social and economic station. The industrialists Anson G. Phelps and William E. Dodge of the Bible Society; the merchants Moses Allen of the Tract Society, John Tappan of the Education Society, and Christopher R. Robert of the Home Missionary Society; the bankers Samuel Ward of the Bible Society and Benjamin B. Comegys of the Sunday School Union; the financier Jay Cooke, also of the

[7] Expressions of benevolence were numerous. For examples, see *Proceedings of a Meeting of the Citizens of New-York and Others, Convened in the City-Hall on the 13th of May, 1816, at the Request of the Board of Managers of the American Bible Society; with the Speeches of George Griffin and Peter A. Jay, Esqrs. Delivered on the Occasion* (New York, 1816), 9-15; American Home Missionary Society, *Report,* VIII (1834), 9-10; American Sunday School Union, *Annual Report,* X (1834), 24-26; American Tract Society, *Annual Report,* XX (1845), 133-35; American Education Society, *Annual Report,* XVII (1833), 26, 65. These five societies had no monopoly on the idea of benevolence. Gilbert H. Barnes, *The Antislavery Impulse, 1830-1844* (New York, 1933), 17-28, correctly stresses that the spirit of benevolence pervaded many other groups, including temperance, peace, and antislavery societies. Only those organizations whose main activity was to evangelize the country are being discussed here.

Sunday School Union; and the lawyers Charles Butler of the Home Missionary Society and Samuel A. Foot of the Bible Society were the type of men who felt themselves best qualified to guide others.

In selecting their presidents, the societies' managers reflected their own political, social, and economic position. As Federalism, with its desired rule by men of wealth, station, and ability, died, members of the party perpetuated their ideas in the benevolent groups. The Bible Society, for example, chose as presidents such staunch Federalists as the wealthy Elias Boudinot of New Jersey, the New York City lawyer Richard Varick, and former United States Supreme Court Chief Justice John Jay.[8] From 1832 until 1845 John Cotton Smith, an equally steadfast Federalist, headed the society. A loyal party member and former governor of Connecticut, Smith had supported the Hartford Convention of 1814, that ill-fated protest to "Mr. Madison's War," and had just as vigorously opposed the disestablishment of the Congregational church in his state.[9] Although Alexander Henry, first president of the Sunday School Union, tried to keep out of politics, his conservative views and his merchant's fortune made him the choice of the managers. Federalists in other groups were Home Missionary Society president Stephen Van Rensselaer, "The Patroon"; the Boston merchant William Phillips and the Boston lawyer Samuel Hubbard of the Education Society; and the merchant and international financier Sampson Vryling Stoddard Wilder, first president of the Tract Society.[10]

When these men died, long after the expiration of Federalism, the managers turned to those who continued the tradition of the direction of society and government by men thought particularly qualified to lead. Theodore Frelinghuysen, Whig politician and

[8] For Boudinot's biography, see George Adams Boyd, *Elias Boudinot, Patriot and Statesman, 1740-1821* (Princeton, 1952); on Varick, see Dixon Ryan Fox, *The Decline of Aristocracy in the Politics of New York* (New York, 1919), 15-16; for Jay's biography, Frank Monaghan, *John Jay* (New York, 1935).

[9] Richard J. Purcell, *Connecticut in Transition, 1775-1818* (Washington, 1918), 291-95, 332-72.

[10] On Henry, see S. Austin Allibone, "Alexander Henry," in Henry Simpson, *The Lives of Eminent Philadelphians* (Philadelphia, 1859), 515-21; on Van Rensselaer, see Fox, *Decline of Aristocracy in the Politics of New York*, 4-5, 32-33, 229-37; on Phillips, see Hamilton A. Hill, *William Phillips and William Phillips, Father and Son, 1722-1827* (reprint from the *New England Historical and Genealogical Register*, April, 1885); for Hubbard's Federalism, see Arthur B. Darling, *Political Changes in Massachusetts, 1824-1848* (New Haven, 1925), 47-48; for Wilder, see *Records from the Life of S. V. S. Wilder* (New York, 1865).

later president of Rutgers College, served from 1842 to 1848 as president of the Tract Society and from 1846 to 1862 as head of the Bible Society.[11] Thomas S. Williams, who followed Frelinghuysen in the Tract Society, was former chief justice of Connecticut. United States Supreme Court Justice and Sunday School Union president John McLean passed through a political spectrum as Democrat, Whig, Know-Nothing, and Republican — whatever allegiance seemed to increase his chances for the national presidency. Through all of these shifts, however, McLean maintained his firm belief that morality and religion were the only bases for proper government. In 1846 he claimed that the country had been declining in moral virtue since the administration of President James Monroe.[12] In the Home Missionary Society, Henry Dwight, wealthy upstate New York banker, followed Stephen Van Rensselaer; Dwight was succeeded by Aristarchus Champion, reputed to be the richest man in Rochester. The third president of the Education Society was Samuel T. Armstrong, a prosperous Boston publisher and a Whig governor of Massachusetts.[13] Before 1861 only two clergymen led the societies: Theodore Dwight Woolsey, president of Yale College and the Home Missionary Society, and Heman Humphrey, president of the Education Society and Amherst College.[14] But clerical or lay, the managers saw in the benevolent groups a hopeful means of keeping society godly and orderly, stable and quiet.

[11] See Talbot W. Chambers, *Memoir of the Life and Character of the Late Hon. Theo. Frelinghuysen* (New York, 1863).

[12] On Williams, see *Congregational Quarterly* (Boston), V (January, 1863), 1-19; for McLean, Francis P. Weisenburger, *The Life of John McLean: A Politician on the United States Supreme Court* (Columbus, Ohio, 1937). See also John McLean to Mr. Harvey, May 1, 1846; McLean to Charles Behne, December 26, 1846, John McLean Papers (Division of Manuscripts, Library of Congress).

[13] For Dwight, see Charles F. Millikin, *A History of Ontario County, New York, and Its People* (2 vols., New York, 1911), I, 360-61; George S. Conover (ed.) and Lewis C. Aldrich (comp.), *History of Ontario County, New York, with Illustrations and Family Sketches of Some of the Prominent Men and Families* (Syracuse, 1893), 278-79; [W. H. McIntosh], *History of Ontario Co., New York* (Philadelphia, 1876), 57. On Champion, see Blake McKelvey, *Rochester, the Flower City, 1855-1890* (Cambridge, 1949), 19-20, 34, 43, 145; Edward R. Foreman (comp. and ed.), *Centennial History of Rochester* (4 vols., Rochester, 1931-1934), I, 177. On Armstrong, see Darling, *Political Changes in Massachusetts*, 190-97.

[14] For Woolsey's life, see Timothy Dwight, *Theodore Dwight Woolsey, D.D. LL.D.: Memorial Address before the Graduates of Yale University, June 24, 1890* (New Haven, 1890); George P. Fisher, "The Academic Career of Ex-President Woolsey," *Century Magazine* (New York), XXIV (September, 1882), 709-17. Brief notice of Heman Humphrey is in American Tract Society, *Annual Report*, XXXVI (1861), 14-15.

The rise of Andrew Jackson's popularity coincided with the founding and early years of all the societies. Thus at their start the managers and their supporters faced first a man and then an administration characterized, as they thought, by everything wrong in the politics of the period. With the success of the Jacksonians and the general continuance of the Democratic party in power after 1829, benevolent men began to deplore unchristian politics and to claim that the perpetuity of the republic depended on the maintenance of evangelical Christianity in the land.

Jackson's popularity after the War of 1812 and his electioneering between 1824 and 1828 made the managers apprehensive even before he took office. In the early fall of 1824 the Reverend Benjamin H. Rice took a quick look at Old Hickory and told the Education Society that the country needed religious guidance. Without it, said Rice, the people would soon become the "slaves of a military despotism." [15] After Jackson's inauguration and the startling presidential reception, many good men trembled. Addressing the Home Missionary Society in May, 1829, the Reverend Jacob Van Vechten claimed that only despotism could rule a people who had forgotten the fear of God. If, as seemed possible, "an excited populace of irreligious men" ruled the country, the nation could not last. In a vivid verbal picture, Van Vechten predicted that in such circumstances laws would be ineffective, justice lacking, churches demolished, thefts and murders rampant, and streets drenched with blood.[16]

As Jackson's terms continued, managers raged and despaired. By 1832 Bible Society secretary John Pintard, a lifelong Federalist, had had three years too many of the General and hoped for his defeat in the coming election. "My very soul," said Pintard, "sickens at the name of Jackson." [17] In 1837 William M. Evarts, then a youth of nineteen but later a prominent Republican and a Bible Society manager, thought that the Jacksonians continued the "Jeffersonian dominion" in politics. Mercenary government officials, a growing party spirit, and the type of men who supported

[15] American Education Society, *Annual Report,* IX (1824), 28-29.

[16] *Home Missionary,* II (June, 1829), 20-21.

[17] John Pintard to Elizabeth Davidson, February 23, 1832, in Dorothy C. Barck (ed.), *Letters from John Pintard to His Daughter, Eliza Noel Pintard Davidson, 1816-1833* (4 vols., New York, 1940-1941), IV, 19.

the Democrats, Evarts lamented, made impossible the election of any man of "talent and great eminence" to the presidency.[18]

Understandably, the most important society leader, Theodore Frelinghuysen, was an outstanding opponent of Jackson. Tall, rugged, bewhiskered, and impressive in appearance, Frelinghuysen was a resolute opponent of new social and political trends. A devoutly religious Presbyterian, but later a member of the Reverend Thomas De Witt's Dutch Collegiate Church in New York City, he served as a vice-president of the Education and Home Missionary societies and the Sunday School Union, and as president of the Bible and Tract societies. From 1829 to 1835 he was a United States senator from New Jersey; and as the Whig vice- presidential candidate in 1844 he undertook to join his Christian talents with the political ability of Henry Clay in the hope of gaining a victory for conservatism.[19] When the Whig ticket met defeat he sought to console Clay with religion. "Vain is the help of man," he wrote, "and frail and fatal all that trust in the arm of flesh." If Clay would seek solace in the Gospel and would trust in the Lord, he would be like "Mount Zion itself, that can never be removed." [20]

Frelinghuysen opposed both Jacksonian philosophy and the policies of the Jackson administration. In the midst of the attack on the United States Bank, he vigorously defended the bank's president, Nicholas Biddle.[21] In discussing the reasons for Jackson's popularity and warning good citizens against the Democrats, Frelinghuysen claimed that Americans had become too proud of their country and their liberties. Speaking in 1835 before the annual meeting of the Sunday School Union, he declared that this pride had resulted in a spirit of independence almost too strong for law. The words "resistance," "liberty," "independence," and "the rights of man" had become so familiar that Americans were likely to forget that these terms, with "the glow of patriotism" and "the love of country," became, without sound principles, the "mere watchwords for licentiousness and all misrule." [22]

The managers knew that from the religiously destitute West

[18] Chester L. Barrows, *William M. Evarts: Lawyer, Diplomat, Statesman* (Chapel Hill, 1941), 12-13.

[19] See Chambers, *Memoir of the Life of Frelinghuysen, passim.*

[20] Theodore Frelinghuysen to Henry Clay, November 9, 1844, *ibid.*, 178.

[21] Arthur M. Schlesinger, Jr., *The Age of Jackson* (Boston, 1945), 114.

[22] American Sunday School Union, *Annual Report*, XI (1835), 9.

had come much of Jackson's support. As the West grew, the prospect of seeing the control of Congress by the Mississippi Valley, within their lifetimes, alarmed them. In 1826 the Bible Society's managers printed with concern part of a report of the Young Men's Bible Society of Baltimore. Areas formerly wilderness, the report said, were now states. Westward migration was swelling and soon these new states would have a population and resources equal to or greater than the Atlantic commonwealths. Political power was passing across the Appalachian Range.[23] Two years later the Education Society predicted that by 1850 the West would have a majority in Congress.[24] Agreeing, the Home Missionary Society frequently printed statistics to show how fast the western states were gaining in relative political power.[25] Summing up the situation, William H. Bulkley, president of the Young Men's Tract Society of Louisville, Kentucky, told the national managers that the political voice of the West would speak out to the nation in "*thunder tones*." [26] By spreading the news of God's mercy and supplying the means of conversion, benevolent men hoped to bring others to Christ and at the same time allay fears of how the growing West would vote.

A combination of reports from the West and their own imaginations gave eastern managers a low opinion of most westerners. In 1831 the Bible Society was told by one of its agents that the "lower classes" from several southern states and Ohio had occupied a large part of Indiana and that many of these people had left "civilized & religious society for the simple purpose of getting out of its restraints." [27] The Reverend John Spaulding of Cincinnati told the Education Society that prejudice, fanaticism, or political ambition easily controlled the western mind: "Its rush is like that of the ocean wave." [28] Similarly warning the Tract Society, the

[23] American Bible Society, *Annual Report*, X (1826), 89-90.

[24] *Quarterly Register and Journal of the American Education Society* (Andover and Boston), I (April, 1828), 61-65.

[25] See *Home Missionary*, XIV (April, 1842), 277-78, and XXIV (July, 1851), 57-58; American Home Missionary Society, *Report*, XXI (1847), 107.

[26] *Proceedings of a Public Deliberative Meeting of the Board and Friends of the American Tract Society, Held in the Broadway Tabernacle, New-York, October 25, 26, and 27, 1842; together with the Documents Presented, and the Sermon Preached on that Occasion* (New York, 1843), 119. For the views of the Sunday School Union, see American Sunday School Union, *Annual Report*, XXIV (1848), 52-55.

[27] M. Fairchild to John C. Brigham, May 20, 1831, American Bible Society Papers.

[28] American Education Society, *Annual Report*, XIX (1835), 61-62.

Reverend John M. Stevenson said that in crossing the mountains easterners often changed character. They lost their culture, polish, and rectitude. Their enjoyments became coarse and their "*passions* violent and barbaric." Law and civil order vanished, he said, and in their places lynch law and border ruffianism reigned.[29]

Easterners responded warmly to such descriptions. In 1830 Theodore Frelinghuysen, deeply worried, told the managers of the Sunday School Union that the West was in danger of losing its public and private virtue and that there was grave danger that this people, "but yesterday born into political existence," would exhibit a "universal degeneracy of manners." With murders, corruption, and disobedience of the laws prevalent, Frelinghuysen said, the only means of checking violence was the "reformation of public sentiment" through religion.[30] Alarmed by this description and by what the Reverend James W. Alexander called the "growing but unformed, chaotic, tumultuating society" in the country,[31] the Union urged the extension of its work. Future judges, senators, and statesmen were now children in the West, said the managers, and should receive proper training in their youth.[32] In 1845 the Home Missionary Society fearfully asserted that without evangelical Protestantism the country's future was dark indeed. Among other evils, "the state will be the synonym of anarchy — Law the refuge and charter of violence — Justice the incarnation of partiality and revenge. Then stations of power will be the prizes of an ambition instinct with outrage and crime." [33]

Although western voting strength disturbed the societies most, their solution for making the Mississippi Valley safe for good government applied to the entire nation. If the voters could be converted to Christ, they would presumably elect to office religious men who would govern wisely. If the rule of the country by the rich, the well-born, and the able was ended, at least the United States might have the government of the moral, the virtuous, and the sanctified.

29 American Tract Society, *Annual Report,* XXXI (1856), 181-82. For typical reports to the Home Missionary Society, see Heman S. Colton (Putnam County, Illinois) to Absalom Peters, October 15, 1836; N. T. Fay (Wood County, Ohio) to Milton Badger, June 7, 1852, American Home Missionary Society Papers.

30 *American Sunday-School Magazine* (Philadelphia), VII (August, 1830), 249-51.

31 James W. Alexander to Frederick A. Packard, December 18, 1840, Samuel C. Perkins Papers (Historical Society of Pennsylvania).

32 American Sunday School Union, *Annual Report,* XXII (1846), 22-23.

33 American Home Missionary Society, *Report,* XIX (1845), 119-20.

In 1827 the Reverend John J. Aikin argued before a Utica, New York, Sunday school convention that great political benefits would be conferred on the country by the establishment of Sunday schools among the poor. "Does not the vote of a poor man at your polls count as much as the vote of a rich man?" Aikin asked. "Is not his example in the sphere in which he moves, whether good or bad, contagious and influential? Dismiss, then, your Sunday-schools; withhold from this interesting and important class of citizens religious instruction — and in vain will you try to fill your halls of legislation with honest and intelligent men." The reins of government would be in the hands of an "unprincipled mob, who care neither for law nor religion." [34] The Education Society claimed that immorality in the electorate begot immorality in officialdom, but that religiously enlightened people elected religiously enlightened rulers.[35] In the middle of Andrew Jackson's second term the Reverend Absalom Peters, secretary of the Home Missionary Society, asserted that amid political fights and financial embarrassments the only safety was in religion: "This alone can restore the conscience of the nation & give efficacy even to human laws." [36]

Managers often contended that the very existence of the republic depended on evangelical Protestantism. In 1843 the Tract Society's executive committee surveyed the country and concluded that the United States had reached the critical point in the experiment of popular government. American liberties had produced national evils. Freedom of the press had degenerated to "unbridled licentiousness and blind partizanship"; freedom of immigration and an easily obtained franchise for foreigners had brought millions of voters who were ignorant of American institutions and laws; freedom of conscience had aided the "spiritual despotism" of Catholicism. According to the Tract Society committee, the remedy for all these ills was not political action but the evangelization of the whole people. Only when there was "absolute dependence on the spirit of God" would the country be safe.[37]

Other societies and their managers agreed. They made the Reformation responsible for America's civil liberty,[38] asserted that with-

[34] *American Sunday-School Magazine*, IV (August, 1827), 243.

[35] American Education Society, *Annual Report*, X (1826), 11.

[36] Absalom Peters to Richard S. Storrs, March 7, 1834 (copy), American Home Missionary Society Papers.

[37] American Tract Society, *Annual Report*, XVIII (1843), 24-26.

[38] John B. Romeyn, *Sermons* (2 vols., New York, 1816), I, 53-54.

out the Gospel the body politic would sicken and decline,[39] and stressed as axiomatic the idea that "moral power" — which the societies promoted — was the only true foundation for a free government.[40] Even after the Whig victory in the election of 1840 many managers were apprehensive. In 1841 the Home Missionary Society warned that still the only hope of the country was in religion.[41] Referring first to the symbolic log cabin used by the Whigs in the election and then to western churches built of logs, the Reverend Leonard Bacon declared that the latter were the "*only log cabins that can save the nation!*" [42]

The millions of immigrants who came to America before the Civil War intensified political problems. Although they looked upon all immigrants as potentially troublesome, the managers considered the Catholics especially dangerous. Opposing them on religious grounds, the societies also feared that the "Romanists" eventually might either control the entire country through the polls or form an alliance with the ungodly and thus make good government impossible. The Reverend Gardiner Spring, well-known Presbyterian divine and for several years a manager of the Bible, Tract, and Education societies, said that Catholics joyfully seized all the civil rights Americans provided, but used these rights only as representatives of the Holy See. Spring claimed that Catholics held the balance of power between American political parties and that in using the franchise these foreigners might decide almost every question on their own terms. In his view, only the Pope would benefit.[43] To other managers, also, Catholicism was anathema; it was a religion essentially opposed to all American civil institutions.[44]

While thousands of Catholics settled in eastern cities, other thousands went to the politically influential Mississippi Valley.

39 American Education Society, *Annual Report*, XIX (1835), 37-38.

40 John McLean to the Board of Officers and Managers of the American Sunday School Union, April 10, 1849, American Sunday School Union, *Annual Report*, XXV (1849), 5-8.

41 American Home Missionary Society, *Report*, XV (1841), 86-88.

42 *Ibid.*, 102-103.

43 Gardiner Spring, *The Danger and Hope of the American People: A Discourse on the Day of the Annual Thanksgiving, in the State of New-York* (New York, 1843), 21-29

44 *Quarterly Register and Journal of the American Education Society*, V (May, 1833), 339. Also Jesse Mann to John McLean, February 10, 1845; McLean to Mann, February 14, 1845; McLean to Robert A. Parrish, March 3, 1855, McLean Papers.

Accounts of their voting strength were alarming. In Ohio, said a report, to curry favor with Catholic voters would-be politicians opposed the Bible, Tract, and Home Missionary societies and thus threatened to leave the people in darkness, a prey alike to demagogues and priests.[45] The Reverend S. E. Miner reported from Madison, Wisconsin, in 1845 that Catholics were steadily becoming more influential and that already they had "crouching whining politicians" as servants.[46] In 1852 the Reverend George Sheldon, Bible Society agent in Indiana, advised the national managers to urge upon both Whig and Democratic nominees for school superintendent the use of the Bible in common schools. But Sheldon thought that with their Catholic allies the Democrats, who did not favor the Bible in schools, would win. Democrats, Sheldon averred, did obeisance to "Romanists and Infidels. . . . The Romanists with the infidelity they carry with them, have the balance of power between democracy and Whigery [*sic*]." [47] The Tract Society, by 1845, thought that the Irish alone constituted a serious threat to American institutions. Estimating their number at between 750,000 and 1,000,000, the managers saw Hibernians everywhere: "crowding our cities, lining our railroads and canals . . . and *electing our rulers*." [48]

While the societies were worrying about the political effects of western growth, they feared also the effect of social change in the East as well as in the West. Society managers trembled at the prospect of an unpacified urban population. In the jammed tenements and narrow streets of Atlantic coastal cities were crowded thousands of low-income workers and poor whom they held responsible for vice and crime, mobs and riots. Easterners had only to walk the streets of Boston, New York, and Philadelphia, or read their newspapers, the managers said, to learn of social unrest along the seaboard. Sunday School Union manager Joseph H. Dulles of Philadelphia looked at the rapidly growing ranks of youths between sixteen and twenty who were rioting in the cities and feared the "growing spirit of libertinism destructive of good order in

[45] S. Buck to Absalom Peters, March 18, 1830, American Home Missionary Society Papers.

[46] S. E. Miner to Milton Badger, March 4, 1845, *ibid.*

[47] George Sheldon to "Dear Brethren," March 10, 1852, American Bible Society Papers.

[48] *General View of Colportage as Conducted by the American Tract Society in the United States, May, 1845* (New York, n.d.), 44-46.

Society & good morals in individuals" which he saw.[49] The Reverend Charles Hall, secretary of the Home Missionary Society, woefully noted that men seemed to "rejoice in casting off restraints & unsettling the foundations of social order."[50] Concerned over the recent riots in Philadelphia and the Dorr Rebellion in Rhode Island, the editors of the Presbyterian New York *Observer*, which had great influence among benevolent men, said in 1844 that such actions were a disgrace to the republic.[51] Maintaining his original Federalist views in 1836, Frederick A. Packard, secretary of the Sunday School Union, was just as irate when he condemned a variety of evils: riotous assemblies, mobs, trade unions, and strikes.[52]

In evangelical Christianity the managers saw a way to stop violence and disorder. Without religion among the people, said Packard, "law and lawful authority are trampled upon," and "riots and tumults" encouraged.[53] By 1843 the Reverend Gardiner Spring was convinced that the American trait of insubordination was increasing in vigor. The characteristics of the age were fearful: "resistance to lawful authority," "clamor about the rights of man," "tumultuous conventions," "arraignment and abuse of the courts of justice," "the bold assumption of the power of the law by an infuriated mob." A free government and the "absurd doctrine of liberty and equality" were responsible for such evils. God and Protestantism, according to Spring, were the only hopes of the American people.[54] President John Cotton Smith of the Bible Society thought that the distribution and reading of the Scriptures would go far toward keeping social peace.[55] The Education Society's managers firmly asserted that religion and religious institutions were sources of quiet in society and proclaimed that ministers should "exercise over the multitude . . . that power which is always the prerogative of superior attainments."[56]

Allied with mobs and riots was crime. In 1841 the Home Missionary Society feared and deplored the great increase in the number

[49] Joseph H. Dulles to Frederick A. Packard, August 20, 1835, Perkins Papers.

[50] Charles Hall to Jepthah Pool, May 20, 1835 (copy), American Home Missionary Society Papers.

[51] New York *Observer*, July 20, 1844.

[52] [Frederick A. Packard], *Thoughts on the Condition and Prospects of Popular Education in the United States* (Philadelphia, 1836), 36.

[53] *Ibid.*, 27-32.

[54] Spring, *Danger and Hope of the American People*, 15-21 and *passim.*

[55] American Bible Society, *Annual Report*, XVI (1832), 98.

[56] American Education Society, *Annual Report*, IX (1824), 6.

of frauds, robberies, and murders. Although the laws forbade killing, said the managers, no statute ever reached the human heart. Only the precepts of religion could establish social tranquillity and "protect our persons from violence."[57] The Sunday School Union, claimed its leaders, did much more than bring children to Christ. Religious training was an excellent way of keeping youths out of the ranks of crime and of bringing them into society as useful, worthy citizens.[58] From the West came similar reports. In December, 1852, Z. M. Humphrey, secretary of the Racine County, Wisconsin, Bible Society, reported that his organization encouraged social order. The Bible was a guard over property and life, he said, for it had the same effect in rural areas that a police force had in cities in keeping down riots and crime.[59]

Often including city immigrants with the poor, the societies ascribed to them a large part of these social sins. In an analysis in 1857 the Bible Society's managers said that poverty was in general the result of ignorance, vicious indulgences, or indolence. The poor forgot the moral virtues in a haste to be rich; they spent their money foolishly on worthless amusements; many of them had an aversion to honest work. Gripped by these evils, the city poor were "congregated in filth and bound together by the horrid ties of vicious and beastly appetities. In their sensual sty the man is transformed into the brute." There was no crime too base for these poor: "Amid these orgies, crimes against society are plotted, and the most savage passions stimulated to action."[60] Viewing the immigrant horde of almost 5,500 foreigners who arrived in New York City on April 21, 1854, the Sunday School Union thought that among these new arrivals were at least 100 whose ideas made them "implacable foes to the best interests of society, if not to its peace and safety," and probably 1,000 private or public paupers.[61]

57 *Home Missionary*, XIII (February, 1841), 217-18.

58 American Sunday School Union, *Annual Report*, I (1825), 15-16.

59 Annual Report of the Secretary [Z. M. Humphrey] of the Racine County Bible Society, December 12, 1852, American Bible Society Papers.

60 *Bible Society Record* (New York), II (September, 1857), 137-38.

61 American Sunday School Union, *Annual Report*, XXX (1854), 10-11. For other analyses of the poor, see American Sunday School Union, *Annual Report*, XXXII (1856), 32-33; American Home Missionary Society, *Report*, XXXI (1857), 110-14; James Milnor, *Address Delivered before the Superintendents, Teachers, and Pupils, of the Sunday Schools Attached to St. George's Church, in the City of New-York; on the Occasion of Their Entering into the Occupation of the Apartments Prepared for Their Accommodation by the Vestry of Said Church, on Sunday, November 9, 1817* (New York, 1817), 6-13; New York *Observer*, July 20, 1844.

The Bible Society's managers saw great social value in the Scriptures. They would show the poor their rights and duties and develop in them "whatsoever is honest, and pure, and of good report." The Bible tended to check the "rampant propensities to low and vicious indulgence" and to "enthrone reason and conscience over the depraved appetities of carnality." Further, it required and supplied motives for honest toil.[62] The Reverend Franklin Y. Vail, city agent of the Tract Society, urged rich men to aid in bringing religion to the common people. Christianity would help to "bridge over the dangerous chasm between the rich and the poor; so that instead of . . . mobs and outbreaks destroying . . . life and property, there will be between these two great classes a reciprocation of confidence and good feeling, as there will be also a ready recognition of their mutual dependence, their harmonious interests, and their immortal brotherhood."[63]

To keep the poor pacified, managers had a ready philosophy. There was nothing wrong with being poverty-stricken, the Sunday School Union told its children:

And if we had riches, they could not procure
 A happy and peaceable mind;
Rich people have troubles as well as the poor,
 Although of a different kind.

. . . .

It signifies not what our stations have been,
 Nor whether we're little or great;
For happiness lies in the temper within,
 And not in the outward estate.[64]

At the annual meeting of the Education Society in 1851 the Reverend Andrew L. Stone extolled the Christian poor and claimed that they had many advantages. Poverty produced piety, humility, and the spirit of self-sacrifice; it made people vigorous, hardy, and rugged, familiar with struggling, and inured to difficulty. For these reasons, Stone said, the best type of minister came from the poorer classes.[65] In a similar but less complimentary vein the Rev-

[62] *Bible Society Record,* II (September, 1857), 137-38.

[63] *Importance and Increasing Liberality of Our American Cities: Annual Report of Rev. F. Y. Vail, General Agent of the American Tract Society for Cities, Etc.* (New York, 1857), 11.

[64] *The Union Spelling Book: Prepared for the American Sunday-School Union, and Revised by the Committee of Publication* (Philadelphia, 1838), 1858 ed., 104-105.

[65] American Education Society, *Annual Report,* XXXV (1851), 44-48.

erend James Drummond told the Home Missionary Society that a man's worldly possessions showed his inherent energies. Those who succeeded in their earthly life had trod the right path; thus those who did not deserve to be rich remained poor.[66]

The social philosophy of the managers provided means for the poor either to bear with their poverty or to improve their condition. Although it was benevolent to help the poor in material ways, said the directors of the Worcester County, Massachusetts, Bible Society, the Scriptures would help prevent extreme poverty, aid the poor in wisely enduring their lot, or enable them to rise to a new social rank.[67] While the precepts of God would neither banish poverty nor end economic inequalities, the Gospel would bring "timely and grateful relief" to the poor and make the different classes more conscious of their mutual dependence.[68] The Tract Society told poor children that the only way to the top of any profession was to start at the bottom, work up step by step and not try to rise too fast, and maintain a Christian character.[69]

If hard work and faith in God were the only ways that people had to improve their condition, other means were wrong. Reports of socialistic communities and Fourierist societies caused great alarm. Managers heatedly condemned as godless all non-religious plans for saving society by changing its general structure. By supporting the Bible Society, said L. Q. C. Elmer, president of a New Jersey auxiliary, good citizens were protesting against "all that heartless deism, revolting socialism, blasphemous pantheism, and withering skepticism" which were the basis of those social reforms.[70] Socialism, Fourierism, and similar ideas were considered anti-Christian and obviously against God's social plans.[71] After receiving a report of socialistic communities in northern Indiana, the Home Missionary Society's managers said that no area needed "the conservative influence of an enlightened ministry" as much as the Mississippi Valley.[72] A speaker before the Tract Society asserted

66 American Home Missionary Society, *Report*, XXXI (1857), 110-14.

67 Report of Directors of Worcester County Bible Society for 1857 (MS. signed by Secretary George P. Smith), American Bible Society Papers.

68 American Sunday School Union, *Annual Report*, XXVIII (1852), 55-56.

69 *Child's Paper* (New York), March, 1861, p. 12.

70 *Bible Society Record*, IV (July, 1859), 97.

71 American Education Society, *Annual Report*, XXX (1846), 45.

72 *Home Missionary*, XVI (August, 1843), 87-88. The report was from the Reverend Christopher Coy to Milton Badger and Charles Hall, June 13, 1843, American Home Missionary Society Papers.

that in their publications the managers had erected barriers against "Popery and Rationalism and Socialism, and every other wild ism and vile ism." [73]

Benevolent men claimed that these schemes were radical and unchristian because they tried to reform society without first changing individuals. It was the original and actual sins of men, said the managers, that produced evils in society, rather than the reverse. God had set forth social principles; men had corrupted them. In 1849, noting an increasing popularity of plans to reform the whole of society at once, the Sunday School Union called these ideas ridiculous and the people who held them misguided and irreligious. The managers would reverse the principle: "Instead of making the invisible, intangible and irresponsible composition which we call SOCIETY the scape-goat for the sins and sufferings of the visible, tangible and responsible individuals who compose it . . . we should . . . hold the individuals to answer for the burdens and griefs of society." [74]

In the West were problems of more immediate concern to the benevolent societies than communal or socialistic villages. The failure of westerners to pay their debts brought losses to eastern creditors. By bringing religion to the Mississippi Valley, the managers hoped to insure economic stability and protect eastern investments. The Home Missionary Society was particularly interested in this problem. During the depression following the Panic of 1837 and at other times, the leaders remarked, western debtors had defrauded many eastern businessmen. By establishing a Christian sense of right in every man, the society would help to decrease in number or abolish these frauds: "Far better," agreed the managers with a missionary, "for the merchant to give his money, not to say his prayers, to make people good, where he intrusts millions of property, than to spend it upon bailiffs, to apprehend his runaway creditors, or to collect his debts among a dissolute people, without

[73] The speaker was the Reverend Alexander Duff. See American Tract Society, *Annual Report*, XXIX (1854), 4, 9. For the views of the Sunday School Union, see American Sunday School Union, *Annual Report*, XXV (1849), 56-57.

[74] American Sunday School Union, *Annual Report*, XXV (1849), 25-29. See also American Education Society, *Annual Report*, XXX (1846), 45-46; William G. T. Shedd, *The Education of a Ministry, the Proper Work and Care of the Churches: A Discourse, Delivered before the American Education Society, May 28, 1855* (Boston, 1855), 17-21; *Home Missionary*, XX (February, 1848), 236-38.

either responsibility or principle. *The Gospel is the most economical police on earth.*"[75]

When the effects of the Panic of 1837 and overextended borrowing caused many western states to repudiate their debts, lay managers called this action fraudulent and enlisted ministers in the cause. Charles Butler, lawyer and manager of the Home Missionary Society, went west to Michigan and Indiana to represent the claims of bondholders.[76] Back in the East men fumed against repudiation. The Reverend William R. Williams, a Tract Society manager, damned state legislatures for "repudiating their plighted word and bond. In the matter of good faith between man and man, as to pecuniary engagements, the wheels of the social machine groan ominously, as if they were . . . ready to tear asunder the fabric of society."[77] From his pulpit the Reverend Gardiner Spring condemned repudiation. Had the forefathers of America been told that such a thing would happen, Spring said, they would have blushed with shame at "this horrid disgrace of their apostate descendants." Evangelical Protestantism and more abundant Christian literature were regarded as safeguards against such financial sinning.[78]

Proper Christianity would also promote general economic stability. The Madison, Indiana, Bible Society, acting on the belief that where people read their Bibles good business conditions existed, argued that to get men of wealth and principle into Indiana the state must first have plenty of Bibles.[79] "Intelligent capitalists," asserted the Reverend Daniel P. Noyes, Home Missionary Society secretary, knew that as essential to the growth of a new town as stores, buildings, and a dam were a church and minister. Moreover, religous institutions were cheaper.[80] In giving money for the propagation of Sunday schools, said the Union's managers, businessmen added to the security and profits of all their other investments.[81]

[75] *Home Missionary*, XI (January, 1839), 209-10; XII (May, 1839), 9-10; XXVII (January, 1855), 212-13. See also American Sunday School Union, *Annual Report*, XXIX (1853), 36-37.

[76] Francis H. Stoddard, *The Life and Letters of Charles Butler* (New York, 1903), 182-206, 222-78.

[77] William R. Williams, *Miscellanies* (New York, 1850), 16-19, 35 ff.

[78] Spring, *Danger and Hope of the American People*, 12-14 and *passim*.

[79] American Bible Society, *Annual Report*, VI (1822), 127-29.

[80] Daniel P. Noyes to Ezra Newton, April 11, 1860 (copy), American Home Missionary Society Papers.

[81] American Sunday School Union, *Annual Report*, XXIX (1853), 36-37.

In May, 1847, Emory Washburn, prominent Massachusetts lawyer and later Bay State governor, spoke on the importance of the Bible Society to the preservation of good order in society. Every day, said Washburn, he saw new social schemes proposed, mobs trampling upon private rights and setting laws aside, and states repudiating their debts. New principles and new ideas contrary to all Christian truth were destroying the whole social structure. The only protection was the Bible. Far better than "every measure of secret espionage to which a Napoleon or a Nicholas may resort," he said, the Bible was a "moral police." If their spirit spread through every family and every school in the country, the Scriptures would cure America's social ills and insure a stable society.[82]

If they were to change the ungodly poor into the Christian poor and make debtors pay by Christian means, these wealthy managers needed a rationale for their high economic position. If they could show that rich Christians had a right to their wealth, they reasoned that there would be no demand from the poor and debtor classes for a share of that wealth. Christians would certainly not rise against Christians; the poor would not desire the rich man's gold. Individuals might choose to feed the hungry, clothe the naked, and provide almshouses, hospitals, and asylums, said the Sunday School Union, but it was obviously no part of God's social plan that a common fund should exist to which the wealthy should contribute and from which the poor should draw.[83] In trying to protect their property from verbal and physical assaults by the poor, the managers stressed the idea of the stewardship of wealth: that every man held what he had in trust from God and thus should always be willing to give some of this substance back to the Lord. Since the societies considered themselves God's agencies, a man could justify his wealth by turning over part of it to them.

In May, 1850, preaching in behalf of the Tract Society, the Reverend Gardiner Spring argued that those who became rich by their own toil and economy had superior intellectual faculties and strength of character. Both they and those who inherited wealth had influence in the community because they deserved to have influence. They were men of "mind," "forethought," "great practical wisdom,"

[82] American Bible Society, *Annual Report*, XXXI (1847), 94-95

[83] American Sunday School Union, *Annual Report*, XXVII (1851), 50-52. See also *ibid.*, 50-53, 57-61.

"energy." With few exceptions, Spring claimed, they were men of integrity and moral virtue. In thus justifying the rich, however, Spring added the important qualification of stewardship. Since money had tremendous influence for either good or evil and since God desired only good, rich men should contribute to Christian causes. Money hoarded was "accursed"; money squandered bought only "shame and a grave"; money used to corrupt others spoke of the "pageantry of vice . . . of the miserable victims of sin and perdition." Wealth meant either selfishness or benevolence and Spring emphasized that only the latter was proper.[84] Similarly, Bradford Sumner told the Education Society that men should be "faithful stewards" of all they held. The greater the wealth, the greater was the accountability to God for its proper use.[85] There was nothing wrong in holding money, houses, and land, according to the stewardship doctrine of the Reverend Heman Humphrey, but rich men had a duty to give away some of their possessions. Although no one should make his sole goal in life the acquisition of property, he could rightfully seek it if he would yield up a part of it.[86]

In 1835 the Tract Society summed up the rules for a Christian merchant. The analysis was as important for what it omitted as for what it included. Stressed were such things as honesty, economy in expenses, accuracy in accounts, the moral and religious supervision of employees, and personal piety. But the managers made no mention of how far the merchant might expand his operations, what constituted a fair profit, and what constituted proper business ethics. Presumably, all these rules were overshadowed by the fourth: "I must pledge my purse, my time, and my influence, for the preservation of order, intelligence, morality and religion in the community." But the amount to be given was not stated; each merchant could salve his own conscience as he pleased.[87]

As they justified, warned, and chastised, as they asserted that a safe future for America lay only in men's obeying God, the Gospel, and the tenets of evangelical Protestantism, the managers were both transmitting and enlarging the heritage of their forebears. From the

84 Gardiner Spring, *Influence: A Quarter-Century Sermon, Preached in Behalf of the American Tract Society, in the Reformed Dutch Church, Lafayette Place, New York, May 5, 1850* (New York, 1850), 15-18.

85 American Education Society, *Annual Report*, IX (1824), 27-28.

86 *Home Missionary*, I (September, 1828), 73-76, and XII (April, 1840), 265-69.

87 The rules appeared in the New York *Observer*, November 14, 1835.

colonial theocrats and Federalism, benevolent men received and continued the idea that only a small number of men of particular attainments were qualified to shape, govern, and lead society. As the theocracies vanished and the growing electorate made impossible Federalism's continuance, the managers believed that religion propagated by the benevolent societies could be made an effective means of controlling a seemingly chaotic society. Their fundamental tenet was that they should dictate right conduct to their fellow citizens. In so believing, benevolent men bequeathed a lasting legacy. Many of the societies' leaders gave to the Republican party much of its often voiced morality. They and others tried to Americanize and mold the immigrant. They and their descendants discouraged dissent from their idealized economic, political, and social order. In their era the societies perpetuated the religio-political tradition in American history which claimed that only those men who met their standards were responsible for establishing the rule of the righteous and the jurisdiction of the just.

A Scheme in Regard to Cyrenaica

BY JAMES A. FIELD, JR.

On August 10, 1875, the summer calm of the State Department was shattered by an alarming cable from the American consul at Tripoli in Barbary: "My home violated by sailors of Ottoman Squadron. Am insulted, am threatened by a crowd. Denial of redress. Slave traffic cause of hostility. Immediate protection desirable." [1]

No time was lost in communicating with the Navy Department. Orders from the Secretary of the Navy to provide the desired protection were at once cabled to the commander of the European Squadron, Rear Admiral John L. Worden, at Southampton. The response of the hero of Hampton Roads was prompt and decisive. The *Congress*, then at Corfu, was ordered to proceed to Tripoli without delay; cables were sent to Port Said, Palermo, and Messina to intercept and divert the *Hartford*, then transiting the Suez Canal on her way home from the Asiatic Station; at Southampton, the *Alaska* and the *Juniata* were ordered to prepare to sail on short notice. By afternoon of August 11 the Admiral's reply was at hand — "*Congress* will be in Tripoli by 15th inst." — and was reported in the State Department's acknowledgment of the consul's cable, together with the hope that that functionary would sustain no "serious injury" and that further information as to the causes of the incident would be forthcoming.[2]

One week later a long despatch from Tripoli was received in Washington. Bearing date of June 22, it contained nothing con-

[1] Michel Vidal to Secretary of State Hamilton Fish, August 7, 1875, Despatches from U. S. Consuls in Tripoli, Records of the Department of State (National Archives).

[2] Admiral John L. Worden to Secretary of the Navy George M. Robeson, August 11 and August 18, 1875, Letters Received by Secretary of the Navy from Commander of European Squadron, Naval Records Collection of Office of Naval Records and Library (National Archives); Acting Secretary of State John L. Cadwalader to Vidal, August 11, 1875, Diplomatic Instructions, Barbary Powers (Tripoli), State Department Records.

cerning either the slave trade or difficulties at Tripoli but seemed at first sight a wordy and anecdotal discussion of the geography, history, and population of Marmarica, the little-known eastern part of the Regency. But the cover sheet of the despatch carried the instruction to the reader to "Use Grille X" for more than half of its forty-two pages. When this device, a paper with fifteen irregularly spaced holes which had been received from the consul some four months earlier, was placed over the pages of the message and the words which were thus made visible transcribed, a somewhat different impression resulted.[3]

> Since the Department [the despatch begins] did me the honor to inform me that my proposition to pave the way for the acquisition by the U. S. Government of a port for a coaling station on this African coast would be taken into serious consideration all my thoughts, energy, and doings were directed towards the furtherance of that patriotic scheme. My first object was to ascertain whether the inhabitants would prove for our Government as an insuperable obstacle to colonization by Christians as it was and is still the case in Algeria for the French [;] the second, whether adequate station could be found in this Regency [;] the third one whether our country would, in consequence of such an acquisition be involved in a war with the Ottoman or any other European government, fourthly, by what means we could bring about that acquisition, and, lastly what benefit the American people would derive from that colonization.

Having thus defined the problem, the consul went on to describe the potentialities of this isolated and almost unknown region. It was subject neither to Tripoli nor to Egypt. It contained two or three suitable ports. It was fertile, and samples of wheat would shortly be forwarded as evidence. The Bedouin were few in number, well-disposed, would welcome the protection of the American flag, and "would be but too happy the day they would see the Ottoman leeches leaving forever their vicinity." Acquisition of this desirable territory would cost but little and would benefit American trade.

Should the Department approve the project, its execution would prove simple. A first step would be to return the relations of the United States and Tripoli to the status ante pacem of 1805, which

[3] Vidal to Assistant Secretary of State William Hunter, March 20, 1875, enclosing the Grille, explained it as designed to permit the transmission of information "of a nature greatly to compromise my person, and possibly to defeat the ends of the Department's policy, should it come to the knowledge of other parties." Despatches, Tripoli, State Department Records.

could be easily accomplished by sending a frigate to visit the capital and to demand the first salute in accordance with Article XIII of the treaty of that year. This action would presumably provoke the Pasha to denounce the treaty, whereupon the same frigate might go from Tripoli "and visit Bombah, Tobrook and Bardiah in the Gulf of Solloon and should the report of the Captain be favorable in regard to the eligibility of the second port a handful of men would be a sufficient force to take possession of it, and keep it against all the Ottoman forces the Bashaw of Benghazy can actually dispose of."

Desirability being demonstrated and feasibility assured, there remained the question of possible complications with the Ottoman Empire, which had reasserted its sovereignty over Tripoli in 1835, or with European powers. The former problem the consul solved by developing a theory of Ottoman federalism under which the Pasha's expected denunciation of the Treaty of 1805 would be the signal for the United States to "come down on the Grand Signior, with a bill of expense for all our losses, expense incurred during that war, and in the meantime take possession of Dernah, Tobrook, &c." Possession would be nine tenths of the law, for Turks and Egyptians lacked the means to prevent the operation, while European opposition was not to be anticipated. Should, however, any government protest the action, a suitable rationale was available in recent American remonstrances against the North African slave trade.[4]

The career of Michel Vidal, the author of this remarkable scheme and the individual for whose protection the United States Navy had just dispatched two warships, had already spanned four continents. Born in Carcassonne, he had emigrated to Texas at the age of twenty-one, arriving in the last months of the Republic's independent existence. Following annexation he had removed to Louisiana where, after engaging in "literary and scientific pursuits," he had turned to journalism. This phase of his life was terminated by his opposition to secession, but the end of the Civil War found him back in Louisiana as a newspaper proprietor, a leader of the Republican party, and member of the state constitutional convention. Entering Congress upon the readmission of his state, Vidal served until March, 1869, at which time, deterred by mob violence from standing for re-election, he petitioned for federal employment. Appointment as one of the commissioners under the Peruvian claims convention

[4] Vidal to Hunter, June 22, 1875, *ibid.*

followed, and in 1870, on his return from South America, he was named consul at Tripoli.[5]

Wholly Americanized, strongly Anglophobe, convinced of the future of the United States and of the decadence of Europe, Vidal brought to his work the unusual combination of a classical French education and the crusading zeal of an American editor, to which was added, presumably as a result of his experiences of Reconstruction, a perhaps excessive appreciation of force as an instrument of reform. His despatches to the Department were fluent and learned, reflecting diligence in research and a considerable knowledge of the history of diplomacy and of international law. If they also embodied the editor's predilection for scoring debating points and the verbosity of the exile, their merits of form and content, the original French Alexandrines and the quotations from Homer, Lope da Vega, and Davy Crockett with which they were ornamented, evidenced an intellectual distinction unusual among the appointees of the Grant administration.

The consulate at Tripoli, where Vidal arrived on September 1, 1870, was one of the finest sinecures in the gift of the President of the United States. The pay was good, $3,000 a year and $800 for expenses; there were no resident Americans and no American merchantman had called within the last generation. The principal imports were of British manufactures; the principal exports such exotics as ostrich feathers, clarified butter, and esparto grass; the principal activities of his predecessor had been the acknowledgment of circular instructions from Washington and the hoisting twice a year, on the Fourth of July and on the anniversary of the Battle of New Orleans, of the largest available national flag. Doubtless these facts were known to the Department, but it was an unusual incumbent who could state in an official despatch that his post might well have been abolished at any date subsequent to the Turkish reoccupation. This Vidal did in February, 1873, but at the same time he solicited reappointment. He had found something to do.[6]

Faced with no problems, blessed with none but routine instructions, too energetic to rust in idleness, the consul perforce developed

[5] Vidal to Hunter, May 14, 1878, *ibid.*; Vidal to Fish, March 13 and March 23, 1869, Appointment Papers, State Department Records. See also *Biographical Directory of the American Congress, 1774-1927* (Washington, 1928), 296, 1650.

[6] Fish to Vidal, May 26, 1870, Instructions, Barbary Powers (Tripoli); Vidal to Hunter, February 10, 1873, Despatches, Tripoli.

his own policy. This policy derived, in the first instance, from his estimate of the European situation. The collapse of France before the Prussian onslaught promised advantages for his country. Old World rulers might dislike the United States, but their peoples held us in high esteem; increasingly, therefore, as the great powers declined the smaller states would look to America for leadership. In this situation no country was more in need of disinterested friendship than the Ottoman Empire: "It is a great relief for Turkey to find in the civilized world one great nation at least which neither wants to despoil her, nor assumes toward her the dreaded part of a tyrannical protector." This was the traditional attitude of sympathy for the rights of weak nations which had informed American policy toward Turkey since the days of Commodore David Porter, and patient reassurance of the Tripolitan Pasha along these lines brought about a minor triumph. In April, 1871, a visit by the steam frigate *Guerrière* had unexpectedly gratifying results: the turnout of all the officers of government together with a brass band and five hundred soldiers, a reception "in semi-regal style," and the presentation by the Pasha to the United States of the anchor of the frigate *Philadelphia* which had just been recovered at a cost of 8,000 piastres after sixty-eight years in the harbor mud.[7]

A year after the grand reception tendered the *Guerrière* a second influence was at work. While the apparent decline of the great powers of Europe had gratified Vidal's patriotism, his observations at Tripoli excited his compassion. There the slave trade, flowing from time immemorial from inner Africa to Constantinople, had received new impetus from the recent proliferation of steamship lines connecting Tripoli, Malta, and the Levant. Accurate information as to the conduct of this traffic was difficult to obtain, but it was clear that the Tripolitan authorities were deeply involved, and a trip to Malta provided convincing evidence that its tragic perpetuation depended on the connivance or negligence of the British authorities. Humanitarian concern was thus reinforced by the pleasures of emphasizing British pharisaism: British praise of Portuguese politeness in accepting protests on the coolie trade moved Vidal to hope that Lord Granville would show equal complaisance in receiving from the American minister the representations regarding affairs at Malta which the Treaty of Ghent and the Con-

[7] Vidal to Hunter, April 10 and May 26, 1871, Despatches, Tripoli.

vention of 1862 made both the right and duty of the United States.[8]

Yet life in Tripoli was not limited to the contemplation of the decline of the West or to the study of man's inhumanity to man. Inevitably, consular society suffered from the tensions which beset those in the competitive business of statecraft when isolated in an alien environment and with little to occupy their time. For the American the situation was aggravated by the anomalous position in which history had placed him. In Barbary, from the very beginning, American consuls had exercised diplomatic functions. Although unauthorized by law, this quasi-diplomatic status had been maintained, as had the special rights deriving from the Tripolitan War, despite the reassertion of Turkish control. As it had with his predecessors, however, Vidal's claim as diplomatic agent to precedence over his consular colleagues resulted in strained relations, while his emphasis on treaty rights antagonized the Pasha. As the situation developed the consul took high ground, in which he was at least partially sustained by the State Department. Although declining to support his claim to precedence, Secretary Hamilton Fish concurred in his contention that Ottoman reconquest had not changed the legal status of Tripoli, and stated that "there can be no doubt that the Treaty of 1805 . . . is still in force," and that "this government is not disposed to surrender its rights under any existing treaties." [9]

Thus on this little stage the traditional anti-European nature of American policy was reaffirmed in difficulties of official and personal intercourse. The hostility of the consuls of England, France, and Spain forced Vidal back upon the society of the representatives of those smaller commercial powers with which Jefferson, in the early days of Barbary diplomacy, had made common cause. History was repeating itself, but with a difference. The Pasha, also resistant to American claims to special status, was now as an Ottoman functionary subject to European pressures by way of Constantinople, and as he and the representatives of the great powers maneuvered in concert against Vidal the latter's early sympathy for the Turks evaporated. In 1871 Turkey had been fortunate to find in the United States a disinterested friend; by 1874 the blight of Europe

[8] Vidal to Hunter, June 30, September 28, and December 21, 1872, *ibid.*

[9] Vidal to Hunter, January 12, 1871, February 19, February 25, and March 20, 1873, *ibid.*; Fish to Vidal, February 28, 1871, and June 20, 1873, Instructions, Barbary Powers (Tripoli); J. C. Bancroft Davis to Vidal, July 10, 1873, *ibid.*

was upon her and the Ottoman Empire was a "rotten fabric" sustained only by the power of Britain.[10]

So microcosm and macrocosm interacted. In the world at large only Britain presented a threat to the United States. In Tripoli the inhuman slave trade depended on British complaisance. A forward American policy in the Mediterranean would be helpful in the great competition. American action against the slave trade would aid the cause of humanity. Quite possibly both aims could be served at once by the American consul at Tripoli.

In one of his early reports on the slave trade Vidal had promised to show how the United States might profit from this British violation of treaty engagements. This undertaking he fulfilled on January 6, 1873, in a despatch of large implications. "I believe," he began, "I do no more than repeat a generally accepted truism, when I state that the only nation in the world with which the United States will have to contend for that supremacy which is their manifest destiny, is the British Empire." Granting this premise, war was sooner or later inevitable, and it behooved America to prepare both for defense and for action overseas. Not only should the Navy be kept up but the existence of Britain's world-wide strategic network of cables, colonies, and coaling stations made it "good policy for the United States to have in various countries of the world, naval stations, such as our great rival . . . has wisely scattered in every possible sea and ocean." A Mediterranean base would help offset British advantages but the problem was complex. European antagonism made a site in the western basin impossible; in the eastern basin British influence ruled out the Turkish islands; the harbor of Syra was suitable but its acquisition would be difficult owing to Greek unwillingness to sell, the hostility of the great powers, and America's own Monroe Doctrine. There remained only Tripoli, with the longest coast line of any of the Regencies, including places "which a powerful Government might perhaps convert into a formidable position." Should the United States desire a footing in the Mediterranean "for military and commercial purposes," on the analogy of Aden or Hong Kong, a vessel should be dispatched to survey the coast, which could be done without exciting suspicion. If a suitable location were found, the means of securing it could

10 Vidal to Hunter, February 19 and March 20, 1873, January 27, 1874, August 25, 1875, Despatches, Tripoli.

then be considered. Perhaps action could be taken, following the British example at Lagos, as a part of the effort to suppress the African slave trade.[11]

For the next year the linked problems of the African naval base, the slave trade, and the nature of American relations with Tripoli marched together in Vidal's despatches. On February 14, 1873, he transmitted a French account of the American Bible Society's work in Bulgaria which linked missionary activity, American interest in the Cretan revolution, and rumored American designs on an island in the Cyclades as evidence of a forward policy in the Levant. The expenditure of so much devotion on such stony ground was to the consul a matter for regret. No profit could accrue to the United States from missionary work in that inland province, he argued, whereas the coast of Africa, home of the amiable Tuareg and potentially a great trading center, would repay serious effort. Five days later Vidal concluded a learned survey of Tripolitan history with the observation that since no Americans were resident in Tripoli and no American merchant vessel had called in thirty years it seemed pointless to maintain a representative in the Regency unless the government was inclined to follow his suggestion regarding a Cyrenaican naval base. In May the need for haste was pointed up by the report of a British scheme for "settlement by Maltese emigrants, and virtual annexation to the British Empire . . . [of] that very District of this Regency, which I had in view when, in despatch No. 32, I alluded to the possibility for the U. S. Government to acquire a naval station in the Mediterranean sea." The fertility of the country, the mildness of the inhabitants, and the value of the seaports were again rehearsed, with emphasis upon Tobruk, "which, according to trusty travellers, is a splendid port, the center of a magnificent country, but without trade of any kind, a sort of San Francisco Bay under the rule of Mexicans."[12]

[11] In a paper submitted to the President and the State Department prior to his appointment to Tripoli, Vidal had suggested American acquisition of one of those Turkish islands which increasing British influence now seemed to have put beyond reach. On the Monroe Doctrine he had positive views: "I beg to be excused for saying that, while it has never done us any good in America, it may in the end, when it is our policy to acquire territory abroad, prove a very nuisance to the American nation." It will be noted that his concept of the Doctrine was precise: while it militated against activity in Greek (i.e. European) territory, it had no relevance in questions concerning the Ottoman Empire (an Asiatic power) or Africa. Vidal to Hunter, January 6, 1873, Despatches, Tripoli.

[12] Vidal to Hunter, February 14, 1873, and enclosed translation of Albert Dumont,

Vidal's early reports on the slave trade had led the Department to query Malta and Constantinople on the subject, and to ask for further detail from Tripoli. In his efforts to comply with this request the consul engaged the Pasha in correspondence regarding the possibility of stationing a consular agent at the port of Benghazi, and enlarged his staff by "Mejbura (a Woman) Spy from Tripoli to Malta" and by two supernumerary cavasses, paid from his private funds. But the search for evidence was tedious, and in July Vidal put forward a plan for "the abolition of slavery in Egypt, Syria, and the Barbaresque Regencies" which had at least the merits of directness. Observing that British consuls had on occasion taken slaves under their protection, he urged that "what had been done occasionally only by British consuls . . . I would like to see the great American nation doing on a grand scale, for the protection and civilization of the thousands of negroes who live on the coast of Barbary and in Egypt." American consuls should be authorized to issue protection papers to all Negroes not Ottoman subjects, a procedure which "would cost the Government no additional expense; is practicable, easy, and in conformity with existing treaties." [13]

While awaiting the Department's reaction to this proposal Vidal continued active in the search for evidence, and attempted with the help of his native agents to "establish an old-fashion underground railroad." Mejbura and one of the men were sent to Malta with orders to identify any slaves among their fellow passengers and to denounce them to the British authorities. So far as liberating the slaves was concerned the plan miscarried, but reports of the episode proved sufficiently alarming to the Ottoman authorities to produce an order from the Tripolitan Pasha in October, 1873, which threatened slavers with severe punishment. The consequent drying up of the traffic at Tripoli encouraged Vidal to continue his offensive and to plan a visit to Benghazi, capital of the eastern section of the Regency and an important outlet for slaves from the interior. Again the two lines of action coincided: "Thence it is my intention to

"Souvenir de la Roumélie," *Revue des Deux Mondes* (Paris), October 1, 1871, February 19 and May 27, 1873, and enclosed copy of the speech of Admiral Lord Clarence Paget at the inauguration of the Clarence Hydraulic Dock, Malta, January 23, 1873, *ibid.*

[13] Fish to George H. Boker, February 10, 1873, Instructions, Turkey, State Department Records; Fish to Vidal, February 10, 1873, Instructions, Barbary Powers (Tripoli); Departmental endorsement on Vidal to Hunter, September 28, 1872, and Vidal to Hunter, March 22, June 2, July 16, and December 31, 1873, Despatches, Tripoli.

visit the Cyrenean section, and thus be in a measure to communicate to the Department reliable information in regard to a country which has been once or twice mentioned in my preceding despatches in connection with a scheme of annexation." [14]

In June, 1874, despite remonstrances from the Pasha as to the hazards of the journey, Vidal took ship for Benghazi. There the provincial pasha proved also obstructionist, but an outbreak of the plague gave the traveler, as he reported, the opportunity to show the inhabitants the "wide difference" between a humanitarian American consul and the extortionate Ottoman functionaries. His advice to the confused authorities and his initiative in supervising the establishment of a *cordon sanitaire* earned him the gratitude of local merchants and ship captains, some favorable publicity in the Mediterranean press, and an official expression of thanks from the Ottoman government to the Department at Washington. These adventures he reported in a despatch written on June 30, preparatory to setting out on his overland journey, in which he described his objectives as the study of the commercial possibilities of the country, an investigation of the Negro slave trade, historical research on the Eaton expedition of 1805, and exploration of the ruins of antiquity. Not wishing to trust important information to the local mails, Vidal stopped there. "I will not," he wrote, "here allude again to the scheme I have mentioned in previous despatches, in regard to Cyrenaica." This discretion was to prove insufficient.[15]

With the plague under control, Vidal set out eastward. Proceeding through the ruins of the Pentapolis, he found at Derna some Arabs who were "still called Americans by their townfolks, on account of their fathers' connection with General Eaton's movements." After a survey of the ports of Bomba and Tobruk, at which latter point his bodyguard turned back, Vidal continued, with only his janissary, a cook, and two camel drivers, past the port of Bardia and along the coast to the Egyptian frontier where he arrived on

[14] Vidal to Hunter, November 6, 1873, Despatches, Tripoli. Extracts from this despatch were communicated to Robert C. Schenck, American minister at London, to be read to Lord Granville, and resulted in an investigation of the conduct of the Malta police regarding the slave trade. Fish to Vidal, February 4 and June 26, 1874, Instructions, Barbary Powers (Tripoli); Fish to Schenck, February 4, 1874, Instructions, Great Britain; Sir Edward Thornton to Fish, March 11, June 19, and October 28, 1874, Notes Received from Foreign Legations, Great Britain, State Department Records.

[15] Vidal to Hunter, June 30, 1874, July 7, 1876 (No. 80), and Enclosures 4-7, and July 8, 1876, Despatches, Tripoli; Gregoire Aristarchi Bey to Fish, September 30, 1874, Notes Received, Turkey.

October 10, exhausted in body but triumphant in spirit, having accomplished a journey made only twice before by Christians in the twelve centuries since the Mohammedan conquest.[16]

In his Benghazi despatch Vidal had predicted that his exploration would be completed in four or five weeks. In this he proved not far wrong, but its completion marked only the beginning of his troubles, for at Matruka the conqueror of the plague in Barbary ran up against the sanitary cordon which the Egyptians had erected against that same disease. Further passage was forbidden him, and he was ordered to return to Tripoli by the way he had come. This order, which in his weakened condition he feared would amount to a death sentence, Vidal attempted to appeal through the American consulate, but the consul was on leave in Europe and the Greek merchant who was acting proved arrogant and unhelpful. The sequel of this remarkable desert journey was consequently almost equally remarkable. After forty days of confinement in one of the forts of Alexandria, the American consul to Tripoli was forcibly embarked on an Ottoman trading schooner, narrowly escaped with his life when this vessel was shipwrecked on the coast of Asia Minor, and finally made his way back via Beirut and Malta to Tripoli, where he arrived on February 5, 1875. In his despatch reporting his return to his post he wrote that, while the man had much to complain of, the journey had been a complete success so far as the consul was concerned. Ever sanguine, he observed that "were I now in Constantinople, and authorized to negotiate, I have an idea that the hopes expressed in my despatch No. 32, might become realized." But whatever the decision of the Department, the journey had been accomplished. "Ashamed of my *far niente* in Tripoli, I sought to make myself useful, and thought, with Tennyson's Ulysses,

> 'How dull it is to pause, to make an end,
> To rust unburnish'd, not to shine in use!' "[17]

Ulysses had returned from his travels, but it was not a happy homecoming. His Penelope was sick, his Telemachus, his only son, was dying, and the consuls and the Pasha were conspiring against him.[18] He had, indeed, succeeded in making himself a conspicuous

16 Vidal to Hunter, April 17 and June 22, 1875, Despatches, Tripoli.

17 Vidal to Hunter, March 1 and April 17, 1875, *ibid.*; N. D. Comanos to Fish, October 30, 1874, and enclosures, and Richard Beardsley to Fish, December 21, 1874, Despatches, Egypt.

18 Vidal to Hunter, April 17, 1875, Despatches, Tripoli.

target. His maneuvers against the slave trade had forced the Tripolitan authorities to issue a proclamation against it in October, 1873.[19] In January of the next year the *Mémorial Diplomatique*, commenting on his argument that Tripoli, although under the suzerainty of the Sultan, was yet independent of the Ottoman Empire, had noted with interest that publication of this despatch in *Foreign Relations* seemed to argue the concurrence of the Washington government.[20] Before departing on his journey of exploration in the spring of 1874, Vidal had thoughtlessly alerted the Pasha by presenting him with a map of the Regency on which Marmarica was designated as independent.[21] At Malta, in January, 1875, he had encountered this same Pasha returning to Constantinople with fourteen slaves, had denounced him to the authorities, and had endeavored to procure his arrest.[22] As if this were not enough, the State Department had printed without deletion his despatches of May 27, 1873, and June 30, 1874, thus publishing to the world his project for an African naval station and his cryptic remarks about a previously mentioned scheme "in regard to Cyrenaica," and reviving European and Ottoman fears of American intervention in the eastern Mediterranean.[23] In Constantinople serious thought began to be given to where all this might be leading. On July 6, 1875, the American minister reported a discussion with the Minister of Foreign Affairs on the subject of Turkey's claim to jurisdiction over Tripoli and asked for instructions. This query reached Washington three days before Vidal's cabled request for protection.[24]

At Tripoli the six months following the consul's return had not been easy ones. Vidal had submerged his personal troubles in con-

[19] Vidal to Hunter, November 6, 1873, and July 8, 1876, *ibid.*

[20] *Mémorial Diplomatique* (Paris), January 17, 1874, enclosed with Vidal to Hunter, July 8, 1876, *ibid.* This article resulted from the publication of Vidal to Hunter, February 25, 1873, in *Papers Relating to the Foreign Relations of the United States in 1873* (3 vols., Washington, 1873-1874), II, 1157-66.

[21] Vidal to Hunter, June 22, 1875, Despatches, Tripoli.

[22] Vidal to Hunter, March 1, 1875, and July 8, 1876, *ibid.*

[23] The despatch of May 27, 1873, with enclosures, is in *Foreign Relations, 1873*, II, 1167-69; that of June 30, 1874, is in *Papers Relating to the Foreign Relations of the United States in 1874* (Washington, 1874), 48-49. Other indications of European concern over the American naval base project are in Dumont, "Souvenir de la Roumélie" (see Note 12 above), and in the *Levant Herald* (Constantinople), September 20, 1875, copy enclosed with Horace Maynard to Fish, December 27, 1875, Despatches, Turkey. See also Vidal to Hunter, December 17, 1873, and March 6, 1876, Despatches, Tripoli; and Arthur J. May, "Crete and the United States, 1866-1869," *Journal of Modern History* (Chicago), XVI (December, 1944), 286-93.

[24] Maynard to Fish, July 6, 1875, Despatches, Turkey.

tinued war against the slaving interests and had used his consular powers to manumit slaves. Following the arrival in June, 1875, of a new governor, Moustapha Phosphor Pasha, so named because of his fiery temperament, the results became apparent in harassment of consular personnel, slights to Vidal himself, and widespread rumors that complaints against the American consul would receive official support. In July, Vidal had a long interview with the Pasha in which he urged that dignitary to prevent the sowing of discord, and a visit from the frigate *Congress* went off well. But both sides were spoiling for trouble and the crisis, when it came, was the result of a sufficiently trivial incident.[25]

Vidal had just moved his family to a seaside villa for the summer when on August 4 a visiting Ottoman naval squadron put a working party ashore nearby to water ship. Soon after lunch a sailor appeared unannounced inside the walled garden, refused to leave when ordered away by a maidservant, and then fled precipitously at sight of Vidal, with the consul in hot pursuit. Failing to overtake the miscreant, Vidal accosted a group of his fellows, was impudently replied to, and shook one of them by the collar. Shortly the garden wall was lined by a gang of sailors, armed with sticks, whose menacing appearance and refusal to disperse forced the family to flee the house.[26]

This affair Vidal interpreted as an attempt by the authorities to steal his despatch box in order to obtain copies of his reports on the slave trade and Cyrenaica.[27] The next day he forwarded to the Pasha a long account of the incident, together with a demand for the court martial of the offending sailors; this protest crossed a curt message from Moustapha calling for an apology to the squadron commander for an assault on Ottoman naval personnel. On August 6, having received no acknowledgment of his protest and learning of attempts to suborn witnesses against him, the consul forwarded a still more detailed statement of charges.[28] But on the next day a

[25] Vidal to Hunter, August 26, 1875, and July 8, 1876, Despatches, Tripoli.

[26] Vidal to Hunter, August 26, 1875, *ibid.*, gives a detailed account of the intrusion. The subsequent history of the crisis is set forth in three despatches (Numbers 71-73) of August 27, 1875, of which Number 71 covers the events of August 5-26 in diary form, Number 72 discusses the presumed motives behind the sailor's action, and Number 73 encloses copies of the correspondence.

[27] Vidal to Hunter, August 21 and August 27, 1875 (No. 72), *ibid.*

[28] Vidal to Moustapha Phosphor Pasha, August 5, 1875; Moustapha to Vidal, August 5, 1875; Vidal to Moustapha, August 6, 1875 (No. 73, Enclosures 1, 2, and 3), *ibid.*

request from the Medjliss el Temiz, a civil "Cleansing Court," that his interpreter be sent to hear testimony, resulted in the astounding discovery that proceedings had been instituted not against the sailor but against the consul, who was alleged to have attacked the Turk with a knife. In the town, officials were reported boasting that they had the American in their power, and a rumor circulated that the consulate had already been offered for rent. Amid rapidly increasing tension Vidal moved his family back to Tripoli, and on August 8, as false testimony continued to pile up at the Medjliss proceeding, he sent his interpreter by ship to Malta to cable the Department for protection.[29] With the court continuing its investigation, and with reports of further subornation of witnesses, Vidal on August 12 demanded in peremptory terms of the Pasha an immediate termination of this "monstruous proceeding." [30]

Thus far both parties had been somewhat reckless in pressing their cases. Sustained, at least at the start, by the European consuls, the Pasha apparently hoped either to intimidate his antagonist or to provoke him to action which would warrant a request for recall. As for Vidal, whether or not he had decided to try to push things to a point that would justify naval intervention and a seizure of Cyrenaican ports, the language of his communications, which demanded that "Mussulmen should be taught by striking examples," was, as Admiral Worden later observed, a departure from "that dignified and courteous language which should characterize all official papers." [31] Among the consuls of the great powers, however, the Medjliss proceeding against a member of the consular corps had stimulated second thoughts, and on August 11 the French dragoman declined to testify.[32] And on the afternoon of the 17th further weight was thrown into the scales on the side of the isolated and embattled American when the *Congress*, commanded by Captain Earl English, steamed in and anchored in the harbor which her original namesake had blockaded seventy years before.[33]

[29] No. 71; Medjliss el Temiz to Vidal, August 7 and August 10, 1875 (No. 73, Enclosures 4 and 5), *ibid.*

[30] No. 71; Vidal to Moustapha, August 12, 1875 (No. 73, Enclosure 6), *ibid.*

[31] Vidal to Moustapha, August 5 and August 12, 1875 (No. 73, Enclosures 1 and 6), *ibid.*, Worden to Robeson, October 20, 1875, and Enclosures B1 and B6, European Squadron Letters.

[32] Vidal to Hunter, August 27, 1875 (No. 71), Despatches, Tripoli.

[33] Vidal to Hunter, August 21, 1875, *ibid.*; Commanding Officer, U. S. S. *Congress* to Commander of European Squadron, August 31, 1875 (Enclosure with Worden to Robeson, October 20, 1875), European Squadron Letters. For Captain English this

Nothing daunted by what had transpired, Vidal took the appearance of the *Congress* as the occasion to remind the Pasha, in accordance with the Treaty of 1805, that the forts were required to salute the warship. Not only was no salute forthcoming, however, but when Captain English landed two officers with instructions to report to the consul they were greeted on the quay by a crowd of boys who howled and shouted and spat, and who followed them to the consulate with cries of "Go on, pig," and "Go on, hog." The result of this further unpleasantness was to occupy the next few days with correspondence concerning the proper treatment of American naval personnel, and to give Captain English an opportunity to bring himself up to date on the history of the consul's difficulties. Contemptuous at first of these new protests, the Pasha was brought around by August 21 to an expression of regret for the actions of the mob, and on the 23rd the head of the municipality and the chief of police apologized formally at the consulate. This day also saw the arrival of reinforcements, as the *Hartford* entered Tripoli and anchored off the starboard bow of the *Congress* "so as to bring her battery to bear on the fortifications." [34]

Affairs had now reached a state of crisis such as even to affect Moustapha Phosphor. All business had been suspended, the bottom had fallen out of the esparto grass market, it was rumored that at the first shot of the bombardment, which Vidal now considered "almost inevitable," the Moslem populace would undertake a massacre of all Jews and Christians. On the evening of August 23 the consul met with the captains of the *Congress* and the *Hartford* to draw up the final American demands: withdrawal by the Pasha of his insulting letters, and an apology; severe punishment for the intruding sailor; dismissal from office of the members of the Medjliss el Temiz for having summoned a consul in violation of law, custom, and treaty; a guarantee that American consular personnel would have the secure enjoyment of the same rights as the protégés of other

was not the first experience of trouble in distant places. As a junior officer he had been wounded during the reduction of the Chinese Barrier Forts; at Osaka, during the last days of the Tokugawa period, he had given refuge on board his ship to the defeated Shogun and his followers. The executive officer of the *Congress* at the time of the Tripolitan affair was Robley D. Evans, who has left a brief account in *A Sailor's Log* (New York, 1901), 203-205. See also *Annual Report of the Secretary of the Navy, 1875* (Washington, 1876), 5.

[34] Vidal to Hunter, August 21 and August 27, 1875 (No. 71), Despatches, Tripoli; Commanding Officer, U. S. S. *Congress* to Commander of European Squadron, August 31 and October 6, 1875, European Squadron Letters.

governments; a national salute of twenty-one guns from the fort. No indemnity was to be required, but a reply was "confidently expected within twenty-four hours after the receipt of this despatch." [35]

At Constantinople the concern about American relations with Tripoli continued unabated, while in the Regency the consuls of the great powers were by now fully engaged, bending every effort to liquidate the crisis without an American diplomatic victory. On August 16 the American minister to the Porte had advised Washington by cable that the Pasha had been instructed to atone for the insult to the consul prior to the arrival of the *Hartford*, adding that Turkey's anxiety in the matter stemmed from her desire to show that Tripoli was under her effective jurisdiction.[36] At Tripoli the French consul general had pressed the Pasha to settle the question of the insult to the American officers so as not to complicate an already difficult situation. On the evening of August 23, while the Americans were concerting their demands, there had been much nocturnal movement between consulates and castle; and the next morning the consuls attempted unsuccessfully to by-pass Vidal and meet secretly with Captain English.[37] The upshot of this activity was the Pasha's reply of August 24 to the American demands, unsatisfactory in content but conciliatory in tone.[38]

It was left for Baron Emile de Testa, the Dutch consul, to whom Vidal had entrusted his duties during his excursion across the desert, to bring the crisis to a satisfactory conclusion. On August 25, armed with the alarming rumor that Vidal was preparing to move his family aboard the *Congress*, Testa called upon the Pasha "in order to make a last attempt to find a pacific solution and spare this city great misfortune," and found a willingness to settle. Moustapha now undertook to have the sailor punished, to dismiss two members of the Medjliss, to refer the question of the salute to Constantinople, and to call in uniform at the consulate to apologize. He was just in time: Vidal and English agreed to accept the compromise, and

[35] Vidal to Hunter, August 27, 1875 (No. 71); Vidal to Moustapha, August 23, 1875 (No. 73, Enclosure 23), Despatches, Tripoli.

[36] Maynard to Fish, August 16 and August 17, 1875, Despatches, Turkey.

[37] Vidal to Hunter, August 27, 1875 (No. 71); Vidal to P. Delaporte, August 21, 1875; Delaporte to Vidal, August 22, 1875 (No. 73, Enclosures 21 and 22); Malta *Times*, September 18, 1875 (enclosed with Vidal to Hunter, September 25, 1876), Despatches, Tripoli.

[38] Moustapha to Vidal, August 24, 1875 (No. 73, Enclosure 24), *ibid.*

the next day the Malta steamer arrived with orders to the Pasha to consent to any demands that might be made upon him.[39]

Vidal was determined to make the apology a memorable one, and a letter from English suggesting that some officers might appropriately be present crossed one of his which expressed the hope that he would see "if not the two Captains themselves . . . at least a great number of officers of both steamers, with about twenty soldiers, drummers, musicians, a standard-bearer &c. We must vindicate the U. S. dignity in as solemn a style as the place can afford." [40] All this he did not get, but he got plenty. At the appointed hour "the Pasha came to the U. S. Consulate in full uniform, and there, in presence of Captain Harmony, and other officers of the Congress, and the Hartford, and the Consul General of the Netherlands, with the Consul of Belgium, he offered an apology for what had taken place. The street on which the Consulate is situated was crowded with people of all nationalities. . . . It was generally noticed how pale with rage were looking the officers and servants forming the escort of the Pasha. As for the latter he was fairly bowed down. After the departure of the Pasha and his train of followers, a brass band, composed of French and Maltese amateurs came unasked to play in honor of the flag and officers of the United States, — a compliment they have never paid to their respective Consulates." [41]

It was a famous victory. The stain of Bainbridge's imprisonment had been washed away. "Read, as one pleases, the annals of diplomacy," wrote the triumphant consul, "it was never heard before, that the head of a Government consented to go in full uniform to the residence of a foreign consul, and there in presence of numerous witnesses of various nationalities, apologize for his wrongs, whatever they might have been." [42]

Indeed it was too good a victory. The Porte was acutely unhappy at a proceeding which so emphasized the American view that the

39 Vidal to Hunter, August 27, 1873 (No. 71); Baron Emile de Testa to Vidal, August 25, 1875, Vidal to Testa, August 25, 1875, and Moustapha to Vidal, August 26, 1875 (No. 73, Enclosures 25-27), *ibid.*; Malta *Times*, September 18, 1875; Vidal to English, August 25 and August 26, 1875, and English to Vidal, August 25, 1875 (Commanding Officer, U. S. S. *Congress* to Commander of European Squadron, August 31, 1875, Enclosures E, F, and 4), European Squadron Letters.

40 English to Vidal, August 25, 1875, and Vidal to English, August 26, 1875 (Commanding Officer, U. S. S. *Congress* to Commander of European Squadron, August 31, 1875, Enclosures 4 and G), European Squadron Letters.

41 Vidal to Hunter, August 27, 1875 (No. 71), Despatches, Tripoli.

42 Vidal to Hunter, August 26, 1875, *ibid.*

Pasha of Tripoli was "the head of a Government," and the consuls of the great powers, while doubtless approving the termination of the court proceeding against a member of their corps, derived no pleasure from so complete an American triumph. The episode had caused a considerable stir in the Mediterranean press, where the division of opinion conformed to Vidal's earlier appreciation of the contrasting attitudes toward the United States that were held by Europe's rulers and by Europe's ruled. The Malta *Public Opinion* praised Vidal for an important service to all Europeans residing in Turkish dominions and urged the consuls of other nations, Great Britain included, to profit by his example. Similar sentiments were put forward by the Malta *Corriere* when expressing the gratitude of Maltese residents of Tripoli.[43] Against all this, however, the authentic voice of European policy was heard when the *Levant Herald* of Constantinople, which had earlier printed a Vidalian version of the crisis, published on September 25 an extremely hostile correction together with editorial animadversions on American policy. The news story accused the consul of pelting the sailors with stones and denied any insult to the officers of the *Congress*; the editorial began with an attack on the American for "having quarrelled with every successive *vali* . . . [and] rendered himself most unpopular with all classes of the inhabitants," and concluded hopefully with the observation that although Vidal had carried the day, "the 'rowdy' character of the proceedings warrants the belief that they will be promptly disavowed." [44]

The attempt of the Porte to demonstrate its sovereignty over Tripoli by promising satisfaction to the United States was followed by further argumentation. A note from Gregoire Aristarchi Bey, the Ottoman minister at Washington, contended that since Tripoli was a province of the empire all complaints should be addressed to the Porte, and requested withdrawal of the warships; at Constantinople the Minister of Foreign Affairs advanced counter complaints

[43] Malta *Public Opinion*, September 8, 1875, and Malta *Corriere*, September 12, 1875, enclosed with Vidal to Hunter, July 7, 1876 (No. 80), Despatches, Tripoli. See also Vidal to Secretary of State William M. Evarts, May 14, 1878, *ibid.*; and Malta *Times*, September 18, 1875, enclosed with Vidal to Hunter, September 25, 1876, *ibid.*

[44] *Levant Herald*, September 20 and September 25, 1875, enclosed with Maynard to Fish, September 27, 1875, Despatches, Turkey; Vidal to Hunter, July 7, 1876 (Nos. 79 and 80), Despatches, Tripoli. At Constantinople the second *Levant Herald* article was thought to have been inspired by the Porte; Vidal considered it the work of the British and French consuls at Tripoli.

against Vidal.[45] To these communications the Department replied ambiguously. While insisting that the United States did not recognize Turkish sovereignty as affecting treaty relations with Tripoli it agreed to withdraw the naval vessels upon a Turkish promise of satisfaction and to take appropriate action should the complaints against the consul prove well founded.[46] This much having been gained, Aristarchi returned to the charge in December, reasserting Turkish sovereignty, claiming that the United States had recognized it through certain acts, accusing Vidal of improper conduct, and requesting his recall.[47]

The consul, in the meantime, had returned to his work. In January he caused an American merchantman to visit the Regency for the first time within the memory of any living man, and he began to cherish aspirations of reviving the trade, "once so lively," between America and Tripoli. In February he granted protection to a Moroccan "Maraboot or Saint" who had incurred the hostility of the French and Italian consuls.[48] In March he began again to employ his consular powers in the struggle against the slave trade, and by June he had emancipated and taken under his protection fifty-five slaves.[49] None of this eased his relations with consuls or Pasha, jealous of his eminence and suspicious of American designs on the coast, but such was the hostility between rulers and ruled in Tripoli that the more he was denounced the more hopes were founded on him by the populace. "Strange as it may sound to American ears," he reported, "there is now on this Barbary coast a whole population, American in feelings and aspirations," and a "revolutionary movement in the well prepared soil of the Berber and Arab populations." Doubtless this news did sound strange, and even alarming, to the ears of the State Department, but to Vidal it had a different meaning: "Not knowing whether the Sick Man will, or will not, breathe his last next spring; whether there will be a general war in conse-

45 Aristarchi Bey to Fish, August 25, 1875, Notes Received, Turkey; Maynard to Fish, September 27, 1875, Despatches, Turkey.

46 Fish to Aristarchi, August 27, 1875, Notes to Foreign Legations, Turkey; Fish to Maynard, October 8 and November 9, 1875, Instructions, Turkey.

47 Aristarchi to Fish, December 9 and December 30, 1875, Notes Received, Turkey.

48 Vidal to Hunter, March 6 and May 16, 1876, Despatches, Tripoli; Mohammed ben Said el Bethoul to Vidal, January 8, 1876, and T. J. Fitzinger, Master of Bark *Robert Morison*, to Vidal, February 10, 1876, enclosed with Vidal to Hunter, July 7, 1876 (No. 80), *ibid.*

49 Vidal to Hunter, May 16 and July 15, 1876 (No. 82), *ibid.* Some of the depositions of emancipated slaves enclosed with Vidal's No. 82 are very moving.

quence of Great Britain taking possession, (as it surely will,) of the Suez Canal; and what kind of attitude the U. S. Government may be compelled to assume during the imbroglio, on these Mediterranean seas, — it cannot hurt, — in case it does no good, — to have on the African coast, and near to Egypt, a population ready to welcome American seamen with open arms." [50]

On the day that this report of a population ripe for revolutionizing reached Washington, Aristarchi Bey again requested Vidal's recall. Ottoman complaints of inadmissible demands, illegal protection of Moroccans, and threats of further visits from American men of war were reported by the minister at Constantinople, and these, with further pressure from Aristarchi, resulted in a request by the Department for explanations.[51] To this Vidal replied in May in two despatches, denying any impropriety, proving by learned citation of treaties and precedents that he was authorized to protect Moroccans, stating that no consul who took seriously his duty to enforce the treaties could ever be persona grata in Tripoli, and affirming that his every action had been based upon the American motto, "First be sure you are right; and then go ahead." [52] These despatches were followed, after a period devoted to research, by seven more, which demonstrated with a wealth of evidence that with all but the Pasha and the consuls the American representative enjoyed great esteem, attributed the allegations of unpopularity to his interference with the slave trafficking of the Pasha and his cronies, argued that the Porte could neither dismiss the American consul at Tripoli nor expel a foreign representative who was persona non grata, and appealed for the support of the Department. "I am doing here a good work; and I dare say that, single handed as I am, I am equal to a whole squadron, as far as the opposing the negro-slave-traffic is concerned." [53]

As to the impropriety of Vidal's conduct opinions doubtless differed, but there could be little doubt that the broad lines of his policy had enjoyed State Department approval. His efforts to maintain the special rights deriving from the Treaty of 1805 had been sup-

[50] Vidal to Hunter, March 6, 1876, *ibid.*

[51] Aristarchi to Fish, April 5, 1876, Notes Received, Turkey; Maynard to Fish, March 27, 1875, and March 30, 1876, Despatches, Turkey; Fish to Vidal, April 22, 1876, Instructions, Barbary Powers (Tripoli).

[52] Vidal to Hunter, May 16, 1876 (Nos. 76 and 77), Despatches, Tripoli.

[53] Vidal to Hunter, July 1, 1876; July 7, 1876 (Nos. 79 and 80); July 8, 1876; July 15, 1876 (Nos. 82 and 83); July 17, 1876, *ibid.*

ported, and his exposition of the dangers to those rights implicit in the proposed court reforms had earned him commendation.[54] A request for leave to study "political questions" at Constantinople had been granted, his reports on the slave trade had been welcomed and the information on connivance at Malta transmitted to Her Majesty's government, his first proposal regarding a North African naval base had been acknowledged with the comment that the suggestion would "be taken into consideration." [55] Despite the total absence of consular business in the Regency the Department had concurred in his plan to appoint an agent at Benghazi, it had commended his effort to liberate slaves at Malta and his proposed visit to Cyrenaica, it had approved the activities described in his despatch from Benghazi and his management of the crisis which followed the summons from the Medjliss el Temiz.[56]

Nor did the consul's activities lack the sanction of important American tradition. The expansion of the area of freedom, with its implicit limitation on the influence of the great powers of Europe, had been one of the major rationales of American territorial growth and of American diplomatic activity generally. The historic rivalry with Britain had received recent emphasis in the diplomacy of the Civil War and its aftermath. In the logic of the reformer, if not in that of the strategist, there was little reason to discriminate between the slave trade of the Atlantic coast of the Dark Continent and that of its Mediterranean shore. The question of the Mediterranean naval station had itself a long history. Proposals to acquire Greek or Turkish islands had come to naught, the ample Spanish and Italian base facilities of ante-bellum days were no longer available, and by the 1870's the European Squadron's logistic infrastructure was limited to a rented warehouse at Villefranche on the French Riviera. In his concern with the base problem, which indeed antedated his appointment to Tripoli, Vidal was not alone, for at the time of his exploration of Cyrenaica the American minister to Turkey had suggested to the government the purchase of an enclave at Bab el Mandeb.[57]

[54] Assistant Secretary of State J. C. Bancroft Davis to Vidal, July 25, 1871; Fish to Vidal, June 20, 1873, and March 17, 1874, Instructions, Barbary Powers (Tripoli).

[55] Hunter to Vidal, August 9, 1872; Fish to Vidal, February 10 and March 27, 1873, and February 4, 1874, *ibid.* See also Note 14 above.

[56] Hunter to Vidal, August 11, 1873; Fish to Vidal, February 4 and August 25, 1874; John L. Cadwalader to Vidal, October 13, 1875, *ibid.*

[57] Vidal to Hunter, January 6, 1873, Despatches, Tripoli; George H. Boker to Fish, June 18, 1874, Despatches, Turkey.

Supported though they had been by the Department, and consistent though they were with traditional policy, Vidal's activities had brought about a crisis which faced Washington with the always unwelcome need for a decision. Had there been any inclination to force the issue with the Turkish authorities, either in connection with the status of the treaties or with the acquisition of a naval station, a better time could hardly have been imagined than the summer of 1876. The Sick Man appeared indeed about to breathe his last, and in July, as dissolution of the Ottoman Empire seemed increasingly imminent, European fears of American intervention brought the British and Italian ministers to the State Department to join their voices with that of Aristarchi in protesting the conduct of Vidal.[58] Revealing though these actions were, they were unnecessary. The decision had been taken, and although the consul's reply to the Turkish complaints had not yet been received, his recall, promised Aristarchi on May 3, had been finally sent on June 20.[59]

Times, after all, were changing as the centenary of American independence approached. American expansion, so vigorous before the Civil War, had stopped after Appomattox with Alaska. Efforts to acquire Santo Domingo and the Danish West Indies had failed, as had plans for the purchase of Greenland and Iceland. In America new forms of energy were revolutionizing manufacturing and transportation, bringing opportunities of wealth beyond the dreams of avarice and far beyond those based on the simple physiocratic exchange of goods on which traditional American foreign policy had been founded. As opportunity at home replaced opportunity on the oceans the new mercantilism became visible, the one world of free trade began to separate into a world of discrete power centers, and the navy of Jefferson to give way to the navy of Mahan. Not only had the application of steam to naval propulsion complicated the logistics of distant squadrons but new troubles were developing in American waters. In November following the crisis at Tripoli the European Squadron was drastically weakened by recall of ships in consequence of the war in Cuba and Secretary

[58] Thornton to Fish, July 18, 1876, Notes Received, Great Britain; Baron Alberto Blanc to Fish, July 26, 1876, Notes Received, Italy.

[59] Fish to Aristarchi, May 3 and June 28, 1876, Notes to Foreign Legations, Turkey; Fish to Vidal, June 20, 1876 (Nos. 61 and 62), Instructions, Barbary Powers (Tripoli).

Fish's famous despatch Number 266 to Spain.[60] Far from demonstrating an interest in the eastern Mediterranean, the Navy Department was planning to shift the headquarters of the European Squadron to Lisbon, and was only deterred by a lengthy and urgent despatch from Admiral Worden emphasizing how gravely this would complicate the problem of supporting the missionaries in Ottoman regions.[61] In diplomatic affairs a similar retrograde tendency was apparent, and 1876 saw American consulates in Italy down-graded to consular agencies, the ministers to Greece and Portugal reduced to chargés d'affaires, and the consulate in Cyprus abandoned.

On July 17 Vidal was deploying his agents in search of evidence of the slave trade when the Malta steamer arrived with his recall, which he received with "an unruffled conscience." Retaining his spirit to the last, he reported on the next day a great pyrrhic victory: dressed in full uniform the Pasha had received the letter of the President addressed to His Highness the Bey (*sic*) of Tripoli, and by so doing had validated the American case concerning the independent status of the Regency.[62] If it was a victory it was one that had to be followed up, but of this there was by now no chance; the twin impulses of expansion and reform were dead. Under pressure from Britain the Department would shortly concede that the Pasha had no right to this title and the credentials of Vidal's successor would be modified accordingly. Fish's instructions to the new consul ruled out both a naval base and the emancipation of slaves and withdrew into the non-participating morality also sanctioned by important American tradition. "Unlike some, at least, of the European Governments," he wrote, "we have no political objects in the Turkish dominions. . . . We covet no occasions to bluster or domineer there, certainly none such as sentimental patronage of benighted Africans would require of us." [63]

In October the new consul arrived and Vidal departed, speeded on his way by touching testimonials from the "benighted Africans,"

[60] *Annual Report of the Secretary of the Navy, 1876* (Washington, 1876), 8, 10; Worden to Robeson, December 8, 1875, European Squadron Letters.

[61] Fish to Benjamin Moran, March 2 and July 10, 1877, Instructions, Portugal; Moran to Fish, April 7 and August 1, 1877, Despatches, Portugal; Worden to Robeson, March 17, 1877, European Squadron Letters.

[62] Vidal to Hunter, July 17 and July 18, 1876, Despatches, Tripoli.

[63] Fish to Edwards Pierrepoint, November 17, 1876, Instructions, Great Britain; Fish to Cuthbert B. Jones, November 16, 1876, Instructions, Barbary Powers (Tripoli).

Moroccans, and Jews whom he had befriended, and from his consular staff.[64] Shortly the several hundred Moroccans and Sudanese whom he had covered with the Stars and Stripes found their apprehensions justified and their protection withdrawn. Under the new management affairs in Tripoli settled back into the status quo ante, there to remain until in 1882 congressional abolition of the consulate wrote an end to a diplomatic history which had begun in London in 1786 when Abdurrahman, the Bashaw's ambassador, had observed to a surprised John Adams that a state of war existed between their countries.[65]

As in diplomatic activity, so it was in naval affairs. Somewhat surprisingly, perhaps, the hydrographic survey of the Tripolitan coast which Vidal had desired was in fact undertaken, and in the summer of 1878, into waters which Preble and Barron had once controlled and to the shore made famous by Eaton's anabasis steamed the side-wheeler *Gettysburg*. But the operation was more symbolic than successful. With the work still uncompleted the ancient ship broke down, and so decrepit was her condition that repairs seemed impracticable and she was sold for scrap at Genoa.[66] As for the problem of the Mediterranean naval base, no solution was attempted. If the Department did not withdraw outside the Straits to Lisbon, neither was an advance made toward Egypt and the Suez Canal. Between journeys to the Levant in support of the missionary effort, increasingly their only function, the ships of the European Squadron continued to base at Villefranche. Whatever the disadvantages from certain larger points of view, it was a location that the liberty parties understandably preferred.

64 Vidal to Evarts, May 14, 1878, and enclosures, Despatches, Tripoli.

65 The correspondence of Cuthbert B. Jones, Vidal's successor, *ibid.*, reflects the change. Secretary of State Frederick T. Frelinghuysen to John T. Robeson, July 8, 1882, Instructions, Barbary Powers (Tripoli), orders the closing of the consulate. The first encounter is reported in John Adams to John Jay, February 17, 1786, Charles Francis Adams (ed.), *The Works of John Adams* (10 vols., Boston, 1850-1856), VIII, 372.

66 See correspondence of the period in European Squadron Letters; Jones to Hunter, May 31, 1878, Despatches, Tripoli. Seaton Schroeder, *A Half Century of Naval Service* (New York, 1922), 105-32, is an account by a participant.

The Brownsville Episode and the Negro Vote

By Emma Lou Thornbrough

By 1900 the number of Negro voters in some northern cities was large enough to constitute the balance of power between the major political parties. Nevertheless, Negroes seldom enjoyed political recognition proportionate to their numbers. Because of their record of unswerving loyalty to the party of Lincoln, Republican leaders tended to take their support for granted, and few Democrats made a serious bid for Negro votes. Although the habit of voting a straight Republican ticket continued into the twentieth century, there were signs of increasing disillusionment among Negroes for the failure of the party to protect their rights in the South. Hopes of Negroes for more equitable treatment were raised temporarily by gestures in favor of racial equality made by Theodore Roosevelt. By dining with Booker T. Washington, by using the Negro educator as an adviser, and by fighting for the confirmation of a Negro as collector of the port of Charleston, South Carolina, Roosevelt won a personal following among Negroes which none of his recent predecessors had enjoyed. But one incident — the discharging from the United States Army without honor of three companies of Negro troops in November, 1906 — threatened Roosevelt's personal popularity and also raised the possibility of a wholesale defection of Negro voters from the Republican party.

The story of the "shooting up" of the town of Brownsville, Texas, the subsequent discharge of the Negro troops stationed at nearby Fort Brown, and the numerous investigations of the affair has been told elsewhere, although some elements of mystery remain.[1] The

[1] See "Report on Brownsville Affray," *Senate Documents*, 59 Cong., 2 Sess., No. 155; James A. Tinsley, "Roosevelt, Foraker, and the Brownsville Affray," *Journal of Negro History* (Washington), XLI (January, 1956), 43-65; Joseph B. Foraker, *Notes of a Busy Life* (2 vols., Cincinnati, 1916), II, 231-327; Henry F. Pringle, *Theodore Roosevelt: A Biography* (New York, 1931), 458-64.

purpose of this article is to consider the political repercussions that followed the presidential order for the discharge, and especially to examine its effect upon Negro voters. The unprecedented mass discharge grew out of the fact that on the night of August 13, 1906, a group of armed men (whose identity was never established) had "shot up" the town of Brownsville, killing one person and wounding two others. White residents, who had previously shown hostility toward the colored soldiers of the Twenty-fifth Infantry, which had recently been assigned to the Brownsville post, immediately charged them with the outrage. Subsequent investigations by military authorities appeared to confirm that soldiers were responsible, but it was impossible to fix the guilt on any individuals. No one in any of the companies would confess, nor would any member reveal the guilty ones. All steadfastly persisted in maintaining their innocence and in denying any knowledge whatsoever of the raid. In the face of this alleged "conspiracy of silence" the Inspector General of the Army recommended that all the members of the three companies be discharged without honor, even though they included men with records of service ranging up to twenty-five years and six who had won medals of honor. The President, after studying the report of the Inspector General, approved its findings and instructed Secretary of War William Howard Taft to carry out the recommendations for the discharge. The order was not released to the public, however, until November 7, 1906, the day after elections in which Republicans retained control of the House of Representatives.

From first to last Roosevelt insisted that his action was in no way influenced by the fact that the troops were colored, and that he would have acted in exactly the same way had they been white. The effect of his action, however, was to arouse a wave of race feeling, in which extreme advocates of white supremacy exulted in the humiliation of the black troops, while Negroes and their white defenders deplored it. Some southern newspapers which had excoriated the President a few years before for entertaining Booker T. Washington at the White House now applauded him.[2] On the other hand, many northern white journals, regardless of their political leanings, were critical of the discharge and especially of its timing. It was widely reported that several Republican congress-

[2] The Atlanta *Journal*, November 8, 1906, for example, termed the discharge "in disgrace" of the entire battalion as "most commendable" because the innocent had tried to shield the guilty.

men, including the President's son-in-law, Nicholas Longworth, could attribute their election to the fact that the discharge was not revealed until after election day. The Waterville (Maine) *Sentinel* declared that in many northern districts colored voters had turned the tide for the Republicans because of their personal devotion to Roosevelt. "They did not care so much for the local candidates. It was a case of 'we are coming brother Theodore, three hundred thousand strong,' but they would have been coming in different temper had they known that on brother Theodore's desk was an order to disgrace and humiliate the entire colored battalion of the 25th infantry." The *Sentinel* charged that the President's action did "more credit to his adroitness than to his frankness, and the picture of a President whose chief merit is supposed to lie in his fearless bravery dodging an issue like this one, until after the votes are counted, is not pleasant to look upon, even though it stamps him as a clever politician." [3]

The Negro press greeted the President's order with unprecedented bitterness. The main point of attack was that the order applied to the innocent and guilty alike. Negro editors defended the refusal of the soldiers to expose the guilty men, even if they had known their identity, on the grounds that to have done so would have been to turn them over to lynch law. The most distinguished Negro paper, the New York *Age*, edited by T. Thomas Fortune, attacked the President's action for its flouting of due process. It declared: "It is carrying into the Federal Government the demand of the Southern white devils that innocent and law abiding black men shall help the legal authorities spy out and deliver practically to the mob black men alleged to have committed some sort of crime. The spirit invoked is not only vicious and contrary to the spirit of our Constitution, but it is an outrage upon the rights of citizens who are entitled in civil life to trial by jury and military life to trial by court martial." The *Age* insisted that "if we cannot get justice in the army, we are not compelled to enter it," and urged that any black man who offered to enlist to fill the place of a discharged soldier should be spurned by other Negroes.[4]

In Washington, D. C., the vitriolic Calvin Chase, editor of the *Bee*, exclaimed: "If this is military discipline, then we say to h__l

[3] Waterville (Maine) *Sentinel*, November 26, 1906. See also Washington *Star*, November 22, 1906.

[4] New York *Age*, November 8, 1906.

with military discipline." He, too, defended the soldiers for not betraying the guilty men, and asserted that "had they known and told who the guilty ones were, and they had been delivered up to the Brownsville civil authorities, there would have been a lynching the next night." Chase was of the opinion that the outcome of the recent elections in the Northeast would have been different if the presidential order had been promulgated earlier, and he predicted that the discharge would have far-reaching political repercussions. The following week he suggested with bitter sarcasm that Roosevelt run for another term "and see how dearly he is loved by the colored citizens of the United States. . . . Jefferson Davis is more honored today than Theodore Roosevelt. Benedict Arnold would have a monument erected to his memory sooner than Theodore Roosevelt." [5]

Richard W. Thompson, whose weekly column appeared in Negro newspapers throughout the country, wrote from Washington that not since the Supreme Court decision in the civil rights cases in 1883 had Negroes been so aroused, and that had the announcement been made a day earlier "there would have been a disastrous slump in the colored Republican vote." Writing privately to Emmett J. Scott, secretary to Booker T. Washington, Thompson expressed sorrow that "Roosevelt has made the mistake of his life in that 25th regiment discharge. . . . The South has bewitched Roosevelt as it did McKinley. . . . He may correct this thing, if he takes it in hand and rescinds the order in time. If he stands pat, his name will be anathema with the Negroes from now on." [6] Other private correspondence arriving at Tuskegee seemed to corroborate this view. From Columbus, Ohio, another Negro newspaperman, Ralph W. Tyler, wrote Booker T. Washington that "the Negroes are depleting the dictionary of adjectives in their denunciation of the President." Another correspondent wrote: "Things in Chicago are at fever heat in the race matter. You cannot find a Negro who is not denouncing the President in frightful terms of abuse. I never saw and heard anything like it. Mass meetings are held in which the President's acts and motives are held up to scorn." [7]

[5] Washington *Bee*, November 10, November 16, 1906.

[6] "Thompson's Weekly Review," Indianapolis *Freeman*, November 17, 1906; Richard W. Thompson to Emmett J. Scott, November 21, 1906, Booker T. Washington Papers (Division of Manuscripts, Library of Congress). All correspondence cited hereinafter is in the Booker T. Washington Papers unless otherwise identified.

[7] Ralph W. Tyler to Booker T. Washington, November 23, 1906; S. Laing Williams to Washington, November 26, 1906.

In pulpits throughout the country colored congregations heard their ministers attack the President. In New York City the minister of the Olivet Baptist Church indirectly threatened political opposition when he declared: "You have often heard me speak in admiration of the President, but now he has yielded to the ungodly prejudice of the South and has acted as he never would have done with white people." At the Abyssinian Baptist Church the minister made an even less veiled political threat. "The President's decree was signed the day after the election," he said. "He shot us when our gun was empty. But we have two years to work, and our slogan shall be a Republican Congress to protect our people in the South, a Democratic President to resent the insult heaped upon us. Thus shall we answer Theodore Roosevelt, once enshrined in our hearts as Moses, now enshrouded in our scorn as Judas." [8]

While ministers, editors, and other would-be race spokesmen were outdoing themselves in denunciation of the President, Booker T. Washington, the best-known and most influential American Negro, was noticeably silent. The situation created by the Brownsville order was not only embarrassing to him but it posed a potential threat to his position as race leader. Although Washington frequently deprecated political activity and disparaged Negro politicians, he himself had become a powerful political figure since Roosevelt had begun to consult him on race matters and southern politics. The fact that the President relied on the educator and ignored Negro political leaders in making appointments aroused resentment among politicians and was one reason for increasing criticism of Washington by members of his own race. At the same time a more fundamental reason for opposition to the "Tuskegee Wizard" was disagreement with his conservatism and his willingness to compromise where the rights of Negroes were concerned. Some of the more intellectual and militant Negroes even charged that his leadership had resulted in betrayal of the best interests of the race.

In spite of Washington's efforts to suppress criticism through control of the Negro press and race organizations, by 1906 opposition to him was becoming organized and vocal. A few Negro newspapers — among which the Boston *Guardian*, edited by Monroe Trotter, a Harvard graduate, was the most virulent — had opened an at-

[8] Boston *Herald*, November 17, 1906; Washington *Post*, November 23, 1906; New York *Times*, November 19, 1906.

tack upon his leadership, while organizations which he could not control were demanding an aggressive fight for civil rights. In the summer of 1905 the Niagara Movement, a forerunner of the National Association for the Advancement of Colored People, had been launched by a group led by W. E. B. DuBois and including Monroe Trotter. The Constitutional League, made up of both whites and Negroes but financed principally by white men, was attempting a fight for recognition of legal and political rights of Negroes. The dominant figure in the League was John E. Milholland, with whom Washington had once been on friendly terms but from whom he was now estranged. The old Afro-American Council, which had been dominated for years by Washington and his friend, T. Thomas Fortune of the New York *Age*, was no longer under his control. Because Washington was known to have influence with Roosevelt, the discharge of the Negro troops created a situation which his opponents (whom Washington privately referred to as "the enemy") might use to embarrass him and to challenge his leadership.

Washington had advance knowledge of the President's decision to discharge the troops and had written to him asking him to reconsider. But Roosevelt replied: "I could not possibly refrain from acting as regards those colored soldiers. You cannot have any information to give me privately, to which I could pay heed, my dear Mr. Washington, because the information on which I act is that which came out of the investigation itself." Although unable to deter Roosevelt, Washington privately circulated information that he had tried to do so. To one friend he sent a copy of the above letter with the remark: "I did my utmost to prevent his taking the action he did. I feel that I did my full duty in the matter which the enclosed copy of a letter from him will show." [9]

After his failure with Roosevelt, Washington turned to Secretary of War Taft, with whom he was on cordial terms and whom he hoped to see nominated for the presidency in 1908 if Roosevelt did not seek another term. Washington urged Taft to hold up the discharge until the President returned from a trip to Panama. He expressed the hope that when the President returned some plan might be worked out which would change the feeling of colored people over the discharge. He explained to Taft: "I have never in all my ex-

[9] Copy of letter of Theodore Roosevelt to Booker T. Washington, November 5, 1906, and Washington to Whitfield McKinlay, November 7, 1906, Carter G. Woodson Collection (Division of Manuscripts, Library of Congress).

perience with the race, experienced a time when the entire people have the feeling that they now have in regard to the administration."[10] Taft complied with the request, but his plea for delay was rejected by the President. Although Taft had no part in the decision to discharge the troops and was at first a victim of Roosevelt's impetuosity, he later asserted that he regarded the discharge as "fully sustained by the facts" and he steadfastly refused to question or criticize the action.[11] When Roosevelt returned to the capital later in November, Washington sent Emmett J. Scott to the White House with a message. The contents of this message were not revealed, but whatever they were they did not cause the President to modify his stand.[12]

Washington realized that his own opponents among the Negroes would try to use the President's action to discredit him. Even though he privately disagreed with that action, he believed that he should not criticize it publicly. He spoke of his dilemma to one of his protégés, Charles Anderson of New York, who owed his appointment by Roosevelt as collector of internal revenue more to the influence of Washington than to the New York politicians. Washington said that it was regrettable that the discharge order had been delayed until after the election and predicted that "the enemy will, as usual, try to blame me for all this. They can talk; I cannot, without being disloyal to our friend, who I mean to stand by throughout his administration." Anderson in reply expressed regret that their "friend" had not acted upon Washington's advice and informed him that "the Milholland crowd" were "making the most" of Roosevelt's action.[13]

Some of Washington's critics even implied that he was responsible for the troop discharge. For example, the Reverend Clayton Powell, in an address in New York City, after denouncing Roosevelt, said: "It is hard to believe that the man with the big stick disarming and crushing the colored soldiers is the same Theodore Roosevelt who three years ago declared that as long as he was president every man should have a 'square deal.' What has caused him to change his stand? Dr. Booker T. Washington is his

[10] Washington to Taft, November 20, 1906.

[11] Henry F. Pringle, *The Life and Times of William Howard Taft* (2 vols., New York, 1939), I, 324-25.

[12] Brooklyn *Eagle*, November 27, 1906; New York *Times*, November 28, 1906.

[13] Washington to Charles Anderson, November 7, 1906; Anderson to Washington, November 10, 1906.

adviser. Some believe that he is responsible for the change in the President's attitude toward the Negro Americans. The awful march of events since the famous Roosevelt-Washington luncheon makes a thoughtful man ask: Has the colored race been sold for a mess of pottage?"[14]

Instead of trying to reply to attacks of this sort Washington began a behind-the-scenes campaign to restrain the denunciation of the President. To Ralph Tyler he wrote: "Of course it was natural that some protest should be made, but I fear there is danger of too much of it. One thing the American people will not stand for any length of time, and that is abuse by any group of people of the President of the United States, and if our people in the North make the mistake of going too far there will be a reaction among the people, and the newspapers who have stood by us. I am doing all I can to check that folly." Shortly thereafter, speaking in a similar vein at a public banquet, he declared: "Civilization soon tires of a race, as of an individual, that continually whines and complains. And, likewise, the country will not tolerate any element in the population abusing and cursing the chief executive." When a group of newspapermen asked him to comment on the discharge of the troops Washington refused, merely saying: "I have nothing to say on that subject. I will not applaud nor condemn."[15]

Although Washington preferred to ignore the Brownsville matter and sought to make Negroes forget about it, the issue would not die so long as other groups and individuals insisted upon keeping it alive. One of these groups was the Constitutional League, which not only sponsored protest meetings but sent Gilchrist Stewart, a colored lawyer who was active in New York politics, to conduct an investigation of the discharge in an effort to obtain more evidence to place before the President.[16] The Afro-American Council also

[14] New York *Times*, December 16, 1906.

[15] Washington to Tyler, December 5, 1906; Springfield *Republican*, December 26, 1906; Pittsburgh *Times*, January 4, 1907. In an editorial in the New Orleans *Democrat*, December 31, 1906, Washington's reticence with regard to the troop discharge was the occasion for sarcastic comment: "It is not the wont of Booker to remain silent when any subject whatsoever is under discussion. . . . Is it possible that the dusky educator does not know 'where he is at?' With the President at one end and the criminal soldiers of his race at the other, is it possible that both ends of the poker are too hot for his handling, and a middle course too confined to give leeway for his utterance?"

[16] Stewart reported evidence which cast doubt as to whether any of the soldiers had been responsible for the shooting and which raised the question whether there was actually a "conspiracy of silence." New York *Evening World*, November 26, 1906; Youngstown *Telegram*, November 27, 1906.

employed a lawyer to take steps to protect the legal rights of the discharged soldiers.

But the individual who more than anyone else was responsible for keeping the Brownsville affair alive and making a political issue of it was Senator Joseph B. Foraker of Ohio. When Congress met in December, Foraker introduced a resolution calling for the secretary of war to turn over to the Senate all the evidence as to guilt of the soldiers which had led to the discharge. In January, as the result of his prodding, the Senate authorized an investigation by the Committee on Military Affairs. Foraker claimed that the evidence on which Roosevelt had acted was flimsy and untrustworthy, and he himself presented to the Senate persuasive evidence to show that not only was there no "conspiracy of silence," but that it would have been impossible for members of the three companies to have perpetrated the outrage.

Foraker's motives for pressing the inquiry were the subject for much speculation. He himself insisted that his only concern was for the discharged soldiers, who, in his opinion, were the victims of an unjust and probably unconstitutional action on the part of the President. But persons interested in politics concluded that Foraker probably had presidential ambitions and that the investigation would win him Negro support and at the same time embarrass Roosevelt in the event he sought another term. The investigation would also have the effect of putting an obstacle in the way of Foraker's fellow Ohioan, Taft, if Roosevelt did not seek the nomination himself. Taft probably accurately analyzed the situation when he told his brother: "Foraker is determined to make the President as uncomfortable as possible, and incidentally eliminate me from the Ohio situation." [17]

Regardless of his motives, Foraker's stand won him enthusiastic support in the Negro press. A few days after the troop discharge had been ordered a Negro paper, the Cleveland *Gazette*, forecast that the senator would take some steps in behalf of the discharged soldiers. At the same time the *Gazette* attacked Taft. "It should not be forgotten these days," it pointed out, "that the secretary of war is an Ohioan, the Hon. William H. Taft of Cincinnati. What kind of a member of the U. S. Supreme Court or president of the United States would he make from a race viewpoint. The dismissal

[17] Taft to Charles P. Taft, December 26, 1906, Pringle, *Life and Times of Taft*, I, 326.

of the three companies of the Twenty-fifth infantry was hatched up in his department." Soon afterward the Washington *Bee* declared: "Mr. Taft may be nominated for President but there is one thing certain, and that is that the colored voters of the country will not support him if nominated." [18]

Any possibilty that Roosevelt would attempt to retreat gracefully from the predicament in which he had placed himself by the discharge order vanished when Foraker entered the fray. Characteristically, the President impugned the motives of the Ohio senator and everyone else who criticized his handling of the affair. Foraker's opposition he described as "simply a cloak to cover antagonism to my actions about trusts, swollen fortunes and the like." Newspapers such as the New York *Sun* which attacked him for discharging the troops did so, he said, because they represented the interests of the "capitalistic reactionaries." The opposition by the leaders of the Constitutional League, John E. Milholland and Andrew B. Humphrey, Republicans who had supported Roosevelt at earlier stages of his political career, he characterized as "wicked and silly agitation" and declared: "These creatures have no place in the Republican party and are entitled to the scorn and abhorrence of every patriotic citizen." He insisted repeatedly that no one who was both honest and intelligent could question the guilt of the soldiers and that anyone who did so was condoning murder and perjury.[19]

While continuing to justify the discharge, Roosevelt insisted that he was utterly indifferent to any political consequences. When he learned that Taft was considering the suspension of the discharge order until he returned from Panama he wired that he cared "nothing whatever for the yelling of either the politicians or the sentimentalists." To a personal friend he wrote: "There has been great pressure not only by sentimentalists but by the northern politicians who wish to keep the negro vote. As you know I believe in practical politics . . . but in a case like this, where the issue is not merely one of naked right and wrong but one of vital concern to the whole country, I will not for one moment consider the political effect." [20]

[18] Cleveland *Gazette*, November 17, 1906; Washington *Bee*, December 22, 1906.

[19] Roosevelt to George Spinney, January 22, 1907, Elting E. Morison (ed.), *The Letters of Theodore Roosevelt* (8 vols., Cambridge, 1951-1954), V, 560; Roosevelt to Herbert Parsons, April 10, 1908, *ibid.*, VI, 999; Roosevelt to Lyman Abbott, May 10, 1908, *ibid.*, 1026.

[20] Roosevelt to Taft, November 21, 1906, *ibid.*, V, 498; Roosevelt to Silas McBee, November 27, 1906, *ibid.*, 509. He wrote several letters in similar vein. See, for example, the letter to Curtis Guild, Jr., November 7, 1906, *ibid.*, 489.

In spite of these protestations the President was not unmindful of political consequences and especially of the damage which Foraker might do to him and Taft. He hit upon a scheme which he thought amusing because it would be beating Foraker at his own game. He wrote to Booker T. Washington asking him to recommend the names of one or two colored Republicans, preferably in the Cincinnati area, who would be worthy of appointment to a position such as a collectorship of internal revenue or a surveyorship. A few weeks later there were newspaper reports that, on the recommendation of Washington, Roosevelt intended to name Ralph W. Tyler of Columbus, Ohio, to the position of surveyor of the port of Cincinnati, Foraker's home city.[21]

Tyler was a part-time journalist and secretary to Robert Wolfe, owner of the Columbus *Ohio State Journal* and the Columbus *Dispatch*, both of which were opposed to Foraker. Neither Foraker nor his colleague, Senator Charles W. F. Dick, had been consulted; but, as one newspaper explained, it was a foregone conclusion that they would vote to confirm the appointment "without visible wincing" because there were about 50,000 colored voters in Ohio. Later it was reported that Roosevelt had changed his mind and would not press the appointment because the proposal gave pain to so many white Republicans in Cincinnati. It was said that his son-in-law, Nicholas Longworth, had protested that the naming of a Negro to such a post in his district would mean his political ruin. The intended appointee himself thought that the President's change of heart was due to the fear that the appointment would hurt Taft's candidacy. He had been informed by his employer, he reported, that Roosevelt did not want to antagonize the two senators and thus make it more difficult for Taft to secure the Ohio delegation in 1908. Tyler did not get the surveyorship, but he was appointed an auditor in the Navy Department in Washington, D. C., where his presence would not offend white voters and where, it was hoped, he would be useful in keeping Negroes faithful to the Republican party.[22]

21 Roosevelt to Washington, December 25, 1906.

22 Tyler to Washington, March 14, 1907; Cumberland (Md.) *Times*, January 31, 1907; Cincinnati *Enquirer*, April 11, 1907. That Washington had a hand in this blow at Foraker and senatorial courtesy was well known. When a Negro witness named Washington was called before the Senate committee investigating the Brownsville affair someone laughingly inquired whether it was Booker T. At this Foraker was reported to have retorted: "No. Booker Washington is too busy attending to his senatorial duties to come here." Montgomery *Advertiser*, February 8, 1907.

A few Negro newspapers gave lukewarm endorsement to the naming of Tyler, but others were openly scornful and suspicious. While the appointment was pending the Cleveland *Gazette* remarked: "There ought not to be, and we trust there is not, a member of the race in Ohio so ungrateful and disloyal as to permit himself to be used by the president of the United States or any other person as a club with which to 'punish' politically the most aggressive and best friend of the race in America today — Senator Foraker — for his efforts in behalf of the race." Later the same paper declared that by naming Tyler the President had "but aggravated the situation in Ohio as far as he and our people are concerned." [23] Calvin Chase, of the Washington *Bee*, in an open letter to Roosevelt declared that the appointment would not influence Negro voters. "If I was Ralph W. Taylor [*sic*]," he said, "and Ralph W. Taylor was editor of the Bee I would inform the President that I object to being used as catspaw or a toady to rebuke a man who has been a friend to my race. This appointment, Mr. President, is not a drop in the bucket. It will only influence one vote in the entire state of Ohio and that vote is no doubt doubtful — Ralph W. Taylor." [24]

The efforts of Booker T. Washington to repair the damage done by the discharge of the troops extended far beyond the recommendation of Tyler. His confidant, Charles Anderson, warned him that members of the Constitutional League were saying that Foraker's fight would kill Roosevelt's aspirations for another term and "thereby knock out 'the Booker T. Washington Cabinet'." In an effort to hold the loyalty of the Negroes to himself as well as to the administration the Negro educator engineered several other appointments. As the result of his influence Roosevelt named two colored lawyers, William H. Lewis of Boston and S. Laing Williams of Chicago, as special attorneys for naturalization affairs in their respective cities. He also arranged numerous lesser appointments. When two Negroes were named to the board for the improvement of the city of Washington, he wrote to Roosevelt to thank him, assuring him that "these appointments will accomplish a great deal of good at this time." [25]

[23] Cleveland *Gazette*, February 9, April 20, 1907. See also New York *Age*, April 18, 1907; Indianapolis *Freeman*, February 9, 1907.

[24] Washington *Bee*, April 20, 1907.

[25] Anderson to Washington, January 4, 1907; Washington to Roosevelt, May 8, 1907. Both Washington and Anderson tried to discredit the Constitutional League in the eyes of the administration. For example, Washington told George B. Cortelyou,

In view of the fact that Negroes took a particular pride in their record of service in the army, Washington began a campaign to show that the discharge of the troops at Brownsville did not mean that Roosevelt and Taft were opposed to colored troops and their advancement. Emmett Scott, his private secretary, began correspondence with the War Department a few weeks after the discharge order, suggesting that Negroes be allowed to qualify as bandmasters in colored regiments, positions heretofore open only to white persons. Taft replied that he would try to arrange that the suggestion be carried out. After the size of the Field Artillery and the Coast Guard was increased by act of Congress, Washington wrote both Roosevelt and Taft for assurance that Negroes would be recruited to fill some of the posts. As a result of his influence a colored chaplain in Ohio, the principal battleground between Taft and Foraker, was elevated to the rank of major — the first Negro to attain that rank in the regular army.[26]

Washington's campaign included arrangements for Taft to speak at a fund-raising meeting for Hampton Institute — a nonpolitical affair at which the Secretary would nonetheless have an opportunity to display his friendship for the colored race. Negro speakers loyal to Washington were also in the field attempting to counteract the attacks upon the administration. For example, Fred R. Moore, the field representative of the Negro Business League, which was completely under Washington's control, spoke in defense of Roosevelt and insisted that he had done too much good for the race to be repudiated for a single act.[27]

In spite of these efforts, there were numerous signs throughout 1907 that Foraker's fight was winning him Negro support, while bitter opposition to Roosevelt and Taft continued to be manifested by the press and by race organizations. Washington himself was attacked because of his support of the administration. Even the New York *Age* (in which Washington had a secret financial in-

secretary of the treasury, that the League was in reality little more than one man, John E. Milholland. Washington to Cortelyou, January 28, 1907.

[26] Scott to Taft, December 12, 1906; Washington to Roosevelt, March 8, 1907; Washington to Taft, May 31, 1907; Indianapolis *Freeman*, February 23, 1907; Philadelphia *Ledger*, September 12, 1907; Cleveland *Plain Dealer*, September 17, 1907. Taft expressed himself as favorable to the creation of a colored artillery unit but insisted that he could not take action so long as he was subject "to the suspicion of being influenced by political motives," while the Foraker investigation was in progress. Taft to Washington, February 5, 1908.

[27] Norfolk (Va.) *Pilot*, January 19, 1907.

terest) criticized the Negro educator for his role in the contest between Foraker and Roosevelt. "In this posture of the contending forces," it said, "we regret exceedingly the wholly selfish use which the President is making of Mr. Washington and the colored people in this battle for political survivorship with Senator Foraker and the powerful interests and classes which he is leading. Neither Mr. Washington nor the colored people of the country can risk the hazard to be moved as mere pawns on this chess board of the President." The Washington *Bee* more bluntly declared: "The colored American will not support President Roosevelt for the Presidency or any man named by him, and if Prof. Washington cares for the good will and support of the people he should not tell them to be patient and support the President and Secretary Taft." [28]

Washington diligently sought to change the tone of the Negro press and was partially successful. In June, 1907, he wrote Arthur I. Vorys of Columbus, Ohio, who was managing the pre-convention campaign for Taft, that he was putting pressure on T. Thomas Fortune, editor of the *Age*, and a few days later wrote that he was "doing some quiet and effective work" with other colored newspapers to quiet the agitation over Brownsville. His efforts with Fortune were so successful that the Cleveland *Gazette* (which was probably subsidized by Foraker) began to charge that the *Age* was being subsidized with Taft money as the result of Washington's influence. It warned: "Politics will yet KILL the great Tuskegee school. *Mark our prediction*! When it does, Mr. Washington will have no one but himself to blame — Taft is too big a load for any person or thing to carry." [29]

Meanwhile there were other signs of disaffection. The national convention of the Afro-American Council, meeting in Baltimore in July, approved an address which deplored the dismissal of the Brownsville soldiers as "subversive of fundamental rights." It praised Foraker for championing the black soldiers "against the enormous and unexampled injustice and wanton abuse of executive authority" and promised to help him in his political fight. Members of the Niagara Movement, meeting in Boston the following month, took a pledge to enter politics and to try to unite the Negro

[28] New York *Age*, February 14, 1907; Washington *Bee*, June 30, 1907.

[29] Washington to Arthur I. Vorys, June 26 and July 8, 1907; Cleveland *Gazette*, July 6, 1907.

race against the Republican party so long as it remained under the leadership of Roosevelt or a Roosevelt man.[30]

Negro ministers continued their attack upon the administration. Resolutions adopted at the New England conference of colored Methodists declared that the discharge of the colored troops had "done more to arouse our just resentment and unite all elements of our people than any act of any President since Emancipation" and predicted that the action would have political consequences.[31] On the other hand, at the national Negro Baptist convention in Washington, D. C., at which Booker T. Washington was one of the principal speakers, attempts to introduce resolutions condemning Roosevelt were sidetracked, although a resolution praising Foraker was adopted. Washington wrote Roosevelt that this convention was the largest and most representative body of Negroes in America and added: "I was very glad to note, that with the exception of a few extreme radicals that the feeling toward you and your administration was kindly. . . . The feeling indicated at this convention, I think is representative of the change that is taking place gradually among our people in most parts of the country." [32]

More significant tests of the political feeling of Negroes were to be found in elections held in some of the cities of the North. Greatest interest centered in Ohio, where Taft and Foraker forces were engaged in a contest looking to control of the state's delegation to the national Republican convention in 1908. Foraker was openly making a bid for Negro support. In May a conference of Negro politicians meeting in Columbus criticized Taft's record on race questions and promised support of Foraker for any office he might seek. As commencement speaker at nearby Wilberforce University, Foraker took advantage of the opportunity to promise to fight for the rights of Negroes. Nevertheless in the Republican primary in Columbus he fared badly. In the pre-election campaign some Negroes attempted to exploit the Brownsville issue, but the Foraker candidate for mayor was reported to have received less than three hundred out of a possible four thousand Negro votes. A Negro

30 Hampton (Va.) *Fishermen's Net*, July 5, 1907; Washington *Bee*, July 6, 1907; Baltimore *Sun*, June 29, 1907; Boston *Transcript*, August 29, 1907.

31 Montpelier (Vt.) *Argus*, July 12, 1907.

32 Washington to Roosevelt, September 19, 1907. See also Washington *Herald*, September 17, 1907; Richmond *Planet*, September 28, 1907.

candidate for the city council who also tried to capitalize on the troop discharge made an extremely poor showing.[33]

The results of the Cleveland election were less encouraging to the Taft forces. There Roosevelt and Taft supported the candidacy of Representative Theodore E. Burton against Tom Johnson for mayor, apparently in the hope that a victory would make Burton a potential contender for Foraker's senatorial seat. In spite of their support Burton was defeated. Of the two wards in which Negroes were most numerous, one went Republican, as it had in the past, but the other gave Johnson a majority. The pro-Foraker Cleveland *Gazette*, which had been urging Negroes to support Johnson, hailed this as a repudiation of Roosevelt and as evidence that Brownsville had not been forgotten.[34]

In Boston, on the other hand, there was no evidence of a drift of Negroes to the Democrats. A Republican mayor was elected for the first time in years, despite strenuous efforts to capitalize on the Brownsville issue. Booker T. Washington, who was in the city during the campaign, wrote Roosevelt that the troop discharge had been "worked for all it was worth," but that it had practically no effect. He assured the President that he no longer thought that the Brownsville affair would hurt Taft's presidential candidacy.[35] In spite of this optimistic report, however, both Washington and Taft's advisers continued to have misgivings and to miss no opportunity to show Taft's interest in the welfare of the colored race. Washington arranged that he and Taft should speak from the same platform at a meeting of the Armstrong Association in Brooklyn. He advised Taft not to dwell on politics or to combat charges which "the enemy" had brought against him, but rather to take "a strong affirmative position" on education and race progress.[36]

Washington was concerned over the effect which the choice of delegates to the Republican convention might have on Negroes. He warned that rumors that Taft intended to rely on a Lily White delegation from Alabama might have an adverse effect in the North. To Vorys he wrote: "I am writing you all the more plainly and frankly on this subject, for the reason that no one knows better than yourself

[33] Cleveland *Gazette*, May 18, 1907; Columbus *Ohio State Journal*, June 21, 1907; Tyler to Washington, September 17, 1907.

[34] Cleveland *Gazette*, November 16, 1907.

[35] Washington to Roosevelt, December 16, 1907; New York *Age*, December 19, 1907.

[36] Washington to Taft, March 9, 1908; New York *Press*, March 17, 1908.

that we *have a hard battle* for ourselves to win the colored people of the North and doubtful states to the Secretary and I am very anxious that nothing be done in this or any other Southern state that will make the effort to overcome the Brownsville influence more difficult than it is." As another step toward winning Negro support Washington had suggested that Charles Anderson be a delegate from New York. Roosevelt's influence resulted in the selection of Anderson as a delegate at large. This was the first instance in which a New York Negro was given such a position and it was regarded as a stroke which would strengthen Taft against Governor Charles E. Hughes in that state.[37]

As Foraker's presidential chances faded and it became evident that Taft would be nominated, Negro opposition to the latter's candidacy evaporated. The dilemma in which members of the race found themselves was expressed by Richard W. Thompson in a private letter to Emmett Scott: "It is still Taft against the field. Foraker seems to be out of it in Ohio, and never was in it elsewhere. The Negroes are in a quandary, but might go to Hughes, if he looks like a winner. They will have to support Taft if he is nominated, and the wisest of them are taking in sail on the bolting question, while there is time to save them from being made ridiculous after next June." [38]

As early as November, 1907, the New York *Age*, which had been trying to start a boom for Hughes, had paved the way for an endorsement of Taft when it declared that it would support him or any other Republican who might be nominated.[39] Washington

[37] Washington to Vorys, December 25, 1907; Washington to Roosevelt, July 23, 1907; Washington to William Loeb, Jr., February 7 and April 3, 1907; Loeb to Emmett Scott, April 16, 1908. Roosevelt was also concerned over the charges that Taft favored the Lily Whites. In writing to a Republican leader in Louisiana, he expressed his regret that there was to be no colored delegate from that state and said that he had personally seen to it that New York sent a colored delegate. He explained: "The very considerations which made me set my face like flint against white and black demagogs who attack me for my action in the Brownsville matter, make me feel that we should be scrupulously careful to do justice to the decent colored man." Roosevelt to Pearl Wight, April 18, 1908, Morison (ed.), *Letters of Theodore Roosevelt*, VI, 1012.

[38] Thompson to Scott, January 30, 1908.

[39] New York *Age*, November 14, 1907. The changed position of the *Age* was made possible by the sudden withdrawal from the paper of T. Thomas Fortune, its editor and co-owner. Fortune's interest was acquired secretly by Booker T. Washington, who nevertheless persistently denied having any financial interest in the *Age* or any other newspaper. Washington's relationship to the *Age* is discussed in Emma Lou Thornbrough, "More Light on Booker T. Washington and the New York *Age*," scheduled for publication in *Journal of Negro History*.

considered the influence of the *Age* greater than that of any other Negro paper, but he sought to impress upon Vorys the importance of getting control of other papers as well. Ralph W. Tyler, who, as an auditor in the Navy Department, continued to do yeoman service for the Taft cause, was given the assignment of rounding up the support of certain journals. In a short time he wrote jubilantly that he had seen Chase of the Washington *Bee* and had brought that paper into the fold in addition to winning over the Indianapolis *Freeman*. He also asserted that "the enemy" would not get control of the Chicago *Conservator* if he could help it — that it "*must* stand as supporter of Dr. Washington and the administration." [40]

In its next issue the *Bee* announced that it was bowing to the will of the majority and would support Taft since it was evident that the country was for him. Although Chase's decision was no doubt due in part to Tyler's powers of persuasion as well as to financial inducements, additional considerations which influenced him and other Negroes were set forth in the editorial: "If the Republican party says Taft, and if the Negroes of this country prefer the Republican party to the party of Tillman, Vardaman, et al., there is nothing left for us to do but to join in the general acclaim. . . . The Bee recognizes that the party is greater than any one man, and that the tail cannot wag the dog. . . . The Bee because of the accursed and relentless opposition of the Democratic party to the race must of necessity stand for the Republican party." [41]

The remaining opposition to Taft did not greatly alarm Washington. The Cleveland *Plain Dealer*, a leading holdout, declared that the colored people of the state were still for Foraker and suspicious of Taft, even after the Republican state convention in Ohio had given its solid support to Taft. Vorys continued to express concern, but Washington was convinced that the danger of an important defection of Negro voters had passed. After addressing conferences of both the African Methodist Episcopal church and the A. M. E. Zion church he reported to William Loeb: "It was very interesting to see how the great bulk of our people are coming around to the point where they understand the President and Secretary Taft and are ceasing to be misled by a few paid agitators [a phrase which both Washington and Roosevelt liked to use to describe members of the

[40] Washington to Vorys, February 26, 1908; Tyler to Thompson, March 26, 1908.

[41] Washington *Bee*, March 28, 1908.

Constitutional League]."[42] After this favorable state of affairs had been reached, Loeb proposed to prepare a statement regarding Brownsville for the Republican campaign textbook; but Washington replied that the less said about that unpleasant subject, the better, since colored people were beginning to forget about it.[43]

By the time of the Republican national convention most Negroes had climbed aboard the Taft band wagon. There was, of course, some resentment over the treatment which their race received at the convention, especially at the seating of Lily White delegations from the South, but, as one newspaper explained: "It was but natural for the colored Republicans to resent the insults, the trickery and fraud perpetrated upon them by the galvanized Republicans who dominated the Chicago convention, but when one considers the record of the Democratic party he must admit that it is out of the question for the colored man to vote for Bryan. The 'Jim Crow' laws of every Democratic State, the exclusion from the jury of almost every southern court, the mockery of a fair trial before every southern tribunal, all stand as brazen reminders of the eternal enmity of the Democracy toward the Negro."[44]

Indeed, the fact that Negroes remained loyal to the Republican party in spite of the Brownsville episode and in spite of the gestures which Taft was making toward the white South was due as much or more to abiding suspicion of the Democratic party and the failure of that party to capitalize on Negro discontent as it was to the conciliatory efforts of the Republicans. Southern champions of white supremacy had not only applauded Roosevelt's discharge of the colored troops but were using the Brownsville affair as justification for proposing new racial disabilities. Both houses of the Tennessee legislature adopted resolutions commending the President for the discharge of the troops. This was followed by similar ac-

[42] Cleveland *Plain Dealer*, April 27, 1908; Vorys to Washington, March 6 and April 3, 1908; Washington to Loeb, May 10, 1908. To Taft he reported a similar change in attitude on the part of a prominent colored Baptist and remarked: "It shows that our best men are gradually taking on sensible views regarding the Brownsville and other incidents. The race has gotten thoroughly sick and tired of John E. Milholland and his crowd." Washington to Taft, May 20, 1908.

[43] Washington to Arthur S. Gray, May 19, 1908. Washington nevertheless wrote a statement in which he pointed out that although the mass of Negroes did not approve of Roosevelt's action with regard to the colored troops, they felt that he would have acted in the same way if the troops had been white. He also cited examples of actions which the President had taken in behalf of Negroes and asserted that it was unfair to condemn him for one act.

[44] Dallas *Express*, quoted in Indianapolis *World*, August 15, 1908.

tions in other southern states. In the border state of Missouri a laudatory resolution was adopted by Democratic votes, with the Republican minority in the legislature voting against it. The people of Brownsville prepared to show their enthusiasm for the presidential order by presenting Roosevelt with a jewel-adorned "big stick." [45]

The conduct of southern Democrats in and out of Congress, which their northern colleagues did nothing to restrain, prevented northern Negroes from joining Democratic ranks. In the debate over the discharge of the troops the Democrats in Congress not only supported Roosevelt against Foraker but even proposed that Negroes be barred completely from enlisting in the army. In support of such a step Representative James L. Slayden of Texas attacked the record of Negro troops in general and especially that of the troops stationed at Brownsville.[46] The attitude of the Democrats caused Roosevelt to confide to his son-in-law: "In my judgment, when the report of the committee [investigating the discharge of the troops] comes in the Democrats of the committee will take such an extreme position as to make the colored men who have even the slightest shred of common sense realize where their real friends are." [47]

Outside of Congress, the Democrats, instead of wooing the Negro voters of the North, followed a course which inevitably had the effect of alienating them. In Maryland a constitutional amendment to disfranchise Negroes by means of a "grandfather clause" was

[45] New York *Age*, January 17, 1907. Even before the Brownsville affair Roosevelt had won a more enthusiastic following among white Democrats than had any of his Republican predecessors. The dismissal of the troops increased this popularity. At a dinner in honor of William Jennings Bryan, John Temple Graves went so far as to propose that Bryan should endorse Roosevelt for the presidency in 1908. The New York *Age*, April 18, 1907, warned: "If the Republicans are not on their guard the Democratic South will grab Theodore Roosevelt and appropriate him to their own uses."

[46] *Cong. Record*, 59 Cong., 2 Sess., 776-80 (January 8, 1907). Another Texan, Representative John N. Garner, introduced a similar measure. A remarkable exception among the southerners heaping praise upon Roosevelt was Senator Benjamin R. Tillman of South Carolina, who attacked the discharge of the troops as lynch law.

[47] Roosevelt to Nicholas Longworth, June 26, 1907, Morison (ed.), *Letters of Theodore Roosevelt*, V, 695. When the Senate Committee on Military Affairs, which had been investigating the troop discharge, made its report on March 11, 1908, the five Democratic members did not file a separate report as Roosevelt had evidently expected. They joined four of the Republican members in a majority report upholding the presidential discharge. A minority report was filed by four Republican members who held that the testimony on which Roosevelt had acted did not establish the guilt of the soldiers beyond any reasonable doubt. The minority asked that the discharged men be reinstated. See *Senate Reports*, 60 Cong., 1 Sess., No. 355.

passed by both houses of the legislature. In a speech in New York City, William Jennings Bryan defended the disfranchisement of southern Negroes and said that the white men of the South were giving Negroes better laws than Negroes would give white men if they were making the laws. The platform adopted at the Democratic national convention made no mention of the Negro and was silent on the subject of disfranchisement. John W. Kern, Bryan's running mate, was reported to have made disparaging remarks about colored voters. There was a story that he attributed his defeat for the governorship of Indiana in 1900 to the fact that his opponent received the Negro vote. At a banquet after the election he said: "I am proud of the fact that I did not receive a Negro vote. I was elected by the white vote but defeated by the ignorant nigger vote." [48]

In view of the record of the two political parties an impartial observer might have concluded that Negroes could expect to gain little from either a Democratic or a Republican victory, but it required considerable rationalizing to decide that a victory by Bryan would be more favorable to the interests of the colored population than would a Taft victory. Nevertheless a few well-known Negroes campaigned for the Democratic candidate. One of them was the president of the Afro-American Council, Bishop Alexander Walters of the A. M. E. Zion church. Together with Monroe Trotter, president of the New England Constitutional and Suffrage League, and William H. Scott, president of the Boston Suffrage League, Walters sent out a call for a national convention of Negroes to decide upon a course of political action. The call declared that the alliance of Roosevelt and the southern nullifiers of the Constitution made such a meeting necessary. It also spoke of "the defaming and discharging in disgrace of more than a hundred soldiers, all colored," and referred to the candidacy of a cabinet member, who in public speeches in the South, had condoned disfranchisement and who had "supinely endorsed in toto the brutal and autocratic discharge of colored soldiers." [49] The convention, which met in Philadelphia in April, was a rather sorry affair, attended by only about forty persons. All those present pledged themselves to support Bryan if Taft were nominated.[50]

[48] Indianapolis *World*, February 29, August 22, 1908; Indianapolis *Freeman*, May 2, 1908.

[49] Indianapolis *Freeman*, February 22, 1908.

[50] *Ibid.*, April 18, 1908.

After the nominating conventions, Walters and Trotter continued to oppose Taft and to work actively for Bryan. Trotter's paper, the Boston *Guardian*, declared: "There is only one proper and sensible thing for colored men to do, then, in real self-interest, and to help save their Southern colored brethren and that is to compass Taft's defeat. To vote for him should be out of the question with any decent colored person." W. E. B. DuBois, another intellectual, agreed. "It is high noon, brethren — the clock has struck twelve," he exclaimed. "What are we going to do? I have made up my mind. You can do as you please — you are free, sane and twenty-one. If between two parties who stand on identically the same platform you can prefer the party who perpetrated Brownsville, well and good! But I shall vote for Bryan." [51]

Few Negroes shared this point of view, and the conduct of Bryan and the Democrats generally caused embarrassment to those members of the colored race who were supporting them. Early in the campaign there were reports that Bryan was eager for Negro support and was hopeful of capitalizing on dissatisfaction over Brownsville. Bishop Walters was reported to have said that Bryan had told a delegation of Negroes that he regarded Roosevelt's discharge of the Negro troops as unjust, and that if elected he would recognize Negroes in appointments to office. But when questioned by a correspondent of the New York *American* about this statement, Bryan said that he had not discussed the matter of Brownsville for publication and did not recall "ever having stated any positive attitude upon either of the questions propounded." He asserted that during the campaign he intended to confine himself strictly to the issues promulgated in the Democratic platform (which did not mention Negroes) and would not discuss Brownsville or Negro appointments.[52] The Negro press did not fail to note that Bryan's statement put Walters in an embarrassing position and, in fact, seemed to cast doubt on his veracity. One paper declared: "It's too bad, and we are awfully sorry. Bishop Walters is a good, able, well intentioned man, but the good bishop lets his passions lead his judgment astray." Another remarked: "Those disgruntled Negroes who have been expecting so much from the Democratic party and

[51] *Ibid.*, July 18, 1908, quoting Boston *Guardian* and *Horizon* (Washington).

[52] Indianapolis *World*, August 1, 1908 (quoting New York *American*); *ibid.*, August 8, 1908 (quoting New York *Herald*).

most especially its nominee for the presidency don't seem to be getting it anywhere but in the neck." [53]

Walters continued to work for Bryan in spite of these rebuffs. To him and a few others the Brownsville issue continued to transcend all other considerations. The Niagara Movement, meeting in Oberlin, Ohio, adopted the following appeal to voters: "Register and vote whenever and wherever you have a right. Remember the conduct of the Republican party toward Negroes has been a disgraceful failure to keep just promises. The dominant Roosevelt faction has sinned in this respect beyond forgiveness. We therefore trust that every colored voter will uphold men like Joseph B. Foraker and will leave no stone unturned to defeat William H. Taft." The appeal continued: "Remember Brownsville and establish next November the principle of Negro independence in voting, not only for punishing enemies, but for rebuking false friends." [54]

To the rank and file the importance of the Brownsville issue declined in the face of fresh evidence of Democratic hostility to racial equality. In August the Democratic state convention of West Virginia adopted a plaform containing two planks which observers predicted would do much to hold Negroes in the Republican party. The first, a demand for a constitutional amendment "to insure the purity of the ballot," declared that the extension of suffrage to "a race inferior in intelligence and without preparation for the wise and prudent exercise thereof" had been a mistake. The second called for a law requiring separate accommodations in transportation for members of the white and colored races. In northern cities Republican party strategists instructed their speakers to answer hecklers who attempted to raise the Brownsville issue by simply calling attention to the Democratic record instead of trying to justify the discharge of the colored troops. They were told to refer to Democratic efforts in Congress to bar Negroes from the army, to the Jim Crow and disfranchisement planks in the West Virginia platform, and to the silence of Bryan on the race question.[55] Writing to Booker T. Washington of this strategy Charles Anderson said that the mere recital of the Democratic record "ought to be a sufficient answer to any men who have the nerve to ask about Brownsville." [56]

[53] *Ibid.*, August 15, 1908, quoting Sumter (S. C.) *Defender* and Hampton (Va.) *Fishermen's Net.*

[54] Cleveland *Plain Dealer*, September 3, 1908.

[55] Indianapolis *World*, August 15, 1908; Cleveland *Journal*, August 8, 1908.

[56] Anderson to Washington, October 7, 1908.

During the campaign Anderson was quoted in the press as saying confidently that "ten out of every fourteen colored voters of this country are wearing Taft buttons or expressing in some way their feelings for Taft." This assertion was promptly challenged by some Negroes as being worthless because it came from a member of the "black bread and butter brigade" of federal officeholders. There continued to be predictions that the mass of Negroes would not vote for Taft — that they would vote for Eugene V. Debs instead if they could not bring themselves to vote for Bryan. Even Theodore Roosevelt privately expressed some pessimism in regard to the Negro vote.[57]

The results of the election seemed to indicate that Anderson had assessed the situation quite accurately. Taft won easily, although neither his popular vote nor his electoral vote was as large as Roosevelt's had been in 1904. From available statistics it is not possible to separate the Negro vote from the white and therefore to state accurately to what extent the difference between the Republican vote in 1904 and 1908 was due to a decline in Negro support. The fact that Taft's margin of victory in certain northern states — Pennsylvania, Ohio, Indiana, and Illinois — was smaller than Roosevelt's may have been due in part to the loss of Negro votes. But the outcome did not reflect a personal antipathy to Taft, since he ran ahead of other Republican candidates in those states. Ohio, where it had been feared that the Negro feeling against him was especially strong, gave him its electoral votes but elected a Democratic governor. Taft also carried the neighboring state of Indiana, where both a Democratic governor and legislature were elected. Moreover, in New York, where efforts to turn Negroes against him had been particularly strenuous, Taft won by a larger margin than had Roosevelt, and he also ran well ahead of the gubernatorial candidate, Hughes. He also carried New Jersey, which had a sizable Negro vote, by a larger margin than had Roosevelt. From all this it appears that the Brownsville episode did not lead to a marked defection of Negroes from the Republican party, nor did Taft appear to have suffered personally because of his part in the affair.[58]

[57] Cleveland *Plain Dealer*, September 27, 1908; Roosevelt to Kermit Roosevelt, October 20, 1908, Morison (ed.), *Letters of Theodore Roosevelt*, VI, 1303-1304.

[58] The fact that Taft's vote in such cities as Cleveland and Indianapolis was smaller than Roosevelt's had been may have been due in part to the loss of Negro votes, but in both cities Taft ran ahead of the Republican candidate for governor.

This does not mean, however, that the discharge of the colored soldiers had not created a real threat to the traditional loyalty of Negroes to the Republican party. There is abundant evidence that the members of the race were aroused over the treatment of the soldiers as they had not been aroused by the action of any other president. That Roosevelt's order did not have the serious consequences that at first threatened was due in part to the record of the Democrats and their failure to take advantage of the opportunity to win Negroes away from their Republican allegiance. It was also due to the fact that in the two-year interval between the discharge of the soldiers and the presidential election the influence of Booker T. Washington had been a guiding factor in the waging of an astute and effective campaign to minimize the effect of Roosevelt's action and to rehabilitate him and Secretary Taft in the eyes of the colored population. Although the general public was unaware of Washington's role, some of the Negro leaders in the campaign recognized the importance of his contribution, and shortly after the election one of them wrote to him: "Without appearing on the stump or giving out any public utterance of more than a general character, you did more than any other dozen men in the country to bring into line for Mr. Taft the Negro masses." [59]

[59] Thompson to Washington, November 22, 1908. See also Vorys to Washington, November 9, 1908, acknowledging the indebtedness which Taft and the Republican party owed to him for his unfaltering support "particularly when the colored race was up in arms against Taft."

The Semicentennial of the Mississippi Valley Historical Association

By James L. Sellers

The founders of this Association, when they met in Lincoln fifty years ago, designed their organization around a common interest in historical study. Their purpose was general and the means had not yet been envisaged in clear outline. The nature and character of the organization, its financial support, its activities, and the selection of its leadership all had to be designed and reconciled to the interests and tastes of its members. The full story cannot be related in a brief paper, but the consideration of a number of events and decisions may help the reader to understand the Association as we know it today.[1] No history is complete, and in this story more is omitted than is related, but the author believes that some of the most important problems in the history of the Association are treated. Future studies may assign more definite credit and responsibility for many of these decisions than would appear appropriate at this time. It seems highly probable that the somewhat vague and uncertain policies and programs of the Association constitute a truly reflected image of the leadership within the Association. They are the product of the inevitable and natural ferment of a democratic organization.

The Lincoln *Star* of October 18, 1907 (then an evening paper), carried the first press account of this Association. It began:

> The Mississippi Valley Historical Association was organized, tentatively, this morning at a meeting of secretaries of the societies of the Mississippi Valley states. The meeting was held in the rooms of The Nebraska State Historical Society in the State University Library Building. It was presided over by F. A. Sampson, Secretary of the Missouri His-

[1] This article is a revision of the paper presented in the session on "The Mississippi Valley Historical Association in Retrospect," at the fiftieth annual meeting of the Association, in Lincoln, on May 2, 1957. The author is indebted to the Secretary-Treasurer for a number of the changes from the paper as delivered at the meeting.

torical Society, and E. R. Harlan, Assistant Curator of the Iowa Historical Department, served as Secretary.[2]

The group had assembled in response to invitations sent out on July 29 by Clarence S. Paine, secretary of the Nebraska State Historical Society, asking the recipients "to meet the secretaries of neighboring historical societies for the purpose of considering plans for effecting a permanent organization for the advancement of historical research and the collection and conservation of historical materials in these western states." [3] Despite the *Star's* mention of the Mississippi Valley states, only six states — Iowa, Kansas, Missouri, Minnesota, Montana, and Nebraska — were represented. Assurance of interest and future participation had been received, however, from the historical societies of Chicago and St. Louis, and from the state societies of Arkansas, Colorado, Illinois, North Dakota, South Dakota, Wisconsin, and the Territory of New Mexico.[4]

In the organization meeting Paine presented a draft of a constitution modeled after the constitution of the Pacific Coast Branch of the American Historical Association. His original draft proposed the name that is still current, but it was temporarily amended to read, "the Mississippi Valley Branch of the American Historical Association." His proposal described the object of the organization to be, "to promote and popularize historical study and research and to provide a plan of co-operation for local and state Historical Societies of the Mississippi Valley." The section on membership limited "active members . . . to those who are officers or heads of departments of local or state historical societies." Honorary members chosen from "persons distinguished for literary or scientific at-

[2] In addition to Sampson and Harlan, those present at this meeting were Clarence S. Paine of the Nebraska State Historical Society, who had extended the invitations to meet in Lincoln, William S. Bell of the Montana Historical Library, George W. Martin of the Kansas State Historical Society, Benjamin F. Shambaugh of the State Historical Society of Iowa, and Warren Upham of the Minnesota Historical Society. Mississippi Valley Historical Association, *Proceedings* (Cedar Rapids), I (1907-1908), 9. See also James L. Sellers, "Before We Were Members — The MVHA," *Mississippi Valley Historical Review* (Cedar Rapids), XL (June, 1953), 4-5.

[3] Paine had been elected secretary of the Nebraska State Historical Society only a few months earlier, and he was conscious of the need for consultation among the directors of societies in the interest of advancing their work.

[4] Lincoln *Star*, October 18, 1907. Paine said that eleven other societies had indicated support; and in addition to the nine named above there are letters in his correspondence from Texas and Wyoming expressing intention of attending the meeting. Mississippi Valley Historical Association Collection (Nebraska State Historical Society, Lincoln), Letter File, Box 1.

tainment or the promotion of historical research" might be approved by the Executive Committee. Two meetings were to be held each year — one in June and the other in connection with the annual meetings of the American Historical Association in December. It was agreed that the completion of plans for a permanent organization should be deferred and that the provisional officers should arrange for a meeting in December at Madison, where the 1907 meeting of the American Historical Association was to be held. Before the Lincoln meeting adjourned it was also agreed that Paine should retain the promotional leadership of the provisional organization.[5]

Correspondence with Charles H. Haskins, secretary of the American Historical Association, revealed that neither the Pacific Coast Branch model nor the limited membership proposed at Lincoln fitted the purposes which the founders wished to realize. At the Madison meeting a number of professors took an active part in the movement. Clarence W. Alvord, along with Paine and Harlan, constituted a committee for revision of the proposed constitution and their report, with some amendments, has served as our basic constitution down to the present day.

This committee returned to the originally suggested name, which eliminated the proposed branch relationship with the American Historical Association. The objective of the Association as stated in this report was, "to promote historical study and research and to secure co-operation between the historical societies and departments of history in the Mississippi Valley." Membership was put on the broad basis of interest and payment of dues, with the proposal for honorary members being eliminated. The organization was very simple, with three officers and two additional members selected to make up an Executive Committee which was "to have general charge of the affairs of the Association." The original constitution specified that all former presidents should also serve as members of the Committee, but this provision was later amended to limit such service to the six years immediately following the expiration of their terms as president. The first Executive Committee chosen consisted of Thomas M. Owen, president, Clarence W. Alvord, vice-president,

[5] Shambaugh urged that no organization be attempted until the Madison meeting, but Paine insisted on the provisional organization to keep the movement alive and to supply leadership for carrying the plans forward at Madison. Paine to Clarence W. Alvord, July 5, 1908, Mississippi Valley Historical Association Collection.

Clarence S. Paine, secretary-treasurer, George W. Martin and Reuben G. Thwaites as elected members, and Francis A. Sampson as former president. At its Madison meeting the Executive Committee outlined five lines of work: (1) to open correspondence with all the historical societies in the Mississippi Valley; (2) to publish lists of each society's materials; (3) to publish a combined list of newspaper files and volumes on western travels; (4) to procure as far as possible through the various historical societies lists of state materials; (5) to publish a bibliography of bibliographies of the Mississippi Valley, to be prepared by Thwaites.[6] The Committee accepted the invitation of Warren Upham to meet in Minnesota, and the first annual meeting was set for June, 1908, at Lake Minnetonka. The President and Secretary were made a committee on program.

Paine's original idea had envisioned a close co-operation among the four secretaries of Iowa, Kansas, Missouri, and Nebraska, with frequent meetings, possibly as often as quarterly. On reflection he had widened its scope, with the small Lincoln meeting resulting from his first efforts.[7] At Madison the character of the organization was changed almost completely.[8] Clarence W. Alvord seems to have become the chief collaborating architect. It is a tribute to Paine's adaptability and readiness to co-operate and enlarge the scope and character of the organization to meet the vision of others that he repeatedly and seemingly eagerly extended the activities and responsibilities of the Association in response to suggestions offered. Alvord and Paine as intellectual types stood at opposite poles, and yet they co-operated most agreeably. The author has yet to discover a recorded criticism of one by the other.

[6] Mississippi Valley Historical Association, *Proceedings*, I (1907-1908), 26-28.

[7] Paine to Alvord, July 25, 1908, Mississippi Valley Historical Association Collection.

[8] The *American Historical Review* (New York), XIII (April, 1908), 439, carried a paragraph on the launching of this new organization. After naming the officers and Executive Committee, it continued: "The object of this new society, which it is understood will stand in some relation of affiliation to the American Historical Association, is to promote mutual consultation among the officers and members of the various organizations already existing and to care in other ways for the interests of special work in the history of this western region. It may be expected that whatever plans are suggested as advisable by the committee named above may find their best means of execution through this new association, which will be able to exercise upon the state historical agencies a strong influence in favor of whatever measures of co-operation may commend themselves to the new organization. The latter, it is expected, will consist largely of the officers of the existing and more local bodies."

Alvord had left Madison before the report of the nominating committe was received. In reply to Paine's notice of election, he commented:

> I can count myself Vice-President and a member of the Executive Committee. Personally I am pleased to occupy this position, and regard it an honor, but if the society is to amount to anything in the world, membership on this first Executive Committee is no sinecure. In fact the Executive Board has got to prove the usefulness of the society. I am aware that there was a good deal of opposition on the part of members of the A. H. A. to forming a new association in the west, and we cannot expect cordial support from that association.[9]

Benjamin F. Shambaugh printed the report of the Madison action, together with the constitution, in the *Iowa Journal of History and Politics* and supplied copies to the Secretary. Alvord was asked to prepare a brochure to be used in seeking new members. As the new vice-president he had a great interest in the enterprise. He had written to Paine that everything depended on the success of the first meeting. But the program was left to the initiative of the President, who announced early in May that he could not attend and asked the Vice-President and Secretary to prepare the program.[10] The Vice-President undertook the well-nigh impossible responsibility, but his nerves were frayed before he saw the program in print. It took the most vigorous urging to get papers from the proper people. He then became panicky about the prospects for an audience. The meeting was too far north, he complained to Paine. The expenses were prohibitive. A more central place must be chosen for the next year. Historians of the West had not responded and there was a real danger that the Association would "die before it is really born." His spirits ran lower. "Perhaps Thwaites was right," he commented. "We have started a movement that can have no life. The only hope was to have a successful meeting this June, and have everything go off with skyrockets. This the Executive Committee has failed to bring about." [11]

As a matter of fact this first program was a remarkably able one. Alvord presided over all the sessions. His own address, "The Study

[9] Alvord to Paine, January 7, 1908, Mississippi Valley Historical Association Collection.

[10] Both Alvord and Paine had received letters from Owen by May 4.

[11] These are scattered phrases from a series of letters, especially Alvord to Paine, May 29, 1908, and June 16, 1908, *ibid.*

and Writing of History in the Mississippi Valley," was an informing and challenging statement. Oliver M. Dickerson's paper on "The British Board of Trade in the Colonies" was a forerunner of his more exhaustive treatment of that topic. Charles M. Mann's "Co-operation among Historical Agencies in the Mississippi Valley" treated in a splendid imaginative fashion the problem of disseminating historical knowledge useful to society. Orin G. Libby, Warren Upham, Louis Pelzer, and Laurence M. Larson all brought fresh knowledge and viewpoints to their audience.[12]

The first printed program carried two pages on the nature and prospects of the Association. A paragraph on publication read: "Publication is the life of an historical association, for by publication the members can be reached and through it alone can research be encouraged. . . . The Executive Committee feels certain that . . . some form of annual or quarterly publication will be developed." [13]

Paine had denied Alvord any money to be used for speakers, with the explanation that he hoped to be able to publish the papers read on this first program. The matter of publication was discussed both in the first business meeting and by the Executive Committee. The Executive Committee named Shambaugh editor for the publication of its *Proceedings*. With the aid of the Secretary-Treasurer, and of John C. Parish and Dan E. Clark of the State Historical Society of Iowa, Shambaugh brought out the Mississippi Valley Historical Association's first volume of *Proceedings* in 147 pages. The Association, with its name on a respectable volume, took its place in the world of historical publishers. The volume was material evidence of the value of membership in the Association. The published history of the founding and activity of the Association gave it a character and identity in the scholarly world. Shambaugh also made the initial arrangement with The Torch Press of Cedar Rapids for our first printing; and the Press has continued to extend patience, credit, and understanding, as well as superior service, over almost fifty years.

The joint meeting with the American Historical Association in December, 1909, failed to materialize. President Orin G. Libby had written officials of the American, but the Secretary reported on May 10, 1910, that he had received no official explanation of the

12 These papers were published in the first volume of the Association's *Proceedings*.

13 Program of First Annual Meeting, Mississippi Valley Historical Association Collection.

misunderstanding.[14] Consequently a meeting of the Association had been called at Lincoln, January 18, 1910, to take care of necessary business. This meeting was sparsely attended, three papers were read, and an amendment was approved dropping the mandatory dates for the meetings. Plans for a May meeting in Iowa City were already well advanced.[15]

The third annual meeting, at Iowa City, was the first occasion on which an enthusiastic local committee had made extensive plans with much publicity and had secured the support of the University and of the state's cultural organizations in making the meetings a prominent event. This did much to give the Association standing and aided it in securing new members. Shambaugh, who had headed the local arrangements committee and was editor of the *Proceedings*, was chosen the new president.

The next two annual meetings, at Evanston-Chicago in 1911 and Bloomington in 1912, were well attended. Presidents Shambaugh, Andrew C. McLaughlin, and Reuben G. Thwaites secured co-operation from able workers in the historical field. Most of the leading historians in the central area of the nation were active on the Association's programs and committees. In addition the Ohio Valley Historical Association and the North Central History Teachers Association were invited to meet with the Association at its fourth annual meeting in Evanston. Through such groups with similar interests the knowledge of the Association's activities was reaching a wider audience. Local historical societies in each of the meeting places joined in sponsoring its programs.

The problem of publications continued to be the most important question to the Association. The single annual volume of *Proceedings* was not enough to sustain the organization and hold its members. There was need for a quarterly to carry the articles, reviews, and historical news of the membership, as well as to give publicity to the program of activities of the Association. A committee on publications, consisting of Alvord, Shambaugh, Paine, Isaac J. Cox, and Frank H. Hodder, had been named at Iowa City. This committee and its successors worked to ascertain the feasibility of a quarterly review. The historians of the area were canvassed

14 Mississippi Valley Historical Association, *Proceedings*, III (1909-1910), 33.

15 Correspondence between Shambaugh and Paine, Mississippi Valley Historical Association Collection.

by questionnaire on three points: (1) Could such a publication succeed? (2) Would each historian contribute articles? (3) Would each prepare reviews? Of the forty-six who replied, only two thought it would fail.[16] There were enough articles promised to fill from eight to twelve numbers, and almost the entire group agreed to prepare reviews.

This was abundant evidence that the literary content for a quarterly review was obtainable, but without a large list of subscribers the cost of printing and publication could not be met. Financing such a publication was the most difficult obstacle. It was agreed that a subscription of $1,500 per year for three years from guarantors was essential before the enterprise could start. This followed the example of the *American Historical Review*, which had not been published at its beginning by the Association but had been sponsored by a separate group of associates during the first three years of its existence.[17] The committee had a report for the December, 1912, Boston meeting, but owing to the small attendance at that distant city action was postponed until the Omaha meeting the following May. Here it was agreed that when a guarantors' fund of $1,500 annually for three years had been subscribed, the publication of the quarterly review might proceed.

The raising of the guarantee fund became the pressing objective. Most of this solicitation was carried on by Alvord and Paine. The former, in the rich state of Illinois and the prosperous center of Chicago, had the more fertile hunting ground. Paine covered much territory in his voluminous correspondence searching for support. In due course the fund was oversubscribed, but collections were never up to date. A number of surprises came to the solicitors, who had expected not to accept less than $100 from a guarantor. When Alvord got only a $50 pledge from Northwestern University, Paine expressed amazement that "with his [Alvord's] nerve he let them off short of $500." When Paine's stock of prospects proved sterile, Alvord suggested that he sell Mr. B—, an easy touch, a life membership as "he would not live more than a year or two at the most." Paine's greatest agony was expressed in connection with the case of Mr. W— who had promised him $200 when Paine did not have a subscription blank, and he included Mr. W— in their printed list

16 These replies are now on file in the Association's Collection.

17 See J. Franklin Jameson, "The American Historical Review, 1895-1920," *American Historical Review*, XXVI (October, 1920), 3-7, 14-16.

of guarantors to encourage other prospects. On seeing the list, Mr. W— exploded and declared he would not give a penny. In writing to Alvord, Paine lamented this loss, but his apology and explanation to Mr. W— finally brought the $200, along with an exhaustive letter on proper business procedure. The collections seldom corresponded with the guarantors' pledges, for it was not unusual for some of the pledges to be in arrears. Nevertheless, the Secretary and the Editor located a generous and faithful group of friends to launch this scholarly enterprise.[18]

At the Omaha meeting in May, 1913, the Executive Committee selected the first board of editors, consisting of Alvord, managing editor, Shambaugh, Eugene C. Barker, Claude H. Van Tyne, Orin G. Libby, Archer B. Hulbert, James A. James, Walter L. Fleming, and Reuben G. Thwaites. The problem of the relation of the *Proceedings* and the *Review* was discussed but not definitely settled. Publication of the *Proceedings* was to be continued for the time being. The relation of the two organs made delicate problems for the two editors. Perhaps one may discern a shade of rivalry between the two enterprises. Shambaugh wrote Paine that he favored the publication of the *Review*, "Provided we could get sufficient guarantee without drawing upon the resources of the Association," but he insisted that "we should see that our obligations to the printers of the Proceedings should be taken care of before additional enterprises are started."[19] He also delineated to Alvord the exact specifications for the printing, paper, appearance, and character of the *Review*. He was opposed to editorializing in a scholarly publication. He thought the reviews should be "confined to American history and foreign histories specifically related to the Mississippi Valley."[20] The Managing Editor adopted a close approximation to his specifications.

The publication of the *Review* raised the problem of subscriptions, dues, and membership in the Association. It was decided to take subscriptions to the *Review* at two dollars per year. Members in the Association might continue without the *Review* for one dollar and receive the *Proceedings*. Members wishing the *Review* would

[18] For lists of guarantors and amounts collected, see *Mississippi Valley Historical Review*, XL (June, 1953), 12.

[19] Shambaugh to Paine, January 7, 1914, Mississippi Valley Historical Association Collection.

[20] Shambaugh to Alvord, January 18, 1914, *ibid.*

pay three dollars, libraries four dollars, and sustaining members and life members would receive both publications. This was complicated. It caused Paine to set up separate accounts for the Association and the *Review*.[21]

The early years of the *Review* were difficult. The separation of offices, with the business office in Lincoln, the editorial office in Urbana, and the printing office in Cedar Rapids, made for uncertain communication and certain delay. Questions as to what should be done where had to be resolved, and this called for much intercommunication. The new journal required time for recognition before it could attain a wide support. The campaign to publicize it put an excessive burden on the Secretary. Seven years of intensive promotion of the Association had worn off the novelty for both Paine and Alvord. In December Alvord wrote: "My dear Paine: You're cracked. Look at your mail. On December 3d you were invited to a meeting of the Board of Editors and on the 7th you accepted. Too much to do is your trouble." [22]

Such a letter did not daunt the Secretary-Treasurer. Six weeks later, when Shambaugh was holding up the printing of the *Proceedings* on the assumption that the Association's funds could not take care of the cost, Paine replied: "Fire the copy in for the volume of *Proceedings* . . . we must get it out, if possible before the New Orleans meeting. I will take care of the finances." [23] But the burdens of the Secretary were more fully revealed in a letter to Alvord relative to the New Orleans meeting.

> It looks as though I could not get to New Orleans [Paine wrote]. I want especially to go because it seems to me that the time has come when some one ought to be found who would be willing to relieve me of this work. I believe that I have done about all that ought to be expected of me. Not but that others might have accomplished more if they would, but it fell to my lot to do it. I have hung on because I did not want to be called a quitter, and I did want to get the Association to a point where it could not fail. In what I have done I have found much pleasure, but it is a luxury I cannot afford to keep up.[24]

The eight years of growth and experience revealed need for change in the organization and practices of the Association, and con-

21 See Financial Reports in *Proceedings*, 1914-1916.

22 Alvord to Paine, December 21, 1914, Mississippi Valley Historical Association Collection.

23 Paine to Shambaugh, February 4, 1915, *ibid.*

24 Paine to Alvord, March 27, 1915, *ibid.*

sideration of some of these adjustments was planned for the 1916 meeting, scheduled to be held in Nashville in April. President Dunbar Rowland announced a nominating committee, with Solon J. Buck as chairman, several weeks in advance, and Buck took up the problem of reconstituting the Executive Committee. He consulted Paine on three possible amendments to the constitution: (1) abolishing the vice-presidents; (2) adding three elective members to the Executive Committee (making nine);[25] (3) having the Executive Committee select a substitute to act for the president in cases of the president's absence. Paine also wished the Executive Committee to choose a chairman who would perform the functions of a vice-president as well as head the Committee, and who would be eligible for re-election. It was thought these changes would do much to stabilize the Executive Committee by eliminating one-year vice-presidents as members, and would provide an added element of experienced leadership in the chairman of the Executive Committee.[26]

Such an amendment was adopted, and Isaac J. Cox was chosen as the first chairman of the Executive Committee at the December meeting in 1916. Many members of the Association are probably not aware of the importance of the services of the chairman of the Executive Committee, in whom is lodged the responsibility for decisions on matters which require attention during the intervals between the regular meetings of the Committee in April and December. The chairmen are selected by the members of the Committee and are eligible for re-election. They have been elected, with two exceptions, from the former presidents, and they usually represent a long service on the Committee. This, along with the extended service of the secretary-treasurer and the managing editor, has been a stabilizing influence in the Association.

The annual meeting of 1916 also changed all active membership dues to three dollars and library dues to four dollars, and retained the sustaining and life memberships. This action lost the Association a few non-subscribing members, but it tended to fix the character

[25] The elected members of the Executive Committee had been increased from two to six by an amendment adopted at the Evanston meeting in 1911. The three-year overlapping terms were also established at that time. Mississippi Valley Historical Association, *Proceedings*, V (1911-1912), 10.

[26] Paine to Solon J. Buck, April 7, 1916, Mississippi Valley Historical Association Collection.

of the membership more definitely. The publications were consolidated under the board of editors of the *Review*, and it was expected that the *Proceedings* would appear as an extra number of the *Review*. But Paine became seriously ill at the Nashville meeting, and on June 14, 1916, he died without having been able to take the initial steps toward putting the new provisions into operation. Frederic L. Paxson, the new president, placed the business of the Association in the hands of a clerk, with Mrs. C. S. Paine doing the work. In December, 1916, the Executive Committee appointed her acting secretary-treasurer, and at the annual business meeting of the following April she was regularly elected to the office. In this position she continued to serve the Association until her illness in August, 1952, compelled her to retire.

It is difficult to appreciate the work and services of Mrs. Paine. The routine of her work for the Association was the collecting of dues, paying of bills, keeping of records, holding on to old members, securing new ones, soliciting guarantors and collecting their pledges, preparing budgets, satisfying editors and officers. In fact, she became a clearing center that was much more than financial. She took over the office at a crucial time in the development of the Association. The changes in organization adopted at Nashville were to be applied, and a new and able, but less experienced, group of leaders was becoming active within the Executive Committee. Her intimate knowledge of her husband's work and her own devotion to the Association enabled her to gather up the work and to carry on in an effective way.

Mrs. Paine's position as secretary-treasurer of the Association was anomalous. Although interested in history, she did not pretend to be a historian. Many members of the Association would not have thought of her as the suitable successor to carry on her husband's work in the organization. Her proficiency with the work and her interest in the Association led the Executive Committee and finally the business meeting of the membership to elect her secretary-treasurer, and to continue her in that office from year to year. It was this test of service through the usual channels of selection that brought a nonprofessional woman to this key position in the organization. Some members of the Association continued to question the advisability of having a woman as secretary-treasurer, but she naturally received staunch support from those who knew her best. Paxson, who saw her work the Association out of its deepest deficit, and early chairmen of the Executive Committee — Cox, Eugene M. Violette, Milo M. Quaife, and William E. Connelley — who knew her work in detail and her devotion to the Association, became her unwavering supporters. The fact that she did not participate in programs other than the business meeting and did not attempt to influence policies except concerning new members and Association finances limited her acquaintance with the scholarly qualities of the various members.

It is doubtful that even those who have been most closely associated with Mrs. Paine in carrying on the work of the Association were ever fully aware of the numerous responsibilities and duties that she cared for in her early years as secretary-treasurer. She was left with limited means and with three children of her own and a step-daughter, ranging in age from five weeks to fourteen years. She put in a long week as librarian for the Nebraska State Historical Society, and took care of the Association's business at night. Often she worked into the morning hours to complete a voluminous correspondence.[27] Among her multiple duties, the business of this Association could easily have received belated attention, but instead its affairs prospered. The correspondence of this period provides abundant evidence that the affairs of the Association were conducted with great care. The President in acknowledging the financial report in November, 1916, could write: "This leaves us entirely out of debt so far as I know. I think you have done well." [28]

In a report which she prepared for the President in December, 1916, Mrs. Paine presented an analysis of the membership situation at this point of transition. According to her tabulation the Association had 523 members paid up to June, 1917; 110 in arrears since June, 1916; 134 one-dollar members, not subscribers to the *Review*; 70 members who were two years in arrears and still on the roll; and 94 had requested cancellation of membership. Delinquents were the subject of much concern to the Secretary, and her correspondence bulges with reminders, inquiries, and appeals to them.[29] Throughout

[27] A series of unfiled letters at the bottom of filed correspondence in the Mississippi Valley Historical Association Collection, 1917-1921, contains much incidental information concerning her personal affairs during those years.

[28] Frederic L. Paxson to Mrs. Paine, November 11, 1916, Mississippi Valley Historical Association Collection.

[29] Secretary to President, December 14, 1916, *ibid.*

the succeeding years the Secretary kept up a vigorous drive for new members. Small pages with half a dozen names as prospects, signed by some member, are common items in the files of the Association. Applications for membership signed by many of our current members are evidence of the effectiveness of this work.

The major problem during the early years of Mrs. Paine's service was that of finding the resources to finance the publication of the *Review.* Despite the vigorous push for members, the Association did did not immediately succeed in accumulating a surplus. The American participation in the World War was a distracting factor. The original three-year pledges of guarantors had expired, and it was difficult to secure their renewal. New guarantors were difficult to find in wartime. University faculties were reduced and graduate students became scarce. The Association's paid memberships declined by approximately one hundred in the war year, but they were restored in the succeeding year and the Association remained on a solvent basis.

The decline in the fund from guarantors was a most serious loss. Mrs. Paine sought to escape dependence upon guarantors by urging a drive for an endowment. Dr. Otto L. Schmidt, one of our most faithful guarantors, pointed out that it would be difficult to obtain endowment contributions because the Association held no real property and prospective donors would have no tangible guarantee of the perpetuity of the organization. Not long after the endowment drive was suggested, however, the American Historical Association initiated its canvass for the same purpose, and the Executive Committee declined to enter a competitive campaign. In fact two prominent members of our Association used our annual business meeting to urge our members to support the drive of the American Historical Association.

Nevertheless, following the war Mrs. Paine's campaign for members and her collections from guarantors did bring the Association a surplus even in the face of highly inflated costs of printing.[30] By 1921 the surplus justified investment, and the Executive Committee was faced with a new and pleasant responsibility. The Treasurer and the Managing Editor were heartened by their success, but because they wished to take advantage of the good times to garner a reserve they continued to collect from the guarantors. At this time

[30] J. L. Powers to Mrs. Paine, May 14, 1919, *ibid.*

Alvord wrote Mrs. Paine: "I have an idea for raising money. University salaries have been generally raised, and prices are going down, so that our professors are fairly well off. Besides them, there are other members of the Association who are well-to-do. Suppose you make a list of these well-to-do's and ask them to guarantee $25 or even $15 a year for two years. I'll start the list with a promise of $25 and I am not among the wealthiest." [31] She asked him to compose the appeal that should be addressed to the professors.[32] Illness prevented him from doing so for several months, but his appeal was a splendid statement of the character and purposes of the Association.

This was one of Alvord's last services to the Association, as his work as editor was drawing toward its close. It is interesting to note that during the last two years of his editorship his attitude toward Mrs. Paine as the secretary-treasurer became more friendly. He and Paine had worked together most congenially, but he seems to have doubted the desirability of a woman for secretary-treasurer. He always addressed the Secretary as "My dear Mrs. Paine." She reciprocated with "My dear Dr. Alvord." She always spoke in the highest respect and praise of his work, but faced him squarely when he made unfounded assumptions that she was attempting to initiate actions on her own responsibility in the Association. In the end he had a very high respect for her work and wrote: "I need not tell you how pleasant have been my relations with both your husband and yourself." [33]

One of Alvord's last official acts as managing editor, however, was to present a request for additional funds for editorial assistance which Mrs. Paine felt that she was not authorized to provide. During the years when the editorial office of the *Review* was at the University of Illinois the expenses ranged from about $275 to $400 per year, but following Alvord's move to the University of Minnesota in 1920 the demands for editorial assistance rose sharply. In 1921-1922 the expenditures amounted to $758, and in 1923 the Executive Committee allotted $600 for editorial and office expenses. Alvord did not attend the annual meeting in Oklahoma City in 1923, but his request to the Executive Committee that Lester B. Shippee of the University of Minnesota be reappointed to the board

[31] Alvord to Mrs. Paine, July 10, 1921, *ibid.*
[32] Mrs. Paine to Alvord, July 20, 1921, *ibid.*
[33] Alvord to Mrs. Paine, June 15, 1923, *ibid.*

MISSISSIPPI VALLEY HISTORICAL ASSOCIATION
FINANCIAL EXHIBIT, 1907-1923 [34]

Year [35]	Receipts			Disbursements				Balance
	Dues etc.[36]	Guaranty	Total	Administra.[37]	Publications	Editorial [38]	Total	
1907-08	$ 80		$ 80	$ 77			$ 77	$ 3
1908-09	184		184	249			249	- 65
1909-10	566		566	218	$ 213		431	135
1910-11	827		827	327	476		803	24
1911-12	1,658		1,658	811	835		1,646	12
1912-13	1,688		1,688	972	746		1,718	- 30
1913-14	1,508	$ 450	1,958	1,528	349	$ 66	1,943	15
1914-15	2,062	1,175	3,237	943	2,016	359	3,318	- 81
1915-16	2,589	2,250	4,839	1,557	2,794	279	4,630	209
1916-17	2,436	1,925	4,361	951	3,113 [39]	282	4,346	15
1917-18	2,137	1,425	3,562	1,062	1,705	348	3,115	447
1918-19	2,473	1,200	3,673	980	1,601	413	2,994	679
1919-20	2,404	1,500	3,904	1,548	1,685	369	3,602	302
1920-21	3,535	1,050	4,585	1,740	2,305	622	4,667	- 82
1921-22	3,359	1,212	4,571	1,879	1,797	758	4,434	137
1922-23	3,822	1,394	5,216	1,698	2,172	650	4,520	696
Totals	$31,328	$13,581	$44,909	$16,540	$21,807	$4,146	$42,493	$2,416 [40]

[34] This table is from a copy of Mrs. Paine's summary, in Mississippi Valley Historical Association Collection, 1923. It follows the original except for the omission of a column showing what per cent of the total disbursements constituted editorial costs for each year after the establishment of the *Review*.

[35] Note by the Secretary: "The fiscal years have varied in length from eleven to thirteen months."

[36] Note by the Secretary: "This heading covers, besides dues and contributions, receipts from advertising, the sale of publications, and miscellaneous items."

[37] Note by the Secretary: "Under 'Administration' is included the salary of the secretary and clerical assistants in her office; her commissions on new members and on the sale of publications; her traveling expenses; postage, express, etc.; office supplies; and miscellaneous printing."

[38] Note by the Secretary: "This heading covers all expenses of the office of managing editor, including postage, stationery, and clerical work, as well as editorial assistance. It does not include the cost of promoting the *Review*, which was considerable in the early years when it was on a subscription basis."

[39] Note by the Secretary: "Includes $300 'Borrowed money repaid.' As this sum is nowhere included among the receipts, it is assumed that someone was reimbursed for bills paid for the Association. Whether these bills were for administrative or editorial expenses or for publications cannot be ascertained from the printed accounts, but the secretary thinks they were for publications."

[40] This figure is the difference between the sums of the deficits and the surpluses for the individual years. It is also the difference between the total receipts and total disbursements shown in this table. The completeness and accuracy of the tabulation are further attested by the fact that the Treasurer's report for the year 1922-1923 shows a balance on hand of $2,415.90 as of March 23, 1923. See Mississippi Valley Historical Association, *Proceedings*, XI (1921-1923), 30.

of editors and be given the title of assistant managing editor was approved. He then wrote directly to the Secretary-Treasurer, asking for an additional $375 for editorial assistance, but Mrs. Paine, convinced that she had no authority to exceed the earlier $600 allotment, referred the request to the chairman of the Executive Committee. Solon J. Buck, the newly elected chairman, felt that before the Committee could act it needed more adequate information concerning the financial history of the Association. He therefore asked the Secretary-Treasurer to prepare a complete recapitulation by items of the Association's financial operations year by year from its inception.

This proved to be a difficult and time-consuming task. In some instances the records were not sufficiently clear for certainty in classifying receipts and expenditures, but Mrs. Paine succeeded in completing the analysis in time to present it at the mid-year meeting of the Committee in December, 1923. Her summary represents an interesting and revealing commentary on the Association's early financial history, and since it has not previously been published it seems appropriate to include it here in approximately the form in which it was prepared. (See page 509.)

Before the compilation of this statement could be completed Alvord had announced his resignation from the managing editorship of the *Review*. On June 15, 1923, he wrote the Secretary that since he was leaving the University of Minnesota and would probably have no further connection with institutions in the Mississippi Valley he could not continue as editor. "I am turning the *Review* over to Mr. Shippee for the rest of the year," he said, "and then the whole matter can be taken up at the spring meeting." [41]

The procedure for selecting a managing editor was not yet a standardized matter, but the primary responsibility was clearly lodged in the chairman of the Executive Committee. The problem of finding a successor to Alvord was not easy or simple. A number of institutions were interested in sponsoring the *Review*, but none offered very high inducements to obtain it. Buck, as chairman of

[41] Alvord to Mrs. Paine, June 15, 1923, Mississippi Valley Historical Association Collection. Following his resignation Alvord went to England for further research in British records, and he continued to live abroad until his death in January, 1928, in Italy. For sketches of his career see Solon J. Buck, "Clarence Walworth Alvord, Historian," *Mississippi Valley Historical Review*, XV (December, 1928), 309-20, and Marion Dargan, "Clarence Walworth Alvord," in William T. Hutchinson (ed.), *The Marcus W. Jernegan Essays in American Historiography* (Chicago, 1937), 323-38.

the Executive Committee, asked that a subcommittee be chosen by mail ballot to canvass the situation and report. The subcommittee, consisting of Buck, chairman, William E. Connelley, and Harlow Lindley, canvassed the Executive Committee members for a preferential vote on the editorship. About half of the members did not express their preference, and the result was nine nominees, with no majority for any of them. After those persons who could not serve had been eliminated, the preference of those who had expressed themselves was for Shippee, and the subcommittee recommended him as its choice to the Executive Committee at its meeting in Louisville in May, 1924. After a thorough study of the possibilities, however, the Executive Committee selected Milo M. Quaife, who was sponsored by the Burton Historical Collection of the Detroit Public Library. It was evident that Quaife could handle the work with much less editorial expense to the Association than had been required in Minnesota.

During the decade of the "prosperous twenties" the Association had to adapt itself to new conditions. While Quaife kept the expenses of the editorial office at an average of less than $100 per year, the cost of the *Review* soared. The editorial board accepted a better quality of paper which became increasingly expensive. The *Review* was enlarged and given a new format. The policy of supplying off-prints to contributors, along with the increased number of copies to supply the growing membership, brought the cost of printing much above previous estimates of the finance committee. This cost suggested the necessity of increasing the dues of members. Thus an amendment raising the annual dues to five dollars was adopted at the Springfield meeting in 1926.

As the changing conditions of the postwar decade brought an increasing need for constructive planning, the rapid turnover in the personnel of the Executive Committee and especially the frequent changes in its chairmanship made it extremely difficult to develop a continuity of policy. Up to 1929, only one chairman had served more than two years, and he had been absent from a number of the meetings. Three had served only one year each. The Secretary-Treasurer almost invariably had to educate the new chairmen on the nature of their duties. In 1926, for example, Chairman Frank H. Hodder could not see any point in adopting an estimated budget for the year's expenses if the items of expenditure were not held within the estimates. Charles W. Ramsdell, who began his long service as chairman after the 1929 meeting, hoping to save on printing costs, meticulously checked the bills against the contract with The Torch Press only to find that no further reductions could be made.

In this postwar era, in which the ideals were largely set by the business executives and the salesmen, some historians were caught by the prevailing trend of expansion. Some members of the Association wanted an overhauling of its organization and a great expansion of its activities. In 1927, in response to these expressions President Joseph Schafer appointed Solon J. Buck a committee of one on policy, with permission to enlarge his committee. In the next year Ramsdell, as president, added Schafer and Eugene C. Barker to the committee, but before this group had gone far in its explorations two new factors affected the direction of its endeavors. Alvord died in 1928 and Buck proposed to utilize his reputation and his relation with the Association for creating a suitable memorial foundation for the promotion of publication, which was one of the insistent demands within the Association. Buck's proposal for the establishment of the Alvord Memorial Commission, which was to raise its own endowment fund and was to operate within the Association under the direction of the Executive Committee with its funds to be handled by the Association's treasurer, was approved at the Chattanooga meeting in 1930; and the commission thus functioned until 1956, when it and its funds were transferred to the Minnesota Historical Society.

The other factor that the policy committee had to consider was the announcement in 1929 that Quaife would resign from the editorship of the *Review*. A committee consisting of Avery O. Craven, Shippee, and Barker was named to report on the editorship at the Chattanooga meeting; but the committee on policy could not ignore the editorial situation in its report. It suggested that the moment seemed opportune for unifying the Association's activities in a single office and appointing a general director who might serve as managing editor of the *Review* along with his administrative responsibilities. Thus when the Executive Committee met at Chattanooga it had before it reports from both of these important committees.

A prompt decision was required in the selection of an editor. A number of institutions were interested in sponsoring the *Review*.

The University of Chicago with Chauncey S. Boucher as its candidate headed the list reported by the committee on the editorship. The State University of Iowa offered Louis Pelzer as its candidate, Western Reserve University Graduate School proposed Arthur C. Cole, and Logan Esarey was sponsored by Indiana University. The Executive Committee put in long night hours in considering the various proposals of the several schools and the relation of those proposals to the policies that the Association wished to follow, and finally accepted the offer of Western Reserve University, with Arthur C. Cole for managing editor.

This action of course disposed of the suggestion of the committee on policy for consolidation of the editorial and administrative activities in one office, but it left numerous other recommendations from that committee to be considered. Although these recommendations were presented in a general form, they involved possible adjustments under six rather specific heads: (1) the clarification of business procedures; (2) the expansion of publication activities; (3) the promotion of investment funds; (4) the promotion of co-operation among historical agencies; (5) the fixing of future headquarters for the Association; and (6) the creation of a membership committee. The last would require adjustment of the arrangement by which the Secretary-Treasurer received compensation for her services.

Of these recommendations, the first did not seem to the Executive Committee to be urgent, in view of the existing auditing arrangement. As for the second, publication activities had absorbed the first collected dues of the Association, and the proposed expansion was in a measure implemented in the new Alvord Memorial Commission. The promotion of investment funds had been urged for years by the Secretary-Treasurer, and the co-operation of historical agencies had prompted Paine to call the original Lincoln meeting. The fixing of future headquarters for the Association was perhaps the most novel and most controversial of the recommendations, and on it the Executive Committee took no action. The question of adjusting the arrangement with regard to the Secretary-Treasurer's compensation, however, was given serious consideration. Hitherto, the holder of that office had received no salary but had been granted the first year's dues from new members and the returns from sales of back publications of the Association as her remuneration. These provided only a limited return, but some members objected to the arrangement despite the fact that the payment of such commissions was a common practice in business promotion. The policy committee did not discuss the question of commissions in its report, but it proposed the establishment of a new committee to operate independently of the Secretary-Treasurer in a continuous campaign for new members. In accord with this suggestion the Executive Committee provided for the creation of a standing committee on membership and authorized the payment of a regular stipend to the Secretary-Treasurer as remuneration for her services and to take care of incidental clerical assistance.[42]

The succeeding decade left the Association in steady hands with effective leadership both in the long-term chairmen of the Executive Committee (Ramsdell for six years and Shippee for five) and with Cole editing the *Review* for the full decade. All of these men had a long acquaintance with the Association and saw in extended perspective the benefits of the organization's undramatic activities. The committee drive for new members with ambitions to enroll the learned professions netted only 131 additions. Of coursc the depression of the 1930's offered a ready explanation. In course of time it became apparent that the *Review* was a professional journal that appealed chiefly to students of American history, and that the prospective members were in the graduate history departments. This was recognized by the adoption of special student membership dues in 1940. In fact, the great growth in membership over the past fifteen years has paralleled the growth of academic and institutional work in history.

The problem of selecting managing editors for the *Review* has continued to be a matter of great concern to the Association. It is well that this is so, for the position is the most important one in the gift of the Association. The first two subcommittees for the selection of managing editors failed to convince the Executive Committee that it should accept their recommendations. The occasion for refilling the position has arisen three times since. In 1940 after ten years as managing editor, Arthur C. Cole resigned. A committee consisting of John D. Hicks, chairman, Homer C. Hockett, Louis Pelzer, James G. Randall, and Jonas Viles was named to recom-

[42] See "Report of the Secretary-Treasurer for the Year 1929-30," *Mississippi Valley Historical Review,* XVII (September, 1930), 312-16, for a summary of the actions taken at the Chattanooga meeting. Copies of the committee reports and correspondence are in Mississippi Valley Historical Association Collection, 1929-1930.

mend a successor. The committee's nomination of Louis Pelzer was accepted by the Executive Committee with the State University of Iowa becoming the sponsor of the *Review*.

The death of Pelzer in 1946 necessitated a new selection. This time Elmer Ellis, chairman, William C. Binkley, Harold W. Bradley, Everett E. Edwards, and Carl F. Wittke constituted the recommending committee. The interest in the *Review* was indicated by proposals from nine universities. The generous offer of Tulane University along with the recognized editorial talent of Wendell H. Stephenson drew the recommendation of this committee, and it was accepted. Again in 1953 the resignation of Stephenson led to the appointment of another committee, composed of Howard H. Peckham, chairman, Ray A. Billington, Dwight L. Dumond, Elmer Ellis, and James L. Sellers. Its recommendation of the present managing editor brings the story down to date. It seems now that the procedure for selecting a managing editor is institutionalized and has become accepted.

There are many other interesting aspects of the Association's history. In recent years it has revived the office of vice-president and has changed the method of filling the office of secretary-treasurer from annual election in the business meeting to appointment for a more extended term by the Executive Committee. Within the last four years it has also changed the procedure for nomination and election of its officers and members of the Executive Committee. It is too soon to say how the present practices will work out. They were designed to provide a fuller participation of the membership in governing the affairs of the Association. The important test is whether they will find the persons that devote themselves to the Association through their faithful attendance to the organization's work throughout their terms of office.

In retrospect, this Association has a remarkable history over its first fifty years. It has grown from seven representatives at its first meeting to more than three thousand members. It has published eleven volumes of *Proceedings* and it is in the forty-fourth volume of the *Review*, which is unrivaled in its own special field. It has resources to undertake new publication ventures. The Prize Monograph Series just announced initiates such an enterprise.

To develop an organization of this scope and character requires a tremendous initiative and continued effort from some source or sources, and it also calls for a consistency of purpose. Such clear objectives may be supplied by the hopes for profits or other financial rewards to promoters; and many organizations hire a manager or director who is responsible for the entire program. But in this Association the compensation for official service is the honor which it brings and the satisfaction that comes from the privilege of participating in the development of a constructive program "for the promotion of historical study and research." This award of honor has been sufficient to attract the services of many of the leading scholars in the field of American history, as the following list of our executive officers over the years so well shows; and the range of places where the Association has accepted invitations to meet indicates how much this organization has endeavored to identify itself with the local history of many communities in this country.

ANNUAL MEETINGS AND EXECUTIVE OFFICERS OF THE ASSOCIATION, 1907-1957 [43]

Year ending [44]	Date of meeting [45]	Place	Presidents	Chairmen of Executive Committee
1907	Oct. 17	Lincoln	Francis A. Sampson [46]	
1908	June 22	Lake Minnetonka	Thomas M. Owen	
1909	June 17	St. Louis	Clarence W. Alvord	
1910	May 26	Iowa City	Orin G. Libby	
1911	May 18	Evanston-Chicago	Benjamin F. Shambaugh	
1912	May 23	Bloomington, Ind.	Andrew C. McLaughlin	
1913	May 8	Omaha	Reuben G. Thwaites	
1914	May 26	Grand Forks	James A. James	
1915	April 22	New Orleans	Isaac J. Cox	
1916	April 27	Nashville	Dunbar Rowland	
1917	April 26	Chicago	Frederic L. Paxson	Isaac J. Cox
1918	May 9	St. Paul	St. George L. Sioussat	" "
1919	May 8	St. Louis	Harlow Lindley	Eugene M. Violette
1920	April 29	Greencastle, Ind.	Milo M. Quaife	Isaac J. Cox
1921	April 14	Madison	Chauncey S. Boucher	Milo M. Quaife
1922	May 11	Iowa City	William E. Connelley	" "
1923	March 29	Oklahoma City	Solon J. Buck	William E. Connelley
1924	May 1	Louisville	Eugene C. Barker	Solon J. Buck
1925	April 30	Detroit	Frank H. Hodder	" "
1926	May 6	Springfield, Ill.	James A. Woodburn	Frank H. Hodder
1927	March 31	New Orleans	Otto L. Schmidt	James A. Woodburn
1928	April 28	Des Moines	Joseph Schafer	" "
1929	April 25	Vincennes, Ind.	Charles W. Ramsdell	" "

(*Continued next page.*)

ANNUAL MEETINGS AND EXECUTIVE OFFICERS OF THE ASSOCIATION, 1907-1957 [43]

Year ending [44]	Date of meeting [45]	Place	Presidents	Chairmen of Executive Committee
1930	April 24	Chattanooga	Homer C. Hockett	Charles W. Ramsdell
1931	April 30	Lexington, Ky.	Louise P. Kellogg	" "
1932	April 28	Lincoln	Beverley W. Bond	" "
1933	April 13	Chicago	John D. Hicks	" "
1934	April 26	Columbia, Mo.	Jonas Viles	" "
1935	April 25	Cincinnati	Lester B. Shippee	" "
1936	April 16	Austin	Louis Pelzer	Lester B. Shippee
1937	April 29	St. Louis	Edward E. Dale	" "
1938	April 28	Indianapolis	Clarence E. Carter	" "
1939	April 20	Memphis	William O. Lynch	" "
1940	May 2	Omaha	James G. Randall	" "
1941	April 24	Milwaukee	Carl F. Wittke	Edward E. Dale
1942	May 7	Lexington	Arthur C. Cole	" "
1943	April 22	Cedar Rapids	Charles H. Ambler	" "
1944	April 20	St. Louis	Theodore C. Blegen	William O. Lynch
1945	No meeting [47]		William C. Binkley	" "
1946	April 18	Bloomington	William C. Binkley	" "
1947	April 24	Columbus	Herbert A. Kellar	William C. Binkley
1948	April 22	Rock Island	Ralph P. Bieber	" "
1949	April 13	Madison	Dwight L. Dumond	" "
1950	April 20	Oklahoma City	Carl C. Rister	" "
1951	April 19	Cincinnati	Elmer Ellis	" "
1952	April 17	Chicago	Merle E. Curti	" "
1953	May 7	Lexington	James L. Sellers	Dwight L. Dumond
1954	April 24	Madison	Fred A. Shannon	" "
1955	April 28	St. Louis	Walter P. Webb	" "
1956	April 19	Pittsburgh	Edward C. Kirkland	George L. Anderson
1957	May 2	Lincoln	Thomas D. Clark	" "

[43] This record has been compiled from the Minute Books of the Secretary, 1907 to date. The following have served as secretary-treasurer during these fifty years: Clarence S. Paine, 1907-1916; Mrs. Clara S. Paine, 1916-1952; Clarence S. Paine II, 1952-1953 (acting); James C. Olson, 1953-1956; William D. Aeschbacher, since 1956.

[44] The official year is the period from one annual meeting to the next. It thus varied in length from eleven to thirteen months in the earlier years, before the time of meeting was standardized to fall in late April or early May. The fiscal year has been established as beginning on April 1 and ending on the following March 31.

[45] These dates indicate the first day of the annual meetings. In 1908 and 1909 two-day meetings were held. Beginning in 1910 the meetings have regularly extended over a three-day period.

[46] Served as provisional president from October 17 until the adoption of the constitution and the election of regular officers in December, 1907.

[47] The meeting which had been scheduled for 1945 had to be canceled because of wartime restrictions on travel. All terms of office were officially extended for one year.

In this Association there seems to be an indigenous interest in things historical that is most manifest at its annual and mid-year (December) meetings. In these gatherings the work of the membership appears in the literary programs and the reports of the numerous committees. Meetings of the Executive Committee devote much time and effort to discussions of problems and policies. The managing editor and editorial board supplement their extensive correspondence by give-and-take discussions. The annual business meeting receives the reports of officers and approves or otherwise registers its reactions to the efforts of its selected agents, and it also selects the officers for continuing the Association's work. Not only the formal aspects of the meetings but the innumerable informal interchanges have been of inestimable value to the profession and to its members.

This organization seems unique in that its management, policy, and control come out of its membership through its Executive Committee. The managing editor and secretary-treasurer are selected by the Executive Committee and paid by other sponsoring institutions. Inasmuch as their salaries do not come out of our organization they do not insist on dominating financial or organizational policies. This is perhaps the ideal relationship for free and uninfluenced historical work and expression. The work of the organization is carried in the main by the voluntary effort of its members. The co-operation of historical institutions and agencies and the interchange and mutual stimulation and cross-fertilization of ideas of historical workers has been greatly facilitated and advanced by this Association. It is an organization with an enviable record. Members attend its meetings eagerly, participate in its programs freely, and feel that the Association is their own.

Under Our Strange Device: A Review of the "Review"

BY JOHN W. CAUGHEY

On plunging into the files of the *Mississippi Valley Historical Review*, my first impression was of "a vast drifting miscellany." The phrase is not original. Charles E. Chapman applied it years ago to the multi-volumed *Works* of Hubert Howe Bancroft.

Vast it certainly is. The forty-three plump volumes stretch out for eight and one-half feet along the shelf. They contain on the order of twenty-five thousand pages and ten million words, something like seven hundred articles and ten thousand book reviews. None of us will turn out any such mass of scholarly production— unless perhaps the editor of the *Territorial Papers*, who has half the residents of the territories for collaborators.

Miscellany is the right word. The spread of subject matter is immense — so immense that no one can be really expert upon it all. The unit parts are small, ranging from a paragraph to one paper that was allowed to run to sixty-seven pages. Oftentimes they deal with a particle of history appropriate for compact treatment. Multiplicity of authorship makes for variety of style, though with a good deal of sameness. The file is rich in incident, in detail, and often in wisdom. An ever-changing cast of characters walks its pages. But it is a work without plot, with no discernible outline, and with little continuity. Its construction, with articles appearing in the order of their writing and books reviewed in the order of their publication, precludes a sequential reading of American history. Not only a miscellany, it is a drifting miscellany.

This character of the back numbers of the *Review* of course was inevitable. They were produced with some expectation of abiding

EDITOR'S NOTE: — This paper was presented as part of the program of the session on "The Mississippi Valley Historical Association in Retrospect," at the fiftieth annual meeting of the Association, in Lincoln, on May 2, 1957.

usefulness, but all along the *Review's* primary characteristic has been as a periodical. Each of the 172 issues was designed as an entity. Each was intended for current reading, in the fall of 1914, the summer of 1935, the winter of 1950, and so on. The journal had to pass muster first of all as a quarterly. I am not unmindful of this immediate purpose, but the appraisal I am about to offer must go mainly to the forty-three volumes as a totality — to the question: What kind of an arsenal of historical scholarship is this opus that the Association has wrought?

Reading on in the files, I became aware that here was a place to view a procession of the historians of America. The roster of contributors was not as large as the membership of the Association, and the by-lines of articles and reviews are not a complete roll call of the fraternity. Some of the brightest lights of our discipline are absent: Charles M. Andrews, Carl Becker, Edward Channing, Samuel Eliot Morison, and Frederick Jackson Turner, to name only a few. Charles A. Beard and Herbert E. Bolton contributed only once, and some of the Association's presidents entered only with their presidential addresses.

But by taking into account the authors of the books reviewed and dipping occasionally into footnotes and news notes, one finds most of the active participants in our chosen study passing in review. Volume by volume new recruits enter the ranks; volume by volume names once familiar cease to appear. Such evidence suggests the life and death of a scholar. Fortunately, these clues are not always infallible. Some of these people veered off into administration; some graduated from the writing of articles to the writing of books; others took a great oath to write no more book reviews. The stately files of the *Review* nevertheless do suggest with tolerable accuracy the personnel of scholarship in American history, as it was in 1914, as it changed year by year, and as it is today. At least two of the contributors to the first volume are still active, and the March, 1957, issue contains an obituary tribute to Eugene C. Barker, whose "The United States and Mexico, 1835-1837" appeared as Article 1 in Volume I, Number 1.

The persevering reader will also begin to get a feel of the pulsations and progressions in the study and writing of American history. Essays on American historians and their writings were in vogue at the outset, became less frequent, and then returned to favor. The theme of urban history makes a well-defined entrance and the onset of popularity for immigration studies is almost as clearly imprinted. The more recent discovery of intellectual history also made its mark. On the whole, the *Review* gives the impression of being impervious to current events and current forces. Once it missed publication because of labor troubles and had to catch up with a double number, but there is not so much as a hint of the wartime paper shortage. For obvious reasons in the early forties special attention began to go to the historian in wartime. The preceding half dozen volumes reflect much less influence of the Great Depression and the last half dozen take almost no note of McCarthyism. I do believe that the *Review* pretty accurately registers the stream of American historiography, moving ponderously, almost glacially.

The glacier is a metaphor that can illuminate further. Bits of scholarship and writing, and historians too, are picked up and carried along. Some get ground down to size; others take on a better polish. Occasionally a finger of the glacier advances and then retreats, leaving a stray boulder such as the Pelzer report on "Projects in American History and Culture,"[1] or a moraine such as the regional surveys of historical activities of the first several volumes, or the Teachers' Section.[2] The *Review* in process had life and movement. The file is perhaps more to be compared to the track of a glacier, with scoured valleys, plowed soil, residual lakes, and rearranged landscapes that testify in part to the work that took place.

Articles have always been the largest component of the *Review*. Across a somewhat arbitrary dividing line are the notes, some of which are indistinguishable from the articles. The documentary material is another shade removed, but perhaps not more than that, for characteristically this source material is well edited and processed almost as far as the material out of which the articles are built. Primary versus secondary is not the criterion. Edward E. Dale's memories of Frederick Jackson Turner[3] quite properly appeared as an article.

A goodly fraction of the articles had initial presentation at the programs of the Association. Some were obviously meant for oral delivery and hardly hold up in print. Occasional articles undertake

[1] XXXI (March, 1945), 499-522. All references in this paper are to the *Mississippi Valley Historical Review*.
[2] XXIII-XXXIII (1936-1946).
[3] XXX (December, 1943), 339-58.

to expound a philosophy, to justify a viewpoint, or to reflect on a trend. This occurs most often, though not exclusively, in the messages from our presidents. The prevailing article is more in the nature of a report on a more intensive but narrower piece of research. Many — probably far more than I recognized — are the outgrowth of directed study for the doctorate. Happily, a number of these articles represent the full fruition of the doctoral dissertation. Indeed, the *Review* and others like it may be making their best contribution to scholarship by publishing such distillations and thereby making unnecessary the publication of the dissertations in their entirety.

Another type of frequent occurrence is the article that shortly thereafter is reproduced as a chapter in a book. Because the book is so much readier for reference and because it contains additional related material, it is almost always preferred for subsequent use and citation. The long-term usefulness of the article thereby goes into quick decline. That, I would submit, does not necessarily mean that no such articles should be published. For one thing, the editor cannot always distinguish such an article from the one that will stand as a better substitute for a book. Also, the quarterly can be counted on to outcirculate many of these books, and, apart from any numerical comparison, it will reach many readers who cannot be counted on to lay hands on the book. All else being equal, the editor probably should choose a paper that is not going to have other publication, but I certainly would not advocate an inexorable rule that no article should be accepted if there is prospect of reissue in a book. Nowhere did I detect an article that was a mere reprint from a published book — one of the favorite devices of the *Review's* most glamorous and affluent competitor, *American Heritage*.

I have no intention of singling out a half dozen articles as the *Review's* all-time best. Because the articles range from expository to argumentative, differ greatly in perspective, and even more widely in point of reference, they are not readily comparable. In the book review section in 1950 I did run across high praise of an article which had appeared ten years earlier. I quote: "The essay on 'The City in American Civilization' is, in my opinion, of the utmost importance and merits a place beside Frederick Jackson Turner's famous essay." [4] My only quarrel with this estimate is

[4] XXXVII (September, 1950), 346.

that Professor Schlesinger had taken some of the edge off his essay by earlier publication of his book, *The Rise of the City*.

Ruminating over the contributions published set me to wondering about the kind of article ideal for the *Review*. It is, I believe, the kind that will be read by the largest number of the clients of the journal. It must strike a chord in the common denominator of reader interest. Preferably it should be interstate rather than narrowly localized. It should involve a matter of importance rather than mere triviality. It should contribute to knowledge, or better still to wisdom, and it should be stimulating though not necessarily provocative. Schlesinger's essay on the city will illustrate. It has a theme that is nation-wide or even broader in its incidence. A high degree of significance is claimed, the appeal is for a correction in interpretation, and it is advanced in such a way as to prompt study and thought.

All that is by no means to say that the editors should seek out this kind of article and no other. Articles of more modest scope can have place. I recall, for example, that the one and only contribution that one distinguished historian made to the *Review* was an article locating the site of La Salle's attempted Gulf Coast colony.[5] Because the colony was a complete failure, the exact location mattered little continentally, not much more to the French empire or the Spanish, and even in Texas had little more than curiosity value. The article, however, was of interest for historical method as well as for content. It turned to Spanish records to answer a question that was French, and it utilized geography and ethnology as well as orthodox historical documentation. The *Review* will do well to salt its fare with such excursions into the smaller confines of American history.

A few years ago a friend of mine got a special appropriation to strengthen the American history section of his college library. I was surprised that his first move was to have an assistant go through the file of the *Mississippi Valley Historical Review* and make out an order card for every book reviewed. Some of the reviews, had they been read, would have warned "don't buy." But on second thought, why should I have been startled? Is there any better place or more reliable way to get the first ten thousand titles for a library of modern works on American history?

The editors of course make no pretense that coverage is absolute,

[5] II (September, 1915), 165-82.

but there is evidence that an effort is made to make this section reasonably comprehensive. For instance, in 1950 there was a reaching back to review a book published in 1945, with this explanation: "Through an oversight this volume was not sent to the *Mississippi Valley Historical Review* for notice at the time of publication. But, given its importance, it has seemed best to review it late rather than not at all."[6] Perhaps it was the emphasis of the argument of better late than never that caused me to recall that four volumes and 2,700 pages earlier there had been an on-time review of this same book. It is, so far as I am aware, the only one accorded the distinction of the double treatment. I bring this episode in as a subtle way of demonstrating that my rereading of the files was not altogether cursory, but more especially to underline the editors' firm purpose that books of importance should be covered.

As a test of comprehensiveness I also ran down a personal list of sixteen titles and found twelve reviewed and four apparently not. Other omissions that I have detected were of Parrington's *Main Currents*, Dorfman's *Thorstein Veblen*, and Miller's *The New England Mind in the Seventeenth Century*. Omissions such as these may be traceable to the book publishers, to the mails, to the editor's underestimate of the importance of the work, or to the failure of the contracting reviewer to deliver. A more systematic test on the coverage could be run, but I am sure the findings would be that over the years the *Mississippi Valley Historical Review* has been by all odds the main reviewing channel for works on American history. Recent issues seem to indicate a deliberate reduction of the space budgeted for reviews. I hope this trend will not get out of hand, because one of the strong points about the *Review* has been its coverage of the pertinent books.

The accumulated notices of ten thousand histories suggests another digression. We the specialists in American history have two things in common. Most of us have the *Mississippi Valley Historical Review* and most of us have the Ph.D. degree. We have learned to depend on the book review section of this journal to keep us informed on current books in our field. To acquire the Ph.D. we had to demonstrate that we had learned to use a couple of foreign languages. How do these things dovetail? There are reviews of books in Spanish, French, German, Dutch, and Danish — all told

[6] XXXVI (March, 1950), 683.

something like a dozen and a half, which means on the average a review of a foreign language book in every tenth issue of the magazine. There may be theoretical justifications for the still prevalent foreign language requirement for the doctorate in American history. But the justification apparently resides hardly at all in twentieth-century scholarship as published. On the basis of the assemblage of reviews all but one fifth of one per cent of the pertinent books come out in workaday English.

A more important consideration is the quality of the reviewing. It impresses me as competent but perhaps not rigorous enough. With insignificant exceptions the reviewers appear to have been well qualified to appraise the book assigned. A few may have stood too close to the author; in student-mentor relationship, for instance. And there were periods when the reviewing staff was perhaps unduly narrowed, as when most Latin American titles were assigned to Isaac J. Cox, and most Mormon titles to William J. McNiff. In the early issues some of the reviews were unsigned. As late as Volume XIV a note stated that the reviewers of half a dozen books "have elected not to advertise their identity." [7] Shortly thereafter almost every review carried a signature.

Occasional reviewers have taken advantage of their assignment to try to educate the author by public horsewhipping, either through a review-long exercise or through a snide or cutting remark. "Mr.—— is no stylist. His sentences are sometimes awkward or 'schoolmasterish'." [8] Or, "The binding is paper and does not appear to be durable. This may prove to be satisfactory because it does not seem likely that great numbers will make use of [this book]." [9] Another example: "To read [this book] and to write about it are unrewarding tasks." [10] Or, sideswiping other critics, "[This book] will be particularly distasteful to the 'war-hawks' of 1941, so many of whom were invincible in peace but invisible in war." [11] It is proper, of course, for the reviewer to warn readers, but I doubt that this kind of barbed criticism is helpful.

The journal has offered examples of brilliant reviewing. I take the liberty of nominating a few: Orin G. Libby's appraisal of

[7] XIV (June, 1927), 133.
[8] XXXIII (December, 1946), 467.
[9] XXXIV (December, 1947), 478.
[10] XXXIX (December, 1952), 581.
[11] XXXV (December, 1948), 534.

Clarence W. Alvord's first volume of the *Centennial History of Illinois*;[12] Alvord's review of the fifth volume of Channing's *History*, in which he speaks in the name of Transappalachia to an author from the remote parts of Cisappalachia;[13] the review of Turner's *Frontier in American History*, including some thoughts that Alvord had been gestating ever since the publication of the famous essay on "The Significance of the Frontier";[14] Milo M. Quaife's pointed criticism of Sandburg's *Lincoln*;[15] Fred A. Shannon's polite disposal of Margaret Leach's *Reveille in Washington*;[16] Roman J. Zorn's review of Schlesinger's *Age of Jackson*;[17] and Frederic L. Paxson's brisk commentary on the Beards' *Rise of American Civilization*.[18]

Several of these reviews are considerably longer than the average. There are those who sigh for the free-flowing, loquacious, essay-type review, yet if the journal is to cover its field of books it cannot afford many such excursions. The Paxson review in particular well illustrates that a vigorous, analytical, knowledgeable review can be done gracefully and eloquently and still in short compass.

Throughout its forty-three years the *Mississippi Valley Historical Review* has performed its function of historical criticism almost exclusively through the individual book review. Seldom if ever has it indulged in review essays. These, to be sure, usually have to be solicited, which is hazardous, and they involve either duplication or canceling out of the normal reviews of the books covered. Other journals find this device useful. It is a possibility that the editor and the board might explore.

A quarterly such as ours has certain conversational possibilities. The back numbers indicate that the most common embracing of this opportunity has been in letters to the editor, in most instances stirred by a book review. The earliest communication was an exception; it urged the Association to support publication of some of the treasures in the nation's archives such as the territorial papers. In Volume X an irate author belabored his reviewer, who answered with dignity. From time to time, thereafter, authors and reviewers

12 VII (March, 1921), 399-401.
13 VIII (March, 1922), 377-80.
14 VII (March, 1921), 403-407.
15 XIII (September, 1926), 287-91.
16 XXVIII (December, 1941), 447-48.
17 XXXII (March, 1946), 590-92.
18 XIV (September, 1927), 233-35.

claimed this privilege, varying the performance by choosing rapiers or bludgeons, pained dignity or zestful asperity. At one point the referee called a halt: "The Editor of this *Review* regrets the dissonance in the views concerning Professor ——'s volume . . . reviewed in the December, 1944 issue (pp. 461-3) and subsequently discussed in the March, 1945 issue (pp. 641-4). Limitations of space preclude further discussion in these pages. Students of this field are referred to the volume itself for further questions and judgments." [19]

Some years later a review called forth an *amicus curiae* rejoinder by a friend of the scholarship represented in the book. Whatever other merits it might possess, this technique did not mellow the reviewer or persuade him to temper his criticism.[20] Alerted by another review which proclaimed that a certain biography would "stand as definitive so long as there is any interest in reading about its central character," a second friend of history entered the lists. He commented: "I do not remember easily a letter to the editor of a professional journal which complained that a book review was too laudatory. . . . But I think that the student of history should be as willing to speak up when the critical faculty is allowed to lie dormant as when it is overextended." [21] The author of the book did not feel called upon to break silence, but his champion, the reviewer, continued the debate.

The Communications column probably is a necessary outlet and a useful protective device in cases of errant criticism. On the basis of most actual uses, however, I am inclined to think that all concerned would have been as well off without it.

More rarely the conversation has proceeded article to article. An instance would be Murray Kane's "Some Considerations on the Safety Valve Doctrine" [22] and Joseph Schafer's rejoinder, "Was the West a Safety Valve for Labor?" [23] Still more fruitful — and perhaps the best example of interchange of views — was the colloquium touched off by Robert S. Henry's "The Railroad Land Grant Legend in American History Texts." [24] David M. Ellis, Richard C. Overton, Robert E. Riegel, Herbert O. Brayer, Chester McArthur Destler,

19 XXXII (September, 1945), 305.
20 XXXVIII (June, 1951), 146-49.
21 XXXIX (June, 1952), 163-64.
22 XXIII (September, 1936), 169-88.
23 XXIV (December, 1937), 299-314.
24 XXXII (September, 1945), 171-94.

Stanley Pargellis, Fred A. Shannon, and Edward C. Kirkland had their say in one of the most illuminating quires that the *Review* has ever printed.[25]

The *Review* is also a purveyor of news. It tells us when and where the next assemblage of historians is to be, notes major acquisitions of historical materials, keeps track of other periodicals, records our comings and goings, and in the end bestows the final accolade. We expect comments such as "The flood of Lincolniana continues unabated," and, "There has been abundant generalization upon the significance of the West. What is now needed is detailed evidence and proof." These remarks might bear the date line 1957. This may shake faith in progress, but as it happens they come from the first volume.[26]

The first several volumes had little news and less gossip. In Volume II, the editor did make reference to "the somewhat tense political situation" that had existed in the American Historical Association. He dismissed it with the remark that "the extreme insurgents found that there was nothing to offset the debit account of personalities which they had run up in the last few months." [27]

Not until the tenth volume did genuinely personal news break through the editorial ice. The first of these personals is about as durable a piece of goods as the editors have ever found. With new names inserted it has appeared time and again in this and kindred journals. "Professor Frederick J. Turner has announced his intention of retiring from teaching at the end of August, 1924, when he will become professor emeritus at Harvard. 'I hope to do some writing when I end my teaching,' Professor Turner remarks." [28] Over the years the news columns have expanded. In part this is merely a matter of keeping pace with the growth of our company and our activities. In part it is a result of more systematic reporting.

Perhaps I missed the entries, but in the first ten volumes I found no obituaries. American historians then were young, they were rugged, and they were not numerous — in its tenth year, 1924, the *Review* had only 279 persons as subscribers.[29] Perhaps no one died. As time went on, death notices became more frequent and some-

25 XXXII (March, 1946), 557-76.

26 I (June, 1914), 161; *ibid.* (December, 1914), 482.

27 II (March, 1916), 619.

28 X (September, 1923), 205.

29 XI (September, 1924), 268.

times more elaborate. The first were formal and limited to a sentence or two. Others included a brief biographical sketch. Still others, written as tributes, ran considerably longer, in one instance to sixteen pages, but a paragraph or two became the norm and has continued so.

In an epoch in which the editorship of scholarly journals frequently has gone begging, the *Review* has been extraordinarily successful in claiming the services of men of outstanding ability. Prevailingly they have been former presidents of the Association; if not, the Association has soon taken appropriate steps to convert them into former presidents.

In the beginning it was Clarence W. Alvord. Ten years later, after a brief interlude in which Lester B. Shippee was in charge as acting managing editor, Milo M. Quaife took over for six years, followed by Arthur C. Cole for ten, and Louis Pelzer for six. William O. Lynch then served as regent until the succession to Wendell H. Stephenson was determined. After seven years Stephenson passed the insignia of office to William C. Binkley, who is now in his fifth year of service. Associate Editors Bertha Josephson of the Western Reserve dispensation and Fred C. Cole of the Stephenson period should also be mentioned. These ten, but especially Alvord, Quaife, and Cole, Pelzer, Stephenson, and Binkley are the ones who deserve chief credit for making and maintaining the *Review* as we know it.

With its first editor the journal got off to a most auspicious start. Alvord was one of the two or three most distinguished scholars in the early ranks of the Association. The *Centennial History of Illinois*, of which he was editor and contributing author, still stands as a model treatment of state history. His *Mississippi Valley in British Politics*, which won him the Loubat Prize, was hailed by Paxson as "perhaps the leading work in erudition and interpretation that our school of western historians has produced." Paxson's comment continues: "But we shall not remember Alvord longest for his *Mississippi Valley*. It is as the great spirit of this *Review*, and as the inspirer of the useful association of scholars whom this *Review* represents, that his service was greatest and will best endure. We cannot forget that he was more nearly our founder than was any other man. He originated the *Review*, and guided it among the financial hazards that have wrecked too many works of scholarship, and among the greater risks of the office that test the sincerity and courage of literary honesty. . . . There will, for a long time, be a need for the exposition and interpretation of the point of view that Alvord represented in Transappalachia."[30]

That point of view was set forth in the editorial with which Alvord launched the *Review*. Thereafter he was exceedingly chary about inserting any editorial comment, and even in his farewell in Volume X he was still reticent about letting anything personal intrude. Those who knew him report a lively, warmhearted man who made new friends readily and held and "intrigued" old friends. As a book reviewer he had no hesitation about letting his personality show through, but as editor he maintained almost complete reserve.

Quaife frequently inserted comments on the American scene. He editorialized on how to keep a local history society alive, on censorial laws, on a Canadian complaint against the inclusion of Longfellow's *Evangeline* in a book of readings, on the proposed renaming of Mount Rainier, on Poavo Nurmi and the exaggerated reputation of the Indians as long-distance runners, on a 1925 novelty — a history lecture by radio, on the Scopes trial, on the discovery of a sixteenth-century manuscript proving that Adam died of the gout, on historical myth making, on the Associated Descendants of Scalpees of King Philip's War, on faculty salaries as compared to Ty Cobb's, on the writing of business history, and on the dubious realism in Rolvaag's *Giants in the Earth*. In June, 1930, Quaife published his farewell — and in the next issue had to add a postscript because his successor had not been ready to take over. Here it is disclosed that the prestige of the journal had grown to the point that five midwestern universities came forward with bids for the editorship.

This running commentary that Quaife kept up during his six-year term was just one of many expressions of his boundless interest and energy. His hand was active also in historical society and library work, in the writing of a number of books, and in the publication of edited documents.

Cole likewise came to the editorship as a well-known scholar. His most widely read book is *The Irrepressible Conflict*. He entered upon his duties with no salutatory and left without a valedictory. Pelzer's background consisted of a long career of dynamic

[30] XV (June, 1928), 153-54.

teaching at Iowa and productive scholarship best represented in his book on *The Cattleman's Frontier*. According to a close friend, the editorship of the *Review* was the climax of his career. Pelzer continued in the Alvord-Cole tradition of unobtrusive editing. Both Stephenson and Binkley are sufficiently contemporary that a resumé of their scholarly achievements is not necessary. Should anyone require an introduction or a review, their Fleming lectures on, respectively, *The South Lives in History* and *The Texas Revolution* will serve. Their school of editing is also the unobtrusive.

The whole file of the *Review* has the hallmark of good editing. Open the set at any page. There is a chance in a thousand that a mistake will be found. A couple were thought serious enough to call for published correction. But it is far more characteristic that the mechanics of scholarship, as represented in the footnotes, will be found in good order, the spelling and punctuation correct, the grammar according to rule, the sentences clear, the paragraphing logical, the rhetoric acceptable. The contributor must be a man of parts — a good craftsman, a good scholar, a good writer. But before jumping to that conclusion I would like to look back of the printed page. I would like to see the manuscript as first submitted, the editor's markings, his correspondence with his consultants and with the author. Perhaps the editors have kept such records. Perhaps not.

The publication and the annual reports of the editors which I have heard have not been communicative on the work that goes on back of the printed page. The standard phrase has been "The four issues of the *Review* are my report." I do know that some contributions have been accepted almost by return mail, that a few have been published without any alterations, and that others have been accepted only after multiplication, circulation to the entire board of editors, and a careful pondering by all concerned. In the volume of J. Franklin Jameson's correspondence recently published are several letters in which he as editor of the *American Historical Review* gave most generously in criticism, guidance, and encouragement to prospective contributors. Editors of other journals have reminisced in similar vein. Ours have not, but I am morally certain that a great deal of such advising and educating has gone on behind the scenes. The paper work for every issue must considerably exceed the finished product. And the paper work is just a fraction of what constitutes editing.

The published file suggests that editorial policy has been conservative. The format provides a hint. Cover design and the type face have been improved but with care to preserve substantial continuity throughout the years. The general make-up of the issue has remained essentially the same. A few tables break the steady flow of textual matter, but only once in the 172 issues has there been a graph, or a map, or an illustration. The journal has grown by accretion, article by article and review by review. Only once has there been a special issue — the cluster of papers marking the Jefferson bicentenary [31] — and here the arrangement probably stemmed more from a program committee than from the editors.

Very few controversial articles have been published. It is not recorded, for example, that the paper on textbooks and railroad land grants was recognized as controversial until after it was published. Another paper which the editor thought might provoke argument was accepted only after the oncoming program chairman had agreed to set up a program session that could be the release for any complaints and objections that the article might occasion. The book reviews, as has been remarked, are generally mild and bland, and since they are written by invitation their tone may reflect the preference of the editors.

A particular evidence of this conservatism can be seen in the minimal response to the wave of anti-intellectualism that has characterized the period of the Cold War. That the Association showed some awareness of what was going on, is indicated in resolutions adopted at several of the annual meetings. In the *American Historical Review*, Guy Stanton Ford periodically commented on these issues and their bearing on the history profession. Our journal contains hardly a hint on any of these problems and stresses of the postwar period. The degree of detachment pretty clearly exceeds that which the majority of contributors could feel. It suggests that the *Review* is more insulated than we are as individuals, and perhaps that the study of history has less relationship to the present than we usually claim for it. The *Review's* glacier-like imperviousness to the Cold War, its complete retention of its own status quo, is a telling evidence of conservatism.

[31] XXX, No. 2 (September, 1943).

Now the editor of a scholarly journal, except in the rare instances when it and its field are his personal creation, is of necessity a middleman. He is a selecter, a smoother, a lubricator. If he is a builder, it is by assembling parts that others have prefabricated. He has much less than full control over what shall comprise the final product. Concern for balance and fairness also pulls him toward the middle of the road. Historians in general are affected by this same gravitational force, because much more than most, history as a discipline puts stress on considering all the evidence and on alertness against bias, while the imponderables we have to deal with also suggest guarded judgments. The staid, non-venturesome character of the *Review* thus derives from the rank and file of its constituents and not just from its editors. In an undertaking as co-operative as our journal the fundamental determinations inevitably flow in large measure from the group.

The *Mississippi Valley Historical Review* came into existence as the organ of the Mississippi Valley Historical Association, founded at Lincoln in 1907 as a sort of congress of seven midwestern state historical societies. Rather quickly the Association took on more of the character of a society of historians, and when the quarterly was launched in 1914 it had only a few reminders of its local-history-society ancestry.

At the outset Alvord declared its devotion to the history of the Valley, generously defined as extending from the Appalachians to the Rockies. Even these limits would not be meanly applied. He promised that the "surrounding regions" would have attention "in so far as they have been historically connected with the westward movement." He also assured that the department of reviews would reach even further afield.[32]

Ten years later Editor Quaife rephrased the definition of the function of the *Review*. It was, he said, to interpret "that comparatively small segment of the past which has had its setting in the Mississippi Valley." [33] Taken literally, this statement indicates a much more restricted field than Alvord had proclaimed. No other editor, to the best of my detection, promulgated a definition of the field of the journal.

As early as my graduate school days I caught on to the fact that

[32] I (June, 1914), 157-58.
[33] XI (September, 1924), 304.

this Association's quarterly was actually nation-wide in scope. I assumed, or perhaps was told, that it had begun with narrower horizons and later had expanded in fulfillment of its manifest destiny. The opening statements of Alvord and especially Quaife would have supported this assumption. But out of my recent rereading of the files comes the intelligence that the *Review* never was as provincial as its name.

Its books reviewed always spread across the nation and beyond. Its articles likewise were chosen on a catholic, national, or even continental basis. The very first item offered — the lead article in the initial number — was on the relations of the United States and Mexico. Other first-year articles dealt with the dispersion of the American Tories, William Walker's designs on Cuba, the Pan-American policy of Jefferson and Wilkinson, McMaster's *History*, Schouler's *History*, and historical activities in the Old Northwest and eastern Canada. So it went in subsequent years with articles appearing on United States legations in Latin America, the statesmanship of President Johnson, the French Council of Commerce and American trade, the doughboy newspapers of World War I, diplomatic attention to Tehuantepec, and federal Indian policy in California.

The contributors, I grant, were mainly from the Valley, and there was attention to the history of the Valley and of its more minute parts. With the launching of the *Hispanic American Historical Review* most of the Latin American articles migrated to it. The *Canadian Historical Review* siphoned others northward, and new state and local journals relieved at the more provincial level. The field of the nation's history remained as the most inviting, and it was a preserve in large part because the *Mississippi Valley Historical Review* had already pre-empted it.

The first strong voice on this point was the "father" of the *Review*, Clarence W. Alvord. In his farewell as retiring editor in 1923, the one piece of advice that he offered was: "The *Review* has become fairly well established and is generally accepted, in spite of its local name, as the representative review devoted to American history. Should its scope not be extended to the limits of its reputation? My answer is Yes and my advice is that there be admitted to its pages articles on all phases of our national development." [34]

[34] X (September, 1923), 212.

Alvord's motion got a second seventeen years later when a reviewer of the cumulative index for Volumes XVI-XXV remarked that the journal was "gradually outgrowing its original title 'Mississippi Valley' " and becoming in reality a United States history review.[35] It might have been more accurate to say that it had already passed over the line. That certainly was a tenable conclusion for Theodore C. Blegen's presidential message in 1944, "Our Widening Province," in which the principal evidence used was the material in the files of the *Review*.[36]

As of today no one could deny that the field of our journal is the nation, not just the Mississippi Valley. My rereading of the files leads me to believe that it began that way, had a partial relapse into provincialism, but long ago staged a recovery and resumed its national character. I would go so far as to say that there never was a time when a national rather than a regional title would not have been more accurate and less misleading.

Half a dozen years ago a proposal was advanced to make the names of the Association and the *Review* accord with the national character of our group and our publication. The move did not succeed. Any student of historians might have known that habit and precedent would not be lightly set aside. And any student of numerology could have pointed out that the time was much too soon. Only after twenty-four years of publication, long after the true nature of the periodical had become clear, did the management add a subtitle that gave a clue to the scope of the contents. When another twenty-four years have gone by — that will be in 1962 — the time may be ripe to let accuracy prevail by conferring on our publication the title it has earned, *Journal of American History*.

Let me emphasize that I make this proposal not as a citizen of far-away California, nor even as a onetime resident of Texas, a sort of illegitimate part of the Mississippi Valley. Rather, I make it as a native of Kansas, someone partly educated in Nebraska, and currently (as of May, 1957) at work in Wisconsin, all of which are in the bosom of the Valley.

Meanwhile, under our strange device, we can carry on, continuing the features in which our journal is excellent, and improving those in which it is merely good.

35 XXVII (December, 1940), 496.
36 XXXI (June, 1944), 3-20.

Book Reviews

British Essays in American History. Edited by H. C. Allen and C. P. Hill. (New York: St. Martin's Press Inc., 1957. x + 348 pp. Bibliography and index. $6.00.)

This book may well be considered a landmark not so much for what it says — although many of the essays in it are very good indeed — as for what it represents. Here are seventeen British scholars, all but one of them teachers at British universities, who are willing to indicate, by this joint exercise, that American history is a study serious enough both to elicit their attention and to include formally in their universities' curriculums.

Of the seventeen, five are professors or lecturers at London University, three are at Cambridge, two at Oxford, two at Manchester, and one each at Glasgow, Edinburgh, Wales, Birmingham, and the Bristol Grammar School. This shows how widely the interest in American studies in Britain has spread; of even more significance is the fact that in the company are eight who hold chairs or lectureships in American history (seven, actually, for the pioneer of them all, Professor H. Hale Bellot of London University, is now retired).

The American should understand that this book and these essayists stand not so much for accomplishment as for promise, and a promise that may turn out to be very impressive before too long. Most of the contributors are young and sustained work from them in American studies still lies before them, although some have already published scholarly works or whole general books, for example, H. C. Allen of London, Marcus Cunliffe of Manchester, Frank Thistlethwaite of Cambridge, Henry Pelling and Max Beloff of Oxford, and D. W. Brogan of Cambridge (the last two are the best known to Americans). As well, the seven who have chairs or lectureships in American history are inevitably committed to the wider inclusion of the study of this field in the programs of their universities and to the training of new generations of scholars.

In Britain, an undergraduate who takes honors in modern history — unlike the major in an American college, whose concentration is not much more than 30 points — is expected to spend almost all his time at the university in preparing for the papers (examinations) in this area alone; in fact, the greater part of the stress is on English history. Of the few papers outside of English history, up to recently not much more than one (and then, as a rule, as an elective) has been wholly on an American theme. That is to say, a British undergraduate could take a first-class degree in modern history and never have studied American history at all. The fact that a subject was being lectured on — as Americans have discovered when they were called to British universities — did not mean that examinations in it were part of the regular syllabus.

Changes in syllabuses have been occurring of late, of course; these are being accelerated because, among other things, of the presence of the seven essayists alluded to, and one has every reason to assume that the British undergraduate — as well as, also, the British schoolboy — in time will know as much of the American past as he does today of the French and German. The impact on better mutual understanding and more cordial Anglo-American relations is one of the obvious gains from such a preoccupation. Thus, every one of the writers in this volume has approached his subject, as well as the general one of American development, seriously and sympathetically; where the writing is critical, it is within the context of the problem set rather than outside of it.

The collection of papers has been put together in effect to make a continuous narrative from 1787 to the present; this was necessary, of course, in order to find a British public for the book. But the writers have had the boldness to follow their own specialized bents, and in consequence have written in a large variety of fields: political (on federalism, by H. Hale Bellot of London), political-philosophical (on Hamilton, by W. R. Brock of Cambridge; on Jefferson, by Esmond Wright of Glasgow; on the radicalism of Jackson, Bryan, and Wilson by C. P. Hill of the Bristol Grammar School), economic (on commercial America by Frank Thistlethwaite of Cambridge and on industrial America by J. Potter of London), military (on the American military tradition by Marcus Cunliffe of Manchester), and in other fields as well.

It is to be hoped that American historians and students will read this book, for many keen insights are to be found in it; it serves, as well, as a directory, in little, of colleagues in the British Isles whose work they should watch for and learn to know.

Columbia University LOUIS M. HACKER

The Life of John Smith, English Soldier. By Henry Wharton. Translated from the Latin Manuscript, with an Essay on Captain John Smith in Seventeenth-Century Literature, by Laura Polanyi Striker. (Chapel Hill: University of North Carolina Press, for the Virginia Historical Society, 1957. xii + 101 pp. Illustrations, notes, appendix, and index. $4.00.)

Dr. Striker has put an end to a fascinating sport — the game of sniping at Captain John Smith. For three hundred years, skeptics have questioned the stature of his achievements and aimed sharp barbs at the credibility of his writings. For some time, however, the credibility of Smith's *American* exploits and writings has been well established. There remained only a small cloud of doubt over his career in southern Europe and Turkey before he came to America in 1607 as one of the founders of Jamestown, Virginia. Dr. Striker has dispelled this cloud over Smith's pre-Jamestown career in her scholarly appendix to Bradford Smith's *Captain John Smith, His Life and Legend* (1953), and in her expansive introduction to Wharton's account. She has conclusively demonstrated that John Smith's adventures in Hungary and Turkey really happened, that they are fact, not myth.

Now for Henry Wharton. His *Vita* of Smith is brilliantly written. It constitutes a substantial "character witness" on behalf of the Captain. As narrative history, however, Wharton's account leaves something to be desired. Clerical historians like Wharton proclaimed themselves to be and strove to be absolutely truthful. But clerics are, by their profession, accustomed to accepting many things on faith which are not always capable of mundane proof. So we may pass over his introductory note — "I pledge my honor that this entire story is true" — as an oath of no particular substance. Many historians of his time, clerical or lay, prefaced their narratives with a similar pledge, sometimes good, sometimes of little value.

Wharton is adequate on who did what and why. He is a little less satisfactory on indicating where some of the events in his story took place, and much more vague as to when they transpired. In fact, there is not a single precise date in his *Vita*, by day, month, or even year. Without supporting notes from modern scholarship, one would frequently be hard put to know just what he was writing about.

To this reviewer, Wharton's life of John Smith has a haunting similarity to another war and adventure narrative of the time, Cotton Mather's *Decennium Luctuosum*, or history of King William's War in New England. Although separated by the Atlantic Ocean, the two men wrote in much the same way. Wharton's biography of Smith, however, is less clogged with obscure allusions to ancient history.

Wharton makes a major error of fact in stating that John Smith came to Virginia *after* the colony had been founded for some time and was in danger of dissolution. He also overstates his case for Smith by portraying the Captain as the one and only hero in Jamestown amidst a horde of complete ingrates and poltroons. So let us salute Henry Wharton as a sincere, honest, and well-intended supporter of Captain John Smith, but offer our major accolade to his editor, Dr. Striker. She has left with us the challenging hypothesis that, in writing this *Vita*, Wharton had the benefit of a contemporary source not now known to us. This reviewer hopes later research may uncover such a helpful document.

McCoy College JARVIS M. MORSE
The Johns Hopkins University

James Logan and the Culture of Provincial America. By Frederick B. Tolles. *The Library of American Biography.* Edited by Oscar Handlin. (Boston: Little, Brown and Company, 1957. xii + 228 pp. Note on the sources and index. $3.50.)

Professor Tolles has written a graceful, perceptive volume, bringing together the widely scattered materials on a leading colonial figure whose importance has never received the individual attention it deserves. Although some of Logan's responsibilities receive more thorough treatment than others, every facet of his varied career is touched upon. The result is a significant book which should encourage the preparation of similar succinct biographies of other colonial statesmen.

Logan came to the Quaker colony in 1699 as secretary to the great William Penn. Logan's earlier career had not been distinguished, although his greatest success was in teaching, a talent he probably inherited from his father along with a love of books and learning. The disappointing monetary rewards of teaching, characteristic it would seem of any age, prompted Logan to try his hand in business, but his initial efforts were less successful than he had hoped. The offer from Penn rescued him from oblivion and set him on the road to wealth and station, his dearest ambition.

While William and Hannah Penn resided in the colony Logan was little more than an aide, but when Penn departed in 1704 to unwind his tangled affairs in England Logan's position greatly improved. His career in Pennsylvania, as Professor Tolles makes clear, reached a turning point in 1709. Before that date he considered himself a temporary resident of Pennsylvania, carrying out the orders of his employer; after that date — partly as the result of a trip to England where he was rebuffed in a marriage proposal by a Quaker family who considered his social and financial position inadequate for their daughter — he determined to seek his fame and fortune in the Quaker colony, to become a colonial. That he had become a powerful figure in Pennsylvania politics before his crucial decision can be seen not only in the significant colonial offices he held but also in the fact that the assembly of Pennsylvania recognized his power. When a dispute over the judicial system erupted, for example, the assembly hurled invectives not at the governor but at Logan, the enemy, so they said, of the "Governor and government of this province."

When Logan reappeared on the Pennsylvania scene after 1709 he quickly demonstrated his commanding economic and political position. These were crowded years. On the personal side, he built a near monopoly of the fur trade, engrossed lands, carried on mercantile affairs, and settled down with a family. In his larger role, he negotiated with the Indians, played a critical part in the public life of the province, and acted generally as the spokesman for the Penn family. During these years Logan was also able to indulge his intellectual interests, particularly in building a reputable library and in conducting scientific experiments, a phase of his career that provides Professor Tolles with his title.

Professor Tolles has packed a remarkable amount of understanding and detail into two hundred pages, but it is fair to suggest, especially for the guidance of scholars who are not close students of the colonial period, that there are three criticisms in particular worth noting: first, a subtle partisanship for Logan runs through the study; secondly, some subjects receive more informed treatment than do others; and thirdly, the emphasis, when certain issues are discussed, seems misplaced.

To be specific: Logan's arguments are usually labeled cogent, informed, and persuasive, while those of his opponents are misleading, full of errors, and, at times, products of demagoguery. As a result, to cite an instance, Logan's eventual triumph over Sir William Keith is described as a "vindication," whereas it would seem to be a triumph of power. Moreover, Professor Tolles claims too much for Logan in certain cases. Verner Crane's investigations years ago, for example, revealed that Logan was not the only colonial, or even the first, to discern that a momentous conflict was taking shape between the French and English on the American frontier, nor was Logan the first to grasp the "imperial" view. The unevenness apparent in the study, is best seen when the concise, remarkably full treatment of political development and change is compared with the scanty, almost impressionistic description of Logan's personal business affairs, especially in relation to his landholding and fur trading activity. Or again, the discussion of individual negotiations with the Indians is almost profuse, but the larger background of Indian relations in New York and the southern colonies (it could be sketched in a paragraph or two) is neglected. This omission together with a failure to fuse the individual strands of fur trading and Indian affairs robs the account of its fullest meaning. So far as the question of misplaced emphasis is concerned another illustration will serve. Much is made, and appropriately, of Logan's immense usefulness to the proprietors, but the significance of the reverse influence, the sponsorship by the Penns, is not only overlooked but down-graded; and in the political narrative the significance of profound constitutional questions is largely lost when the impression is given that a battle of personalities, Logan versus his opponents, is in progress rather than a basic institutional conflict.

The points mentioned above do not seriously detract from the undeniable virtues of this volume. Every reader will profit from Professor Tolles's insight into colonial development and will delight in his clarity of style and apt quotations. What is more, his volume helps to illuminate that critical but neglected period of maturation and change, the first half of the eighteenth century.

Northwestern University CLARENCE L. VER STEEG

The Carolina Chronicle of Dr. Francis Le Jau, 1706-1717. Edited by Frank J. Klingberg. *University of California Publications in History*, Volume 53. (Berkeley: University of California Press, 1956. viii + 220 pp. Illustrations and index. $3.50.)

Francis Le Jau was a young Huguenot dissenter living in the vicinity of La Rochelle at the time that the French government canceled the last remaining liberties of the nonconformists. In 1706, when he entered upon his duties in South Carolina as a missionary of the English Society for the Propagation of the Gospel, he was a mature man, somewhat over forty years of age. Little is known of the circumstances under which Le Jau escaped from France, transferred his allegiance to the Church of England, pursued his studies at Trinity College in Dublin, became a canon of St. Paul's Cathedral, and, while still holding this title, served for eighteen months as a rector in the English colony on St. Kitts; but the letters from his pen which are now made available in print give a remarkably complete account of his life from the day of his arrival in Charleston to a time within a few weeks of his death in 1717. The record is that of a gentle, tactful Christian who labored with considerable success to bring the benefits of religion to the men and women of various creeds and different races whom fate had suddenly brought together in the little parish of St. James, Goose Creek.

But these letters are more than a personal record. In one written on December 2, 1706, Le Jau tells us: "Upon my first Landing I saw the Inhabitants rejoycing: they had kept the day before holy for a thanksgiving to Almighty God for being safely delivered from an Invasion from the French and Spaniards." In another letter dated some nine years later is found the first of a long series of reports on the destructive Yamassee War. And in the interval between these two crises in the history of South Carolina there were few events of any importance that escaped the attention of the faithful reporter. In more than one instance it is doubtful that a better contemporary account can be produced.

One of the duties of the S.P.G. missionary was to keep the central office informed regarding conditions in the field, and Le Jau was never unmindful of this obligation. The result was long passages in his letters devoted to the customs of the Indians, the manner in which the trade between these natives and the white settlers was conducted, the relationships between masters and slaves, the efforts of the provincial government to establish schools, and a number of other subjects. Because he often chose to extend his observations beyond the limits of his own parish, Le Jau has provided us with a description of the social scene in the South Carolina colony in the closing years of the proprietary period.

By adding another volume to his list of excellent editions of documents selected from the archives of the Society for the Propagation of the Gospel and of the Bishop of London, Dr. Klingberg has increased the debt owed him by his fellow historians. These records have long been recognized as source material of great value, but it is obvious that they will never be effectively used until they are annotated, indexed, and printed.

South Carolina Archives Department J. H. EASTERBY

Counterfeiting in Colonial America. By Kenneth Scott. (New York: Oxford University Press, 1957. xii + 283 pp. Illustrations, bibliography, and index. $5.00.)

The author of this interesting and informative work on colonial counterfeiting is a professor of modern languages and a frequent contributor to numismatic journals. It is as a numismatist that he has produced this survey of early American counterfeiting. After a few pages on Indians who made imitation wampum, and a brief discussion of the forgeries of the seventeenth century, the major portion of the book is devoted to the illicit production of money during the eighteenth century. The author competently escorts his reader throughout the hiding places of counterfeiters in every section of the American colonies and introduces him to the men and women, seemingly from all strata of society, who "uttered" forged currency.

From the point of view of the historian the most serious failure of the book is its lack of perspective. One hopes in vain for a picture of the nature of the specie and the currency of the colonial period. The author constantly reiterates that counterfeiters were hard to convict and seldom was the punishment nearly as severe as the law permitted. Did the bogus money fill a lack of the real commodity or was the laxity of enforcement a reflection of low moral tone? No answer to these questions is offered. Many laymen would appreciate a discussion of the techniques of the counterfeiter whether in coin or currency. Assuredly many of the bills were crudely forged and easily detected. Although there is some discussion of the counterfeiting efforts of Able Buell and Samuel Casey, there is no indication that both of these men were capable engravers who had earlier been engaged to make official plates for colonial currency.

Mr. Scott has covered the sources for his field thoroughly. The professional historian will lament the lack of footnotes. A brief critical essay on the materials used in the preparation of this monograph would have helped supply that lack. Unfortunately, the brief list of books and articles, largely the author's previous publications, does not reflect the wealth of material consulted.

In spite of these defects, *Counterfeiting in Colonial America* is a worthwhile supplement to the colonial bookshelf. Historians will find it a useful addition to criminological and legal history. The story has been told with considerable charm and it is a book which may be read for its entertainment value as well as for the information which it adds to a neglected chapter of American colonial history.

United States Air Force Academy CARLOS RICHARD ALLEN, JR.

Franklin and His French Contemporaries. By Alfred Owen Aldridge. (New York: New York University Press, 1957. 260 pp. Notes and index. $4.75.)

Writing to his wife, Franklin observed whimsically in 1773 that the engraver of his portrait in the latest Paris edition of his works had given him "so French a Countenance, that you would take me for one of that lively Nation." Something very like this happened to his reputation during the years of his diplomatic mission in France. French contemporaries — philosophers, men of letters, journalistic hacks — created a Franklin myth, which personified the eighteenth-century Gallic myth of America. Professor Aldridge, an able critical student of Franklin and his French admirer, Dubourg, as he has shown in a series of articles, now provides us with the first detailed study of the literary elements in that extraordinary compound of fact and fiction, of reality and symbol, the wartime vogue of Franklin in France.

Long since, the solid basis of his continental fame had been laid in his scientific prestige, though Professor Aldridge is disposed to minimize its popular diffusion; and for a decade past the physiocrats had claimed him, no doubt exaggerating the similarities in their economic principles. From English sources, moreover, Frenchmen had recently been persuaded that the American Revolution was chiefly his handiwork. Two main elements in his reputation were linked in Turgot's superb epigram: *Eripuit coelo fulmen, sceptrumque tyrannis.* A third, which Aldridge rightly recognizes as most distinctively a Gallic transmutation, was the popular identification (shrewdly encouraged by Franklin himself) of this subtle, sophisticated, politician with his fictional character of *Bonhomme Richard.* Few Franklin writings were known in France, and those chiefly of this genre: one of them was "a hoax concerning Indians . . . in the literary tradition of the imaginary voyage," whose authorship Professor Aldridge has recently determined; another, better known from widely circulated French translations, was his selections from Poor Richard in *The Way to Wealth.* Missing out on his tongue-in-cheek irony, Frenchmen read them all as serious expositions of a code "of sublime morality," and assimilated them to their own romantic, primitivistic dream of America.

Aldridge's study is an important contribution to the history of Franco-American cultural relations — and also, though less directly, to the history of political relations, for which it supplies context. The ground it covers was barely scratched in Edward Everett Hale's classic volumes on *Franklin in*

France; in contrast to Bernard Faÿ's flashy narrative it is accurate and judicious. From contemporary writings in manuscript as well as in books, pamphlets, and memoirs, and from journals, poems, dramas, eulogies, and anecdotes, the author skillfully reconstructs the "literary character" imputed to Franklin by French contemporaries. Much that he offers is either new in detail, or supplements and corrects previous scholarship.

Most of my expectations from this study have been amply met; but I would add a hope that Professor Aldridge may elsewhere round out his rather summary treatment of Franklin's own literary and journalistic activities during his years in France. There is an excellent, rather full, discussion of the so-called "bagatelles." There is nothing about such characteristic political hoaxes as the purported supplement to the Boston *Independent Chronicle*, or the letter on the sale of the Hessians. (Is this certainly a Franklin piece? What is its relation to current satires on the same theme, specifically to the *Lettre du Landgrave de Hesse*?) And surely one paragraph is short measure for the importance in Franklin studies of Genet's propaganda periodical, *Affaires de l'Angleterre et de l'Amérique*, the organ of the foreign office. The Franklin Papers contain revealing letters between the editor and his principal American contributor, who furnished both news and extracts of letters from America, and (for reprinting) a number of his own writings, not all of them yet satisfactorily identified. And this periodical contains references to Franklin of the sort that Aldridge has sought out diligently elsewhere. For instance, in Number 33 appears the assertion, though in a fictional setting, that the same pen which wrote the "edict by the King of Prussia" composed "MATROCO, Drame burlesque," performed in the court theater at Fontainebleau, November 13, 1777, and here characterized as a satire on the boastings of Johnny Burgoyne. Is this merely a hoax within a hoax?

There are a few minor blemishes: some awkward translations, or texts misread. But this is a substantial work of scholarship — and by the same token deserves a more adequate index.

University of Michigan VERNER W. CRANE

Joseph Reed: A Moderate in the American Revolution. By John F. Roche. *Columbia Studies in the Social Sciences*, Number 595. (New York: Columbia University Press, 1957. xii + 298 pp. Illustration, notes, bibliography, and index. $5.00.)

The Revolutionary generation was fortunate in having an immediate posterity which exerted itself to commemorate the great figures and stirring events of the Revolutionary period. But indiscriminate adulation, special pleading, inaccurate transcriptions, and unnoted excisions in early biographies and collected works presented a sometimes distorted view of the period. Recent biographical treatments of the major Revolutionary figures have done much to rectify the distortions of filiopietistic devotion, but the work cannot be completed until more attention is given to the secondary figures. Mr. Roche, in this capable biography of Joseph Reed, is therefore entering a fruitful field of historical research and writing. It is to be hoped that other scholars will follow in his path.

Roche presents Reed as a typical "moderate" of the Revolutionary period. Born of a substantial New Jersey family, he studied law at the Middle Temple and made connections with important people in England. After hopes of a career there were dashed by family misfortunes at home, he returned to America, brought order to the family affairs by dint of considerable effort and sacrifice, and established a flourishing law practice in Philadelphia. The onset of the Revolutionary agitation in 1774 placed him in a somewhat equivocal position. On one hand he sympathized entirely with the colonial objection to Parliamentary taxation; on the other he valued his English connections and held a high regard for the imperial relation. This ambivalence led him simultaneously to play an important part in organizing the resistance movement in Pennsylvania and to send friendly letters of advice and information to his English friends. But the developing crisis forced him into the radical camp; he joined the army and was appointed adjutant general by Washington. Hesitant still, however, he hoped for compromise and even as late as the summer of 1776 frowned on the idea of independence. Becoming dissatisfied with military life, he resigned his commission to enter Pennsylvania politics and expand his law practice. Successful in both objectives, he became a leader of the state bar and served three years as president of Pennsylvania. But in state politics the "moderate" propensities he had shown during the early years of the Revolution involved him in serious inconsistencies. These aroused bitter animosities and scurrilous controversy which darkened the last years of his life.

Using the voluminous Reed Papers in the New-York Historical Society as his main source, Mr. Roche has constructed his biography in a very workmanlike fashion. But if by historical standards he has done a capable job, by the standards of biography his work leaves something to be desired. Mr. Roche's treatment of Reed's personality is much less convincing than his account of Reed's political career. The Reed Papers exhibit a man of marked contradictions, a man who could be by turns decisive and vacillating, courageous and pusillanimous, generous and grasping. The "moderateness" of Reed appears often not so much a matter of policy as of equivocation. The main flaw of this otherwise commendable book, then, is the conventionalized consistency which Roche imparts to the somewhat erratic Joseph Reed.

University of North Carolina ELISHA P. DOUGLASS

Revolution in America: Confidential Letters and Journals, 1776-1784, of Adjutant General Major Baurmeister of the Hessian Forces. Translated and annotated by Bernhard A. Uhlendorf. (New Brunswick: Rutgers University Press, 1957. xvi + 640 pp. Illustrations, maps, notes, and index. $9.00.)

The use of mercenaries, whose services were purchased by England from the German princes, was not an unheard-of practice in the eighteenth century. During the reign of George II they had been employed in 1739, 1740, and 1742 to bolster British forces on the Continent. In 1746 they had fought on British soil when they participated in the Battle of Culloden. Therefore, in 1775 when recruiting a force to subdue the American colonies proved unpopular in England and Catherine the Great decided to keep her Russians at home, it was only natural that the ministry of George III turn once again to the German princes to hire an army.

With the first of these so-called Hessians to arrive in America in the summer of 1776 was Major Carl Leopold Baurmeister, subject and soldier of Frederick II, Landgrave of Hesse-Cassel. Baurmeister, who served primarily as a staff officer, was more active with his pen than his sword. His military position was such that he was never privy to the dispatches from the field, yet it was not so minor that he did not receive the benefit of headquarters gossip. From 1776 to 1783 he periodically recorded his impressions of the war and dispatched them as information bulletins to the Baron von Jungkenn, who at one time was serving as Frederick II's minister of war. Notwithstanding the fact that his service never carried him south of Philadelphia or north of New York, Baurmeister assiduously reported every action that came to his attention. At times the conflict was painted with broad strokes; at others he cluttered his reports with the minutest of details. Too much of his information was based on rumor, which the gullible Major reported as fact. Occasionally he corrected earlier mistakes, but even then he sometimes succeeded in only compounding his original errors.

Any student of the American Revolution who has examined the von Jungkenn Papers in the William L. Clements Library and shuddered at the formidable Teutonic scrawl, will always be grateful to Dr. Uhlendorf for his translation. On the other hand, a sense of frustration is sometimes experienced with the annotation. Any volume of this size necessarily limits the activities of, and presents an initial problem to, an editor: should he attempt to confine his comments to a correction of the author's mistakes of fact, or should he limit his primary efforts to identification? Dr. Uhlendorf chose the latter course, and his identification of major and minor characters has indeed been masterful. By allowing the author's errors to remain, however, the editor has left himself open to criticism and the volume becomes useful only to the specialist. Even the informed must use the work with caution, for the unqualified acceptance of Baurmeister's observations would be, to say the least, hazardous.

The publisher has also been unkind to the editor, albeit unintentionally, by declaring on the jacket that Baurmeister's account is "one of the most unbiased, comprehensive, and informed of the contemporary accounts of the Revolution." In such a statement lies danger, particularly in view of Baurmeister's tendency to expand and elaborate.

Nevertheless, certain positive values in this book cannot be ignored. Baurmeister's pictures of garrison life in New York are good, and he adds valuable details for the few engagements in which he did participate. Even his critical observations of the British conduct of the war give an insight into the mind of the Hessian soldier of that day. Many of his observations add a few more tiles to the mosaic of the whole, but they must be fitted into place by utilizing all the skill of the craftsman.

By way of introduction, Dr. Uhlendorf has prepared an essay on "The Hessians and the Revolution." This excellent account brings together many of the actual contract negotiations not easily found elsewhere. A new selection of illustrations provides a pleasant contrast to those which have been irritating the eyes in every book on the Revolutionary War for the past few years. The index is excellent, and the volume has been put together in an attractive package by the publishers.

Tulane University HUGH F. RANKIN

The Life and Times of King Cotton. By David L. Cohn. (New York: Oxford University Press, 1956. x + 286 pp. Illustration and index. $5.00.)

David L. Cohn presents in this book an account of the great white staple from its introduction in America to the present. Combining considerable research, wide reading, and an excellent, readable style, he relates cotton to the destinies of all persons who were affected by it and seeks to place cotton in its role as a factor in American history. He makes high drama of King Cotton and demonstrates understanding as well as a remarkable talent for pin-point expression.

Cohn begins with an account of the invention of the cotton gin and traces the effect of the new machine on the coastal states. He follows the development of the new southwestern cotton kingdom to and across the Mississippi, relating this story to the rise of the cotton aristocracy, to the slave trade, and to the commercial developments necessary to market the ever-increasing crop. Using standard authorities, he pithily summarizes the role of the "Cotton is King" philosophy in the political and diplomatic maneuvering before and during the Civil War, and expresses feelingly the plight of the agrarian postwar South under industrial dominance. The chapter on the migration of cotton to the Southwest and California, entitled "Cotton Is a Frontier Crop," is one of the most interesting in the book. From the standpoint of both area and time covered this volume was ambitious.

This is a distinctly useful volume, similar to many others of the last decade in that it is designed to fill informational gaps for the general reader. For historians it offers sound opinions and striking observations but does not provide an informational crutch. Mr. Cohn's errors, if any, are difficult to check since there are no footnotes or citations. Ulrich B. Phillips, Lewis C. Gray, Matthew B. Hammond, and other scholars certainly were studied; but some of the other authorities mentioned are not of the same importance. For example, I have doubts that Margaret Coit is an authority on southern history; and the overworked clichés of Frederick Law Olmsted on life in the South arouse in me a sensation similar to that of discovering a marked deck in a poker game.

In some of his best writing Mr. Cohn describes the cotton aristocracy. Perhaps in a more detailed study it would be necessary to state the criteria used in this classification. While such an aristocracy may have flourished to a degree at different times in portions of South Carolina, Mississippi, and Louisiana, it is difficult to see such a group measuring up to any uniform criteria. These individuals or groups may have been as important as inverted history indicates, but they left no mark of superior breeding, intelligence, or even of extraordinary energy. It is difficult to see just for what reasons yeomen who acquired wealth should be termed aristocrats. If they achieved culture, a way of life, good manners, gentility, and breeding in the seventy years between the invention of the cotton gin and the Civil War, perhaps they should be termed the "rabbit aristocracy." Did the acquisition of objects and slaves either require or indicate taste, manners, or comprehension? It is probable that the cotton aristocracy, taken generally, will be remembered longer for its failure to contribute to our culture than for any achievement. William Johnson, for one, found many of them virtual savages in velvet breeches. Certainly, one of the principal claims to fame of the so-called southern aristocracy was that its pedigree was determined and graded in accordance with the number of human beings kept in bondage.

Cohn is correct in his emphasis on cotton as a key factor in American history, however much each reader may differ with the various extensions of his thesis. His volume may serve to stimulate interest in the subject and its interrelationships. Perhaps, too, it will supply our busy writers with a usable reference book on which they may depend instead of turning to those dusty old records that have been awaiting examination for many decades.

University of Kentucky BENNETT H. WALL

Homicide in American Fiction, 1798-1860: A Study in Social Values. By David Brion Davis. (Ithaca: Cornell University Press, 1957. xviii + 346 pp. Notes, bibliography, and index. $5.00.)

This interesting and thought-provoking book by an intellectual historian will probably shock historians who pride themselves on their conservatism, because it employs literary and social science as well as historical disciplines. But since it represents an important new departure in techniques and materials, it may excite some younger minds even if it pains some older ones.

The study uses as source material not only the fascinating sensationalism of violent fiction, but also the works of moral philosophers, psychiatrists, and legal theorizers, and it explores the relations between them all during the period from the beginning of the American novel to the Civil War.

Dr. Davis' book shows a complex structure of four parts and eleven chapters. Parts One and Two present separate chapters on human nature and insanity as they relate to murder, followed by chapters which analyze similar subjects in American fiction. Part Three explores the psychological relationship in fiction between sex and death and the accompanying themes of jealousy and vengeance. Part Four includes consideration of the question whether a country without an authoritarian government can produce a moral code which effectively holds down violence. There are chapters on dueling and lynching and on attitudes favoring or opposing capital punishment. Some themes also run through all sections of the work. These include: (1) the shift from sensationalist psychology to emphasis upon an intuitive moral sense; (2) uncertainty over the role and status of women; (3) the attempts to find in the situational structure of fiction the rationalizations of violence; and (4) the tensions between the American fear of conspiratorial threats to society and a belief in human nature which would include even the conspirators.

This book has a number of virtues. The many theories Dr. Davis presents are handled with an admirable clarity and concision. Probably even more impressive are the analyses of the novels — usually brief, always penetrating, and generally convincing. The author's use of depth psychology in exploring the latent meaning of situations, plots, and characters is both sophisticated and sensible. So there are excellent expositions of the attitudes in works of Brockden Brown, Cooper, Simms, Melville, and Poe. (Hawthorne is less convincingly interpreted.) Moreover the boldness of his generalizations shows an imaginative power which is of a high order.

Yet despite Dr. Davis' undoubted scholarship and insight, there is still a feeling, not easily to be downed, of something lacking which prevents this good book from being as good as its best parts. It is not the style, which is fluent and avoids jargon. It is rather that one level of generalization has been omitted between the broadest and the most specific. Probably because this form of history has not been thoroughly enough explored for a complete pattern to have been developed, Dr. Davis emphasizes the psychological factor at the expense of the sociological and political. One would like to see him include, as terms in the analysis, the political and social affiliations of the authors whom he treats, for example. But this is the defect of a pioneering work and one which can be remedied if Dr. Davis should decide to continue his valuable analysis into the period after the Civil War.

State University of Iowa ALEXANDER C. KERN

The Territorial Papers of the United States. Volume XXII, *The Territory of Florida, 1821-1824.* Compiled and edited by Clarence Edwin Carter. (Washington: United States Government Printing Office, 1956 [published in 1957]. xiv + 1129 pp. Tables, facsimile, map, notes, and index. $8.25.)

This is the first of several volumes of the official papers of the Territory of Florida, the originals of which are located principally in the National Archives. Of necessity, the volume is limited to a portion of the available material and the editor explains the basis of his selection in the preface. Papers previously edited and published are in general excluded, as is also routine correspondence of slight significance. Documents which contain duplicating information are reduced by selecting the best account of a given situation and citing the others in footnotes. Effort has been made to sustain as the "cohesive theme" of the volume the problem of establishing administrative techniques in a newly acquired region that, since its discovery, had existed under an alien pattern. A broad construction enables the editor to include reports on geography, resources, people, economic development, and military installations. He deserves praise for the judgment shown in making the selection. Most collections of this type are dull except to those seeking specific information; this volume, on the contrary, holds one's attention as two years of evolution amid confusion unfold.

The papers are divided into four parts. Part I relates to the transfer of Florida from Spanish to American hands. The dilatory practices of the Spanish authorities and their appropriation of portions of the archives important for the settlement of land claims are well known. Less well known, probably, is the geographical spread from which the first appointed officials were drawn. From the beginning Florida acquired population from all sections of the United States.

Part II deals with the administration of Andrew Jackson as "Commissioner and Governor" of Florida until he became disgusted with the region and its problems and returned to Tennessee, whence he resigned on November 13, 1821. Later, stung by criticism of his actions, he asked to take back his resignation but it had already been accepted. Even to a less irascible disposition than Jackson's the situation would have been discouraging. Both Pensacola and St. Augustine were in a dilapidated condition. American officials were slow, even reluctant, to arrive. The Spanish population appeared bewildered and unsure of their status, and well they might be, for the fitting together of Spanish and American ways was confusing. Meanwhile personality conflicts flared and various newcomers greedily pursued their own advantage. Conditions among the Florida Indians were troublesome. It was Jackson's advice to pack them off to Georgia from where most of them or their ancestors had come. Equally arresting is his dismissal of the Florida peninsula, now the most populous and productive part of the state, as quite useless.

After Jackson had emptied Florida sand from his boots, the region was placed under the direction of the two secretaries, now become acting governors: William G. D. Worthington in East Florida and George Walton in West Florida. Finally, in March, 1822, as related in Part III, Congress organized Florida as a territory, but even then it was months before an actual organization was set up and the new officials reached their posts. There was some evidence of dissatisfaction over the joining of East and West Florida rather than continuing the separation which had existed under Spanish rule.

William P. Duval was the first territorial governor. By June, 1822, he had taken his seat, and Part IV is devoted to the first two years of his administration. Originally from Kentucky, Duval had come to East Florida as a judge in 1821. With the establishment of the territorial government new problems arose. Commissioners attacked the question of validating land claims. The problem of what to do with the Florida Indians required solution. They were eventually moved, with a few exceptions, to that "useless" part of Florida, the peninsula, and a watchful garrison settled in the Tampa Bay area.

The problem of distance — still a plague for Florida — was a critical one for the young territory; this led to the building of a road from Pensacola to St. Augustine and the founding of a permanent capital, Tallahassee, midway between them. When this volume ends, territorial Florida, which to the people of that day meant the region between the Perdido River and the Atlantic Ocean, was bursting with land controversies and political quarrels, and with unsolved problems of Indian affairs, immigration, and internal improvements. They are topics of territorial growth which were to continue well beyond the terminal date of this volume.

Winter Park, Florida KATHRYN ABBEY HANNA

British Emigration to North America: Projects and Opinions in the Early Victorian Period. By W. S. Shepperson. (Minneapolis: University of Minnesota Press, 1957. xvi + 302 pp. Illustrations, tables, notes, appendixes, bibliography, and index. $5.00.)

Till recently, nineteenth-century British emigration to North America has not been studied in detail. Mr. Shepperson tries to remedy the historians' neglect of the Old Country background by attempting "to set forth the views of the British people as well as the attitudes of Westminster on the controversial subject of emigration" between 1837 and 1861. He ranges widely, but decided, whilst attempting "interpretation and explanation," to give "most space to a recording of information." Much of the material comes from periodicals, publications of propagandists, and government and parliamentary sources.

The first part, "The Emigration Movement," has sections on the farmers, the Welsh, the gentry, the laborers, American land agents, and on opposition to agrarian emigration; on private, group, trade union, and communal industrial (or urban) emigration, and opposition to it; and on emigration promotion by humanitarian and religious groups.

There is much of interest, and many people whose activities are described were Dickensian in their lunacy or roguery. Various points of criticism arise, however. Individual emigration gets only six pages, yet Mr. Shepperson's accounts of particular efforts to organize emigration, entertaining as some are, rarely merit the space accorded them — for example, seven of the ten pages on "Agricultural Laborers" deal with one abortive scheme of 1839-1842. The relevance of these promotional activities to the main theme is often obscure. Moreover, the propaganda of these people seems to be accepted as sufficient evidence of the motives and attitudes of the actual emigrants, and of conditions in Britain. Most of these episodes ended in failure, but their importance is seldom assessed and the scale of this activity does not appear clearly — thus, in the section on state, provincial, and private land agents, no notion is given of the total then at work, or how typical these examples are. In the industrial field the extent of trade union interest is exaggerated partly by listing as active, union emigration schemes that never or seldom functioned, and the motives behind the desultory attention paid by some unions to emigration tend to be simplified and distorted.

The second part, "The Emigration Movement as a Public Issue," discusses the business views of shipping companies, emigrant suppliers, railroads, and Texas land owners; ideas about the creation of markets, investment opportunities, and raw material supplies; and the unfavorable views of people like those of the Anti-Corn Law League. These are interesting and important subjects, sometimes deprived of lengthy treatment by the space afforded descriptions of short-lived schemes of doubtful relevance.

The next chapter deals with instances of government assistance to emigration, legislative and administrative action to improve emigrants' conditions, and the laissez-faire or lethargic government attitude toward advocates of a more positive policy, whether Radicals, Wakefieldians, those seeking personal assistance, or those desirous of British expansion on the American Pacific coast. Mr. Shepperson brings out the contradiction between the Radicals' desire for colonial responsible government and their wish for a central imperial emigration program. This section contributes most usefully to Mr. Shepperson's theme, though one hopes that he will tell us more about all these aspects. Some tables, a useful bibliography, and an index complete the volume.

Manchester, England ROGER V. CLEMENTS

William T. Porter and the "Spirit of the Times": A Study of the Big Bear School of Humor. By Norris W. Yates. (Baton Rouge: Louisiana State University Press, 1957. xii + 222 pp. Illustrations, notes, bibliography, and index. $5.00.)

The twofold value of this study of the "Big Bear school of humor" is implicit in the author's stated purpose: to demonstrate "the part played by the 'Tall Son of York' . . . and by the *Spirit* in promoting the regional writing of the Old Southwest and assisting the comic realists of this area to reach a national public." By ably performing both halves of this worthy task, Mr. Yates has shown not only how important an outlet for ante-bellum southern humor Porter's *Spirit* was for more than a quarter-century, but also how broadly significant were both this type of narrative and the southerners who created it. It would be difficult to say which of these closely related values is the more fully realized by the author, although his work reveals both the strengths and the limitations of the source materials on which it is based and is least successful in analyzing the character of Porter himself.

Porter, the man — his personal habits, tastes, attitudes, aims, editorial methods, and social relations — remains as shadowy a figure here as in the biography written nearly a century ago by his brother-in-law, Francis Brinley. Having to rely chiefly on the meager information furnished in Brinley's *Life* and in a handful of letters extant in the Henry Carey Baird and Porter Papers, none of which offer a very substantial basis for establishing accurate judgments concerning Porter's literary successes and failures, Mr. Yates is obliged to speculate a good deal about these matters. His inferences occasionally lead to such questionable assumptions as (a) that Porter would have broken much more ground for American realism "had he not had an English thoroughbred — imported by a gentleman slaveowner — hitched to his editorial plow"; and (b) that "it was the social attitude of the *Spirit*, not its literary policy, that finally broke the magazine." Few southern scholars would accept these and other similarly pat conclusions which, taking too much for granted on the basis of insufficient evidence, make Mr. Yates's first two and final chapters the weakest and least satisfying in the book.

On the other hand, in his analysis of the comic realism published in the *Spirit* itself over a thirty-year period, Mr. Yates stands on firmer ground. That vast storehouse of comic lore, containing at a conservative estimate well over a thousand pieces of Southwest frontier narrative, affords the enterprising scholar an almost inexhaustible variety of source material for evaluating the impact of this type of writing upon American literary culture; and the author makes the most of his opportunity. In his four main chapters, covering the *Spirit* and its writers, the social types and kinds of frontier experiences treated in their stories, and the techniques and variations of the tall tale printed in the *Spirit*, he is at his best, demonstrating the stages in the growth of comic narrative, comparing and contrasting the work of various writers (his discussion of C. F. M. Noland and Philip B. January is particularly noteworthy), differentiating the kinds of humor present in their anecdotes and tall tales, and illustrating with copious examples the manifold connections between these yarns and the roistering frontier background from which they sprang. Mr. Yates can take justifiable pride in the work of these chapters, while his book as a whole is praiseworthy for having brought together much valuable information about the *Spirit*, hitherto available only in many separate studies. Carefully documented and unpretentiously set forth, as well as attractively designed and illustrated, this book deserves a hearty welcome from all students of American literature, particularly those in southern educational institutions.

Alabama Polytechnic Institute EUGENE CURRENT-GARCIA

Half Horse, Half Alligator: The Growth of the Mike Fink Legend. Edited by Walter Blair and Franklin J. Meine. (Chicago: University of Chicago Press, 1956. x + 289 pp. Illustrations and bibliography. $5.00.)

Among the first character types to become established in the American tradition were the keelboatmen, described by Mark Twain as "rough and hardy men; rude, uneducated, brave, suffering terrific hardships with sailor-like stoicism; heavy drinkers, coarse frolickers in moral sties like Natchez-under-the-hill of that day, heavy fighters, reckless fellows every one, elephantinely jolly, foul witted, profane, prodigal of their money, bankrupt at the end of the trip, fond of barbaric finery, prodigious braggarts; yet, in the main, honest, trustworthy, faithful to promises and duty, and often picturesquely magnanimous."

Though these men attracted considerable attention from western travelers during the first two decades of the nineteenth century, they mostly remained anonymous. An exception was Mike Fink, who became known throughout the Mississippi Valley and the Rocky Mountains as a marksman, a strong man, and a trickster. He was reintroduced to the American public in 1933 by Blair and Meine in a book entitled *Mike Fink: King of Mississippi Keelboatmen.* This book presented the Mike Fink of tradition. It was, as described by the authors, a mixture of fiction, "biography, history, legend, and at rare intervals, poetry."

The present work is a reprinting of the main sources of the Mike Fink legend, arranged chronologically under two headings, "The Growth of an American Legend," and "Accounts of Mike Fink's Death." Aside from furnishing information concerning Fink as a folk character, the chief value of the work is the light it throws upon the development of legendary characters in a literate society. The character first attains local fame. His exploits are recounted in groggeries, in village squares, on river boats, and wherever men gather. They are heard and recorded by travelers and journalists in search of copy. Incidents that originally had no connections with the character become attached to him; fictionists introduce him into their works, giving free play to invention.

The editors have done much to separate fact from fiction, the probable from the improbable, but it is doubtful that the real Mike Fink can ever be recovered.

University of Texas MODY C. BOATRIGHT

Revivalism and Social Reform in Mid-Nineteenth-Century America. By Timothy L. Smith. (Nashville: Abingdon Press, 1957. 253 pp. Notes, critical essay on sources, and index. $4.00.)

This is an important work which should be read by anyone who is trying to understand nineteenth-century America. It will be of especial interest to students of church history, intellectual history, and social reform.

Dr. Smith states his thesis and his frame of reference with refreshing directness. He believes that the ideas of the comman man merit study and that the historian should avoid emphasis upon "the learned and sophisticated minority" as well as upon "the crackpot fringe." He believes also that the strength of American Protestantism in the nineteenth century was in the cities rather than on the frontier. Within this explicit framework his thesis is that the revivalism and perfectionism of the ante-bellum period contributed fully as much to the development of the social gospel as did the industrialization, urbanization, and concomitant social pressures of a later period. "The discovery that the doctrine of sanctification and the methods of mass evangelism played an increasingly important role . . . *after* 1842 compels a revaluation of their impact," he says, and it provides "an evangelical explanation of the origins of the social gospel" (p. 149).

Dr. Smith examined a mass of material, including sermons, church periodicals, and "doctrinal and biographical tracts," much of which has been neglected by historians. In the first eleven chapters and the final chapter he discusses the revivalism which spread throughout the country between 1830 and "the Awakening of 1858," showing that it was not limited to the West, and describes the spread of holiness and perfectionist theories through various denominations, the controversy over sanctification, and the identification of the nationalistic concept of America's sacred mission with the theological concept of millenarianism. Unfortunately, Dr. Smith broke the unity of his book by inserting two rather superficial chapters on abolitionism, in which he contributes nothing to the extant literature. Certainly he is correct, however, in pointing out the fact that historians have given more attention to the social influence of Christianity in the last third of the nineteenth century than in the period 1825-1860, and that we have tended to neglect such important figures as Stephen H. Tyng, Charles G. Finney, and Edward N. Kirk.

Excellent as this study is, the author has failed to grasp an important aspect of his subject. Belief that man should strive toward perfection and that the attainment of a state of sanctification or sinlessness not only was possible but was the goal toward which all Christians aspired created an attitude of totality, of completeness, which Smith fails to emphasize. Such men as Charles G. Finney preached a literal application of the idea that the soul must be entirely holy or it would be lost in sin. As Smith states it, "true conversion made one entirely free from sin" (p. 113). Social and political friction inevitably must result from any theory that sin and perfection are absolutes and that the sinless cannot tolerate the existence of imperfection. Dr. Smith, in his comments on abolitionism, shows some understanding of this fact, but he either does not recognize or chooses to ignore the wider implications of the theory.

The layman must move carefully into any discussion of theological terms, but since Smith, in his excellent preface, expresses a hope that his work will be read by laymen, it is proper to suggest that theologians should not ignore the difficulties inherent in the use of technical terms. Such expressions as "Christian perfectionism," "entire sanctification," and "second work of grace" may be current among the clergy, but an author who hopes to enlighten the lay reader should define his terms. Few laymen (and probably not all clergymen) will understand such a sentence as this: "John Swannell Inskip, was sanctified in 1864 while preaching on the experience in his own pulpit in Newark, a year after his wife had found it at Sing Sing camp meetings" (p. 127).

Dr. Smith's personal interest in pentecostal, holiness, and millenarian beliefs shows clearly throughout the book and his distaste for the Princeton brand of Calvinism is thinly disguised. A few typographical errors and an inexcusable reference to the abolitionists as "screwballs" (p. 179) should have been eliminated. The critical essay on sources is very helpful.

Vanderbilt University HENRY LEE SWINT

Inside the Confederate Government: The Diary of Robert Garlick Hill Kean, Head of the Bureau of War. Edited by Edward Younger. (New York: Oxford University Press, 1957. xxxii + 241 pp. Illustration, notes, and index. $5.00.)

Late Sunday night, September 15, 1861, after returning from five days' picket duty, Robert G. H. Kean made the first entry in his diary. Few men in the Confederacy were as well qualified to write as he. Reared in a family of teachers, Kean made a brilliant record in classics, modern languages, and sciences at the University of Virginia. After receiving his law degree from the same institution, he settled in Lynchburg, married, and was a prominent young attorney at the time of John Brown's raid. With other aroused citizens he joined the Lynchburg home guard, which later became Company G of the 11th Virginia infantry regiment.

Kean's first recordings reflect concerns of enlisted men: food, inaction, boredom, ignorance of military plans, and rare social events away from camp. Although he won promotions by merit, it was his wife's uncle, Secretary of War George Wythe Randolph, who brought him to Richmond to head the Bureau of War. There he remained for the duration in close association with John A. Campbell, former associate justice of the United States Supreme Court, now serving as assistant secretary of war in the Confederate government.

Kean is not a faithful diarist. His entries average less than one per week, and for eight months in 1862 he kept no record. He is, however, an interesting and capable chronicler of events, personalities, and opinions. He admires few Confederate civil or military officials, and is severely critical of most of them. Kean repeats the gossip of the garrulous Campbell and ranks Campbell with "Uncle" Randolph as his civilian heroes. General Longstreet fares well, and Stonewall Jackson is a splendid commander with "a character of antique beauty, simple and severe" (p. 61). After Gettysburg, Kean loses his faith in Lee, for the diarist believes the battle poorly planned and "worse in execution than in plan" (p. 84).

Kean's forte is caustic criticism. Joseph E. Johnston is a "*very little man*, has achieved nothing, full of himself . . . eaten up with morbid jealousy of Lee" (p. 50). Davis is a slow worker, who favors West Point graduates, and "is not a comprehensive man . . . the worst judge of men in the world, apt to take up with a man of feeble intellect or character, and when he has done so, holds on with unreasoning tenacity — for instance, Huger, Holmes, Mallory,

Benjamin, Memminger, etc. etc." (p. 72). "This war has produced no more emphatic failure than [Henry A.] *Wise*, not even in the regular army" (p. 102). The "officers of the United States Army (regular) as a class are the most inferior men in their profession and the most ignorant out of it, of any profession with which I have ever come in contact" (pp. 102-103). Civilians such as "Brown, Toombs, Stephens and their set — are the most pestilent demagogues in the land, more injurious than the North Carolina buffaloes because more able and influential" (p. 140).

This diary, which is a most valuable addition to Confederate literature, will bear repeated quotation. It does not, however, overshadow the accounts of Mrs. Mary Boykin Chesnut and John Beauchamp Jones. At times Kean is disappointing, for he is often in error and his knowledge of what transpires is limited. Commendable are the editor's clear and informative introduction, his scholarly detachment in evaluating the diarist, and his helpful footnotes.

University of Florida REMBERT W. PATRICK

When the World Ended: The Diary of Emma Le Conte. Edited by Earl Schenck Miers. (New York: Oxford University Press, 1957. xviii + 124 pp. Illustration, notes, and index. $4.00.)

Vizetelly Covers the Confederacy. By W. Stanley Hoole. *Confederate Centennial Studies,* Number 4. (Tuscaloosa: Confederate Publishing Company, 1957. 173 pp. Illustrations, notes, bibliography, and index. $4.00.)

Books on the Civil War continue to roll off the nation's presses. Two recent publications are *When the World Ended* and *Vizetelly Covers the Confederacy.* The former is the diary of Emma Florence Le Conte, a seventeen-year-old girl of Columbia, South Carolina. Emma's diary records the tragic events that occurred in her home town during the winter and spring of 1865 while General Sherman was applying "total war" in its fullest to the Carolinas.

"The horrible picture" that Columbia would eventually fall to the enemy was constantly before the young girl's mind. As fear becomes reality, on February 17, she relates in vivid terms the sacking and burning of the undefended and deranged city. The devastation visited upon South Carolina by the victorious Northern army served merely to intensify Emma's hatred of the Yankees. It certainly failed to produce in her a defeatist psychology — an aim of "total war." She refused to believe the South's cause hopeless even after Appomattox and Bennett's Farm House. Only upon the news of President Davis' capture did this young girl concede defeat: "This is dreadful . . . because it gives the final blow to our cause. . . . I think I have given up hope at last, at least for the present. We will be conquered."

The original of this diary has been in the Southern Historical Collection of the University of North Carolina Library for more than fifteen years and has been used by many Civil War scholars and by researchers in southern history. Mr. Miers is to be commended, however, for making it available to the general public as a revealing commentary on the Confederacy's last days.

A more extended view of operations within the Confederacy is presented in W. Stanley Hoole's book on Frank Vizetelly, a special artist and war correspondent for the *Illustrated London News*. For a year this young Englishman had covered the conflict from the Northern side, but in the summer of 1862 he slipped away to the Confederate lines. From this time until the end of hostilities Vizetelly reported and sketched war activities in the South. Although an allegedly neutral correspondent, this Englishman never tried to conceal with pen or brush his strong Southern sympathies.

Vizetelly was both an able reporter and a competent artist. His contribution to our knowledge of the Civil War, however, rests primarily upon his artistic work. The author of the Vizetelly story points out that had it not been for this young man, "the only special correspondent who covered the Army of the Confederate States of America," the South's side of the conflict "would never have been illustrated for posterity."

Mr. Hoole's brief volume is an interesting account of a relatively unknown figure, but it adds little that is new to our knowledge of the Civil War. Of most interest to this reviewer were the thirty Vizetelly sketches interspersed throughout the text.

Virginia Military Institute JOHN G. BARRETT

Louisiana Sugar Plantations during the American Civil War. By Charles P. Roland. (Leiden: E. J. Brill, 1957. x + 150 pp. Notes, bibliography, and index. 15 guilders.)

Before the Civil War, in some twenty-three Louisiana parishes, King Cotton yielded precedence to sugar. Sugar plantations were more complex than those producing cotton, requiring more capital and more industrial skill. Small farmers were unable to compete in the sugar industry, and in this region wealthy planters probably were more dominant than in the Delta or the Black Belt. Prosperity tended to make them prefer to endure the rantings of the abolitionists rather than to risk secession. Unionism persisted strongly until Louisiana seceded.

In this attractively printed, small volume Professor Roland presents a well-written account of what happened to this segment of Dixie during the war, basing his findings principally on diaries, journals, and personal papers. He is concerned with both those who experienced the ruin of war and those who might be considered the authors of the ruin. Altogether it is a valuable addition to the historiography of the Civil War.

The monograph begins with an engaging description of the cane country, the operation of sugar plantations, and of the people involved. Producing sugar was a manufacturing process as well as an agricultural one, involving expensive machinery and depending heavily on intelligent use of slave labor. Some of the problems were similar to those on rice, cotton, or tobacco plantations, but many were unique in the plantation economy.

Early in 1862, following the greatest harvest in history, and while much of the sugar remained unmarketed, the miseries of war came to the sugar country. When Federal ships moved up the river to New Orleans many planters evacuated their homesteads to take refuge in Texas, taking with them such of their property as they could conveniently transport. Most of the Creoles, and a few Unionists endured the hazards and humiliations of military occupation and attempted to carry on their normal routine. The occupation was made easy through the use of the waterways that penetrated the whole region. During these trying times sugar prices dropped steeply, marketing became almost impossible, and credit was not available. Barter became commonplace. Gradually the destructiveness of war reduced most of the country to poverty. Soldiers from both sides foraged and impressed whatever they needed. They camped in deserted homes and used rail fences for fuel. The slaves were unpredictable, and often destructive of the property of their masters. Levees deteriorated or were broken by troops. Even seed cane became scarce. Wandering Negroes, stragglers from both armies, and guerrillas added terror to devastation. Despite optimistic reports sent to Washington, Federal efforts to use free black labor to produce sugar failed miserably. Planters who co-operated with the occupying forces and tried to operate their plantations found conditions intolerable.

When the war had run its course sugar plantations had dropped in number from almost twelve hundred to less than two hundred, and sugar production from 459,410 hogsheads in 1861-1862 to approximately 10,000 in 1864-1865. The economic structure of the region was in ruins. Sugar planters either sold their property for what little they could get, or had it foreclosed and taken from them. Northern men attempted to restore production with free Negro labor. Under them the plantation survived, but it was not the same. The fury of war and the humiliation of defeat had left an indelible mark on the land along the rivers and bayous.

This dramatic phase of the Civil War is well recorded by Professor Roland, and his work will contribute significantly to the understanding of the grim tragedy suffered by this gay and colorful region.

Vanderbilt University HERBERT WEAVER

Lincoln's Supreme Court. By David M. Silver. *Illinois Studies in the Social Sciences,* Volume 38. (Urbana: University of Illinois Press, 1956. x + 272 pp. Illustration, notes, appendix, bibliography, and index. Paper, $3.00; cloth, $4.00.)

This is the first book to devote itself exclusively to an analysis of President Lincoln's relations with the Supreme Court and of the Court's judicial and political role during the Civil War. It is a good, concise, scholarly treatment, based upon extensive use of the manuscript collections of Robert Todd Lincoln, of the justices, and of contemporary political figures. The approach is basically historical rather than legalistic (in the James Randall tradition), although attention is given to the Court's major decisions during and immediately following the war.

From the outset Dr. Silver makes it clear that there was a fundamental "pattern of conflict" between Lincoln and the more conservative justices led by Chief Justice Taney. Lincoln, with the support of Congress and the majority of the northern people, was determined that the American Union would be maintained at all hazards, while Taney, and perhaps some of his associates, "deemed a peaceful separation of the North and the South preferable to a Union that was made possible only by military force and coercion." Lincoln and some Republicans criticized the Supreme Court for attempting to dictate governmental policy while certain justices insisted that a "government of laws" must prevail even amidst a great civil war.

Dr. Silver's study constitutes another confirmation of the significant fact that Lincoln and his cabinet largely directed the war for the Union, with only minor interference from either Congress or the Supreme Court. There was severe criticism of some of the President's actions, both privately and publicly, but his presidential dictatorship continued unhampered. After the Court, by a very close vote, upheld the President's broad authority in the Prize Cases (1863) it seemingly was willing to await the restoration of peace before attempting to resolve most other great constitutional issues growing out of the war. Moreover, both Lincoln and Attorney General Edward Bates took pains to keep certain crucial issues from reaching the Court during the war.

The major contribution of this book is the careful analysis of the political forces at work in the reorganization of the federal circuit courts during the war and of the political factors involved in Lincoln's appointments to the supreme bench. The manuscript sources throw new light upon these appointments, including that of Chief Justice Chase in 1864, and emphasize the fact that Abraham Lincoln was the consummate politician as well as the pre-eminent statesman of the Civil War.

From this reviewer's standpoint the only mar upon this fine book is the exaggerated effort to "absolve" Taney from the condemnation of many of his contemporaries and from the criticism of certain historians. Dr. Silver insists that Taney was not really wrong when he opposed Lincoln's broad presidential powers — he was only indiscreet and untimely — and that the Milligan decision was a clear-cut vindication of the Chief Justice's position. But during the Civil War, time was certainly of the essence and history has pretty definitely supported Lincoln in his all-out effort to maintain the Union even by the "imperative demands of military necessity." Perhaps the Union could have won without resort to such unprecedented exercise of power, but certainly there was no assurance of this fact at the time. As Justice Davis pointed out, the Milligan decision would not and could not have been enunciated if the war had been still in progress. It has been good in recent years to have Taney's reputation resurrected from the dishonor which engulfed it, but the hard fact remains that he was unwaveringly committed to constitutional doctrines which were unacceptable to most northerners and which were being swept away by the revolutionary nature of the Civil War.

Wayne State University WINFRED A. HARBISON

Orville H. Browning: Lincoln's Friend and Critic. By Maurice G. Baxter. *Indiana University Publications, Social Science Series,* Number 16. (Bloomington: Indiana University Press, 1957. viii + 351 pp. Notes, bibliography, and index. $4.50.)

James G. Randall once suggested that scholars should write the biographies of Lincoln's associates as a means of illuminating some aspects of the President's life. This advice produced a number of significant works. Although future doctoral candidates might have to content themselves with Isaac N. Arnold, Gustave Koerner, and Norman B. Judd, Mr. Baxter has been able to study a man of sufficient interest and importance to merit a biography. Orville Browning has been of special interest because of the extensive diary he kept for nearly thirty years. The author correctly describes it as "informative, though sometimes wearisome," but it is invaluable as a source for the period. Naturally he has used it extensively.

Browning was a leader in both the Whig and Republican parties before Reconstruction, but he held only a few public offices. The first third of the book carries his career to 1861. During that time he served briefly in the Illinois legislature and made three unsuccessful efforts to get elected to Congress. Baxter discusses his activities in connection with state and national politics, explains his position on various legislative matters, follows his itinerary during the canvasses, and summarizes his views as set forth in his speeches. His connection with Lincoln was no greater than that enjoyed by many other prominent Illinois leaders. Actually, in 1860 he preferred Edward Bates for the presidency.

The second third of the volume covers Browning's career in the Senate, to which he was appointed in 1861 to replace Douglas, and his services as secretary of the interior under Johnson. His position on wartime legislation is traced in detail; his relations with Lincoln and with other congressmen are also elaborated. In 1864 Browning was still not convinced that Lincoln was the best choice but "thought he might get through, as many a boy through college, without disgrace, and without knowledge." For the period of his service in Johnson's cabinet the author concentrates on land and railroad problems which Browning faced.

The final third of the book deals with Browning's later career as a lawyer. He was regarded, Baxter says, as one of the finest legal minds in Illinois. As an attorney for the Burlington Railroad his most important legal work arose in connection with the Granger Cases, and he was among the first to suggest the use of the Fourteenth Amendment as a protection for American business. In 1869 he was a delegate to the convention which drafted a new Illinois constitution, and his work at the meeting is traced with much detail.

In the preparation of this work the author has made extensive use of many manuscript collections, pertinent government and state publications, selected newspapers, and the monograph material which was relevant to a study of the period and subject. It is a straightforward, clearly written piece of research, complete with fifty pages of notes inconveniently placed at the back of the book. But the publisher must bear the blame for this as well as the failure to include a single illustration, even of Browning.

Mr. Baxter has written a valuable study for students of local political history. It is possible to follow the intricate shifts of politics in Illinois before the Civil War. To Lincoln scholars the book should be of value, illuminating as it does the career of a prominent conservative. It is a balanced account, which does not overemphasize the importance of Browning in either the national or state picture.

Baxter's goal was to describe "all the significant, ascertainable facts of his life." He has succeeded in doing that to a large degree. My only criticism is that he fails (at least for me) to bring the subject to life. The reader is never brought to an understanding of Browning the man. I missed much information on his character and personality, his family life, his daily activities, and even on the formative "bib and porridge" years. Browning's life was surely more than political rallies, speeches, legal briefs, and legislative sessions, which this book emphasizes.

Kansas State College, Manhattan — William F. Zornow

Negro Militia and Reconstruction. By Otis A. Singletary. (Austin: University of Texas Press, 1957. xii + 181 pp. Illustrations, notes, bibliography, and index. $3.75.)

In this short but provocative study of the use of Negro militia during the Radical Reconstruction period in the South, Professor Singletary has adequately filled in one of the voids of southern history. It has long been understood by historians that these troops were organized by the Reconstruction governments as defensive forces to perpetuate Radical rule; but, ironically, the movement was not only a failure but it actually aided in the destruction of the very political interests it was created to protect. This was due to the inevitable conversion of the militia forces into aggressive political instruments, leading to depredations, disturbances, social annoyances, and the expressed hostility of the Conservative whites. The racial affront, however, was at the core of the white man's hatred of the Negro militia, and this bitterness led to racial conflicts and violence that erupted until white supremacy was restored.

Professor Singletary has sought to show how the troops were organized, armed, and trained, and what were their major activities. Militia forces were not active in all southern states, for Virginia, Georgia, Alabama, and Florida did not utilize them; and contrary to usual belief they were not made up exclusively of Negro troops. Arms were acquired first by state and private purchases, but later Congress authorized the distribution of federal arms in 1873. The author contradicts the Dunning school of historical thought that the militiamen were "arrogant, swaggering bullies bent on a rapacious campaign of violence against and humiliation of the South," while at the same time he refuses to accept the revisionist summation that the militia activities were "little more than a series of playful pranks committed by a troop of benevolent comics." Instead, he generalizes that the crimes of violence committed were so infrequent that they can be dismissed as the inevitable concomitant of protracted military activity — that instead of being horrified at the excessive number of unlawful acts committed one should be surprised that there were not more.

Life in the militia passed through two distinct phases. The first was the period of organization, when enthusiasm was exceedingly high and participation was merely the extension of the social and political life of the community. This was due to a number of factors: the novelty of the experience; participation by the Negro in a crusade on his own behalf; the welcome relief which muster and drills furnished from the boredom of routine plantation life; the association of recreation and entertainment with militia exercises; and the Negro's delight in the trappings of military life. The second phase began when the unit was called up for active service. Mobilization was almost always accompanied by a gradual deterioration of morale. Discipline was forgotten or ignored and equipment lost, misplaced, sold, or stolen. Other problems included violation of the chain of command, desertion (deliberately encouraged by the whites in an attempt to place the militia in an unfavorable light), a haphazard manner of paying the troops, and the omnipresent evidence of Conservative enmity.

Throughout the entire period of Negro militia activities the southern white Conservatives bitterly opposed the program. Militia laws were challenged in the state legislatures and courts as being sinister political maneuvers. The troops were charged with every conceivable crime by the white-controlled press; were subjected to warnings, bribes, and seizure of equipment; and were threatened with direct retaliation such as refusal to rent land or give employment to Negro militiamen. Impeachment was another weapon used, primarily against Radical governors. Abortive attempts were made against Powell Clayton of Arkansas and Henry C. Warmoth of Louisiana. Governor Adelbert Ames of Mississippi was impeached but allowed to resign, while William W. Holden of North Carolina was convicted and removed from office after the so-called "Kirk-Holden War."

The reviewer is in general agreement with the conclusions and synthesis of Professor Singletary, but feels that the study is based too much on the older secondary accounts. Too little use was made of the primary printed and manuscript materials connected with the subject, and the more recent monographs and publications were not adequately consulted. The author is to be commended, however, for making his study into a very readable and interestingly written volume. It is also an example of good craftsmanship in book-making and reflects credit on the University of Texas Press. Above all, it is most timely in view of fears of resurgence of racial violence in the South today.

Tennessee Polytechnic Institute HORACE W. RAPER

Pioneer Years in the Black Hills. By Richard B. Hughes. Edited by Agnes Wright Spring. (Glendale: The Arthur H. Clark Company, 1957. 366 pp. Illustrations, notes, appendixes, and index. $10.00.)

In April, 1876, Richard B. Hughes, then twenty years of age, completed teaching a term of district school near West Point, Nebraska, and a few days later in company with two companions left for the Black Hills. This region was sacred ground to the Sioux and had been guaranteed to them by solemn treaty with the government of the United States. But it had recently become a subject of interest to a great part of the country because of reports sent out by the Custer expedition of 1874 of "gold at the roots of the grass." The nation was then in the throes of a depression and since in the eyes of the average frontiersman no Indian had any rights that a white man was bound to respect, the miners began to infiltrate into the Hills. Orders from Washington forbade trespass on the Sioux reservation and the army made a conscientious effort to enforce those orders, but still the prospectors continued to come despite the efforts of the army and the opposition of the Indians.

In these reminiscences, written from a diary kept at the time, Hughes details the hardships and dangers of the trip to Custer and then on to Deadwood, and the incidents of daily life after his arrival. Prospecting was the business for which he and his partners had come, and the author describes the various trips which they made in the hope of locating abundant quantities of the precious yellow metal. The town of Deadwood, a site located only a short time before Hughes's arrival, soon became the objective of all travel to the Hills, and began to acquire all the appurtenances of frontier civilization: saloons, gambling houses, and dance halls coming first, to be followed by theaters, newspapers, and law offices. In June, 1876, the first newspaper, *The Pioneer*, came into existence, to be followed by several others, with the result that rivalry became intense and "personal journalism" reached a high degree of development. It was on *The Pioneer* that Hughes, who had had previous journalistic experience, soon obtained employment, since the wages that he earned were necessary to permit him and his partners to continue prospecting.

This book is a mine of information for the social historian of the frontier. Troubles with the Indians, as well as the depredations of the "road-agents" who later infested the region, are well described, and the shooting of "Wild Bill" Hickok by Jack McCall, and the latter's trial and acquittal by a miners' court, are ably presented. (Seen in this connection the subsequent trial, conviction, and execution of McCall in Yankton was undoubtedly an early case of double jeopardy.) While considerable attention is given the seamier side of Deadwood's history, Hughes has an explanation for it. But the other side of the picture receives its share of attention, as witness the description of the mail distribution in the early days, when fifty cents was the price of every letter handed out and no one could ask for mail for more than one person at a time. Hughes became a member of the first legislature following the admission of South Dakota as a state, and he gives a good description of the successful fight that kept the state School of Mines in existence.

The editing by Mrs. Spring is beyond reproach, the illustrations are judiciously chosen, and several appendixes add value to the book. The index is adequate, and in format and composition the volume attains that degree of excellence that one has come to expect from the Arthur H. Clark Company. The only criticism that can be made is to note the complete absence of maps. A good map of the local area around Deadwood, giving the various streams and places mentioned in the text, would have been a great help to persons not too well acquainted with the geography of the region. So, too, a general map of South Dakota would have been helpful. But these are trifling faults in a volume of the excellence of this, which is one that no historian of the American West can afford to miss.

Eastern Washington College EDGAR I. STEWART

Anglo-American Understanding, 1898-1903. By Charles S. Campbell, Jr. (Baltimore: The Johns Hopkins Press, 1957. x + 385 pp. Map, notes, appendixes, bibliographical note, and index. $5.50.)

The purpose of this study is to show how, during the five years 1898-1903, relations between Britain and the United States changed, with comparative suddenness, from a long record of mutual hostility into one of close friendship and collaboration. To sharpen the reader's sense of almost miraculous though enduring change, Mr. Campbell in his opening pages reviews the evidence of implacable hostility felt, especially on the American side, in the period between the Civil War and the Venezuela boundary dispute of 1895. While it would be possible to cite countervailing evidence to suggest that Mr. Campbell has exaggerated the contrast, there is no doubt but that a basic change did take place in the attitudes of the two nations toward each other. This was emphasized and explained at some length by Lionel M. Gelber nearly twenty years ago in his book, *The Rise of Anglo-American Friendship: A Study in World Politics, 1898-1906.* In its conception and in its conclusions Mr. Campbell's book does not differ substantially from Mr. Gelber's. But, whereas Gelber relied on printed sources, Campbell has utilized a wealth of manuscript material unavailable, for the most part, in the 1930's but calculated to render his book definitive. This material is suitably listed and discussed in a bibliographical note at the end of the volume. Both Gelber and Campbell employ the common Anglo-American realization of the mutuality of their interests in the Far East in 1898 as their point of departure, but whereas Gelber carries his study through to the Russo-Japanese War, which he sees as the peak of Anglo-American understanding in the Far East, Campbell stops with the Alaska boundary settlement of 1903 as marking the end of the last serious trouble between the two countries.

Mr. Campbell's book does not, in this reviewer's opinion, supersede Mr. Gelber's, but it does enrich the record with a good deal of illuminating detail. Furthermore, it can be read to great advantage in company with Howard K. Beale's recent important volume, *Theodore Roosevelt and the Rise of America to World Power*, published also by the Johns Hopkins Press. Campbell lays at final rest the legend that John Hay's China policy originated in the British Foreign Office or with Alfred Hippisley, who was a member of the Chinese civil service. This legend may have started with a casual remark by Alfred L. P. Dennis in his *Adventures in American Diplomacy, 1896-1906*, but in any event it was taken up and enlarged upon by A. Whitney Griswold, Thomas A. Bailey, Samuel F. Bemis, and perhaps others. Campbell is also very effective in identifying various American foreign policies with certain special-interest groups, a skill which he demonstrated in his previous book on *Special Business Interests and the Open Door Policy.* Thus the small town of Gloucester, Massachusetts, through Senator Lodge and his son-in-law in Congress, Robert Gardner, exercised a veto power over the settlement of the North Atlantic fisheries dispute; while in the case of the Alaska boundary dispute certain business groups in the Pacific Northwest states, eager to monopolize the trade of the Klondike, made things difficult.

In sum, Mr. Campbell has written a meaty little volume. Specialists in American diplomatic history will be rewarded by a perusal of his transcripts of certain British Foreign Office documents printed in the appendixes.

University of Southern California RICHARD W. VAN ALSTYNE

National Tuberculosis Association, 1904-1954: A Study of the Voluntary Health Movement in the United States. By Richard Harrison Shryock. (New York: National Tuberculosis Association, 1957. 342 pp. Illustrations, table, bibliography, notes, and index. $3.50.)

In 1954 the National Tuberculosis Association looked back over fifty years of activity and decided it was time to have a full-fledged history of the organization. Unlike some organizations which leave the history writing to a participant or a member of the staff, the Association turned to a professional medical historian to recapture the story of this important voluntary health movement.

The resulting volume bears the stamp of this selection. The search for the cause of tuberculosis is set against the broad background of all science through the centuries. The scientific, social, and economic conditions leading to the establishment of the Association are explained. The basic aims of the Association's public health program — arousing the public, stimulating informed persons to create voluntary societies which would then campaign for necessary laws and institutions — are clearly defined.

The Association had three major problems, whether it should (1) use the medical or social approach, (2) concentrate on private or public programs, and (3) entrust control of the Association to the central or local groups. Dr. Shryock analyzes the ensuing battles with comprehension.

The dramatic arrival from Denmark of the idea of selling Christmas seals marked the most important development in the history of the antituberculosis movement. After the Red Cross had established the program of Christmas seals, the NTA took over, and in 1920, registered the double-barred cross as a trade mark, thereby curbing the activities of local organizations which wanted to place their own seals on the market and retain all the profits.

With money in the bank, the Association continued to grow in size and influence, and became an important element of the public health movement in the United States. The Association's increasing activities, its internal reorganizations, its relations with local and international bodies, and its changing policies are set down in factual form.

But the very sameness of the presentation leaves the reader groping for something. Many of the medical terms like "pneumothorax therapy" are unexplained for the lay reader, the characters seldom come to life, and a crisis is sometimes glossed over with a phrase, "friction developed," or so-and-so became "involved in difficulties." Perhaps it is an inherent problem for the historian writing about an organization such as this, but throughout the book, there is little feeling for the drama of the situation. A sound, competent, history of the Association, the book nonetheless will appeal more to those vitally concerned with the movement than to the outside reader.

State Historical Society of Wisconsin DONALD R. MCNEIL

Dry Farming in the Northern Great Plains, 1900-1925. By Mary Wilma M. Hargreaves. (Cambridge: Harvard University Press, 1957. xii + 587 pp. Maps, charts, notes, bibliographical note, and index. $10.00.)

The title of this treatise is deceptive. It leads one to assume that the author is concerned with the evolution of dry-farming techniques whereas she is actually concerned with the use which regional promoters made of these techniques to convince prospective settlers that they could farm the western plains. As she summarizes on page 220, "The essence of the dry-farming movement was not the discovery and promulgation of new techniques or new crop varieties which assured successful cultivation of the semiarid lands, but rather the organized effort to attract settlers into the region."

Within this orientation, Mrs. Hargreaves makes a notable contribution to our understanding of the history of the Northern Great Plains. The study is confined to the western Dakotas and eastern Montana. After reviewing the mid-nineteenth-century concept of the Great American Desert, she notes that the railway companies, the realtors, the bankers, the merchants, and the millers seized upon dry farming as a propaganda device to destroy this concept as it related to the northern plains. They organized the Dry Farming Congress and used it as an agency to convince unwary settlers that new agricultural practices had been discovered that would enable them to farm these western lands without irrigation. The railroads employed Hardy W. Campbell and Thomas Shaw to demonstrate and to advertise the efficacy of dry-farming techniques. Although some of the state agricultural experiment station agronomists opposed this misleading propaganda, most of them contributed to it. Unfortunately, they had not had time to test these techniques and only in the field of plant adaptation did they have sufficient experience to offer tested counsel. Nor did the promoters permit the development of a suitable land policy. Rejecting classification of western lands, they demanded policies which would dispose of the public domain as rapidly as possible. This attitude also affected the disposal of both state and railroad lands.

The final section of the book, entitled "Dry-Land Settlement," describes the key problems of the plains pioneers, namely, schools, county government, transportation, water supply, fuel, fencing, farm power, capital, and markets.

This study is extremely well organized; the research is accurate and extensive although I miss references to the agricultural press and to the manuscript files of the state extension services. In addition to the chapters on dry-farming propaganda, the sections on settlement problems, the development of drought-resistant cereals and grasses, and the disposal of state, Indian, and railway lands are outstanding. They present additional evidence of the influence of the humid areas upon the retardation of the adaption of institutions and techniques to the plains.

In spite of its excellence, this volume leaves room for a supplemental book-length study of the evolution of dry-farming methods from the standpoint of agricultural scientists and farmers, a study which will stress the creation of a new agricultural complex adapted to the needs of the region. Such a study will emphasize the fact that although many of the elements which went into this complex were old, the combination was new. It will relate the experimentations and the gropings of both scientists and farmers. It will stress instead of minimize the efforts of F. B. Linfield, director of the Montana Agricultural Experiment Station, in withstanding the propaganda of the promoters. It will emphasize the role of the drought of 1917-1921 in forcing the adoption of dry-farming practices and the efforts of the Montana Extension Service in helping distressed settlers to survive on the dust-blown plains of northern Montana.

Montana State College ROBERT G. DUNBAR

Lowden of Illinois: The Life of Frank O. Lowden. Two volumes. By William T. Hutchinson. (Chicago: University of Chicago Press, 1957. Vol. I: *City and State.* xiv + 381 pp. Vol. II: *Nation and Countryside.* vii + pp. 383-767. Illustrations, notes, and index. $15.00.)

Frank O. Lowden's life was long, rich, and active. Swift success as a young lawyer was followed by decades of varied, purposeful effort and by impressive accomplishment. His chief claim upon posterity's attention rests upon his participation in the politics of Chicago, Illinois, and the nation. The political side of his career has been treated with masterly skill. Seldom have conditions underlying pre-primary, primary, and election campaigns been related as fully and lucidly to the events on the surface. The book affords a better understanding than has before been possible of Lowden's experience in Congress, his role in the Republican convention of 1912, his service as Illinois' war governor, his campaign for the Republican nomination in 1920, his rejection of that party's nomination for the vice-presidency in 1924, and his virtual repudiation of the convention of 1928.

Lowden's interests ranged far beyond politics. This biography shows how he cultivated them. At the turn of the century he delved into corporate mergers and management. He speculated in land and mining ventures. He was happiest in the role of farmer, which in his case consisted of decades of experimentation with husbandry and farm management in Illinois and eastern Arkansas. Among his numerous public-spirited endeavors, the combining of professional research with practical experience in attacking major problems of public administration, penology, and rural economy receives attention in an interesting chapter. Lowden became a member of innumerable boards, committees, commissions, societies, associations, and clubs. The number of his acquaintances was enormous; his travels and speeches, many and lengthy.

Any career as long, energetic, and varied as Lowden's is extremely difficult to portray in detail without sacrificing the sense of unity and movement. By sagacious organization and by deftly linking related matter, the author achieves clarity without forfeiting either unity or momentum. Despite the two long volumes, the book is not a "life and times." The focus on Lowden is invariably sharp. It is assumed that the reader already knows enough of the background. Sources cited are preponderantly Lowden's own papers, those of his family, and particularly the diary of his remarkable wife. Footnote references to the principal historical works concerning Lowden's period are scanty. Yet in balance, perspective, and scrupulous regard for accuracy of detail, the book is a distillation of the literature on that period.

Some of the potential zest of the story has been sacrificed. The mass of detail dilutes dramatic episodes. The author's enthusiasm for his subject is kept under close control. He has a certain fondness for clichés, in particular that about "throwing one's hat into the ring." Offsetting such traits are a discerning eye for the ironical without resort to petty cynicism, and occasional flashes of pleasing wit. He shows a sympathetic appreciation of Lowden's abilities, exploits, failings, and disappointments. Above all, his objective thoroughness inspires trust when he summarizes evidence or characterizes persons and events.

Perhaps a dramatized, short biography laced with satirical comment would win more readers today than a lengthy example of meticulous scholarship is likely to claim. This reviewer believes, however, that in the long run Lowden's reputation will be better served by Professor Hutchinson's book, where teachers and historians will find the basis for giving "Lowden of Illinois" his exact due.

Washington, D. C. GEORGE F. HOWE

The Roots of American Communism. By Theodore Draper. (New York: Viking Press, 1957. xii + 498 pp. Illustrations, notes, and index. $6.75.)

This is the first of a series of studies on "Communism in American Life" sponsored by the Fund for the Republic, under the editorship of Clinton Rossiter. It is certainly one of the best of the many studies of American radicalism that have appeared in recent years, and it sets a high standard for the volumes to follow. The author, a journalist, is identified by the publisher as a former Communist. This fact has to be noted only because it should be said that no visible scars from that experience are evident. His rejection of Communism is complete, but it is the kind of dispassionate rejection to be found among thoughtful observers in all parts of the free world, and it does not show the marks of a personal crisis.

One of Mr. Draper's most important contributions is to show how the problems and point of view of early American Communism were determined by the heritage of Left Wing Socialism out of which it emerged. The interplay between that domestic tradition and the authority of Bolshevism exercised through the Comintern furnishes his fundamental theme. The Left Wing had tended toward syndicalism and sectarian purity with respect to partial reforms, and this heritage fixed the initial character of American Communism. But as the prospect of world revolution receded after 1919 the Comintern switched to the united front and denounced Left Wing "infantilism" — the first instance of the successive changes of line which, if nothing else, were admirably calculated to test the organizational fidelity of Communists throughout the world.

A second theme is furnished by the ethnic composition of American Communism. The foreign language federations, especially Finnish, Russian, and Lettish, supplied a large portion of the party membership in the early years. But an English speaking (or writing) leadership was always necessary. The federations were composed of first-generation immigrants or transients completely isolated from the main currents of American life; the party leadership with its Left Wing or IWW background was already well screened to eliminate any who might be inclined toward the temptation to recruit a mass following by offering a practical reform program. The result was sectarian futility, intensified by the policy of persecution adopted by A. Mitchell Palmer, which drove Communism underground. Incidentally, the effectiveness of this kind of persecution, says Mr. Draper tersely, is a "particularly ignorant illusion."

Many Communists seem to have enjoyed the conspiratorial atmosphere of the underground, which confirmed their romantic impressions of their own Bolshevik orthodoxy. They came above ground in 1922 only upon peremptory orders from the Comintern. Mr. Draper's history stops at this point. He plans a further volume to carry the party's history down to 1945.

As one of a series of studies on Communism in American life this volume suggests some intriguing questions. One of the most striking conclusions that one draws from it is that Communism prior to 1922 had virtually nothing to do with American life. This fact makes it possible for Mr. Draper to concentrate on the Communist movement as upon something occurring in a vacuum, without reference to American life. Its orientation was toward the Soviet Union, not toward the United States. The excellent brief biographical sketches of Reed, Fraina, Browder, Foster, and the other early leaders, tracing the path by which each of them arrived at Communism, throws some light on this question without fully clarifying it. Did a change subsequently occur, and if so, when and under what circumstances? After reading this first volume of the series one might well wonder whether it would not have been more illuminating to reverse the perspective and investigate American life and Communism.

State University of Iowa STOW PERSONS

American Immigration Policy, 1924-1952. By Robert A. Divine. (New Haven: Yale University Press, 1957. x + 220 pp. Notes, appendixes, bibliographical essay, and index. $4.00.)

This unhappy little volume purports to survey American immigration policy between the adoption of the National Origins Quota system and its latest codification in the McCarran-Walter Act. Unfortunately, the book falls far short of its mark.

Errors of commission and of omission and dubious interpretations mar it throughout. When Henry P. Fairchild is described as a "disinterested observer" (p. 11) and the Junior Order of United American Mechanics becomes a patriotic society (p. 38), when Edward Lewis' racist tract is praised as "temperate and carefully reasoned" (p. 49), and the heartless refugee policy of the 1930's emerges as "a major humanitarian achievement" (p. 104), one can only marvel at the shallowness of the author's judgments. But when the founders of the Immigration Restriction League are incorrectly listed (p. 3) and the *Abstracts* are referred to as "a useful summary" of the Dillingham Committee Report (p. 197) the inadequacy of the research on which those judgments rest is clear.

More important still, a narrow conception of the legislative process renders this study entirely worthless. Mr. Divine believes that congressmen and senators represent districts in which their constituents are moved by different interests and ideas. The legislators debate the issues, but vote in reflection of the will of those who elect them. The enactment of a law by Congress shows what "a majority of the American people" want (p. 49).

To ascertain what happened, therefore, it is sufficient to follow the records of debates and hearings in Congress. This view is entirely inadequate. It leaves Mr. Divine no comprehension whatever of the elements that formed public opinion; it is astounding to read an account of the legislation of the 1920's with no reference to the Ku Klux Klan or to the anti-Catholicism and anti-Semitism of the decade. For the same reason, the shift in the attitude of labor between 1924 and 1952 remains a mystery to this author. But then he has made no effort at all to investigate the agencies and the media of communication that influenced the development of ideas on immigration.

Nor can a sound view of the problem be derived from an account which concentrates on the official development of legislation. An enormously complicated bill, like the McCarran-Walter Act, was not framed by legislative debate; most of the senators who voted for it had only a foggy notion of its contents. Indeed, the permanent staff of the Senate Judiciary Committee had more influence upon the form of the law than did any member of Congress. These are considerations of an order which Mr. Divine ignores entirely.

Finally, this conception of legislation compels the author to treat all legislators as if they were on the same plane and acted out of equally disinterested motives. Although he approves of the national origins scheme (p. 51), Mr. Divine makes an elaborate profession of objectivity. The restrictionists made a strong case (p. 78) it is true, while the anti-restrictionists delivered "emotional tirades" (p. 82). But "both sides were guilty of extreme overstatement" (p. 130) and both were equally honest — simply furthering their own interests.

Now this is the most violent distortion of all. It simply is not true that Senator McCarran was an "eminent jurist" who "rarely compromised on matters of principle" (p. 135). A little inquiry into the matter of the Basque sheepherders might have qualified that description. Nor is it true that opponents of the McCarran Act were moved by the "special group interests of ethnic blocs in the Northeast" (p. 188). Jews, for instance, continued to argue for a liberal immigration policy after 1948 when there were no longer significant numbers of their co-religionists seeking admission to the United States.

The whole process was far more complicated than Mr. Divine realizes; and it included many more elements of irrationality and demagoguery, as well as of idealism, than he is willing to admit.

Harvard University OSCAR HANDLIN

The New Age of Franklin Roosevelt, 1932-45. By Dexter Perkins. *The Chicago History of American Civilization*. Edited by Daniel J. Boorstin. (Chicago: University of Chicago Press, 1957. x + 194 pp. Bibliography and index. $3.50.)

The Price of Power: America since 1945. By Herbert Agar. *The Chicago History of American Civilization*. Edited by Daniel J. Boorstin. (Chicago: University of Chicago Press, 1957. xii + 200 pp. Bibliographical note and index. $3.50.)

One subseries of *The Chicago History of American Civilization* treats particular problems in cross section; another, including these volumes, furnishes a chronological narrative. Writers of such volumes must condense to save space. They do so either by giving a full narrative at the expense of adequate descriptive detail, or by sacrificing parts of the narrative in order to draw a larger picture. They must also exercise rare judgment in selection. If they include too much, the layman becomes confused and the professional frustrated, expecting more than the author has room to tell. If they include too little, the layman receives an oversimplified view, while the professional looks unhappily for things he fails to find.

The authors of these two volumes merit high marks for brief and intelligent narrative. Professor Perkins seeks neither to defend nor to condemn, but to understand the Roosevelt years. His account of domestic affairs takes the reader through the hectic Hundred Days into the maze of alphabetical agencies which both gained and lost friends for the New Deal. It shows the second New Deal's increasing appeal to the less privileged, contributing to the towering Rooseveltian victory in 1936, and then the descending curve to 1938, when international matters moved upstage. Perkins views the New Deal as evolutionary rather than revolutionary. In foreign affairs he portrays the President initially reflecting rather than molding the American mood. Indicating the failure to oppose the isolationism of the mid-1930's, the author points out Roosevelt's increasing international awareness in the Quarantine speech and the message of 1939, following which he moved by fits and starts toward full involvement in European hostilities prior to Pearl Harbor. The military and diplomatic story continues beyond the President's death.

In terms of the dilemma posed above, Perkins leans toward inclusiveness. This compels him to an extreme brevity in describing individual events — which disappoints the professional — but enables him to present an occasional bit of brilliant condensation, such as his account of Japanese relations in 1941. This reader would have liked to learn more about the economic aberrations of the early New Deal, the confusion accompanying the magnificent wartime industrial effort, the political implications of Winston Churchill's "underbelly" scheme, and the naïveté of American planners in refusing to consider any but immediate military objectives. Playing these in a low key, however, is in line with the author's stout determination to achieve objectivity; here he is easily in the van among his contemporaries.

A greater urgency animates Mr. Agar, who makes no great effort to be objective. The apt phrase and caustic comment enliven his chronicle of growing maturity, painfully won. Eschewing any attempt to be all-inclusive, he nevertheless creates a sharply lighted picture of a decade filled with tensions and ending in bitter disillusionment. Passing lightly over legislative history, he credits the Republicans with adopting, perforce but reluctantly, the heart of New Deal social and fiscal policies. Playing up the sensational Hiss, MacArthur, and McCarthy episodes, he leaves little hide on McCarthy, but gives some credit for his success to President Eisenhower, who learned eventually that failure to assume executive leadership paid no dividends, either from the Senator from Wisconsin or from a power-hungry Congress.

In foreign affairs, Agar condemns much more vigorously than Perkins the American failure to recognize the relationship between power and policy in the late-war period, but he admits wryly that greater sophistication would hardly have won greater concessions from the U. S. S. R. He blames President Truman for not taking Congress into his confidence as he courageously inaugurated the Korean "police action," but ridicules Douglas MacArthur's doctrine of all-out war. His contempt for John Foster Dulles grows with the narrative, but he fails to mention one of Dulles' major accomplishments, the Japanese Peace Treaty. Indeed, the index of this book fails to list a number of important developments of the first half-decade: Indo-China, EDC, SEATO, the Bagdad Pact, each of which deeply enlisted American concern. Agar's choice of creating a picture at the expense of detail, like Perkins' decision to be inclusive, draws attention again to the well-nigh insoluble dilemma of the writer of condensed history.

Rutgers University L. ETHAN ELLIS

Imprints on History: Book Publishers and American Frontiers. By Madeleine B. Stern. (Bloomington: Indiana University Press, 1956. xii + 492 pp. Illustrations, notes on sources, and index. $7.50.)

Imprints on History is an attempt, and a very successful one indeed, to interpret the development of publishing and bookselling in the United States during the nineteenth century in terms of its cultural and social relationships. In a broad sense it applies the Turner thesis of the influence of the frontier to the history of publishing and bookselling. It is not a strictly chronological narrative, nor is it an encyclopedic compilation such as the works of Frank Luther Mott; rather it achieves its effect by focusing the presentation upon a limited group of key figures in the world of publishing, each of whom illustrates a particular social or cultural phenomenon, force, or influence. The frontiers, of which some seventeen have here been identified, are grouped into two major categories: the frontiers of space and the frontiers of the mind.

The first group treats of such frontiers as the East, the ante-bellum South, and the Middle West; the second includes, among others, the success and failure of rugged individualism, railroads and railroad literature, and the immigrant and the book. A concluding chapter traces nineteenth-century survivals in the present century, and there is an excellent and extremely useful supplement which lists alphabetically and chronologically 191 publishing firms surviving from before 1900. Finally, the notes on sources are unusually full. The book, therefore, is not only good history but also a welcome reference work.

Miss Stern is admirably qualified to write such a book as this. She has enjoyed a long association with the rare book trade, and in addition she is the author of numerous specialized monographs on the publishing history of the nineteenth century and a trilogy of American biographies. The present volume, therefore, represents the climax of her research in the publishing field. She writes with an easy, flowing style which displays erudition without ponderousness, and is a delight to read.

The literature of printing, bookselling, and publishing in the United States is meager at best. Lawrence C. Wroth's *Colonial Printer*, Isaiah Thomas' *History*, the writings of Frank Luther Mott, the unfinished work of Douglas C. McMurtrie, and that of Albert Johannsen on the dime novel — these are not only the landmark works, they represent almost the entire literature on the subject. Miss Stern, therefore, has not only performed a particularly useful service in bringing together much information hitherto not readily available, but to her must also go the credit for attempting its integration with contemporary social and cultural history. In short, her treatment is itself something of a frontier in that little world of scholarship which has dealt with the history of bookselling and publishing during the first century of the Republic.

School of Library Science J. H. SHERA
Western Reserve University

American Nationalism: An Interpretative Essay. By Hans Kohn. (New York: The Macmillan Company, 1957. xii + 272 pp. Notes and index. $5.00.)

Professor Kohn, eminent authority on nationalism, here reflects upon the nature of the American variety. When a mature scholar and specialist shares insights acquired through long years of research, the study of history moves forward.

In this series of five lectures (for the Norman Wait Harris Foundation) given at Northwestern University in April, 1956, Professor Kohn discusses problems encountered in the study of American nationalism as these appear to a student of other nationalisms. He makes no attempt to present a complete history. Far too much basic work on American nationalism remains to be done before any definitive history can be written. Much more systematic work has been done by American scholars on other Western nationalisms and even Eastern than on the nationalism of the United States. Beyond the work of a few historians (Curti, Potter, Savelle, and the reviewer, for example) many painstaking studies are needed which delve into the voluminous American primary sources, both literary and documentary. Professor Kohn opens pathways for future studies. Some day a historian, on the basis of these, will write a major work on the subject. It is surprising that American historians have so far done so little work upon it.

With copious quotations from a wide variety of American and European newspaper and magazine writers, novelists and poets, politicians, and historians, Kohn elaborates on the theme that American nationalism has been peculiarly characterized by liberty in diversity, by "the universalization of the English tradition of liberty, which the early settlers had brought with them." The United States, he believes, as a free nation has never been "an entirely uniform nation nor an entirely politicized nation." From its beginning the nationalism of the United States has varied from the usual pattern, and throughout its history it has continued to deviate. Perhaps it is too early to judge whether the theme of liberty in diversity will carry the weight of the story of American nationalism. The theme provides unity in this treatment and produces some provocative hypotheses. The United States is a nation of several nations and races, a country of great diversities. Certainly this is one of its permanent peculiarities and one key to its national development. Its immense and thinly populated territory made continued diversity (as in federalism) possible, and the land plus the millions of immigrants afforded wealth of talents and realization of potentialities.

One may differ with Kohn on several points, on, for instance, his view that in 1940 Franklin Roosevelt provided "only scant leadership in foreign affairs," his characterization of the sociologists Ross and Fairchild as "progressives," or his statement that after 1918 patriotic societies other than the Ku Klux Klan "amounted to nothing," with combined memberships never surpassing 25,000. About the main theme, that the United States has meant liberty, few on this side of Berlin will disagree. Kohn is at his best when he compares the American with other nationalisms. His amazing knowledge of the literature of European and Eastern nationalisms brings forth sharp contrasts that enlighten us, make us ask new questions. This reviewer would have liked more of Kohn on nationalism and less on foreign policy and other subjects. He wishes also that the author had quoted less and given us more of his own imaginative and informed thinking. But always his comments as well as his obiter dicta are worth hearing and reading, and when Hans Kohn speaks on nationalism he speaks with the authority of a master.

American Historical Association BOYD C. SHAFER

Book Notes

The American Way. By Dexter Perkins. (Ithaca: Cornell University Press, 1957. vi + 141 pp. $2.75.) The five essays included in this volume are based on lectures delivered by Professor Perkins at Cornell University. "They are brief but, I hope, suggestive comments on some aspects of American history," he says in a prefatory note. "More than this I do not claim for them." The first four essays concern the role in American life of conservatism, liberalism, radicalism, and socialism. The concluding essay deals with the outstanding characteristics of "the American way," characteristics identified by the author as libertarianism, empiricism, and the faith of Americans in the values of a fluid society. It is Professor Perkins' belief that "so long as the libertarian spirit exists, so long as Americans retain their strong preference for what works as against some doctrine of what ought to work, so long as the sources of American vitality are refreshed and invigorated through our schools and our colleges, we need not fear for the future."

Interpreting Our Heritage: Principles and Practices for Visitor Services in Parks, Museums, and Historic Places. By Freeman Tilden. (Chapel Hill: University of North Carolina Press, 1957. xviii + 110 pp. Illustrations and index. $3.50.) Teachers of history and members of historical societies are among those who will find in this small book helpful suggestions, clearly presented, on methods of "interpreting" our parks, museums, and historic places in order to increase the understanding and appreciation of the millions who visit them each year. Numerous photographs, supplementing the text, illustrate the manner in which many adults and children already have been given a deeper feeling for "our common heritage in history and science and nature." The work was undertaken under the guidance of the National Park Service. The author's earlier training in literature shows to good advantage in the writing.

New Light on Washington's Fort Necessity: A Report on the Archeological Explorations at Fort Necessity National Battlefield Site. By J. C. Harrington. (Richmond: Eastern National Park and Monument Association, 1957. xii + 139 pp. Maps, illustrations, notes, appendixes, and references. $2.00.) As a means of more adequately interpreting the Battle of Great Meadows, which occurred on July 3, 1754, near Fort Necessity, to the public, the National Park Service began an archeological exploration of the site in 1952. The results of the exploration are here reported and interpreted in the light of available recorded information. Close examination of the archeological evidence revealed that documentary accounts of the location, size, and shape of the fort were erroneous. Reconstruction of the fort on the basis of the new evidence has been completed. The author concludes: "the excavating revealed the correct picture of the physical structures involved; it prevented an entirely erroneous reconstruction from being perpetuated; and it furnished the evidence for a worthwhile educational exhibit."

Parson Clapp of the Strangers' Church of New Orleans. Edited by John Duffy. (Baton Rouge: Louisiana State University Press, 1957. xii + 191 pp. Illustrations, facsimiles, notes, and index. $5.00.) Professor Duffy presents in this volume a new edition of the autobiographical sketches and recollections of a New England parson who in 1822 was called to the pulpit of the First Presbyterian Church of New Orleans. During a period when the Unitarians of New England were fanning the sparks of abolitionism and the Presbyterians of the South were fashioning the theological rationale for the "peculiar institution," Clapp evolved from a Presbyterian into a proslavery Unitarian. Cast out of the Mississippi presbytery because of this Unitarian heresy, the magnetic clergyman carried his congregation with him and made "Dr. Clapp's Church" — a non-sectarian body without creed, Bible class, Sunday school, prayer meeting, or anything else except Parson Clapp — one of the most popular places of worship in New Orleans. One of the South's most remarkable divines, he was known for his love of the renowned gaiety of New Orleans and, with special favor, for the manner in which he ministered tirelessly to the dead and dying during the grim visitations of cholera and yellow fever. Professor Duffy has prefaced his edition of these sketches — first published in 1858 — with three informative chapters on Parson Clapp's life and services.

The Catholic Church in Maine. By William Leo Lucey. (Francestown, New Hamphire: Marshall Jones Company, 1957. xvi+ 372 pp. Illustrations, bibliographical notes, and index. $3.95.) A record of the Catholic church in Maine since colonial times, this publication by Father Lucey of Holy Cross College was initiated in connection with the observance of the centenary of the diocese of Portland. As expressed in the foreword, the book "was not conceived to be a detailed recitation of events to cover local parochial and institutional growth over the years, but rather as a broad adaptation of the Church's life in general as affected by the eras and circumstances in which over three hundred and fifty years she found herself." Although the author states that he has not projected "a complete history" of the Catholic church in Maine, the coverage appears to be thorough and detailed. The bibliographical notes are in the nature of a critical bibliography.

The Exploration of the Colorado River. By John Wesley Powell. Edited by Wallace Stegner. (Chicago: University of Chicago Press, 1957. xxii + 138 pp. Illustrations. $3.75.) Originally published as a series of articles in *Scribner's Monthly* in 1874 and 1875, this account of John Wesley Powell's Colorado River explorations is a valuable addition to western exploration literature. Major Powell and his party of ten men, financed primarily by contributions from several Illinois educational institutions, set out from Green River, Wyoming, in May, 1869, and explored the Green and Colorado rivers to the junction of the Colorado and Virgin rivers in Arizona. In this narrative Powell relates the experiences of the hazardous boat trip down the Green and Colorado rivers. Also included is an account of a later expedition by which Powell reached the Grand Canyon in Arizona on foot. Powell writes with dramatic and artistic skill, but he is not always reliably accurate, often twisting facts for the sake of the story. The scientific portion of Powell's report is not reprinted here, the topographical and geological details having been, according to the editor, "superseded as science and . . . never intended for literature."

America and the British Left: From Bright to Bevan. By Henry Pelling. (New York: New York University Press, 1957. xii + 174 pp. Notes, biographical index, and general index. $3.50.) "This book," in the author's words, "is an attempt to illustrate the attitude to the United States of the members of the British Left — first Liberal and Radical, later also Socialist — in the period since the American Civil War and up to the present day." Certain British political controversies, such as the struggle for the Reform Act of 1867 and the adoption by the Liberal party of the convention system, are selected and treated in greater detail because of their value in throwing light on the contemporary view of America. Mr. Pelling, the author of *Origins of the Labour Party* (London, 1954), treats the period before 1914 with greater thoroughness and with more authority than he does the period after 1914.

The author gives the following reasons for the change in the attitude of the British Left from admiration of America in the nineteenth century to extreme criticism in the mid-twentieth: "the enormous growth of American industry after the Civil War, which put an end to the Jeffersonian ideal of a commonwealth based on rural simplicity; the increasing participation of the United States in world politics, which deprived its statesmen of the reputation for disinterested diplomacy derived from the policy of isolation; and the increasing restrictions placed upon immigration, which signified the closing of the 'golden door' mentioned in the inscription on the Statue of Liberty." In addition, "the growth of Socialist influences among the Radicals and in the Labour movement gave rise to suspicion of any country whose economy was founded on economic laissez-faire, however democratic its institutions." The study rests on numerous periodical articles and manuscript material from both Great Britain and the United States, as shown by the extensive footnotes.

Evolution or Revolution: The United Nations and the Problem of Peaceful Territorial Change. By Lincoln P. Bloomfield. (Cambridge: Harvard University Press, 1957. xii + 220 pp. Notes and index. $4.50.) Writing from what he calls a "pragmatic and utilitarian bias," the author traces the attempts to effect international changes peacefully by the League of Nations and the United Nations, concentrating on the latter. A significant contribution of the work is the supplying of additional information on official United States policy in the drafting of the United Nations charter. In the chapter on United States foreign policy the author sums up the dilemma of the American policy toward peaceful change in these words: "First, the United States, as a matter of self-preservation, must defend and preserve the *status quo* of Western civilization against the onslaught of revolutionary communism. Second, the United States recognizes the necessity of accommodating the *status quo* to those forces of change that are armed with legitimate grievances. . . . And, third, at the same time the United States itself desires to see altered the territorial *status quo* established by communist power across the map of Europe and Asia." Mr. Bloomfield was formerly State Department planner on United Nations problems.

No Frontier to Learning: The Mexican Student in the United States. By Ralph L. Beals and Norman D. Humphrey. (Minneapolis: University of Minnesota Press, 1957. xiv + 148 pp. Notes, tables, appendix, and index. $3.25.) Taking a group of approximately fifty Mexican students in several California universities as the nucleus of their study, the authors carefully analyze the students' cultural background, their reaction and adjustment to the United States, and their problems on returning to their home country. The authors, both professors of anthropology and sociology, relied on extensive interviews with ten students at the University of California at Los Angeles and tests and questionnaires from all fifty students for the basic data. Studies of Japanese and Indian students having already been made in this series, the authors were enabled to make some comparisons of the relative adaptability of Mexican, Japanese, and Indian students to American life. They conclude that Mexican students better adapted themselves to life in the United States, perhaps because they were better informed, and consequently better prepared for adjustment. A general conclusion is that "The Mexican concedes the United States' great technological superiority, greater order, and more effective political democracy, but . . . is convinced that Mexican culture offers a deeper meaning to human existence and provides a more satisfactory pattern of social relationships."

The Historical Thinking of Charles A. Beard. By Elias Berg. *Skrifter Utgivna av Statsvetenskapliga Foreningen i Uppsala,* XXXVIII. (Stockholm: Almqvist and Wiksell, 1957. 83 pp. Notes and bibliography. 3 kronor.) The major part of this short volume presents an analysis of Beard's "economic interpretation" and of his "historical relativism." An introduction contains basic facts about his life and publications, and concluding pages deal with "Charles A. Beard as Historical Thinker." The author concludes that Beard "was not a systematic or penetrating thinker. His historical theories were fragmentary, vague, ambiguous, and sometimes contradictory. Nor were they original, except — and this is significant — in their application to the study of concrete historical events. Yet his theoretical contribution to American historiography was important: acting as a kind of popularizer of more original and profound — but frequently less sensible — thinkers, he emphasized essential aspects and problems which had previously been neglected by American historians."

More Confederate Imprints. Two volumes. By Richard Harwell. (Richmond: Virginia State Library, 1957. Vol. I: *Official Publications.* xxxvi + 158 pp. Vol. II: *Unofficial Publications.* Pp. 159-345. Illustrations, appendix, and index. $2.50 per volume; $5.00 for set of two volumes.) *More Confederate Imprints* lists 1,773 items, including books, maps, broadsides, almanacs, sheet music, and official government documents, published in the Confederacy during its separate existence. It is the first supplement to Marjorie Lyle Crandall's *Confederate Imprints,* which was published in 1955 and which listed 5,121 items. Crandall's list is based on the collection of Confederate literature at the Boston Athenaeum; the present work depends primarily on the large collection of previously uncatalogued Confederate imprints at the Virginia State Library but includes holdings from over 120 libraries throughout the country. Items in the volume of official publications are listed alphabetically according to the departments of government, and according to the separate state governments. Unofficial publications are arranged in six parts: "Military, Historical, and Economic Publications," "Belles-Lettres," "Sheet Music," "Educational Publications," "Religious Publications," and "Charitable and Fraternal Publications and Almanacs." The appendix records publications listed in *Confederate Imprints* which are in Richmond libraries. In the introduction Mr. Harwell, the author of *Confederate Belles-Lettres* (1941) and *Confederate Music* (1950), writes an entertaining and informative essay on the literary output of the South during the Civil War.

Guide to the Manuscripts of the State Historical Society of Wisconsin, Supplement Number One. By Josephine L. Harper and Sharon C. Smith (Madison: State Historical Society of Wisconsin, 1957. xii + 222 pp. Index. $5.00.) Supplementing the *Guide to Manuscripts of the Wisconsin Historical Society* published in 1944, this additional guide describes manuscript collections acquired from 1941 through May, 1956. The collections are divided into two groups, organized and unprocessed. Approximately 700 of the 790 recently acquired collections have been organized, and the authors describe their contents in considerable detail in this book. Two collecting projects, one in labor history and the other in medical history, have brought to the Society outstanding collections of records of Wisconsin labor organizations and records of the history of medicine and dentistry in Wisconsin. The provenance of each collection is published in the quarterly accession reports in the *Wisconsin Magazine of History* and is not repeated in this book.

Studies in Enterprise: A Selected Bibliography of American and Canadian Company Histories and Biographies of Businessmen. Compiled by Lorna M. Daniells. (Boston: Baker Library, Harvard University Graduate School of Business Administration, 1957. xiv + 169 pp. Appendixes and indexes. $4.50.) An informative essay by George S. Gibb on the development of business history introduces this bibliographical guide to company histories and business biographies, a field of writing which has attracted an increasing number of historians in recent years. The bibliography is an expanded edition of an earlier guide compiled by the Baker Library and printed in 1948. The greater part is devoted to the literature on United States companies and businessmen, followed by a separate brief section on those of Canada. Company histories and biographies are grouped separately — normally without annotation — under the several major headings into which the bibliography is divided. These main, classified headings are comprised of: Agriculture and Fishing, Contract Construction, Manufacturing, Transportation, Public Utilities, Distribution, Finance, Insurance, Real Estate and Colonial Land Companies, and Services (including Hotels and Amusements). Entries — over two thousand, serially numbered — include periodical references as well as published books. Special lists, printed as appendixes, cover other bibliographies, Newcomen publications, collective histories, and materials on business history research and writing. The index is in three parts: companies and businessmen, authors, and periodicals and serial publications cited.

Historical News and Comments

Affairs of the Association

The program for the joint session of the Mississippi Valley Historical Association and the American Historical Association in New York on the morning of December 28, will be devoted to "The Nineteen-twenties." Arthur S. Link of Northwestern University will present a paper entitled "The 1920's: Was Progressivism Dead?" This paper will be discussed by John M. Blum, Yale University, and Frank Freidel, Harvard University. The chairman of the session will be R. Carlyle Buley of Indiana University.

The address at the dinner meeting of the Association, on the evening of December 28, will be given by Bert J. Loewenberg of Sarah Lawrence College on the topic "Darwin, Darwinism, and History." William T. Hutchinson of the University of Chicago, the vice-president of the Association, will preside.

Philip D. Jordan, chairman of the committee on local arrangements for the annual meeting of the Association, to be held April 24-26, 1958, at Minneapolis, has announced that the Hotel Nicollet will be the headquarters for the meeting.

Personals

At Harvard University, Frederick Merk and Michael Karpovich have retired from active service, effective July 1, 1957. Crane Brinton is on leave of absence for 1957-1958 for work in the Institute for Behavioral Sciences at Stanford University. Klaus W. Epstein has been promoted to assistant professor of history at Harvard, and new appointments include H. Stuart Hughes, formerly of Stanford, as professor, and James H. Billington as instructor in history.

George A. Hoar, a doctoral candidate at the University of Michigan, has been appointed instructor in history at Tufts College.

New appointments at Boston University include Frederick S. Allen and John B. Armstrong as instructors and Joseph George, Jr., as lecturer in history. Robert V. Bruce has been granted leave of absence for the year 1957-

1958, and Herbert Moller is on leave for the first semester. Warren O. Ault retired in June after forty-three years of service at the University.

At Williams College, Charles R. Keller has been appointed Brown Professor of History and Robert C. L. Scott has been named as the J. Leland Miller Professor of American History. Donald G. Rohr has been promoted to assistant professor, and John G. Sproat, formerly of Michigan State University, has been appointed lecturer in history.

Gerald N. Grob, formerly of City College, New York, and more recently in United States Army service, has been appointed instructor in history at Clark University.

At the University of Maine, John J. Nolde and Thomas W. Parker have been promoted to associate professors of history, and Charles J. Bayard and George A. Billias to assistant professors. Herbert J. Bass, formerly at Clark University, and Edward Grant, a doctoral graduate of the University of Wisconsin, have been appointed instructors in history.

Willard A. Fletcher and Jean Davison have been promoted to assistant professors of history at the University of Vermont, and Thomas J. Spinner and Jeremy Felt have been added to the staff as instructors.

John Morton Blum of the Massachusetts Institute of Technology has been appointed professor of history at Yale University. E. David Cronon, Richard Herr, Firuz Kazemzadeh, and Robert H. L. Wheeler have been promoted to assistant professors, and new appointments as instructors include Ivo J. Lederer, formerly at Princeton, Robin W. Winks, formerly at Connecticut College, Martin B. Duberman, formerly at Harvard, and Lawrence W. Chisolm, Hector G. Kinloch, and William H. Goetzmann, who were assistants in history at Yale last year. Whitfield J. Bell, Jr., associate editor of the Papers of Benjamin Franklin, has been appointed research associate in history.

Columbia University has announced the appointment of Charles F. Mullett, of the University of Missouri, and C. Vann Woodward, of Johns Hopkins University, as visiting professors of history for the year 1957-1958. Fritz Stern has been promoted to associate professor and granted a year's leave of absence. David Donald and William E. Leuchtenburg are also on leave of absence for the year.

At New York University, Bayrd Still has been made head of the newly created all-University history department, and Oscar J. Falnes named assistant chairman of the history department of Washington Square College. A. William Salomone has been promoted to professor of history, Vincent P. Carosso to associate professor, and Chester C. Tan and Thomas P. Robinson to assistant professors. John W. Wilkes of Pomona College has been added to the staff as assistant professor. Brooke Hindle has been granted a leave of absence for 1957-1958.

Walter M. Simon has been promoted to associate professor of history at Cornell University and granted a leave of absence for the year, and Curtis P. Nettels is on leave of absence for the first term. Thomas T. Helde, formerly at Carnegie Institute of Technology, has been appointed visiting assistant professor for 1957-1958.

Leo A. Loubere, formerly at the University of Tennessee, has been appointed assistant professor of history at the University of Buffalo.

Rosemary Husband of St. Andrews University, Scotland, has been appointed visiting lecturer in history at Keuka College for the current year.

At Princeton University, leaves of absence have been granted to Assistant Professors Robert A. Lively, Merrill D. Peterson, and Gordon B. Turner for the year, to Associate Professor Elmer A. Beller for the fall term, and to Professor Cyril E. Black for the spring term. Rowland T. Berthoff has been promoted to assistant professor, and David C. Gordon, Donald A. Limoli, and Peter F. Sugar, all previously graduate students at Princeton, have been appointed instructors in history.

Robert C. Johnson, formerly at Southwest Texas State College, has been appointed assistant professor of history at Temple University. James A. Barnes is on leave of absence for the year.

Warren W. Hassler and Clark C. Spence have been promoted to assistant professors of history at Pennsylvania State University, and Harry Harootunian, from Oklahoma State University, and Richard B. Sherman, a doctoral candidate at Harvard, have been added to the staff as instructors.

Charles M. George, formerly at the University of Washington, Seattle, has been appointed assistant professor and Harry R. Beck, of Elizabethtown College, as instructor in history at the University of Pittsburgh, and Harold J. Gordon has been promoted to assistant professor.

At the University of Maryland, Earl S. Beard and Patrick W. Riddleberger have been promoted to assistant professors of history; Albert D. Mott from the University of California, Berkeley, and Helen A. Rivlin of the Harvard Middle East Institute have been appointed as new assistant professors; and Gerald G. Eggert, a doctoral candidate at Michigan, William F. McKee, a doctoral candidate at Wisconsin, and Kenneth B. O'Brien, formerly instructor at Stanford University, have been appointed instructors in history.

At American University, Ernst Posner has been granted a leave of absence for the year. Arthur A. Ekirch is serving as acting chairman of the department during his absence.

Paul M. Gaston, from the University of North Carolina, and David A. Williams, from Queen's College, North Carolina, have been appointed instructors in history at the University of Virginia. Professor Edward Younger is on leave of absence for the year to serve as Fulbright lecturer at the Allahabad University, India.

W. Harrison Daniel has been promoted to assistant professor of history at the University of Richmond.

At Duke University, John R. Alden has been named chairman of the department to succeed E. Malcolm Carroll, who continues to serve as the James B. Duke Professor of History. Harold T. Parker has been promoted to professor and Joel G. Colton to associate professor. William R. Rock and John Stark, doctoral candidates at Duke, and R. Don Higginbotham, a doctoral candidate at the University of Nebraska, have been appointed instructors in history. Professor William B. Hamilton has become editor of the *South Atlantic Quarterly*.

At the University of North Carolina, Cornelius O. Cathey and Frank W. Klingberg have been promoted to professors of history, and Elisha P. Douglass and George V. Taylor to associate professors. Clifford M. Foust, Jr., of the University of Chicago, has been added to the staff as assistant professor, and Robin D. S. Higham, from the University of Massachusetts, and Richard B. Barlow, from the University of Pennsylvania, as instructors in history. Professor James L. Godfrey of the history department has been appointed dean of the faculty at the University.

North Carolina State College has announced the promotion of Philip M. Rice and Stuart Noblin to professors of history, Marvin L. Brown and Abraham Holtzman to associate professors, and Burton F. Beers to assistant professor.

Richard Bardolph has been promoted to professor of history at the Woman's College of the University of North Carolina.

Clarence B. Carson, a doctoral graduate of Vanderbilt University, has been appointed assistant professor of history at Elon College. Horace H. Cunningham, chairman of the department at Elon, has been appointed dean of the College.

At the University of South Carolina, William B. Hesseltine of the University of Wisconsin is serving as visiting professor of history for the fall term, and Bruce Wernham of New College, Oxford University, will be visiting professor in the spring term. Professor Arney R. Childs retired in June.

Florida State University has announced the appointment of Charles W. Arnade, formerly of the University of Tampa, Richard A. Bartlett, a doctoral graduate of the University of Colorado, and Coburn V. Graves, from Southwest Texas State College, as assistant professors of history, and of William I. Hair, a doctoral candidate at Louisiana State University, as instructor. Venila Lovina Shores, who has been at the University since 1922, and who was head of the department for fifteen years, retired from active service on July 1, 1957.

Wilbur D. Jones and C. Jay Smith have been promoted to associate professors of history at the University of Georgia. Lothar L. Tresp, from Birmingham-Southern College, has been appointed assistant professor, and Walter S. Hanchett, from Columbia University, appointed instructor in history.

At Emory University, Ross H. McLean retired in August, 1957, after thirty-eight years of service. Bell I. Wiley and James Z. Rabun are on leave of absence for the year. George C. Rogers of Hunter College has been appointed acting assistant professor and Douglas A. Unfug of Williams College and Ovid Futch, Emory graduate student, have been appointed instructors in history.

Gerald Strauss, a doctoral graduate of Columbia University, has been appointed assistant professor of history at the University of Alabama.

Henry C. Randall, a doctoral candidate at the University of North Carolina, has been appointed assistant professor of history at Birmingham-Southern College.

Robert A. Naylor has been promoted to assistant professor of history at Alabama Polytechnic Institute, and Edward C. Williamson from the Air

University, Montgomery, Richard W. Griffin from Athens College, and Thomas A. Belser from Jacksonville (Alabama) State Teachers College have been added to the staff as assistant professors.

At Louisiana State University, Walter Prichard retired on July 1, 1957, after thirty-eight years of service. Frank L. Byrne, a doctoral graduate of the University of Wisconsin, has been appointed instructor in history. John L. Loos has been promoted to assistant professor and granted a leave of absence for the second semester, and George B. Tindall is on leave for the year.

Charles T. Davis has been promoted to assistant professor of history at Tulane University, and new appointments include Robert C. Reinders, a doctoral graduate of the University of Texas, as assistant professor and Henry A. Kmen, doctoral candidate at Tulane, as instructor. W. Burlie Brown is on leave of absence for the year.

W. Magruder Drake has been promoted to associate professor of history at Southwestern Louisiana Institute, and Paul K. Conkin, a doctoral graduate of Vanderbilt University, and Roy V. Scott, doctoral graduate of the University of Illinois, have been added to the staff as assistant professors.

At the University of Mississippi, John H. Moore has been promoted to associate professor of history, Allen T. Green of Emory University has been appointed assistant professor, and Margaret DesChamps Moore, formerly at Agnes Scott College, is serving as an acting assistant professor for 1957-1958.

Emmett B. Fields, formerly at the Jacksonville (Alabama) State Teachers College, has been appointed assistant professor of history and associate dean of the College of Arts and Science at Vanderbilt University, effective in September, 1957. Paul H. Hardacre has been granted leave of absence for the year for research at the Huntington Library, and Alexander Marchant is on leave for the first semester for research in Portugal and England.

At the University of Tennessee, Galen Broeker, a doctoral graduate of the University of Minnesota, has been appointed assistant professor of history, and Douglas W. Houston, from New York University, and Robert G. Russell, from Southern Illinois University, have been made instructors. Lawrence F. Silverman has been promoted to assistant professor and granted a leave of absence for the year.

Frank B. Williams has been promoted to professor of history at East Tennessee State College, and James E. Sutton has been promoted to associate professor and granted a leave of absence for the year. Morton A. Brown, doctoral candidate at Harvard, and Willard B. Gatewood, doctoral graduate of Duke University, have been appointed assistant professors of history.

At the University of Kentucky, J. Merton England has been promoted to professor of history, Rhea A. Taylor and Holman Hamilton to associate professors, and Ross A. Webb and Gerhard L. Weinberg to assistant professors. W. Clement Eaton is on leave of absence for the year to serve as Fulbright lecturer in the University of Innsbruck.

Wesley M. Bagby and Mortimer Levine have been promoted to assistant professors of history at West Virginia University.

Milton S. Cushman has retired after thirty-four years of service as professor of history and chairman of the department at Concord College (Athens, West Virginia) and has accepted an appointment as acting associate professor at King College (Bristol, Tennessee).

Harold J. Grimm, chairman of the history department at Indiana University, has been appointed chairman of the history department at Ohio State University as of February 1, 1958, succeeding Professor Foster Rhea Dulles. Harvey Goldberg has been promoted to associate professor of history at Ohio State, and Paul W. Bamford to assistant professor. Appointments as instructors have been given to George E. Etue, Alan D. Harper, Edwin T. Layton, Lillian B. Silver, John G. Sperling, Rudolph J. Vecoli, Walter R. Weitzmann, and Edward F. Yurick.

Marvin B. Becker, from Baldwin-Wallace College, has been appointed assistant professor of history at Western Reserve University.

Robert S. Fletcher has been made chairman of the history department at Oberlin College, succeeding Frederick B. Artz.

Ohio University (Athens) has announced the appointment of Harry R. Stevens from Duke University as associate professor of history, Robert L. Daniel from Cornell University as assistant professor, and Richard A. Thompson from the University of Wisconsin as instructor.

At the University of Toledo, Willard A. Smith has been promoted to professor of history and Lloyd B. Lapp to associate professor. Appointments as instructors have been given to Arthur R. Steele, formerly at the New York State College for Teachers, Buffalo, and Bruce W. Bugbee, a doctoral candidate at the University of Michigan. Cecil E. Cody has been granted a leave of absence to accept a Fulbright grant for research and teaching in the Women's University of the Philippines.

At the University of Michigan, Caroline Robbins of Bryn Mawr College has been appointed as the Alice Freeman Palmer Visiting Professor of History for the second semester. Other appointments include Paul J. Alexander of Brandeis University as professor of history, effective in February, 1958, Alexander DeConde of Duke University as associate professor, Finley A. Hooper of Michigan State University as visiting assistant professor, and John P. Spielman of the University of Wisconsin as instructor. Leaves of absence have been granted to William B. Willcox and Sidney Fine for the year, and to Dwight L. Dumond for the first semester.

John A. Garraty has been promoted to professor of history at Michigan State University. Charles R. Crowe from the College of William and Mary has been appointed assistant professor and George B. Baehr from Notre Dame University as instructor in history.

At Indiana University, Ssu-yu Teng has been promoted to professor of history and Piotr S. Wandycz to assistant professor. James E. Sutton, of East Tennessee State College, has been appointed visiting assistant professor for 1957-1958. Warren H. Carroll, a doctoral candidate at Columbia University, and Jack M. Sosin, a doctoral candidate at Indiana, have been appointed lecturers in history. C. Leonard Lundin is on leave of absence for the year, and Arthur R. Hogue, Robert E. Quirk, and Piotr S. Wandycz will be on leave during the second semester.

At the University of Illinois, Norman A. Graebner, formerly at Iowa State College, has been appointed professor of history, and Oscar H. Dodson, formerly in the Navy, and Francis L. Loewenheim, from the College of William and Mary, have been appointed to the staff as assistant professors. Robert M. Sutton, Deno J. Geanakoplos, and Theodore S. Hamerow have been promoted to associate professors.

Stuart W. Bruchey, formerly of Dickinson College, has been appointed assistant professor of business history and Raymond H. Robinson, from Northeastern University, has been made lecturer in business history in the School of Business of Northwestern University.

David A. Shannon of Teachers College, Columbia University, and William A. Williams of the University of Oregon have been appointed assistant professors of history at the University of Wisconsin. George L.

Mosse has been promoted to professor of history, and Rondo E. Cameron and Philip D. Curtin to associate professors. Robert W. Johannsen of the University of Kansas is a visiting lecturer in history at Wisconsin for the first semester.

Jack H. Hexter of Queen's College has been appointed professor of history and chairman of the department at Washington University (St. Louis).

The State University of Iowa has announced the appointment of Robert M. Kingdon, from the University of Massachusetts, Alan B. Spitzer, from Boston University, and Arthur P. Mendel, from Roosevelt University, as assistant professors of history, and the promotion of Giles Constable to an assistant professorship.

At the University of Minnesota, Robert S. Hoyt has been promoted to professor of history, Paul L. Murphy from Ohio State University has been appointed assistant professor, and William E. Wright of the University of Colorado appointed instructor. Harold C. Deutsch is on leave of absence for the year as a Fulbright Research Fellow in Germany. Professors Alfred L. Burt and Ernest S. Osgood retired in June after twenty-seven and thirty years, respectively, of continuous service in the University.

Robert P. Wilkins has been promoted to associate professor of history and John L. Harnsberger to assistant professor at the University of North Dakota.

At the University of Nebraska, Stanley R. Ross has been promoted to associate professor of history and Aubrey C. Land has been granted a leave of absence for research in England on Fulbright and Guggenheim grants. Peter J. Coleman, a Social Science Research Council Fellow at Harvard during the past year, is serving on a temporary appointment as assistant professor during Professor Land's absence.

A. Stanley Trickett, formerly executive director of the Association of Non-Tax-Supported Colleges and Universities, has been appointed professor of history and chairman of the department at the University of Omaha.

Robert W. Johannsen and William Gilbert have been promoted to associate professors and Elmo R. Richardson, a doctoral graduate of the University of California at Los Angeles, has been appointed instructor in history at the University of Kansas. Oswald P. Backus is on leave of absence on a Fulbright appointment in Finland, and Robert G. Colodny, a doctoral graduate of the University of California at Berkeley, has been appointed visiting assistant professor for 1957-1958 to teach his courses at Kansas.

Eugene L. Asher of the University of California at Los Angeles and Thomas T. Hamilton of the University of Georgia have been appointed assistant professors of history at the University of Wichita, and Albert R. Parker has been promoted to associate professor.

At the University of Oklahoma, Arrell M. Gibson, formerly of Phillips University, has been appointed assistant professor of history and director of the Archives and Manuscript Division of the University Library. Edwin C. McReynolds has been promoted to professor of history, and Donnell M. Owings is on leave of absence on a Fulbright appointment to New Zealand.

At the University of Texas, Robert A. Divine, Otis A. Singletary, David D. Van Tassel, and Philip L. White have been promoted to assistant professors of history, and George G. Arnakis from Texas Christian University has been added to the staff as associate professor.

Katherine F. Drew and Edward H. Phillips have been promoted to associate professors of history at Rice Institute.

Edwin A. Miles, Stanley E. Siegel, and Richard D. Younger have been promoted to associate professors of history at the University of Houston, and Allen J. Going from the University of Alabama has been added to the staff as associate professor.

Ralph L. Lynn has been promoted to professor of history at Baylor University, and Rufus B. Spain, a doctoral graduate of Vanderbilt University, has been appointed assistant professor.

Dorothy P. Clarke, lecturer in United States and British colonial history in Queen's University, Belfast, North Ireland, is serving as visiting professor of history at Texas Christian University under the sponsorship of the John Hay Whitney Foundation and the State Department. New appointments at Texas Christian include Edward L. Cannan from the University of Texas as assistant professor, and Eugene McCluney from the University of New Mexico and Ben H. Procter from Harvard as instructors in history.

Lester F. Sheffy, head of the department, and Hattie M. Anderson have retired at West Texas State College (Canyon) where they had been members of the history department since 1918 and 1920 respectively. Lowell H. Harrison has been promoted to professor of history and made head of the department, and new staff members include Mary Elizabeth Davidson, doctoral candidate at the University of Pennsylvania, Robert F. Heflin, doctoral candidate at Vanderbilt University, John K. Kahler, doctoral candidate at the University of Chicago, and John S. Goff, doctoral candidate at the University of Southern California, all appointed as instructors.

Edwin Lieuwen, formerly at the University of California, Berkeley, and more recently in United States Government service, has been appointed associate professor of history and chairman of the department at the University of New Mexico.

Herman E. Bateman has been promoted to associate professor of history at the University of Arizona.

Eugene E. Campbell has been promoted to professor of history at Brigham Young University, and George M. Addy, doctoral graduate of Duke University, DeLamar Jensen, doctoral graduate of Columbia University, and Paul V. Hyer, doctoral candidate at the University of California at Berkeley, have been added to the staff as instructors.

David H. Stratton of Baylor University is serving as acting assistant professor of history at the University of Wyoming during the current academic year.

Morton Borden, formerly at Ohio State University, has been appointed assistant professor of history at Montana State University.

Allan H. Kittell from Stanford University and Dwane W. Hill from the University of Omaha have been appointed assistant professors of history and government at Montana State College.

At the University of Washington (Seattle), Robert E. Burke from the University of Hawaii and Howard Kaminsky from the Milwaukee Center of the University of Wisconsin have been appointed assistant professors of history, and Kenneth MacKirdy from Queen's University, Kingston, Ontario, appointed acting assistant professor. Scott H. Lytle has been promoted to associate professor, and Edith Dobie has retired from teaching and will do research work in England in 1957-1958.

At the University of Nevada, Russell R. Elliott has succeeded Charles R. Hicks as chairman of the department of history and political science. Wilbur S. Shepperson has been promoted to associate professor, and Don W. Driggs and Harry M. Chase to assistant professors.

Gerald E. Wheeler, from the United States Naval Academy, Gladys H. Waldron, formerly at Tulane University, and Lawrence B. Lee, from the Northwestern University School of Business, have been appointed assistant professors of history at San Jose State College (California).

Henry C. Meyer has been promoted to professor of history at Pomona College, and Elizabeth Bruchholz and William A. Smith have been appointed instructors.

The University of Redlands has announced the promotion of Gilbert Becker and David G. Poston to professors of history and of Henry G. Dittmar to associate professor, the appointment of John L. Groom and Louise H. Jennings as assistant professors, and the granting of a leave of absence for 1957-1958 to Joseph D. Applewhite.

Walton E. Bean has been promoted to professor of history at the University of California at Berkeley, and Charles Jelavich and Armin Rappaport have been promoted to associate professors. Nicholas V. Riasanovsky from the State University of Iowa has been appointed associate professor, T. G. Percival Spear from Selwyn College, Cambridge University, visiting professor, and Richard E. Drinnon from the University of Minnesota and James R. Scobie from the University of Maryland, instructors in history.

At the University of California at Los Angeles, John S. Galbraith has been promoted to professor of history. Marie Boas from Brandeis University and Harold M. Hyman from Arizona State College have been added to the staff as assistant professors of history.

Members of the historical guild who have recently crossed over to executive's row are S. Walter Martin of the University of Georgia, who has accepted appointment as president of Emory University; Glenn S. Dumke of Occidental College, who has become president of the San Francisco State College; and Paul F. Sharp of the University of Wisconsin, who has been elected president of Hiram College.

George Newman Fuller, former executive secretary of the Michigan Historical Commission, died on February 8, 1957, at the age of eighty-three. Following the receipt of the Ph.D. degree from the University of Michigan in 1912 he was primarily responsible for the establishment of the Michigan Historical Commission, and from 1916 until his retirement in 1946 he served as its executive secretary. His *Economic and Social Beginnings of Michigan*, published in 1916, is still an authoritative work on early Michigan. For thirty years (1916-1946) he was the editor of *Michigan History*, published under the joint auspices of the Commission and the Historical Society of

Michigan. Active also in the early work of the Mississippi Valley Historical Association, he served on its executive committee from 1921 to 1924.

Albert Tangeman Volwiler, professor of history at Ohio University, Athens, died on June 18, 1957, at the age of sixty-eight. A native of Cincinnati, he was graduated from Miami University in 1910, received the M.A. degree at the University of Chicago in 1911, and the Ph.D. at the University of Pennsylvania in 1922. After several years as professor of history and chairman of the department at Wittenberg College, he went to Ohio University in 1933, and from 1947 to 1955 served as chairman of the department of history. His published works include *George Croghan and the Westward Movement* (1926) and *Correspondence between Benjamin Harrison and James G. Blaine* (1940), in addition to articles in numerous historical journals. He had completed the first volume of a projected two-volume biography of Benjamin Harrison, and it is expected that this study will be published. He had been president of the Ohio Academy of History, a member of the Ohio War History Commission, and a member of the editorial board of the *Ohio Historical Quarterly*, and from 1946 to 1949 he served as a member of the executive committee of the Mississippi Valley Historical Association.

Charles Henry Ambler, professor emeritus of history at West Virginia University and a former president of the Mississippi Valley Historical Association, died on August 31, 1957, at the age of eighty-one. He was a native of Ohio, a graduate of West Virginia University, and received the Ph.D. degree in history at the University of Wisconsin in 1908. From 1908 to 1917 he was professor of history at Randolph-Macon College, and in 1917 he went to West Virginia University, where he served as professor until his retirement in 1947 and as head of the department of history from 1929 to 1946. He was president of the Mississippi Valley Historical Association in 1942-1943, an elected member of its executive committee from 1939 to 1942, and ex officio member of the committee from 1943 to 1950.

Professor Ambler's intensive research in regional history resulted in the publication of twelve important books, including *Sectionalism in Virginia from 1776 to 1861* (1910); *Thomas Ritchie* (1912); *Life and Diary of John Floyd* (1918); *Letters and Papers of Robert M. T. Hunter* (1918); *History of Transportation in the Ohio Valley* (1932); *George Washington and the West* (1936); and five studies dealing more directly with men and events in West Virginia history. From 1908 to 1917 he was editor of the *John P. Branch Papers of Randolph-Macon College*, and after going to West Virginia University he initiated the program for the collection of historical source materials which led to the establishment of a manuscripts division in the University library in 1933. He also took an active interest in public affairs, serving as sheriff of his home county in his early years, and two terms as a member of the West Virginia legislature following his retirement.

Robert Glass Cleland, professor emeritus of history at Occidental College and a member of the staff of the Henry E. Huntington Library, died in Pasadena, California, on September 4, 1957, at the age of seventy-two. Born in Kentucky, he went with his parents to California in the early 1890's. He was graduated from Occidental College in 1907, and received the Ph.D. degree in history from Princeton University in 1912. Becoming a member of the Occidental faculty in 1912, he served as the Norman Bridge professor of history and dean of the faculty for many years and for a short time as vice-president of the College. Upon his retirement in 1943 he joined the staff of the Huntington Library, where he enjoyed ten fruitful years of writing and lecturing and administered, with Rockefeller Foundation support, an effective program of research in American history, with emphasis on the West and California.

A major portion of his research was concerned with California's development from a frontier wilderness into an agricultural and industrial empire, and among more than a dozen books from his pen, the best known are such general accounts as *A History of California: The American Period* (1922); *The Cattle on a Thousand Hills, 1850-1870* (1941); *From Wilderness to Empire* (1944); *California Pageant* (1946); *California in Our Time* (1947); and *That Reckless Breed of Men* (1953). He also wrote several detailed studies of particular areas within Southern California, and in collaboration with Juanita Brooks he edited the two-volume *Mormon Chronicle: The Diaries of John D. Lee* (1955). Through his teaching, his direction of research projects, and the scope and vigor of his own writing he played an important part in determining the character and emphasis of historical writing on California and the American Southwest.

Arthur Cecil Bining, associate professor of history at the University of Pennsylvania, died on September 30, 1957, at the age of sixty-three. A native of Wales, he came to the United States as a young man, and after several years of employment in the steel industry entered the University of Pennsylvania as a student. Following his graduation in 1927 he taught in high school for one year and returned to the University in 1928 for graduate study. He became an instructor in history in 1929 and following the receipt of the Ph.D. degree in 1932 was advanced through the ranks to associate professor. More interested in problems of the teaching of history than in research, he was active in both regional and national organizations for teachers. He was president of the Middle States Council for the Social Studies in 1945-1946 and served as editor of *Social Studies* from 1935 to 1950. He had been a member of the council of the Pennsylvania Historical Association since 1934 and was president of the Association from 1942 to 1945. In addition to collaborating with others in the writing of textbooks in American history, and of works on the teaching of history and the social studies in secondary schools, he was the author of *The Rise of American Economic Life* (1943; revised edition, 1954), and of *Pennsylvania's Iron and Steel Industry* (1954), and co-compiler of *Writings on Pennsylvania History: A Bibliography* (1946).

Grants and Awards

John Simon Guggenheim Memorial Fellows for 1957-1958 include the following scholars in American history and related fields: Arthur J. A. Anderson, curator of the New Mexico Museum, Santa Fe, Aztec accounts of Spanish settlement in the Americas; W. Burlie Brown, Tulane University, American architectural thought and expression, 1865-1914; Robert V. Bruce, Boston University, the 1877 railroad strikes and labor riots in the United States; Lawrence A. Cremin, Columbia University, history of American educational thought, 1880-1940; Sidney Fine, University of Michigan, relationship between the National Recovery Administration and the automobile industry, 1933-1935; Louis L. Gerson, University of Connecticut, impact of American immigrant groups on foreign policies of the United States; Howard J. Graham, Los Angeles County Law Library, history of the Fourteenth Amendment; Robert V. Hine, University of California, Riverside, biographical studies of Edward, Richard, and Benjamin Kern, explorers of the American West, 1845-1863; Herbert H. Hyman, Columbia University, comparative study of public opinion on civil liberties in the United States and Great Britain; W. Turrentine Jackson, University of California, Davis, British contributions to the development of the American West; Weymouth T. Jordan, Florida State University, scientific agriculture in the Old South; Aubrey C. Land, University of Nebraska, the merchant-planter class of the Chesapeake colonies; Leonard W. Levy, Brandeis University, provisions against compulsory self-incrimination in Anglo-American law; Robert A. Lively, Princeton University, Herbert Hoover and American enterprise; Richard Lowitt, Connecticut College, life and times of Senator George W. Norris; Redding F. Perry, Alexandria, Virginia, history of the Second Armored Division in World War II; Bessie L. Pierce, University of Chicago, history of the city of Chicago; Frederick Rudolph, Williams College, history of higher education in the United States; Paul F. Sharp, University of Wisconsin, influence of humanitarian sentiment upon public policy after the Civil War; Helen Clapesattle Shugg, Chicago, the part played by the search for health in westward migration in the United States; Alice E. Smith, State Historical Society of Wisconsin, Scottish leadership and capital in the development of the lower Lake Michigan area in the nineteenth century; Watt Stewart, New York State College for Teachers, Albany, business activities of Minor Cooper Keith in Costa Rica; George B. Tindall, Louisiana State University, history of the South, 1913-1946; J. Chalmers Vinson, University of Georgia, the United States Senate and American foreign policy, 1931-1941; Bell I. Wiley, Emory University, studies toward a history of the Confederate States of America, 1861-1865.

Grants were also made to the following American scholars for projects in other fields of history: Joseph O. Baylen, Delta State College; Ernest J. Burrus, St. Louis University; John L. Clive, Harvard University; Joel G. Colton, Duke University; Durand Echeverria, Brown University; Donald J. Greene, University of California, Riverside; Oscar Halecki, Fordham University; Paul H. Hardacre, Vanderbilt University; J. Jean Hecht, Haverford College; Benjamin B. Hoover, University of Washington; Paul O. Kristeller, Columbia University; Paul L. MacKendrick, University of Wisconsin; Frank E. Manuel, Brandeis University; Arthur J. Marder, University of Hawaii; Juan A. J. Marichal, Bryn Mawr College; Ernst M. Posner, American University; Marc Raeff, Clark University; Walter M. Simon, Cornell University; Samuel E. Thorne, Harvard University; Klemens von Klemperer, Smith College; Herbert C. Youtie, University of Michigan.

The Southern Fellowships Fund has announced the following awards for advanced study in the field of history for 1957-1958: James D. Barber, Stetson University; James R. Connor, Washington and Lee University; Leonard P. Curry, University of Kentucky; John L. Ferguson, Conway Baptist College; Thomas F. Harwood, University of Texas; Paul E. Isaac, David Lipscomb College; Clifton H. Johnson, LeMoyne College; Billy B. Lightfoot, University of Texas; Lawrence F. Silverman, University of Tennessee; Frank L. Turner, University of North Carolina; Arda S. Walker, Maryville College; Robert B. Walz, East Texas State College; Evelyn V. Wiley, Birmingham-Southern College; and Burleigh T. Wilkins, Shorter College.

Grants-in-aid for research during the summer were awarded to the following: Martin L. Abbott, Oglethorpe University; John G. Barrett, Virginia Military Institute; Mildred C. Beckwith, Winthrop College; John H. Beeler, Woman's College of the University of North Carolina; Sin-ming Chiu, Centenary College; Robert G. Crawford, East Tennessee State College; Marvin R. Farley, Western Carolina College; Marshall W. Fishwick, Washington and Lee University; Edward H. Gibson, Brenau College; Abraham A. Kreusler, Randolph-Macon Woman's College; Dun Jen Li, Wiley College; H. Grady McWhiney, Millsaps College; Richard Megargee, The Citadel; W. Hugh Moomaw, Randolph-Macon College; Joseph H.

Parks, Birmingham-Southern College; Walter B. Posey, Agnes Scott College; James A. Rawley, Sweet Briar College; Lothar L. Tresp, Birmingham-Southern College; Philip A. Walker, Mississippi Southern College; and Howard Zinn, Spelman College.

Fulbright awards for advanced research abroad have been made to the following American historians for the academic year 1957-1958: Oswald P. Backus, University of Kansas, at the University of Helsinki; Harold C. Deutsch, University of Minnesota, at the University of Munich; Aubrey C. Land, University of Nebraska, at the University of London; Robert S. Lopez, Yale University, at the University of Rome; C. Leonard Lundin, Indiana University, at the University of Helsinki; T. Francis Mayer-Oakes, Wayne State University, at Tokyo University; Ernst M. Posner, American University, at the University of Rome; Lloyd R. Sorenson, University of Oregon, at the Free University, Berlin; Edward C. Thaden, Pennsylvania State University, at the University of Helsinki; Klemens von Klemperer, Smith College, at the University of Vienna; and Joseph F. Wall, Grinnell College, at the University of Edinburgh.

Lecturing appointments for the year have been made to the following: J. Cutler Andrews, Chatham College, at the University of Helsinki; Reginald F. Arragon, Reed College, at the Universities of Lille and Rennes; Walter E. Bezanson, Rutgers University, at the University of Liège; Henry J. Browne, Catholic University, at the University of Naples; Henry S. Commager, Amherst College, at the University of Aix-Marseilles; Wallace E. Davies, University of Pennsylvania, at the University of Manchester; Elisha P. Douglass, University of North Carolina, at the University of Göttingen; W. Clement Eaton, University of Kentucky, at the University of Innsbruck; Kent Forster, Pennsylvania State University, at the University of Helsinki; Walter Johnson, University of Chicago, at Oxford University; Paul I. Miller, Hiram College, at the University of Ceylon; Katharine F. Nutt, Kansas State College (Fort Hays), at Isabella Thoburn College (India); Donnell M. Owings, University of Oklahoma, at Auckland University College (New Zealand); Cornelius Penner, Baldwin-Wallace College, at Wilhelmshaven (Germany); Martin H. Schaefer, Valparaiso University, at the University of Cologne; William L. Spalding, Vassar College, at Osaka University; William B. Willcox, University of Michigan, at Oxford University; Edward E. Younger, University of Virginia, at Allahabad University (India).

Historical Activities

The Library of Congress reports that approximately 8,000 pieces have been added to the papers of Senator Thomas J. Walsh of Montana by his daughter.

The new material, which is dated from 1921 to 1933, is largely concerned with the World Court at The Hague. Papers of John E. Erickson for the two years he served in the Senate as Walsh's successor (1933-1935) have been given to the Library by Mrs. Erickson. The 9,000 items are chiefly related to the Flathead River project, farm legislation, and federal farm loans in Montana.

Additional papers of Harold L. Ickes, totaling approximately 2,000 items, have recently been presented to the Library by Mrs. Ickes. This addition is composed primarily of his personal correspondence from 1933 to 1952.

An important addition to the Library's holdings of manuscripts relating to the history of the Negro in America has been made in the acquisition of the papers of Judge Robert H. Terrell, who was appointed by President Harrison as the first Negro to become chief of a division in the federal government in Washington, and who served for twenty-three years as a judge in the municipal court of the District of Columbia.

The first volume of the projected ten-volume edition of the Papers of Henry Clay, edited by James F. Hopkins and Mary W. M. Hargreaves, has been announced for publication in 1958 by the University of Kentucky Press.

Robert W. Johannsen of the University of Kansas has been engaged for the past year on a project to collect and edit the letters of Stephen A. Douglas for publication. He will appreciate information concerning the location of any Douglas letters, especially those in private possession or among the papers of his contemporaries in public or private institutions. Until February 1, 1958, he may be reached in care of the Department of History, University of Wisconsin, Madison; after that date he should be addressed at the Department of History, University of Kansas, Lawrence.

The Nebraska State Historical Society held its seventy-ninth annual meeting on September 28, 1957, in Lincoln. Maurice Frink, executive director of the State Historical Society of Colorado, addressed the luncheon session on the topic, "Hoosier on the High Plains"; and the speaker at the annual dinner was Herbert S. Schell, professor of history and dean of the Graduate School, University of South Dakota, on "The American Leviathan: A Historical View."

The tenth annual meeting of the Alabama Historical Association was held in April on the campus of Alabama College at Montevallo. The program included nineteen formal papers on varied subjects in Alabama history, and the presidential address, by Charles G. Summersell of the University of Alabama, was on "Alabama and the Supreme Court: The First Case."

The Minnesota Historical Society has announced the appointment of Robert C. Wheeler, a former field representative of the Ohio Historical Society, to the position of assistant director.

The State Historical Society of Wisconsin announces the appointment of William Haygood, a novelist and a graduate of the Emory University School of Library Science, as editor of the *Wisconsin Magazine of History*, and Lawrence Burnett, formerly of Washington and Lee University and more recently field editor for Charles Scribner's Sons, as book editor for the Society.

The July and August numbers of *Wi-Iyohi*, the monthly bulletin of the South Dakota Historical Society, contain a listing of approximately nine hundred newspapers which have been published within the area of the present state of South Dakota. The entries are arranged in the alphabetical order of the names of towns, and each item includes the date of founding and for those not now being published the date when publication ceased.

The Agricultural History Society has announced the establishment of an annual award for the best book-length manuscript dealing with a subject in agricultural history, beginning in 1958. The winning manuscript will be published by the University of Illinois Press and the author will receive a standard royalty contract.

The resignation of D. A. Brown as editor of *Agricultural History* has been accepted by the executive committee, and C. Clyde Jones, the present associate editor, has been appointed to succeed him, effective with the April, 1958, number of the magazine. The editorial office will continue to be located at the University of Illinois.

The program of the twenty-first annual meeting of the Society of American Archivists, held in Columbus, Ohio, October 2-4, 1957, included sessions on "Manuscripts and Business Records in Archival Depositories," "The Archives of Canada," and "Trends in Archives." The following officers were elected for the year 1957-1958: William D. Overman, Firestone Archives, president; Oliver W. Holmes, The National Archives, vice-president; Dorothy C. Renze, state archivist of Colorado, secretary (re-elected); and Leon de Valinger, Jr., state archivist of Delaware, treasurer.

Shortly before the adjournment of Congress in August, the Senate and House of Representatives approved a concurrent resolution which "urges the governors and legislatures of the several states and the state historical commissions and archival agencies, as well as appropriate libraries, historical societies, colleges and universities, business corporations, foundations, civic and other non-profit organizations, and individuals to co-operate with the National Historical Publications Commission" in the program for the publication of the basic source materials of American history. In a statement presented at a House committee hearing on the measure, held on June 5, 1957, Philip M. Hamer, executive director of the Commission, listed the following ten projects for which such co-operative plans have been arranged: (1) Adams Family Papers, sponsored by the Massachusetts Historical Society and Harvard University, and financed by a grant from Time, Inc., through *Life* magazine; (2) Bishop Francis Asbury Journal and Letters, sponsored by the Association of Methodist Historical Societies; (3) Archbishop John Carroll Papers, sponsored by the American Catholic Historical Association; (4) John C. Calhoun Papers, sponsored by the University of South Carolina, Clemson College, and the South Carolina Archives Department; (5) Henry Clay Papers, sponsored by the University of Kentucky; (6) Benjamin Franklin Papers, sponsored by Yale University and the American Philosophical Society, and financed by grants from the American Philosophical Society and Time, Inc.; (7) Alexander Hamilton Papers, sponsored by Columbia University, and financed by grants from the Rockefeller Foundation and Time, Inc.; (8) Rutherford B. Hayes Papers, sponsored by the Hayes Memorial Library, and financed by the Rutherford B. Hayes and Lucy Webb Hayes Foundation; (9) Andrew Johnson Papers, sponsored by the Tennessee Historical Commission and the University of Tennessee; (10) James Madison Papers, sponsored by the University of Chicago and the University of Virginia, and financed by grants from the Ford Foundation, the Rockefeller Foundation, and a biennium appropriation by the Virginia legislature.

Recent Articles of General Interest

Agricultural History — July, 1957: "Letters from a Sugar Plantation in Antigua, 1739-1758," ed. by Richard B. Sheridan; "Colonial Agriculture in New Spain," by Richard J. Morrisey.

American Archivist — July, 1957: "The Overseas Record Program of the Department of State," by Frances T. Bourne; "Editing the Henry Clay Papers," by James F. Hopkins.

American-German Review — June-July, 1957: "Trouble at Manila Bay: The Dewey-Diederichs Incident," by Joachim Remak.

American Historical Review — July, 1957: "Trends of United States Studies in Latin American History," by Charles Gibson and Benjamin Keen; "The James Gallatin Diary: A Fraud?" by Raymond Walters, Jr.

American Quarterly — Summer, 1957: "Can 'American Studies' Develop a Method?" by Henry Nash Smith.

Historian — August, 1957: "Pearl Harbor in Pacific Strategy, 1898-1908," by Willis E. Snowbarger; "The Mission of Lansing Bond Mizner to Central America," by Mary Patricia Chapman.

Journal of Mississippi History — July, 1957: "Jefferson Davis and Ambrose Dudley Mann," by J. Preston Moore.

Journal of Negro History — July, 1957: "The New England Anti-Slavery Society: Pioneer Abolition Organization," by Roman J. Zorn; "The Niagara Movement," by Elliott M. Rudwick.

Journal of the History of Ideas — June, 1957: "Charles Eliot Norton on Art and Morals," by Edward H. Madden.

Military Affairs — Summer, 1957: "Military History: A Civilian Caveat," by Arthur A. Ekirch, Jr.; "The Case for Military History and Research," by Tyson Wilson; "The United States Navy and the Japanese 'Enemy,' 1919-1931," by Gerald E. Wheeler; "American Shipbuilding and Russian Naval Power, 1837-1846," by Frederick M. Binder.

Ohio Historical Quarterly — July, 1957: "Social History: A Nation Announcing Itself," by Philip D. Jordan.

Pacific Historical Review — August, 1957: "Their Majesties the Mob: Vigilantes Past and Present," by John W. Caughey; "The United States Navy's Dilemma in the Pacific, 1906-1909," by William R. Braisted; "An Anthropologist Looks at History," by A. L. Kroeber.

Pennsylvania History — July, 1957: "Origins of the Interstate Commerce Act of 1887," by Gerald D. Nash.

Political Science Quarterly — September, 1957: "The Dubious Democrat: Thomas Jefferson in Bourbon France," by R. R. Palmer; "Notes on Roosevelt's 'Quarantine' Speech," by Dorothy Borg.

William and Mary Quarterly — July, 1957: "Captain John Smith's Route through Turkey and Russia," by Philip L. Barbour.

Recent Articles Concerning the East

Maryland Historical Magazine — September, 1957: "George William Brown and His Influence on the Johns Hopkins University," by Hugh D. Hawkins; "Gunpowder Production in Post-Revolutionary Maryland," by Arlan K. Gilbert; "Kent Island: Part II, Settlement and Landholding under the Proprietary; Part III, Kent Fort Manor," by Erich Isaac; "Lafayette's Letters to Eliza Ridgely of Hampton," ed. by James W. Foster.

New-York Historical Society Quarterly — July, 1957: "The Diary of a Union Soldier in Confederate Prisons," ed. by James J. Heslin; "War, Profit, and Privateers along the New Jersey Coast: Letters of 1782 Relating to an Obscure Warfront of the American Revolution," ed. by Richard J. Koke; "The Military Association of the Sons of Liberty," by Roger Champagne; "The Recollections of John Ferguson Weir (1841-1926)," Part II, ed. by Theodore Sizer.

Pennsylvania History — July, 1957: "James D. Harris and William B. Foster, Jr., Canal Engineers," by Hubertis M. Cummings; "A Note on Scalp Bounties in Pennsylvania," by Henry J. Young; "'When Once the Ball Is Commenced . . .': A Pennsylvania Irishman at Fort Sumter," ed. by Rowland T. Berthoff; "Origins of Iroquois Neutrality: The Grand Settlement of 1701," by Anthony F. C. Wallace; "Colonial Houses and the Stephen Moylan Press," by Paul A. W. Wallace.

Pennsylvania Magazine of History and Biography — July, 1957: "William Birch: His 'Country Seats of the United States'," by Martin P. Snyder; "James Buchanan and Public Office: An Appraisal," by Robert E. Carlson; "Henry C. Carey and the Republican Tariff," by Arthur M. Lee; "Gifford Pinchot's 1914 Campaign," by M. Nelson McGeary.

Western Pennsylvania Historical Magazine — Summer, 1957: "Louis Kossuth's Visit to Pittsburgh in 1852," by Robert D. Ilisevich and James H. Mast; "Favorite American Foods and the Role They Have Played in History," by Ruth M. Stoehr; "Two Local Newspapers and Agriculture; 1869, 1911, and 1949," by Phil R. Jack; "The Pennsylvania Germans," by Ralph Charles Wood; "The Story of Ross Mountain Club: A Vanishing Type of American Summer Resort," by Elizabeth Reed Orr.

William and Mary Quarterly — July, 1957: "The Apologia of Governor Lawrie of East New Jersey, 1686," by John E. Pomfret; "The Maryland Gentry and Social Mobility, 1637-1676," by William A. Reavis.

Recent Articles Concerning the South

Agricultural History — July, 1957: "David Dickson's 'System of Farming' and the Agricultural Revolution in the Deep South, 1850-1885," by Chester McArthur Destler; "Thomas Affleck: Missionary to the Planter, the Farmer, and the Gardener," by Robert W. Williams; "Black's Bend Grange, 1873-77: A Case Study of a Subordinate Grange of the Deep South," by Robert Partin.

Alabama Review — April, 1957: "Comer, Smith, and Jones: Alabama's Railroad War of 1907-1914," by James F. Doster; "Conservatism in

Old Montgomery, 1817-1861," by Clanton W. Williams; "Tustunugee Hutkee and Creek Factionalism on the Georgia-Alabama Frontier," by James C. Bonner; "The Letters of Captain Joab Goodson, 1862-1864," ed. by W. Stanley Hoole.

July, 1957: "Alabama and the Supreme Court: The First Case," by Charles G. Summersell; "The Alabama Historical Association, 1947-1957," by James F. Sulzby, Jr.; "Oscar W. Underwood: An Aristocrat from the Bluegrass," by Evans C. Johnson; "The Letters of Captain Joab Goodson, 1862-1864," Part II, ed. by W. Stanley Hoole.

Arkansas Historical Quarterly — Autumn, 1957: "Arkansas' First 'Wonder Working Wire'," by John E. Sunder; "Some Notes on Robert Crittenden," by Farrar Newberry; "William Byers of Batesville," by Paul T. Wayland; "Pleasant Hill Methodist Church, Carroll County, 1853-1894," by Boyd W. Johnson; "Diary of Private John P. Wright, U. S. A., 1864-1865," ed. by Ralph R. Rea.

Filson Club History Quarterly — July, 1957: "Patty Smith Hill, Louisville's Contribution to Education," by Frances Farley Gwinn; "Old Kentucky Iron Furnaces," by J. Winston Coleman, Jr.; "Stephen Theodore Badin: Priest of Frontier Kentucky," by David R. Driscoll, Jr.; "A Law Student at Transylvania University in 1810-1812," by Clement Eaton; "William Shreve Bailey, Kentucky Abolitionist," by Will Frank Steely.

Florida Historical Quarterly — July, 1957: "Birthplaces of the Conquistadors," by Karl A. Bickel; "The Florida Ship Canal Project," by Benjamin F. Rogers; "Florida and Iowa: A Contemporary View," by Franklin A. Doty; "Gavino Gutierrez and His Contributions to Tampa," by Jesse L. Keene; "The Woman Suffrage Movement in Florida," by A. Elizabeth Taylor.

Georgia Historical Quarterly — September, 1957: "The New Departure Democrats of Georgia: An Interpretation," by Judson Clements Ward, Jr.; "Four Slave Trials in Elbert County, Georgia," by E. Merton Coulter; "Ben: Perley Poore's Stay in Athens," by John E. Talmadge; "The Letter Book of Thomas Rasberry, 1758-1861," Part V, ed. by Lilla M. Hawes; "With Sherman through Georgia: A Journal," ed. by David J. de Laubenfels; "Letters of James Longstreet Relative to His Position of United States Marshal in Georgia," ed. by George P. Perros; "Leaves from a Travel Diary: A Visit to Augusta and Savannah, 1882," ed. by Samuel Proctor; "The Journal of Ebenezer Hazard in Georgia, 1778," ed. by Fred Shelley.

Journal of Mississippi History — July, 1957: "Logging and Rafting Timber in South Mississippi, 1840-1910," by Nollie W. Hickman; "A Brief History of Delta State College," by William Marion Kethley.

Journal of Negro History — July, 1957: "Cassius M. Clay and John G. Fee: A Study in Southern Anti-Slavery Thought," by David L. Smiley.

Journal of Southern History — August, 1957: "Sectional Conflict and Medical Education in Louisiana," by John Duffy; "Virginia Railroads in April, 1861," by Angus J. Johnston, II; "'The Cave of the Winds' and the Compromise of 1850," by Holman Hamilton; "The Mississippi Constitutional Convention of 1832," by Winbourne Magruder Drake.

North Carolina Historical Review — July, 1957: "John Lawson's Alter-Ego — Dr. John Brickell," by Percy G. Adams; "The Dugger-Dromgoole Duel," by Henry W. Lewis; "Gifford Pinchot at Biltmore," by Harold T. Pinkett; "The Idea of Cotton Textile Industry in the South, 1870-1900," by Herbert Collins; "Simms's Views on National and Sectional Literature, 1825-1845," by John C. Guilds; "Tryon's 'Book' on North Carolina," ed. by William S. Powell.

Register of the Kentucky Historical Society — July, 1957: "Kentucky's Linn Boyd and the Dramatic Days of 1850," by Holman Hamilton; "Election Year — Kentucky, 1828," by Leonard P. Curry; "Mexican War Journal of Leander M. Cox," Part II, ed. by Charles F. Hinds.

South Carolina Historical Magazine — July, 1957: "Letters of Morris & Brailsford to Thomas Jefferson," ed. by Richard Walsh; "Letters of Thomas Pinckney, 1775-1780," continued, ed. by Jack L. Cross.

Southwestern Historical Quarterly — July, 1957: "The Butterfield Overland Mail Road across Texas," by J. W. Williams; "Operation Camel: An Experiment in Animal Transportation in Texas, 1857-1860," by Frank Bishop Lammons; "Edward M. House and the Governors," by Rupert N. Richardson; "Saluria, Fort Esperanza, and Military Operations on the Texas Coast, 1861-1864," by Lester N. Fitzhugh; "The Rainmakers in Duval," by John C. Rayburn; "The Texas Cotton Acreage Control Law of 1931-1932," by Karl E. Ashburn; "Calendar of the Letters of Antonio Martinez, Last Spanish Governor of Texas, 1817-1822," Part VII, ed. by Virginia H. Taylor.

Tennessee Historical Quarterly — September, 1957: "Some Phases of the State of Franklin," by Paul M. Fink; "Timothy Demonbreun," by Wirt Armistead Cate; "Holding the Tennessee Line: Winter, 1861-1862," by Peter Franklin Walker; "A Tennessean, Texas, and Camels: The Diary of James H. Holman, June 11 to August 25, 1860," ed. by Beatrice Milhous Rees and William T. Alderson; "Letters over the Water: The European Tour of Henry Maney, 1851-1852," ed. by Alfred Leland Crabb.

Virginia Magazine of History and Biography — July, 1957: "The Smith-Pocahontas Story in Literature," by Jay B. Hubbell; "Biographer's

Notebook [on Captain John Smith]," by Bradford Smith; "The Tufton Manuscripts and the Virginia Connection," ed. by Felix Hull; "Captain John Smith in the Light of Styrian Sources," by J. Franz Pichler.

West Virginia History — July, 1957: "The Martyrdom of John Brown," by Charles A. Jellison; "A Check List of West Virginia Imprints, 1790-1863," by Delf Norona; "A Background and History of the W. H. H. Cook Memorial Baptist Church of Pineville, West Virginia," by Elizabeth B. Kuhn.

William and Mary Quarterly — July, 1957: "Alexander Whitaker: Cambridge Apostle to Virginia," by Harry Culverwell Porter; "Sir William Berkeley's 'A History of Our Miseries'," ed. by Wilcomb E. Washburn; "John White and the Sarsaparilla," by Edmund S. Morgan.

RECENT ARTICLES CONCERNING THE MIDDLE WEST

Agricultural History — July, 1957: "Hiram Smith (1817-1890)," by W. H. Glover.

Bulletin of the Historical and Philosophical Society of Ohio — July, 1957: "Moses Dawson, Chronic Belligerent," by Virginius C. Hall; "The Paddy's Run Papers," by Murat Halstead, ed. by Robert Herron; "Have Lily, Will Travel: Oscar Wilde in Cincinnati," by Robert Herron.

Chronicles of Oklahoma — Summer, 1957: "Grand Seal of the Territory of Oklahoma," by Muriel H. Wright; "The Big Pasture," by Charles M. Cooper; "Uncle Sam's Horse-Race for Land: The Opening of the 'Cherokee Strip'," by J. S. Wade; "The Founding of Ponca City," by Louis Seymour Barnes; "The Lost Colonel," by George H. Shirk.

Indiana Magazine of History — September, 1957: "Log-Cabin Canvass, Hoosier Style," by Robert G. Gunderson; "Elements of Culture in the Old Northwest," by Logan Esarey; "Cultural History of Indianapolis: Music, 1875-1890," by Eva Draegert.

Iowa Journal of History — July, 1957: "Iowa and the Battle of Shiloh," by Mildred Throne.

Journal of the Illinois State Historical Society — Summer, 1957: "Normal University Centennial Number": "Education in Illinois before 1857," by Robert Gehlmann Bone; "The Town and the Gown," by Helen E. Marshall; "The School Extends Its Influence," by John A. Kinneman; "A Library Grows Up," by Eleanor Weir Welch; "Special Education — Then and Now," by Theodore Sands and Rose E. Parker.

Kansas Historical Quarterly — Summer, 1957: "A Free-Stater's 'Letters to to the Editor': Samuel N. Wood's Letters to Eastern Newspapers, 1854," ed. by Robert W. Richmond; "Theatre in Kansas, 1858-1868: Background for the Coming of the Lord Dramatic Company to Kansas, 1869," concluded, by James C. Malin.

Mennonite Quarterly Review — July, 1957: "The Oak Grove–Pleasant Hill Amish Mennonite Church in Wayne County, Ohio, in the Nineteenth Century (1815-1900)," by John Umble.

Michigan History — June, 1957: "Lewis Cass, Jr. and Pope Pius IX, 1850-58," by Sexson E. Humphreys; "Quincy Mine: The Old Reliable," by William H. Pyne.

September, 1957: "Michigan State Party Chairmen, 1882-1956," by John W. Lederle and Rita Feiler Aid; "The Legislative Recount of 1934," by Robert G. Scigliano; "Nathan M. Thomas: Michigan Pioneer," by Robert L. Kincaid.

Mid-America — July, 1957: "The Decline of Wisconsin Progressivism, 1911-1914," by Herbert F. Margulies; "Ignatius Donnelly and the Greenback Movement," by Martin Ridge; "Bryan and the Urban Progressives," by Paul W. Glad; "Thomas P. Gore and the Election of Woodrow Wilson," by Monroe Billington.

Minnesota History — September, 1957: "The Alliance Party and the Civil War," by Carl H. Chrislock; "Letters of a Union Officer: L. F. Hubbard and the Civil War," by N. B. Martin; "The Alexander Faribault House," by Kenneth Bjork.

Missouri Historical Review — July, 1957: "Major General Samuel Ryan Curtis — City Engineer [St. Louis]," by John P. Dietzler; "The First Steamboats on the Missouri: Reminiscences of Captain W. D. Hubbell," ed. by Vivian K. McLarty; "A Peoria Indian States His Case," by James W. Covington.

Nebraska History — September, 1957: "Back to Normal [Nebraska, 1918-1921]," by R. E. Dale; "The Kearney Cotton Mill — A Bubble That Burst," by Charles Jenkins; "Fort Atkinson at Council Bluffs," by Sally A. Johnson.

North Dakota History — April, 1957: "North Dakota in the 1890's: Its People, Politics, and Press," by D. Jerome Tweton; "Lord Selkirk and the Canadian Courts," by Gene M. Gressley.

North Dakota Quarterly — Summer, 1957: "Middle Western Isolationism: A Re-examination," by Robert P. Wilkins.

Northwest Ohio Quarterly — Summer, 1957: "John Eaton and the Freedmen," by Leo K. Siegel; "The Last Gathering under the Old Council Elm: A Selection from the Dresden W. H. Howard Papers," ed. by Robert F. Bauman; "The Scott Nearing Controversy in Toledo, 1916-1917," Part II, by Elliott J. Anderson.

Ohio Historical Quarterly — July, 1957: "A Surgeon's Mate at Fort Defiance: The Journal of Joseph Gardner Andrews for the Year 1795," Part III, ed. by Richard C. Knopf; "Commerce and Culture: The Pattern in Ohio," by Harlan Hatcher; "The Rubber Industry in Ohio," by William D. Overman; "Ohio's Industrial Growth, 1900-1957, and Some Possibilities for Study," by Robert E. Holmes.

Palimpsest — June, 1957: "The Spirit Lake Massacre," by William J. Petersen.

July, 1957: "The Fourth of July in Iowa," by William J. Petersen.

September, 1957: "The Manchester & Oneida Railway," by Frank P. Donavan, Jr.

Recent Articles Concerning the Far West

Colorado Magazine — July, 1957: "Charles Autobees," by Janet Lecompte; "Railway Equipment as Historic Exhibits," by Agnes Wright Spring; "Nathaniel P. Hill Takes Ore to Swansea, Wales," ed. by Agnes Wright Spring; "[Oliver] Loving Proposed Expedition against Indians and Denver," ed. by Agnes Wright Spring; "Bent's Fort in 1846," by Edgeley W. Todd; "W. Arthur Dier, Pioneer Teacher and Lawyer," ed. by Agnes Wright Spring.

New Mexico Historical Review — July, 1957: "Kearny's Route from the Rio Grande to the Gila River," by George Ruhlen; "Exit Axtell: Enter Wallace [as territorial governors]," by Philip Rasch; "Across the Plains in 1866," by Thomas A. Muzzall; "The *Apuntes* of Father J. B. Ralliere," concluded, by Florence Hawley Ellis and Edwin Baca.

Oregon Historical Quarterly — September, 1957: "Nathaniel Wyeth's Fort Hall," by Richard G. Beidleman; "The Discovery and Cartographical Recognition of Shoalwater Bay," by Jean Hazeltine.

Pacific Northwest Quarterly — July, 1957: "Northwest Region — Fact or Fiction?" by John H. Binns; "George Abernethy, Pioneer Merchant," by Arthur L. Throckmorton; "The West, States' Rights, and Conservation: A Study of Six Public Land Conferences," by Lawrence Rakestraw; "Caxton Printers, Ltd., Regional Publishers," by Paul E. Johnston.

Directory of Contributors

Clifford S. Griffin is an instructor in history in Lake Forest College.

James A. Field, Jr., is associate professor of history in Swarthmore College.

Emma Lou Thornbrough is associate professor in the department of history and political science in Butler University.

James L. Sellers is professor of history in the University of Nebraska.

John W. Caughey is professor of history in the University of California at Los Angeles and managing editor of the *Pacific Historical Review*.

The Mississippi Valley Historical Review

PUBLISHED QUARTERLY BY THE MISSISSIPPI VALLEY HISTORICAL ASSOCIATION

VOL. XLIV, NO. 4 — MARCH, 1958

Correspondence concerning contributions, books for review, and all editorial matters should be addressed to William C. Binkley, Managing Editor, Tulane University of Louisiana, New Orleans 18, Louisiana. Annual membership dues are $5.00. Student membership dues are $3.00 annually. Correspondence concerning membership dues and all business matters should be addressed to the Secretary, William D. Aeschbacher, 1500 R Street, Lincoln, Nebraska. The *Review* is sent to all members of the Association. Single numbers and back files may be obtained from the Secretary.

The Mississippi Valley Historical Association disclaims responsibility for statements whether of fact or of opinion made by contributors.

Entered as second-class matter, May 22, 1914, at the post office in Cedar Rapids, Iowa, and Lincoln 8, Nebraska, under the Act of August 24, 1912. Printed by The Torch Press, Cedar Rapids, Iowa.

Contents

Andrew Jackson versus the Historians. By Charles Grier Sellers, Jr. . 615
The Dismissal of Lord Sackville. By Charles S. Campbell, Jr. . . . 635
Books and Reading on the Ohio Valley Frontier. By Howard H. Peckham 649
Business Disunity and the Progressive Movement, 1901-1914. By Robert H. Wiebe 664
The Louisville and Portland Canal Company, 1825-1874. By Paul B. Trescott 686

Book Reviews

Roseboom, *A History of Presidential Elections*, by Cortez A. M. Ewing 709
Schmidt, *The Liberal Arts College*, by Frederick Rudolph 710
Garraty, *The Nature of Biography*, by Jacques Barzun 711
Ellis *et al.*, *A Short History of New York State*, by Howard D. Williams . . . 713
Gaustad, *The Great Awakening in New England*, by James Fulton Maclear . . . 714
Meade, *Patrick Henry: Patriot in the Making*, by John R. Alden 716
Mitchell, *Alexander Hamilton: Youth to Maturity, 1755-1788*, by Clarence L. Ver Steeg . 717
Robinson, *William R. Davie*, by Lee N. Newcomer 719
Walters, *Albert Gallatin: Jeffersonian Financier and Diplomat*, by Anthony F. Turhollow 720
Hammond, *Banks and Politics in America from the Revolution to the Civil War*, by Thomas P. Govan 721
Overmyer, *America's First Hamlet*, by Martin S. Shockley 724
Smith (ed.), *The Journals of Welcome Arnold Greene*, by J. Orin Oliphant . . 725
Moore, *The Frontier Mind*, by F. Garvin Davenport 726
McReynolds, *The Seminoles*, by Kenneth Wiggins Porter 728
Cox, *The Columbia River* (ed. by Stewart), by William L. Davis 729
Meyers, *The Jacksonian Persuasion*, by Robert E. Riegel 730
Gunderson, *The Log-Cabin Campaign*, by Glyndon G. Van Deusen 731
Mooney, *Slavery in Tennessee*, by Stanley J. Folmsbee 733
Zornow, *Kansas: A History of the Jayhawk State*, by Raymond C. Miller . . . 734
Riddle, *Congressman Abraham Lincoln*, by Charles H. Coleman 735
O'Dea, *The Mormons*, by Leland H. Creer 737
Mulder, *Homeward to Zion: The Mormon Migration from Scandinavia*, by William J. McNiff . 738
Hamilton, *From Wilderness to Statehood: A History of Montana, 1805-1900* (ed. by Burlingame), by Lola M. Homsher 739
Korn, *The American Reaction to the Mortara Case, 1858-1859*, by Donald L. Kinzer . . 740
Fehrenbacher, *Chicago Giant: A Biography of "Long John" Wentworth*, by Maurice G. Baxter . 742
Silver, *Confederate Morale and Church Propaganda*, by Frank W. Klingberg . . . 743
Merrill, *The Rebel Shore: The Story of Union Sea Power in the Civil War*, by Charles G. Summersell 744
Ames (comp.), *Chronicles from the Nineteenth Century* (2 vols.), by Hans L. Trefousse . 745
Grodinsky, *Jay Gould: His Business Career, 1867-1892*, by Richard C. Overton . . 747
Thorp, *Spirit Gun of the West*, by Harold E. Briggs 749
Pannill, *The Religious Faith of John Fiske*, by Ira V. Brown 751
Tansill, *America and the Fight for Irish Freedom, 1866-1922*, by H. C. Allen . . . 752
Doster, *Railroads in Alabama Politics, 1875-1914*, by Jean E. Keith 754
Holder, *McIver of North Carolina*, and Wilson, *The University of North Carolina, 1900-1930*, by Allen J. Going 755
Taylor, *The Woman Suffrage Movement in Tennessee*, by LeRoy P. Graf . . . 757
Mott, *A History of American Magazines*, Vol. IV, *1885-1905*, by W. Burlie Brown . . 758
Buehrig (ed.), *Wilson's Foreign Policy in Perspective*, and Link, *Wilson the Diplomatist*, by Ernest R. May 759
Bickel, *The Unpublished Opinions of Mr. Justice Brandeis*, by Paul L. Murphy . . 761
Shideler, *Farm Crisis, 1919-1923*, by Homer E. Socolofsky 762
Foreign Relations of the United States: Diplomatic Papers, 1942: China, by Richard W. Leopold 763
Barzun and Graff, *The Modern Researcher*, by Stanley Pargellis 765

Book Notes 766
Historical News and Comments 777
Directory of Contributors 794

Andrew Jackson versus the Historians

By Charles Grier Sellers, Jr.

Andrew Jackson's masterful personality was enough by itself to make him one of the most controversial figures ever to stride across the American stage. "It can hardly be expected that the present generation will do justice to the character of Jackson," complained the compiler of his funeral eulogies in 1846, for "his opponents have ever been most bitter enemies, and his friends almost his worshippers." [1] And when James Parton sat down fifteen years later to attempt the first impartial biography of Old Hickory, he despairingly concluded from the mountain of conflicting sources before him that his subject "was a patriot and a traitor. He was one of the greatest of generals, and wholly ignorant of the art of war. A writer brilliant, elegant, eloquent, without being able to compose a correct sentence, or spell words of four syllables. The first of statesmen, he never devised, he never framed a measure. He was the most candid of men, and was capable of the profoundest dissimulation. A most law-defying, law-obeying citizen. A stickler for discipline, he never hesitated to disobey his superior. A democratic autocrat. An urbane savage. An atrocious saint." [2]

Such radical opposites could not be reconciled simply by splitting the difference; Parton and all who followed him on this difficult terrain have been forced pretty substantially either into the Jackson camp or into the camp of Jackson's enemies. Indeed, Parton's lament could almost stand today as the conclusion to a review of Jacksonian historiography.

The reasons for such continuing disagreement run far deeper than the individual characteristics of any historical personality. Andrew Jackson was intimately identified with the full flowering of American democracy; and as long as democracy remains pre-eminently the

1 Benjamin M. Dusenbery (comp.), *Monument to the Memory of General Andrew Jackson: Containing Twenty-five Eulogies and Sermons Delivered on Occasion of His Death* (Philadelphia, 1846), 32.

2 James Parton, *Life of Andrew Jackson* (3 vols., New York, 1861), I, vii.

distinguishing feature of our society, the period and symbol of its triumph will remain controversial.

While American democracy emerged victorious on the plane of political ideology around 1776 or 1800, and on the plane of political practice around 1828, it did not achieve respectability in American historiography (for all George Bancroft's efforts) until about 1900. From the Jacksonian era to the end of the nineteenth century the writing of American history was dominated, as Charles H. Peck observed in 1899, by men "who were educated under the sway of the Whiggish culture of the country."[3] This "Whig" school of Jacksonian historiography included the first two important Jackson biographers, James Parton and William Graham Sumner; the authors of the first two detailed American histories extending to the Civil War, Hermann E. von Holst and James Schouler; and Moisei Ostrogorski, author of the enormously influential study of *Democracy and the Organization of Political Parties.*

These writers, in effect, stamped the partisan fulminations of Jackson's political enemies with the cachet of scholarly authority. If Henry Clay had pronounced Old Hickory "ignorant, passionate, hypocritical, corrupt, and easily swayed by the base men who surround him," von Holst could similarly pronounce him an "arrogant general" whose "mind was as untrained as his passions were unbridled" and who was "like wax in skillful hands." Sumner thought him a "barbarian" who "acted from spite, pique, instinct, prejudice or emotion"; Schouler flatly declared him "illiterate"; Ostrogorski expatiated on his "autocratic policy"; and Parton, despite a grudging admiration for some aspects of Jackson's character, lamented "the elevation to the presidency of a man whose ignorance, whose good intentions, and whose passions combined to render him, of all conceivable human beings, the most unfit for the office."[4]

Yet it was not fundamentally Jackson's personality that turned the Whig historians against him, nor was it the general policies he pursued as president. These writers were all liberals of the nine-

[3] Charles H. Peck, *The Jacksonian Epoch* (New York, 1899), 328.

[4] Calvin Colton (ed.), *The Private Correspondence of Henry Clay* (Boston, 1856), 368-69; Hermann E. von Holst, *The Constitutional and Political History of the United States* (8 vols., Chicago, 1876-1892), II, 2, 3, 30; William Graham Sumner, *Andrew Jackson as a Public Man: What He Was, What Chances He Had, and What He Did with Them* (Boston, 1882), 25, 278-79; James Schouler, *History of the United States of America under the Constitution* (Rev. ed., 6 vols., New York, 1894-1904), II, 439; M. Ostrogorski, *Democracy and the Organization of Political Parties* (2 vols., New York, 1902), II, 46, 65; Parton, *Jackson*, III, 694-700.

teenth-century stripe and actually approved the laissez-faire tendencies of most of the Jacksonian measures. Sumner was outraged that Jackson had "unjustly, passionately, ignorantly, and without regard to truth assailed a great and valuable financial institution," for the Yale economist was a stout champion of sound money and vested interests. But Sumner was an even more strenuous champion of Herbert Spencer's doctrine of unfettered individual enterprise, and his philosophy compelled him to admit that "it came in Jackson's way to do some good, to check some bad tendencies and to strengthen some good ones." Parton went further in approval of Jackson's policies, defending not only the objectives but also the aggressive tactics of the Jacksonian assault on the national bank. An admirer of Jefferson, Parton was also one of the earliest American Spencerians, and he considered Jackson an instinctive disciple of both his ideological heroes.[5] And all the Whig historians were ardent nationalists and applauded Jackson's bold stand against the South Carolina nullifiers.

How, then, could Parton say that "notwithstanding the good done by General Jackson during his presidency, his election to power was a mistake"? How could von Holst speak of "the frightful influence . . . which he exercised during the eight years of his presidency"? A clue may be found in the abhorrence with which the Whig historians uniformly treated Jackson's policy of removing his political enemies from federal office and replacing them with his friends. Indeed, for these scholarly mugwumps, the institution of the spoils system on a large scale became almost the distinguishing feature of Jackson's administration. "If all his other public acts had been perfectly wise and right," said Parton, "this single feature of his administration would suffice to render it deplorable."[6]

Yet the spoils system was only a symptom of the real disease — the new system of democratic politics that both Jackson and the spoils system symbolized. "Popular sovereignty," said von Holst, would be "a dreadful condition of things"; and Schouler lamented

5 Sumner, *Jackson*, 279, 339; Parton, *Jackson*, III, 693-94. Jackson, said Parton, "had a clear perception that the toiling millions are not a class in the community, but *are* the community. He knew and felt that government should exist only for the benefit of the governed; that the strong are strong only that they may aid the weak; that the rich are rightfully rich only that they may so combine and direct the labors of the poor as to make labor more profitable to the laborer. He did not comprehend these truths as they are demonstrated by Jefferson and Spencer, but he had an intuitive and instinctive perception of them." *Jackson*, III, 699.

6 Parton, *Jackson*, III, 692, 694; von Holst, *History*, II, 29-31.

the fact that, all too often, "the great body of our American democracy . . . slips back unconsciously into the mire whence the poverty-stricken millions emerge and falls too easy a prey to vice and ignorance." Ostrogorski got to the heart of the Whig historians' case against Jacksonian Democracy when he complained that it "excluded men of sterling worth and high principles from public life." Von Holst similarly argued that since Jackson "the people have begun to exchange the leadership of a small number of statesmen and politicians of a higher order for the rule of an ever increasing crowd of politicians of high and low degree, down even to the pothouse politician and the common thief, in the protecting mantle of demagogism." And as a result, said Parton, "the public affairs of the United States have been conducted with a stupidity which has excited the wonder of mankind." [7]

It is important to remember that the Whig historians all came from eastern or European middle-class or upper-middle-class families with traditions of education, prestige, and public service, the kind of families that had claimed social and political leadership as their natural right during the early days of the republic. By the time these men began to write the history of Jacksonian Democracy, however, their kind had been largely ousted from political leadership by the professional politicians and new-style parties that had arisen as the institutional embodiments of the Jacksonian democratic revolution. They were writing, moreover, in the era of Grantism in national politics and Tweedism in local politics, when the least lovely aspects of democracy were most conspicuous. Whig historiography, indeed, was a facet of "patrician liberalism," the movement that sought to restore the pristine purity of American politics by destroying the spoils system, breaking the bosses' power, ending the unholy alliance between government and business, and placing gentlemen in public office. What could be more natural, then, than for the Whig historians to find in Jacksonian Democracy the origin of the features of American life they most deplored? These scholars displayed, in short, the class bias of an elite displaced from leadership by a vulgar and frequently corrupt democracy.

By the 1890's patrician liberalism was giving way to the broader movement which under the name Progressivism was soon to effect a

[7] Von Holst, *History*, II, 77-79; Schouler, *History*, III, 198-99; Ostrogorski, *Democracy and Political Parties*, II, 50, 69-70; Parton, *Jackson*, III, 149-50, 698, 700.

profound shift in the mood and direction of American life. A corresponding shift in the mood of American historiography was signaled in 1893, when the young Wisconsin historian, Frederick Jackson Turner, read his famous paper emphasizing "The Significance of the Frontier in American History." Yet Turner's real significance lies less in his controversial frontier thesis than in his influence as leader of the massive shift of American historiography to a pro-democratic orientation. A whole new generation of young historians — men like Woodrow Wilson, William E. Dodd, John Spencer Bassett, Charles A. Beard, and Vernon L. Parrington — stood ready to echo Turner's vibrantly sympathetic description of democracy emerging "stark and strong and full of life, from the American forest." [8]

Two facts should be especially noted about these young scholars who were to transform the writing of American history. One is that nearly all of them came from rural or small-town backgrounds in the West or South, and this in itself brought a new point of view into a field previously dominated by the urban Northeast. The second significant fact is that though they came from substantial middle-class families, they lived in a period when middle-class Americans, and particularly middle-class intellectuals, were being swept into the current of reform. The Progressive campaign to preserve the traditional values of American society in the threatening new context of industrialism and urbanism was made possible by a revival of faith in the possibilities of the whole people, and the Progressives characteristically devoted much of their energy to making the democratic process work more effectively. Small wonder, then, that the young scholars of the Progressive era responded enthusiastically to Turner's reaffirmation of the long-tarnished democratic faith of an earlier day.

Andrew Jackson and his Democracy were naturally among the leading beneficiaries of the new pro-democratic orientation of American historiography. Out of the "frontier democratic society" of the West, said Turner, "where the freedom and abundance of land in the great Valley opened a refuge to the oppressed in all regions, came the Jacksonian democracy which governed the nation after the downfall of the party of John Quincy Adams." This

[8] Frederick Jackson Turner, *The Frontier in American History* (New York, 1920), 216.

Jacksonian Democracy was "strong in the faith of the intrinsic excellence of the common man, and in his capacity to share in government." [9]

Turner's contemporaries quickly took up the refrain. John W. Burgess enthusiastically acclaimed Jackson as "the noblest Roman of them all"; while William E. Dodd thought of the "brave and generous" Old Hickory as "a second Jefferson," whose mission it was "to arouse the people to a sense of their responsibility." In the eyes of that rather romantic nationalist, Woodrow Wilson, Jackson represented the "forces of health" that were to "nationalize the government." Though Jackson's policies "temporarily ruined the business of the country" and "permanently demoralized our politics," Wilson nevertheless regarded his election as "a great democratic upheaval," which "did the incalculable good of giving to the national spirit its first self-reliant expression of resolution and of consentaneous power." [10]

The earliest major product of the democratic school of Jacksonian historiography was John Spencer Bassett's *Life of Andrew Jackson*, published in 1911. Bassett was the first scholar since Parton to work thoroughly through the extant Jacksonian sources, which now seemed to reveal "a man who was great, spite of many limitations." Bassett was generally sympathetic to Jackson's purposes and policies, but he was not uncritical, and his final chapter remains the most successful attempt to appraise Jackson's baffling character. Jackson had plenty of shortcomings — "lack of education, his crude judgments in many affairs, his occasional outbreaks of passion, his habitual hatred of those enemies with whom he had not made friends for party purposes, and his crude ideas of some political policies" — yet, for Bassett, "all lose some of their infelicity in the face of his brave, frank, masterly leadership of the democratic movement which then established itself in our life. . . . Few American Presidents have better lived up to the demands of the movement which brought them into power." [11]

The transitional indecision of a few scholars was best represented by William MacDonald, whose volume on the Jackson period for

[9] *Ibid.*, 192, 302.

[10] John W. Burgess, *The Middle Period, 1817-1858* (New York, 1905), 135; William E. Dodd, *Expansion and Conflict* (Boston, 1915), 3, 36; Woodrow Wilson, *Division and Reunion, 1829-1909* (New York, 1910), 25, 115.

[11] John Spencer Bassett, *The Life of Andrew Jackson* (2 vols., Garden City, 1911), I, xi; II, 750.

the American Nation Series fell squarely between the Whig and Democratic positions. Though MacDonald described Jackson as "an untrained, self-willed, passionate frontier soldier," he admonished his readers that "It was as idle then as it is now to bemoan" his election, for "this predominance of the masses" is "the price of popular government." It almost seems that MacDonald was unconsciously making the same accommodation to democracy as a Whig historian in 1906 that Daniel Webster had made as a Whig politician in 1840.[12]

But most American historians embraced the democratic orientation with only slight hesitation, and even the Spencerians capitulated to Jackson. The anti-democratic Whiggery that had made Parton and Sumner so critical of Old Hickory, despite their sympathy for his laissez-faire policies, had little effect on their fellow Spencerian, John Fiske. Though Fiske boggled a bit at the spoils system, he concluded that Jackson's "sounder instincts prompted him to a course of action quite in harmony with the highest political philosophy," as contained in the works of Herbert Spencer. For Jackson had checked "a tendency toward the mollycoddling, old granny theory of government, according to which the ruling powers are to take care of the people, build their roads for them, do their banking for them, rob Peter to pay Paul for carrying on a losing business, and tinker and bemuddle things generally."[13]

What a dramatic shift in interpretation the democratic orientation could effect was demonstrated even more strikingly when Carl Russell Fish, writing in 1904, almost made a Jacksonian virtue of the spoils system in his study of *The Civil Service and the Patronage*. By careful scholarship Fish showed that the civil service had needed some ventilation in 1829, and that the irresistible pressures for the spoils system must have triumphed regardless of who was president. But it was Fish's democratic frame of reference rather than his research that produced his most startling conclusions. "The spoils system paid for the party organization . . . which established a 'government of the people' in the United States in 1829," he declared, and in so doing, "it served a purpose that could probably

12 William MacDonald, *Jacksonian Democracy, 1829-1837* (New York, 1906), 42, 311-12. The influence of Turner is conspicuous in MacDonald's volume. See, for example, p. 314.

13 John Fiske, *Essays Historical and Literary* (2 vols., New York, 1902), I, 286, 310-11.

have been performed in no other way, and that was fully worth the cost." [14]

While the new democratic orientation was winning converts, another influence was finally making itself felt in Jacksonian historiography: the cult of objectivity. In 1903 Ralph C. H. Catterall produced a study of the Second Bank of the United States that was a masterpiece. Though Catterall's personal sympathies were unquestionably Whiggish — he regretted, for example, that the influence of "enlightened business men" and other members of "the intelligent class" on public affairs "has always been inconsiderable, partly because they are not interested in politics, partly because they are themselves objects of suspicion to the democratic masses" — he nevertheless granted Jackson's complete sincerity and reported his position fully and fairly.[15]

The desire for objectivity had less fortunate results in the case of John Bach McMaster, whose habit of quoting copiously from the contemporary arguments on both sides of every question, while scrupulously withholding his own judgments and interpretations, made an arid waste of his multi-volume history. Yet the reader can discern that by 1900, when he reached the Jackson period, he had gone over to the democratic camp, for he described in great detail the democratic reform movements of the era, he relieved Jackson from responsibility for the spoils system, and he acclaimed Old Hickory's victory of 1828, with unwonted enthusiasm, as "indeed a great uprising of the people, a triumph of democracy, another political revolution the like of which the country had not seen since 1800." [16]

The pro-democratic orientation that transformed Jacksonian historiography at the turn of the century has continued to be the dominant influence on writings about the Jackson period ever since. It permeated Marquis James's impressive Jackson biography of the 1930's, as well as the extensive studies of the Jackson period by Claude G. Bowers in the 1920's and Arthur M. Schlesinger, Jr., in the 1940's. More significantly, it has controlled the interpreta-

[14] Carl Russell Fish, *The Civil Service and the Patronage* (Cambridge, 1904), 75-78, 155-57.

[15] Ralph C. H. Catterall, *The Second Bank of the United States* (Chicago, 1903), 168 and *passim.*

[16] John B. McMaster, *A History of the People of the United States from the Revolution to the Civil War* (8 vols., New York, 1883-1913), V, 518, 522, and V-VI *passim.*

tions of Jacksonian Democracy to be found in nearly all the general works on American history written in the twentieth century, from the widely influential accounts of Vernon L. Parrington and Charles and Mary Beard to the most obscure textbooks. Political scientists have joined in the chorus of approval, with such writers as John W. Burgess, Wilfred E. Binkley, and Leonard D. White praising Jackson and his followers for strengthening the presidency and developing the new-style political party as an indispensable democratic institution.[17]

Despite this widespread acceptance, the twentieth-century democratic school of Jacksonian historiography has attained neither the unchallenged hegemony nor the unity of outlook that the Whig school enjoyed in the nineteenth century. For one thing, the Whig interpretation would not play dead.[18] Most embarrassing to the democratic view of Andrew Jackson has been the interpretation of Old Hickory's role in early Tennessee politics advanced by Thomas P. Abernethy. Abernethy presents Jackson as a frontier nabob who took sides against the democratic movement in his own state. Actually, this leader of the democratic movement in national politics was a demagogic aristocrat, says Abernethy, an "opportunist" for whom

[17] See, for example, Marquis James, *The Life of Andrew Jackson* (2 vols. in 1, Indianapolis, 1938), 720-24 and *passim*; Claude G. Bowers, *The Party Battles of the Jackson Period* (Boston, 1922); Arthur M. Schlesinger, Jr., *The Age of Jackson* (Boston, 1945); Vernon L. Parrington, *Main Currents in American Thought: An Interpretation of American Literature from the Beginnings to 1920* (3 vols., New York, 1927-1930), II, 146; Charles A. and Mary R. Beard, *The Rise of American Civilization* (2 vols., New York, 1927), I, 557; Burgess, *Middle Period*, 282-83; Wilfred E. Binkley, *The Powers of the President: Problems of American Democracy* (Garden City, 1937), 67-88; Wilfred E. Binkley, *American Political Parties: Their Natural History* (2nd ed., New York, 1954), 141; Leonard D. White, *The Jacksonians: A Study in Administrative History, 1829-1861* (New York, 1954), 17, 48-49, 566.

[18] Jackson's most inveterate scholarly foe in the twentieth century has been Richard R. Stenberg, who undertook "an extensive critique of Jackson's career and character" to be entitled *The Insidious Andrew Jackson.* Though the book never appeared, Stenberg's point of view gained some currency through a series of articles: "Jackson, Anthony Butler, and Texas," *Southwestern Social Science Quarterly* (Austin), XIII (December, 1932), 264-86; "The Texas Schemes of Jackson and Houston, 1829-1836," *ibid.*, XV (December, 1934), 229-50; "Jackson, Buchanan, and the 'Corrupt Bargain' Calumny," *Pennsylvania Magazine of History and Biography* (Philadelphia), LVIII (January, 1934), 61-85; "Jackson's Neches Claim, 1829-1836," *Southwestern Historical Quarterly* (Austin), XXXIX (April, 1936), 255-74; "Andrew Jackson and the Erving Affidavit," *ibid.*, XLI (October, 1937), 142-53; "Jackson's 'Rhea Letter' Hoax," *Journal of Southern History* (Baton Rouge), II (November, 1936), 480-96; "The Jefferson Birthday Dinner, 1830," *ibid.*, IV (August, 1938), 334-45; "President Jackson and Anthony Butler," *Southwest Review* (Dallas), XXII (Summer, 1937), 391-404; "A Note on the Jackson-Calhoun Breach of 1830-31," *Tyler's Quarterly Historical and Genealogical Magazine* (Holdcroft, Va.), XXI (October, 1939), 65-69.

"Democracy was good talk with which to win the favor of the people and thereby accomplish ulterior objectives." [19]

The Whig interpretation has received its fullest modern application to the Jackson movement as a whole in Charles M. Wiltse's impressive biography of Calhoun. Wiltse sees the reality of Jacksonian politics as a selfish struggle for office and federal subsidy. Jackson was in many respects "a frontier bully," and "in a growing, expanding, gambling, ebullient country like the United States of the 1820's and 30's, the frontier bully was a national hero." [20]

Yet the democratic historians have suffered less from these dissenting views than from their own inability to make clear just what they mean by "democracy." The men of Turner's generation who originated democratic historiography conceived of the democratic process in a characteristically middle-class, Progressive way. Hating monopoly and plutocracy, they rejoiced in the egalitarian, antimonopolistic tradition that stemmed from Jacksonian Democracy. But hating the class consciousness of Populism and Socialism as much or more, they shrank from any interpretation of the American past that smacked of social conflict. Their enthusiasm for democracy rested on an essentially romantic faith in the whole people, whom they saw as an undifferentiated mass, virtually free of inequalities and conflicts. Democracy, in the view which informed both Progressive politics and Turnerean historiography, was the process by which the whole people's fundamentally virtuous impulses were translated into public policy.

Thus Turner was careful to assert that "classes and inequalities of fortune played little part" in frontier democracy. It "did not demand equality of condition," he declared, for it believed that the

[19] For Abernethy's view of Jackson see: "Andrew Jackson and the Rise of Southwestern Democracy," *American Historical Review* (New York), XXXIII (October, 1927), 64-77; *From Frontier to Plantation in Tennessee: A Study in Frontier Democracy* (Chapel Hill, 1932), especially 238-49; and *Dictionary of American Biography* (21 vols., New York, 1928-1944), IX, 526-34.

Even the most democratically oriented historian had no choice, without an independent study of Tennessee political history, but to accept Abernethy's interpretation as sound and adjust his own interpretation of Jackson to it as painlessly as possible. Arthur M. Schlesinger, Jr., for example, was driven to argue that "No amount of inference based on what Jackson was like before 1828 can be a substitute for the facts after 1828." *Age of Jackson*, 44.

Abernethy's interpretation of Jackson's role in Tennessee politics is criticized in Charles G. Sellers, Jr., "Banking and Politics in Jackson's Tennessee, 1817-1827," *Mississippi Valley Historical Review* (Cedar Rapids), XLI (June, 1954), 61-84.

[20] Charles M. Wiltse, *John C. Calhoun* (3 vols., Indianapolis, 1944-1951), II, 234-35 and *passim.*

"self-made man had a right to his success in the free competition which western life afforded." Mere inequality of condition was a negligible consideration to Turner, alongside the more spiritual brand of equality that the frontier process had guaranteed. "Mere success in the game . . . gave to the successful ones no right to look down upon their neighbors," he insisted, and he clung passionately to his conviction that the abundance of free land made it impossible for "the successful ones . . . to harden their triumphs into the rule of a privileged class." [21]

However plausible this view of democracy may have been for the early nineteenth century, the free land was undeniably gone by Turner's day, while inequality of condition had become so gross that its danger to democracy could no longer be ignored. The successful ones now threatened either to harden their triumphs into the rule of a privileged class, or to provoke a bitter class struggle, and both possibilities disturbed middle-class Americans. It was this apparent crisis of democracy that produced both the Progressive movement and the democratic school of historians.

Turner mirrored one mood of his generation in his desperate efforts to believe that there was no crisis, that the great monopolists themselves were products of the democratic West and, by a quasi-Lamarckian inheritance of acquired characteristics "still profess its principles." [22] But the more typical response of the democratic historians was to rely upon a revival of democracy, a movement of the whole people; and they were in effect supplying a historical tradition for Progressivism when they described the democratic upheaval of Jackson's day as an amorphous force, arising with no specific cause or particular program from the creative western forest, and spreading over the East by contagion.

The democratic historians' aversion to social conflict was a major factor in causing them to supplement the frontier thesis with a heavy emphasis on sectionalism. Conflict was simply too obvious in

21 Turner, *Frontier*, 302-303, 342-43.

22 Turner virtually staked the future of democracy on the fact that Andrew Carnegie had built up his fortune in Pittsburgh, "then a distinctively Western town," and whatever the tendencies of his Steel Trust, "there can be little doubt of the democratic ideals of Mr. Carnegie himself." Carnegie had after all written a book entitled *Triumphant Democracy*, Turner pointed out, in which the steel master rejoiced that America's vast resources were "in the hands of an intelligent people, the Democracy, to be used for the general good of the masses, and not made the spoils of monarchs, courts, and aristocracy, to be turned to the base and selfish ends of a privileged hereditary class." Turner, *Frontier*, 264-65.

the Jackson era to be ignored, but Turner and his followers muted the discordant note of class struggle by transposing it into conflict between distinct geographical sections. Thus, alongside the Jacksonian rise of the whole people, we find in their writings a three-way contest among the democratic West (epitomized by Jackson), the capitalist Northeast, and the planting and increasingly aristocratic South.[23] Beard and Parrington, to be sure, made social conflict central to their interpretations. But even their dramas of struggle against privileged minorities were grounded on the same Rousseauistic concept of the whole people as the conventional democratic interpretation; and more often than not they, too, fell back upon oversimplified sectional categories.

This vague conception of democracy remained prevalent in Jacksonian historiography until 1945, when Arthur M. Schlesinger, Jr., published *The Age of Jackson*. Schlesinger's thesis was that "more can be understood about Jacksonian democracy if it is regarded as a problem not of sections but of classes." Defining the central theme of American political history to be the efforts "on the part of the other sections of society to restrain the power of the business community," he interpreted Jacksonian Democracy as a movement "to control the power of the capitalistic groups, mainly Eastern, for the benefit of noncapitalist groups, farmers and laboring men, East, West, and South." Schlesinger traced the movement to the economic hardships of the 1820's, and he saw the East and the workingmen as playing the crucial roles in the Jacksonian coalition.[24]

Schlesinger not only provided a sharper definition of the democratic movement and a clearer explanation of its origins, but he also stirred up a warm debate which prompted other historians to offer alternative definitions. The attack on *The Age of Jackson* was launched by a scholarly official of the Federal Reserve Board, Bray Hammond, who was irritated in the first instance by Schlesinger's failure to appreciate the central banking functions that

[23] Frederick Jackson Turner, *The Rise of the New West, 1819-1829* (New York, 1906); F. J. Turner, *The United States, 1830-1850: The Nation and Its Sections* (New York, 1932); Wilson, *Division and Reunion*; Bassett, *Jackson*; Dodd, *Expansion and Conflict.* Edward Channing in his *A History of the United States* (6 vols., New York, 1905-1925), V, 380-402, follows von Holst's odd interpretation, which makes Jackson a representative of the southern planters.

[24] Schlesinger, *Age of Jackson*, 208-209, 263, 505; Arthur M. Schlesinger, Jr., "Communication," *American Historical Review*, LIV (April, 1949), 785-86.

the national bank had exercised so beneficially before it was attacked by Jackson. Emphasizing the role of the state banks in fomenting the Jacksonian assault on the national bank, Hammond insisted that the real animus of Jacksonian Democracy was not against business but against the exclusion of new entrepreneurs from business opportunities. Schlesinger "represents the age of Jackson as one of triumphant liberalism," he complained, "when it was as much or more an age of triumphant exploitation." [25]

Hammond was quickly joined in his criticism of Schlesinger by a group of historians at Columbia University. Joseph Dorfman argued that the "labor" spokesmen whom Schlesinger had emphasized did not represent a genuine labor movement, and that their views were far from anti-business.[26] Richard B. Morris contended that Jackson was anti-labor rather than pro-labor,[27] while several of Morris' students attempted, with questionable success, to demonstrate that workingmen did not vote for Jackson.[28]

[25] Bray Hammond, "Jackson, Biddle, and the Bank of the United States," *Journal of Economic History* (New York), VII (May, 1947), 1-23. See also his review of the *Age of Jackson*, *ibid.*, VI (May, 1946), 79-84. In another article, "Banking in the Early West: Monopoly, Prohibition, and Laissez Faire," *ibid.*, VIII (May, 1949), 1-25, Hammond contended that hard-money sentiment, which Schlesinger attributed mainly to eastern labor circles, was actually as strong or stronger in the West. In a recent book review Schlesinger agrees that he did not sufficiently emphasize the central banking functions of the national bank; he also suggests that he now believes that "The men in Jackson's day who were most nearly right from the viewpoint of economic growth were neither the Bank advocates nor the hard money theorists but the soft money men of the West." *American Historical Review*, LIX (October, 1953), 140-41.

[26] Joseph Dorfman, *The Economic Mind in American Civilization* (3 vols., New York, 1946-1949), II, 601; Joseph Dorfman, "The Jackson Wage-Earner Thesis," *American Historical Review*, LIV (January, 1949), 296-306. For Schlesinger's reply to Dorfman's article see *ibid.*, LIV (April, 1949), 785-86.

[27] Richard B. Morris, " 'Old Hickory' Jackson Was No FDR," *Labor and Nation* (New York), V (May-June, 1949), 38-40; Richard B. Morris, "Andrew Jackson, Strikebreaker," *American Historical Review*, LV (October, 1949), 54-68.

[28] William A. Sullivan, "Did Labor Support Andrew Jackson?" *Political Science Quarterly* (New York), LXII (December, 1947), 569-80; Edward Pessen, "Did Labor Support Andrew Jackson? The Boston Story," *ibid.*, LXIV (June, 1949), 262-74; William A. Sullivan, *The Industrial Worker in Pennsylvania, 1800-1840* (Harrisburg, 1955), 159-207. These studies are criticized in a review by Joseph G. Rayback, *Mississippi Valley Historical Review*, XLIII (September, 1956), 311-12, and in Robert T. Bower, "Note on 'Did Labor Support Jackson? The Boston Story,' " *Political Science Quarterly*, LXV (September, 1950), 441-44.

In a recent article Pessen has retreated from some of the positions formerly maintained by the Columbia historians. He concedes that the workingmen's political organizations, newspapers, and spokesmen were closely identified with a genuine labor movement and that their anti-business views may properly be called radical, though not necessarily anti-capitalist. He also shows that the specifically workingmen's political organizations usually remained independent of, and sometimes hostile to, the

These historians showed a considerable affinity for the Whig view of Jackson personally, especially in the version advanced by Thomas P. Abernethy. Their own interpretation of the Jackson movement was expressed best, perhaps, by Richard Hofstadter, who described it as "a phase in the expansion of liberated capitalism," and as "closely linked to the ambitions of the small capitalist." [29]

Thus the recent historiography of Jacksonian Democracy has been dominated by the debate over Schlesinger's "class-conflict" or "labor" thesis on the one hand and the "entrepreneurial" thesis put forward by Schlesinger's critics on the other. Schlesinger and his supporters picture the democratic impulse largely as a movement of protest against the unfair privileges claimed by an exploitative business elite, while the Columbia historians defend the diametrically opposed view that the democratic movement was itself strongly capitalist in spirit and objected only to any limitation on free entry into the game of capitalist exploitation.

Yet closer examination reveals some significant affinities between the two interpretations. They share, for one thing, a common origin. It was the socialist publicist Algie M. Simons who staked the first effective claim of real significance for Jacksonian labor.[30] Using

Democratic party. It must be remembered, however, that these organizations rarely attracted the votes of more than a small minority of the workingmen, and the question of how "labor" at large voted remains open. Edward Pessen, "The Workingmen's Movement of the Jacksonian Era," *Mississippi Valley Historical Review*, XLIII (December, 1956), 428-43.

[29] Richard Hofstadter, *The American Political Tradition and the Men Who Made It* (New York, 1954), 58. For a convenient summary of the views of this group of historians, see the preface to the volume of Jackson documents compiled by another Columbia scholar: Harold C. Syrett, *Andrew Jackson: His Contribution to the American Tradition* (Indianapolis, 1954).

[30] Though Simons was the first to develop the labor thesis fully, it had been foreshadowed by, of all people, William Graham Sumner. An admirer of those earlier sound-money men, the labor-oriented Loco Focos, Sumner declared that their "sound and imperishable ideas . . . first put the democratic party on the platform which . . . it had been trying to find." Sumner, *Jackson*, 373. Very different assumptions prompted Sumner's perennial antagonist, the socialist-influenced economist Richard T. Ely, to claim a few years later that "the Democratic party from 1829 to 1841 was more truly a workingmen's party than has been the case with any other great party in our country." *The Labor Movement in America* (New York, 1886), 42-43. And a sympathy with popular causes that has never been adequately recognized induced John B. McMaster to include in his *History* at the turn of the century the first full account of the Jacksonian labor movement. *History*, V, 82-108; VI, 100-103, 181-82, 220-23, 364-70. For a clear indication of the reformist sympathies that never became explicit in McMaster's *History*, see his *The Acquisition of Political, Social, and Industrial Rights of Man in America* (Cleveland, 1903), especially 96-110 for the Jacksonian labor movement. It was apparently through this little book that Simons became acquainted with Jacksonian labor.

data first turned up by John B. McMaster, Simons argued that the labor movement not only was an important part of the democratic upsurge of Jackson's day, but "measured by the impress it left, was the most important event in American history." [31]

After John R. Commons and his associates published their monumental *Documentary History of American Industrial Society*, labor's importance in the Jackson era could no longer be ignored. Even Turner gave the eastern workingmen a minor place in the Jackson movement, and a few scholars went further. In 1913 a textbook writer, Willis Mason West, assigned labor equal weight with the West and asserted that for some years the Democratic party "remained in large degree a workingmen's party." Ten years later Arthur M. Schlesinger, Sr., used West's treatment as the basis for an essay on Jacksonian Democracy that dealt briefly with many of the points subsequently developed in the younger Schlesinger's *Age of Jackson*.[32]

Labor historians were following the same line,[33] but general American historians remained largely unshaken in their devotion to the frontier-sectional interpretation set by Turner. It is rather remarkable, in fact, that the growing vogue of economic interpretation did not produce a greater emphasis on economic class interests in the Jackson period. Even Charles and Mary Beard treated the Jacksonian conflicts as mainly sectional in their *Rise of American Civilization*, an approach which belied their chapter title, "Jack-

[31] A. M. Simons, *Social Forces in American History* (New York, 1911), 188. Simons' discovery of the Jacksonian labor movement from a reading of McMaster is interestingly illustrated in a series of his writings: *Class Struggles in America* (Chicago, 1903); "The Rise of Labor in America," *International Socialist Review* (Chicago), V (September, 1904), 143-49; *Class Struggles in America* (Rev. ed., Chicago, 1906). In 1903 he knew nothing of the Jacksonian labor movement, interpreting this period of American history in slavishly Turnerean terms. The 1904 article reveals his reading of McMaster, and in 1906 he revised his earlier pamphlet to make a major place for Jacksonian labor. *Social Forces in American History* is an expansion of the 1906 revision.

[32] Turner, *Frontier*, 216, 303; Willis Mason West, *The Story of American Democracy, Political and Industrial* (Boston, 1922), 438; Arthur M. Schlesinger, *New Viewpoints in American History* (New York, 1922), 200-19. I have quoted from the 1922 edition of West's textbook rather than the 1913 edition which Schlesinger used.

[33] John R. Commons and others, *History of Labour in the United States* (2 vols., New York, 1918), I, 459, 461, 465; Selig Perlman, *A History of Trade Unionism in the United States* (New York, 1922), 9-10, 27-28; Nathan Fine, *Labor and Farmer Parties in the United States, 1828-1928* (New York, 1928), 12, 15; Philip S. Foner, *History of the Labor Movement in the United States: From Colonial Times to the Founding of the American Federation of Labor* (New York, 1947), 143-66; Foster Rhea Dulles, *Labor in America: A History* (New York, 1949), 25, 37-38, 45-46.

sonian Democracy — A Triumphant Farmer-Labor Party," as well as their over-all interpretation of American history.[34]

The entrepreneurial thesis, like the labor thesis, found its first full statement in the socialist tracts of Algie Simons, where it appeared as a gloss on Turner's frontier thesis. "The 'frontier' which is spoken of as being in the ascendent under Jackson was distinctly individualistic and small capitalistic in its instincts, rather than proletarian," Simons declared. Jacksonian Democracy was "neither frontier, nor wageworking, or even purely capitalist in its mental make-up." It was the "democracy of expectant capitalists." Throughout Simons' account there runs a note of Marxian distaste for this greedy democracy of "petit bourgeois," an attitude which, at one remove from its Marxian roots, may be detected in later expositions of the entrepreneurial thesis.[35]

The striking fact that both the labor thesis and the entrepreneurial thesis found their first full development in Simons invites a further examination of their affinities. Both, it is clear, are indebted to Marxian analysis and represent a "realistic" approach to history, the one maintaining a detached, analytical attitude, which occasionally betrays an implicit distaste for the middle-class norms of American democratic capitalism, and the other viewing democratic liberalism as being perennially sustained and advanced by anti-business elements in American society, class-conscious and organized for social and political struggle. This "realism" explains the hostility of both to the diffuse Turnerean conception of democracy, but it does not account for the fact that writers of both schools are consistently critical of agrarian elements and seek to de-emphasize their importance in our history. These latter facts, when correlated with the personal origins and sympathies of the writers involved, suggest the belated emergence of the city as a major influence on American historical scholarship.

[34] Beard, *Rise of American Civilization,* I, 542-57.

[35] Simons, *Class Struggle* (1903 ed.), 10; Simons, *Social Forces,* 210. Turner was quite sensitive to Simons' viewpoint, for he had recognized on occasion that the conflict between Clay and Jackson reflected a larger conflict between two elements in western life: "the industrial forces (town-makers and the business builders), on the one side and the old rural democracy of the uplands on the other." Yet Turner was never able to clarify this ambiguity in his conception of western democracy, and he reacted defensively to Simons' interpretation. "If this . . . Jacksonian democracy, was, as its socialist critics have called it, in reality a democracy of 'expectant capitalists'," Turner declared, "it was not one which expected or acknowledged on the part of the successful ones the right to harden their triumphs into the rule of a privileged class." Turner, *Frontier,* 172-73, 342-43.

Thus we are reminded once again of the profound influence of frames of reference. Indeed the historians of Jacksonian Democracy might best be classified by the social and intellectual environments that seem so largely to control their interpretations. In place of the simple categories of a Whig school and a democratic school, we might distinguish three main groups.

First, a "patrician" school of historians, drawn from eastern or European upper-middle-class backgrounds, dominated Jacksonian historiography until the end of the nineteenth century. Resenting the vulgar democracy and the equally vulgar plutocracy that were displacing their kind of social and intellectual elite from leadership, these men spoke for the conservative, semi-aristocratic, mugwumpish liberalism of the Gilded Age.

Around 1900 the patrician historians were displaced by an "agrarian democratic" school, drawn from western and southern middle-class backgrounds and reflecting the revival of old-fashioned democratic dogmas in the Progressive era. Fearful of both class antagonism and monopoly capitalism, these men effected a reorientation of American historiography around the concept of an agrarian-derived democracy of the whole people.

Finally, in recent years, we have seen the emergence of a school of "urban" scholars, drawn from eastern cities, who find the agrarian democratic theme naïve or otherwise unsatisfactory. Most of these urban historians came to maturity during the New Deal years, and they often manifest a greater sympathy for industrial labor than for farmers and middle-class businessmen. Their stance seems to be that of self-conscious intellectuals and critics, expressing through their detached, "scientific," faintly ironic, "realistic" analysis an alienation from the middle-class mainstream of American life that is reminiscent of the patrician school. The entrepreneurial thesis is the most characteristic product of this group, though the labor thesis grows out of many of the same influences.

Actually, Arthur M. Schlesinger, Jr., the leading proponent of the labor thesis, emphasizes entrepreneurial elements in Jacksonian Democracy far more than his critics appear to realize; indeed, he sees the western Jacksonians as almost wholly entrepreneurial in spirit. Basically, however, his *Age of Jackson* seems to represent a marriage of the agrarian democratic and the urban points of view, in much the same way that Simons seemed to mix Populism with Marxism. Schlesinger's semi-Marxist "realism" is solidly urban, but the democratic idealism with which he combines it is clearly in the tradition of Turner.[36]

But what of Old Hickory himself and Jacksonian Democracy? What are we to conclude when, after a century of scholarship, historians still squarely contradict each other about the essential nature of both the man and the movement? Has the frame of reference cut us off from the past as it actually was? Do historical writings tell us more about their authors than they do about their purported subjects?

Before accepting these disheartening conclusions, it may be well to remind ourselves that an interpretation is not necessarily wrong merely because a writer seems to have been impelled toward that interpretation by a particular frame of reference. The conclusions of honest men, working within limits set by an abundance of reliable and relatively unmalleable evidence, must have some basis in the reality of the past they seek to interpret. This may suggest that each school of Jacksonian historiography has been correct up to a point, and that the real problem of interpreting Jacksonian Democracy is to define the proper relationship among the various elements emphasized by the different schools.

Several recent writers, in attempting to do just this, have concluded that the Jacksonian movement was essentially paradoxical. Louis Hartz describes the American democrat of the Jackson era as a hybrid personality — both a class-conscious democrat and an incipient entrepreneur — at once the "man of the land, the factory, and the forge . . . who has all the proletarian virtues that Marx was forever contrasting with the pettiness of the petit-bourgeois," and "an aggressive entrepreneur, buying 'on speculation,' combining 'some trade with agriculture,' making 'agriculture itself a trade'." He had "a certain smallness of entrepreneurial preoccupation which has never been glamorous in Western thought," Hartz concludes, but at the same time he was involved in "two heroic dramas, the covered wagon drama of the American frontier and the strike-ridden

[36] Schlesinger, it should be remembered, is deeply indebted to his father, who came out of Turner's "valley of democracy" to proclaim the city as the great new frontier for historical scholarship. The elder Schlesinger's essay on Jacksonian Democracy is even more obviously composed of equal parts of Turnerean and labor themes.

Of course, the three schools as defined above represent central positions, leaving some historians on the fringes. Woodrow Wilson, for example, shows both patrician and agrarian democratic tendencies, while Parrington and the Beards reveal urban tendencies in a context that is mainly agrarian democratic.

drama of a rising labor movement, so that when we come to men like Jackson and Leggett we are never quite sure whether we are dealing with a petty hope or a glorious dream." [37]

Another scholar has defined the paradox of Jacksonian Democracy somewhat differently. Judging from Jackson's own public papers, says Marvin Meyers, the Jacksonians appealed "not to some workingman's yearning for a brave new world; not to the possibilities of a fresh creation at the western limits of civilization; not to the ambitions of a rising laissez-faire capitalism — not to any of these so much as to a *restoration* of old virtues and a (perhaps imaginary) old republican way of life." Meyers states the paradox thus: "The movement which in many ways cleared the path for the triumph of laissez-faire capitalism and its culture in America, and the public which in its daily life acted out that victory, held nevertheless in their conscience an image of a chaste republican order, resisting the seductions of risk and novelty, greed and extravagance, rapid motion and complex dealings." Still another scholar, John W. Ward, has found confirmation for this mood of Old Republican restorationism in the symbolic uses to which Jackson was put by his generation.[38]

If these scholars are right about the paradoxical character of the Jacksonian democratic impulse, then it is easy to see why historians, in emphasizing different elements of the paradox, have reached such different interpretations. Viewed in this light, the frame of reference has served a valuable purpose after all, by leading historians to the different elements of the complex Jacksonian past out of which an over-all synthesis must eventually be constructed.[39]

[37] Louis Hartz, *The Liberal Tradition in America: An Interpretation of American Political Thought since the Revolution* (New York, 1955), 89-138, especially 115-16.

[38] Marvin Meyers, "The Jacksonian Persuasion," *American Quarterly* (Philadelphia), V (Spring, 1953), 3-15; John W. Ward, *Andrew Jackson: Symbol for an Age* (New York, 1955).

[39] This utility of the frame of reference is especially evident in the case of a historian caught between several contexts. Strangely enough it was Vernon L. Parrington — so wrong about so many things — who first described the contradictory character of the American democrat in the Jackson period. Parrington lived early enough in the twentieth century to share the agrarian-derived democratic faith of Turner and company, but late enough to embrace the hard-headed "critical realism" that was soon to displace their rather romantic nostalgia. His heart yearning for an agrarian democracy that his head told him was doomed, he defined the essential meaning of the American democratic impulse as paradoxical. Inspired by both Turner and Simons, Parrington found in Jacksonian Democracy a growing, and to him fatal, entrepreneurial spirit on the one hand, and a delaying action by an anti-aristocratic, anti-business alliance of farmers and workingmen on the other. *American Thought*, II, v, 137-52. Cf. Arthur A. Ekirch, Jr., "Parrington and the Decline of American Liberalism," *American Quarterly*, III (Winter, 1951), 295-308.

Yet the succession of frames of reference and the multiplication of hypotheses can distort as well as amplify the past, and our current wealth in hypotheses about the Jackson period suggests that we are poor in the data by which our hypotheses must be checked. The sources, moreover, can force upon our notice factors to which our frames of reference might never lead us.[40] But the melancholy truth is that from Parton's day to our own, hardly more than a half-dozen scholars have worked thoroughly through the available Jackson material. Consequently few phases of American history offer historians a greater challenge to research and synthesis.

Looking back over a century of scholarship, students of Jacksonian Democracy may well rejoice that their subject has been so central to defining the American experience as to become a major focus for each succeeding reorientation of historical interpretation. New frames of reference have steadily yielded new insights, and the critical spirit in which frames of reference are increasingly used is itself a momentous advance in historical technique. The course from Parton to Turner to our present indecision between labor thesis and entrepreneurial thesis may not look like a straight-line approach to Truth. "Objective reality" we know we can never altogether reach, but we need not apologize for assuming it is there, or for believing that our zigzag course brings us swinging in on a circle of ever closer vantage points for discerning its salient features.[41]

[40] Few scholars, for example, can ever again possess the Jeffersonian frame of reference that led Parrington to discover the profound influence of Old Republican ideology on the Jacksonian generation. Arthur Schlesinger, Jr., had to discover the same thing from the sources themselves; in fact, he had some difficulty reconciling it with his central hypotheses.

The findings of Meyers and Ward suggest the value of devising new ways to start from the sources as well as from our hypotheses. Meyers analyzed the value content of Jackson's public papers by a technique akin to literary criticism, while Ward recovered the revealing "public image" of Old Hickory from a wide variety of contemporary sources. Previous scholars seem to have missed the important feature of Jacksonian America yielded by these novel techniques simply because it was not significantly related to any modern frame of reference.

[41] Unfortunately, two major contributions to Jacksonian historiography have appeared barely too late for discussion here: Bray Hammond, *Banks and Politics in America from the Revolution to the Civil War* (Princeton, 1957), and Marvin Meyers, *The Jacksonian Persuasion: Politics and Belief* (Stanford, 1957). Each author has brought added richness and authority to the important interpretation that he had previously adumbrated in the articles discussed above. Though I have not done full justice to these interpretations as they are now developed in book-length statements, I believe I have indicated fairly adequately the authors' essential positions, on the basis of their earlier articles.

The Dismissal of Lord Sackville

By Charles S. Campbell, Jr.

One of the dramatic incidents in American political and diplomatic history of the 1880's was the Cleveland administration's abrupt dismissal of the British minister, Lord Sackville (as Sir Lionel Sackville-West had just become), on the eve of the presidential election of 1888. American historians, quite properly, have blamed the Englishman for his unwise letter to "Murchison." They have also, less properly, defended the action of the United States government, or at least refrained from criticizing it. In his biography of President Cleveland, Allan Nevins says flatly: "In this [dismissing the envoy] Cleveland did right." [1] The whole tenor of Charles C. Tansill's long account is distinctly favorable to the President and Secretary of State Thomas F. Bayard and highly critical of Sackville and Great Britain.[2] Although Thomas A. Bailey refers to the "indecent haste" with which the imprudent Englishman was sent on his way, Samuel F. Bemis and Julius W. Pratt consign their accounts of the incident to footnotes critical only of the minister.[3] British historians as well appear loath to censure the United States. It is true that Lady Gwendolen Cecil asserts (not altogether cor-

[1] Allan Nevins, *Grover Cleveland: A Study in Courage* (New York, 1932), 430. Robert McN. McElroy, *Grover Cleveland, The Man and the Statesman: An Authorized Biography* (2 vols., New York, 1923), I, 296-97, seems to approve of the dismissal, as does Denis T. Lynch, *Grover Cleveland: A Man Four-Square* (New York, 1932), 366-67.

[2] Charles C. Tansill, *The Foreign Policy of Thomas F. Bayard, 1885-1897* (New York, 1940), Chap. XI.

[3] Thomas A. Bailey, *A Diplomatic History of the American People* (New York, 1955), 442; Samuel F. Bemis, *A Diplomatic History of the United States* (New York, 1955), 108; Julius W. Pratt, *A History of United States Foreign Policy* (New York, 1955), 355. Samuel E. Morison and Henry S. Commager, *The Growth of the American Republic* (2 vols., New York, 1950), II, 232, refer to Sackville's "incredible stupidity" but not to his dismissal. Ellis P. Oberholtzer, *A History of the United States since the Civil War* (5 vols., New York, 1937), V, 62-63, does mention "the requirements of a rampant struggle for party power," but explains the dismissal partly on the ground of "no action being in immediate contemplation by Lord Salisbury."

rectly) that "In November, its [the American] Government had dismissed Sir Lionel Sackville West . . . from Washington with the most summary brutality and without any consultation with his own Government, on the ground of his having interfered in American domestic politics." [4] But perhaps Lady Gwendolen felt obligated to vindicate her famous father. A present-day British writer, Harry C. Allen, unencumbered by such filial ties, instead of finding fault with the United States condemns Great Britain: "neither the original action of its representative, nor the subsequent actions of the British Government can be excused." [5]

The main developments leading to the dismissal are well known. In the presidential election of 1888, which promised to be close, the Irish-American vote could be decisive. President Cleveland, already suspected of British leanings because of his low-tariff propensity, had to handle the Irish with the utmost care. He was held suspect, too, because of the recent Bayard-Chamberlain treaty over the Canadian fisheries, negotiated with Joseph Chamberlain, known to all true sons of Erin as their arch-enemy. After a Republican Senate refused to ratify the treaty, the President attempted to boost his stock by recommending drastic retaliation against Canada for allegedly persecuting American fishermen; but he remained extremely vulnerable to charges of being pro-British.

The Republicans, eager to discredit Cleveland in the eyes of the Irish, found what they wanted in the inept conduct of Sackville. The minister had received a letter signed "Charles F. Murchison" (George Osgoodby), purportedly a naturalized Englishman, in which the writer expressed bewilderment over the retaliation policy, and asked for advice on whether British interests called for the election of Cleveland or Harrison.[6] Most injudiciously, Sir Lionel in effect came out for Cleveland. His reply to Murchison, which fell into the hands of the Republican party, was published in a west-coast newspaper on October 21, and throughout the country within the next two days. It created a sensation. Advice came to the White

[4] Gwendolen Cecil, *Life of Robert, Marquis of Salisbury* (4 vols., London, 1921-1932), IV, 116.

[5] Harry C. Allen, *Great Britain and the United States: A History of Anglo-American Relations* (New York, 1955), 522. Robert B. Mowat, *The Diplomatic Relations of Great Britain and the United States* (London, 1925), in an inaccurate account (pp. 240-45), does not censure the American government but blames Salisbury for not immediately recalling Sackville.

[6] Regarding the episode see Tansill, *Bayard*, Chap. XI.

House that only strong action would save the Irish vote.[7] And nine days after the first publication of the correspondence, Secretary Bayard sent the British minister his passport.[8]

The administration had moved with unusual haste in dismissing the minister, but it defended its action on three grounds. First, it explained, it had acted only after giving Great Britain ample opportunity to recall Lord Sackville. Second, Sackville did not make public retraction of interviews which cast aspersions upon the Senate and the President. Third, according to international law, a request for recall should meet with immediate compliance, with no right on the part of the envoy's government to demand prior explanation; and since Great Britain refused to recall Sackville, the United States was justified in dismissing him. The case thus presented may have impressed the administration, but it was not so strong as it appeared.

The first of these points — that Great Britain had been afforded ample opportunity to recall her minister — was expressed by President Cleveland in explaining the incident to Congress. In his annual message on December 3, the President, doubtless still embittered over Sackville's contribution to his recent downfall at the polls, justified the summary dismissal in the following terms:

> Having first fulfilled the just demands of international comity, by affording full opportunity for Her Majesty's Government to act in relief of the situation, I considered prolongation of discussion to be unwarranted

[7] See Papers of Grover Cleveland (Division of Manuscripts, Library of Congress), Vol. 221, Doc. 7295, for an important telegram from John Boyle O'Reilly, editor of the Boston *Pilot*, to the President, October 25, 1888: "British Minister's letter regarded as deep offense his withdrawal ought to be the consequence." After reading this telegram Cleveland wrote Bayard as follows: "I am very much concerned about this [Sackville] matter and almost feel that if this stupid thing does not greatly endanger or wreck our [election] prospects, it will only be because this wretched marplot is recalled. John Boyle O'Reilly of the Boston Pilot who is doing good work will falter or worse if this is not done and I am afraid it is too much just what the enemy wants to have him remain here." Cleveland to Bayard, October 26, 1888, Papers of Thomas F. Bayard (Division of Manuscripts, Library of Congress), Vol. 131, Doc. 26793.

[8] Cleveland's willingness to manipulate foreign affairs for domestic votes is apparent also from his handling of a bill introduced by Representative William L. Scott, restricting Chinese immigration. Although Bayard, who had recently negotiated an immigration treaty with China which was still unsigned, protested against the bill, Cleveland approved it on October 1, 1888. He could not have been heedless of advice just received that approval would give him the west coast in the coming election. The incident provides a neat parallel to the Sackville affair, in which Cleveland was angling for the Irish vote, concentrated on the east coast. For the Scott bill see Tansill, *Bayard*, Chap. V.

> and thereupon declined to further recognize the diplomatic character of the person, whose continuance in such function would destroy that mutual confidence which is essential to the good understanding of the two Governments, and was inconsistent with the welfare and self-respect of the Government of the United States.[9]

But did the United States, as Cleveland asserted unequivocally, afford "full opportunity" to Great Britain to recall her envoy? The only instructions regarding recall that reached Edward Phelps, the American minister in London, before Sackville's dismissal on October 30 were two telegrams from Secretary Bayard. The first, dated October 25, asked Phelps to "bring the matter [of Sackville's "interference . . . in our domestic issues"] to the attention of Lord Salisbury [the Prime Minister], and say that this government confidently relies upon disapproval action of British Minister." The second, sent the following day, stated that Sackville's "usefulness here has ended," and that "no time should be lost in letting Lord Salisbury understand the necessity of immediate action." [10] In neither telegram did Bayard explicitly demand recall, and as a matter of fact he specifically denied, about that same time, having asked for it at all. In a memorandum written on the night of October 26, after the second telegram — the last one prior to dismissal — had been dispatched, the Secretary made note of an unexpected visit from the agitated British minister. "He asked me if I had asked for his recall," Bayard noted, "and I told him I had not made the request." [11]

The second telegram called for "immediate," though undefined, action by Great Britain. It may be that Bayard, desiring recall but unwilling for some reason to express himself plainly, wanted Phelps to read between the lines and guess his intent. If so, his wish was granted, for Phelps interpreted the instructions in the two telegrams "by their substance and intent rather than by their literal phrase-

[9] *Papers Relating to the Foreign Relations of the United States, 1888* (Washington, 1889), Part 1, p. xii. Michael Herbert, the British chargé d'affaires at Washington, wrote to Lord Salisbury: "It is somewhat significant that the reading in the House of Representatives of the passages explaining the reasons for Lord Sackville's dismissal was received with laughter by the Democrats as well as by the Republicans." Herbert to Salisbury, December 14, 1888, Public Record Office (London), Foreign Office 5:2020. See also Bayard's report to Cleveland, October 29, 1888, *House Exec. Docs.*, 50 Cong., 2 Sess., No. 150, p. 7; and Bayard to Edward Phelps, October 31, 1888, Instructions, Great Britain, State Department Records (National Archives).

[10] Bayard to Phelps, October 25 and 26, 1888, Instructions, Great Britain, State Department Records.

[11] Bayard Memorandum, October 26, 1888, Bayard Papers, Vol. 131, Doc. 26787.

ology" [12] and bluntly asked Prime Minister Salisbury to recall Lord Sackville.[13] There is nothing, however, in the diplomatic correspondence suggesting that Phelps conveyed the feeling of urgency. Indeed, why should he have done so? Two short telegrams worded so uncertainly that their author could say he had not requested recall, and Phelps that he had had to interpret their meaning, could not be expected to convey a sense of crisis either to Phelps or through him to Salisbury.

Even had Bayard's instructions been altogether forthright, even had Phelps brought home to Salisbury the need for quick action, one would still have to entertain grave doubts as to the correctness of Cleveland's implication that Britain's procrastination justified the sudden American move. The plain fact is that unless London had acted with almost headlong speed it simply could not have recalled Sackville before Washington dismissed him. Phelps did not broach Washington's complaints to the British government until he spoke to Lord Salisbury late at night on Saturday, October 27, at Hatfield House, where the Prime Minister was spending the week-end.[14] Had there been a grave emergency, Salisbury could no doubt have consulted the Queen (who was in Scotland) and his colleagues that very night or early the next day, and have sent a telegram on Sunday recalling Sackville forthwith. But in the circumstances one can hardly blame him for not disrupting the week-end. Equally true it is that Salisbury could have acted on Monday the 29th. But that was the only regular working day on which it would have been possible to recall the minister before Bayard dismissed him on the 30th. A delay of one day, when no sense of urgency had been made known in London, does not justify the United States in putting the onus on Britain on the ground that, having afforded "full opportunity for Her Majesty's Government to act in relief of the situation," it could wait no longer for the unwelcome diplomat to be recalled.

A second defense of the administration's action centered about statements made by Sackville to reporters two days after the publication of the Murchison correspondence. "On the 23d of October," Bayard informed Phelps, "Lord Sackville held an interview with a

12 Phelps to Bayard, November 10, 1888, *ibid.*, Doc. 26935.

13 Salisbury to Sackville, October 27, 1888, Public Record Office, F. O. 5:2031.

14 Salisbury to the Queen, October 28, 1888, George E. Buckle (ed.), *The Letters of Queen Victoria, Third Series* (3 vols., New York, 1930-1932), I, 444.

reporter of the New York Tribune — which was published in that journal on the 24th — in which he distinctly impugned the sincerity of the President and the Senate and, in phrases of disrespect and derision, aspersed the integrity of both."[15] Sackville did give an interview to a *Tribune* reporter and, according to the newspaper, he did charge the President and Senate with insincerity. But both verbally and in a letter he several times insisted to Bayard that he had been misrepresented. In his written denial of the accuracy of the *Tribune's* report he told the Secretary: "I remark that my words are so turned as to impugn the action of the Executive. I beg to emphasize that I had no thought or intention of doing so."[16] Since it would have been absurd for the administration to defend the dismissal on the basis of a newspaper article, especially an article repudiated by Sackville — and still more absurd, an article in the New York *Tribune*, which was practically an official mouthpiece of the Republican party and which had steadily belabored Cleveland as pro-British — Bayard could contend only that Sackville had made no "disavowal or modification . . . through the channels in which his statements first found publicity."[17]

The Secretary was correct. Instead of replying through the press, Sackville had sent his explanation and denial to Secretary Bayard. But this was what Bayard himself had recommended. In the Secretary's papers is a memorandum he wrote regarding the Englishman's visit at the State Department on the morning of October 26, two days after the *Tribune* report of the interview. The following excerpt from this memorandum is especially revealing:

> I [Bayard] then said: "Sir; I wish to say to you that this Tribune interview, affects me even more than your letter [to Murchison]."
>
> He said he had been misrepresented.
>
> "Well," I said; "that is a thing I can understand. You will learn after

[15] Bayard to Phelps, October 31, 1888, Instructions, Great Britain, State Department Records. Sackville also gave interviews to the New York *Times* and the New York *Herald*, but Bayard did not complain about them. The *Tribune* attributed much more offensive language to Sackville than did the other papers.

[16] Sackville to Bayard, October 27, 1888, Bayard Papers, Vol. 131, Doc. 26806. See also Sackville's denials in Sackville to Salisbury, October 31, 1888, Public Record Office, F. O. 5:2020; and Herbert to Salisbury, November 9, 1888, enclosing a statement by Sackville dated November 8, 1888, *ibid.*

[17] Bayard's report to Cleveland, October 29, 1888, *House Exec. Docs.*, 50 Cong., 2 Sess., No. 150, p. 6. Sackville wrote Salisbury that "the assertion of Mr. Phelps, that such insinuations had been made by me, rests entirely upon the distorted statements of newspaper reporters under the influence of strong political partizanship." Sackville to Salisbury, December 13, 1888, Public Record Office, F. O. 5:2031.

a time the great insecurity of allowing these newspaper men to approach you unless you are going to see in advance what they will publish. You had better read again, Sir, the statements of that paper, which I consider highly exceptionable, and if you choose after reading that interview to address me a private note, stating what you can in your own exoneration, it will do you no harm."

He said he would do so.

He then remarked — "A private, personal note?"

I told him it was the first time I had the opportunity to tell him of the interview in The Tribune, and having drawn his attention to it [if? (word missing)] he had anything to say to show that he had been misrepresented by that paper I would receive it in a note.[18]

Having by his own admission made specific request for a private retraction, Secretary Bayard was not entitled to blame Lord Sackville for failing to make a public one. Three months later the Secretary shifted his ground somewhat and contended that the note did not completely repudiate the *Tribune* article.[19] But this new assertion, the accuracy of which is questionable, appears to have been an afterthought; certainly it formed no part of any recorded reason for deciding on dismissal. Although one can find fault with the way Sackville worded his note, there is no doubt that he believed it met Bayard's request.[20]

No more convincing was the administration's attempted justification of dismissal on the ground that, by well-recognized international law, Great Britain, when asked to recall her envoy, should have acted at once without requiring an explanation. In the first place, some of the argument's force is lost by the fact that Bayard, who made the argument, had denied having requested recall; but since the American minister did make the request, the point need not be pressed. More pertinent are the opinions of authorities on international law as to the legal obligations regarding dismissal and recall.

Writing to Lord Salisbury some weeks after the dismissal, Minister Phelps, himself a former professor of law at Yale University,

18 Bayard Memorandum, October 26, 1888, Bayard Papers, Vol. 131, Doc. 26791.

19 Bayard to Phelps, January 30, 1889, *House Exec. Docs.*, 50 Cong., 2 Sess., No. 150, p. 56. In this letter Bayard repeated his complaint that Sackville's denial "was contained in a personal note to me, as if the issue was personal in its nature between his lordship and myself."

20 Sackville to Salisbury, October 31, 1888, Public Record Office, F. O. 5:2020. See also Herbert to Salisbury, November 9, 1888, enclosing a statement by Sackville dated November 8, 1888, *ibid.*; and Sackville to Salisbury, December 13, 1888, *ibid.*, F. O. 5:2031.

explained that "the Government of the United States assumed that such request [for recall] would be sufficient for that purpose, whatever consideration the reasons for it might afterwards demand or receive." [21] But the Prime Minister refused to accept this explanation. He replied on December 24: "It is, of course, open to any Government, on its responsibility, suddenly to terminate its diplomatic relations with any other State, or with any particular Minister of any other State. But it has no claim to demand that the other State shall make itself the instrument of that proceeding, or concur in it, unless that State is satisfied by reasons, duly produced, of the justice of the grounds on which the demand is made." [22]

From the beginning Salisbury had consistently refused to recall without having an opportunity to judge the professed grievances. Regarding his talk with Phelps at Hatfield House the Prime Minister had written Sackville that "to recall on a formal request from the Government of the United States, made under circumstances of considerable publicity, was a course which implied the censure of two Governments, and, therefore, before acceding to any such request, Her Majesty's Government were bound, in justice to you, to satisfy themselves of the objectionable character of the language you had uttered." [23] Although Sackville himself asked to be recalled,[24] Salisbury stood firm: no recall without examination of the complaint.

Unwilling to leave office with the Prime Minister's statement of December 24 as the last word in the record, and perhaps uneasy about the part he himself had played, Secretary Bayard prepared a detailed defense of the administration's action, in the course of which he argued at length in support of Phelps's, and against Salisbury's, reading of international law. He based his argument in large part on "the high authority of Calvo," who had written in *Le Droit International*: "The government which asks for the recall may or may not, at its pleasure, communicate the reasons on which it bases

[21] Phelps to Salisbury, December 4, 1888, *House Exec. Docs.*, 50 Cong., 2 Sess., No. 150, p. 41. See also Phelps to Bayard, November 10, 1888, Bayard Papers, Vol. 131, Doc. 26936.

[22] Salisbury to Phelps, December 24, 1888, Public Record Office, F. O. 5:2031.

[23] Salisbury to Sackville, October 27, 1888, *ibid.*

[24] Sackville to Salisbury, October 28, 1888, Public Record Office, F. O. 5:2021: "To allay excitement, may I say I am recalled?" Salisbury's determination not to recall without explanation must have been reinforced by a telegram from Queen Victoria: "I trust Lord Sackville will *not* be allowed to say he is recalled." The Queen to Salisbury, October 30, 1888, Buckle (ed.), *Letters of Victoria, Third Series*, I, 444.

its request; but such an explanation can not be required. It is sufficient that the representative is no longer acceptable. In this case international courtesy prescribes his immediate recall; and if, notwithstanding, the other government does not comply with the request, the dismissal of the agent follows as a necessary consequence, it is effected by a simple notification and the sending of his passport." [25]

Calvo's statement of the law was unequivocal, and it appears at first sight to justify fully Bayard's position. But the statement has a serious weakness. It came straight from General Henry W. Halleck's treatise; and Halleck in turn had based his statement mainly on an opinion of Caleb Cushing, former Attorney General of the United States — an opinion which does not sustain Halleck's conclusion.[26] In invoking Calvo's "high authority" on this matter, Secretary Bayard would seem to have stood upon shaky ground.

[25] Bayard to Phelps, January 30, 1889, *House Exec. Docs.*, 50 Cong., 2 Sess., No. 150, p. 58. See Carlos Calvo, *Le Droit International, Théorique et Pratique* (4 vols., Paris, 1880-1881), I, 496.

[26] That Calvo simply reproduced Halleck is apparent from a comparison of his wording with Halleck's. Halleck wrote: "The government asking such a recall may, or may not, at its own option, state the reasons for the request; they cannot be required. It is sufficient that he is no longer acceptable. In such a case international courtesy would require his immediate recall. If, however, the request should not be complied with, his dismissal would follow as a matter of course. This is done by a simple notification and the offer of his passport." G. Sherston Baker (ed.), *Halleck's International Law* (2nd ed., 2 vols., London, 1878), I, 307. See also William E. Hall, *A Treatise on International Law* (5th ed., Oxford, 1904), 305; and Hannis Taylor, *A Treatise on International Public Law* (Chicago, 1901), 350-51. Calvo did not mention his indebtedness to Halleck. The opinion of Attorney General Cushing which Halleck cited had reference to an incident involving another British minister to the United States, John Crampton; Cushing advised that a diplomat who had enlisted soldiers in the United States for his government could be expelled or, after a demand for his recall, dismissed by the President. John B. Moore, *A Digest of International Law* (8 vols., Washington, 1906), IV, 535.

The position taken by the United States, before 1888, as regards recall had occasionally been similar to that taken by Bayard. Especially similar to Bayard's contention was a statement written by Secretary of State Hamilton Fish in 1871. With reference to the Russian minister to the United States, Catacazy, Fish wrote: "The official or authorized statement that a minister has made himself unacceptable, or even that he has ceased to be *persona grata*, to the government to which he is accredited, is sufficient to invoke the deference to a friendly power and the observance of the courtesy and the practice regulating the diplomatic intercourse of the powers of Christendom for the recall of an objectionable minister. The declaration of the authorized representative of the power to which an offending minister is accredited is all that can properly be asked, and all that a self-respecting power could give." Fish to Andrew G. Curtin, November 16, 1871, Instructions, Russia, State Department Records. Fish, however, gave Russia over five months to recall her envoy. For United States practice as regards recall and dismissal, see Moore, *Digest of International Law*, IV, 484-549.

Moreover, no other authority than Calvo (reproducing Halleck) is known to have written, before 1888, on the subject of a government's obligation, or lack of obligation, to recall an envoy on mere request. This doubtless explains why Salisbury cited not even one authority. There simply had not been enough controversies about recall to stimulate much speculation regarding the legal principles.

Bayard had every right, of course, to cite the Halleck-Calvo contention. But this solitary and dubious opinion strengthened his case very little, if at all, and certainly did not justify his assertion that Great Britain was obligated by international law to recall her envoy without explanation.

After Sackville's dramatic dismissal, legal experts began to examine the point debated by Bayard and Salisbury, and to make up their minds as to which statesman had been correct. Is a government obliged to recall an envoy on mere request, or not? All authorities on international law who discussed this question after 1888, it is believed, have pronounced a verdict in favor of the position taken by Lord Salisbury. A government is *not* obliged, they have agreed, so to act. Thus Hannis Taylor wrote that "There is no reasonable foundation for the position . . . that a state is in duty bound to recall an envoy who has become unacceptable to the government to which he is accredited simply upon its statement that he is so; and that such state has no right to ask for reasons to be assigned why such envoy has become unacceptable."[27] Edwin Maxey, writing shortly after Taylor, was in agreement: "A state is not under obligations to recall its diplomatic agent merely upon request from another state. It has a right to know what are the charges against him and whether or not those charges are supported by a reasonable amount of evidence. If, in its judgment, either of these is insufficient, it may rightly refuse to recall him."[28] Sir Ernest Satow was equally categorical: "any Government has the right of asking for the recall of a foreign diplomatic agent . . . and the Government which has appointed him has an equal right of declining to withdraw him."[29] And Amos S. Hershey expressed the general conclusion that "Lord Salisbury properly declined to act until he had received Lord Sackville's explanation."[30]

[27] Taylor, *International Public Law*, 350-51.
[28] Edwin Maxey, *International Law* (St. Louis, 1906), 111.
[29] Ernest M. Satow, *A Guide to Diplomatic Practice* (2 vols., London, 1917), I, 406.
[30] Amos S. Hershey, *The Essentials of International Public Law* (New York,

Granted, however, that the diplomat's government is not obliged to recall on mere request, is not the offended government entitled to dismiss? Authorities have always agreed, of course — whether writing before or after 1888 — that a government does have the right to dismiss; but the general opinion has been that the right should not be exercised except under serious circumstances. Those writers on international law who have discussed the particular question of Sackville's dismissal have contended that the United States did not have sufficient grounds for its hasty action. In contrast to the judgment of historians, they have therefore disapproved of the dismissal. One authority, Thomas J. Lawrence, wrote that "it did not become the country [the United States] . . . to hurry him [Sackville] out of its territory before his own government had an opportunity of examining the evidence against him." [31] According to Amos S. Hershey, "The British Minister was undoubtedly guilty of an indiscretion, but it cannot be seriously maintained that his offence was of such a character as to justify a dismissal or even a demand for recall." [32] And another expert, Charles G. Fenwick, stated: "Dismissal is an extreme measure. . . . The dismissal of the British minister . . . by the United States in 1888 . . . has met with general disapproval by writers on international law." [33]

If, then, the United States did not give Great Britain time to recall Lord Sackville before it dismissed him, if it was not justified in censuring the minister because he failed to retract publicly statements printed in the newspapers, and if Great Britain was not obliged by international law to recall her envoy on mere request, what can be said in defense of Secretary Bayard? That he acted under pressure from Cleveland is certain. The imminent election, the Irish pressure, the President's anxiety not to appear pro-British,

1912), 284; see also *ibid.*, 281-82. For similar statements to those of Hershey and the other authorities cited, see Charles G. Fenwick, *International Law* (New York, 1924), 369; Hall, *International Law*, 305; Thomas J. Lawrence, *The Principles of International Law* (4th ed., Boston, 1910), 304. John W. Foster, although apparently in agreement with the above writers, was less forthright. He wrote: "It is usually sufficient to allege that a minister is *persona non grata* to secure his recall, but this is not always the case." See his *The Practice of Diplomacy* (Boston, 1906), 180. In his *Diplomatic Memoirs* (2 vols., Boston, 1909), II, 265, Foster mentioned the "unseemly haste in the dismissal of Sackville-West," an opinion no doubt colored by Foster's strong Republican sympathies. In any event, Foster was not an expert on international law.

31 Lawrence, *Principles*, 306.

32 Hershey, *International Public Law*, 284.

33 Fenwick, *International Law*, 369, 371.

these matters have been mentioned. Doubtless they suffice to explain the dismissal as far as Cleveland was concerned. But the Secretary of State was not only a scrupulously honorable man but one with a sentimental attachment to Great Britain and a deep desire to improve Anglo-American relations.[34] One may wonder whether he would not have hesitated, notwithstanding the virtual insistence of President Cleveland for early action, had he known that the envoy's dismissal would anger London even to the point of delaying appointment of a successor until the Democrats left office in March, 1889.

In all probability the Secretary labored under the misapprehension that the British government would welcome dismissal as a means of relieving it from the disagreeable task of deciding about recall. It is undeniable that he was misinformed by Phelps. After the talk with Salisbury on October 27 at Hatfield House, Phelps telegraphed Bayard: "He [Salisbury] will only act on receipt of the language charged to have been used and after hearing from Minister [Sackville]. . . . He intimated that you can send him away for which there are precedents. Says a recall by British Government would terminate Minister's career. Not necessarily so if dismissed by the Government of the United States. . . . If you deem the case to require effectual action, I advise that you act upon the hint of Secretary of State for Foreign Affairs and terminate matters at once." [35] And on the 29th he reiterated the suggestion: "All the London papers this morning agree that British Minister must leave. You need not hesitate to act." [36] With these assurances at hand, Bayard must have prepared the note of dismissal on the 30th with an easy conscience.

But Minister Phelps's conscience, before many days passed, became troubled. Apparently alarmed by signs of resentment in Britain,[37] he confessed that: "I inferred . . . that the British Government would prefer that action should be taken, if at all, by the Government of the United States. It is proper, however, to add that this inference was based only upon the remark above quoted [Salisbury's statement "that a recall by his own Government would

[34] See Bayard's revealing letter to Phelps, November 19, 1888, Bayard Papers, Letter-Book No. 9.

[35] Phelps to Bayard, October 28, 1888, Bayard Papers, Vol. 131, Doc. 26813.

[36] Phelps to Bayard, telegram, October 29, 1888, *ibid.*, Doc. 26818.

[37] Phelps to Bayard, November 2, 1888, *ibid.*, Doc. 26887.

be ruinous to Lord Sackville, whereas such a result would not necessarily follow if he was dismissed"], and though I believe it to be correct, was not justified by any more direct expression of Lord Salisbury." [38]

The minister had good reason for concern. That his information had been incorrect and his recommendation bad soon became evident when the British government and the British press, far from approving Sackville's dismissal, denounced it roundly. Perhaps they would not have done so had the United States moved with calm deliberation, after giving Britain time to assess the evidence. Phelps, however, had advised Bayard to act "at once" and that he "need not hesitate." In a stiff letter Salisbury criticized the undignified haste with which the United States had moved. "There was nothing in Lord Sackville's conduct," he observed, "to justify so striking a departure from the circumspect and deliberate procedure by which in such cases it is the usage of friendly States to mark their consideration for each other." [39] As for the press, the London *Times*, though moderate in tone in comparison with some other journals, reflected the general verdict: "Lord Sackville was summarily and unceremoniously dismissed by the Government of President Cleveland, when . . . only half their complaint against him had been brought to the knowledge of the British Government, and that not the more important half." [40]

What a mountain of trouble may have been piled high upon Phelps's unwarranted inference! His culpability in advising — by his own admission, on inadequate evidence — that Lord Salisbury desired dismissal and that it could advantageously take place "at once," is evident. In a matter of such moment he would have done well to exercise a diplomat's customary sense of caution, especially since the instructions he received from Bayard were themselves not explicitly phrased. No one can say, of course, that had Phelps not misinformed Bayard, Sackville would have been permitted to re-

38 Phelps to Bayard, November 2, 1888, *House Exec. Docs.*, 50 Cong., 2 Sess., No. 150, p. 11.

39 Salisbury to Phelps, December 24, 1888, Public Record Office, F. O. 5:2031. Salisbury had already reprimanded Phelps for not giving him needed information: "Nothing [regarding the reasons for the requested recall] has been made known to me except what you did me the honour to communicate on Saturday evening [at Hatfield House]: and by that communication I was only made acquainted with the interpretation which Mr. Bayard put upon certain speeches made by Lord Sackville." Salisbury to Phelps, November 1, 1888, *ibid.*

40 London *Times*, November 7, 1888.

main at his post. Indeed, the probability is that political considerations would have dictated otherwise. But one may well wonder whether Bayard, if correctly informed as to London's attitude, would not have stood against the summary decision to dismiss the blundering diplomat, just possibly with sufficient resolution to have saved the country from a discreditable act.

Books and Reading on the Ohio Valley Frontier

By Howard H. Peckham

The general verdict about the dearth of books in frontier society is deceptively logical. We have assumed that in a rude society which had little time for reading there was no incentive to acquire books, and thus that the exceptional frontiersman who might wish to read found it difficult to obtain reading matter. Our attitude is reinforced, for example, by stories of young Abraham Lincoln eagerly borrowing books from his neighbors. But what we remember is the scarcity of books in the Lincoln cabin, rather than the fact that his Indiana neighbors had books to lend. Commonly, also, little distinction is drawn between frontier farms and frontier hamlets. It is probably true that log-cabin farmers on the edge of the wilderness, with occasional exceptions, owned few books. But the frontier was more than isolated farms; it was also small new communities. To look in on a few representative communities in the Ohio Valley is to discover an unexpected level of reading interest and availability of books.[1]

Not everyone who moved to the West went for the purpose of taking up land. There were many, perhaps more, who wanted to get started professionally, to be merchants or innkeepers, or to practice their trades. They were the town builders. They were physicians, lawyers, ministers, and teachers. They were tanners, tailors, printers, carpenters, blacksmiths, masons, glaziers, millers, bakers, shoemakers, coppersmiths, saddlers, hatters, tinners, silversmiths, brewers, surveyors, butchers, tobacconists, clockmakers, and practitioners of other forgotten crafts. They were pioneers just as much as the farmer on his isolated section. The great difference be-

[1] In slightly different form this paper was presented as the presidential address at the annual meeting of the American Association for State and Local History in 1956.

tween them is obvious: the nearness of neighbors and the spirit of community that encouraged joint enterprises.

Immediate results were town government, lodges, churches, a newspaper, social entertainments, schools, and then a library. Schools meant books, and in general town living meant time and houseroom for books. The farmer's isolated cabin, containing only the family Bible, an almanac, a book on the care of animals, perhaps a religious tract or an out-of-date newspaper, is part of the picture, but only a part. Frontier communities, at least in the Ohio Valley, offered a much wider range of reading matter.

The Ohio Valley is used as a convenient and perhaps typical region, particularly as it was in 1810. No one can deny the right of the people then living in that valley to be called pioneers. The northern parts of Ohio, Indiana, and Illinois were almost unbroken wildernesses, as was western Kentucky. The Indians were firmly planted in this area and although they had maintained a sullen kind of peace since General Anthony Wayne's Treaty of Greenville in 1795, they were far from being subdued; and at the moment the Shawnee Chief Tecumseh was fomenting a conspiracy to resist white advancement. A second war with Great Britain was only two years away. Yet the Ohio River was alive with flatboats and keelboats carrying the migrants, or "movers," into the new country. Kentucky and Ohio were now states of the Union; Indiana and Illinois were organized as territories.

Spotted along that irregular and convoluted line of the frontier some respectable towns were flourishing by 1810. Pittsburgh was actually an old town with a population of 4,800. Down river, Marietta counted perhaps 1,000 inhabitants, and Cincinnati, 2,300. Dayton contained 380, and Chillicothe, the capital, had about 800. Across the river in Kentucky, Lexington boasted of a college and a population of 2,800 whites. Louisville was younger, but it had almost 1,000 inhabitants, while Frankfort had 700. On the Indiana shore, Madison contained less than 100 persons, but Jeffersonville counted 215 and nearby Clarksville added another 100. Over on the Wabash, the old French town of Vincennes had a mixed population of about 700. In Illinois the largest town was Shawneetown on the Ohio with a population of more than 800, followed by Cahokia with 670 and Kaskaskia with 575. Across the Mississippi and just to the north was the booming cosmopolitan center of St.

Louis with 2,000 people. To complete the picture to the north, isolated Detroit, which had already observed its centennial and survived a disastrous fire, counted a population of 1,650.

These people were by no means existing in a bookless wilderness. A remarkable characteristic of the westward migration was the speed and intensity with which the pioneers sought to reproduce the culture they had left behind. They had brought with them not only clothes, some utensils, and pieces of furniture, but their crafts and tools, a few books, a familiarity with self-government, and a determination to provide for the education of their children. The log cabin was a temporary home, and in the towns some newcomers immediately built frame houses. Cincinnati, for instance, consisted of 171 houses in 1805, of which less than one third were log cabins.[2]

The immigrants into the Ohio Valley, in contrast to those who crossed the Great Plains later, traveled for the most part by boat from Pittsburgh, and some of them had reached that fork by boat. More household goods, including books, could be carried on boats than in covered wagons, and freight boats were available to carry extra chests and cartons and crates. The pioneers of the Ohio Valley who headed for the new towns by no means arrived empty-handed. Books were companions as frequently as dogs, and sometimes as frequently as the rifle or ax. Even the explorer sometimes found room in his pack or pocket for an octavo or duodecimo.

When Daniel Boone first penetrated Kentucky in 1769, with John Stuart, he lost his furs to the Indians and was warned to get out of the country. Boone was of no mind to depart, especially as his brother Squire had promised to join him later. The brothers happened to meet near the end of the year, and Squire brought with him a companion, Alexander Neeley. The four men made a winter camp near the junction of the Red River with the Kentucky in east central Kentucky. How did they pass the long winter nights in camp? By reading. Neeley had with him a copy of *Gulliver's Travels* which he read aloud to the others. Once they were roused by the Indians and drove them off. Neeley remarked that they had disposed of the Lulbegruds. This literary allusion pleased them so much that they named the little stream near them Lulbegrud Creek, by which it is still known today.[3]

[2] *The Cincinnati Directory* (Cinncincinnati, 1819), 29 n.

[3] John Bakeless, *Daniel Boone* (New York, 1939), 55. Even earlier, back in 1764, Captain Thomas Morris of the British Army was dispatched from Lake Erie up the

In the communities which later pioneers founded in the Ohio Valley, merchants were quick to recognize that their success depended on procuring merchandise which their customers wanted. Books were one of the items in demand, and most of the general stores stocked them, along with dry goods, sugar, tea, coffee, chinaware, and medicines. Although schools provided the only market for textbooks, religious works, self-help manuals, literature and history books were all salable in the stores. In 1788 no less than six merchants in Lexington, which then had a population of only 700, advertised books for sale in the *Kentucky Gazette*.[4] For the most part they were Bibles and testaments, confessions of faith and catechisms, hymnbooks and sermons, grammars, spellers, and primers. But John Duncan showed broader interests. Besides his dry goods and groceries, he stocked "books of divinity, law and physic; several entertaining histories; some English and Latin school books; a variety of books for the instruction and entertainment of children; American magazines and museums of the latest dates." Three years later he was advertising the Greek and Roman classics. In Cincinnati in 1796 — then a town of some 500 inhabitants — both William Maxwell, the printer of the *Centinel of the North-West Territory*, and David Ziegler's dry goods store were advertising books.[5]

Philadelphia printers and importers seem to have been the chief source of supply of books for the Ohio Valley. The road from Philadelphia to Pittsburgh was well traveled by carters, and the Ohio River flowed through the heart of the new settlements. The New Englanders who migrated at the behest of the Ohio Company, however, naturally favored goods from Boston.

But a substantial part of the reading matter available to the townsmen was printed locally. New communities attracted printers, and the printer-editor of the town newspaper was also a publisher. He issued pamphlets for the various religious denominations, proceedings of lodges, state laws — virtually anything for which he

Maumee River to test the friendship of the Ottawa and Miami Indians after the collapse of Pontiac's uprising the year before. Captain Morris did not find the Indians exactly glad to see him, but at the rapids an Ottawa chief presented him with some melons and sold him a volume of Shakespeare! Journal of Thomas Morris, Gage Papers (William L. Clements Library, University of Michigan).

[4] Lexington *Kentucky Gazette*, July to December, 1788, *passim.*

[5] *Centinel of the North-West Territory* (Cincinnati), March 28, 1796. An auction in Cincinnati in 1794 featured some books. *Ibid.*, June 24, 1794.

could get paid. He also risked his meager capital on a few titles he thought he could sell. His office was another bookstore where reading matter could be purchased. Pittsburgh printers had published probably 175 books alone by 1815, not counting broadsides. Up to the same date, Kentucky's printers issued 647 titles of all kinds. Ohio printers put out 590 items through 1820. Indiana printers produced 601 books, pamphlets, and broadsides through 1835. Illinois printers published 474 non-official titles through 1840.[6]

There were thus three sources of supply for books, all operating simultaneously. The steady flow of migrants brought books with them. The early merchants kept importing books from the eastern seaboard for sale. And the Ohio Valley printers were publishing locally. Distribution into the back country may have been faulty and meager, but books in the little towns were not merely adequate but probably plentiful. When William Blane reached St. Louis in 1822, he found "several gentlemen" who "had not only read all the first Waverley novels, but even the last one, the *Fortunes of Nigel*, which had only been published a short time before I left England."[7]

Yet these fountainheads do not tell the whole story. They say nothing of reading habits or circulation. Information on these subjects may be found in the records of numerous libraries founded in the small towns of the frontier. By the time the War of 1812 began, eleven towns of Kentucky and ten in Ohio had libraries.[8] Indiana had at least two. In addition, each of the half-dozen colleges in the region possessed a library, but these are excluded from this survey.

Settlement of Kentucky had begun in 1775, although it fell off and was almost wiped out during the Revolution. When the westward surge began again, Lexington, which had been founded in 1779, grew rapidly. By 1795 it had a population of about 1,000, a

[6] Douglas C. McMurtrie and Albert H. Allen, *Check List of Kentucky Imprints, 1787-1810* (Louisville, 1939), and *Check List of Kentucky Imprints, 1811-1820* (Louisville, 1939); John W. Townsend, *Supplementary Check List of Kentucky Imprints* (Louisville, 1942); *A Check List of Ohio Imprints, 1796-1820* (Columbus, 1941); Cecil K. Byrd and Howard H. Peckham, *A Bibliography of Indiana Imprints, 1804-1853* (Indianapolis, 1955). For Pittsburgh imprints I am indebted to the Carnegie Library of Pittsburgh for a typed list of local imprints, and to Ernest J. Wessen of Mansfield, Ohio, for a much longer manuscript catalogue of Pittsburgh imprints.

[7] John F. McDermott, "Private Libraries in Frontier St. Louis," Bibliographical Society of America, *Papers* (New York), LI (1st quarter, 1957), 19.

[8] William H. Venable, *Beginnings of Literary Culture in the Ohio Valley* (Cincinnati, 1891), 129-31, quoting Reuben T. Durrett; Beverley W. Bond, *Civilization of the Old Northwest* (New York, 1934), 432.

college, and several stores selling books. In this year a subscription library was formed. A committee raised the staggering total of $500 for the purchase of books in Philadelphia. Five years later the library contained 750 volumes. In that year, 1800, subscription libraries were formed also in Georgetown and Danville, the population of the former amounting to 225 and of the latter only 170. Other library groups were incorporated at Lancaster in 1804, Paris in 1808, New Castle, 1809, Shelbyville and Winchester, 1810, Washington, 1811, and Versailles and Frankfort in 1812. These towns ranged in size from 100 to 800.[9]

Across the river in Ohio, where settlement began in 1787, the New England immigrants not only brought books with them but quickly turned their attention to schools, newspapers, and libraries. The first library was formed in Belpré, just north of Marietta, in 1796. This was not a town, but a rural township and the organizers were farmers. Colonel Israel Putnam had brought part of his father's library to the new country and with his neighbors established "The Belpré Farmers Library," with shares of stock at $10 each. A librarian was appointed and the books were kept at his house. In 1815 the library was dissolved, and the books divided among the shareholders.[10]

One of the shareholders, Amos Dunham, recalled his use of the library at the turn of the century. "The long winter evenings were rather tedious, and in order to make them pass more smoothly, by great exertion I purchased a share in the Belpré library, 6 miles distant. From this I promised myself much entertainment, but another obstacle presented itself — I had no candles; however, the woods afforded plenty of pine knots — with these I made torches by which I could read, though I nearly spoiled my eyes. Many a night have I passed in this manner till 12 or 1 o'clock reading to my wife, while she was hatchelling, carding or spinning." [11]

When the town of Cincinnati was thirteen years old, in 1802, but only six weeks after it received a charter, some of its 800 citizens met at Yeatman's Tavern to promote a public library. Twenty-five subscribers purchased thirty-four shares of stock at $10, some of them taking two shares. Although it is known that books were

[9] Venable, *Beginnings of Literary Culture in the Ohio Valley*, 129-31.

[10] Cornelius E. Dickinson, *A History of Belpré, Washington County, Ohio* (Parkersburg, W. Va., 1920), 174-76.

[11] Henry Howe, *Historical Collections of Ohio* (Cincinnati, 1847), 349.

purchased with the initial $340, little else is known about the operations or duration of the library.[12] A new one was organized in 1813.

One of the more unusual ventures resulted from a meeting in 1803 of the farmers of Ames Township, west of Marietta. They had gathered to discuss roads, but ended with plans for a library similar to that of their neighbors in Belpré. Lacking cash for the enterprise, however, they agreed to trap and hunt during the winter for furs to be carried to Boston the following spring by Samuel Brown. The planners were still enthusiastic in February, 1804, when they met again to organize formally and adopt regulations. Their preamble was formidable: "Considering the many beneficial effects which social libraries are calculated to produce in societies where they are established both as a source of rational entertainment and instruction; we, the subscribers wishing to participate in these blessings agree to form ourselves into a society for this purpose under the title of the Western Library Association in the Town of Ames." Shares were offered for sale at $2.50, and each member was to be assessed 25 cents annually to provide more books. While Samuel Brown went east with the fur assets of the association, some money was raised locally. Twenty-four persons took shares the first year, a few buying more than one share. In Boston, Brown raised $70 from the sale of furs and invested it in fifty-one books, chosen with the help of Manasseh Cutler, one of the Ohio Company founders, and the Reverend Thaddeus Harris. He returned to Ohio in November of 1804, and the new library was in business. Owing to its origin it became known as the Coonskin Library, and many of the books survive. Ephraim Cutler, son of Manasseh Cutler, was named the first librarian. A bookcase was purchased in 1807. The library continued to operate until 1861, when the directors sold it off.[13]

The fourth Ohio library was established at Dayton in 1805, when the town was ten years old and contained a population of about 100. Known as "The Social Library Society of Dayton" the subscribers or proprietors purchased shares at $3.00 each. The books were kept at the post office. The society had one peculiar rule, that all books must be returned four times a year: the first Monday

12 James McBride, *Pioneer Biography* (2 vols., Cincinnati, 1869-1871), I, 43, 104.

13 Sarah J. Cutler, "The Coonskin Library," *Ohio Archaeological and Historical Quarterly* (Columbus), XXVI (January, 1917), 58-77.

in January, April, July, and October. The library continued in existence until 1835, when it was dispersed at auction.[14]

Five other libraries in Ohio, founded at New Town, Wooster, Poland, Zanesville, and Lebanon, followed a similar pattern. The plan adopted at Cleveland, however, was different, the charter members forming a reading circle library to pass around the books they had brought with them. This plan, drawn up in 1811, was appropriate for the size of the town, which then consisted of two taverns, two stores, one school, and a population of 64, of whom 16 (25 per cent) joined in the organization of the library.[15]

The two libraries in Indiana were at Vincennes and Madison. The Vincennes Library was incorporated by the territorial legislature in 1806 and organized with local contributions of 210 books. The town was then seventy-five years old, but it had been almost entirely French until 1788. Now it was the capital of Indiana Territory and had a population of 700. A lottery for the benefit of the library was authorized in 1810, but apparently was not held. The library seems to have lapsed, for the legislature reaffirmed the incorporation in 1813. Thereafter it flourished, and one of Governor William Henry Harrison's sons was librarian for a number of years before his death in 1830, and the books were kept at the Harrison mansion. The library went out of existence in 1860 and the surviving books were turned over to Vincennes University.[16]

Madison was only six years old and had just been platted when a group of easterners met at an inn in 1811 under the leadership of Alexander Meek, an attorney, and formed the Madison Society Library. Twenty-four subscribers, who must have included every man in town, paid in $5.00 each. The books purchased were kept first at the inn, and later were moved into a store building. After the Civil War it became a county library and then merged into the Madison Public Library.[17]

Illinois did not have a library organization until 1819, when two were established — one at Albion and the other at Edwardsville.[18]

[14] "Constitution of the Social Library Society of Dayton," reproduced in appendix to Dayton Public Library and Museum, *Sixty-first and Sixty-second Annual Reports* (Dayton, 1922).

[15] Harlan Hatcher, *Lake Erie* (Indianapolis, 1945), 206.

[16] Francis S. Philbrick (ed.), *The Laws of Indiana Territory, 1801-1809* (Indianapolis, 1931), 202, 547; Venable, *Beginnings of Literary Culture in Ohio Valley*, 263-64.

[17] *Indiana: A Guide to the Hoosier State* (New York, 1941), 380.

[18] Edgar L. Dukes, *Yester-years in Edwards County, Illinois* (Albion, 1946), 117-18;

However, the early Catholic priests who had founded a mission post at Cahokia brought books with them and imported more. As early as 1724 a library of 90 volumes, primarily religious, existed there, although the circulation may have been small in view of the percentage of illiteracy among the French habitants. At Kaskaskia, Father Gibault began assembling a library upon his arrival in 1769. By the time of his death in 1802 it amounted to 243 volumes, which were afterwards sold.[19]

These are examples of a movement that became contagious throughout the Ohio Valley. After the War of 1812, libraries spread like a rash; the number in Ohio alone grew to 160 by 1840. The interesting aspect of the development is how early in the life of a community libraries were thought of and considered necessary.

These glimpses of the quantity of books available to pioneer settlers in the Ohio Valley arouse curiosity as to the kind of books they were reading. First, the locally produced books may be classified. An attempt has been made to segregate from the many books printed in each of the Ohio Valley states those which represent risk publications on the part of the printer. In such ventures the printers supply us with a guide to public taste and interest of the time, for it goes without saying that they would consider most carefully what was likely to sell in their communities before committing any time or money in production. They might issue any kind of book or pamphlet for which they were paid, by an individual, a church, lodge, or other organization, or a branch of the government — this is job printing — but their success as publishers depended on how accurately they gauged what the new settlers wanted to read.

In the absence of a regional bibliography, western Pennsylvania as a whole cannot be considered, but only Pittsburgh. In the period from 1786, when the first press was brought to Pittsburgh, to 1815, approximately 160 books were issued at the risk of the printers. Fifty-two, or almost one third, were almanacs. Thirty-four, or about one fifth, were religious works — interpretative, argumentative, and inspirational, including a Bible in 1815. Twenty-eight

W. T. Norton, "Early Libraries in Illinois," *Journal of the Illinois State Historical Society* (Springfield), VI (July, 1913), 246-51 (Courtesy of Dorothy G. Bailey, Illinois State Library).

[19] John F. McDermott, "The Library of Father Gibault," *Mid-America* (Chicago), XVII (October, 1935), 273-75.

of the books were instructional. They included twelve textbooks for children, four descriptive books of travel, three gazetteers, and nine editions of a navigation guide for the Ohio River compiled by Zadok Cramer, himself one of the principal printers. Obviously, Cramer had written a best seller. As belles-lettres there should be included five novels, one of them — Goldsmith's *Vicar of Wakefield* — published twice; six books of poetry; eight biographies; and five volumes of essays. Political disquisitions account for ten more books.

Books on religion or affording practical information should not surprise us as pre-eminent choices, from what we know of the early settler. Grouped together, however, they form an amusing juxtaposition under what might be considered as technology: how to get along in this world, and how to get along in (or at least make sure of) the next. More revealing, perhaps, is the fact that the local printers thought they could sell so many novels, essays, and poetry. Some settlers were reading for pleasure.

Following the Ohio River downstream to the second area of settlement west of the Alleghenies, in Kentucky by 1815 about 179 books had been published for general sale. The largest number were religious in nature, amounting to fifty-three or 30 per cent, exceeding the interest in Pittsburgh. With them might be classified nine books of reform: anti-slavery or anti-corruption (in government). Almanacs and gazetteers, a kind of bread-and-butter publication for the early printer, totaled forty-three, or 24 per cent. There were thirty-four instructional titles — textbooks, self-help manuals, and general educational works. For literature, there were twelve books of poetry (twice as many as in Pittsburgh), one local autobiography, a novel, a play, and a book of essays — sixteen all told. A dozen historical items, half a dozen hymnbooks, two philosophical works, and the story of an Indian captive complete the roster.

If the religious books reflect the general concern of the time and the instructional books are to be expected on the frontier, the strong showing of literature and history cannot be accounted for on any such grounds. They are evidence of cultural interests, outside religion and without practical application.

In examining the field of publishing within Ohio the terminal date has been pushed forward to 1820, since printing did not begin until 1796, approximately ten years after it started in western

Pennsylvania and Kentucky. About 142 books were issued at the printers' risk in this period. Almanacs and gazetteers proved most popular, with fifty-four published, or 38 per cent. Religion, especially its controversial aspects, accounted for twenty-three titles. The category of instruction included twenty-five items. Music books numbered thirteen, all of them hymnals except two that taught singing. The printers of Ohio had much less confidence in poetry than those of Kentucky, as they published only three books against Kentucky's twelve. Fiction and biography ran almost the same: three and two, making a total of eight in general literature. However, in Ohio seven sensational books were published as against Kentucky's single Indian thriller. Whether this means violence and scandal were more prevalent on the north side of the Ohio, or so rare as to arouse more public interest, I am not prepared to say. These Ohio books dealt with confessions of criminals and victims of capture. History books made a showing with seven titles.

Printing was begun in Vincennes, Indiana, in 1804 by a man trained at Lexington, Kentucky. For ten years he had no competition in Indiana and he stuck to his newspaper and job printing. The first publishing venture was made in 1818, with a biography of Napoleon. And if we carry the investigation through 1835, only about sixty-five published works are found. Either the Indiana printers found plenty of job printing, or they were afraid to risk their money in speculative publishing.

There was one unusual development in the history of Indiana publishing that prevents it from being considered a typical frontier state. Robert Owen's New Harmony community began operating in 1825, and it had a press that started publishing immediately and prolifically. As one consequence, we have to count eighteen scientific titles issued before 1836 in the fields of conchology, mineralogy, entomology, and geology. Although it is true that the press was somewhat subsidized, its products were advertised and sold to the public. These eighteen titles happen to equal the eighteen religious pamphlets and books published.

Instructional works issued by Indiana printers amounted to ten, and only five almanacs or gazetteers could be identified in this period. Besides the biography of Napoleon, three books of poetry, one novel, and an edition of Aesop's fables made up the section on belles-lettres. Two criminal confessions appeared. One book of

English history and one book of dances contrast with the several historical and musical books issued in Ohio and Kentucky.

Printing in Illinois began in 1814 at Kaskaskia, and speculative publishing lagged eight years behind. The state cannot be regarded as typical of the region, since it was the last to introduce printing and last to fill up with American settlers, who by that time had many centers in the Ohio Valley, as well as St. Louis, where books could not only be purchased but produced. If we follow printing in Illinois through 1840, only a meager thirty-two books appear to have been published. Almanacs and gazetteers, twelve in number, led the way. They contained local information and would be bought from the nearest source. Four sermons and a Mormon journal made up the religious offerings. No fiction at all was published, but three books of bad poetry and two biographical sketches of local figures were issued. Four sensational items were undoubtedly more popular: a trial, a confession, the story of the Alton riots, and an account of some Mormon murders. Three legal works appeared, and two political speeches — one by young A. Lincoln.

In summary, then, the printer-publishers of the Ohio Valley issued a grand total of 567 books in the pioneer period. Almanacs and gazetteers accounted for 29 per cent of the total, while religious works made up 23 per cent of the output. In third place were the instructional books, amounting to 17 per cent. Literary works were a poor fourth, accounting for 12 per cent. The remaining 19 per cent of production was scattered principally among history, music, science (almost all from Indiana), and sensational stories.

To check on how accurately the printers reflected public taste, their publications should be compared with what the pioneers themselves bought for their subscription libraries. Some of these first libraries printed lists, or catalogues, of their holdings very early, either as broadsides or as pamphlets. Such catalogues exist for the libraries already mentioned at Lexington, Kentucky, and Ames and Cincinnati in Ohio. There is also one for the State Library in Columbus, founded in 1817, and for the library at Edwardsville, Illinois, founded in 1819.[20] The total of all books listed in the five

[20] *Catalogue of Books Belonging to the Lexington Library* (Lexington, 1804). For the Ames library see analysis in Cutler, "The Coonskin Library," *Ohio Archaeological and Historical Quarterly*, XXVI (January, 1917), 58-77. Among the extant contemporary lists are: *A Systematic Catalogue of Books Belonging to the Circulating Library Society of Cincinnati* (Cincinnati, 1816); *Catalogue of Books in the State*

libraries in these early years amounts to 3,082. Since many of them represent multiple-volume works, the total number of titles is probably not more than 2,000.

Subject categories indicate that 30 per cent of the books — the largest group — were literary. Next, 15 per cent were legal and political works, owing to the preponderance of law books in the Ohio State Library. Thirteen per cent were history, only 7 per cent religious and reform titles, 6 per cent books of travel, and 3 per cent scientific. These groups total 74 per cent. The remaining 26 per cent were encyclopedias and periodicals in the fields of philosophy, economics, and a few scattered topics. We know also that the Vincennes Library was strong in literature, law, history, science, and philosophy, but we have no figures.

These library holdings present some interesting contrasts with local publishing. Sensational books are not found, and few instructional works or almanacs. The reasons are obvious: the first category was not quite respectable, and instructional books were either for children or they were manuals one would want to own personally for study or quick reference; almanacs were likewise of personal and recurrent use, and once out of date were considered useless. Interestingly enough, the library organizers seem to have purchased few books of religious controversy. Perhaps they could not agree on what should be included and ended by excluding most of them. Perhaps they found that the local presses provided enough of this type of reading matter.

On the positive side, when the people got together to form libraries, their main interest was in literature — novels, plays, poems, and essays. Their literary appetite was something that local printers did not come close to satisfying, and scholars who have studied only state imprints have missed this interest among the pioneers. Nor were they reading trash. The favorite authors were Goldsmith and Pope, Shakespeare, Sterne and Swift, Burns and Scott, Joel Barlow, Maria Edgeworth, and Jane Porter. These are respectable choices, the ladies perhaps excepted. Byron was the first of the romantic poets to become a rage. Lord Byron himself confided to his diary on December 5, 1813: "Dallas' nephew (son to the American attorney general) is arrived in this country, and tells Dallas that my

Library (Columbus, 1823); *A Complete Catalogue of All the Books . . . Edwardsville Library* (Edwardsville, 1819).

rhymes are very popular in the United States. These are the first tidings that have ever sounded like *Fame* to my ears — to be redde on the banks of the Ohio." [21]

Reasons for the failure of the Ohio Valley printers to publish more literary works can only be surmised. They may never have realized the market was there. Copyright obligations did not deter them, for the pirating of popular books continued until after the middle of the century. Possibly the eastern printers were flooding the market with American editions of English best sellers which the frontier settlers brought with them or which formed the stock of the early book merchants in the Ohio Valley.

The early library organizers, though they sought mainly for literary works, betrayed a noticeable weakness for books of travel and description. We might think that in opening new country themselves they would have fulfilled their dreams and satisfied their urge for learning about distant places. We consider that books of travel appeal more to stay-at-homes than to travelers. Yet they seemed eager to read about Lewis and Clark, Zebulon Pike, and Jonathan Carver, as well as about the Holy Land, Europe, and Asia. Possibly they gloried in making comparisons with their own vistas.

Finally, it might be pointed out that these early libraries do not differ markedly from our public libraries today. The American Library Association recommends that 30 per cent of a public library's holdings be in adult fiction, the same percentage that these first libraries devoted to fiction, biography, and essays. The other recommendations are 45 per cent non-fiction and 25 per cent children's books — the last a category almost unknown to the early settlers. An American Library Association buying guide for small libraries suggests scientific titles amounting to 3 per cent and history books aggregating 9 per cent, compared to 3 per cent and 13 per cent in the pioneer institutions.[22]

We shall never know how many books the early settlers of the Ohio Valley brought with them. Storekeepers, we have seen, imported books along with other commodities. Printers manufactured books. Yet all these sources were not sufficient to meet the demand. The printed word cast its spell over the frontier as it had over the

[21] Rowland E. Prothero (ed.), *Letters and Journals of Lord Byron* (6 vols., London, 1922), II, 360. See also Venable, *Beginnings of Literary Culture in Ohio Valley*, 271.

[22] *Post-War Standards for Public Libraries* (Chicago, 1943); Orrilla T. Blackshear, *Buying List for Small Libraries* (Chicago, 1954).

old seaboard colonies and the home country. Interest in reading had little to do with the size or age of a community. It was manifest in towns of less than 100 population and in those of more than 1,000. It showed itself in subscription libraries organized from one to fifteen years after the founding of a town. In short, people who had formed the habit of reading did not let frontier conditions deprive them of this pleasure. Books were the solace, the inspiration, the entertainment, and the teacher of the pioneer as they had been of their ancestors. Books seemed to rank with utensils and weapons as necessary accompaniments of the westward movement.

The reader who knows well the story of young Abe Lincoln in Indiana trudging weary miles in 1825 to borrow books should remember also Amos Dunham in the Ohio wilderness, twenty-five years earlier, joining a library association and borrowing books when he could not afford candles.

Business Disunity and the Progressive Movement, 1901-1914

By Robert H. Wiebe

Histories of post-Civil War America, describing the rise of an industrialized society, stress businessmen's common characteristics at the expense of their differences and seldom uncover any appreciable diversity in their response to broad economic and political issues. In the standard interpretations, the businessmen appear as a united force, determined to protect group interests against all assaults. The only common exception to this treatment is to point out the antagonism between small business and big business, although even here historians tend to reunite many of these businessmen in a community of interests. In some studies the assumption of a single business outlook seems to have served primarily as a convenience to the writer. When entrepreneurs act as a group, furnishing counterpoint for other themes, their unity helps to produce a sharper, more effective narrative.[1] In some other histories a homogeneous community develops naturally from the particular selection of business representatives — either a few prominent and verbal entrepreneurs or certain politicians, lawyers, and theorists — who presumably speak for the mass of less articulate businessmen.[2]

Editor's Note: — This article received honorable mention in the competition for the 1957 Pelzer Award.

[1] Examples dealing with the Progressive period are George E. Mowry, *Theodore Roosevelt and the Progressive Movement* (Madison, 1946), Chap. I; Russel B. Nye, *Midwestern Progressive Politics: A Historical Study of Its Origins and Development, 1870-1950* (East Lansing, 1951), 258-59. Among the survey treatments in which business unity is assumed are Charles A. and Mary R. Beard, *The Rise of American Civilization* (2 vols., New York, 1927), II, Chaps. XX, XXV, XXVII, and XXIX; Harry J. Carman and Harold C. Syrett, *A History of the American People* (2 vols., New York, 1952), II, Chaps. IV, XI, XII, and XIV.

[2] See Chester McA. Destler, "Opposition of American Businessmen to Social Control during the 'Gilded Age'," *Mississippi Valley Historical Review* (Cedar Rapids), XXXIX (March, 1953), 641-72; Gordon Harrison, *Road to the Right: The Tradition and Hope of American Conservatism* (New York, 1954); Edward C. Kirkland, *Dream and Thought in the Business Community, 1860-1900* (Ithaca, 1956); James W. Prothro, *The Dollar Decade: Business Ideas in the 1920's* (Baton Rouge, 1954).

However valid this analysis may be for other periods of American history, an examination of businessmen's reactions to the Progressive movement indicates that far from forming a cohesive group they differed widely over the proper solution to America's problems and expended a large portion of their energies in internal conflicts.

The thirteen years between Theodore Roosevelt's ascent to the presidency and the outbreak of a general European war contained an exceptional number of public challenges to the business community's accustomed way of life.[3] Flanked by the relative complacency of the Gilded Age and the 1920's, the Progressive era stood as a period of concentrated reform. Campaigns to make government more responsive to the voters' wishes, to allow the underprivileged a larger share of the nation's benefits, and to regulate the economic system so that it would better serve the public interest were all parts of a general movement, heavy with the accumulation of past discontent, which matured in the Progressives' reform program of the early twentieth century. To integrate the several parts of this program required guidance from the federal government, now more alert to cries for change than it had been in the nineteenth century. Thus the widespread desire for reform gained respectability and momentum during the Roosevelt administrations, grew restive in the interlude of William Howard Taft's presidency, and finally culminated in Woodrow Wilson's New Freedom.

The common denominator for this mixture of campaigns was an attempt to create a more equitable balance of privilege and power in American society. Because the roots for so many Progressive problems lay in the previous half-century's rapid industrialization, businessmen, who had acted as the overseers of this economic revolution, found their interests involved or their behavior attacked in virtually all aspects of the reform process. No area caused them deeper concern or elicited a more complicated response than the attempts to supervise America's economic system. This issue raised not only the delicate problem of governmental control but also intricate questions of readjusting privilege among the entrepreneurs themselves. Three separate parts of this reform goal — the movement for banking and currency reorganization, the campaign for

[3] More accurately, the Progressive period should also include the last two years of Woodrow Wilson's first administration, but the material treated in this article adapts itself to the shorter time-span. The best survey of the full Progressive movement is Harold U. Faulkner, *The Quest for Social Justice* (New York, 1931).

railroad rate regulation, and the control of trusts—illustrate how the business community split into hostile factions over problems which threatened a redistribution of power among its members.

At the turn of the century, businessmen were operating within a banking and currency framework suited to the needs of a departed age. The national banking laws of 1863, 1864, and 1865 had created a system which was admirable for its uniformity at the time it passed but which became dangerously decentralized and inflexible as the economy grew increasingly national and complex.[4] These measures had tied the issuance of currency to a bank's holdings of government bonds, a regulation which made the banking structure unrelated to seasonal or exceptional fluctuations in the demand for credit. Combined with the absence of any established method of over-all co-ordination, this regulation meant that banks could neither expand their note issue to alleviate periodic currency and credit stringencies nor contract at times of overexpansion. While this arrangement was especially vulnerable to panics, it also failed annually to meet the economy's normal credit requirements. Trussed in an archaic financial system, the bankers themselves led the search for changes which would offer them greater freedom and security.

In 1902, Representative Charles N. Fowler, an outspoken Republican from New Jersey, combined two ideas then current among financiers into the first important reform program of the Progressive era. The heart of his plan was the replacement of the government-bond currency with one based upon the amount of a bank's liquid assets, an index to varying credit needs. Then, in an effort to provide more uniformity in interest rates, he advocated full legalization of branch banking, which had been prohibited by the earlier legislation.[5] Urban bankers, especially those from the Midwest, endorsed the proposal, seeing in it possibilities for flexibility and expansion.[6] Midwestern country bankers, however, formed a solid phalanx of opposition. To these smaller entrepreneurs, branch banking meant an annihilating invasion of their domains from the large

[4] For background information, see Paul Studenski and Herman E. Krooss, *Financial History of the United States* (New York, 1952), 154-55, 178-80.

[5] "Address of Hon. Charles N. Fowler of New Jersey," *Proceedings of the American Bankers' Association* (1902), 99-113. For earlier references to these ideas, see *Proceedings of the American Bankers' Association* (1901), 149-56; *Iron Age* (New York), LXVIII, No. 24 (December 12, 1901), 30.

[6] See *Proceedings of the American Bankers' Association* (1902), 132-34, 144, 175-76; (1906), 142-55, 165-99; (1907), 109-13. See also F. Cyril James, *The Growth of Chicago Banks* (2 vols., New York, 1938), II, 747.

urban centers, and the assets scheme, which did not recognize rural credits, promised a continuing city monopoly in currency. During the next few years, the country bankers, headed by Andrew J. Frame, a tireless campaigner from Waukesha, Wisconsin, remained hostile to each variation of the proposal suggested by their city colleagues. They preferred instead an emergency currency which the federal government would authorize local clearing houses to issue in times of crisis and which the government would then retire with a steeply graduated tax as conditions returned to normal.[7] While these forces battled in public, the New York money powers moved more cautiously. They frowned upon the Fowler plan as too revolutionary, with no safeguards for their dominant role in the nation's finances, and, although they gave a measure of backing to a later assets bill, they gravitated more and more to a banker-controlled central bank as the ideal solution.[8] Through 1907, recognition of a need for reform produced only dissension. With urban financiers divided East and West and their country colleagues suspicious of both, the epigram of a west coast observer summed up these early years: "[The] bankers are still divided, while the public and politicians look on, and smilingly say, 'Who shall decide when doctors disagree?' "[9]

The Panic of 1907 abruptly ended this period of leisurely debate. Warmed by the sun of prosperity, the bankers had not felt pressed to act. The chill of crisis, however, produced a new sense of urgency

[7] For examples of country banker opposition to the Fowler plan, see *Proceedings of the Minnesota Bankers' Association* (1902), 142-43; *Proceedings of the Iowa Bankers' Association* (1902), 78-84; *Commercial West* (Minneapolis), V, No. 34 (August 22, 1903), 12. Typical alternative programs which they supported are given in *Proceedings of the American Bankers' Association* (1903), 163; *Proceedings of the Kansas Bankers' Association* (1903), 138-42; *Wall Street Journal* (New York), September 29, 1905.

[8] For opposition to the Fowler plan, see James W. Stillman to Theodore Roosevelt, August 14, 1903, Papers of Theodore Roosevelt (Division of Manuscripts, Library of Congress). Their support for a 1906 assets currency bill is described in *Report of the Currency Commission to the American Bankers' Association and Remarks by Hon. A. B. Hepburn* ([New York, 1907]), 1-3; *Proceedings of the American Bankers' Association* (New York, 1907), 107-16. The growth of central bank sentiment is indicated by *Forty-ninth Annual Report of the Corporation of the Chamber of Commerce of the State of New York* (1906-1907), 15-37, 40-57; Charles A. Conant, *A History of Modern Banks of Issue* (6th ed., New York, 1927), 437-40. For further New York-Chicago differences, see James H. Eckles, *The Financial Power of the New West* (n. p., 1905); "Why Chicago Bankers Opposed Aldrich Bill," *Commercial West*, V, No. 10 (March 7, 1903), 15.

[9] Miles C. Moore, "Address of the President [of the Washington State Bankers' Association]," reprinted in *Financial Age* (New York), VIII (August 17, 1903), 265-67.

in their discussions.[10] While city financiers tried to muster strength behind a new version of their assets currency program, Congress, in an attempt to assuage public fears, passed a temporary measure, the Aldrich-Vreeland Act.[11] This expedient authorized an emergency currency which regional associations of national banks could distribute in times of special stress. Having favored this type of reform earlier, a respectable number of country bankers, with Andrew Frame again in the forefront, applauded the bill.[12] The urban financiers who demanded a general overhauling could only complain in futile opposition and base their future hopes upon the National Monetary Commission, a congressional body which the Aldrich-Vreeland Act had established to study permanent reorganization.

City bankers emerged from the Panic of 1907 with far greater unity. The crisis of that year, by underlining the constant danger of decentralized reserves, had brought leading urban financiers from East and West into agreement upon the necessity of a central bank.[13] In order to conduct a successful campaign on this principle, they needed the allegiance of businessmen generally, who had tended to favor much milder reforms, and of the country bankers, whose vocal opposition had seriously hampered them in the past.[14] Such a

[10] The Panic also accentuated the city-country split, as smaller financiers accused their city correspondents of freezing rural bank deposits when local currency needs were greatest. George W. Peltier, "President's Address," *Proceedings of the Iowa Bankers' Association* (1908), 18-25; *Transactions of the Arkansas Bankers' Association* (1908), 14.

[11] City banker efforts to replace the Aldrich-Vreeland bill with an assets plan are described in House Committee on Banking and Currency (60 Cong., 1 Sess.), *Hearings and Arguments on Proposed Currency Legislation* (Washington, 1908), 82-86; James, *Growth of Chicago Banks*, II, 775, 778. Western urban financiers, with some justification, accused big New York bankers of supporting the Aldrich-Vreeland bill despite its weaknesses, because the East monopolized the bonds upon which its currency would be based. "West against Aldrich," *Rand McNally Bankers' Monthly* (Chicago), XXXVI (February, 1908), 78-80.

[12] House Committee on Banking and Currency, *Hearings and Arguments on Proposed Currency Legislation*, 235-58; Charles E. Warren, "President's Annual Address," *Proceedings of the New York State Bankers Association* (1908), 9-17; *Proceedings of the Missouri Bankers Association* (1908), 189-90.

[13] Among the many evidences of the western city bankers' conversion, see George E. Roberts, "A Central Bank of Issue," *Proceedings of the Colorado Bankers' Association* (1908), 42-65; George M. Reynolds, "Annual Address of the President," *Proceedings of the American Bankers' Association* (1909), 69-80; Paul M. Warburg to Nelson W. Aldrich, December 24, 1909, Papers of Nelson W. Aldrich (Division of Manuscripts, Library of Congress); *Commercial West*, XIII, No. 4 (January 25, 1908), 7-8. For different interpretations of this period, see Nathaniel W. Stephenson, *Nelson W. Aldrich: A Leader in American Politics* (New York, 1930), 362-63; James, *Growth of Chicago Banks*, II, 773-74.

[14] Businessmen's suspicions of earlier city bankers' programs are shown in *Pro-*

project required tight organization behind a carefully selected plan.

After two years of preliminary propaganda, the city bankers received their concrete program early in 1911 from Senator Nelson W. Aldrich, the National Monetary Commission's chairman who had dominated its work under guidance from powerful New York financiers.[15] The Aldrich plan, while camouflaged by general and sometimes deceptive language, called for a central banking institution, with branches, which bankers would own and operate and which would regulate the issuance of assets currency.[16] By prearrangement, a special Business Men's Monetary Conference, sponsored by the National Board of Trade, met the day after the announcement, and, with Aldrich's chief financial mentor, Paul M. Warburg, as floor manager, the Conference gave the plan full endorsement. It also began work toward establishing the National Citizens' League, meant to serve as propaganda headquarters in the coming drive for business support.[17]

Founders of the Citizens' League tried hard to surround it with an aura of nonpartisanship. They chose Chicago as its home in order to avoid the "animosities and jealousies" associated with New York, and then announced as their open-minded goal "an improved

ceedings of the National Board of Trade (1906), 268-69; *Iron Age*, LXX (November 20, 1902), 30-31; New York *Journal of Commerce and Commercial Bulletin*, October 16, 1906. After the Panic, however, these men expressed a far livelier interest in general reform. See, for example, F. B. DeBerard to Buck's Stove and Range Co., August 1, 1908, Papers of Daniel A. Tompkins (Southern Historical Collection, University of North Carolina); also *Eighteenth Annual Report of the Trades League of Philadelphia* (1908), 105-108.

15 Stephenson, *Aldrich*, Chap. XXIV; Thomas W. Lamont, *Henry P. Davison: The Record of a Useful Life* (New York, 1933), 92-102; Frank A. Vanderlip (in collaboration with Boyden Sparkes), *From Farm Boy to Financier* (New York, 1935), 210-19.

16 "Suggested Plan for Monetary Legislation Submitted to the National Monetary Commission by Hon. Nelson W. Aldrich," *Senate Docs.*, 61 Cong., 3 Sess., No. 784. Newspapers uncritically accepted Aldrich's word that his plan was not centralized. Washington *Post*, January 18, 1911, and New York *Times*, January 18, 1911. Aldrich later made some additional concessions toward banker control, described in Stephenson, *Aldrich*, 389-92, and *Journal of the American Bankers' Association* (New York), III (May, 1911), 643-48, before perfecting his plan. For its final form, see *Publications of the National Monetary Commission* (24 vols., Washington, 1911-1912), XXIV (*Report of National Monetary Commission*).

17 *Fifty-fourth Annual Report of the Corporation of the Chamber of Commerce of the State of New York* (1911-1912), 146-51; *Proceedings of the National Board of Trade* (1911), 184-207; New York *Times*, January 19, 1911. For details on the establishment of the National Citizens' League, see *The National Citizens' League for the Promotion of a Sound Banking System: The Origins of the League* (Chicago, [1911]); Harry A. Wheeler, "From the President," *Annual Report of the Chicago Association of Commerce* (1911), 11-14.

banking system for the United States." [18] Beneath this veneer of impartiality, however, the Citizens' League worked diligently for the Aldrich plan, saturating the business community with speeches and literature in an effort to allay suspicions of a centralized banking system. Country bankers and other small businessmen received the most delicate handling, with constant stress placed upon the plan's supposed freedom from Wall Street domination.[19] The combination of a definite program and efficient organization achieved remarkable results during a few months of intensive campaigning. Few hazarded open criticism, while a wide assortment of approving resolutions and statements created the semblance of broad business unity behind the plan.[20]

No matter how well city bankers marshaled their business support, they could achieve final victory only by an act of Congress. In early 1912 the nation was poised on the brink of a political upheaval which would sweep reform-minded Democrats into full federal power. Democrats and progressive Republicans, crying out against privileged money powers, already controlled Congress. In such a climate no program associated with Aldrich and New York's great financiers could possibly succeed, and bills based upon the plan died one by one in committee.[21] The façade of business unity which the urban financiers had labored so hard to construct crumbled with the removal of its major prop, the Aldrich plan. Smaller

[18] *The Commercial Club of Chicago Year-Book* (1914-1915), 73; *The National Citizens' League for the Promotion of a Sound Banking System: Constitution and By-Laws* (Chicago, 1911). See also Stephenson, *Aldrich*, 381.

[19] The League's commitment is divulged by its director in "Statement by Prof. J. Laurence Laughlin" (n. d.), Papers of James Laurence Laughlin (Division of Manuscripts, Library of Congress); Laughlin to James B. Forgan, August 13, 1911, quoted in part in Laughlin, *The Federal Reserve Act: Its Origins and Problems* (New York, 1933), 48. After its first important months as propaganda co-ordinator, the League ran afoul of the old Chicago-New York hostilities, which eventually sapped its strength. Laughlin to Wallace D. Simmons, January 15, 1914, Laughlin Papers; Laughlin, *Federal Reserve Act*, 44-47; H. Parker Willis to Carter Glass, November 29, 1912, Papers of Carter Glass (Alderman Library, University of Virginia). Examples of the special treatment accorded smaller bankers and businessmen are *The National Reserve Association: Advantages It Will Give the Smaller Banks and Their Communities* ([Chicago, 1912]); "Address of Mr. Charles A. Conant," *Proceedings of the National Association of Manufacturers* (1911), 206-12; Laughlin, *Federal Reserve Act*, 79; Stephenson, *Aldrich*, 392-94.

[20] Among the rare open dissents are Daniel A. Tompkins, "Disadvantages of the Aldrich Plan," *American Industries* (New York), XI, No. 10 (May, 1911), 17-18; Andrew J. Frame, "Diagnosis of the National Monetary Bill" (Copy), Papers of William Howard Taft (Division of Manuscripts, Library of Congress).

[21] A general description of the Aldrich plan's failure in Congress is given in Stephenson, *Aldrich*, 401-404.

bankers, no longer cowed by organized pressure, now poured forth alternative proposals, most of which recommended thoroughly decentralized systems, with a sprinkling of suggestions for a government-controlled central bank.[22] In this confusion of plans and counterplans, the city financiers suddenly found themselves on the defensive, forced to wait until the Wilson administration had decided upon its choice of reform.

The Democrats' solution, gradually molded by various factions of the party, represented a compromise on the question of centralization, but it rejected banker control over the new system's policy or currency.[23] The Glass-Owen bill, through which the Federal Reserve system originated, authorized twelve regional institutions under loose supervision by a politically appointed Federal Reserve Board. It also provided for the replacement of the government-bond currency with one based upon a bank's asset structure, ultimately backed by the government. Many smaller bankers and businessmen, especially in the West and South, praised this proposal as a wise one which would satisfactorily protect their interests. "We are more willing to take our chances with the Government," explained one Wisconsin country banker.[24] On the other hand, urban financiers who believed in the banker-controlled centralization of the Aldrich plan were naturally unhappy. Yet, de-

[22] Smaller urban bankers joined in this display of opposition to centralization. The most popular plan came from a minor New York financier, James G. Cannon. See his *Clearing Houses and Currency No. 1* (Syracuse, 1913), copy in Papers of Woodrow Wilson (Division of Manuscripts, Library of Congress). See also House Subcommittee of the Committee on Banking and Currency (62 Cong., 3 Sess.), *Banking and Currency Reform, Hearings* (Washington, 1913), 337-40, 447-51; Leslie Butler, "Address of the President," *Oregon State Bankers Association Proceedings* (1913), 12-14.

[23] The details of this intraparty struggle are described in Arthur S. Link, *Wilson: The New Freedom* (Princeton, 1956), Chap. VII. It is important to point out, however, that Professor Link has ascribed too much unanimity to city banker opinion throughout the Glass-Owen bill's development, ignoring in the process the very real conflicts among those financiers who wanted to alter the measure. To the Wilson administration, these banker differences may have sounded like minor variations on a single theme of total opposition, but to the financiers they represented a clear and significant rift within the banking community, which the hostile forces found extremely difficult to reconcile.

[24] Senate Committee on Banking and Currency (63 Cong., 1 Sess.), *Hearings on H. R. 7837 (S. 2639)* (4 vols., Washington, 1913), II, 1549. See also *ibid.*, II, 2070, 2096; [D. A. Tompkins], "The Glass Currency Bill" (Copy), Papers of Daniel A. Tompkins (Division of Manuscripts, Library of Congress); "Address of W. H. Manly, President," *Proceedings of the Alabama Bankers' Association* (1913), 21-36. Excellent sources for this viewpoint are cited in Link, *Wilson: The New Freedom*, 224.

spite their common disappointment, the city bankers themselves divided sharply over the proper opposition tactics to follow.

Chicago's two strongest bankers, James B. Forgan and George M. Reynolds, led the two major factions of urban financiers. Forgan, with support from certain big New York financiers and from the officers of the American Bankers' Association, condemned the bill as "unworkable, impracticable and fundamentally unsound," and wanted to scrap it entirely.[25] Reynolds, whose followers decidedly outnumbered Forgan's irreconcilables, countered with a conciliatory plea for moderation, arguing that the bankers faced a practical, not a theoretical, situation and could win concessions only by working within the framework of the administration measure.[26] The two forces met for a test of strength in August, 1913, at a Chicago conference called by the American Bankers' Association's Currency Commission, where the conciliationists won a clear victory.[27] Joined by an equally moderate group from the infant United States Chamber of Commerce, a committee from the Chicago conference moved to Washington to negotiate the best adjustment possible with Congress.[28]

In all probability, the bankers' mission was a predestined failure. By the time the Wilson administration had mollified the diverse

[25] Quoted in *Financial Age*, XXVIII (August 30, 1913), 344. Other elements of Forgan's intransigeants are described in Senate Committee on Banking and Currency, *Hearings on H. R. 7837*, I, 680-81; Wallace D. Simmons to the Members of the Banking and Currency Committee of the United States Chamber of Commerce, January 10, 1914, Laughlin Papers; Arthur Reynolds, "Annual Address of the First Vice-President," *Proceedings of the American Bankers' Association* (1913), 54-65.

[26] The evolution of the conciliationist group can be seen from A. Barton Hepburn to Carter Glass, December 19, 1912; H. Parker Willis to Glass, December 31, 1912, January 18, 1913; George M. Reynolds to Glass, April 18, 1913; all in Glass Papers; House Subcommittee of the Committee on Banking and Currency (62 Cong., 3 Sess.), *Banking and Currency Reform, Hearings*, 357-62 and *passim*; John V. Farwell to Woodrow Wilson, July 22, 1913, Wilson Papers. Willis and Reynolds, trying to separate those bankers who would co-operate with Congress, warned Glass of the threat from intransigeants such as Forgan and officers of the American Bankers' Association.

[27] Chicago *Tribune*, August 24, 25, 1913. New York *Times*, August 23, 24, 1913. Its conclusions are given in *Report Unanimously Adopted by a Conference Held at Chicago, August 22 and 23, 1913* ([1913]), copy in Wilson Papers.

[28] For the Chamber's moderate approach, see *Nation's Business* (Washington), I, No. 13 (July 15, 1913), 4-6; No. 16 (October 15, 1913), 3; supplemented by the friendly letters of its president, Harry A. Wheeler, to J. Laurence Laughlin, August 19, 1913, Wilson Papers, and to Carter Glass, August 8, 1913, Glass Papers; also reprinted in Henry Parker Willis, *The Federal Reserve System: Legislation, Organization, and Operation* (New York, 1923), 417-21.

Democratic factions, it was in no mood to grant city financiers any major concessions.[29] But the bankers, as a fitting climax to their Progressive record, exhibited one final show of disunity. At Chicago, the urban leaders had been so involved in reconciling their own differences that they brusquely ignored their sensitive country colleagues, who now followed the conference delegation to Washington and broadcast their grievances. One irate Arkansas financier described the Chicago proceedings to amused congressmen: "That committee was stacked; that was the coldest deal I ever went against in my life. We were invited there simply and solely to set the stage, to have a crowd, to carry a spear and sing a song and dance around, so that the stage would be full while the bigwigs could have the spot lights played on them." [30] While the city financiers scurried to put their house in order, Congress applied the final touches to the Glass-Owen bill.[31] At the end as at the beginning of the Progressive period, the bankers had found their internal conflicts a more powerful force than their desire to reform the financial system.

As in the case of banking reform, the lag of legislation behind America's industrial realities provided the background for the battles of businessmen over railroad regulation. During the latter part of the nineteenth century, entrepreneurs had extended and consolidated the network of existing lines into national transportation systems, forming a skeleton for the country's remarkable commercial growth. Closely limited by court decisions, state attempts to control these private empires had proved ineffectual. Congress finally made a beginning toward regulation with the Interstate Commerce Act of 1887, but its failure to buttress the law against the weakening effect of judicial interpretations left the Interstate Commerce Com-

[29] Link, *Wilson: The New Freedom*, 226-27, shows that the distinction between intransigeants and conciliationists did not impress the Wilson administration, which viewed the Chicago conference results as proof that no co-operation with the urban bankers was possible. As tactless as they seem to have been, these resolutions were not meant to be an ultimatum, rather a complete list of ideals toward which these men hoped to move Congress.

[30] Senate Committee on Banking and Currency, *Hearings on H. R. 7837*, II, 1566. See also *ibid.*, 1539-65, and McLane Tilton, Jr., to Glass, September 3, 1913, Glass Papers.

[31] These efforts included an extraordinary country bankers' session, as well as some difficult maneuvering among full supporters and adamant opponents of the administration bill, during the regular American Bankers' Association sessions. *Proceedings of the American Bankers' Association* (1913), 75-91, 95-99, 101-16.

mission with little more power than the states to cope with major transportation problems.[32]

Few businessmen were satisfied with the rate structure which had evolved during those years of free interplay between the railroads as carriers and their customers as shippers. For the carriers, the worst abuses lay in an intricate rebate system to which a number of the bigger railroads had resorted as a result of unbridled rail competition and under pressure from giant industries. Business shippers, for their part, felt that the exorbitant transportation rates, which the railroads staunchly defended, constituted the basic evil. During the Progressive era, as the federal government experimented with various techniques of rate control, the carriers and shippers engaged in a continuous struggle, each group maneuvering to protect its special interests.

At the beginning of the century, the shippers, divided occupationally and scattered geographically throughout the nation, had no way of pressing their cause as a group. Their one national spokesman was the Interstate Commerce Law Convention, founded in 1900 by a handful of midwestern grain merchants and millers.[33] Insignificant in size, this organization gained prominence through the incessant activity of its leader, Edward P. Bacon, a politically ambitious grain dealer from Milwaukee, who set himself the task of rallying the country's diversified shippers behind a bill that would give the Interstate Commerce Commission the power to establish reasonable rates. Dubbed a "Peter the Hermit" by his enemies, Bacon began his crusade by taking his bill to Washington in hopes of attracting sufficient attention to launch a broad shippers' movement.[34] With some difficulty, he found sponsors for his measure in 1902, only to lose control of his campaign through bad strategy. Railroad leaders were simultaneously backing anti-rebate legislation, and, in a move to dull the point of Bacon's attack, they lured him into joining his proposal with theirs as the revised Elkins bill.

[32] I. L. Sharfman, *The Interstate Commerce Commission: A Study in Administrative Law and Procedure* (4 parts, New York, 1931-1937), Part I, 13-19; William Z. Ripley, *Railroads: Rates and Regulation* (New York, 1912), 456-86.

[33] *Forty-fourth Annual Report of the Chicago Board of Trade* (1901), lxxiv-lxxv; *Railway Age* (Chicago), XL (September 8, 1905), 280-82.

[34] Senate Committee on Interstate Commerce, *Regulation of Railway Rates, Hearings on Bills to Amend the Interstate Commerce Act* (*Senate Docs.*, 59 Cong., 1 Sess., No. 243; 5 vols., Washington, 1906), III, 2503. For early recognition of Bacon's importance, see *Commercial and Financial Chronicle* (New York), LXXIV (February 8, 1902), 291-92.

Bacon worked unstintingly for the combination measure, then stood impotently by as the Senate cut away his sections of the bill and passed only the Elkins Anti-Rebate Act of 1903. In defeat, Bacon grimly promised "to follow this up by vigorous effort . . . at the next session of Congress." [35]

His prospects brightened considerably as Progressive spokesmen, with the magnetic President Roosevelt prominent among them, made rate regulation a central part of their program. Shippers whom Bacon alone could never have reached now became enthusiastic members of his Interstate Commerce Law Convention.[36] Riding the crest of a Progressive wave, he decided in 1905 to call another meeting of the Convention in preparation for the final thrust. Bacon gambled everything upon the appeal of his richest asset, the Roosevelt name, requiring a pledge from each prospective delegate that he would support the President's rate reforms.[37]

This second strategic error proved fatal. While many shippers willingly responded to his call, an equally strong countermovement arose among businessmen wary of the federal powers connected with Roosevelt and reform. These dissidents had an aggressive and capable leader in David M. Parry, president of the National As-

[35] Edward P. Bacon to John C. Spooner, February 9, 1903, Papers of John C. Spooner (Division of Manuscripts, Library of Congress). For details of Bacon's labors, see Bacon to Spooner, December 2, 23, 1901, June 26, July 3, 1902, January 3, 24, 1903, and Robert Eliot (for the Milwaukee Chamber of Commerce) to Spooner, April 2, 1902, *ibid.* In rare instances a railroad executive agreed that some rate control powers should be given to the Interstate Commerce Commission. The president of the Pennsylvania Railroad, for example, explained that he supported some government control "because we believe that it is better policy to assist in framing and passing a reasonable measure now than to have a more drastic and perhaps a seriously injurious one forced upon us by public clamor." Alexander J. Cassatt to Theodore Roosevelt, April 1, 1902, Roosevelt Papers. See also Destler, "Opposition of American Businessmen to Social Control," *Mississippi Valley Historical Review*, XXXIX (March, 1953), 666-67, for corroboration in an earlier period. Hans Thorelli, *The Federal Antitrust Policy: Origination of an American Tradition* (Baltimore, 1955), 538-49, provides a broader background for the Elkins Act. Sharfman, *Interstate Commerce Commission*, I, 36-37, indicates railroad backing for the rebate portions.

[36] The best general account of this phase of the railroad regulation movement is John M. Blum, *The Republican Roosevelt* (Cambridge, 1954), Chap. VI. *Proceedings of the Interstate Commerce Law Convention* (1904), 27-38, indicates the broadening membership of the Convention while showing that its primary strength still lay in the Midwest. Although Bacon capitalized upon progressive Republican propaganda, he proved totally unable to influence the course of its policy. See Bacon to Spooner, May 4, August 5, 1904, Spooner Papers, for his failure to encourage a stronger Republican stand on regulation during the 1904 campaign; and Bacon to Roosevelt, August 15, 1904; Roosevelt to Bacon, August 19, 1904; Bacon to Roosevelt, August 23, 1904; all in Roosevelt Papers, for Roosevelt's easy mastery over his admirer.

[37] Edward P. Bacon [open letter], September 18, 1905, copy in Roosevelt Papers.

sociation of Manufacturers and a determined opponent of railroad regulation.[38] When the Interstate Commerce Law Convention met in October, 1905, Parry's followers refused to sign the necessary pledge, and Bacon, fearing that they would pack his meeting, hastily hired armed guards to bar dissenters from the Convention conference hall.[39] The rebels promptly marched a few blocks away to hold their own sessions, claiming that they were the legitimate voice of business. The farce of two meetings, approximately the same size, allegedly representing the same economic group, yet proclaiming diametrically opposed programs, ruined the effectiveness of Bacon's convention; and thus the victory went to Parry and his associates.[40]

Temporarily the shippers reverted to their earlier state of disorganization. In the final months before Congress acted upon the rate question, shippers, lacking a national representative, had to plead their cause individually or through local groups. The railroads, assisted by their own business allies, redoubled their efforts against rate regulation with a degree of success.[41] Despite the fact that the Hepburn Act of 1906 gave the Interstate Commerce Commission the right to pass judgment upon the carriers' tariffs, the railroads still retained broad use of court review before the Commission's rulings could go into effect. There matters stood until the Panic of 1907 spurred both carriers and shippers to new action. The railroads, trying to capitalize upon a measure of business sympathy for their financial plight, proposed general rate advances in the

38 Although Parry, as a carriage and car manufacturer, was ostensibly a shipper, he had considerable railroad investments. Albert K. Steigerwalt, Jr., "The National Association of Manufacturers: Organization and Policies, 1895-1914" (Ph.D. dissertation, University of Michigan, 1952), 175.

39 Chicago *Tribune*, October 25, 26, 1905. New York *Times*, October 27, 1905. Bacon had had ample warning of the rising opposition. See, for example, a widely circulated public letter from David M. Parry to Bacon, January 3, 1905, copy in Papers of Francis G. Newlands (Division of Manuscripts, Yale University Library).

40 *Proceedings of the Federal Rate Regulation Association* (1905), 3-18, 22-28, 51-52; *Proceedings of the Interstate Commerce Law Convention* (1905), 11-12, 18-19, 60, 66, 99-100. Soon after this fiasco, Bacon disappeared as a factor in the regulation movement, and the Convention disintegrated.

41 The central railroad argument was presented by railroad presidents Samuel Spencer and David Willcox in House Committee on Interstate and Foreign Commerce, *Hearings on Bills to Amend the Interstate-Commerce Act* (*House Docs.*, 58 Cong., 3 Sess., No. 422; Washington, 1905), 239-63. For other business advocacy of the carriers' arguments, see *ibid.*, 139-44, and Senate Committee on Interstate Commerce, *Regulation of Railway Rates, Hearings* (*Senate Docs.*, 59 Cong., 1 Sess., No 243), I, 169-71, 486-91.

midst of the crisis. The move backfired. Faced with loud and widespread denunciation from business organizations, the carriers withdrew their plan, and simultaneously the threatened shippers organized once more to defend themselves.[42] This time they built their new association, the National Industrial Traffic League, upon a foundation of powerful midwestern commercial organizations, whose professional traffic managers directed the Traffic League's technical work. Firmly grounded, in contrast to the personalized Interstate Commerce Law Convention, the Traffic League prepared to match railroad arguments before the Interstate Commerce Commission and to encourage new legislation which would strengthen the Commission's powers.[43] The Panic period had accentuated shipper-carrier differences without satisfying either of the antagonists.

In 1910 these strained relations produced a major crisis. The first phase involved the Mann-Elkins Act, which allowed the Interstate Commerce Commission to suspend proposed rate changes and placed its rulings in effect before court review. Since the measure embodied two major planks in the shippers' platform, it received enthusiastic and consistent support from the Traffic League.[44] The railroads, perhaps sensing defeat, repeated their 1908 mistake by trying to slip in over-all rate advances before the bill could pass, but once again they were forced to retreat. Threatened with antitrust prosecution if they did not comply, the carriers agreed in conference with President Taft to postpone the question of increases in return for tacit assurances of an Interstate Commerce Commission hearing as soon as Congress acted on the Mann-Elkins bill.[45] The railroads now centered their primary hopes for relief upon a favorable ruling by the Commission.

42 For examples of the national protest, see *Seventeenth Annual Report of the Trades League of Philadelphia* (1907), 53-56; *Fifty-ninth Annual Report of the Cincinnati Chamber of Commerce and Merchants' Exchange* (1907), 42; *Board of Directors Minutes of the National Association of Manufacturers* (May 18, 1908); *The Members' Annual of the Los Angeles Chamber of Commerce* (1909), 26.

43 James C. Lincoln, *The National Industrial Traffic League* ([Chicago], 1908); Edward F. Lacey, "The National Industrial Traffic League: Organization and Development" (Typed copy in Bureau of Railway Economics Library, Washington, D. C.), 5; House Committee on Interstate and Foreign Commerce (61 Cong., 1 Sess.), *Hearings on Bills Affecting Interstate Commerce* (2 vols., Washington, 1910), I, 395-98.

44 House Committee on Interstate and Foreign Commerce, *Hearings on Bills Affecting Interstate Commerce, passim.*

45 For the story of the government's action, see *Bulletin of the American Iron and Steel Association* (Philadelphia), XLIV (July 1, 1910), 59; New York *Times*, June 7, 8, 1910; "Railroad Rate Agreement" (Copy), Taft Papers; Ripley, *Railroads*, 561-62.

Once Congress passed the Mann-Elkins Act, the scene shifted to the Interstate Commerce Commission hearings and the second phase of this shipper-carrier struggle. By then, the shippers had reached their apex of organization. To accompany the midwestern strength of the Traffic League, eastern commercial associations representing shipping interests banded together to hire the brilliant Boston lawyer, Louis D. Brandeis, as their spokesman, and an assortment of local and national business groups contributed what force they could in creating a solid front of shippers to oppose the increases.[46] The railroads were not able to present sufficient evidence to counteract the combined efforts of Brandeis and well-informed traffic managers, and in February, 1911, the Commission ruled against the rate increases sought by the carriers.[47]

These defeats, as extensive as they were, did not leave the railroads helpless. At the very time shipper unity was approaching its peak of effectiveness, the carriers were in the process of undermining it. In the period of the Panic of 1907 a few alert railroad leaders had initiated a public relations movement which, after 1910, became a concerted campaign to woo the public and divide the hostile shippers. Special agents, friendly industrialists, and railroad executives canvassed the business community, probing the weakest spot in their antagonists' armor, a need for regular, efficient service. Time and again, these men warned that in a period of rising costs unchanged rates would bankrupt the roads and produce transportation chaos.[48] By 1913 the carriers were prepared to try again for rate advances.

In that year, the Interstate Commerce Commission granted the

[46] The general development and extent of shipper power can be seen from "Resolutions Unanimously Adopted by a Convention of Shippers and Representatives of Shipping and Commercial Organizations Held at Chicago, Ill., May 17, 1910," ICC Docket No. 3400; Louis D. Brandeis, *Brief on Behalf of Traffic Committee of Commercial Organizations of the Atlantic Seaboard* (Washington, 1911), ICC Investigation and Suspension No. 3; "Testimony" (August 29, 1910), 5-48, ICC Investigation and Suspension No. 4; all in Records of the Interstate Commerce Commission (National Archives, Washington).

[47] *Decisions of the Interstate Commerce Commission of the United States* (Washington), XX (1911), 243-399. See also Alpheus T. Mason, *Brandeis: A Free Man's Life* (New York, 1946), 315-51.

[48] For the development of this new diplomacy, see William W. Finley, *Addresses and Statements, 1907-1910* (Washington, n. d.), *passim*; Edward P. Ripley, "The Railroads and Public Approval," *First Annual Dinner, Railway Business Association* (1909), 30-34; J. Hampton Baumgartner, *The Railroads and Public Relations* (n. p., 1913); Eric F. Goldman, *Two-Way Street: The Emergence of the Public Relations Counsel* (Cambridge, 1948), Chap. I.

railroads a rehearing of their case for increases. This time the carriers' propaganda had neutralized or converted so many erstwhile shipper foes that there was no chance of re-creating the 1910 battle lines. On the contrary, the railroads dominated the hearings to such an extent that the Commission complained: "There appears to have been a set purpose to convince us that the people were of one mind respecting the very important questions involved in the case, and that, in order to satisfy every public requirement, there remained nothing for the Commission to do but to register this consensus of opinion by immediately entering an order permitting the carriers to make their proposed charges effective." [49] Although it first rejected the carriers' request, the Commission partially reversed itself later in 1914 and allowed the eastern roads their increases.[50] Many shippers, meanwhile, were regretting their temporary moderation. Even during the truce they had emphasized that they remained firm defenders of the existing regulatory laws and that they would scrutinize every future railroad request with critical care.[51] The earlier animosity had mellowed but had certainly not disappeared. As difficult as it was for the diversified shipping interests to achieve and maintain a working unity, their common concern over reasonable rates set them apart as the natural business antagonists of the railroads throughout the Progressive period.

The struggle over rate levels had proceeded along obvious lines of economic self-interest. The debate among businessmen over trust control, on the other hand, suffered from hazy definition and from blurred demarcation among opponents. Part of this confusion resulted from the sudden burst of business consolidation, beginning after the election of 1896, which gave the old question of supervising industrial enterprises new dimensions of complexity and

[49] *Decisions of the Interstate Commerce Commission*, XXXI (1914), 425-26. For the hard core of continuing shipper opposition, see *ibid.*, 357. Typical examples of the railroad leaders' success in neutralizing their former enemies are given in F. A. Delano to E. E. Clark, May 12, 1913, and H. C. Barlow to John H. Marble, October 22, 1913, ICC Docket No. 5860, Records of the Interstate Commerce Commission; *Report of the Boston Chamber of Commerce* (1913), 38-39; "National Industrial Traffic League," *Railway Age-Gazette* (Chicago), LV (November 21, 1913), 962-64.

[50] *Decisions of the Interstate Commerce Commission*, XXXI (1914), 351-454; XXXII (1914), 325-54.

[51] *National Industrial Traffic League: Proceedings* (July, 1912), 18; (August, 1914), 29-31; (November, 1914), 3-7. This strictly limited shipper acceptance of railroad requests is also illustrated by their unanimous refusal to allow carriers an increase in spotting charges even during the 1914 truce. See the hundreds of letters in "Protest" Files of ICC Docket No. 5860, Records of the Interstate Commerce Commission.

public concern.[52] The problem of trust control became a symbol of the Progressive period's general worry over unfamiliar bigness and the decline of competition. Into this stream of unrest flowed the specific enmity of those businessmen who felt oppressed by large enterprises because of direct competition, the price of trust products, or the uncertain future of smaller entrepreneurs in an economy of giants.[53] The exact problem was usually ill-defined, but the business conflicts were nonetheless acrimonious.

Business arguments over trust regulation remained diffuse until the Roosevelt administration dramatically placed itself in the midst of the controversy. In 1902, the government gave its basic regulatory weapon, the Sherman Antitrust Act of 1890, fresh prestige by prosecuting one of the nation's major combinations, the Northern Securities Company.[54] Then, in the wake of this surprise, came the establishment of the Bureau of Corporations as a general investigating agency within the Department of Commerce and Labor. The smaller businessmen whose hostility toward trusts had been frustrated for lack of a satisfactory outlet now flooded the administration with pleas to champion their causes, whether they be battles with the country's great corporations or conflicts with various price-fixing retail leagues.[55] Big-business leaders, on the other hand, concentrated upon coming to terms with this potential enemy, the federal government. Led by Elbert H. Gary, chairman of United States Steel's board of directors, the more discerning of these went directly to the source of their trouble and tried to negotiate private agreements with the administration, by which the corporations would co-operate in investigations in return for undefined but presumably lenient treatment.[56]

52 For general information on this subject, see Harold U. Faulkner, *The Decline of Laissez Faire, 1897-1917* (New York, 1951), 153-63.

53 For background concerning this sentiment, see Thorelli, *Federal Antitrust Policy*, 149, 350-51. See also *Official Proceedings of the Trans-Mississippi Commercial Congress* (1902), 244.

54 For the legal status of the Sherman Act in 1902, see Thorelli, *Federal Antitrust Policy*, 592, 599-604.

55 See, for examples, Sam H. Harris to James R. Garfield (concerning the American Tobacco Co.), January 7, 1905; Kelso and Anglin Correspondence (concerning a Cleveland lumber dealers' association); E. D. Beebe Correspondence (concerning the National Association of Retail Druggists); Ross E. Parks to Theodore Roosevelt (concerning a grain dealers' organization), July 13, 1906; all in Records of the Federal Trade Commission (National Archives).

56 The arrangements are described in "Conference at White House, Evening of November 2, 1905"; "Memorandum of Interview In Re *International Harvester Company*, on January 18, 1907"; "Memorandum In Re Second Interview with In-

These efforts to commit the government to one side or the other in trust prosecution, however, did not actively involve the majority of businessmen. Although the scandals of 1905 and 1906 concerning life insurance companies and food industries shocked many businessmen and quickened their reform impulses, most of them refused to endorse programs which might someday be turned upon them.[57] As a result, the popular solution among mixed business organizations, such as the National Association of Manufacturers and the National Board of Trade, was a national incorporation law, elastic enough to satisfy both those desiring tighter control and those hoping for a relaxation of the Sherman Act's ban on restraint of trade.[58]

Out of the Panic of 1907 emerged a proposal which helped to clear the lines dividing the business community. A group of powerful industrialists decided that their salvation lay in transforming the Sherman Act into an ally instead of a hovering threat. To achieve this, they formulated a plan whereby businessmen would submit their projects for expansion and communities of interest to the Bureau of Corporations which, after a thorough investigation, could immunize them from future prosecution by issuing a protective stamp of approval.[59] With valuable help from President Roosevelt, they were able in early 1908 to bring their proposal before Congress as the Hepburn amendments to the Sherman Act.[60] An opposition among lesser businessmen solidified immediately. While speaking most vigorously against certain peripheral labor

ternational Harvester Company on January 19, 1907"; all in Records of Federal Trade Commission. These loose understandings slowly deteriorated until antitrust suits against U. S. Steel and International Harvester officially terminated them. See Edgar A. Bancroft to Luther Conant, Jr., September 10, 1912, *ibid.*

57 For examples of indignant business reactions to insurance and food scandals, see N. B. Coffman, "Some Unwise Tendencies in Banking as Viewed from the Standpoint of a Country Banker," *Proceedings of the Washington State Bankers' Association* (1905), 75; *Seventy-third Annual Report of the Philadelphia Board of Trade* (1906), 24-25; *Proceedings of the National Board of Trade* (1906), 271; *The Members' Annual of the Los Angeles Chamber of Commerce* (1906), 19.

58 *Proceedings of the National Association of Manufacturers* (1906), 34-39; *Proceedings of the National Board of Trade* (1904), 80-93.

59 The background to this proposal is given in *Proceedings of the National Conference on Trusts and Combinations under the Auspices of the National Civic Federation* (1907), 454-55, 465.

60 Roosevelt's role in this process is indicated by Roosevelt to Seth Low, April 1, 1908, in Elting E. Morison (ed.), *The Letters of Theodore Roosevelt* (8 vols., Cambridge, 1951-1954), VI, 986-87; and Low to Roosevelt, April 11, 1908, Records of the Federal Trade Commission. See also Gordon M. Jensen, "The National Civic Federation: American Business in an Age of Social Change and Social Reform, 1900-1910" (Ph.D. dissertation, Princeton University, 1956), 277.

clauses in the bill, these smaller entrepreneurs made it patently clear to congressmen that they would not tolerate any differentiation between "reasonable" and "unreasonable" restraint of trade, no matter what else the bill might contain. To these dissenters, such a law would invite a few mammoth corporations to dominate the economy with governmental assistance.[61] The Hepburn amendments failed in an election year sensitive to big-business privileges, but its advocates did not abandon their objective.

For a time the debate waned as the nation entered an unstable transition between Roosevelt's Square Deal and Wilson's New Freedom. Businessmen tensely watched the Supreme Court for their next guidepost. In 1911 the Court issued its long-awaited decisions on the Standard Oil and American Tobacco Company antitrust suits, ruling against the legality of each but, in its famous gloss on the Sherman Act, officially separating reasonable from unreasonable restraint of trade. Once announced, these decisions somehow seemed anticlimactic. For smaller businessmen who had opposed this distinction in 1908, the Court's interpretation naturally constituted a defeat, and even for the powerful corporations, who were theoretical victors, the decisions provided little solace.[62] If each large enterprise had to undergo the ordeal of a judicial test in order to survive, who would be next? United States Steel received the unpleasant answer in October, 1911, in the form of an antitrust suit, and International Harvester followed it into court a few months later. These prosecutions underlined the big-business conviction that only a new, liberal law could offer permanent relief.

During the Progressive ferment of 1912, industrial leaders reopened the campaign which had stalled with the 1908 defeat of the

[61] For the core of smaller business opposition, see House Subcommittee of the Committee on the Judiciary (60 Cong., 1 Sess.), *An Act to Regulate Commerce, Etc., Hearings on House Bill 19745* (Washington, 1908), 153-64, 167-68; Senate Subcommittee of the Committee on the Judiciary (60 Cong., 1 Sess.), *Amendment of Sherman Antitrust Law, Hearings on the Bill (S. 6331) and the Bill (S. 6440)* (Washington, 1908), 60-62; "New York Board of Trade and Transportation Petition, April 8, 1908" (Copy), Records of the Federal Trade Commission, with an analysis in Roosevelt to Herbert Knox Smith, April 14, 1908, *ibid.*, partially reprinted in Morison (ed.), *Letters of Theodore Roosevelt*, VI, 1007-1008. The industrialists backing the Hepburn amendments would have been happy to drop the labor provisions which superficially aroused the strongest small-business opposition. Jensen, "National Civic Federation," 285-86.

[62] For smaller businessmen's continuing rejection of this viewpoint, see "Report of Mr. P. A. Peterson, President," *Reports of the Illinois Manufacturers' Association* (1911), 3-23; "Address of President Harry H. Pond," *Proceedings of the New Jersey Bankers' Association* (1912), 86-92.

Hepburn amendments. They altered their advice-and-consent formula to include an interstate trade commission, similar in status to the interstate commerce commission, as well as stricter criminal liability laws, but the goal remained government sanction for business consolidation and co-operation.[63] With this revised edition of their plan in hand, the big businessmen prepared to meet the challenge from the Wilson administration, which had been elected on a platform and in an atmosphere averse to bigness. The Democrats, too, wanted clarification of the Sherman Act, but in the Clayton bill of 1914 they chose a path opposite from the one corporation magnates followed.[64] Instead of liberalizing the anti-trust statute, the Clayton omnibus measure promised stiffer governmental control, designating specific corporate practices as destructive of competition and henceforth illegal. Although certain sections, especially those dealing with interlocking directorates and interlacing stock ownership, appealed to many entrepreneurs whose operations were more limited in scope, the measure as a whole seemed to be "a strait-jacket upon American business" which large and small businessmen joined in denouncing.[65]

The companion Democratic proposal for a Federal Trade Commission, however, contained potentially the exact solution big industrialists had sought since the days of the Hepburn amendments. Leading a far larger segment of business than before, these men concentrated their efforts upon constructing a trade commission which would serve as a business guardian. The thrust of their argument, as presented in the Chicago Association of Commerce's "Chicago Plan," by-passed the Clayton bill's approach by rejecting "further detailed definition of 'restraint of trade' or unfair practices," but at the same time embodied the contradictory complaint that "nothing hampers business like uncertainty." The reconcilia-

[63] See proposals offered by the National Civic Federation, Elbert H. Gary, and George W. Perkins, in Senate Committee on Interstate Commerce (62 Cong., 2 Sess.), *Hearings Pursuant to S. Res. 98* (3 vols., Washington, 1912), I, 515-24, 693-95, 1091-92. See also Nelson B. Gaskill, *The Regulation of Competition* (New York, 1936), 37.

[64] The best analysis of the Democrats' evolving trust program is given in Link, *Wilson: The New Freedom*, Chap. XIII.

[65] *The Cleveland Chamber of Commerce* (1915), 155. See also *Fifty-sixth Annual Report of the Corporation of the Chamber of Commerce of the State of New York* (1913-1914), 182-83; *Eighty-second Annual Report of the Philadelphia Board of Trade* (1915), 10-18. For the mixed reaction to interlocking directorates and stock ownership, see the results of a United States Chamber of Commerce referendum reported in *Nation's Business*, II, No. 7 (July 15, 1914), 3.

tion lay in a friendly Federal Trade Commission "to which we can submit business practices" and which would then "decide in advance as to the propriety, fairness and benefits of such proposed arrangements, each upon the merits of that particular case."[66]

Smaller industrialists who had steadily fought this concept recognized their old enemy in its latest disguise.[67] From their standpoint, none of the measures before Congress could benefit them, and therefore, with the National Association of Manufacturers in the vanguard, they organized a business drive to pressure Congress into immediate adjournment. "The Country Is Suffering from *Too Much Law*," they protested; let us "Free Business from Political Persecution."[68] With these notes of negativism echoing throughout the debates, Congress passed a modified Clayton Act and established the Federal Trade Commission without the advisory or directive powers outlined in the "Chicago Plan." Suspicions which had persistently kept businessmen from uniting on a trust regulation program left them neutralized in 1914 while Congress enacted legislation unsatisfactory to either of the opposing forces.

The business community had split over trust control, as it had over banking and railroad legislation, into factions shaped according to the dictates of particular economic interests. Yet, beyond motives of self-interest, these specific internal contests formed a broader pattern of business conflict. Its first thread was an urban-rural rift, most clearly shown by the battle between city and country bankers over financial reform. Another thread, in some respects similar, involved a division between businessmen of the East and those of the West and South. While the urban-rural split was related to the regional division, due to a concentration of cities in the East, special sectional characteristics separated the second as a unique strand. Thus urban bankers in Chicago and New York competed

[66] *The Chicago Plan* ([Chicago, 1914]).

[67] This hostility, now diminished because many former opponents supported a commission in order to escape the Clayton Act's controls, is indicated by another U. S. Chamber of Commerce referendum, reported in *Nation's Business,* II, No. 6 (June 18, 1914), 5-6, and analyzed in Senate Committee on Interstate Commerce (63 Cong., 2 Sess.), *Interstate Trade, Hearings on Bills Relating to Trust Legislation* (2 vols., Washington, 1914), II, 688-94.

[68] These are two samples of the stickered slogans which the National Association of Manufacturers offered in unlimited quantities to all applicants. National Association of Manufacturers to Associations, July 30, 1914, Wilson Papers. See also Simmons Hardware Company's widely distributed circular letter of June 9, 1914, *ibid.*; *Report of the Boston Chamber of Commerce* (1914), 48; John M. Glenn, *Urge Congress to Adjourn* ([Chicago, 1914]).

during this time for financial leadership and prestige; city bankers in the Democratic South more readily accepted Wilsonian reform than did their northern — and largely Republican — counterparts; and urban businessmen in the West, where shippers predominated, fought their eastern colleagues who controlled the railroads. Cleavages according to size provided a third thread, which dominated the debate over trust regulation and which also paralleled the city-country rift among bankers. Finally, functional divisions underlay the contest between shippers and carriers over rate levels and made it difficult for bankers to rally other types of businessmen, who were their customers, behind reform programs favorable to the financiers. Interwoven in various ways depending upon the time and the issue, these four strands outlined the quarrels among businessmen over the reform programs of the period. These battles, considered as a group, give consistent testimony that conflict, not co-operation, typified the business community's reaction to crisis during the Progressive era.

The Louisville and Portland Canal Company, 1825-1874

By Paul B. Trescott

The corporation which built and long controlled the Louisville and Portland Canal, a two-mile passage around the falls of the Ohio River at Louisville, enjoyed a unique and turbulent history. Born in the midst of political intrigue, it was involved in controversy throughout its lifetime. The Kentucky legislature chartered it as a private company in 1825 in the face of strong public sentiment in favor of a state project. When financial difficulties threatened to overcome it, the federal government stepped in and purchased a large amount of its stock, thus transforming it into a mixed corporation. Once completed, the canal made large profits, yet the stockholders ultimately bought themselves out through an intricate financial arrangement designed to convert it into a federal government enterprise. But the completion of this arrangement was delayed because of congressional reluctance to accept the canal and its financial responsibilities, and the company remained for twenty years nominally a private corporation under the jurisdiction of the state of Kentucky, managed by individuals not subject to formal federal control, yet in fact owned by the United States and operated for public purposes. This anomalous state marks it as a predecessor of the modern "government corporation," and the story of its peculiar relations to both state and federal government provides an illustration of the changing attitude toward private versus government enterprise in the nineteenth century.

The settlement and growth of Louisville were due largely to a geological circumstance: the obstruction of the Ohio River at the site of the city by a ledge of limestone rock, producing a falls twenty-five feet high which could not be navigated except for a few weeks during high water in the spring. This was the only serious obstruction in the river's thousand-mile course. As the Ohio became a major route of transportation in the early nineteenth century, a considerable business developed in transshipping cargoes around the falls. While this brought profits to Louisville merchants, it meant serious inconvenience to the users of the river. Shippers and boatmen complained of the time and expenses involved in broken voyages, and farmers up-river objected to the wide fluctuations in prices which resulted from the seasonal glut of the New Orleans produce markets every spring when heavy shipments were concentrated in the short period of high water.[1]

Projects for a canal around the falls were formulated as early as 1805, marked from the start by competition between proponents of a canal on the Kentucky side and those proposing a canal on the Indiana or north side. Those who favored an Indiana canal received much support from Cincinnati, reflecting keen commercial rivalry between that city and Louisville. Kentucky and Indiana each chartered a canal company in 1805, but nothing came of either venture. In 1818, the two states again chartered rival companies. The Indiana company made some preliminary excavations, but the panic and depression which descended in 1819 halted both projects.[2]

Since these early companies sought the aid of the federal government, the subject was frequently under consideration in Washington. In 1808, Secretary of the Treasury Albert Gallatin's "Report on Roads and Canals" urged the importance of a canal and recommended a federal subscription to the stock of the Kentucky corporation.[3] In 1810 and 1811 the Senate passed bills to make a contingent subscription, but these died in the House.[4] In 1817, committees of

1 For background see Archer B. Hulbert, *The Ohio River* (New York, 1906), 265-79; Alvin F. Harlow, *Old Towpaths* (New York, 1926), 289-91; Benjamin Casseday, *The History of Louisville* (Louisville, 1852); "Report . . . [on] the Navigation of the Ohio and Mississippi Rivers," *House Reports*, 18 Cong., 1 Sess., No. 98 (1824).

The author wishes to thank the Social Science Research Council for a grant-in-aid which made possible the completion of this study, and Miss Mary Verhoeff for permitting the use of her newspaper collection.

2 See Louis C. Hunter, *Steamboats on the Western Rivers* (Cambridge, 1949), 182-83; Logan Esarey, *Internal Improvements in Early Indiana* (Indianapolis, 1912), 65-69; Heber P. Walker, "Louisville and Portland Canal," *Indiana Magazine of History* (Bloomington), XXVIII (March, 1932), 21-23; Leslie S. Wright, "The Origin and History of the Louisville and Portland Canal" (M.A. thesis, University of Louisville, 1939), 1-16; *American State Papers, Miscellaneous* (2 vols., Washington, 1834), I, 821-26.

3 *American State Papers, Miscellaneous*, I, 732, 741.

4 *Annals of Congress*, 11 Cong., 2 Sess., 626 (March 26, 1810), 633 (March 29,

both houses of Congress endorsed a program of federal subscriptions to road and canal companies, including a falls canal on the Kentucky side.[5] But proposals to aid the two companies recently chartered did not reach the floor of Congress until 1820, and there they made no progress.[6]

As the country recovered from the financial disorganization attending the panic, interest in a canal revived, and by late 1823 the subject was widely debated in Kentucky and other interested states. Although some Louisville businessmen feared loss of trade if the need to transfer cargoes by land should be eliminated, most sentiment in Louisville and in Kentucky apparently favored a canal. Controversy centered on whether the state should charter another private company or do the job itself. Articulate public opinion appears to have been favorable to a state project, and was in some cases overtly hostile to creating a private company.[7]

When the Kentucky legislature convened in November, 1823, approval of a state project seemed likely. Governor Joseph Desha strongly endorsed it in his annual message, and the appropriate committees of the legislature also approved it. Prospects for enactment were strengthened by the likelihood of financial aid from the state of Ohio and the federal government.[8] But the proposal became snarled in the bitter political fight then raging in Kentucky. The state had attempted to mitigate the severity of the depression by

1810), 1679 (March 29, 1810), 1699 (March 31, 1810); *ibid.*, 11 Cong., 3 Sess., 37 (December 27, 1810), 94 (January 11, 1811), 1110 (March 3, 1811).

[5] *American State Papers, Miscellaneous*, II, 422, 425.

[6] *Annals of Congress*, 16 Cong., 1 Sess., 437 (February 22, 1820), 440-42 (February 23, 1820), 1738-40 (April 4, 1820).

[7] The grand jurors of Montgomery County argued that giving the project over to a private corporation would be "utterly hostile to the true interest of the state, as well as its Treasury. If that mode involves the necessity of investing the corporators with power to tax and toll the commerce of the country, *without limit of duration*, [we] . . . protest against it as an alarming innovation, and a dangerous precedent. . . . [We] are against any corporation, whether the charter is limited in time or not." Louisville *Public Advertiser*, September 22, 1824. See also Louis A. Tarascon, "Canal at the Falls of the Ohio," in a pamphlet entitled *Considerations on Some Matters to Be Acted on, or Worth Acting on, at the Next Session of the General Assembly of Kentucky* (Louisville, 1824), 36-38; Louisville *Public Advertiser*, September 22, October 13, 27, November 3, December 15, 1824.

[8] Kentucky Legislature, *House Journal*, 32 Sess. (1823-1824), 454-56, and 33 Sess. (1824-1825), 13-14, 142-50, 256-73; *Senate Journal*, 33 Sess., 271-78. *House Reports*, 18 Cong., 1 Sess., No. 98 (1824), 3, recommended that $100,000 of federal funds be paid to the state. "It is difficult," the report explained, "to elicit the investment of private capital in a fund which must be fluctuating and uncertain in its productiveness, and, though the sum required to perform the work is inconsiderable, it is more than the states of Ohio and Kentucky, distressed as they have been . . . can now command."

a "relief" program, but one of its key measures, a replevin law, had just been declared unconstitutional by the state supreme court. Governor Desha and most of the legislators had been elected in 1824 pledged to overturn this ruling. When an attempt to remove the offending justices from office narrowly failed of the required two-thirds vote, the "relief" party pushed through a measure in December, 1824, to abolish the existing court altogether and create a new one to which new justices could be appointed.[9]

One of the incidental effects of this controversy was the defeat of the proposal for a state canal. Conservative opinion, long hostile to the relief program, was outraged by the court reorganization. Consequently the "old-court" group in the legislature voted heavily against the state-canal proposal. Since the opinion of "new-court" legislators was divided on the canal issue, the proposal was defeated. On January 3, 1825, the bill to authorize the state to construct and manage the canal was defeated in the house, 49 to 38. "New-court" legislators supported it, 28 to 20, but the "old-court" forces voted 26 to 8 against it.[10] One of the eight was Charles M. Thruston, of Louisville. Thruston immediately introduced a bill to charter a private corporation, which passed the house on January 5 without incident.[11] On January 10, the senate, probably influenced by the house actions, defeated the bill for a state project, 23 to 12. All eleven "old-court" men voted against the bill, while known "new-court" men voted 12 to 11 in its favor (one unknown).[12] The following day the senate passed the private charter bill, and on January 12 the governor signed it. Two years later, in his annual message, Governor Desha added an epilogue to the incident:

It will ever be a subject of deep regret, that in a moment of excitement,

[9] See Arndt M. Stickles, *The Critical Court Struggle in Kentucky, 1819-1829* (Bloomington, Ind., 1929).

[10] Vote on the canal bill in Kentucky Legislature, *House Journal*, 33 Sess., 520-21; old court-new court alignments ascertained from votes on the removal bill and the reorganization bill, pp. 436-37 and 454. Five representatives voted for removal but against reorganization and are therefore excluded from the above calculation. Two of these favored and three opposed the state canal. All three representatives from Jefferson County (Louisville) voted for the bill. In the debates, opposition centered on grounds of economy and the risk of inadequate return on the state's money, while it was argued that "eastern capitalists have offered any amount of money if the Legislature will incorporate a private company." *Argus of Western America* (Frankfort), January 12, 1825.

[11] Kentucky Legislature, *House Journal*, 33 Sess., 522, 532, 538-39.

[12] Kentucky Legislature, *Senate Journal*, 33 Sess., 413-17, 431; compare votes on removing judges, p. 290. The senator from Jefferson County voted against the state canal.

> the legislature gave into private hands the digging of the canal . . . and thus threw away a source of revenue as lasting as that noble river. . . . The controversy about old court and new court is finally settled . . . but the benefits to the state in the making of the Louisville canal, which the feelings originating in that controversy induced the legislature to throw away, can never be reclaimed.[13]

The charter of the Louisville and Portland Canal Company authorized a capitalization of $600,000. Its management was to consist of a president and four other directors chosen annually by the stockholders.[14] The charter established the basic toll rate at twenty cents a ton, but permitted the company to increase it if the annual profits after operating expenses, repairs, and improvements, should fall short of 12½ per cent of the capital. On the other hand, the state legislature reserved the right to reduce the toll if the profits exceeded 18 per cent.[15] No other limitations were placed on the valuable privilege granted the company, except the customary requirements, later waived, that the canal be begun and completed by certain dates. There was no time limit on the charter, no provision for subsequent purchase or participation by the state.[16]

In March, 1826, subscriptions to the capital stock were opened, and pledges totaling about $350,000 were received. The Louisville *Public Advertiser* noted with satisfaction that "there is no longer a doubt of the success of the proposed canal. So large a share of the stock is, and will be owned *out of the state*, that no one is now apprehensive of any imprudent or unjust interference on the part of the Legislature."[17]

Subsequently, additional pledges of about $150,000 were received. Much of the capital came from Philadelphia investors.[18]

13 Kentucky Legislature, *House Journal*, 36 Sess. (1827-1828), 18. In 1835, Representative Patrick H. Pope of Kentucky stated in Congress: "The motives of those who passed the act of incorporation were pure and praiseworthy. . . . They were aware that there was no surplus local capital, and it was to tempt the employment of foreign means in the undertaking that the act . . . was passed." *Cong. Globe*, 23 Cong., 2 Sess., 202 (February 5, 1835).

14 *Acts Passed at the First Session of the Thirty-third General Assembly for the Commonwealth of Kentucky* (1824-1825), 167-73.

15 Toll charges were based on "measured tonnage." See Hunter, *Steamboats on the Western Rivers*, 642, on this concept. The 12½ to 18 per cent proviso had also been in the charter of 1818. Kentucky Legislature, *Acts* (1817-1818), 418-26.

16 The state senate rejected a proposal to reserve to the state the right to buy out the canal at a 10 per cent premium. Kentucky Legislature, *Senate Journal*, 33 Sess., 431.

17 Louisville *Public Advertiser*, March 30, 1825.

18 *History of the Ohio Falls Cities and Their Counties* (2 vols., Cleveland, 1882), I, 48. The list of stockholders for 1845 shows 56 private accounts, of which 38 repre-

There is considerable circumstantial evidence that the Bank of the United States, which had its main offices in Philadelphia and a branch in Louisville, served as an informal channel for bringing outside funds into the project. Several of the leading Philadelphia investors were connected with the Bank.[19] In Louisville, officers of the branch bank formed a large part of the canal company management.[20]

In 1824, there were predictions that the canal would be constructed in one summer for about $300,000.[21] They proved pathetically over-optimistic. Both cost and construction time far exceeded estimates, and the company, in consequence, passed through a series of financial crises. In December, 1825, contracts were arranged providing for completion within two years at a cost of $375,000, and work began in March, 1826. It soon appeared that the canal would have to be dug through solid rock, raising costs and delaying completion.[22] This discouraged many stockholders. By the end of 1826 the company had to admit that $160,000 in pledges

sented Philadelphians, holding 3,540 of the 5,312 shares then privately owned. "Louisville and Portland Canal," *House Docs.*, 28 Cong., 2 Sess., No. 94 (1845), 2-3. Stockholders for 1851 are listed in "Report of the Secretary of the Treasury . . . in Relation to the Louisville and Portland Canal," *Senate Docs.*, 32 Cong., 1 Sess., No. 39 (1852), 16-17.

[19] On the basis of the stockholder lists for 1845 and 1851, and the names of company directors for earlier years listed in the annual reports, it appears that the principal stockholders were Thomas, Peter, and John Hulme, James and Richard Ronaldson, Elihu Chauncey, William Short, William Duane, Thomas C. Rockhill, Thomas McEwen, and James C. Fisher, all of Philadelphia; John Shackford, of Portsmouth, New Hampshire, and John Mullanphy of St. Louis. Of these, James Ronaldson, Chauncey, Rockhill, Fisher, Mullanphy, and Duane had some connection with the Bank of the United States. However, Nicholas Biddle's Letter Books as president of the Bank (Division of Manuscripts, Library of Congress) show no concern with the canal company.

[20] The first president of the canal company, and a director until 1830, was James Hughes, president of the branch bank. Edward Shippen, cashier of the branch, served as company president in 1827 and was a director until 1830. Nicholas Berthoud, another original canal director, was a director of the branch bank. John I. Jacob, first treasurer of the canal company, was then a director and later president of the branch bank. See Louisville *Public Advertiser*, November 3, 1824, and November 7, 1827; James Craik, *Historical Sketches of Christ Church, Louisville* (Louisville, 1862), 26, 34; *History of Ohio Falls Cities*, I, 254; *Biographical Encyclopedia of Kentucky* (Cincinnati, 1878), 321-22.

[21] Louisville *Public Advertiser*, October 13, 1824.

[22] *Fourth Annual Report of the Louisville and Portland Canal Company* (Louisville, 1829), and *Fifth Annual Report* (1830). A complete set of the printed original reports is in the Fiscal Section of the National Archives. Most of the reports were reprinted in the Kentucky legislative documents. See Adelaide R. Hasse, *Index of Economic Material in Documents of the States of the United States: Kentucky, 1792-1904* (Washington, 1910), 109-10.

had been defaulted, chiefly, it appears, by people in the locality who were best aware of the difficulties.[23]

The company was saved by assistance from another quarter. In May, 1826, Congress voted to subscribe $100,000 to the stock.[24] The financial obstacles of the depression years to such action had passed. The increase in agricultural population and production in the Old Northwest and the farmers' sense that the Ohio River navigation was vital as a marketing channel for their products supplied the political push needed for the measure.[25] The government's purchase of stock converted the company into a mixed corporation. But this made no difference in its management, for federal officials made no effort to influence the policies of the company.

Despite this windfall, financial problems continued as construction difficulties mounted. The course of the canal was changed, requiring additional work.[26] In 1828, the stockholders, hoping to surmount the difficulties by getting expert advice, elected as a director Canvass White, of Philadelphia, one of the leading canal engineers of the country. He visited Louisville several times to give technical advice.[27] Nevertheless at the end of 1828 the contractors failed, and new arrangements had to be made to complete the canal, at higher costs.[28]

In 1829 all the stockholders' pledges had been called in, and the company was running out of money. Once again the federal government came to the rescue. In March, Congress approved the purchase of the remaining forfeited stock, amounting to $133,500.[29] This kept the company going only until the end of the year. Then

[23] "Report Relative to the Purchase of Individual Stock in the Louisville and Portland Canal Company," *House Docs.*, 28 Cong., 2 Sess., No. 66 (1845), 3-4, 10; *Second Annual Report* (1827). The stockholder lists show that very little stock was locally owned.

[24] *Statutes at Large of the United States*, IV (1824-1835), 162. Three other canal companies received federal subscriptions at this time. The idea of purchasing stock was developed as a means of circumventing the constitutional objections of President Monroe and others to outright federal construction and control of internal improvements. See Leonard D. White, *The Jacksonians* (New York, 1954), 479-81; Carter Goodrich, "National Planning of Internal Improvements," *Political Science Quarterly* (New York), LXIII (March, 1948), 34-36.

[25] See *House Reports*, 18 Cong., 1 Sess., No. 98 (1824).

[26] *Fifth Annual Report* (1830).

[27] *Dictionary of American Biography* (21 vols., New York, 1928-1944), XX, 93; Increase Lapham's Diary (Photostat, Filson Club, Louisville), entries for May 16 and August 19, 1828.

[28] *The Louisville Directory for the Year 1832* (Louisville, 1832), 110.

[29] *Statutes at Large*, IV (1824-1835), 353.

the directors sought aid from the state legislature, which amended the charter to permit an increase of $100,000 in the capitalization, but did not accept the company's proposal that the state should buy the added stock.[30] Again the directors sought aid from Washington, and for the third time, Congress responded, voting this time to buy the additional $100,000 of stock. But President Andrew Jackson vetoed the bill and denounced the practice of subscribing federal funds to private corporations which were not under effective federal control and which were permitted to charge tolls for services provided partly with public funds.[31] This put an end to federal stock purchases.

Unable to secure government funds or to market more stock privately, the company turned to large-scale borrowing. It obtained $154,000 in loans in 1830, giving the lenders the option of receiving stock in payment.[32] This sum was sufficient to get the canal opened in December, 1830, but it was still unfinished and the company had to borrow more money in 1831. In December, 1831, the Kentucky legislature amended the charter to permit the capitalization to be increased by any amount needed to complete the canal, including interest on loans. On this basis, the company issued a stock dividend of 26 per cent to its stockholders.[33]

The company was still $190,000 in debt, but it was now open for business, and people soon realized that it would be a lucrative enterprise. Most of the creditors were willing to accept stock in settlement of their claims, and $172,000 worth was issued in that manner. Sales of stock to the public brought the total capitalization of the company to an even $1,000,000, of which the federal government held $290,000.[34]

30 Kentucky Legislature, *House Journal*, 38 Sess. (1829-1830), 73, 95; "Report on the Louisville and Portland Canal," *House Misc. Docs.*, 40 Cong., 2 Sess., No. 83 (1868), 3-4.

31 *Sixth Annual Report* (1831); Jackson's Annual Message, *House Docs.*, 21 Cong., 2 Sess., No. 2 (1830), 9-12.

32 *Sixth Annual Report* (1831).

33 The company distributed stock amounting to $156,000 par value, of which the United States received $57,000. The legislature had authorized the company "to extend their capital stock to such an amount as will be sufficient to pay all the cost and expenses of constructing said canal, and the interest on the sums [so] expended." *House Docs.*, 28 Cong., 2 Sess., No. 66 (1845), 6-7. Part of the stock dividend was calculated as "accrued interest" at 6 per cent due the stockholders. Although this was probably not what the legislature had in mind, no criticism seems to have been directed at this action.

34 *Eleventh Annual Report* (1836); *House Misc. Docs.*, 40 Cong., 2 Sess., No. 83 (1868), 34-35.

Upon completion, the canal was two miles long. It had three lift locks, each with a lift of slightly over eight feet, a length of 183 feet, and a width of 50 feet. The imposing sloping banks rose more than 100 feet above the bottom of the canal bed, and were 200 feet apart at the top.[35] The canal was the first major improvement to be successfully completed on the great central river system of the United States. By comparison with the Erie Canal and other eastern projects, it was gigantic in dimensions (save length, of course) — "having a capacity equal to that of 25 common canals" — and became a cynosure of tourist interest.[36] Huge it had to be to cope with the emerging shape of the western steamboat and the great variations in the level of the river, which flowed into its upper end without any barrier. Yet the canal was scarcely open before evolving steamboat technology had rendered it practically obsolete.

The opening of the canal does not appear to have had much economic impact. Undoubtedly it contributed to lower freight rates, but it was only one of many such factors, among which technical improvements in the steamboat were more important. Freight rates on the Ohio had been declining in the 1820's, but no notable reductions accompanied the opening of the canal. The differential in prices of commodities between Cincinnati and New Orleans was being steadily reduced during this period, but appears to have fallen more in the quinquennium preceding the canal's opening than in that following it.[37] The rapid increase in the canal's toll rate wiped out much of the saving achieved by avoiding transshipment, and the inadequate size of the canal soon presented shippers with the unpleasant alternatives of either foregoing the superior efficiency of large boats or reverting to transshipment around the falls.[38]

[35] *Fifth Annual Report* (1830); see also *House Docs.*, 28 Cong., 2 Sess., No. 66 (1845), 10.

[36] *Fifth Annual Report* (1830). It continues: "we may not be considered extravagant in drawing the comparison between the work in this and that in 70 or 75 miles of common canalling." For a tourist's report, see John Starkey's Diary, 1829 (Photostat, Filson Club), 6.

[37] Thomas S. Berry, in his exhaustive study of western prices and commodity markets, does not connect the canal with any observable changes in prices or freight rates. His apparent opinion of the canal is indicated by his description of it as a "narrow little ditch." *Western Prices before 1861* (Cambridge, 1943), 40. On freight rates, see *ibid.*, 46, 55; on price differentials, pp. 106, 113. Note that Cincinnati's "terms of trade" (prices received relative to prices paid) showed a large improvement in 1831 (p. 564).

[38] By 1840 transshipment by land had revived. Berry, *Western Prices before 1861*, 40.

Business was slow for the canal company during the first two years, partly because the canal was not fully completed until 1833. The company management discovered that the toll rate of twenty cents a ton would not yield the profits permitted by the charter, so the rate was increased to forty cents in 1832 and to sixty cents in 1837.[39] In 1833, the canal hit full stride, carrying 1,585 boats totaling 170,000 tons, and yielding $61,000 gross revenue. Cash dividends of 6 per cent were paid in 1834, 1835, and 1836, and the stock reached par. Higher toll rates and the boom of the late 1830's brought a tidal wave of profits, reaching a peak in 1839 when boats totaling 300,000 tons passed through the canal. They left behind $180,000 in tolls that year, of which $136,000 was divided among the stockholders. For the entire period 1831-1842 the company collected $1,120,000 in tolls and paid out $823,000 in dividends plus $43,000 interest.[40] Yet this did not give the stockholders windfall gains, considering the whole period — it represented a return to the original stockholders of less than 8 per cent a year, counting the early years when no dividends were paid.

The canal was scarcely open when boatmen and shippers began to complain about the high tolls. By 1833 the average boat paid about $40 to get through the canal; by 1838 it paid nearly $80. Petitions descended on Congress urging that the government buy out the stockholders and reduce the tolls.[41] Even the Kentucky legislature passed a resolution asking the United States to take over.[42] Some of the stockholders, noting the hostility to the company underlying this movement and fearing that the federal government might take over anyway, indicated their willingness to sell out at a reasonable figure.[43]

39 "[Report] from the Committee on Roads and Canals, on . . . the Louisville and Portland Canal," *Senate Docs.*, 22 Cong., 2 Sess., No. 25 (1833), 3; *Tenth* and *Twelfth Annual Reports* (1835, 1837).

40 *House Misc. Docs.*, 40 Cong., 2 Sess., No. 83 (1868), 34. The federal government received $255,000 in cash dividends during this period.

41 See "Memorial of Sundry Inhabitants of Pennsylvania," *Senate Docs.*, 22 Cong., 2 Sess., No. 11 (1832); "Memorial of Sundry Inhabitants of St. Louis," *ibid.*, No. 5; *Senate Journal*, 22 Cong., 2 Sess., 24, 26, 31, 37, 43, 81; "Memorial of Sundry Inhabitants of Cincinnati," *Senate Docs.*, 23 Cong., 1 Sess., No. 6 (1833); "Petition of Sundry Individuals," *Senate Docs.*, 23 Cong., 2 Sess., No. 94 (1835). The Cincinnati memorialists pointed out that "the company was . . . vested with perpetual jurisdiction and the power of taxing the immense commerce that must . . . pass through the canal, *ad libitum*; for, although they are restricted to dividends of eighteen per cent per annum, there is no limit to the amount of capital that they may invest in it."

42 "Resolutions of the Legislature of Kentucky," *House Docs.*, 23 Cong., 2 Sess., No. 159 (1835).

43 *Senate Docs.*, 22 Cong., 2 Sess., No. 25 (1833).

Committees of both houses of Congress endorsed the move to buy out the private stockholders and reduce tolls.[44] In June, 1836, the Senate passed such a bill, but it died in the House.[45] The proposal continued to echo in Congress but made no headway against determined resistance.[46] One source of opposition consisted of Indiana interests, whose hostility to the canal dated from the earliest discussions of the project and continued to plague the company throughout its existence. Indiana had chartered a new canal company in 1836, but it accomplished nothing.[47] To this group were added opponents who took a constitutional stand that buying the canal would be an invasion of state rights. It was also argued that government operation of the canal would be less efficient than private operation.[48]

[44] *Ibid.*; "Louisville and Portland Canal," *House Reports*, 23 Cong., 1 Sess., No. 307 (1834); "Report . . . [on] the Louisville and Portland Canal Company," *Senate Docs.*, 24 Cong., 1 Sess., No. 117 (1836). In supporting the measure on the floor of the House, Representative Pope of Kentucky cited complaints against "the exaction of a corporation almost wholly irresponsible . . . a corporation most improvidently clothed with extraordinary powers, and possessed of that pernicious gift, perpetual existence." Pope declared: "I do solemnly believe that it is, or will be the most profitable stock in the United States. The stockholders are possessed of the most valuable charter in the country, and they know it." He insisted that the bill was not "a trick put on foot by designing stockholders for selfish purposes." *Cong. Globe*, 23 Cong., 2 Sess., 202-203 (February 5, 1835).

[45] *Senate Journal*, 24 Cong., 1 Sess. (1835-1836), 136, 382, 398, 402; *House Journal*, 24 Cong., 1 Sess., 958, 962, 1215; *Cong. Globe*, 24 Cong., 1 Sess., 416-17 (June 2, 1836).

[46] See *House Misc. Docs.*, 40 Cong., 2 Sess., No. 83 (1868), 5-6, 18; "Letter from the Secretary of the Treasury . . . Relative to the Louisville and Portland Canal," *House Docs.*, 28 Cong., 1 Sess., No. 154 (1844); *Cong. Globe*, 25 Cong., 2 Sess., 230 (March 8, 1838); *ibid.*, 26 Cong., 1 Sess., 79 (December 24, 1839), 158-59 (February 3, 1840).

Considering that financial questions involving the canal were before Congress so often, it is worth noting that three men listed as stockholders in 1845 served in the House of Representatives — John Sergeant, of Philadelphia (1815-1823, 1827-1829, 1837-1841); William Drayton, of South Carolina (1825-1833), later of Philadelphia; and Samuel F. Vinton, of Gallipolis, Ohio (1823-1837, 1843-1851). *Dictionary of American Biography*, V, 448; XVI, 588-89; XIX, 284; Madelene Vinton Dahlgren, "Samuel Finley Vinton," *Publications of the Ohio State Archaeological and Historical Society* (Columbus), IV (1895), 231-62. None held much stock, and none played any recorded role in proceedings involving the canal (except voting), although Vinton long served on the Committee on Roads and Canals.

[47] Esarey, *Internal Improvements in Early Indiana*, 69; "Resolutions of the General Assembly of Indiana," *Senate Docs.*, 24 Cong., 2 Sess., No. 117 (1837).

[48] According to Representative Albert G. Hawes, of Kentucky, "it was improper for the General Government to appropriate money for improvements within the States. Besides, the Government was incapable of carrying on and superintending this canal so as to produce any practical good or benefit." *Cong. Globe*, 23 Cong., 2 Sess., 205 (February 5, 1835). Representative John Y. Mason, of Virginia, added: "the very moment that individuals ceased to be interested in it as their own private property, that very moment all security for that vigorous and constant attention which

The stockholders observed with apprehension the movement for a new canal on the Indiana side of the river. In a memorial to the Kentucky legislature in 1842 they expressed their alarm at "the repeated applications to Congress for another canal, the hostility exhibited to the company from various quarters, and the apathy with which propositions to destroy its rights are entertained in Congress and elsewhere"; noted "the general expectation that the thoroughfare for the navigation of this important section of the Union should be free"; and concluded that they would be willing to sell out for "a sum much below the intrinsic value of their stock." [49]

In this memorial the stockholders proposed an ingenious scheme: if Congress would not buy them out they would buy themselves out — with Congress's money. Instead of paying dividends, the company would use its net income to redeem all the private shares at a substantial premium plus interest. Thus the government's share of the dividends would be diverted into the hands of the private stockholders in payment for their shares. The shareholders would receive a tidy profit and the United States would wind up with the canal.

At the company's request, the Kentucky legislature amended the charter to authorize the canal managers to use the company's net income in this way. They were directed to purchase the stock at the lowest possible price, not to exceed $150 per share in the first year, but with 6 per cent interest to be added each subsequent year. The directors were to hold in trust the stock so purchased until all had been acquired; then the canal was to be "transferred to the Government of the United States, on condition of said government levying tolls . . . only sufficient to keep the [canal] . . . in repair and pay all necessary . . . expenses, and make all necessary improvements." [50]

works of this nature required would be lost." *Ibid.*, 205. Others argued that the project was not truly national in importance, and that buying it might commit the government to similar action with other companies in which it held stock. *Ibid.*, 203-205.

49 Quoted in *House Docs.*, 28 Cong., 2 Sess., No. 66 (1845), 42.

50 Act of January 21, 1842, reprinted in "Report of the Committee on Finance . . . [on] the Bill Providing for the Payment of the Bonds of the Louisville and Portland Canal Company," *Senate Reports*, 43 Cong., 1 Sess., No. 270 (1874). A Kentucky resolution of 1844 promised to cede jurisdiction to the United States when it should assume ownership. *House Misc. Docs.*, 40 Cong., 2 Sess., No. 83 (1868), 4. In a letter in 1844, Thomas Hulme, who held the largest private block of stock in the company, took credit for devising the plan. He added: "I and my family . . . are willing to make any reasonable sacrifice for the purpose of rendering the navigation of the

The stockholders approved this policy in 1842, with the federal government taking no part in the decision. The canal board then began buying stock, and no further regular dividends were paid. After buying a few shares at prices of $125 to $130, the board settled upon regular purchases at the maximum price of $150 per share plus interest from January, 1843, of $9.00 annually, not compounded.

The financial strength of the company had already been demonstrated by continued high profits in the depression years from 1840 to 1842. Tolls reached their nadir in 1842, at $95,000, but expenses were only $19,000. That year the management voluntarily lowered the toll from sixty to fifty cents per ton, where it remained until 1855. By 1843, revenues were again increasing and soon poured in as they had in the 1830's. In consequence, the company was able to make substantial purchases of stock each year until the task was completed in 1855. A total of $1,419,000 was paid to the stockholders after 1842, representing redemption of $709,000 par value of stock (for which the company had received about $620,000 cash originally), plus premiums of $354,000, plus interest of $356,000.[51] The federal government's share in this money would have been about $400,000, so the remaining million dollars would presumably have gone to the stockholders anyway. They received nearly four fifths of the total canal revenue during the period 1842-1855, giving them a return of about 20 per cent a year on the original cost of the stock. One stockholder commented in 1854: "Thus are my individual interests all *retired* from that company, and I fear I shall never be able to find as good an investment for the money as that has been. And I understand that another year will pay off all the private stockholders, when I suppose the concern will fall into the hands of some democrat pet of the Government, and of course go to the dogs." [52]

By 1842 the inadequate size of the canal was as serious a subject

Ohio River *free*; because we think it *ought to be free*." Printed in *House Docs.*, 28 Cong., 1 Sess., No. 154 (1844).

[51] *House Misc. Docs.*, 40 Cong., 2 Sess., No. 83 (1868), 35.

[52] J. Cleves Short to Charles W. Short, January 8, 1854, Short Family Papers (Division of Manuscripts, Library of Congress). Their correspondence indicates that by 1848 the president and superintendent ran the company without significant interference from stockholders or the other directors. See letters from Charles to Cleves Short, January 4 and 6, 1848, January 1, 1849; Cleves to Charles, December 9, 1848, and January 5, 1851.

of complaint as that of excessive tolls. Although the company's 1830 report described the canal as "intended for steamboats of the largest class," the steamboats soon outgrew the canal. Many new boats could not pass through it at all, while others suffered delays and risked damage because the canal was too narrow and shallow. There was also complaint that the lower end of the canal was located at a point where the river was narrow and moved too swiftly.[53] The inadequacy of the canal was demonstrated by the failure of canal traffic to increase appreciably during the 1850's, despite the great growth of river traffic.[54]

During the 1840's pressure was again exerted on Congress to pay off the remaining private stockholders, reduce the tolls, and enlarge the canal. Even the company management urged such action.[55] But again the movement got no further than an occasional favorable committee report.[56] Jefferson Davis stated the prevailing view of opponents when he argued that the proposal "presents another means of multiplying Federal officers and stretching the influence of the Federal Government still further over the States. . . . I have no doubt also that the work would be more economically improved by the company than by the Federal Government." [57]

In January, 1855, the canal directors informed Secretary of the Treasury James Guthrie that they had purchased all the private stock save one share held by each director as a formality required by the charter, and that "the canal is now ready to be transferred to the custody of the general government." [58] They expressed willing-

[53] *House Docs.*, 28 Cong., 2 Sess., No. 66 (1845), 3-4; Hunter, *Steamboats on the Western Rivers*, 184-86; "Letter from the Secretary of the Treasury . . . Relative to the Louisville and Portland Canal," *House Docs.*, 34 Cong., 1 Sess., No. 74 (1856), which notes that by 1853 few boats could get through the canal in less than five hours.

[54] Hunter, *Steamboats on the Western Rivers*, 185-86.

[55] *Senate Docs.*, 32 Cong., 1 Sess., No. 39 (1852), 11-12.

[56] *House Docs.*, 28 Cong., 1 Sess., No. 154 (1844); *Cong. Globe*, 28 Cong., 2 Sess., 77 (December 31, 1844); *ibid.*, 31 Cong., 2 Sess., 114-16 (December 22, 1850). In 1851 a bill designed to placate both the state-rights sentiment and the Indiana interests proposed that the United States buy out the private stockholders, cede the canal to Kentucky, and build another on the Indiana side. See *House Misc. Docs.*, 40 Cong., 2 Sess., No. 83 (1868), 8; "Canal Around the Falls of the Ohio River," *House Reports*, 32 Cong., 1 Sess., No. 166 (1852). The Kentucky legislature repeatedly indicated that Kentucky did not want the canal.

[57] *Cong. Globe*, 31 Cong., 2 Sess., 116 (December 23, 1850).

[58] Quoted in *House Misc. Docs.*, 40 Cong., 2 Sess., No. 83 (1868), 20. James Guthrie of Louisville, who served as secretary of the treasury from 1853 to 1857, had been associated with the canal company in its early years and was later to become its president. His name appeared in the original charter as one of the men authorized to supervise formation of the company, and he later served as lawyer for it. His name

ness to continue to manage it but urged the necessity of enlarging its facilities. Guthrie asked them to remain in charge pending formal government action.[59] At his suggestion they reduced the toll from fifty to twenty-five cents. He authorized them to use surplus canal revenues for certain minor improvements in canal facilities, but instructed them to refrain from enlarging the locks.[60]

It seemed only a matter of form for Congress to accept full control of the canal. Yet it was nearly twenty years before this was done, during which time the corporation remained, as it were, suspended in mid-air. In 1854, when the management had nearly finished redeeming the stock, the Senate passed a bill authorizing the President to take formal possession of the canal, but this failed to pass the House.[61] From 1854 until 1860, bills to take over the canal and improve it were continually under discussion in Congress, but none passed.[62] Objections on grounds of constitutionality, economy, and efficiency were reiterated in the debates.

In a lengthy speech, Representative Humphrey Marshall of Kentucky bitterly paid tribute to the opposition forces.

> Year in and year out [he said] the Representative from the city of Louisville has been before Congress with this offer made by the company, asking that an appropriation may be made to make the Louisville and Portland Canal "equal to the wants of commerce," so that the United States might become the proprietor of the work, in conformity with the Kentucky statute; and year by year the constitutional scruples of gentlemen on the Democratic side of the House have prevented that being done. Year by year, when I have attempted to get an appropriation for this purpose, these same Indiana gentlemen have proposed to acquiesce in it with the condition that the Government of the United States, in appropriating money to make the Louisville and Portland canal equal to the wants of commerce, should also appropriate money to build another canal on the Indiana side of the river.[63]

does not appear on the stockholder lists of 1845 and 1851, however, and the claim that he was "the controlling force" in the canal seems exaggerated. See *Dictionary of American Biography*, VIII, 60-62. Guthrie later achieved prominence as president of the Louisville and Nashville Railroad.

59 *House Misc. Docs.*, 40 Cong., 2 Sess., No. 83 (1868), 20-21.

60 *Ibid.*, 21; "Report of the Secretary of the Treasury Respecting the Louisville and Portland Canal," *Senate Docs.*, 34 Cong., 3 Sess., No. 44 (1857).

61 *Cong. Globe*, 33 Cong., 1 Sess., 2039 (August 1, 1854).

62 *Ibid.*, 34 Cong., 1 Sess., 2160 (August 15, 1856); 3 Sess., 988-89 (March 3, 1857); 35 Cong., 1 Sess., 1125-28 (March 15, 1858); "Louisville and Portland Canal," *House Reports*, 34 Cong., 1 Sess., No. 327 (1856); "Report . . . [on] Enlarging and Improving the 'Louisville and Portland Canal'," *Senate Reports*, 34 Cong., 3 Sess., No. 371 (1857).

63 *Cong. Globe*, 35 Cong., 1 Sess., 1126 (March 15, 1858). Indiana had chartered

Marshall went on to accuse the Indiana and Cincinnati interests of attempting to prevent the company itself from making any improvements. That opposition, plus the constitutional argument, he said, had prevented the federal government from improving the canal. In 1860, however, Senator Lazarus W. Powell, also of Kentucky, argued that "the only reason why the Government of the United States has not long since taken charge of the canal, is the fear that there would be a demand on the national Treasury to enlarge it." [64]

The company directors, despairing of federal funds, pressed for freedom to proceed on their own with the needed improvements. In 1857 they persuaded the Kentucky legislature to amend the charter "to authorize said company to construct, with the revenues, and on the credit of the corporation, a branch canal sufficient to pass the largest class of steam vessels navigating the Ohio River." [65] The Army Engineers endorsed the proposed improvements, but Secretary of the Treasury Howell Cobb directed the company to make no expenditures on improvements pending congressional action.[66]

Congress finally adopted the only measure that was politically feasible — it formalized the status quo. Instead of taking over the canal, it voted to keep the corporation in existence and to permit it to undertake the proposed major improvements.[67] This was done in May, 1860, by a joint resolution which essentially repeated the phrasing of the Kentucky resolution of 1857, with the added provisions that the company was not to "use or pledge the faith or credit of the United States," that "the Government of the United States shall not be in any manner liable for said enlargement and

still another abortive canal company in 1849. William J. Ball, *Canal around the Falls of the Ohio* (Cincinnati, 1850).

64 *Cong. Globe*, 36 Cong., 1 Sess., 1175 (March 15, 1860).

65 Quoted in *House Misc. Docs.*, 40 Cong., 2 Sess., No. 83 (1868), 4.

66 *Ibid.*, 14-15, 24-25.

67 The situation was well described by Representative David Ritchie of Pennsylvania: "We have this company in the very act of applying the tolls now collected for the enlargement of the canal on the Kentucky side. If let alone, they will, in my judgment, have a canal there in a short time, which will probably answer the purpose of the commerce of the river. . . . I see no hope in the present state of the national finances and in the present aspect of the political forces in this House and in the Senate, with the constitutional scruples of the Democratic majorities, of getting money from the National Government for this purpose. . . . I therefore go for what I consider the only practical measure . . . and that is to permit the men, who have now the Louisville canal, to go on collecting their tolls and to enlarge the present canal." *Cong. Globe*, 35 Cong., 1 Sess., 1127 (March 15, 1858).

construction," and that when the improvements were completed and paid for, "no more tolls shall be collected than an amount sufficient to keep the canal in repair, and pay for all necessary superintendence and management."[68] The measure assuaged the objections of the economy bloc and appeased the state-rights advocates and the Indiana interests.[69] Robert Toombs, senator from Georgia, raised the pertinent objection, however, that the canal directors were being granted great power without any real check on how it was to be used.[70]

The resolution of 1860 inaugurated a new phase in the canal company's existence, which may well earn it the designation as the first real federal government corporation, an honor usually reserved for later creations.[71] True, it was not chartered by the United States, nor did it originate as a government corporation. But from 1855 it was de facto owned by the federal government. Futhermore, the resolution of 1860 was a measure intended to continue the company's peculiar organization as a deliberate means of achieving desirable objectives without the political, constitutional, and administrative difficulties which might otherwise arise.

Prior to 1855, the federal government had exercised little influence over the policies of the canal. Liaison with the company was maintained by the secretary of the treasury, but the government always gave the incumbent management authority to act as its proxy, and the only substantive subject of correspondence between the government and its proxies was accruing dividends. The government's stock was voted in favor of the maneuver of 1842, but the subject was not mentioned in the prior correspondence.[72]

After 1855, liaison between the Treasury Department and the company was closer, reflecting at first Guthrie's presence in the Treasury post. Guthrie's interest in the canal led him to urge re-

[68] *Statutes at Large*, XII (1860-1863), 116.

[69] See statements by Powell, Jefferson Davis, and Jesse D. Bright, senator from Indiana, all in *Cong. Globe*, 36 Cong., 1 Sess., 1174-75 (March 15, 1860).

[70] "It is for the Government to hold the legal title," Toombs said, "and to allow five gentlemen, who elect themselves directors . . . to govern it as they please; to borrow money on the tolls, and doubtless, when they get in debt, they will expect the Government to pay it." *Ibid.*, 1174.

[71] See John A. McDiarmid, *Government Corporations and Federal Funds* (Chicago, 1938), 22. The honor usually goes to the Panama Railroad Corporation, included in the purchase of the Canal Zone in 1904.

[72] The correspondence to 1852 is contained in *Senate Docs.*, 32 Cong., 1 Sess., No. 39 (1852). All of it to 1867 is summarized in *House Misc. Docs.*, 40 Cong., 2 Sess., No. 83 (1868), 18-25.

duction of tolls and to indicate what sort of improvements the company might undertake. His successor, Secretary Cobb, also intervened in company policy when he instructed the directors in 1858 to suspend work on improvements.[73] They complied, but they also registered strong objection to being given orders by the government. They pointed out that the government owned outright only the shares acquired before 1842. The shares bought up after that date were held in trust by the company directors and did not entitle the government to any additional control in the management of the company. They added: "The United States can only acquire the proprietorship of the property in the whole canal upon the basis established by said act [of 1842]; and, with all respect to Congress, it does seem to the undersigned that a reasonable period within which the election might have been made has already transpired." [74]

The company was now, as many contemporary observers noted, an anomaly. The federal government owned, in fact if not in law, 99.95 per cent of the stock, while the management, holding the other 0.05 per cent, retained operating control. To be sure, the directors acknowledged their responsibility to act in the interests of the government — but they were to be the interpreters of that interest. Congress, of course, had the power to assume control at any time — but only by assuming the financial responsibility for the canal. From 1855 until Congress did decide to assume control the board of directors retained great autonomy. The directors consisted of Louisville residents recruited apparently by co-option. They published no further annual reports and made no reports at all to Congress after 1860.

From 1860 to 1867 Congress ignored the canal, and the directors concentrated on enlarging it. The plan was to build a new set of large locks branching off from the existing canal to enter the river at a better point.[75] In addition, the old locks were to be improved in a manner that would permit continued use of the canal during construction. The company arranged a contract for the branch canal which stipulated a cost of $865,000 — more than the original canal had cost. A contract for enlarging the old locks was let for

[73] See quotations in *House Misc. Docs.*, 40 Cong., 2 Sess., No. 83 (1868), 20-25; "Letter from the Secretary of the Treasury on the Condition of the Louisville and Portland Canal Company," *House Docs.*, 35 Cong., 1 Sess., No. 131 (1858), 5-7.

[74] *House Misc. Docs.*, 40 Cong., 2 Sess., No. 83 (1868), 24-25; see also pp. 46-50.

[75] *Ibid.*, 12-13.

$443,000. The contractors agreed to accept 6 per cent mortgage bonds of the company in payment as the work progressed.

Work began in 1860, but the Civil War soon interfered seriously with the ambitious building program. Reduced river traffic cut current revenues sharply in the first year of the war, and the company reacted by raising the toll back to fifty cents. Traffic revived strongly in 1863 and after, so that current revenues averaged better than $160,000 annually through 1866. But more serious difficulties arose as the contractors found themselves pinched between a declining market for bonds and rapidly rising costs, both reflecting wartime financial conditions. Their contracts were revised upward in 1863 and 1864, and the size of the new locks was reduced slightly. But when they sought another revision in 1865, the canal directors canceled the contract. The directors managed to keep the construction going through other arrangements until the end of 1866, but financial difficulties then brought it to a halt.[76] Nearly two million dollars had been spent and still more was needed for completion. The company was $1,600,000 in debt, faced with increasing interest charges, and could sell 6-per cent bonds for no more than 80 per cent of par. The old locks were still in use, but were now in bad condition, and the tolls were again too high to suit the canal users.[77] As before, the only apparent way out of the difficulty was to secure aid from the government. Fortunately for the company, the political obstacles to such aid had been largely removed by the war. The spirit of economic nationalism, which had been widespread when the canal first sought federal aid, was then enjoying a postwar revival and promised to provide the proper atmosphere for the renewal of government interest.

The first government body to reflect the new spirit was the Army Corps of Engineers, which became a supporter of the canal company's hope for government assistance. Late in 1866, the canal was inspected by W. Milnor Roberts, the officer in charge of the Ohio River improvement program of the Army Engineers. Roberts commented: "I had an opportunity of examining the magnificent new locks of the unfinished enlarged canal. They are on the grandest scale, and superior in workmanship to any I have ever seen. . . . The masonry of these immense locks is entirely finished, but a large

[76] *Ibid.*, 31, 34-35, 43-44.

[77] See "Memorial from the Cincinnati Chamber of Commerce," *House Misc. Docs.*, 41 Cong., 2 Sess., No. 122 (1870).

amount of work still remains to be done, including lock gates, rock excavation, &c., which the late chief engineer . . . estimated would, at present high prices, cost a million of dollars." According to Roberts, the old locks were "literally worn out, out of date, behind the age, and entirely inadequate to the present business of the river." He concluded that "the government ought to take this important work in hand and complete it at the earliest period possible." [78]

The prompt response of Congress to the suggestions of the Engineers and the river interests indicated the extent to which the climate of opinion concerning federal aid had changed. In 1867 it authorized the Army to prepare surveys and estimates both for completing the improvements of the old canal and for building another on the Indiana side.[79] The latter proposal was shown, as usual, to involve excessive expense and was again rejected. The Engineers also drew up an improvement plan for the river channel at Louisville, and started to execute it in 1869. Work was begun on the canal improvement in 1870, using funds from a discretionary appropriation of April, 1869. Congress acquiesced in this by passing subsequent explicit appropriations for the canal as more funds were needed, without apparent political controversy,[80] and without taking formal possession of the canal.

Work on the enlarged branch of the canal proceeded rapidly, and in November, 1871, water was let into the new locks and a few boats passed through. But the pressure of the water dislodged the miter sills on which the lock gates rested, and the new section had to be blocked off again for repairs.[81] It was reopened successfully in February, 1872, although the improvements were not entirely completed until two years later. The government's expenditure to complete the improvements was about $1,300,000.[82]

The new branch contained two locks, each 390 feet long and 90

[78] "Report by the Chief of Engineers Respecting Certain Public Works," *House Docs.*, 39 Cong., 2 Sess., No. 56 (1867), 317-18.

[79] *Statutes at Large*, XV (1867-1869), 25.

[80] "Report Relative to a Ship Canal Around the Falls of the Ohio River," *House Docs.*, 40 Cong., 2 Sess., No. 181 (1868). The river and harbor appropriation bills of 1868 and 1869 did not specify sums for individual projects. The law of July, 1870, appropriated $250,000 "for improvement of the falls of the Ohio River and Louisville canal," the first such specific appropriation. *Statutes at Large*, XV (1867-1869), 174; XVI (1869-1871), 44, 225.

[81] On progress of the work, see the annual reports of the Chief of Engineers, 1868-1874, in *House Documents*, as listed in *Tables of and Annotated Index to the Congressional Series of United States Public Documents* (Washington, 1902), 324.

[82] "Report [of the] Committee on Commerce [on] . . . the Bill . . . Providing for

feet wide, with lifts of twelve and fourteen feet respectively.[83] The effect on the river economy of opening the new branch was probably as great as that of the original opening of the canal nearly half a century earlier.[84] By 1877 the canal was passing three times as much tonnage as it had ever carried before the improvement. But the nature of the river trade had changed greatly over the preceding half-century. In the early years of the canal, the Ohio was the great marketing outlet and a major avenue of supply for northwestern farmers. By 1860, trade in farm products and supplies had been diverted to more direct East-West transport media, chiefly the railways. Failure to improve the canal in the 1840's and 1850's undoubtedly helped promote this shift in trade routes. After the Civil War the river became, and still is, chiefly a medium for transporting heavy, low-value industrial supplies and products. Most of the canal's business consisted of barge shipments of coal, salt, and iron ore.[85]

While the Engineers were working on the canal improvements they were involved in a running controversy with the canal company management over the precise relationship between the federal government and the company.[86] In March, 1873, Congress at last faced that issue squarely, authorizing the secretary of the treasury to assume control and management of the canal and appropriating the necessary funds.[87] The secretary demurred, however, on grounds that the government could not assume jurisdiction until all the company's bonds were paid off — and some of them were not due until 1886.[88] Congress decided that assurance of payment was good enough. In May, 1874, it passed a bill authorizing the Army

the Payment of the Bonds of the Louisville and Portland Canal Company," *House Reports*, 43 Cong., 1 Sess., No. 218 (1874), 13-14.

[83] *House Docs.*, 39 Cong., 2 Sess., No. 56 (1867), 264-65, 317.

[84] "River traffic was thereby given a new lease on life (it had languished since 1861 as a result of railway competition). The maximum size of boats plying above and below Louisville was increased from six or seven hundred to seventeen hundred tons, and rates on coal, by that time the principal cargo, sank as low as one twentieth of a cent per ton-mile." Berry, *Western Prices before 1861*, p. 41.

[85] *Ibid.*, 277-79, 295 ff. See also Major Godfrey Weitzel's annual reports on the canal, 1874-1880, in *Senate Documents*, as listed in *Tables of and Annotated Index to the Congressional Series of United States Public Documents*, 453.

[86] See annual reports of the Chief of Engineers, 1869, pp. 47-49; 1872, pp. 444-52; 1873, p. 535; "Letter from the Secretary of War . . . Relative to the . . . Louisville and Portland Canal," *Senate Docs.*, 42 Cong., 3 Sess., No. 1 (1872), 4-9.

[87] *Statutes at Large*, XVII (1871-1873), 563.

[88] "Report of the Secretary of the Treasury on the State of the Finances for the Year 1873," *House Docs.*, 43 Cong., 1 Sess., No. 2, xxxvi-xxxviii.

to take over the canal, and instructing the Treasury Department to pay off the company's bonds and to purchase the last five shares of stock from the directors.[89]

On June 11, 1874, the Louisville and Portland Canal Company passed out of existence, and the canal became formally the property of the United States government. Tolls were reduced to ten cents by the law of 1874, and were cut further by the Army in 1878 and 1879. In May, 1880, half a century of agitation by river interests came to a successful conclusion when Congress voted to make the canal free of toll and to pay its expenses out of the federal treasury.[90]

The company's ghost lingered a bit longer through its unpaid bonds, of which about $1,172,000 were outstanding in 1874. The treasury paid the interest on all until they matured (at a total cost of $464,000), and redeemed them at par upon maturity in 1876, 1881, and 1886.[91] The total direct cost to the government of improving and acquiring the canal, deducting dividends received, was only about $3,000,000.

The fate of the Louisville and Portland Canal Company testifies to the limitations on the ability of private interests to exploit a monopolistic position which adversely affected broad public interests. It is true that the stockholders relinquished control under circumstances favorable to themselves, but they were undoubtedly influenced somewhat by fear of adverse government action (of which there was never very much real danger). Some were probably influenced by a sense of public obligation as well, although this did not extend to the point of willingness to put up more money for the improvement of the canal in the 1840's.

The company's history also furnishes a good example of how the pressure of private interests — the canal's customers — led to the substitution of government for private ownership and control of the canal. But before the government assumed full ownership and control, the halfway expedient of a government-owned but largely autonomous corporation evolved as a compromise between the de-

89 *Statutes at Large,* XVIII (1873-1875), 43-45.

90 See Weitzel's annual reports; also *Statutes at Large,* XXI (1879-1881), 141. Hunter, *Steamboats on the Western Rivers,* 373, notes that "relief came too late to be of much help to the declining steamboat interest." For the subsequent history of the canal, see Wright, "Origins and History of the Louisville and Portland Canal," 102 ff.

91 See the annual volumes of "Receipts and Expenditures of the United States," 1874-1886, in *House Documents,* as listed in *Tables of and Annotated Index to the Congressional Series of United States Public Documents,* 620.

mands of the canal users and the objections to complete government ownership on grounds of constitutionality, expense, efficiency, or sectional interest. Then, after the Civil War, the drive of economic nationalism spurred Congress to override the old objections and operate the canal in the public interest.

During its lifetime the company was the target of bitter criticism by river interests because of high tolls and inadequate facilities.[92] But it is by no means obvious that the conduct of the company merits censure. To the contemporary student, the stock dividend and the high returns reaped by stockholders after 1842 might deserve disapproval. But the high returns were a reward for bearing a substantial risk, and could have been obtained by anyone willing to buy the stock at par or below any time before 1834. The returns were not out of line with those received by successful firms in commerce, banking, or manufacturing.

In 1872, Joshua F. Speed, then president of the company, wrote: "For years the duties of the board have been arduous, responsible, without profit to themselves, and thankless. . . . To keep up the credit of the company, and the canal open to commerce, they have repeatedly been compelled to pledge their individual credit for large sums."[93] Although Speed's assertion may be exaggerated, the judgment of contemporaries was that the management had done a good job of fulfilling their trust in the years after 1855.[94] Yet, because of the delay in completing the improvements, and because the government eventually had to step in to complete and help pay for them, it cannot be said that this first experiment with the government corporation device was an unqualified success. The company's failure to complete the canal improvements was the result of unusual circumstances rather than poor management or other defects in the corporate device itself. The experiment demonstrated that the corporate device could compromise the incompatible elements of government versus private ownership and control, but it also showed its limitations when applied to an objective with a high cost and a large political significance.

[92] One historian has referred to it as the "notorious Portland Canal." *Dictionary of American Biography*, VIII, 61.

[93] *House Docs.*, 42 Cong., 3 Sess., No. 1, Part 2 (1872), 449-50.

[94] Representative Marshall stated in 1858 that "there are no more honorable men on the face of the earth than those five men." *Cong. Globe*, 35 Cong., 1 Sess., 1126 (March 15, 1858). In 1868, Major Weitzel of the Engineers added: "I think that the directors . . . are entitled to the thanks of the community for their praiseworthy efforts to improve the canal." *House Docs.*, 40 Cong., 2 Sess., No. 181 (1868), 12.

Book Reviews

A History of Presidential Elections. By Eugene H. Roseboom. (New York: The Macmillan Company, 1957. viii + 568 pp. Notes, bibliography, and index. $8.50.)

The problems involved in writing a single-volume history of American presidential elections are multitudinous and of differing degrees of solution. The limitations of space serve always to reduce the treatment of the individual contests until the end result is likely to resemble the bare bones of historical skeletons. Only a scholar with a particular hypothesis on the operations of the American political democracy at the national level could hope to cover all the elections, but such treatment would not constitute a real history of those quadrennial pageants. It would be little more than the use of historical materials to support a thesis.

Mr. Roseboom has no pronounced hypothesis on American presidential elections. He presents history to prove what history will prove. And he does an excellent job, so far as I am able to judge, in setting forth the important issues of the campaigns. His discussion is gemmed with the personal factors, the precedents, and the voting statistics of the various campaigns. In that sense, he has contributed a welcome work to American scholarship. A young student or a tired teacher may profitably consult it for the basic facts of a particular campaign. But the work will be of slight value to scholars working in the field of American political history. There is practically no bibliographical guidance, and no critical evaluations of sources. A selective bibliography of some 250 items is appended to the discussion, but it includes only a small fraction of the sources which the scholar must consult for even one of the forty-three elections.

The methodological approach to the problem necessitates that the author remain far removed from the actual elbowing in the campaign. He views the landscape, but ignores many of the individual phenomena of which it is composed. He almost never goes to the country, except in key states of particular campaigns, though he does give intelligent attention to sectional influences.

The treatment of particular campaigns would have been improved if party totals had been given in tabular form for each state. There is no tracing of trends in sections or states at any period. Each campaign tends to start as a new adventure, though, as everyone knows, the sins of the fathers in politics are often visited upon the offspring. The memories of voters are tenacious, and especially in regard to the snubbings of former years. As coalitions, political parties experience difficulty in making the programmatic adjustments necessary for the welding together of disparate groups in a strong party organization. These are the vital forces in political campaigns, and not the characters, speeches, or reputations of candidates for high office.

The finest parts of this study are the discussions on the pre-convention availability of individual candidates for presidential nomination. The author moves with a deft hand among the many hopefuls, pointing out the sources of real strength or of weakness. His characterization of William Jennings Bryan is especially good, but those of Grover Cleveland, Theodore Roosevelt, Woodrow Wilson, and Franklin D. Roosevelt — to mention only a few — are effective and equally informative. Sketches of many of the "also-rans," especially those of James M. Cox and Wendell Willkie, are well motivated.

The purists in American political theory will disagree heartily with the author's practice of using "radical" and "liberal" interchangeably through his discourse on the issues of the campaigns after the emergence of the People's party. He treats the non-ideological aspects of the party struggle with confidence and success, but he never quite achieves a fine understanding of the minor-party mission, and especially of La Follette Progressivism, which is such a formidable factor in American politics.

The book as a whole is the best that we have on the subject. Its merits far outweigh its shortcomings.

University of Oklahoma CORTEZ A. M. EWING

The Liberal Arts College: A Chapter in American Cultural History. By George P. Schmidt. (New Brunswick: Rutgers University Press, 1957. x + 310 pp. Illustrations, notes, bibliographical note, and index. $6.00.)

This study is a pleasant and diverting account of the career of the liberal arts college in the United States. Professor Schmidt devotes approximately half of his space to the history of the American college prior to 1875, and he tells that story with a knowledge and charm that characterize no other recent attempt to provide a brief general survey of the subject. The rest of his book charts the path of the old classical college as it became submerged in the university structure or became engaged in competition with the university. This second half is less successful: the proportion is unbalanced, the non-university-connected college is all but lost sight of, and the final chapters become less historical and more topical.

On the whole Professor Schmidt has taken a warm and sometimes witty look at the liberal arts college, and the truth of the matter is that regardless of its failings his book fills a need for a general survey of an important aspect of American education. But within the narrow compass of this small book he has not in any significant way added to the scholarship of higher education in the United States. His approach varies with his materials and his subjects. A discussion of the old-time college president and an account of the curricular experiences of the liberal arts college are informed and scholarly; they are based on the author's previously published work. But such important matters as alumni societies, Greek-letter fraternities, athletics, and finance are treated, variously, with whimsy or mild indignation or bemusement, but in any case only slightly. Many of his generalizations have the ring of authority; others are clearly a matter of unsupported opinion.

The book is written from what might be called the administrative point of view. In a brief bibliographical note Professor Schmidt observes that if he had been writing the history of a single college "the faculty minutes, the trustees' minutes, and the annual reports of administrative officers would have been the first line of investigation." While such sources are revealing, they do not reveal everything and they even conceal much that is important. Surely the bit of folklore that "the old American college was the lengthened shadow of the president" does not bear up under the weight of scholarship which makes important the line of investigation of what the students and alumni and society at large were doing to shape the American college.

And it is a serious error to claim, as the author also does, that the undergraduate extracurriculum is largely a response to the appearance of the heterogeneous and impersonal university. A study less oriented toward administration and curriculum would have discovered that the extracurriculum is almost as old as the liberal arts college, that well before the middle of the nineteenth century such groups as fraternities, literary societies, science clubs, and the like were enabling undergraduates to define the nature of the American college. Intercollegiate athletics, moreover, are a product of the classical college, not of the burgeoning university.

There are some errors of fact, as there are bound to be in a book that attempts to cover so much territory, but it is difficult to understand the appearance of errors that would have been avoided by a not particularly taxing reading of recent books which are mentioned in the footnotes and referred to in the bibliographical note.

Williams College FREDERICK RUDOLPH

The Nature of Biography. By John A. Garraty. (New York: Alfred A. Knopf, Inc., 1957. xiv + 289 + xii pp. Essay on sources and index. $5.00.)

Professor John A. Garraty, whose lives of Woodrow Wilson and Henry Cabot Lodge I am not competent to judge, has written a discussion of biography that appears to be addressed to the general educated reader. It consists of three parts: the first, entitled (like the whole book) "The Nature of Biography," tries to state in thirty pages what biography includes and entails;

the second, much longer, sketches the development of the genre; and the last, still longer, purports to discuss method. There is in addition an "Essay on Sources," balancing the first one in length.

The author tells us in the Foreword that he began the research for this book by studying psychology on a foundation fellowship and pursued his investigations with the aid of a three-year grant from the Social Science Research Council; in all, the book ripened during five years. It is presented, enticingly enough, with the promise that new notions and devices will be explained and assessed in the later chapters.

The book unfortunately does not live up to the promise; and what is worse, its deficiencies make one regret the time and money that have gone into it. For one thing, the bulk of the book is a cento of quotations from secondary sources. In skillful hands the making of such a compendium might have acquired value; but the present work is marred by poor arrangement and clumsy expression. Not only will it not enlighten the uninformed but in all likelihood it will not hold their attention.

As for the more demanding readers, it will annoy them by its failure to come to grips with any of the traditional issues it raises. Beyond telling us that the Rorschach test doesn't help the biographer but graphology and psychoanalysis may, the author has nothing to contribute that we can properly ascribe to the workings of his mind. Just as in the chapters on the history of the genre Mr. Garraty depends on Stuart, Stauffer, and Dunn, so in the meandering discussions of form, personality, and what he persists in calling methodology (though all he means is method), he relies on what has been said by various practitioners of biography from Plutarch to Freud.

His inadequacy does not prevent him from being frequently toplofty toward writers who should inspire him with humility. Carlyle is manhandled in the ignorant, conventional way; Lockhart is dismissed; Parton is but a preserver of anecdotes; and R. F. Harrod, the greatly gifted biographer of Keynes, is given a patronizing pat and then put in his place with mysterious words about his "archaic structure." Perhaps a few random examples of Mr. Garraty's looseness of diction, technique, and thought will suggest the inutility of his book for any conceivable intellectual purpose.

We are told about Brantôme (as to whom I take leave to doubt Mr. Garraty's firsthand knowledge) that he was "absolutely fascinated by scandal" and "showed real talent." In the same vein of mature reflection we read that "perhaps Freud made sex too important," which strictly analyzed means nothing whatever. Such remarks recur too often to pass for mere slips. How interpret, for instance, the would-be judicious observation that in a certain essay, Professor Gottschalk "confined himself to an analysis of general historical technology"? Or solve the puzzle of "Many biographies are the result of mutual interest"?

Speaking of "technology," one deplores finding a mention of *The History of King Richard the Third* without reference to the possibility of its being defamatory propaganda; one notes with surprise the total omission of Pierre Bayle; one goggles at seeing Boswell's *Johnson* called "a great work of art"; one gags at the cheap mocking of nineteenth-century biography, a mockery unrelieved by any sign that the author has sampled it fairly and critically; one is shocked to find Francis Steegmuller taken to task for *O Rare Ben Jonson*, his first book, written in college, without a word about his later *Flaubert*, *Maupassant*, or *Grande Mademoiselle*. This is on a par with calling Clark's edition of *Aubrey's Lives* "perhaps the best," eight years after the appearance of the text by Oliver Lawson Dick.

The list of misdemeanors and crimes does not stop there. Of explanations for these shortcomings, "perhaps the best" is that the author was out of his element: he may, for all I know, be an excellent biographer, but he is neither theorist nor historian of biography.

Columbia University JACQUES BARZUN

A Short History of New York State. By David M. Ellis, James A. Frost, Harold C. Syrett, and Harry J. Carman. (Ithaca: Cornell University Press, in co-operation with New York State Historical Association, 1957. xiv + 705 pp. Illustrations, maps, tables, bibliographical note, and index. $7.75.)

This volume, published under the sponsorship of the New York State Historical Association, is the fruition of a project begun ten years ago to bring within the covers of one book a comprehensive treatment of the history of the Empire State. Heretofore, one had to rely on Alexander C. Flick's collaborative ten-volume *History of the State of New York* (1933-1937), which still stands as a monument to the scholarship of its time though its size tends to discourage all but the most interested readers. The *Short History*, despite its 653 pages of text, makes available an excellent summary which meets a longfelt need and will prove very useful to students and teachers of the subject.

The preparation of this work afforded an opportunity for selecting, condensing, and reassessing a vast amount of material and for bringing the account down to date. The authors were well qualified for their task and in general have accomplished it most commendably. They have kept a good chronological balance in dividing the book about equally between the periods before and after 1865. The broad topical coverage embraces such items as dairying, immigration, religions, schools and colleges, reform movements, and the arts, as well as political, constitutional, and economic developments and military activities. Though one might like a little fuller treatment of each author's specialty, whatever it may be, a valuable survey is provided within the allotted space.

The approach is objective and non-parochial but a slightly wider focus would at times have been helpful for relating events in the colony and state to movements within the British Empire and the United States. Interpretation, especially in some of the chapters covering the complex post-Civil War period, is minimized in favor of facts which tend to overwhelm the reader. The tortuous currents of politics throughout the state's entire development are lucidly presented. Vignettes of outstanding governors of the more recent period, such as Hughes, Smith, Franklin D. Roosevelt, Lehman, and Dewey, are well drawn.

The difficult problem of identifying a distinct New York culture plagued the authors in the last two chapters and perhaps it is one for which there is no solution. Their emphasis on New York City's influence on intellectual and artistic developments, however, gives little opportunity for discussing accomplishments elsewhere within the state.

Thirty-two pages of illustrations, placed in the center of the book, and a substantial number of maps and charts supplement the text. A very useful critical bibliographical essay and an inadequate index conclude the book.

All students of New York history, as well as of American history in which the state has taken an important role for over three centuries, must be grateful to the authors for providing this convenient and attractive volume which will be a standard for many years. It was well worth waiting for.

Colgate University HOWARD D. WILLIAMS

The Great Awakening in New England. By Edwin Scott Gaustad. (New York: Harper and Brothers, 1957. xiv + 173 pp. Illustrations, notes, bibliography, and index. $3.00.)

A competent study of the Great Awakening in New England has long been overdue. Though we have had useful monographs on the religious revival in the middle colonies and in Virginia, this is the first adequate retelling of the New England story. This is a slender volume, but with the exception of a somewhat unsatisfying introductory chapter the job has been well done. The author devotes the first four chapters to a detailed account of the progress of the movement: its beginnings in the Connecticut Valley awakening associated with Jonathan Edwards, its triumph through the work of such great itinerants as Whitefield and Tennent, and its ultimate evaporation in recrimination and controversy. The last three chapters, more valuable to historians interested in the broader aspects of New England's institutional and intellectual history, discuss the aftermath of the revival and include both New England's troubled self-appraisals and the author's own judgments. Skillful use has been made of newspapers and theological and polemical literature, and the story is told with economy and pace. Parenthetically, a reviewer must regret the casualness of the proofreading: one meets such errors as "Whiefield" (p. 50), "Edinburg" (p. 88), "sevententh" and "goverment" (p. 110).

The author reaches interesting conclusions, some of which discredit common assumptions concerning the revival. He sees little connection between the Connecticut Valley movement of the mid-1730's and the more general awakening farther east in 1740-1742. He dismisses the epidemic which preceded the frontier revival as of slight significance. He challenges a popular modern view that differing reactions to the Awakening reflected social cleavage by showing that at first revivalists and anti-revivalists were found in all strata of provincial society. The last chapters are especially valuable to an understanding of the eventual dissolution of the old order with the coming of theological and ecclesiastical division and with the rise of the radical and protesting element, chiefly Baptist, which was to play a significant role in New England history until Jeffersonianism absorbed its energies. In these chapters, also, a thesis which runs throughout the book becomes explicit. The author contends that the two main streams of New England religious thought, rationalistic and pietistic, represented by Chauncy and Edwards respectively, took their rise in the Great Awakening. This largely accounts for its "persistent appeal." "For nowhere else in the western world did the double reaction against the devotional decline and theological pedantry of the seventeenth century focus on a single movement" (p. 138).

The thesis has its merits, but one criticism may be voiced: to prevent distortion it should be properly related to previous tradition. At the opening of the revival New England's intellectual baggage included both rationalistic and pietistic strains which were, of course, greatly intensified and altered by the revival and by the discussion it aroused. The controversialists themselves recognized this continuity with an older Puritanism. Advocates of the revival discovered "a renewed taste for those old pious and experimental writers" such as Hooker, Shepard, and Owen, while its opponents pointedly combated the antinomian heresy of the 1630's. For this reason the book could have profited by greater analysis of relevant themes in theology and piety on the eve of the Awakening. Such analysis would have been more helpful than the hasty survey of Puritan history, doctrine, and polity which fills the first chapter. It would also have brought the revival's place in the entire sweep of New England's intellectual history into sharper focus. Yet even with this disappointment, this study is a valuable and illuminating work.

University of Minnesota (Duluth) JAMES FULTON MACLEAR

Patrick Henry: Patriot in the Making. By Robert Douthat Meade. (Philadelphia: J. B. Lippincott Company, 1957. xiv + 431 pp. Illustrations, facsimiles, notes, bibliography, and index. $7.50.)

There has long been a need for a detailed and scholarly biography of Patrick Henry, and the appearance of the first half of Robert Douthat Meade's study of the "forest-born Demosthenes" is therefore an interesting event. In this volume Professor Meade narrates Henry's career to the outbreak of the War of Independence; in another to follow, he will deal with Henry's later years.

It is, of course, too early to attempt a close estimate of Professor Meade's achievement. However, it is apparent enough that the first part of the biography is as full as a lengthy search of the records will permit, and that it is highly reliable in terms of fact. Moreover, the author displays suitable and laudable caution in his handling of the memoirs and traditions which cluster about Henry. It may safely be conjectured that Professor Meade's second volume will have these same fine qualities.

Patrick Henry: Patriot in the Making contains no startling revelations of fact. Among other useful contributions, however, Professor Meade proves that Henry's background, which he traces in Scotland as well as Virginia, was not so humble as it is commonly thought to have been, and that the orator's education was less limited than most of us have fancied. He also offers some solid information concerning Henry's early legal career. More important, he demonstrates that Henry's defiance of Britain in the House of Burgesses in the closing days of May, 1765, was very nearly as forthright as it has been in general American opinion.

It cannot be asked that a historian supply major new data not contained in the available documents, and the author is hardly to be condemned because he has not been able to offer a much fuller account of the first four decades of Henry's life than have earlier biographers. If he has not given us as much as he might have, it is principally because he has confined himself very largely to narrative. Henry does not come to life. Moreover, the author avoids clear commitment with respect to Henry's character, abilities, and behavior. He carefully says there was a "touch of" demagoguery in the orator's conduct in the Parson's Cause, but he does not say that Henry was or was not addicted to demagoguery. He offers no precise estimate of Henry's intellectual powers. Was Henry a champion of the yeoman farmers against the Tidewater aristocracy? Professor Meade is mildly inclined toward a belief that he was.

Perhaps the author will tell us much more certainly in his second volume what he thinks regarding Henry. If anyone can speak with some authority concerning the questions often asked about Henry, Professor Meade should be that man. He will not finish the task he set for himself unless he lets his readers know that he believes Henry had or had not intellectual and moral warts. Certainly Henry's reputation is deservedly so great that it is quite unnecessary to avoid discussion of the supposed weaknesses which able contemporaries and respectable historians have found in him. The lawyer from Hanover will ever be a commanding figure.

Duke University JOHN R. ALDEN

Alexander Hamilton: Youth to Maturity, 1755-1788. By Broadus Mitchell. (New York: The Macmillan Company, 1957. xvi + 675 pp. Illustration, notes, bibliography, and index. $8.75.)

This, the first volume of what is to be a two-volume biography of Hamilton, is such an unusual amalgam that a reviewer scarcely knows whether to praise or condemn the author; for, on the one hand, his detailed treatment adds to our knowledge of this early statesman, but, on the other, his presentation contains a number of impressions that appear misleading and confusing. Certainly this biography goes beyond that of Nathan Schachner, and it is far superior to Louis Hacker's recent *Alexander Hamilton in the American Tradition.*

As the title indicates, the Hamilton story is covered from his humble origins and background through the exciting period of the Constitutional Convention. The most space is devoted to Hamilton's military career — almost half of the book. His early life, his education, and his career in New York from 1783-1788, each receives Professor Mitchell's attention in several chapters. Somewhat more space is devoted to the period when Hamilton approaches the national scene as a receiver of taxes in New York and as a fledgling delegate to the Continental Congress, while a still larger section is appropriately taken up with Hamilton's agitation for, and his successful advocacy of, a change in government.

Some phases of this biography are especially strong. If there is any part that can approach the adjective "definitive" it is the description of Hamilton's obscure beginnings. The author writes about it with candor and balance, after a discriminating review of the existing sources and an on-the-spot check of the physical survivals in the islands where Hamilton grew up. Balance is also a good word to describe his discussion of Hamilton's courtship and marriage to Elizabeth Schuyler, where the author is persuasive that it was Hamilton's heart that guided him rather than his ambitions. The author's scholarship in the Hamilton material also reveals itself when he analyzes the influence of Malachy Postlethwayt upon Hamilton's thinking, where his assessment seems more reasonable than others who have consulted the same evidence. In addition, the multi-volume character of this study enables Professor Mitchell to give a fuller treatment to several episodes in his subject's military career, and his diligence enables him to set aright the chronology of Hamilton's full life.

It is not accidental that the foregoing examples, where the special merit of Professor Mitchell's account is noted, relate almost exclusively to Hamilton personally, not to the larger events of which he was a part. Indeed, where Hamilton's career intersects with major events or trends the narrative is often disappointing, and, at times, significantly misleading. It stems from what, for a better word, can be called a lack of "knowledgeableness" about the period, due perhaps in large measure to the fact that the author has not taken advantage of some of the standard historical literature and the most recent writing on the Revolutionary era. When discussing the military phase of Hamilton's career, for example, Christopher Ward, John R. Alden, and Douglas Southall Freeman scarcely receive a nod, while most of the recent writing on political and financial developments — two of the essential elements in Mitchell's discussion — is ignored. Even studies of figures pertinent to the main story are not consulted, the most obvious being the chapter on "Witness to Treason," where the most recent and best biography of Arnold, by Willard Wallace, is never mentioned.

What is the result? Hamilton's role in public affairs is not presented in perspective, claims are made that seem dubious, and the commentary in many cases does not appear to be warranted. The point of departure in discussing his military experience, to choose an outstanding example, is based on the assumption that Hamilton, to use the author's phrase, acted as the alter ego of Washington, a grossly extravagant claim, as a casual reading of Freeman will readily document; and later, when Hamilton takes on a small task as receiver of taxes in New York, he immediately becomes, in Mitchell's account, the co-equal partner of Morris whereas, in fact, the New Yorker was as yet on the fringes of influence while Morris was at the center. No one would question that Hamilton's military and political career from 1776 to 1783 was important to *him* and to his education and growth, but to assign him an extremely influential role in public policy during these years is a highly dubious judgment. Yet, it is this approach that the author stresses — a common fault of Hamilton's biographers — rather than Hamilton's maturation.

The misrepresentation of the larger themes touches a great number of smaller incidents and episodes, either as background or as an essential part of the story: the discussion of executive departments is uninformed because it fails to take into account the work of Jennings Sanders and others; the discussion of Washington's decision with respect to the Chesapeake campaign appears to depart, in some particulars, from the accepted one without evidence to sustain it; the background of the impost is so inadequate that it is not understandable; and the long background to funding the public debt, so essential in evaluating the Hamilton story, constitutes a complete void.

A final word should be said about the footnotes and the organization of the material within the chapters. The footnotes, though informative at times, too often border on the extraneous; and the abbreviations used — Louis Gottschalk (editor), *Letters of Lafayette to Washington*, becomes LOLTW — are sometimes disconcerting, even to those well acquainted with the sources. In addition, a number of chapters include a change of pace so abrupt as to be distracting. The most obvious example is in "Affairs of State and Morristown Romance" where, on the heels of a discussion of Hamilton's economic ideas, the story turns, without warning, to his marriage. There are seeds of irony here, but it is clear that the author did not intend to be that subtle.

In summation, it can be seen that, though this biography is not definitive, especially where the role of Hamilton in public affairs is concerned, it is an advance in Hamiltonian scholarship and future biographers will build upon it.

Northwestern University CLARENCE L. VER STEEG

William R. Davie. By Blackwell P. Robinson. (Chapel Hill: University of North Carolina Press, 1957. xiv + 495 pp. Illustrations, map, appendixes, notes, bibliography, and index. $6.00.)

Fordyce Hubbard's century-old biography of Davie is now supplemented by Blackwell P. Robinson's, sponsored by the North Carolina Society of the Cincinnati. To Hubbard's readers Davie appeared as an exciting example of a self-made man, a southerner who by wise devotion to the public service endeared his memory to the state whose honor he so faithfully guarded. To Mr. Robinson's readers Davie will appear as a somewhat less exciting man — Hubbard's southern natonalism is of course subdued — but still a man to be remembered: partisan war hero, commissary general under Nathanael Greene, "father" of the University of North Carolina, Federalist governor, and diplomat to France. On some subjects, notably military, the book is detailed; on others, for example religion or the Masons, it is scant; on still others, such as the Cincinnati, it is a blank.

Mr. Robinson has found little material on Davie the man, or on what made the man. Was it Woodmason's Piedmont or Witherspoon's Princeton? Since Davie is a "commanding, almost marmoreal figure" from the beginning, this is no real life drama. Neither is it a life and times; it is more akin to a life and letters. Documents, allowing Davie to speak for himself, are the real heart of the book. Such an arrangement has its occasional hazards. In explaining his stand against Chisholm *v.* Georgia, for instance, a Davie letter, quoted at length, explains nothing.

Though many of his sources are the same as Hubbard's, Mr. Robinson cuts loose from the earlier biographer, in at least one case unwisely. Hubbard, describing a battle for an enemy camp, has men taking shelter behind "trees and brush huts" while Robinson, reading the same Davie handwriting, comes up with "trees and bush heaps." Apparent errors of this type are infrequent, although one startling sentence catches James Iredell "repudiating the compact theory."

At important points, standard sources are used almost exclusively, Farrand on Davie at the Federal Convention, Elliot on ratification, and McRee's *Iredell* on everything. While strictly on his guard concerning Hubbard, Mr. Robinson takes McRee's editorial work at face value. Until the day when all great manuscript collections are on microfilm, the historian will have an excuse to travel, to spend his substance on journeys to distant depositories. Mr. Robinson, working in the great historical collections of North Carolina, firmly put aside any such temptations. As a consequence his work is weakest on the periods when Davie worked with men from outside the state.

Davie, like his biographer, carried a map of North Carolina in his head, but to the reader who may not know Currituck from Cherokee the one map here reproduced is practically valueless.

This reviewer would like to have had a review of Davie's own book, *Instructions to Be Observed for the Formation and Movements of the Cavalry.* But Davie has undoubtedly been given his due. Like a Federal Writers' Project *Guide*, Mr. Robinson gives us a volume at once trustworthy, dispassionate, parochial, and brimful.

Memphis State University LEE N. NEWCOMER

Albert Gallatin: Jeffersonian Financier and Diplomat. By Raymond Walters, Jr. (New York: The Macmillan Company, 1957. x + 461 pp. Notes, bibliography, and index. $7.00.)

Albert Gallatin, widely recognized by his contemporaries, well known to scholars, yet unknown to Americans today, is presented by Dr. Walters in a study which if not definitive is at least now the standard biography.

There are a variety of reasons for the neglect of Gallatin by our age, but the most important is the manner in which his papers have been handled until recently. Blessed like his famous contemporaries with a historical sense, Gallatin accumulated over twenty thousand documents which were left in charge of his family. In 1877, approximately twenty years after his death, the Gallatin family commissioned Henry Adams to prepare a selection of the papers and a biography. With other documents gathered from government archives and private collections, *The Writings of Albert Gallatin* in three volumes, plus a single-volume *Life* appeared in 1879. A later biography, published in the American Statesmen Series in 1884 by John Austin Stevens, a family connection, is inadequate. The Gallatin papers, although deposited with the New-York Historical Society, were until recently closed to the public. Ten years ago, however, the Gallatin family, belatedly aware of its responsibilities, had the collection catalogued and made available to selected scholars.

Walters capitalized on this opportunity to study Gallatin and now, after a decade of work, has presented this full-length biography which, based on thorough research and written with superior skill, will be welcomed by scholars and the general public. He portrays "a man unique and invaluable in any age or land, a superbly able and almost completely selfless public servant." In the early nineteenth century Gallatin was foremost in public finances, second only to John Quincy Adams in diplomacy, and surpassed only by Jefferson among early American ethnologists. In his enthusiasm Walters belittles Jefferson; the perspicacious Gallatin himself never did.

As the only Jeffersonian whose understanding of fiscal matters was comparable to Hamilton's, Gallatin was the natural choice of both Jefferson and Madison for secretary of the treasury, and in that position he sought through financial measures to promote a Jeffersonian society. As the most realistic of the Republicans, however, he persuaded his colleagues to follow a course "midway between the conceptions now known as Hamiltonianism and Jeffersonianism." In 1813 he left the Treasury and embarked on a career in diplomacy to secure peace and other objectives which he believed necessary to promote the best interests of the United States. His career as a diplomat between 1813 and 1829, matching his role as financier, met with amazing success. Walters' biography is most useful for its full account of this side of Gallatin's life. Gallatin's greatest triumphs were in laying the foundations for the American reciprocity program of the early nineteenth century and his handling of the northwest boundary question which established the basis for acquisition of the Pacific Northwest in 1846.

Walters acknowledges that Chapters 12 through 20 of his study owe much to Adams' *History*, and the entire piece invites a comparison with Adams' *Life of Albert Gallatin*. The strong forte of both biographies is documentation, but where Adams' work suffers from a distracting weight of documentation imperfectly blended into the exposition, Walters, by a proper use of sources, produces a lively, readable, and scholarly account. Adams, by concentrating on the public career of Gallatin, presented a less human and less objective picture than does Walters, who presents the complete man.

Loyola University of Los Angeles ANTHONY F. TURHOLLOW

Banks and Politics in America from the Revolution to the Civil War. By Bray Hammond. (Princeton: Princeton University Press, 1957. xii + 771 pp. Notes, bibliography, and index. $12.50.)

Money, credit, and banks have been the source of some of the most crucial political controversies in the United States from the colonial period to the present day. But there has been no other area of political debate in which there has been so much ignorance, prejudice, and misunderstanding exhibited both by those who have made the effective decisions and by historians. Bray Hammond's study of banks and politics is thus doubly needed. First and most importantly it is needed as a guide for those who will make decisions about money and credit in the future, and secondly as a corrector of erroneous interpretations of the American past. The preface, perhaps the whole book, should be required reading for every person who attempts to study and understand the history of the United States, for in it the author correctly indicts the great body of historical literature, including the work of the most noted scholars, as inadequate and misleading.

The accepted view of American history divides the people into two groups, the poor farmers who are always in debt, and the rich businessmen who are creditors. This view, in which Jefferson and Jackson are the defenders of the poor, whereas Hamilton, Webster, Clay, and Biddle are spokesmen for the rich, Hammond rightly designates as an unfounded myth. "Typical accounts," he observes, "read as if it were to be taken for granted that Americans have borrowed only when they have been in trouble, that debtors have all been poor agrarians, and that a chronic and significant condition of American life has been the distress of agrarian debtors, their oppression by creditors, and their struggles for relief." And yet it is entirely obvious, as Robert Morris with complete accuracy said in 1785, that America has grown rich by borrowing. The chronic and significant condition has not been the distress of the agrarian debtor, but rather "the prosperous use of borrowed funds," and the debtors "who are of most economic and political importance are and always have been business men and business corporations" among which must be numbered the banks.

The author does more than dispel the myth of the poor debtor; but he has written so much about so many things that it is impossible to do more than describe roughly and inadequately the scope of the book. He has covered the whole history of money, banking, and credit, and the political conflicts these subjects engendered in the American colonies and in the United States down to the formation of the national banking system during the Civil War. He has also included a discussion of the parallel, though sometimes contrasting, economic and political history of Canada, and has related the particular circumstances about which he is writing to the general history and theory of money, credit, and banking in other areas and times.

The sheer mass of material at times overwhelms the reader and the genuinely revolutionary treatment of many important episodes is unfortunately obscured. But what the author has to say is of such great significance that this additional labor on the part of the reader is well worth the effort required. One of the most valuable contributions of the book is the reinterpretation of the roles of Alexander Hamilton and Nicholas Biddle, and the author has wisely devoted more space and attention to them and to the first and second

Bank of the United States than to any other subjects. The one serious omission is any adequate discussion of agricultural credit, and here, it seems, Mr. Hammond's acceptance of another unfounded historical myth is the reason for his neglect of this important area. He has accepted the view that "until fairly well along in the 19th century farmers did not wish to borrow and lenders did not consider agriculture a very good credit risk"; and he says that the political conflicts in this period were between two rivals, agrarianism and business enterprise, that "these two fought about banks," and that enterprise won "because banks provide credit, and credit is indispensable to enterprise."

This analysis of American political and economic conflicts, which separates agriculture from all other forms of economic activity and divides the farmers from the other producers, is as mythical a view as that which says all debtors are poor. Farmers were just as dependent upon credit and banks as the other economic groups. They raised crops for sale in distant markets and some means had to be provided for them to obtain the proceeds of these sales. They also needed credit to finance them during the long growing season, and above all they needed a circulating currency which, in the period under discussion, could be furnished only by banks. The responsible spokesmen of the farmers all over the country defended banks and their currency, and, when there were no banks in a particular area, created them. Numerous attempts were made, some with success, to organize institutions to provide long-term loans for the purchase of land, but their need for this kind of credit did not mean that the farmers had no use for short-time loans, either directly or through mercantile intermediaries, from the ordinary commercial banks.

The political conflicts in the early nineteenth century were centered on economic questions but the division was seldom if ever along economic lines. Party interest and party loyalty were the principal sources of political division among politicians, and rival theories of political economy were the principal subjects of debate. The attacks upon banks were made by men of all parties and diverse occupations who believed that the only proper (the term "moral" could be used) currency was silver or gold, and their reason for believing this was the teaching of the classical liberal economists. Other interests and political theories were involved in the attacks upon the national banks, but at no time were the farmers united on this or any other political question or in support of a single political party.

Hammond's great contributions to the reinterpretation of the American past should not be undervalued because he has accepted this view that "the conflict of farmer and entrepreneur for dominance over American culture provoked much of the basic political controversy between the Revolution and the Civil War." This oft-repeated but erroneous theory has had little effect upon his treatment of the basic material, and what he has to say concerning the actual developments in the history of banks, money, and credit, is so refreshingly honest, clear, and helpfully corrective that the appearance of the book should be a cause for enthusiastic rejoicing.

New York City THOMAS P. GOVAN

America's First Hamlet. By Grace Overmyer. (New York: New York University Press, 1957. 439 pp. Illustration, notes, appendix, bibliography, and index. $7.50.)

American school children all know that "Home Sweet Home" was written by John Howard Payne, and many of them will add the folklore tag, "who never had a home"; most college students know that the famous song comes from the opera *Clari*, and drama majors learn that Payne wrote several successful stage pieces and was himself an actor of note both in England and the United States; some students can identify Payne as an American diplomat, but fewer persons know that this versatile man was also a leading nineteenth-century champion of civil rights, and was himself persecuted for his liberal views and humane actions.

This is the fifth biography of John Howard Payne (1791-1852). The first, written by Gabriel Harrison, appeared twenty-three years after Payne's death. It was followed ten years later by "a biographical sketch" by Charles Brainard, occasioned by the removal of Payne's remains from Tunis to Washington, where on June 9, 1883, the ninety-second anniversary of Payne's birth, his reinterment was made a national ceremony. In 1913, Willis Tracy Hanson published *The Early Life of John Howard Payne*, and in 1930 Rosa Pendleton Chiles published the most ambitious biography to precede this one.

Miss Overmyer takes pains to lay the fiction that Payne was homeless; she gives lengthy details of family background (his father was a schoolmaster), boyhood, education, and stage triumphs as a child prodigy. In Boston he played Hamlet to Elizabeth Arnold Poe's Ophelia, becoming "the first American ever to enact the role." The major portion of this biography is devoted to Payne's career as player and playwright of the British stage. He acted with varying success the major roles of contemporary stage favorites in the shadow of Kemble and Kean. Serving the fashions of the day, he adapted the works of German, French, and English authors into such successes as *Thérèse*, *Brutus*, *Charles II* (with Washington Irving), and of course *Clari*. Of these, *Clari* is presented in greatest detail, and "Home Sweet Home" is given the full treatment. Admittedly no rival to Sheridan or Shaw, Payne deserves recognition as the author of half a dozen successful plays which place him among the most important American playwrights of his century.

Returning to the United States in 1832, Payne enjoyed some successes, theatrical and literary, but the most noteworthy episode was his championing of the cause of the Cherokees which led to his capture and imprisonment by the Georgia militia — a scene which might have come from one of his own melodramas. His last years as a diplomat in Tunis were sad. Here he served competently in the minor sinecure which was considered appropriate provision for a man of letters in nineteenth-century America.

His reputation, personal as well as literary, has fared poorly. This biography seeks to rescue him from both personal disfavor and literary neglect. Montrose J. Moses dismissed him as inconsequential; Arthur Hobson Quinn considers him an important link between the American and English theaters; had he written about the Cherokees instead of about Brutus and Charles II, he might have become a more significant figure in American literature. Fourteen volumes of his notes for a projected history of the Cherokee nation are in the Newberry Library.

Miss Overmyer adds considerably to Payne scholarship. She is respectful toward facts, thorough in use of source materials, and she strives constantly to picture the man in relation to his period. Admittedly seeking to counteract "a widespread prejudice against Payne," she probably protests too much; but this volume will help to rehabilitate its subject, who deserves a better reputation than he has had.

North Texas State College MARTIN S. SHOCKLEY

The Journals of Welcome Arnold Greene: Journeys in the South, 1822-1824. Edited by Alice E. Smith. (Madison: State Historical Society of Wisconsin, 1957. x + 278 pp. Illustration, map, notes, and index. $5.00.)

This book consists of journals, hitherto unpublished, of three journeys of Welcome Arnold Greene, a young Quaker merchant of Rhode Island. The first of these journeys, made in 1822, took Greene to Charleston, South Carolina, thence to Savannah by way of Augusta, and then home by way of Washington, Baltimore, and Philadelphia. The second and the third journeys took him by ship to New Orleans and thence by steamboat up the Mississippi River. On the second journey, made in 1823, he ascended the Ohio River to Wheeling and then proceeded overland through Pennsylvania to the East. On the third journey, made in 1824, he ascended the Cumberland River to Nashville and returned home by way of New Orleans.

These journeys Greene made partly for reasons of business and partly for the purpose of seeking information about an uncle who had disappeared in the back country of Georgia in 1806. For knowledge about these purposes, however, we are less indebted to his journals than to the researches of his editor. Because Greene said little about the objects of his travels, our evaluation of his journals has to turn not upon his skill as a salesman or as a detective, but upon his ability to observe closely and to report accurately what he saw as a traveler.

We must, I think, conclude that Greene, a man of broad interests, of catholic tastes, and of charitable disposition, was a competent observer and an accurate reporter of both things and behavior. Consequently, the book embodying his journals, although it makes no striking contribution to our knowledge of American history, is worthy of our serious attention. It should be classed with the better "travel books" — books containing information of the sort that social and intellectual historians are eager to lay hold of. Among other things Greene has given us an excellent description of New Orleans in 1823; he has also given us numerous close-up views of Kentucky society in that same year; and he has limned for us sharply etched pictures of cultural activity in the Ohio Valley in 1823 and in the Cumberland Valley in 1824. His interest in what was to be seen about him never flagged. Whether he was in the East, in the South, or in the West, his eyes were always wide open to observe economic change, political and social behavior, cultural growth, and pretty women.

Like other good diarists, Greene has told us much about himself. His enthusiasm for collecting geological specimens apart, he has let us know that he was a moderate man; that he had an amateurish interest in archeology and anthropology; that he read numerous books of divers sorts; that he walked steadfastly in the Quaker way; that he held no inflated opinion of himself; that he knew that whited sepulchers do exist; and, finally, that his well-developed sense of humor was as dry as sometimes it was sly.

This book is competently edited and attractively printed.

Bucknell University J. ORIN OLIPHANT

The Frontier Mind: A Cultural Analysis of the Kentucky Frontiersman. By Arthur K. Moore. (Lexington: University of Kentucky Press, 1957. xii + 264 pp. Notes and index. $5.00.)

It should be stated at the outset that this is no ordinary book about the frontier and no short review will do justice to the many ideas that it projects or to the central theme that it develops. The main objective of the study is to suggest with rather impressive argument that the American frontier interfered with the development of an original cultural pattern of high order and that the high-minded buckskin hero never existed at all. Dr. Moore points out that while there were small groups of cultured people along the frontier, this minority weakened and retreated before the barbaric impact of the frontier mind. The history of Transylvania University is cited as a good example of the defeat of the intellectuals. Under the influence of Horace Holley, Transylvania rose to the heights of educational experimentation in the 1820's only to succumb under an avalanche of sectarian disputes and anti-intellectualism.

It was this anti-intellectualism of the West that created an atmosphere unfriendly to the development of an important, native literature. In developing this idea, the author takes the opportunity to re-examine the "somewhat battered frontier theory of Frederick Jackson Turner" (p. 242), and to reject it as far as American literature is concerned. In like manner he disposes of the work of J. B. Hubbell and Walter Prescott Webb, perhaps with some degree of injustice. This, of course, is a matter of opinion.

One of the most interesting contributions of the book is the analysis of the Kentucky frontiersman and his role in the history of American culture. There were two types of frontiersman: one, the Indian fighter, and the other, the "half alligator, half horse" riverman who worked the keelboats on the inland waterways. In discussing the first type, Dr. Moore dissolves some of the glamour from the legendary Boone by claiming that Alexander McConnel was a tougher man and actually killed more Indians than Boone. In this same section, the author compares the frontier adventurer Simon Kenton with Beowulf, which is rather startling until one gets used to the idea. As a matter of fact, there are numerous comparisons of this type in the book and references to Greek mythology, medieval history, and English literature are common. One cannot help but admire an author who can swing with apparent ease from the jug-toting frontiersman on the Ohio to Homer's nectar-sipping characters on the Aegean and back again by way of medieval scholasticism and the eighteenth-century Enlightenment. Prototype Mike Fink never dreamed that one day he would be the inspiration for learned probing on the part of twentieth-century scholars.

The second frontier type, the "alligator-horse," is presented as a liquor-drinking, cabbage-eating, eye-gouging, wenching savage who was interested in many things but never in education or institutionalized society. These uncouth rivermen terrorized the more genteel people from Pittsburgh to New Orleans. In passion and arrogance, according to Dr. Moore, they were like the Goths who descended on Rome, but unlike the Goths they preferred trading to looting. The people of Louisiana associated all that was unrefined with the Kentucky boatmen. Most southerners agreed with the Kentuckian's description of himself when, in the midst of a brothel brawl at Natchez-under-the-Hill, he announced that he had bear's claws, alligator's teeth, and the devil's tail. In such an atmosphere the high-minded, idealistic buckskin hero of legend and romantic history fades into a thin, pale wraith.

The book is original, erudite, and controversial. That it rests too much on literature and literary concepts to the exclusion of political, social, and religious forces can be justified on the basis that the author is a literary scholar. He has chosen to emphasize that which he knows best.

Monmouth College F. GARVIN DAVENPORT

The Seminoles. By Edwin C. McReynolds. (Norman: University of Oklahoma Press, 1957. xvi + 397 pp. Illustrations, maps, notes, bibliography, and index. $5.75.)

The Seminoles is a pioneer work. Until its publication, the Seminoles, alone of the Five Civilized Tribes, were without any pretense to a complete history. Students interested in their history had to collect it in scattered, fragmentary, and very incomplete form from a few pages in John R. Swanton's ethnological work, *Early History of the Creek Indians and Their Neighbors*, and from the pertinent chapters in Grant Foreman's *Indian Removal* and *The Five Civilized Tribes.* And for the period after 1860 there was nothing easily accessible except anthropological and sociological studies of the Florida Seminoles and occasional references in histories of Oklahoma. Professor McReynolds' book goes far to fill this serious and longfelt gap.

Certain weaknesses in organization, proportion, and to some extent in information prevent it, however, from being a final answer to the need for a full-scale history of the Seminoles. There is undue attention to such extraneous matters as early Spanish Florida, Lafitte, the Battle of New Orleans, Peggy Eaton, and Jackson's Florida governorship, and, on the other hand, the periods which most needed attention — the earliest and more recent — are still the weakest. The Cowkeeper, Seminole chief whom Swanton regards as the founder of the tribe, is, for example, mentioned only once in passing. The history of the Seminole people from 1865 to the present is dealt with in little over fifty pages — in which the Florida Seminoles never appear. Except for a slight reference to the oil boom of the 1920's there is nothing at all about the Seminoles during the half-century of Oklahoma statehood — nothing, for example, about their reaction to the substitution of state for tribal government. The use of a comparatively small body of available monographic literature accounts for some of the factual errors, but others result from dependence on such outmoded authorities as Giddings and Parton instead of on recent monographs unmentioned in the useful bibliography.

The treatment of the Seminoles for the approximate century from the 1770's through 1865, despite certain omissions and questionable statements, is in general excellent. The relations between the Seminoles and their agents are particularly well handled. Professor McReynolds' sympathies are naturally and properly with the Seminoles, but he gives full credit to agents and army officers caught in the dilemma between duty and humanity. The chapter on the Civil War is a distinctive and especially welcome contribution — as indeed, despite space limitations, are the chapters on the post-Civil War generation. The author's attention to the highly important but usually neglected Seminole Negro element is notable. Such contributions make the book one which will be welcomed by all students of American Indian history and of United States Indian policy.

University of Illinois KENNETH WIGGINS PORTER

The Columbia River, or Scenes and Adventures during a Residence of Six Years on the Western Side of the Rocky Mountains among Various Tribes of Indians Hitherto Unknown: Together with "A Journey across the American Continent." By Ross Cox. Edited by Edgar I. Stewart and Jane R. Stewart. (Norman: University of Oklahoma Press, 1957. xxxiv + 398 pp. Illustrations, notes, maps, tables, appendix, and index. $5.75.)

The Columbia River is Volume 24 in the American Exploration and Travel Series and the third therein on the early history of the Pacific Northwest. The original work was first published in London in 1831 and in New York in 1832, and the present reprinting is a fine piece of bookmaking which makes available another early classic of western Americana. Moreover, the editors have included an excellent introduction which places the book in its proper milieu.

The author's narrative opens with an account of the voyage of the *Beaver* from New York to Astoria in 1811-1812, via Cape Horn and the Sandwich Islands. This is followed by a lengthy discussion of the fate of the *Tonquin* and briefer notices of the site of Fort Astoria, of the establishment of Fort Okanogan, and of the straggling arrival of Hunt's overland party. Only with the opening of Chapter 6 do we encounter the interior ventures of the Astorian fur traders. And it is from this point that the deficiencies of the editors come to the surface.

Between June 29, 1812, when Cox set out from Fort Astoria on his first trading voyage up the Columbia and into the interior, and April 16, 1817, when he left Fort George on his final voyage up the river and outward via Athabaska Pass, he made eight round trips up and down the Lower Columbia; that is, he journeyed sixteen times between Celilo Falls and the Lower Cascade Rapids through one of the most difficult and romantic stretches of waterway in all of North America. He not only described the natural features and the Indians but also listed the trade goods and explained the methods of conducting a brigade along the route. The editors, however, have failed, in their use of explanatory notes, to make these pages live for the present-day reader. There is no map of this waterway, no mention of the Lower, Middle, and Upper Cascade Rapids; The Dalles are not discussed, and Celilo Falls are there in high or low water. Bradford Island is not exactly located, nor is its importance then or now distinguished. Further, no reference is made to the Journal of Major Osborne Cross which includes a number of remarkable sketches of this part of the river, nor to Howard M. Corning's *Dictionary of Oregon History* (1956), nor to Lewis A. McArthur's *Oregon Geographic Names* (1944).

Once Cox left the river he came either to Fort Okanogan or to Spokan

House and inland stations. On these land journeys the editors do no better; for they do not furnish us with a map of the country, and, of the two given, that of Cox's meanderings in 1812 is useless while that of Fort Okanogan is copied without acknowledgment. Not a word is said of the excavation of the sites of Fort Spokan and Fort Okanogan by the National Park Board under the direction of Louis R. Caywood. As to the location of Boat Encampment the editors are equally vague. They do not inform us how Cox and his party made their way from the Canoe River to the Wood, which they state is "a tributary of the Canoe River" (p. 281, n. 6). Neither do they make any reference to the literature on these important geographical features, nor to the surveys of the Inter-Provincial Boundary Commission. In fact, the editors do not provide us with a bibliography at all.

The same deficiencies are found in the treatment of the Indians. Not a single tribe is clearly identified, nor are any of the chiefs, such as "a young chief, of fine figure" (p. 202). This fault is particularly annoying with regard to the tribes along the Lower Columbia. The Cayuse are never mentioned, and the Bureau of American Ethnology's *Bulletin 30* is never cited. As to the traders associated with Cox, we find again a woeful want of exact and recent information, despite the fact that many of them have been listed in the biographical appendixes of Volumes I and IV of the Hudson's Bay Series. In sum, one puts this volume down regretfully; the tools for a good job were at hand, but they simply were not used.

Gonzaga University WILLIAM L. DAVIS

The Jacksonian Persuasion: Politics and Belief. By Marvin Meyers. (Stanford: Stanford University Press, 1957. viii + 231 pp. Notes, appendixes, bibliography, and index. $5.00.)

Andrew Jackson has persistently remained one of the most controversial figures in American history. Starting with the vituperation of his own day, to which Jackson himself made notable contributions, violent differences of opinion have been commonplace. Even modern historical scholarship has brought no basic agreement, so that at one extreme the Jackson political message "is discounted as the largely meaningless babble of demagogues; at the other it is blown up into the prophetic utterance of a modern welfare ideology" (p. 91).

The Meyers interpretation is certainly no laudation of Jackson, whose "presidential messages are ragged political philosophy, tendentious accounting, crude policy" (p. 12), and who was politically successful because he was "a national hero, combining dramatic flair with the common touch" (p. 11). Jackson's central philosophy — and the word may well be too pretentious — was conservative, with the desire to tear down recent developments and to return to the Jefferson ideal of the simple and independent yeoman. The Democratic party of Jackson was no more the originator of political democracy than was the Whig party of Clay, but it accepted new instruments and methods with greater facility. Both parties appealed to roughly the same people, with no obvious class splits, even though the Whigs probably attracted a few more of the commercial and manufacturing classes than did the Democrats. The main difference was that "the Whig party spoke to the explicit hopes of Americans as Jacksonians addressed their diffuse fears and resentments" (p. 9). Meyers notes that Jackson's vetoes were more vigorous than his positive proposals, and then adds that Jackson's excoriations concerned mainly such vague groups as the money power, the monied aristocracy, and special privilege, thus permitting even rich men to enlist under his banner.

Meyers' technique stresses sampling rather than complete coverage, and his organization is intriguingly unusual. The book concerns banks and paper money almost exclusively, with little more than passing references to other subjects of Jackson's concern. The conclusions are presented in the first chapter, after which comes a general discussion of Jacksonian ideology based on two contemporary writers, Tocqueville and Cooper, with almost ecstatic approval of Tocqueville. Then follows a description of the actual situation of banks and paper money, succeeded by accounts of Jacksonians of varied views — Van Buren, Sedgwick, Leggett, and Rantoul; Van Buren is described as a better Jacksonian than Jackson. Finally there is a case study of the political history of New York state.

Both in contents and in style, Meyers' book illustrates a current trend in American historical writing. Materials and techniques of other disciplines are used intelligently — maybe in part because of the year the author spent at the Center for Advanced Study in the Behavioral Sciences. A definite philosophic-psychological approach is apparent, accompanied by considerable subtlety of thought and wording. The style is good, with sparklingly quotable phrases here and there. Any reader will probably regret the omissions of certain material and want to modify certain generalizations, but such criticisms are not worth making in any general evaluation. The outstanding impression of at least this reader is of an imaginative job well done.

Dartmouth College ROBERT E. RIEGEL

The Log-Cabin Campaign. By Robert Gray Gunderson. (Lexington: University of Kentucky Press, 1957. xii + 292 pp. Illustrations, notes, bibliographical note, and index. $7.50.)

Every writer on the Jacksonian era is inspired to describe, sometimes with malicious relish, the color and drama of the presidential campaign of 1840.

Professor Gunderson has dealt with practically every immediate aspect of this famous political jamboree. Beginning with the Whig Young Men's ratifying convention of May 4, 1840, he gives us a detailed account of the doings of political bosses, politicians and statesmen, publicists, voters, and candidates in this contest which ended Van Buren's presidential career and brought Harrison, and Tyler, to the White House.

The author's approach to his task is scholarly, in the sense that he has faithfully used a formidable array of source materials. It is also a literary approach. He writes well, and in his pages one sees brought to life the spirit of raucous, rabble-rousing, political battle. Here is research data organized and molded into a living narrative.

To praise this book is not to say that it is a perfect work of history. That it is written with obvious sympathy for the Democratic side of the argument is perhaps not a great fault. Few of us write in a political vacuum. A graver criticism is that the author slights some of the significant background of the campaign. He does not bring out clearly enough the Democracy's failure, during the twelve years preceding the campaign, to develop a constructive attitude toward the economic needs of a rapidly developing country. He does not clearly indicate that Democratic monetary policy had been inadequate, nor that the party had taken an equivocal and therefore unsatisfactory stand toward the developing corporate form of business activity. He does not indicate the evil consequences of destroying the Second Bank of the United States, to say nothing of other party measures that had helped to bring on the Panic of 1837. These were factors in 1840 just as certainly as were Van Buren's lack of personal appeal, the depression itself, and unscrupulous Whig tactics in the campaign.

Professor Gunderson seems to feel that the parties were poles apart in their social and political orientation; that the Whigs represented the classes and the Democrats the masses. This reviewer believes that the parties were very evenly balanced, save for 1840, in popular appeal; that many laboring men voted Whig and many capitalists voted Democratic; and that, while Whiggery had the stronger appeal for the "haves," both parties were oriented around a middle class norm. It may also be added that the book's exhaustive description of campaign activities at times palls upon the reader, and that there is missing at its end, after the tumult and the shouting has died away, a summing up or analysis of the historical significance of the campaign.

It is not fair to Professor Gunderson, however, to end this discussion of his book on a critical note. He has written an honest and spirited monograph, to which all subsequent writers on the campaign of 1840 must turn for information. It is not likely that we shall soon see another volume devoted solely to the contest between "Tippecanoe" and "Sweet Sandy Whiskers."

University of Rochester GLYNDON G. VAN DEUSEN

Slavery in Tennessee. By Chase C. Mooney. *Indiana University Publications, Social Science Series,* Number 17. (Bloomington: Indiana University Press, 1957. xii + 250 pp. Map, appendixes, notes, bibliography, and index. $4.50.)

Nearly twenty-five years ago the late Frank L. Owsley, with the collaboration of his wife and a corps of graduate students at Vanderbilt University, inaugurated a project of re-evaluating the social and economic structure of the pre-Civil War South. As a basic part of their source material they used the individual census returns of 1850 and 1860, which had recently been made available on microfilm, supplemented by many types of state, county, and personal records. Most historians are familiar with the new interpretation which resulted, with its rediscovery of the large and respectable middle class of the ante-bellum South.

The author of *Slavery in Tennessee,* now a professor at Indiana University, was one of the graduate students engaged in that project. Some of his findings have already appeared in article form in the *Tennessee Historical Quarterly* and the *Journal of Southern History,* but the Indiana University Press is to be congratulated for making the study available in print in its entirety, even though the use of a flimsy paper cover is regrettable. The notes are placed in the back of the book, but running heads giving groups of page numbers facilitate their use.

Professor Mooney has successfully exploded several hoary traditions regarding slavery in Tennessee, as has been done by his confreres for other states. He has shown that "planters," defined as those who owned thirty or more slaves and five hundred or more acres of improved land, constituted "islands" in an ocean of small farmers. More than two thirds of the slaveowners held fewer than ten slaves each in both 1850 and 1860, with their holdings totaling more than a fourth of the slave population. The number of nonslaveholding landowners actually increased between 1850 and 1860, thus contradicting the traditional claim that "the slaveowners were driving the nonslaveowners from the good lands and reducing them to a position of economic and political vassalage."

The research procedure adopted, as was the case with other similar studies, was the sampling technique. Fifteen counties, carefully selected to represent adequately the several physiographic regions of the state, were subjected to intensive statistical analysis. The result naturally revealed wide disparity between aspects of the institution of slavery in different parts of the state. To supplement this statistical treatment the author analyzed exhaustively legislation concerning slavery, information about the hire, sale, flight, and theft of slaves, antislavery sentiment, and slave life. Especially in regard to the last-named topic, the author betrays the fact that at heart he is, as was his mentor, a "true Southerner." Although the treatment of slaves was not as harsh in Tennessee as in the Lower South, the slaves' existence could not have been as nearly idyllic as the author's chapter seems to imply. That slavery was basically and morally wrong receives scant mention. Even so, it is perhaps appropriate in view of present issues to have called to our attention the fact that in 1860 there was more segregation on the basis of race and color in the free states than in the South.

University of Tennessee STANLEY J. FOLMSBEE

Kansas: A History of the Jayhawk State. By William Frank Zornow. (Norman: University of Oklahoma Press, 1957. xii + 417 pp. Illustrations, maps, notes, bibliography, and index. $4.95.)

This is one of our superior state histories. Written frankly for the adult audience, it avoids the deadly infection of textbookishness and the patronizing tone of the book for young people. On the other hand, the author resists sturdily the lure of the picturesque and the anecdotal which has marred and distorted too many state histories. I hope Kansas adults appreciate and buy it.

The author maintains an admirable balance and proportion throughout, and that is not easy, for Kansas has had its flaming moments and its flamboyant characters. It required deliberate effort to hold to 20 per cent the proportion of the book which predates statehood, for that is not the tradition in Kansas historical writing. John Brown, Jim Lane, Jerry Simpson, Mary Ellen Lease, Will White, Carry Nation, Lizzie Wooster, Doctor Brinkley, and a score of other colorful Kansans are not easy to contain.

The result of this self-discipline is the inclusion of otherwise neglected material. "Bleeding" Kansas is thrown against its proper background of frontier turbulence and land grabbing. The movement of the Indian tribes to the territory, and then from the state, is developed with admirable economy of words, as is the story of what happened to their lands. The cattle industry appears as an industry, and the cowboy as a believable workman at a hazardous trade. The cow towns themselves will never be believable. The space limitations probably prevented a fuller account of railroad organization and consolidation, with attendant land-grabbing operations. It would have been helpful to have had a summary of the actual operation of our land system.

It is always hard to write local history. It must be sketched against the background of national events, for emotions, fears, and economic forces are not respecters of state lines. (The author has maintained an acceptable balance here, also.) The chapters on politics, especially those covering events before 1918, succeed in giving the sense of a Kansas divergence from a national political norm.

It must be confessed that the final chapters are the least successful of the work, only because the last quarter-century has almost wiped out the state as a peculiar entity, separable from other states. The chapter on urbanization is hardly more than a state gazetteer. The chapter on culture is an afterthought. The chapter on industry must have shocked state loyalty as it revealed how extensively Kansas industrial expansion depended on federal subsidy and federal purchase. Kansas farmers were saved by the New Deal, were made unprecedentedly prosperous by World War II and the mechanizing revolution which came with it, and survived in diminishing numbers since because federal law made it possible.

The politics which came out of this in the last third of a century makes no sense. Traditional emotional party associations suddenly contradicted direct interest, and new economic issues proved divisive and frustrating. It is a record of political evasion, double talk, and consequent factional feuding which the author presents coldly and without emphasis — but the dominant Republican party of Kansas should have sued to suppress this book, on the ground that it constitutes indecent exposure.

The author has done a great deal of work in the extensive newspaper collections of the state, and in the conventional materials of the State Historical Society, but the remarkable feature of the work is the skill with which he has utilized the unexpectedly vast body of scholarly work presented to universities in the state and outside by candidates for advanced degrees.

The University of Oklahoma Press has given this book a handsome dress, the illustrations are well chosen, and the maps are adequate. The errors noted were few and unimportant. This is an excellent book, of which the state should be proud.

Wayne State University RAYMOND C. MILLER

Congressman Abraham Lincoln. By Donald W. Riddle. (Urbana: University of Illinois Press, 1957. x + 280 pp. Notes, bibliography, and index. $4.50.)

Professor Riddle has placed all members of the Lincoln fraternity in his debt by this scholarly and detailed account of Lincoln's one term in Congress. The study begins where the author's earlier book, *Lincoln Runs for Congress*, ends and carries the story of Lincoln's political career through his failure to win a seat in the United States Senate in February, 1855. The reviewer hopes that Professor Riddle has in mind (if not in progress) a third volume, "Lincoln Runs for the Senate," to carry the story through 1858.

The first fourteen chapters deal with Congressman Lincoln, the last three with ex-Congressman Lincoln. Riddle finds that Congressman Lincoln "demonstrated praiseworthy industry and much better than average ability. . . . He was a faithful party man. He missed few roll calls, and never 'skulked' a vote on touchy issues. He served well and conspicuously in his committee assignments." Lincoln took an active part in debate, and in two formal speeches he ably presented his party's case. Perhaps of greater importance were the lasting friendships he made and the fact that he "learned much of inestimable value to him in his subsequent political career" (pp. 3-4).

Why then did Lincoln come short of success as a member of Congress? Seeing the political scene from a national viewpoint, Lincoln was influenced by eastern and southern party leaders and lost contact with his constituents. This led him to make three serious political errors: his "Spot resolutions," his affirmative vote on the Ashmun amendment, and his full-length speech on the Mexican War. All three were highly critical of the war, which was very popular among Whigs as well as Democrats in Illinois. It was this position on the war that aroused resentment among his constituents and led to his temporary political eclipse. Riddle observes that Lincoln "for the first time in his life was completely mistaken in his estimate of a political situation" (p. 69). As a result his congressional career came to an end and his party was defeated in his district in the next election.

The author examines Lincoln's voting record on the slavery issue and finds it confusing. "Lincoln maintained the principle that there should be no extension of slavery into the areas where it did not then exist," but his votes "show that he had no clear conception of how this was to be accomplished." Riddle concludes that "the most conspicuous feature of Congressman Lincoln's course with reference to slavery is his discreet silence" (pp. 178-79). It is in the chapter on slavery that the only serious error is noted. Riddle summarizes the provisions of Lincoln's proposals in the short session for the gradual abolition of slavery in the District of Columbia (p. 171), but comparison with the text in *The Collected Works of Abraham Lincoln* (which he cites) shows a serious misreading of the first three sections of Lincoln's eight-section proposals.

In the matter of patronage, Congressman Lincoln "maintained a standard of political ethics which merits the highest praise" (p. 181). Riddle gives a detailed treatment of ex-Congressman Lincoln's unsuccessful effort to obtain the commissionership of the Land Office, and concludes that his "fairness to his rival and his consideration for [Secretary] Ewing are the measure of unstinted magnanimity" (p. 221). Professor Riddle has also given us a complete and documented account of the two Oregon appointments offered to Lincoln and observes that "the governorship, not the minor . . . secretaryship, of Oregon Territory, was the measure of the Taylor administration's value of Lincoln" (p. 235). As for Lincoln's "retirement" from politics following his term in Congress, it is the author's conclusion that "he was involuntarily retired, by reason of the widespread and lasting unpopularity" of his Mexican War record in Congress.

Eastern Illinois University CHARLES H. COLEMAN

The Mormons. By Thomas F. O'Dea. (Chicago: University of Chicago Press, 1957. xii + 289 pp. Notes, bibliography, and index. $5.00.)

This brilliantly written monograph is a penetrating study of the Mormons by a Catholic scholar. It is also a book by one whose background is exclusively eastern about a people who are westerners. Throughout, the author has striven to combine intellectual objectivity with intelligent human sympathy. He has succeeded magnificently.

The book is divided into two parts. The first, embracing the first five chapters, deals with the historical evolution of Mormonism and the impact of the western frontier upon this development. The last four chapters examine the theological, political, and economic implications of Mormon group life and analyze the sources of strain and conflict which these factors have precipitated. The author's major contribution lies in this section, for it affords him an opportunity to apply his talents in his chosen fields of philosophy and sociology.

In a penetrating analysis of the Mormon prophet Joseph Smith the author offers the explanation that Smith "was a normal person living in an atmosphere of religious excitement that influenced his behavior as it had many thousands of others and . . . led him from necromancy into revelation, from revelation to prophecy, and from prophecy to leadership of an important religious movement" (p. 24). And he adds: "To one who does not accept the work [the Book of Mormon] as a divinely revealed scripture, such an explanation on the basis of evidence at hand seems by far the most likely and safest." The Prophet was martyred at the Carthage jail in June, 1844, and thereafter for thirty-three years Brigham Young became the acknowledged leader. Under his direction, and steeled by the rigors of persecution and conflict against both man and nature, the Mormons prospered and became the most orderly American community in the great West.

In his analysis of Mormon theology the author presents a surprisingly lucid picture of Mormon views on the origin and nature of the universe; God, His nature and place in the universe; man and his place in the universe; and the Restoration. The Mormon conception of God connotes a progressive, ever-changing deity, a God who has risen to Godhead by His own labor. Joseph Smith said: "God himself was as we are now and is an exalted man and sits enthroned in yonder heavens." Man, in Mormon theology, is not only eternal, "but he is also the possessor of Godlike attributes which need only cultivating, improving, developing, and advancing by a series of progressive changes to arrive at the climax of Divine Humanity." The Restoration is interpreted to be the renewal of communication between God and man and the re-establishment of the original Church of Christ.

Mormon achievements in fields other than theology also receive their due share of attention. Pointing out that by 1865 there were in Utah 1,043 miles of canals, irrigating 153,949 acres and valued at $1,766,939, Mr. O'Dea says: "The thousands of miles of canals and ditches were built by the farmers and operated by the farmers. They constituted one of the greatest and most successful community or co-operative undertakings in the history of America" (p. 202). He shows, also, that such co-operative effort has continued into the twentieth century, citing especially the inauguration in 1936 of the Mormon Church Welfare Plan which, disdaining federal relief during the depression years, provided aid and employment for some 300,000 persons.

In his final chapter the author considers the dilemmas of strain and conflict within the Mormon Church. The greatest of these is the conflict with secular thought. The conservative group seems now in control of the Church, and the principles of Church organization "make the advancement of liberals into Church leadership very unlikely in the next several years. Yet it is these very liberals, shut out from leadership, who in the Church's educational system are saving many of the youth from apostasy."

Despite the general excellence of the volume, the text contains some errors of fact. For example, Beaver (or Mackinac) Island is incorrectly located (p. 71); the year 1869, not 1867, marks the date of the coming of the railroad (p. 87); Miles Goodyear was never in the employ of the Hudson's Bay Company, and neither he nor anyone else ever received a land grant from the Mexican government in the Great Basin area (p. 88). The reviewer is at a loss to understand the lack of emphasis with regard to the basic causes of the important Utah War (p. 101), and questions the use of statements made by John D. Lee, self-confessed murderer and leader in the crime at Mountain Meadows, as basic evidence in proof of the alleged practice of Blood Atonement. The footnote citations are revealing and helpful. A brief but adequate bibliography is appended.

University of Utah LELAND H. CREER

Homeward to Zion: The Mormon Migration from Scandinavia. By William Mulder. (Minneapolis: University of Minnesota Press, 1957. xiv + 375 pp. Notes, bibliography, and index. $7.50.)

This book most agreeably goes far beyond its title. On the migration itself it goes deeply into the multiplicity of factors that caused men, women, and children to leave the Scandinavian countries to settle the desert and deserted areas of Utah. The author discusses conditions in Norway, Denmark, and Sweden during the last half of the nineteenth century which made those areas a fruitful orchard for Mormon missionaries. Economic factors receive full study. But, as Mr. Mulder's work shows, much emphasis was placed on the religious utopia to be found in Zion. The evidence here is treated fully and sympathetically and understandingly. The intangibles of religious belief receive their due. The ups and downs of the Mormon missionaries and converts, the social ostracism, the official attitude of the governments, including that of the United States (mostly hostile), the financial problems, difficulties with other sects — all these receive balanced treatment. The author shows what happened to many a Scandinavian convert when the lure of the American West had added to it the pull of a religious crusade. Skillfully the author portrays the emigrant drawn between the Scylla of economic desire and the Charybdis of a religious haven for the oppressed of all lands. The account shows the changing attitudes of the Mormon leaders toward the problem of gathering to Zion. At first, all were urged to come; later, those desirous of coming received full warning of the difficulties to be encountered, both on the way and in Utah itself.

The niche of the Scandinavian in the Mormon Church and in Utah is fully and competently treated. The author describes how the Olsens, Nelsons, and Hansens fitted into a community of New Englanders and converts from Old England as artisans, farmers, elders, deacons, and group leaders. In other words, this is a case study of the American melting pot in action — that is, if a group of over 40,000 immigrants can be classified as a case study. But the Mormon emigrant was frequently melted by a religious fervor and belief that makes this study more than the usual immigrant or emigrant saga. The book adds much to the knowledge of Mormon recruiting methods, or converting methods, if you wish. It displays full understanding of the intangible factors involved in a religious movement, for this movement of peoples undoubtedly had such an aspect. It also treats fairly those who opposed the Mormon migration from Scandinavia. The work is an outstanding contribution to the history of Mormonism as well as a thorough study of why thousands of Scandinavians came to the Zion of Utah.

Miami University WILLIAM J. MCNIFF

From Wilderness to Statehood: A History of Montana, 1805-1900. By James McClellan Hamilton. Edited by Merrill G. Burlingame. (Portland, Oregon: Binfords and Mort, 1957. xvi + 620 pp. Illustrations, end map, references, and index. $6.00.)

James McClellan Hamilton arrived in Montana in 1889, the year Montana achieved statehood. For the next half century he was an instrumental figure in the development of the educational system of the state, as a member of the state board of education, vice-president of Montana State University, and later president, a professor, and dean of men at Montana State College. As a pioneer he had the opportunity to know socially and professionally the territorial leaders of Montana, and over a period of half a century he gathered, sifted, and interpreted the stories of the frontier history of the state.

The present volume was the first of two projected volumes, the second of which Dean Hamilton was unable to complete before his death in 1940. Volume I was to have covered the pre-territorial and territorial history and Volume II the later period of statehood. Since he had finished only one chapter of the second volume, "Making Montana a State," the editor of this volume has included it as a closing chapter.

From Wilderness to Statehood is written in eleven parts, none of which have been designated as chapters. Each division could be considered as a separate dissertation, and as such would stand alone. As a consequence there is a certain amount of repetition to supply background information in each section. Part One recounts the history of the Lewis and Clark expedition across present Montana. The following sections successively relate the story of the fur trade, military explorations, early immigration, acquisition of the Indian lands, mining, government, agriculture and business development, Indian wars, and the development of the educational, social, and religious institutions of the territory, ending with the early days of statehood.

If this reviewer were to make a suggestion for improvement it would be the addition of maps which could be easily read. The only map in the book is the end map drawn by W. W. deLacy for the use of the first legislature of Montana Territory, showing the mining discoveries to January 1, 1865. The high reduction ratio of the map makes for great difficulty in readability, and unless the reader is well acquainted with the geography and political subdivisions of Montana as they exist today he occasionally becomes lost in this third-largest state in the Union. Several unfortunate typographical errors appear in dates and in names.

Definitive histories of the Rocky Mountain states have yet to be written, for their history, in point of time, is in general not far enough removed from the present for the historian to gain an objective view. Dean Hamilton has made a definite and a much-needed contribution to Montana history. He has with understanding and insight traced the growth of Montana through the various phases of its history and emphasized the evolution of the economic and social aspects through the various pressures of a new frontier and the meeting and solving of problems unique to the frontier and to Montana.

Wyoming State Archives and Historical Department LOLA M. HOMSHER

The American Reaction to the Mortara Case, 1858-1859. By Bertram Wallace Korn. (Cincinnati: The American Jewish Archives, 1957. xii + 196 pp. Illustrations, facsimiles, appendixes, notes, and index. $4.00.)

In June, 1858, Edgardo Mortara, a seven-year-old Jewish child was removed from his parents' home in Bologna by uniformed officials and taken to a catechumen's home in Rome. He never returned to his parents. Bologna was at the time within the Papal States, and Church authorities explained that the "kidnapping" was the consequence of a valid baptism during an infant illness. Jewish protests to the papacy were taken up by Jews and Protestants throughout Europe, while Italian nationalists used the incident in their campaign for Italian unity.

Mr. Korn has chosen to investigate the American reaction to this incident which coincided with the floundering of Know-Nothingism in the immediate pre-Civil War years. The case was publicized and agitated by the several American Jewish communities with the objective of obtaining an official protest to the papacy from President Buchanan. In this they failed, although they did obtain a personal expression of sympathy from Buchanan and Secretary of State Cass. Korn assesses the attempts to make partisan use of the sensational and pathetic aspects of the case which were meat to the secular press. He suspects that the publicity gave a slightly longer lease on life to Know-Nothingism, and shows the manner in which Protestant and Catholic newspapers reacted to attack or to defend.

The particular contribution of the book lies in its illustration of one phase of Jewish history in the United States, and in its comparative portrayal of the operation of religious prejudice. Their ineffective appeals to Buchanan for intercession showed American Jewish communities that they lacked a common voice. Directly out of the Mortara incident there developed plans for the first national representative Jewish organization which, though it was eventually replaced by a more effective body, did perform for a time as a central council. Despite the fact that the Mortara incident was the kind that might have revived bitter anti-Catholic prejudice, Mr. Korn shows that with only a few exceptions American Jews did not permit their criticism to degenerate into bigotry, but directed it toward the ideal of personal freedom. Consequently, anti-Catholicism was not revitalized by Jews, although American Catholics regarded the agitation, whether it came from Jewish or Protestant sources, as a continuation of vicious prejudice and were bitterly anti-Jewish and anti-Protestant in defense.

Mr. Korn has based his study principally on contemporary periodicals. He has used the Jewish, Protestant, Catholic, and secular press. The book is clearly written and logically organized. Moreover, it is moderate in detailing an emotion-laden subject. It is a welcome addition to the small body of temperate historical literature on the general subject of religious prejudice in United States history.

University of Delaware DONALD L. KINZER

Chicago Giant: A Biography of "Long John" Wentworth. By Don E. Fehrenbacher. (Madison: American History Research Center, 1957. x + 278 pp. Illustrations, notes, bibliographical note, and index. $4.50.)

The history of Chicago in the mid-nineteenth century is connected to a great extent with the fascinating career of John Wentworth, a New Hampshire youth who arrived there in 1836 and was prominent in the city's affairs until his death in 1888. Founder and proprietor of the Chicago *Democrat*, for twenty-five years Wentworth used his colorful newspaper to advance party causes and personal ambitions. From the first, like many editors of the day, he was primarily interested in politics. "Long John," as his contemporaries named him, was a familiar figure at conventions, mass meetings, and caucuses. Though frequently furnishing comic relief to the proceedings, owing to his sense of humor, his style of expression, and his unique appearance, he displayed unusual ability in maneuver and manipulation.

Sent to Congress at an early age, he was a dedicated Jacksonian Democrat who understandably departed from orthodoxy on internal improvements, especially river-and-harbor legislation to benefit his home town. Altogether, he served as a representative for six terms, one of which was during the Reconstruction period. Never distinguishing himself as an orator or a statesman, he was nevertheless an effective spokesman for free soil in the territories when the slavery controversy intensified. Reluctantly he abandoned the Democracy of Douglas and Buchanan to become a Republican in 1856. Here his path joined that of equally reluctant Whigs, such as Lincoln. Among the many squabbles that Wentworth had with his Northern Illinois rivals was a bitter one with Norman B. Judd, Lincoln's campaign manager of 1858 and aspirant for the governorship in 1860. The Judd-Wentworth struggles threatened to divide the Republican leadership by drawing in David Davis, Leonard Swett, and Orville Browning. Fortunately, Lincoln's good sense prevented this.

In Chicago "Long John" was always a prominent figure. Twice he was mayor of this burgeoning western city, whose growth he understood sufficiently to make a fortune in lands but whose development surpassed his social outlook. He clung to the unyielding principle of low taxation when urban society required expensive services and utilities. By the 1860's his *Democrat* was behind the times in contrast to the competing *Tribune*, as journalism in America was assuming its modern shape. Yet he adopted quite progressive agricultural methods at his large estate, the Summit, a retreat to which he often retired from his headquarters in a downtown hotel. Even in his last years, as an "old-timer," his fellow citizens found him an exciting topic of conversation.

Mr. Fehrenbacher adeptly weaves into his biography the many patterns of

Wentworth's life: frontier journalism, scientific agriculture, local matters, Illinois politics, and shifting party affiliations. The research for the book is exhaustive but required some ingenuity since Wentworth materials were destroyed by the great fire of 1871. There is just the needed amount of general history to give the work clarity — an enviable accomplishment. The skillful, compact writing could attract that elusive individual, the general reader.

Indiana University MAURICE G. BAXTER

Confederate Morale and Church Propaganda. By James W. Silver. *Confederate Centennial Studies*, Number 3. (Tuscaloosa: Confederate Publishing Company, 1957. 120 pp. Notes, bibliography, and index. $4.00.)

This perceptive, richly illustrated, and pungent analysis of religious thought and Confederate morale is a welcome contribution to the studies on the intellectual history of the South. The author measures the influence of the southern clergy against the faith of a people who generally acknowledged "the hand of God in every event." This mass creed was "based on the assurance of personal salvation and divine interposition in everyday affairs, buttressed by a literal reading of the Scriptures." Slavery had long been defended in the South as part of God's plan and "if Southerners as a whole could be convinced that the Confederacy and the war were also of divine inspiration, they might well build up an indestructible morale."

While acknowledging that unanimity in thought and deed was never achieved among the peoples of the many-regioned South, Mr. Silver supports with trenchant evidence his major conclusions. The overwhelming majority of southern clergymen were in the vanguard of the secession movement. They were initially quite successful in helping the people to identify "God, the right, and the destiny of history with slavery, the Confederacy, and the war." By personal example and by supplication the clergy exerted a tremendous pressure on individual conduct, steadfastly supported the Davis administration, and retained in the hour of despair and despondency a higher degree of morale than they were then able to instill into their parishioners.

In ministerial prose, to fight without stint or moral reservation became a religious duty. The war "was the holiest battle of all time, a fight for home, fireside, family, freedom, civilization, and religion." The Confederacy was founded on the "immutable laws of God," and the cause was pre-eminently "the cause of God himself." When the shock of invasion comes "*the Lord will be here* to repel it."

Military setbacks were rationalized in religious terms. Violation of the Sabbath, intemperance, demagoguery, corruption, luxury, impiety, greed and avarice, lewdness, skepticism, private immorality, profanity, a proud and haughty spirit, speculation, bribery, covetousness, were sins of the southern people undermining the war effort. Failure to administer the institution of slavery in conformity with the teachings of the Bible was a particularly virulent evil. Slaveholders must give religious instruction to the Negroes, insist on the sacredness of marriage and parent-child relationships, observe the laws designed to protect slaves against harsh and cruel masters, and allow the slaves to observe the Sabbath.

Mr. Silver's evidence has been collected from a broad analysis of sermons, church newspapers, and the minutes of denominational organizations. The work is not a study of religion as such, but an analysis of the church as a powerful social organization. The research covers well-known and heretofore obscure religious leaders in and out of the military forces. The style is polished, the treatment balanced, and the conclusions are thoughtful and well reasoned.

In the last analysis "it is difficult to see how the religious leaders or the people themselves, believing as they did in the intervention of the Lord in human affairs, could have come to any other conclusion than that the outcome of the war was God's will." It seems clear that the southern clergy perceived the mote in a brother's eye, but considered not the beam that was in their own.

University of North Carolina FRANK W. KLINGBERG

The Rebel Shore: The Story of Union Sea Power in the Civil War. By James M. Merrill. (Boston: Little, Brown and Company, 1957. x + 246 pp. Illustrations, bibliographical essay, and index. $4.75.)

Because the Confederates won most of the big battles and lost the war, explanations of Confederate defeat have been sought in recent years by exploring activities apart from the field of battle. The author of *The Rebel Shore,* in finding reasons for ultimate Union victory, has gone back to the battlefields and studied amphibious attacks in which the Federal army and navy generally won victories against Confederate coastal installations. The book logs the course to Union victory at sea, and makes sharp appraisals of errors. Focus is upon Union activities, and properly so, as the Federals held the initiative, but the Confederates and their innumerable mistakes are not neglected. New light is shed on local defense as a problem of the Confederacy.

Union success in amphibious operations is not altogether a new idea to readers of such works as Soley, Scharf, Boynton, and the *Official Records.* Yet *The Rebel Shore* is a book which will be welcomed by specialists because the sources are subjected to criticism, distilled into narrative form, and pointed up with numerous and specific conclusions. It includes intriguing essays on some little-known subjects, such as the failure of "the Rathole Squadron," commando raids and sneak attacks, picket boats, mine warfare, submarines, torpedo boats, Port Royal as a liberty port, logistic support of the "beef boat" run, and inter-service rivalry. In this book naval assaults, usually amphibious, proceed from Hatteras Inlet to Port Royal, Fort Pulaski, Roanoke Island, New Orleans, Charleston, Galveston, Mobile Bay, Fort Fisher, and lesser points. Because blockading was the chief purpose behind the seizure of Confederate coastal forts, in a sense it may be said that the entire book treats the blockade. In a more literal sense a single chapter, a very good one, is devoted to blockade routine.

Yet praise for *The Rebel Shore* is not intended to be a blanket endorsement of all the numerous interpretations. It is unfortunate that there are no footnotes, especially as the book is based on extensive research. Furthermore, nowhere does *The Rebel Shore* describe the operation of the Union blockaders in guarding foreign ports, such as Bermuda, Nassau, Matamoros, and Havana, although this was one of the most effective means of enforcing the blockade. It comes as something of a surprise to read that the Federal navy had "no precedents to follow in damming up Rebel harbors" (p. 67), when there were the precedents of the Mexican War in which so many of the Civil War seniors had participated, to say nothing of the navy's acquaintance with British precedents. This reviewer believes that the Confederates were reacting to more than a "Naval bluff" when they evacuated Pensacola. Because this port lacked adequate interior transportation facilities, a matter overlooked in *The Rebel Shore*, the Confederate decision to move troops from Pensacola to Mobile was probably sound. It was an error of the Confederates that they did not provide stronger defenses of more highly selected harbors. This might have been done if the Confederates had known as much about sea fighting as they did about land fighting. Economy of force, as practiced on the battlefields of Virginia, would have been useful to the defenders of the long coastline of the Confederacy.

These criticisms, however, are minor when measured against the solid worth and lively prose of Professor Merrill's book.

University of Alabama CHARLES G. SUMMERSELL

Chronicles from the Nineteenth Century: Family Letters of Blanche Butler and Adelbert Ames. Two volumes. Compiled by Blanche Butler Ames, 1935. (Privately issued; copyright by Jessie Ames Marshall [Jamaica Plain, Massachusetts], 1957. Vol. I, *1861-1874*: xiv + 719 pp. Vol. II, *1874-1899*: vi + 689 pp. Index. $10.00 per set.)

Some forty years ago Jessie Ames Marshall performed a great service for scholars by publishing the Civil War correspondence of her grandfather, General Benjamin F. Butler. Now once again she deserves the thanks of the profession for making possible the publication of the correspondence (originally compiled by her mother in 1935) of her parents, General and Mrs. Adelbert Ames.

Adelbert Ames was a West Point graduate who had a distinguished career during the Civil War. Brevetted a major general at the age of twenty-nine, he went south with the army after Appomattox. He is generally remembered as the Yankee governor of Mississippi in whose administration Radical Reconstruction reached a climax. After the conservatives' recapture of the state government, he left Mississippi, not to re-enter public service until the Spanish-American War, when he served as a brigadier general in the Cuban campaign. In 1870, he married Blanche Butler, the General's daughter, whose political and financial connections were helpful to him.

The letters included in the two volumes reflect General Ames's career between 1861 and 1899. Although the portions dealing with the Civil War are very incomplete, no future student of Reconstruction will be able to overlook the important material bearing on the Ames administration in Mississippi. The General's struggle with James L. Alcorn, his scalawag rival, his efforts to make the Fifteenth Amendment more than a dead letter, his bitterness about Grant's refusal to send federal troops in 1874 (he accused the President of seeking southern support for a third term), and his compromise with the conservatives concerning the Negro militia, all are vividly covered in his correspondence. Even Dunbar Rowland, the Magnolia State's conservative historian, admits that Ames, unlike other Radical governors, was personally honest. Therefore the publication of his correspondence is of special interest to those for whom the researches of David Donald and Vernon L. Wharton have already pointed a way toward a reinterpretation of traditional accounts of the horrors of Reconstruction in Mississippi. Moreover, the letters dealing with the Spanish-American War not only reveal once again the gross inefficiency of many responsible participants, but also contain interesting references to the partial healing of Civil War wounds in 1898.

The portions of the collection which pertain to Blanche Butler Ames are less important. Mainly concerned with her private affairs and her happy married life, they shed little new light on her father's activities. It is disappointing not to find more than one or two letters dealing with some of the most important events of General Butler's career — the impeachment of Johnson, the crucial gubernatorial campaigns of 1878 and 1879, the single term as governor of Massachusetts, and the final try for the presidency in 1884. Judicious editorial work would not only have avoided some of these shortcomings, but would also have resulted in additions to the explanatory notes which, at present, are inadequate.

In spite of these criticisms, *Chronicles from the Nineteenth Century*, with its excellent index, constitutes a valuable addition to the documentation of the Reconstruction period. It is to be hoped that Mrs. Marshall will see her way clear in the future to publishing some additional excerpts from her family's voluminous correspondence.

Brooklyn College HANS L. TREFOUSSE

Jay Gould: His Business Career, 1867-1892. By Julius Grodinsky. (Philadelphia: University of Pennsylvania Press, 1957. 627 pp. Illustration, maps, notes, tables, bibliographical note, and index. $10.00.)

Between 1879 (perhaps sooner) and his death in 1892, Jay Gould wielded so much influence in the fields of security trading and railways (except in the Southeast) that any serious study of that period devoted to those subjects must take him into account. Hence this volume is of prime importance because it sheds more light on this incredible figure than any previous combination of books or articles.

Except for the author's final conclusion in Chapter XXX, of which, I feel sure, one may be respectfully skeptical without in the least impugning the far-reaching value of the book, this is an illuminating, fact-packed, and disarmingly candid account based on primary sources. Mr. Grodinsky diligently unravels the hitherto hopelessly snarled skein of Gould's multifarious (and often nefarious) activities; this in itself is a great service. Of even more significance, he singles out and establishes beyond question the underlying motive that possessed Gould with compulsive force throughout his life, thus providing a logical common denominator for actions that have often been regarded at best as contradictory, and at worst as sadistically malicious.

In his seven-line preface Mr. Grodinsky announces clearly that this is "an examination of the policies of a businessman *in the field of speculative or equity capital*. . . . It is not a biography" (p. 7, italics supplied). Nor, he might have added, is it primarily railway history; it *does*, in full justification of its sub-subtitle, "The Expansion of America's Railroad Empire," throw voluminous and invaluable light on the intimate workings of railway strategy and the men who guided it, but only in so far as that strategy involved Gould or his opponents. This, of course, covers a lot of territory, and in respect to some roads (such as the Missouri Pacific, Wabash, and Union Pacific) this volume provides a tolerably continuous account for the years covered. There are also excellent thumbnail sketches of Adams, John Dillon, Perkins, Sage, Vanderbilt, and others, and shrewd commentaries on construction companies, refinancing, and the like. But the spotlight throughout is deliberately on Gould the trader, the manipulator of capital.

Why? For two excellent reasons: First, both Gould's abilities and interest "lay largely in the field of corporate negotiation and security trading" (p. 22); his business activities, specifically including those involving railways, "were subsidiary to his stock market operations" (p. 479). Thus the book's approach is logical, however surprising this may appear to those who think of Gould as primarily a railroader. Intrinsically he was no such thing; to him railways were merely vehicles to advance his trading ambitions. In driving this point home, the author puts Gould in proper focus and thereby makes a major contribution. Secondly, Mr. Grodinsky, himself a keen student of security markets and a knowledgeable trader therein, is plainly fascinated by Gould's ingenious techniques. Because this fascination is combined with sophisticated comprehension of what Gould was trying to do, we pedantic laymen are treated to a fast-moving ringside account that fairly crackles with know-how and excitement. Don't mistake me: Mr. Grodinsky is no blind partisan. He misses nary a foul by "his boy," and calls each by its right name. But his all-out enthusiasm for Gould's fertile imagination and technical wizardry gives the book an adventure-like air. Were this not so, 610 pages devoted largely to clever skulduggery, beguiling prevarication, successful bribery, and brazen swindling could, conceivably, be dull.

Space limitations here preclude even a summary of this volume's wide-ranging factual content. Suffice it to say that it discusses in orderly fashion Gould's railway buccaneering in the East, Midwest, and Southwest; his successful capture of Western Union and Manhattan Elevated (from which he derived most of his fair-sized fortune), and his ups and downs as a stock market trader. With genuine craftsmanship these activities are linked throughout to Gould's driving determination to outsmart his competitors by skillful trading and manipulation.

Only in that context, I am persuaded, can Gould be understood, and only in those respects could he be termed a "success." Even on his chosen ground he occasionally met his match: Vanderbilt in the East and Perkins in the West eventually stopped him cold in his tracks. But on balance and, I think, at huge cost to the nation's economy then and since, he generally won — or escaped relatively unscathed from — each competitive battle. Otherwise, as Mr. Grodinsky convincingly shows, Gould's record was dismal. He was a failure as a corporate manager, as a railway strategist, as an interpreter of economic trends, and even as a judge of the market. His business ethics, which contrasted sharply with his exemplary behavior at home, were, even for his day, unpardonable.

In his closing chapter, Mr. Grodinsky suggests that Gould, quite unwittingly, made substantial long-run contributions to society (1) by forcing the construction of vast railway mileage, thus providing additional service; (2) by permanently lowering railway rates, thus speeding industrial and agricultural development; and (3) by cashing his paper profits, thus channeling much-needed capital into productive investments. I confess I cannot accept this reasoning. To my thinking, duplicate railway facilities, many if not most of which were unnecessary even then, constituted an intolerable financial burden and economic waste; depression of rates below a compensatory level not only drove countless companies into bankruptcy and ruined investors but resulted in widespread undermaintenance and execrable service, notably on Gould's own lines; mobilization of capital, however worthy in itself, was hardly a benefit when used for predatory and uneconomic ends. If any monuments are to be raised to Gould, they might conceivably honor his ingenuity (however misguided), but more importantly his horrible example which led responsible railroaders to close ranks and to take effective steps against his more outrageous schemes and methods and to assume greater responsibility toward their corporate and public obligations.

But to cavil unduly at Mr. Grodinsky's personal conclusions is to distort the picture. This is an extremely valuable book about an unquestionably influential person; it goes a long way toward filling a major gap in post-Civil War economic and business history. Since it is based almost wholly on primary sources, an extended note on the fifteen collections consulted replaces the usual bibliography. Documentation of the text, though delightfully unconventional, is adequate. The maps, however, which sacrifice schematic lucidity for physiographic accuracy, are very hard to read. The index is satisfactory.

This is not a book for laymen, for it assumes that the reader has a considerable familiarity with security trading and railway development. Nor is it, in spots, particularly easy reading. But from now on no one interested in this period can afford to overlook it. Mr. Grodinsky has, I am sure, made a lasting contribution.

Bureau of Railway Economics RICHARD C. OVERTON

Spirit Gun of the West: The Story of Doc W. F. Carver, Plainsman, Trapper, Buffalo Hunter, Medicine Chief of the Santee Sioux, World's Champion Marksman, and Originator of the American Wild West Show. By Raymond W. Thorp. (Glendale: Arthur H. Clark Company, 1957. 266 pp. Illustrations, notes, bibliography, and index. $8.50.)

This work is the seventh volume of the Arthur H. Clark Western Frontiersmen Series and deals with the life of a man who could boast of having been buffalo hunter, medicine chief, world's champion marksman, and originator of the wild West show. Born in Winslow, Illinois, in 1840, William Frank Carver, usually known as "Doc," ran away from home at the age of seventeen and lived in Minnesota with the Santee Sioux tribe of Indians for a period of three years. He was called "Spirit Gun" because of his shooting ability. Going into Missouri, Arkansas, and Nebraska in the early sixties, he soon gained a wide reputation as a buffalo hunter and became acquainted with numerous well-known frontier characters of the period, among whom were "Wild Bill" Hickok, Jack McCall, and William F. Cody, commonly known as "Buffalo Bill."

Leaving the buffalo country about 1870, Carver specialized in shooting at flying targets with a rifle and soon became well known as an expert marksman. He challenged all of the best shots in this country and in Europe, won most of his contests, and claimed to be the champion marksman of the world. Carver was a large man of great strength and engaged in endurance shooting contests, some of which lasted from six to ten days.

In the spring of 1882, Carver and Cody organized a wild West show in partnership, with Cody as manager and Carver putting up the necessary money. Cody's experience as an actor in such traveling western plays as *The Scout of the Border* and *Life on the Plains* probably influenced Carver in consenting to the arrangement. The partnership was soon dissolved, however, and Carver took charge of the show. Cody joined forces with Nate Salsbury, a man of considerable wealth, and for a time two wild West shows were in operation. Attempts by Carver to obtain payment of the money owed him by Cody led to a series of lawsuits in which Carver apparently won a technical victory but was forced to close his show. Carver did a special shooting act with the Adam Forepaugh Circus for a time, and in 1888 signed a contract with Fred Whitney to organize a wild West show and to tour Europe and Australia. Cody and Salsbury were in Europe with their show at the same time. After returning from Australia, Carver traveled with a stage play, *The Scout*, and by 1896 was ready to "hang up his guns." The last thirty years of Carver's life, during which time he presented trained-horse acts at state and county fairs and carnivals, are barely mentioned. He died at his California ranch in 1927.

Based largely upon sixteen volumes of Carver's manuscripts and scrapbooks, this work makes an important contribution to the history of the beginnings of the American wild West show and of exhibition shooting in the United States and Europe during the last quarter of the nineteenth century. The portions of the book dealing with these activities are well documented. The professional historian will doubtless be irritated by what appear to be exaggerated statements regarding some of the activities of Carver. They are either not substantiated or are based on Carver's own account. This is not a serious matter, however, when compared with the positive contributions in the volume. The paper, printing, and binding of the book are excellent, as is characteristic of Arthur H. Clark publications.

Southern Illinois University HAROLD E. BRIGGS

The Religious Faith of John Fiske. By H. Burnell Pannill. (Durham: Duke University Press, 1957. xiv + 263 pp. Notes, bibliography, and index. $5.00.)

The name of John Fiske is well known to American historians, but probably few know much about him. As a popular reconciler of evolution and religion and as the author of a series of widely read volumes on early American history, he has a secure — if secondary — place in the national annals. It is odd that there has been no biography of him since John Spencer Clark's *Life and Letters*, published in 1917. There is need for a modern evaluation of Fiske's achievement.

The present work, however, is likely to prove a disappointment to historians. It is not history or biography, but a study in the philosophy of religion. It originated as a doctoral thesis at Duke University, and the author, an ordained minister, is professor of philosophy and dean of men at Randolph-Macon College. In six topical chapters, Dr. Pannill analyzes and evaluates Fiske's thought in the light of current theology. The first chapter outlines rather briefly the highlights of Fiske's life. This is followed by four chapters dealing in turn with the roots of Fiske's thought, his philosophy of history, his view of God, and his view of man. Chapter VI is a critique of Fiske's religious system, written essentially from a neo-orthodox point of view. The discussion of Fiske's historical writings occupies a rather minor place.

Dr. Pannill's account of the various intellectual influences which molded Fiske's thinking is perhaps the most significant aspect of the book. New England transcendentalism as represented by Emerson and Parker, Comtean positivism, Alexander von Humboldt's *Cosmos*, and Herbert Spencer's *Synthetic Philosophy* were major sources of Fiske's "Cosmic Philosophy." Evolutionary science was used only as a bulwark to support his fundamental faith. The central thesis of this study is that in the last analysis the roots of Fiske's evolutionary optimism are to be found in his intuitive confidence in man's potentialities. The origins of this faith, either in Fiske's personality or in the nineteenth-century American setting, are not fully explored.

John Fiske was convinced that history was the story of "the triumph of good over evil" and that its culmination would be the establishment of the Kingdom of God on earth. With Matthew Arnold he regarded God as "an Eternal Power, not ourselves, that makes for righteousness." He considered morality the essence of religion, and he sincerely believed that the process of evolution involved ethical progress. Man was slowly but surely throwing off his brute inheritance. "We cannot fail to see," he wrote, "that the final extinction of warfare is only a question of time." It is difficult to defend such a creed in these days, and Dr. Pannill does not attempt to do so. In general Fiske comes off rather badly in the course of this study. A historian, however, may raise the question of whether it would not have been fairer to treat Fiske more sympathetically within the context of his own time.

The study was based chiefly on Fiske's collected works in twenty-four volumes; no manuscripts appear in the bibliography. The author might well have made more use of secondary materials on other contemporary figures and movements. Another weakness is that Fiske does not emerge as a person. A recent list in the *American Quarterly* indicates that two other Ph.D. theses on John Fiske are in progress. The candidates need not abandon their work.

Pennsylvania State University IRA V. BROWN

America and the Fight for Irish Freedom, 1866-1922: An Old Story Based upon New Data. By Charles Callan Tansill. (New York: The Devin-Adair Company, 1957. xii + 489 pp. Illustrations, notes, appendix, bibliography, and index. $7.50.)

I could wish that this book had been sent for review to one of Professor Tansill's compatriots — an American, I mean, not an Irishman — for although an English historian of Anglo-American relations should be technically well equipped to review a work on *America and the Fight for Irish Freedom* he may, particularly if he holds strong views on the supreme necessity for Anglo-American friendship, be emotionally very ill-suited for the task. And no historian can escape altogether from the emotions engendered by his background and environment. But it is our first duty as historians to seek the truth, which necessitates a constant struggle against our natural bias, and even though this review may be open to a *tu quoque* (a *tu quoque, O Anglice*, what is more), it must be said that what is wrong with this history is that it is extraordinarily biased.

This might be less pernicious if the preface openly avowed its Irishry, but it comes no nearer to this than a statement that "many critics . . . will sharply disagree with my interpretation. . . . It will not be the first time I have stirred up controversy and I hope it will not be the last," which is a sort of Irish challenge to battle with all and sundry. Professor Tansill's failure explicitly to proclaim his predilections might be forgiven if his feelings did not so obviously keep breaking in; so much so indeed that it is remarkably hard to remember that this is a history of events which took place more than thirty-five years ago, for it reads as passionately as a contemporary tract, and one is at a loss to know with which particular points one can best illustrate this blinkered approach. (It certainly would be a waste of space with a historian of Professor Tansill's experience, industry, and smartness to spend time on small points of content and method, when the great defect of partiality sticks out from the work on every side.)

It is not surprising that the first sentence of the text is about British imperialism, nor that in Ireland Britain could do no right in the author's eyes, for few Britons today are proud of their over-all record in Ireland in the nineteenth and early twentieth centuries; but it does seem to be "stretching it a little" to say that, in February, 1920, "The reign of terrorism that existed in Ireland was in many cases worse than the regime of murder and oppression now associated with Russian rule behind the Iron Curtain." It is odd, too, that in all the discussion of the Black and Tan atrocities there is virtually no mention of Irish terrorism, and, earlier, no emphasis on the fact that Britain herself was fighting for her life between 1914 and 1918. Nor is it surprising that no recognition whatever is given to the case of Ulster, in refusing to be forced *out* of a body politic — the United Kingdom — of which Protestant Irishmen, whatever the views and the unhappy lot of their Southern countrymen, had been a willing part for almost as long as the United States had been an independent country. It is not even surprising, perhaps, to find that a President who could rejoice in his Scots-Irish ancestry is castigated in a way that can only be justified by gross omissions of evidence; it certainly had never occurred to me before that Wilson (not one of my own heroes) "felt deeply dedicated to the complete support of British foreign policy no matter what the cost might be in terms of American lives and treasure."

But it really is astonishing, even to a member of the race that has had the experience of being embroiled with the Irish people for three-quarters of a millennium, to realize that these are incidental themes, and that the real thesis of the work is a defense of one faction of Irish-American supporters of Irish freedom, not only against other Irish-Americans, but even against a large section of the Irish people themselves, headed by their first leader, De Valera. And when, in the face of the violent, insensate, and persistent divisions among the Irish, one finds Professor Tansill quoting, apparently in solemn disapproval, the words of the English Catholic Bishop Keating, "The Home Rule question is not the fault of England, but of Ireland. If Ireland can only agree upon an acceptable form of Government, England will . . . gladly grant it. The trouble is that what suits one faction will not suit another, and each wishes to impose its ideas upon the others," one's astonishment knows no bounds. But when one reflects further, that at the very time when Professor Tansill is writing with so much emotion, individual citizens of Eire are still engaged in armed attacks across the Ulster border, perhaps one's astonishment at the violence of a mere historical narrative may seem unjustified.

University of London H. C. ALLEN

Railroads in Alabama Politics, 1875-1914. By James F. Doster. *University of Alabama Studies*, Number 12. (University: University of Alabama Press, 1957. x + 273 pp. Maps, notes, bibliography, and index. $5.00, cloth bound; $4.00, paper bound.)

As the author himself states, narratives which would reveal the inner workings of the various railroads of Alabama have not yet been published. Perhaps, for that reason, a synthesis of railroad participation in Alabama politics is premature. Written in the main from Alabama newspaper files, from the records of various state officials and agencies, and from other contemporary published sources, this book necessarily tells an external story.

The result is at times tantalizing. Too often the real flavor of the period is buried in the numerous informational footnotes. We are told repeatedly of "violent objections," of "personal attacks," of "intemperate denunciations," but little or none of this scurrilous correspondence or debate finds its way into the text. Expecting to plunge immediately into a lively discussion of economic pressures and political countermeasures, we find instead that the first half of the book contains elementary background material on court decisions, outline histories of each railroad that passed through the state, and an explanation of railroad rates and traffic problems.

The second half of the book shapes up around two major contenders, the governor of Alabama, Braxton Bragg Comer, and the president of the Louisville and Nashville Railroad, Milton Hannibal Smith. An unduly cautious approach to the two protagonists robs this part of the book of much of its punch. Smith, an empire-building mogul who successfully defied the Interstate Commerce Commission of the United States, a man to whom power and the manipulation of the affairs of state was the measure of success, is presented as "a man of energy, integrity, vision, perseverance, and judgment." No clear definition of the character of Comer emerges. Was he a political opportunist who used the anti-railroad sentiment to raise himself successively to the positions he desired, or was he a man dedicated to deliver his people from the enemy? The author believes both to be true. In evaluating these two men, he finds that it is very hard to say who was in the right, "for the differences between what was right and what was wrong lack sharp shadings of tone when seen in the perspective of time."

Other conclusions are more controversial. One that hardly seems substantiated by the evidence is that "without the interference of the Fourteenth Amendment and the federal courts people and railroads in Alabama might have been able to work out their differences to their mutual satisfaction, for their interests in common were far greater than their differences. People who need each other ought to be able to work out their differences without the intervention of trouble-making third parties."

If this book has been attempted too soon, it still has the merit of drawing attention to a field of study which has only recently been explored objectively, the interrelationships of corporations with society. From the stimulus provided by this pioneering work, intensive research into railroad company archives should undoubtedly ensue. For those who desire to do so, the meticulously selected bibliography in this book provides an excellent starting point.

Historical Division JEAN E. KEITH
U. S. Army, Corps of Engineers

McIver of North Carolina. By Rose Howell Holder. (Chapel Hill: University of North Carolina Press, 1957. xvi + 283 pp. Illustrations, notes, and index. $5.00.)

The University of North Carolina, 1900-1930: The Making of a Modern University. By Louis R. Wilson. (Chapel Hill: University of North Carolina Press, 1957. xxii + 633 pp. Illustrations, notes, appendixes, and index. $7.50.)

North Carolina's leadership and pioneering efforts for better educational facilities in the South have long been recognized, and these two books treat important phases of that story. They are virtually in chronological sequence since the greater part of McIver's activities occurred before 1900. Although the methods, materials used, and writing styles of the two authors differ noticeably, their general themes are the same, the development of higher education in North Carolina; and in both some of the same personalities and problems appear.

Charles Duncan McIver, of a staunch, North Carolina Scotch Presbyterian family, was graduated from the University of North Carolina in 1881. While there, he, along with his fellow students, Edwin A. Alderman, James Y. Joyner, and Charles B. Aycock, acquired an early concern for the educational plight of the state. As a teacher in the public schools and at Peace Institute in Raleigh, McIver began to exercise his talents as a public speaker and lobbyist to obtain better schools and teacher training. His efforts contributed to an accelerated program for the establishment of normal schools and institutes in North Carolina and to the establishment in 1892 of a state-supported institution of higher learning for women, now known as the Woman's College of the University of North Carolina. McIver had often said, "Educate a man and you educate an individual; educate a woman and you educate a family." Thus it was altogether fitting that he should devote the remaining fourteen years of his life to the presidency of the Woman's College. He also continued an active interest in the education crusade as one of three district directors for the Southern Education Board.

Mrs. Holder has presented a well-balanced, chronological account of this energetic, determined, and affable man who was loved by practically all and deeply devoted to the cause of blazing new paths in education. Not particularly appealing to this reviewer is the free-wheeling, journalistic style of writing which too often strains for cleverness at the expense of clarity. The book is not well documented. The few notes indicate that most of the information came from McIver's personal papers, and apparently the author did not consult the vast amount of pertinent manuscript material in the Southern Historical Collection at the University of North Carolina.

Professor Wilson's history of the University of North Carolina is an exhaustive account of the thirty-year period which saw the emergence of the institution from a good, small college with about five hundred students to a fully developed university. Following an introductory chapter, the book is divided into three parts in which are traced the development and problems of the University during the administrations of three different presidents. Francis P. Venable (1900-1914) assembled a highly qualified faculty, initiated a steady building program, provided an orderly administration, and emphasized good scholarship. Under Edward K. Graham (1914-1919) the institution continued to grow along sound lines, but his principal contribution was in personifying and firmly establishing the intangible spirit of democracy, idealism, and respect for learning that has continued to pervade Chapel Hill. North Carolina experienced its most rapid growth in enrollment, financial support, and broadening activities during the presidency of Harry W. Chase (1919-1930), who ably steered a course that brought the University to a position of leadership in the South and recognition as one of the best universities in the nation.

The author's thorough treatment probably will most interest those who have had some connection with the University. Here they will encounter many familiar names and discover the origins of such distinctive traditions and institutions as the Kenan professorships, the Institute for Research in Social Science, a strong student government, a large and efficiently run library, and complete freedom of thought and expression. The book sheds considerable light on the entire history of the institution because of its frequent references to the periods before 1900 and after 1930. Based on a thorough use of manuscript and published materials, it is further enhanced by the firsthand knowledge and insights of the author himself who, as librarian, first director of the press, and founder of extension services, played a prominent role in the University's growth. The general reader would perhaps better appreciate the University of North Carolina's history and significance through a more compact, interpretative, and less repetitious work. Wilson's detailed treatment, however, is supplemental to, and complemented by, two other recently published histories: *The Campus of the First State University*, by Archibald Henderson, and *Impressions of Men and Move-*

ments at the University of North Carolina, by Henry M. Wagstaff. Perhaps from these and earlier works there will some day appear a single-volume account of the development of the nation's first state university.

University of Houston ALLEN J. GOING

The Woman Suffrage Movement in Tennessee. By A. Elizabeth Taylor. (New York: Bookman Associates, 1957. 150 pp. Notes, bibliography, and index. $3.50.)

Studies of reform movements at the state level, such as Dr. Taylor's volume on the efforts of Tennessee women and their male associates to get the vote for women, are worthy topics of research for Ph.D. candidates. With commendable brevity, agreeable lucidity, and neat (as well as sound) arrangement of her material, Dr. Taylor has presented the story of the organizations which worked toward woman suffrage in Tennessee. Dutifully she treats of the quarrels among the suffragettes, of their efforts to prod the state legislature into making concessions, and of the final satisfaction of seeing Tennessee the thirty-sixth state to ratify the Nineteenth Amendment, which made it certain that women throughout the nation would have an opportunity to help elect Warren G. Harding. In a particularly entertaining chapter she presents, often quoting at length, some of the anti-suffragists' arguments which now seem both specious and amusing. Dr. Taylor has done well what she set out to do, and her study will be referred to for years to come.

But one wonders whether there aren't contributions which such a state study could and should make which are not found in this book. The relationship with the national crusade is always shadowy. Even though the book focuses on the state arena, this reader felt that examination of materials in the records of the National American Woman Suffrage Association would have helped to place the Tennessee effort in the framework of the larger movement. Students of the national effort have introduced us to the type of woman who devoted her energies to leadership at that level. Dr. Taylor tells us the names of the women who occupied offices in local or state organizations, but these women who were the very soul of the movement never come alive. They emerge as mere names who, with other names, hold meetings, pass resolutions, lobby, bicker, and finally produce ratification. What little biographical information the author offers about these women is shunted into the footnotes, which unfortunately are relegated to the back of the book. But the reader wants to know so much more about the participant that it is regrettable that a study like this does not appease his curiosity. What were the backgrounds of women like Mrs. James M. McCormack of Memphis, Mrs. L. Crozier French of Knoxville, Mrs. Guilford Dudley of Nashville? Why were they active in this movement? In what other activities did they engage? What was their standing in their communities? These and similar questions may not be easy to answer, but we must have the answers before the story of the movement as a whole can come alive for the reader.

Relying especially on newspapers, publications of the organizations, and manuscript materials available in Tennessee, Dr. Taylor has written a careful account of the activities of woman suffrage organizations in that state. It is to be hoped that some day she will write about the women who animated those organizations.

University of Tennessee LEROY P. GRAF

A History of American Magazines. Volume IV, *1885-1905.* By Frank Luther Mott. (Cambridge: The Belknap Press of Harvard University Press, 1957. xxii + 858 pp. Illustrations, notes, and index. $12.50.)

In 1939 Volumes II and III of this history won the Pulitzer Prize. Already it had become recognized as "the standard work" and its scholarly, urbane, and often delightful pages a treasured possession of historians whose interests involved the use of American periodicals. Thus to describe the latest volume as up to the caliber of the earlier ones, and following the same arrangement of contents, should be a sufficient critical judgment and description for the initiated.

There are, however, two reasons for venturing further. First, the twenty-year period covered in this volume comprises the Golden Age of American magazines. It was a time of great editors: Richard Watson Gilder, Walter Hines Page, Edward W. Bok, Henry M. Alden, S. S. McClure, Albert Shaw, John Brisben Walker, and B. O. Flower; of distinguished magazines: *Forum, Arena, Review of Reviews, World's Work,* and a good many others; of vastly expanded circulation; of the rise of national advertising; and of a greatly increased emphasis on current affairs. The importance of the magazine in the life of the nation in this period gives this volume a special relevance.

A more important reason exists for not ceasing with an endorsement of the value and excellence of Mr. Mott's work, conceded on all sides. It deserves all the adjectives of encomium that have been heaped upon it, save one — "definitive." Apart from the manifest absurdity involved in applying this word to any work on such a subject, this ill-considered plaudit does Mr. Mott a great injustice. The greatest value of these four fine volumes lies precisely in the opposite direction. They open almost unlimited vistas for future scholarship — more, they *incite* further investigation. It is impossible for anyone with the bent of a historian to immerse himself in these provocative pages without coming away with a nagging desire to plunge into dozens of avenues of investigation of which the author has given him a fascinating but tantalizingly incomplete glimpse.

Reading Mott is like going on an exploring party covering a vast area filled with a multitude of phenomena, each of which demands long years of study, with an enormously competent and articulate guide whose enthusiasm and sensitivity to all of it is highly contagious. Editors, publishers, and writers that live in these pages beckon biographers. The careers of magazines, sketched brilliantly in the second half of each volume, invite full-length portrayal. Trends in publishing (illustration, advertising, marketing) and types of periodicals (local, trade, religious, professional) dealt with in the first half of each volume suggest fruitful areas of further research. Finally, the content analysis of the magazines that Mr. Mott provides, forming as it does a continuous series of fleeting glimpses of the American mind, like a landscape viewed from a window of a speeding train, must exercise an irresistible fascination for the historians of our social, cultural, and intellectual past and force them to learn more.

This, in many ways, is a far greater achievement in the cause of historical scholarship than the production of "the definitive work."

Tulane University W. BURLIE BROWN

Wilson's Foreign Policy in Perspective. Edited by Edward H. Buehrig. (Bloomington: Indiana University Press, 1957. 176 pp. $4.50.)

Wilson the Diplomatist: A Look at His Major Foreign Policies. By Arthur S. Link. *The Albert Shaw Lectures on Diplomatic History*, 1956. (Baltimore: The Johns Hopkins Press, 1957. xiv + 165 pp. Notes and index. $4.00.)

Wilson's Foreign Policy in Perspective contains lectures given at Indiana University for the Woodrow Wilson centennial. Charles Seymour, Edward H. Buehrig, Harold M. Vinacke, Samuel Flagg Bemis, and Sir Llewellyn Woodward were the five speakers, and their topics were respectively the role of Colonel House, the concept of collective security, Wilson's Far Eastern policy, his Latin American policy, and his later reputation in England. All five essays have the virtues of the lecture form: they are thoughtful, suggestive, and untrammeled. Professor Bemis', comparing Wilson's Latin American and European policies, is especially provocative. If the centennial had not produced so many good lectures and essays, these five might become permanent references. As it is, the volume is almost certainly doomed to obscurity on shelves already creaking with commemorative literature.

Arthur S. Link's *Wilson the Diplomatist* is ephemeral in a different sense. Containing the Albert Shaw lectures for 1956, it is certain eventually to be superseded by successive volumes of Link's magisterial biography of Wilson. It does, however, have a value quite apart from its temporary utility as a forecast of the chef-d'oeuvre. When compared with the first volume of the biography, published in 1947, with Link's contribution to the New American Nation Series (*Woodrow Wilson and the Progressive Era*), printed in 1954, and with the second volume of the biography, which appeared in 1956, it indicates the progress of Link's thought about Wilson.

Wilson: The Road to the White House was coldly and detachedly critical. In the New American Nation volume, which extended to the presidential years, there began to appear a more favorable appraisal of Wilson. One obtained more sense, at any rate, of the forces that limited the President's initiative and of the complexity of his problems. The man who emerged had greater moral vigor and more capacity for leadership. In the second volume of the biography, *Wilson: The New Freedom*, these traits came more sharply into view. Although Link was still ruthlessly critical whenever the President's ideals and acts were at variance, the total image seemed somehow deeper, more sympathetic, more understanding — more a Rembrandt than a Goya.

In *Wilson the Diplomatist* this development continues. The essays deal with Wilson's neutrality diplomacy, his decision for war, the development of his peace program, and the struggles at Versailles and after. In them Link is less critical of the President's neutrality and peace policies than he appeared to be in the New American Nation volume, and Wilson seems more a prisoner of circumstances, himself nobler in thought and more realistic in diplomacy. The earlier book had no real explanation of the President's decision to opt for war instead of armed neutrality. In *Wilson the Diplomatist*, on the other hand, an eloquent chapter demonstrates that no other choice was possible if the President were to strive for the ideal peace that he envisioned. Dealing with the war and the treaty, which were not touched in the earlier book, Link seems equally sympathetic. He is not quite prepared to praise the Versailles treaty as R. G. McCallum did in *Public Opinion and the Last Peace*, but he writes: "for Woodrow Wilson the Paris Peace Conference was more a time of heroic striving and impressive achievement than of failure." Though granting that Wilson underestimated home opposition, Link finds it understandable that the President should have erred and that he should have fought as he did. The one reticence in *Wilson the Diplomatist* has to do with Wilson's refusal to compromise when the treaty battle was all but lost. Although Link suggests explicit alternatives, he is still hesitant to pass judgment.

Taken as part of the corpus of Link's writings, *Wilson the Diplomatist* may have an unintended permanence. It shows a mind working on the themes and materials that absorb it; it is printed evidence of thought in progress. It draws, of course, upon almost incredibly comprehensive research. The indications of Link's increasing sympathy for his subject are not evidences of declining rigor in critical scholarship or of any slackening in his determination to be detached, objective, and judicious. They are rather signs of the real truth in the vinegared adage, *tout comprendre c'est tout pardonner.*

Harvard University ERNEST R. MAY

The Unpublished Opinions of Mr. Justice Brandeis: The Supreme Court at Work. By Alexander M. Bickel. (Cambridge: The Belknap Press of Harvard University Press, 1957. xxvi + 278 pp. Illustrations, notes, appendix, table of cases, and index. $6.00.)

The great justices in the history of the United States Supreme Court have more often been those who evidenced not just loyalty to the Court and its traditions, but who came to that body with a felt mission of making it an instrument in molding and shaping American institutions and who saw their goals at least partially realized. Brandeis was one. His mission was both to set an example in employing an enlightened and realistic approach in the analysis of social and economic conditions and to educate subtly those of his judicial brethren to whom example alone was not sufficient. This collection of eleven unissued opinions, although, disappointingly, not including civil liberties materials, does illustrate nicely Brandeis playing his chosen dual role as regards judicial self-restraint, the maintenance of an intelligent federal balance, and the combating of "the curse of bigness."

The opinions, all fully completed, went unannounced for a variety of curious reasons. In fact, much of the interest of the book lies here. In at least four instances, by being circulated far in advance they were instrumental in producing the ruling Brandeis sought but feared strongly would not result. These situations involved such important subjects as the liability of labor under the Sherman Act and the permissibility of state taxation under the commerce clause. In another instance the scope of a decision was materially altered, and in yet another Justice Pitney was made to see the justification for state workmen's compensation laws even though he was initially instinctively opposed to such legislation. Furthermore, the opinions, plus their contextual setting, make more plausible Brandeis' strong belief in observing every jurisdictional and procedural limitation on the Court's authority in order to avoid "great" constitutional decisions, and they illustrate his fear of giantism and his feeling that it was a controllable phenomenon.

The volume, *in toto*, however, also serves a most useful function in revealing Brandeis' creative processes at work, and the Court's backstage procedures become more clear, as do the personal relationships between justices. Brandeis' association with Taft, who had fought so vigorously his appointment to the bench, shows well the process of education at work. Taft could be reached, although as by a "drawbridge over a wide gulf," and Brandeis, well aware of the climate of opinion of his day, was willing in two instances at least to let Taft have credit for a view which he had put forward, since "they will take it from Taft but wouldn't take it from me." Others of his philosophically diametric colleagues could also be swayed, although the process was seldom completely rewarding, since lessons learned for the occasion were too often lessons forgotten by the time the next one arrived. The case introduced to illustrate his relationship with his supposed soulmate, Holmes, on the other hand, brings out strongly the divergencies between the two, both in psyche and in legal approach.

Professor Bickel has given us an interesting fragment of Brandeisiana, although, as Professor Paul A. Freund points out in his introduction, "a more rounded picture of the Court during this period requires a study of materials more extensive than these." Further, Professor Bickel's introductions and comments, although essential for correlative purposes, occasionally tend to compound the already technical legal confusion. It could be wished that he might have emulated that quality he admires in Brandeis of penetrating "an intricate business situation with the expertness of one directly engaged in it, and [laying] bare, for the densest layman to see, the exact spot at which the shoe pinched."

University of Minnesota PAUL L. MURPHY

Farm Crisis, 1919-1923. By James H. Shideler. (Berkeley: University of California Press, 1957. x + 345 pp. Bibliography, notes, and index. $5.00.)

Professor Shideler in *Farm Crisis, 1919-1923,* deals with a significant turning point in American agricultural history. The period was one of almost unparalleled frustration for American farmers; one in which the traditional, individualistic pattern of farm production and marketing was upset by economic forces over which the farmers themselves had little control. They turned first, individually, to self-help solutions. They stressed efficiency of operation, diversification, and drastically reduced standards of living. Next, they turned to collective efforts with results that were almost as futile. Agricultural co-operatives gained important advantages for certain specialty crops, but progress fell far short of goals. The farmers then turned to politics, and in Congress the nonpartisan "farm bloc" organized to bolster their cause. When the "return to normalcy" policies of the Harding administration failed to provide a satisfactory solution to the farm crisis, the farm interests "led a movement away from laissez faire to government participation in business affairs, one of the great economic changes of the twentieth century."

Farm legislation of the crisis years suggests a basic respect for agricultural fundamentalism, a belief that agriculture was a basic industry and that damaged purchasing power here would impair prosperity in business and industry. But the new laws did little to alleviate the farm crisis. For example, when the Federal Intermediate Credit Act was finally passed in 1923 it was no longer possible to save orderly marketing. In many cases the legislation pushed through Congress by the farm bloc was "too little — too late." The farmers had a sympathetic spokesman in Secretary of Agriculture Henry C. Wallace, and through him they had access to the President, but Harding was under control of eastern conservatives. During 1923 the prestige of Wallace's position declined and Coolidge, on his succession to the presidency, was inclined to rely on Secretary of Commerce Hoover for economic advice.

Despite efforts made in Washington, agricultural distress was not relieved. Various political solutions, including voluntary action, government aid, and the Peek-Johnson plan for a subsidized disposal of surpluses, were suggested. The two-price system was later accepted in part and the ideas of Peek and Johnson, frequently identified as the McNary-Haugen bill from its birth in the hectic early twenties, have never really died. While the farm crisis occupies the stage in this book, the author is cognizant that these problems did not operate in a vacuum. We are reminded that farm problems had to "compete for attention with sharp issues" of the period.

Of special value for this study were the files of the Secretary of Agriculture, 1919-1925, and the records and files of other government agencies. Pertinent material was gleaned from the manuscript collections of Wilson, Coolidge, and Hoover, and of Henry C. Taylor, Chester C. Davis, William M. Jardine, Frank O. Lowden, Arthur M. Hyde, Peter Norbeck, Arthur Capper, and the national office of the American Farm Bureau Federation. Many of the principals of this period were contributors through interviews or correspondence.

For the lay reader, this book should provide a useful understanding of the unique position of agriculture in the economy. The serious student will find that it keeps close to sources and is profusely footnoted, although in a difficult form for ready use.

Kansas State College, Manhattan HOMER E. SOCOLOFSKY

Foreign Relations of the United States: Diplomatic Papers, 1942: China. (Washington: United States Government Printing Office, 1956. vi + 782 pp. Notes and index. $3.75.)

Although several volumes for the years 1939, 1940, and 1941 remain to be published, the State Department is pushing ahead with a program, adopted at the urging of the Senate Committee on Appropriations, of compiling two special categories within its highly respected *Foreign Relations* series. One, dealing with the wartime meetings of the heads of governments between 1941 and 1945, will consist of about seven volumes; and the initial offering, the much publicized *Conferences at Malta and Yalta, 1945*, has already been reviewed in this journal (XLIII, 517). The second, relating to China in the years from 1942 to 1949, will require perhaps fifteen volumes; and the present collection of papers, issued on December 1, 1956, is the first to appear.

As is customary, the documents are arranged chronologically under various topical divisions. Those of greatest interest cover Sino-American relations generally and the problem of assisting the Chinese war effort (pp. 1-190), the political conditions within China and the threatened Kuomintang-Communist conflict (pp. 191-267), and the negotiations for the relinquishment by the United States of its extraterritorial rights (pp. 268-418). There is also abundant material on the $500,000,000 credit granted on March 21, 1942, on the Lend-Lease Agreement of June 2, 1942, and on the delivery of vital supplies by circuitous routes (pp. 419-623).

Both scholars and those seeking political scapegoats will undoubtedly concentrate on the reports emanating from the embassy in Chungking and on the memoranda of the Far Eastern experts in Washington. Neither set of documents substantiates, at least so far as 1942 is concerned, the facile generalization that China was lost to the free world because the United States refused to support Chiang Kai-shek wholeheartedly and favored instead his Communist rivals. To be sure, the estimates of Ambassador Clarence R. Gauss, Counselor John Carter Vincent, Second Secretary John Paton Davies, and Third Secretary John Stewart Service frequently deplored the confusion and corruption within the Kuomintang regime; and many of these papers, read today, will irritate the officials on Formosa. But it cannot be said that those men manifested an implacable hostility toward the Generalissimo, and they freely conceded that, with all his faults, he alone could weld China into an effective fighting force. There was no question in 1942 of supplanting him or compelling him to form a coalition with the Communists. If anything, the State Department was too reluctant to bring pressure on his government. Certainly Chiang had staunch friends in Stanley K. Hornbeck, Adviser on Political Relations, and Maxwell M. Hamilton, Chief of the Division of Far Eastern Affairs. The views of President Roosevelt, Secretary Hull, and Under Secretary Welles show less clearly in these pages, for China was not foremost in their minds at this critical stage of the war.

As with the Yalta volume, the editors in the Historical Division have been obliged to go beyond the State Department's files to tell their story. Several papers from the Franklin D. Roosevelt Library have been printed, but only in cases where the documents, or copies thereof, should have come to rest in the archives in the first place. Since the purpose of the *Foreign Relations* series is to present a substantially complete documentary record and not an exhaustive historical account, it has been decided to include outside materials only where the State Department was directly concerned with an issue and where its files are now inadequate. This principle is a reasonable compromise between the unwisdom of printing nothing but papers retained by the Department and the impracticability of searching for every manuscript, whether in private collections or in other governmental agencies, that bears upon the matter at hand. Unlike the Yalta volume, this one lacks the elaborate introduction, the statement of editorial practices, the list of documents, and the illustrations, maps, and bibliographical data. This difference is justified by the fact that the installment on Yalta was printed out of chronological sequence, while the present offering follows closely upon the release of two of the three volumes for 1940 and 1941 devoted to the Far East.

Northwestern University RICHARD W. LEOPOLD

The Modern Researcher. By Jacques Barzun and Henry F. Graff. (New York: Harcourt, Brace, and Company, 1957. xiv + 386 pp. Figures, notes, bibliography, and index. $6.00.)

Begin a book review with a baited opening sentence. Such is the advice of the authors of this manual for writers of all kinds of reports. Report writing, which has become fundamental in the conduct of affairs today, must follow the standards and methods developed by historians. Any reporter should know how to do research, how to verify facts, how to distinguish between facts and ideas, and how to write.

It needs scarcely be said that any book with which Jacques Barzun has had something to do will lay out familiar materials in a fresh way, will sparkle, and will please. Young historians should read and re-read those parts of this book of which they are most in need. Older historians who have passed through the ABC stage will profit most from the final part, on writing. All of us use jargon and clichés; a list of fifty forbidden words which includes "basic," "essential," "major," "background," and "factors" ought to help us end lazy writing habits. Every teacher knows that it often takes hours to show a student how to rewrite a single paragraph. Both are served by the advice in Chapters 11, 12, and 13 on "Organizing," "Plain Words," and "Clear Sentences," as well put and as sound as can be found in a modern book.

The investigator who writes a report for his office on new chemical industries in an area will wonder just how much of this book is for him. Chapters on causation, on the philosophy of history, on the difference between historians in Europe and America, and on the social sciences will seem to him remote from his needs. Why so much space given in a book of this kind, he might ask, to a defense of history against those who doubt its value? Others than the business report writer may doubt whether a book that addresses itself to him, to the graduate student in any subject which involves the use of prose, to the mature scholar, and to any free-lance writer who does research, has not sought too wide an audience to produce the desired effect upon each of its parts. Badly in need of reform as business reports are, writers of them will not be aided by advice which suggests that no difference exists between them, biography, and multi-volumed history. Does every report writer address "the whole educated community"?

With two of the authors' assumptions historians trained in an older school might disagree. The "notion of an absolute past," of events that actually occurred as seen by a "divine mind," does not appear harmful to them, who conceive it their task to approach as closely as they can that impossible goal. Older historians also believe, as the authors nowhere expressly state, that the great scholars do not chase down facts on some single subject alone, looking straight ahead, refusing to be diverted by alluring byways. They follow any lead that seems interesting and possibly fruitful. They steep themselves in source-materials, the papers and books they write are deliberately made part of a whole, and their final "report" has taken a lifetime to prepare.

The Newberry Library STANLEY PARGELLIS

Book Notes

American Fiction, 1851-1875: A Contribution toward a Bibliography. By Lyle H. Wright. (San Marino: The Huntington Library, 1957. xx + 413 pp. Illustration and title index. $7.50.) In 1948 the author, head of the Huntington Library's reference department, published *American Fiction, 1774-1850.* The present volume, covering the next quarter century, is a bibliography of "fiction written for adults by Americans and published in the United States between 1851 and 1875." Among other events or topics reflected in the fiction of the period are slavery, the Civil War, the westward movement, and reform interests of the time. Almost 3,000 titles are recorded in serially numbered entries arranged according to author, and supplemented by a title index. The author has intended the work as "a guide to the books of American fiction rather than as a complete bibliographical description of them." Notes are employed where needed for additional bibliographical information, or to show the content or special nature of a work. Though not regularly given, the notes which show this special nature — for example, "Anti-Catholic," or "A temperance tale," or "Ridicules Lincoln's Civil War policies" — will be of particular value to historians.

Diary of America: The Intimate Story of Our Nation, Told by 100 Diarists. Edited by Josef and Dorothy Berger. (New York: Simon and Schuster, 1957.

xviii + 621 pp. Sources and acknowledgments. $6.95.) This "intimate story" of the nation is, more plainly, a sampler of American diaries kept by "public figures and plain citizens, natives and visitors," from Columbus to Will Rogers. It is designed to resurrect for a wide public numerous eyewitness accounts which have been "gathering the sad dust of infinite disuse," and to make the country's past come "astonishingly alive."

The Witness of William Penn. Edited by Frederick B. Tolles and E. Gordon Alderfer. (New York: The Macmillan Company, 1957. xxx + 205 pp. Notes and bibliographical note. $3.75.) The image of William Penn which emerges from this selection of his writings is more complex than the simple, portly figure standing "under the great elm at Shackamaxon, eternally dispensing peace and yard goods to the Indians." The general reader, for whom this book is designed, becomes acquainted with Penn, "The Apostolic Christian," and Penn, "The Christian Statesman." The editors present selections from a dozen or so of Penn's works — "he published over a hundred separate works during his lifetime, from broadsides to full-length books" — ranging from *No Cross, No Crown* (written in its original form in the Tower of London where Penn was imprisoned in 1668 and 1669) to *Some Fruits of Solitude* (1693) and *Fruits of a Father's Love* (1702). Of special interest are Penn's plan of union for the American colonies (1696) and his *Essay towards the Present and Future Peace of Europe* (1693). The publisher has found this volume worthy of a number of "firsts," such as "the first broadly representative selection of William Penn's writings since 1825." The "firsts," however, are not all of the same quality — witness "the first edition annotated to explain occasional obscure words and to elucidate historical references." The editorial work itself is more sophisticated, and does "place Penn's writings in the context of his career and of the intellectual life of his time."

Cradle of Culture: The Philadelphia Stage, 1800-1810. By Reese Davis James. (Philadelphia: University of Pennsylvania Press, 1957. 156 pp. Illustrations, appendixes, and index. $5.00.) This book centers about Philadelphia's Chestnut Street Theatre from its opening in December, 1799, to 1810 — a period during which the American theater was gaining respectability as a cultural medium. The author writes of the actors and actresses (many of whom were distinguished English thespians), the plays, the theatrical music of the period, advances in scenery design, and the operations of the theater managers. The growth of the Philadelphia theater is linked with the cultural development of the city and nation. Among other persons responsible for this cultural expansion had been George Washington, whose interest in things theatrical is credited with furthering interest on the part of others.

Samuel McIntire: A Bicentennial Symposium, 1757-1957. Edited by Benjamin W. Labaree. (Salem, Massachusetts: The Essex Institute, 1957. viii + 118 pp. Illustrations, drawings, notes, and bibliography. $4.00.) This commemorative volume originated with the Essex Institute's celebration in 1957 of the bicentennial of Samuel McIntire's birth. McIntire, "one of America's first distinguished architects," was also well known for his decorative carving and wood sculpture. His work was done in Salem, where a number of houses which he designed may still be seen, and where he died in 1811. Contributors to this volume include Abbott Lowell Cummings, on "Samuel McIntire and His Sources"; Dean A. Fales, Jr., on "The Furniture of McIntire"; Nina Fletcher Little, on "Carved Figures by Samuel McIntire and His Contemporaries"; Mabel Munson Swan, on "A Factual Estimate of Samuel McIntire"; and Oliver W. Larkin, on "Samuel McIntire and the Arts of Post-Colonial America." The bibliography was prepared by Benjamin W. Labaree. The numerous illustrations testify to the high quality of McIntire's work.

The President — Office and Powers, 1787-1957: History and Analysis of Practice and Opinion. Fourth revised edition. By Edward S. Corwin. (New York: New York University Press, 1957. xiv + 519 pp. Notes, table of cases, and index. $6.50.) This fourth edition, the author states, is a substantial reworking of the last edition, published in 1948. The central theme remains the same: "the development and contemporary status of presidential power and of the presidential office under the Constitution." This theme is worked out in seven chapters under the titles: Conceptions of the Office; Apparatus of the Presidency; Administrative Chief; Chief Executive; Organ of Foreign Relations; Commander-in-Chief in Wartime; and Legislative Leader and "Institution." Professor Corwin's approach is "partly historical, partly analytical and critical." The text is completed at page 313, and is followed by 180 pages of "Notes," which make good reading in themselves.

Manners and Customs of Several Indian Tribes Located West of the Mississippi. By John D. Hunter. (Minneapolis: Ross and Haines, Inc., 1957. 402 pp. $8.75.) While a young boy the author of this narrative was captured by a band of Kickapoo Indians. After living with the Kickapoos, and later with the Osage and Kansas Indians for approximately fifteen years, he rejoined white society in 1816 and assumed the name John D. Hunter. He published this account of his experiences and observations in 1823. The first part of the book, covering some 130 pages, is autobiographical. One of the principal features of this section is an account of a hunting expedition which took Hunter and his thirty-odd Kansas Indian companions across the Rocky Mountains to the Pacific Coast. In the remaining 260 pages Hunter presents his impression of the religious beliefs, medical practices, warring and hunting techniques, educational practice, and, in general, the manners and customs of the Indian tribes with which he came into contact.

History of the Ojibway Nation. By William W. Warren. (Minneapolis: Ross and Haines, Inc., 1957. 527 pp. Illustrations, notes, and index. $8.75.) William W. Warren, whose father was a Wisconsin fur trader and Indian agent, completed this study shortly before his death in 1853 at the age of twenty-eight. It was first published, with notes and additions, by the Minnesota Historical Society in 1885. The present work, a reprint of the 1885 publication, is one of the volumes in the Mid-America Series of Classic Americana Reprints. Warren's long residence among the Ojibways of Lake Superior and the Upper Mississippi and his intimate knowledge of the Ojibway language and legends strengthen his claim to have written the study "from purely Indian sources." In describing the chronological detail, however, Warren had access to published works; but the important digressions on Ojibway customs and beliefs depend on the author's personal observations and study.

Three Years among the Comanches: The Narrative of Nelson Lee, the Texas Ranger. (Norman: University of Oklahoma Press, 1957. xvi + 179 pp. Illustration. $2.00.) After several years in the United States Navy, Nelson Lee settled in Texas where he was occupied alternately as a horse trader and Texas Ranger. Captured by the Comanches in 1855 while on a horse-trading expedition to California, he finally made his escape three years later, and with the help of an unknown editor wrote this account of his adventures within sixty days of his arrival in New York. It is now reprinted, with an introduction by Walter P. Webb, as Volume IX in the Western Frontier Library series. According to Webb, "There is no better description of the life of the Texas Rangers than that given by Nelson Lee," and "the information he conveys about how the Comanches lived before they were affected by the white man is invaluable."

A Glimpse of Iowa in 1846: or, The Emigrant's Guide, and State Directory, with a Description of the New Purchase. Second edition. By J. B. Newhall. (Iowa City: State Historical Society of Iowa, 1957. xxii + 106 pp.) "This reprint of a little-known rare Iowana volume," according to William J. Petersen's introduction, "is being published by the State Historical Society of Iowa to familiarize Iowans with the work of John B. Newhall — the most influential promoter of Iowa to 1850." The second edition, which was originally published in 1846, was chosen for reprinting because it contains "about one-third more material than the original edition." After a general description of Iowa, including its climate, soil, and resources, Newhall devotes some fifty-five pages to brief descriptions of the important counties and cities. For ten cities he includes a brief city directory. Other sections concern the system of government, prevailing prices, and advice to immigrants.

Storm over Sumter: The Opening Engagement of the Civil War. By Roy Meredith. (New York: Simon and Schuster, 1957. viii + 214 pp. Map, illustrations, bibliography, and index. $3.95.) This is a detailed narrative of the engagement that opened the Civil War, with an account of the background to that fateful episode. The author draws primarily on published contemporary diaries, journals, and letters to present an exposition of the conflict of ideologies and personalities that led to the battle. The volume ends with an essay on the character of Major Robert Anderson, commander of Fort Sumter, which pictures him as a loyal and courageous officer torn between a sense of duty to the Union and love for his native South.

A Civil War Artist at the Front: Edwin Forbes' Life Studies of the Great Army. Edited by William Forrest Dawson. (New York: Oxford University Press, 1957. [xii + 81 pp.]. Illustrations. $6.50.) In 1861 Edwin Forbes was assigned as a staff artist for *Frank Leslie's Illustrated Newspaper* to cover the activities of the Army of the Potomac. The twenty-two-year-old artist followed the Union troops from the occupation of Manassas to the siege of Petersburg, creating pictures primarily of the earthy, day-to-day scenes of military life. The present volume is a collection of these drawings. They are accompanied by a lively commentary prepared by the editor from Forbes's writings, and from memoirs and other contemporary records.

Manton Marble of the New York World. By Sister Mary Cortona Phelan. (Washington: Catholic University of America Press, 1957. viii + 135 pp. Notes, appendixes, essay on sources, and index. $1.50.) Manton Marble was editor and proprietor of the New York *World* from 1862 until 1876, a time when the troubled state of politics, in New York and in the nation, provided spectacular copy for politically minded editors. The present study, a dissertation prepared at the Catholic University of America, surveys Marble's political attitudes, with emphasis on "the issues of conflicting interpretations of the United States constitution, of the legal and political problems of the Civil War and Reconstruction, and of the social and economic forces in post-Civil War America." In addition, considerable biographical material is included, although the author observes that her work "makes no pretense of being a definitive biography, nor of covering all the aspects of Marble's many-sided career."

Baltimore: A Picture History, 1858-1958. Commentary by Francis F. Beirne. (New York: Hastings House, 1957. vi + 153 pp. Illustrations, facsimiles, and maps. $5.00.) Compiled under the auspices of the Maryland Historical Society, this volume presents an attractive, historical panorama of Baltimore — its landmarks, celebrities, beautiful women, a bill of fare for 1858, some oyster canners of 1880, and a Goucher fencing class of 1904. Despite the conglomerate nature of his subject, Mr. Beirne, author of *The Amiable Baltimoreans*, has managed to convey a sense of continuity in a highly readable commentary.

Indian Territory: A Frontier Photographic Record. By W. S. Prettyman. Edited by Robert E. Cunningham. (Norman: University of Oklahoma Press, 1957. xii + 174 pp. Illustrations, map, and index. $5.95.) In the early 1880's William S. Prettyman opened a photographic gallery in Arkansas City, near the southern border of Kansas, and began a remarkable series of photographic expeditions into Indian Territory. He took pictures of nearly all the tribes and important chiefs who had recently been moved into the area. When, in the 1890's, the Indian lands were gradually opened to white settlement, Prettyman photographed the crowds of "boomers" gathering in southern Kansas, the several land rushes, and the establishment of homesteads. As the years passed he recorded by photographs the passing of the cattleman's era, the fusion of the two civilizations, and the mushroom growth of cities and towns. In this book Mr. Cunningham, a photographer and engraver by profession, reproduces over a hundred of Prettyman's best photographs. In addition to supplying pithy captions Mr. Cunningham provides a competent historical introduction and a biographical sketch of Prettyman.

The Jews of Des Moines: The First Century. By Frank Rosenthal. (Des Moines: Jewish Welfare Federation, 1957. xvi + 213 pp. Illustrations, facsimile, notes, and index. $3.75.) "The focus of this story," according to the foreword, "is upon the religious, economic, and social development of the Jew as part of his religious community and also as part of his general community." Except for a period of uneasiness between old and new immigrants, it is a story of steady progress toward greater unity and more effective organization of the Jewish community in religious, educational, and charitable activities. Much of the information on the numerous Jewish charitable organizations comes from the unpublished memoirs of Rabbi Eugene Mannheimer, a leader of Des Moines Jewry from 1905 until his death in 1952. The author concludes that "the Jews of Des Moines speedily developed a natural and full social program among themselves and for each other without curtailing their wider civic interest, or withdrawing from close, personal contact with non-Jewish friends and neighbors" (p. 154).

The National Policy and the Wheat Economy. By Vernon C. Fowke. (Toronto: University of Toronto Press, 1957. x + 312 pp. Notes, bibliography, and index. $5.50.) This volume is the seventh in a series "Social Credit in Alberta," sponsored by the Canadian Social Science Research Council and edited by S. D. Clark. The author, an economist at the University of Saskatchewan, points out to begin with that the term "National Policy," to Canadians, refers specifically to the policy of tariff protection initiated in 1879; as used in this book, however, the term "comprises collectively that group of policies and instruments which were designed to transform the British North American territories of the mid-nineteenth century into a political and economic unit." The study then centers about the origins and development of the national policy, with particular reference to the growth of the wheat economy; grain marketing problems in western Canada in the period from 1900 to 1920; and the course of the open market system for Canadian wheat and the manner in which "The Dominion government became heavily involved in the marketing of wheat with the onset of the depression in the early 1930's and has continued so to the present time." An essential part of the study deals with the relation of railway, land, and immigration policies to the wheat economy.

The Federal Lands: Their Use and Management. By Marion Clawson and Burnell Held. (Baltimore: The Johns Hopkins Press, 1957. xxi + 501 pp. Illustrations, appendixes, notes, and index. $8.50.) Both Mr. Clawson and Mr. Held are associated with Resources of the Future, "a nonprofit corporation for research and education to advance development, conservation, and use of natural resources." Their aim is to describe in complete factual detail the uses of federal lands (except Indian lands, which are not owned by the federal government, and military reservations) and how they are managed. In describing the uses of national parks, national forests, wildlife refuges, grazing districts, and other federal lands, the authors are primarily concerned with the pricing processes, revenues, and expenditures connected with federal lands. Numerous charts, tables, and graphs supplement the text and emphasize their economic viewpoint. The authors do not attempt "to present a critical over-all appraisal of federal land management" although they think "some of the data included should be helpful in such an appraisal." Nevertheless, they suggest that the present system of federal land management is incapable of meeting present-day problems and that it should be overhauled. In the concluding chapter they offer several solutions; one is the establishment of a federal land corporation.

The Supreme Court and State Police Power: A Study in Federalism. By Ruth Locke Roettinger. (Washington: Public Affairs Press, 1957. viii +

252 pp. Sources, index of cases cited, and index. $4.50.) The state police power, a subject of continuing interest in view of Supreme Court decisions of recent years, is the subject of this constitutional study. The author, a member of the department of government at Sweet Briar College, has confined the book primarily to an examination of the Court's decisions since 1930, which she discusses in the light of the state's role in the federal Union and the role of the Court in our constitutional system. She finds some evidence that "the Court has been moving full circle back to Taney's conception of the nature and reach of the police power as that ultimate authority over local polity reserved to the states as a fundamental feature of our federal system." But "the decisions of the Court in the segregation and sedition cases stand out in glaring conflict" with this trend, and may "portend a swing of the judicial pendulum away from Taney's balance under a federal system and toward the consolidation of a national state."

Desegregation and the Law: The Meaning and Effect of the School Segregation Cases. By Albert P. Blaustein and Clarence Clyde Ferguson, Jr. (New Brunswick: Rutgers University Press, 1957. xiv + 333 pp. Notes, table of cases, and index. $5.00.) The authors of this volume, faculty members of the Rutgers University Law School, have undertaken the significant task of presenting, in terms intelligible to the layman, an account of "the most important legal decision of the twentieth century." Focusing on the segregation cases decided by the Supreme Court in 1954, and writing from "the advantages of three years of hindsight," the authors have ranged back to Dred Scott (back, too, to John Marshall) and on beyond 1954 to the "avoidance, evasion and delay" which the Court's ruling has engendered. The role of the Supreme Court in government, the course and customs of constitutional interpretation, and judicial precedents in the field of civil rights are some of the subjects discussed. Considerable emphasis is given to public comment, both northern and southern, about the segregation cases. The authors have evidently aspired to write — on a subject which has occasioned much intemperate comment — in "an atmosphere cleared of personal predilections and prejudgment."

One House for Two: Nebraska's Unicameral Legislature. By Adam Carlyle Breckenridge. (Washington: Public Affairs Press, 1957. xii + 98 pp. Charts, tables, bibliography, appendixes, and index. $2.50.) Alone among the forty-eight states, Nebraska is governed by a unicameral legislature, which was adopted by the voters in 1934. "This book is about Nebraska's experiment in government, how it does its work, and some inquiry into the political environs which produced it and now maintain it." The author, professor of political science at the University of Nebraska, has written a rather brief survey of the subject (some sixty pages of text), which describes and appraises the work of the Nebraska legislature. Appendixes include a printing of the rules of the Nebraska legislature and a list of lobbying organizations.

The Volunteers: Means and Ends in a National Organization. By David L. Sills. (Glencoe, Illinois: The Free Press, 1957. xx + 320 pp. Tables, charts, appendixes, references, and index. $6.00.) As the title may imply, this book is concerned with the nature of voluntary associations in America, although largely in terms of one association, the National Foundation for Infantile Paralysis. It is not a history of the Foundation, but "is concerned chiefly with the local organization of the Foundation and their Volunteer members"—who these members are, and why they became members, and similar questions. The author, of the Bureau of Applied Social Research at Columbia University, states that "although it is essentially an institutional analysis, rather than a critique of voluntary associations generally, it constitutes in the very nature of the case one further attempt to explain the proliferation of voluntary activity in America, and to trace out some of the consequences of this activity for American society."

Balloons to Jets: A Century of Aeronautics in Illinois, 1855-1955. By Howard L. Scamehorn. Illinois State Historical Society, *Occasional Publications*, Number 52. (Chicago: Henry Regnery Company, 1957. xiv + 271 pp. Illustrations and index. $5.00.) Without entering into the "purely scientific or technical side of aeronautics" the author here traces the history of flight in Illinois. Personalities are emphasized. The book centers on Illinoisans who have contributed to the advancement of aviation and on aeronautical enthusiasts who conducted experiments or exhibitions in Illinois. One chapter is devoted to Octave Chanute, an engineer who retired in 1888 to turn his attention to aeronautics, and the relationship of his experiments to those of the Wright brothers. In general, an attempt is made to relate the achievements made in Illinois or made by Illinoisans to the general development of flight. There are additional chapters on the aviation industry, air mail, military aeronautics, commercial air transport, airports, and government regulation of aeronautics—all covering national developments but centering on Illinois. Mr. Scamehorn covers the early experiments with heavier-than-air machines, such as those by Chanute, with greater thoroughness than he does the complex and multiple advances in aviation after 1920.

A History of the United States Air Force, 1907-1957. Edited by Alfred Goldberg. (Princeton: D. Van Nostrand Company, 1957. x + 277 pp. Illustrations, maps, charts, bibliography, and index. $6.75.) The year 1957 marks the fiftieth anniversary of military aviation in the United States and the tenth anniversary of the United States Air Force, and so has inspired this history. Photographers and writers have shared the pages about equally. The nature of the contents is evident from the section headings: From the Balloon to the B-17, 1907-1939; World War II, 1939-1945; The Establishment; The Missions; The Men; The Tools; The Deeds. Emphasis has been placed on the decade after the establishment of the USAF in 1947, particularly appropriate in view of the earlier coverage of the World War II period in the *Army Air Forces in World War II.* A total of eight contributors, in addition to the editor, receive mention on the title page and the table of contents shows authorship by chapter. The individual authors, according to the preface, "were chosen from among the historians in both the Washington and Air University offices of the USAF Historical Division." Other credits in the preface, along with a foreword by the Chief of Staff, USAF, testify further to the official character of the work. A kind of postscript to the preface indicates that this history originally appeared in *Air Force Magazine*, and furthermore that it was the responsibility of the editors of that periodical "to perform the final editing, select the illustrations, write the captions, and shepherd the material through final design and layout." The whole work, in short, seems to be the product of a rather complex command.

Northwest Africa: Seizing the Initiative in the West. By George F. Howe. *United States Army in World War II: The Mediterranean Theater of Operations.* (Washington: Office of the Chief of Military History, 1957. xxiv + 748 pp. Maps, illustrations, notes, note on sources, tables, glossary, code names, basic military map symbols, and index. $7.75.) *Northwest Africa* is the first volume to be published of the proposed six-volume subseries on the Mediterranean theater. It explains the reasons for the decision to invade Northwest Africa, describes the preparation for the attack and the three-pronged attack of November 8, 1942, on Casablanca, Oran, and Algiers, and follows with a detailed account of the final expulsion of the Germans and Italians from Northwest Africa in May, 1943. This volume is noteworthy for its extensive coverage of enemy intelligence, enemy war plans, and enemy problems — resulting in a balanced account of the fighting.

The Education of a Bibliographer: An Autobiographical Essay. By Thomas James Holmes. (Cleveland: Western Reserve University Press, 1957. xii + 54 pp. Bibliography and index. $2.50.) In the first chapter of his brief autobiographical essay Mr. Holmes relates his experiences as an apprentice bookbinder in England, where he was born in 1874, and describes the reading he did as a youth. The rest of the sketch is devoted to his experiences in the United States, to which he migrated in 1902. Mr. Holmes's work as librarian of the William G. Mather Collection, as compiler of bibliographies of Cotton and Increase Mather, and as director of the restoration of the Armed Forces Medical Library, is briefly described. The bibliography of Mr. Holmes's own publications, printed at the end of the book, includes twenty-nine books and articles, primarily on books of the Mathers.

Foreign Policy and the American Spirit: Essays by Dexter Perkins. Edited by Glyndon G. Van Deusen and Richard C. Wade. (Ithaca: Cornell University Press, 1957. xiv + 254 pp. Notes. $3.75.) The dozen essays collected in this volume, half or more of them previously published, are presented in honor of Professor Perkins. Not all are confined to diplomatic history. In point of time they range from an address on "The Constitution and the American Spirit," delivered at Rochester in observance of Constitution Day in 1937, to his 1956 presidential address before the American Historical Association — "We Shall Gladly Teach." The larger part of the volume, however, consists of essays chosen by the editors to illustrate two ideas about diplomatic history which have especially concerned Professor Perkins. The one is, as the editors state it, "the notion that there *is* a uniquely American approach to foreign affairs"; the other, "that 'revisionist' writing on the two world wars of this century, though stimulating, is essentially 'history by hypothesis' and, as such, often misleading and dangerous." The seven essays selected to illustrate these themes are entitled: "What Is Distinctively American about the Foreign Policy of the United States?"; "The American Attitude toward War"; "Open Diplomacy and Its Critics"; "The Department of State and American Public Opinion"; "American Wars and Critical Historians"; "Was Roosevelt Wrong?"; and "The State Department Speaks."

Reporting the Wars. By Joseph J. Mathews. (Minneapolis: University of Minnesota Press, 1957. x + 322 pp. Illustrations, notes, and index. $6.50.) American experience forms only part of this broad history of modern war news, which covers the last two hundred years and principally the period from the Napoleonic Wars to World War II. "During this period the subject matter of the news, the ways of transmitting it, and the audience all changed character." The term "war news" itself is difficult to define although its core is "information about battles and about people who participate in them." As the author points out, the term may now include production statistics and weather reports, and concern civilians as well as people in uniform — so that "war news has tended to merge with news in wartime." The present account, however, "does not wander far from the battlefield." Numerous illustrations, mostly from contemporary newspapers and periodicals, are included. The final chapters deal with censorship and associated news controls, official war news, and the profession and literature of war correspondence.

Historical News and Comments

Affairs of the Association

The fifty-first annual meeting of the Mississippi Valley Historical Association will be held on April 24, 25, and 26 in Minneapolis, with headquarters at the Hotel Nicollet.

The program committee, under the chairmanship of Gilbert C. Fite, of the University of Oklahoma, has arranged for the presentation of forty-six papers distributed among nineteen sessions, in addition to one luncheon and two dinner addresses. Such session themes as Science and the Organization of Learning in American Culture; History of American Higher Education; History of Philanthropy and Social Work; American Legal and Constitutional History; American Foreign Policy; Publishing; Historiography; and Some Aspects of Turner's Thought offer a good variety of general subjects for discussion.

There will also be sessions on such regional or period topics as The West; Current Problems in the South (sponsored by the Southern Historical Association); Railway Development in the Great Northwest (sponsored by the Lexington Group); Mexico — History and Literature; Eighteenth-Century Colonial America; The "Era of Good Feelings"; The Civil War; The Repatriated Immigrant (sponsored by the American Studies Association); and New Deal Agricultural Policy (sponsored by the Agricultural History Society). The Teachers Section of the Association has planned a session on "The Teaching of History in School and College — Co-existence or Cooperation," with George B. Carson, of the American Historical Association's Service Center for Teachers of History, as the speaker; and the American Association for State and Local History has a group of papers on Writing State History.

At the luncheon meeting on Thursday, sponsored jointly by Phi Alpha Theta and the Forest History Foundation, James W. Silver, of the University of Mississippi, will speak on "Writing a Business History: An Excursion into Frustration." The presidential address, "A Quarter Century of American Historiography," will be given by Wendell H. Shephenson, of the University of Oregon, at the annual dinner meeting on Thursday evening; and Senator John F. Kennedy of Massachusetts will speak on "Historians and Politicians" at the dinner meeting on Friday evening.

All meetings will be held in the headquarters hotel.

Personals

Lawrence C. Wroth, librarian of the John Carter Brown Library, Brown University, since 1923, has retired from active service but will continue his association with the Library in an honorary capacity as librarian emeritus. Thomas R. Adams has been appointed to succeed him as librarian.

Richard H. Shryock will retire in June, 1958, as director of the Institute of the History of Medicine at Johns Hopkins University. He has been appointed librarian of the American Philosophical Society and part-time professor at the University of Pennsylvania.

Wallace E. Davies has been promoted to associate professor of history at the University of Pennsylvania; Richard S. Dunn, from the University of Michigan, has been appointed assistant professor; and Jeannette P. Nichols has accepted an interim appointment as associate professor.

At Columbia University, David H. Donald has been promoted to professor of history, and Frederick D. Kershner, formerly at Ohio University (Athens), has been appointed associate professor of history in the Teachers College.

Donald R. McCoy, formerly at New York State Teachers College (Cortland), has been appointed assistant professor of history at the University of Kansas.

James N. Primm of the University of Missouri has been named dean of the faculty and professor of history at Hiram College.

At the University of Chattanooga, James W. Livingood, professor of history, became dean of the College of Arts and Sciences on September 1, 1957, and Jane W. Harbaugh, a doctoral graduate of the Fletcher School of Law and Diplomacy, has been appointed instructor in history.

At Southwest Texas State College, William C. Pool has been promoted to professor of history and Emmie Craddock to associate professor. Elizabeth Seymour, a doctoral candidate at the University of Chicago, has been appointed assistant professor of history, and David Conrad, a doctoral candidate at the University of Oklahoma, and Edward Swinney, doctoral candidate at Pennsylvania State University, have been appointed as instructors.

Jay Luvaas, from Duke University, has been appointed assistant professor of history at Allegheny College, and Russell E. Vance, from Indiana University, has been appointed instructor in history.

Paul A. W. Wallace has resigned from the editorship of *Pennsylvania History*, and John M. Coleman, professor of history at Lafayette College, has been named as his successor.

James L. Sellers, professor of history at the University of Nebraska, has been elected president of the Nebraska State Historical Society.

Richard A. McLemore, formerly professor of history and dean at Mississippi Southern College, has become president of Mississippi College at Clinton, Mississippi.

At Denison University, Morton B. Stratton has been named chairman of the department of history for a three-year term, Robert Seager has been promoted to associate professor, and William P. Preston and David S. Watson promoted to assistant professors.

Alfred D. Low, of Marietta College, has been appointed associate professor of history at Youngstown University.

Samuel R. Spencer, professor of history at Davidson College, has resigned to become president of Mary Baldwin College.

Sidney Ratner has been promoted to professor of history at Rutgers University.

Thomas Starling Staples, professor emeritus of history at Hendrix College, died on July 15, 1957, at the age of seventy-eight. A native of Georgia and a graduate of Emory College, he received the Ph.D. degree at Columbia University in 1923 as one of the last of the distinguished group of southerners who worked under the supervision of William A. Dunning. After a brief service as instructor at Central College, he became professor of history at Hendrix College in 1908 and was made dean of the College in 1928, serving in both capacities until his retirement in 1949. He was the author of *Reconstruction in Arkansas* (1923) and of *Political History of Arkansas, 1865-1908* (1930), and was a member of the executive council of the Southern Historical Association from 1937 to 1940.

Elinor Shafer (Mrs. James A.) Barnes, former assistant editor of *Pennsylvania History*, died in Philadelphia on August 22, 1957. In addition to her editorial services, she had taught in Wisconsin and in Washington, D. C., and had written a number of articles on Philadelphia history.

Colin Brummitt Goodykoontz, professor emeritus of history at the University of Colorado, died on January 6, 1958, at the age of seventy-two. A native of Indiana, he received his collegiate education at the University of Colorado, earned a master's degree from the University of California (1914), and received the Ph.D. degree at Harvard (1921). He was an instructor at Bowdoin College in 1918-1919, and at Yale in 1919-1920; and in 1921 he became an assistant professor of history at the University of Colorado, where he taught until his retirement in 1954.

In addition to his *Home Missions on the American Frontier* (1939), which has become one of the standard studies on frontier religion, he edited the *Papers of Edward P. Costigan Relating to the Progressive Movement in Colorado* (1941), and was co-editor with James F. Willard of *Experiments in Colorado Colonization* (1926) and of *The Trans-Mississippi West* (1930).

A member of the Mississippi Valley Historical Association since 1920, he was a frequent participant in the programs of its annual meetings and served on many of its standing and special committees. He was a member of the executive committee of the Association from 1941 to 1944, chairman of the program committee for the 1950 meeting, and a member of the board of editors of the *Review* from 1950 to 1953. He served as president of the Pacific Coast Branch of the American Historical Association in 1953 and was for several years a member of the editorial board of the *Pacific Historical Review*.

A quiet, precise, and completely controlled person, he will be remembered by his graduate students as a conscientious teacher who was stern and exacting in his requirements, but thoroughly kind and understanding in all academic and personal problems.

Historical Activities

The Library of Congress has received as a gift from Queen Elizabeth II of England a microfilm copy of an album, the original of which is in the Royal Library at Windsor Castle, containing correspondence of John Jay during the period from 1776 to 1794. Many of the fifty-five letters in the volume are relatively unknown to scholars. They include letters written to Jay by George Washington, Thomas Jefferson, John and John Quincy Adams, Benjamin Franklin, Alexander Hamilton, the Marquis de Lafayette, and other statesmen, as well as retained copies of Jay's letters to several of these correspondents.

Donald R. Richberg has given the Library the first installment of his personal papers. The present gift of approximately 2,500 items reflects his career as a lawyer and his service during the Roosevelt administration as general counsel to the National Recovery Administration, executive director of the National Emergency Council, and special assistant to the Attorney General.

A collection of thirty-six volumes of headquarters records kept by General

U. S. Grant on the battlefields of the Civil War has been given to the Library by his grandson, General U. S. Grant III. This collection supplements the sixty-two volumes of similar records received from the same donor two years ago.

The Library has also received a large collection (approximately 5,400 manuscripts) of personal and business correspondence of the Hoe family, which for more than a century and a half has loomed large in the history of printing in America. In addition to depicting the origin and growth of Hoe and Company, the correspondence includes interesting comments by members of the family on political and other events of the nineteenth century. When the papers have been organized they will be available for use in the Manuscript Division.

Other recent manuscript acquisitions by the Library include: a group of personal papers (about 300 items) of Horace H. Lurton, Confederate veteran and associate justice of the United States Supreme Court; a collection of letters (about 150 items) written by Benjamin Perley Poore, newspaper correspondent, editor, and author, to William W. Clapp, editor of the Boston *Journal*, and a related group (about 200 items) of confidential letters written to Clapp by his son-in-law, E. B. Wight, who was a colleague of Poore in the Washington bureau of the *Journal*; a substantial addition (about 4,000 items) to the papers of Willie P. Mangum, senator from North Carolina in the 1830's and 1840's; a collection of the personal papers of Stuart M. Crocker, relating to his secretaryship of the American delegation in the 1924 and 1929 committees of experts which drafted the Dawes Plan and the Young Plan; additions to the Woodrow Wilson papers, including letters, copies of letters, and dispatches sent to the White House during the period immediately preceding the United States entry into World War I and selections from Mrs. Wilson's correspondence (to be consulted only with special permission); a collection of the personal papers, chiefly correspondence, of Florence Jaffray (Mrs. J. Borden) Harriman, relating to her political activities and her service as minister to Norway; transcriptions from stenographic notes of speeches made by Charles Evans Hughes in the presidential campaign of 1916; and an organized collection (approximately 6,000 items) of early records of the National Consumers' League.

The personal papers of William B. Greeley, one of the leaders in the American forestry and conservation movements, and chief of the United States Forest Service from 1920 to 1928, have been placed in the manuscripts collection of the University of Oregon Library. These papers, which include diaries, more than 5,000 letters, pictures, unpublished works, speeches, and other records, will provide a valuable complement to Greeley's official papers in the Department of Agriculture records in the National Archives.

The State Historical Society of Wisconsin has established a new department, the Mass Communications History Center, to collect and preserve the materials which throw light on the development and influence of radio, television, movies, and other means of mass communication, and to promote historical research in that field. Among the initial acquisitions made for this collection are the papers of Hans V. Kaltenborn, radio and television news analyst, and of Louis P. Lochner, Pulitzer Prize winning newsman and commentator. The Center has also received a collection of the early cartoons of Gluyas Williams, selections from the comic strips of Frank King ("Gasoline Alley") and Carl Anderson ("Little Henry"), and some of the scripts and documents of early movie companies organized in the period before World War I by Harry and Roy Aitken, and through which most of the stars of silent pictures came to be known.

Among recent acquisitions of the Manuscripts Division of the University of Virginia Library is a collection (about 3,000 items) of documents to be added to the Cocke Family Papers. Consisting chiefly of correspondence during the middle years of the nineteenth century, the collection includes letters from Henry St. George Tucker, Andrew Stevenson, John Tyler, and John C. Calhoun, as well as from numerous former slaves of the Cocke family writing from Liberia.

Columbia University has recently obtained an unusually valuable collection of papers and letters of John Jay. Numbering over 2,000 items, the collection includes letters to and from more than 250 men during the colonial, revolutionary, and early national periods.

The American Historical Association has received a grant from the Council on Library Resources, Inc., to prepare a Guide to Photographed Historical Materials in the United States and Canada. The Canadian Historical Association is co-operating in the project. The American Historical Association's Committee on Documentary Reproduction will supervise the work, which will be directed by Professor Richard W. Hale, Jr., Boston University. Preparation of the Guide will take about two years, and publication will follow.

Those who wish to make suggestions or obtain further information should write to Dr. Richard W. Hale, Jr., Boston University, Copley Square Campus, 84 Exeter Street, Room 401, Boston 15, Massachusetts.

The Second Supplement to the *Dictionary of American Biography* will be published in May, 1958, by Charles Scribner's Sons. The volume will contain 584 articles sketching the lives of all distinguished Americans whose deaths occurred between 1935 and the end of the year 1940. This Supplement has been edited by Robert Livingston Schuyler, in association with Edward T. James. The American Council of Learned Societies is the sponsor of this volume, as of the original twenty-one volumes of the work.

Announcement has been made of the establishment of a new international quarterly, *Comparative Studies in Society and History*, to be published by Mouton of The Hague, with several American universities as sponsors. The purpose of the journal is to serve as a clearing house for substantive work on problems that are common to any two or more of the numerous branches of study dealing with man's life in society. It will treat any subject that bears on the explanation of stability or change within a social structure, including ways of thought or expression, and it will deal with forms of cultural interchange. It is not the intention of the editors merely to popularize work that is already well known to specialists. They invite contributions from fresh research in which the problems at issue are clearly formulated. They hope to achieve some testing of the ideas of the theoretical social sciences in regard to longer intervals of time and larger social units than is customary. Comparison, if not drawn within an article can be attained by setting together articles on comparable material. The first issue is scheduled to appear in October, 1958.

The editorial board has been drawn from twelve universities in America and from seven in Europe, and is representative of various fields of history and the social sciences. Correspondence regarding contributions should be directed to the Editor, Sylvia L. Thrupp, Box 222, Faculty Exchange, University of Chicago, Chicago 37, Illinois.

The sixth Conference on Early American History, held at Williamsburg, Virginia, on November 22 and 23, 1957, had as its general theme research and writing in local and regional history for the colonial, revolutionary, and early national periods. Clarence L. Ver Steeg of Northwestern University, John R. Alden of Duke University, and Thomas P. Abernethy of the University of Virginia, who are writing the volumes dealing with these periods for the History of the South series, discussed problems they have encountered in their own work; and Esther Forbes, who is currently writing a community study of Salem, Massachusetts, during the era of the witchcraft trials, dealt with similar problems in the writing of New England history.

The Second International Congress of Historians of the United States and Mexico will be held on November 4-6, 1958, at the University of Texas. This Congress will be a part of the celebration of the seventy-fifth year of the University of Texas. Its sponsors in the United States are the University of Texas, the American Historical Association, and the Texas State Historical Association; the Mexican sponsors are the University of Mexico, the Institute of Anthropology and History, and the Academy of Historical Sciences of Monterrey. Distinguished scholars from Argentina, Brazil, Spain, France, Britain, and the British Commonwealth, as well as from the United States and Mexico have been invited to participate.

The program will include sessions on such topics as "Pre-Hispanic Peoples of the United States and Mexico"; "Mexican and American Conceptions of the Frontier"; "Society and Culture in the United States and Mexico — The Texas Ranch and the Mexican Hacienda"; "The Great Frontier Concept, 1500-1950"; and "The Historian's Task from the American and Mexican Viewpoint."

Inquiries concerning the conference should be directed to Archibald R. Lewis, Secretary General, Second International Congress of Historians of the United States and Mexico, University of Texas, Austin 12, Texas.

The 1957 annual meeting of the Society of American Archivists was held in Columbus, Ohio, on October 2-4, and that of the American Association for State and Local History on October 4-6, with the program of the overlapping date arranged as a joint meeting of the two organizations. Among the speakers on the program of the archivists' meeting were William S. Jenkins of the University of North Carolina, who discussed the State Records Microfilm Project which he had directed; W. Kaye Lamb, national librarian and archivist of Canada, who described the progress of the Canadian program for concentrating under one roof the materials necessary for the study of the history of Canada; and Lester J. Cappon, director of the Institute of Early American History and Culture, whose presidential address, "Tardy Scholars among the Archivists," took archivists, particularly in the states, to task for the small amount of publication being done by them.

The joint program on October 4 included a luncheon address by Roy F. Nichols, University of Pennslyvania, entitled "Alice in Wonderland after Eighteen Years"; a dinner address by Thomas D. Clark, University of Kentucky, on "The Present World of History"; and a panel discussion of "Acquisition Policies of Presidential Libraries," with David C. Mearns of the Library of Congress, Herman Kahn of the Franklin D. Roosevelt Library, Howard H. Peckham of the William L. Clements Library (whose paper was read in his absence by S. K. Stevens), and Stephen T. Riley of the Massachusetts Historical Society as the principal participants.

The program of the American Association for State and Local History included a session on "The Historical Society as an Educational Institution," with Richard P. McCormick of Rutgers University, Phyllis H. Winkleman of the Nebraska State Historical Society, and Everett Walters of Ohio State University as the speakers; one on "The Artifact in History," with papers by

William B. Hesseltine of the University of Wisconsin, J. C. Harrington of the National Park Service, and Anthony N. B. Garvan of the University of Pennsylvania; and one on "Significant Developments in Local History," with papers by James M. Smith of the Institute of Early American History and Culture, Francis P. Weisenburger of Ohio State University, and Philip D. Jordan of the University of Minnesota.

The fifth series of the J. P. Young Lectures in American History, sponsored by Memphis State University, was delivered by Rembert W. Patrick of the University of Florida on October 27, 28, and 29, 1957. The general theme was "Social Changes in the New South: Patterns of Southern Society"; and the titles of the individual lectures were: "The Aristocratic-Slave Myth"; "Twilight and New Patterns"; "The Fruit of Ignorance"; and "The Historian and His Sources."

The twenty-third annual meeting of the Southern Historical Association was held in Houston, Texas, November 7-9, 1957. The program included sessions on European and Latin American history as well as those on southern and general American history. The presidential address, by Robert S. Henry of the Association of American Railroads, was entitled "West by South." The Charles W. Ramsdell Award, made by the Association for the best article published in the *Journal of Southern History* during the two preceding calendar years, was given to Robert R. Russel of Western Michigan College for his "What Was the Compromise of 1850?" which appeared in the August, 1956, issue.

Walter B. Posey, of Agnes Scott College and Emory University, was elected president of the Association for 1958; T. Harry Williams, of Louisiana State University, vice-president; and Bennett H. Wall, of the University of Kentucky, re-elected secretary-treasurer. New members of the executive council for the terms ending in 1960 are Rembert W. Patrick of the University of Florida and Alfred B. Sears of the University of Oklahoma. The 1958 meeting of the Association will be held in Nashville, Tennessee, in November.

At the fiftieth annual meeting of the Pacific Coast Branch of the American Historical Association, held in San Francisco, December 27-29, 1957, announcement was made of the award of the Pacific Coast Branch Prize for the best book published by a member during the year to Don E. Fehrenbacher of Stanford University for his *Chicago Giant: A Biography of "Long John" Wentworth* (Madison: American History Research Center, 1957). The Louis Knott Koontz Award for the best article in the *Pacific Historical Review* went to John W. Caughey of the University of California at Los

Angeles for his "Their Majesties the Mob," published in the August, 1957, issue.

Officers elected for 1958 are: John W. Caughey, president; Raymond J. Sontag, University of California, Berkeley, vice-president; John A. Schutz, Whittier College, secretary-treasurer (re-elected); and James G. Allen, University of Colorado, Solomon Katz, University of Washington, and Abraham P. Nasatir, San Diego State College, members of the executive council for three-year terms.

Recent Articles of General Interest

Agricultural History — October, 1957: "Early Agricultural Editors and Their Farm Philosophies," by George F. Lemmer.

American Historical Review — October, 1957: "George Canning, Great Britain, and the United States, 1807-1809," by Bradford Perkins; "The Movement to Abolish Capital Punishment in America, 1787-1861," by David Brion Davis.

American Jewish Archives — October, 1957: "The War between the States: Reminiscences of Edward Rosewater, Army Telegrapher."

American Quarterly — Fall, 1957: "Music and Class Structure in the United States," by Charles Seeger; "Thomas Nast and the American Political Scene," by J. Chal Vinson; "Law and Colonial Society," by George L. Haskins.

Colorado Quarterly — Autumn, 1957: "John Chamberlain and American Liberalism," by Louis Filler.

Filson Club History Quarterly — October, 1957: "Rise of the American People, 1750-1775," by Willard R. Jillson.

Historian — November, 1957: "Is Liberalism Dead?" by Max Savelle; "The Divine Art and Its Uses," by Stanford E. Lehmberg; "Henry Adams: A Sketch and an Analysis," by Thomas N. Bonner.

Journal of Negro History — October, 1957: "National Negro Conventions of the Middle 1840's: Moral Suasion vs. Political Action," by Howard H. Bell; "The Negro in Who's Who in America, 1936-1955," by Richard Bardolph.

Journal of Politics — November, 1957: "Emigration as a Theoretical Doctrine during the American Revolution," by William S. Livingston.

Journal of the Presbyterian Historical Society — September, 1957: "Ashbel Green, 1762-1848 — Preacher, Educator, Editor," by Robert E. Lewis.

December, 1957: "Franklin and the Presbyterians," by Leonard W. Labaree; "The German Reformed Church during the French and Indian War," by Glenn Weaver.

Maryland Historical Magazine — December, 1957: "Brantz Mayer, Man of Letters," by Jerry E. Patterson; "John Surratt and the Lincoln Assassination Plot," by Alfred Isacsson.

Mennonite Quarterly Review — October, 1957: "Joseph Funk, Early Mennonite Printer and Publisher (with a Bibliography)," by Irvin B. Horst.

Mid-America — October, 1957: "Eugene Debs and the Socialist Campaign of 1912," by H. Wayne Morgan.

Nebraska History — December, 1957: "The American Leviathan: A Historical View," by Herbert S. Schell.

New England Quarterly — September, 1957: "Ben Butler in the Civil War," by Robert S. Holzman; "Harriet Beecher Stowe and New Orleans: A Study in Hate," by Joseph P. Roppolo; "Mark Twain and the American Labor Movement," by Paul J. Carter, Jr.

New-York Historical Society Quarterly — October, 1957: "Congressional Junket in Japan: The Taft Party of 1905 Meets the Mikado," by Elsie C. Parsons; "The Third Assassination [McKinley]," by Kenneth R. Walker.

North Carolina Historical Review — October, 1957: "Woodrow Wilson: The Evolution of a Name," by George C. Osborn.

Pacific Historical Review — November, 1957: "Robert Lansing's Proposed Bargain with Japan," by Burton F. Beers.

Southwestern Social Science Quarterly — September, 1957: "Jackson, the Bank War, and Liberalism," by Harold J. Plous.

Virginia Magazine of History and Biography — October, 1957: "England's Tobacco Trade in the Reign of Charles I," by Neville Williams; "Volumes from George Sandys's Library now in America," by Richard Beale Davis.

William and Mary Quarterly — October, 1957: "William Wirt and the Legend of the Old South," by William Robert Taylor; "The House of Lords, Edward Randolph, and the Navigation Act of 1696," by Michael G. Hall; "Louisburg and the Peace of Aix-la-Chapelle, 1748," by Jack M. Sosin.

Recent Articles Concerning the East

Delaware History — September, 1957: "The Delaware College Lotteries, 1818-1845," by Jane N. Garrett; "Merchants, Millers, and Ocean Ships: The Components of an Early American Industrial Town [Wilmington]," by Peter C. Welsh; "The Political History of Delaware during the Civil War: Part III, A Divided House," by Harold Bell Hancock.

Maryland Historical Magazine — December, 1957: "Union Mills, the Shriver Homestead," by Frederic Shriver Klein; "Daniel Defoe and Maryland," by George E. Gifford, Jr.

New England Quarterly — September, 1957: "Governor Berkeley and King Philip's War," by Wilcomb E. Washburn.

New-York Historical Society Quarterly — October, 1957: "Alexander Hamilton's First Court Case: Elizabeth Rutgers *v.* Joshua Waddington," by Louis Ottenberg; "Custom House Patronage under Lincoln," by William Hartman; "The Recollections of John Ferguson Weir (1841-1926)," Part III, ed. by Theodore Sizer.

Pennsylvania History — October, 1957: "Penn's Charter of Property of 1701," ed. by Edwin B. Bronner; "The Schwenkfelders of Pennsylvania," by Selina G. Schultz; "Thomas Brothers, Anti-Capitalist Employer," by Edward Pessen; "The Baltimore Riots, April, 1861," by Edward G. Everett.

Pennsylvania Magazine of History and Biography — October, 1957: "The New Penn Portraits," by R. N. Williams II; "Benjamin Franklin and the Pennsylvania Chronicle," by John J. Zimmerman; "Christopher Ludwick, the Patriotic Gingerbread Baker," by William Ward Condit; "The Gilpins and Their Endless Papermaking Machine," by Harold B. Hancock and Norman B. Wilkinson; "Leigh Hunt and His Pennsylvania Editor," by David Kaser.

Western Pennsylvania Historical Magazine — Fall, 1957: "Down the Rivers: A Rafting Journal of 1859 — from Warren, Pa., to Louisville, Ky.," ed. by Ernest C. Miller; "Frank H. Shiras Letters, 1862-1865," ed. by Wallace F. Workmaster; "Washington (Pa.) Newspaper Battles, 1817-1825," by George H. Roadman; "Galusha Grow — Pennsylvania's Champion of the Homestead Act," by Robert D. Ilisevich.

William and Mary Quarterly — October, 1957: "Benjamin Franklin and the Pennsylvania Germans," by Glenn Weaver; "Suffrage and Representation in Massachusetts: A Statistical Note," by J. R. Pole.

RECENT ARTICLES CONCERNING THE SOUTH

Agricultural History — October, 1957: "Noah B. Cloud and the *American Cotton Planter*," by Weymouth T. Jordan.

American-German Review — October-November, 1957: "A Century of German Song in Texas," by Martha and Earl W. Fornell.

American Jewish Archives — October, 1957: "Kronikals of the Times: Memphis, 1862," by A. E. Frankland, ed. by Maxwell Whiteman.

Filson Club History Quarterly — October, 1957: "Colonel John Floyd, of Kentucky: A Story," by Walter Distelhorst; "Kentucky, 1790-1815: As Seen by Bishop Francis Asbury," ed. by Walter B. Posey; "Thomas Duche Mitchell (1791-1865)," by V. F. Payne; "Kentucky Looks at Old New Orleans," by R. W. Buskirk.

Florida Historical Quarterly — October, 1957: "Blockade Runners," by Alice Strickland; "The Civil War Letters of Augustus Henry Mathers, Assistant Surgeon, Fourth Florida Regiment, C.S.A.," ed. by Franklin A. Doty; "Civil War Operations in and around Pensacola," by Edwin C. Bearss.

Georgia Historical Quarterly — December, 1957: "The Toombs Legend," by William Y. Thompson; "The Myth of Dade County's Seceding from Georgia in 1860," by E. Merton Coulter; "Duche, the Potter," by E. D. Wells; "The Letter Book of Thomas Rasberry, 1758-1761," Part VI, ed. by Lilla M. Hawes; "Fanny Cohen's Journal of Sherman's Occupation of Savannah," ed. by Spencer B. King, Jr.; "A Georgia Authoress Writes to Her Editor: Mrs. Mary E. Bryan to W. W. Mann (1860)," ed. by James S. Patty.

Historian — November, 1957: "The Spirit of Carlyle in the Old South," by Gerald M. Straka.

Journal of Mississippi History — October, 1957: "The Public Manners of Ante-Bellum Southerners," by Walter B. Posey; "The Revolution of 1800 in Mississippi," by Robert V. Haynes; "Cassius M. Clay and the Mississippi Election of 1875," by David L. Smiley; "The Vicksburg Campaign as Viewed by an Indiana Soldier," ed. by William A. Russ, Jr.

Journal of the Presbyterian Historical Society — September, 1957: "Colonial Presbyterianism in the Valley of Virginia, 1726-1775," Part II, by Robert F. Scott.

Military Affairs — Fall, 1957: "A Prussian Observer with Lee," by Jay Luvaas; "Irregular but Effective: Partizan Weapons Tactics in the American Revolution, Southern Theatre," by Jac Weller.

North Carolina Historical Review — October, 1957: "Cherokee Pre-History," by David H. Corkran; "Counterfeiting in Colonial North Carolina," by Kenneth Scott; "Joseph Seawell Jones of Shocco — Historian and Humbug," by Edwin A. Miles; "Childhood Recollections of My Father [Calvin H. Wiley]," by Mary C. Wiley.

Register of the Kentucky Historical Society — October, 1957: "Louisville and the Confederate Invasion of 1862," by Charles K. Messmer; "A Transcendentalist in Old Kentucky," by Derek Colville.

South Carolina Historical Magazine — October, 1957: "Letters from South Carolina, 1821-1822," ed. by P. J. Staudenraus; "The 'Periclean Age' of Beaufort," by Gilbert P. Voigt; "Letters of Thomas Pinckney, 1775-1780," Part III, ed. by Jack L. Cross.

Southwestern Historical Quarterly — October, 1957: "Barbed Wire in Texas," by Henry D. McCallum; "George H. Giddings and the San Antonio-San Diego Mail Line," by Emmie Giddings W. Mahon and Chester V. Kielman; "Highlights of Early Harrison County," by Sallie M. Lentz; "Cotton Ginning in Texas to 1861," by Raymond E. White; "The 1850 Affair of the Brownville Separatists," by Frank H. Dugan; "Calendar of the Letters of Antonio Martinez, Last Spanish Governor of Texas, 1817-1822," concluded, ed. by Virginia H. Taylor.

Virginia Magazine of History and Biography — October, 1957: "Virginia in 1632," ed. by Robert C. Johnson; "Archer's Hope and the Glebe," by Charles E. Hatch, Jr.

West Virginia History — October, 1957: "Maryland — West Virginia, Western Boundary," by Harold Bruce Fortney; "Harpers Ferry National Monument: A Sketch of Its History and Proposed Development," by Herbert H. Kissling; "The History of the County Unit in West Virginia," by Roy C. Woods.

Recent Articles Concerning the Middle West

Agricultural History — October, 1957: "Dairy Journalism: Studies in Successful Farm Journalism," by John T. Schlebecker; "The Development of the Capper Farm Press," by Homer E. Socolofsky; "Suggested Research on Railroad Aid to the Farmer, with Particular Reference to Iowa and Kansas," by Mildred Throne; "Railroads and Agricultural Development of the Red River Valley of the North, 1870-1890," by Stanley N. Murray; "The Burlington Railroad and Agricultural Policy in the 1920's," by C. Clyde Jones.

Bulletin of the Historical and Philosophical Society of Ohio — October, 1957: "Cincinnati: From Keelboat to Steamboat," by Ophia D. Smith; "The Tafts Went to Texas," by Gene North; "The Earliest Map of Cincinnati (1792)," by Arthur G. Kind; "News from North Bend: Some Early Letters," ed. by Lee Shepard.

Chronicles of Oklahoma — Autumn, 1957: " 'The Wedding of Oklahoma and Miss Indian Territory'," by Muriel H. Wright; "Senator Thomas P. Gore," by Monroe Billington; "Joseph Samuel Murrow, Apostle to the Indians," by Frank A. Balyeat; "Two Notable Women of the Creek Nation," by Carolyn Thomas Foreman; "Leasing of Quapaw Mineral Lands," by A. M. Gibson.

Indiana Magazine of History — December, 1957: "The Rise of Albert J. Beveridge to the United States Senate," by John Braeman; "The Mexican War Journal of Henry S. Lane," contributed by Graham A. Barringer.

Iowa Journal of History — October, 1957: "Proslavery Sentiment in Iowa, 1838-1861," by Joel H. Silbey; "Reminiscences of Jacob C. Switzer of the 22nd Iowa," ed. by Mildred Throne.

Journal of the Illinois State Historical Society — Autumn, 1957: " 'Won, 1880 — One, 1884': The Courtship of William Jennings Bryan and Mary Elizabeth Baird," by Paolo E. Coletta; "Charles E. Hovey, Educator and Soldier," by Helen E. Marshall; "John Henry Rauch and Public Health in Illinois, 1877-1891," by F. Garvin Davenport.

Journal of the Presbyterian Historical Society — September, 1957: "Letters of William Hamilton, 1811-1891 [missionary to Indians]," ed. by Charles A. Anderson.

December, 1957: "Journal of Comfort I. Slack, 1863-64 [missionary in Iowa]," ed. by Charles A. Anderson.

Kansas Historical Quarterly — Autumn, 1957: "The Lecompton Constitutional Convention: An Analysis of Its Membership," by Robert W. Johannsen; "Thomas Benton Murdock and William Allen White," by Rolla A. Clymer; "The Story of Fort Larned," by William E. Unrau; "Notes on Two Kansas Impeachments [Josiah Hayes, 1874, and Theodosius Botkin, 1891]," by Cortez A. M. Ewing; "Traveling Theatre in Kansas: The James A. Lord Chicago Dramatic Company, 1869-1871," Part I, by James C. Malin.

Mid-America — October, 1957: "The Failure of North Dakota Progressivism," by Charles N. Glaab.

Missouri Historical Review — October, 1957: "Boyhood Impressions of the Lexington, Missouri, Area, 1858-1863," by George A. McKee; "Clay County," by Floyd C. Shoemaker.

Nebraska History — December, 1957: "Val Kuska, Agricultural Development Agent," by C. Clyde Jones.

North Dakota Quarterly — Fall, 1957: "North Dakota: A Two-Party State?" by Ross B. Talbot; "America's Elusive Welsh Indians: A Ghost Is Laid to Rest," by Donald M. Gillmor.

Ohio Historical Quarterly — October, 1957: "Ohio's Germans, 1840-1875," by Carl Wittke; "Samuel A. Hudson's Panorama of the Ohio and Mississippi Rivers," by Joseph Earl Arrington; "Cleveland's Johnson: The Cabinet," by Eugene C. Murdock; "Howells' Campaign Biography of Rutherford B. Hayes: A Series of Letters," ed. by Leo P. Coyle.

Wisconsin Magazine of History — Autumn, 1957: "In the Footsteps of Draper," by Bennett H. Wall; "The Election of 1920 in Wisconsin: The Return to 'Normalcy' Reappraised," by Herbert F. Margulies.

RECENT ARTICLES CONCERNING THE FAR WEST

Colorado Magazine — October, 1957: "Colorado's Earliest Settlements," by Forbes Parkhill; "Tilford Stillings, Pioneer Mail Carrier to Brown's Park," by Lulita Crawford Pritchett; "Charles Autobees," Part III, by Janet Lecompte; "W. Arthur Dier, Pioneer Teacher and Lawyer," continued, ed. by Muriel Wright Spring.

New Mexico Historical Review — October, 1957: "The Crown's Participation in the Founding of New Mexico," by George P. Hammond and Agapito Rey; "Father Gottfried Bernhardt Middendorff, S. J., Pioneer of Tucson," by Theodore E. Treutlein; "The Janos, Jocomes, Mansos, and Sumas Indians," by Jack Douglas Forbes; "Cordero's Description of the Apache, 1796," ed. by Daniel S. Matson and Albert H. Schroeder.

Pacific Historical Review — November, 1957: "Gaylord Wilshire and Socialism's First Congressional Campaign," by Howard H. Quint; "The Stagecoach in the Southern San Joaquin Valley, 1854-1876," by William Harland Boyd.

Pacific Northwest Quarterly — October, 1957: "Washington's Blanket Primary Reviewed," by Claudius O. Johnson; "Story of Coal at Newcastle," by Marilyn Tharp; "Writing the History of Forest Industries," by Elwood R. Maunder; "Mountain Challenge, 1857: Journal of Lt. August V. Kautz on Mount Rainier," ed. by Aubrey L. Haines; "Witness of

Indian Religion: Present-Day Concepts of the Guardian Spirit," by June Randolph.

RECENT ARTICLES CONCERNING CANADA

Canadian Historical Review — September, 1957: "The Forty-ninth Degree of North Latitude as an International Boundary, 1719: The Origin of an Idea," by Max Savelle; "Opposition to the Founding of the Elgin Settlement," by William H. Pease and Jane H. Pease; "The Cape Breton Landfall, 1494 or 1497: Note on a Letter from John Day," by L. A. Vigneras.

December, 1957: "The Canadian Offer of Troops for Hong Kong, 1894," by Guy R. MacLean; "Criminal Extradition Menaces the Canadian Haven for Fugitive Slaves, 1841-1861," by Roman J. Zorn; "The Political Testament of Papineau in Exile, 1837," by Ronald F. Howell.

Colorado Quarterly — Autumn, 1957: "American Investment in Canada," by John Manning.

Mennonite Quarterly Review — October, 1957: "Nonresistance in the Early Brethren in Christ Church in Ontario," by E. Morris Sider.

North Dakota History — July, 1957: "The British North American West and the Civil War," by Robin W. Winks.

Directory of Contributors

Charles Grier Sellers, Jr., is an assistant professor of history in Princeton University.

Charles S. Campbell, Jr., is an assistant professor of history in Johns Hopkins University.

Howard H. Peckham is director of the William L. Clements Library and associate professor of history in the University of Michigan.

Robert H. Wiebe is an instructor in the department of humanities in Michigan State University.

Paul B. Trescott is associate professor of economics in Kenyon College.

Index

ABERNETHY, Thomas P., and Jackson historiography, 623, 624 n., 628
Abrams, Richard M., on Wilson and Congress, 219-20
Adair, James, Indian trader, and travel accounts, 5
Adams, John Quincy, rep., and Oregon boundary question, 300
Advance Agents of American Destiny, by Roy F. Nichols, revd., 130-31
Aeschbacher, William D., "Report of the Secretary-Treasurer for the Year 1956-1957," 411-19
Africa, North, U. S. interests in, art. on, 445-68
Afro-American Council, and Brownsville episode, 474, 476, 482, 489
Agar, Herbert, *The Price of Power: America since 1945*, revd., 574-76
Age of Roosevelt: The Crisis of the Old Order, 1919-1933, by Arthur M. Schlesinger, Jr., revd., 379-80
Agricultural Adjustment Act, and National Progressive party, 89
Agriculture, Dept. of, and Teapot Dome investigation, 247, 248-49, 252, 253, 265
Aikin, John J., on Sunday schools, 433
Alabama, and Blair bill, 276, 278, 281, 287 n.; railroads and politics in, book on, revd., 754-55
Alaska, and Harding conservation policies, 247, 248-49, 250, 252-53, 256, 265
Albert Gallatin: Jeffersonian Financier and Diplomat, by Raymond Walters, revd., 720-21
Alden, John R., revs., 716-17
Alderfer, E. Gordon (co-ed.), *The Witness of William Penn*, noted, 767
Aldrich, Nelson W., sen., and banking legislation, 669-70, 671
Aldrich-Vreeland Act, and business disunity, 668
Aldridge, Alfred O., *Franklin and His French Contemporaries*, revd., 543-44; revs., 335-36
Alexander, Archibald, on plenary inspiration, 69 n.
Alexander, James W., and religious needs of West, 432
Alexander Hamilton: Selections Representing His Life, His Thought, and His Style, ed. by Bower Aly, noted, 386
Alexander Hamilton: Youth to Maturity, 1755-1788, by Broadus Mitchell, revd., 717-19
Alexander Hamilton in the American Tradition, by Louis M. Hacker, revd., 343-44
Alfonsi, Paul R., and National Progressive party, 89
Alien and sedition laws, book on, revd., 344-46
Allen, Carlos R., Jr., revs., 542-43
Allen, H. C., on dismissal of Lord Sackville, 636; revs., 752-53; (co-ed.), *British Essays in American History*, revd., 536-37
Allen, Max P., discussion of history teaching, reported, 332
Allen, Moses, and Tract Society, 426
Allen, William, sen., and 54-40 slogan, 295, 296, 301 n., 302-303, 306
Allison, William B., biog. of, revd., 159-61
Almanacs, and reading on frontier, 650, 657, 658, 659, 660
Alsop, Em Bowles, and Wilson historiography, 210
Alvord, Clarence W., and MVHA, 311-12, 496-99, 500-508, 510, 512; ed. of *MVHR*, 502, 510, 529-30, 531, 533-34
Alvord Memorial Commission, and MVHA, 512, 513
Aly, Bower (ed.), *Alexander Hamilton*, noted, 386
Ambler, Charles H., deceased, 597-98
America and the British Left: From Bright to Bevan, by Henry Pelling, noted, 581-82
America and the Fight for Irish Freedom, 1866-1922, by Charles C. Tansill, revd., 752-53
American Bankers' Association, and Progressive banking reforms, 672, 673 n.
American Bible Society, and religious benevolence, 423 ff.
American Conscience, by Roger Burlingame, noted, 180
American Education Society, and religious benevolence, 423 ff.
American Fiction, 1851-1875: A Contribution toward a Bibliography, by Lyle H. Wright, noted, 766
American Forestry Association, and Harding conservation policies, 251-52, 255
American Historical Association, and be-

ginnings of MVHA, 495-96, 497 n., 498, 499, 507
American Historical Review, and founding of *MVHR*, 501, 531, 532
American Home Missionary Society, and religious benevolence, 423 ff.
American Immigration Policy, 1924-1952, by Robert A. Divine, revd., 573-74
American Indian and White Relations to 1830: Needs and Opportunities for Study, by William N. Fenton, revd., 337-39
American Industry and the European Immigrant, 1860-1885, by Charlotte Erickson, revd., 369-70
American Labor party, and National Progressive party, 75-76, 86
American Nationalism: An Interpretative Essay, by Hans Kohn, revd., 577-78
American Reaction to the Mortara Case, 1858-1859, by Bertram W. Korn, revd., 740-41
American Revolution, and foreign travelers, 8; books on, revd., 340-41, 544-47
American Sunday School Union, and religious benevolence, 423 ff.
American Tobacco Company, and trust control, 682
American Tract Society, and religious benevolence, 423 ff.
American Way, by Dexter Perkins, noted, 579
American Whig Review, on 54-40 slogan, 308
America's First Hamlet, by Grace Overmyer, revd., 724-25
Ames, Adelbert, letters of, revd., 745-47
Ames, Blanche B. (comp.), *Chronicles from the Nineteenth Century*, revd., 745-47
Ames Township (Ohio), frontier library in, 655, 660
Anaconda Copper Company, and conservation movement, 50, 51, 56
Anburey, Thomas, account of cotton gin, 22
Anderson, Charles, and Negro in politics, 475, 480, 485, 491-92
"Andrew Jackson versus the Historians," by Charles G. Sellers, Jr., 615-34
Andrews, J. Cutler, paper on teaching history on television, reported, 332
Anglo-American Understanding, 1898-1903, by Charles S. Campbell, Jr., revd., 567-68
Annals of Kansas, 1886-1925, ed. by Kirke Mechem, revd., 373-74
Antitrust legislation, and business disunity, 680-85; and interpretations of Wilson, 217, 219
Aristarchi, Gregoire, Turkish minister, and U. S. interests in Cyrenaica, 462, 463, 464, 466
Arkansas, and Blair bill, 276, 282
Armstrong, Samuel C., opposes Blair bill, 283
Armstrong, Samuel T., and Education Society, 428
Army Corps of Engineers, and Louisville and Portland Canal, 701, 704-705, 706
Arthur, Chester A., and federal aid to education, 272
Atchison, David R., sen., and Oregon boundary question, 293, 303 n., 305
Athearn, Robert G., *Sherman and the Settlement of the West*, revd., 155-56; revs., 342
Auburn prison, foreign visitors to, 20, 21
Auraria: The Story of a Georgia Gold-Mining Town, by E. Merton Coulter, revd., 141-42
Austria-Hungary, and Wilson's foreign policy, 229

BACON, Edward P., and railroad rate regulation, 674-76
Bacon, Leonard, and religious benevolence, 434
Bacon's Rebellion: The Contemporary News Sheets, ed. by Harry Finestone, noted, 173-74
Bailey, Thomas A., on dismissal of Lord Sackville, 635; and Wilson historiography, 221, 223, 234
Bailyn, Bernard, revs., 339-40
Baker, Ray S., and Wilson historiography, 209, 211, 234
Baker's Dozen: Thirteen Unusual Americans, by Russel B. Nye, revd., 129-30
Ballinger, Richard A., sec. of interior, and conservation movement, 35, 44, 55, 239, 242, 247, 262
Balloons to Jets: A Century of Aeronautics in Illinois, 1855-1955, by Howard L. Scamehorn, noted, 774
Baltimore: A Picture History, 1858-1958, by Francis F. Beirne, noted, 771
Bancroft, Frederic, book on, revd., 383-85
Bancroft, George, and 1844 election, 295, 297-98
Bank, national, in 1844 election, 296, 297 n.
Bank of the United States, and Jackson's advisers, 96, 97, 101, 103, 104, 105; in Jackson historiography, 617, 622, 627; and Louisville and Portland Canal, 691
Banking reform, and business disunity, 665-73, 684-85
Banks and Politics in America from the Revolution to the Civil War, by Bray Hammond, revd., 721-24
Baptists, and religious benevolence, 423; Negro, and Brownsville episode, 483
Barbour, John S., sen., on federal aid to education, 290
Barker, Charles A., on intellectual history, 58

Barker, Eugene C., and MVHA, 502, 512, 520
Barnes, Elinor S., deceased, 779
Barnhart, John D., revs., 131-32
Barrett, John G., *Sherman's March through the Carolinas*, revd., 150; revs., 558-59
Barrow, Alexander, sen., and 54-40 slogan, 306
Barzun, Jacques, revs., 711-13; (co-auth.), *The Modern Researcher*, revd., 765-66
Bassett, John Spencer, and Jackson historiography, 619, 620
Bate, William B., sen., opposes Blair bill, 287
Bates, J. Leonard, "Fulfilling American Democracy: The Conservation Movement, 1907 to 1921," 29-57
Baurmeister, Carl L., letters and journals of, revd., 546-47
Baxter, Maurice G., *Orville H. Browning*, revd., 562-63; revs., 742-43
Bay Psalm Book: A Facsimile Reprint of the First Edition of 1640, ed. by Zoltán Haraszti, revd., 116-17
Bayard, Thomas F., sen., opposes Blair bill, 282, 284; sec. of state, and dismissal of Lord Sackville, 635, 637-41, 642-44, 645-48
Beale, Howard K., *Theodore Roosevelt and the Rise of America to World Power*, revd., 162-63
Beals, Ralph L. (co-auth.), *No Frontier to Learning*, noted, 582-83
Beard, Charles A., and Jackson historiography, 619, 626; and *MVHR*, 520, 526; historical thinking of, book on, noted, 583
Beaton, Kendall, *Enterprise in Oil*, noted, 391
Beatty, W. Donald, revs., 130-31
Beck, James B., sen., on Blair bill, 285, 286, 287
Beekman Mercantile Papers, 1746-1799, ed. by Philip L. White, revd., 123-25
Beekmans of New York in Politics and Commerce, 1647-1877, by Philip L. White, revd., 123-25
Beidler, Xavier, vigilante, book on, noted, 389
Beirne, Francis F., *Baltimore: A Picture History*, noted, 771
Belcher, Wyatt W., revs., 371-72
Bell, Herbert C. F., and Wilson historiography, 221
Bell, John R., capt., journal of, revd., 350-52
Beloff, Max, on Wilson's foreign policy, 229
Belpré (Ohio), frontier library in, 654
Bemis, Samuel F., on dismissal of Lord Sackville, 635
Benevolent societies, and social control, art. on, 423-44
Benghazi, Vidal's interest in, 453-54, 465
Benson, Elmer A., gov., and National Progressive party, 75, 77 n.
Benton, Thomas H., as Jackson adviser, 97, 98, 99, 100, 104; and Oregon boundary question, 303-304, 306
Berg, Elias, *The Historical Thinking of Charles A. Beard*, noted, 583
Berger, Josef and Dorothy, *Diary of America*, noted, 766-67
Berry, Thomas S., on Louisville and Portland Canal, 694 n.
Berthoff, Rowland T., revs., 369-70
Berthoud, Nicholas, and Louisville and Portland Canal, 691 n.
Berthrong, Donald J. (co-ed.), *Joseph Reddeford Walker and the Arizona Adventure*, revd., 152-53
Bertsche, William H., Jr. (co-ed.), *X. Beidler, Vigilante*, noted, 389
Beveridge, Albert J., on Oregon boundary question, 292; and conservation movement, 32-33
Bible, views on, in American thought, 69, 70; and reading on frontier, 650, 652, 657; and religious benevolence, 424, 435, 436, 437, 438, 441, 442
Bickel, Alexander M., *The Unpublished Opinions of Mr. Justice Brandeis*, revd., 761-62
Biddle, Nicholas, defended by Theodore Frelinghuysen, 430
Bill of Rights and What It Means Today, by Edward Dumbauld, noted, 386
Billington, Ray A., and MVHA, 515
Bingham, Harold J., communication from, 203-204
Bining, Arthur C., deceased, 598-99
Binkley, Wilfred E., and Jackson historiography, 623
Binkley, William C., ed. of *MVHR*, 529, 531
Biography, nature of, book on, revd., 711-13
Birney, James G., and 1844 election, 296, 297
Birr, Kendall, revs., 168-70
Black Hills, book on, revd., 565-66
Blair, Francis P., as Jackson adviser, 98, 99, 102 n., 104; and Oregon boundary question, 293
Blair, Henry W., sen., and federal aid to education, 267 ff.
Blair, Walter (co-ed.), *Half Horse, Half Alligator: The Growth of the Mike Fink Legend*, revd., 554-55
Blair bill, and South, art. on, 267-90
Blake, Nelson M., revs., 121-23
Blane, William, and reading on frontier, 653

Blaustein, Albert P. (co-auth.), *Desegregation and the Law*, noted, 773
Blegen, Theodore C., and scope of *MVHR*, 535
Bloom, John P., paper on soldier life, reported, 325
Bloomfield, Lincoln P., *Evolution or Revolution*, noted, 582
Blum, John M., *Woodrow Wilson and the Politics of Morality*, review discussion of, 207 n., 208, 230-33
Boatright, Mody C., revs., 554-55
Bolitho, Hector, visit to U. S., 25
Bollaert, William, writings on Texas, revd., 134-37
Bolton, Herbert E., and *MVHR*, 520
Bond, Beverley W. (ed.), *The Intimate Letters of John Cleves Symmes and His Family*, revd., 131-32
Bone, Scott, gov., and Harding conservation policies, 248 n., 249 n.
Bonner, Thomas N., *Medicine in Chicago, 1850-1950*, revd., 372-73; revs., 381-82
Book publishers, and frontiers, book on, revd., 576-77
Book reviews, *MVHR*, appraisal of, 522, 523-27, 532, 533, 534
"Books and Reading on the Ohio Valley Frontier," by Howard H. Peckham, 649-63
Boone, Daniel, and reading on frontier, 651
Bornet, Vaughn D., *California Social Welfare*, noted, 390
Boston, supplies books for frontier, 652, 655; and Negro vote, 484
Boston *Guardian*, and Brownsville episode, 473, 490
Boucher, Chauncey S., and MVHA, 513
Boudinot, Elias, and Bible Society, 427
Bowers, Claude G., and Jackson historiography, 622
Boyle, Robert, views on nature, 64, 65
Bracken, Dorothy K. (co-auth.), *Marks of Lincoln on Our Land*, noted, 389
Bradley, Harold W., and MVHA, 515; revs., 375-77
Brandeis, Louis D., and railroad rate regulation, 678; and Wilson's progressive thought, 213, 217; opinions of, book on, revd., 761-62
Brant, Irving, *James Madison, the President, 1809-1812*, revd., 348-49
Breckenridge, Adam C., *One House for Two: Nebraska's Unicameral Legislature*, noted, 773-74
Breese, Sidney, sen., and Oregon boundary question, 297 n., 303
Bridges, Hal, paper on robber barons, reported, 317
Briggs, Harold E., revs., 749-50
British Emigration to North America: Projects and Opinions in the Early Victorian Period, by Wilbur S. Shepperson, revd., 552-53
British Essays in American History, ed. by H. C. Allen and C. P. Hill, revd., 536-37
British Indian policy, paper on, reported, 323-24
British travelers, views of U. S., 6-7, 8, 10, 16, 26
Brown, A. Theodore, paper on Kansas City historiography, reported, 318
Brown, Aaron V., rep., and Oregon boundary question, 300
Brown, D. Alexander, revs., 148-49
Brown, Ira V., revs., 751-52
Brown, Joseph E., sen., favors federal aid to education, 269, 276, 287
Brown, Samuel, and reading on frontier, 655
Brown, W. Burlie, revs., 758-59
Browning, Orville H., biog. of, revd., 562-63
Brownsville (Texas), and discharge of Negro troops, 469-70, 481, 488
"Brownsville Episode and the Negro Vote," by Emma Lou Thornbrough, 469-93
Bruce, Robert V., *Lincoln and the Tools of War*, communications on, 202-204
Bruchey, Stuart W., *Robert Oliver, Merchant of Baltimore*, revd., 347-48
Bryan, T. Conn, revs., 141-42
Bryan, William J., and Negro vote, 487, 488 n., 489-92; in Wilson historiography, 213, 221, 223; paper on, reported, 328-29
Bryant, R. C., and Harding conservation policies, 240, 250-51
Buchanan, James, sec. of state, and Oregon boundary question, 301
Buck, Solon J., and MVHA, 504, 510-11, 512
Buehrig, Edward H., and Wilson historiography, 226, 227; (ed.), *Wilson's Foreign Policy in Perspective*, revd., 759-61
Bulkley, William H., on western political power, 431
Buranelli, Vincent (ed.), *The Trial of Peter Zenger*, revd., 125-26
Burgess, John W., and Jackson historiography, 620, 623
Burleson, Albert S., and conservation movement, 54
Burlingame, Merrill G. (ed.), *From Wilderness to Statehood: A History of Montana*, by James M. Hamilton, revd., 739-40
Burlingame, Roger, *The American Conscience*, noted, 180
Burnside, Ambrose E., sen., favors federal aid to education, 271

Burton, Theodore E., and Negro vote, 484
Business, in Jackson historiography, 626, 627, 628; and politics, papers on, reported, 316-18
"Business Disunity and the Progressive Movement, 1901-1914," by Robert H. Wiebe, 664-85
Business histories, bibliog. of, noted, 584
Butler, Benjamin F., atty. gen., as Jackson adviser, 104
Butler, Charles, and Home Missionary Society, 427, 441
Butler, Matthew C., sen., opposes Blair bill, 282, 284, 286 n.
Butler, Ruth L. (co-ed.), *William Bollaert's Texas*, revd., 134-37
Bykofsky, Joseph (co-auth.), *The Transportation Corps: Operations Overseas*, noted, 392
Byron, Lord, and reading on frontier, 661

CABLE, George W., favors Blair bill, 279, 280
Cahokia (Ill.), and books on frontier, 650, 657
Calhoun, John C., sen., and Oregon boundary question, 295, 298 n., 304
California, naval oil reserves in, 244, 245, 246, 248, 258, 260, 261; and National Progressive party, 80, 88, 92
California Gold Rush Merchant: The Journal of Stephen Chapin Davis, ed. by Benjamin B. Richards, noted, 174
California Social Welfare, by Vaughn D. Bornet, noted, 390
Call, Wilkinson, sen., favors Blair bill, 276
Calvinism, and religious benevolence, 424-26
Calvo, Carlos, on diplomatic recall, 642-44
Campbell, Charles S., Jr., "The Dismissal of Lord Sackville," 635-48; *Anglo-American Understanding, 1898-1903*, revd., 567-68
Canadian fisheries, and Cleveland's British policy, 636
Canadian Historical Review, and scope of *MVHR*, 534
Candler, Allen D., rep., and Blair bill, 282
Capers, Gerald M., paper on Douglas, reported, 327-28
Capitalism, in Jackson historiography, 626, 628, 630, 631, 633
Capper farm press, paper on, reported, 326
Caribbean, and New Orleans, paper on, reported, 320
Carlisle, John G., rep., opposes Blair bill, 282
Carman, Harry J. (co-auth.), *A Short History of New York State*, revd., 713-14
Carolina Chronicle of Dr. Francis Le Jau, 1706-1717, ed. by Frank J. Klingberg, revd., 541-42
Carolinas, under Spanish rule, book on, revd., 114-16; Sherman in, book on, revd., 150
Carter, Clarence E. (ed.), *The Territorial Papers of the United States*, Vol. XXII (Florida), revd., 550-51
Carter, Harvey L., revs., 350-52
Carver, William F., biog. of, revd., 749-50
Cass, Lewis, as Jackson adviser, 103, 105; and 1844 Democratic national convention, 294; and Oregon boundary question, 306
Castañeda, Carlos E., paper on Spanish Southwest, reported, 325
Cathcart, Charles W., rep., on 54-40 slogan, 300 n.
Catholic Church in Maine, by William L. Lucey, noted, 580
Catholic history, docs. on, revd., 113-14
Catholics, and Protestant religious societies, 434-35
Catterall, Ralph C. H., and Jackson historiography, 622
Cattle industry, book on, revd., 158-59
Caughey, John W., paper on *MVHR*, reported, 312; "Under Our Strange Device: A Review of the 'Review'," 519-35
Cecil, Lady Gwendolen, on dismissal of Lord Sackville, 635-36
Chamber of Commerce (U. S.), and Progressive banking reforms, 672
Chamberlain, Joseph, and Cleveland's British policy, 636
Chambers, Clarke A., revs., 379-80
Champion, Aristarchus, and Home Missionary Society, 428
Chandler, Alfred D., Jr., *Henry Varnum Poor*, revd., 143-44
Channing, Edward, and *MVHR* book reviews, 526
Charles, Joseph, *The Origins of the American Party System*, revd., 127-28
Chase, Calvin, and Brownsville episode, 471-72, 480, 486
Cherokees of the Old South: A People in Transition, by Henry T. Malone, revd., 133-34
Cherry Hill prison (Philadelphia), book on, revd., 353-54
Chicago, travelers' views of, 16-17; and business disunity in Progressive era, 669, 670 n., 672, 673, 683-84; books on, revd., 371-73
Chicago Giant: A Biography of "Long John" Wentworth, by Don E. Fehrenbacher, revd., 742-43
Chicora, and Spanish rule in Carolinas, book on, revd., 114-16
China, and Wilson's foreign policy, 222,

223-24; diplomatic papers on, revd., 763-65
Chronicles from the Nineteenth Century: Family Letters of Blanche Butler and Adelbert Ames, comp. by Blanche B. Ames, revd., 745-47
Cincinnati, and culture in Ohio Valley, 650, 651, 652, 654, 660; and Louisville and Portland Canal, 687, 693, 701
Civil War, books on, revd., 146-54, 363-66, 557-62, 743-47
Civil War Artist at the Front: Edwin Forbes' Life Studies of the Great Army, ed. by William F. Dawson, noted, 770
Clark, Dan E., and MVHA *Proceedings*, 499
Clark, Thomas D., "The Great Visitation to American Democracy," 3-28
Clawson, Marion (co-auth.), *The Federal Lands*, noted, 772
Clay, Henry, criticizes Jackson, 616, 630 n.; and 1844 election, 291, 296, 297, 298, 430; biog. of, revd., 356-57
Clayton Anti-Trust Act, and business disunity in Progressive era, 683, 684; Wilson's attitude on, 214, 217
Cleland, Robert G., deceased, 598
Clemenceau, Georges, and Wilson's Far Eastern policy, 224
Clements, Judson C., rep., favors Blair bill, 276
Clements, Roger V., revs., 552-53
Cleveland, frontier library in, 656; and Negro vote, 484, 492 n.
Cleveland, Grover, and Blair bill, 275; and dismissal of Lord Sackville, 635-38, 640, 645-46, 647; and conservation movement, 32
Cleveland *Gazette*, and Negro vote, 477-78, 480, 482, 484
Cleveland *Plain Dealer*, and 54-40 slogan, 307
Cobb, Howell, sec. of treasury, and Louisville and Portland Canal, 701, 703
Cobb, Rufus W., gov., opposes Blair bill, 283
Cochran, Thomas C., paper on economic history, reported, 322-23
Coddington, Edwin B., revs., 365-66
Cohn, David L., *The Life and Times of King Cotton*, revd., 547-48
Cokers of Carolina: A Social Biography of a Family, by George L. Simpson, Jr., revd., 154-55
Cole, Arthur C., ed. of *MVHR*, 513-14, 529, 530-31
Cole, Fred C., assoc. ed. of *MVHR*, 529
Coleman, Charles H., revs., 735-36
Coleman, Peter J., paper on New Zealand progressives, reported, 328
Colonial America, travelers in, 3-8; books on, revd., 114-28, 537-47; papers on, reported, 313-16
Colonial Records of South Carolina: The Journal of the Commons House of Assembly, September 10, 1745–June 17, 1746, ed. by J. Harold Easterby, revd., 126-27
Colquitt, Alfred H., sen., favors Blair bill, 287
Columbia River, or Scenes and Adventures during a Residence of Six Years on the Western Side of the Rocky Mountains, by Ross Cox, revd., 729-30
Columbus (Ohio), and Negro vote, 483
Colyar, Arthur S., and Blair bill, 277, 287
Comanche Indians, book on, noted, 769
Comegys, Benjamin B., and Sunday School Union, 426
Coming of the Civil War, revised ed., by Avery Craven, noted, 388-89
Commager, Henry S., views on Wilson, 212
Common Frontiers of the Social Sciences, ed. by Mirra Komarovsky, noted, 179
Commons, John R., and Jackson historiography, 629
Communism, American, book on, revd., 572-73
Communists, and National Progressive party, 76, 87
Confederacy, books on, revd., 151-52, 557-59, 743-44
Confederate imprints, bibliog. of, noted, 583
Confederate Morale and Church Propaganda, by James W. Silver, revd., 743-44
Confederate property, U. S. claims to, paper on, reported, 320-21
Congregationalists, and religious benevolence, 423, 424 n.
Congress, travelers' views of, 10-11; and Oregon boundary question, 293, 300, 301-308; and Louisville and Portland Canal, 686, 687-88, 692-93, 695-97, 699-701, 703, 705, 706-708; and Blair bill, 267 ff.; and business disunity in Progressive era, 668, 670, 673, 676, 677-78, 684; Wilson's relations with, 216, 220, 235; and conservation movement, 36-37, 42, 44-45, 47, 51, 54; and Teapot Dome investigation, 238, 252, 254, 262, 264-65
Congress, the, and Cyrenaican naval base scheme, 445, 457, 458-62
Congressman Abraham Lincoln, by Donald W. Riddle, revd., 735-36
Connelley, William E., and MVHA, 506, 511
Conner, Daniel E., *Joseph Reddeford Walker and the Arizona Adventure*, revd., 152-53
Conservation movement, art. on, 29-57; and Teapot Dome investigation, 237-66
Constitutional League, and Brownsville episode, 474, 476, 478, 480, 487

Cook, James H., *Fifty Years on the Old Frontier*, reprint, noted, 175
Cooke, Jacob E., *Frederic Bancroft, Historian*, revd., 383-85
Cooke, Jay, and Sunday School Union, 426
Coolidge, Calvin, and conservation movement, 47
Cooper, Oscar H., opposes Blair bill, 283
Corbitt, David L. (ed.), *Public Addresses, Letters, and Papers of William Kerr Scott*, noted, 391-92
Cornish, Dudley T., *The Sable Arm: Negro Troops in the Union Army*, revd., 146-47; revs., 363-65
Corporations, Bureau of, and trust control, 680, 681
Corwin, Edward S., on Wilson as president, 216; *The President — Office and Powers*, noted, 768
Cotton, hist. of, book on, revd., 547-48
Coulter, E. Merton, *Auraria*, revd., 141-42
Counterfeiting in Colonial America, by Kenneth Scott, revd., 542-43
Courtship of Mr. Lincoln, by Ruth P. Randall, revd., 144-46
Cox, Isaac J., and MVHA, 500, 504, 506, 525
Cox, Mildred C., paper on urban history, reported, 319
Cox, Ross, *The Columbia River*, ed. by Edgar I. and Jane R. Stewart, revd., 729-30
Cradle of Culture: The Philadelphia Stage, 1800-1810, by Reese D. James, noted, 767
Craig, William B., rep., and conservation movement, 52
Cramer, Zadok, and reading on frontier, 658
Crane, Verner W., revs., 543-44
Craven, Avery O., *The Coming of the Civil War*, revised ed., noted, 388-89; and MVHA, 512
Credit Mobilier, paper on, reported, 316-17
Creer, Leland H., revs., 737-38
Cronon E. David, revs., 377-78
Crossroads of Freedom: The 1912 Campaign Speeches of Woodrow Wilson, ed. by John W. Davidson, review discussion of, 207 n., 209, 218-19
Cultural Life of the American Colonies, 1607-1763, by Louis B. Wright, revd., 120-21
Cummins, Cedric C., discussion of history teaching, reported, 332
Cunningham, Noble E., Jr., revs., 343-44
Cunningham, Robert E. (ed.), *Indian Territory*, by William S. Prettyman, noted, 771
Currency reform, in Progressive era, and business disunity, 665-71
Current-Garcia, Eugene, revs., 553-54
Curry, J. L. M., and Blair bill, 269, 270, 277, 279
Curry, Roy W., and Wilson historiography, 222, 223-24
Curti, Merle, on intellectual history, 58
Cushing, Caleb, and diplomatic recall, 643
Cutler, Ephraim, and reading on frontier, 655
Cutler, Manasseh, and reading on frontier, 655
Cyprus, and U. S. Mediterranean policy, 467
Cyrenaica, Vidal's plan for base in, art. on, 445-68

DAIRY press, paper on, reported, 326
Dakota Territory, book on, revd., 565-66
Dale, Edward E., and MVHA, 521
Damon, Ethel M., *Sanford Ballard Dole and His Hawaii*, revd., 375-77
Dana, James D., on science and religion, 70
Daniel, John W., rep., favors Blair bill, 276
Daniells, Lorna M. (comp.), *Studies in Enterprise*, noted, 584
Daniels, Josephus, sec. of navy, and conservation movement, 49, 52-54; and naval oil reserves, 244-45, 256-57, 258, 261
Daring Diplomacy: The Case of the First American Ultimatum, by Andor Klay, noted, 174
Dark Missouri, by Henry C. Hart, noted, 389
Darwin, Charles, views on nature, 64, 65
Darwin, Erasmus, views on nature, 66, 67
Darwinism, and intellectual history, 71
Dauer, Manning J., revs., 127-28
Davenport, F. Garvin, revs., 726-27
Davenport, Odessa (co-ed.), *Joseph Reddeford Walker and the Arizona Adventure*, revd., 152-53
Davidson, John W. (ed.), *Crossroads of Freedom: The 1912 Campaign Speeches of Woodrow Wilson*, review discussion of, 207 n., 209, 218-19
Davie, William R., biog. of, revd., 719-20
Davies, Godfrey, deceased, 395-96
Davis, David B., *Homicide in American Fiction, 1798-1860*, revd., 549-50
Davis, Jefferson, sen., and Louisville and Portland Canal, 699
Davis, Stephen C., journal of, noted, 174
Davis, William L., revs., 729-30
Dawson, N. H. R., favors Blair bill, 277
Dawson, William F. (ed.), *A Civil War Artist at the Front*, noted, 770
Day, Donald, and Wilson historiography, 209
Dayton (Ohio), frontier library in, 650, 655
Debo, Angie, revs., 133-34
Debs, Eugene V., and Negro vote, 492

Deism, and 18th-century thought, 62, 70, 71
Delaware, and Blair bill, 268, 281
Democracy, in U. S., travelers' views of, 10, 11, 21; and Jackson historiography, 615-16, 619-26, 628-29, 631, 632; and conservation movement, art. on, 29-57
Democratic national convention (1844), and Oregon question, 294-95, 298, 300, 302, 308; (1908), and Negro vote, 489
Democratic party, and religious benevolence, 429, 430, 435; and 54-40 slogan, 292-309; and Blair bill, 267 ff.; and Brownsville episode, 469, 484, 486-93; and conservation movement, 32, 42, 44-45, 48-50, 52-54; and National Progressive party, 75 ff.
Denby, Edwin, and conservation movement, 44; and Teapot Dome investigation, 242, 245-46, 257, 261
Desegregation and the Law: The Meaning and Effect of the School Segregation Cases, by Albert P. Blaustein and Clarence C. Ferguson, Jr., noted, 773
Desha, Joseph, gov., and Louisville and Portland Canal, 688-89
Detroit Public Library, sponsor of *MVHR*, 511
Diamond, William, and Wilson historiography, 212, 221 n.
Diary of America: The Intimate Story of Our Nation, ed. by Josef and Dorothy Berger, noted, 766-67
Dickerson, Oliver M., and beginnings of MVHA, 499
Different Valor: The Story of General Joseph E. Johnston, by Gilbert E. Govan and James W. Livingood, revd., 147-48
Dimock, Marshall E., and Wilson historiography, 221 n.
Diplomacy, and Vidal's Cyrenaican scheme, 445-68; and dismissal of Lord Sackville, 635-48; and southern politics, papers on, reported, 320-21
Diplomatic relations, papers on, revd., 763-65
"Dismissal of Lord Sackville," by Charles S. Campbell, Jr., 635-48
Divine, Robert A., *American Immigration Policy, 1924-1952*, revd., 573-74
Dixon, Joseph M., and conservation movement, 51, 56
Documents of American Catholic History, ed. by John Tracy Ellis, revd., 113-14
Dodd, William E., and Jackson historiography, 619, 620; and Wilson historiography, 209
Dodge, William E., and Bible Society, 426
Doheny, Edward L., and conservation movement, 50, 51; and Teapot Dome investigation, 253, 255, 258, 260, 261
Dole, Sanford B., biog. of, revd., 375-77
Donelson, Andrew J., as Jackson adviser, 98, 99, 100, 102 n., 103, 104, 105-106
Donnelly, Ignatius, as Greenbacker, paper on, reported, 328-29
Dorfman, Joseph, and Jackson historiography, 627
Doster, James F., *Railroads in Alabama Politics, 1875-1914*, revd., 754-55
Douglas, Paul H., and National Progressive party, 80
Douglas, Stephen A., paper on, reported, 327-28
Douglass, Elisha P., revs., 544-45
Dowd, Clement, rep., favors Blair bill, 276
Downey, Joseph T., reminiscences of, noted, 174-75
Draper, Theodore, *The Roots of American Communism*, revd., 572-73
Drayton, William, rep., and Louisville and Portland Canal, 696 n.
Drummond, James, on wealth and religion, 439
Dry Farming in the Northern Great Plains, 1900-1925, by Mary W. M. Hargreaves, revd., 569-70
Duane, William J., sec. of treasury, and Jackson cabinet, 101
Du Bois, W. E. B., and Niagara Movement, 474; and 1908 election, 490
Duffy, John (ed.), *Parson Clapp of the Strangers' Church of New Orleans*, noted, 580
Dulles, Foster R., *The Imperial Years*, revd., 374-75
Dulles, Joseph H., and religious benevolence, 435-36
Dumbauld, Edward, *The Bill of Rights and What It Means Today*, noted, 386
Dumond, Dwight L., and MVHA, 515
Dunbar, Robert G., revs., 569-70
Duncan, John, and reading on frontier, 652
Dunham, Amos, and reading on frontier, 654, 663
Dunne, Peter M., deceased, 186
Dupree, A. Hunter, *Science in the Federal Government*, revd., 168-70
Dwight, Henry, and Home Missionary Society, 428
Dwight, Timothy, views on nature, 62
Dyer, Brainerd, paper on Confederate property, reported, 320-21
Dyer, John P., revs., 147-48

Early Jackson Party in Ohio, by Harry R. Stevens, revd., 355-56
Easterby, J. Harold (ed.), *The Colonial Records of South Carolina*, revd., 126-27; revs., 541-42
Eaton, Clement, *Henry Clay and the Art of American Politics*, revd., 356-57
Eaton, John, and federal aid to education, 270 n., 277

Eaton, John H., as Jackson adviser, 98, 104
Eaton affair, and Jackson cabinet, 95, 97, 99 n., 101
Eaves, T. C. Duncan (co-ed.), *The Letters of William Gilmore Simms*, Vols. IV-V, revd., 362-63
Echeverria, Durand, *Mirage in the West*, revd., 335-36
Economic history, paper on, reported, 322-23
Education, travelers' views of, 19-20; federal aid for, art. on, 267-90
Education of a Bibliographer: An Autobiographical Essay, by Thomas J. Holmes, noted, 775-76
Edward Palmer: Plant Explorer of the American West, by Rogers McVaugh, revd., 157-58
Edwards, Everett E., and MVHA, 515
Edwardsville (Ill.), frontier library in, 656, 660
Election, congressional, of 1906, and Brownsville episode, 470-71, 475
Election, presidential, of 1840, book on, revd., 731-32; of 1844, and 54-40 slogan, art. on, 291-309; of 1888, and dismissal of Lord Sackville, 635, 636, 645; of 1908, and Negro vote, 479-93
Elections, presidential, hist. of, revd., 709-10
Eliot, Charles W., and conservation movement, 36
Elkins Anti-Rebate Act, and business disunity, 674-75
Ellis, David M. (co-auth.), *A Short History of New York State*, revd., 713-14
Ellis, Elmer, and MVHA, 515
Ellis, John Tracy (ed.), *Documents of American Catholic History*, revd., 113-14
Ellis, L. Ethan, revs., 574-76
Elmer, L. Q. C., on social reforms, 439
Ely, Richard T., and Jackson historiography, 628 n.
Emigration, British, to North America, book on, revd., 552-53
Empire of the Columbia: A History of the Pacific Northwest, by Dorothy O. Johansen and Charles M. Gates, noted, 386-87
Engineers, Army, and Louisville and Portland Canal, 701, 704-705, 706
English, Earl, capt., and Cyrenaican naval base scheme, 458-61
Enigma of the Bay Psalm Book, by Zoltán Haraszti, revd., 116-17
Enterprise in Oil: A History of Shell in the United States, by Kendall Beaton, noted, 391
Episcopalians, and religious benevolence, 423
Erickson, Charlotte, *American Industry and the European Immigrant, 1860-1885*, revd., 369-70
Erie Canal, paper on, reported, 324-25
Errand into the Wilderness, by Perry Miller, revd., 117-19
Esarey, Logan, and MVHA, 513
Evans, George, sen., and 54-40 slogan, 306
Evarts, William M., on Jackson politics, 429
Evjue, William T., and National Progressive party, 89 n., 90
Evolution, and intellectual history, 64, 66, 67
Evolution or Revolution: The United Nations and the Problem of Peaceful Territorial Change, by Lincoln P. Bloomfield, noted, 582
Ewing, Cortez A. M., revs., 709-10
Exploration of the Colorado River, by John W. Powell, noted, 581

Fable, Fact, and History, by Willis Thornton, noted, 179
Fall, Albert B., and conservation movement, 55, 56; and Teapot Dome investigation, 237 ff.; paper on, reported, 317-18
Far West and the Rockies, 1820-1875, Vol. VI, revd., 350-52
Farm Crisis, 1919-1923, by James H. Shideler, revd., 762-63
Farm press, papers on, reported, 326-27
Farmer-Labor parties, and National Progressive party, in Iowa, 80, 88; in Minn., 75, 76, 86; in Wis., 89, 91
Federal Convention, and West, paper on, reported, 323
Federal government, and Louisville and Portland Canal, 686, 687-88, 692-93, 695-703, 704, 705, 706-708; and aid to education, 267-90; and science, book on, revd., 168-70
Federal Lands: Their Use and Management, by Marion Clawson and Burnell Held, noted, 772
Federal Reserve system, origins of, and business disunity, 671; and Wilson, 214, 215, 216, 217
Federal Trade Commission, and trust control, 683-84; and Wilson, 217
Federalism, and religious benevolence, 423, 426, 427, 444
Fehrenbacher, Don E., *Chicago Giant: A Biography of "Long John" Wentworth*, revd., 742-43
Fenton, William N., *American Indian and White Relations to 1830*, revd., 337
Fenwick, Charles G., on dismissal of Lord Sackville, 645
Ferguson, Clarence C., Jr. (co-auth.), *Desegregation and the Law*, noted, 773
Ferguson, Eugene S., *Truxtun of the Constellation*, revd., 132-33
Ferrell, Robert H., on Wilson's foreign policy, 229

Ferris, Scott, rep., and conservation movement, 52-53
Ficklin, Orlando B., rep., on 54-40 slogan, 300 n.
Fiction Fights the Civil War, by Robert A. Lively, revd., 153-54
Field, James A., Jr., "A Scheme in Regard to Cyrenaica," 445-68
Field, Matthew C., *Prairie and Mountain Sketches*, ed. by Kate L. Gregg and John F. McDermott, revd., 359-60
Fifield, Russell H., and Wilson historiography, 223-24
"Fiftieth Annual Meeting of the Mississippi Valley Historical Association," by Oscar O. Winther, 310-34
" 'Fifty-four Forty or Fight' — An American Political Legend," by Edwin A. Miles, 291-309
Fifty Years on the Old Frontier as Cowboy, Hunter, Guide, Scout, and Ranchman, by James H. Cook, reprint, noted, 175
Fight for Fluoridation, by Donald R. McNeil, revd., 381-82
Filings from an Old Saw: Reminiscences of San Francisco and California's Conquest, ed. by Fred B. Rogers, noted, 174-75
Filler, Louis, revs., 352-53
Finestone, Harry (ed.), *Bacon's Rebellion*, noted, 173-74
Fink, Mike, book on, revd., 554-55
Finney, Edward C., and Teapot Dome investigation, 259-60
Fish, Carl R., and Jackson historiography, 621
Fish, Hamilton, sec. of state, on relations with Tripoli, 450, 467; on diplomatic recall, 643 n.
Fisher, Walter L., sec. of interior, and conservation movement, 35
Fiske, John, and Jackson historiography, 621; religious faith of, book on, revd., 751-52
Fite, Gilbert C. (co-auth.), *Opponents of War, 1917-1918*, revd., 378-79
Fleming, E. McClung, paper on decorative arts, reported, 332
Fleming, Walter L., and *MVHR*, 502
Florida, territorial papers of, revd., 550-51; and Blair bill, 276, 278
Folmsbee, Stanley J., revs., 733-34
Foot, Samuel A., and Bible Society, 427
Foraker, Joseph B., sen., and Brownsville episode and Negro vote, 477-84, 486, 488, 491
Forbes, Edwin, Civil War artist, book on, noted, 770
Ford, Guy S., ed. of *American Historical Review*, 532
Foreign policy, and post-Civil War expansionism, 466; of Wilson, review discussion of, 221-29, 236; books on, revd., 162-63, 165-66, 759-61
Foreign Policy and the American Spirit: Essays by Dexter Perkins, ed. by Glyndon G. Van Deusen and Richard C. Wade, noted, 776
Foreign Relations of the United States: Diplomatic Papers, 1942: China, revd., 763-65
Forest Service, and conservation movement, 33, 34, 41, 44; and Teapot Dome investigation, 237, 247, 248-52, 253-54, 255
Forgan, James B., and Progressive banking reforms, 672
Forman, Henry C., *Tidewater Maryland Architecture and Gardens*, noted, 176
Forsyth, John, as Jackson adviser, 105 n.
Fortune, T. Thomas, and Brownsville episode, 471, 474, 482, 485 n.
Fourierism, views of religious societies on, 439
Fowke, Vernon C., *The National Policy and the Wheat Economy*, noted, 772
Fowler, Charles N., rep., and Progressive banking reforms, 666, 667
Fox, George, early travel account of, 4
Frame, Andrew J., and Progressive banking reforms, 667, 668
France, and Benjamin Franklin, book on, revd., 543-44
Frank, Glenn, and Wis. Progressive party, 90
Frankfort (Ky.), frontier library in, 654
Franklin, Benjamin, book on, revd., 543-44
Franklin, John Hope, *The Militant South, 1800-1861*, revd., 140-41; *From Slavery to Freedom*, 2nd ed., noted, 176-77
Franklin and His French Contemporaries, by Alfred O. Aldridge, revd., 543-44
Frantz, Joe B., revs., 158-59
Frazier, E. Franklin, *The Negro in the United States*, revised ed., noted, 177
Frederic Bancroft, Historian, by Jacob E. Cooke, revd., 383-85
Freedom's Fetters: The Alien and Sedition Laws and American Civil Liberties, by James M. Smith, revd., 344-46
Freiberg, Malcolm, paper on Gov. Thomas Hutchinson, reported, 314, 316
Frelinghuysen, Joseph S., sen., and Harding, 241
Frelinghuysen, Theodore, and religious societies, 427-28, 432; and 1844 election, 430
French travelers, views of U. S., 8, 10, 16
Frink, Maurice (co-auth.), *When Grass Was King*, revd., 158-59
From Slavery to Freedom: A History of American Negroes, by John Hope Franklin, 2nd ed., noted, 176-77
Frontier, Ohio Valley, books and reading on, art. on, 649-63

Frontier Mind: A Cultural Analysis of the Kentucky Frontiersman, by Arthur K. Moore, revd., 726-27
Frontier thesis, and Jackson historiography, 619, 624-25, 629, 630
Frost, James A. (co-auth.), *A Short History of New York State*, revd., 713-14
"Fulfilling American Democracy: The Conservation Movement, 1907 to 1921," by J. Leonard Bates, 29-57
Fuller, George N., deceased, 596-97
Fuller, Harlin M. (co-ed.), *The Journal of Captain John R. Bell*, revd., 350-52

GABRIEL, Ralph H., views on Wilson, 212-13
Gallatin, Albert, and Louisville and Portland Canal, 687; biog. of, revd., 720-21
Gara, Larry, *Westernized Yankee: The Story of Cyrus Woodman*, revd., 142-43
Gardiner, C. Harvey, paper on American-Mexican relations, reported, 331
Garfield, James A., favors federal aid to education, 272
Garfield, James R., and conservation movement, 35
Garland, Augustus H., sen., favors Blair bill, 276
Garraty, John A., *Woodrow Wilson*, review discussion of, 207 n., 208, 211, 232-33; *The Nature of Biography*, revd., 711-13
Gary, Elbert H., and trust control, 680
Gates, Charles M. (co-auth.), *Empire of the Columbia*, noted, 386-87
Gates, Paul W., revs., 143-44
Gaustad, Edwin S., *The Great Awakening in New England*, revd., 714-15
Gazetteers, and reading on frontier, 658, 659, 660
Geiser, Samuel W., revs., 157-58
General George B. McClellan, Shield of the Union, by Warren W. Hassler, Jr., 365-66
George, Alexander L. and Juliette L., *Woodrow Wilson and Colonel House*, review discussion of, 207 n., 208, 211, 233-35
George, Henry, influence on conservationists, 30, 40, 41
George, James Z., sen., favors Blair bill, 276, 280, 287
Georgia, and Blair bill, 276, 278, 287
German Culture in America: Philosophical and Literary Influences, 1600-1900, by Henry A. Pochmann, revd., 109-12
German-Language Press in America, by Carl Wittke, revd., 336-37
German travelers, views of U. S., 10
Germany, and Wilson's foreign policy, 226-29
Gerson, Louis L., and Wilson historiography, 229
Gibault, Father, and books on frontier, 657
Gibb, George S. (co-auth.), *The Resurgent Years, 1911-1927: History of the Standard Oil Company (New Jersey)*, revd., 164-65
Gibbs, Sir Phillip, visit to U. S., 25
Gibson, Randall L., sen., on federal aid to education, 281
Gilbert, Benjamin F., *Pioneers for One Hundred Years*, noted, 390
Glaab, Charles N., paper on Kansas City, reported, 319
Glad, Paul W., paper on Bryan, reported, 328-29
Glass, Carter, and New Freedom, 219; and Progressive banking reforms, 672 n.
Glass-Owen bill, and business disunity, 671, 673
Glenn, Hugh, and Sante Fe trade, paper on, reported, 325
Glimpse of Iowa in 1846: or, The Emigrants' Guide, and State Directory, by John B. Newhall, noted, 769-70
Glover, Thomas, early travel account of, 4
Going, Allen J., "The South and the Blair Education Bill," 267-90; revs., 755-57
Goldberg, Alfred (ed.), *A History of the United States Air Force*, noted, 774-75
Goldman, Eric F., on 1912 election, 213, 214
Goodykoontz, Colin B., paper on Federal Convention, reported, 323-24; deceased, 779-80
Gould, Clarence P., revs., 347-48
Gould, Jay, book on, revd., 747-49
Govan, Gilbert E. (co-auth.), *A Different Valor: The Story of General Joseph E. Johnston*, revd., 147-48
Govan, Thomas P., revs., 721-24
Graebner, Norman A., revs., 357-59
Graf, LeRoy P., revs., 757-58
Graff, Henry F. (co-auth.), *The Modern Researcher*, revd., 765-66
Graffenried, Baron Christoph von, early travel account of, 4
Grant, Charles S., revs., 340-41
Grant, Ulysses S., favors federal aid to education, 272; book on, revd., 148-49
Granville, Lord, and U. S. interests in Cyrenaica, 449, 454 n.
Gray, Wood, revs., 129-30
Great Awakening in New England, by Edwin S. Gaustad, revd., 714-15
Great Britain, and Oregon boundary question, 292-93, 295, 299, 302-304, 307; and U. S. interests in Cyrenaica, 450-52, 453, 462, 464, 465, 467; and dismissal of Lord Sackville, 635-48; and Wilson's neutrality policy, 226, 227; and U. S., book on, revd., 567-68
"Great Visitation to American Democracy," by Thomas D. Clark, 3-28

Greece, and U. S. Mediterranean policy, 465, 467
Greeley, Horace, on 1844 election, 297 n.
Greeley, William B., on conservation movement, 239 n., 247 n.
Green, Duff, as Jackson adviser, 98, 99, 101, 104
Green, Fletcher M., paper on Credit Mobilier, reported, 316; revs., 140-41
Greene, Howard (co-ed.), *The Journals of Welcome Arnold Greene*, revd., 349-50
Greene, John C., "Objectives and Methods in Intellectual History," 58-74
Greene, Welcome Arnold, journals of, revd., 349-50, 725-26
Gregg, Kate L. (co-ed.), *Prairie and Mountain Sketches*, by Matthew C. Field, revd., 359-60
Gregory, Thomas W., atty. gen., and conservation movement, 52, 53, 54
Griffin, Clifford S., "Religious Benevolence as Social Control, 1815-1860," 423-44
Griffin, Robert S., adm., and Teapot Dome investigation, 257, 260
Groce, George C. (co-auth.), *The New-York Historical Society's Dictionary of Artists in America, 1564-1860*, noted, 172-73
Grodinsky, Julius, *Jay Gould: His Business Career*, revd., 747-49
Guide to the Manuscripts of the State Historical Society of Wisconsin, Supplement Number One, by Josephine L. Harper and Sharon C. Smith, noted, 584
Gunderson, Robert G., *The Log-Cabin Campaign*, revd., 731-32
Guns on the Early Frontiers: A History of Firearms from Colonial Times through the Years of the Western Fur Trade, by Carl P. Russell, revd., 342
Guthrie, James, sec. of treasury, and Louisville and Portland Canal, 699-700, 702

Hacker, Louis M., *Alexander Hamilton in the American Tradition*, revd., 343-44; revs., 536-37
Hafen, LeRoy R., paper on Mormon migration, reported, 330-31; (co-ed.), *The Journal of Captain John R. Bell*, revd., 350-52
Haight, Raymond, and National Progressive party, 80, 88, 92
Half Horse, Half Alligator: The Growth of the Mike Fink Legend, ed. by Walter Blair and Franklin J. Meine, revd., 554-55
Hall, Charles, and religious benevolence, 436
Halleck, Henry W., and diplomatic recall, 643-44
Halligan, John, capt., and Teapot Dome investigation, 257, 260
Hamilton, Alexander, books on, revd., 343-44, 717-19
Hamilton, James A., as Jackson adviser, 103
Hamilton, James M., *From Wilderness to Statehood: A History of Montana*, ed. by Merrill G. Burlingame, revd., 739-40
Hamilton, Thomas, British traveler, view of U. S., 9
Hammond, Bray, *Banks and Politics in America from the Revolution to the Civil War*, revd., 721-24; and Jackson historiography, 626-27, 634 n.
Hamor, Ralph, *A True Discourse of the Present State of Virginia*, noted, 173
Hampton, Wade, sen., favors Blair bill, 276
Handlin, Oscar, *Race and Nationality in American Life*, revd., 382-83; revs., 573-74
Hanna, Kathryn Abbey, revs., 550-51
Hannegan, Edward A., sen., and Oregon boundary question, 303, 304-305, 306
Haraszti, Zoltán, *The Enigma of the Bay Psalm Book*, revd., 116-17; (ed.), *The Bay Psalm Book*, revd., 116-17
Harbison, Winfred A., revs., 561-62
Harding, Warren G., and conservation movement, 47; and Teapot Dome investigation, 237 ff.
Hargreaves, Mary Wilma M., *Dry Farming in the Northern Great Plains*, revd., 569-70
Harlan, Edgar R., and founding of MVHA, 495, 496
Harper, Josephine L. (co-auth.), *Guide to the Manuscripts of the State Historical Society of Wisconsin*, noted, 584
Harper, William R., and travelers' views of Chicago, 17
Harrington, Fred H., revs., 165-66
Harrington, J. C., *New Light on Washington's Fort Necessity*, noted, 579-80
Harris, Dixie R. (co-auth.), *The Signal Corps: The Test*, noted, 392
Harris, Isham G., sen., opposes Blair bill, 287
Harris, Robert J., revs., 366-68
Harris, Thaddeus, and books on frontier, 655
Harrison, Benjamin, and Blair bill, 274; and 1888 election, 636
Hart, Henry C., *The Dark Missouri*, noted, 389
Hartley, E. N., *Ironworks on the Saugus*, revd., 339-40
Hartz, Louis, and Jackson historiography, 632
Harwell, Richard B., *More Confederate Imprints*, noted, 583

Haskins, Charles H., and MVHA, 496
Hassler, Warren W., Jr., *General George B. McClellan*, revd., 365-66
Hawes, Albert G., rep., and Louisville and Portland Canal, 696 n.
Hawgood, John A., paper on Americans in Mexican Calif., reported, 330-31
Hayes, Rutherford B., favors federal aid to education, 272
Haygood, Atticus G., and Blair bill, 279
Haywood, William H., sen., on Oregon boundary question, 304-305, 306
Heckscher, August, and Wilson historiography, 209-10
Hedges, James B., revs., 123-25
Heil, Julius P., and Wis. politics, 91
Held, Burnell (co-auth.), *The Federal Lands*, noted, 772
Hennepin, Louis, early travel account of, 4
Henry, Alexander, and Sunday School Union, 427
Henry, Patrick, book on, revd., 716-17
Henry, Robert S., and *MVHR* article, 527
Henry Clay and the Art of American Politics, by Clement Eaton, revd., 356-57
Henry Varnum Poor: Business Editor, Analyst, and Reformer, by Alfred D. Chandler, Jr., revd., 143-44
Hepburn Act, and railroad rate regulation, 676
Hepburn amendments, to Sherman Anti-Trust Act, 681-83
Herschel, William, views on nature, 62
Hershey, Amos S., on dismissal of Lord Sackville, 644, 645
Hesseltine, William B., paper on political history, reported, 321-22
Hicks, John D., and MVHA, 514
Higham, John, on intellectual history, 58, 74
Hill, C. P. (co-ed.), *British Essays in American History*, revd., 536-37
Hill, Isaac, as Jackson adviser, 98, 99, 104
Hill, Jim Dan, revs., 134-37
Hispanic American Historical Review, and scope of *MVHR*, 534
Historians, and use of travel accounts, 6, 22; interpretation of Jackson, art. on, 615-34; on dismissal of Lord Sackville, 635, 645; and interpretations of Wilson, art. on, 207-36; and *MVHR*, 520, 528, 533, 535
Historical method, book on, revd., 765-66
Historical societies, and founding of MVHA, 495, 497, 500, 533
Historical Thinking of Charles A. Beard, by Elias Berg, noted, 583
History of American Magazines, Vol. IV, *1885-1905*, by Frank L. Mott, revd., 758-59
History of Chicago, Vol. III, *The Rise of a Modern City, 1871-1893*, by Bessie L. Pierce, revd., 371-72
History of Presidential Elections, by Eugene H. Roseboom, revd., 709-10
History of the Ojibway Nation, by William W. Warren, noted, 769
History of the United States Air Force, 1907-1957, ed. by Alfred Goldberg, noted, 774-75
History teaching, papers on, reported, 332-33
Hitchcock, Edward, on science and religion, 70
Hoar, George F., rep., and federal aid to education, 271
Hockett, Homer C., and MVHA, 514
Hodder, Frank H., and MVHA, 500, 511
Hofstadter, Richard, and Jackson historiography, 628; and Wilson historiography, 213, 230
Holder, Rose H., *McIver of North Carolina*, revd., 755-57
Hole, S. Reynolds, view of Chicago, 16
Hollon, W. Eugene (co-ed.), *William Bollaert's Texas*, revd., 134-37
Holmes, Justice Oliver Wendell, book on, revd., 366-68
Holmes, Thomas J., *The Education of a Bibliographer*, noted, 775-76
Homeward to Zion: The Mormon Migration from Scandinavia, by William Mulder, revd., 738-39
Homicide in American Fiction, 1798-1860: A Study in Social Values, by David B. Davis, revd., 549-50
Homsher, Lola M., revs., 739-40
Hones, K. W., on National Progressive party, 85
Hoole, W. Stanley, *Vizetelly Covers the Confederacy*, revd., 558-59
Hoover, Herbert, and conservation movement, 29, 43; and Harding cabinet, 253; on National Progressive party, 85
Hopkins, Samuel, and idea of benevolence, 425
Horsman, Reginald, paper on British Indian policy, reported, 323-24
House, Edward M., in Wilson historiography, 233-34
Howard, Perry H., *Political Tendencies in Louisiana, 1812-1952*, noted, 387
Howe, George F., *Northwest Africa: Seizing the Initiative in the West*, noted, 775; revs., 570-71
Howe, Mark DeWolfe, *Justice Oliver Wendell Holmes*, revd., 366-68
Hubbard, Samuel, and Education Society, 427
Hudson, T. S., on U. S. newspapers, 19
Huey Long's Louisiana: State Politics, 1920-1952, by Allan P. Sindler, revd., 167-68

Hugh-Jones, E. M., and Wilson historiography, 208
Hughes, Charles E., and 1908 election, 485, 492; and Harding cabinet, 253, 256-57, 258
Hughes, James, and Louisville and Portland Canal, 691 n.
Hughes, Richard B., *Pioneer Years in the Black Hills*, ed. by Agnes W. Spring, revd., 565-66
Hughes, William H. (co-ed.), *Robert Russa Moton of Hampton and Tuskegee*, revd., 377-78
Hulbert, Archer B., and *MVHR*, 502
Hulme, Thomas, and Louisville and Portland Canal, 697 n.
Humphrey, Andrew B., and Negro vote, 478
Humphrey, Heman, and religious benevolence, 428, 443
Humphrey, Norman D. (co-auth.), *No Frontier to Learning*, noted, 582-83
Humphrey, Z. M., on Bible Society, 437
Hunter, John D., *Manners and Customs of Several Indian Tribes Located West of the Mississippi*, noted, 768-69
Huntington, Samuel P., *The Soldier and the State*, noted, 385-86
Hurst, James W., *Law and the Conditions of Freedom in the Nineteenth-Century United States*, revd., 170-71
Hutchinson, Thomas, gov., paper on, reported, 314-15, 316
Hutchinson, William T., *Lowden of Illinois*, revd., 570-71
Hymnbooks, and reading on frontier, 652, 658, 659

Ickes, Harold L., sec. of interior, on Ballinger-Pinchot controversy, 247
Idaho, National Progressive party in, 88
Illinois, and culture in Ohio Valley, 650, 653, 656-57, 660; and Negro vote in 1908 election, 492; and National Progressive party, 88; aviation in, book on, noted, 774
Illinois, University of, sponsor of *MVHR*, 508
Illiteracy, in South, and Blair bill, 267, 268, 270, 279, 280 n., 286, 290
Immel, Ralph, and National Progressive party, 88
Immigrants, and religious societies, 434, 437, 444
Immigration, and travel accounts, 5, 7, 15, 18; studies of, and *MVHR*, 521
Immigration policy, book on, revd., 573-74
Imperial Years, by Foster R. Dulles, revd., 374-75
Imprints on History: Book Publishers and American Frontiers, by Madeleine B. Stern, revd., 576-77
Index to the Writings on American History, 1902-1940, comp. by David M. Matteson, noted, 172
Indian Territory: A Frontier Photographic Record, by William S. Prettyman, noted, 771
Indiana, and culture in Ohio Valley, 649, 650, 653, 656, 659-60; and Louisville and Portland Canal, 687, 696-97, 699 n., 700-701, 702, 705; and 1844 election, 296, 298-99; and Negro vote in 1908 election, 489, 492
Indians, French travelers' views of, 8; relations with whites, book on, revd., 337-39; Cherokee, book on, revd., 133-34; Seminole, book on, revd., 728; Sioux, paper on, reported, 330
Inside the Confederate Government: The Diary of Robert Garlick Hill Kean, ed. by Edward Younger, revd., 557-58
Intellectual history, art. on, 58-74; and *MVHR*, 521
Interior, Dept. of, and Teapot Dome investigation, 241 ff.
International Harvester Company, and trust control, 681 n., 682
International law, and dismissal of Lord Sackville, 637, 641-45
Interpreting Our Heritage: Principles and Practices for Visitor Services in Parks, Museums, and Historic Places, by Freeman Tilden, noted, 579
Interstate Commerce Commission, and railroad rate regulation, 673-74, 675 n., 676-79
Interstate Commerce Law Convention, and railroad rate regulation, 674-76, 677
Intimate Letters of John Cleves Symmes and His Family, ed. by Beverley W. Bond, revd., 131-32
Iowa, National Progressive party in, 80, 88, 89, 92; and founding of MVHA, 495, 497
Iowa, State University of, sponsor of *MVHR*, 513, 515
Ireland, and U. S., book on, revd., 752-53
Irish-American vote, and dismissal of Lord Sackville, 636, 637, 645
Ironworks on the Saugus: The Lynn and Braintree Ventures of the Company of Undertakers of the Ironworks in New England, by E. N. Hartley, revd., 339-40
Italy, and U. S. Mediterranean policy, 467

Jackson, Andrew, and advisers, art. on, 94-108; historians' views on, art. on, 615-34; and Louisville and Portland Canal, 693; and religious societies, 429-31, 433; book on, revd., 730-31
Jackson, Howell E., sen., and Blair bill, 280, 287
Jackson, Thomas J., gen., biog. of, revd., 363-65
Jackson, W. Turrentine (co-auth.), *When Grass Was King*, revd., 158-59

Jacksonian Persuasion: Politics and Belief, by Marvin Meyers, revd., 730-31
Jacob, John I., and Louisville and Portland Canal, 691 n.
James, James A., and MVHA, 502
James, Marquis, and Jackson historiography, 622
James, Reese D., *Cradle of Culture: The Philadelphia Stage, 1800-1810*, noted, 767
James K. Polk, Jacksonian, 1795-1843, by Charles G. Sellers, Jr., revd., 357-59
James Logan and the Culture of Provincial America, by Frederick B. Tolles, revd., 539-40
James Madison, the President, 1809-1812, by Irving Brant, revd., 348-49
Jameson, J. Franklin, ed. of *American Historical Review*, 531
Japan, and Wilson's foreign policy, 222-25, 227 n.
Jay, John, and Bible Society, 427
Jay Gould: His Business Career, 1867-1892, by Julius Grodinsky, revd., 747-49
Jefferson, Thomas, and foreign visitors, 8, 12; views on nature, 62, 65; in Jackson historiography, 617, 620, 634 n.
Jeffries, William W., revs., 132-33
Jews of Des Moines: The First Century, by Frank Rosenthal, noted, 771
Jim Crow laws, and Negro vote in 1908 election, 487, 491
Johansen, Dorothy O. (co-auth.), *Empire of the Columbia*, noted, 386-87
Johnson, Reverdy, sen., and Oregon boundary question, 306-307
Johnson, Richard M., and Oregon boundary question, 292
Johnson, Tom L., and Negro vote in Cleveland, 484
Johnston, Joseph E., biog. of, revd., 147-48
Jones, C. Clyde, paper on Burlington Railroad, reported, 329
Jones, Charles W., sen., favors Blair bill, 276
Jordan, Philip D., paper on social history, reported, 322; revs., 372-73
Joseph Reddeford Walker and the Arizona Adventure, by Daniel E. Conner, revd., 152-53
Joseph Reed: A Moderate in the American Revolution, by John F. Roche, revd., 544-45
Josephson, Bertha, assoc. ed. of *MVHR*, 529
Journal of Captain John R. Bell, Official Journalist for the Stephen H. Long Expedition to the Rocky Mountains, 1820, ed. by Harlin M. Fuller and LeRoy R. Hafen, revd., 350-52
Journals of Welcome Arnold Greene: Journeys in the South, 1822-1824, ed. by Alice E. Smith, revd., 725-26
Journals of Welcome Arnold Greene: The Voyages of the Brigantine Perseverance, 1817-1820, ed. by Howard Greene and Alice E. Smith, revd., 349-50
Justice, Dept. of, and Harding conservation policies, 243
Justice Oliver Wendell Holmes: The Shaping Years, 1841-1870, by Mark DeWolfe Howe, revd., 366-68

Kane, Murray, and *MVHR* article, 527
Kansas, annals of, revd., 373-74; and founding of MVHA, 495, 497
Kansas: A History of the Jayhawk State, by William F. Zornow, revd., 734-35
Kansas City, papers on, reported, 318-20
Kant, Immanuel, views on nature, 63-64, 65
Kaskaskia (Ill.), and reading on frontier, 650, 657, 660
Kean, Robert G. H., diary of, revd., 557-58
Keith, Jean E., revs., 754-55
Kendall, Amos, as Jackson adviser, 97 n., 98, 99-100, 102, 103, 104, 105-106
Kendrick, John B., sen., and conservation movement, 51; and Teapot Dome investigation, 258-59, 261, 263
Kennan, George F., and Wilson historiography, 228-29; *Soviet-American Relations, 1917-1920*, Vol. I, revd., 165-66
Kent, William, rep., and conservation movement, 33-34, 51, 56
Kentucky, and culture in Ohio Valley, 650, 651, 653-54, 658-60; and Louisville and Portland Canal, 686-90, 693, 695, 697, 700, 701; and Blair bill, 268, 278, 281, 282, 283; and frontier mind, book on, revd., 726-27
Kern, Alexander C., revs., 549-50
Kern, John W., and Negro vote, 489
Kershner, Frederick D., Jr., paper on midwestern small towns, reported, 329
King, John F., rep., favors Blair bill, 276
King, Judson, and Harding conservation policies, 253
King, William H., sen., and Teapot Dome investigation, 250-51
Kinzer, Donald L., revs., 740-41
Kitchen Cabinet, art. on, 94-108
Klay, Andor, *Daring Diplomacy*, noted, 174
Klein, Felix, view of Chicago, 16
Klingberg, Frank J. (ed.), *The Carolina Chronicle of Dr. Francis Le Jau*, revd., 541-42
Klingberg, Frank W., revs., 743-44
Klinkowström, Baron Axel, on American prisons, 20
Knowlton, Evelyn H. (co-auth.), *The Resurgent Years, 1911-1927: History of the Standard Oil Company (New Jersey)*, revd., 164-65

Koch, Adrienne, revs., 344-46
Kohn, Hans, *American Nationalism*, revd., 577-78
Komarovsky, Mirra (ed.), *Common Frontiers of the Social Sciences*, noted, 179
Korn, Bertram W., *The American Reaction to the Mortara Case*, revd., 740-41

Labaree, Benjamin W. (ed.), *Samuel McIntire*, noted, 768
Labor, in Jackson historiography, 626, 627-30, 631, 632 n., 633, 634; and National Progressive party, 76, 85, 86
La Follette, Philip F., and National Progressive party, art. on, 75-93
La Follette, Robert M., sen., and conservation movement, 37, 38, 45-48, 53-54, 57; and Teapot Dome investigation, 244, 246-47, 255-57, 258, 259, 261-65; in Wilson historiography, 213
La Follette, Robert M., Jr., sen., and National Progressive party, 78, 81-82, 88
La Guardia, Fiorello, and National Progressive party, 80, 87
Lamar, Lucius Q. C., sen., favors Blair bill, 287
Lambert, Robert S., on 54-40 slogan, 300 n.
Land Called Chicora: The Carolinas under Spanish Rule with French Intrusions, 1520-1670, by Paul Quattlebaum, revd., 114-16
Lane, Franklin K., sec. of interior, and conservation movement, 49, 54-55; and naval oil reserves, 244
Lansing, Robert, in Wilson historiography, 224 n., 226 n., 227
Laplace, Pierre Simon, and 18th-century view of nature, 61
Larson, Harold (co-auth.), *The Transportation Corps: Operations Overseas*, noted, 392
Larson, Laurence M., and MVHA, 499
Lathrop, John E., and Teapot Dome investigation, 257 n., 260
Latin American policy, in Wilson historiography, 215, 221
Law and the Conditions of Freedom in the Nineteenth-Century United States, by James W. Hurst, revd., 170-71
Law of the Commonwealth and Chief Justice Shaw, by Leonard W. Levy, revd., 360-61
Lawrence, Thomas J., on dismissal of Lord Sackville, 645
League of Nations, in Wilson historiography, 209, 210, 224, 227, 232, 233 n.
Le Conte, Emma, diary of, revd., 558-59
Lee, Gordon C., on federal aid to education, 268
Lee, Henry, as Jackson adviser, 103
Lee, Nelson, *Three Years among the Comanches*, noted, 769
Le Jau, Francis, Carolina chronicle of, revd., 541-42
Lemke, William, rep., on National Progressive party, 87
Lemmer, George F., paper on agricultural editors, reported, 326
Lenroot, Irvine L., sen., and conservation movement, 36, 37, 45-46
Leopold, Richard W., and Wilson historiography, 225, 226; revs., 763-65
Letters of William Gilmore Simms, Vols. IV-V, ed. by Mary C. Simms Oliphant and T. C. Duncan Eaves, revd., 362-63
Lever, Asbury F., rep., and conservation movement, 52
Levy, Leonard W., *The Law of the Commonwealth and Chief Justice Shaw*, revd., 360-61; revs., 170-71
Lewis, John L., and third party movement, 77
Lewis, McMillan, and Wilson historiography, 211
Lewis, William B., as Jackson adviser, 98, 99, 101, 102 n., 103, 104, 105
Lewis, William H., and Negro in politics, 480
Lexington (Ky.), and culture in Ohio Valley, 650, 652, 653, 660
Li, Tien-yi, and Wilson historiography, 222
Libby, Orin G., and beginnings of MVHA, 499, 502; and *MVHR* book reviews, 525-26
Liberal Arts College: A Chapter in American Cultural History, by George P. Schmidt, revd., 710-11
Liberalism, paper on, reported, 313
Liberals, and National Progressive party, 76-80, 82, 85-89, 92-93
Liberty party, and 1844 election, 296
Libraries, and culture in Ohio Valley, 650, 653-57, 660-63
Lieber, Francis, on travelers in U. S., 27
Life and Times of King Cotton, by David L. Cohn, revd., 547-48
Life of John Smith, English Soldier, by Henry Wharton, revd., 537-38
Lily White delegates, and Republican national convention (1908), 484, 485 n., 487
Lincoln (Neb.), and founding of MVHA, 494-95
Lincoln, Abraham, and reading on frontier, 649, 660, 663; and Republican party, paper on, reported, 327; books on, revd., 144-46, 735-36
Lincoln and the Tools of War, by Robert V. Bruce, communications on, 202-204
Lincoln Finds a General: A Military Study of the Civil War, Vol. IV, by Kenneth P. Williams, revd., 148-49
Lincoln's Supreme Court, by David M. Silver, revd., 561-62

Lindley, Harlow, and MVHA, 511
Lindsey, Ben B., and conservation movement, 36, 51
Link, Arthur S., *Wilson: The New Freedom,* review discussion of, 207 n., 208, 214-33; *Wilson the Diplomatist,* revd., 759-61
Linnaeus, Carolus, views on nature, 62, 65, 66
Lippman, Walter, and Wilson historiography, 210
Lively, Robert A., *Fiction Fights the Civil War,* revd., 153-54
Livingood, James W. (co-auth.), *A Different Valor: The Story of General Joseph E. Johnston,* revd., 147-48
Livingston, Edward, as Jackson adviser, 98, 99, 100, 103, 105
Lloyd George, David, and Wilson's foreign policy, 224
Loeb, William, and Negro vote, 486-87
Logan, James, book on, revd., 539-40
Log-Cabin Campaign, by Robert G. Gunderson, revd., 731-32
Long, Huey P., and La. politics, book on, revd., 167-68
Long expedition, to Rocky Mountains, journal of, revd., 350-52
Longaker, Richard P., "Was Jackson's Kitchen Cabinet a Cabinet?" 94-108
Longworth, Nicholas, rep., and Brownsville episode, 471, 479
Louisiana, and Blair bill, 276, 278; politics in, book on, revd., 167-68
Louisiana Sugar Plantations during the American Civil War, by Charles P. Roland, revd., 559-60
"Louisville and Portland Canal Company, 1825-1874," by Paul B. Trescott, 686-708
Lovejoy, Arthur O., and intellectual history, 59
Lowden of Illinois: The Life of Frank O. Lowden, by William T. Hutchinson, revd., 570-71
Lucey, William L., *The Catholic Church in Maine,* noted, 580
Lynch, William O., acting ed. of *MVHR,* 529; deceased, 187

McClellan, George B., gen., book on, revd., 365-66
McCoy, Donald R., "The National Progressives of America, 1938," 75-93
McDermott, John F. (co-ed.), *Prairie and Mountain Sketches,* by Matthew C. Field, revd., 359-60
MacDonald, William, and Jackson historiography, 620-21
McDuffie, George, sen., and Oregon boundary question, 304
McGee, W J, and conservation movement, 34, 36, 39-40, 57
McIntire, Samuel, book on, noted, 768
McIver of North Carolna, by Rose H. Holder, revd., 755-57
McKelvey, Blake, *Rochester: The Quest for Quality,* revd., 161-62; revs., 353-54
McLaughlin, Andrew C., and MVHA, 500
McLean, John, on Jackson and advisers, 106; and Sunday School Union, 428
Maclear, James F., revs., 714-15
McMaster, John B., and Jackson historiography, 622, 628 n., 629
McNeil, Donald R., *The Fight for Fluoridation,* revd., 381-82; revs., 568-69
McNiff, William J., revs., 738-39
McReynolds, Edwin C., *The Seminoles,* revd., 728
McReynolds, James C., atty. gen., and conservation movement, 52
McVaugh, Rogers, *Edward Palmer: Plant Explorer of the American West,* revd., 157-58
Madison (Ind.), frontier library in, 650, 656
Madison, James, book on, revd., 348-49
Magazines, American, book on, revd., 758-59
Malone, Henry T., *Cherokees of the Old South,* revd., 133-34
Mamatey, Victor S., on Wilson's foreign policy, 229
Mammoth Oil Company, and conservation movement, 51; and Teapot Dome investigation, 258, 259-60, 262
Mangum, Willie P., papers of, revd., 138-39
Mann, Charles M., and beginnings of MVHA, 499
Mann, James R., rep., and conservation movement, 42
Mann-Elkins Act, and railroad rate regulation, 677-78
Manners and Customs of Several Indian Tribes Located West of the Mississippi, by John D. Hunter, noted, 768-69
Manton Marble of the New York World, by Sister Mary C. Phelan, noted, 770
Mark Twain of the Enterprise: Newspaper Articles and Other Documents, 1862-1864, ed. by Henry Nash Smith, revd., 368-69
Marks of Lincoln on Our Land, by Maurine W. Redway and Dorothy K. Bracken, noted, 389
Marshall, Humphrey, rep., and Louisville and Portland Canal, 700-701
Martin, George W., and founding of MVHA, 495 n., 497
Marx, Karl, and intellectual history, 66
Marxism, and Jackson historiography, 630, 631
Maryland, and Blair bill, 268, 281; disfranchisement of Negroes in, 488
Mason, John Y., rep., and Louisville and Portland Canal, 696 n.

Massachusetts, colonial governors in, papers on, reported, 314-15
Massey, Mary E., revs., 144-46
Mather, Cotton, and idea of benevolence, 425
Mathews, Joseph J., *Reporting the Wars*, noted, 776
Matteson, David M. (comp.), *Index to the Writings on American History, 1902-1940*, noted, 172
Maury, Matthew F., on science and religion, 70 n.
Maxey, Edwin, on diplomatic recall, 644
Maxey, Samuel B., sen., opposes Blair bill, 282, 286 n.
Maxwell, William, and reading on frontier, 652
May, Ernest R., revs., 759-61
Mayo, Amory D., favors Blair bill, 277, 279
Meade, Robert D., *Patrick Henry: Patriot in the Making*, revd., 716-17
Mechem, Kirke (ed.), *The Annals of Kansas, 1886-1925*, revd., 373-74
Medary, Samuel, and 54-40 slogan, 294-95, 296
Medicine in Chicago, 1850-1950: A Chapter in the Social and Scientific Development of a City, by Thomas N. Bonner, revd., 372-73
Mediterranean, and U. S. interests in Cyrenaica, 451, 456, 465, 467, 468
Meek, Alexander, and reading on frontier, 656
Meine, Franklin J. (co-ed.), *Half Horse, Half Alligator: The Growth of the Mike Fink Legend*, revd., 554-55
Meredith, Roy, *Storm over Sumter*, noted, 770
Merrill, James M., *The Rebel Shore*, revd., 744-45
Messages of the Governors of Tennessee, Vol. IV, *1845-1857*, ed. by Robert H. White, noted, 387-88
Methodists, and religious benevolence, 423; and Blair bill, 279
Mexico, relations with U. S., papers on, reported, 331
Meyers, Marvin, and Jackson historiography, 633, 634 n.; *The Jacksonian Persuasion*, revd., 730-31
Miers, Earl S. (ed.), *When the World Ended: The Diary of Emma Le Conte*, revd., 558-59
Mighty Stonewall, by Frank E. Vandiver, revd., 363-65
Miles, Edwin A., "'Fifty-four Forty or Fight'—An American Political Legend," 291-309
Milholland, John E., and Negro vote, 474, 475, 478, 481 n., 487 n.
Militant South, 1800-1861, by John Hope Franklin, revd., 140-41
Miller, Charles T., paper on midwestern small towns, reported, 329
Miller, Jacob W., sen., and 54-40 slogan, 305
Miller, Perry, and intellectual history, 59, 72; *Errand into the Wilderness*, revd., 117-19
Miller, Raymond C., revs., 734-35
Milner, Samuel, *Victory in Papua*, noted, 178
Miner, S. E., on Wis. politics, 435
Ministers, and religious benevolence, 424, 426, 441; Negro, and Brownsville episode, 473, 483
Minnesota, Farmer-Labor party in, 75, 76, 86; and founding of MVHA, 495
Minnesota, University of, sponsor of *MVHR*, 508, 510, 511
Mirage in the West: A History of the French Image of American Society to 1815, by Durand Echeverria, revd., 335-36
Mirror for Gotham: New York as Seen by Contemporaries from Dutch Days to the Present, by Bayrd Still, revd., 121-23
Mississippi, and Blair bill, 276, 278, 287
Mississippi Valley, and religious societies, 431, 432, 435, 439, 440
Mississippi Valley Historical Association, presidential address, 3-28; annual meeting, 310-34; report of secretary-treasurer, 411-19; history of, art. on, 494-518; officers and meeting places listed, 516-17; Prize Monograph Series, announced, 181-83
Mississippi Valley Historical Review, art. on, 519-35
Missouri, and Blair bill, 268, 271, 281; and founding of MVHA, 495, 497
Missouri River, book on, noted, 389
Mitchell, Broadus, *Alexander Hamilton: Youth to Maturity*, revd., 717-19
Modern Researcher, by Jacques Barzun and Henry F. Graff, revd., 765-66
Montana, and founding of MVHA, 495; book on, revd., 739-40
Mooney, Chase C., *Slavery in Tennessee*, revd., 733-34
Moore, Arthur K., *The Frontier Mind*, revd., 726-27
Moore, Fred R., and Brownsville episode, 481
Moore, Margaret DesChamps, revs., 154-55
More Confederate Imprints, by Richard B. Harwell, noted, 583
Morgan, John T., sen., and Blair bill, 281, 282, 283, 284, 286, 287 n.
Morgenthau, Hans, on Wilson's foreign policy, 228
Mormon migration, paper on, reported,

330; from Scandinavia, book on, revd., 738-39
Mormons, by Thomas F. O'Dea, revd., 737-38
Morrill, Justin S., sen., and federal aid to education, 272, 273 n.
Morris, Richard B., and Jackson historiography, 627
Morris, Thomas, capt., and books on frontier, 651 n.
Morrow, Dwight W., mission to Mexico, paper on, reported, 331
Morse, Jarvis M., revs., 537-38
Mortara case, American reaction to, book on, revd., 740-41
Moton, Robert R., book on, revd., 377-78
Mott, Frank L., *A History of American Magazines*, Vol. IV, revd., 758-59
Moustapha Phosphor, Pasha of Tripoli, and U. S. interests in Cyrenaica, 457, 459-62, 463, 467
Mulder, William, *Homeward to Zion: The Mormon Migration from Scandinavia*, revd., 738-39
Murchison letter, and dismissal of Lord Sackville, 635, 639, 640
Murdoch, Richard K., revs., 114-16
Murphy, Paul L., revs., 761-62
Murray, Stanley N., paper on railroads and agricultural development, reported, 330
Myers, William Starr, and Wilson historiography, 212

NATIONAL Association of Manufacturers, and business disunity, 675-76, 681, 684
National bank, as issue in 1844 election, 296, 297 n.
National Board of Trade, and business disunity, 669, 681
National Citizens' League, and Progressive banking reforms, 669, 670
National Conservation Association, and conservation movement, 36-37, 46, 47, 49, 53, 238, 249 n.
National Education Association, and federal aid, 269-70, 276
National Farmers' Union, and National Progressive party, 85
National Forest Commission, and conservation movement, 33
National Industrial Traffic League, and railroad rate regulation, 677, 678
National Monetary Commission, and business disunity, 668, 669
National Policy and the Wheat Economy, by Vernon C. Fowke, noted, 772
National Progressive party, art. on, 75-93
"National Progressives of America, 1938," by Donald R. McCoy, 75-93
National Tuberculosis Association, 1904-1954: A Study of the Voluntary Health Movement in the United States, by Richard H. Shryock, revd., 568-69
Nationalism, American, book on, revd., 577-78; and Erie Canal, paper on, reported, 324-25
Nature, ideas of, and intellectual history, 60-71
Nature of Biography, by John A. Garraty, revd., 711-13
Naval oil reserves, and Teapot Dome investigation, 237, 243-46, 248, 253-62
Navy, and U. S. interests in Cyrenaica, 447, 451, 467; Union, in Civil War, book on, revd., 744-45
Navy, Dept. of, and U. S. interests in Cyrenaica, 445, 467; and Teapot Dome investigation, 243-46, 258-60
Navy Surgeon in California, 1846-1847: The Journal of Marius Duvall, ed. by Fred B. Rogers, noted, 388
Nebraska, and founding of MVHA, 495, 497
Neeley, Alexander, and reading on frontier, 651
Negro and Southern Politics: A Chapter of Florida History, by Hugh D. Price, noted, 177
Negro in the United States, by E. Franklin Frazier, revised ed., noted, 177
Negro Militia and Reconstruction, by Otis A. Singletary, revd., 563-65
Negro newspapers, and Brownsville episode, 471, 473, 477, 480, 482, 486, 490
Negro vote, and Brownsville episode, art. on, 469-93
Negroes, travelers' views of, 15; in Union army, book on, revd., 146-47; and Blair bill, 268, 269, 270, 276, 277, 279, 280, 281, 289-90; southern, disfranchisement of, 488-89
Neu, Irene D., revs., 142-43
Nevins, Allan, on dismissal of Lord Sackville, 635
New, Harry S., sen., and Harding conservation policies, 250
New Age of Franklin Roosevelt, 1932-45, by Dexter Perkins, revd., 574-76
New Deal, and National Progressive party, 75-78, 81, 85-87, 89
New England, Great Awakening in, book on, revd., 714-15
New Freedom, in Wilson historiography, 213, 216-19, 223, 231, 232
New Harmony (Ind.), and culture in Ohio Valley, 659
New Jersey, and Negro vote in 1908 election, 492
New Light on Washington's Fort Necessity, by J. C. Harrington, noted, 579-80
New Nationalism, in Wilson historiography, 213, 214, 217-19, 220 n., 232
New Orleans, travelers' views of, 16; and Louisville and Portland Canal, 687, 694; and Caribbean, paper on, reported, 320

New York, travelers in, 13, 16; and 1844 election, 297; and Negro vote, 485, 492; hist. of, revd., 713-14
New York *Age*, and Brownsville episode, 471, 481-82, 485-86, 488 n.
New York City, book on, revd., 121-23; and business disunity in Progressive era, 669-70, 672, 684
New-York Historical Society's Dictionary of Artists in America, 1564-1860, by George C. Groce and David H. Wallace, noted, 172-73
New York *Tribune*, and dismissal of Lord Sackville, 640-41
New Zealand, progressive movement in, paper on, reported, 328
Newcomer, Lee N., revs., 719-20
Newhall, John B., *A Glimpse of Iowa in 1846*, noted, 769-70
Newsome, Albert R., and 54-40 slogan, 301 n.
Newspapers, travelers' views of, 18-19; and reading on frontier, 650, 652, 654; and 54-40 slogan, 306-309; and Teapot Dome investigation, 250-52, 258-59, 260; Negro, and Brownsville episode, 471, 473, 477, 480, 482, 486, 490; southern, and Blair bill, 277, 283-84, 286, 287
Newton, Isaac, and 18th-century view of nature, 61, 62-64
Niagara Movement, and Negro in politics, 474, 482, 491
Nichols, Jeannette P., revs., 159-61
Nichols, Roy F., *Advance Agents of American Destiny*, revd., 130-31
No Frontier to Learning: The Mexican Student in the United States, by Ralph L. Beals and Norman D. Humphrey, noted, 582-83
Noggle, Burl, "The Origins of the Teapot Dome Investigation," 237-66
Norris, George W., sen., and conservation movement, 47 n., 57; on National Progressive party, 85
North Africa, U. S. interests in, art. on, 445-68
North Carolina, and Blair bill, 268, 276, 278, 279, 280; higher education in, books on, revd., 755-57
North Dakota, National Progressive party in, 88
Northern Securities Company, and trust control, 680
Northwest Africa: Seizing the Initiative in the West, by George F. Howe, noted, 775
Norwegian-American Studies and Records, Vol. XIX, ed. by Carlton C. Qualey, noted, 177-78
Notter, Harley, and Wilson historiography, 221
Noyes, Daniel P., on religious needs of West, 441
Nullification proclamation, and Jackson's advisers, 100, 102, 103, 105
Nye, Russel B., *A Baker's Dozen: Thirteen Unusual Americans*, revd., 129-30

OAKES, Pauline M. (co-auth.), *The Signal Corps: The Test*, noted, 392
"Objectives and Methods in Intellectual History," by John C. Greene, 58-74
O'Dea, Thomas F., *The Mormons*, revd., 737-38
Ohio, and culture in Ohio Valley, 650, 653-56, 658-60; Jackson party in, book on, revd., 355-56; and Louisville and Portland Canal, 688; in 1844 election, 294-95, 296; and Brownsville episode and Negro vote, 477, 479-80, 481, 483, 485, 486, 492
Ohio River, and Louisville and Portland Canal, 686-87, 692, 694, 701, 704, 706
Ohio Valley frontier, books and reading on, art. on, 649-63
Oil, and conservation movement, 31, 46, 48, 55; and Teapot Dome investigation, 237, 243-46, 248, 253-62
Oil industry, book on, revd., 164-65
Ojibway Indians, book on, noted, 769
Oliphant, J. Orin, revs., 725-26
Oliphant, Mary C. Simms (co-ed.), *The Letters of William Gilmore Simms*, Vols. IV-V, revd., 362-63
Oliver, Robert, book on, revd., 347-48
Olmsted, Frederick E., and Harding conservation policies, 249-50
Olson, James C., and MVHA meeting, 310, 334
One House for Two: Nebraska's Unicameral Legislature, by Adam C. Breckenridge, noted, 773-74
O'Neal, Edward A., gov., opposes Blair bill, 283
Opponents of War, 1917-1918, by H. C. Peterson and Gilbert C. Fite, revd., 378-79
Oregon, National Progressive party in, 88
Oregon boundary question, and 54-40 slogan, art. on, 291-309
Origins of the American Party System, by Joseph Charles, revd., 127-28
"Origins of the Teapot Dome Investigation," by Burl Noggle, 237-66
Orr, Gustavus J., favors federal aid to education, 269-70
Orville H. Browning: Lincoln's Friend and Critic, by Maurice G. Baxter, revd., 562-63
Osgood, Robert E., and Wilson historiography, 227 n., 228 n.
Ostrogorski, Moisei, and Jackson historiography, 616, 618
Ottoman Empire, and U. S. interests in Cyrenaica, 445 ff.
Overmyer, Grace, *America's First Hamlet*, revd., 724-25

Overton, Richard C., revs., 747-49
Owen, Robert, and books on frontier, 659
Owen, Robert Dale, rep., and Oregon boundary question, 293
Owen, Thomas M., and MVHA, 496

PACIFIC Northwest, book on, revd., 729-30
Packard, Frederick A., and religious benevolence, 436
Paine, Clarence S., and MVHA, 495-99, 500-503, 504, 505
Paine, Mrs. Clarence S., and MVHA, 505-508, 510
Paine, Thomas, and foreign visitors, 8; views on nature, 62
Pakenham, Richard, British minister, and Oregon boundary question, 301-302
Paley, William, views on nature, 62, 69 n.
Palmer, A. Mitchell, atty. gen., and conservation movement, 54-55
Palmer, Edward, biog. of, revd., 157-58
Palmer, Thomas W., Jr., deceased, 186
Pan-American Petroleum Company, and conservation movement, 50, 51; and Teapot Dome investigation, 260
Pannill, H. Burnell, *The Religious Faith of John Fiske*, revd., 751-52
Papers of Willie Person Mangum, Vols. III-V, ed. by Henry T. Shanks, revd., 138-39
Pardee, George C., gov., and conservation movement, 51
Pargellis, Stanley, revs., 765-66
Parish, John C., and MVHA *Proceedings*, 499
Parrington, Vernon L., and Jackson historiography, 619, 623, 626, 632 n., 633 n., 634 n.
Parry, David M., opponent of railroad regulation, 675-76
Parson Clapp of the Strangers' Church of New Orleans, ed. by John Duffy, noted, 580
Parton, James, and Jackson historiography, 615-18, 621, 634
Patent medicines, paper on, reported, 330
Patrick, Rembert W., revs., 557-58
Patrick Henry: Patriot in the Making, by Robert D. Meade, revd., 716-17
Patterson, Frederick D. (co-ed.), *Robert Russa Moton of Hampton and Tuskegee*, revd., 377-78
Paul, Rodman W., revs., 368-69
Paxson, Frederic L., and MVHA, 505-506; and *MVHR* book reviews, 526, 529; on Clarence W. Alvord, 529-30
Payne, John Howard, biog. of, revd., 724-25
Peabody Education Fund, and federal aid to education, 269, 270, 277
Peck, Charles H., and Jackson historiography, 616
Peckham, Howard H., "Books and Reading on the Ohio Valley Frontier," 649-63; and MVHA, 515
Pelling, Henry, *America and the British Left*, noted, 581-82
Pelzer, Louis, and MVHA, 499, 513, 514; report on projects in U. S. history, 521; ed. of *MVHR*, 515, 529, 530
Pelzer Award essay, 423-44
Penn, William, book on, noted, 767
Pennsylvania, and Negro vote in 1908 election, 492
Penology, and Cherry Hill prison, book on, revd., 353-54
Perce, Legrand W., rep., favors federal aid to education, 271
Perkins, Bradford, revs., 348-49
Perkins, Dexter, *The New Age of Franklin Roosevelt, 1932-45*, revd., 574-76; *The American Way*, noted, 579; *Foreign Policy and the American Spirit*, noted, 776; revs., 374-75
Persons, Stow, revs., 572-73
Pessen, Edward, and Jackson historiography, 627 n.
Peters, Absalom, and religious benevolence, 433
Peters, H. F., revs., 109-12
Peterson, Horace C. (co-auth.), *Opponents of War, 1917-1918*, revd., 378-79
Phelan, James D., sen., and conservation movement, 54
Phelan, Sister Mary C., *Manton Marble of the New York World*, noted, 770
Phelps, Anson G., and Bible Society, 426
Phelps, Edward, minister to Great Britain, and dismissal of Lord Sackville, 638-39, 640 n., 641-42, 646, 647
Philadelphia, supplies books for frontier, 652, 654; and Louisville and Portland Canal, 690, 691
Philadelphia *Dollar Newspaper*, and 54-40 slogan, 306
Phillips, William, and Education Society, 427
Pierce, Bessie L., *A History of Chicago*, Vol. III, revd., 371-72
Pillow, Gideon J., and nomination of Polk, 295
Pinchot, Gifford, and conservation movement, 30 ff.; and Teapot Dome investigation, 237 ff.
Pintard, John, criticizes Jackson, 429
Pioneer Years in the Black Hills, by Richard B. Hughes, revd., 565-66
Pioneers for One Hundred Years: San Jose State College, 1857-1957, by Benjamin F. Gilbert, noted, 390
Pioneers in Service: The History of the Associated Jewish Philanthropies of Boston, by Barbara M. Solomon, noted, 178
Pittman mineral leasing bill, and conservation movement, 46, 53, 54

Pittsburgh, and culture in Ohio Valley, 650, 651, 652, 653, 657-58
Pletcher, David M., paper on American-Mexican relations, reported, 331
Plumb, Preston B., sen., and Blair bill, 289
Plumer, William, gov., paper on, reported, 314
Pochmann, Henry A., *German Culture in America*, revd., 109-12; revs., 336-37
Poland, and Wilson's foreign policy, 229
Political history, paper on, reported, 322
Political History of the Texas Republic, 1836-1845, by Stanley Siegel, revd., 134-37
Political Party Patterns in Michigan, by Stephen B. and Vera H. Sarasohn, noted, 178-79
Political party system, origins of, book on, revd., 127-28
Political Tendencies in Louisiana, 1812-1952, by Perry H. Howard, noted, 387
Politics, and pre-Civil War banking, book on, revd., 721-24; in mid-19th century, papers on, reported, 327-28; in Jacksonian era, book on, revd., 730-31; and business, papers on, reported, 316-18; and Brownsville episode, art. on, 469-93
Polk, James K., as Jackson adviser, 98, 99; and Oregon boundary question, 291, 294-99, 301-305, 307-309; book on, revd., 357-59
Pomfret, John E., revs., 117-19
Poor, Henry V., biog. of, revd., 143-44
Pope, Patrick H., rep., and Louisville and Portland Canal, 690 n., 696 n.
Populism, in Jackson historiography, 624, 631
Porter, Kenneth W., revs., 728
Porter, William T., and *Spirit of the Times*, book on, revd., 553-54
Portugal, and U. S. Mediterranean policy, 467
Powell, Clayton, on Brownsville episode, 475
Powell, John W., and conservation movement, 34, 40; *The Exploration of the Colorado River*, ed. by Wallace Stegner, noted, 581
Powell, Lazarus W., sen., and Louisville and Portland Canal, 701
Prairie and Mountain Sketches, by Matthew C. Field, revd., 359-60
Pratt, Julius W., on dismissal of Lord Sackville, 635; revs., 162-63
Presbyterians, and religious benevolence, 423, 424 n.
Presidency in the Courts, by Glendon A. Schubert, Jr., noted, 179-80
President — Office and Powers, 1787-1957: History and Analysis of Practice and Opinion, by Edward S. Corwin, noted, 768
Presidential address, MVHA, 3-28
Pressly, Thomas J., revs., 383-85
Prettyman, William S., *Indian Territory*, ed. by Robert E. Cunningham, noted, 771
Price, Hugh D., *The Negro and Southern Politics*, noted, 177
Price, Overton, and conservation movement, 33, 36 n.
Price of Power: America since 1945, by Herbert Agar, revd., 574-76
Priestley, Joseph, and plenary inspiration, 69 n.
Prison at Philadelphia, Cherry Hill: The Separate System of Penal Discipline, 1829-1913, by Negley K. Teeters and John D. Shearer, revd., 353-54
Prize Monograph Series (MVHA), announced, 181-83
Proceedings, MVHA, publication of, 499, 500, 502, 503, 505, 515
Professors and Public Ethics: Studies of Northern Moral Philosophers before the Civil War, by Wilson Smith, revd., 352-53
Progressive movement, and business disunity, art. on, 664-85; and conservation, 30, 32, 38, 44-45, 49, 54-55
Progressives, and National Progressive party, 75, 80-82, 85, 87, 89, 90-91, 92
Progressivism, and Jackson historiography, 618, 619, 624, 625, 631; and Wilson historiography, 212-14, 217-19, 220 n., 236; papers on, reported, 328-29
Protestantism, evangelical, and religious benevolence, 423-25, 432, 433, 441, 443
Public Addresses, Letters, and Papers of William Kerr Scott, Governor of North Carolina, 1949-1953, ed. by David L. Corbitt, noted, 391-92
Public lands, and federal aid to education, 271, 272, 275, 287; and conservation movement, 31, 38, 53, 56
Publishers, and books on Ohio Valley frontier, 652-53, 657-60, 661, 663
Pugh, James L., sen., favors Blair bill, 276, 287 n.
Pullman cars, foreign travelers' views of, 24-26
Puritanism, book on, revd., 117-19; and intellectual history, 72
Puritans, and idea of benevolence, 425, 426
Putnam, Israel, and reading on frontier, 654

QUAIFE, Milo M., and MVHA, 506; ed. of *MVHR*, 511, 512, 529, 530, 533-34
Qualey, Carlton C. (ed.), *Norwegian-American Studies and Records*, Vol. XIX, noted, 177-78
Quarles, Benjamin, revs., 146-47
Quattlebaum, Paul, *The Land Called Chicora*, revd., 114-16

Quint, Howard H., revs., 378-79
Quintanilla, Luis, on Wilson and Pan-Americanism, 210

Race and Nationality in American Life, by Oscar Handlin, revd., 382-83
Radicals, and National Progressive party, 76, 77, 85
Railroad rate regulation, and business disunity, 666, 673-79, 685
Railroads, foreign travelers' views of, 25-26; and Louisville and Portland Canal, 706; and agricultural development, papers on, reported, 329-30
Railroads in Alabama Politics, 1875-1914, by James F. Doster, revd., 754-55
Ramsdell, Charles W., and MVHA, 512, 514
Randall, James G., and MVHA, 514
Randall, Ruth P., *The Courtship of Mr. Lincoln,* revd., 144-46
Range cattle industry, book on, revd., 158-59
Rankin, Hugh F. (co-auth.), *Rebels and Redcoats,* revd., 340-41; revs., 546-47
Raper, Horace W., revs., 563-65
Ray, John, views on nature, 63, 65
Reading, on Ohio Valley frontier, art. on, 649-63
Reagan, John H., sen., opposes Blair bill, 282
Rebel Brass: The Confederate Command System, by Frank E. Vandiver, revd., 151-52
Rebel Shore: The Story of Union Sea Power in the Civil War, by James M. Merrill, revd., 744-45
Rebels and Redcoats, by George F. Scheer and Hugh F. Rankin, revd., 340-41
Reconstruction, and schools in South, 268, 269, 271 n., 285; and Negro militia, book on, revd., 563-65
Records, Ralph H., deceased, 185-86
Redway, Maurine W. (co-auth.), *Marks of Lincoln on Our Land,* noted, 389
Reed, Joseph, biog. of, revd., 544-45
Reid, James W., rep., and Blair bill, 274, 276
Reinoehl, John H., revs., 349-50
Reis, Alvin, and National Progressive party, 82
Religion, and Great Awakening, book on, revd., 714-15
"Religious Benevolence as Social Control, 1815-1860," by Clifford S. Griffin, 423-44
Religious Faith of John Fiske, by H. Burnell Pannill, revd., 751-52
Religious thought, and intellectual history, 68-72
Reporting the Wars, by Joseph J. Mathews, noted, 776
Republican party, and Lincoln, paper on, reported, 327; and federal aid to education, 269, 271-72, 274, 275, 277, 278, 286, 288-90; and Brownsville episode and Negro vote, 469 ff.; and conservation movement, 32, 42, 45, 48-50, 54-55; and Teapot Dome investigation, 237, 238, 242, 263, 264; and National Progressive party, 75, 79, 82, 84, 85, 87, 90, 91, 92
Research methods, book on, revd., 765-66
Resurgent Years, 1911-1927: History of the Standard Oil Company (New Jersey), by George S. Gibb and Evelyn H. Knowlton, revd., 164-65
Revivalism and Social Reform in Mid-Nineteenth-Century America, by Timothy L. Smith, revd., 555-57
Revolution in America: Confidential Letters and Journals, 1776-1784, of Adjutant General Major Baurmeister of the Hessian Forces, ed. by Bernhard A. Uhlendorf, revd., 546-47
Reynolds, George M., and Progressive banking reforms, 672
Rice, Benjamin H., and Education Society, 429
Richards, Benjamin B. (ed.), *California Gold Rush Merchant,* noted, 174
Riddle, Donald W., *Congressman Abraham Lincoln,* revd., 735-36; paper on Lincoln and Republican party, reported, 327
Riddleberger, Harrison H., sen., favors Blair bill, 276
Ridge, Martin, paper on Ignatius Donnelly, reported, 328
Riegel, Robert E., revs., 730-31
Ritchie, David, rep., on Louisville and Portland Canal, 701 n.
Ritchie, Thomas, and 54-40 slogan, 302, 303
Rives, John C., on Jackson and advisers, 107
Roach, George W., on 54-40 slogan, 300 n.
Robber barons, idea of, paper on, reported, 317
Robert, Christopher R., and Home Missionary Society, 426
Robert Oliver, Merchant of Baltimore, 1783-1819, by Stuart W. Bruchey, revd., 347-48
Robert Russa Moton of Hampton and Tuskegee, ed. by William H. Hughes and Frederick D. Patterson, revd., 377-78
Roberts, W. Milnor, on Louisville and Portland Canal, 704-705
Robinson, Blackwell P., *William R. Davie,* revd., 719-20
Robison, John K., adm., and Teapot Dome investigation, 261
Roche, John F., *Joseph Reed,* revd., 544-45

Rochester: The Quest for Quality, 1890-1925, by Blake McKelvey, revd., 161-62
Roettinger, Ruth L., *The Supreme Court and State Police Power*, noted, 772-73
Rogers, Fred B. (ed.), *Filings from an Old Saw*, noted, 174-75; *A Navy Surgeon in California, 1846-1847*, noted, 388
Roland, Charles P., *Louisiana Sugar Plantations during the American Civil War*, revd., 559-60; revs., 167-68
Rolle, Andrew F., revs., 152-53
Roosevelt, Franklin D., and National Progressive party, 75, 76, 77-81, 84, 85 n., 86-87, 89, 92; books on, revd., 379-80, 574-76
Roosevelt, Theodore, and Brownsville episode and Negro vote, 469-93; and conservation movement, 29 ff.; and trust control, 680, 681, 682; in Wilson historiography, 213, 214, 216, 219, 227; book on, revd., 162-63
Roosevelt, Theodore, Jr., asst. sec. of navy, and Teapot Dome investigation, 245-46
Roots of American Communism, by Theodore Draper, revd., 572-73
Roppolo, Joseph P., revs., 362-63
Roseboom, Eugene H., *A History of Presidential Elections*, revd., 709-10; revs., 355-56
Rosenthal, Frank, *The Jews of Des Moines*, noted, 771
Ross, Stanley R., paper on Morrow's mission to Mexico, reported, 331
Rowland, Dunbar, and MVHA, 504
Rudolph, Frederick, revs., 710-11
Russell, Carl P., *Guns on the Early Frontiers*, revd., 342
Russia, relations with U. S., book on, revd., 165-66

Sable Arm: Negro Troops in the Union Army, 1861-1865, by Dudley T. Cornish, revd., 146-47
Sackville, Lord, dismissal of, art. on, 635-48
Sage, Leland L., *William Boyd Allison*, revd., 159-61
St. Louis, and reading on frontier, 650-51, 653, 660
Salisbury, Lord, and dismissal of Lord Sackville, 635 n., 636 n., 638-39, 641-42, 644, 646-47
Sampson, Francis A., and founding of MVHA, 494, 497
Samuel McIntire: A Bicentennial Symposium, 1757-1957, ed. by Benjamin W. Labaree, noted, 768
Sanders, Helen F. (co-ed.), *X. Beidler, Vigilante*, noted, 389
Sanford Ballard Dole and His Hawaii, by Ethel M. Damon, revd., 375-77
Sarasohn, Stephen B. and Vera H., *Political Party Patterns in Michigan*, noted, 178-79
Satow, Sir Ernest, on diplomatic recall, 644
Saugus (Mass.) Ironworks, book on, revd., 339-40
Saulsbury, Eli, sen., opposes Blair bill, 282
Savelle, Max, paper on liberalism, reported, 313
Saveth, Edward N., revs., 382-83
Sawyer, William, rep., and 54-40 slogan, 308
Scales, Alfred M., gov., and Blair bill, 278
Scamehorn, Howard L., *Balloons to Jets*, noted, 774
Scandinavia, Mormon migration from, book on, revd., 738-39
Schafer, Joseph, and MVHA, 512; and *MVHR* article, 527
Scheer, George F. (co-auth.), *Rebels and Redcoats*, revd., 340-41
"Scheme in Regard to Cyrenaica," by James A. Field, Jr., 445-68
Schlebecker, John T., paper on dairy press, reported, 326
Schlesinger, Arthur M., and Jackson historiography, 629, 632 n.; essay on city, 523
Schlesinger, Arthur M., Jr., and Jackson historiography, 622, 624 n., 626-29, 631, 632 n., 634 n.; *The Age of Roosevelt*, revd., 379-80
Schmidt, George P., *The Liberal Arts College*, revd., 710-11
Schmidt, Otto L., and MVHA, 507
Schouler, James, and Jackson historiography, 616, 617
Schubert, Glendon A., Jr., *The Presidency in the Courts*, noted, 179-80
Schutz, John A., paper on Mass. colonial governors, reported, 315, 316; revs., 125-26
Science in the Federal Government: A History of Policies and Activities to 1940, by A. Hunter Dupree, revd., 168-70
Scientific thought, and intellectual history, 68, 69-71
Scott, Emmett J., and Negro vote, 472, 475, 481, 485
Scott, Kenneth, *Counterfeiting in Colonial America*, revd., 542-43
Scott, William H., and Negro vote, 489
Sears, Barnas, favors federal aid to education, 270
Seay, Thomas, gov., and Blair bill, 278
Sectionalism, travelers' views on, 5, 14; in Jackson historiography, 625, 626, 629; and conservation movement, 42, 50-53
Sellers, Charles G., Jr., *James K. Polk, Jacksonian, 1795-1843*, revd., 357-59;

"Andrew Jackson versus the Historians," 615-34
Sellers, James L., and MVHA, 515; "The Semicentennial of the Mississippi Valley Historical Association," 494-518
"Semicentennial of the Mississippi Valley Historical Association," by James L. Sellers, 494-518
Seminoles, by Edwin C. McReynolds, revd., 728
Sergeant, John, rep., and Louisville and Portland Canal, 696 n.
Sevier, Ambrose H., sen., on 54-40 slogan, 305
Seymour, Charles, and Wilson historiography, 208-209, 221, 236
Shafer, Boyd C., revs., 577-78
Shambaugh, Benjamin F., and beginnings of MVHA, 495 n., 496 n., 498, 499-500, 502, 503
Shanks, Henry T. (ed.), *The Papers of Willie Person Mangum*, Vols. III-V, revd., 138-39
Shannon, Fred A., and *MVHR* book reviews, 526
Shaw, Lemuel, book on, revd., 360-61
Shaw, Ronald E., paper on Erie Canal, reported, 324-25
Shearer, John D. (co-auth.), *The Prison at Philadelphia, Cherry Hill*, revd., 353-54
Sheldon, George, and religious societies, 435
Shell Oil Company, hist. of, noted, 391
Shepperson, Wilbur S., *British Emigration to North America*, revd., 552-53
Shera, Jesse H., revs., 576-77
Sherman, E. A., and Teapot Dome investigation, 250
Sherman, William T., and West, book on, revd., 155-56
Sherman Anti-Trust Act, and trust control in Progressive era, 680-83
Sherman's March through the Carolinas, by John G. Barrett, revd., 150
Sherwin, John C., rep., and federal aid to education, 273, 290
Shideler, James H., *Farm Crisis, 1919-1923*, revd., 762-63
Shippee, Lester B., and MVHA, 508, 512, 514; acting ed. of *MVHR*, 510-11, 529
Shippen, Edward, and Louisville and Portland Canal, 691 n.
Shipton, Clifford K., revs., 120-21
Shirley, William, gov., paper on, reported, 315-16
Shockley, Martin S., revs., 724-25
Short History of New York State, by David M. Ellis *et al.*, revd., 713-14
Shryock, Richard H., *National Tuberculosis Association, 1904-1954*, revd., 568-69
Siberian expedition, and Wilson foreign policy, 224
Siegel, Stanley, *A Political History of the Texas Republic*, revd., 134-37
Signal Corps: The Test (December 1941 to July 1943), by George R. Thompson *et al.*, noted, 392
Silliman, Benjamin, on science and religion, 70
Sills, David L., *The Volunteers*, noted, 774
Silver, David M., *Lincoln's Supreme Court*, revd., 561-62
Silver, James W., *Confederate Morale and Church Propaganda*, revd., 743-44
Simms, William G., letters of, revd., 362-63
Simons, Algie M., on Jacksonian labor movement, 628-29, 630, 631, 633 n.
Simpson, George Lee, Jr., *The Cokers of Carolina*, revd., 154-55
Sinclair, Harry F., and conservation movement, 51; and Teapot Dome investigation, 258, 259
Sindler, Allan P., *Huey Long's Louisiana*, revd., 167-68
Sing Sing prison, foreign visitors to, 20
Singletary, Otis A., *Negro Militia and Reconstruction*, revd., 563-65
Sioux Indians, paper on, reported, 330
Sitterson, J. Carlyle (ed.), *Studies in Southern History*, noted, 176
Sitting Bull, Champion of the Sioux: A Biography, by Stanley Vestal, noted, 175
Slamm, Levi D., and 54-40 slogan, 305
Slattery, Harry A., and conservation movement, 35-37, 43, 46-47, 49-50, 53; and Teapot Dome investigation, 237 ff.
Slave trade, and U. S. interests in Cyrenaica, 445-47, 449, 451-54, 456-57, 463-65, 467
Slavery, travelers' views on, 13-15
Slavery in Tennessee, by Chase C. Mooney, revd., 733-34
Slayden, James L., rep., and Brownsville episode, 488
Smith, Alice E. (ed.), *The Journals of Welcome Arnold Greene*, revd., 349-50, 725-26
Smith, Claude C., deceased, 185
Smith, Culver H., revs., 138-39
Smith, Daniel M., and Wilson historiography, 226 n.
Smith, Sir Frederick E., view of Chicago, 17
Smith, Henry Nash (ed.), *Mark Twain of the Enterprise*, revd., 368-69
Smith, Hoke, sec. of interior, and conservation movement, 32
Smith, James M., *Freedom's Fetters*, revd., 344-46
Smith, Capt. John, and U. S. travel accounts, 3-4; book on, revd., 537-38
Smith, John Cotton, and religious benevolence, 427, 436
Smith, Robert, rep., on 1844 election, 301

Smith, Sharon C. (co-auth.), *Guide to the Manuscripts of the State Historical Society of Wisconsin*, noted, 584
Smith, Timothy L., *Revivalism and Social Reform in Mid-Nineteenth-Century America*, revd., 555-57
Smith, Wilson, *Professors and Public Ethics*, revd., 352-53
Smoot, Reed, sen., and conservation movement, 55; and Teapot Dome investigation, 262-64
Snell, John L., and Wilson historiography, 228-29
Social Darwinism, and Progressive movement, 30, 40
Social history, paper on, reported, 322
Social sciences, and intellectual history, 73-74
Socialism, views of religious societies on, 439-40; and Jackson historiography, 624; and National Progressive party, 76, 87
Society of American Foresters, and conservation movement, 251
Socolofsky, Homer E., paper on Capper farm press, reported, 326; revs., 762-63
Soldier and the State: The Theory and Politics of Civil-Military Relations, by Samuel P. Huntington, noted, 385-86
Solomon, Barbara M., *Pioneers in Service*, noted, 178
South, travelers' views of, 6, 10, 14-15; and conservation movement, 42-43, 50, 52, 56; book on, revd., 140-41
"South and the Blair Education Bill," by Allen J. Going, 267-90
South Carolina, and Blair bill, 271, 276, 279, 281, 287 n.; books on, revd., 126-27, 541-42
Southern Congressmen, and New Freedom, 219-20
Southern politics, and diplomacy, papers on, reported, 320-21
Southern Race Progress: The Wavering Color Line, by Thomas J. Woofter, noted, 390-91
Southwest, Spanish, papers on, reported, 325
Soviet-American Relations, 1917-1920, Vol. I, *Russia Leaves the War*, by George F. Kennan, revd., 165-66
Spaeth, J. Duncan, and Wilson historiography, 212
Sparks, William A. J., and conservation movement, 32
Spaulding, John, on western political power, 431
Specie Circular, and Jackson's advisers, 96, 97, 100, 104
Speed, Joshua F., and Louisville and Portland Canal, 708
Spencer, Herbert, and intellectual history, 65; in Jackson historiography, 617, 621
Spirit Gun of the West: The Story of Doc W. F. Carver, by Raymond W. Thorp, revd., 749-50
Spirit of the Times, and William T. Porter, book on, revd., 553-54
Spoils system, in Jackson historiography, 617, 618, 621, 622
Spring, Agnes W. (co-auth.), *When Grass Was King*, revd., 158-59; (ed.), *Pioneer Years in the Black Hills*, by Richard B. Hughes, revd., 565-66
Spring, Gardiner, and religious benevolence, 434, 436, 441, 442-43
Standard Oil Company, and trust control, 682; of New Jersey, book on, revd., 164-65
Stansifer, Charles L., revs., 373-74
Staples, Thomas S., deceased, 779
Steamboats, and Louisville and Portland Canal, 694, 699
Stegner, Wallace (ed.), *The Exploration of the Colorado River*, by John W. Powell, noted, 581
Stenberg, Richard R., and Jackson historiography, 623 n.
Stephenson, Wendell H., ed. of *MVHR*, 515, 529, 531
Sterling, Everett, paper on Sioux Indians, reported, 330-31
Stern, Madeleine B., *Imprints on History*, revd., 576-77
Stevens, Harry R., *The Early Jackson Party in Ohio*, revd., 355-56; paper on Hugh Glenn and Sante Fe trade, reported, 325
Stevenson, John M., on religious needs of West, 432
Stewart, Edgar I. (co-ed.), *The Columbia River*, by Ross Cox, revd., 729-30; revs., 565-66
Stewart, Gilchrist, and Brownsville episode, 476
Stewart, Jane R. (co-ed.), *The Columbia River*, by Ross Cox, revd., 729-30
Still, Bayrd, *Mirror for Gotham*, revd., 121-23; revs., 161-62
Stone, Andrew L., on poverty and religion, 438
Storm over Sumter: The Opening Engagement of the Civil War, by Roy Meredith, noted, 770
Stratton, David H., paper on Teapot Dome controversy, reported, 317-18
Striker, Laura P. (trans.), *The Life of John Smith, English Soldier*, by Henry Wharton, revd., 537-38
Stuart, Alexander H. H., and federal aid to education, 270
Stuart, H. A., and Teapot Dome investigation, 260-61
Stuart, John, and reading on frontier, 651
Stuart-Wortley, Lady Emmeline, visit of to U. S., 12
Studies in Enterprise: A Selected Bibliography of American and Canadian

Company Histories and Biographies of Businessmen, comp. by Lorna M. Daniells, noted, 584
Studies in Southern History, ed. by J. Carlyle Sitterson, noted, 176
Sugar plantations, in La., book on, revd., 559-60
Summersell, Charles G., revs., 744-45
Sumner, Bradford, on religious benevolence, 443
Sumner, William G., and Jackson historiography, 616, 617, 621, 628 n.
Sunday schools, and religious benevolence, 433, 441
Supreme Court, under Lincoln, book on, revd., 561-62; and Brandeis, book on, revd., 761-62; and trust control in Progressive era, 682
Supreme Court and State Police Power: A Study in Federalism, by Ruth L. Roettinger, noted, 772-73
Swanson, Claude A., sen., and conservation movement, 52
Swem, Charles L., records Wilson's speeches, 218
Swint, Henry L., on intellectual history, 58; revs., 555-57
Swisher, Carl B., revs., 360-61
Symmes, John Cleves, letters of, revd., 131-32
Syrett, Harold C. (co-auth.), *A Short History of New York State*, revd., 713-14

Taft, William H., and Brownsville episode and Negro vote, 470, 474-75, 477-79, 481-82, 484-87, 489-93; and conservation movement, 35, 36, 42, 44, 45, 239, 242-44; and railroad rate regulation, 677
Taney, Roger B., as Jackson adviser, 98, 99, 100, 103, 104, 105-106
Tansill, Charles C., on dismissal of Lord Sackville, 635; *America and the Fight for Irish Freedom*, revd., 752-53
Tappan, John, and Education Society, 426
Tariff, and federal aid to education, 272, 275, 286, 287; and Wilson, 215, 216, 219
Taylor, A. Elizabeth, *The Woman Suffrage Movement in Tennessee*, revd., 757-58
Taylor, Edward T., rep., and conservation movement, 52
Taylor, Hannis, on diplomatic recall, 644
Taylor, Robert L., gov., and Blair bill, 278
Teapot Dome investigation, origins of, art. on, 237-66; and conservation movement, 47, 56; paper on, reported, 317-18
Teeters, Negley K. (co-auth.), *The Prison at Philadelphia, Cherry Hill*, revd., 353-54
Television, and teaching of history, paper on, reported, 332
Tennessee, in Jackson historiography, 623, 624 n.; and Blair bill, 277, 278, 281, 287; slavery in, book on, revd., 733-34; woman suffrage movement in, book on, revd., 757-58
Tennessee Valley Authority, and foreign travelers, 15
Terrett, Dulany (co-auth.), *The Signal Corps: The Test*, noted, 392
Territorial Papers of the United States, Vol. XXII, *The Territory of Florida, 1821-1824*, ed. by Clarence E. Carter, revd., 550-51
Testa, Emile de, and U. S. interests in Cyrenaica, 460
Texas, as issue in 1844 election, 292, 293-99, 300, 301, 302; and Blair bill, 268, 281, 283, 287; and National Progressive party, 88; books on, revd., 134-37
Thackwell, Helen W., and Wilson historiography, 211
Theodore Roosevelt and the Rise of America to World Power, by Howard K. Beale, revd., 162-63
Thomas, Charles S., sen., and conservation movement, 43, 54
Thomas, Norman, on National Progressive party, 86
Thompson, George R. (co-auth.), *The Signal Corps: The Test*, noted, 392
Thompson, Jacob, rep., on 1844 election, 300 n., 301
Thompson, Lawrence S., revs., 153-54
Thompson, Richard W., and Brownsville episode, 472, 485
Thornbrough, Emma Lou, "The Brownsville Episode and the Negro Vote," 469-93
Thornton, Willis, *Fable, Fact, and History*, noted, 179
Thorp, Raymond W., *Spirit Gun of the West*, revd., 749-50
Three Years among the Comanches: The Narrative of Nelson Lee, the Texas Ranger, noted, 769
Thruston, Charles M., and Louisville and Portland Canal, 689
Thwaites, Reuben G., and beginnings of MVHA, 497, 498, 500, 502
Tidewater Maryland Architecture and Gardens, by Henry C. Forman, noted, 176
Tilden, Freeman, *Interpreting Our Heritage*, noted, 579
Tocqueville, Alexis de, on federal system, 10
Tolles, Frederick B., *James Logan and the Culture of Provincial America*, revd., 539-40; (co-ed.), *The Witness of William Penn*, noted, 767
Toombs, Robert, sen., and Louisville and Portland Canal, 702
Torch Press, and publication of *MVHR*, 499, 512

Transcendentalism, and intellectual history, 70-72
Trans-Mississippi West, papers on, reported, 330
Transportation Corps: Operations Overseas, by Joseph Bykofsky and Harold Larson, noted, 392
Travelers, foreign, in U. S., art. on, 3-28
Treasury, Dept. of, and Louisville and Portland Canal, 702-703, 707
Trefousse, Hans L., revs., 745-47
Tregle, Joseph G., Jr., revs., 356-57
Trelease, Allen W., revs., 337-39
Trescott, Paul B., "The Louisville and Portland Canal Company, 1825-1874," 686-708
Trial of Peter Zenger, ed. by Vincent Buranelli, revd., 125-26
Tripoli, U. S. interests in, art. on, 445-68
Trotter, Monroe, and Brownsville episode, 473-74; and Negro vote, 489-90
True Discourse of the Present State of Virginia, by Ralph Hamor, noted, 173
Trust control, and business disunity, 666, 679-85
Truxtun of the Constellation: The Life of Commodore Thomas Truxton, U. S. Navy, 1755-1822, by Eugene S. Ferguson, revd., 132-33
Tulane University, sponsor of *MVHR*, 515
Tumulty, Joseph, in Wilson historiography, 232 n.
Turhollow, Anthony F., revs., 720-21
Turkey, and U. S. interests in Cyrenaica, 447, 449, 450-51, 456, 460, 462-63, 465, 466
Turner, Frederick J., and Jackson historiography, 619-20, 621 n., 624-26, 629, 630, 632, 633 n., 634; in *MVHR*, 520, 521, 522, 526, 528
Turner, Lynn W., paper on N. H. governors, reported, 314
Turney, Hopkins L., sen., and Oregon boundary question, 303
Tyler, John, and Oregon boundary question, 299
Tyler, Ralph W., and Negro in politics, 472, 476, 479-80, 486

UHLENDORF, Bernhard A. (ed.), *Revolution in America*, revd., 546-47
"Under Our Strange Device: A Review of the 'Review'," by John W. Caughey, 519-35
Underwood, Oscar W., rep., and New Freedom, 219
United Nations, book on, noted, 582
United States Army in World War II series, vols. of, noted, 178, 392, 775
United States Steel Company, and trust control, 681 n., 682
University of North Carolina, 1900-1930: The Making of a Modern University, by Louis R. Wilson, revd., 755-57
Unpublished Opinions of Mr. Justice Brandeis: The Supreme Court at Work, by Alexander M. Bickel, revd., 761-62
Unterberger, Betty M., and Wilson historiography, 224
Upham, Warren, and founding of MVHA, 495 n., 497, 499
Urban, C. Stanley, paper on New Orleans and Caribbean, reported, 320
Urban history, and *MVHR*, 521; papers on, reported, 318-19

VAIL, Franklin Y., on wealth and religion, 438
Van Alstyne, Richard W., revs., 567-68
Van Buren, Martin, as Jackson adviser, 98, 99, 100, 101, 103, 104, 107; and 1844 Democratic national convention, 294, 295
Van Deusen, Glyndon G. (co-ed.), *Foreign Policy and the American Spirit*, noted, 776; revs., 731-32
Van Hise, Charles R., on National Conservation Association, 37
Van Rensselaer, Stephen, and Home Missionary Society, 427, 428
Van Tyne, Claude H., and *MVHR*, 502
Van Vechten, Jacob, on religion in Jackson era, 429
Vandiver, Frank E., *Rebel Brass: The Confederate Command System*, revd., 151-52; *Mighty Stonewall*, revd., 363-65
Varick, Richard, and Bible Society, 427
Versailles Treaty, in Wilson historiography, 223, 229, 231, 232
Ver Steeg, Clarence L., revs., 539-40, 717-19
Vestal, Stanley, *Sitting Bull, Champion of the Sioux*, noted, 175
Victoria, Queen, and dismissal of Lord Sackville, 639
Victory in Papua, by Samuel Milner, noted, 178
Vidal, Michel, U. S. consul at Tripoli, and Cyrenaican naval base scheme, art. on, 445-68
Viles, Jonas, and MVHA, 514
Vincennes, and culture in Ohio Valley, 650, 656, 659
Vinton, Samuel F., rep., and Louisville and Portland Canal, 696 n.
Violette, Eugene M., and beginnings of MVHA, 506
Virginia, and Blair bill, 276, 278
Vizetelly Covers the Confederacy, by W. Stanley Hoole, revd., 558-59
Volunteers: Means and Ends in a National Organization, by David L. Sills, noted, 774
Volwiler, Albert T., deceased, 597

Von Holst, Hermann E., and Jackson historiography, 616, 617-18
Vorys, Arthur I., and Negro in politics, 482, 484, 486

WADE, Richard C. (co-ed.), *Foreign Policy and the American Spirit*, noted, 776
Wagner, Henry R., deceased, 186-87
Walker, Joseph R., book on, revd., 152-53
Wall, Bennett H., revs., 547-48
Wallace, David H. (co-auth.), *The New-York Historical Society's Dictionary of Artists in America*, noted, 172-73
Wallace, Henry C., sec. of agriculture, and Harding conservation policies, 247 n., 251-54
Walsh, Thomas J., sen., and conservation movement, 51-52, 53, 55; and Teapot Dome investigation, 263-64
Walters, Alexander, and Negro in politics, 489-91
Walters, J. Bennett, revs., 151-52
Walters, Raymond, *Albert Gallatin*, revd., 720-21
Walthall, Edward C., sen., favors Blair bill, 287
Warburg, Paul M., and Aldrich banking plan, 669
Ward, John W., and Jackson historiography, 633, 634 n.
Ward, Lester F., influence on conservationists, 30, 40
Ward, Samuel, and Bible Society, 426
Wardell, Morris L., deceased, 186
Warren, William W., *History of the Ojibway Nation*, noted, 769
"Was Jackson's Kitchen Cabinet a Cabinet?" by Richard P. Longaker, 94-108
Washburn, Emory, on Bible Society, 442
Washington (D. C.), travelers' views of, 13
Washington, Booker T., and Brownsville episode and Negro vote, 469 ff.
Washington, George, and foreign visitors, 8, 11-12
Washington *Bee*, and Brownsville episode, 471-72; and Negro vote, 478, 480, 482, 486
Watson, Richard L., Jr., "Woodrow Wilson and His Interpreters, 1947-1957," 207-36
Watterson, Henry, opposes Blair bill, 283-85, 286, 287
Weaver, Herbert, revs., 559-60
Webb, Walter P., paper on teaching of history, reported, 333
Weber, Max, and intellectual history, 59
Webster, Noah, views on nature, 65
Welliver, Judson, and 1920 election, 238
Wells, Philip P., and conservation movement, 35, 36, 37, 40-41, 46-47, 53, 254, 256
Welty, Raymond L., revs., 155-56
Wentworth, John, biog. of, revd., 742-43
West, and religious societies, 430-32, 435, 437, 440; and conservation movement, 42, 43, 50-53, 56; papers on, reported, 323-24, 330; books on, revd., 155-59, 342, 359-60, 749-50
West, Willis M., and Jackson historiography, 629
West Virginia, and restrictions on Negro, 491
Western Reserve University, sponsor of *MVHR*, 513
Westernized Yankee: The Story of Cyrus Woodman, by Larry Gara, revd., 142-43
Wharton, Henry, *The Life of John Smith, English Soldier*, revd., 537-38
Wheeler, Joseph, rep., and Blair bill, 274, 276
When Grass Was King: Contributions to the Western Range Cattle Industry Study, by Maurice Frink *et al.*, revd., 158-59
When the World Ended: The Diary of Emma Le Conte, ed. by Earl S. Miers, revd., 558-59
Whig interpretation, in Jackson historiography, 616-18, 621, 622, 623-24, 628, 631
Whig party, and religious societies, 434, 435; and Oregon boundary question, 293, 298-99; and 54-40 slogan, 308-309
White, Canvass, and Louisville and Portland Canal, 692
White, Hugh L., sen., as Jackson adviser, 99
White, Leonard D., and Jackson historiography, 623
White, Philip L., *The Beekmans of New York*, revd., 123-25; (ed.), *Beekman Mercantile Papers*, revd., 123-25
White, Robert H. (ed.), *Messages of the Governors of Tennessee*, Vol. IV, noted, 387-88
White, William Allen, and Wilson historiography, 230
Whitehead, Alfred North, and intellectual history, 59
White House Conference (1908), and conservation movement, 34, 36, 40
Wiebe, Robert H., "Business Disunity and the Progressive Movement, 1901-1914," 664-85
Wilder, Sampson V. S., and Tract Society, 427
Wilderness to Statehood: A History of Montana, 1805-1900, by James M. Hamilton, revd., 739-40
William Bollaert's Texas, ed. by W. Eugene Hollon and Ruth L. Butler, revd., 134-37
William Boyd Allison: A Study in Practical Politics, by Leland L. Sage, revd., 159-61
William R. Davie, by Blackwell P. Robinson, revd., 719-20

William T. Porter and the "Spirit of the Times": A Study of the Big Bear School of Humor, by Norris W. Yates, revd., 553-54
William Tecumseh Sherman and the Settlement of the West, by Robert G. Athearn, revd., 155-56
Williams, Howard D., revs., 713-14
Williams, Kenneth P., *Lincoln Finds a General*, Vol. IV, revd., 148-49
Williams, S. Laing, and Negro in politics, 480
Williams, Thomas S., and Tract Society, 428
Williams, William A., and Wilson historiography, 222 n., 225 n.
Williams, William R., and religious benevolence, 441
Williamson, Harold F., revs., 164-65
Willis, Albert S., rep., and Blair bill, 274, 276
Willis, H. Parker, and Progressive banking reforms, 672 n.
Wilson, Louis R., *The University of North Carolina, 1900-1930*, revd., 755-57
Wilson, Woodrow, and interpreters, art. on, 207-36; opposes Blair bill, 283; and Jackson historiography, 619, 620, 632 n.; and business disunity, 665, 671, 672, 682-83, 685; and conservation movement, 45, 47, 48-50, 52-55, 244; foreign policy of, books on, revd., 759-61
Wilson: The New Freedom, by Arthur S. Link, review discussion of, 207 n., 208, 214-33
Wilson the Diplomatist: A Look at His Major Foreign Policies, by Arthur S. Link, revd., 759-61
Wilson's Foreign Policy in Perspective, ed. by Edward H. Buehrig, revd., 759-61
Wiltse, Charles M., and Jackson historiography, 624
Winther, Oscar O., "The Fiftieth Annual Meeting of the Mississippi Valley Historical Association," 310-34
Winthrop, Robert C., favors federal aid to education, 270, 277
Wisconsin, and National Progressive party, 75 ff.
Wisconsin State Historical Society, guide to manuscript collections, noted, 584
Wise, George D., rep., favors Blair bill, 276
Wish, Harvey, revs., 113-14
Witness of William Penn, ed. by Frederick B. Tolles and E. Gordon Alderfer, noted, 767
Wittke, Carl F., and MVHA, 515; *The German-Language Press in America*, revd., 336-37
Woman Suffrage Movement in Tennessee, by A. Elizabeth Taylor, revd., 757-58
Woodbury, Levi, as Jackson adviser, 103, 106
Woodman, Cyrus, biog. of, revd., 142-43
Woodrow Wilson: A Great Life in Brief, by John A. Garraty, review discussion of, 207 n., 208, 211, 232-33
Woodrow Wilson and Colonel House: A Personality Study, by Alexander L. and Juliette L. George, review discussion of, 207 n., 208, 211, 233-35
"Woodrow Wilson and His Interpreters, 1947-1957," by Richard L. Watson, Jr., 207-36
Woodrow Wilson and the Politics of Morality, by John M. Blum, review discussion of, 207 n., 208, 230-33
Woodruff, George W., and conservation movement, 35
Woody, Robert H., revs., 126-27
Woofter, Thomas J., *Southern Race Progress*, noted, 390-91
Woolsey, Theodore D., and Home Missionary Society, 428
Worden, John L., adm., and Cyrenaican naval base scheme, 445, 458, 467
World War I, opposition to, book on, revd., 378-79; in Wilson historiography, 218, 220-21, 225-28, 231
World War II, U. S. Army in, books on, noted, 178, 392, 775
Wright, Louis B., *The Cultural Life of the American Colonies, 1607-1763*, revd., 120-21; revs., 116-17
Wright, Lyle H., *American Fiction, 1851-1875*, noted, 766
Wright, Nathan H., and Teapot Dome investigation, 260-61
Wright, Silas, sen., and 1844 Democratic national convention, 295
Wyman, Walker D., revs., 359-60

X. Beidler, Vigilante, ed. by Helen F. Sanders and William H. Bertsche, Jr., noted, 389

YATES, Norris W., *William T. Porter and the "Spirit of the Times,"* revd., 553-54
Yates, Richard E., revs., 150
Young, J. Harvey, paper on patent medicines, reported, 330
Young, Otis E., discussion of history teaching, reported, 332
Younger, Edward (ed.), *Inside the Confederate Government*, revd., 557-58

ZENGER, Peter, trial of, book on, revd., 125-26
Ziegler, David, and books on frontier, 652
Zorn, Roman J., and *MVHR* book reviews, 526
Zornow, William F., *Kansas: A History of the Jayhawk State*, revd., 734-35; revs., 562-63